the study of

psychology

the study of
psychology

Joseph Rubinstein

the dushkin publishing group inc.
guilford, connecticut

Library of Congress Catalog Card Number: 74-30681

Manufactured in the United States of America.

Second Edition, Second Printing

preface

The popular media regularly expose us to dramatic new developments they say may change our lives. Many students hope to learn more about such findings in the introductory psychology course. *The Study of Psychology* was written to help satisfy this hope, but in a way that does not compromise the scientific aspects of the discipline.

The Study of Psychology is intended to help students become sophisticated consumers of psychological information. To this end, I have followed these guidelines:

1. PRESENT AN OVERVIEW OF THE DISCIPLINE IN ITS FULL RANGE. This involved the development of relatively independent units that could be classified at various levels of behavior, ranging from social to biological and across a number of perspectives. The general plan is to show that psychology can be mostly empirical in method, largely behavioristic in strategy and basically humanistic in its aims.

2. DEVELOP EACH UNIT WITH THE SAME GENERAL ORGANIZATION. The concern here was to provide a basic structure on which to impose information so that the reader would be able to organize the information in advance. The concept of the advance organizer is a principle of educational psychology shown to be helpful in retaining information. Each unit in *The Study of Psychology* has six common sections.

3. HELP THE READER DEVELOP SKILLS IN DISCOVERING AND EVALUATING PSYCHOLOGICAL INFORMATION. Despite its diversity, there is a common core in psychological information: the way psychologists ask questions, develop hypotheses and seek evidence to accept or reject their hypotheses. The heart of each unit is this progression from questions through hypothesis to evidence.

4. PRESENT INFORMATION BASIC TO CERTAIN TOPICS IN A WAY THAT WILL MAKE THE RELATIONSHIPS OBVIOUS. Students in introductory psychology often wonder why they should study topics that apparently concern only the professional. For example, rather than treat these topics as separate units, intelligence testing is used in *The Study of Psychology* to introduce the unit on *intelligence,* personality measurement to introduce the unit on personality, and anatomy and physiology are distributed where most appropriate throughout the units that come under the general heading of *Biology and Behavior.*

5. PREPARE A TEXT WHICH COULD BE UTILIZED IN BOTH TRADITIONAL AND P.S.I. MODES OF INSTRUCTION. The modular format of the text is particularly well suited to this goal. In addition, a unit-mastery workbook with behavioral objectives is available, and the instructor is aided by a carefully-prepared set of unit tests obtainable from the publisher upon adoption.

The Study of Psychology follows a happy year of using its predecessor. Many users, including myself, found that students seemed to be grasping concepts and developing reading and comprehension skills more readily than students using other texts. We also found that some descriptions could be further enhanced with explanatory graphics. In this revision you will find many new illustrations, including new flow diagrams summarizing each unit.

A major addition to the book is a brief issue-oriented essay following each unit. These essays were written by Dr. Ian Robertson, who received a doctorate from Harvard University and has taught and lectured in England and the United States.

Finally, a major role in producing *The Study of Psychology* was played by Rick Connelly of the Dushkin Publishing Group, who initiated it, spoke with the many users of the earlier edition, coordinated all operations and contributed his good judgment throughout.

Joseph Rubinstein

Purdue University
West Lafayette, Indiana

note to students

"The new education must teach the individual
how to classify and reclassify information, how
to evaluate its veracity, how to change categories
when necessary, how to move from the concrete
to the abstract and back, how to look at problems
from a new direction—how to teach himself."
—Herbert Gerjuoy, in *Future Shock* by Alvin
Toffler, 1970

This book is an invitation to explore behavior from a new direction and to sample a wide range of psychology. It demonstrates processes that enable us to move between subjective and objective information. This book says something about how we know about people and other animals.

How do we know about people? We often feel deeply about people and events that touch our lives. These feelings are a rich source of information—yet often lead to misconceptions. Whether others agree with these feelings often has little bearing on how we behave. Our long-range behavior and planning, however, tend to be based on predictable events rather than on subjective feelings.

How does the psychologist know about people? The training of the psychologist involves developing skills in obtaining and interpreting *objective* evidence about behavior. What psychologists have in common is a way of asking questions about behavior that will produce *testable* answers. Their approach includes an openness to new sources of information and an ability to evaluate that information objectively. It is this approach to information that you are invited to share in these pages.

This book is organized by topic units that are interesting to most of us and of special interest to psychologists. Each unit is written to stand alone and can be read independently. As you read you should become aware of the interrelationships of various areas as each unit suggests the web that ties them all together.

To help you see these interrelationships, each of the units follows the same organization. We believe this common organization will help you to find the contents easier to understand. The six sections of each unit are: *Introductory Graphic, Definition and Background, Questions and Evidence, Putting it Together, What's Accepted and What's Debated* and *Issue*. As this organization becomes familiar to you, it should become the principal apparatus for organizing your review of the text.

In addition, built into each unit are five different types of summaries that should be helpful for study purposes:

The *Schematic Outline* on the opening page of each unit provides a preview of the unit. The *Introductory Graphics* facing the Schematic Outline preview the content in terms of experiences you should recognize. The *tabular representation* of questions, hypotheses, and evidence (the *"evigram"*) organizes and summarizes information pertaining to each question. Taken together, the evigrams within a unit serve to organize the major portion of content. Each hypothesis named in the evigram may be found easily in the text that follows, since it always appears in *italics*. The results of each investigation appear in colored type. This distinguishes results from interpretations and conclusions made about the results. The flow diagram, *Putting It Together,* appearing near the end of the unit, organizes the principles discussed in the text as they relate to each other. *What's Accepted and What's Debated* lists principles discussed in the text on the basis of the acceptability of the evidence to most psychologists.

In addition to these built-in summaries, a workbook has been prepared to aid you in mastering the information presented in the text. This should be available in your bookstore.

contents

Preface   v

Note to Students   vi

1. Social Behavior . . . Relating to Others

1. The Study of Psychology   2
2. Self-Fulfilling Prophecy   32
3. Helping Others   46
4. Hurting Others   60
5. Morality   74
6. Sexuality   90
7. Love   106
8. Prejudice   120
9. Groups and Leaders   138
10. Social Influence   152
11. Therapy in Groups   168

II. Individual Behavior . . . Being A Unique Person

12. Intelligence   186
13. The Disordered Mind   206
14. Using Language   226
15. Personality   244
16. Children's Thinking   266
17. Signs of Emotion   282
18. Problem Solving and Creativity 296
19. Hypnosis   312
20. Therapy for Individuals   326

III. Processes Underlying Behavior . . . Basic Operations

21. Motivation   346
22. Concept Learning   370
23. Perceiving   384
24. Paying Attention   406
25. Memory   422
26. Pavlovian Conditioning   444
27. Operant Conditioning   458

IV. Biology and Behavior . . . Basic Relationships

28. Stress and Anxiety   482
29. Genes and Their Nurture   498
30. Built-in Behavior   516
31. The Senses   534
32. Sleep and Dreams   554
33. Brain Storage   568
34. Brain Stimulation   584
35. Biofeedback   602
36. Psychoactive Drugs   620

Bibliography   x

Glossary   xxviii

Index of Names   xxxix

General Index   xlii

Credits   xlix

Acknowledgments   lii

Part I
social behavior . . .
relating to others

1. The Study of Psychology

Although barely a century old as a formal discipline, today *The Study of Psychology* covers a very broad range. Psychologists are involved in virtually every area of human endeavor, and while their particular fields of concentration may vary, they do share a basic interest in the explanation of behavior and in special methods for studying it.

2. Self-Fulfilling Prophecy

3. Helping Others

4. Hurting Others

Many of the critical events in our society can be traced to the motives and forces underlying how people behave toward one another. One concept that has emerged from the study of these interactions is *Self-Fulfilling Prophecy,* the capacity for people's expectations and preconceived ideas to create reality in their own image. The wide-scale social consequences of such prophecies are still largely unrecognized and unexplored. Perhaps the two most important kinds of behavior that result from social motives in general are *Helping Others* and *Hurting Others.* In modern psychology, neither helping nor hurting is attributed to any single motive or cause, but to a variety of explanatory concepts involving both one's past experiences and characteristics of the immediate situation.

5. Morality

6. Sexuality

7. Love

The social interactions that each of us experiences during infancy and childhood are crucial determinants of our social behavior later on. This is true for developing a conscience and individual principles of *Morality,* for developing the capacity to *Love,* and for developing the behavior associated with our *Sexuality.* Sex-role behavior derives from physical and biological differences, differences in parental treatment and cultural traditions and values—which have inspired social protest and the women's liberation movement.

8. Prejudice

9. Groups and Leaders

Social psychologists have intensively studied *Prejudice.* Though most of us identify prejudice with racial and ethnic bigotry, in some ways prejudice and stereotypes are inevitable byproducts of the way human beings process information, the way we deal with the world. This fact makes prejudice no less evil but perhaps more comprehensible. Another way in which human beings process information is in committees and conferences where *Groups and Leaders* try to deal collectively with problems that are beyond the capacities or responsibilities of one individual. How people in a group interact and how the group functions to accomplish its purpose present social psychologists with some of their most complex problems for analysis.

10. Social Influence

11. Therapy in Groups

People's reactions to each other are often described in terms of communications, emotions, or judgments. Most of us tend not to consider these reactions as attempts to control others' behavior, but people do influence and control each other all the time. *Social Influence* is most obvious in situations involving persuasion, advertising and salesmanship, but people also influence each other in many ways that are often subtle or latent in their effects. The capacity for social interactions to influence an individual and even alter his behavior is demonstrated by those psychiatrists and clinical psychologists who use *Therapy in Groups* to help mental patients and others with serious problems. There is little doubt that the social influences that take place in group therapeutic situations can have powerful effects on disturbed behavior.

Unit 1

The Study of Psychology

OVERVIEW

An introduction to the field, its historical development, applications, and its methods, this unit describes past and present schools of psychology and details the scientific method of investigation. A section on using statistics is included.

UNIT OUTLINE

A. What Is Psychology?
B. What Do Psychologists Do?
C. A Brief History of Psychology
    1. Structuralism
    2. Functionalism
    3. Behaviorism
    4. Gestalt psychology
    5. Psychoanalytic theory
D. Today's Psychology
    1. Humanism
E. The Method of Psychology
    1. The Scientific Method
        a. Hypotheses
        b. Theories
    2. From Question to Evidence
    3. Types of Evidence
    4. Experimental Control
F. Using Statistics
G. What's Accepted and What's Debated
H. Social Responsibility
I. A Brief Encounter with Statistical Analysis

IMPORTANT CONCEPTS

	page
behavior	4
behaviorism	11
control group	21
correlation	25
correlation coefficient	25
dependent variable	21
descriptive evidence	20
deviation, standard and average	25
experimental evidence	21
experimental group	21
functionalism	9
Gestalt psychology	12
humanism	15
hypothesis	18
independent variable	21
introspection	9
mean	25
median	25
mode	28
operational definitions	18
organism	4
psychoanalysis	13
psychology	4
reliability	15
scientific method	15
structuralism	8
theory	18
validity	15
variable	21

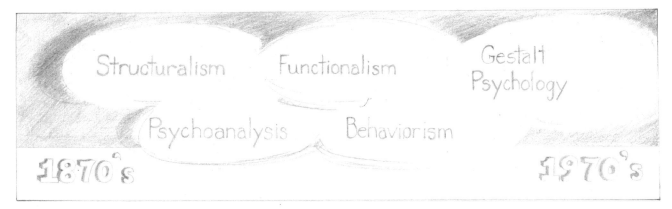

Psychology as an empirical science traces its roots back less than 100 years and has been strongly influenced by a number of historical schools of thought.

Today psychologists, no longer characterized by specific schools, pursue a broad range of interests.

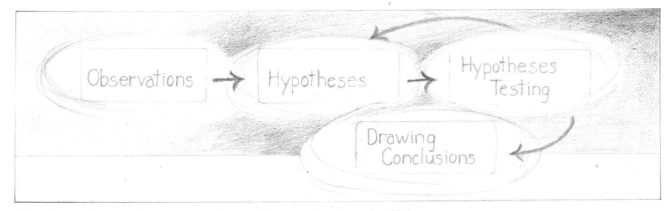

What all psychologists do have in common is a scientific approach to the study of behavior.

WHAT IS PSYCHOLOGY?

What images come to your mind when you hear the word "psychology"? Do you first think of people behaving abnormally? Or do you perhaps imagine people "using psychology" at carnivals, on automobile lots or in political campaigns? Or do you conceive of psychologists as running rats through mazes, or as learning "what makes people tick"?

Taken together, all these conceptions of psychology contain an element of truth. For example, one type of psychologist, called a clinical psychologist, is primarily concerned with treating mental disorders and personality problems. Another, the social psychologist, may specialize in investigating the sources of persuasion and social motivation. Salesmen persuading others to buy their products are applying techniques that may interest social psychologists. Experimental psychologists, comparative psychologists and learning theorists, among others, use a variety of animals to test their hypotheses. So the image of psychologists working with rats is also appropriate.

What all psychologists have in common is a basic training in the methods of finding out why animals, including humans, behave the way they do. Therefore, learning "what makes people tick" is probably the more accurate popular conception of psychology. A DEFINITION of psychology accepted by most psychologists is *the science of the behavior of organisms*.

Stated this way, the definition covers an extremely wide range of subject matter. As it is used in this definition, the term *organism* refers to any living animal, either human or subhuman. Basically, psychology is concerned with the behavior of human beings, but much about human behavior can be learned from studying the behavior of other organisms, including cats, monkeys, pigeons, chimpanzees, and even the lowly flatworm. Taken literally, psychology means the "science of the mind," but the word "mind" is difficult to define objectively. Contemporary psychologists usually find it more fruitful to talk about behavior. By *behavior*, psychologists mean, first of all, any observable activity of an organism. This includes the activity of muscles, glands and other body parts, as well as the total, organized, goal-directed behavior patterns that characterize an organism. But *behavior*, to most psychologists, also means observable mental processes, those processes such as thinking and emotional reactions that go on inside the organism and can be inferred from observable behavior.

Psychology, however, is not just a science, it is also a scholarly discipline, and a profession. The American Psychological Association in its publication, *A Career in Psychology*, describes the field as follows:

> Psychology is at one time a scholarly discipline, a scientific field, and a professional activity. Its overall focus is on the study of both animal and human behavior and related mental and physiological processes.
>
> As a *scholarly discipline*, psychology represents a major field of study in academic settings, with emphasis on the communication and explanation of principles and theories of behavior.
>
> As a *science*, it is a focus of research through which investigators collect, quantify, analyze and interpret data describing human and animal behavior, thus shedding light on the causes and dynamics of behavior patterns.
>
> As a *profession*, psychology involves the practical application of knowledge, skills and techniques for the solution or prevention of individual or social problems; the professional role also provides an opportunity for the psychologist to develop further his understanding of human behavior and thus to contribute to the science of psychology.

WHAT DO PSYCHOLOGISTS DO?

The discipline of psychology covers a remarkably broad range of interests. You will find psychologists in biochemistry laboratories, in school systems, in college classrooms, in clinics, in industry, in government—in virtually every area of human endeavor. (See Figure 1.) This is both one of the attractions of the field and one of the challenges in preparing a coherent introduction to it. One psychologist may be absorbed in the refinement of a laboratory technique while another is concerned solely with the problems of reducing international tensions: they may be so separated by the nature of their particular areas that neither appears even to be in the same field as the other. All psychologists do share the same basic interest in the explanation of behavior, but they pursue their interests at many different levels and from a variety of perspectives at each level.

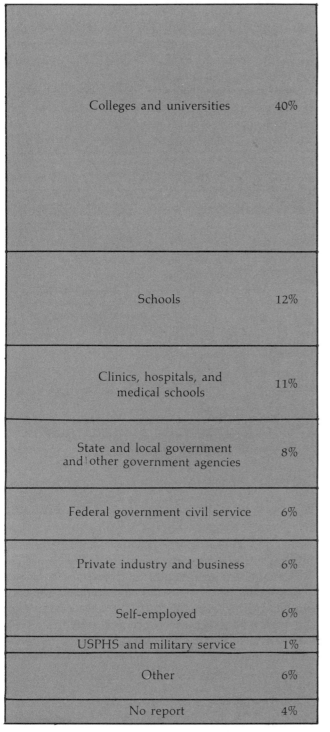

Figure 1. Employers of psychologists. Psychologists will be found in a wide range of occupations and employment settings. Source: A.P.A. *A Career in Psychology* 1971.

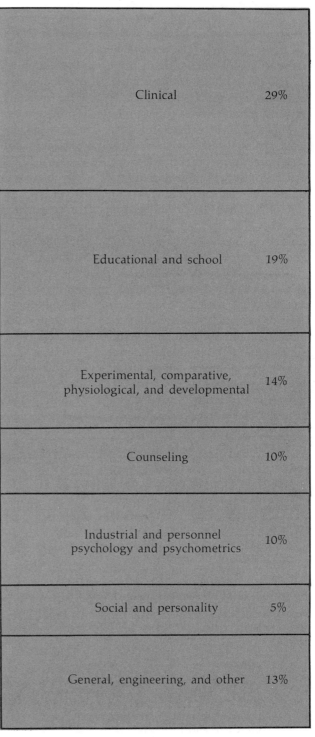

Figure 2. Subfields of psychology. Psychology is a broad discipline with many branches. Source: A.P.A. *A Career in Psychology* 1971.

As Figure 2 indicates, the greatest number of psychologists in any single field practice *clinical psychology*. After receiving their doctoral degrees, they usually serve at least a year's internship in an institution for individuals with severe psychological problems. This training prepares them to serve in mental hospitals, prisons, mental health clinics, schools for the retarded and juvenile corrective programs. The clinical psychologist may establish an office and engage in private practice. People often confuse the clinical psychologist with the psychiatrist. A psychiatrist is trained in medicine and holds an M.D. degree. He can, if he chooses, prescribe drugs or even perform surgery. The psychologist, on the other hand, is trained in methods of research and clinical practice and very rarely holds an M.D. along with his Ph.D.

Closely related to clinical psychology is *counseling and guidance psychology*. Professionals in these fields usually work with individuals who have some problems of personal or social adjustment. These psychologists are often consulted by individuals in need of educational or vocational guidance.

Educational psychologists are likely to do research on such problems as efficiency of learning, including motivation to learn. They usually work in university schools of education. *School psychologists* usually work directly with children, teachers and school administrators. They often give intelligence and other psychological tests and interpret the scores. They also work with problems of child behavior and often hold the Doctor of Education (Ed.D.) degree.

Experimental psychologists usually work in colleges or universities or in special laboratories where they carry on basic research concerned with behavior. Such work often involves the use of animals as

---

PSYCHOLOGIST IN A UNIVERSITY
Alan Stuart, Ph.D., *social psychologist* . . . Employed by a large state university as an associate professor of psychology, introduction to social psychology, group dynamics, and specialized topics of social psychology . . . Chairs departmental committees on undergraduate curriculum and graduate examinations . . . Sits on university committee on institutional goals . . . Is conducting research program on group reactions to the introduction of deviant members and supervising related thesis research of two master's degree students . . . Is member of dissertation committees of several doctoral candidates . . . Is consulting editor for the *Journal of Personality and Social Psychology*.

PSYCHOLOGIST IN COMMUNITY MENTAL HEALTH CLINIC
Peter Newman, Ph.D., *clinical psychologist* . . . Conducts individual and group psychotherapy . . . Meets in 50-minute sessions with several adults . . . Is co-therapist with two graduate students from a local university in group therapy sessions, one with adolescent boys, the other with three sets of parents . . . Confers with other psychologists and with psychiatrists and social workers on planning and evaluation of community programs . . . Maintains contact with representatives of school, correctional, and welfare systems . . . Collaborates with a psychiatrist in providing consultation of community committees evaluating preschool enrichment programs and studying riot prevention.

---

subjects (*comparative psychology*) and very precise instruments and techniques of research.

Social psychologists, as the name implies, are concerned with problems of behavior in social settings. They may be especially concerned with the child's learning to live with other children and with adults and his general intellectual and physical growth (*developmental psychology*). One area of special interest is the measurement and evaluation of the characteristics that make up the unique individual (*personality psychology*). Sometimes social psychologists work in the fields of public opinion surveys and market research.

Today considerable attention is being given to what might be called *environmental psychology*, which is

PSYCHOLOGIST IN UNIVERSITY
COUNSELING CENTER
Robert Franklin, Ph.D., counseling psychologist . . . Interviews and tests students
to assess ability, motivation, and interests
. . . Works intensively with students who
are having serious difficulty adjusting to
college or are experiencing emotional
problems which hamper their college
work . . . Conducts group meetings in
reading and study skills . . . Supervises
three interns enrolled in the university's
doctoral program in counseling psychology . . . Teaches undergraduate courses
in child psychology, psychology of personality, and tests and measurements . . .
Is faculty adviser to a group of student
volunteers in mental hospitals.

closely related to social psychology. Workers in this field are concerned with man's use of space. How does environment influence choice of locality for a home? What is the effect on behavior of prolonged sensory deprivation as man explores outer space and ocean depths? These psychologists are concerned with the general problem of ecology. Their field may be called *human ecology* or *behavioral ecology*.

Psychologists interested in the general area of business are often spoken of as *industrial psychologists*. They often work in personnel offices. Related specialties are called *consumer psychology* and *engineering psychology*.

Most of the qualified psychologists in the United States belong to the American Psychological Association (not to be confused with the American Psychiatric Association). The purpose of this organization is "to advance psychology as a science and as a means of promoting human welfare." It was founded in 1892 as a general organization of psychologists. Today, members may belong to various divisions, depending on their specialized interests. (See Figure 4.) The association encourages professional standards by awarding its diplomas to individuals who meet certain high standards of training and experience.

PSYCHOLOGIST IN PUBLIC
SCHOOL SYSTEM
Frank Wright, Ph.D., school psychologist
. . . Employed by an urban school system
of 6 high schools, 14 junior high schools,
and 45 elementary schools . . . Supervises
two psychologists who administer and
interpret individual tests and conduct a
standardized testing program for entire
system . . . Plans and conducts frequent
workshops for teachers on such skills
and techniques as effective classroom
management, diagnosis of learning
problems, and role playing . . . Acts as
consultant to system-wide committee
planning preschool programs for inner-
city children . . . Currently experimenting
with computer-assisted instruction in
1 elementary school and advising two
graduate students on related thesis
research.

PSYCHOLOGIST IN
INDUSTRIAL PLANT
Judith Simmons, Ph.D., industrial psychologist . . . Consults on selection and
placement of employees and training
of employment interviewers and personnel
specialists . . . Is conducting a study to
evaluate new interview techniques . . .
Confers with department heads, union
representatives, and foremen on criteria
for performance evaluation . . . Advises
management on questions of employee
morale . . . Supervises applied research
program to reduce accidents and worker
fatigue . . . Is developing a special training
program for workers from disadvantaged
backgrounds.

A BRIEF HISTORY OF PSYCHOLOGY

The efforts of mankind to understand human behavior may date back to the origin of the human
species. We can easily trace our curiosity and speculation about the behavior and mental activities of man

Divisions of the APA

The numerous interests and activities of psychologists are currently represented in the APA by 33 divisions.

1 General Psychology
2 Teaching of Psychology
3 Experimental Psychology
5 Evaluation and Measurement
6 Physiological and Comparative Psychology
7 Developmental Psychology
8 Personality and Social Psychology
9 The Society for the Psychological Study of Social Issues
10 Psychology and the Arts
12 Clinical Psychology
13 Consulting Psychology
14 Industrial and Organizational Psychology
15 Educational Psychology
16 School Psychology
17 Counseling Psychology
18 Psychologists in Public Service
19 Military Psychology
20 Adult Development and Aging
21 The Society of Engineering Psychologists
22 Psychological Aspects of Disability
23 Consumer Psychology
24 Philosophical Psychology
25 Experimental Analysis of Behavior
26 History of Psychology
27 Community Psychology
28 Psychopharmacology
29 Psychotherapy
30 Hypnosis
31 State Psychological Association Affairs
32 Humanistic Psychology
33 Mental Retardation
34 Population
35 Psychology of Women

Figure 4. Divisions of the American Psychological Association. There are currently 33 divisions in the A.P.A. which represent the numerous interests and activities of psychologists. Divisions 34 and 35 were added in 1974. (There is no Division 4 or 11.)

to the biblical writer who asked, "What is man that Thou art mindful of him?" Like all sciences, psychology developed from philosophy, which through the centuries had tried to understand the ultimate nature of the world.

Before the days of the scientific approach to psychology, the ancient philosophers were concerned with many of the same problems confronting psychologists today. As knowledge increased, persons who would formerly have been spoken of as philosophers came to be known as scientists.

The problem of the relationship of mind and body runs far back in history. Socrates, for example, believed that the one true kind of knowledge was knowledge of the self. Plato for the first time made a clear-cut distinction between mind and matter, but Aristotle found no sharp distinction between the two. Later, Rene Descartes (1596-1650) argued that there are two substances in the world and termed them "thinking substance" and "extended substance." He considered that these two interacted as mind and body.

Although it was the philosophers who laid the groundwork for the study of behavior, today's identification of psychology as an empirical science is most often associated with the opening of what was probably the first psychological laboratory by Wilhelm Wundt in Leipzig, Germany in 1879. (See Unit 24, Paying Attention.)

From the 1800s to the 1930s five important schools of psychology greatly influenced the development of the emerging science of psychology. These schools were: (1) structuralism (2) functionalism (3) psychoanalysis (4) behaviorism and (5) Gestalt psychology.

STRUCTURALISM

In 1874, Wilhelm Wundt (1832-1920), a professor of philosophy, published the landmark edition of *Physiological Psychology,* stating in the preface: "the work which I here present to the public is an attempt to mark out a new domain of science." Five years later he opened his laboratory.

Wundt proposed that the proper study of psychology should be man's conscious experience, and he argued that the basic approach of the new science should be, as with all other sciences, analysis. He reasoned that if you want to know what man's experience is, you ask him. He trained the subjects at

Figure 5. Wilhelm Wundt (1832–1920), the first scientist to devote himself almost exclusively to psychological research. Through his extensive, methodological research on a wide range of sensory experience, he helped gain acceptance of psychology as a science and influenced the founding of structuralism.

Figure 6. E. B. Titchener (1867–1927), considered the founder of the structuralist school of psychology. He was greatly influenced by his years of work with Wundt. He trained subjects to analyze their own sensory experience through the method of introspection. He strongly opposed the functionalist approach.

his laboratory to analyze their conscious experiences into smaller, more basic elements, so that he might then examine these elements to see how they fit into a "composite psychical compound." He postulated that these experiences consisted of sensations, images and feelings of which only the person himself is aware. *Structuralism* as a system of psychological study grew out of Wundt's work.

Edward Titchener (1867-1927), a British psychologist, is considered the founder of the structuralist school of psychology. He studied for his Ph.D. under Wundt at Leipzig and introduced structuralism to the United States at Cornell where he taught for thirty-five years. He, like Wundt and the growing ranks of other structuralists throughout Germany, England and America, studied the contents of the conscious experience of the mind through a method known as *introspection*. According to these structuralists, introspection required the dispassionate analysis and reporting of one's own conscious experience at a given time after stimulation by some object or event.

FUNCTIONALISM

Prior to and during the development of structuralism, the scientific world was reformulating some of its traditional ideas about the behavior of organisms. The publication in 1859 of Charles Darwin's (1809-1882) *Origin of Species* profoundly influenced the course of thinking in almost every scientific discipline. Perhaps most significant for psychology was Darwin's *principle of natural selection:* those organisms survive that are best adapted to their environment and its requirements for living. By emphasizing the organism's ability *to adapt* to its environment, he focused attention on the adaptive value of man's own behavior and mental activity as well as on individual differences among members of a species. (See Unit 17, Signs of Emotion.)

It was this emphasis on the individual organism's responses to its environment that laid the groundwork for *functionalism*, which developed in opposition to structuralism. Where structuralists concerned themselves with what composed the mind (the elements of consciousness), functionalists studied *why*

Figure 7. Charles Darwin (1809–1882), through his evolutionary theories changed the course of thinking in almost every scientific discipline. His emphasis on the capacity of an organism to function effectively in order to survive considerably influenced the development of functionalism.

Figure 8. William James (1842–1910), while convinced that the goal of psychology was the study of consciousness, rejected the notion that this could be accomplished by structuralism's attempts to reduce the mind to elements. He regarded consciousness as an ongoing process or stream in continuous interaction with the environment. Through his writings, he had profound impact on the development of the functionalist school.

and *how* the mind worked, and argued that the mind was the most important organ for man's adaptation to his environment.

Perhaps the most important precursor of the functionalist school was William James (1842-1910). Regarded by many as the greatest of American psychologists, James' practical or functional approach to the study of the mind derived from Darwin's theory of evolution. He believed that consciousness had developed like all other human functions, to aid the human species in its fight for survival. James stated that while the goal of psychology was the study of consciousness, this could not be accomplished as the structuralists suggested, by reducing the mind to elements. Rather, consciousness must be regarded as an ongoing process or stream. The mind, as expressed in habits, learning and perception, is in continuous interaction with the environment; its primary purpose is to facilitate adjustment to the environment. James

rejected the attempts of Titchener and the structuralists to subject human consciousness to scientific analysis.

James described human consciousness as having four characteristics. First, it is highly personal and unique to each individual. Second, it is forever changing. Because mind is a cumulative process, it is modified by each new sensory experience. Therefore, should the same sensory experiences recur, the mind that confronts it is not the same as it was previously. Third, it is continuous: changes in consciousness do not occur suddenly, but evolve over time. Finally, James held that consciousness is selective, choosing from the environment on the basis of what is most "relevant" to the organism's adaptation.

John Dewey (1859-1952), who was considerably influenced by the writings of William James and Charles Darwin, is generally regarded as the individual most responsible for establishing functionalism as a movement in American psychology. Originally trained in philosophy, he became increasingly convinced that philosophy must concern itself with man as he struggles for survival in the environment. His article on the reflex arc, published in 1896, attacked the views of Wundt and Titchener. He claimed that human experience cannot be understood by attempting to reduce it to ever simpler and more basic units. Dewey maintained that the reflex was an indivisibly integrated unit, comprised of a stimulus and a response, neither part of which had any function without the other. He went on to state that the reflex, like all other forms of behavior and experience, should be interpreted in terms of its significance for human adaptation. In establishing these principles, Dewey set forth the first statement of the functionalist doctrine.

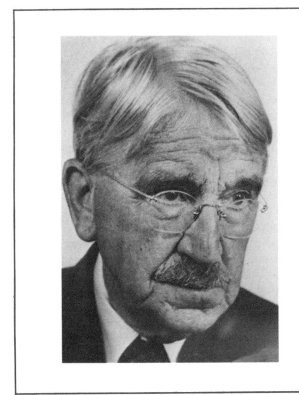

Figure 9. John Dewey (1859–1952) is generally regarded as the individual most responsible for establishing functionalism as a movement in American psychology. Through his work, he changed the direction of psychology from academic and abstract to practical and functional. His work has had a profound impact on American education.

Although functionalists did not entirely reject the introspective methods of the structuralists, their emphasis was more on objective testing of theories. Functionalism as a well-defined school of psychology no longer exists, but its point of view greatly influenced the development of scientific psychology.

To indicate the influence of the functionalists in psychology, it is interesting to note that William James was president of the American Psychological Association in 1894 and 1904, and John Dewey was president in 1899.

BEHAVIORISM

In 1906, Ivan Pavlov, a Russian physiologist, addressed the Charing Cross Medical School in London. (See Unit 26, Pavlovian Conditioning.)The title of that address, one of the most significant events in modern experimental psychology, was *Scientific Study of the So-called Psychical Processes in the Higher Animals.* There Pavlov described how he measured the amount of saliva secreted by a dog whenever the dog was signaled that food would come to its mouth. Pavlov had experimentally measured observable behavior, drops of saliva, rather than the dog's mental content, its expectation. This provided the impetus for John B. Watson (1878-1958), who received his Ph.D. under Dewey at the University of Chicago, to start the *behaviorist* movement. Although he approved of the functionalists' concern for responsiveness to the environment, he felt that there was no place for mentalism in science. In 1913 he published an article called *Psychology as the Behaviorist Views It.* He wrote, "The time seems to have come when psychology must discard all reference to consciousness; when it need no longer delude itself into thinking that it is making mental states the object of observation . . . there is no longer any guarantee that we all mean the same thing when we use the terms now current in psychology. . . . I believe we can write a psychology and never go back on our definition. Never use the terms of habit formation, habit integration and the like . . . In a system of psychology completely worked out, given the stimuli, the response can be predicted." Watson would take a *stimulus-response approach,* believing only objective, observable behavior to be the proper study of psychology.

Figure 10. John B. Watson (1878–1958) was the father of what has come to be known as the "behaviorist revolt." He declared that psychology should be limited to the study of behavior and concern itself with stimulus-response connections. He stressed objective methods of measurement. His impact on psychology is most prominent today in the work of B. F. Skinner, who has greatly expanded and popularized Watson's behavioristic theories.

Following the turn of the century, this image of science as measuring only the observable, such as the substance in a test tube, was obviously *too* limiting for the interests of psychologists. Watson had to expand the current concept of what observable behavior consisted of. This gave rise to an emphasis on implicit behavior: secretions of glands, nerve impulses, small contractions of muscles that could be measured only with special instruments, etc. Watson measured small movements of the larynx, tongue and lips. His study of such small units of behavior was similar to the structuralists' in this respect. Where the structuralists were interested in combinations of sensations, the behaviorists studied combinations of conditioned reflexes. Watson eventually came to study the activity of the mind, a word he threw out of his dictionary by defining thinking as "implicit speech movements."

In 1915, Watson became president of the American Psychological Association.

GESTALT PSYCHOLOGY

While functionalism and behaviorism were thriving in America, structuralism was still strong in Germany. But several German psychologists were concerned about the multitude of problems that simply could not be handled by combining small elements. Their battle cry became, "the whole is more than the sum of its parts." They became known as *Gestaltists,* from the German word *Gestalt* which means "form" or "configuration" and refers to their emphasis on the entire new pattern that emerges when an organism perceives or responds to the environment.

Although the Gestalt point of view was primarily a reaction against the piecemeal approach to consciousness of the structuralists, it also absorbed contemporary functionalism's concern for responding to the environment and protested as well against behaviorism's revival of the small unit for analysis.

Gestalt psychology's leaders were Max Wertheimer (1880-1943) (See Unit 23, Perceiving), Kurt Koffka (1887-1967) and Wolfgang Kohler (1887-1967) (See Unit 18, Problem Solving and Creativity). Although he was not one of the original founders, Kurt Lewin (1890-1947) is often considered one of the principal figures in this movement (See Unit 9, Groups and Leaders). Wertheimer was concerned with the perception of apparent movement, as when our perception of a sequence of still pictures gives rise to the illusion of moving pictures. Koffka, the chief spokesman for the Gestaltists, developed the Gestalt laws of organization and published the definitive statement of their position in a 1922 article for the *Psychological Bulletin.* Kohler was interested in the phenomenon of transposition, whereby we can recognize a melody even if it is transposed to a new key. This concern for the configuration that arises from the *relationship* among stimuli was an important contribution to our understanding of problem solving. Lewin's contribution was in the area of relationships among people in groups, and he developed his theory of group dynamics into a complex mathematical or "topological" theory of human motivation.

All of these Gestalt leaders fled from Nazi Germany to America where they contributed mightily to the rise of psychology as an experimental discipline. In 1959, at the age of 72, Wolfgang Kohler became president of the American Psychological Association.

New ideas about individual differences would also come from a doctor in Vienna. In 1896 the word "psychoanalysis" was first used to name a form of treatment for mental patients. Since psychoanalysis was originally conceived of as a medical treatment, its effect on the experimental disciplines was not felt until much later, when it had developed into a general theory of personality.

The moving force behind psychoanalysis, both as treatment and as a personality theory, was Sigmund Freud (1856-1939). (See Units 6, Sexuality; 15, Personality; 20, Therapy for Individuals.) Where the structuralists were satisfied to *describe* human consciousness, Freud explored the root causes, daring even to suggest that we are motivated by *unconscious* forces which are not easily retrieved through ordinary introspective means. The techniques of the therapy included free association and the interpretation of dreams. The theory emphasized forgotten childhood experiences and sexual conflicts.

Freud's ideas were shocking to many medical prac-

titioners, and he was not widely accepted. Recognition of his theories in the academic world came in 1909 when he was invited to give a series of lectures at Clark University in Massachusetts. One year later the International Psychoanalytic Association was founded.

The concepts of psychoanalysis foreshadowed the concern for individual differences that would develop among the functionalists, the concern for "the whole person" that was later to develop among the Gestaltists, and for the notion that mental disorders can be described in terms of cause and effect that was to influence all of psychology.

TODAY'S PSYCHOLOGY

The influence of each of these historical movements is still felt today. Structuralism's introspection and mentalism have been cautiously revived, tempered by behaviorism's insistence upon objective definitions and functionalism's interaction with the environment. Evolutionary theory may be seen in the animal laboratories and in speculative theories about continuity among the species. Behaviorism's influence is especially strong in modern psychotechnology, especially in the practice of behavior modification (See Unit 27, Operant Conditioning) and in social learning theory (See Units 3, Helping Others; 4, Hurting Others; 5, Morality; 13, The Disordered Mind). The influence of Gestalt psychology remains in our concepts of perceiving, problem-solving, memory and group dynamics. Psychoanalytic therapy is barely breathing in its orthodox form, but the theory pervades most of psychology, either in provoking active rejection or eager acceptance. Perhaps the greatest contribution of psychoanalysis is in the multitude of hypotheses it still generates and in the research that follows the hypotheses. Functionalism's concern for the relationship between the organism and the environment also pervades most of psychology and has had a profound effect on our educational systems.

All of these "isms" have been fairly well integrated into modern psychology. No longer characterized by specific schools of thought, psychology is divided today into specialties such as social psychology, educational psychology, clinical psychology and physiological psychology.

Figure 11. Sigmund Freud (1856–1939), shown in this photo (bottom left), taken in 1909 at Clark University, with G. Stanley Hall, Carl Jung (front row) and A. A. Brill, Ernest Jones and Sandor Ferenczi (back row), is generally considered the founder of psychoanalysis.

THE BACKGROUND INFLUENCES IN CURRENT PSYCHOLOGY

APA PRESIDENT

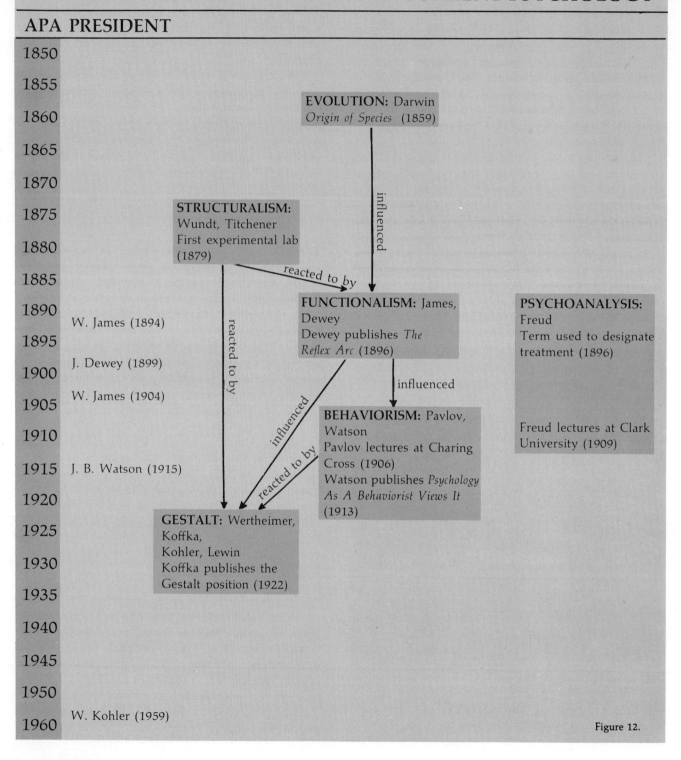

1850
1855
1860
1865
1870
1875
1880
1885
1890
1895
1900
1905
1910
1915
1920
1925
1930
1935
1940
1945
1950
1960

W. James (1894)

J. Dewey (1899)

W. James (1904)

J. B. Watson (1915)

W. Kohler (1959)

EVOLUTION: Darwin
Origin of Species (1859)

influenced

STRUCTURALISM:
Wundt, Titchener
First experimental lab
(1879)

reacted to by

reacted to by

FUNCTIONALISM: James,
Dewey
Dewey publishes *The Reflex Arc* (1896)

influenced

influenced

reacted to by

BEHAVIORISM: Pavlov,
Watson
Pavlov lectures at Charing
Cross (1906)
Watson publishes *Psychology As A Behaviorist Views It* (1913)

GESTALT: Wertheimer,
Koffka,
Kohler, Lewin
Koffka publishes the
Gestalt position (1922)

PSYCHOANALYSIS:
Freud
Term used to designate
treatment (1896)

Freud lectures at Clark
University (1909)

Figure 12.

HUMANISM

The humanistic movement, representing an approach rather than a school, is rather strong today. It has its own division within the American Psychological Association and its own association which meets annually. Humanism is considered a third force because it rejects the powerful influences of behaviorism and psychoanalysis. It quarrels with their determinism, their emphasis on controlling factors in human behavior which, the humanists claim, neglect people's acceptance of responsibility for their own destinies.

The influence of humanism may be seen in our current theories of helping behavior (Unit 3), personality (Unit 15) and motivation (Unit 21).

In a 1971 article in *The Humanist*, Floyd Matson wrote: "Whereas behaviorism placed all its stress upon the external environment (that is, upon stimuli from the outer world) as the controlling factor in behavior, psychoanalysis placed its emphasis upon the internal environment (upon stimuli from within, in the form of drives and instincts)." His explanation of what humanistic psychology is:

> Humanistic psychology tries to tell it not like it is, but like it ought to be. It seeks to bring psychology back to its source, to the *psyche,* where it all began and where it finally culminates. But there is more to it than that. Humanistic psychology is not just the study of "human being"; it is a commitment to human becoming.

THE METHOD OF PSYCHOLOGY

The aim of any science, whether psychology, biology, physics or sociology is the acquisition of knowledge about the world. Yet to study the world is difficult, for the subject matter is full of highly variable factors, factors so closely interrelated that alterations in any one are likely to affect the nature of others.

Like all sciences, psychology generally begins with *observation.* Correct observation is a most difficult task. Few of us observe correctly, because we are unconsciously biased. We tend to see what we *want* to see or what we think we *ought* to see. Past experience, "common sense," or our relationships with others can be subtle obstacles to correct observation. For instance, if we are convinced, because of our past experience or because someone has told us so, that a

person is basically "good," we are likely to find that, indeed, that person is good. On the other hand, if we are convinced that a person is basically evil, we are likely to observe that person's behavior as evil. To complicate our observation, people tend to behave in accordance with how they perceive our convictions, providing yet additional evidence to support those convictions. It is extremely hard to get rid of such unconscious bias and to see just what is there, no more and no less.

Psychology's task as a science is to seek out principles of behavior that exist independently of our individual experience and that are untainted by unconscious biases.

THE SCIENTIFIC METHOD

The *scientific method* is the process that allows psychologists to do this. Through the scientific method, science makes a deliberate attempt to come to agreement about how things really are. However, scientists do not go around constantly nodding their heads in agreement. The scientific process of knowing is just that, a process. It is *not a final knowing.*

What distinguishes scientific knowledge from personal opinion is a *prearranged agreement that criteria, external to the individual and communicable to others, must be established for each set of observations referred to as fact.* Thus, in order to bring observations out of the realm of personal opinion and into the realm of fact, the standards for any judgment about the observations must be agreed to beforehand. We refer to such a judgment as *valid.*

If several other people, conforming to the same standards, are able to make the same judgment about the observations, we consider the judgment *reliable.* Validity and reliability are the important characteristics of knowledge that tend to lead to agreement.

One psychologist, Filmore Sanford, has defined fact as *"an agreed-upon perceptual relation between an observer and an event."* This definition makes fact an agreement about an observation. It says nothing about truth or reality. It is, in essence, a statement of limitations, a statement defining the process by which some of us have agreed to obtain knowledge. This definition implies that *absolute* truth is outside the realm of science, that science deals with *relative* truth. It is an acknowledgment of limitations.

Figure 13. What do you see? To test your observation powers, look at the rather familiar scene above and then try answering the questions below. You'll find the answers at the bottom of the page, and you may be surprised to find that you see more in the scene than is actually there.

Which of the following statements is true, false, or cannot be answered based on the information presented?

	T	F	?
1. The Danford family owns a TV set.	( )	( )	( )
2. There are four people in the room.	( )	( )	( )
3. They have a pet dog.	( )	( )	( )
4. Mrs. Danford is a blond.	( )	( )	( )
5. They are watching an evening television program.	( )	( )	( )
6. The Danfords have two children.	( )	( )	( )
7. The father is reading the newspaper.	( )	( )	( )

In many ways the legal process of obtaining knowledge is similar to the scientific process. It is an attempt to establish agreement among observers. The available evidence is presented, and then a number of individuals (the jury) attempt to come to agreement on what the evidence indicates. Having established the criteria for judgment, the juror's verdict is an agreement on truth beyond a reasonable doubt. The juror, like the scientist, reports on what is *believed* to be the truth.

In 1974 Americans were exposed to this legal process of attempting to establish facts as the House Judiciary Committee held its proceedings on the impeachment of Richard Nixon. These proceedings were the first step in the legal process. The roll call votes of the members of the committee represented their effort to establish the criteria for judgment. The articles for impeachment were the agreed-upon criteria for judgment, necessarily preliminary to any final judgment.

The special characteristics of both the legal and scientific process provide the greatest possible opportunity for cautious, skeptical people to arrive at an agreement and so establish "facts" upon which to build still more "facts." These same characteristics

The picture does not provide enough information to answer True or False to any of the statements. Therefore, all the answers should be question marks.

COMMITTEE ON THE JUDICIARY
HOUSE OF REPRESENTATIVES
93D CONGRESS
ROLL CALL
ARTICLE 1

REPUBLICANS	Ayes	Nays	DEMOCRATS	Ayes	Nays
Mr. Hutchinson		X	Mr. Donohue	✓	
Mr. McClory		X	Mr. Brooks	✓	
Mr. Smith		X	Mr. Kastenmeier	✓	
Mr. Sandman		X	Mr. Edwards	✓	
Mr. Railsback	✓		Mr. Hungate	✓	
Mr. Wiggins		X	Mr. Conyers	✓	
Mr. Dennis		X	Mr. Eilberg	✓	
Mr. Fish	✓		Mr. Waldie	✓	
Mr. Mayne		X	Mr. Flowers	✓	
Mr. Hogan	✓		Mr. Mann	✓	
Mr. Butler	✓		Mr. Sarbanes	✓	
Mr. Cohen	✓		Mr. Seiberling	✓	
Mr. Lott		X	Mr. Danielson	✓	
Mr. Froehlich	✓		Mr. Drinan	✓	
Mr. Moorhead		X	Mr. Rangel	✓	
Mr. Maraziti		X	Ms. Jordan	✓	
Mr. Latta		X	Mr. Thornton	✓	
			Ms. Holtzman	✓	
	6	11	Mr. Owens	✓	
			Mr. Mezvinsky	✓	
			Mr. Rodino, *Chairman*	✓	
				21	0
Total				27	11

Figure 14. This roll call vote of the House Committee on the Judiciary was an example of the legal process of coming to agreement on the criteria for judgment to determine if Richard Nixon had committed impeachable offenses.

From *Herblock Special Report* (W. W. Norton and Company, Inc., 1974).

© Herblock in The Washington Post

The other cover-up

Figure 15. An example of observational bias. In the legal process, as in the experimental process, we must guard against biases which can affect the way we observe.

extend the scientist's means of learning about the world beyond the way of knowing called "common sense."

Common sense observation tells us, after all, that the world is flat and that the sun revolves around the earth. Common sense is the method of explaining reality that is confined by and to our own viewpoint. The scientific process is a strategy designed to extend beyond the limits of mere common sense, and to minimize errors made by individual observers. We must take particular care when we wish to observe ourselves.

Let us consider how this strategy develops. Scientists ask questions, and psychologists ask questions about behavior. A scientifically productive question produces hypotheses and specifies observations that generate answers. These answers should permit an interested person to agree or disagree about their validity and meaning. Most of us view the world and observe how events seem to fit together in some meaningful way. We may accept these perceived relationships as "truth" or "fact," or we may be more tentative and accept them only as a more personal *hunch.* Sometimes we call this feeling intuition.

1. The Study of Psychology   **17**

HYPOTHESES

The scientist usually gets his ideas in much the same way, but he distrusts the finality of his hunch. Instead, he makes a statement of probability. He may say, "I'll *bet* that hair color and personality are related." His statement implies his awareness of the possibility that he may be wrong and that he is prepared to test this possibility. The scientist may search further for some organization in the relationship. He may decide to bet that the genetic structures responsible for hair color are also responsible for personality characteristics. Stated in this organized fashion, his hunch has been developed into a *hypothesis. A hypothesis is a hunch or educated guess stated in a way that can be tested.* A hypothesis may be stated in a variety of ways, but the most testable form is a statement of relationship between variables (any changeable characteristics or conditions) that can be tested. If an event is not directly observable, then the variables must be defined by the operations by which they will be measured. These definitions are referred to as *operational definitions.* For example, "intelligence" may be operationally defined as a score on an IQ test, and "excitability" may be defined as sudden shifts in activity of the autonomic nervous system.

"Remember, son, if at first you don't succeed, re-evaluate the situation, draw up various hypotheses for your failure, choose reasonable corrective measures, and try, try again."

Figure 16. The scientific method is a continuing process of hypothesis testing.

The scientist now can generate a number of related hypotheses. In order, from the least precise to the most precise, they are: 1. hair color and personality are related; 2. the genetic structures responsible for hair color are also responsible for personality characteristics; 3. the genetic structure responsible for hair color is also responsible for the activity of the autonomic nervous system.

THEORIES

Stated as precisely as possible, known facts can help the observer look for highly specific relationships. Now let us suppose that investigation eventually provides evidence to support the hypothesis in question. But the evidence is so specific that, at best, it supports only a small part of the more general statement. Precision has its price. When many related hypotheses at various levels of precision are supported by the evidence, we are fairly confident that the most general statement is being supported. When some hypotheses are supported and others are not, we may have enough information to revise the most general, least precise statement. These very general statements, which are more useful in generating research, are called *theories.* There is a continuum between theory and hypothesis. Sometimes a theory can be distinguished from a hypothesis only by asking, "Is this statement being used to generate more hypotheses or does it lead directly to research?"

This process of making and testing hypotheses is a strategy used by psychologists for getting information. A theoretical or hypothetical statement helps to develop agreement, and therefore it is useful. But this strategy is also limited and leaves out something vital. We employ comparisons because they have utility. But they remain comparisons—X is *like* Y—and not identifications—X *is* Y. The observer must be constantly aware that he is delicately balancing the utility of his strategy against its limitations. If he loses sight of this delicate balance, his answers become inappropriate to his question.

In this book, similar hypotheses may appear in a number of locations. For example, the *locus of control* hypothesis appears several times in response to different questions. Each time, it is stated so that it may generate information pertinent to a specific question. It is therefore appropriate to consider each hypothesis specifically in terms of the question which generated it.

We have stated our hypotheses so that they will be oriented toward existing evidence. Most hypotheses are designed to make new observations rather than to examine observations that have already been made. However, it is also a common procedure to search the professional journals for investigations already made before launching a new investigation. This is what we have done. It may be reasonable to consider this book an initial search of the literature, designed to stimulate your search for further evidence.

Still, they are not quite specific enough to obtain direct evidence. It is now necessary to specify what operations will be used to make measurable observations and thereby provide appropriate scientific evidence for these hypotheses.

The progression from question to evidence is from the abstract to the concrete. Because concrete statements cover less than highly abstract statements, it takes a great variety of evidence to cover most hypotheses and most questions. The productivity of a question—or a theory, for that matter—may be measured by the number of hypotheses and consequent

QUESTION   1. HOW DO OUR BELIEFS AFFECT OUR OWN AND OTHERS' BEHAVIOR?

HYPOTHESES	LOCUS OF CONTROL	EXPECTANCY FOR ACHIEVEMENT	SOCIAL ATTRACTION
DESCRIPTIVE EVIDENCE	ASSESS: relation between locus of control and academic achievement		
EXPERIMENTAL EVIDENCE		VARY: teacher expectations MEASURE: students' academic performance	VARY: impressions of like or dislike MEASURE: attitudes, cooperative responses

This is an example of an *evigram*, used throughout the text as a summarizing device. For each question, the hypotheses discussed within the text are presented, and evidence classified either descriptive or experimental is summarized.

FROM QUESTION TO EVIDENCE

The following are examples, taken from Unit 2, of hypotheses that might lead to some evidence bearing on our initial question:

QUESTION: How do our beliefs affect our own and others' behavior?

HYPOTHESES: locus of control; expectancy for achievement.

The *locus-of-control hypothesis* states that people who believe they are in control of the events in their own lives are more likely to achieve high performance than people who believe their lives are controlled by luck or by other people.

The *expectancy-for-achievement hypothesis* states that expectations held by administrators will direct the quality of achievement of those whose performance they administer.

Both of these hypotheses are more concrete and specific than the question from which they derive.

amount of evidence it produces. You will note that the two hypotheses above are quite independent of one another. However, the various hypotheses designed to answer questions need not be mutually exclusive.

Throughout this book, the hypotheses deriving from a question usually complement one another, providing varieties of evidence. It is a common scientific practice, however, also to develop mutually exclusive hypotheses. The debates that follow from the development of hypotheses that are antagonistic to one another strengthen the learning process and provide much of the excitement in science.

Although we chose to emphasize variety rather than sets of alternative hypotheses in this book in order to provide a wider scope of psychological information, you should not forget that evidence is rarely considered conclusive, and constant reinter-

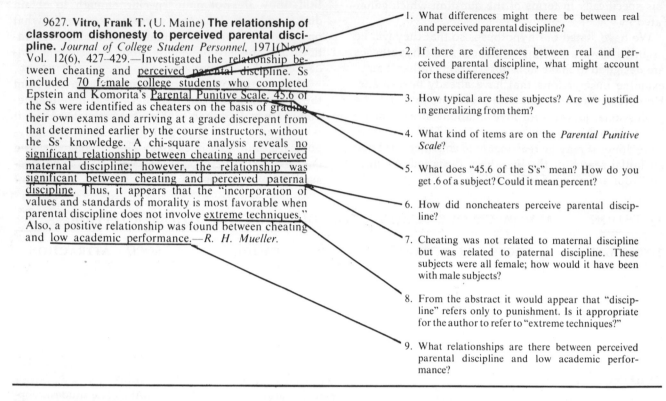

9627. **Vitro, Frank T.** (U. Maine) **The relationship of classroom dishonesty to perceived parental discipline.** *Journal of College Student Personnel,* 1971(Nov), Vol. 12(6), 427–429.—Investigated the relationship between cheating and perceived parental discipline. Ss included 70 female college students who completed Epstein and Komorita's Parental Punitive Scale. 45.6 of the Ss were identified as cheaters on the basis of grading their own exams and arriving at a grade discrepant from that determined earlier by the course instructors, without the Ss' knowledge. A chi-square analysis reveals no significant relationship between cheating and perceived maternal discipline; however, the relationship was significant between cheating and perceived paternal discipline. Thus, it appears that the "incorporation of values and standards of morality is most favorable when parental discipline does not involve extreme techniques." Also, a positive relationship was found between cheating and low academic performance.—*R. H. Mueller.*

1. What differences might there be between real and perceived parental discipline?

2. If there are differences between real and perceived parental discipline, what might account for these differences?

3. How typical are these subjects? Are we justified in generalizing from them?

4. What kind of items are on the *Parental Punitive Scale*?

5. What does "45.6 of the S's" mean? How do you get .6 of a subject? Could it mean percent?

6. How did noncheaters perceive parental discipline?

7. Cheating was not related to maternal discipline but was related to paternal discipline. These subjects were all female; how would it have been with male subjects?

8. From the abstract it would appear that "discipline" refers only to punishment. Is it appropriate for the author to refer to "extreme techniques?"

9. What relationships are there between perceived parental discipline and low academic performance?

Figure 17. A textbook can report original investigations only in abbreviated form. When we attempt to review the literature on specific investigations, we use a kind of catalogue to find the original reports. The catalogue for most psychological literature is called *Psychological Abstracts* which contains summaries of investigations reported in psychological journals. These abstracts are similar to the summaries of investigations in this book, except for the terminology which allows more information to be condensed into a smaller space.

This is an example of one of these abstracts, along with questions a reader might ask to find more information. Compare this abstract with a summary of the same study in Unit 5, Morality. Developing skills in raising this type of question is an initial step in learning to evaluate evidence from scientific journals as well as from the news media.

pretation is the essence of the scientific process. In fact, some scientists consider that genuine proof in science does not exist because better explanations may be forthcoming at any time. The strongest kind of inference occurs when a number of alternative and mutually exclusive hypotheses are made for the same questions. In this way, the acceptance of some hypotheses and the rejection of others reinforce each other in terms of the inferences that can be made.

TYPES OF EVIDENCE

We may roughly divide the various kinds of evidence into descriptive on the one hand and experimental on the other. Some topics seem to lend themselves predominantly to one kind of evidence.

Descriptive evidence includes uncontrolled studies that allow one to assess the degree of relationship between variables but provide little insight into which variables are the cause and which the effect. *Surveys,* for example, that may involve, among other things, a kind of census taking or measurement of attitudes, generally involve the observation and measurement of two or more variables (for example, income level and voting preference) to see how closely changes in one variable may be predicted by changes in the other. The stronger the observed relationship, the better the prediction. Descriptive evidence may also include *naturalistic observation* and the *case study* approach. Field observations of both animal and human behavior can be valuable starting points for more sophisticated types of research, and case studies or clinical observations of individuals can also be important sources of data and hypothesis generation.

Koniček-Kaufman

"KEEP AN EYE ON THE KIDS FOR AWHILE, WILL YOU, JEAN?"

Figure 18. Much psychological research begins in a naturalistic setting. Jean Piaget began his work by observing his own children.

Experimental evidence includes studies where conditions are carefully controlled and measurements taken in a way that permits cause-and-effect relationships among variables to be inferred. An experiment involves arranging for something to happen and observing the effect on something specific. More precisely, what the researcher arranges to happen beforehand through experimental manipulation is called the *independent variable*, and what he observes later on is called the *dependent variable*. In designing an experiment to test a hypothesis, one must decide exactly how he will *vary* the independent variable and how he will *measure* the dependent variable. The hope is that at the conclusion of the experiment it will be reasonable to infer that the independent variable caused the dependent variable to change as the hypothesis predicted.

EXPERIMENTAL CONTROL

An essential part of any experiment that enables inferences to be made about causation is *experimental control*. One wants to isolate just the variable under investigation while holding all other variables constant. The ability to control extraneous variables is the major distinction between evidence generated experi-

mentally and evidence derived through descriptive techniques. To produce this needed control, both an *experimental group* (which is usually subjected to some special treatment) and a *control group* (which does not receive this special experimental treatment) are used. A control group consists of subjects who are as similar as possible to the subjects in the experiment group and whose treatment differs only in the manner designated by the independent variable.

In some studies, the *same* subjects are used to compare both control and experimental conditions, and the sequence of conditions is randomized.

Using these procedures, differences in the dependent variable between the two groups or conditions may be attributed to the manipulation of the independent variable.

Since we have information about conditions under which the differences do *not* occur (control conditions), we can infer what *did* cause the differences to occur.

Because we cannot ethically manipulate such variables as intelligence or genes or infantile malnutrition or chronic severe stress in humans, we use lower animals for many experimental studies that follow from descriptive investigations with humans. As you read you will occasionally find that very similar studies are called *descriptive* when they are done with humans and *experimental* when they are done with lower animals. This is because some variables can only be measured in humans while they can be deliberately manipulated in lower animals. For example, a researcher may note that in humans, exposure to certain kinds of stress is consistently associated with ulcers. It is unlikely, however, that he will be able to measure these relationships in enough varied circumstances to determine whether ulcer-prone people tend to get themselves into stressful situations or whether the stressful situations cause ulcers. He can, however, control the complete life histories of lower animals and then subject them to stressful situations (as discussed in Unit 28, Stress and Anxiety). The amount of ulceration in experimental animals is then compared with the amount of ulceration in control animals.

Another common problem in research on behavior is that the causative agent for a phenomenon might involve a complex cluster of variables, and the experimental isolation of single variables might obscure the phenomenon. Ulcers, for example, might result from

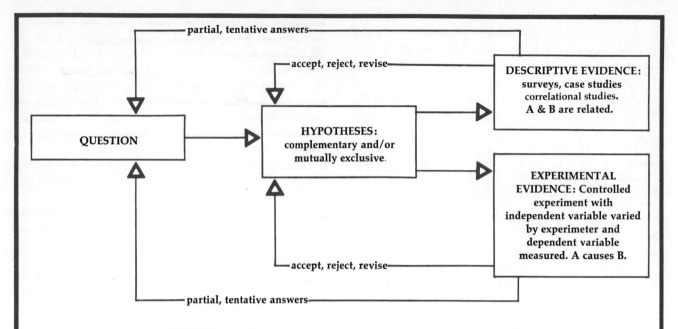

PUTTING IT TOGETHER: The Scientific Method

The flow diagram above describes the relationships among questions, hypotheses and evidence as they are treated in the evigrams throughout this book. First, a basic *question* is asked. Then *hypotheses* are developed to generate evidence that will serve in some way to answer the initial question. When a number of hypotheses are developed from a single question, they may complement each other so that enough evidence may be generated to provide a fuller range of answers than any single hypothesis could generate. Sometimes, hypotheses might be mutually exclusive, in which case the evidence would indicate that one hypothesis might be acceptable and other hypotheses might be unacceptable, providing stronger evidence on which to base conclusions.

Descriptive evidence includes a number of ways of observing how variables may be related. As a rule, it involves careful observations of variables which vary in nature but are not specifically varied by the researcher. However, studies are considered to provide descriptive evidence when some variables are manipulated by the researcher but no controlled comparisons are made. Descriptive evidence indicates that variables are related but does not indicate what causes what to happen.

Experimental evidence comes from a controlled study in which the researcher varies the independent variables, measures the dependent variable and compares the measurement obtained under a variety of conditions. Since experimental evidence gives information about circumstances under which some variables do not change, as well as those under which they do change, it allows us to infer which variables cause others to change.

When statistical analysis indicates that measured differences are probably not due to chance, both the descriptive and experimental evidence are useful for indicating whether it is appropriate to accept the hypotheses generating the evidence. When the analysis indicates that hypotheses should be rejected, the usual procedure is to revise hypotheses until the evidence allows the researcher to accept them.

Since questions are usually stated in abstract or general terms, and since research evidence is usually quite specific, only partial, tentative answers are obtained. These complex relationships among questions, hypotheses and evidence are responsible for the ongoing, continuous process of information-seeking that rarely yields final answers.

a combination of genetic predisposition, infantile experience, motivation and specific situation. Isolating any one of these variables might give us irrelevant information. Frequently, irrelevance is the price we pay for precision.

Descriptive and experimental evidence deserve equal respect, but for different reasons. It is a mistake to consider either one more meaningful than the other. Ideally, descriptive evidence and experimental evidence balance one another in providing information about nature. The value of the evidence is more a function of logic and accuracy than it is of the setting from which it was derived. Each method has its own advantages and disadvantages. Observing nature without interfering with it permits us to describe certain characteristics and behavior of organisms as they normally function without artificial interruption, but the absence of control does not allow us to make strong inferences about what causes what. At the other extreme, precise laboratory investigations are designed to enable us to make inferences about causation, but they may be so specific and narrow that they do not permit inferences that can be easily generalized to nature. Getting evidence that allows us to understand the causes of events in their natural settings can be quite tricky.

An interesting case in point is discussed in Unit 30, Built-in Behavior: Konrad Lorenz had reported descriptive evidence several decades ago indicating that goslings formed permanent attachments to the first moving objects they saw after hatching. Subsequent experimental studies in American laboratories had indicated that such attachments were *not* permanent. The experimental investigations were carefully controlled so that the birds were incubated and hatched in isolation. The data from descriptive and experimental studies seemed to indicate that the attachments are permanent when they occur in nature but reversible when they occur in the laboratory. Eckhard Hess, who had conducted many laboratory investigations, decided to place sophisticated recording equipment in natural settings to investigate the reasons for the discrepancies between the descriptive and the experimental evidence. He concluded that vocal interaction between the mothers and the unhatched birds was an important variable in forming attachments and that carefully controlled experimental studies had actually deprived the birds of this important interaction.

The determination and isolation of the important variables occurring in nature are often a matter of ingenuity. As you read about investigations throughout this book you will find yourself thinking about new descriptive studies to check on relevance and about new variables to isolate through controlled experiments. It is the nature of empirical investigation that each study suggests variables that have previously been overlooked. It would be quite possible for you to think of more definitive research on a question raised in this book than anyone else has thought of before.

Many studies combine both descriptive and experimental techniques for obtaining data. Because it is useful for you to consider the various kinds of inferences and generalizations you can make from different types of evidence, we have classified the evidence for most studies reported here as either descriptive or experimental. At times complicated research designs make such classification arbitrary. Our criteria for making these classifications included the following:

1. If independent variables were *selected*, it was considered descriptive (e.g., human intelligence). If independent variables were *manipulated*, it was considered experimental (e.g., the administration of shock).

2. If the experimental independent variables could be specifically designated and the results compared with controls, it was considered experimental (e.g., comparing academic performances between two groups of students whose teachers were given different expectations about their performances). If no comparisons were made between conditions, it was considered descriptive (e.g., observing social behavior under crowded living conditions).

The first question in Unit 2 is responded to with descriptive evidence for one hypothesis and experimental evidence for another.

In our example a descriptive study is used to investigate the locus-of-control hypothesis. Materials in this study involve a questionnaire called a locus-of-control scale that had been used in a number of previous investigations, achievement tests designed to measure general knowledge, and school grades. Because none of the variables can be manipulated by the experimenter, the status of the subjects can only be measured, described and analyzed statistically. How-

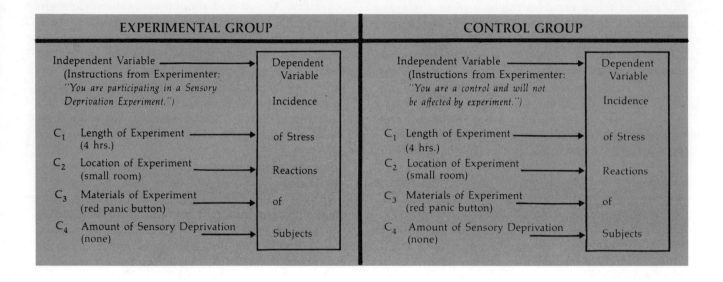

EXPERIMENTAL GROUP		CONTROL GROUP	
Independent Variable (Instructions from Experimenter: *"You are participating in a Sensory Deprivation Experiment."*)	Dependent Variable Incidence	Independent Variable (Instructions from Experimenter: *"You are a control and will not be affected by experiment."*)	Dependent Variable Incidence
C_1 Length of Experiment (4 hrs.)	of Stress	C_1 Length of Experiment (4 hrs.)	of Stress
C_2 Location of Experiment (small room)	Reactions	C_2 Location of Experiment (small room)	Reactions
C_3 Materials of Experiment (red panic button)	of	C_3 Materials of Experiment (red panic button)	of
C_4 Amount of Sensory Deprivation (none)	Subjects	C_4 Amount of Sensory Deprivation (none)	Subjects

Figure 19. An example of an experimental design. All variables (indicated by C's) are the same (controlled,) for both the experimental group and the control group. This allows the researcher to determine the effect of the independent variable by having it differ in the experimental group.

ever, the analysis indicated that the evidence does not justify any conclusion about what causes what. A number of possible implications are reported in the unit, each of which might constitute another hypothesis for gathering further evidence.

The study investigating the expectancy-for-achievement hypothesis used an experimental approach in which teachers were told exactly what to expect by the experimenters, and student academic performance was measured as the dependent variable. As reported in the unit, the evidence supports the hypothesis only in part. Although the type of evidence allows causal inferences to be made, the results suggest a number of new hypotheses worthy of further exploration.

Specifications for this study as they are presented in Unit 2 indicate the title of the article in which the information appeared, the names of the investigators and a description of the subjects and materials. Throughout the book, wherever sex of the subject is not specified, it may be assumed that both males and

females were used. In this case subjects were all students in elementary, junior high and high schools. When considering the implications from any evidence it is well to consider how reasonable it is to generalize beyond the kind of subjects used in the study.

USING STATISTICS

Throughout this book we have reported the results of investigations by using such phrases as "the experimental subjects made more errors than the control subjects," or "the subjects preferred the familiar pattern to the unfamiliar pattern." When we base such statements on our everyday experiences, we are usually talking about our subjective impressions, and we run the risk of being inaccurate because we have a tendency to ignore any evidence inconsistent with what we already believe or wish to believe. For this reason, statistical analyses are usually based on data collected in a scientific investigation. Thus, when we make such statements in this text, they have a specific meaning in the language of statistical analysis. We may have confidence that the differences between these measurements are greater than they would be if chance alone were responsible. And there is a generally agreed-upon level of confidence. If the differences could have occurred by chance less than 5 times out of 100, the results may be used to accept any hypothesis predicting those differences. If the differences could have occurred by chance more than 5 times out of 100, we would reject the hypothesis. When the differences reach this accepted level of confidence, we refer to them as being statistically significant. In this case, the term "significant" does *not* refer to the absolute magnitude of the differences nor to their importance. What is socially significant may have nothing to do with what is statistically significant.

In many studies using descriptive evidence, the investigators are primarily concerned with the relationship between two or more sets of measurements. In such cases, the statistical analysis used is referred to as the *coefficient of correlation*. Suppose, for example, we are interested in determining the validity of an IQ test, and our criterion for validity is its ability to predict grades during the first year of college. We would first obtain IQ scores from a large number of people before they enter college. After these people had completed one year of college, we would compare their IQ scores with their college grades. We would then apply the statistical formula for the coefficient of correlation to determine to what extent these two groups of scores vary together. If there were a perfect relationship between these two scores, indicating that the higher the IQ score the higher the college grades, the analysis would yield a correlation of +1.00. If there were absolutely no relationship whatsoever, the correlation would be 0.00. Of course, any correlation between 0.00 and 1.00 might be due to chance, or it might be statistically significant, and again the size of the correlation would have to be analyzed to determine whether it met our predesignated level of confidence to decide that the IQ test is valid.

A correlation might also yield a strong *inverse* relationship between two groups of measurements. For example, if we were to measure relationships between the number of children in a family and the size of a family's bank account, the correlation might be high, but in a negative direction. In such cases, the fact that the relationship is inverse would be reflected in the negative sign before the number. Inverse correlations, therefore, yield scores ranging between 0.00 and −1.00.

It is especially important in using these statistics to remember that they are rarely used to describe an individual case. If you are a female Presbyterian, the average IQ score of all female Presbyterians tells us nothing about your IQ score. By their nature, statistics must describe variations in groups of measurements. The inferences to be made, therefore, are predictive and should not be confused with the unique condition of individuals. As a rule, psychologists work with distributions of scores. For example, if 1,000 students took a 60-item examination in psychology, the scores would be arranged in a distribution indicating how many students received each score.

Many large universities score such examinations by computers that statistically analyze the data and report the mean and standard deviation. The *mean* of a distribution of scores, sometimes called the average score, is derived by adding up all obtained scores and dividing by the number of students taking the test. This mean is then used to get some idea about what kind of a score is representative of all the scores. It tells us how well or how poorly students in general did on this examination.

The mean is the most commonly used score to provide this kind of information. It is called a measure of *central tendency* because it tells us where the scores tend to centralize. Another measure of central tendency is the *median*, which divides the distribution in half by indicating the middle score when all the scores in the distribution are arranged from highest to lowest. A third measure of central tendency is the *mode*, which is simply that score obtained by most of the people in the distribution.

The mean is favored among these measures of central tendency because it is derived from information about every score in the distribution, whereas the other measures may ignore some scores.

Any student could now compare his obtained score with the mean to determine how high his score is relative to the representative score. But he cannot tell from the mean alone how much his score deviated from the representative score. That is to say, we need still another statistic to tell us *how* representative the mean score is. An *average deviation* may be determined by measuring the deviation of each score in the distribution from the mean and calculating the average of the deviations. The *standard deviation* is a slightly more complicated statistic, very much like the average deviation, which is most commonly used to determine how representative the mean of a distribution is. At this point the student may determine his standing in the original distribution by calculating how many standard deviations his test score is from the mean.

The mean and standard deviation form the basis for some of the more sophisticated statistical analyses used in behavioral research.

WHAT'S ACCEPTED AND WHAT'S DEBATED

Richard Feynman, a theoretical physicist, wrote:
" . . . We find that the statements of science are not of what is true and what is not true, but statements of what is known to different degrees of certainty: 'It is very much more likely that so and so is true than that it is not true'; or 'such and such is almost certain but there is still a little bit of doubt;' or at the other extreme—'well, we really don't know.' Every one of the concepts of science is on a scale graduated somewhere between, but at neither end of, absolute falsity or absolute truth.

It is necessary, I believe, to accept this idea, not only for science, but also for other things; it is of great value to acknowledge ignorance. It is a fact that when we make decisions in our life we don't necessarily know that we are making them correctly; we only think that we are doing the best we can—and that is what we should do."

We would feel more comfortable knowing the "truth" of a statement. Nevertheless, as information grows we revise our strategies and reject statements we once accepted as "facts." Therefore it is more appropriate to present statements that are generally accepted by mainstream psychologists than it is to state what is "true." In this text, we have therefore summarized each unit by listing statements that are accepted and questions that are still being debated.

SOCIAL RESPONSIBILITY

In recent decades scientists have become increasingly concerned about accepting responsibility for the use of the information they provide. Psychologists are becoming increasingly concerned with the contributions they might be able to make to human welfare.

Probably the single most debated issue in psychology involves the extent to which applications should be made of our knowledge of how behavior may be controlled. Conditioning techniques are used in social settings as therapy for patients in mental hospitals, for training retarded children, for rehabilitating prisoners and also as educational procedures in higher education. Brain stimulation is used to enable some epileptic patients to control their own behavior. Psychosurgery is used to reduce aggressive behavior in some people. The accuracy of genetic information is often hotly debated because it is used by many people to encourage racist attitudes and behavior. Child-rearing practices, daycare centers and school systems are being affected by information coming out of psychological laboratories.

It becomes increasingly apparent that information about human behavior may be used constructively for promoting human welfare; or it may be used for the comfort of a few to the detriment of the many. The ultimate application of psychological principles can no longer be entrusted to an elite few. The future must be everybody's business.

A BRIEF ENCOUNTER WITH STATISTICAL ANALYSIS

Because much of psychology relies heavily on statistical techniques and methods, it's important that you understand some of the basic terminology of statistics. Our concern here is with *measures of central tendency, variability* and *correlation*. Since these techniques are used to *describe* the results of research, you will encounter references to them throughout the book.

Let's assume that a psychology instructor gives a ten-item examination to the twenty-one students in her class (they all attended class that day). The students could receive a score on a scale from 0-10. (This is referred to as a ratio scale of measurement as indicated in Table 2.)

The scores on this hypothetical examination are given in column A of Table 1 and are ranked from high score to low. A look at column A gives us a feeling for the distribution of scores, but it doesn't tell us much about the performance of the group as a whole. What the instructor would probably do is express the average performance or *central tendency* of the group using one or more of the following measures:

Table 1. Statistical Analysis of a Hypothetical Examination

	A	B	C	D	E	F	G
Student Name	Score on Test	Current Grade Point Average	Deviation from Mean Score				
	(X)	(Y)	$(X - \overline{X} = x)$	x^2	X^2	Y^2	XY (X times Y)
Carol	10	4.0	3.1	9.61	100	16.00	40.0
Bob	10	3.3	3.1	9.61	100	10.89	33.0
Dick	9	3.6	2.1	4.41	81	12.96	32.4
Pat	9	3.0	2.1	4.41	81	9.00	27.0
Sue	8	3.0	1.1	1.21	64	9.00	24.0
Denise	8	2.8	1.1	1.21	64	7.84	22.4
George	8	3.2	1.1	1.21	64	10.24	25.6
Joe	8	2.5	1.1	1.21	64	6.25	20.0
Jim	8	2.7	1.1	1.21	64	7.29	21.6
Rick	8	2.4	1.1	1.21	64	5.76	19.2
Glen	7	2.6	.1	.01	49	6.76	18.2
Barbara	7	2.4	.1	.01	49	5.76	16.8
Miriam	7	2.8	.1	.01	49	7.84	19.6
John	7	2.5	.1	.01	49	6.25	17.5
Marie	6	2.4	−.9	.81	36	5.76	14.4
Mart	6	2.2	−.9	.81	36	4.84	13.2
Tim	5	2.6	−1.9	3.61	25	6.76	13.0
Pete	5	2.1	−1.9	3.61	25	4.41	10.5
Alice	4	2.0	−2.9	8.41	16	4.00	8.0
Ray	3	1.8	−3.9	15.21	9	3.24	5.4
Terry	2	2.0	−4.9	24.01	4	4.00	4.0
N = 21	$\Sigma X = 145$	$\Sigma Y = 55.9$	$\Sigma x = 0$	$\Sigma x^2 = 91.81$	$\Sigma X^2 = 1093$	$\Sigma Y^2 = 154.85$	$\Sigma XY = 405.8$

I. Measures of Central Tendency

Mean—the sum of the scores in a set (ΣX) divided by the number of scores in a set (N). In our example above:

$$\text{Mean } (\overline{X}) = \frac{\Sigma X}{N} \text{ or } \frac{145}{21} = 6.9$$

Median—the score that divides a set of ranked scores in half. In our example above:

Median = 7

Mode—the score that occurs most frequently in a set of scores. In our example above:

Mode = 8

II. Measures of Variability

Range—the highest score minus the lowest score. In our example above:

Range = 10 − 2 = 8

Variance—the sum of the mean squared distance of the scores from the mean. In our example above:

$$\text{Variance}(\sigma^2) = \frac{\Sigma x^2}{N} = \frac{91.81}{21} = 4.37$$

Standard deviation—the square root of the variance. In our example above:

Standard deviation (σ)

$$= \sqrt{\sigma^2} \text{ or } \sqrt{\frac{\Sigma x^2}{N}} = \sqrt{4.37} = 2.09$$

III. Measure of Correlation

Correlation Coefficient—a measure of the degree to which two variables are related. In our example above:

r XY (the correlation between X and Y)

$$= \frac{N\Sigma XY - (\Sigma X)(\Sigma Y)}{\sqrt{[N\Sigma X^2 - (\Sigma X)^2][N\Sigma Y^2 - (\Sigma Y)^2]}}$$

r (the correlation between score and grade point average)

$$= \frac{(21)(405.8) - (145)(55.9)}{\sqrt{[(21)(1093) - (145)^2][(21)(154.85) - (55.9)^2]}}$$

r = + .841

Table 2. Four Basic Types of Scales Used in Measurement

Properties of Scale	Nominal Scale[1]	Ordinal Scale[2]	Interval Scale[3]	Ratio Scale[4]
CLASSIFICATION	X	X	X	X
ORDER		X	X	X
EQUAL UNITS			X	X
ABSOLUTE ZERO				X
Examples:	Numbers on baseball jerseys Social Security numbers	House numbers Order of finish in a race	Calendar Thermometer	Page numbers Ruler

[1]Nominal Scale —Numbers merely differentiate one item or individual from another without indicating any meaningful order.

[2]Ordinal Scale —Numbers differentiate items or individuals and indicate order but do not indicate amount of difference between items.

[3]Interval Scale —Numbers differentiate items or individuals, indicate order, and indicate equal differences between one number and the number preceding or following it, but do not indicate ratio of numbers. (e.g. One item cannot be twice as much as another.)

[4]Ratio Scale —Numbers differentiate items or individuals, indicate equal differences between one number and the numbers preceding or following it, and since it contains an absolute zero it indicates ratio of numbers.

The Mode

The mode is the most easily obtained measure. It is simply the score that occurs most frequently. In our example there are six students with a score of 8. Since this is a higher number of students than at any other score, the mode in our distribution is 8. With more complex data it might be necessary first to construct a frequency distribution table (as in Table 3). Frequency of distribution can also be expressed graphically as in Figure 20.

The Median

The median is another simply arrived-at measure. It is the score that divides the distribution of scores in half. In our example the midpoint score is 7. 50% of the students scored above this number and 50% scored at or below this number.

The Arithmetic Mean

If our measurement scale is interval or ratio we can use still a third measure of central tendency. The arithmetic mean ($\bar{X}$) is simply the total of all the scores (ΣX in Table 1) divided by the total number of scores (N in Table 1). A single score is given the symbol X. The Greek letter sigma (Σ) is a symbol for "sum of," so ΣX is the sum of all scores. A simple way to indicate the mean of a group of scores is $\bar{X}$. It indicates that the score is an average and not an individual score.

As we can see, the mean, median and mode can differ. The mean score in our example is 6.9, the median score is 7 and the modal score is 8. How do we know which of these different measures to use? There is no clear rule, except that only the mode can be used with a nominal scale. A median can be calculated for ordinal scales or higher, and a mean score can be

Score (X)	Frequency (F)
10	2
9	2
8	6
7	4
6	2
5	2
4	1
3	1
2	1
1	0
0	0
	$\Sigma F = 21 = N$

Table 3. Tabular representation of the distribution of examination scores.

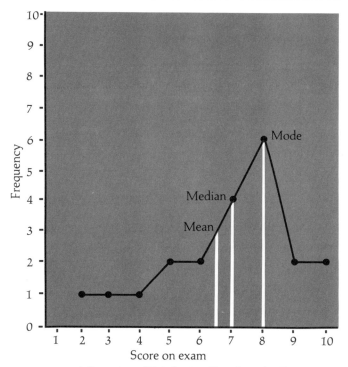

A Frequency Distribution Based on the Data

Figure 20. Graphic representation of the distribution of examination scores.

determined for interval or higher scales of measurement. Another important point is that the mean is quite sensitive to very high or very low scores, particularly in distributions where the N (number of cases) is small. In general, the type of distribution and the kind of information we want determine the measure of central value that is most telling for us.

Normal Distribution

In a normal distribution all measures of central tendency are the same. A normal distribution, as represented by the bell curve in our Figure 21, is the most important distribution in statistics, because so many psychological factors are normally distributed. In a small *sample* of a population, a normal distribution is very infrequently obtained, but the closer the sample approximates the size of the total population, the closer the distribution will approach the bell curve (assuming of course that the variable being measured is normally distributed in the total population). Distributions can also be *skewed*. In our example the distribution is skewed left. (See Figure 20.)

Measures of Variability

Since humans typically vary, psychologists use statistical devices that measure the degree of variability within a given distribution.

The simplest measure of variability is *range*. This is the difference between the largest and the smallest score. To calculate the range we subtract the lowest score from the highest. In our example the range is 8 (10-2). This reflects little about the distribution of other scores, however.

A better, and much more commonly used method is *standard deviation*. By this method every score in the distribution is taken into account. It is based on every score's deviation from the mean, and is arrived at by taking the *square root of the mean of the squared distance from the mean of all the scores*.

The mean *squared* distance is used instead of the mean distance, because by the very nature of the mean the sum of all differences will be *zero*. (See column C in Table 1.) In our example the standard deviation is 2.09. This was determined by calculating the deviation from the mean for each score (column

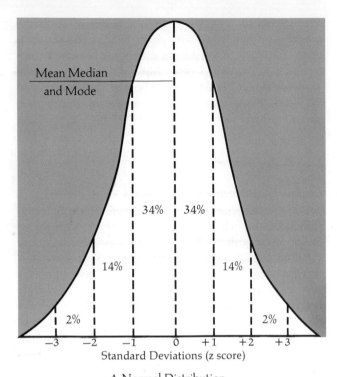

Mean Median
and Mode

34%   34%

14%   14%

2%   2%

−3   −2   −1   0   +1   +2   +3
Standard Deviations (z score)

A Normal Distribution

Figure 21. A normal distribution as represented by the bell curve.

C) by squaring this deviation for each score (column D), by calculating the mean of the sum of these squared deviations (referred to as the *variance*) and then by taking the square root of this sum (*variance*). The greater the size of the standard deviation, the greater the variability of the scores.

In a normal frequency distribution, if we know the mean and the standard distribution we can calculate the percentage of cases falling within various areas of the distribution. Figure 21 indicates the approximate percentage of cases that fall within the mean, and one standard deviation, and two standard deviations and three standard deviations. The range of scores goes from a low of −3 deviations to a high of +3 deviations (this covers nearly the entire population). A z score (standard deviation score) is a conversion of a score into its standard deviation from the mean. For example, a score that falls −2 deviations from the mean has a z score of −2.

Measures of Correlation

Where the measures of central tendency and variability are used to describe a single distribution of scores, *the correlation coefficient is used to describe the degree of relationship between two distributions of scores.*

In our example the instructor, after determining the mean and standard deviation for the students' scores on the examination, might want to determine the relationship (if any) between how the students performed on the examination (their scores) and their current grade point averages (as indicated in column B of Table 1). She might want to determine how these variables vary together. By creating a scatter diagram for the scores and grade point averages she can determine that there is a degree of positive relationship (see Figure 22). To determine the coefficient of correlation between score and grade point average she might do the calculation as indicated in Table 1. The correlation coefficient for these two sets of scores is +.841. This shows a high degree of relationship

Scatter Plot of Data

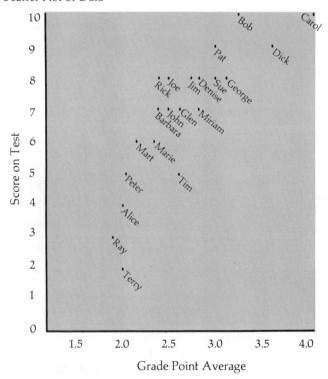

Figure 22. A scatter diagram of examination scores and current grade point averages of 21 students taking the examination.

between the students' scores and their current grade point average.

The correlation coefficient can range from −1.00 (perfect negative correlation) to +1.00 (perfect positive correlation). Figure 23 shows hypothetical scatter diagrams for high positive, high negative and zero correlations.

If a psychologist determines to test a hypothesis about a general population, he follows a basic procedure. He first *defines the population* (or universe); he then draws a *sample* from this universe. The most common method of drawing a sample is called *random sampling*. (Each member of the population must have the same chance of being selected, and the probability

Scatter Plots of Three Correlations

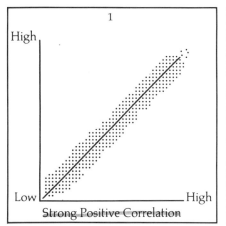
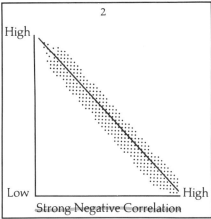
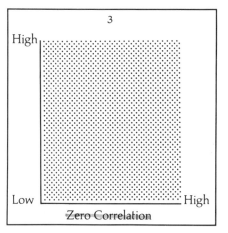

Figure 23. Scatter diagrams showing (1.) strong positive, (2.) strong negative, and (3.) zero correlation.

Inferential Statistics

The measures described above are all examples of statistics used to describe the results of particular research. They fall within the category termed *descriptive statistics*. But psychologists, like other scientists, need to make general statements regarding the large population from which a particular case (research) is drawn. They need to infer information about a population from a sample drawn from that population.

To do this they use methods which are referred to as *inferential statistics*. It is the use of these statistical procedures that allow psychologists to generalize.

of each member being selected must not be affected by some other member's selection or non-selection.) After drawing the sample, the psychologist then *measures* the sample, *computes* one or more descriptive statistics for that sample and then makes inferences from the sample to the population. As you can easily imagine, all these steps require careful control.

Your instructor may decide to introduce you to additional statistical methods, determined perhaps by your mathematical background. However, if you are familiar with the basic concepts presented here, you will have no difficulty with any statistical references made in the text.

Unit 2

Self-Fulfilling Prophecy

OVERVIEW

People's own expectations play a role in influencing their decisions and the lives of other people, and their expectations can create the very situation that is expected to occur. For example, the self-fulfilling prophecies of teachers can affect their students' academic performance, or the expectations of both experimenters and their subjects can affect the outcome of behavioral research. The Issue section presents the concept of "Labeling" and its implications for the study of deviance.

<table>
<tr><td>

UNIT OUTLINE

DEFINITION AND BACKGROUND
1. *Definition:* self-fulfilling prophecy is a preconceived expectation or belief about a situation that evokes behavior resulting in a situation consistent with the preconception.
2. *Background:* William I. Thomas (1863–1947).

QUESTIONS AND EVIDENCE
1. How do our beliefs affect our own and others' behavior?
Hypotheses:
  a. *Locus-of-control:* those individuals who perceive themselves to be internally controlled are more likely to be successful than individuals who perceive themselves to be externally controlled. **36**
  b. *Expectancy-for-achievement:* the expectancies held by an individual administratively responsible for the achievement of others will affect achievement in the direction of his expectations. **36**
  c. *Social-attraction:* an individual's conception of how others feel about him will initiate behavior that is likely to produce those feelings in others and thereby strengthen that conception of the individual. **37**
2. How can expectations influence behavioral research?
Hypotheses:
  a. *Demand-characteristics:* subjects' motivation to perform well and do what they believe the experimenter wants them to do may strongly influence the results of behavioral experiments. **40**
  b. *Experimenter-bias:* the expectations of the researcher can also influence the outcome of an investigation. **40**

</td><td>

IMPORTANT CONCEPTS

	page
attitude	34
demand characteristics	39
experimenter bias	40
halo effect	36
locus of control (external, internal)	36
Rosenthal effect	35
self-fulfilling prophecy	34
sensory deprivation	40

</td></tr>
</table>

Preconceptions about the behavior of others may serve as a focus for relationships with them.

Behavior in accord with these preconceptions may affect the expectations and self-concepts of others.

There is evidence that such relationships may serve to mold reality out of the preconceptions.

DEFINITION AND BACKGROUND

Convinced that he is going to fail an examination, a student spends more time worrying than studying and consequently fails. A clinician decides that a patient is schizophrenic and places him in a state institution. The patient is treated as schizophrenics are treated and his behavior becomes increasingly psychotic. An experimenter, certain that his theory is right, goes looking for evidence that will prove it is right. A white legislator becomes convinced that blacks do poorly in school and consequently refuses to vote funds for improving educational facilities for blacks, who then do poorly in school. All these examples illustrate self-fulfilling prophecies in action. The DEFINITION of a self-fulfilling prophecy is *a preconceived expectation or belief about a situation that evokes behavior resulting in a situation consistent with the preconception.* Self-fulfilling prophecies are important because they appear to influence many kinds of human activity—from personality development to community relations, from business enterprise to the "objective" deliberations of doctors and scientists.

This unit will FOCUS on the role that self-fulfilling prophecies play in social, academic, and even behavioral research settings.

BACKGROUND: WILLIAM ISAAC THOMAS (1863–1947)

W. I. Thomas was an American social scientist who made important contributions to the beginnings of social psychology early in this century. He was, for example, one of the first psychologists to emphasize human attitudes and their influence on behavior. In a classic five-volume work entitled *The Polish Peasant in Europe and America* (1918–1920, with Florian Znaniecki), Thomas helped establish the study of attitudes as one of the central concerns of social psychology for decades to follow (see Unit 10).

The roots of the notion that the manner in which people view events has an impact on those events can be traced to the writings of Thomas. His theory of social behavior, which focused on the complex interaction of a person's characteristics and his environment, was loosely woven but influential. Thomas believed that how a person behaves in a particular situation is determined both by his attitudes, which

Figure 1. William I. Thomas, a pioneer in social psychology, insisted on scientifically oriented research procedures and stressed the influence of human attitudes on behavior.

have been created by his previous experiences, and by his subjective definition of the present situation. This notion—the basic idea behind self-fulfilling prophecy—can be formulated as the "Thomas theorem," which states that if persons define situations as real, they are real in their consequences.

Robert Merton (1957) has given an example of how the Thomas theorem might work with respect to racial discrimination. A fair-minded white man may support a policy that excludes blacks from his labor union not as an expression of any racial prejudice but as a result of his knowledge of some apparent facts: relative to whites, the blacks who are trying to get jobs appear less disciplined, have a lower standard of living, and are more likely to be admitted strikebreakers. But this white man does not realize that, by excluding blacks from the same opportunity he enjoys, he is creating the very reality that he objects to. For when the blacks discover they can work only by taking jobs from strikers, they will seize the only opportunity open to them. Thus, social fact is created by social fiction.

Although the Thomas theorem seems to possess a compelling validity, at the time of its statement it was mostly ignored, perhaps because, by today's standards, Thomas' contemporaries lacked social consciousness. Today, however, the basic notion of self-fulfilling prophecy is enjoying a substantial revival in social psychology and is finding application in other areas of psychology as well. Generally, it is now recognized that there is an ever-greater need for objectivity in interpreting today's very complex world. Because they have become more sensitive to the possibility that the same situation can have several "interpretations," psychologists are becoming more and more aware that an individual's views may dictate reality in a variety of situations.

The concept of self-fulfilling prophecy in psychology reemerged as the result of several independent but convergent trends that became well-known in the 1960s. One trend was the work of Robert Rosenthal, whose studies on experimenter bias in research and teacher expectancies in academic settings were quoted so often that the generalizations from his findings have become known as the "Rosenthal effect"—self-fulfilling prophecies perpetrated by academic people. Another trend was the development of measures of subtle dimensions of personality related to expectations, like locus of control, discussed below. A third trend was the growing dissatisfaction of some psychologists with certain categorical and classificatory aspects of diagnostic systems in clinical psychology: once a label like "schizophrenic" is attached to a person's behavior, does the label with all its implications influence the person's behavior—and how he is treated by others?

Figure 2. During the Great Depression of the 1930s, people who expected the banks to fail withdrew their money and thereby contributed to the failure—a self-fulfilling prophecy.

QUESTIONS AND EVIDENCE

1. How do our beliefs affect our own and others' behavior?
2. How can expectations influence behavioral research?

1. HOW DO OUR BELIEFS AFFECT OUR OWN AND OTHERS' BEHAVIOR?

Some people believe that their own behavior determines their success; others believe that success is in the hands of fate and that nothing they do will affect the outcome; still others see the control of destiny as

QUESTION	1. HOW DO OUR BELIEFS AFFECT OUR OWN AND OTHERS' BEHAVIOR?		
HYPOTHESES	**LOCUS OF CONTROL**	**EXPECTANCY FOR ACHIEVEMENT**	**SOCIAL ATTRACTION**
DESCRIPTIVE EVIDENCE	ASSESS: relation between locus of control and academic achievement		
EXPERIMENTAL EVIDENCE		VARY: teacher expectations MEASURE: students' academic performance	VARY: impressions of like or dislike MEASURE: attitudes, cooperative responses

lying somewhere between these extremes. Where we see this control to be located is referred to as locus of control. At the extremes, a person with an internal locus of control believes that outcomes are related to how he acts, while a person with external locus of control believes that outcomes are determined by luck or chance—that is, by factors external to himself. The *locus-of-control hypothesis* states that those individuals who perceive themselves to be internally controlled are more likely to be successful than individuals who perceive themselves to be externally controlled.

The 1966 report of the Coleman Commission (which had investigated the nature of unequal educational opportunities for minorities) concluded that "a stronger relationship to achievement than . . . all the 'school' factors together, is the extent to which an individual feels he has some control over his own destiny."

This statement is an assertion that the locus-of-control hypothesis is accurate in the case of minority students. That the Coleman Commission came to this conclusion tends to support the hypothesis but does not offer direct evidence for it. Some direct evidence of an informal nature might be found in the Coleman Report itself. However, the following investigation of nearly 1,000 students did turn up direct evidence for this hypothesis.

DESCRIPTIVE EVIDENCE

Investigators: P. E. McGhee and V. C. Crandall
Source, Date:"Beliefs in Internal-External Control of Reinforcements and Academic Performance," 1968
Location: Ohio State University and Fels Research Institute
Subjects: 923 elementary, junior-high, and high-school students
Materials: Locus-of-control test, 2 achievement tests, report-card grades

Locus of control can be tested by asking the individual to check as true or false a number of attitudinal self-descriptive statements. Some of these reflect an internal locus of control: for example, "Hard work will assure me success," "People only get out of life what they put into it," and "People who cause trouble should be dealt with sternly." Other statements reflect external locus of control: for example, "The only reliable rewards in life are those which come from higher beings," "Advancement in my job is not determined by the quality of my work," and "There is very little justice in the world."

Subjects were administered a locus-of-control test and an achievement test designed to measure their level of knowledge. The scores on the locus-of-control test were then compared with achievement-test scores and report-card grades.

The results indicated that those subjects who perceived themselves to be internally controlled (as measured by their scores on the locus-of-control test) had significantly higher report-card grade averages and generally scored higher on the achievement tests. The data may indicate any combination of the following implications: (1) An individual's perceived locus of control may be relatively independent of actual abilities except to influence his motivation to try to succeed. (2) Locus-of-control scores may reflect realistic appraisals by the students of their own ability to achieve in school and thereby to control academic success. (3) Perceived locus of control may reflect the realities of an individual's specific social environment. Unfortunately this kind of research cannot indicate whether an individual's perceived locus of control precedes or follows experience with academic success.

Studies that concentrate on an individual's locus of control emphasize the individual's role in fulfilling his prophecies. However, in the real world, most kinds of success ultimately depend on the outcome of our interactions with others. Many students, for example, make a special attempt to perform well in the first examination given by a new teacher in order to make a good impression. The notion that first impressions color subsequent impressions is often referred to as the *halo effect*. To what extent do the beliefs, and therefore, the expectations of others affect our behavior and nurture our own abilities?

The *expectancy-for-achievement hypothesis* states that the expectancies held by an individual administratively responsible for the achievement of others will affect achievement in the direction of his expectations.

In the following experiment, the researchers explored the effect a teacher's expectations might have on his students' intellectual growth.

EXPERIMENTAL EVIDENCE

Investigators: R. Rosenthal and L. F. Jacobson
Source, Date: "Pygmalion in the Classroom: Teacher Expectations and Pupils' Intellectual Development," 1968

Location: San Francisco
Subjects: Elementary school pupils from 18 classrooms
Materials: Flanagan Tests of General Ability

Most of the subjects were from lower-class families who received welfare payments. The six grades in the school were "tracked" according to above-average, average, and below-average scholastic achievement. The investigators told the school's personnel that they were obtaining data to validate a "new" kind of test —the "Test of Inflected Acquisition"—which ostensibly was able to predict academic "blooming" or sudden intellectual gains in students. They informed the teachers that the data would be sent to Harvard University for evaluation. The actual test used was a new, and therefore unfamiliar to the teachers, intelligence test known as Flanagan Tests of General Ability.

On a particular day each student in grades kindergarten through five was given the test. Prior to the reopening of school in the fall, the experimenters randomly designated 20 percent of the children in the school as "potential academic spurters." Although no outside criteria had in fact been applied to these children, who were distributed about five to each classroom, each teacher was casually informed that specific children in their classes had done well in the "Harvard study." Thus, at the beginning of the academic year the only difference between the experimental (20 percent) and control (80 percent) groups was in what the teacher "expected" from each. The children were retested after four months of school, at the end of the year, and in May of the following year.

Although the test results revealed that the children from whom teachers expected intellectual gains did in fact show such gains, this finding was not uniform. In the tests administered at the end of the first year students in the first and second grades demonstrated greatest gains. During the second year the most significant gains were made by the sixth graders, who had been just beginning the fifth grade when they were designated as "spurters."

It is not clear why the expectancy effect was most pronounced in lower grades during the first year and in older children during the follow-up year. The researchers suggest the possibility that younger children, having less well-established school reputations, may be easier to change and that older children needed longer contact with teachers for the effect to be manifested.

Following the completion of the first year of study, each teacher was asked to describe the behavior of his students. The descriptions of members of the experimental group indicated that the teachers saw them as having greater chances of success in later life and as being happier, more curious, and more interesting than the other children. The teachers also described these students as more appealing and affectionate and as demonstrating greater adjustment to life. A surprising result occurred in the ratings of the children in the control group, however. Although many of them also gained in IQ scores during the year, the more they gained the less favorably they were rated. The teachers seemed especially prone to rate children who had begun in the school-designated "slow learner" group in this manner. Apparently unpredicted intellectual gains may be seen in some cases as involving undesirable behavior.

In examining the ways in which teacher expectancies affect student intellectual growth, the researchers feel that teachers probably communicate their expectations to students through facial expression, tone of voice, touch and posture. These expectations then lead to positive self-evaluations on the part of the student.

It appears then that what teachers expect in student achievement may also affect the degree of attraction they feel toward students. How is social attraction between individuals affected by the impression one has of how well liked he is by another?

The *social-attraction hypothesis* states that an individual's conception of how others feel about him will initiate behavior that is likely to produce those feelings in others and thereby strengthen that conception of the individual.

Is it true that we tend to live up to (or for that matter live down to) the expectations of others, accepting them and enforcing them for ourselves? Do you find evidence for this hypothesis in the following experiment?

EXPERIMENTAL EVIDENCE

Investigators: S. C. Jones and D. Panitch
Source, Date: "The Self-Fulfilling Prophecy and Interpersonal Attraction," 1971

Location: Cornell University
Subjects: 28 male and 28 female undergraduate students
Materials: Interviews, false attitude data, game, question-
naire

Subjects were randomly paired off with strangers of the same sex. After being introduced they were told that the experiment concerned the nature and accuracy of one person's impressions of another. Their instructions indicated that one member would be asked to form an impression of his partner after observing him being interviewed by the experimenter and after playing a game with him.

One subject was then picked at random and was interviewed for ten minutes while the second subject observed. They were then taken to separate rooms to answer questionnaires, and the observer recorded his initial impressions of his partner. Later the experimenter gave his interviewed subject (the "receiver") a contrived set of "impressions" that he said was written by the observer (the "sender").

The subjects were then brought together to play a bargaining game. They could make either cooperative choices, where they could expect to gain .5 point and their partners 1.5 points, or competitive choices, where they could gain 1 point and their partner 0 points. On each trial the subjects made their choices privately and the experimenter announced the choices and the number of points won by each partner. Each point was worth five cents and the game consisted of two sets of fifteen trials. After the first set of trials, the sender again was asked to record his impressions of his partner and the receiver was again given a prearranged contrived impression.

There were two experimental conditions. In the "like" condition, the receiver was told that the sender said he was very likable and that the two of them were compatible. In the "dislike" condition the receiver was told just the opposite.

The number of cooperative responses made in a set of fifteen trials was recorded. After the game the subjects were separated and administered a questionnaire that required them to assess their attitudes toward one another. The experimenters report: "Both male and female receivers had more positive attitudes toward the sender in the Like than the Dislike condition. However, whereas males played more cooperatively with the sender in the Like condition, females tended, if anything, to play more cooperatively in the Dislike condition. Nevertheless, female differences between the two conditions were not statistically significant. This pattern of results suggests that there were sex differences in the degree of consistency between a subject's feelings for his partner and how cooperatively he behaved toward him."

In general, these results tend to agree with the social-attraction hypothesis: once a person has some idea about how another regards him, the person's behavior tends to strengthen the preconception.

In the past fifteen years, several psychiatrists and psychologists have also become very concerned that self-fulfilling prophecies may operate when mental patients are categorized or labeled as such. For example, a British psychiatrist, R. D. Laing, has argued that the symptoms of mental disturbance may be produced in an individual by his family's insistence that he is mentally ill. This interpretation is not totally new, but the considerable publicity Laing's ideas have received may help alleviate some of the anxiety and hostility aroused by the term "mental illness."

It is possible that the attitudes that the general public holds toward a person diagnosed as mentally ill

TABLE 1.   Results of Jones and Panitch Study

	Sender "likes" Receiver	Sender "dislikes" Receiver
Receiver Responses	Males and females have more positive attitudes toward Sender; Males play more cooperatively with Sender.	——— ———

Source: Adapted from S. C. Jones and D. Panitch, "The Self-Fulfilling Prophecy and Interpersonal Attraction," *Journal of Experimental Social Psychology,* 7 (1971), 356–366.

can negatively influence that person's behavior. Most persons diagnosed as mentally ill are still regarded with fear, distrust, and hostility by the general public. There's little real reason for this feeling—extremely few mental patients are dangerous to other people; more often they are dangerous only to themselves. In a famous paper entitled "The Myth of Mental Illness" (1960), Thomas Szasz, a New York psychiatrist, argued that the use of the term "mental illness" to describe a person results in unfair and inaccurate categorization, that the label in essence creates the self-fulfilling prophecy that the person requires medical help in order to "get well." In actuality, the individual may not require medical help at all, but simply changes in his social environment (see Unit 13). Most often, according to Szasz, a "symptom" of mental illness is tied not to physiological observations but to social contexts.

These very recent arguments about effects of self-fulfilling prophecy in dealing with mental illness are still controversial, and there is little hard evidence to support the very broad conclusions made by writers such as Laing and Szasz. Although Szasz's opinions were once dismissed as "out in left field," more and more psychologists and psychiatrists are paying attention to his and Laing's basic contentions. Research may eventually show that the diagnostic and classification system that clinicians use causes as many problems as it supposedly solves.

It is to the highest degree probable that the [subject's] general attitude of mind is that of ready complacency and cheerful willingness to assist the investigator in every possible way by reporting to him those very things which he is most eager to find, and that the very questions of the experimenter . . . suggest the shade of reply expected . . . Indeed . . . it seems too often as if the subject were now regarded as a stupid automaton.

Experimenters are still trying to come to grips with the issues involved in this challenge. Martin Orne, who has explored the problem for a number of years, coined the term "demand characteristics" to refer to all those aspects of an experiment that artificially change its results by influencing the subjects' expectations of what the situation demands. According to Orne, the roles of subject and experimenter are well defined and well understood in our culture. The subject implicitly agrees to perform submissively for prolonged periods of time, often with complete willingness to endure discomfort. To illustrate his point, Orne reports the following:

A number of casual acquaintances were asked whether they would do the experimenter a favor; on their acquiescence, they were asked to perform five push-ups. Their response tended to be amaze-

QUESTION 2. HOW CAN EXPECTATIONS INFLUENCE BEHAVIORAL RESEARCH?

HYPOTHESES	DEMAND CHARACTERISTICS	EXPERIMENTER BIAS
DESCRIPTIVE EVIDENCE		
EXPERIMENTAL EVIDENCE	VARY: instructions from experimenter MEASURE: incidence of stress reactions	VARY: expectancies of rats' performances MEASURE: actual performance of rats

2. HOW CAN EXPECTATIONS INFLUENCE BEHAVIORAL RESEARCH?

In 1908, when experimental psychology was still a fledgling discipline, A. H. Pierce offered a cogent warning:

ment, incredulity and the question "Why?" Another similar group of individuals were asked whether they would take part in an experiment of brief duration. When they agreed to do so, they too were asked to perform five push-ups. Their typical response was "Where?"

The *demand-characteristics hypothesis* states that subjects' motivation to perform well and do what they believe the experimenter wants them to do may strongly influence the results of behavioral experiments. (See Figure 3.)

A case in point, according to Orne, is the sensory-deprivation experiment in which the subject is placed in a small soundproofed room. Usually he is asked to lie down, and his arms and hands are covered with cardboard, he is blindfolded, and he wears earphones that block out auditory stimuli. After several hours of this experience, most subjects report visual and/or auditory hallucinations. Sensory-deprivation studies have indicated that individuals cannot tolerate prolonged periods of complete sensory deprivation without temporary but severe disruptions of the nervous system as well as psychological disturbances (see Unit 31). Orne has hypothesized that overly cautious treatment of subjects, careful screening for mental or physical disorders, awesome release forms, and the presence of a panic button to signal the subject's desire to be released from the experiment might be more important in producing these effects than the actual diminution of sensory input.

In order to test the demand-characteristics hypothesis, Orne created laboratory conditions for two groups of subjects that differed only in the fact that one group was given demand characteristics and the other group was not. He then postulated that any differences in the reactions of the groups should be the result of the demand characteristics.

EXPERIMENTAL EVIDENCE

Investigator: M. T. Orne
Source, Date: "On the Social Psychology of the Psychological Experiment: With Particular Reference to Demand Characteristics and Their Implications," 1962
Location: Harvard Medical School
Subjects: 20 volunteer subjects
Materials: Experimental room, microphone, addition task

The experimental subjects were told that they were participating in a sensory-deprivation experiment. Each was taken to a small room that had all the paraphernalia for sensory-deprivation experiments, including release forms and a red panic button. However, it was well lighted and equipped with two comfortable chairs, a pitcher of ice water, and a

sandwich. The experiment lasted four hours, during which the subject did not have a watch. No attempt was made to create any sensory deprivation, however; the experimental room was not even soundproofed. A second group of subjects received identical treatment, but they were informed that they were controls and were not expected to be affected by the experiment.

The experience of the two groups was identical, then, except for the demand characteristics. When fourteen different tests commonly used in sensory-deprivation experiments were administered to each subject before and after the experiment, thirteen showed that the experimental subjects reported more stress than did the control subjects. Six of these thirteen indicated highly reliable and sizable differences between the groups. The subjects who perceived the demand characteristic of the experiment to be that they would experience stress dutifully experienced it.

It is difficult to eliminate demand characteristics entirely from research, but they can be minimized by carefully pretesting experimental procedures and by providing appropriate instructions and explanations. Extensive questioning of subjects after the experiment may also be useful. Orne has concluded that an increased understanding of the demand characteristics intrinsic to laboratory research will enable the experimental method to become a more effective tool for predicting behavior in other contexts.

The subject's tendency to have reactions consistent with the demands of the investigator is not the only possible source of error in psychological research. The biases of the investigator may also affect the results. Research that has been colored in this fashion has been called "research with an objective" as opposed to "objective research," although usually the investigator is not aware that he is expressing his bias.

The *experimenter-bias hypothesis* states that the expectations of the researcher can also influence the outcome of an investigation. Researchers do not intentionally distort or misrepresent their data. But they may, in subtle and sometimes almost unnoticeable ways, communicate their hypotheses and expectations to their subjects. (See Figure 3.)

This problem was first analyzed by a group of German investigators at the turn of the century (reported by Rosenthal, 1971). Their observations centered on Clever Hans, a remarkable horse reportedly

Figure 3. The attitudes of both experimenter and subject can influence the results of behavioral experiments. Experimenter bias (1.) refers to the influence of the researcher's expectation on the outcome of an investigation, demand characteristics (r.) to a subject's motivation to perform according to the perceived expectations of the experimenter.

able to add, subtract, multiply, and divide (not only integers but also fractions), to read, and to identify musical notes. All of his answers were presented in a numerical code that he stomped out with one of his front feet. Clever Hans was quite an attraction in his day, and on September 12, 1904, thirteen men, including the eminent psychologist Carl Stumpf, risked their professional reputations by certifying that he was receiving no intentional cues from his owner or any other questioner. They then formed a committee to investigate the origins of his cleverness.

First they established that Hans was just as clever with or without the presence of his owner. But his performance was severely impaired by two manipulations. He could not solve problems to which the asker himself did not know the answers, nor could he answer a question if he could not see the questioner. These clues seemed to indicate that his ability was dependent on some kind of visual information. From this point it took only the time needed for many small trial-and-error experiments to settle the matter. A clever animal indeed, Hans was responding to the angle of the questioner's head. After asking a question, the questioner would inevitably look down at Hans' feet; this was the signal to begin. If the head was bent far down, as if anticipating a long chain of tappings, Hans tapped at a much faster rate than if it was only bent slightly. As the end of the chain approached, the observer would gradually raise his head, and when the last correct step had been given, he would lift it entirely. That would be the signal to stop.

This revelation is relevant to experimentation with

human beings in several respects. The conveying of cues from experimenter to subject may be extremely subtle and complex—and most college student subjects are even cleverer than Hans. Thus, the possibilities for unintended communication are vast. A logical and consistent attack on the problem may uncover more such influences. Most importantly, informative cues can be transmitted even when the sender is actively trying not to communicate them. Indeed, the sender and receiver may be complete strangers, perhaps not even members of the same species.

Robert Rosenthal has devised a number of procedures to test the experimenter-bias hypothesis. Most of these involve placing the subjects in the role of experimenters and giving subjects various biases in doing experiments that are otherwise identical. Then any variations in the results of the experiments can be traced, in large measure, to the biases.

EXPERIMENTAL EVIDENCE

Investigators: R. Rosenthal, K. L. Fode
Source, Date: "The Effect of Experimenter Bias on the Performance of the Albino Rat," 1963
Location: Harvard University
Subjects: 12 student experimenters, 206 introductory psychology students
Materials: Rats, maze

Twelve student researchers were actually the subjects in this experiment but did not realize it. They were told that, to gain experience in duplicating experimental results, they were to run five rats through a simple maze ten times each day for five days. Half of the subjects were informed that their rats were quite "bright" and should learn easily and quickly. The remaining six subjects were told that their animals were "dull." All the rats had in fact been randomly drawn from a homogeneous rat colony. The "experimenters" then recorded each of the 250 trials and noted when the rats made the correct response (going to the darker of two platforms).

Analysis of the data revealed that on any one day the "bright" rats made 2.3 correct responses while the "dull" animals made only 1.5 correct responses. This difference was statistically significant. Rosenthal and Fode concluded that it was the result of experimenter bias. Others have suggested that it might have come about because the "bright" animals were handled gently; the "dull" animals roughly.

Theodore X. Barber has argued that the problem of experimenter bias is not as severe as Rosenthal's work apparently suggests. He maintains that the size of the effect is really quite small and that appropriate steps can be taken to minimize it (Barber and Silver, 1965). Experimenters can learn through experience to suppress the smiles, gestures, tones of voice, or persistent attention that may tell a subject that he is performing "successfully" and the frowns or terse readings of instructions that indicate that the subject should respond differently. In some cases an experiment can be run by a researcher who is unfamiliar with the hypothesis being tested. Because neutral researchers are not always possible to find, however, other techniques can be used. For example, one experimenter may read the instructions and another actually supervise the procedure without knowing the experimental condition of each subject. Tape-recorded instructions can also be used, and the whole experiment can be run by a computer or some other mechanical device.

The problem may never be fully solved as long as psychology depends on human experimenters, but careful planning of instructions, tasks, and procedures limits the possibility that research will be seriously hampered by self-fulfilling prophecies. In the long run, the relatively simple, straightforward experiment may be the best deterrent to bias. Subjects should not be forced into positions where they must make guesses about how they should respond in this or that situation. The more a subject knows and understands about the situation, the less likely he will be to try to "psych it out." Subjects should be encouraged to ask any questions, and the experimenter should bring as few expectations as possible to the investigation.

In fact, these problems are common to almost any form of reactive research. Whether it be the chemist standing close enough to a test tube to change its temperature or a political researcher asking questions for a survey, the person is a potential contaminating variable in research.

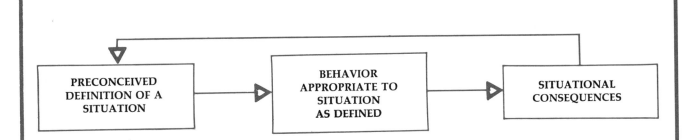

| PRECONCEIVED DEFINITION OF A SITUATION | → | BEHAVIOR APPROPRIATE TO SITUATION AS DEFINED | → | SITUATIONAL CONSEQUENCES |

PUTTING IT TOGETHER: Self-Fulfilling Prophecy

The concept of self-fulfilling prophecy involves a process beginning with a preconceived definition of a situation. People usually plan their behavior to be appropriate to situations as they define them. Our behavior may be responsible for structuring the continuing nature of a variety of situations. When the situational consequences are consistent with our preconceptions, those preconceptions are "confirmed" and may be accepted as "true," regardless of their accuracy.

Following are a number of examples of the self-fulfilling prophecy in a variety of situations:

In social interactions the preconception that an individual is in control of his own destiny may lead to energetic striving behavior with consequent achievement. The preconception that one is liked or disliked by others may initiate behavior towards other people that causes one to like or dislike the initiator.

In educational situations, a teacher may expect some students to be "late bloomers" and therefore change the quality of his or her behavior with the students in ways that may improve their school performance.

In behavioral research, a subject may understand that the experimenter wants him to behave in some specific way. In response to the demand characteristics as he understands them, he may produce data the experimenter hopes to get. If an experimenter believes her hypothesis to be "true," she may treat her subjects differently or analyze and interpret the data so that the experimenter's biases are confirmed.

1. WHAT'S ACCEPTED . . .

1. An individual's belief that he is internally or externally controlled will normally be related to his academic success.

2. An individual's beliefs about another's feelings about him can generate actual feelings congruent with those beliefs.

3. Teachers' expectancies about how well a child will perform can generate teacher behavior that realizes that expectancy.

4. Demand characteristics and experimenter bias can influence the outcomes of psychological experiments.

2. WHAT'S DEBATED . . .

1. How an individual's locus of control is related to achievement behavior—which causes which.

2. To what extent teacher expectancies operate in real-life classroom settings.

3. The utility of diagnostic labels and the validity of diagnostic techniques.

4. To what extent demand characteristics and experimenter bias affect the outcomes of psychological research in general.

There is little disagreement that the concept of the self-fulfilling prophecy has significant implications for psychological research. It has sensitized social scientists to an awareness that they may unknowingly influence the behavior of their experimental subjects. Researchers today guard against this danger by using various methods, often including taking care to ensure that the subjects do not discover the true purpose of the experiment, and having some independent observer check the findings without prior knowledge of the hypothesis being tested.

But the self-fulfilling prophecy has implications that reach far beyond the laboratory, into the home, the classroom, the workplace—anywhere that people interact with other people. For instance, how might you react if told that someone you were about to meet had just been released from a mental hospital?

The chances are that your perceptions of the person would be significantly affected. You might observe and analyze the person's behavior rather differently from how you might have without the background information. And if enough people were to treat the former inmate on the basis of his or her past record, the result could well be that the person would ultimately be returned to the institution. If one expects former patients to be disordered, one tends to interpret what they say and do in the light of this preconception. In consequence, the former inmate may be unable to function effectively in society. The resulting stresses may easily drive him back to his earlier behavioral patterns of mental illness. And as the prophecy is fulfilled, those who labeled the former inmate as "ill" might say, "I told you so."

The concept of the self-fulfilling prophecy has profound implications for human behavior, and social scientists are very concerned that indiscriminate labeling may contribute to deviance, personality disorder, and academic or personal failure. Many of these attributes may not be intrinsic to the individual, but instead learned over a period of time through acceptance of labels applied by other people.

One of the strongest proponents of this labeling concept is Howard S. Becker, who suggests that labeling and the subsequent self-fulfilling prophecy is the basis for much socially deviant behavior. Traditionally, society has tended to regard deviance as a character defect located in the individual—the delinquent is naturally "bad," the homosexual basically "degenerate," and so on. Becker argues, however, that deviance is not so much an attribute of an individual as the result of a social process of labeling: "the deviant is someone to whom the label has been successfully applied." Many other people also engage in socially deviant behavior (such as dodging taxes), but because they are not discovered and labeled as deviants, they do not regard themselves as criminal.

Most individuals, Becker points out, explore some form or another of deviant behavior, such as adolescent homosexuality or petty theft. Usually this behavior is short-lived and passes unnoticed by others. But if significant members of society—parents, friends, policemen—notice the behavior, they may label the individual as a "deviant" or a "homosexual" and begin to treat him accordingly. Gradually, the person comes to accept the label and to define himself as a delinquent or a homosexual. He constructs his choices and experiences in accordance with this self-definition, and becomes a permanent deviant. This label becomes prophetic, and the prophecy is fulfilled.

Thomas Scheff has used the concepts of labeling and self-fulfilling prophecies to account for the origins of some forms of mental disorder. At times, we all behave in irrational, apparently disordered ways, perhaps losing our tempers, or talking to ourselves, or even becoming hysterical. Sometimes a person may engage in this kind of behavior for prolonged periods—perhaps hours, days or months—simply because he or she is unable to deal effectively with some difficult and stressful social situation. Relatives and friends, however, are often quick to apply the label of "mentally ill" to the person concerned. And perhaps the person, involuntarily, unconsciously, finds it convenient to accept this label, because when someone is defined as "sick," he or she is excused from normal responsibilities and escapes the difficult situation. But the label is more easily taken on than cast aside. Anxious associates continue to interpret the individual's behavior in accordance with their belief that he or she is ill, and scrutinize even the most normal behavior with apprehension. Eventually, suggests Scheff,

the individual may fully accept the label of mental illness, and the disordered behavior becomes permanent.

So far, most of the research on self-fulfilling prophecy concerns the undesirable effects of the process—bad school grades, deviant behavior and personal disorders. In the future, psychologists may explore more fully the positive potential of labeling. Their findings could be a new force for constructive social change in many areas, especially early human development. It might be possible, for example, to use positive labeling as a means of enhancing the self-image of deviant and disadvantaged people. The likelihood of success would be greatest for young people, since they are less likely to have become the permanent victims of earlier negative labeling. In the schools, in the family, in therapy, and in the treatment of juvenile offenders, the use of self-fulfilling prophecies designed to improve self-concept and personal confidence may offer immense potential.

Unit 3

Helping Others

OVERVIEW

What are the motives and circumstances under which people help other people? The first part of the unit deals with factors that tend to increase the likelihood of people displaying helping behavior. The second part deals with the particular personality characteristics that apparently make some individuals more helpful than others. The Issue section focuses on helping behavior or the lack of it in crowded urban settings.

UNIT OUTLINE

DEFINITION AND BACKGROUND
1. *Definition:* helping is any behavior that has the effect of benefiting another.
2. *Background:* Carl Rogers (1902–   ).

QUESTIONS AND EVIDENCE
1. Under what conditions do people help others?
Hypotheses:
   a. *Guilt:* helping behavior can be generated by the feeling of discomfort or psychological distress that comes from knowing one has harmed another person or committed a "sinful" act. **50**
   b. *Modeling:* people are more likely to help after they have seen someone else do so. **51**
   c. *Responsibility:* a bystander who is alone is more likely to intervene in an emergency than a bystander who is in a group, because the lone bystander bears all the responsibility for helping. **51**
   d. *Empathy:* people help other people in order to experience their pleasure empathically. **53**
2. What kind of people are helpful?
Hypotheses:
   a. *Dependency:* dependent people tend to be more helpful than independent people. **54**
   b. *Internal-control:* internally-controlled people are more helpful than those who are externally controlled. **55**
   c. *Empathy:* empathic people are more helpful than unempathic people. **55**

IMPORTANT CONCEPTS

	page
altruism	48
client-centered therapy	49
dependence	54
diffusion of responsibility	52
empathy	53
guilt feelings	50
imitation	51
locus of control	55
models	51

Our experience with helping behavior may include being helped or observing people helping others.

Willingness to help others in need is influenced by each individual's relationship to a specific situation.

There is evidence that personal empathy and having previously observed people help leads to helping others.

DEFINITION AND BACKGROUND

In the history of ideas, helping traditionally has been the concern of religious leaders and ethical philosophers. They have treated helping as a value, and debated whether people have a moral obligation to make sacrifices for the sake of others. Most theologians and philosophers have defended the value of helping others, but some have argued against it. Nietzsche, for example, asserted that people have a moral obligation only to look after themselves. He objected to what he called the "slave morality" of the Christian ethic, arguing that Christians preach self-sacrifice because *they* need help, and they want others to make sacrifices for them.

As theoreticians or researchers, psychologists do not treat questions about helping as moral questions. They observe people, see that some of them do sometimes help others, and ask questions like: what kind of people are most likely to help others and under what circumstances?

One possible DEFINITION of helping is *any behavior that has the effect of benefiting another*. The helping behaviors most frequently studied by psychologists are sharing, giving aid to someone in distress, helping someone do a task, making donations to charity, and foregoing the chance to win in order to increase someone else's chances of winning.

Helping behavior has the effect of benefiting another person, but note that it need not be aimed solely at doing so. A young man may mow his grandmother's lawn because he hopes she will remember

him in her will; a woman may wash and iron her husband's clothes because she knows he will be angry if she does not. Behavior motivated by a *desire* to benefit another person rather than oneself is called altruistic behavior; altruistic behavior is always meant to be helpful, but helping behavior is not always altruistic. In fact, it may never be. Some people argue that man is by nature motivated to do only that which he sees as being in his own best interest, and that people are therefore incapable of true altruism.

This unit will FOCUS on some of the causes of helping behavior, and on some of the personality characteristics of helpful people.

BACKGROUND: CARL ROGERS (1902—   )

The life of Carl Rogers, a leading figure in the humanistic psychology movement and the originator of nondirective or client-centered therapy, exemplifies the link between religious values and an interest in helping behavior referred to at the start of this unit. Born in 1902, Rogers grew up in a strict Protestant family. He studied for the ministry at college and began postgraduate work at Union Theological Seminary. Then he dropped out and switched to the study of psychology, specializing at first in work with delinquent and underprivileged children and later in psychotherapy. He abandoned the ministry, he says, partly because of a six-month visit to China with the World Student Christian Federation, which brought him into contact with people who held sincere religious beliefs very different from his own. This experience was a critical one for Rogers, for it shook his faith in the idea that his was the "one, right way." Indeed, for him, it seemed to demolish the idea that *any* one way is *the* way. A profound respect for opposing points of view and for each person's capacity to make his own choices is a key characteristic of Rogers' approach to psychology.

Rogers is generally regarded as the first American to pose a serious challenge to the more pessimistic theories of Sigmund Freud. In Freud's view the irrational forces in man's nature are so strong that rationality has little chance against them, on either an individual or a social level. In *Civilization and Its Discontents*, Freud expressed the belief that people would never be able fully to control or rechannel their destructive impulses. One consequence, he thought, was that wars are an inevitable part of human exist-

Figure 1. Carl Rogers, founder of client-centered therapy, whose view of human nature as basically positive and healthy contrasted sharply with Sigmund Freud's more pessimistic theories of human irrationality.

ence. Rogers' view of human nature is as positive as Freud's is bleak. To Rogers, it is a mistake to see consciousness as "the watchman over a dangerous and unpredictable lot of impulses": people's basic impulses are healthy and positive, and "very satisfactorily self-governing when not fearfully guarded."

This approach is illustrated in client-centered therapy, which Rogers originated (see Unit 20). It rejects the notion that a person with problems should be thought of as a "patient" with a "disease" that an "expert" will cure. Rather, the person is a "client" who solves his problems in his own way, assisted by an accepting and nondirective "counselor." The counselor's job is to create a free, open atmosphere of trust so that the client will feel free to explore himself and his problems, and to become gradually the kind of person he truly is. The stress on acceptance, Rogers says, is not due to a hypersensitivity about the client's ability to withstand criticism but to "the conviction, based on experience, that if I can free him as completely as possible from external threat, then he can begin to experience and to deal with the internal feelings and conflicts which he finds threatening within himself."

"My interest in psychotherapy," Rogers wrote in *On Becoming a Person* (1961), "has brought about in me an interest in every kind of helping relationship"—not only counselor/client but parent/child, teacher/student, and just plain person/person. Rogers' interest in helping relationships is based on the conviction that helping others to be fully themselves is an essential part of one's own self-realization. Although Rogers has done some empirical research, chiefly on the effectiveness of various therapies, his main contribution to the study of helping relationships is his descriptive and theoretical writings in which he often supports his points by citing research performed by other psychologists. In *On Becoming A Person*, for example, he describes studies showing that helping relationships are:

1. *Accepting*. Children of parents with a democratic, accepting attitude show faster intellectual development, more originality, and more emotional security and control than those from other types of homes (Baldwin et al., 1945).
2. *Personal*. Physicians working with hospitalized schizophrenic patients have most success when they focus on the meaning a patient's behavior has for the patient himself rather than on seeing the schizophrenic as a walking case study or diagnostic category (Betz and Whitehorn, 1956; Whitehorn and Betz, 1954).
3. *Trustful*. Patients who have been helped by various types of therapy say that the important factor was not the therapist's particular technique but the patient's feeling that the therapist was trustworthy, understanding, and willing to have the patient make his own decisions and choices (Heine, 1950).

Rogers is one of the "grand old men" of humanistic psychology. Now on the staff of the Center for Studies of the Person in La Jolla, California, he is an enthusiastic participant in the encounter-group movement. Most such groups stress two aspects of behavior that Rogers considers essential to helping relationships: *honesty*—the need to be "dependably real"; and *expressiveness*—the ability to communicate one's "real self" of the moment in an unambiguous fashion. A person whose behavior lacks these qualities may be rigidly consistent, but he does not come across as fully trustworthy and thus will have trouble helping others to be as they truly are.

Much of Rogers' work is based on his own experiences as a therapist and in other capacities. Clearly he himself is a very "helping" kind of person. Most people, whether they have met him or have only read his books, cannot help liking him, and most psychologists regard him as an important theorist, even though not all of them accept his ideas. Some consider his optimism about human nature naive; others think that a full understanding of the psychology of helping is more likely to come from research data than from any theory. Our next step, then, is to examine some empirical evidence on the reasons for helping behavior.

QUESTIONS AND EVIDENCE

1. Under what conditions do people help others?

2. What kind of people are helpful?

The first question asks what external events cause the average person to help others; that is, it is aimed at identifying factors that affect the helping behavior of people generally. The second question asks what personal characteristics make it likely that a person will help others; that is, it is aimed at identifying

HYPOTHESES	GUILT	MODELING	RESPONSIBILITY	EMPATHY
DESCRIPTIVE EVIDENCE				
EXPERIMENTAL EVIDENCE	VARY: degree of need of student left unaided MEASURE: willingness of "helper" to donate blood	VARY: opportunity to observe a motorist helping a woman fix a flat tire MEASURE: number of motorists stopping to help a woman fix a flat tire	VARY: number and familiarity of people present during an emergency MEASURE: speed and frequency of helping	VARY: experience of person attended to MEASURE: number of pages scored for experimenter

factors that affect the helping behavior of particular individuals.

1. UNDER WHAT CONDITIONS DO PEOPLE HELP OTHERS?

Many of the reasons people help others seem obvious. We help because it is our duty; or because we want others to help us; or because it makes us feel good; or because we like people and want them to like us. But many reasons for helping others are more subtle than they seem. Social psychologists have investigated a large variety of possible determinants of helping. Among the most interesting are feelings of guilt, the desire to imitate or conform to the behavior of others, a feeling of responsibility, and a sense of empathy with other people.

The *guilt hypothesis* states that helping behavior can be generated by the feeling of discomfort or psychological distress that comes from knowing one has harmed another person or committed a "sinful" act. The power of a guilty conscience is well known to income-tax authorities, who receive thousands of anonymous "donations" each year. It also has been suggested that many "philanthropists" donate to charity to relieve the guilt associated with the way they earned their fortunes.

EXPERIMENTAL EVIDENCE

Investigators: R. B. Darlington and C. E. Macker
Source, Date: "Displacement of Guilt-produced Altruistic Behavior," 1966
Location: University of Minnesota
Subjects: 26 female college students

Materials: 3 dummy tasks; blood-donation appeal

As each subject arrived for the experiment, she was introduced to a man who, she was told, was another subject. Actually the man was a confederate of the experimenters. The subject was told that she was taking part in a study on cooperation, and that the man was her "partner." The two of them would be given a number of pencil and paper tasks, and the success of one member of the pair would help the other gain credits that could be used to increase his grade in a course. As each subject in the experimental group waited for the experiment to begin, the confederate told her a hard-luck story intended to increase her feeling that it was important to gain credits for him during the experiment. He said that he had had to drop out of school for a year to work. During that time he had married, and his wife was expecting a baby. He was having a hard time making ends meet, had to work twenty hours a week, and as a result was failing his psychology course.

To the subjects in a control group, the confederate said he was auditing the psychology course. Therefore, the credits the subject could earn him were of little importance.

The pencil-and-paper tasks were, in fact, impossible; thus, the subjects were unable to do them and thought they had failed to gain points for their partner. Each was told, however, that the partner had succeeded in gaining points for her. At the end of the experiment, while the subjects were waiting (they thought) for the experimenter to give them a questionnaire, a girl entered the room and asked if they would volunteer to donate blood to the University Hospital Blood Bank. As expected, more of the subjects who had heard the hard-luck story volunteered to donate blood than did those in the control group. The experimenters interpreted this result in terms of "displaced guilt," suggesting that the subjects in the experimental group were more willing to volunteer in order to assuage the guilt they experienced for not helping their needy partner.

Other studies have induced guilt and measured its effect on helping in other ways. Carlsmith and Gross (1969) found that subjects who had been induced to deliver what they thought were electric shocks to other subjects were more prone to volunteer to help save redwood trees in California than subjects who had delivered a buzzer sound. In 1967 Freedman, Wallington, and Bliss found that subjects who had been induced to tell a lie to an experimenter were more likely to volunteer for another experiment than subjects who had not. They even found that subjects who had knocked over a stack of index cards were more prone to volunteer for an experiment than subjects who had not.

One of the strongest influences on what we do is what we see other people do. Observing another person act helpfully draws our attention to his helping behavior and reminds us that we too could help. In a strange situation, people are often uncertain about what to do, and they look to other people for guidance. They especially tend to imitate the behavior of those they admire. Also, they learn from the mistakes of others. If a person sees someone helping another and suffering for it, he is less likely to imitate him.

Copying the behavior of another individual is called "imitation" or "modeling." Copying the behavior of a group of other people is usually called conforming. Everyone has experienced the pressure to conform to the norms of groups. Of all the experiments done on helping behavior, by far the largest number have investigated the *modeling hypothesis*. The modeling hypothesis predicts that people are more likely to help after they have seen someone else do so.

EXPERIMENTAL EVIDENCE

Investigators: J. H. Bryan and M. A. Test
Source, Date: "Models and Helping: Naturalistic Studies in Aiding Behavior," 1967

Location: Northwestern University
Subjects: Several thousand automobile drivers
Materials: 1965 Ford Mustang, 1965 Oldsmobile

Bryan and Test parked two cars with flat left-rear tires by the side of a Los Angeles road about a quarter of a mile apart. One car was a 1965 Ford Mustang beside which stood an inflated spare tire and a girl apparently in distress. The other car was a 1965 Oldsmobile parked ahead of the Mustang, raised on a jack; a girl, apparently its owner, stood by watching a man change the tire.

The question was, how many people would stop to help the girl with the Mustang? As a control condition, Bryan and Test reran the experiment using only the Mustang, so that they would know how many motorists stopped when they had no model (the man helping the girl with the Oldsmobile) to imitate.

Bryan and Test conducted the experiment on two successive Saturday afternoons. Each day they waited until 1,000 cars had passed in the experimental condition (Mustang plus Oldsmobile) and 1,000 cars had passed in the control condition (Mustang alone).

They found that fifty-eight motorists who saw both cars stopped, but only thirty-five who saw the Mustang alone stopped. The researchers concluded that someone who sees another person help is more likely to help in a similar situation than someone who has seen no model.

Imitation, however, is a two-edged sword, for seeing other people *fail* to help seems to increase the probability of *not* helping. On a March night in 1964, Kitty Genovese was beaten and murdered as she was returning from work to her home in Queens, New York, at 3 A.M. Her assailant took over half an hour to kill her. During that time, thirty-eight of her neighbors heard her screams, came to their windows, and watched—but failed to come to her assistance. None of them even called the police (*The New York Times*, March 27, 1964).

This event created a journalistic sensation and subsequently led several psychologists to investigate the circumstances in which witnesses to emergencies do or do not help the victims. Their work tends to confirm not only the tendency to conform to the nonhelping behavior of others but also the tendency for responsibility to diffuse over the members of a group. The *responsibility hypothesis* states that a bystander who is alone is more likely to intervene in an emergency than a bystander who is in a group, because the lone bystander bears all the responsibility for helping. For example, he gets all the credit if he helps and all the blame if he does not.

EXPERIMENTAL EVIDENCE

Investigators: B. Latané and J. Darley
Source, Date: "Group Inhibition of Bystander Intervention in Emergencies," 1969
Location: Columbia University
Subjects: College students
Materials: Tape recordings (in most of the studies)

Different subjects waited in a room alone, with a friend, or with a stranger to participate in what they thought would be a market research study. Some of the strangers were actually confederates of the experimenters, who had been told to act passive and not to respond to the "emergency" to come. While waiting, the subjects heard from the next room the sounds of a woman climbing onto a chair, a loud crash and a scream, followed by moaning. Actually, the sounds were on a tape recording. After slightly more than two minutes, the woman seemed to struggle to the door and let herself out.

Over 70 percent of the students who were waiting alone went to help the "victim" before she left the room. When friends waited together, at least one of them responded 70 percent of the time. However, only 13 percent of those who waited with a stranger and 7 percent of those who waited with a passive confederate of the experimenters responded. With respect to speed of responding, the subjects who waited alone reacted fastest; next those who waited with friends; then those waiting with strangers; and, finally, those with passive confederates, many of whom did not respond at all.

In another experiment, two undergraduates staged a total of ninety-six "robberies" at a liquor store. In each instance, they stole a case of beer while the "proprietor" (another confederate of the experimenter) was out of the room. Half the robberies were staged while one customer was in the store, the other half when two customers were present. While 65 percent of the single witnesses reported the theft to the proprietor, only 56 percent of the pairs did.

In a third experiment, each of one hundred female college subjects was ushered into a room where, supposedly, she would take part in a discussion of the personal problems of students. She was informed that, "in order to avoid embarrassing anyone," the discussion would be conducted not face-to-face but over intercoms. Each student would present her problems to the group and then comment on the others' problems. Some of the subjects were told that only they and one other person were taking part in the discussion, while others thought there were three or six students in the group. Some of the subjects in the larger groups were led to think that a friend was taking part in the discussion; others thought the other people were strangers.

Actually, the "others" taking part in the discussion were prerecorded voices. When the discussion began, the first speaker was the "victim." He mentioned with embarrassment that he was prone to seizures. Then each of the other "participants" (if any) spoke, with the real subject going last. When it was again time for the victim to speak, the recording gave the impression that he was having an epileptic fit.

All—100 percent—of the subjects who thought they were alone with the victim reported his plight, but only 62 percent of those who thought they were part of a six-member group ever did so. The subjects who believed they were part of a three-member group with a friend as the third member responded faster than those who thought the third member was a stranger.

The inhibiting effect of other bystanders seems to follow a clear pattern: a stranger who does not react is the most inhibiting, a neutral stranger next, and then a friend. Latané and Darley have attributed this effect to "diffusion of responsibility": it is easier to accept one-sixth or one thirty-eighth of the blame for not responding than to accept all the responsibility. They have also suggested several other possible explanations for the lack of action by individuals in a group. For instance, the apparent lack of concern shown by other bystanders may lead a person to regard a situation as less serious than it actually is. If you see a man collapse on the street, you may think he is having a heart attack, but if all the other pedestrians keep right on walking, you are likely to downgrade your diagnosis and figure he is probably just drunk. In situations like the murder of Kitty Genovese, there is also the factor of risk—though that hardly explains why no one managed to call the police during the

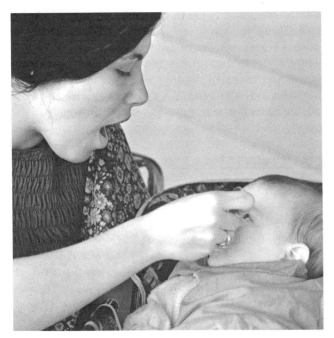

Figure 2. Empathy is feeling and sharing another person's experience, as in this mother's reaction to her baby during feeding.

attack. Perhaps each bystander was assuming that someone else had already done so, or would.

One reason the apparent apathy of bystanders to emergencies is surprising is that, as we all know from experience, we tend to feel bad when we see other people suffering. We empathize with them—we feel bad when they feel bad and good when they feel good. The *empathy hypothesis* states that people help other people in order to experience their pleasure empathically (or to relieve empathically experienced pain).

EXPERIMENTAL EVIDENCE

Investigators: D. Aderman and L. Berkowitz
Source, Date: "Observational Set, Empathy, and Helping," 1970
Location: University of Wisconsin
Subjects: 120 male college students
Materials: Tape-recorded interviews; instructions; scoring task; mood (empathy) questionnaires

Subjects were asked to listen to a tape-recorded conversation between a student in need of help and a helper. Half of the subjects were instructed to pay particular attention to the student and the other half to pay attention to the helper. The experimenters assumed that attending to one speaker or the other would encourage empathy with him. The two groups were then divided into three sub-groups, each of which listened to a different taped conversation. In the first, the helper failed to help the student. In the second, he helped but was not thanked; and in the third he helped and was thanked. At the end of the experiment, all subjects were asked to fill out a "mood questionnaire" concerning their feelings about the two people they had listened to on the tape. Finally, the experimenter nonchalantly asked the subjects to help him score some papers.

The subjects' helping scores were determined by the number of pages they graded during a ten-minute period. The results are summarized in Table 1. Of the subjects who attended to the student, the most helpful were those who thought the student had not been helped. Of those attending to the helper, the most helpful were those who had heard the helper help and be thanked.

TABLE 1.   Mean Number of Pages Scored by Subjects

Subjects Attending to Person in Need		Subjects Attending to Helper
"No help" outcome	73	56
"Help" outcome	65	63
"Help plus thanks" outcome	66	74

Source: Adapted from D. Aderman and L. Berkowitz, "Observational Set, Empathy, and Helping," *Journal of Personality and Social Psychology*, 14 (1970), 141–148.

The mood questionnaire tended to show that a "pleasurable empathic experience" led the subjects who attended to the thanked helper to help the experimenter. They empathized with the helper and felt pleasure when he was thanked, which increased their willingness to help the experimenter after the experiment. The subjects who attended to the student who got no help also empathized with him. They experienced *unpleasant* feelings when he did not receive help, and these feelings decreased their willingness to instill similar feelings in the experimenter. Therefore, they also helped more. The subjects in the other four sub-groups felt less empathy and therefore were less inclined to help.

In examining research on the conditions under which people help others, we have paid no attention to the personality characteristics of the subjects in the experiments. The conclusions drawn concerned the responses of the average subject under this or that set of circumstances. The next question, in contrast, focuses on the personality characteristics that are typical of individual helpful people.

Before the subjects for this experiment were selected, sixty-three boys in seven nursery-school classes were given eighteen pieces of candy and three plastic bags. They were told to divide the candy between themselves and "the two children in the nursery school you like best." The children were given a generosity score on the basis of the number of candies they gave to the other children. The boys who gave many candies

QUESTION 2. WHAT KIND OF PEOPLE ARE HELPFUL?

HYPOTHESES	DEPENDENCY	INTERNAL CONTROL	EMPATHY
DESCRIPTIVE EVIDENCE	ASSESS: relationship between dependency needs, and number of candies given away	ASSESS: relationship between feelings of control over one's own fate and willingness to volunteer for civil rights work	ASSESS: relationship between empathy score and willingness to help another win money
EXPERIMENTAL EVIDENCE			

2. WHAT KIND OF PEOPLE ARE HELPFUL?

The evidence on this question is descriptive and correlational rather than experimental; that is, it shows that certain personality characteristics tend to be found in people who help, but it does not show that those characteristics *cause* helpfulness. Not surprisingly, however, there is a rough correspondence between the characteristics of situations that encourage helping behavior and the personality characteristics of helpful people. It has been pointed out, for example, that people are likely to help when they see others help; that is, they tend to help in conformity situations. We might expect, then, that a conforming person would probably be more helpful than a nonconforming person. Dependency is one personality characteristic of many conforming people. Dependent people are concerned with pleasing others, and one of the best ways of pleasing others is to do things for them. The *dependency hypothesis* states that dependent people tend to be more helpful than independent people.

DESCRIPTIVE EVIDENCE

Investigators: E. Rutherford and P. Mussen
Source, Date: "Generosity in Nursery School Boys," 1968
Location: San Jose State College
Subjects: 22 nursery-school boys
Materials: Candy, doll-play task, competitive racing game

away were called highly generous boys, and the boys who gave away only a few were called selfish.

The twelve boys in the highly generous category and ten boys in the selfish category became the experimental subjects. They were given several dolls —a mother, a father, and a child—and asked to act out endings for seven incomplete stories. In one, for example, the parent dolls were in their bed, and the child was in his. The boys were told, "It is late at night; everyone is asleep. Suddenly the boy has a bad dream and wakes up very frightened. What do you think he will do?" The responses of each boy to these situations were scored for the presence or absence of dependency.

After the boys had completed the doll-play task, they were asked to participate in a racing game. The experimenter gave the boy a doll and kept one himself. He told the boy that they (the experimenter and the boy) would race their dolls along the length of a yardstick. The experimenter moved his slowly and steadily in order to allow the child to win the race. The margin by which each boy chose to win was translated into a competitiveness score.

The experimenters found that the boys in the highly generous group were more dependent and less competitive than the boys in the selfish group. At least at this age, dependent and noncompetitive children were the most helpful.

In discussing the modeling or conformity hypothesis, it was mentioned that people tend to conform to the unhelpful as well as the helpful behavior of others. You are not likely to get a ladder and retrieve a kitten from a tree if there are a dozen other people around who are acting unconcerned (unless it happens to be your cat). In such a situation, the helpful person may be not the dependent or conforming one but the one who relies on himself and is accustomed to assuming control.

Julian Rotter has developed a "locus-of-control" scale to measure the extent to which a person perceives himself as having control over his fate rather than being controlled by others or by chance. People who score high on this scale are called "internally controlled," and those who score low on the scale are called "externally controlled." The *internal-control hypothesis* states that internally controlled people are more helpful than those who are externally controlled, especially in situations that call for action (rather than, say, generosity, as in the preceding experiment).

DESCRIPTIVE EVIDENCE

Investigators: P. M. Gore and J. B. Rotter
Source, Date: "A Personality Correlate of Social Action,"
1963
Location: Ohio State University
Subjects: 62 male and 54 female students at a black college in
Florida
Materials: Locus-of-control scale; questionnaire

The experimenters entered three psychology classes at a southern black college and asked all students to take the Rotter locus-of-control test. The test includes such statements as "Capable people who fail to become leaders have not taken advantage of their opportunities" and "Trusting to fate has never turned out as well for me as making a decision to take a definite course of action." People who score high on internal control usually agree with those statements and disagree with others, such as "Without the right breaks one cannot be an effective leader" and "I have often found that what is going to happen will happen."

Four weeks after the subjects had taken the locus-of-control test, a student confederate of the experimenters went into their classes and said, "Thank you, Doctor, for allowing me this time. I would like to ask

the cooperation of each of you in a Students for Freedom Movement. To that end, I will pass out slips for you to fill out and hand back to me as you leave." The slip is shown in Figure 3.

```
Students for Freedom Rally
Please check any or all aspects of our program in which
you would be willing to participate.
I would be interested in:                    Check here:

    (A)  Attending a rally for civil rights.        _____

    (B)  Signing a petition to go to local
         government and/or news media calling
         for full and immediate integration
         of all facilities throughout Florida.      _____

    (C)  Joining a silent march to the capitol
         to demonstrate our plea for full and
         immediate integration of all facilities
         throughout Florida.                        _____

    (D)  Joining a Freedom Riders' Group for
         a trip during the semester break.          _____

    (E)  I would not be interested in par-
         ticipating in any of the foregoing.        _____

Signature: _____

Address: _____

Telephone No.: _____
```

Figure 3. Questionnaire completed by subjects in the experiment conducted by Gore and Rotter (1963) which found that subjects with high internal-control scores were more willing to volunteer for civil-rights work than subjects with low scores.

Answers to the questions were scored according to the students' willingness to take part in social action, which was used as a measure of their helpfulness. At the time of the study (1963) large numbers of civil-rights workers were being put in jail for participating in marches similar to the one suggested in the questionnaire. Subjects who volunteered to march or join a Freedom Riders' group, then, expected that their action might entail considerable self-sacrifice.

The results of the study showed a strong positive relationship between a high internal-control score and a willingness to volunteer for civil-rights action. Probably, internally controlled students were more willing to help than the externally controlled students because they were more inclined to believe that their actions would have an effect.

Both dependency and internal control are traits of the helper; they have little to do with the needs of the one who is helped. The final personality trait that we will examine, empathy, is more closely tied to the needs of the other person. The *empathy hypothesis* states that empathic people are more helpful than unempathic people. Recall that it has been found that conditions that arouse feelings of empathy in people make it more likely that they will help; it follows that people characterized by the personality trait of empathy will be more helpful than others.

DESCRIPTIVE EVIDENCE

Investigator: D. Krebs
Source, Date: "The Effect of Prior Experience on Generosity—Role Taking or Modeling," 1972
Location: Harvard University
Subjects: 36 college students
Materials: A roulette game, the Hogan Empathy Scale

The empathy of each subject was measured on a test developed by Hogan (1968). It consists of sixty-four, true-false statements, some of which have a clear relation to empathy ("As a rule I have little difficulty in 'putting myself in other people's shoes'" and "I have seen some things so sad that I almost felt like crying") and others of which do not ("I liked *Alice in Wonderland* by Lewis Carroll"). Hogan has validated the test in several ways, and it seems to be an accurate measure of empathy.

After taking the empathy test, the subjects were escorted one by one to a room behind a one-way mirror. Through it, they watched a confederate of the experimenter play roulette. They saw the experimenter tell the player that there would be one last bonus trial on which he had a chance to win a great deal of money. Privately, the experimenter told each subject that he, too, had a chance to win a lot of money, and that he would be allowed to define the odds of winning and losing both for the roulette player and for himself. The catch was that the better odds a subject gave the player, the worse odds he had to give himself.

The results of the experiment were straightforward. The higher the subjects scored on Hogan's Empathy Scale, the more willing they were to give the roulette player favorable odds. The study supports the idea that highly empathic people are helpful.

Figure 4. Helping behavior is determined by external events as well as the personality traits of the people exposed to those events. Observing other people help and believing that one has control over one's fate increase the probability of helping.

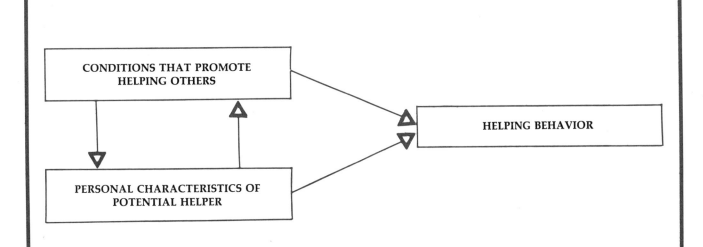

PUTTING IT TOGETHER: Helping Others

When people help one another, there is an interaction between the *conditions* under which the event occurs and the *personal characteristics* of the helpful people. Some of the conditions that promote *helping behavior* in the average person are the production of guilt that arises from harming others, observing other people help, bearing sole responsibility for helping and being asked to attend to the feelings of another. People who are dependent, internally controlled and empathic tend to be more helpful than other people, at least in certain situations.

One might reasonably suppose that most helping would occur when there is a correspondence between events and personality characteristics and the least helping when there is not.

External events as well as specific personality traits put people in particular psychological states which determine their helping behavior. Dependent people are more affected by events that elicit conformity. People who believe they control their fate are more affected by situations that demand the taking of responsibility. People who are empathic are more influenced by the pain and pleasure of others.

1. WHAT'S ACCEPTED . . .

1. Unintentionally harming another person increases the probability of helping.

2. Observing other people help increases the probability of helping.

3. A lone bystander is more likely to help during an emergency than people in groups.

4. Drawing the average person's attention to the pain and pleasure of another seems to arouse a state of empathy that increases the probability that the observer will help another.

5. When helping corresponds to conformity, dependent people are more prone to help than independent people.

6. People who believe that they have control over their fate are more prone to help others.

7. Empathic people tend to be more helpful in face-to-face situations than unempathic people.

8. External events and the personality traits of the people exposed to them combine to determine helping behavior.

2. WHAT'S DEBATED . . .

1. What helping behaviors, if any, are altruistic.

2. Whether the helping that follows unintentional harm to others is a result of guilt or other factors (such as shame).

3. Whether the helping that follows the observation of another person helping is due to conformity, the increased salience of social values, information about the consequences of the observed course of action, identification with the person observed, or something else.

4. What situations increase the probability that people with various personality traits will help.

As we have seen, people in crowds are relatively unwilling to help others. For this reason, the psychological implications of urban crowding are critically significant. According to the 1970 Census, over 70 percent of us now live in metropolitan areas, and that proportion is expected to rise rapidly to 90 percent by 1980. In fact, the future of the entire human species seems likely to be an urban one. By the end of this century most of mankind will live in cities, and overpopulated countries like India will contain urban concentrations with as many as 30 million inhabitants.

The psychological implications of crowding are not yet fully understood. Man has inhabited the planet earth for well over a million years, but he has lived in cities for little more than 6000 years. The huge impersonal city of over one million inhabitants is barely a century old. As a species, we evolved in small communities of perhaps a few dozen members, in which every individual knew every other individual. Some theorists suggest that man is not evolutionarily adapted for existence in the new urban form, and that his biological being is ill-prepared for the subtle but constant stress of the crowded city environment. Others take the view that man is an infinitely adaptable creature, fully capable of taking a wide range of environments in his stride without undue psychological consequences. Most psychologists take the latter view—but they cannot be certain.

Many who have lived in a large city are familiar with the phenomenon of bystander apathy. A man or woman may be sprawled on the sidewalk—drunk, or ill, dying, or dead—while crowds of people pass hurriedly by with scarcely a glance, much less an offer of help. The psychology of crowding is no mere armchair exercise, unrelated to the real world. We live its consequences every day.

What is it about the urban environment that makes people so much more unconcerned about the plight of their fellows? Much of the problem seems to stem from the impersonality of the city. In the teeming mass of inhabitants, most human contacts are based on functional rather than emotional needs. Interactions take place in terms of segmental roles: the city dweller relates to others as barbers or bus drivers, but not as whole people. As Stanley Milgram has suggested, the barrage of stimuli in the modern city is so intense that we have to "screen out" most of them—including appeals for help.

But the impersonality of the city may not only make us resistant to appeals for help, it may also encourage actively anti-social behavior. To test this hypothesis, Philip Zimbardo left two cars unattended in two very different locations, the small California community of Palo Alto, and New York City. (Compare this to Bryan and Test's experiment.) Both cars were made to look abandoned by the removal of the license plates and the raising of the hood. The cars were then kept under observation from a hidden vantage point for some 64 hours. What happened?

The abandoned car in Palo Alto was touched only once. When it started to rain, a passer-by thoughtfully lowered the hood to prevent the engine from getting wet. The fate of the New York car was markedly different. Within ten minutes of its abandonment, it had been vandalized by a family of four out on an evening stroll. Yet this was only the first of a grand total of 24 separate acts of theft and vandalism which reduced the car to a wreck by the end of the observation period. Zimbardo concluded that the relative anonymity of New York was an important factor in accounting for the different fates of the two cars. Anonymity made it unlikely that the thieves would be recognized or that anybody would assume the responsibility for helping the owner by reporting the vandals to the police. (This study will be discussed further in the next unit.)

It is clearly established that population density correlates very highly with a variety of social problems, including crime, violence, juvenile delinquency, physical and mental illness, and suicide. Indifference to others and anti-social behavioral patterns of almost every kind are more common in urban than in rural areas. But we cannot be sure that crowding as such is the critical factor. Poverty also correlates with these social problems, and it may be that poverty, not crowding, is the cause of the high rates of homicide, alcoholism, sexual variance or heroin addiction in the cities.

The cities of America are gradually joining together into great, continuous urban sprawls, like the megalopolis of 40 million people that stretches from Boston to Washington D.C. By the end of the century, most of us will live in these densely populated areas. An imperative task of psychology in the years ahead will be to shed light on the relationship between crowding, anonymity, stress, apathy, and the willingness to help others.

Unit 4

Hurting Others

OVERVIEW

The work psychologists have done to determine the root causes of violence and aggression in individual human beings is described. The first part of the unit deals with significant environmental and social factors that tend to increase aggressive tendencies in all of us, even in our everyday lives. The second part of the unit describes those developmental and learning factors that tend to make some individuals chronically violent and dangerous to others. Zimbardo's recent imprisonment study, and its implications for prison reform, is discussed in the Issue section.

UNIT OUTLINE

DEFINITION AND BACKGROUND
1. *Definition:* hurting others is what happens when people direct aggression and violence toward one another.

QUESTIONS AND EVIDENCE
1. Under what conditions do people hurt other people?
Hypotheses:
   a. *Obedience:* people are willing to hurt others when they are ordered to do so by a credible authority. **63**
   b. *Anonymity:* a person will be more willing to hurt others when his identity is unknown than when he is identifiable. **64**
   c. *Overcrowding:* the denser the population, the greater the tendency toward violence and aggression. **65**
   d. *Imitation:* people are more likely to hurt after they have seen someone else do so. **67**

2. Why are some people more violent than others?
Hypotheses:
   a. *Early-experience:* deprivation of certain essential relationships during infancy and childhood can lead to violent and aggressive elements in an adult's personality and behavior. **68**

IMPORTANT CONCEPTS

	page
aggression	62
early experience	68
imitation	67
models	67
psychic overload	66
social learning	67

Our experience with hurting behavior may include being hurt or observing people hurting others.

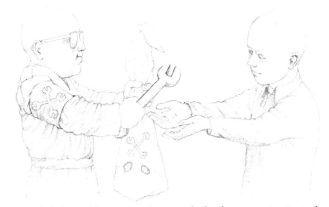

The conditions that increase the probability of hurting others include the opportunity to be anonymous and the presence of authority figures commanding obedience.

Evidence indicates that hurting others is more likely to occur in overcrowded situations and when anonymity is maintained.

DEFINITION AND BACKGROUND

Virtually all of the world's religions and philosophies rest on concepts of good and evil. The conflict between such forces is an inescapable part of human life: Freud, for example, structured his theory of personality upon the competing characteristics of creative and destructive urges. The modern psychologist, with his emphasis on observable behavior, can translate these vast ideas into the more restricted concepts of "helping" others and "hurting" others.

People do hurt each other. At times they may act in self-defense, or because someone "deserves" punishment, or in the name of freedom or justice. But at other times the hurting may be for sheer "kicks," or to strike back at an alienating world, or in reaction to frustration and intolerance. A working DEFINITION might state that hurting others is what happens when people *direct aggression and violence toward one another.* On a small scale, a person might merely punch someone else in the nose for driving over a flowerbed. On a larger scale, entire societies may engage in war, massacre, and mass murder.

This unit will FOCUS on the conditions that cause individuals to hurt other people. Some of these conditions are immediate and circumstantial, but others are more subtle and have their roots in the past experience and personalities of certain individuals.

BACKGROUND

Research in the phenomenon of hurting others is so new that it is impossible to ascribe the historical antecedents to any one individual. Academics have largely confined their activity to commiserating over the notion that people are just put together that way.

William James, physician, philosopher, and psychologist, published an essay in 1911 entitled "The Moral Equivalent of War," which was essentially a proposal for a kind of peace-corps activity to channel the aggressive tendencies of young people into constructive work. In this proposal he stated, "Our ancestors have bred pugnacity into our bone and marrow, and thousands of years of peace won't breed it out of us."

In 1932, on invitation from the League of Nations, Albert Einstein wrote a letter to Sigmund Freud about the reason for our endless wars in which he said, "Only one answer is possible . . . Because man has within him a lust for hatred and destruction." But, Einstein continued, "Is it possible to control man's mental evolution so as to make him proof *against* the psychoses of hate and destructiveness?" In his reply, Freud offered only this hope: We may rest on the assurance that "whatever makes for cultural development is working also against war." Behind these pronouncements by some of the geniuses of our century is the elusive shadow of hope that man will gain control of his tendencies to destroy his own kind.

Indeed, though man's history tells us every generation has known war, a glance at anthropology tells us that some cultures have escaped. In 1934 anthropologist Ruth Benedict wrote that it was impossible to discuss warfare with the Mission Indians of California because their culture provided no basis that allowed them to understand the very idea of war. Apparently war and human nature are not inextricably intertwined.

If we ascribe wars to human nature, we imply that war is inevitable and indirectly we sanction behavior that is designed to fulfill our prophecy. Black leader H. Rap Brown has reminded us of the cultural support for aggression in his well-publicized statement: "Violence is as American as cherry pie."

Robert Ardrey, commentator on man as an animal, wrote (1970):

> Action and destruction are fun. The concerned observer who will not grant it indulges in a hypocrisy which we cannot afford. He who regards a taste for violent action as a human perversion will not likely make any great contribution to the containment of our violent way.

Whether you accept Ardrey's point of view or not, understanding and controlling violence and aggression can be viewed as one of the tasks of psychology and other social sciences that is most important for the survival and well-being of mankind.

QUESTIONS AND EVIDENCE

1. Under what conditions do people hurt other people?

2. Why are some people more violent than others?

HYPOTHESES	OBEDIENCE	ANONYMITY	OVERCROWDING	IMITATION
DESCRIPTIVE EVIDENCE			ASSESS: social distribution and behavior in a developing rat colony confined to small living space	
EXPERIMENTAL EVIDENCE	VARY: credibility of an authority figure MEASURE: intensity of shock delivered to victim	VARY: anonymity and "niceness" of victim MEASURE: duration of shock to victim		VARY: realism of aggressive models MEASURE: aggressive play behavior

1. UNDER WHAT CONDITIONS DO PEOPLE HURT OTHER PEOPLE?

The *obedience hypothesis* states that people are willing to hurt others when they are ordered to do so by a credible authority. The real-life examples of this phenomenon, ranging from Adolf Eichmann to Lieutenant Calley, need not be detailed here. Experimental validation of the hypothesis was provided by a social psychologist who actually suspected that he would disprove it: he thought that his subjects would refuse to obey his orders to harm other people.

EXPERIMENTAL EVIDENCE

Investigator: S. Milgram
Source, Date: "Some Conditions of Obedience and Disobedience to Authority," 1965
Location: Yale University
Subjects: Male adults from all socioeconomic classes
Materials: Fake shock generator, paired-associate lists

The subjects were led to believe they were participating in an experiment designed to study the effects of punishment on memory. Arriving in pairs, each was immediately paid $4.50 for participating, and then a drawing was held to choose which of the two subjects would be the "teacher" and which the "learner." Actually, the drawing was rigged so that the real subject was always the teacher and the other subject—in fact a confederate of the experimenter—the learner. After the learner had been strapped in a chair in an adjacent room, the teacher was told that his task was to teach him a list of word pairs, to test him on the list, and to punish him whenever he erred. Punishment was to be delivered in the form of electric shocks administered by a generator whose thirty switches ranged from 15 to 450 volts at 15-volt intervals. The subject was instructed to increase the intensity of the shocks by one switch every time the learner erred.

As the experiment progressed, the subject was able to hear the protests of the learner. At 75 volts he began to moan, at 150 volts he demanded to be let out, at 180 he cried that he could no longer stand the pain, and at 300 volts he refused to go any further and demanded to be freed. (These responses were actually a tape recording, and no shocks were ever delivered.) Whenever the subject expressed a desire to stop or said he could not go on hurting the learner, the experimenter—standing behind him—told him to disregard the learner's protest: "You have no choice, the experiment requires that you continue."

The degree of obedience was measured by the number of shocks (switches) a subject would deliver before refusing to continue. Also, before the learning trials began, the subjects were themselves given a shock identified as 45 volts so that they would have some idea how much such a shock hurts.

Despite this knowledge, 65 percent of the subjects went all the way to the 450-volt limit, disregarding the cries and protests of the learner. Milgram cogently described his impressions of one of them:

Despite his numerous, agitated objections, which were constant accompaniments to his actions, the subject unfailingly obeyed the experimenter, proceeding to the highest shock level on the generator. He displayed a curious dissociation between work and action. Although at the verbal level he had resolved not to go on, his actions were fully in accord with the experimenter's commands. This subject did not want to shock the victim, and he found it an extremely disagreeable task, but he was unable to invent a response that would free him from E's authority.

Milgram thought that the Yale University setting, with its aura of prestige and authority, might have helped make the subjects so obedient. To test this possibility, another study of the same sort was conducted in Bridgeport, Connecticut, by a fictional organization called "Research Associates of Bridgeport." Unlike the Yale study, which took place in an impressive psychological laboratory, the Bridgeport study was done in a run-down building—respectable, but just barely—in the downtown shopping area. Here 48 percent of the subjects delivered the maximum shock. Thus, although the setting may have made some difference, almost half of the subjects were still obedient even when it meant hurting another person.

Similar experiments have largely verified these findings. Some indicated that the closer the learner was placed to the subject, the more often the subject would defy the experimenter. For example, 60 percent of the subjects who were only one-and-a-half feet from their "victims" refused to continue. Another study showed that the farther away the experimenter stood from the subject, the greater the likelihood that the subject would refuse to go on.

Aggression or hurting others needn't only take place when someone gives orders, however. One cynical idea all of us have had at one time or another is that people in general might be more mean and cruel if they "could get away with it"—if no one else were around to punish or condemn them for their hurting behaviors, either legally or socially. This is the basic idea underlying the *anonymity hypothesis*, which states that a person will be more willing to hurt others when his identity is unknown than when he is identifiable.

EXPERIMENTAL EVIDENCE

Investigator: P. G. Zimbardo

Source, Date: "The Human Choice: Individuation, Reason, and Order vs. Deindividuation, Impulse, and Chaos," 1970

Location: Stanford University

Subjects: 8 female introductory psychology students

Materials: White lab coats and hoods, name tags, tape recordings, fake shock equipment

One group of four subjects wore large lab coats and hoods to maintain anonymity; none of them knew the other subjects, and names were never used. The four subjects in the second group wore name tags, were greeted and addressed by name, and could identify all other members in the group.

The experiment was conducted under the pretense of assessing the subjects' empathic responses to strangers. Initially, all the subjects listened to a tape-recorded interview between the experimenter and two future "victims" (one potential victim at a time). The first was portrayed as being nice, sweet, and altruistic, while the second was presented as obnoxious, conceited, and self-centered. These impressions were verified by having the subjects rate each victim's warmth, sincerity, genuineness, and honesty after listening to the tape.

As part of the pretense of the experiment, the subjects were told that, in order for them to become actively involved with each of the victims, and since the victims were paid subjects going through a series of conditioning studies anyway, the two experiments would be combined: the subjects would deliver a series of electric shocks to the victims. The subjects in each group were led to believe that only two of them would actually deliver the shocks while the other two observed. To reinforce this assumption, they drew lots, but the conditions were rigged so that each subject thought that she and one other girl were to deliver the shocks.

The subjects were then separated into individual cubicles so they could not see the reactions of the others. Each was then given a real sample of the strong electric shock the victim would supposedly receive, and the procedure for delivering the shocks was described. A signal light indicated when the subject was to depress her shock key, and a green light, which remained lit for a maximum of 2.5 seconds, indicated when the shock was supposedly being transmitted. The subjects were led to believe that the experimenter could not tell which of the two subjects was delivering the shock.

The subjects could view the victim through a one-way mirror as she interacted with the experimenter.

With each supposed shock the victim reacted with symptoms of severe pain. After the tenth trial, the victim reacted so strongly to the presumed shock that her hand ripped out of the electrode strap. On each of a total of twenty trials, the experimenter recorded whether or not each subject actually "delivered" a shock and how long it lasted.

The results show that anonymity substantially affected the delivery of shocks to the victim. The anonymous subjects continued the shocks twice as long as the identifiable subjects. Anonymity apparently had a much greater effect than whether the victim was "nice" or not: the anonymous group increased the duration of the shocks for both nice and obnoxious victims, whereas the identifiable subjects tended to increase the duration of shocks for the obnoxious victim but to decrease it for the nice victim. On the other hand, all subjects were equally obedient to the experimenter, averaging seventeen shocks out of twenty trials in both conditions.

The experimenter concluded that "conditions which induce feelings of remoteness lead to lowered self-consciousness, less embarrassment, and reduced inhibitions about punishing the victim." Unlike the procedure in Milgram's experiments, no one attempted to coerce the subjects to behave cruelly. However, each girl knew that even if she didn't deliver the shock, another subject might.

One of the best ways to achieve anonymity is to live in a large modern city. Urban analyst Jane Jacobs has explained that "great cities are not like towns, only larger. They differ from towns and suburbs in basic ways, and one of these is that cities are, by definition, full of strangers." It might be expected that indifference would thrive in such a setting. The *overcrowding hypothesis* states the denser the population, the greater the tendency toward violence and aggression. A classic laboratory experiment has demonstrated the behavioral effects of overcrowding in rats.

DESCRIPTIVE EVIDENCE

Investigator: J. B. Calhoun
Source, Date: "Population Density and Social Pathology," 1962
Location: National Institute of Mental Health, Washington
Subjects: 40 male, 40 female rats
Materials: 10 x 14 room divided into 4 pens by an electrified fence, with each pen supplied with dwellings, food, and water; pens are interconnected so that 2 end pens have only 1 entrance each, middle pens have 2

The experimental apparatus, shown in Figure 2, was capable of housing forty-eight rats comfortably (twelve in each pen). However, when thirty-two rats

Figure 1. Zimbardo's study showed that anonymity had a greater effect on aggression (shock duration) than whether the "victim" was nice or obnoxious. Does anonymity also affect the behavior of the Ku Klux Klan member?

were allowed to interact and interbreed freely for over sixteen months, the population gradually leveled off at about eighty or more adult rats.

The majority of the rats developed certain "abnormal" behavior patterns in response to the overcrowded conditions. For example, single dominant male rats took control of the end pens after a status struggle. These dominant males established a harem of females and prevented other males from entering by guarding the single entrance at all times. Of all the male rats, the dominant males appeared to be the most "normal" throughout the study. In the middle pens, dominance of males shifted frequently during battles for control.

At the same time, a "middle" class of males arose. These rarely contended for dominance and developed "abnormal" sexual patterns: they were sexually active but could not discriminate between males and females.

A bottom class of male "dropouts" also developed. Although these rats were fat and sleek, unscarred by combat, they were ignored by all the other rats, were sexually inactive and ate only when the others were asleep.

With further crowding, the middle pens developed into what Calhoun called a "behavioral sink," so that most rats ate and drank together in large groups, never alone. A new class of male rats, which Calhoun called the "probers," appeared. These animals never contended for dominance with the larger males but were essentially an active "criminal" class. They moved about in groups, were hypersexual and bisexual, frequently ate infant rats. Their sexual behavior completely ignored ordinary rat courtship rituals: they chased females until they caught and subdued them.

The disorder of the middle pens also disrupted normal female behaviors. Nest building fell off until, during the last half of the experiment, no new nests were built at all. Infants were scattered, abandoned, or eaten. Whereas the infant death rate was about 50 percent in the end pens, it rose to 96 percent in the middle pens. Strangely, females in the protected harems of the dominant males sought the middle pens when in estrus (heat), without interference from their dominant masters.

There is no simple way to generalize the effects of overcrowding in rats to human behavior. But Stanley

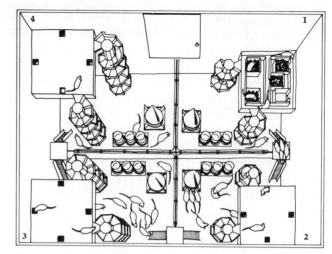

Figure 2.   Rats raised in Calhoun's apparatus developed abnormal behavior patterns under overcrowded conditions. The apparatus, a 10 x 14 room divided into 4 pens (numbered 1 to 4, clockwise from door) by an electrified fence, could comfortably house 48 rats, but actually held 80 or more. Each interconnected pen was supplied with food (the conical objects,) water (trays with 3 bottles,) and dwellings (elevated burrows reached by winding stairways, each with 5 nest boxes as shown in pen 1). Pens 1 and 4 had only one entrance ramp each, the middle pens had 2 ramps. Single dominant male rats (sleeping near ramps) took control of pens 1 and 4, establishing a harem of females, and prevented other males (see 3 "probers" on ramp to pen 1) from entering. The middle pens (2 and 3) developed into a "behavioral sink," with severe disruptions of normal activities and a 96 percent infant death rate. Adapted from Calhoun (1962).

Milgram, in an article entitled "The Experience of Living in Cities," provided some cogent explanations of the overcrowding hypothesis for humans. In addition to anonymity, Milgram discussed the distrust of strangers, the lessened consciousness of courtesy and civilities, and the relatively faster pace of life that characterizes cities. He subsumed all of these factors, and others as well, under a general concept of "psychic overload." Such an overload occurs as a result of human inability to process inputs from the environment because there are too many of them or because they come at too rapid a pace.

Faced with the possibility of such psychic overload, city dwellers make certain adaptations that can be regarded as typical of urban life. The individual may allocate less time to each input (perhaps possessing more acquaintances but fewer close friends) or disregard inputs of low priority (ignoring the sick drunk on the crowded sidewalk). The boundaries of social transaction may be redrawn (the bus driver no longer

Figure 3. Anonymity. Hitler understood very well that it is easier to assure the blind following of authority when individual identity is submerged in a crowd.

Figure 4. The tendency for people to behave aggressively can increase with anonymity or with overcrowding. Is bystander apathy a result of anonymity, overcrowding in cities, or that combination of factors Milgram calls "psychic overload?"

makes change for riders) or possible receptions or disruptions may be blocked (people may obtain an unlisted telephone number). At the community level, there is a tendency to create new institutions to alleviate the potential overload (a welfare department takes over care of the indigent).

Milgram concluded: "The ultimate adaptation to an overloaded social environment is to totally disregard the needs, interests, and demands of those whom one does not define as relevant to the satisfaction of personal needs."

At its extreme, such adaptation may lead to active violence and aggression of the sort revealed by Calhoun's dominant and criminal rats. But anonymity and overcrowding cannot fully account for the hurt some human individuals inflict on others. The modern social psychologist sees such behavior as learned and focuses on the effects of childhood experiences as well as the effects of social models on an individual's hurting behavior.

The *imitation hypothesis* states that people are more likely to hurt after they have seen someone else do so. Recently, much research on this hypothesis has focused on the possibility that violent TV programs may "teach" such behavior. Although the issue is still controversial, the evidence tends to confirm the relationship.

EXPERIMENTAL EVIDENCE

Investigators: A. Bandura, D. Ross, and S. A. Ross
Source, Date: "Imitation of Film-mediated Aggressive Models," 1963
Location: Stanford University
Subjects: 48 boys and 48 girls, 3-6 years old
Materials: Live models, filmed models, and cartoon models; Bobo, a large inflated doll

The subjects were divided into four groups. The first three groups were the experimental groups: they watched adult models (male and female) behave aggressively toward a large, inflated "Bobo" doll. The adults sat on the doll, punched it in the face, hit it on the head with a mallet, threw it in the air and kicked it while shouting things like "Sock him in the nose!" "Kick him!" and "Pow!" One experimental group observed actual adult models; the second watched a film of the same models; and the third was shown cartoon models. The fourth group, a control group, did not watch any aggressive behavior.

When the observation period was over, the children were taken one at a time into another room, which contained a Bobo doll and various other toys. Each child spent twenty minutes with the toys, while an experimenter watched his or her behavior and rated it for different kinds of aggressive responses.

On the average, the experimental subjects displayed almost twice as many aggressive responses as the control subjects. In general, the boys exhibited more aggression than the girls. The form of the model had no significant effect. That is, the film and the cartoons as well as the live performance increased the frequency of aggression. The models also seemed to shape the form of the subjects' aggressiveness. Many of the children repeated the very same actions that they had seen the models perform.

In a similar study using college-age subjects, Leonard Berkowitz found that those who observed a violent boxing film where a "bad guy" was beaten up were likely to give a greater electric "shock" (no real shock was used in the experiment) to another subject than those who viewed the same film but were told the protagonist of the film was a "good guy." Presumably, aggressive tendencies were aroused when the protagonist "deserved" his beating, but sympathetic, nonaggressive responses were aroused when the protagonist of the film did not deserve such treatment.

Berkowitz concluded that the strongest effects of filmed violence occur immediately after seeing the film. The viewer, still attuned to a violent atmosphere, may decide that he himself is justified in attacking someone who has angered him.

The long-term effects of observing filmed violence have not been firmly established. However, a recent study by L. D. Eron, M. M. Lefkowitz, L. R. Huesmann, and L. O. Walder showed some positive correlation between boys' (not girls') preferences for violent TV programs in the third grade and peer ratings of their aggressiveness ten years later. These results support the notion that watching violent TV programs may lead to more aggressive behavior over time. The evidence is correlational, however, and other interpretations are possible. It could be that the third-grade boys' preference for violent TV programs and their aggressiveness later were both caused by some third factor. For example, the boys could have been imitating the preferences and behavior of their fathers.

HYPOTHESIS	EARLY EXPERIENCE
DESCRIPTIVE EVIDENCE	ASSESS: background characteristics of child-abusing parents
EXPERIMENTAL EVIDENCE	VARY: social deprivation in infancy of monkeys MEASURE: monkey mothers' later reactions to their own infants

2. WHY ARE SOME PEOPLE MORE VIOLENT THAN OTHERS?

The *early-experience hypothesis* states that deprivation of certain essential relationships during infancy and childhood can lead to violent and aggressive elements in an adult's personality and behavior. Research in this area can begin with perhaps the most unfortunate example of hurting others in our society: parents who beat, maim, and sometimes even murder their own infants. More than 700 children and infants are killed by their parents every year in the United States, and 40,000 more are seriously tortured or beaten by parents and relatives. Psychologists have traced such nearly incomprehensible behavior to certain kinds of events and deprivations that the parents experienced during their own infancy and childhood.

DESCRIPTIVE EVIDENCE

Investigators: B. F. Steele and C. B. Pollock
Source, Date: "A Psychiatric Study of Parents Who Abuse Infants and Small Children," 1968
Location: University of Colorado School of Medicine
Subjects: 60 families in which well-documented abuse of infants or small children occurred
Materials: Interviews, home visits, psychological tests

Over a period of five-and-a-half years, an attempt was made to reach as deeply as possible into the abusing parents' personalities, experiences, and backgrounds. The information was obtained through therapeutic interviews, home visits by social workers, and, whenever possible, interviews with parents and relatives. A battery of psychological tests was also administered to most of the parents. The duration of contacts with families varied widely, but the majority of parents were seen over a period of many months.

This comprehensive study revealed consistent behavior patterns and traits among abusing parents. Characteristically, they made premature demands and had overly high expectations for the infant's performance. These tendencies were coupled with a disregard for the infant's needs, limitations, and helplessness. Although their standards were similar to those of most parents—in terms of obedience, respect, thoughtfulness, submission—they sought compliance with these standards when their infants were at an inappropriately early age, and implemented their demands with extreme intensity. Many of them seemed to treat their children as though they were adults who were capable of providing security and love.

Without exception, the results of this study also showed that abusing parents had been reared according to the patterns they themselves now used. All of them had experienced continuous, extreme parental demands, accompanied by constant criticism and sometimes beatings. Deprived as children of basic "mothering"—the awareness and consideration of

their needs as infants, tenderness, appropriate emotional interactions—they later lacked the quality of motherliness themselves. They showed little or no confidence and felt that it was useless to turn to family and friends for need-satisfying relationships.

Living a life that is relatively asocial and isolated, the potentially abusing parent turns to his or her child in a desperate, last-ditch attempt to satisfy the needs for love and comfort. Because the young infant cannot actively and purposefully satisfy such demands, the parent experiences frustration and lack of fulfillment.

The psychiatric interviews also indicated that the persistent demands and criticism that abusing parents experienced during their own childhoods lead to a lack of integration of concepts of self. For example, it is not unusual for an abusing parent to see the infant who is attacked or abused as representing his "bad" self.

Despite a number of campaigns calling attention to it, child abuse remains one of the least visible problems in our society. Most people simply do not, quite understandably, wish to be reminded of it. Equally repellent but harder to avoid thinking about are political assassinations—perhaps the most frighteningly inescapable signs of violence today.

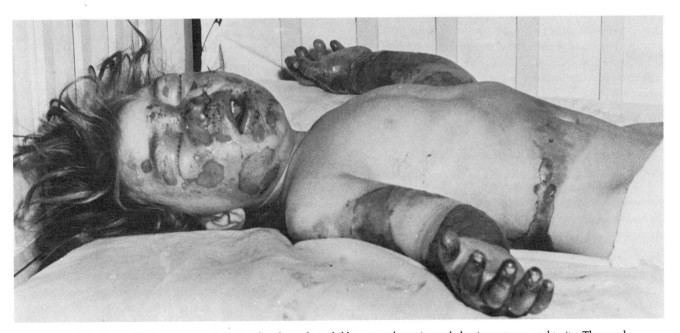

Figure 5. A baby burned by her parents. Parents who abuse their children reveal consistent behavior patterns and traits. They make premature demands, have overly high expectations, and disregard their infant's needs, limitations, and helplessness. Significantly, abusive parents were themselves abused as children, experiencing continuous demands accompanied by constant criticism and, sometimes, beatings.

In 1969 A. E. Weisz and R. L. Taylor studied the available medical and sociological literature on presidential assassins and identified a number of common background characteristics. The typical assassin is a male Caucasian, between twenty-four and forty years of age, who in childhood and adulthood has been lonely and alienated. He has few friends and is often a bachelor. Perhaps because of his severe isolation and asocial character, he is often subject to delusions, to the point where he might be considered severely disturbed mentally. The assassin is also likely to have experienced "downward social mobility" (such as the loss of a job), especially just prior to the assassination attempt. Often, the assassin has given up working months or even years before the attempt.

The behavior of psychopathic assassins, like that of child-abusing parents, can probably be traced to deprivation of certain kinds of critical emotional and social experiences during childhood. The word "probably" must be used because the evidence from such studies is descriptive and correlational. It has enabled researchers to identify some of the experiences and psychological characteristics that are associated with violence and aggression, but it does not prove that the experiences or characteristics cause the behavior.

One way to establish cause and effect is to conduct an experiment that includes a control group. The study described below, for example, compares the adult behavior of monkeys deprived of mothering and affection during infancy with that of mothers raised normally.

EXPERIMENTAL EVIDENCE

Investigators: B. Seay, B. K. Alexander, and H. F. Harlow
Source, Date: "Maternal Behavior of Socially Deprived Rhesus Monkeys," 1964
Location: University of Wisconsin
Subjects: 13 female rhesus monkeys and their infants
Materials: A playpen area surrounded by 4 controlled cages

Four female rhesus monkeys were raised without mothers or any social contact for the first eighteen months of life and thereafter lived in pairs in cages. These socially deprived animals subsequently became "motherless mothers" (the MM group), and their reactions to their own infants were compared with behavior of normally reared females who also had infant monkeys. These observations were made under controlled conditions at periodic intervals, when the mother monkeys were permitted to interact with their infants.

Figure 6. Female monkey rejecting her baby. Females in Harlow's study raised without mothers acted so aggressively toward their young—ignoring and punishing them—that the infants would have died without human intervention. Presumably the mothers had never learned how to behave toward children because they had themselves been deprived of mothering.

All four MMs acted toward their infants in such a hostile manner that the young monkeys would not have survived if the laboratory staff had not intervened to protect them. The mothers either ignored the infants or, when the infants tried to cling to the mothers' bodies (as they did repeatedly), punished them. The experimenters judged the four MMs to be totally inadequate mothers with these first infants. However, the MMs that had second infants cared for them in a normal, motherly fashion.

These findings and others suggest that maternal behavior in monkeys is partly innate and partly learned. Early social deprivation apparently can prevent innate components from being integrated into normal maternal behavior. But even an unsuccessful experience with a first infant can "trigger" and integrate the maternal response network, just as normal mothering during an MM's own infancy would have. Thus, MMs are able to behave normally toward their second infants.

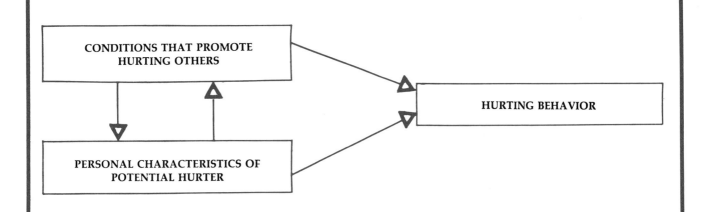

PUTTING IT TOGETHER: Hurting Others

When people resort to hurting others, there is an interaction between the *conditions* under which the event occurs and the *personality characteristics* of the people involved. Some of the conditions that promote *hurting behavior* are: being ordered by credible authorities, being guaranteed anonymity, overcrowding, and observing people hurt others.

Those most likely to respond to these conditions are usually people who have had childhood experiences involving continuous parental demands, constant criticism, frequent beatings, or deprivation of adult affection. Often they are lonely, alienated people.

1. WHAT'S ACCEPTED . . .

1. The tendency for a person to behave aggressively can increase with anonymity or with overcrowding.

2. Many people tend to believe and obey credible authority figures, even when called upon to hurt another person.

3. Overcrowding in some species tends to produce destructive behavior.

4. Observing violence can heighten aggressive tendencies for a short period of time.

5. Pathological social behavior, such as abusing children, is often related to early childhood experiences and deprivations of affection.

6. Aggressiveness and violent behavior can be learned through imitation and observation.

2. WHAT'S DEBATED . . .

1. The various ways in which individuals can achieve anonymity and, consequently, act more aggressively.

2. How violence and aggression in cities are related to overcrowding.

3. The usefulness of a concept such as "psychic overload" to account for the psychological factors that lead to violence and aggression in cities.

4. The extent to which violent and aggressive tendencies in animals can be used to explain human behavior.

5. The effects of observing violence on long-term behavior.

We have seen in this unit how many of us behave in ways that hurt others if we are placed in the right situation. In particular, Stanley Milgram's disturbing experiments have shown how ordinary citizens may act in unusually hurtful ways when they are playing roles that seem to demand aggressive conduct. In the light of this research, the behavior of many officials of Hitler's Germany becomes clearer to us, as does the killing of women and children by American troops acting "under orders" at My Lai in Vietnam.

Psychologist Philip Zimbardo believes that our prisons may also lock people into hurtful roles. Guards and prisoners, he believes, quickly become resentful and aggressive toward one another, and hostility builds up to the point where the prison's main task, that of restoring the convict to constructive activity, becomes practically impossible. Since no less than 70 percent of all convicts are convicted again within five years of their release, our prisons are clearly failing to rehabilitate. Zimbardo's views, then, are worth taking seriously.

Zimbardo developed this belief when he got some unexpected and frightening results from an experiment that he had originally designed merely to judge the psychological effects of imprisonment. He set up a mock prison and advertised for volunteers to live in it for two weeks, some as prisoners and some as guards. From a large number of applicants, Zimbardo chose two dozen young men, all of them emotionally stable and mature college students without any criminal record. The volunteers were well paid for taking part in the experiment.

Zimbardo divided his subjects at random into "prisoners" and "guards." The guards were equipped with uniforms, wrap-around sunglasses, and whistles. They were made fully aware of their responsibility of maintaining order in the prison and preventing escapes, and were allowed to make up their own rules for the smooth running of the prison. The prisoners, meanwhile, were picked up at their homes by a city policeman and taken to the local police station. There they were booked, fingerprinted, searched, and handcuffed. They were then taken blindfolded to the mock prison. Here they were stripped, disinfected, put into uniform, given numbers, and placed in cells. Zimbardo then waited to see what happened.

The results were so frightening that Zimbardo had to close the prison down after six days. Most of the subjects rapidly lost all sense of where their roles ended and where reality began. Most seemed to consider themselves as "real" prisoners or guards. Zimbardo reported: "In less than a week the experience of prison undid . . . a lifetime of learning; human values were suspended, self-concepts were challenged, and the ugliest, most base, pathological side of human nature surfaced. We were horrified because we saw some of the boys (guards) treat others as if they were despicable animals, taking pleasure in cruelty, while other boys (prisoners) became servile, dehumanized robots who thought only of escape, of their individual survival and of their mounting hatred for the guards."

Within the first four days, Zimbardo had to release three of his twelve prisoners because they had sudden traumatic reactions, such as confusion in thinking, hysterical crying, and severe depression. Others pleaded for parole from the prison, and nine of the twelve were prepared to give up all the money they had earned if they could be released. When the request for parole was denied, the prisoners returned meekly to their cells, obviously having forgotten that they were student volunteers in an experiment which they could legitimately have demanded to leave at any time.

About a third of the guards, meanwhile, became tyrannical and abused their power over the prisoners. They purposely invented a number of techniques for humiliating and breaking the spirit of the prisoners in their charge. Blankets were often taken away at night and some prisoners were locked in a closet under "solitary confinement." A few of the guards attempted throughout to be friendly but firm. These guards, however, never once interfered with the other guards. They never told them to ease off because it was only an experiment, and they never complained to Zimbardo about the abuses of authority.

Zimbardo explains why he abruptly ended the experiment: "I called off the experiment not because of the horror I saw out there in the prison yard, but because of the horror of realizing that *I* could have changed places with the most brutal guard or become the weakest prisoner full of hatred at being so powerless that I could not eat, sleep or go to the toilet without permission of the authorities. I could have become Calley at My Lai, George Jackson at San Quentin, one of the men at Attica."

As Zimbardo points out, we all carry around a favorable self image. We think of ourselves as basically just, fair, humane, understanding, and incapable of causing pain to others—especially to others who have done us no harm. Yet, concludes Zimbardo, "Many people, perhaps the majority, can be made to do almost anything when put into psychologically compelling situations—regardless of their morals, ethics, values, attitudes, beliefs or personal convictions." And as for our prisons, Zimbardo suggests, the implications are both very clear and very serious: "The prison situation, as presently arranged, is guaranteed to generate severe enough pathological reactions in both guards and prisoners as to debase their humanity, lower their feelings of self-worth and make it difficult for them to be part of a society outside of their prison." Zimbardo's research puts our widespread prison riots and lack of success at reforming criminals into new perspective. And perhaps more immediately, it may shock us into examining just how much—or how little—it takes to make each of us cause others pain.

Unit 5

Morality

OVERVIEW

What is known about how children develop ethical principles? This relatively new area of research in developmental psychology is described. Moral development in children involves both cognitive development (progressive stages and a dependence on thinking abilities) and important learning experiences (such as parental discipline, imitation, and social learning.) Apparent moral regression is discussed in the Issue section.

UNIT OUTLINE

DEFINITION AND BACKGROUND
1. *Definition:* morality is the assimilation of society's standards of conduct so that one may react to others in accord with these accepted standards and resist the temptation to go beyond the rules of acceptable behavior.
2. *Background:* Hugh Hartshorne (1885–1967) and Mark May (1891–   ).

QUESTIONS AND EVIDENCE
1. How are thinking processes involved in the development of morality?
Hypotheses:
   a. *Stages:* moral development occurs as a series of cognitive stages. 78
2. How is social learning involved in the development of morality?
Hypotheses:
   a. *Modeling:* children learn moral behavior by imitating the behavior of the adults around them. 81
   b. *Association:* much of what is called moral behavior is affected by its association with external rewards and punishments. 83
   c. *Early-discipline:* moral development is related to early parental disciplining of the child. 85

IMPORTANT CONCEPTS

	page
association	83
conscience	79
hedonism	79
imitation	81
modeling	81
moral dilemma	79
morality	77
objective responsibility	81
role taking	86
social contract	79
social learning	80
subjective responsibility	81

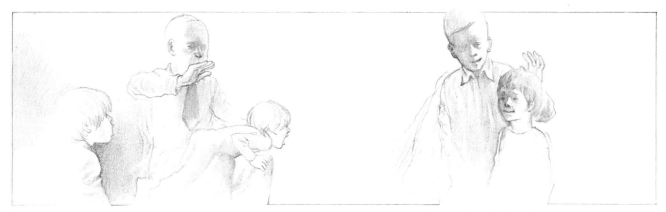

The origins of moral development include observing the behavior of others and type of early discipline.

Situations requiring moral judgments initiate a variety of behaviors among individuals.

Evidence indicates that different people may make the same moral decisions for different reasons depending upon the stage in the sequence of moral development to which each individual has progressed.

DEFINITION AND BACKGROUND

A hermit probably spends little of his time puzzling over the differences between right and wrong. When we interact with other people, however, we are immediately confronted with many ethical choices. Trying to decide which is the moral, ethical, or just choice among numerous alternatives has been a major preoccupation in our time. Consider the situations that make headlines: Vietnam, civil rights, the Calley trial, Watergate, abortion. All these involve ethical issues of such complexity that they have sparked intense debate within the country—revealing the existence of deep internal divisions.

As we grow up, all of us have to come to terms with questions of morality—from such early problems as whether to invade Grandma's cookie jar to the far more serious matters of adolescent and adult years. Attempts to analyze morality are much older even than those of Aristotle, who said one of man's greatest challenges was to be both "happy" and "good."

Psychologists define morality in a number of different ways depending on which aspect of the problem attracts their interest. Morality includes behavioral, emotional, and judgmental components; the degree to which each component is emphasized affects the definition. Psychoanalytic theory, discussed in Unit 15, suggests that people are what they feel. Therefore, the psychoanalytic approach to morality emphasizes the processes by which we acquire *feelings* of guilt and shame. Social-learning theory provides a *behavioral* emphasis, looking primarily at how people act when they are faced with temptations to be unethical. The cognitive developmentalists take another theoretical position, focusing on *judgment* rather than on feelings or behavior. They might define morality as the ethical principles used by an individual to judge his own behavior and the behavior of others. How do ethical

Figure 1. Both Watergate and Prohibition represent ethical failures. The Watergate affair involved complex moral issues for all Americans in the 1970s, while during the Prohibition era illegal liquor was so common that the law was repealed. Cognitive (judgmental) development is necessary but not sufficient for moral development. Morality includes components of feelings and behavior as well as judgment.

From *Herblock Special Report* (W. W. Norton and Company, Inc., 1974).

principles and moral judgments change as we develop? Where do we get our ethical principles from?

Producing an overall DEFINITION under which all theoretical positions can be subsumed is not an easy task, but one might say that morality is the assimilation of society's *standards of conduct so that one may react to others in accord with these accepted standards and resist the temptation to go beyond the rules of acceptable behavior.* This unit will FOCUS, in part, on the relative importance to this definition of the three components of morality we just mentioned.

BACKGROUND: HUGH HARTSHORNE (1885–1967) AND MARK MAY (1891–   )

The first efforts to subject moral behavior to scientific analysis came in the late 1920s. The 1920s, a decade of much change and complexity, seemed to have had more than its share of moral dilemmas. Hollywood with its host of new movie stars was creating a way of life that challenged the small-town Main Street ethos of church, courthouse, and corner store. Bootleg whiskey and bathtub gin were making a mockery of Prohibition—still considered by many people to be the culmination of a great crusade. In this setting, religious educator Hugh Hartshorne and psychologist Mark May led a team that attempted to study practical ways of evaluating the influence of religion, education, and other factors in developing moral behavior in children.

To this end, Hartshorne and May designed a vast study, carried out in American schools between 1928 and 1930 and later described in a three-volume work called *Studies in the Nature of Character.* In effect they offered thousands of children of different ages (five to eleven) and social backgrounds a number of opportunities to cheat, lie, and steal. For example, the experimenters would have the teacher leave a classroom during a test, placing the children in a situation where cheating was easy, would be advantageous to the children, and would, as far as the children could tell, go undetected. They found some behavior differences that at the time seemed difficult to evaluate. Cheating seemed to occur less frequently among well-mannered children and also less among richer children and children who went to fewer movies than their peers. In general, however, the researchers

Figure 2. Hugh Hartshorne and Mark May (above), early investigators of moral behavior, studied practical ways of evaluating the factors influencing the ethical behavior in children. Focusing on conduct, they defined morality as behavior that conformed to general societal norms.

found some deceptive behavior among all categories of children studied. Whether cheating occurred or not seemed to depend less on the "moral character" (or any other trait) of the child in question than on characteristics of the situations in which the children found themselves. Knowledge of right and wrong, frequent attendance at Sunday school, avowed adherence to the Boy Scout oath, and other common measures of conventional morality seemed to have no particular influence on a child's tendency to lie, cheat, or steal. A child who cheated in one situation was neither more nor less likely than another child to cheat in other situations. A child who cheated in a game did not necessarily cheat on a school test, or steal from a store, or lie to his mother; a child might steal money from a bus driver but not from his friends, or from his father's pockets but not from a bus driver. Virtually all the children were dishonest some of the time, particularly in situations in which being dishonest was made to appear self-beneficial, safe, and easy.

For the religious educators who sponsored the study in the first place, Hartshorne and May's findings raised some disturbing questions. Did the study mean, for example, that religious or moral training had no carry-over to real life? Is there even such a thing as moral character?

Hartshorne and May defined moral behavior as conduct that conformed to general societal norms. Cheating on a school task, in their study, was considered unethical. Because they found that a child who was "ethical" in one situation might be "unethical" in another, their findings were interpreted by some as meaning that there were no such things as general moral character traits. Because teaching people about morality had little effect, it seemed that the way to keep people honest would be to place them in situations where their behavior was strongly controlled.

Note, however, that Hartshorne and May focused on one aspect of morality: conduct. Jean Piaget, a Swiss psychologist, began studying morality from a very different perspective. Piaget's approach was to ask children themselves what they thought about certain behavior and to observe how their opinions varied over time according to chronological age, apparent intelligence, training, and so forth. Many psychologists would say that Piaget made the problem of morality *dynamic* rather than *static* (as in Hartshorne and May's experiments, for example) by con-

centrating more on development and less on the factors that influenced morality on particular occasions. He also approached the problem chiefly from a cognitive rather than a behavioral point of view, being more interested in children's judgments and reasoning processes than in their actions.

QUESTIONS AND EVIDENCE

1. How are thinking processes involved in the development of morality?

2. How is social learning involved in the development of morality?

1. HOW ARE THINKING PROCESSES INVOLVED IN THE DEVELOPMENT OF MORALITY?

The *stages hypothesis* states that moral development occurs as a series of cognitive stages. Research on this hypothesis focuses on children's *cognitive judgments* rather than on their overt behavior, as the Hartshorne and May study did. This approach to moral development is based on stages in the development of children's thinking as described by Piaget (see Unit 16).

Lawrence Kohlberg has been the most important figure in the study of the development of moral stages. Out of his research has come a useful set of methods and approaches, many of which were developed in a longitudinal study of a group of American

QUESTION	1. HOW ARE THINKING PROCESSES INVOLVED IN THE DEVELOPMENT OF MORALITY?
HYPOTHESIS	STAGES
DESCRIPTIVE EVIDENCE	ASSESS: Progress of moral development through childhood in U.S. and other countries
EXPERIMENTAL EVIDENCE	

boys over a twelve-year period, beginning when they were between ten and sixteen years old. Later, boys from other cultures were studied as well.

DESCRIPTIVE EVIDENCE

Investigator: L. Kohlberg
Source, Date: "Development of Character and Moral Ideology," 1964
Location: University of Chicago; later, Harvard
Subjects: 75 American boys, ages ten to sixteen at start of study; additional boys from Great Britain, Canada, Taiwan, Mexico, and Turkey
Materials: Stories with a "moral dilemma"

Each subject was presented with stories that embodied a "moral dilemma"—a situation or problem that required a moral decision or judgment. From his observations and studies, Kohlberg gradually developed a set of nine dilemmas, of which the following is typical:

> In Europe, a woman was near death from a special kind of cancer. There was one drug that the doctors thought might save her. It was a form of radium that a druggist in the same town had recently discovered. The druggist was charging ten times what the drug cost him to make. He paid $200 for the radium and charged $2,000 for a small dose of the drug. The sick woman's husband, Heinz, went to everyone he knew to borrow the money, but he could get together only about $1,000. He told the druggist that his wife was dying and asked him to sell cheaper or let him pay later. The druggist said: "No, I discovered the drug and I'm going to make money from it." So Heinz got desperate and broke into the man's store to steal the drug for his wife. Should the husband have done that? Why or why not?

Accompanying each dilemma was a set of questions designed to elicit the subject's moral reasoning about that particular issue. These nine dilemmas, with the appropriate questions, were administered to the subjects during interviews and then readministered at periodic intervals over the twelve-year period.

What emerged from Kohlberg's analyses of their responses was a progressive pattern of the develop-

ment of moral judgment. It showed a fixed sequence of three general levels and six distinct stages:

Level I. Premoral Orientation: Awareness of rules and "good" and "bad," but interpretation of them exclusively in terms of physical actions and reward and punishment.

Stage 1. Punishment and Obedience Orientation: Avoidance of punishment and unquestioning deference to authority. (A possible answer: "No, because he'll get caught and punished.")

Stage 2. Naive Instrumental Hedonism: "Right" is what gives the child pleasure and satisfies his needs. ("He should steal the drug because he needs his wife to clean his house for him.")

Level II. Conventional Morality: Conformity to, and maintenance of, expectations of other people, accepted standards, and social orderliness.

Stage 3. Seeking Approval: A concern for social acceptability either by society in general or by a specific reference group. ("He should steal the drug if he truly loves his wife.")

Stage 4. Maintaining Authority: Ethics centered on respect for authority, doing one's duty, maintaining social order. ("Stealing is against the law. If everyone lived by his own private rules there would be chaos.")

Level III. Postconventional Morality: Individual moral principles, which include and recognize conventional morality but at the same time recognize that disobeying conventional standards can be an ethical act.

Stage 5. The Social Contract Point of View: Recognizes that moral values are often arbitrary but necessary contracts between people. Respect for individual rights in the context of socially agreed-upon obligations. ("In most instances it is probably best to obey the law, but here it might be right to steal because life is not the same as property and life takes precedence.")

Stage 6. Individual Principles of Conscience: Decisions based on rational principles considered to be just and equitable principles for all people to follow. The following example of a stage 6 response is taken from Kohlberg:

> [Should the husband steal the drug to save his wife? How about for someone he just knows?]:
> "Yes. A human life takes precedence over any

other moral or legal value, whoever it is. A human life has inherent value whether or not it is valued by a particular individual."

[Why is that?] "The inherent worth of the individual human being is the central value in a set of values where the principles of justice and love are normative for all human relationships."

Kohlberg, like Piaget, sees the changes in moral cognitions that occur during development as signaling the emergence of distinct stages. More mature stages arise and replace less mature stages because the individual, as he experiences the world more and interacts with more people, finds that his earlier ways of thinking cannot deal with all of the situations he encounters and therefore develops more adequate ways of dealing with the world.

Kohlberg finds that the sequence of stages appears to be universal, 1 always coming before 2, 2 before 3, and so forth. In addition, the stages themselves seem to be universal. When Kohlberg used translations of his nine moral dilemmas with subjects from Great Britain, Canada, Taiwan, Mexico, and Turkey, the same six stages were found among boys in each of the cultures studied, regardless of economic class or religious differences. However, children from rural and/or "primitive" societies appeared to advance through the stages at a much slower rate than American middle-class children. Also, in every culture examined, middle-class children were found to be more advanced in moral reasoning, on the average, than lower-class children (here "class" refers only to differences in income). In other words, all children went through the same stages, but some went through them at a slower rate than others. According to Kohlberg's theory, the opportunity to assume various social roles and thus to learn how other people feel is an important factor in moral development. Possibly, the slower development of lower-class and rural children may occur because they have fewer social role-taking opportunities than the average middle-class child or because they do not get as much exposure to different ways of viewing the world. More research, however, is needed in order to interpret the class and cultural differences in moral development that Kohlberg found.

A study by R. L. Krebs (1967) suggests that there may be a developmental explanation for the findings of Hartshorne and May. A major finding of theirs, you will recall, was the low predictability of ethical behavior in different situations, indicating that there may not be individual dispositions, or character traits, that govern ethical conduct. Piaget (Unit 16) and Kohlberg have approached the problem of morality by studying how individuals reason when confronted with ethical issues. The Krebs study asked if there is a relationship between ethical conduct and the maturity of moral judgment.

Krebs allowed both sixth-grade children and college students to cheat in an experimental situation that allowed him to detect the cheaters. In both groups he found that most cheating was done by the subjects who had reached only premoral and conventional-morality levels (stages 1 through 4). Relatively less cheating occurred among principled-level subjects (stages 5 and 6) in both groups. Perhaps Hartshorne and May were unable to find honest subjects because the children studied were too young. They used subjects between five and eleven, which Kohlberg finds to be the typical ages of premoral- and conventional-level morality. At those stages, Kohlberg says, a good deal of behavior is situationally determined.

Kohlberg's theory stresses the importance of interaction with others to a child's moral development, but it does not particularly emphasize the importance of parental practices. That emphasis is more characteristic of psychoanalytic theory and, to a lesser extent, social-learning theory. Freud's theory of personality development is covered in Unit 15; here, it will be enough to merely point out that, according to psychoanalytic theory, a child's moral character is formed primarily through his identification with the parent of his own sex at about age six after resolution of the Oedipus complex in boys and the Electra complex in girls. At that time, the child internalizes the moral standards of the parent and tries to behave as those standards dictate.

2. HOW IS SOCIAL LEARNING INVOLVED IN THE DEVELOPMENT OF MORALITY?

Moral development does not occur in a vacuum. It takes place in a social context, in which the individual is constantly interacting with his parents and peers, meeting new people, and discovering new points of view. Social-learning theorists, for example, argue

2. HOW IS SOCIAL LEARNING INVOLVED IN THE DEVELOPMENT OF MORALITY?

HYPOTHESES	MODELING	ASSOCIATION	EARLY DISCIPLINE
DESCRIPTIVE EVIDENCE			ASSESS: 1. Relation between cheating and severity of parental discipline 2. Relation between moral maturity and type of parental discipline
EXPERIMENTAL EVIDENCE	VARY: presence of models and compliments MEASURE: changes in moral judgments	VARY: task instructions and control of rewards and punishments MEASURE: self-criticism and concern for corrective behavior	

that moral development takes place as a gradual accumulation of bits and pieces of knowledge learned by observing and imitating older people, not in a series of qualitatively different cognitive stages. According to social-learning theory, the child interacts less actively with the world than cognitive developmentalists think he does; he is a relatively passive recipient of adult teachings. The *modeling hypothesis* states that children learn moral behavior by imitating the behavior of the adults around them.

EXPERIMENTAL EVIDENCE

Investigators: A. Bandura and F. J. McDonald
Source, Date: "Influence of Social Reinforcement and the Behavior of Models in Shaping Children's Moral Judgments," 1963
Location: Stanford University
Subjects: 78 boys, 87 girls from five to eleven years of age
Materials: 36 pairs of stories presenting situations for moral judgments

The pairs of stories, (based on stories of Piaget's) demonstrated two forms of moral judgment: *objective responsibility,* in which the badness of an action is judged according to the amount of material damage done, and *subjective responsibility,* in which the badness of an action is judged by what was intended rather than by what actually happened (See Figure 3). According to Piaget, subjective responsibility is the more mature type. Here is a sample pair of stories:

> 1. John was in his room when his mother called him to dinner. John went down and opened the door to the dining room. But behind the door was a chair, and on the chair was a tray with fifteen cups on it. John did not know the cups were behind the door. He opens the door, the door hits the tray, bang go the fifteen cups, and they all get broken.
> 2. One day when Henry's mother was out, Henry tried to get some cookies out of the cupboard. He climbed up on a chair, but the cookie jar was still too high, and he couldn't reach it. But while he was trying to get the cookie jar, he knocked over a cup. The cup fell down and broke.

The task of the subjects in the experiment was to explain, fot stories like these, who had done the naughtier thing and why they thought so. A child who argued that John was naughtier than Henry because John broke fifteen cups but Henry broke only one was said to be in the objective stage of moral development. A child who felt that Henry was naughtier because he was trying to steal some cookies whereas John didn't mean to break the cups was in the subjective stage of development.

Of the 165 children, 48 gave subjective responses (that is, they said that the person who intended to be

Figure 3. According to Piaget, if a child considers John (l.) naughtier because he broke more cups, he is said to be at the *objective* stage of moral development. If a child considers *Henry* (r.) naughtier because he was being sneaky, he is said to be at the *subjective* stage of moral development.

naughty was the naughtier) to ten of the twelve stories; 36 children made objective responses to ten of the twelve stories; the rest tended to switch back and forth and therefore were omitted from the next part of the experiment.

In the second part of the study, the "subjective" and "objective" children were divided into three "training groups." In the first group, adult models were present, and they told each child that they disagreed with the child's previous position. For example, if the child had responded in the pretest by saying that John was naughtier, the model indicated that he thought Henry was naughtier. If the child then chose the type of response that the model had indicated, the experimenter praised him. In the second group, adult models were present and acted the

same as with the first group, but the child received no compliments from the experimenter. Members of the third group had no models.

When the children were retested on twelve new pairs of stories, the results indicated that the children exposed to the models tended to change their responses. Under the model's influence, most young children were willing to switch from objective to subjective judgments, and older ones would revert to objective judgments. These findings suggest that children at a given age level make *both* objective and subjective judgments rather than just one type of judgment that is dependent on their stage of development. Also, the models alone without the experimenter's compliment were as effective in changing the children's choices as providing praise along with the model. Both the model and model-plus-praise conditions were more effective than the condition in the third group where no model was provided.

The ease with which the moral stage of the child was changed by the adult model presents a problem for cognitive-developmental theory. This theory sees change as a slow process resulting from considerable interpersonal interaction, general experience, and construction of new cognitive structures. The Bandura and McDonald study, however, has been subjected to some criticism. All the subjects were posttested immediately after the training session with the models. It is reasonable to ask how long the changes induced by imitation of an adult model last.

Cowan, Langer, Heavenrich, and Nathanson (1969) replicated (reran) the Bandura and McDonald study, but also added several new conditions. In one condition half the subjects were posttested immediately; the other half received the posttest two weeks later.

Cowan and his colleagues found the same results as Bandura and McDonald on the immediate posttest but not on the delayed posttest. Two weeks after training, the subjects who had shifted from an objective responsibility position to a subjective one in response to training retained the change. But the subjects who had been trained to shift from a subjective position to an objective one tended to revert to their original subjective orientation. (Remember that, according to cognitive-developmental theory, the subjective position is the more mature one.)

The fact that changes from objective to subjective positions were retained, but not the reverse, raises a problem for social-learning theorists. If the acquisition of morality is a habit learned by imitating adults, why is it easier to change habits in one direction than in the other? Perhaps the Bandura and McDonald study indicates that subjectively oriented children may comply with adult expectations for short periods of time without really changing their manner of thought (in this case, their moral stage). Because the Cowan study is one of a kind, however, further investigation needs to be made before any definitive conclusions can be made.

Not all social-learning theorists use a modeling approach in their efforts to understand morality. The *association hypothesis* states that much of what is called moral behavior is affected by its association with external rewards and punishments. Even though these social-learning theorists recognize the importance of internal events like thoughts and memories, they still insist that all behavior is under at least indirect control by external events.

EXPERIMENTAL EVIDENCE

Investigator: J. Aronfreed

Source, Date: "The Effects of Experimental Socialization Paradigms Upon Two Moral Responses to Transgression," 1963

Location: University of Pennsylvania

Subjects: 57 fifth-grade girls about ten years old drawn from a large urban school system

Materials: Rectangular composition board, 24 plastic soldiers, a wooden doll, a cloth-padded cardboard box, an instrument called a "pusher," and a box of tootsie rolls

The experimental task involved pushing the doll into the box beneath the table and out of supposed danger. To do this, however, the pusher had to be pushed through the array of soldiers to the doll. The idea was to knock down as few soldiers as possible while completing the task. (It was impossible to avoid knocking over at least a few.) (See Figure 4.) Two different procedures were used, differing only in degree of cognitive structure and control of punishment. In the high cognitive structure–high control group, the children were continually told how important it was to be extremely careful and gentle when moving the doll to safety. They were also asked to evaluate their own performance by deciding how many tootsie rolls they needed to give up from the pile they had been given. In the low cognitive structure–low control group no warnings were made concerning the delicacy of the task, but this time the experimenter decided how many tootsie rolls would be taken away. (See Table 1.) After each group went through ten learning trials, a test trial was set up that involved the unexpected breaking of the doll as it hit the cardboard box beneath the table. The experimenter at this point, looking quite surprised, made such reflective statements as "Gee, I wonder why it broke" and "Well, now that it's broken, I wonder what we should do." The first statement was used as an indirect verbal stimulus intended to elicit a self-critical response; the second was supposed to bring out responses indicating modes of correction (reparative responses). A response was classified as self-critical if the child, in

High cognitive structure-High control group

". . . Push off the nurse and knock down as few soldiers as you can. And be as careful and gentle as you can. All right, go ahead."

"All right. You knocked down some soldiers, so you decide how careless and rough you've been. Take as many Tootsie Rolls as you think is right and put them in the box."

Low cognitive structure-Low control group

". . . Push off the nurse and knock down as few soldiers as you can. All right, go ahead."

"All right. You knocked down some soldiers, so I'll have to take—let's see [one, two, three] Tootsie Rolls."

Figure 4. In Aronfreed's study, the experimental task involved pushing the female doll standing behind the toy soldiers into a box under the table and out of supposed danger. The subjects, all fifth-grade girls, had to use the "pusher" (a small hoe) to move the doll and could not avoid knocking down at least a few of the soldiers. The experimenter sat to one side of the table. As Table 1 shows, with one group of subjects, the experimenter constantly warned how important it was to be gentle and careful. These subjects were asked to evaluate their own performance and to decide how many candies they needed to give up from the pile they had been given. With the other group of subjects, the experimenter gave no warnings, but decided how many candies would be taken away. It was found that subjects in the first group made more self-critical and reparative responses. Adapted from Aronfreed (1963).

accounting for the doll's breaking, referred to her behavior in pushing it (for example, any response indicating that she had not pushed the doll "the right way"). Responses were classified as reparative when they indicated the child's perception that the effects of the wrongdoing could be corrected through self-initiated action.

As Aronfreed had predicted, the results showed that both self-critical and reparative responses were more likely to occur when cognitive structure and the child's control over punishment had been maximized. This indicates that, in the absence of external punishment, the nature of an individual's response after committing a "no-no" is a function of his previous training and socialization. Aronfreed claims that a child who had been encouraged to make corrective responses to his socially unacceptable behavior would be expected to more frequently resolve subsequent inadequacies through critical and reparative actions than one who has previously experienced the consequences of inappropriate actions in events outside of his own control. When you do something wrong and are punished for it (getting a zero on a test because you were caught cheating), the initial *behavior* (cheating) that brought on the punishment becomes a warning that elicits anxiety. When this anxiety is no longer contingent on the actual presence of punishment (the instructor has left the room—your friends won't tell), it can be considered an internal moral response to inappropriate behavior. The anxiety can now be reduced by making responses that were instrumental in avoiding punishment in the original socializing situation. In fact, we have just described a learning process with two aspects that correspond to varieties of conditioning, discussed in Units 28 and 29.

The *early-discipline hypothesis* of moral development states that moral development is related to early parental disciplining of the child. It argues that differences in people's moral maturity or moral judgment are related to differences in their early childhood experiences with their parents.

DESCRIPTIVE EVIDENCE

Investigator: F. T. Vitro
Source, Date: "The Relationship of Classroom Dishonesty to Perceived Parental Discipline," 1971
Location: University of Maine

Subjects: 70 college girls
Materials: 3 biology exams; self-reports on parental discipline

The students were given what appeared to be a routine biology exam. After the papers had been collected (and the number of wrong answers on each exam secretly tabulated), they were then turned back to the students with the bogus explanation that the professor had not had time to grade them. The girls were asked to grade their own papers and hand in the corrected tests.

The change in the number of wrong answers was recorded for each girl. Tests were administered on three different occasions with the same girls using the same procedure. The data revealed that a total of 34 girls (45.6 percent) were consistent cheaters.

Two-thirds of girls who cheated were found, according to self-reports, to have been raised either by very harsh or by very lenient parents, while two-thirds of the honest girls said they had been raised with moderate discipline. Although there are problems with this data (the self-reports may not have been accurate, and the girls' definitions of harsh, moderate, and lenient discipline may have differed), other studies have confirmed that harsh discipline in the form of physical punishment leads to less guilt—and thus, presumably, to moral behavior at a lower stage—than does psychological punishment in the form of withdrawal of love and explanations to the child of why his behavior was wrong.

DESCRIPTIVE EVIDENCE

Investigators: M. L. Hoffman and H. D. Saltzstein
Source, Date: "Parent Discipline and the Child's Moral Development," 1967
Location: Merrill-Palmer Institute, Detroit
Subjects: 444 seventh-grade children (about age twelve) and their parents
Materials: Pencil-and-paper tests, ratings

The investigators used pencil-and-paper tests and ratings by parents, teachers, and peers to assess several aspects of the seventh-grade children's moral maturity, including guilt, internalization of moral judgments, and conducts. In addition, the children's parents were interviewed concerning their method of discipline. The parents' usual mode of discipline was placed in one of three categories: power assertion (use of force or threat), love withdrawal (ignoring child, not speaking to him), and induction (explaining to the child the consequences of his actions for others).

The overall finding was that power assertion is related to weak moral development while the inductive reasoning approach is related to mature moral development. In other words, parents who explained to the child the consequences his behavior had for other people had children who were morally more mature than did parents who used the physical punishment. However, this relationship held only for middle-class parents and children. For lower-class parents and children, no consistent relationship between method of discipline and moral maturity was found.

Why is induction (that is, explaining to the child the consequences of his act for others) a powerful means of increasing moral maturity? This question can be answered adequately by both social-learning and stage theory. It is in accord with Aronfreed's position that verbal explanations help the child internalize moral standards by providing him with thoughts that he associates with reward or punishment. Also, since induction techniques encourage the child's ability to empathize (see Unit 3), this interpretation is consistent with Kohlberg's notion that role-taking abilities are stimulants to moral development.

A good informal illustration of the connection between role taking and ethical conduct is provided by the following anecdote. The speaker is a New York cab driver; notice his emphasis on the victim's plight as his reason for returning the lost pocketbook:

Once I found a pocketbook full of credit cards, and one of them was Unicard. That is just like finding cash. I tried to call the woman up . . . But when I was calling her from a restaurant over on Twenty-eighth Street, a guy approached me. The word had got around that I had found this pocketbook. He said "I'll give you four hundred dollars for the cards." *It was Friday evening—you know what they would do to that woman? They would have buried her, because she had no way of calling anybody.* He offered me four hundred dollars to get these cards, but I told him, I says, "Look, if you ever as much as speak to me, I'm going to have you locked up." The guy is still there. He hangs around there.

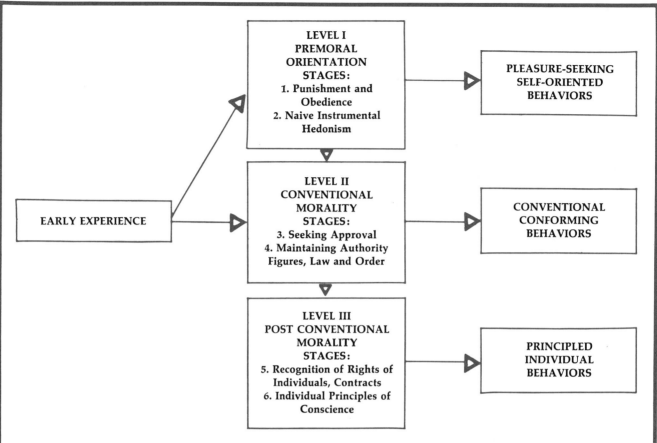

LEVEL I
PREMORAL
ORIENTATION
STAGES:
1. Punishment and
Obedience
2. Naive Instrumental
Hedonism

PLEASURE-SEEKING
SELF-ORIENTED
BEHAVIORS

EARLY EXPERIENCE

LEVEL II
CONVENTIONAL
MORALITY
STAGES:
3. Seeking Approval
4. Maintaining Authority
Figures, Law and Order

CONVENTIONAL
CONFORMING
BEHAVIORS

LEVEL III
POST CONVENTIONAL
MORALITY
STAGES:
5. Recognition of Rights of
Individuals, Contracts
6. Individual Principles of
Conscience

PRINCIPLED
INDIVIDUAL
BEHAVIORS

PUTTING IT TOGETHER: Morality

Various developmental theorists emphasize different aspects in the development of morality. All would probably agree that a child's *early experiences* initiate the process and aid in the socialization of moral behavior. The psychoanalytic and social-learning theorists emphasize the influence of authority figures who provide models to imitate, the association of "correct" or "incorrect" behavior with reward and punishment, and the type of parental discipline employed.

The social-learning theorists assert that moral behavior is specific to each situation and dependent upon what has been learned in similar situations. On the other hand, the cognitive developmentalists say that people develop through an irreversible sequence of stages consistent with the way they think.

Piaget roughly divided the stages into objective responsibility, during which an individual concerns himself only with material harm, and the more mature subjective responsibility, during which behavior is judged by one's intentions. Kohlberg's *three levels of moral judgment, each with two stages,* is more widely used today. Kohlberg and his colleagues have gathered impressive evidence that this sequence is universal. His early stages correspond with Piaget's objective responsibility. As the basis of moral judgment becomes more internal, the stages correspond more with Piaget's subjective responsibility.

Behaviors following from each of the levels of moral judgment are respectively, *pleasure-seeking self-oriented behaviors, conventional conforming behaviors, and principled individual behaviors.*

WHAT'S ACCEPTED AND WHAT'S DEBATED

1. WHAT'S ACCEPTED . . .

1. There are stages of moral development that have cross-cultural validity.

2. Cognitive development is necessary but is not sufficient for moral development.

3. The kinds of discipline a child receives may affect his moral maturity.

4. Moral behavior is to some extent learned through imitation and rewards/punishments.

2. WHAT'S DEBATED . . .

1. Whether a stage of development can be easily altered or reversed by simple learning procedures.

2. The nature of the transitional phase between stages.

3. The reasons for social class and cultural variations in the rate of moral development.

4. The relative impacts of various influences on morality: the development of thinking processes, rearing practices, modeling, rewards and punishments.

ISSUE: "RASKOLNIKOV REGRESSION"

As we have seen in this unit, Lawrence Kohlberg's research on morality (1964) indicates a fixed sequence of stages in the development of moral judgment. However, in 1969, Kohlberg discovered that those stages may not always conform to the originally stated sequence. Take the case of the folksinger, Bob Dylan. Bob Dylan captured the imagination of a generation. He came to epitomize the fierce moralism of the early sixties, when the civil rights movement emerged as one of the great moral crusades of American history. The old order was challenged everywhere as hypocritical and unjust, and a committed youth movement sought major social change in the name of the highest ethical principles. Dylan's songs—dedicated, principled, morally absolute—captured the feelings of the young and were sung and quoted across the nation.

But within a few years, Dylan changed. The high moral tone began to disappear from his lyrics. Instead, he frankly admitted to his doubts. Issues of right and wrong no longer seemed so clear to him. To the dismay of many of his followers, the folksinger seemed uncertain of his principles and no longer applied them to his lyrics. Instead, his songs became increasingly hedonistic, preaching a "do your own thing" morality of hedonism and instant gratification. He renounced any moral leadership in the movement he had helped shape, and his piercing social criticism was heard no more.

There is growing evidence that what happened to Dylan has happened to a great many young people. After achieving a high, postconventional level of moral reasoning (stages 5 or 6 in Kohlberg's system), they seem to lapse back into an earlier, premoral level of reasoning (stage 2 in Kohlberg's system). They renounce their earlier principles and instead embrace a more egoistic, self-gratifying morality, at least temporarily. This phenomenon poses severe problems for Kohlberg's system, because the stages are supposed to be an invariant sequence. That is, an individual should advance forward stage by stage, skipping none and never regressing.

The first indication that this sequence might not hold in every case came in the course of research conducted by Kohlberg and one of his associates in 1969. While interviewing a young man, they were surprised to find that he was fully capable of reasoning at a postconventional level, but he rejected this form of reasoning as an appropriate guide to his own behavior and instead adopted a premoral, stage 2 level of reasoning. Normally, an individual cannot understand reasoning a stage or two above his own, so it should not have been possible for this young man at stage 2 to use postconventional reasoning. The only possible explanation was that he had already reached and comprehended the postconventional level, but had then regressed to an earlier one. Kohlberg termed the phenomenon "Raskolnikov Regression," after a character in Dostoyevski's *Crime and Punishment* who renounces his high principles and commits a crime he knows to be morally wrong. Research by Kohlberg and others has shown, however, that the regression is usually temporary. Most regressives eventually revert to the higher level of reasoning within a few months or years.

How can we account for this apparent regression and subsequent reversion to principled reasoning? No consensus has yet developed among psychologists, but it is probable that two quite separate processes are involved, each affecting particular individuals.

In the first case, a person who has recently achieved a postconventional stage of high moral reasoning confronts the world and attempts to reshape it in the image of his ideals. But the world is not so easily changed in reality as it is in the imagination. After repeated but unsuccessful attempts to apply their principles, some people become disillusioned, even cynical: they fail to "keep the faith." As a result they become deeply frustrated, abandon the seemingly fruitless principles, and regress to an earlier premoral stage in which they merely gratify their own hedonistic impulses. But the individual knows at heart that this way of life is ultimately unsatisfactory and unfulfilling. It represents, after all, a stage that he had rejected long ago for precisely that reason. Gradually, then, he reverts back once more to a higher, postconventional level of reasoning, although his morality this time has perhaps more realism and less youthful passion.

The second case concerns persons who become confused at the very point at which they are moving from a conventional to a postconventional level of moral reasoning. Essentially, they are leaving a world of secure, taken-for-granted morality and charting an uncertain course in personal moral autonomy. They suddenly find themselves confronted with a number of competing viewpoints—different religions, different ethical systems, different moral choices. In this confusion they can find no clear guide to principled action and relapse defeated into a "do your own thing" morality as the only possible solution to the problem. Yet they, too, find no real comfort in this form of reasoning, which seems an inappropriate basis for adult relationships. Eventually the regressives begin to move, this time more cautiously, back to a postconventional form of reasoning.

Research on student unrest at colleges has shown that student protestors are drawn almost exclusively from two stages of the six in Kohlberg's system: the postconventional stage 6 and the premoral stage 2, with many of the latter apparently being temporary regressives. The protestors consist, then, of two distinct groups: students who are protesting on the grounds of high ethical principles, and students who come along just for "kicks," but have no real commitment to any moral outcome.

Kohlberg's system provides an interesting model to account for the failure of negotiations in so many campus confrontations. The student negotiators are arguing at two different stages of reasoning, stages 2 and 6. The college administrators, however, tend to argue at the conventional stage 4, and are more concerned about practicalities such as the disruption of classes than about the principles behind the confrontation. Liberal faculty members, meanwhile, are arguing at stage 5, attempting to balance conflicting interests and opinions. Since people usually do not comprehend reasoning on a stage above their own, it is hardly surprising that the parties to the confrontation often seem to be talking at crosspurposes, with different groups wondering "what do these people really want?" The difference in the levels of reasoning of the parties may make a negotiated settlement very difficult to achieve, especially when most of the participants do not realize that it is the level rather than the content of their opponents' reasoning which is the stumbling block to mutual understanding and agreement. Kohlberg's model can provide a sharp insight into the turmoil of the real world.

Unit 6

Sexuality

OVERVIEW

Research on sex differences and those factors—whether physiological, experimental, or cultural—that contribute to the development of sex-role differences are described. The first part of the unit deals with child development and such influences as parental behavior and cultural expectations. The last part of the unit discusses sex-role differences in adulthood and how cultural evaluations of sexuality tend to affect the behavior of individuals. The controversial issue of homosexuality is examined.

UNIT OUTLINE

DEFINITION AND BACKGROUND
1. *Definition:* sexuality encompasses all those roles, activities, expectations, and attitudes that are thought to be specific to being male or female.
2. *Background:* Sigmund Freud (1856–1939).

QUESTIONS AND EVIDENCE
1. What are some influences on the development of sex-role behavior?
Hypotheses:
    a. *Parental-behavior:* differential sex roles are produced and reinforced by parental attitudes and actions. 94
    b. *Cultural expectations:* given the general norms of our culture, girls tend to be more stable in their degree of passivity and dependence than boys. 95
    c. *Children's preferences:* children of either sex find traditional masculine roles more desirable and important than feminine ones. 96
2. What are some influences on sex-role differences during adulthood?
Hypotheses:
    a. *Hormones:* there are genetic-biological differences between the sexes that affect emotional behavior. 97
    b. *Need-for-achievement:* in our culture women are expected to have less need for achievement than men. 98
    c. *Discrimination:* in our culture women are consistently rated as inferior to men.

IMPORTANT CONCEPTS

	page
achievement drive	98
anxiety	98
dependence	94
double bind	100
Electra complex	93
homosexuality	93
hormones	97
latency period	92
Oedipus complex	92
projective test	98
sex role	92
socialization	96

While genetic inheritance determines the gender of the individual, social development and cultural expectations define the sex role.

During the course of development hormonal changes modify and enhance gender differences, but current research indicates that expectations for achievement and success involve socially controlled sex roles.

Evidence indicates that in our culture traditional sex-role socialization has favored assertive behavior in males and passive behavior in females.

DEFINITION AND BACKGROUND

The DEFINITION of sexuality must encompass *all those roles, activities, expectations, and attitudes that are thought to be specific to being male or female.* This unit will FOCUS on the processes by which such characteristics are acquired and maintained. It will emphasize the particular biological, experiential, and cultural factors that are implicated in the development of sex roles, especially in our society.

BACKGROUND: SIGMUND FREUD (1856–1939)

In most everyday matters Freud was a conventional man of the turn of the century leading a respectable life. Yet his work and writings probably did more than those of anyone else to shatter respectable conventions about sex. When he published *Three Essays on the Theory of Sexuality* in 1905, he was forty-nine

Figure 1. The works and theories of Sigmund Freud, father of psychoanalysis, attracted a larger following—and more controversy—than any other psychologist's.

years old and had considerable clinical experience treating "hysterical" patients. He had also been psychoanalyzing himself for several years. On the basis of his own and his patients' earliest childhood memories, he concluded that human sexuality does not begin with the onset of puberty but much earlier, in infant and childhood experiences.

According to Freud, an infant normally develops in fairly distinct stages (see Unit 15). Up to age three or four, male and female development is quite similar. Then physical and genital differences begin to separate boys and girls and to direct their development toward different sex roles in later life. A boy begins to associate his feelings of arousal with an attraction for his mother, the person who usually gives him the closest attention and who is therefore seen as the primary source of gratification and pleasure. But he now becomes a rival of his father for his mother's attentions. Furthermore, he becomes aware of his penis as the organ of pleasure and of the fact that his mother or sisters or other little girls do not have one. According to Freud, this leads him to fear that he might lose his penis, and when that fear is combined with his rivalry with his father, the child comes to believe that his father might castrate him if he tries to satisfy his attraction to his mother. Thus, the young boy is faced with conflicting feelings—fear of his father as a more powerful rival and attraction toward his mother that must remain unfulfilled for fear of castration. Freud called this conflict the *Oedipus complex,* named for the Greek myth about a son who discovers that he has killed his father and married his mother.

In normal development, according to Freud, the boy resolves the Oedipal crisis with consequences less tragic than in the myth. He wishes to be like his father, with whom he identifies. Stifled and anxious about feelings of love and hate, a boy is forced to "repress" his sexual feelings. He then enters a period of sexual latency or disinterest that lasts until puberty, when sexual feelings reappear as a normal, active interest in girls of his own age. In this way the male sex-role characteristics of adulthood develop. In Freudian theory, an interruption in the successful resolution of the Oedipal complex could be used to explain such abnormal sexual developments as inhibitions and homosexuality.

Freud was less clear about the development of

sexuality in females. He proposed the term *Electra complex* to describe the sexual dilemma a girl suffers early in childhood. She notices that boys and her father have a penis—something she does not have—and she fears she might have lost a penis and begins to desire one (what Freud called penis envy). This discovery turns the girl away from her mother, who does not have a penis, toward her father. She is also in conflict between a desire for, and fear of, penetration by her father. The girl's envy and fear, however, are very slowly resolved relative to the resolution of the Oedipal complex. She gradually shifts her desire for a penis to a "more realistic" wish for a child, especially a little boy.

To Freud, girls must then assume a passive role, giving up active manipulation of the clitoris and developing, after latency, an adult sexuality fulfilled through vaginal sexual orgasm. Other than the idea that behavior of women was a resolution of their unfulfilled penis envy, he offered little insight, aside from the obvious genital differences, into female sexuality. Unsatisfactory resolutions of the Electra complex accounted for difficulties or abnormalities in adjusting to the adult female role. Freud noted that women seemed to be passive and men active, but he emphasized this difference only in conjunction with sexual relations, not in all of behavior.

When first proposed, Freud's theory of the development of sexuality was considered outrageous. It violated the sexual taboos of the time and questioned the myth of childhood innocence. But recent work in psychology and physiology has pointed out its inadequacy in other respects. One psychologist, in describing her search for a research topic while a graduate student and young mother, summed up a central criticism: "To a woman who had spent the preceding three years with an obstetrician and who was spending most of a 28-hour day nurturing two small children, the idea that pregnancy and infant nurturance were motivated by an unresolved search for male genitals was nonsense beyond belief" (Bardwick, 1971).

Child psychologists have found personality differences between the sexes at as early an age as six months. There is no doubt that the female's unique capacities for menstruation, childbearing, suckling, and other experiences help to differentiate the sexes and their roles. But social and cultural factors, especially child-rearing practices and social conventions, have been given more attention than biological differences in the study of sex-role development.

QUESTIONS AND EVIDENCE

1. What are some influences on the development of sex-role behavior?

2. What are some influences on sex-role differences during adulthood?

QUESTION	1. WHAT ARE SOME INFLUENCES ON THE DEVELOPMENT OF SEX-ROLE BEHAVIOR?		
HYPOTHESES	PARENTAL BEHAVIOR	CULTURAL EXPECTATIONS	CHILDREN'S PREFERENCES
DESCRIPTIVE EVIDENCE	ASSESS: relation of infant behaviors to parental treatment	ASSESS: relationship of sex roles and long-range stability of dependent behavior	ASSESS: childhood preferences for sex roles
EXPERIMENTAL EVIDENCE			

1. WHAT ARE SOME INFLUENCES ON THE DEVELOPMENT OF SEX-ROLE BEHAVIOR?

Until quite recently most Americans and Europeans believed that women are "by nature" more passive and dependent than men. Although some primate studies have suggested that this difference may be due to innate biological sex differences, any attribution of the characteristics of some nonhuman species to men and women is not only questionable, it is misleading. Cultural and environmental factors may possibly override any biological predispositions that may exist.

What, then, can account for the development of sex roles? Psychologists have been devoting particularly close attention to the attitudes of parents and to the general culture as well as to the tastes and dispositions displayed by young children.

The *parental-behavior hypothesis* states that differential sex roles are produced and reinforced by parental attitudes and actions. Almost two centuries ago novelist Mary Wollstonecraft complained that "the child is not left a moment to its own directions, *particularly a girl*, and thus rendered dependent—dependence is called natural." Many recent studies confirm her point.

DESCRIPTIVE EVIDENCE

Investigators: M. Lewis and his colleagues
Source, Date: "Culture and Gender Roles: There's No Unisex in the Nursery," 1972
Location: Fels Research Institute
Subjects: Male and female infants at ages 3, 6, and 13 months; their mothers
Materials: A room marked off into squares and containing a number of toys and a chair

The researcher visited the homes of the three- and six-month-old infants to observe mother-child interaction during the course of a normal day; the thirteen-month-old infants were placed in a controlled setting for observation. In the case of the latter, the mother was asked to sit in a chair in a special room for fifteen minutes watching her child play. Observers recorded the amounts of vocalization, "looking at," and physical contact that occurred between mother and child during this time. The distance (in number of squares) the infant ventured from his mother and the amount of time he spent away from his mother were also recorded. After fifteen minutes, a barrier was placed between the child and his mother, and the infant's subsequent behavior was observed and recorded.

It was found that at as early as twelve weeks the girl infants were looked at and talked to by their mothers more than the boys were. For the first six months the boys received more physical contact from their mothers than did the girls, but after that point the situation was reversed. At thirteen months boys ventured farther away from their mothers and stayed away longer than girls. Boys also talked less to their mothers and played more vigorously with toys and more frequently with nontoys (such as doorknobs and light switches). When the barrier was placed between mother and child, the boys characteristically attempted to get around it, while girls stood in the middle of the room and cried. It would seem that by six months of age, boys are already being moved from the world of bodily contact with the mother out into the physical environment to explore and master it, while girls are expected to exhibit more passive behavior.

Although differential treatment of the sexes during infancy is a comparatively new area of study, there is a multitude of data exploring differing attitudes of parents toward children's sex role at later ages. It appears, for example, that mothers may tend to show more permissiveness and attention toward their sons, while fathers do the same for daughters. Thus, adult sex roles may not result from the simple expectation that boys should behave like boys and girls like girls.

There are also intellectual differences between the sexes. In general, women do better at verbal and social tasks, while men excel in the mathematical-spatial areas. In creativity, boys and men can restructure problems better than girls and women, who are better as "divergent" thinkers. But researchers have attributed these differences variously to personality factors, parental attitudes, or brain and biological distinctions, and at this time there is still no consensus on any one, clear-cut set of causative factors.

Other adults besides parents—adults of both sexes—still accept the idea that "man does while woman is." And many of them are still shocked by shifts of the sort expressed in one of Dorothy Parker's most pointed lyrics:

In youth, it was a way I had
    To do my best to please,
And change, with every passing lad,
    To suit his theories.
But now I know the things I know,
    And do the things I do,
And if you do not like me so,
    To hell, my love, with you!

At least one woman, Dorothy Parker, says here that "woman does," as well as man. Was she stating the norm for women, or only expressing her own independence?

Contrary to Dorothy Parker's position, the *cultural-expectations hypothesis* states that, given the general norms of our culture, girls tend to be more stable in their degree of passivity and dependence than boys.

This hypothesis is consistent with the parental-behavior hypothesis, adding cultural expectations to those of parents in the establishment of stable sex-role behavior.

DESCRIPTIVE EVIDENCE

Investigators: J. Kagan and H. A. Moss
Source, Date: "The Stability of Passive and Dependent Behavior From Childhood Through Adulthood," 1960
Location: Fels Research Institute
Subjects: 27 male and 27 female adults born between 1930 and 1939
Materials: Narrative reports of direct observation of childhood behavior; interviews with child and mother; interview ratings; perception test

The subjects had been studied throughout childhood, and there were fairly complete longitudinal records of each of them from ages three to ten, including reports of direct observations of childhood behavior in a variety of situations and summaries of interviews with the children and their mothers. This material on each subject was studied and rated according to four vari-

Figure 2. Dress of three generations ago, emphasizing the differences between men and women, contrasts with the "unisex" look of today. Different learning experiences and expectations have altered the concept of sex identity and will doubtless alter it further in future generations.

ables: passivity, general dependence, affection seeking, and instrumental assistance seeking (asking for help in doing something).

In addition, all the subjects, who at the time of this report were between the ages of twenty and twenty-nine, were given a variety of tests and a personal interview lasting about five hours. One of the tests involved the perception of pictures of dependent and aggressive scenes, and six of fifty-nine variables on which the interviewer rated each subject dealt specifically with passive-dependent behaviors. The major overall conclusion was that passive and dependent behaviors had remained fairly stable from childhood to adulthood in females but not in males.

There is no way of knowing to what extent genetic-biological factors may have contributed to these tendencies, but the researchers concluded that the different cultural expectations experienced by children of different sexes were a more important consideration for stable passivity in women and the growing independence that marked the men's development. Overt passivity had been discouraged in boys but not in girls. And assertive-aggressive behavior had been discouraged in girls but not in boys. Thus behavior that was contrary to sex-role expectation seemed to have been discouraged and did not show continuity from childhood to adulthood.

Whatever natural functions the distinctions between passive, nurturant, and submissive girls and dominant, aggressive, and forceful boys may have served in the past have certainly disappeared from contemporary living. Jo Freeman has cogently summed up the situation:

> The characteristics we observe in women and men today are a result of socialization practices that were developed for survival of a primitive society. The value structure of male superiority is a reflection of the primitive orientations and values. But social and economic conditions have changed drastically since these values were developed. Technology has reduced to almost nothing the importance of muscular strength. In fact, the warlike attitude which goes along with an idealization of physical strength and dominance is proving to be positively destructive.

Compelling as such arguments may be, they are so broad that they are ultimately untestable. Some descriptive evidence has been gathered, then, to support the parental-behavior and cultural-expectations hypotheses of the molding of children's distinctive sex-role behavior. This behavior expresses preferences and attitudes the children have developed.

Studies of such sex-role preferences have yielded some specific evidence to support the *children's preferences hypothesis,* which states that children of either sex find traditional masculine roles more desirable and important than feminine ones.

DESCRIPTIVE EVIDENCE

Investigator: D. G. Brown
Source, Date: "Masculinity-Femininity Development in Children," 1957
Location: A Pleasanton, California, elementary school
Subjects: 613 boys and girls from ages five to twelve
Materials: IT Scale for Children

The IT Scale for Children uses thirty-six picture cards of objects, figures, and activities defined by contemporary American culture as associated with either male or female roles. Each subject makes a series of choices among these pictures, but not directly for himself or herself. Instead, the selections are made for the "IT"—a child figure drawn so ambiguously that it can be taken to be either masculine or feminine. This procedure encourages the child to structure the choices in terms of how he or she views the sex role rather than his or her personal preferences.

Each subject was asked to choose eight possible toys for IT from sixteen pictures of boys' and girls' toys. Similar choices were made between eight pairs of pictures matched to present male and female role alternatives: for example, "Would IT rather be an Indian chief or an Indian princess?" From four pictures, subjects chose "the kind of child IT would like to be"—boy, girl, girlish boy, or a boyish girl. Finally, each subject was asked whether IT would rather be a mother or a daddy when IT grows up.

In line with their own roles, boys chose more masculine pictures than feminine ones, and girls chose more feminine ones, overall. But boys showed a much stronger preference for the male role than girls showed for the female role: in the first through fourth grades 63 percent of the boys chose masculine pictures almost exclusively and a mere 4 percent showed a preference for pictures defined as feminine, whereas only 17 percent of the girls chose exclusively feminine pictures as against 40 percent who chose masculine pictures almost exclusively. At the fifth-grade level, however, girls showed a stronger preference for feminine pictures, probably as a result of stronger changes toward female sex-role preferences as girls reach adolescence.

This finding has been confirmed by studies showing that about 3 percent of male adults say that they have at some point had a desire to be female, while between 20 and 31 percent of women report having had a desire to be male. Our culture may allow girls to be tomboys to some degree, but there are strong prohibitions against "sissy" boys. Even while young children are learning to express the approved role preferences, they can survey the social world and see that "masculine" activities are generally approved whereas "feminine" doings are often belittled. Consequently, a larger proportion of both sexes taken together prefer the male role if given a choice. Girls may relinquish this orientation as they grow older and experience social and cultural preferences. The data from Brown's study are from 1957, and preferences may have changed somewhat since that time.

ences between men and women. However, the significance of whatever physiological (internal, hormonal, cyclical) distinctions exist is much less apparent. Some supporters of women's liberation argue that the anatomical differences have been obscured by an emphasis on "mysterious" physiological processes. As Germaine Greer puts it, "The vagina is obliterated from the imagery of femininity in the same way that the signs of independence and vigor in the rest of her body are suppressed." Such suppression is again related to cultural expectations, and both the patterns of achievement and sexual discrimination in our society have received increasing attention from psychologists.

Whatever the effects of such suppression, the role anatomical distinctions must play in determining adult sex differences is recognized. The hormones hypothesis states that there are genetic-biological differences between the sexes that affect emotional behavior. Some animal data on this matter have been obtained, but they cannot be reliably transferred to human behavior. And psychological research on the question has barely begun. Several studies have opened fresh vistas of descriptive evidence, however, in tending to support the hormones hypothesis.

QUESTION	2. WHAT ARE SOME INFLUENCES ON SEX-ROLE DIFFERENCES DURING ADULTHOOD?			
HYPOTHESES	HORMONES	NEED FOR ACHIEVEMENT	DISCRIMINATION
DESCRIPTIVE EVIDENCE	ASSESS: relations among menstrual cycle, mood swings, and psychological needs	ASSESS: relations of achievement needs of women to fears about success	
EXPERIMENTAL EVIDENCE			VARY: apparent qualifications and sex of candidate MEASURE: evaluation of the candidate (according to sex of subjects)

2. WHAT ARE SOME INFLUENCES ON SEX-ROLE DIFFERENCES DURING ADULTHOOD?

But what about biology? Surely that is the basis for adult sex-role. No one can deny the anatomical differ-

DESCRIPTIVE EVIDENCE

Investigators: J. M. Bardwick and M. Ivey
Source, Date: "Her Body, the Battleground," 1972
Location: University of Michigan

Subjects: 26 female college students
Materials: A simple projective test; interviews

In four separate interviews, each subject was asked to tell about any experience she had had and to talk about it spontaneously for five minutes. These talks were tape-recorded over two menstrual cycles, one at each ovulation (midcycle) and one at premenstruation. Each story was scored for indications of verbal anxiety on themes of death, mutilation, separation, low self-esteem, guilt, shame, and so on.

It was found that these subjects expressed the most anxiety over death, mutilation, and separation during the interview before menstruation. On the other hand, themes of high self-esteem and confidence were expressed the most often at ovulation.

Each subject was also asked whether, before her menstrual period, she felt any symptoms by which she could anticipate the onset of the period (such as breast swelling, irritability, weight gain, cramps, or backache). When these reports were compared with accounts of how the subjects were treated when sick as children, it was discovered that the more menstrual symptoms reported by the woman, the more likely it was that she had felt great gratification at being sick or bitter about being neglected during childhood illnesses. Bardwick concluded: "It appears that those who, as children, received extra love and attention when they were sick, continue to seek this gratification with premenstrual symptoms. Those who, as children, were unduly neglected when they were sick, reacted by demanding attention with premenstrual symptoms. In either case the young woman used her reproductive system in acting out a psychological need."

Female physiology may affect a woman's expressiveness and emotionality but there is little convincing evidence that differences in physiology are very important for cognitive or intellectual performances. Achievements in this area are strongly affected by cultural expectations, which generally tend to favor men's activities and preferences. As the noted anthropologist Margaret Mead pointed out: "In every known society, the male's need for achievement can be recognized. Men may cook, or weave or dress dolls or hunt humming-birds, but if such activities are appropriate occupations of men, then the whole society, men and women alike, votes them important.

When the same occupations are performed by women, they are regarded as less important." Some critics of contemporary society term this "domination" and relate it to the most debilitating myths of our culture. Eldridge Cleaver has stated this viewpoint with great force: "The myth of the strong black woman is the other side of the coin of the myth of the beautiful dumb blond. The white man turned the white woman into a weak-minded, weak-bodied, delicate freak, a sex pot, and placed her on a pedestal; he turned the black woman into a strong self-reliant Amazon and deposited her in his kitchen . . . The white man turned himself into the Omnipotent Administrator and established himself in the Front Office."

Exaggerated as this allegory may be, as long ago as 1953 researchers found that though the need "to do well in any achievement-oriented situation involving intelligence and leadership" was a strong motivating factor in men, women's behavior could not be predicted on this basis. The need-for-achievement hypothesis states that in our culture women are expected to have less need for achievement than men. This hypothesis, which points up the strength of cultural expectations in sex-role differences in our society, is supported, for example, by the evidence of the following investigation.

DESCRIPTIVE EVIDENCE

Investigator: M. S. Horner
Source, Date: "Fail: Bright Women," 1969
Location: University of Michigan
Subjects: 90 female and 88 male college freshmen and sophomores
Materials: Thematic Apperception Test (TAT); a story-completion item; a behavioral task

The TAT projective test is simply a series of pictures of people and objects in commonplace situations; the subject is asked to "write a story" about each picture. These particular subjects were asked to write a story based on the following opening line: "After first-term finals, John [Ann] finds himself [herself] at the top of his [her] medical school class." The female subjects were asked to write about Ann, the males about John.

Careful analysis of the stories showed that 65 percent of the girls expressed negative or fearful

Self-esteem	Hostility	Death Anxiety	Mutilation Anxiety
Ovulation			
. . . so I was elected chairman . . . I remember one particularly problematic meeting and afterwards, L. came up to me and said, "You really handled the meeting well." In the end it came out the sort of thing that really bolstered my confidence in myself.	. . . talk about my trip to Europe. It was just the greatest summer of my life. We met all kinds of terrific people everywhere we went, and just the most terrific things happened.	We just went to Jamaica and it was fantastic, the island is so lush and green . . . and the place is so fertile and the natives are just so friendly.	We took our skis and packed them on top of the car and then we took off for up north. We used to go for long walks in the snow, and it was just really great, really quiet and peaceful.
Premenstruation			
They had to teach me how to water-ski. I was so clumsy it was really embarrassing, 'cause it was kind of like saying to yourself you can't do it, and the people were about to lose patience with me.	. . . talk about my brother and his wife. I hated her. I just couldn't stand her . . . I used to do terrible things to separate them.	I'll tell you about the death of my poor dog M . . . oh, another memorable event, my grand-parents died in a plane crash. That was my first contact with death and it was very traumatic.	. . . came around a curve and did a double flip and landed upside down. I remember this car coming down on my hand and slicing it right open and all this blood was all over the place. Later they thought it was broken because every time I touched the finger, it felt like a nail was going through my hand.

Source: Reprinted from *Psychology Today* Magazine, February, 1972. Copyright © Ziff-Davis Publishing Company.

Table 1. Bardwick and Ivey's research indicates that feelings change through the hormonal fluctuations of the menstrual cycle. Themes of high self-esteem and confidence were expressed most often by subjects at ovulation. Before menstruation, the subjects expressed most anxiety over death, mutilation, and separation.

imagery about Ann's success. Some of them felt that it would lead to failure in personal relationships—particularly an inability to marry—and others attributed the heroine's success to luck. On the other hand, only 10 percent of the boys expressed such doubts about the hero's achievement; most of them predicted a thoroughly successful future for John.

Moreover, women who exhibited anxiety over achievement in this study also performed more poorly on a task in competition with men than they did on the same task alone. Conceivably, women who respond in this way are subject to a "double bind." If they are not successful, they fail to live up to their own standards. But if they do achieve success, they are violating the "normal" expectations of our culture. On the basis of this research, Horner suggests that a woman's desire for achievement is contaminated by a motive to avoid success. Exactly what is expected of women in our culture may be indicated by a recent survey of the attitudes expressed in a substantial sample of television commercials. The results, summarized in Figure 3, speak for themselves.

At the social level, there is an abundance of evidence to support the *discrimination hypothesis, which states that in our culture women are consistently rated as inferior to men. Note that this hypothesis does not state who rates women as inferior to men*. It has been shown in the following experiment, for example, that members of both sexes tend to evaluate men more highly than women.

EXPERIMENTAL EVIDENCE

Investigators: K. Deaux and J. Taynor
Source, Date: "Evaluation of Male and Female Ability: Bias Works Two Ways," 1971
Location: Purdue University
Subjects: 47 male and 50 female college students
Materials: Tape-recorded interviews; rating scales

The subjects were asked to evaluate supposed candidates for a study-abroad program. Each listened individually to a tape recording of an interviewer's review of the applicant's transcript and language proficiency followed by the interview, in which the candidate was asked ten questions about the history, government, and geography of Switzerland, the country he or she hoped to visit.

The subjects were randomly assigned to one of the four groups. For one group, the candidate was a male who was highly qualified for the program: he maintained a 3.85 out of 4.00 grade average, was familiar with three languages other than English, and answered most of the interviewer's questions correctly and confidently. The second group of subjects heard exactly the same information and qualifications about a female candidate. For a third group of subjects, the candidate was a male but poorly qualified: he maintained a 2.13 grade point average, was slightly familiar with two languages other than English, answered only two interview questions correctly, and lacked confidence. A fourth group of subjects heard exactly the same information and qualifications as the third group, but for a female.

Each subject was asked to rate the candidate on an eleven-point scale for general competence, intelligence, knowledge of current events, adjustment, attractiveness, probability of being a good representative, and probability of future success and then to decide whether or not the scholarship should be awarded.

Although the highly qualified candidates received

TABLE 2. When Equality Isn't Equal

Income	Men	Women
Overall		
Median Income	$ 7,529	$5,618
Income by Occupation		
Professional and technical workers	$ 9,868	$6,705
Clerical workers	7,006	5,570
Skilled blue-collar workers	6,452	3,668
Service workers	5,778	3,272
Income by Education		
Less than 4 years of high school	$ 5,660	$3,132
High school diploma	7,362	5,500
1 to 3 years of college	8,310	5,608
4 years or more of college	10,726	6,862

Source: Adapted from *The New York Times*, March 26, 1972.

Table 2. Two officials in the Census Bureau found that women between 30 and 44 who had worked consistently since leaving school had lower incomes than men of the same age, with the same education, holding the same type of jobs.

In 24.3%
SUBMISSIVE

In 33.9% —
DEPENDENT ON MEN

In 22.7% —
DEMEANED HOUSEKEEPERS

In 37.5% —
DOMESTIC ADJUNCTS

In 42.6% —
HOUSEHOLD FUNCTIONARIES

In 17.1% —
UNINTELLIGENT

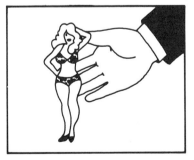

In 16.7% —
SEX OBJECTS

Figure 3. How women are portrayed in 1,200 T.V. commercials. (Adapted from *The New York Times,* May 28, 1972).

much higher ratings overall than did the poorly qualified candidates, the highly qualified male was seen as more competent and more intelligent than the equivalent female. Surprisingly, the poorly qualified male candidate was seen as less intelligent and less competent than the equivalent female. Male and female subjects did not evaluate differently, and both the highly qualified male and the equivalent female were recommended for the scholarship equally often.

The researchers explained this by postulating that the subjects were reluctant to take a course of overt action that would leave them open to charges of discrimina-tion. But the ideology of masculine superiority in our culture may be double-edged, working to the ad-vantage of highly qualified males as compared to females but to the disadvantage of poorly qualified males.

The subjects of this experiment, although both male and female, were limited to college students. Do you think similar results would be obtained for most other male and female groups in our culture? It is often difficult to judge how broadly, if at all, the results of experiments can be generalized beyond the specific kind of subjects of the experiment itself.

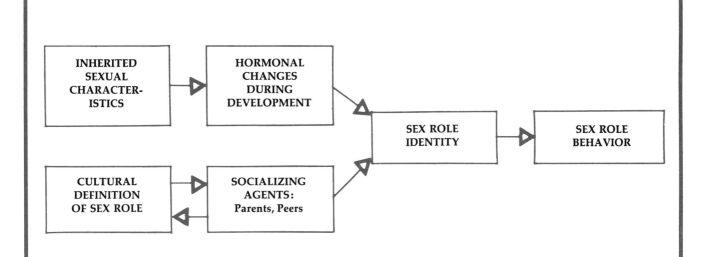

PUTTING IT TOGETHER: Sexuality

The *inherited sexual characteristics* that each individual possesses determine, at the very least, the anatomical differences between the sexes and *hormonal changes during development*. The cultural definition of the sex role is carried or modified by such *socializing agents* as parents or peers.

These socializing agents in combination with the biological differences in the individual determine the *sex role identity* that the individual develops during childhood. This includes passivity and dependence, need for achievement, self-evaluation and confidence.

Out of these differences in sex role identity arise the *behaviors* associated with the differences in sex role.

WHAT'S ACCEPTED AND WHAT'S DEBATED

1. WHAT'S ACCEPTED . . .

1. Behavioral differences between the sexes result from the interaction of genetic, physiological, and cultural factors.

2. The parents of a child are the most important socializing agents for the development of sex-role identification and differences.

3. Many behavioral differences between the sexes not present at an early age develop as a child becomes socialized.

4. Social learning experiences result in the accentuation of some behaviors and the elimination of others in a manner consistent with culturally accepted sex-role norms.

5. The demands and expectations imposed by cultural pressures affect the individual's self-evaluation and the evaluation of others, in terms of sexuality.

2. WHAT'S DEBATED . . .

1. Whether hormonal differences between males and females result in central nervous system differences.

2. The degree to which the causes of nonhuman sex differences are generalizable to parallel sex differences in humans.

3. The proportion in which different kinds of factors—genetic, physiological, cultural—contribute to sex-role differences.

4. The relationships between sex-role identity, achievement, and anxiety, especially in women.

Figure 4. Adults often select children's toys on the basis of sex-role stereotype. These selections in turn probably influence sex-role behavior of the developing child.

ISSUE: HOMOSEXUALITY

As we have seen in this unit, the study of which factors influence sexuality and sex-role behavior will go on for a long time, for there are precious few definite answers. One of the most controversial areas of sexual research is homosexuality, (sexual attraction between members of the same sex), and one of the most controversial modern protest movements is Gay Liberation. Homosexuals all over America are insisting that they are basically normal and that their sexual choices represent another life style, not a failure of personal development. They are demanding that the social and legal prejudices surrounding their sexual expression be erased. One of the main targets for their efforts has been the American Psychiatric Association, which for years included homosexuality in its official list of mental disorders. As long as the disapproval of homosexuality receives approval from psychology, argue homosexuals, there can be no real hope for reform of oppressive laws against a "crime" that has no victim.

The Gay Liberation movement has forced a new examination of homosexuality by social scientists—sociologists and anthropologists as well as psychologists. In the past few years there has been a flood of research published on the subject. The evidence, contrary to popular belief, is that the human species is not biologically programmed to respond to particular sexual stimuli, heterosexual or otherwise. There may be a basic sex drive, but the way in which it is expressed is learned through socialization. (Similarly, there is a basic hunger drive, but we have to learn what is edible, what is inedible, and what is edible but forbidden—like pork for Jews, or fish for Zulus.) Harry Harlow has shown that the same is probably true even of rhesus monkeys. If they are prevented from observing the sexual behavior of other monkeys, they are later incapable of sexual intercourse, and it is almost impossible to teach them to perform it—although they commonly discover masturbation on their own. Sociologist Kingsley Davis, a lifelong expert on marriage and the family, contends that "Sexual activity must be learned. Without socialization, human beings would not even know how to copulate." All of us, then, would seem to have the potential to be heterosexual, homosexual, or bisexual. Our ultimate sexual orientation depends on the prevailing norms of our society and on our learning experiences as individuals.

Psychologists have been particularly interested in anthropological evidence about sexual behavior in other societies, because this evidence reveals how learning experiences can encourage or discourage homosexual behavior. After a survey of all the societies on which information was available, Clellan S. Ford and Frank A. Beach found that while some societies punish homosexuality by ridicule or even death, sixty-four percent of the societies studied regard it as normal and socially acceptable—sometimes for all members of society at all times, sometimes for all members of society at some times, and sometimes only for minorities. But although homosexuality may be permitted heterosexuality is the dominant norm in virtually all societies, because it preserves the species. It would be difficult for any society to survive if it did not institutionalize heterosexuality as the most approved outlet, although exceptional cases are not

unknown. The Marind-anim of New Guinea are a fundamentally homosexual culture and place a total taboo on heterosexual intercourse for all but a few days of the year. They maintain their population by raiding neighboring tribes and kidnapping their children.

Psychological research has cast doubt on the popular assumption that an individual is either heterosexual or homosexual. Instead, it seems, there is a continuum of sexual preferences. Alfred C. Kinsey, who conducted the most extensive research into sexual behavior ever undertaken, proposed a seven-point rating scale, with true bisexuality in the middle and exclusive heterosexuality or homosexuality at either end. Kinsey found that one American male in six has at least as much homosexual as heterosexual experience. About 5 percent of the male population, he discovered, was exclusively homosexual, and some thirty-seven percent of males had experienced homosexual activity to the point of orgasm after the onset of adolescence. For reasons that are not fully understood, the incidence of female homosexuality appears to be significantly lower. Subsequent studies using smaller samples have almost exactly duplicated Kinsey's findings on the incidence of homosexuality.

Research has so far failed to yield any convincing evidence of physiological or genetic differences between predominantly homosexual and predominantly heterosexual individuals. Although homosexuality is sometimes associated with "effeminacy" in men and "butchness" in women, there is no evidence that these supposed characteristics are any more common in homosexuals than heterosexuals. And not only are homosexuals difficult to distinguish by any physical criterion, but research has also indicated that there are no consistent personality differences between homosexuals and heterosexuals other than that of sexual orientation.

The evidence that homosexual activity falls within the biologically normal (if socially abnormal) range of potential human behavior has become so weighty that in 1974 the American Psychiatric Association reconsidered its listing of homosexuality as a mental disorder. After a long and often bitter debate, the Association voted by a large majority to remove homosexuality from the list. They still recognize, however, that social reactions to homosexuals may lead to psychological stress.

Unit 7

Love

OVERVIEW

Love is a topic that has received only scanty interest from psychologists until recent decades. Largely due to Harlow's pioneering studies with monkeys in the 1950s, the experiences and behaviors associated with love and affection are now receiving attention from developmental and social psychologists. Differences between childhood and adult loving are discussed.

UNIT OUTLINE

DEFINITION AND BACKGROUND
1. *Definition:* love can be described as profound feelings of attraction or affection between individuals.
2. *Background:* Harry F. Harlow (1905–   ).

QUESTIONS AND EVIDENCE
1. How is the capacity for love developed in childhood?
Hypotheses:
    a. *Maternalism:* the female of the species, relative to the male, is biologically determined to exhibit behavior more favorable to the care and feeding of the young. 110
    b. *Socialization:* peer and play relationships are necessary for the development and maintenance of normal "loving" social and sexual relationships in adult-hood.111
2. How are liking and love developed in adulthood?
Hypotheses:
    a. *Similarity:* people will like each other to the extent that they resemble one another.113
    b. *Esteem-gain:* an individual's liking for another person may result from an improvement in the other person's appreciation of him or her.114
    c. *Two-component:* an emotional state first occurs as physiological arousal (increased heart rate, heavy breathing, flushed skin, and so on) that is then attributed, largely on the basis of cultural definitions, to "love" for another person.115

IMPORTANT CONCEPTS

	page
arousal	115
contact comfort	109
interpersonal attraction	108
love	108
maternalism	110
self-esteem	115
socialization	111
surrogate	109

The capacity for love develops out of early social interactions.

As we grow older, we are usually attracted to others who are similar to us in important ways.

There is evidence that we tend to be especially attracted to people whose esteem for us has increased over what it once was.

DEFINITION AND BACKGROUND

Few concepts in the history of man have been defined in as many ways as love. Intense experiences of loving things, nature, life, lower animals, and people seem to have a different quality for each attraction. Describing the communication of one human's love for another, Meerloo (1952) pointed out that the simple words "I love you" might express any of the following meanings: I want you sexually. I hope you love me. Maybe we can love each other. I hate you. I want to feel cozy and at home with you. My self-love goes out to you. I want through you to correct the mistakes I have made in human relations. In this unit, we will use a DEFINITION of love as *profound feelings of attraction or affection between individuals.*

Historically a favorite topic of philosophers, poets, and novelists, the intense human experience of love has been paradoxically neglected by psychologists as a suitable topic for their investigations. In 1957 Abraham Maslow, who was to become president of the American Psychological Association eleven years later, lamented: "The sad thing is that most students come into psychology with humanistic interests. They want to find out about people; they want to understand love, hate, hope, fear, ecstasy, happiness, the meaning of living. But what is so often done for these high hopes and yearnings? Most graduate, and even undergraduate training turns away from these subjects, which are called fuzzy, unscientific, tender-minded, mystical. (I couldn't find the word 'love' indexed in any of the psychology books on my shelves, even the ones on marriage.)"

Perhaps the intensity, variety, and subjectivity of love as an experience are responsible for the fact that psychologists shied away from its study for so long. It is difficult to remain objective about some experiences and they sometimes seem best left within the province of literary writers. The idea of searching for uniform relationships among variables in order to derive laws of behavior seems to squeeze the heart out of love. Recently, however, less reluctant investigators have begun to say more about the "phenomenon" of love. Realizing the practical impossibility of analyzing love and all its facets in any simple fashion, a number of psychologists are asking meaningful questions about love and affection that can be answered through research. The FOCUS of this unit is

on this research and its possible implications for the average person's notions about where love comes from and what it is.

Much of the psychological research on the nature of love in recent years has indicated that the capacity of love is best understood by studying relationships among individuals as they develop from infancy. Because we cannot manipulate relationships among human beings as they develop, these investigations are most commonly done with monkeys, phylogenetically our closest relatives. So if you look up "love" in the index of the research journals, it is very likely that you will find references to research with monkeys. To find out what research has been done concerning the nature of human love, it is necessary to look into a popular research area in social psychology often referred to as studies in "interpersonal attraction."

BACKGROUND: HARRY F. HARLOW (1905–   )

In 1958, one year after Maslow complained that he couldn't find the word "love" indexed in any of his psychology books, Harry Harlow of the University of Wisconsin delivered his presidential address to the American Psychological Association, entitled "The Nature of Love." In this address, he also complained

Figure 1. Harry F. Harlow, director of the primate Lab at the University of Wisconsin, has conducted pioneering research with rhesus monkeys in the areas of learning and motivation, early experience, adult-infant interaction, with important implications for human behavior.

that "Psychologists, at least psychologists who write textbooks, not only show no interest in the origin and development of love or affection, but they seem to be unaware of its very existence."

For a long time many psychologists thought that the origins of love in childhood were bound up with the fact that a mother provides nourishment to the newborn infant. According to this idea, the bond between an infant and his mother develops from the infant's associating the source of food (his mother) with the satisfaction of his nutritive needs. Even Freud echoed this view in his description of the first or "oral" stage in infant development.

In the middle 1950s, it occurred to Harlow that the touch and contact that an infant receives from his mother might be at least as important as feeding. His problem was to verify this idea. How could he pit the value of feeding to the infant against the value of physical contact?

Let him choose! Harlow raised two groups of infant monkeys with artificial surrogate mothers. One of the surrogate mothers offered only a wired surface, while the other was padded and covered with soft terry cloth. For some monkeys, one "mother" in each pair fed the infant monkey with a bottle embedded in its chest. With some monkeys, the terry-cloth mother did the feeding; with others, the wire mother did the feeding. In this way an infant monkey presented with two mothers could choose which mother to become attached to—wire versus cloth, feeding versus contact comfort.

There was little doubt about the results of this study: except for actual feeding time, an infant monkey spent much more time on the cloth mother, regardless of whether it provided milk. Clearly, not only was contact comfort as important as feeding, but it seemed to be the only thing that really mattered to the monkeys. Harlow's simple experiment dispelled the old "nutritional" theories in one fell swoop. In addition, new questions could be asked, and new methods similar to Harlow's surrogate mothers could be used to answer further questions about the development and maintenance of love in infancy.

Perhaps one of the most important of these questions was how crucial these early touch and contact experiences are for later development. A host of data soon began to show that they are extremely important, that deprivation of early maternal and social experiences has drastic consequences for later social and sexual behaviors in adulthood. In other words, an infant must learn to love—it's not just a matter of "doing what comes naturally."

Figure 2. Harlow's infant monkeys preferred cloth-covered surrogate mothers over wire mothers, even when a monkey was fed only by the wire mother.

QUESTIONS AND EVIDENCE

1. How is the capacity for love developed in childhood?
2. How are liking and love developed in adulthood?

Drawing an inference that because two groups, like
lower primates and man, have many similar characteristics, another characteristic of the first group,
lower primates, also holds for the second group, man,
is known as an argument by analogy. Unless many
basic points of close similarity between the groups are

QUESTION 1. HOW IS THE CAPACITY FOR LOVE DEVELOPED IN CHILDHOOD?

HYPOTHESES	MATERNALISM	SOCIALIZATION
DESCRIPTIVE EVIDENCE		
EXPERIMENTAL EVIDENCE	VARY: type of early social interactions among monkeys MEASURE: reactions, by sex, to an infant monkey	VARY: amount of social deprivation among monkeys MEASURE: effects on later sexual and aggressive behaviors

1. HOW IS THE CAPACITY FOR LOVE DEVELOPED IN CHILDHOOD?

From the touch and contact provided by his mother
the infant discovers immediately that a presence is
almost always there to see to his needs for nourishment and warmth and to come when he is in distress.
Such early affection is extremely important for later
development. The *maternalism hypothesis* states that
the female of the species, relative to the male, is
biologically determined to exhibit behavior more favorable to the care and feeding of the young.

Mankind has always recognized that mothers usually take special care with their own offspring. Some
twenty-four centuries ago Aristotle attributed this
characteristic to physiological-psychological causes:
"This is the reason why mothers are more devoted to
their children than their fathers: it is that they suffer
more in giving them birth and are more certain that
they are their own." It is possible that the sources of
maternalism can be traced back even further, to
genetic and consequent biological factors. But the
hypothesis cannot be tested directly for human beings, because it would be unethical to manipulate the
hereditary and environmental conditions of a baby for
experimental purposes alone. Again, we must rely on
studies of primate life.

found, and the inferred similarity is intimately related
to the other similarities and is not accidental, arguments by analogy are likely to be very weak or even
misleading. See how strongly you think the following
experiments support the maternalism hypothesis by
analogy.

EXPERIMENTAL EVIDENCE

Investigators: A. Chamove, H. Harlow, and G. Mitchell
Source, Date: "Sex Differences in the Infant-Directed Behav-
ior of Preadolescent Rhesus Monkeys," 1967
Location: University of Wisconsin
Subjects: 15 male-female pairs of preadolescent rhesus mon-
keys averaging two years in age
Materials: A one-month-old female rhesus monkey placed in
a playpen area surrounded by cages

The pairs of monkeys were matched for age, kind of
social rearing, and the experimenter who handled
them. The three experimental conditions involved
seven pairs who had interacted only with peers (no
mothers) since birth, four pairs who had been raised
with mothers but no peers, and four pairs who had
had both maternal and peer experiences. All these

monkeys were tested individually for their reactions to a one-month-old infant monkey. Initially, each monkey was allowed to view the infant for an adaptation period of twenty-four hours. Afterward, the infant was placed in the cage with a subject monkey for a fifteen-minute testing period, during which both animals were observed. Their responses were scored into categories (sexual, grooming, fear, hostility, and so on) by an observer.

Regardless of previous social experiences, female subjects typically exhibited "maternallike" reactions to the infant monkey (contact, caressing, cuddling), and males primarily displayed hostility or indifference.

Harlow extended his thesis to human responses by projecting a photograph of a young monkey on a screen before different college audiences (See Figure 3). Females typically responded with "oohs" and "aahs" while males remained completely silent—when audiences were all female or all male. With mixed audiences, however, the "feminine ecstasy" response was noticeably lessened, apparently inhibited by the presence of males. Yet the fact that maternalism in human females seems to be parallel to or comparable with responses in other primate species does not prove that it arises from the same causes. In humans maternalism is probably determined just as much by sociocultural factors as by biological predispositions.

This leads to another argument by analogy from monkeys to children and gives rise to a hypothesis that supplements the maternalism hypothesis for a more complete understanding of how human capacity for love develops.

As an infant monkey develops, it usually begins to achieve some independence and exploratory curiosity at about two months of age. In fact, by the seventy-fifth day of normal infancy the mother animal displays almost no protectiveness unless the infant is in danger. By five months the mother avoids or rejects it even more strongly. Thus, the transitional stage that starts as gentle punishment increases in frequency and intensity until it actively forces independence on the infant.

The gradual achievement of independence is normal and necessary in the developing infant monkey. Artificial mother "surrogates" never provide the appropriate rejection, and their failure to promote in-

Figure 3. Nonhuman females apparently are biologically programmed to exhibit behavior favorable to infants, such as cuddling and caressing, while males tend to display hostility or indifference. This picture, when exhibited to humans in one of Harlow's experiments, elicited the "female ecstasy response." Maternalism in humans is probably determined just as much by sociocultural factors as biological predisposition.

dependence in their "children" inhibits their later social development and behaviors.

Such a transitional stage, beginning with toilet training at about age two, is also a normal part of human development in Western cultures. Psychoanalyst Erich Fromm sees it as a fundamental problem: "The mother-child relationship is paradoxical and, in a sense, tragic. It requires the most intense love on the mother's side, yet this very love must help the child grow away from the mother, and to become fully independent" (Fromm, *The Art of Loving*).

The *socialization hypothesis* states that peer and play relationships in childhood are necessary for the development and maintenance of normal "loving" social and sexual relationships in adulthood. It can best be assessed by depriving infants of all social contacts during early development.

EXPERIMENTAL EVIDENCE

Investigators: H. F. Harlow, W. D. Joslyn, M. G. Senke, and A. Dopp

Source, Date: "Behavioral Aspects of Reproduction in Primates," 1966

Location: University of Wisconsin

Subjects: Rhesus monkeys of both sexes

Materials: Individual and double cages

Male and female monkeys were raised in individual cages, where they were deprived of the affection and contact obtained through normal interactions with a mother or with peers. When these monkeys attained adulthood, they were paired with monkeys of the opposite sex who had been raised normally. The behavior of the deprived monkeys was then observed and compared with that of other pairs of monkeys who had been raised with both mother and playmate interactions.

The deprived males were and remained extremely aggressive. They made more threats than normal males and often carried them out with brutal treatment of the females. They thus were unable to establish any affectionate relationships with their normal female partners.

At first the deprived females also displayed aggressive behavior toward their partners, but strong retaliation from the larger normal males rapidly suppressed these tendencies. Although they were in proximity to the normal males as often as normal females were, they consistently avoided any contact lasting longer than one minute.

None of the deprived monkeys was able to carry out the mechanics of sex normally, though the males were apparently more crippled in this respect than females. Even if they appeared to recognize their mate's sexual behavior, they simply became puzzled. Deprived females exhibited presexual postures as often as normal females, but they were unable to support the male and carry the sexual act to completion.

In the normal family or colony the young monkey, whether male or female, develops the normal sexual patterns of his species through the experiences of playing with his parents and peers. Aggressiveness within the social structure of monkey colonies is usually intermittent and highly controlled.

Figure 4. Harlow's studies have shown that normal social and heterosexual interactions during monkey childhood are necessary for the later emergence of normal, adult relationships.

Figure 5. Children's cooperative play relationships with peers are probably important precursors to adult love in humans.

Can you think of characteristics of socially deprived children that are similar to the responses of deprived monkeys, supporting the socialization hypothesis by analogy? Or have you observed evidence that tends to directly support this hypothesis on a descriptive basis? Although animal data should not be generalized by analogy in any simple fashion to human behaviors, there is enough evidence to conclude that peer and play relationships are just as important for developing

the capacity to love in human beings as they are for other primates.

2. HOW ARE LIKING AND LOVE DEVELOPED IN ADULTHOOD?

Sex is not identical to "love" in human beings. As Bertrand Russell put it, "Love is something far more than the desire for sexual intercourse; it is the principal means of escape from the loneliness which afflicts most men and women throughout the greater part of their lives." Whether deprived monkeys feel such loneliness we shall never know, but human beings do, and the need to relieve it, through friendship as well as romantic love, seems to be a fundamental aspect of the human character.

There is some confusion in common parlance about the affinities that characterize "liking." One old saying declares that "birds of a feather flock together"; another states that "opposites attract." But there is actually very little evidence to support the latter cliché. Although it has been shown that, under certain circumstances, people do sometimes form relationships that fulfill their complementary needs, the pattern is not common. Thus many psychological investigations have been concerned with the *similarity hypothesis,* which states that people will like each other to the extent that they resemble one another. This is a difficult idea to test with full objectivity. If the subjects are given even the slightest clue about the purpose of the experiment, they may consciously try to influence or change its end results. Consequently, psychologists investigating the similarity hypothesis often use procedures in which the subjects are deliberately misinformed until the end of the study.

QUESTION	2. HOW ARE LIKING AND LOVE DEVELOPED IN ADULTHOOD?		
HYPOTHESES	SIMILARITY	ESTEEM GAIN	TWO-COMPONENT
DESCRIPTIVE EVIDENCE			
EXPERIMENTAL EVIDENCE	VARY: degree of perceived similarity in attitudes MEASURE: amount of liking for the other	VARY: perceived gains, losses, or constancy of esteem MEASURE: amount of liking for the other	VARY: perceived changes in one's own heart rate MEASURE: pictures rated as attractive

EXPERIMENTAL EVIDENCE

Investigator: D. Byrne

Source, Date: "Interpersonal Attraction and Attitude Similarity," 1961

Location: University of Texas

Subjects: 36 male and 28 female introductory psychology students

Materials: Attitude rating scales and counterfeit ratings; attraction and evaluation rating scales

The subjects were asked first to rate, on a seven-point scale, their agreement with opinions concerning twenty-six issues such as integration, premarital sex, classical music, and politics and then to indicate their choice of the thirteen least and thirteen most important of those issues. Two weeks later they were told that, as "part of a study of interpersonal prediction," they would be given the responses of another class to the same twenty-six issues, in order to determine "how much they could learn about one another from the information."

But these ratings were actually counterfeits prepared by the experimenter. One-quarter of the subjects received ratings that were identical to their own; one-quarter received ratings exactly opposite to theirs; one-quarter received ratings similar on the most important issues but dissimilar on the least important ones; and the last quarter received ratings dissimilar on the most important issues but similar on the least important issues. After examining this information, the subjects were asked to indicate on seven-point scales each of the following characteristics about the "person" whose ratings they had received: to what extent he thought he would like the person; to what extent he thought he would enjoy working with the person as a partner in an experiment; the intelligence of the person; his knowledge of current events; his morality; and his adjustment.

The group with identical counterfeit ratings indicated a greater liking for the "other person" than did the group with opposite ratings. They also rated the "other person" higher on intelligence, knowledge of current events, morality, and adjustment. Similar results were obtained for the subjects who received ratings similar to their own on important issues but dissimilar on the less important ones.

Other studies (many of them performed by Byrne and his associates) have confirmed that liking tends to be related to the degree to which people are similar in attitudes, values, beliefs, personality traits—or whatever. But the fact that similarity seems to be one important factor in general interpersonal attraction does not mean that other considerations are not operative. For example, other investigations have shown that competent people are generally liked more than incompetent people and that people who are "nice" tend to be liked in general.

What about immediate interpersonal attraction—or, in more familiar terms, love at first sight? It is generally assumed that this is primarily a physical response, and there is no evidence to contradict the assumption. When two strangers suddenly become aware of each other across a crowded room the enchantment of the evening is based on the only information available to them: how they look physically. At least one study (Walster *et al.*, "Importance of Physical Attractiveness in Dating Behavior," 1966) found that the sole determinant of a college student's "liking" for his blind date was her physical attractiveness. No other measures of compatibility, including those reflecting personality or intelligence, were significantly related to interpersonal liking.

If such an attraction is to last longer than one evening, it will probably involve other components like mutual similarity. After all, the couple will eventually have to talk to one another about something besides their good looks. A good first impression of "liking" is probably also increased considerably by any kind of immediate rewards received from a person one encounters. We usually like people more from whom we receive compliments, gifts, or expressions that they like us. On the social level, the most obvious forms of regard are expressions of respect, esteem, and admiration received from other people, and such expressions are apt to make one like these people.

The *esteem-gain hypothesis* states that an individual's liking for another person may result from an improvement in the other person's appreciation of him or her. The implication is that, although a relatively high and stable degree of esteem may be related to liking, increases in esteem will have even stronger effects on liking.

EXPERIMENTAL EVIDENCE

Investigators: E. Aronson and D. Linder

Source, Date: "Gain and Loss of Esteem as Determinants of

Interpersonal Attractiveness," 1965
Location: University of Minnesota
Subjects: 80 female undergraduate college students
Materials: Cover tasks and stories; rating scales

In the context of a "cover" experiment whose only purpose was to disguise the true purpose of this study, the subjects talked during seven separate meetings with another "subject," who was actually a confederate of the experimenters. After each meeting, each real subject learned how the confederate regarded her in terms of "impressions" from the conversation. These "impressions" were systematically varied over the seven sessions to form four "impression" conditions:

1. Negative-negative: The confederate always, throughout the seven sessions, said "uncomplimentary" things about the subject, such as she was a dull conversationalist, unintelligent.

2. Positive-positive: The confederate said only "nice" things about the subject; she seemed intelligent, a good conversationalist, and so on.

3. Negative-positive: The confederate started out saying negative things but said only positive things in the last three sessions.

4. Positive-negative: The confederate started out saying positive things but ended up saying negative things in the last three sessions.

At the end of all the sessions, the subjects were asked to rate their "liking" for the confederate on a twenty-one point scale.

The subjects generally liked the confederate whose affections were apparently hard to win (negative-positive) even more than they liked the one who appeared to like them from the very beginning (positive-positive). They disliked to an equal degree the confederates who went from positive to negative, and those who stayed negative.

In terms of self-esteem, psychologists have found that college subjects with low opinions of themselves are more receptive to a person offering affection than those having higher self-regard (Walster, "The Effect of Self-Esteem on Romantic Liking"). The general

supposition is that a person with little self-esteem is less demanding and at the same time more in need of admiration and affection; consequently, he or she is less likely to reject another for his or her negative attributes. "Love on the rebound" often takes this form. This hypothesis was confirmed in another study that found college students with low self-acceptance tended to marry spouses whom they perceived as less desirable than other mates (Murstein, "Self-Ideal-Self Discrepancy and Choice of Marital Partner").

Given the vast array of personality factors that enter into any given instance of romantic love, it is virtually impossible to develop a general definition of the physical experience. Everyone seems to be able to identify it, yet poets and philosophers disagreed about what sort of state it is and what it does to or for the human beings for centuries before professional psychologists appeared on the scene. About all that can be said with certainty at this point is that it is a recognizable emotion that is manifested by certain behavioral signs. The two-component hypothesis states that such an emotional state first occurs as physiological arousal (increased heart rate, heavy breathing, flushed skin, and so on) that is then attributed, largely on the basis of cultural definitions, to "love" for another person.

Studies that use subjects who are about to fall in love are understandably rare, so the two-component hypothesis has little direct supporting experimental evidence for love. However, the following investigation dealing with sexual attractiveness is provocative if you can accept that being sexually attracted and falling in love are somehow related.

EXPERIMENTAL EVIDENCE

Investigator: S. Valins
Source, Date: "Cognitive Effects of False Heart-Rate Feedback," 1966
Location: University of North Carolina
Subjects: 60 male introductory psychology students
Materials: Recordings of heartbeats; slide projector and pictures of seminude females

Four groups of subjects viewed ten photographs from Playboy magazine. Two experimental groups were told that as they looked at the pictures their heartbeats would be monitored and that they would be able to hear them through earphones. Actually, the "heart-beat monitoring" was manipulated by the experimenter in such a way that one of these groups heard their supposed heartbeats increase in rate as five of the ten pictures were shown, while the other experimental group heard heart-rate decreases with half the pictures. Two control groups of subjects heard the same sounds as the experimental groups but were told that they were irrelevant noises coming from the tape recorder. (See Figure 6.)

Immediately after the experiment, the experimental subjects rated as most attractive those photographs that had been associated with either increases or decreases in perceived heart rate. For the control subjects, no relationship between sound and attractiveness was found. Similarly, when the subjects were asked to choose one of the photographs as renumeration for participating in the experiment, the experimental subjects tended to choose the pictures that had been presented during heart-rate changes. Moreover, about four weeks later, when the experimental subjects were asked to rank the same ten photographs in order of preference, their highest awards went to those originally presented with heart-rate changes.

This finding may relate to the traditional description of love as a form of blindness or madness. But it is hardly the last word on the subject. As discussed in Unit 17, it is possible that cognitive appraisal of the particular situation may actually precede the arousal that is labeled "love," as well as follow it.

Figure 6. Subjects in Valins' study were especially attracted to photographs when they thought they were hearing their own heart rate change.

Probably romantic love can occur and develop in a number of different ways that have not yet been described or investigated objectively—perhaps in as many ways as there are different kinds of love. On this subject, it seems particularly advisable to follow one of the basic principles of the scientific approach: Always keep the path to inquiry open.

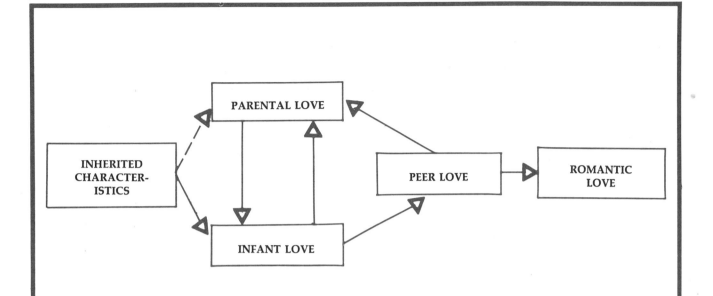

PUTTING IT TOGETHER: Love

Most experiments on the relationship between childhood experiences and adult love have been done with monkeys and compared with descriptive evidence from human behavior. Present evidence indicates that there are *inherited characteristics* in both species contributing to the development of love relationships: Females seem to have an inherited tendency to care for the very young, and infants have a need for contact comfort, leading to snuggling, cuddling and hugging. The development of love apparently has its origin in the mutual satisfaction of needs between mother and infant and the subsequent continuing relationship between *parental love* and *infant love.*

As the child develops, the socialization process involves cooperative play with other children, and *peer love.* These relationships may grow into a fully mature romantic love between adults or they may lead to parenthood and another cycle of fulfilled needs in the love interaction between parents and infants. Parental love or romantic love may be experienced independently of the other. For example, it is possible for two people to marry, have children, and love their children—and at the same time never experience "real" romantic love. On the other hand, a lack of parental love during parenthood is likely to occur only as the result of a lack of the socializing experiences and peer relationships characteristic of peer love.

Romantic love may start from liking other people with similar characteristics. The growth of esteem that one develops towards another individual may also initiate a liking or loving relationship between them. Evidence also indicates that sexual attraction, like many emotions, may involve a personal interpretation of experienced physiological arousal.

WHAT'S ACCEPTED AND WHAT'S DEBATED

1. WHAT'S ACCEPTED . . .

1. "Contact comfort" is an infant need that lies at the heart of infant love.

2. Infant-childhood experiences affect one's ability to form love relationships in later life.

3. One important factor in "liking" another person is similarity in virtually any dimension.

4. Physical attractiveness is an important factor for how men and women interact in meeting, dating, and even marrying.

5. Individuals tend to like more those people who reward them, whether materially or with respect, esteem, and the like.

2. WHAT'S DEBATED . . .

1. Whether or not the human female is biologically programmed to exhibit behavior favorable to infants, as nonhuman females apparently are.

2. To what extent the damage from early social deprivations is permanent: Can the effects be corrected through remedial action?

3. How romantic love comes about, and what it really involves.

4. The relationship of physiological arousal and cognitive appraisal in romantic love.

ISSUE: LOVE AND SCIENCE

Love is probably the most moving, mysterious and profound of all human emotions. It is perhaps for this reason that what's accepted from the research on the topic is so fragmentary. The very sacredness of love seems to defy attempts to categorize, measure, and experiment with it. As a result, modern psychologists find themselves in almost complete disagreement about the dynamics of what is perhaps our most fundamental emotion.

As we have learned, much of the research has focused on early interaction between mother and infant. The message of this research seems clear: unless warm, affectionate bonds are established early in an infant's life with one or more concerned and caring adults, severe and sometimes irreversible emotional damage may result. Lack of love in infancy may not only have adverse effects on intelligence, motivation and other personality attributes in later years, it may also stifle the capacity to love in return. Studies comparing children reared in institutions with children reared in foster homes have shown that the foster home group is relatively less retarded in both cognitive and social development, and has less difficulty forming emotional relationships later in life. The evidence from these studies has had considerable impact on the organization of orphanages and other childrens' institutions. In the past, it was believed that adequate nutrition, health care and toys to keep the child occupied could lead to normal development. Today, every effort is made in progressive institutions to give emphasis to meeting the affective (emotional) needs of infants and children. Adults spend as much time as possible in intimate interaction with them. The capacities to give and receive love are basic to the healthy personality, and early childhood experience with love appears crucial for this capacity to be fully developed.

Recently, psychologists have been looking further afield into their research into love. For example, they are asking whether the word "love" might in fact cover a wide range of somewhat different emotions, each with rather different dynamics and origins. They are asking how people make romantic and marital choices, and whether feelings of romantic love can be shared among a number of people. At a time when many Americans are pioneering forms of "group marriage" that are foreign to our entire Western experience, psychological research on the possibilities of shared romantic love seems especially relevant.

Can group marriage work? Professor Bernard I. Murstein, a leading researcher into the phenomenon of love, believes that the prospects for group marriage are not very hopeful: "I don't really see the group marriage becoming a viable alternative to monogamy in our culture . . . It's no easy thing for even two people to live together harmoniously in a society that emphasizes as heavily as ours does the importance of individuality . . . The possibilities of three or four people being married to each other and making a success of it decreases almost geometrically. I don't know of any marriages of more than six people that have lasted even a few months." This area is still largely unexplored by psychologists, however. For example, there is practically no research data available on how successful the many hundreds of "free love" communes spread all over the United States have been.

Another aspect of interpersonal attraction that is capturing the attention of researchers is the relationship of love to hate. Psychoanalyst R. D. Laing believes the two are intimately connected: "The initial act of brutality against the average child is the mother's first kiss." This view is an extreme one; but the fact remains that a large percentage of homicides committed in the United States every year involve family arguments or romantic entanglements. We still know very little about how love may turn to hate, or tenderness to violence. And psychologists are becoming interested in other, more passive forms of violence associated with love—the parent "smothering" a child with love and retarding the child's development of independence and emotional maturity; or the lover whose possessive jealously becomes oppressive and confining to the one who is loved.

Edward Zigler, professor of child development at Yale University, has forcefully argued that we neglect the development of our children's affective responses, in both the family and the school. Zigler points out that parents often experience the rearing of children as a stressful and perilous task, so that both parent and child derive less joy from the experience than they might. Parents, Zigler maintains, are misled by the publishers of educational books and the makers of educational toys into believing that their childrens' intellectual achievement is the all-important aspect of their development. Mothers and fathers, he contends, once went to a toy shop to buy a toy that would bring delight to the child. Today they are more likely to seek out the toy that promises to be "educational" in preference to the toy that is enjoyable. Similarly, parents often display more concern over a child's academic progress at school than over his or her emotional progress. Zigler believes the parents are making a grave mistake: "By what divine wisdom do we assert that the child with a straight-A report card is superior to the child with artistic ability, to the child with athletic prowess, or the child who is considerate, kind, and a pleasure to have around? Parents should love each of their children for what that child uniquely is."

Zigler fears that in contemporary American society, the child is coming to be regarded as little more than a computer programmed by a parent, and that over-emphasis on the training of the intellect is leading to a distorted view of parental responsiblities. Only when parents direct their energies and love toward nurturing affective development as well as the development of other capacities will the finest development of the childrens' personalities become possible. Psychologists also must share some of the blame for this narrow focus on academic achievement. In the past, experimental work has concentrated heavily on the cognitive and intellectual rather the affective and emotional aspects of personality. The new research interest in love, however, seems likely to correct this imbalance in the future.

Unit 8

Prejudice

OVERVIEW

Research findings are described on how prejudice, especially racial prejudice, develops, how it is maintained, and how it might be reduced. Some of the important processes implicated in the development and maintenance of prejudice are parental behaviors, displacement of aggression, and stereotyping. Prejudice can be reduced through contacts between mutual outgroups as well as by making people more aware of the inconsistencies between their beliefs and their behavior.

UNIT OUTLINE

DEFINITION AND BACKGROUND
1. *Definition:* prejudice is an attitude in which a person holds unfavorable and essentially unjustifiable beliefs and feelings toward members of a group, especially an ethnic group, to which he does not belong.
2. *Background:* D. Katz (1903–   ).

QUESTIONS AND EVIDENCE
1. How does prejudice develop?
Hypotheses:
    a. *Parental-identification:* children acquire prejudices by learning and adopting the attitudes and behavior patterns of their parents and other authority figures.
    b. *Displacement:* prejudice develops when anxiety, frustration and hostility are directed against available outgroups (or a scapegoat) rather than their true sources. **126**
    c. *Belief:* prejudices arise from perceived differences in belief systems. **127**
2. How is prejudice maintained?
Hypotheses:
    a. *Stereotypes:* prejudice resists change because human perception tends to group similar percepts together into categories or stereotypes. **129**
    b. *Personality:* prejudice resists change because it tends to be consistent with other character traits and to serve an individual's needs to reduce anxiety and frustration. **130**
3. How can prejudice be reduced?
Hypotheses:
    a. *Contact:* prejudice is reduced by interactions and cooperation with outgroup members. **131**
    b. *Awareness-of-inconsistency:* prejudice can be reduced by making a person conscious of apparent discrepancies among his own attitudes and values. **132**

IMPORTANT CONCEPTS

	page
aggression	124
anxiety	126
attitude	125
authoritarian personality	125
displacement	126
ethnocentrism	126
frustration	124
identification	125
outgroups	126
prejudice	122
social contact	131
stereotype	129

In learning from others to categorize information we also learn ways of categorizing people.

Prejudgments of other people on the basis of stereotyped categories may be maintained through personal frustrations.

Evidence indicates that prejudice may be reduced through constructive contact with people whose behavior is in conflict with the stereotype.

DEFINITION AND BACKGROUND

In the broad sense, prejudice refers to judgments made without knowledge of the facts. But as commonly used today and as a subject for psychological study, it can be confined to a more restrictive DEFINI-TION: *Prejudice is an attitude in which a person holds unfavorable and essentially unjustifiable beliefs and feelings toward members of a group, especially an ethnic group, to which he does not belong.*

Prejudice and its effects have been studied extensively by sociologists, political scientists, and historians, usually in terms of the social effects of racism or discrimination. The FOCUS here will be that of psychologists who look at the characteristics of the individual who is prejudiced and the functions that prejudice serves. One such function is to provide an economical way of processing information: prejudice evades the continual need to make new decisions in situations with apparently similar characteristics. Broad generalizations from minimal information act as a stereotype that not only initiates behavior but may serve to justify actions or attitudes adopted for other reasons. This unit will also focus on the ways prejudice is developed and maintained in individuals and on the various means by which it might be combated.

BACKGROUND: D. KATZ (1903-   )

The classic study of American stereotypes, conducted by Katz and Braly in 1933, used a simple procedure to determine attitudes about various ethnic and racial groups. A short booklet handed out to one hundred Princeton undergraduates began with a list of eighty-four adjectives like "brilliant," "aggressive," "honest"—a mixed bag of words and phrases that could be taken as representing personal characteristics. On succeeding pages, the students were asked to pick from the list and write down those characteristics they thought best described each of ten groups: Americans, Chinese, English, Germans, Irish, Italians, Japanese, Jews, Negroes, and Turks. After completing this exercise, the students were to go back over their choices, indicating the five characteristics "most typical" of each group considered.

A surprising degree of uniformity appeared in the

Figure 1.   Daniel Katz, whose studies have included research on stereotyping and attitude measurement.

students' attitudes toward each group. More than 75 percent of them ascribed certain specific traits to Jews, Negroes, and Germans. For example, Jews were rated as "shrewd"; Negroes, "superstitious" and "lazy"; and Germans, "scientifically minded." Germans were also considered "industrious" by 65 percent (incidentally, Hitler became German chancellor in 1933). Other characteristics were commonly ascribed to other groups: the Chinese were classified as "superstitious" (34 percent) and "sly" (29 percent), the Irish as "pugnacious" (45 percent) and "quick-tempered" (39 percent), and the Turks as "cruel" (47 percent), "very religious" (26 percent), and "treacherous" (21 percent).

The students were also asked to list which groups they preferred to associate with, and their choices generally followed the same pattern as the ascribed characteristics. The highest preferences went to Americans, the English, and Germans; the lowest to Negroes and Turks. It may have occurred to you that a Princeton man in 1933 would have had, at most, limited personal acquaintance with Turks. This was, of course, true—and significant, since by and large the students tended to attribute unfavorable characteristics to unfamiliar groups.

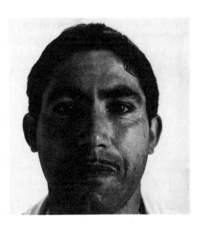

Figure 2. Differences in appearance among racial and ethnic groups help maintain behavioral stereotypes.

Some other irregularities and curiosities revealed by the Katz and Braly experiment were a higher "intelligent" ranking for Americans than for Germans (47 versus 32 percent) and, compared to Americans, a higher "industrious" ranking for Germans (17 percent more of the students applied this adjective to Germans).

Modern psychologists find the study superficial in many ways. For example, there was little statistical analysis, which would be required in current investigations. Furthermore, Katz and Braly made no attempt to discover the basis for the judgments and attitudes expressed by the students: whether they came from experience with the groups, misinformation, vague impressions, or what. Despite these limitations, however, the survey did show that stereotyped judgments and prejudice are very common even in intelligent subjects and, most importantly, that the content of those stereotypes could be measured and described. Similar questionnaires have

been used again and again to evaluate patterns and changes in prejudice, and methods similar to those of Katz and Braly became commonplace in research on intergroup relations.

In another classic study, of a simple empirical sort, Hovland and Sears correlated the number of lynchings of blacks in the South between 1882 and 1930 (a fairly common event during that period) and the price of cotton for each year. Their findings confirmed their suspicions: as the price of cotton went down the number of lynchings went up. This correlation was a reasonable indication not only that aggressive behavior resulted from frustration but also that the target of aggressive behavior is highly predictable from known stereotypes. (See Figure 3.)

In 1950 the study of prejudice was advanced significantly by the publication of *The Authoritarian Personality*, a monumental report on studies of prejudiced individuals by T. W. Adorno and his colleagues. The thrust of this work was that extreme prejudice

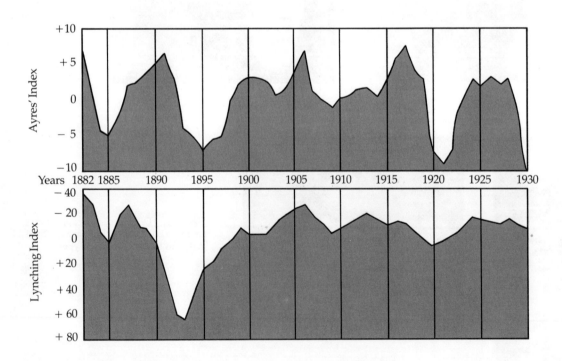

Figure 3. Relation between the frequency of lynchings and a composite economic index based on the price of cotton (Ayres Index). Adapted from Hovland and Sears (1940).

does not exist as an isolated attitude or conviction but is usually an integral part of an "authoritarian" personality structure that both contains and reinforces prejudiced attitudes. Following this work, other studies in the 1950s began to examine in more detail the origins and childhood causes of such a personality.

QUESTIONS AND EVIDENCE

1. How does prejudice develop?

2. How is prejudice maintained?

3. How can prejudice be reduced?

dices develop. Psychologists often draw hypotheses directly from such everyday beliefs or common-sense opinions, although the source obviously has no bearing on the truth or falsehood of the hypothesis. The *parental-identification hypothesis* states that children acquire prejudices by learning and adopting the attitudes and behavior patterns of their parents and other authority figures.

A comprehensive and intensive study like the following, involving many children and their parents, should tend to turn up evidence proving or disproving a broad hypothesis of this kind.

QUESTION   1. HOW DOES PREJUDICE DEVELOP?

HYPOTHESES	PARENTAL IDENTIFICATION	DISPLACEMENT	BELIEF
DESCRIPTIVE EVIDENCE	ASSESS: personality traits of prejudiced vs. unprejudiced children, and their parents		
EXPERIMENTAL EVIDENCE		VARY: amount of frustration MEASURE: attitudes toward irrelevant outgroups	VARY: belief congruence and race of stimulus teenager profiles MEASURE: friendliness and social distance

1. HOW DOES PREJUDICE DEVELOP?

The attempt to understand prejudices raises many difficult questions: How are these unfavorable attitudes, involving so many unjustifiable beliefs and feelings, born in an individual? To what extent are the individual and the people around him involved in the initiation and growth of prejudice? How do some people escape becoming prejudiced, even when they live surrounded by prejudiced groups?

Everyone is familiar with the notion that attitudes and beliefs, including prejudice, are passed on from one generation to the next as a result of the training and teaching parents give their children. This widespread, common-sense explanation is the basis for one hypothesis that attempts to explain how preju-

DESCRIPTIVE EVIDENCE

Investigator: E. Frenkel-Brunswik

Source, Date: "Prejudice in Children," 1948

Location: Institute of Child Welfare, University of California, Berkeley

Subjects: 120 boys and girls from eleven to sixteen years; their parents

Materials: Attitude and personality tests; interviews with the children and their parents

About 1,500 children were administered a "prejudice scale" containing items about attitudes toward five minority groups—Japanese, Jews, Mexicans, Negroes, and "outgroups" in general. The statements on the scale covered such situations as eating in the same

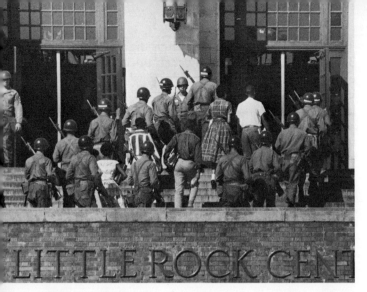

Figure 4. Black students had to be escorted to school in order to prevent riots when some areas first complied with the Supreme Court decision of 1954 to end segregation in the schools.

restaurant, living in the same neighborhood, participating in the same social affairs, and so on. From the large sample, 120 boys and girls were chosen as representing the polar extremes on the scale—"prejudiced" or ethnocentric versus "unprejudiced" or liberal. They were given personality tests, and both they and their parents were interviewed.

The many comparisons made showed that the prejudiced child generally tends to glorify his own group and aggressively reject any outgroup or foreign country. This ethnic prejudice was found to be already firmly established in even the youngest subjects studied, who were eleven years old. The following are a few of the statements that unprejudiced children tended to reject but with which prejudiced children agreed:

1. If we keep on having labor troubles, we may have to turn the government over to a dictator who will prevent strikes. [Rejection of outgroups]
2. People who do not believe that we have the best kind of government in the world should be kicked out of the country. [Selfish acceptance of the ingroup]
3. Only people like myself have a right to be happy. [Selfishness]
4. The world would be perfect if we put on a desert island all the weak, crooked, and feeble-minded people. [Rejection of weakness]
5. Girls should only learn things that are useful around the house. [Rigid sex-role attitudes]
6. Might makes right; the strong win out in the end. [Admiration of power]
7. It would be better if teachers would be more strict. [Submission to authority]

The parents of ethnocentric children were found to be highly concerned with social status. Often they were socially marginal and urgently wished to belong to the "privileged" class or groups. Thus they tended to be intolerant of any action that might keep them or their children from reaching their social goals. Also the parents of prejudiced children used more harsh and rigid types of discipline than did parents of the liberal children. The children learned to submit to, rather than accept, this authority because of fear of punishment. Such submissiveness can lead to admiration of power, success, and prestige. The child comes to identify with the aggressor, whom he envies, and to feel contempt for weakness and exhibit a generalized rejection of anything or anyone that is different.

Although outwardly the prejudiced child appears to idealize his parents, he often reveals an underlying resentment of authority, a feeling of being deprived and victimized. This resentment must be repressed because of fear of retaliation, and when the child is unable to express his truly felt hostility and to integrate his real feelings, a narrow and inflexible personality structure is formed. The repressed resentment that cannot be expressed outwardly against its source is eventually turned against "inferior" and "foreign" groups.

This repression of strong resentment in a person that is later expressed against others has formed the basis for another hypothesis about the development of prejudice. The *displacement hypothesis* states that prejudice develops when anxiety, frustration, and hostility are directed against available outgroups (or a scapegoat) rather than their true sources.

EXPERIMENTAL EVIDENCE

Investigators: N. E. Miller and R. Bugelski
Source, Date: "Minor Studies of Aggression: II. The Influence of Frustrations Imposed by the In-Group on

Attitudes Expressed Toward Out-Groups," 1948
Location: Yale University and University of Buffalo
Subjects: 31 men between the ages of 18 and 20
Materials: Long, dull, difficult tests; attitude-rating scales

The subjects, all of whom were working at a summer camp, were required to take several long, dull tests that were purposely made so difficult that most of the men would fail them. In addition, the tests deliberately ran far overtime so that the subjects missed their chance to go to the local movie theater, the only interesting event scheduled that week.

Before taking the tests, the subjects filled out an attitude scale listing ten desirable and ten undesirable traits that were to be indicated as present or absent in the average "foreigner." Half the subjects completed the scale for Japanese and the other half for Mexicans. The scales were given again after the testing session was over, but this time the subjects who had earlier completed the scale for Japanese now completed the scale for Mexicans, and vice versa. On another occasion, a control group was given the same two scales to complete, separated by an equal amount of time, but without the tests.

The spontaneous comments made by the subjects after the sessions showed that they were angry with the camp officials and experimenters, confirming the assumption that frustration arouses aggression. When the results of the two attitude scales were compared, it was found that the average number of favorable items checked had decreased from one administration to the other—for both Mexican and Japanese scales. This suggests that the aggression elicited by frustration can be displaced against stereotyped groups who have no relation to the particular situation.

But not all prejudice is quite so "blind." It is sometimes based on accurately perceived differences in beliefs and values that seem to challenge an individual's most deep-rooted convictions.

Such a perceived dissimilarity in views has certainly been a factor in the highly publicized "generation gap," which has focused obsessively on a central symbol. As Germaine Greer, women's liberation advocate, explains:

> When men began to grow their hair in our generation they were not acting motivelessly, as they

afterwards tried to maintain. Their hair was a sign that they did not accept the morality of the crop-haired generation of bureaucrats which sired them.

The *belief hypothesis*, developed in 1960 by the prominent social psychologist Milton Rokeach, states that prejudices arise from perceived differences in belief systems.

EXPERIMENTAL EVIDENCE

Investigators: D. D. Stein, J. A. Hardyck, and M. B. Smith
Source, Date: "Race and Belief: An Open and Shut Case," 1965
Location: University of California, Berkeley
Subjects: 44 white fourteen-year-old ninth graders (male and female) from working-class homes
Materials: Values questionnaire, attitude ratings

Two months before the experiment, the subjects completed a questionnaire concerning values in which the question, "Do you think teenagers in general ought to . . . ?" was followed by choices such as:

1. Try to please their parents by the things they do.
2. Try to get average grades, not go "all out" for "A's."
3. Be sincerely religious.
4. Be honest and trustworthy.
5. Live up to strict moral standards.

The responses were indicated in terms of degree of agreement on a five-point scale. The subject's responses to these items formed the basis for constructing a group of hypothetical "stimulus teenagers"—two like the subject in values, two unlike him.

The actual experiment used a test booklet, which explained that the "stimulus teenagers" were profiles from students in other parts of the country who had filled out the same questionnaire. Each booklet indicated how the "profiled" teenagers had responded to the value questions but also stated the race of each of them. For each subject one "like" and one "unlike" teenager were specified as white, while the other "like" and "unlike" teenagers were specified as black. Following the description of each teenager, there were several questions designed to measure friendliness and social distance. For example, the question designed to measure friendliness read as follows: "If you met this teenager for the first time, what would your immediate reaction be?" . . . "I think I would feel":

0. Quite friendly
1. A little friendly
2. Nothing either way
3. A little unfriendly
4. Quite unfriendly

The final results showed that the subjects felt most friendly toward white peers with similar values and least friendly toward black teenagers with unlike values. In the middle range, black-like was ranked above white-unlike. Thus, although both race and congruence of belief made a difference overall, the similarity of values had noticeably larger effects than race.

The results concerning social distance also indicated that belief was a strong factor. The effects of race were apparent only on three items ("Live in the same apartment house," "Invite him home to dinner," and "Have him date my sister"). Other data showed that when white subjects were given no information at all about a teenager other than that he was black, they simply assumed that his beliefs and values were different from their own.

These data support Rokeach's theory that "the prejudiced person does not reject a person or another race, religion, or nationality because of his ethnic membership per se but rather because he perceives that the other differs from him in important beliefs and values." When information concerning beliefs is not available, then subjects react in terms of race, but on the basis of assumptions concerning the beliefs of the other race. The belief hypothesis does not contradict the other hypotheses about how prejudice develops, but rather adds a role for value attitudes and beliefs in the formation of prejudices.

Recent research has tended to qualify the theory. For example, one investigation (Dienstbier, 1972) showed that the relationship between belief differ-

Figure 5. Aggressiveness results from frustration, and the target of aggressive behavior is highly predictable from known stereotypes. Once a prejudice has been acquired, it serves to reinforce an individual's convictions about belief differences. Prejudiced attitudes affect the way an individual perceives people in outgroups, which in turn maintains or strengthens his prejudice.

ences and racial prejudice is probably mutual rather than one-directional. Once the prejudice itself has been acquired, it serves to reinforce the individual's convictions about belief differences. This circular manner in which prejudiced attitudes, once developed, affect the way in which the individual perceives people in outgroups, which in turn maintains or strengthens his prejudice, brings us to the next major question.

2. HOW IS PREJUDICE MAINTAINED?

Strongly held beliefs, or convictions, often affect the way people observe others. Sometimes people react to a stranger as if he possessed all the characteristics attributed to the group he supposedly belongs to. This process of *stereotyping* can be totally unjustified and, as such, makes an important contribution to the maintenance of prejudice. But, to some degree, the

---

QUESTION   2. HOW IS PREJUDICE MAINTAINED?

HYPOTHESES	STEREOTYPES	PERSONALITY
DESCRIPTIVE EVIDENCE		ASSESS: relations between prejudice and social mobility, feelings of deprivation, other insecurities
EXPERIMENTAL EVIDENCE	VARY: labeling or no labeling of different line lengths MEASURE: judgments of line lengths	

Figure 6. Prejudice can be based on perceived dissimilarity of beliefs and attitudes. It can be substantially reduced by increased contact or by making a person conscious of discrepancies in his own stereotyped attitudes and values.

tendency to use stereotypes is simply the inevitable result of the way humans process information, the methods they use to categorize and deal with reality. The *stereotypes hypothesis* states that prejudice resists change because human perception tends to group similar percepts together into categories or stereotypes. A clear demonstration of this cognitive, nonemotional, categorizing feature of stereotypic behavior was provided in the following investigation.

EXPERIMENTAL EVIDENCE

Investigators: H. Tajfel and A. L. Wilkes
Source, Date: "Classification and Quantitative Judgment," 1963
Location: University of Oxford
Subjects: 61 volunteer students (male and female) from Oxford and Manchester universities and Westminster Training College
Materials: Lines varying in length

Eight lines, each a slightly different length from the others, were shown one by one to each subject. The lines were presented six times in successive random orders, and the subjects were asked in turn to estimate the absolute length of each line by calling out their judgments, which were recorded.

There were three experimental groups. For the first the lines were presented alone, without labels. For the second group some of the lines were labeled A and others B, on a purely random basis. For the third each of the four shorter lines was labeled A, while each of the four longer lines was labeled B; thus the categories were related to the length dimension that the subjects were judging.

It was found that subjects in the third group, relative to the other two, exaggerated the differences in length between lines labeled A or B. In other words, they tended to judge lines labeled A as shorter than they really were and those labeled B as longer than they really were. Thus their judgments of simple, physical quantities showed the kind of stereotyping that is characteristic of human responses.

Although stereotyping may be an inescapable adjunct to the human activity of labeling and classifying, it hardly seems adequate to explain the stubborn persistence of some prejudices. Perhaps prejudices continue because they play an active role in certain personalities. The *personality hypothesis* states that prejudice resists change because it tends to be consistent with other character traits and to serve an individual's needs to reduce anxiety and frustration.

Free-ranging interviews designed to expose the deep feelings and needs of people and relate these to their prejudices do not provide a controlled experimental setting. Such interviews have been used, however, to gather descriptive evidence relevant to the personality hypothesis.

DESCRIPTIVE EVIDENCE

Investigators: B. Bettelheim and M. Janowitz
Source, Date: "Dynamics of Prejudice," 1950
Location: University of Chicago
Subjects: 150 Army veterans who returned to civilian life
Materials: Interviews in which free association and spontaneous expression of feelings were encouraged

The subjects, representing all economic classes, were interviewed by social workers trained in psychiatry. The interview sessions lasted from four to seven hours, during which a wide range of personal data, including attitudes toward ethnic minorities, were

Figure 7. Extreme prejudice is often linked with a cluster of personal characteristics, including a need to reduce anxiety and frustration by displacing hostility toward others.

recorded. The content of each interview was subjected to statistical and content analysis of various kinds.

This investigation revealed that, although a subject's actual Army experiences were not related to his prejudices, his evaluation of those experiences was. The men who reported feelings of deprivation and who felt they had been given "bad breaks" were those most inclined to hold hostile attitudes toward Negroes and Jews.

Social mobility—as determined by noting moves up or down on the socioeconomic scale when the subject's present employment was compared to his civilian employment prior to military service—was also found to be related to intolerance. Subjects who had moved down in their social standing were more hostile toward Negroes and Jews than those who were upwardly mobile. Apparently, the "threats to the self" experienced in downward social mobility augmented prejudicial feelings. The subjects' attitudes toward four representative social institutions—the administration of veterans' affairs, the political party system, the federal government, and the economic system—were compared with their degree of anti-Semitism. It was found that subjects who were hostile toward Jews tended to reject social institutions more than did those who were tolerant toward Jews. (This finding is in marked contrast to the findings for college students, where rejection of authority and institutions is often accompanied by liberal attitudes toward minority groups.)

Other research has shown that the outstanding feature of subjects rated high on anti-Semitism was a restricted, narrow personality, with an extremely conventional conscience. Beneath a surface interest in social status and uncritical devotion and obedience to parents and authority in general, anti-Semites were highly aggressive. They also displayed a high degree of social anxiety, deriving security from following strict morals. The repressed aggressive impulses were often expressed indirectly through displacement to outgroups.

In summary, it appears that prejudice may serve an important function in certain forms of personality integration. This knowledge does not excuse prejudice, but it can help us to recognize it for what it is and understand it better. Such knowledge can lead, eventually, to the discovery of ways to effectively diminish or control prejudices.

and work with groups toward which they are unsympathetic. Real-life situations do occasionally offer the opportunity to study the effects of forced contacts between outgroups, however. This was the case in the following classic study of interracial housing.

DESCRIPTIVE EVIDENCE

Investigators: M. Deutsch and M. E. Collins
Source, Date: "Interracial Housing," 1951
Location: New York University
Subjects: 100 white and 25 black housewives in each of two integrated public housing projects in Newark; 24 black and white boys and girls in one project in Newark, one in New York
Materials: Interviews

The housing projects were matched as closely as possible in such respects as ratio of blacks to whites and average family income. The interviews, which

---

QUESTION 3. HOW CAN PREJUDICE BE REDUCED?

HYPOTHESES	CONTACT	AWARENESS OF INCONSISTENCY
DESCRIPTIVE EVIDENCE	ASSESS: effects of interracial housing on racial attitudes	
EXPERIMENTAL EVIDENCE		VARY: awareness of inconsistency in attitude-value system MEASURE: apparent changes in attitudes; response to NAACP solicitation

---

3. HOW CAN PREJUDICE BE REDUCED?

The *contact hypothesis* states that prejudice is reduced by interactions and cooperation with outgroup members.

Because prejudice itself creates barriers that make contact and cooperation unlikely, creating the conditions under which such interactions occur in order to study them is rather difficult. People don't usually join

lasted between one and two hours, focused on five areas of concern:

1. Attitudes toward living in the project, feelings toward the people there.
2. Attitudes toward blacks, feelings about them in general, feelings about living in the same project with them.
3. Amount of contact and friendliness with other women in the project.

4. Social supports for attitudes: for example, how the housewife's family and friends would react to her being friendly with blacks.
5. Characteristics of the housewife herself: age, number of children, etc.

When the reactions of the women in the segregated housing projects were compared with those of housewives from the integrated projects, it was found that the latter generally experienced friendlier, more neighborly contacts between blacks and whites. The social atmosphere in the integrated housing in general was more favorable to friendly interracial associations, and the project community was more closely knit; that is, white housewives were not only more friendly with black housewives, but with other white housewives in the same project as well.

The housewives in the integrated projects were also more friendly toward blacks in general, although this difference was not as extensive as the positiveness of attitudes toward specific blacks in the project. In addition, the reduction in prejudice toward the Negroes was apparently accompanied by less prejudiced feelings toward the Chinese. On the whole, the researchers concluded, "The integrated project, by creating more opportunities for close, social contacts between Negroes and Whites and by stimulating a social atmosphere more conducive to friendly racial relations, exposes its tenants to the kinds of experiences which are likely to change prejudicial attitudes."

Later research by R. K. Young (1970) agreed with these findings. Through surveys in 1955, 1958, and 1964 at the University of Texas, Young found that the more social contact between blacks and whites, the more favorable the attitudes. Young used his statistical data to compile "portraits" of those who would most likely hold attitudes unfavorable or favorable toward blacks. For example, a student who would likely be unfavorable toward blacks would be "a Baptist who attends church about twice a month, who is a business major with a below C average. He belongs to a fraternity and his father, who lives in West Texas, has an income in excess of $30,000 a year." A student who would tend to be favorable toward blacks would be one "who does not belong to any religious group, and who never goes to church.

He is a B plus social science major from outside the South. He does not belong to a fraternity and his father makes less than $30,000 a year."

If increased contact is effective but unlikely, what are other means of reducing prejudice? The *awareness-of-inconsistency* hypothesis suggests that prejudice can be reduced by making a person conscious of apparent discrepancies among his own attitudes and values. During recent years Milton Rokeach and his colleagues have devised some fascinating explorations of attitude changes brought about in this way.

EXPERIMENTAL EVIDENCE

Investigators: M. Rokeach and colleagues
Source, Date: "Long-Range Experimental Modification of Values, Attitudes, and Behavior," 1971
Location: University of Western Ontario
Subjects: 366 freshmen at several colleges
Materials: Value-ranking scale; charts; "pep talk"

Two large groups of students (tested in groups of twenty to twenty-five) were asked to rank values, including equality and freedom, in order of the importance they personally attached to them. The subjects were then asked to state in writing their attitudes toward civil-rights groups. At this point, one group of subjects (control) was dismissed and the other (experimental) was shown the following list, illustrating the average rankings of the values obtained in a previous study:

1. Freedom
2. Happiness
3. Wisdom
4. Self-respect
5. Mature love
6. A sense of accomplishment
7. True friendship
8. Inner harmony
9. Family security
10. A world at peace
11. Equality
12. An exciting life
13. A comfortable life
14. Salvation

15. Social recognition
16. National security
17. A world of beauty
18. Pleasure

Then the members of the experimental group were given a "pep talk," which pointed out that freedom had been ranked first but equality eleventh. Thus, the students seemed to be more interested in their own freedom than in the freedom of others, such as minority groups. The subjects were asked to compare their own rankings of freedom and equality and then to indicate the degree of their sympathy with the aims of the civil-rights movement and demonstrators. Next a chart was presented that indicated average rankings of freedom and equality for people with various positions on civil-rights issues (see Table 1).

example, some discovered that although they cared about civil rights, they had placed a low value on equality. Information about their awareness of such inconsistencies was obtained by asking them to rate, on an eleven-point scale, how satisfied or dissatisfied they were with what they had discovered about their own values and attitudes, as compared with the rankings of the eighteen values in particular.

The ultimate question was whether such awareness would affect subsequent behavior. Specifically, would the experimental subjects, relative to the controls, alter their attitudes and behavior to be more favorable toward blacks and civil rights, or at least so that their values for freedom and equality would be closer to each other? After the experiment, subjects filled out questionnaires, and other measures of behavior indicating attitude change were taken. Subjects were also

TABLE 1. Average Ranking of Freedom and Equality For and Against Civil Rights in Previous Tests

	YES, sympathetic and have participated in a demonstration	YES, sympathetic but have not participated in a demonstration	NO, not sympathetic to civil rights
Freedom	6	1	2
Equality	5	11	17
Difference	+1	−10	−15

Source: M. Rokeach, "Long-range Experimental Modification of Values, Attitudes, and Behavior," *American Psychologist,* 26 (1971), 453–459.

Another talk pointed out that people who are against civil rights seem really to be indifferent to the freedom of others, while the supporters of civil rights want freedom for others as well as for themselves. The students were again invited to compare their rankings of equality and freedom and their own positions on civil rights with those shown in the table.

By means of this procedure, about 40 percent of the experimental subjects became aware of apparent inconsistencies in their value and attitude systems. For

asked to rank the original values once again. The results showed that the experimental subjects' rankings for both equality and freedom increased overall—the rankings showed no changes for control subjects.

A more interesting measure was the number of responses to a direct solicitation from the National Association for the Advancement of Colored People (NAACP), which was received by all subjects three to five months and again fifteen to seventeen months after the experiment was over. Joining the NAACP involved payment of $1 and returning a signed form. When the results from these two solicitations were combined, only 69 out of 366 subjects (about 20 percent) had joined, but 51 of these were from the experimental group, only 18 from the control.

Rokeach's methods can apparently cause people to reexamine their attitudes and values with respect to other races and minorities. None of the subjects was coerced to alter his opinions: attitude change stemmed from the individual's perceptions of relationships within his own value-attitude framework. The experimenter never suggested that the students were prejudiced but simply asked them to compare the rankings and "think about it."

But should social scientists be "permitted" to change or influence attitudes and values at all? Rokeach himself has responded to this:

> Every teacher I have ever met who takes professional pride in his work would like to think that his teaching somehow changes the values, attitudes and behavior of his students in some significant way . . . I believe that educational institutions have always been in the business on the one hand of transmitting knowledge and, on the other, of shaping the values of students in certain directions . . . if we agree that educational institutions are also in the business of shaping values, then we should encourage scientific research on better ways of shaping values.

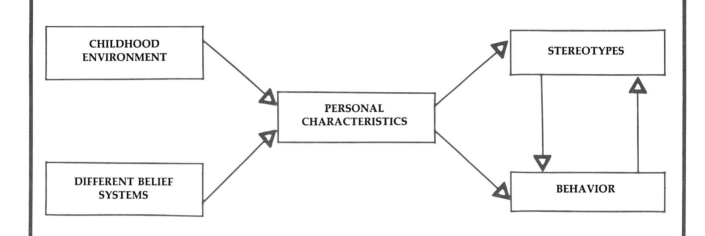

PUTTING IT TOGETHER: Prejudice

An individual's initial exposure to prejudice usually involves parents and other authority figures with whom he or she identifies in his or her *childhood environment*. A prejudicial attitude towards people from other groups is likely to focus on perceived *differences in basic belief systems*.

The highly prejudiced individual is likely to display a number of *personal characteristics* consistent with his or her prejudice, including a need to reduce anxiety and frustration by displacing hostility towards other people.

The normal tendency to group and categorize information is exaggerated by the highly prejudiced person, who easily develops *stereotypes* about people as members of groups. *Behavior* towards others usually is consistent with prejudiced attitudes, which may be reduced by constructive contact with people who conflict with their stereotypes.

1. WHAT'S ACCEPTED . . .

1. Prejudice can be acquired from parents and other authority figures.
2. Prejudice can be based on perceived dissimilarity of beliefs and attitudes.
3. Extreme prejudice is often linked with an identifiable cluster of mutually reinforcing personality traits.
4. Prejudice can be reinforced by an individual's needs to reduce anxiety and express aggression through displacement.
5. To some degree, stereotyping is an inevitable result of how human beings perceive and categorize their world.
6. Contact can reduce prejudice substantially.

2. WHAT'S DEBATED . . .

1. To what extent prejudice causes or is caused by perceived differences in beliefs.
2. To what extent stereotypes may represent some "kernel of truth" about an outgroup.
3. To what extent stereotypes really serve as a ground or maintainer of prejudice.
4. The degree to which individuals feel that their stereotypes are "correct"—that is, how much value or importance they really attach to them.
5. The relationships between prejudice and actual discriminating behaviors.
6. To what extent cognitive inconsistency can actually bring about genuine changes in attitudes or values.

Of all the areas of human behavior studied by psychologists, few are more important to the future of mankind than racial and ethnic prejudice.

The problem of race prejudice is one of the most critical in the modern world. It hurts relationships between nations and relationships between groups within nations. It creates hatred, conflict and war, and limits the opportunities of entire peoples, sometimes for centuries. The United States, for all its high ideals, has a long and sorry history of racial prejudice by the whites against minority groups—a prejudice which contributed to the virtual killing off of the American Indian, and which has deprived generations of black Americans of equal opportunity in the land of their birth. But racial prejudice is not, as is sometimes supposed, mainly a characteristic of those whites who feel a superiority over all other peoples: it is an almost universal phenomenon. Across the range of the Sahara desert where the arabic peoples of the north merge with the negroid peoples of the south, the two groups are to be found even in the seventies engaged in the systematic slaughter of one another for no reason other than a difference in racial background. In fact, it is only within the last few decades that racism has ceased to be respectable. Hitler's war, inspired by a pathological belief in the innate superiority of the "aryan" race, has forever made racism utterly disreputable, but at a terrible cost in human life.

Any light that psychological research can shed on the problem of racial prejudice is therefore of immense practical value. The studies that have been conducted point overwhelmingly to one conclusion: racial prejudice is a learned form of irrational behavior. Prejudice is ingrained in the individual through the process of socialization, and is founded on myth, not truth, on stereotypes, not reality. The racially prejudiced person is ethnocentric—that is, he automatically assumes that his own group and its values are superior to all other groups and their values. He is incapable of seeing the virtues or point of view of other peoples, and perceives them all in terms of rigid stereotypes. Jews are miserly, blacks are lazy, Chinese are inscrutable, say the stereotypes, and they are applied indiscriminately to all members of the group in question. Even when the prejudiced person meets a member of an outgroup who does not conform to the stereotype, he does not see this as a reason for modifying his view—instead, the person is defined as "the exception that proves the rule."

Psychological research has forcefully shown just how irrational racial prejudice really is. In one classic study, subjects were presented with a list of different minority groups and asked to express attitudes toward them. The list included such familiar minorities as Jews, blacks, and chicanos, but it also included unfamiliar groups like the Danireans, the Piraneans, and the Wallorians. The study showed that a very high proportion of those who expressed negative attitudes to Jews and blacks also strongly disliked the other, lesser-known groups. They even recommended restrictive measures against the Danireans, Piraneans, and Wallorians, arguing that they should not be allowed to immigrate to the United States and that those already here should be deported to their original countries. The point of the experiment was this: the Danireans, Piraneans, and Wallorians do not exist. They were dreamed up by a psychologist to see whether racially prejudiced people would extend their prejudices to purely imaginary minority groups.

Another classic experiment, by Gordon W. Allport, has shown that prejudiced people will believe any statement that conforms to and feeds their prejudices, even if several of these statements are mutually contradictory. In a comprehensive scale designed to measure attitudes towards Jews, Allport purposely placed random propositions that were contradictory. He found that prejudiced people were quite prepared to accept the truth of these contradictory propositions. Here are two such pairs of contradictions:

*Much resentment against Jews stems from their tending to keep apart and exclude gentiles from Jewish social life.
*The Jews should not pry too much into Christian activities and organizations nor seek so much recognition and prestige from Christians.

And:

*Jews tend to remain a foreign element in American society, to preserve their old social standards and resist the American way of life.
*Jews go too far in hiding their Jewishness, especially such extremes as changing their names, straightening their noses, and imitating Christian manners and customs.

Allport found that roughtly three-quarters of those who accuse Jews of keeping to themselves also accuse them of being too intrusive. People who disliked them for having too much money also disliked them for begging from others. People who disliked them because they are capitalistic and control business also dislike them because they are communistic and subvert the capitalist system. People who dislike Jews for being so superior also dislike them for having a group inferiority complex. Clearly, genuine group characteristics are not at issue; the results of the experiment merely reveal a deep-seated prejudice seeking any means to justify itself.

Psychological research on the nature of prejudice has done a great deal to create a climate in which prejudice is negatively valued. So long as it was possible to see prejudice as stemming from the genuine characteristics of an outgroup, it could still remain respectable, but this is no longer so. The main task of psychology in the future will be to clarify our understanding of exactly how racial prejudice is learned, and to develop and refine methods that can be used in public education to unlearn prejudice—or to prevent it from being learned in the first place.

Unit 9

Groups and Leaders

OVERVIEW

The factors affecting how groups make decisions, how they influence individuals in the group, and what makes some people emerge as group leaders are described. The unit stresses the importance of taking into account both individual and situational factors in group activity, where the outcome depends on a complex interaction of several sets of factors. The Issue section discusses the phenomenon of groupthink.

UNIT OUTLINE

DEFINITION AND BACKGROUND
1. *Definition:* group behavior refers to the collective behavior of several people working together, or the behavior of an individual as it is affected by group membership.
2. *Background:* Kurt Lewin (1890–1947).

QUESTIONS AND EVIDENCE
1. How does decision making in a group affect the decision?
Hypotheses:
    a. *Risky-shift:* groups will make decisions that involve a higher degree of risk than do the decisions that the individuals in the group would make alone.
    b. *Cautious-shift:* in making decisions involving widely held values that support caution, the group as a whole will tend to be more conservative than the average individual member. **143**
2. What are some of the ways that groups influence individual behavior?
Hypotheses:
    a. *Conformity:* group membership may modify the opinion-stating behavior of participant individuals to conform with a generalized group standard. **144**
    b. *Sensitivity-training:* training in human relations can help the members of a group learn to trust and accept each other. **145**
3. Why do some people become leaders of groups?
Hypotheses:
    a. *Leadership-characteristics:* some people become leaders as a function of a specific cluster of characteristics that draw them into leadership positions.
    b. *Leadership-situation:* environmental variables may thrust authority on an individual, almost regardless of his personal characteristics. **146**
    c. *Person-situation:* leadership results from the interaction between individual characteristics and situational or task variables. **147**

IMPORTANT CONCEPTS

	page
authoritarian leader	140
autokinetic effect	144
cautious shift	143
conformity	144
democratic leader	140
empathy	145
encounter groups	145
feedback	145
group dynamics	143
laissez faire leader	140
leadership	146
risky shift	142
sensitivity training	145
social-emotional leader	148

When a decision is to be made in a group, a leader usually emerges who meets the specific needs of the decision.

Social support in groups may tend to shift decisions toward greater extremes of risk or caution than most individual members would use.

With effective leadership complex decisions can be made while maintaining group cohesiveness.

DEFINITION AND BACKGROUND

Groups often make different decisions than would their individual members working alone. A jury, for example, may arrive at a final decision that is quite different from the sum of the separate opinions of its members when they leave the courtroom. Membership in a group can influence an individual's behavior toward (or away from) conformity to group expectations, and make it easier (or harder) for the individual to perform a specific task. This unit concerns group behavior, which can have two DEFINITIONS: *the collective behavior of several people working together or the behavior of an individual as it is affected by group membership.* The unit will FOCUS on the dynamic process of interaction among group members, especially during the decision-making process. The dynamics of group leadership are also considered.

BACKGROUND: KURT LEWIN (1890–1947)

The work of Kurt Lewin, the originator of "field theory" as a psychological concept and founder of the group-dynamics movement, revolutionized the study of social psychology. The impact of his work on social psychology is sometimes compared to that of Freud's on the study of personality. Lewin began his career as a teacher at the University of Berlin, where he became the colleague of Max Wertheimer (see Unit 23) and other Gestaltists. A former mathematics and physics student, Lewin began to think of psychological events as occurring in a kind of space roughly analogous to physical space. Instead of attempting to identify quantitative laws of human behavior, which was the aim of many of his fellow psychologists, Lewin thought in nonquantitative, spatial terms. He suggested that human behavior should be viewed as *psychological motion toward goals within defined regions of life space,* a position that raised several questions—for example, what are the goals toward which psychological motion occurs? and what barriers interfere with the movement? His early experimental work on these questions fell chiefly in the fields of motivation and personality, but as time went on it focused more and more on social psychology.

Lewin fled to the United States when the Nazis

Figure 1. Kurt Lewin studied human motivation extensively and applied his theories to practical social problems.

came to power, working first at the University of Iowa and later at MIT. Much of his work concerned questions relevant to the rise of Nazism, such as problems of group leadership, the effects of varying social climates of opinion, and the efficiency of different governing styles. A pioneering study of group dynamics, conducted by Lewin and his associates during the late 1930s, can be used to illustrate his approach.

The purpose of the experiment was to investigate the reactions of groups of ten-year-old boys to three leadership styles: authoritarian, democratic, and laissez-faire. The boys met once a week in groups of five to work on various hobbies they were interested in—building models, making masks, playing games, and whatever other projects the group decided on.

Though the activities and materials were virtually the same for all the groups, the leaders of each behaved very differently. The authoritarian leader was dictatorial and aloof, giving orders about required activities without consulting the boys and passing out praise or blame to individuals in an autocratic fashion. The leader was a leader only; he refrained from participation in the boys' projects. The democratic leader encouraged group decision making through discussion and voting, let the group decide who was to work on what, and participated in group activities (without "taking over"). When conflict or indecision arose, he usually confined himself to looking for the facts and suggesting alternative lines of action. The laissez-faire leader made very few suggestions of any sort unless a boy came to him with a question. After outlining the activities and materials available, he allowed each group member to go his own way.

The authoritarian groups got a lot accomplished and apparently operated well when under tight control. But when the leader was out of the room their activities tended to become less focused and there was a general slackening in performance. The boys seemed not to be having a very good time: they bickered among themselves, were sometimes destructive, and were unfriendly toward other groups. The democratic groups got slightly less done than the authoritarian ones, but their motivation and interest were higher. They indulged in little more than roughhousing when the leader left the room. When an outsider criticized their work, group members stuck together and usually argued back in defense of the group. The laissez-faire groups got the least done, "played" most, and seemed to lack cohesiveness. Though most members appeared to enjoy "doing their own thing," group objectives were seldom set or achieved.

On balance, Lewin and his associates concluded, authoritarian leadership was less efficient than it looked, since group tasks were often left undone in the absence of the strong leader. Democratic leadership resulted in less aggressiveness and better, more stable performance from group members.

Although this study was criticized on two counts (first, its results might not hold true for large social bodies like nations, and second, the boys in the study, being Americans, may have had a built-in bias toward democratic techniques), the large number of behavioral differences brought about by the three leadership styles was intriguing. Lewin's early experiments and those of his students remain the prototypes for much of the research in group dynamics being conducted today.

QUESTIONS AND EVIDENCE

1. How does decision making in a group affect the decision?
2. What are some of the ways that groups influence individual behavior?
3. Why do some people become leaders of groups?

It is often said that no one man should be entrusted with the responsibility for launching nuclear weapons, the implication being that such a decision should be left to the sanity and conservatism of a group. On the other hand, it has been pointed out that no one man ever lynched another. Research into the effects of group processes on decision making has developed hypotheses to account for both these statements, which are really opposite sides of the same coin.

QUESTION	1. HOW DOES DECISION MAKING IN A GROUP AFFECT THE DECISION?	
HYPOTHESES	RISKY SHIFT	CAUTIOUS SHIFT
DESCRIPTIVE EVIDENCE		
EXPERIMENTAL EVIDENCE	VARY: whether subject makes decision as individual or as group member MEASURE: riskiness of decision	VARY: values widely held; individual vs. group MEASURE: relative risk or caution of decision

1. HOW DOES DECISION MAKING IN A GROUP AFFECT THE DECISION?

The ~~risky-shift hypothesis~~ states that groups will make decisions that involve a higher degree of risk than do the decisions that the individuals in the group would make alone. Even if you yourself feel that a 1962 station wagon cannot carry you safely all the way across the country, the fact that you're planning the trip with friends can make a big difference: the thing may break down, but then again, it may not—and if it does, the group will cope somehow.

Much of the research concerning this hypothesis stemmed from the work of J. A. Stoner (1961), who devised a series of dilemmas to test it. The Stoner problems follow the pattern of this example:

> Mr. E. is president of a light metals corporation in the United States. The corporation is quite prosperous, and Mr. E. has strongly considered the possibility of expanding his business by building an additional plant in a new location. The choice is between building the plant in the United States, where there would be a moderate return on the initial investment, or building it in a foreign country, where lower labor costs and easy access to raw materials would mean a much higher return on the initial investment. The problem is that there is a history of political instability and revolution in the foreign country under consideration. In fact, the leader of a small minority party is committed to nationalization of all foreign investments.
>
> Imagine that you are advising Mr. E. Listed below are several probabilities or odds of continued political stability in the foreign country under consideration. Please check the LOWEST probability that you would consider acceptable for Mr. E's corporation to build in that country.

1. The chances are 1 in 10 that the foreign country will remain politically stable.
2. The chances are 3 in 10 that the foreign country will remain politically stable.
3. The chances are 5 in 10 that the foreign country will remain politically stable.
4. The chances are 7 in 10 that the foreign country will remain politically stable.
5. The chances are 9 in 10 that the foreign country will remain politically stable.
6. Mr. E's corporation should *not* build a plant in the foreign country, no matter what the probabilities.

EXPERIMENTAL EVIDENCE

Investigators: M. A. Wallach, N. Kogan, and D. J. Bem
Source, Date: "Diffusion of Responsibility and Level of Risk Taking in Groups," 1964
Location: University of Colorado
Subjects: 336 male and female undergraduates
Materials: 10 decision-making problems

Each subject was told that he was to answer five questions and that he could choose their level of difficulty. (The higher the level of difficulty, the greater the risk.) As an incentive, the subjects were told that they could win up to $15, depending on the level of difficulty chosen and the number of correct responses. That is, the higher the risk level, the more they would win for correct answers. This part of the experiment told the experimenters how much risk each subject would take on his own.

Next, the experimental subjects were divided into a number of groups. Some of the groups were asked to reach group decisions, working in threes, on the level of difficulty of five additional questions. The results showed that the groups made decisions involving considerably more risk than the group members alone had been willing to take. In one condition, the group decisions averaged 12.5 percent riskier than the individual judgments. The experimenters interpret this result in terms of diffusion of responsibility.

Other investigators have offered different explanations of this effect. One of the more interesting rests on the fact that a willingness to take risks is perceived as a leadership trait. In an effort to gain leadership, then, group members sometimes try to look more willing to take chances than they really are. Similarly, a dominant, risk-taking leader can influence the outcome of group deliberations.

Whatever the mechanism that accounts for this phenomenon, it raises some significant questions about the decisions made in, for example, meetings of the Joint Chiefs of Staff. Should the President isolate himself from the Cabinet in order to avoid disastrously dangerous actions? As research in this area gathered momentum during the mid-1960s, it seemed to many psychologists that its implications for international peace were not only frightening but real. It should be remembered, however, that the experimental groups were small, informal, leaderless, and artificial. Moreover, the problems were artificial, the range of possibilities predetermined, and the decision had to be unanimous.

The crucial decisions made by groups like the National Security Council often involve moral as well as purely political questions. Research by Nordhoy (1962) and other psychologists has focused on the *cautious-shift hypothesis,* which states that in making decisions involving widely held values that support caution, the group as a whole will tend to be more conservative than the average individual member.

EXPERIMENTAL EVIDENCE

Investigator: J. A. Stoner
Source, Date: "Risky and Cautious Shifts in Group Decision: The Influence of Widely Held Values," 1968
Subjects: 212 young adults living in the Harvard-MIT area
Materials: Value-ranking and relative-riskiness instruments; 12 life-situation problems

Six typical risky- and cautious-shift dilemmas were presented along with six other problems that involved widely held values—both risky and cautious in nature. These values generally related the dilemma directly to a family or home situation (for example, emphasizing that the money to be risked had been saved for a child's college education or was needed for an important operation for the man's wife).

The results showed that a shift in group decision making toward either greater risk or greater caution depends largely on the cultural values involved. If the importance of getting ahead, making a large amount of money, and so on, is emphasized, the group tends to shift toward greater risk taking. But if physical danger or family responsibility is emphasized, the group decision shifts toward greater conservatism.

The implications of findings on risky and cautious shifts for political decisions are, unfortunately, very unclear. For one thing, there is the problem of decid-ing whether a risky decision is really riskier than a cautious one. A decision to do nothing may seem, in general, to be the cautious course, but is it? Doing nothing about urban problems, for example, is quite risky: it can lead to the further decay of cities, to riots, and so on.

It is much easier to evaluate political decisions after the fact than to figure out some "optimum level of risk" in advance. Take, for example, the decision to invade Cuba at the Bay of Pigs—the action is widely recognized as a disaster; the decision, as much too "risky." That decision, made in 1961 by President Kennedy and a small circle of advisers, has recently been analyzed in a book by Irving Janis (1973), a social psychologist from Yale. Janis interprets the decision as the product of what he calls "groupthink." He points out, for example, that the Kennedy advisers constituted a highly cohesive in-group. Because of its cohesiveness, and also because of the euphoria that prevailed in the early days of the Kennedy Administration, the group tended to feel (1) that, as a group, it was invulnerable, and (2) that voicing dissent should be avoided if possible, because it might damage the group's sense of unity. Janis' analysis of the Bay of Pigs decision does not lead him to suggest that important political decisions be made by a single person, but he does suggest that an awareness of the pitfalls of groupthink might help group members guard against them and, perhaps, make better decisions.

The Bay of Pigs decision, however, can be examined from a different perspective. That is, instead of asking how decision making in a group affected the decision, one could ask how being a member of the group affected the behavior of each individual. All of us belong to many groups—family, school or college class, perhaps athletic teams, clubs, political organizations, and so on—and each of us, at one time or another, has probably done something with a group that he would never have dreamed of doing alone. A person who enjoys strolling in the woods may join a hiking club and eventually find himself scaling steep rock faces; a person who loves mountain climbing, after joining a different, quieter hiking club, may come to agree with his new friends that it is silly to risk one's life if one doesn't have to. The following section examines some of the influences of groups on individual behavior.

HYPOTHESES	CONFORMITY	SENSITIVITY TRAINING
DESCRIPTIVE EVIDENCE	ASSESS: tendency to conform to perceptual judgment of group	ASSESS: changes in perception of self and others after training
EXPERIMENTAL EVIDENCE		

2. WHAT ARE SOME OF THE WAYS THAT GROUPS INFLUENCE INDIVIDUAL BEHAVIOR?

The *conformity hypothesis* states that group membership may modify the opinion-stating behavior of participant individuals to conform with a generalized group standard. This effect can readily be observed during an election year. A person who is convinced that one candidate is best for the office may find his political commitment shaken when he discovers that all of his friends are supporting the opponent.

An early demonstration of conformity was provided in M. Sherif's famous investigations (1936) involving the "autokinetic effect"—the illusion of movement that arises when a tiny dot of light is projected in an otherwise completely darkened room. Although everyone succumbs to this illusion, Sherif found that subjects working alone reported more movement of the dot than they did after working in groups. When subjects worked together, conformity of judgment within the group led to greater similarity of decisions.

When Solomon Asch encountered these experiments, he hypothesized that although the conformity of judgments may have occurred because the subjects wanted to be correct and were convinced that their own judgments were wrong, it was also possible that the individual subjects wanted to avoid being out of line with the group and therefore consented to the majority judgment. He devised a further series of studies to test this idea.

DESCRIPTIVE EVIDENCE

Investigator: S. E. Asch
Source, Date: "Opinions and Social Pressure," 1955
Location: Swarthmore College
Subjects: 123 male college students (run in groups of 7 to 9)
Materials: Cards with printed vertical lines

Groups of subjects were shown a series of paired cards: one with a single vertical black line (the standard) and the other with three lines (a line of the same length as the standard plus two that were substantially different). Each subject was asked to choose the line of the same length as the standard.

Only one person in each group was really a subject. The others were confederates who had been instructed to give the same wrong answers to certain sets of lines. On the first two trials the confederates unanimously chose the correct line, but on the third and fourth trials they chose incorrectly. On later trials, the confederates occasionally chose correctly. The uninformed subject was thus placed in a position of conflict: he knew what he saw, but he was often confronted with a unanimous and opposing choice from his peers. In addition, he had to state his opinion publicly.

A considerable percentage of the subjects yielded to the majority opinion even when it was incorrect. When individually presented with the same task, they made errors on only 1 percent of the trials, whereas a rate of 36.8 percent occurred in groups. All errors were in agreement with the confederates.

Asch reported that whether or not a particular subject yields to the majority depends in part on what kind of person he is. A subject who will not succumb even over many trials is independent relative to others. On the other hand, some of the extremely yielding subjects felt that they had been wrong and the group right. Others said they had gone along with the group judgment "in order not to spoil the results of the experiment."

Further experiments by Asch isolated two other variables that effect conformity: the size and the unanimity of the majority. When only one or two people contradicted them, most subjects still answered correctly. But when the size of the majority increased to three, subjects made many errors. If they were given the support of only one other member, though, the subjects answered incorrectly only one-fourth as often as under the pressure of a unanimous majority.

Group membership does not always affect people adversely, making them into conformists and dupes. Indeed, some groups are specifically designed to increase each member's willingness to express and understand his own feelings and to enhance his sensitivity to the feelings of others. The *sensitivity-training hypothesis* states that training in human relations can help the members of a group learn to trust and accept each other. Sensitivity-training groups, called T-groups, are the prototypes for the many kinds of encounter groups and other "intensive group experiences" that have become so popular in recent years. Such groups bear some resemblance to therapy groups (see Unit 11), but they are meant to enrich the life experiences of normal people rather than to serve as therapy for troubled ones.

Unlike the subjects in the experimental groups considered so far, the members of sensitivity groups have no specific tasks. They are encouraged to express their feelings about whatever they wish and to learn by trying things out. The learning experience depends heavily upon *feedback* from the other members in the group, which tells the individual how his behavior makes others feel. Over the course of training, such a group develops specific norms or standards of behavior, and individuals gain insight into the behavior of other members as well as their own.

One of the major questions about T-groups is whether or not they add anything to what an individual could achieve on his own or with the help of a human-relations counselor. Proponents of sensitivity training argue that the value of the group lies in the confrontations among individuals who are not "experts in behavior."

DESCRIPTIVE EVIDENCE
Investigators: R. L. Burke and W. G. Bennis
Source, Date: "Changes in Perception of Self and Others during Human Relations Training," 1961
Location: National Training Laboratory in Group Development, Bethel, Maine
Subjects: 84 delegates and one leader
Materials: Group Semantic Differential

In this study, the members of six T-groups were tested with the Group Semantic Differential (GSD) in the middle of the first week and at the end of the third week of training. The GSD is a test to measure perceptions of a variety of concepts relevant to group functioning and member behavior. The three concepts rated were expressed as "The way I actually feel in this group," "The way I would like to feel in this group," and "The way I feel about each individual in the group." Each member of the group was asked to rate his feeling on these matters on a series of nineteen dimensions, such as strong-weak, bad-good, cool-warm, active-passive.

The group members' ratings showed that, with training, the participants became more satisfied with their perceptions of themselves, that their actual perceptions of themselves moved in the direction of their perception of their ideal selves, and that they came to see other members of the group more as those people saw themselves.

Over time, group conformity based on perceived similarity resulted in the formation of group norms or standards. It is not inconceivable that social standards in general are formed in much the same manner.

QUESTION 3. WHY DO SOME PEOPLE BECOME LEADERS OF GROUPS?

HYPOTHESES	LEADERSHIP CHARACTERISTICS	LEADERSHIP SITUATION	PERSON SITUATION
DESCRIPTIVE EVIDENCE	ASSESS: characteristics of leadership	ASSESS: behavior of "old" leaders in "new" groups	ASSESS: relation between personal and situational characteristics in effective leadership
EXPERIMENTAL EVIDENCE			

3. WHY DO SOME PEOPLE BECOME LEADERS OF GROUPS?

One of the most interesting characteristics of groups is that, one way or another, they always seem to have leaders. Structured groups usually designate their leaders formally, as when a club elects a president, but even in unstructured groups like a group of friends, one or more leaders usually emerge as the group interacts. The nature of people's response to leadership has fascinated analysts of every sort. In the sixth century B.C. Confucius wrote, "The superior man is easy to serve and difficult to please." Robert Townsend, the former president of Avis Rent-A-Car, took a somewhat more cynical view: "Since most people per se are mediocre, the true leader can be recognized because, somehow or other, his people consistently turn in superior performances."

What makes a leader—the man, or the moment, or both? That is, is effective leadership the result of the individual leader's behavioral or personality traits? Is it called forth by the demands of a particular situation? Or, in most cases, does the interplay between the two factors account for the emergence and performance of a leader? Social psychologists have been adding their research to the speculations of philosophers, historians, and business administrators about these questions.

The *leadership-characteristics hypothesis* states that some people become leaders as a function of a specific cluster of characteristics that draw them into leadership positions. One of the more fruitful avenues of research on the personal characteristics of successful leaders has centered on the behavior of effective military leaders. In 1969 Cecil Gibb rephrased some of the leadership characteristics established by a 1952 study of U.S. Army personnel by J. H. Carter. Gibb found that the most effective leaders tended to be able to do seven things: perform professional and technical specialties; know their subordinates and show consideration for them; keep channels of communication open; accept personal responsibility and set an example; initiate and direct action; train the men as a team; and make decisions.

DESCRIPTIVE EVIDENCE

Investigators: A. W. Halpin and B. J. Winer

Source, Date: "The Leadership Behavior of the Airplane Commander," 1952
Subjects: College students
Materials: Questionnaires

The subjects were presented with a list of nine characteristics generally considered important to leadership and were asked to rate the importance of each. The ratings of all of the subjects were combined and analyzed to find common elements.

The data revealed agreement on four essential leadership characteristics: consideration (leader shows warmth, consideration of others, and willingness to listen), initiating structure (leader organizes and defines clearly the relationships between himself and his subordinates), production emphasis (leader stresses getting the job done), and sensitivity (leader demonstrates social awareness). The first two were thought to be much more important than the last two, supporting the interesting notion that the primary components of leadership are not task-oriented abilities but interpersonal skills.

On the other hand, the *leadership-situation hypothesis* states that environmental variables may thrust authority on an individual, almost regardless of his personal characteristics. To pick a simple example, controlled studies of randomly constituted small groups such as juries have shown that seating position often determines who will be the leader. Juries are apt to select as a foreman one of those sitting at the ends of a rectangular table. It is possible that "natural leaders" tend to assume the physical locations of power, but evidence on this point is weak. In essence, the situation hypothesis suggests that the leader in one setting will not necessarily be a leader in another.

DESCRIPTIVE EVIDENCE

Investigator: F. Merei
Source, Date: "Group Leadership and Institutionalization," 1949
Location: University of Pécs, Hungary
Subjects: Boys
Materials: Play rooms

After observing a group of boys in a play situation, Merei selected those who exhibited leadership dominance. Two of the main criteria for the selection were that suggestions from the "leader" were generally carried out by other boys in the group and that the dominant boys tended to enforce group rules.

The less dominant boys were then formed into smaller groups, where they could develop their own norms and find new leaders. The dominant boys were excluded from these groups for between three and six meetings in order to let the new groups become well established.

When one dominant boy was introduced into each of the new groups, none of them reemerged as a natural leader. Their suggestions were either modified or ignored, and the other group members actively opposed any attempt on their part to violate the new group traditions. Very few of the previous leaders ever succeeded in reestablishing their dominance over the groups, presumably because the groups had developed their own well-entrenched rules.

An interesting side result of this study was that a few of the previously dominant boys adopted what Merei termed "diplomat roles" within the new groups. They became the chief guardians of the new group norms and soon began to interpret and change the norms in various ways. This pattern provides

some support for the *person-situation hypothesis*, which states that leadership results from the interaction between individual characteristics and situational or task variables. This rather obvious point hardly needs laboring: the "natural leader" of a feminist consciousness-raising group is no more likely to flourish in the neighborhood sewing circle than the conventional fraternity president is in the midst of a radical political committee.

Research into the questions of what kinds of leaders emerge in what kinds of groups and what effect various kinds of leadership have on group behavior

Figure 2. Personality traits and situational factors combine to account for the emergence of such leaders as first lady, Eleanor Roosevelt, Senator Edward Kennedy, and New York Jets quarterback Joe Namath.

has taken three main directions. The first focuses on leadership style and group productivity: the classic example is Kurt Lewin's study of authoritarian, democratic, and laissez-faire groups, described at the start of this unit. Second, Robert Bales and his colleagues have used a procedure known as Interaction Process Analysis (IPA) to collect data showing that, although the characteristics of leaders vary slightly from situation to situation, most of them score very high on items such as "gives suggestion," "asks opinion," "gives help," and "gives agreement." Perhaps more importantly, Bales' research suggests that two basic leadership styles are active in most groups: "task leaders" maintain group activity and supervise general productivity, while "social-emotional leaders" tend to be more interested in maintaining cohesiveness (which also can lead to increased productivity).

Almost all these studies have shown, among other things, that leaders are not always the most popular members of a group. A third experimental tradition has examined this factor very closely. F. E. Fiedler's "contingency model of leadership effectiveness" predicts that unpopular leaders—those scoring high on a Least Preferred Coworker (LPC) scale—will be strongly task-oriented and will function most effectively in very simple or very complex tasks, while popular—low on LPC scale—and "relationship-oriented" leaders will be most effective in tasks of intermediate complexity.

DESCRIPTIVE EVIDENCE

Investigator: F. E. Fiedler
Source, Date: "Validation and Extension of the Contingency Model of Leadership Effectiveness: A Review of Empirical Findings," 1971
Location: University of Washington, Seattle
Materials: 15 experiments interrelating leadership effectiveness and LPC scores in various kinds of tasks

Taken together, the data from Fiedler's fifteen experiments spanning eight years provide impressive support for the notion that leadership effectiveness is determined by having the right kinds of leaders in the right kinds of settings.

Evidence of one sort comes from field studies of actual situations. A detailed series of investigations in

military groups and athletic teams showed that the most effective leaders of groups with either very difficult or very easy assignments were those who scored very high on the LPC scale—that is, they were unpopular. The leaders in moderately complex tasks were most effective when they were more popular. (See Figure 3.) Evidence from artificially composed groups in laboratory experiments, Fiedler reported, was not adequate to support his model, suggesting that it needs further refinement. In both real and artificial settings, however, Fiedler has concluded that sensitivity-training groups function best under low LPC leadership. Such groups apparently respond to leaders who are predominantly relationship-oriented, regardless of the complexity of the situation. Although Fiedler faces some major problems in quantifying leadership effectiveness, popularity, and task complexity, his model is furthering the development of a technology of group leadership that may ultimately identify the optimal leadership style required for different groups.

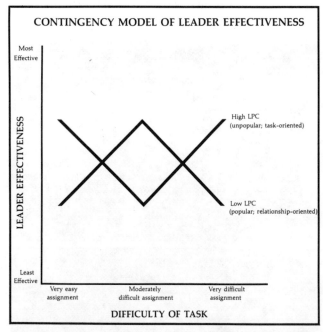

Figure 3. Fiedler's research on leader effectiveness and its relation to difficulty of task indicates that the most effective leaders of groups with either a very easy assignment or a very difficult assignment were those who scored very high on the LPC scale—that is, they were unpopular. Leaders in moderately favorable situations were most effective when they were more popular. Adapted from Fiedler (1971).

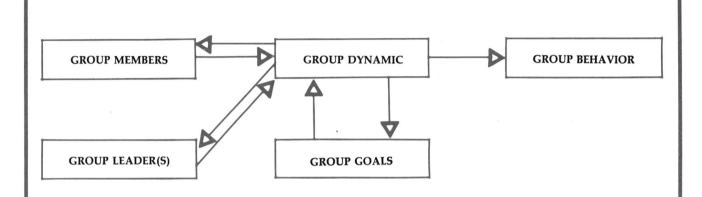

PUTTING IT TOGETHER: Groups and Leaders

Any particular group is composed of its *members* and, usually, a *leader* who is chosen or imposed on the group because of his personality, the group goals or some relationship between the two. Group members can influence the leader and vice versa, and either of these can influence goals through a *group dynamic* that emerges from the process of developing leadership. The *goals* (for example, pleasure, problem-solving, task completion,) define the purpose of the group and influence to some extent the behavior of both leaders and members through the group dynamic, which includes decision-making.

As part of the group dynamic, individual members may shift their positions to conform with majority opinions or behavior. Also, participation in sensitivity training can lead to greater acceptance among group members. In situations with an element of risk, the group dynamic might shift the group decision in the direction of greater risk than any of the individual members would be willing to take. In situations where moral responsibility is stressed, group decisions are likely to shift in a conservative direction.

The resultant *group behavior* may be quite different from what might be predicted from the behavior of each individual considered separately.

1. WHAT'S ACCEPTED . . .

1. Decisions made in groups may differ from those that would be made by most participant individuals.

2. A unanimous majority can influence some individuals to conform.

3. Sensitivity training can enhance perception of the self and of others.

4. Effective leadership characteristics are in part dependent upon situational factors.

2. WHAT'S DEBATED . . .

1. The role of norms and values in group decision making.

2. The relative weight of individual and situational variables in leadership.

3. The factors that influence the direction and degree of risky and cautious shifts in group decision making.

4. Whether experimental groups reflect decision-making proceses in real-life situations.

As we have seen, a group situation may help, or it may hurt the judgment of its individual members. Every group exerts the pressure to conform, and perhaps the most dangerous shape this conformity can take is "groupthink."

Irving Janis, developer of the concept of "groupthink," argues that the Pearl Harbor disaster (which caused the United States to enter World War II), could have been avoided. But groupthink was operating in the U.S. Navy, and it created an unquestioning loyalty to the group. It discouraged any individual member from raising awkward questions. Plenty of evidence of the coming Japanese attack was available. Only a few days before, for example, radio contact with the Japanese aircraft carrier fleet had been lost. The obvious conclusion was that the Japanese were maintaining radio silence for some secret purpose. But the U.S. Navy assumed that Pearl Harbor could not be attacked and expected the Japanese to share that assumption, so the conclusion was not drawn. Raising the alarm would have meant presenting unwelcome arguments against the myth of Pearl Harbor's security. As a result, the Japanese were able to pull off their incredible gamble, cripple the U.S. fleet, and sweep on practically unchallenged to a series of military victories in Southeast Asia and the Pacific.

Janis believes that groupthink involves "a deterioration of mental efficiency, reality testing and moral judgment that results from in-group pressures." When groupthink is operating, the group's discussions focus on a few choices without full consideration of the range of options available. Members of the group make little attempt to obtain sound, relevant information from outside experts, and so make their decisions in ignorance of vital factors. They respond selectively to the information and judgments that are available to them, and accept only those facts and opinions that support the policy they prefer. They fail to work out contingency plans to cope with unforeseen setbacks, and they tend to consider loyalty to the group as the highest morality. Group loyalty prevents individual members from raising controversial matters or ethical issues. In fact, argues Janis, "symptoms of groupthink will be found most often when a decision poses a moral dilemma, especially if the most advantageous course requires the policy makers to violate their own standards of humanitarian behavior." The decision-makers have a need to retain each other's approval, even at the cost of critical thinking.

Groupthink can have very serious results, especially when it affects the national leadership. Janis contends that many foreign policy disasters, like the Bay of Pigs invasion of Cuba in 1961 (discussed earlier in the unit), resulted from groupthink. The invasion of the Bay of Pigs was doomed before it started, as any critical examination of the evidence would have revealed. Instead, an ill-equipped invasion force was sent to land at a coastal spot that was entirely unsuitable for a military landing, and was soon routed by a Cuban force far superior in numbers and armaments. President Kennedy and his advisors had somehow assumed that the world would not suspect the American authorship of the invasion, and the State Department did not trouble to inform the U.S. ambassador to the United Nations that his country was involved. The ambassador received the news while he was in the midst of a speech strongly denying to the assembled representatives of the nations of the world that the U.S. was in any way involved, and America's humiliation was complete. Interestingly, several of the aides and advisors who participated in the decision to invade Cuba had severe private misgivings about the venture. But not one dared to express them.

How can groupthink be avoided? Janis suggests several safeguards. (1) The leader of a group should encourage each member to evaluate policy critically, and give high priority to airing doubts. (2) The leader should be impartial at first, and should not attempt to influence the decision in the early stages of the process. (3) The organization should establish several independent evaluation groups, each under a different leader, so that the possibility of overall groupthink is eliminated. (4) Qualified outgroup members should be invited to the group's deliberations and encouraged to challenge the views of the in-group members. (5) At every meeting, one member should play "devil's advocate," automatically challenging those who support the majority position. (6) Whenever the policy issue involves a rival nation or organization, due care must be taken to survey all warning signals and construct alternative "scenarios" to handle different contingencies. (7) After an initial decision has been

taken, the group members should have a "second chance" meeting to express any lingering doubts. As Alfred P. Sloan, a former chairman of General Motors, once told a meeting of policymakers: "Gentlemen, I take it we are all in complete agreement here. Then I propose we postpone further discussion until our next meeting to give ourselves time to develop disagreement and perhaps gain some understanding of what the decision is all about."

Groupthink is a very old phenomenon. According to the historian Herodotus, even the ancient Persians were aware of it, and whenever they made a decision in a sober, rational frame of mind, they always reconsidered the matter later while drunk. But the insights of Janis have given us a more precise formulation of the problem and of possible solutions to it. Knowledge derived from psychological research on group decision-making processes could be very valuable to corporate executives and public officials who make important economic and political decisions, usually in complete ignorance of group processes that might distort their rational judgment. Better decisions might emerge if there were general public education to the fact that in any group of individuals there is a group dynamic that transcends the individual participants. This principle could readily, and fruitfully, be incorporated into school civics lessons as part of a general training in citizenship and leadership responsibilities.

Unit 10

Social Influence

OVERVIEW

What are some of the factors underlying the capacity of individuals to persuade each other and change each other's opinions and attitudes? The first part of the unit looks at both the sources of influence (such as information and credibility) and what makes people susceptible to influence (such as the need to belong and locus of control.) The next part of the unit describes some techniques found to be effective in getting people to change their attitudes and opinions. The last part examines the use of persuasion techniques to sell anything from cigarettes to presidential candidates.

UNIT OUTLINE

DEFINITION AND BACKGROUND
1. *Definition:* social influence is the process by which people form and change the attitudes, opinions, and associated behavior of others.
2. *Background:* Carl I. Hovland (1912–1961).

QUESTIONS AND EVIDENCE
1. What are some effective sources of social influence?
Hypotheses:
    a. *Information:* a person's attitudes toward situations and people reflect what he has been taught—by teachers, parents, books, and the news media—especially during childhood. **156**
    b. *Credibility:* the persuasiveness of a message depends both on the status and experience of the person stating the message and on the believability of its content. **157**
2. What characteristics of people make them susceptible to social influence?
Hypotheses:
    a. *Need-to-belong:* a person tends to adopt the attitudes held by groups he joins or wishes to join. **158**
    b. *Locus-of-control:* people with an external locus of control are more susceptible to persuasion than those with an internal locus of control. **159**
3. What are some effective techniques for changing opinions and attitudes?
Hypotheses:
    a. *Subtlety:* a persuasive message is more effective when the audience is not aware of the persuader's true purposes. **161**
    b. *Presenting-both-sides:* stating and refuting the opposing viewpoint is a more persuasive technique than presenting only one side of a question (unless the audience is already firmly on the speaker's side). **161**
    c. *Dissonance-reduction:* when a person's attitudes and behavior are inconsistent with one another, his attitudes tend to shift in the direction of behavior. **162**
    d. *Commitment:* once an individual has accepted a persuasive message slightly, the probability increases that he will accept it fully later. **163**

IMPORTANT CONCEPTS

	page
attitude	**154**
cognitive dissonance	**162**
credibility	**157**
locus of control	**159**
persuasion	**157**
propaganda	**162**
sleeper effect	**157**
social influence	**154**

Behavior is most likely to be influenced by people who are credible sources for specific information.

Responsiveness to social influence is related to the strength of social needs.

Susceptibility to behavior control through social influence varies with personal characteristics of individuals.

DEFINITION AND BACKGROUND

Without beliefs and opinions most people would find the world incomprehensibly confusing and complicated. Indeed, firmly held attitudes are often crucial to effective action. As Adam Clayton Powell once remarked, "Mix a conviction with a man and something happens." One thing that usually happens is that the individual attempts to persuade others to share his beliefs.

All of us constantly try to convince other people to adopt certain opinions, to change their minds. One useful DEFINITION of social influence is *the process by which people form and change the attitudes, opinions, and associated behavior of others.* The concept of attitude is central here. An attitude is a relatively enduring organization of beliefs and feelings about an object or situation that predisposes one to respond in a certain way. An *opinion* is an attitude expressed verbally.

An attitude is not the same thing as a value, which social psychologists regard as an even deeper, more meaningful standard of judgment and action held by a person. In most cases, values influence and help determine attitudes rather than the other way around.

This unit will FOCUS on some of the things that affect attitude change and persuasion, processes that lie at the heart of social psychology. It will emphasize the characteristics of people and situations that make social influence inevitable (though not always desirable).

BACKGROUND: CARL I. HOVLAND (1912–1961)

It wasn't until the 1930s and 1940s that truly systematic approaches for analyzing processes of social influence began to emerge. One important contribution to this emerging trend was Kurt Lewin's dynamic study of small groups of individuals (see Unit 9). But the single most important impetus came from a group of psychologists who gathered around one central figure, Carl I. Hovland of Yale University. During World War II, Hovland did some significant work in human learning, which aroused his interest in how mass media affect and change people's attitudes. His initial contribution was to introduce sound experi-

mental methods into research on mass media, interpersonal communication, and persuasion.

Near the end of World War II, Hovland ran a study in which a large number of American soldiers were asked to guess how long the war would last. Then they were divided into two groups. One group heard arguments explaining why the war with Japan would be much longer than the one in Europe. The other group heard those same arguments, but they also heard the other side—discussions of the possibility that the war in the Pacific might end almost immediately after the European conflict.

Then the soldiers were again asked to estimate when the war would end. It turned out that about 59 percent of the men in both groups now believed that the war would last at least another year and a half, as compared to about 37 percent before the arguments had been presented. It became apparent that the one-sided argument was most effective with those soldiers who already believed the war would last quite

Figure 1. Carl I. Hovland, social psychologist and originator of scientific research into attitude change, mass media, persuasion and interpersonal communication.

Figure 2. One of the many World War II posters that had a strong influence on Americans. Processes for analyzing social influence began to be developed during the 1930s and 1940s.

consider the state of mind of the person to be persuaded. Many of the most important experiments and principles that came from the work of the group led by Hovland were discussed in a book by Hovland, Lumsdaine, and Sheffield published in 1949.

In the 1950s Hovland turned to problems in concept formation and computer-simulation research, leaving further explorations of persuasion and attitude change largely to his Yale colleagues. The impact of Hovland's approach was felt at institutions other than Yale, and to this day research on attitude change continues to be one of the most active areas in social psychology. Besides introducing greater experimental rigor, Hovland's group showed that attitudes are dynamic rather than static and unchanging and helped focus the attention of social psychologists on attitude *change*.

a long time. With soldiers who originally thought that the war would end soon, the argument that presented both sides of the question was more effective.

Findings of this sort indicated that studies of the effectiveness of persuasive communications should

QUESTIONS AND EVIDENCE

1. What are some effective sources of social influence?

2. What characteristics of people make them susceptible to social influence?

3. What are some effective techniques for changing opinions and attitudes?

QUESTION   1. WHAT ARE SOME EFFECTIVE SOURCES OF SOCIAL INFLUENCE?

HYPOTHESES	INFORMATION	CREDIBILITY
DESCRIPTIVE EVIDENCE	ASSESS: relation of political attitudes of children to content of textbooks and social class	
EXPERIMENTAL EVIDENCE		VARY: credibility of source and time following presentation MEASURE: attitude toward message and attitude change

1. WHAT ARE SOME EFFECTIVE SOURCES OF SOCIAL INFLUENCE?

Politicians, advertising men and others sometimes use the principles of social influence for their own selfish purposes, thereby giving social influence a bad name. On the other hand, some form of influence is essential to the survival of any group of people living together cooperatively. Societies are preserved by the attitudes their members share, and these attitudes are maintained by education, information, even indoctrination. The *information hypothesis* of social influence states that a person's attitudes toward situations and people reflect what he has been taught—by teachers, parents, books, and the news media—especially during childhood.

DESCRIPTIVE EVIDENCE

Investigator: E. Litt
Source, Date: "Civic Education, Community Norms and Political Indoctrination," 1962
Location: Boston College
Subjects: 301 Boston-area schoolchildren
Materials: Content analyses of civics texts; civics courses

The subjects were chosen from three different communities. One was a politically active upper-middle-class town, the second was a moderately active lower-middle-class town, and the third was a relatively inactive working-class town. The "class" of each community was established by the percentages of its workers in professional, management, sales, clerical, skilled, semiskilled, and unskilled labor positions (as determined from census records). Political activity was measured by median voter turnout in the five most recent gubernatorial elections: 67.8 percent for the upper-middle-class town, 43.8 percent for the lower-middle-class town, and 32.1 percent for the working-class town.

Litt developed a set of content analyses of the textbooks used in civics courses in the three communities during the preceding five years. These were obtained by counting the number of times certain specific political themes appeared. The five major themes, briefly summarized, were: emphasis on citizen political participation (references to voting); political chauvinism (glorified treatment of American political institutions or public figures); the democratic creed (references to rights of citizens and minorities to influence governmental policy); emphasis on political process (references to politics as an arena where politicians and officials interact and influence each other); and emphasis on politics as the resolution of group conflict (references to political conflicts resolved within political rules of the game).

In all three towns, Litt found that the different textbooks used emphasized the democratic creed and deemphasized political chauvinism. However, only the textbooks used by the upper-middle-class community placed strong emphasis on the political process.

The students' political attitudes were measured before and after they took the civics courses in the three communities. The method of measurement was an attitude survey consisting of statements either supporting or not supporting the five major textbook themes.

It was found that the attitudes of the students changed in the direction that one might expect from the content of their textbooks. In all three communities the students' beliefs in the democratic creed increased; their chauvinistic opinions about the American political system were weakened; and their attitudes toward citizen participation did not change. Only the students in the upper-middle-class community, however, came to see politics as involving people, power, and conflict resolution.

Litt concluded that some children were being taught to be politically passive, while others were being taught to become actively involved. It must be noted that the administrators who chose these textbooks and planned the educational programs were probably unaware, for the most part, of the subtle differences in education among communities differing in social class. Furthermore, one cannot conclude that social-class differences in political behavior are determined by textbook differences. However, the fact that the educational system apparently responds to the class differences may have serious consequences for national political involvement and activity.

From a somewhat different point of view, Litt's study demonstrates a central principle of social influence. One way to persuade different groups of people to do different things is to vary the content of the message subtly without altering its apparent purpose.

A textbook looks authoritative, and most students are inclined to accept what it has to say. Its authors are experts in their field, and their experience and academic standing lend respectability to their statements. But if the book does not square with the facts as students perceive them, it and its authors lose credibility. This principle also applies to opinions expressed by parents, friends, and political leaders. The *credibility hypothesis* states that the persuasiveness of a message depends both on the status and experience of the person stating the message and on the believability of its content.

EXPERIMENTAL EVIDENCE

Investigators: H. C. Kelman and C. I. Hovland
Source, Date: "'Reinstatement' of the Communicator in Delayed Measurement of Opinion Change," 1953
Location: Johns Hopkins University and Yale University, respectively
Subjects: 273 summer high-school students
Materials: Attitude questionnaires; recall survey; prearranged radio program

Three different groups of high-school students listened to a speaker on a radio program argue for leniency in the treatment of criminals. The content of the discussion was identical, but each speaker was introduced to a group in a different way, and he played his role accordingly. For the first group he was a highly trained judge from a juvenile court ("positive credibility"). To the second group he was described as a member of the studio audience chosen at random ("neutral credibility"). To the third group he was portrayed as an obnoxious character, a former juvenile delinquent currently free on bail after being arrested for dope peddling ("low credibility").

A questionnaire assessing opinions on treatment of criminals was administered to all students immediately after the program and again three weeks later. (Actually, alternate forms of the questionnaire were used, so that its uniformity would not be apparent.) Each student was asked to check on a five-point scale the extent to which he agreed with a variety of statements ranging from the extremely lenient "Punishment is never justified" to the extremely harsh "Intense physical pain is the only way to make people fear the law." Information was also collected on how the students evaluated the program itself and on how well each of them could remember specific facts included in the presentation.

Before listening to the radio program, the three groups did not differ appreciably in their attitudes about juvenile delinquency. Immediately after the program, the leniency attitude that conformed to the speaker's point of view was found to be greatest for the first ("positive credibility") group and least for the third ("low credibility") group. The first group responded most favorably to the program, and the third group most negatively, with the opinions of the second group falling between the two extremes.

However, when the questionnaire was administered again three weeks later there were no longer any major differences in the leniency of the attitudes of the three groups. Rather, there was a leveling effect. That is, the third group, which earlier had a negative view of the program now expressed opinions that did not differ significantly from those of the first group, whose more positive opinions were also moderated. The experimenters concluded that the subjects had forgotten their original assessment of the source of information. The tendency for credibility effects to diminish over time is known as the *sleeper effect*.

Not everyone is equally susceptible to social influence. Some people refuse to change their minds regardless of what they are told or who tells them; others seem ready to agree with virtually any side of any argument. What accounts for these variations in susceptibility? Two important factors are a person's need to gain the approval of a peer group, and his sense of control over his own life.

HYPOTHESES	NEED TO BELONG	LOCUS OF CONTROL
DESCRIPTIVE EVIDENCE	ASSESS: relation of individual's attitudes to reference group attitudes, and attitude change	
EXPERIMENTAL EVIDENCE		VARY: strength of influence attempt with locus of control MEASURE: amount and kind of reaction to influence attempt according to locus of control and sex

2. WHAT CHARACTERISTICS OF PEOPLE MAKE THEM SUSCEPTIBLE TO SOCIAL INFLUENCE?

The attitudes of even the most independent adults can often be predicted from a knowledge of who his friends are and what they think. The opinions heard in the country-club lounge on a Saturday evening are likely to be different from those expressed in the downtown neighborhood bar. The *need-to-belong hypothesis* states that a person tends to adopt the attitudes held by groups he joins or wishes to join.

DESCRIPTIVE EVIDENCE

Investigator: T. M. Newcomb
Source, Date: "Persistence and Regression of Changed Attitudes," 1963
Subjects: Hundreds of Bennington College female students
Materials: Preference surveys, questionnaires, interview data

This long-range study has become a classic in the field of attitude research. Most of the information was obtained from the students and their parents through preference questionnaires and personal interviews. Of special interest was the relationship between the political attitudes expressed by the students and their parents' opinions.

The study began with the discovery that Ben-

nington juniors and seniors were markedly more liberal than first-year students in their attitudes toward many of the public issues of the day, including the New Deal policies of President Roosevelt. For example, in 1936 when 66 percent of the students' parents preferred the Republican presidential candidate Landon over Roosevelt, 62 percent of the first-year students, 43 percent of the sophomores, and only 15 percent of juniors and seniors supported Landon in a mock political election.

When Newcomb compared this pattern of voting with results from other colleges, he discovered that the degree of progression of increasingly liberal attitudes with each year of college was unique to Bennington. To check his results, he followed individual students through their four years at college and found the same pattern. It should be noted that during the 1930s Bennington was a new school and most of the students came from well-to-do conservative homes.

Personal interviews conducted throughout the four-year period revealed over and over again that most of the students were aware that they were making a choice between the attitudes of their families and those of their college peers. Surveys of their backgrounds and school activities also showed that the acquisition of liberal attitudes was associated with participation in campus life, with respect from others, and with personal involvement with the college as an institution. Those students who remained politically conservative were rated as dependent and socially isolated by their teachers and peers. The influence of reference groups (peers) on attitudes apparently can be very powerful, even after childhood.

In 1961 Newcomb was able to contact, interview, and retest about 130 of the Bennington graduates that he had surveyed in the 1930s. He found that ninety-five of them had remained consistently liberal or conservative since graduation, whereas the attitudes of the other thirty-five had changed in one direction or the other. In general, the Bennington graduates were much more liberal than a representative sample of white, middle-aged, upper-middle-class, Protestant women in the United States. About 60 percent of them preferred John F. Kennedy for President in 1960, while only 30 percent of their ''peers'' supported him.

Most of the Bennington women, Newcomb found, had married men whose economic backgrounds were similar to their parents' but whose political preferences matched their own. The few women whose views differed from their husbands' were those whose opinions had changed most over the more than twenty years since graduation.

A good many women have become more independent-minded in recent years, politically and in other ways. To explain this phenomenon, one might suggest that, for some women, the women's liberation movement has encouraged a shift from external to internal locus of control.

A person with an external locus of control believes that his fate is controlled by something outside himself—by chance, or by other people more powerful than he. A person with an internal locus of control believes that he controls his own fate, and that the rewards he receives are the result of his own actions. According to the *locus-of-control hypothesis* of social influence, people with an external locus of control are more susceptible to persuasion than those with an internal locus of control.

EXPERIMENTAL EVIDENCE

Investigators: J. Biondo and A. P. MacDonald, Jr.
Source, Date: "Internal-External Locus of Control and Response to Influence Attempts," 1971
Location: West Virginia University
Subjects: 144 introductory psychology students
Materials: Rotter Internal-External Locus of Control Scale; grading materials

The Rotter scale of locus of control was administered to all subjects about one week before the actual experiment. The scores were used to determine

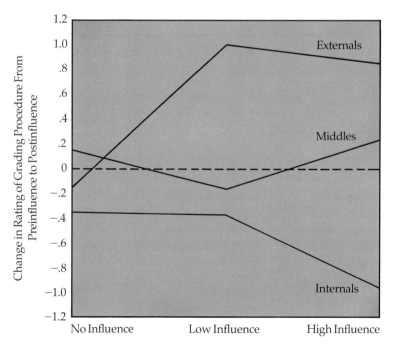

Figure 3. In Biondo and MacDonald's study (1971) subjects with external locus of control were affected by both low- and high-influence attempts. Subjects with internal locus of control were unaffected by low-influence attempts and resisted high-influence attempts.

whether a subject has internal, middle, or external locus of control.

A week later all subjects were asked to rate—on a ten-point scale—a grading procedure that might be used by the school administration. (The particular grading procedure had previously received a relatively neutral rating by other students [not in this study] and was selected because it allowed room for movement in either direction under influence conditions.)

Next, using the explanation that another graduate student needed more information "for research," the experimenter handed out printed matter containing additional information about the grading procedure that had just been rated. This new information was varied in three ways: the "no influence" communication was essentially the same as in the original hand-out; the "low influence" communication ended with a statement that "This grading procedure has been widely accepted at other universities and appears to be one of the best ever used"; the "high influence" information ended by saying "Taking everything into consideration, it is obvious that this is a very good procedure. I don't see how you have any choice but to rate this procedure highly." Then all subjects were again asked to rate the grading procedure on a ten-point scale from "very poor" to "very good." Thus three levels of locus of control were crossed with three levels of influence, making a total of nine experimental conditions. Each condition contained sixteen subjects, eight of each sex.

The results of this study appear in Figure 3 where the dependent or response variable is the amount of change in the ratings as a function of the experimental conditions. The graph shows that the subjects with external locus of control conformed under both high and low levels of persuasive influence. On the other hand, those with internal locus of control reacted negatively to the high-influence attempt (but not to the low-influence attempt). (The sex of the subject made no difference, incidentally.) Stated more generally, individuals who attribute power to authority figures rather than themselves are more likely to be swayed by a persuasive attempt, while people who tend to see control as located in their own persons are more likely to react negatively to obvious attempts at persuasion.

QUESTION   3. WHAT ARE SOME EFFECTIVE TECHNIQUES FOR CHANGING OPINIONS AND ATTITUDES?

HYPOTHESES	SUBTLETY	PRESENTING BOTH SIDES	DISSONANCE REDUCTION	COMMITMENT
DESCRIPTIVE EVIDENCE				ASSESS: buying behavior after getting a small verbal commitment
EXPERIMENTAL EVIDENCE	VARY: awareness of intentions of persuader MEASURE: amount of expressed attitude change	VARY: one- vs. two-sided argument; exposure to counterpropaganda MEASURE: amount of attitude change	VARY: labeling disliked vegetable as high or low in food value; amount of disliked vegetable actually eaten MEASURE: amount of attitude change	

3. WHAT ARE SOME EFFECTIVE TECHNIQUES FOR CHANGING OPINIONS AND ATTITUDES?

The self-serving politicians and advertising men mentioned earlier in this unit are well aware of the characteristics that make people susceptible to their influence. But they also realize that a hard sell appealing directly to, say, the need to belong can have double-edged effects. As Erich Fromm has noted, "Like the effect of advertising upon the customer, the methods of political propaganda tend to increase the feeling of insignificance of the individual voter." To overcome customer or voter apathy, the persuaders often conceal their purposes with various subtle techniques, including presentations of both sides of the case. They also realize the important effects that actual behavior can have on attitudes, especially when the behavior implies at least a partial commitment.

Mark Antony's funeral oration in Shakespeare's *Julius Caesar* is perhaps the most famous example of subtle crowd manipulation. By ironically praising Brutus and the other conspirators as "all honourable men," Antony gradually leads his audience of "friends, Romans, countrymen" to perceive the plot against Caesar from exactly his viewpoint. The *subtlety hypothesis* states that a persuasive message is more effective when the audience is not aware of the persuader's true purposes.

EXPERIMENTAL EVIDENCE

Investigators: J. Allyn and L. Festinger
Source, Date: "The Effectiveness of Unanticipated Persuasive Communications," 1961
Location: Stanford University
Subjects: 53 female and 34 male high-school students
Materials: Opinion questionnaires; two sets of instructions; a speech on teenage driving

Teachers were asked to distribute a "youth survey" among their students. The questionnaire included a number of statements with which the students could "agree strongly," "agree slightly," "disagree slightly," or "disagree strongly." Four of the statements concerned tighter controls on teenage driving—the issue involved in the experiment.

Two weeks later the students assembled to receive booklets and instructions. Half of them were given booklets with "opinion-oriented" instructions. The other half received "personality-oriented" instructions. The opinion-oriented instructions said that they were about to hear a speaker who was an expert and who would try to influence their opinions. The personality-oriented instructions said they were about to hear a speaker who was an expert and asked them to evaluate his personality with no forewarning of his intent.

The speaker's talk on the need for stronger legal measures to restrict teenage driving expressed opinions stronger than any of those expressed by the students on the first administration of the questionnaire. After the speech, the students filled out questions in the booklet, which included the same four questions about teenage driving they had answered previously. Thus the dependent variable was the amount of expressed attitude change from the pretest to the posttest on the four items on teenage driving.

The results showed clearly that the group of students who had not been forewarned about the speaker's persuasive purpose changed their opinions in the direction advocated by the speaker more than the other group of students.

Besides neglecting to explain to an audience that he is trying to talk them into something, a speaker can make his argument more persuasive by presenting the counterargument as well.

According to the *presenting-both-sides hypothesis*, stating and refuting the opposing viewpoint is a more persuasive technique than presenting only one side of a question (unless the audience is already firmly on the speaker's side).

EXPERIMENTAL EVIDENCE

Investigators: A. A. Lumsdaine and I. L. Janis
Source, Date: "Resistance to 'Counterpropaganda' Produced by One-Sided and Two-Sided 'Propaganda' Presentations," 1953
Location: Yale University
Subjects: 197 high-school students
Materials: Attitude questionnaires; two recorded programs

All of the students listened to "radio programs" arguing that Russia would not be able to produce a large number of atomic bombs in the next five years. However, some of them heard only a one-sided statement that explained why Russia could not manufacture many bombs. Others heard a two-sided presentation that also stated counterarguments. One week later, half of the subjects from each group heard a one-sided counterpropaganda program arguing that Russia could produce many bombs in the next five years. Thus the subjects fell into the four experimental conditions shown in Figure 4.

One-sided program, no later counter propaganda	One-sided program, with later counter propaganda
Two-sided program, no later counter propaganda	Two-sided program, with later counter propaganda "immunization"

Figure 4. Experimental conditions of the study by Lumsdaine and Janis (1953).

Both before and after the experiment all subjects filled out questionnaires that assessed their opinions on Russia's atomic-bomb capabilities. One of the key items was "About how long from now do you think it will be before the Russians are really producing *large numbers* of atomic bombs?

The results showed that one-sided and two-sided programs were about equally effective in forming opinions supporting the persuasive argument. For the subjects exposed to counterpropaganda, however, the two-sided program was highly superior in maintaining the position argued on the original program. That is, the two-sided argument seemed to "immunize" the students who heard it against counterarguments.

Although the two-sided approach is superior when an audience is likely to hear counterarguments later, other studies have shown that one-sided statements are more effective when the entire audience is already on the speaker's side, so that he need only reinforce the beliefs they already hold. The contrast between the two approaches can be seen, for example, in the differences between the rousing speech a political candidate gives at a rally attended by his supporters and his more "measured" statements during a nationwide television interview.

The *dissonance-reduction hypothesis* states that when a person's attitudes and behavior are inconsistent with one another, his attitudes tend to shift in the direction of behavior. This insight is part of Leon Festinger's theory of "cognitive dissonance," one of the most influential concepts in modern social psychology. In essence, this theory proposes that people prefer to feel that their beliefs, feelings, and actions are harmonious or "consonant" with each other. When the individual perceives (or is made to perceive) that his attitudes appear to contradict his actual behavior, he experiences a feeling of discomfort or disequilibrium that demands resolution. The reduction of this cognitive dissonance may take some surprising forms. One of the main contributions of Festinger's theory is that it can be used to explain some otherwise puzzling behavior. For example, it explains why a person who is induced to perform a disliked action tends to *increase* his liking for the behavior.

EXPERIMENTAL EVIDENCE

Investigators: J. W. Brehm
Source, Date: "Attitudinal Consequences of Commitment to Unpleasant Behavior," 1960
Location: Yale University
Subjects: Eighth-grade students
Materials: Questionnaires; "dreaded" vegetables

All students were asked to rate how much they liked each of thirty-four vegetables. Later, each was asked individually to estimate the food value ("vitamin content") of one of the vegetables he had reported earlier he disliked. Then each was randomly offered one of the following three conditions: The "low eating" subjects were each persuaded to eat one small dish of his or her dreaded vegetable for an immediate reward of movie tickets or phonograph records. The "high eating" subjects received the same reward but

One cancer you can give yourself.

Horrible isn't it?

AMERICAN CANCER SOCIETY

American Cancer Society

Figure 5. Antismoking campaigns provide dissonance for established smokers.

had to eat the vegetable four or five times in the course of several weeks—a little more each time. The control subjects rated the vegetables and answered the same questions as the others but did not eat the vegetable or receive a reward.

After these conditions had been established, half of each of the three groups was exposed to information in support of eating the disliked vegetable (for example, they were told it was "strong" in vitamins, that one serving furnished 95 percent of daily body-building requirements, etc.). The other half received nonsupporting information (for example, the vegetable was said to be "weak" in vitamins, to contain only 5 percent of body-building nutriments, etc.). All these written statements concerned the "food value" or "vitamin content" of each individual's specific vegetable. Finally, the subjects again completed a questionnaire about the food value of the vegetables and indicated how much they now liked the vegetable.

As dissonance theory predicts, the subjects in the "high eating" condition tended to raise—or at least to resist lowering—their estimates of the food value of the vegetables more than those in the control and "low eating" conditions. In other words, the students tended to believe the supporting information and

disbelieve the nonsupporting information in proportion to the amount of eating to which they were already committed. Their attitudes generally shifted in the direction of their behavior.

The eaters of dreaded vegetables should beware, for the *commitment hypothesis* states that once an individual has accepted a persuasive message slightly, the probability increases that he will accept it fully later. The hypothesis has been confirmed in one of the most interesting reported instances of the application of persuasive techniques to the world of business and selling.

DESCRIPTIVE EVIDENCE

Investigator: J. A. Varela
Source, Date: "Influencing Attitudes and Changing Behavior" by P. Zimbardo and E. B. Ebbesen, 1969
Location: Montevideo, Uruguay
Subjects: Merchandise retailers
Materials: Samples of material, slides, charts, and signs

In April 1968, Juan Diuk, the manager of an upholstery firm in Montevideo, Uruguay, wanted to reduce his inventory of fabric and to sell ready-made curtains to retailers. But retailers traditionally bought new upholstery material only in September. Furthermore, because the sizes of windows in Uruguay are not standardized, most people had their curtains custom-made. Facing these formidable problems, Diuk consulted psychologist Jacobo Varela, who designed a sales program to open up the market. The program involved three main phases.

The first was *getting a foot in the door.* This phase was designed to obtain a minor commitment from the prospective retailer-buyer. Under Varela's supervision, each salesman went to a retail store and asked as a small favor, to display a small sign in the window reading "Coming soon, Pronti-Cort." The sign was not explained to the retailer nor his customers, who regularly asked about it. Thus at the very least some curiosity was aroused. One week later the salesman asked the retailer for a slightly more important favor, namely that he should come to the wholesaler's showroom to learn about the meaning of the sign. In this way, the retailer's behavior was gradually "shaped" by the salesman, and the curtain company gained more and more control of the situation.

Next came *control of the environment.* Once the retailer was in the wholesaler's showroom, the salesman had almost full control of his activities. Well-planned and persuasive presentations could be used and the potential buyers' behavior was closely observed. Whenever a retailer looked favorably impressed, he was immediately asked to express his opinions, thus giving further verbal commitment to his favorable feelings.

The last phase was *getting the buyer to ask a favor.* Although Diuk wanted to sell uncut fabric as well as the ready-made curtains, Varela's sales force did not let the buyers know of this situation, but the fabrics used in the demonstration pictures were purposely quite unusual, and most buyers asked to see the actual cloth. The salesmen acted as if this were an unusual request but, after preplanned hesitation, eventually "gave in" to the "demand." After putting the salesman to "all that trouble" the retailer was almost committed to actual buying.

As a result of this application of psychology to hucksterism the firm, which had sold only 11,000 units in previous Aprils and only 30,000 during the previous September (the traditional buying season), sold 34,000 units in one month. This was far greater than the optimistic estimate of the experienced sales staff when the plan was originally described to them.

Faced with such scientific pitchmen, the retailer was reduced almost to insignificance. Education is perhaps the best counter to these techniques, for most of them are rendered ineffective once the recipient has become aware of what the persuader is doing.

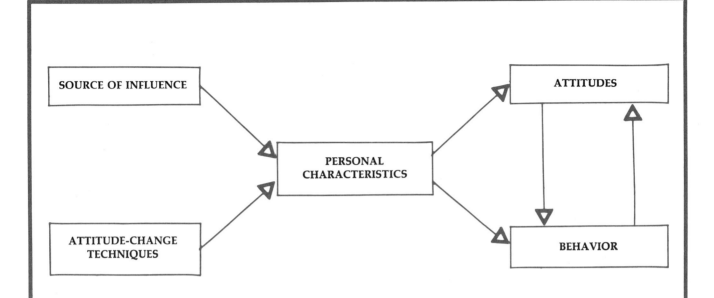

PUTTING IT TOGETHER: Social Influence

How an individual responds to persuasive sources of social influence depends upon the nature of the source of influence and the techniques used.

Those characteristics of *sources of influence* which affect their persuasive power are the selection of information to which the individual is exposed and the credibility of the source, or the authoritativeness with which the source is viewed. There seems to be a leveling effect over a period of time, during which credibility of the source is relatively unimportant if the message got through at all. This phenomenon is referred to as the sleeper effect.

Attitude-change techniques include being subtle about persuasive intentions, presenting both sides of a question, producing behavior which is dissonant with attitudes and obtaining some small commitment in the direction of the desired goal.

The specific effect of various influence sources and persuasive techniques depend upon the *personal characteristics* of the individual concerned. Among these are the need to belong and locus of control. If an individual has strong affiliation with specific reference groups, the attitudes adopted by those groups is highly predictive of attitudes that will be adopted by the individual. If a person perceives himself to be externally controlled, he will be more easily influenced than if he sees himself as being internally controlled.

The resultant *attitudes or behavior* may influence each other. Attitudes are usually thought of as a predisposition to behave in a specific way, but sometimes an individual may behave in ways that are not consistent with his attitudes. In such cases there may be a shift in attitudes to justify the behavior. This attitude shift is one of the possible consequences of dissonance between an individual's attitudes and behavior.

1. WHAT'S ACCEPTED . . .

1. Attitudes can be formed and maintained through conformity to group pressures.

2. The effectiveness of a persuasive attempt depends on the credibility of the source.

3. Prevailing attitudes are related to education and social class.

4. Susceptibility to social influence will depend upon personality characteristics such as locus of control, and affiliation with specific reference groups.

5. In general, presenting both sides of an argument is more effective for persuasion than just presenting one side unless the audience is already committed to a specific viewpoint.

6. Attitudes determine behavior, but behavior also affects attitudes.

7. Persuasion is more effective if you can get the recipient to commit himself a little in favor of the persuasive message.

2. WHAT'S DEBATED . . .

1. In persuasion, how credibility interacts with message characteristics to affect the recipient.

2. Just how "consistent" human behavior really is with attitudes.

3. Under what conditions cognitive dissonance or conformity pressure is primary in attitude change.

4. How much cognitive dissonance individuals can tolerate—especially when they're not aware of inconsistencies between their beliefs and actions.

Psychologists are placed in a difficult position by the fact that modern advertising relies very heavily on the findings of psychological research like that discussed earlier in this unit. As psychologists refine our understanding of the processes of social influence, advertisers will apply these findings, and advertising techniques will become steadily more sophisticated and effective. Unless public representatives or consumer movements such as those founded by Ralph Nader are able to bring about legislative changes to ensure more ethical advertising, psychologists could well find their research into social influence being put to morally questionable purposes by advertisers.

When Richard Nixon decided to run for the Presidency in 1968, his private opinion polls indicated that his prospects for success were bleak. The surveys showed that Nixon's public image was not a favorable one. He was regarded as a "loser," as a dirty campaigner, and as untrustworthy. His advisors recommended that in order to combat this image he should campaign not on his past record, but rather on the basis that he was "a new Nixon." Nixon used the phrase repeatedly during the election, and hired a television expert, Roger Ailes, to put across the message via the mass media.

Ailes recognized that he had a difficult task. As he put it, "Let's face it, a lot of people think Nixon is dull . . . They look at him as the kind of kid who always carried a bookbag . . . Now, you put him on television, you've got a problem right away. He's a funny-looking guy. He looks like someone hung him in a closet overnight and he jumps out in the morning with his suit all bunched up and starts running around saying, 'I want to be President.' I mean, that's how he strikes some people. That's why these shows are important. To make them forget all that." Ailes and his professional advertising assistants coordinated every part of the campaign, carefully "packaging" their candidate and his message for highest public impact. Nixon's final national TV marathon, for example, was arranged to give the impression that the candidate was spontaneously answering questions prepared by his staff and carefully rehearsed. He won the presidency after outspending his opponent by 12.6 million dollars to 7.1 million dollars in media advertising.

Whether the result of the election would have been any different without the attempt to influence the voters by these advertising techniques can never be established. But the issue does highlight the question of the extent to which we are subject to manipulation by media advertisers. The average American spends no less than nine full years of his life watching a television set, during which time he is bombarded with practical applications of most of the principles of mass persuasion that have been identified by psychologists. To what extent are we manipulated by advertisers?

The advertisers certainly believe that they can influence our choices and decisions—it is this belief that keeps the mass media in business. But not all advertising is successful. Some of it unaccountably backfires or has no significant effect. We do know, however, that the method has to be appropriate for the product or viewpoint that is being promoted. Dramatic advertising works best for emotionally neutral products, such as electric toothbrushes, but gentle persuasion works better than drama for changing someone's political attitudes. Militant political or religious groups often neglect this simple fact, and antagonize rather than persuade the public by using language that the hearer does not understand or regards as offensive.

A great deal of advertising in America is more or less dishonest. We are told, for example, that government tests have proved that no other aspirin is more effective than brand X. What the advertiser does not tell us is that the same government test showed that no brand of aspirin was any better or any worse than any other brand. Or we are told that the bread made by a certain manufacturer contains "fewer calories" per slice than the loaves of other manufacturers. What the advertiser does not tell us is that the bread is sliced thinner than the competitor's—the calorie count per loaf is the same.

A good deal of advertising is not really dishonest, but attempts to sell an "image" of the product rather than the product itself. Sometimes this is achieved by using slogans that are appealing but essentially meaningless. For example, potential auto buyers have been urged to invest in a new Pontiac in order to experience the mysterious pleasures of "wide-tracking before you're too old to know what it's all about." Another common method of selling an "image" is to associate the product, which normally would not excite any particular response, with some other quite irrelevant feature, such as a pretty girl, which excites a strong response.

One method of advertising, however, is considered so dangerous and unethical that it has been banned in the United States and most other countries. Termed "subliminal advertising," the method consists of presenting a message so quickly that it is not consciously perceived by the subject. If subliminal advertisements for chocolate are inserted into a film being shown in a movie theatre, chocolate sales are sure to soar during the next intermission.

But we are not so easily manipulated by advertisers as some people might think. Psychologists have found strong evidence that people are very selective in what they perceive and retain; they tend to respond only to information that is consistent with their interests and attitudes. Smokers, for example, are much less likely than nonsmokers to pay attention to anti-smoking advertisements. These advertisements are watched by 60 percent of nonsmokers, compared with 32 percent of smokers. The effect of advertising depends on a whole variety of factors, including the nature of the message, the type of medium employed, the interests and attitudes of the audience, and the prevailing state of public opinion.

Unit 11

Therapy in Groups

OVERVIEW

Various forms of therapy for groups of disturbed individuals are described, and evidence is presented bearing on their actual effectiveness. Four types of therapy are discussed, including traditional group psycho-therapy, psychodrama, token economies, and therapeutic communities. In general, the picture presented by the evidence as well as by the experiences of individual clinical therapists speaks well for group therapeutic methods. The popular encounter group movement is analyzed in the final section.

UNIT OUTLINE

DEFINITION AND BACKGROUND
1. *Definition:* therapy in groups is a form of psychotherapy designed for the treatment of recognizable mental disorders in which personal interaction among group members is the primary therapeutic vehicle.
2. *Background:* J. L. Moreno (1892–1974).

QUESTIONS AND EVIDENCE
1. Do group therapies work?
Hypotheses:
   a. *Psychodrama:* acting out one's problems with other role players can relieve emotional tensions and improve mental well-being. 172
   b. *Group-therapy:* the expression of feelings in emotionally disturbed people to members of a group organized for that purpose may produce personality changes beneficial to mental well-being. 173
2. Can principles be applied in group living to help disturbed individuals make normal adjustments?
Hypotheses:
   a. *Token-economy:* beneficial changes in the behavior of disturbed individuals can be achieved through the proper use of rewards and punishments in a controlled social setting. 176
3. Are therapeutic communities more effective than hospitalization?
Hypotheses:
   a. *Therapeutic-community:* a sheltered but relatively normal environment for disturbed people provides more help with normal adjustment than the artificial environment of a mental hospital. 177

IMPORTANT CONCEPTS

page

depression	170
group therapy	170
hypochondriasis	174
psychodrama	170
role playing	170
sociogram	171
therapeutic community	177
token economy	176

Patients receiving therapy in groups bring with them a variety of backgrounds and personal burdens.

Therapy consists of some form of social interaction with other patients under the general guidance of a therapist.

Maladaptive behavior is frequently brought under control through group cohesiveness and the development of hope and personal confidence.

DEFINITION AND BACKGROUND

Small group sessions usually composed of eight to twelve patients and one or two therapists are often used along with (sometimes instead of) individual psychotherapy. By interacting with a group, a person may learn things about his feelings and behavior that would be much harder to learn by interacting only with a single therapist. For example, a patient may make fine progress in individual therapy exploring his relations with authority figures but need a group of "people like him" to learn more about his feelings toward his brothers, sisters, and other contemporaries.

For this discussion, our DEFINITION of therapy in groups is *a form of psychotherapy designed for the treatment of recognizable mental disorders in which personal interaction among group members is the primary therapeutic vehicle.* The unit will FOCUS not only on traditional group therapies where member interactions are closely guided by a therapist but also on less conventional therapies such as psychodrama, the application of principles of learning, and therapeutic communities as an alternative to hospitalization. Individual therapies are discussed in Unit 20; sensitivity training, which is sometimes described as "therapy for normal people," is covered in Unit 9.

BACKGROUND: J. L. MORENO (1892–1974)

Although group methods did not really come into vogue in the United States until after World War II, there had been several noteworthy experiments with "collective" techniques before that time. In 1905, for example, a Boston physician gave a series of lectures to groups of tuberculosis patients in an effort to relieve their depression. To the doctor's surprise, patients said that, though the health tips offered in the lectures were all well and good, the positive impact of the experience came mainly from being brought together in groups—that is, from realizing that they were not alone and could still enjoy themselves.

A more deliberate attempt at group therapy came in 1910 or so, when J. L. Moreno, a Viennese medical student in his early twenties, began group counseling with children, prostitutes, and displaced persons from World War I. An inventor and experimenter as well as a trained psychotherapist, Moreno introduced some

Figure 1. Jacob L. Moreno, founder of the form of group therapy known as psychodrama.

imaginative innovations into his professional practice, teaching, and clinical work. In a precedent-setting venture in 1921, he staged Vienna's first "Theater of Spontaneity"—actors presented dramas without rehearsal, improvising their parts as they went along.

After settling in the United States in 1925, Moreno founded the "Impromptu Theatre" at Carnegie Hall. He began to publish a magazine called *Impromptu,* and he experimented with other forms of avant-garde art (one project was called the "living newspaper"). He also invented "radio film," electromagnetic sound recordings that were, in principle at least, a precursor of today's tape recordings. And, last but not least, he devised two procedures that had a significant influence on the study and practice of group dynamics: psychodrama and the sociogram.

Psychodrama is a form of group therapy in which a patient is given the "leading role" and urged to act out, or live through, certain real-life situations, problems, fantasies, fears, or whatever occurs on the spur of the moment. The lead role is totally unrehearsed, and a supporting cast—usually trained assistants of the therapist but also unrehearsed—reacts to the lead's spontaneous actions or remarks through responses improvised on the spot.

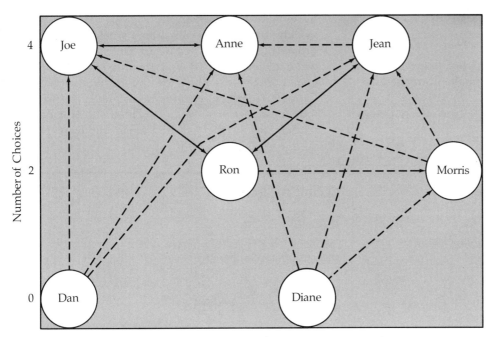

Figure 2. A sociogram: arrows indicate responses to the question "which three people do you like the most?" in a small group of seven people. (Dotted arrows indicate one-way liking, solid arrows two-way liking.) Sociogram can provide information about the structure of a group depending on what question is asked.

Often, the patient plays himself, but sometimes the therapist asks him to take the role of someone with whom he has problems—father, mother, wife—while another "actor" plays the patient. Some explosive situations result. Ideally, the patient develops considerable insight—he can hardly avoid gaining some understanding of the position of the person he is playing or fail to benefit from the chance to see his own behavior, as portrayed by someone else, from a perspective other than his own. The therapist serves as stage director, guiding or simply following the action on stage as the situation seems to demand.

According to Moreno and his followers, the therapeutic value of psychodrama comes from the process itself. Like the interplay of character and event in any well-designed drama, the main character and the cast work through staged but nevertheless vividly real problems. The patient causes others to react to him, learns to evaluate his relations and reactions to others, and gradually gains freedom of expression and personal insight. Psychodrama also raises questions that the patient and the therapist or the group can discuss after each session: "How did you feel when your father lashed out at you? You stepped back so far I thought you were going to fall off the stage." "When he said you'd married a slut, why didn't you get mad?"

Group therapy itself has developed along many lines besides those initiated by Moreno, and the particular characteristics of the person and his problem dictate which method is selected. Group therapy can be used with children, adolescents, or adults; with hospitalized persons or outpatients; with people suffering from psychoses, neuroses, or even less chronic problems of functioning in family or marriage situations. As long as the basic ingredients of support, sense of community, and increased personal responsibility remain, a therapeutic group experience can help bring about a speedy recovery. Although critics sometimes maintain that the relationships formed in such groups are apt to be transitory and superficial, many group therapies have had very promising outcomes. In addition, they provide real economies of time and money for both patient and therapist.

QUESTIONS AND EVIDENCE

1. Do group therapies work?

2. Can learning principles be applied in group living to help disturbed individuals make normal adjustments?

3. Are therapeutic communities more effective than hospitalization?

Seventy-two patients participated in thirty-nine weekly, one-hour psychodrama sessions. The typical group (the groups varied in size and membership from week to week) consisted of about twenty-five patients and a dozen members of the hospital ward staff. Patients from other wards occasionally participated. After the sessions, eight psychiatrists who had not participated in the psychodramas but were respon-

QUESTION   1. DO GROUP THERAPIES WORK?

HYPOTHESES	PSYCHODRAMA	GROUP THERAPY
DESCRIPTIVE EVIDENCE	ASSESS: effects of role playing on adjustment	ASSESS: changes in MMPI scores after group psychotherapy
EXPERIMENTAL EVIDENCE	VARY: opportunity to role-play MEASURE: change in smoking behavior	VARY: group vs. no therapy; ward organization MEASURE: personality change

1. DO GROUP THERAPIES WORK?

The idea that the spectator's emotional responses to a drama can release his inner tensions and fears (catharsis) has been a major part of dramatic theory since Aristotle first introduced it in the fourth century B.C. Freud explored the psychoanalytic implications of the idea in his studies of the Oedipus complex, but Moreno was the first to apply it to clinical practice. By making the untrained and unrehearsed spectator the major character in his dramas, he went a step beyond Hamlet's famous plan of action: "The play's the thing/wherein I'll catch the conscience of the king." The *psychodrama hypothesis* states that acting out one's problems with other role players can relieve emotional tensions and improve mental well-being.

DESCRIPTIVE EVIDENCE

Investigators: M. L. Solomon and K. C. Solomon
Source, Date: "Psychodrama as an Ancillary Therapy on a Psychiatric Ward," 1970
Location: Jewish General Hospital, Montreal, Canada
Subjects: 72 hospitalized mental patients also undergoing individual therapy
Materials: Questionnaires; process notes taken down during sessions.

sible for the patients' individual psychotherapy answered questionnaires on whether psychodrama had improved the patient's emotional expressiveness, contact with reality, social functioning, sexual identification, insight into his own problems, and so on.

Information was also obtained from "process notes" taken down largely verbatim by an observer during the psychodrama sessions. A patient's responses in psychodrama were classified under three headings—affective (emotional), relational, and social. Affective responses were divided into two categories, those focused on oneself (a "happy-sad" scale) and those directed toward others (a "love-hate" scale). Thus, euphoria, laughter, and satisfaction were scored H plus, whereas guilt, despair, and depression were scored H minus; tenderness, compassion, and "support of others" were rated L plus, whereas rejection and hostility were rated L minus. Relational responses, which referred to the patient's attitudes were similarly categorized. Social responses were categorized according to whether a patient's role playing concerned a family, hospital, or community context.

Although this investigation did not isolate the effects of psychodrama from those of individual therapy and general hospital treatment, and therefore cannot support any firm conclusions, the results did indicate that psychodrama had been helpful, especially to patients who discussed the experience later with their therapists and to those who had participated actively. For example, the more emotional and realistic the patient's behavior seemed to have been during the psychodrama sessions, the more improvement his psychiatrist found in his general behavior. The helped group (forty-seven out of the seventy-two subjects) tended especially to have expressed more emotion during the psychodramas, including both negative and positive feelings; the not-helped group was less expressive and the process notes showed lower scores on both the happy-sad and the love-hate scales. In the next experiment, a "psychodrama" was used not as therapy for disturbed patients but to test the effects of emotional role playing on a particular behavior: heavy smoking.

EXPERIMENTAL EVIDENCE

Investigators: I. L. Janis and L. Mann
Source, Date: "Effectiveness of Emotional Role Playing in
*   Modifying Smoking Habits and Attitudes," 1965*
Location: Yale University
Subjects: 26 women 18–23 years old
Materials: Attitude questionnaires; information about the
*   dangers of smoking*

To maximize the emotionality of the situation, fourteen women who each smoked at least fifteen cigarettes a day were asked to play the chief character in five scenes involving a person who discovers she has lung cancer. Through a clever arrangement of conditions and careful wording of information, none of the subjects was ever aware that she was participating in a psychological study. The experimenter played the role of a physician and directed the conversation. The twelve other women, who served as controls, did not role play but were given the same information about the dangers of smoking (in pamphlets and so on) that the "physician" used in the experimental group.

Before the experiment, all the subjects filled out an attitude questionnaire containing fifteen items about smoking and lung cancer. At the end of the experi-

ment, they all answered the same questions again, this time in a larger questionnaire that disguised its real purpose. Finally, two weeks after the experiment was over, the investigators telephoned each subject to "talk about the study" (whose real purpose was still unknown to the subjects) and, as if it were an afterthought, asked whether the subject's own smoking behavior had changed in any way.

At the beginning the two groups did not differ significantly in their opinions. But the postexperimental data indicated that the women in the experimental group had not only changed their attitudes toward smoking on the questionnaire but had actually decreased their cigarette consumption by an average of 10.5 cigarettes per day. This result was not attributable to a few extreme cases: most of the fourteen women were smoking less. The control group had also decreased its average consumption, but by only 4.8 cigarettes. The investigators concluded that the fear and anxiety aroused by their role-playing experiences led the experimental subjects to cut down their smoking. These results were obtained without any suggestions to the subjects that they "should" reduce their smoking or change their attitudes.

The methods used in this study might be very useful in further investigations of psychodrama. Although not much research has been done on it, psychodrama has spread and has many devotees in the professional community. Most therapists who use it claim that the emotionality of the situation brings about effective changes in personality.

As the Janis-Mann study shows, role playing is not restricted to the specifically theatrical structure of psychodrama. One of the major advantages of group therapy is that it gives the patient an opportunity, missing in individual treatment, to try out various ideas and modes of behavior on a sympathetic group. Once a person's "problem" has been isolated, he will probably be encouraged by the other members of the group to express his feelings in their presence. The group-therapy hypothesis states that the expression of personal feelings in emotionally disturbed people to members of a group organized for that purpose may produce personality changes beneficial to mental well-being. One big advantage of group therapy is that finding out that other people have problems like—or worse than—your own reduces anxiety and encourages the open exploration of sensitive areas.

DESCRIPTIVE EVIDENCE

Investigator: L. C. Mone
Source, Date: "Short-Term Psychotherapy with Postcardiac Patients," 1970
Location: American Foundation of Religion and Psychiatry, New York
Subjects: 12 male, 2 female postcardiac patients
Materials: MMPI scales, personal interviews

Fourteen patients who had recently experienced heart attacks attended ninety-minute group sessions once a week for ten weeks. Before and after these sessions the patients took the Minnesota Multiphasic Personality Inventory (MMPI), which measures a variety of personality characteristics ranging from introversion and extroversion to schizophrenic tendencies. (See Unit 15.)

At first the group as a whole refused to talk about death or the heart. But as the sessions progressed, a few themes—fear of death, helplessness, depression, and abandonment—repeatedly came up and were explored thoroughly. Comparison of the two MMPI administrations indicated a definite decrease in the participants' hypochondriasis (physical complaints) and depression scores over the ten-week period. Later interviews of individual patients led Mone to conclude that short-term group therapy can facilitate the rehabilitation of depressed cardiac patients.

The next experiment went farther—comparing the effects of different forms of social interaction on the behavior of disturbed patients under carefully controlled conditions.

EXPERIMENTAL EVIDENCE

Investigators: W. H. Coons and E. P. Peacock
Source, Date: "Interpersonal Interaction and Personality Change in Group Psychotherapy," 1970
Location: Ontario Hospital, Hamilton, Ontario, Canada
Subjects: 28 male, 28 female mental patients
Materials: Wechsler Adult Intelligence Scale, Rorschach inkblot test, Hospital Adjustment Scale

In this well-controlled study, mental patients were randomly assigned to four experimental groups for a six-week period, with seven males (or seven females) in one group of each type. By carefully varying two factors—whether or not a patient received formal group psychotherapy sessions and whether his or her everyday interactions with other patients in the ward were organized or random (organized, as in most mental hospitals)—the specific groups shown in Figure 3 were formed.

Random, **With therapy**	**Organized,** **With therapy**
Random, **No therapy**	**Organized,** **No therapy**

Figure 3. Experimental conditions of the study by Coons and Peacock (1970).

The goal of such group activities as eating together, sleeping in the same dormitory, and participating in recreational and occupational therapy together under the direction of a staff nurse among the organized ward interaction groups was to promote and develop high group cohesiveness outside the formal psychotherapy milieu.

Both before and after the experimental period all patients took the Wechsler Adult Intelligence Scale (a standard adult IQ test) and the Rorschach inkblot test. In addition, ward staff members who were familiar with the day-to-day behavior of specific patients filled out the Hospital Adjustment Scale (HAS)—a list of ninety statements describing hospitalized behavior to which they indicated "true," "false," or "does not apply" relative to each patient.

The HAS has been shown to be effective in distinguishing patients approaching discharge from a mental hospital from those who are still very disturbed.

The overall results showed that formal group therapy alone was more effective in producing beneficial change on all three criterion measures than was any other treatment or combination of treatments. Moreover, the patients in the therapy groups themselves reported that they were less depressed and felt better. Whether a ward was organized in its activities or left uncontrolled apparently made no difference. A possible reason for this would be that the professional group therapist and staff nurses had somewhat conflicting goals: ward staff tend to view "good patients" as those who conform to rules and regulations; pro-

therapy is better for all patients than individual therapy is.

To the relief of hospital administrators, group therapy also provides a way to ease the burden on mental hospitals. Given the shortage of trained personnel and the vast number of patients, state institutions provide minimal comforts at best. They rarely offer any consistent, effective encouragement for specific behavior patterns or achievements (though open physical aggression is always prohibited). Patients frequently lose hope when they discover that there is no generally accepted "method" of gaining discharge from the hospital. Their behavior may deteriorate as a result, and they may gradually move to the "back wards" containing many patients who cannot even take care of their own physical and sanitary needs.

QUESTION	2. CAN LEARNING PRINCIPLES BE APPLIED IN GROUP LIVING TO HELP DISTURBED INDIVIDUALS MAKE NORMAL ADJUSTMENTS?
HYPOTHESIS	TOKEN ECONOMY
DESCRIPTIVE EVIDENCE	ASSESS: discharge rate where token economy is used
EXPERIMENTAL EVIDENCE	VARY: token economy vs. hospital ward MEASURE: behavior change

fessional therapists tend to define improvement in terms of greater independence of action.

Many other studies support the contention that group therapy is an effective way of dealing with problems and emotional difficulties. It is a very popular method for treating disturbed adolescents, perhaps because people of that age are extremely responsive to the reactions of their peers. On the whole, the research seems to offer a more positive picture for group than for individual psychotherapy, though that conclusion, even if correct, does not mean that group

2. CAN LEARNING PRINCIPLES BE APPLIED IN GROUP LIVING TO HELP DISTURBED INDIVIDUALS MAKE NORMAL ADJUSTMENTS?

Much of the overload problem in mental hospitals stems from a lack of funds and professional staff, but an increasing number of mental-health workers have recently begun to criticize the system itself. They point out, for example, that nurses and other ward attendants may inadvertently encourage psychotic behavior because it is the only kind they pay attention to. On a busy ward, a patient tends to be ignored when he goes about his business in a relatively normal, untroublesome manner. But when he "acts crazy," people respond: if a patient refuses to feed himself, a nurse feeds him; if he throws things, an orderly stops him; if he talks about voices that threaten him, someone may lend a sympathetic ear. This sort of attention can maintain the very behavior that the hospital wants the patient to stop displaying.

In a pioneering study done in 1959, Ayllon and Michael tried to reverse this situation by training ward nurses to reinforce approximations of normal behavior instead of psychotic acts. For example, the nurses were told to ignore the delusional statements of a certain patient, since their efforts to be kind or helpful by listening seemed to be encouraging the patient's psychotic talk, and instead to respond with interest and pleasure whenever the patient made a normal remark. The technique was remarkably effective; similar ones were used to encourage self-feeding and to discourage a number of disruptive behaviors. (A similar experience by Ayllon is described in Unit 27.)

The use of reward and punishment need not be restricted to individuals. Groups of persons as well as individuals can be rewarded, punished, condemned, and provided with appropriate models. Sociologists and social psychologists have long stressed the desirability of viewing individual behavior within its broader social context. The *token economy hypothesis* states that beneficial changes in the behavior of disturbed individuals can be achieved through the proper use of rewards and punishments in a controlled social setting.

For example, a mental hospital ward can be reorganized so that each patient is expected to "work" (that is, to behave in relatively desirable ways) for the things he receives—food, clothing, privileges, and the like. Instead of simply being granted them by the staff, he must earn them. The term "token economy" is used to describe such plans. For instance, if a patient makes his bed in the morning, he receives a token that he can trade for breakfast, cigarettes, outdoor privileges, and so on. A system of this kind is therapeutic because it encourages patients to assume greater responsibility and to develop more normal behavior patterns that may eventually lead to discharge from the hospital.

DESCRIPTIVE EVIDENCE

Investigators: J. M. Atthowe, Jr., and L. Krasner
Source, Date: "The Systematic Application of Contingent Reinforcement Procedures (Token Economies) in a Large Social Setting: A Psychiatric Ward," 1968
Subjects: 60 chronic schizophrenic male patients
Materials: Tokens

This investigation took place in a "closed" ward—one that severely restricts the movements of seriously disturbed patients. Many of the patients in the ward had been hospitalized for more than twenty-five years. The experimenters designed a token economy that affected virtually every aspect of the patients' lives. It included both rewards for good behavior and fines for undesirable behavior like bedwetting.

Before the eleven-month program began, it was carefully explained to the patients. At first, tokens were given immediately when a patient did something desirable; social behaviors and activities that approximated work were especially highly rewarded. Later, a delayed-reward system was instituted, so that each patient was "paid" only once a week. If a patient earned enough tokens, he was even awarded a "credit card," which he could use for such things as special passes that allowed him to leave the ward.

During the eleven-month period, it was possible to discharge twice as many patients from the ward as had been discharged in the preceding eleven months. The use of passes quadrupled; one man was able to leave the hospital grounds for the first time in forty years. In addition, infractions of hospital rules declined sharply and attendance at group meetings and group-therapy sessions increased.

Another experiment along the same lines compared a traditional ward with an experimental one where a token economy was in effect.

EXPERIMENTAL EVIDENCE

Investigator: G. W. Fairweather and colleagues
Source, Date: "Social Psychology in Treating Mental Illness," 1964
Location: Veterans Administration Hospital, Palo Alto, Calif.
Subjects: Two wards of seriously disturbed male patients
Materials: Questionnaires; observed behavioral changes

The two wards were matched for such variables as diagnosis and length of hospitalization of their patients. In the control ward, the established hospital patterns prevailed, but the experimental ward was divided into four groups and managed by the patients themselves. In each group, the patients were responsible for administering their own treatment and for "managing" one another's behavior. "Money" (tokens) was distributed by the hospital staff for "acceptable" behavior. Each patient could increase his earnings by moving up through "levels" that demanded ever more rational behavior. In addition to the individual rewards, each group as a whole was

There are still few such programs, and they are all relatively new. Furthermore, it is difficult to separate the effects of tokens themselves from the accompanying social rewards: a patient may develop a better relationship with a staff member who rewards him. And because the rate of return to the hospital after participation in a token economy is not always low, some question remains whether this kind of treatment effectively prepares patients for the "real world." Nevertheless, it seems more useful than many of the established methods of treatment—and considerably better than mere custodial care, which is all that many patients get.

QUESTION 3. ARE THERAPEUTIC COMMUNITIES MORE EFFECTIVE THAN HOSPITALIZATION?

HYPOTHESIS	THERAPEUTIC COMMUNITY
DESCRIPTIVE EVIDENCE	ASSESS: effects of therapeutic living on self-care abilities
EXPERIMENTAL EVIDENCE	VARY: therapeutic community vs. hospital living MEASURE: attitudes toward authority; observed adjustment

rewarded for the overall plans it developed, adding certain social rewards to the straightforward token economy.

The experiment lasted twenty-seven weeks, with a six-month follow-up. It showed that experimental patients spent fewer days in the hospital, stayed out a greater length of time, and achieved better employment records than those from the control ward. A questionnaire given to all patients revealed that those in the experimental ward thought, more often than other patients, that they had been helped in the hospital principally by their fellow patients. Severely disturbed individuals who had vegetated for years in the regular hospital environment were brought back to contact with reality and changed their behavior to more acceptable modes.

3. ARE THERAPEUTIC COMMUNITIES MORE EFFECTIVE THAN HOSPITALIZATION?

Perhaps it would be better for some patients not to be hospitalized at all. The *therapeutic-community hypothesis* states that a sheltered but relatively normal environment for disturbed people provides more help with normal adjustment than the artificial environment of a mental hospital.

Although the concept of a therapeutic community is not new, there has been a rebirth of interest in it in recent years, partly stimulated by the community-health movement. The members of a therapeutic community take as much responsibility as possible for deciding what behavior is acceptable to the group, and for figuring out how to persuade people to live up to the group standards. Professional doctors, nurses, and aides serve as advisers and resource personnel, not as absolute authorities. Group and individual therapy may be available, but only as optional aids, not as primary treatments. The idea is to gear the patients' life to reality rather than to the isolated conventions of a hospital setting.

One research team found a model for such a community in the Hutterites, an isolated, Anabaptist religious sect who live in the American Midwest. Descended from German stock, the Hutterites advocate pacifism, adult baptism, communal ownership of property, and simple living without luxuries, which they regard as sinful.

How does the Hutterite culture deal with mental illness? Although it does not prevent mental disorders, it provides a highly therapeutic atmosphere for their treatment. The onset of a symptom serves as a signal to the entire community to demonstrate support and love for the patient. Hutterites do not approve of the removal of any member to a "strange" hospital except for short periods to try shock treatments. All patients are looked after by the immediate family. They are treated as ill rather than "crazy." They are encouraged to participate in the normal life of their family and community, and most are able to do some useful work . . . No permanent stigma is attached to patients after recovery. The traumatic social consequences which a mental disorder usually brings to the patient, his family, and sometimes his community are kept to a minimum by the patience and tolerance with which most Hutterites regard these conditions. [Eaton Weil, 1967]

Figure 4. A halfway house for drug rehabilitation functions on principles of the therapeutic community. Members of such communities take as much responsibility as possible for deciding what behavior is acceptable to the group, and for determining how to persuade members to live up to group standards.

Not all therapeutic communities are as gentle as the one the Hutterites provide. At Synanon and some other communities for drug addicts, for example, the members are required to play the "Synanon game," in which the people in a group challenge each other to admit—and to give up—the games they have played all their lives. Scorn and contempt are legitimate techniques in the Synanon game, which often reduces people to tears. And yet Synanon, like other therapeutic communities, provides a highly supportive environment and has made it possible for many "hopeless cases" to lead active) useful lives.

DESCRIPTIVE EVIDENCE

Investigators: G. W. Fairweather and colleagues
Source, Date: "Community Life for the Mentally Ill:
    Alternative to Institutional Care," 1969
Location: Portland, Oregon
Subjects: Mental patients
Materials: Observations of behavior changes, self-sufficiency

On a given day a group of institutionalized patients who had volunteered to do so moved from the mental hospital to a lodge within the community. In early stages, a researcher acted as a supervisor, but later, as the group made progress, he was replaced by a layman. The patients assumed total responsibility for running the lodge, getting food, cooking, making money, and monitoring each other's behavior.

Finally, as the group adjusted more and more to the community and their situation in it, it was decided that a handyman service would be the project for the entire group. At first the "outside" community resisted their service, but the business was gradually accepted and earned a total of $50,000 in its first three years of operation. The group became completely self-sufficient, and each man secured his share on the basis of his productivity and responsibility. Importantly, the lodge society significantly increased their employment level and length of time out of the hospital. Of special interest is the fact that although long-term mental-hospital patients in traditional aftercare settings do not usually fare well, in the lodge setting they reached a relatively high level of self-support.

The following study directly compared traditional and innovative methods—the effects of therapeutic community treatment versus those of hospital ward treatment.

EXPERIMENTAL EVIDENCE

Investigator: A. Miles
Source, Date: "Changes in the Attitudes to Authority of
    Patients with Behavior Disorders in a Therapeutic
    Community," 1969
Location: A hospital in Southampton, England
Subjects: About 60 male patients with personality disorders
Materials: Questionnaires; personal interviews; psycho-
    metric data

All of the patients had long-term behavior problems and had, at some time in their lives, been convicted of criminal offenses, mostly stealing and sexual offenses. One of their major difficulties was coping with authority figures, whether policemen or hospital staff personnel. At the start of the study, forty patients were placed in the experimental community and given complete authority over their own ward. Another twenty patients with similar backgrounds (the control group) stayed in a ward of a traditional mental hospital. Psychometric measures, questionnaires, and personal interviews with the patients were administered before the start of the study and one year later.

Although none of the control subjects showed changes on any of the measures used over the one-year period, the attitudes of the experimental subjects altered noticeably. Their responses to authority figures—especially the staff—improved considerably. In their interviews and on questionnaires, they showed much more understanding of the function of the staff in relation to themselves.

The traditional hospital ward setting can be dehumanizing and demeaning to the individual. By labeling him as "sick," the hospital often fosters just such an attitude within himself; a patient who believes he is a chronic schizophrenic is likely to act like one (see Unit 2). On the other hand, if a disturbed person is able to interact with others socially and to behave "normally," he may fulfill a different set of expectations. Mental-health professionals have just begun to tap the full range of responsibilities that can be accepted by people with severe emotional problems.

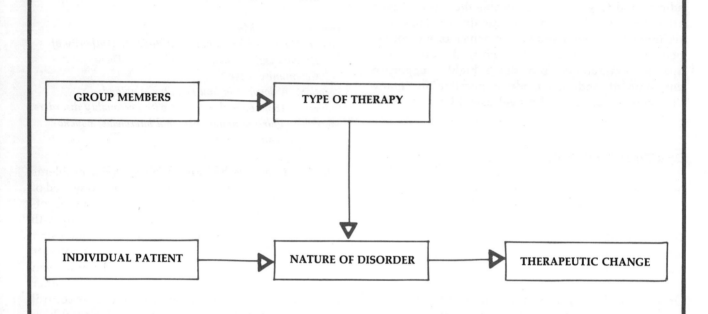

PUTTING IT TOGETHER: Therapy in Groups

Group psychotherapy for an *individual patient* may be viewed primarily as interaction among each patient and other *members of the group*.

The nature of the interaction depends upon the *type of therapy* used. Some forms of group therapy focus on developing insight. These include psychodrama, role playing and sensitivity training. Other forms of group therapy are directed at modifying behavior. These include token economy and the therapeutic community.

The effectiveness of any specific therapy is dependent upon how well the group members interact and the *nature of each individual's disorder*.

Therapeutic change in group therapy usually involves a strengthening of personal confidence and hope in the future.

WHAT'S ACCEPTED AND WHAT'S DEBATED

1. WHAT'S ACCEPTED . . .

1. Role playing can help to change behavior and relieve emotional tensions.

2. Group psychotherapy is an effective means of treating mental disorders.

3. Principles of instrumental learning and reward are effective in changing the behavior of groups of disturbed individuals toward normal life adjustment.

4. Self-management and patient-centered responsibility are much preferable to custodial care for mental patients.

2. WHAT'S DEBATED . . .

1. In what precise way, with what processes, social interactions actually succeed in helping patients.

2. Whether learning and rewards change behavior without resolving the patient's deeper problems; that is, whether changes are temporary or permanent.

ISSUE: ENCOUNTER GROUPS

As we have seen in this unit, therapy in groups is accepted as an effective method for treating psychological problems. A recent development, the encounter group, originally intended as a means of therapy for disturbed individuals, has lately become so popular that many people now see it as a social movement, a massive cult of the American middle class. All over the country, people who regard themselves as basically normal are flocking to encounter groups. Their motives differ. College students are using the experience as a means of increasing awareness of self and others. Feminists are using the groups to exchange information on their own personal experiences and to build sisterhood. Corporations are packing off their executives to encounter groups as weekend retreats, in the hope that the businessman can be "humanized" to meet the demands of changing social values. Prisons and halfway houses for juvenile delinquents are using encounter groups as a means of lending mutual support to those who seek personal improvement.

Encounter groups vary a great deal in their methods and goals, but there are certain common features. An encounter group must be relatively small to be effective. The best size seems to be about a dozen people. An encounter group usually has an experienced leader, someone who has a clear idea of the goals of the group and the best means of achieving them. The styles of leaders differ considerably. One study reported that "some of the leaders believe passionately in love; others just as passionately in hatred . . . Some leaders depended solely on talk-therapy; others used music, lights, the touch of human bodies . . . The leader of one group . . . believed that a person must experience basic rage. He was skilled at including this state, and he had an uncanny ability to sense what would provoke a particular person to anger . . . The onslaught looked like sheer madness, but the leader of this group was a skilled tactician who knew what to do, when to do it, and when to stop."

Many of those who have participated in encounter groups regard them as a profoundly liberating and enlightening experience through which they have learned more about themselves and others. They hold a deep faith that the group experience was a significant and important part of their lives, one that helped solve personal problems and provided ways of solving other problems in the future. But not everyone praises encounter groups.

One critic, Sigmund Koch, regards the encounter group with contempt: "The group movement is the most extreme excursion thus far of man's talent for reducing, distorting, evading and vulgarizing his own reality . . . It seems to court spontaneity and authenticity by artifice; to combat instrumentalism instrumentally, to provide access to experience by reducing it to a neuter-pap commodity; to engineer autonomy by group pressure; to liberate individuality by group sharing." Another critic, Kurt W. Back, regards the encounter movement as an outgrowth of a large, rich bored middle class that has no particular beliefs in anything and is running out of ways to get excitement. He sees the rush to encounter groups as a modern crusade. The old shrines, such as the churches, have lost their magic, but people still seek some quasi-mystical experience and hope to find it in group encounters.

One aspect of the groups that deeply concerns psychologists and psychiatrists is the so-called "casualty rate." In many if not most groups, there are people who find the intensive soul-searching and group examination of innermost secrets deeply disturbing. Some of these people drop out of the groups, but others struggle on and may be severely damaged in the process. A lifetime of carefully constructed defenses against emotional pain may be stripped away, and none replaced, and the person may leave the group in far worse condition than before.

Morton Lieberman, Irvin Yalon and Matthew Miles paid particular attention to the "casualty rate" when they conducted an extensive survey of the successes and failures of encounter groups. They found that some 9 percent of the participants could be classified as failures. This is a disturbingly high rate. It means that on the average there is a casualty in practically every group. In fact, the casualty rate may be much higher, because the researchers used very conservative standards in defining casualties. Group members were included in this category only if they showed evidence of serious psychological harm six to eight months after the group experience, and only if this harm could reasonably be attributed to what had happened in the group. The researchers were also very worried when they found that the judgment of the group leaders about casualties was extremely unreliable. In fact, ordinary group participants were much better than group leaders at identifying the members who were getting hurt.

Lieberman and his associates found that some 19 percent of the group members experienced negative changes as a result of their experience. This figure would indicate that the number of group members whose problems were worsened is nearly twice as high as in traditional psychotherapy. And although 65 percent of group members interviewed immediately after the encounter believe that lasting positive change has taken place, the belief seemed to be short-lived in many cases. Half of the subjects interviewed six to eight months later rated it useless or worthless.

Although most psychologists admit that encounter groups can be very valuable, they would probably agree with Lieberman's feelings about the future of the movement: "Encounter groups are less effective than individual psychotherapy in changing individuals and somewhat more likely to cause damage . . . Encounter groups present a clear and evident danger if they are used as radical surgery to produce a new man. The danger is even greater if the leader and the participants share this misperception. If we no longer expect groups to produce magical lasting change and if we stop seeing them as panaceas, we can regard them as useful, socially sanctioned opportunities for human beings to explore and express themselves."

Part II
individual
behavior . . .
being a unique person

12. Intelligence

13. The Disordered Mind

Intelligence and mental illness are among the most familiar concepts in psychology. Though the measurement of *Intelligence* is often considered a major accomplishment, psychologists are not sure precisely what intelligence is. Research has generated controversy over group differences in measured intelligence and the relative contributions of heredity and environment. Similar controversy surrounds the concept of mental illness, or *The Disordered Mind*. Many factors affect the genesis of mental disturbances, including genetic and physiological anomalies, abnormal upbringing, deprivations in early infancy and maladaptive learning experiences. Presently, social and interpersonal development form the largest group of known determinants of mental disorders. However, many questions remain about the basic causes of even some of the most common mental disturbances.

14. Using Language

15. Personality

16. Children's Thinking

The growing and maturing child progresses from simplicity and dependence to complexity and independence. The development of the capacity for *Using Language* results from the interaction of maturing internal processes with the child's linguistic environment. During child development many factors, internal, environmental and social, contribute to the gradual formation of *Personality,* the constellation of traits and behaviors that uniquely distinguish each individual. Intellectual development during childhood proceeds through a number of stages until *Children's Thinking* eventually reaches the highly abstract and complex operations of adult thinking.

17. Signs of Emotion

18. Problem Solving and Creativity

Feelings are often plainly expressed as *Signs of Emotion* in one's face, gestures and bearing. Though we may not ordinarily think of these signs as information, each of us reacts to such signs (in ourselves and others) in terms of the meanings and interpretations we assign to them. Thus, signs of emotion can serve as nonverbal communications that both enrich and complicate our lives. Information processing also occurs within the brain during *Problem Solving and Creativity,* thinking and reasoning directed toward some desired solution or toward generating unique ideas. Such thinking apparently involves many different factors operating at once, including perceiving, attending, learning, remembering and using language.

19. Hypnosis

20. Therapy for Individuals

Most of us don't like to think of our behavior as being controlled, but sometimes a degree of external control is desirable or necessary. With *Hypnosis,* control usually comes about with the individual's permission. Though modern psychology has brought hypnosis into the laboratory for study, many basic questions—what it is, how it works—remain largely unanswered. When the individual can no longer control his behavior within the range of behaviors that society considers acceptable, one recourse is to seek professional help from clinical psychologists or psychiatrists specializing in the many kinds of *Therapy for Individuals* who are mentally disturbed.

Unit 12

Intelligence

OVERVIEW

What are some of the things that psychologists have learned about intelligence since they first began to devise accurate ways to measure it about seventy years ago? The unit ranges over tests and measurements, how intelligence changes over time, and the genetic versus environmental controversy with respect to racial and ethnic differences in intelligence as it is measured by tests.

UNIT OUTLINE

DEFINITION AND BACKGROUND
1. *Definition:* intelligence is general mental ability, especially the ability to think rationally, use memory and knowledge, and adapt to new situations.
2. *Background:* Alfred Binet (1857–1911).

QUESTIONS AND EVIDENCE
1. What do intelligence tests really measure?
   Hypotheses:
   - a. *Two-factor:* intelligence consists mostly of a single general ability, with secondary or "special" abilities that are peripheral to this general factor. **191**
   - b. *Multifactor:* intelligence consists of a number of independent special abilities.
2. Can intelligence be changed?
   Hypotheses:
   - a. *Stability:* measured intelligence stays about the same throughout an individual's lifetime. **193**
   - b. *Genetic:* intelligence is inherited. **195**
   - c. *Environmental:* variations in surroundings will produce predictable differences in intelligence. **196**

3. Do races and ethnic groups differ in intelligence?
   Hypotheses:
   - a. *Racial-genes:* observable intellectual differences between races are genetically determined. **197**
   - b. *Deprivation:* blacks are largely deprived in childhood of the cultural materials that would challenge and stimulate their mental potential. **199**
   - c. *Ethnic-pattern:* ethnic groups show different patterns of mental abilities, and different levels of ability within groups are determined by socioeconomic position. **201**

IMPORTANT CONCEPTS

	page
chronological age (CA)	**188**
correlation	**191**
cross-sectional study	**194**
factor analysis	**192**
general intelligence	**191**
intelligence	**188**
intelligence quotient (IQ)	**188**
longitudinal study	**194**
mental age (MA)	**188**
reliability	**190**
Stanford-Binet Intelligence Scale	**189**
validity	**190**
WAIS	**190**
WISC	**190**

Genetic endowment and environmental events interact in intellectual performance.

Intelligence may be defined in many ways and tests can be created to measure any definition of intelligence.

The mental abilities displayed by an individual are dependent upon the tests used, motivation, and the nature of the testing situation.

DEFINITION AND BACKGROUND

Defining intelligence is a perpetual problem for psychologists. Some refuse to call it more than "whatever IQ tests measure." Others provide this DEFINITION: intelligence is *general mental ability, especially the ability to think rationally, use memory and knowledge, and adapt to new situations.* All agree that intelligence is not an absolute measure of a person's ability, much less a yardstick of his worth. It remains a theoretical construct, whether it is defined operationally, as a test score that is compared to other test scores, or conceptually, as general mental ability. IQ (Intelligence Quotient) is an indication of how well a person performs on a standardized intelligence test. It is arrived at by dividing the mental age (MA), determined by the person's performance on the test, by the chronological age of the person and multiplying by 100. The formula for arriving at the IQ, then is $\frac{M.A.}{C.A.} \times 100$. It is important to remember that IQ is a measure of relative performance. Unlike the more measurable attribute of weight—which can be determined by the pound—intelligence is measured by comparison. FOCUS in this unit will be on how psychologists have gone about conceptualizing and testing intelligence and on variations in IQ over time and from group to group. The last section of the unit examines the controversy, flamed anew in the 1970s, regarding the social implications of inferences made from IQ test scores.

BACKGROUND: ALFRED BINET (1857–1911)

In 1904, the government of France appointed a commission to work on the problem of subnormal children in schools. The government wished to identify and eliminate from the "normal" schools those children who could not benefit from further instruction. Binet, a leading psychologist at the time, became active in the commission's work.

His initial interest in developing standardized "norms" originated from his observations of a confusing variability when doctors tried to group and educate school children, and when administrators were asked to help with such decisions or come up with plans for improvement or reform. Trained in medicine, fascinated by palmistry and other arcane practices, Binet came to disagree with the direction re-

Figure 1. French psychologist Alfred Binet developed the first standardized test to measure school children's intelligence, as distinct from acquired knowledge.

search on the measurement of intelligence had taken. Most people in the field were investigating sensorimotor measures of mental ability: strength of hand pressure, quickness of hand movement, time taken to react to a sound, judgment of time elapsed, and the like. These measures proved to be unfruitful as predictors of what most people considered intelligent behavior. Particularly bright people did not turn out to be especially quick-handed, and particularly quick-handed people did not turn out to be especially bright. Binet also wondered why, for example, his own two daughters, both doing well in school, nevertheless went about their studies very differently and achieved different kinds of success.

Collaborating with a team of colleagues at the Sorbonne, Binet established age grading as an essential criterion for a direct test of intelligence. In other words, he noted that, on the average, children's intelligence increased with age—eleven-year-olds seemed more intelligent than ten-year-olds, ten-year-olds than nine-year-olds, and so on. The experimenters therefore designed tests to identify the apparent average ability for each age. Then they assumed that those who performed below the average for their age were less intelligent, and those who performed above, more intelligent.

Binet realized that one kind of test was not enough, given differing forms of intellectual aptitude. His research team went on to develop a battery of test items, thirty in all, graded for difficulty. The most basic item tested a child's ability to follow a lighted match as it was moved across his field of vision. Others tested ability to imitate movements or to construct sentences including three words ("Paris," "gutter," and "fortune," for example). To establish the average ability for each group, Binet used this scale with fifty children of each age from three to eleven. Then he arranged the items in such a way that, for example, a normal five-year-old could pass only the first fourteen items, and a retarded five-year-old, only the first eight.

Known eventually as the *Binet-Simon scale* (in recognition of the assistance of psychiatrist Theophile Simon), this test proved to be a genuine scientific breakthrough. It provided a relatively quick, simple, and inexpensive measure of intelligence that could be used to predict the probable success of a child in school and to reveal which children might need special schooling. Tests modeled on Binet's came to be used around the world. The intelligence quotient (IQ), developed later by Wilhelm Stern, is a well-known adaptation of Binet's successful attempt to measure intelligence.

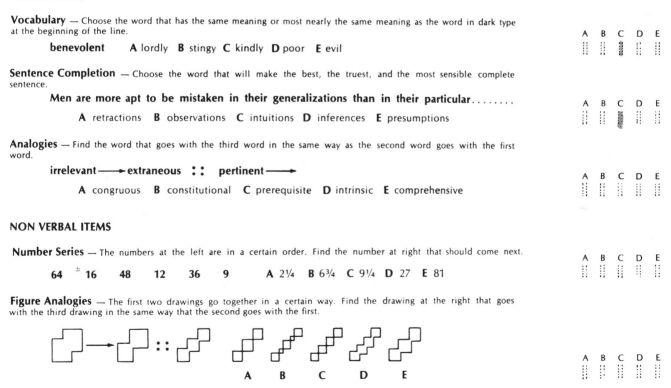

VERBAL ITEMS

Vocabulary — Choose the word that has the same meaning or most nearly the same meaning as the word in dark type at the beginning of the line.

benevolent   A lordly B stingy C kindly D poor E evil

Sentence Completion — Choose the word that will make the best, the truest, and the most sensible complete sentence.

Men are more apt to be mistaken in their generalizations than in their particular........

A retractions B observations C intuitions D inferences E presumptions

Analogies — Find the word that goes with the third word in the same way as the second word goes with the first word.

irrelevant ⟶ extraneous ∷ pertinent ⟶

A congruous B constitutional C prerequisite D intrinsic E comprehensive

NON VERBAL ITEMS

Number Series — The numbers at the left are in a certain order. Find the number at right that should come next.

64   16   48   12   36   9   A 2¼ B 6¾ C 9¼ D 27 E 81

Figure Analogies — The first two drawings go together in a certain way. Find the drawing at the right that goes with the third drawing in the same way that the second goes with the first.

A   B   C   D   E

Figure 2. Sample items on a group-administered intelligence test illustrating a small portion of the variety of abilities tested.

Courtesy Irving Lorge, Robert Thorndike and Houghton Mifflin Company.

QUESTIONS AND EVIDENCE

1. What do intelligence tests measure?
2. Can intelligence be changed?
3. Do different races and ethnic groups differ in intelligence?

Before we attack the problem of what IQ tests measure, it is necessary to explain something about how they are scored and about the criteria used to evaluate the quality of psychological tests. The Stanford-Binet Intelligence Scale for Children (SBIS), the American version of Binet's test, includes a number of items appropriate to each chronological age (CA). The test for each age group starts with items below the subject's CA level and works toward more difficult items until the subject misses a number of problems in a row. The subject's mental age (MA) is then calculated by assigning month credits for correct answers, each correct answer adding slightly more mental age. The design of such tests is a challenge over which generations of researchers have labored, and the simple lists of problems are the highly polished work of many people.

If a test is a good one, (as the Stanford-Binet Scale is), it has been tried and retried until it conforms to a number of exacting criteria. First of all, the test must fit the people who take it. A test that involves putting differently shaped blocks in the appropriate holes will reveal little about a group of twelve-year-olds, while a vocabulary test using such words as "apocryphal" or "Machiavellian" will be of no use with a group of kindergarteners. To prevent this kind of inaccuracy, a good test is *standardized*: each item on the Stanford-Binet has been administered to a large number of children of different ages and then carefully age-graded according to the average age of the children who get it right.

Furthermore, each item on the test must contribute consistently to the score. This is called *discrimination power*. If the item is relatively difficult, most of the average or below-average children should get it wrong. If an item is supposed to be easy, all but the dullest must answer it correctly.

The test must also be reliable. *Reliability* is a term used by psychologists to describe the consistency of a test. A good test should yield consistent scores over time: a person should get nearly the same score if he takes the test on two different occasions. In addition, the test should have internal consistency: a person should score about the same on, say, the odd-numbered and the even-numbered items.

Note that the circumferences of your toes could be a reliable measure of your intelligence, as long as they remained the same from day to day. If you were subject to a swollen big toe during occasional attacks of gout, the test would not be reliable. And, in any case, the toe-test would not meet the final criterion of a good test: validity. *Validity* refers to the extent to which a test measures what it is supposed to measure. If, like most intelligence tests, a test is meant to measure ability to succeed in school, then it must actually do so. One way to assess the validity of a test is to observe the behavior of the people tested and see if it corresponds to predictions based on their scores. The Stanford-Binet IQ test, assessed that way, turns out to be a highly valid test. That is, IQ test scores are excellent predictors of school performance.

Another widely used IQ test is the *Wechsler Adult Intelligence Scale (WAIS),* devised by David Wechsler in the 1930s. It is structured differently from the Stanford-Binet, for it includes six subtests on a verbal scale and five on a nonverbal performance scale. This scale is the individual test most often used to test adults' intelligence; there is also a Wechsler Intelligence Scale for Children (WISC) patterned after the WAIS. These tests, like the Stanford-Binet, meet all four criteria of a good test.

Today, IQ tests are no longer scored exactly as they were in Binet's day. The test scores are now called *deviation IQs,* which means that a person's score is calculated in terms of how far his raw score (simply the number of correct answers) deviates from the average raw score of the normative sample (adult Americans, say). The average raw score of the normative sample at each age level is 100, simply because psychologists have chosen the number as a convenient and traditional average value. So, if a subject scores 100 on the test, it means that his score falls in the middle of the distribution of scores: he did better than 50 percent of the normative sample. The relation between IQ scores and actual percentile (the percentage of normative sample below the subject's score) is given in Figure 3. For example, an IQ of 115 on the SBIS means that the subject did better than about 84 percent of the normative sample.

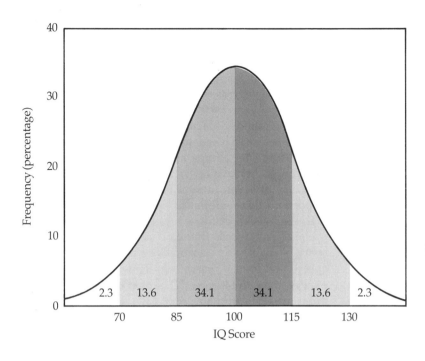

Figure 3. Normal distribution of IQ. IQ tests are constructed so that the average score of the population is 100. This distribution shows percentages of people scoring above and below the average.

QUESTION	1. WHAT DO INTELLIGENCE TESTS MEASURE?	
HYPOTHESES	**TWO FACTOR**	**MULTIFACTOR**
DESCRIPTIVE EVIDENCE	ASSESS: correlations between pairs of ability tests	ASSESS: correlation between each ability test and all the others taken as a whole
EXPERIMENTAL EVIDENCE		

1. WHAT DO INTELLIGENCE TESTS MEASURE?

As it is measured today, then, IQ is basically the expression of a statistical procedure. But what property of the mind do the tests measure, and what does it do?

An intelligent person seems to be able to solve all kinds of problems quickly and easily. He has the power to perform well no matter what the circumstances. He is able, he has the power, he can perform, he has great ability. Then the mental property of intelligence may be ability.

The *two-factor hypothesis* states that intelligence consists mostly of a single general ability, with secondary or "special" abilities that are peripheral to this general factor.

DESCRIPTIVE EVIDENCE

Investigator: C. Spearman
Source, Date: "The Abilities of Man," 1927
Location: University of London
Subjects: Many groups of subjects over many years of study
Materials: Variety of mental-ability tests

Spearman began with the observation that if someone does well on one intelligence test, he is likely to do well on another: the scores will correlate highly. He set himself the task of explaining such correlations, which occurred not only between scores on apparently similar tests but between scores on tests of such different abilities as mathematical ability and "creativity."

When there were only two tests, only one correlation was necessary. But if there were, say, twenty tests, each test had to be correlated with every other test, and the mass of correlations had to be organized meaningfully. Spearman used factor analysis to reduce the complex field to a set of groups (or "factors"). He then restudied his original test items to determine the primary ability that underlay each factor.

Ultimately, Spearman decided that one ability, which he labeled *g* (for "general ability") was consistently related to many tests in his battery. He therefore proposed that *g* is at the heart of intelligence. But he also noted that, although some tests demand a lot of *g*, others do not. The latter tests tend to tap special abilities in such areas as mechanics. These were labeled *s,* and Spearman concluded that intelligence as a whole consists of only two measurable factors, *g* and *s.*

On the face of it, however, isn't Spearman's "general ability" component of intelligence abstract and hard to pin down? Given that intelligence is basically such a general ability under any conditions, how is it related to such special abilities as mathematical and mechanical abilities? These abilities can be observed, but who has observed general ability? Perhaps intelligence is no more than many special abilities.

The *multifactor hypothesis* states that intelligence consists of a number of independent special abilities.

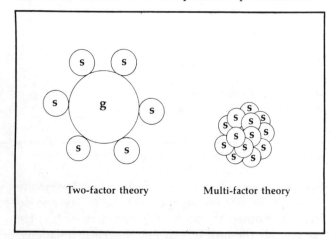

Two-factor theory   Multi-factor theory

Figure 4. Psychologists have offered varying theories of intelligence. The *two-factor* theory proposes that intelligence consists mostly of a single general ability (g), with secondary or "special" abilities peripheral to this general factor. The *multi-factor* theory proposes that intelligence consists of a number of independent special abilities.

DESCRIPTIVE EVIDENCE

Investigator: L. L. Thurstone
Source, Date: "Primary Mental Abilities," 1938
Location: University of Chicago
Subjects: Many groups of subjects over many years
Materials: A large variety of ability tests

By 1938 methods of factor analysis more complex than those Spearman used ten years earlier made it possible to consider a huge number of test correlations in one comprehensive operation. Thurstone argued that a battery of seven mental tests summarized the most important dimensions of general intelligence. He identified seven primary mental abilities: verbal comprehension, word fluency, number manipulation, space visualization, associative memory, perceptual speed, and logical reasoning. This is a more complex picture than the single IQ score, because the seven different tests are not very highly correlated; however, they still correlate well enough that a high score on one tends to predict a high score on another. Thurstone's work, though it does not disconfirm the existence of Spearman's *g*, is usually interpreted as implying that intelligence is not a single factor but a number of independent ones, each of equal value.

Thurstone's results are an advance on Spearman's in the sense that they reflect a more sophisticated level of test design and mathematical analysis. Further refinements have recently been made by J. P. Guilford, who has used a much greater vocabulary of test items and factor analytic methods. In 1967 Guilford, whose more ambitious research aims to find the "structure of the intellect," proposed that intelligence consists of 120 independent abilities. In Figure 5, they are catalogued according to the three dimensions of his structure:

1. *Contents:* Tasks or problems to be solved. They may be spatial, symbolic, semantic, or social.

2. *Operations:* The methods by which the contents are processed by the intellect. This category includes cognition (discovery), memory, judgment, and convergent and divergent production. The last two terms, which are also being used in other fields of psychology, refer to two different sorts of problems. Convergent production is used with a problem that has only one correct answer, as when two figures are multiplied. Divergent production is involved when many different answers must be provided, as in naming possible uses of a brick.

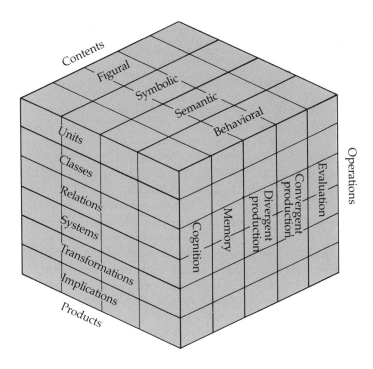

Figure 5. Guilford's structure of the intellect (1967), catalogued in three dimensions. *Contents* are tasks or problems to be solved. *Operations* are the methods by which the contents are processed by the intellect. *Products* are the results of operating on the contents. Guilford proposed that intelligence consists of 120 independent abilities, although only 82 had been discovered and described in 1967. His theory has influenced the practical design of intelligence tests.

3. *Products:* The results of operating on the contents. These range from simple units, classes, and relations to more complex systems, transformations, and implications.

Though Guilford's work has had an impact on the practical design of tests, its theoretical nature is revealed by the fact that only 82 of the 120 postulated abilities had actually been discovered and described by 1967. The model itself is a somewhat arbitrary but imaginative arrangement of the data.

With more improvements in methodology and test items, an energetic researcher might soon demonstrate that intelligence consists of 500 or 1,000 factors. In any case, it is clear by now that intelligence tests can and do measure a wide range of specific abilities, whether one general ability underlies them or not.

2. CAN INTELLIGENCE BE CHANGED?

If intelligence consists essentially of a general ability or of only a few primary abilities, it might be part of the skeleton structure of the mind, unchanging and perhaps inherited. If, however, intelligence consists of numerous specific abilities—like social ability, cognitive ability, and logical ability—some or all of these might be affected markedly by the individual's experience.

The *stability hypothesis* states that measured intelligence stays about the same throughout an individual's lifetime. IQ tests themselves are designed to have high reliability when used over short periods of time, but what happens to an individual's IQ over a period of, say, twenty years?

QUESTION	2. CAN INTELLIGENCE BE CHANGED?		
HYPOTHESES	**STABILITY**	**GENETIC**	**ENVIRONMENTAL**
DESCRIPTIVE EVIDENCE	ASSESS: changes in measured intelligence over time	ASSESS: correlations of twins and siblings raised together and raised apart	
EXPERIMENTAL EVIDENCE			VARY: 1. environment for maze-bright and maze-dull rats 2. teaching programs MEASURE: 1. maze learning performance 2. school and IQ test performance

DESCRIPTIVE EVIDENCE

Investigators: N. Bayley and colleagues
Source, Date: "Behavioral Correlates of Mental Growth:
Birth to 36 Years," 1968
Location: University of California at Berkeley
Subjects: 54 adults over 36-year period
Materials: Variety of ability measures, including the WAIS

Whereas most research in intelligence compares different age groups at the same time (cross-sectional studies), this famous investigation is longitudinal. It began early in the 1930s with an assessment of the intellectual abilities of fifty-four infants. At the ages of sixteen, eighteen, twenty-one, and twenty-six these fifty-four subjects took the Wechsler-Bellevue Tests of Adult Intelligence, a predecessor of the WAIS, which they took at thirty-six. This long-term survey yielded the following general conclusions:

1. Intelligence varied considerably in the infant and early childhood years, with females being somewhat more consistent than males. (One reason for this may be that children's IQ tests measure different kinds of abilities at different periods of development, though that leaves unexplained the relative stability of the girls' scores.)

2. The only ability factor in infancy that was related to later intellectual level was a "verbal knowledge" or "vocalization" factor—tested, for example, by instructing a subject to place a block "in," "on," "under," or "behind" something. This factor was predictive for females only—but it was predictive all the way to thirty-six years of age.

3. From ages sixteen to thirty-six verbal IQ increased slightly, while performance IQ increased from sixteen to twenty-six, then declined slightly. Overall IQ stayed the same (Figure 6).

Bayley's work is not without weaknesses. One is that her subjects were all generally above average in their test scores, which casts some doubt on the accuracy of her results for the population as a whole. In another study she found that very intelligent subjects actually tend to rise in intelligence from one test to the next, even into old age. Whatever the interpretive problems of some of this research, however, this and other studies have shown that IQ usually remains very stable over long periods of time.

Many permanent human properties run in families, so there are such family resemblances as general appearance and color of hair and eyes. Sometimes

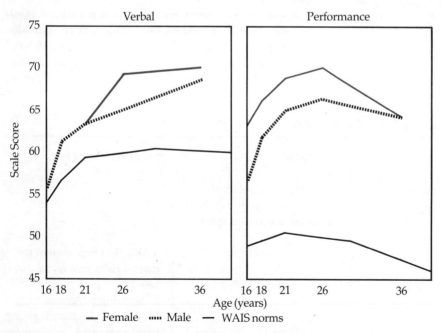

Figure 6.   Data from the Berkeley Growth Study: as subjects grew older, their verbal IQs tended to rise slightly, while performance IQs tended to decline after age twenty-six. Adapted from Bayley (1968).

individual family members may be strikingly different, too. So it makes sense to ask whether or not the stable abilities of intelligence run in families.

The *genetic hypothesis* asserts that intelligence is inherited. This idea is a difficult one to test, because anyone old enough to take a test is already a complex product of inherited traits and learned behavior. The classic, and perhaps the only convincing, way of approaching this problem is by comparing the IQs of identical twins raised together and those of identical twins raised apart from birth. Identical twins raised together have the same genetic inheritance and, it is assumed, the same experiences; identical twins raised apart have the same inheritance but different environmental experiences. If intelligence is inherited, it should be as similar in twins raised apart as it is in twins raised together. In fact, if genetics is the *only* factor involved, the IQs of identical twins should always be identical.

DESCRIPTIVE EVIDENCE

Investigators: L. Erlenmeyer-Kimling and L. F. Jarvik
Source, Date: "Genetics and Intelligence: A Review," 1963
Location: Columbia University
Subjects: 99 pairs of subjects, from previous studies
Materials: Correlational data from 52 previous studies

The 99 pairs of subjects included identical twins (twins from a single egg), fraternal (two-egg) twins, and siblings. The studies that were analyzed used many different measures of intelligence and derived their data from samples varying in size, age, ethnic composition, and socioeconomic class. The data had been collected in eight countries on four continents, and it covered two generations of subjects.

Although the data presented some difficulties—for example, there was no way of knowing how different the various environments of the subjects were—the results of this survey showed some important consistencies (Figure 7). In general, the studies showed that the closer the genetic link between individuals, the closer their IQ scores will be. In particular, it stated that the correlation of IQs for identical twins raised together is plus .87; for those raised apart, it is plus .75. Correlation is measured on a scale of minus 1 to plus 1; if two groups of people have identical IQ scores, the correlation between their scores is plus 1.00. These high positive correlations for identical twins suggest that they have nearly the same intelligence, whether raised together or not.

This evidence does *not* show that IQ is totally

Figure 7. Summary of data from 52 studies: the correlation of intelligence between pairs of people tends to rise as they share closer genetic relationships. Adapted from Erlenmeyer-Kimling and Jarvik (1963).

Category		Correlation Coefficients	Groups Included
Unrelated persons	Reared apart		4
	Reared together		5
Foster parent, child			3
Parent, child			12
Siblings	Reared apart		2
	Reared together		35
Twins — Two-egg	Opposite sex		9
	Like sex		11
Twins — One-egg	Reared apart		4
	Reared together		14

inherited, however, nor that surroundings are powerless to affect IQ. For example, the surroundings of the identical twins raised apart apparently influenced their IQs enough to make them correlate less strongly than those of identical twins raised together.

The evidence *does* support the inference that heredity is a more accurate predictor of IQ than upbringing. If one thinks of heredity as potential ability, one can say that environment determines the extent to which that potential is fulfilled, setting the upper limit to actual intellectual growth. Then heredity and environment are not opposed principles but different factors that interact to make people what they are.

The *environmental hypothesis* states that variations in surroundings will produce predictable differences in intelligence. Generations of rats pass much more quickly than human generations, and selective breeding of rats and restriction of their environments can be controlled to an extent taboo with human subjects. So rats were used in the following experiment on the relative effects of genetic and environmental factors on learning ability.

EXPERIMENTAL EVIDENCE

Investigators: R. M. Cooper and J. P. Zubek
Source, Date: "Effects of Enriched and Restricted Early Environments on the Learning Ability of Bright and Dull Rats," 1958
Location: University of Manitoba, Canada
Subjects: Two strains of inbred rats
Materials: Mazes

One of the two strains of rats was "maze-bright," or clever at finding its way through a maze, while the other was "maze-dull." After several generations of breeding bright with bright and dull with dull rats, each strain was divided into three groups. One group was raised in a restricted environment with little variation or stimulation, another in a moderately stimulating environment (regular laboratory cages), and the third in a stimulating environment filled with colored objects and playthings. Then, as adults, all the rats were tested in mazes.

As Figure 8 shows, the rats from the normal laboratory cages reflected hereditary differences in learning the mazes. The bright strain averaged only 120 errors as against 168 for the dull strain. But significantly closer scores were recorded for the other

two environmental groups. Both strains from the restricted environment made about 170 errors, and both strains from the stimulating environment averaged between 110 and 120 errors. The study demonstrates very clearly the interdependence of heredity and environment: extreme environments can override genetic factors, while a moderately stimulating environment seems to give much freer rein to hereditary factors.

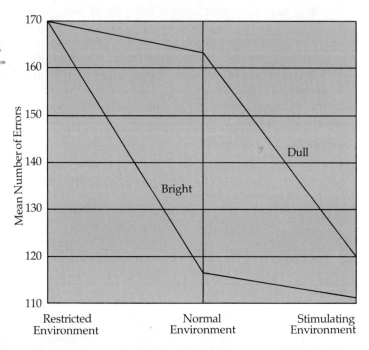

Figure 8. The interaction between genetic potential and environment is expressed in these results from the experiment by Cooper and Zubek (1958). When rats are raised in a normal environment, the genetically maze-bright rats make fewer errors than maze-dull rats. But when the rats are raised in restricted or stimulating environments, genetic differences between strains of rats seem to make little difference for maze performance.

Still, rats are not people, maze-brightness is not intelligence, and laboratory cages are not "real life." The practical, human significance of the nature-nurture question appears in the problem of improving the intellectual abilities of children growing up in a disadvantaged environment—living conditions in which children are not exposed to many challenging objects and experiences.

EXPERIMENTAL EVIDENCE

Investigator: M. B. Karnes
Source, Date: H. H. Spicker, "Intellectual Development Through Early Childhood Education," 1971
Location: University of Illinois
Subjects: Preschool children

Karnes measured the effects of five different kinds of teaching or "intervention" programs for "disadvantaged" children in Illinois. When the children started instruction, all were four years old. Instruction continued for one year, with each child in one of the following programs (italics indicate the crucial differences):

1. Traditional preschool. The familiar nursery school curriculum: unstructured free play, arts and crafts, storytelling, games; *incidental and informal opportunities for learning.*
2. Community integrated. The same as the traditional preschool, except the children who attended included *not only disadvantaged but middle-class children.*
3. Montessori. An emphasis on the *development of perceptual and motor skills and visual discrimination* through a series of tasks in which the child manipulates toys and other materials; little emphasis on language or verbal training.
4. Ameliorative. A cognitive approach that seeks to develop *intellectual and verbal skills* by solving problems in language, memory, and conceptual thinking.
5. Direct verbal. An approach emphasizing *pattern drills and rote* in the areas of language, arithmetic, and an initial teaching alphabet.

The results showed that three programs—those using traditional, ameliorative and direct verbal methods—produced statistically significant IQ and language gains compared with community integrated and Montessori programs. These differences probably reflect the amount of emphasis placed on verbal interaction between teacher and child. By the second year the children in the improved groups were at the same grade level as their middle-class peers. It appears that IQ is malleable to some degree, at least in early childhood, and that some methods are more effective than others.

When the question of intelligence among the "disadvantaged" is coupled with observed racial differences, it becomes heavily laden with emotional and social implications. It is essential to remember that studies in this area—whether they deal with genetic factors, environmental quality, or socioeconomic considerations—always deal with averages. They say nothing whatsoever about any particular individual.

3. DO RACES AND ETHNIC GROUPS DIFFER IN INTELLIGENCE?

The *racial-genes hypothesis* states that observable intellectual differences between races are genetically determined.

DESCRIPTIVE EVIDENCE

Investigator: W. A. Kennedy
Source, Date: "A Follow-up Normative Study of Negro Intelligence and Achievement," 1969
Location: Florida State University
Subjects: 1,800 black children in five Southern states
Materials: IQ tests; IQ test norms for white children

QUESTION	3. DO RACES AND ETHNIC GROUPS DIFFER IN INTELLIGENCE?		
HYPOTHESES	RACIAL GENES	DEPRIVATION	ETHNIC PATTERN
DESCRIPTIVE EVIDENCE	ASSESS: 1. black-white IQ difference 2. black-white differences in specific learning skills	ASSESS: relation of environmental deprivations to black-white IQ differences	ASSESS: relation of ability patterns of different ethnic groups to socioeconomic classes
EXPERIMENTAL EVIDENCE			

The average IQ test score of white children was found to be 101.8. The average score of the black children tested in the study was 80.7 (see Figure 9). A follow-up study showed that the IQ differences did not change over a five-year period.

In 1966, A. M. Shuey published a survey of 380 studies containing data on the IQs of blacks and whites. The studies revealed that the white average consistently exceeded the black average by ten to fifteen IQ points. The larger difference found in the Kennedy study may be due to the fact that he compared the test scores of Southern black children with those of white children from all parts of the country; on the average, both Southern blacks and Southern whites score lower than blacks and whites from other regions.

The existence of an average black-white IQ difference is not heavily debated, but the real question remains: What accounts for it? (The black-white difference is used here mainly because the article described below helped stimulate a tremendous amount of interest in it. It should be pointed out that there are also average IQ differences between other groups—not only South/North, as mentioned above, but middle class/lower class, and city/suburban/rural.)

DESCRIPTIVE EVIDENCE

Investigator: A. R. Jensen
Source, Date: "How Much Can We Boost IQ and Scholastic
*   Achievement?" 1969*
Location: University of California, Berkeley
Materials: Data from many previous studies using IQ tests

In a hotly debated article in the *Harvard Educational Review*, Jensen proposed that the black-white IQ difference stems from a difference in learning abilities that is genetically determined.   He reportedly found that black children seem to be better at associative and rote learning, whereas white children are better at more abstract reasoning and learning. One of the

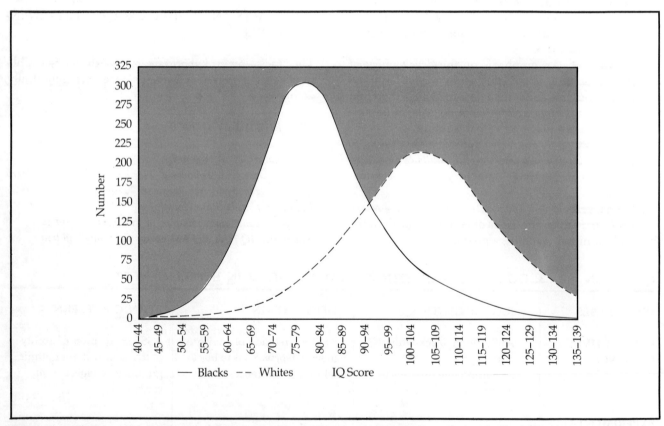

Figure 9. Difference in IQ distributions for black vs. white children, from a study by Kennedy (1969). The difference in means for the two distributions is about 21 points, one of the most extreme differences reported.

central points that he tried to make was that this kind of genetic difference could explain why so many Head Start programs had failed.

This article stirred up immediate and violent reactions. Though its arguments are largely based on complexities of genetic theory, a few of Jensen's points can be summarized here. It appears that the IQ difference persists even when comparisons are made between whites and blacks of the same socioeconomic status. Furthermore, the gap between American Indians, despite poor schooling, and whites is not as pronounced as that between blacks and whites. Jensen also noted that American schools are geared to the very sort of learning that white children are best equipped to handle. But he still argued that genetic factors are responsible for the lower black educational potential. Jensen's study has been severely criticized by a number of social and behavioral scientists. They question the data on which Jensen based his conclusions. This data was largely taken from the reports of

other investigators, some from as far back as 1943. Many have also questioned the statistical methods by which he drew his inferences.

The general feeling among many people—psychologists, educators, government officials, and laymen alike—runs contrary to the racial-genes hypothesis. The differences in IQ, in this view, are likely the result of environmental effects, including a multitude of social, historical, and socioeconomic conditions. This view stresses that whatever a person's genetic endowment, it develops from potential into performance only through interaction with the environment.

The *deprivation hypothesis,* which fits with this view, holds that blacks are largely deprived in childhood of the cultural materials that would challenge and stimulate their mental potential. A variation on this theme refers not to deprivation but to *cultural differences.* Many blacks in the United States belong to a subculture with its own values, beliefs, and goals,

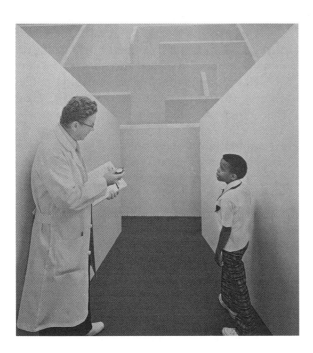

Figure 10. Children from minorities attend schools oriented toward white, middle-class values. In this white world IQ tests are constructed by white people, geared toward white values, and administered primarily by white personnel.

which are different from those of the white middle class. Perhaps because of their different values, black children may not feel that IQ is very important and, consequently, may not try as hard on the tests as white children. Perhaps the black culture stresses accomplishments other than the verbal and abstract skills that figure so largely in white-oriented schools and tests. Perhaps the tests, standardized primarily on whites, are unfairly biased against other racial groups. Many possible environmental arguments, which support and extend the deprivation hypothesis, can be based on evidence like the following.

DESCRIPTIVE EVIDENCE

Investigators: W. Bodmer and L. L. Cavalli-Sforza
Source, Date: "Intelligence and Race," 1970
Location: Stanford University School of Medicine
Materials: Data from previous studies

This alternative to Jensen's genetic argument uses most of the same data. Its rebuttal to Jensen's points about the matching of black socioeconomic status with white and about American Indian test results gives the gist of its position.

It is difficult to see how blacks and whites can be compared even when they are from the same socioeconomic class, say the researchers, for "It is impossible to accept the idea that matching for (socioeconomic) status provides an adequate, or even a substantial, control over the most important environmental differences between blacks and whites." Furthermore, American Indians "typically go to schools where whites are in the majority, which is not the case for most of the schools attended by black children." According to the Coleman Report, a major survey of educational achievement published in 1966, attending a school where more than half the students come from middle-class homes (which almost always means a predominantly white school) is *the* major factor in determining whether the achievement of the average black child at the school matches that of the average white (Coleman, 1966).

The report noted some facets of the black environment that might affect test scores. IQs of blacks are usually higher when tested by blacks. The white test administrators might be prejudiced, or their presence may intimidate the black children. Furthermore, the tests themselves may be culturally biased, since they are designed by whites and standardized on white children.

Bodmer and Cavalli-Sforza also point out that socioeconomic differences are correlated with dietary deficiencies in the lower classes. Such deficiencies affect brain growth and therefore probably intellectual development, they argue. It is also possible that the cultural heritage of slavery and continued discrimination affects the home environment of black children to such an extent that their mental growth is seriously stunted. Family emotional climate is particularly crucial in early childhood.

It is difficult to conclude that environmental deficiencies can explain *all* the differences between blacks' and whites' IQs. After all, very little is known about the effect of various facets of the environment on individual development. The social implications of the question are summed up by Richard Goldsby, a black biologist from Yale, in his book *Race and Races:* "It is not extreme to suggest that whichever hypothesis is correct, a belief in the environmental one is likely to lead to social policies aimed at the expansion of opportunities and the inclusion of racial minorities whereas subscription to the genetic one could produce a policy of contraction and exclusion."

Further observations have provided evidence for quite a different hypothesis than those stressing either genetic or environmental determination of IQ. The various abilities involved in intelligence may be assembled in different potential combinations inherited by different ethnic groups and their actualization determined by socioeconomic factors. This is the *ethnic-pattern hypothesis,* which states that ethnic groups show different patterns of mental abilities, and that different levels of ability within groups are determined by socioeconomic position.

DESCRIPTIVE EVIDENCE

Investigators: G. S. Lesser, G. Fifer, and D. H. Clark
Source, Date: "Mental Abilities of Children from Different Social Class and Cultural Groups," 1965
Location: New York City

Subjects: 80 Chinese, 80 Jewish, 80 Negro, and 80 Puerto Rican six- and seven-year-old children
Materials: 4 mental ability tests

Each group of eighty subjects was divided into two subgroups according to socioeconomic status—forty middle-class children and forty lower-class children. Four mental ability scales were developed for use in the study, to test verbal skill (vocabulary), reasoning, numerical ability (arithmetic), and space conceptualization (for example, jigsaw puzzles). The experimenters went to great lengths to assure that the tests were not culturally biased: the instructions were translated into each language, reading and writing were not required as part of the test, and the test administrator was always from the same ethnic group as the child tested. Exhaustive tryouts of the vocabulary items certified cross-cultural equivalence.

As the results shown in Figure 11 demonstrate, the different groups did show different patterns of abili-

ties. For example, Chinese children did best on reasoning and spatial abilities; Jewish children did best on verbal and numerical abilities. Note, however, that the differences in pattern are larger when one compares the lower-class children in the four groups than when one compares the middle-class children, and that within each group the middle-class children consistently scored higher than did the lower-class children. The biggest difference between socioeconomic levels occurred among the black children, where the middle-class group surpassed the performance of the lower-class group by a wide margin. A final interesting finding is that, within each ethnic group, the ability patterns of boys differed from those of girls.

The origin of these ability pattern differences is not a factor in this experiment. But the prospect of replacing the traditional single IQ score with a more complex profile of mental abilities is promising—and reminiscent of the work by Spearman and Thurstone with which this discussion of intelligence began.

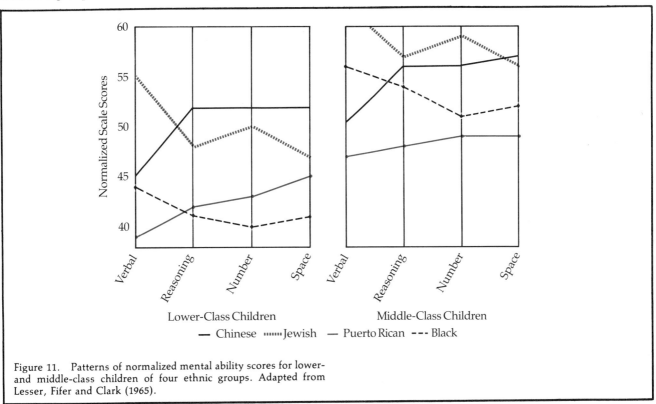

Figure 11. Patterns of normalized mental ability scores for lower- and middle-class children of four ethnic groups. Adapted from Lesser, Fifer and Clark (1965).

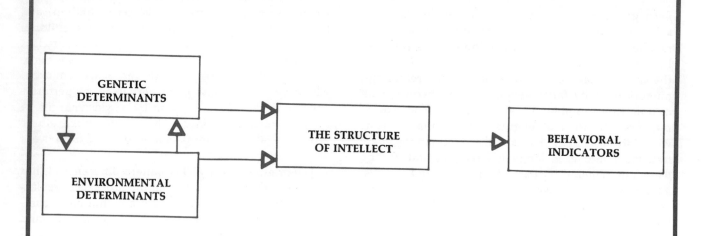

PUTTING IT TOGETHER: Intelligence

Intelligence is more easily defined abstractly than concretely. There is general agreement that intelligence is the ability to think rationally, use information and adapt to new situations, but there is considerable disagreement about what activities represent these constituents of intelligence. When constructed appropriately, intelligence tests serve as fair predictors of performance for specific activities within the culture for which they are devised.

Taken together, most evidence indicates that *genetic and environmental determinants* interact to form intelligence, which remains fairly stable after early childhood. When comparing racial and ethnic groups, statistical differences in intellectual patterns emerge, but debates continue about whether these differences reflect genes, early environmental deprivations or cultural emphases.

There are several points of view concerning *the structure of intellect*, ranging from Spearman's two-factor notion to Thurstone's primary mental abilities and Guilford's proposal of 120 abilities that can be catalogued in three dimensions.

While debates rage about the structure of intellect and its determinants, we continue formally or informally to make inferences and predictions about people's mental abilities from such *behavioral indicators* as IQ test scores, school performance and occupational abilities.

WHAT'S ACCEPTED AND WHAT'S DEBATED

1. WHAT'S ACCEPTED . . .

1. Intelligence is a term that summarizes many different abilities taken together. Guilford's model is as good a scheme as we have for describing intelligence, though many psychologists find Piaget's system, described in Unit 16, more to the point conceptually.
2. Measured IQ predicts success in school and general occupational level as a corollary.
3. IQ is somewhat plastic in early childhood but stable in later years.
4. Genetic factors contribute to IQ.
5. IQ can be enhanced or stunted by environmental conditions.
6. There are some average-IQ differences between various groups, including black/white and middle class/lower class.
7. There are patterns of intellectual abilities related to cultural-ethnic background.

2. WHAT'S DEBATED . . .

1. Whether IQ tests measure a broad capacity or set of capacities worthy of the name "intelligence" or something considerably narrower.
2. How best to conceptualize discrete mental abilities.
3. What the best methods are for maximizing intellectual development.
4. The relative contribution of genetic endowment and environment to IQ.
5. The causes of differences in ethnic and male/female patterns of ability.
6. The degree to which social class determines IQ, and how.

ISSUE: THE I.Q. CONTROVERSY

As a college student, you probably have an I.Q. considerably above the national average. But try some of these simple items from a recent I.Q. test, and see how you fare (correct answers below):

1. A "handkerchief head" is   (a) a cool cat
    (b) a porter
    (c) an Uncle Tom
    (d) a hoddi
    (e) a preacher.

2. What are the "Dixie hummingbirds"?
    (a) part of the KKK
    (b) a swamp disease
    (c) a modern gospel group
    (d) a negro paramilitary group
    (e) deacons.

3. A "gas head" is a person who has a
    (a) fast-moving car
    (b) stable of "lace"
    (c) "process"
    (d) habit of stealing cars
    (e) long jail record for arson.

Answers: 1—(c); 2—(c); 3—(c).

The chances are that, unless you are black, you scored zero.

These test items are drawn from a "culture bound" test for black Americans constructed by black psychologist Adrian Dove. The test, while only half-serious, makes an important point: all I.Q. tests are to some extent culturally biased. No matter how carefully constructed, a test must assume knowledge. In the items above, knowledge of the words in which the questions are asked is assumed. The knowledge which a test assumes may not be equally available to all groups and individuals in a given society. A child reared in a white, middle class environment should have little difficulty in selecting the "odd one out" from a group of farm animals. A child of similar age in Harlem, denied experience of rural areas and access to picture books, may be unable to perform this task correctly. This inability would not reflect the intelligence of the Harlem child so much as his or her cultural background.

Many psychologists are becoming increasingly dissatisfied with traditional I.Q. tests, and are worried that laymen perceive them as an absolute, objective measure of "intelligence." I.Q. testing is in fact rife with difficulties. The same individual may achieve markedly different scores on different occasions. Blacks score significantly better if tested by a black than if tested by a white. Early childhood tests, often used for tracking purposes in schools, may encourage a self-fulfilling prophecy: the "bright" child gets more encouragement, better teachers, and thus achieves higher grades. Many tests even contain items that can be correctly answered in several ways, although only one answer is acceptable to the tester. Some tests for young children, for example, ask, "Who discovered America?" The right answer would seem to be Christopher Columbus. But what happens to the bright child who is familiar with recent evidence that America was discovered by the Scandinavian explorer Leif Erikson? Or the American Indian child who quite reasonably considers that America was discovered by the Indians many centuries before Columbus? An item on one test scores a child "right" for selecting as "pretty" a white, prim-looking woman. The child is scored wrong for selecting a woman with negroid features and slightly unkempt hair. A further problem with I.Q. tests is that they test only a narrow range of human intellectual abilities—primarily those most necessary for academic success. But what of other intellectual abilities—the capacity to compose music, to write poetry, to create art? If I.Q. tests included measures of these abilities, we might all score rather differently. Ex-Beatle drummer Ringo Starr was a low-I.Q. school dropout. He might have reached genius level on an I.Q. test that substituted musical for mathematical ability. Both abilities after all, are complex intellectual gifts, and the inclusion of one and the exclusion of the other is an entirely arbitrary feature of I.Q. tests.

Difficulties like these have led psychologists to search for other means of measuring intellectual capacities. One interesting innovation is the use of electronic equipment to monitor brainwaves. Canadian psychologist John Ertl has developed a test of intelligence which involves flashing a light in the eyes of the subject. The light causes tiny changes in the brainwaves, and the speed of this response appears to indicate the intelligence of the subject—the quicker the response takes place, the brighter the subject seems to be on a battery of other tests.

Ertl points out that his test does not require the subject to read, write or even speak, so that ethnic or cultural background cannot distort the results. All the subject has to do is attach a helmet-like apparatus to his head, so that electronic equipment can detect and measure his brain waves, and then sit in a darkened room and watch a flashing light. The entire procedure takes about 5 minutes, as compared to about an hour for conventional tests. At the end of the period, a computer prints out the subject's score. Much more research is needed on the method to determine its accuracy and also precisely what aspects of intelligence it measures. Preliminary findings suggest that the technique gives an indication of an individual's *potential* to solve problems rapidly. It is still too early to predict what the ultimate uses of the brainwave monitor will be, but Ertl is already concerned that "it will be used to pigeonhole people, just as the I.Q. test was."

The traditional I.Q. test, of course, still has its uses. It remains the best predictor, other than the social class of one's parents, of an individual's academic success and future economic status. But many big city school systems have abandoned the tests because they believe that scores for minority group students are misleading, sometimes branding bright students as dull simply because they do not have a fluent command of language. A recent Supreme Court ruling has also made it difficult to use I.Q. tests as part of the hiring procedure in commerce and industry, on the grounds that the tests are racially biased and discriminate against minority group members.

Unit 13

The Disordered Mind

OVERVIEW

This unit summarizes information about the origins of mental disorders and the main types of disorders that exist. Psychoses, neuroses, personality disorders, and suicidal behavior are reviewed and related to the primary causal factors discussed by psychologists — genetic and constitutional factors, childhood experiences, Freudian theory, and social learning theory. The views of Thomas Szasz and R. D. Laing are discussed in the Issue section.

UNIT OUTLINE

DEFINITION AND BACKGROUND
1. *Definition:* mental disorder is a mental condition that leads to behavior that deviates from what society regards as normal.
2. *Background:* Emil Kraepelin (1856-1926).

QUESTIONS AND EVIDENCE

1. What causes psychosis?
Hypotheses:
- a. *Constitutional:* psychosis results from inherited anomalies. **212**
- b. *Social-learning:* psychosis results from detrimental psychological and social experiences, especially during childhood. **213**

2. What causes neuroses and chronic anxiety?
Hypotheses:
- a. *Social-learning:* neurotic behavior is acquired in much the same manner as any other behavior pattern: through conditioning and modeling (imitation).
- b. *Psychodynamic:* the major determinants of neurotic behavior are intrapsychic events and unconscious motivations. **217**

3. Why do some individuals display antisocial behavior patterns?
Hypotheses:
- a. *Indifference-to-punishment:* it is because the conditioning process has broken down that the psychopath, though he can distinguish right from wrong, feels no guilt or remorse about antisocial behavior. **219**
- b. *Parental-rejection:* a child who is rejected by his parents learns to hate instead of to love; consequently, he reacts to social standards and authority with violence and aggression. **219**

4. Why do people attempt suicide?
Hypotheses:
- a. *Alienation:* people who commit suicide (or try to) lack or have lost interpersonal relationships. **221**
- b. *Depression:* a relatively calm withdrawal behavior in an individual may mark the onset of suicidal depression. **221**

IMPORTANT CONCEPTS

	page
alienation	**221**
anxiety	**215**
delusion	**211**
dementia praecox	**209**
depression	**211**
hallucination	**211**
manic-depressive reaction	**211**
neurosis	**215**
normal	**208**
Oedipus complex	**217**
phobia	**216**
psychopath	**218**
psychosis	**209**
schizophrenia	**209**
social learning	**213**
unconscious	**217**
withdrawal	**221**

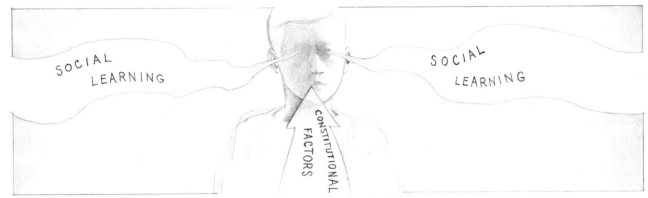

Constitutional factors and social learning interact to determine an individual's orientation to life.

Intense feelings, such as rejection, guilt, or confusion, may be triggered by specific events.

Difficulties in coping with these feelings may lead to a variety of mental disorders.

DEFINITION AND BACKGROUND

Aberrant behavior has puzzled and intrigued men in every society throughout history. For many centuries, possession by spirits was offered as an explanation; only a few hundred years ago, remember, Americans were burning "witches" at the stake. Today, a wide range of psychological and chemical factors are being studied in an effort to learn the bases of mental disorders.

One DEFINITION of mental disorder is *a mental condition that leads to behavior that deviates from what society regards as normal.* Note that the word "normal," though basically a statistical term ("normal" behavior is the behavior typical of most people in a given group), also connotes a *social judgment.* In our Western society, we are more likely to use the term "abnormal" to describe a person who cannot hold a job despite fine training and a wealth of opportunities than we are to use it for a compulsive worker. This is especially true if the compulsive worker produces a major achievement, like Thomas Edison or Beethoven or Bobby Fischer, all of whom would probably be thought of as "abnormal" if it were not for their outstanding success in their chosen fields of endeavor. In this society we also place a high value on personal happiness; partly for that reason, we are particularly inclined to suspect mental disorder in a person who not only behaves oddly but also seems to be suffering.

This unit will FOCUS on the major classifications of mental disorder—psychoses, neuroses, and psychopathic behavior—and on their causes and origins. The problem of suicide, which can occur as the result of a number of different psychological states, but is most closely associated with severe depression, also receives attention.

BACKGROUND: EMIL KRAEPELIN (1856–1926)

Originally trained in medicine, Kraepelin studied under Wilhelm Wundt (see Unit 24), who in 1879 established in Leipzig the earliest known psychological laboratory. In a series of experiments that can be said to mark the beginning of the scientific study of mental disease, Kraepelin and his assistants tried to induce mild mental disorders in human subjects by means of alcohol, fatigue, and hunger. Word-association tests were then used to assess the effects of these disturbing influences. Not too surprisingly, as a subject became more disturbed, there was an increase in the number of associative responses that had little or no apparent relation to the stimulus word.

Kraepelin's most important contribution was his attempt to classify mental disorders into a descriptive system. His goal was to apply the procedures of the natural sciences to thousands of psychiatric case histories by grouping together those patients who shared the same symptoms and whose disorders followed similar courses over time. So began the "Kraepelin era," when naming and classifying disorders became a major concern of psychiatry. The idea was that if mental illnesses could be diagnosed as precisely as physical ones, equally precise cures could be found and applied. Today, a good many psychologists and psychiatrists doubt that is true—indeed, they question the validity of any system that compares mental disorders to physical disease—but many others continue to work with and refine the classification scheme that Kraepelin devised.

Kraepelin's classifications, first outlined in a survey published in 1883, when he was twenty-seven, were

Figure 1. Emil Kraepelin classified psychiatric disorders by onset, symptoms, development, and outcome.

continually revised throughout his career. In the 1890s Kraepelin identified two major categories of disorders: *manic-depressive psychosis* and *dementia praecox*. Manic-depressive psychosis was characterized by periodic alternations of extreme nervous activity with deeply depressed moods. Dementia praecox subsumed many previously known disorders on the basis of similarity of such symptoms as hallucinations, delusions, deficient attention, and gradual mental and behavioral deterioration. Unlike manic-depressive psychosis, dementia praecox was thought by Kraepelin to stem from organic brain damage, perhaps a disease of brain metabolism, and to follow a clinical course that often ended in incurable insanity.

Several modifications of Kraepelin's system were introduced by some of his contemporaries, notably Eugene Bleuler (1856–1935) and Adolf Meyer (1866–1950). Bleuler emphasized the presence of psychological versus physiological factors in dementia praecox, which he labeled *schizophrenia,* the term still used today. Meyer, who brought Kraepelin's general classification system to the United States, believed that mental disorders were not entirely physical in origin but were "psychobiological" reactions.

The initial reactions of the medical and psychological professions to Kraepelin, Bleuler, and Meyer's categories were quite positive. This kind of system answered many puzzling questions and gave order and stability to the concept of "madness." Viewing mental disorders in terms of organic-physiological bases brought them into the domain of the medical profession and, therefore, within the realm of scientific scrutiny. These early efforts evolved into our current psychiatric nomenclature for the diagnosis and classification of mental disorders.

On the other hand, some of Kraepelin's work received criticism even in his time. His objective approach was sometimes called depersonalized and inhuman, and certain aspects of it were soon modified and replaced by the Freudian approach, which emphasized the psychodynamics of individual cases. Although only some of Kraepelin's concepts and terms are still in use, his and his followers' work can nevertheless be seen as the first empirical scientific attempt to study disordered behavior.

QUESTIONS AND EVIDENCE

1. What causes psychoses?

2. What causes neuroses and chronic anxiety?

3. Why do some individuals display antisocial behavior patterns?

4. Why do people attempt suicide?

The term *psychosis* is used to describe serious pathological conditions in which a person's ability to relate to what most people accept as reality is badly impaired. Psychoses are traditionally divided into *organic psychoses* and *functional psychoses.* Organic psychoses are those associated with known physiological damage; senile dementia (extreme "senility" caused by a deterioration of brain tissues) is an example. Functional psychoses are those without any known physiological cause. Three of the most common func-

TABLE 1.   Major Psychoses

Type	General Symptoms	Subtype	Dominant Symptoms
SCHIZOPHRENIA	Disturbance of thought, social withdrawal	Simple	Social withdrawal
		Catatonic	Physical rigidity, unresponsiveness
		Paranoid	Delusions with confusion
		Childhood	Unresponsiveness to people
		Chronic undifferentiated	Mixture of above
AFFECTIVE DISORDERS	Disturbance of mood, emotionality	Involutional melancholia	
		Manic-depressive	Depression of old age
			Long-range, periodic mood swings
PARANOID STATES	Specific thought disturbance, with lack of impairment in other respects	Paranoia	Encapsulated, highly structured delusions, impervious to change
		Involutional paranoid state	Delusional thinking

Source: Based on *Diagnostic and Statistical Manual of Mental Disorders* (Washington: American Psychiatric Association, 1968).

Figure 2. Although mentally disturbed people are more often portrayed as strait-jacketed fiends rather than as pitiful, withdrawn creatures, the latter are more typical of seriously disturbed people. (Photographs from the drama *Marat/Sade*.)

tional psychoses are *schizophrenic reactions, manic-depressive reactions,* and *paranoid reactions.*

It has been estimated that half or more of the patients in mental hospitals are schizophrenics, but it would be a mistake to assume that all schizophrenics are hospitalized. Some people with fairly pronounced schizophrenic tendencies are able to lead relatively normal lives, and some chronic schizophrenics still manage, one way or another, to stay out of the hospital. If you live in a large city, you have almost surely encountered people riding the subway or walking down the street who are carrying on a spirited conversation with some unseen companion; passersby often assume that these people are drunk or brain-damaged from chronic alcoholism, but some of them are actually hallucinating schizophrenics.

Hallucinations and delusions are fairly common symptoms of schizophrenia. Other symptoms include inappropriate emotional reactions, as when a person speaks of a tragic or extremely upsetting event with no visible emotion at all; withdrawal, which can take the extreme form called a catatonic stupor, in which a person may hold a single rigid position for days on end; thought disturbances, often reflected in apparently incoherent speech related to the person's fantasies; peculiar and repetitive gestures (also related to the person's fantasies); and disorientations about time, place, and person. One man who underwent a schizophrenic episode said later that the first symptom he recalled was his discovery, one morning, that his hat no longer seemed to be the same size as his head; later, when he had recovered enough to go bowling occasionally, he had a hard time directing the ball properly because it kept changing its size and sometimes acquired corners, like a cube, when it was halfway down the alley.

In Greek, the word *schizin* means "to split" and *phren* means "mind," but the split referred to is between the thought processes and the emotions, not between two or more "multiple personalities" as in *The Three Faces of Eve* or *Dr. Jekyll and Mr. Hyde.* (Multiple personality is a dissociative reaction classified as neurotic.) It is this split between thought and feeling that accounts, for example, for the inappropriate emotional reactions mentioned above.

Manic-depressive reactions are extreme disturbances of mood. Some people alternate between mania and depression, but most alternate either between normalcy and mania or between normalcy and depression. A person entering a manic psychosis is very energetic and enthusiastic; he may talk excitedly about sailing around the world and, if no one stops him, try to buy a sea-going yacht and a home at each of his projected ports of call. A person in the depressive phase feels totally worthless and unable to do anything. He is likely to talk with great effort if at all and to have trouble eating, sleeping, even moving around. An extremely depressed patient may be bedridden and have to be fed intravenously.

A person with a manic-depressive psychosis does not usually stay manic or depressed for an indefinite period of time but goes through recurrent cycles. A typical manic episode might last three months and be followed by almost a year of normal behavior. Depressive episodes usually last longer, about nine months according to one estimate, but they too tend to end on their own, even without treatment (though they often recur at some future time).

Paranoid reactions are much rarer than either schizophrenic or manic-depressive reactions but often can show the most dramatic symptoms. They are generally marked by bizarre delusions, usually of the grandeur or persecution variety. A paranoid patient may tell you that he is Jesus or Henry Kissinger and spin quite a tale to prove it; equally possible, he may have the delusion that a group of evil individuals is conspiring against him in a plot to oust him as president of General Motors. Except for this delusional system, however, the paranoid psychotic usually shows no disorder in thinking; he appears normal until something happens to precipitate the delusional thinking. Surprisingly, the delusional system is well worked out, and it even seems plausible at times. The intact thinking and the more or less logical delusions are in marked contrast to the disordered thinking encountered in the variety of schizophrenia that is labeled paranoid.

How do such disorders begin? Researchers have pursued two general orientations in the search for the causes of psychotic mental disorders—constitutional and social learning. They are by no means mutually exclusive.

HYPOTHESES	CONSTITUTIONAL	SOCIAL LEARNING
DESCRIPTIVE EVIDENCE	ASSESS: relation of genetic ties to occurrence of schizophrenia	ASSESS: relationship of childhood schizophrenia to family interaction patterns
EXPERIMENTAL EVIDENCE		

1. WHAT CAUSES PSYCHOSES?

The *constitutional hypothesis* states that psychosis results from inherited anomalies. This is a very old notion, stemming largely from the observation that psychosis often seems to run in families. In certain families there is a high incidence of disturbed individuals over several generations. "Grandma was psychotic, and so was her sister; Dad's brother was psychotic and now two of my cousins." Of course observing a few families informally is quite inadequate from a scientific standpoint. It took Franz Kallman to formalize the genetic study of mental disorders, particularly schizophrenia.

DESCRIPTIVE EVIDENCE

Investigator: F. J. Kallman
Source, Date: "The Genetics of Schizophrenia," 1938
Subjects: 1,087 schizophrenics and their relatives
Materials: Hospital records, interviews, statistics

Kallman reasoned that if schizophrenia was genetically caused he should be able to predict, following Mendelian principles, its appearance in earlier generations of a given patient's family. Using an original sample of 1,087 schizophrenic patients, he surveyed 3,279 parents and husbands and wives (for corroborative data); 3,384 direct descendants; 3,920 brothers, sisters, half-brothers, and half-sisters; and 2,194 nephews and nieces (by blood) of schizophrenic patients. His total sample was fairly representative of the population of northern Germany, where his study was conducted.

As the results shown in Table 2 indicate, almost nine out of ten identical twins of schizophrenics themselves develop schizophrenia, and the disorder is found more often among other blood relatives of schizophrenics than it is in the general population. In a more recent review of the literature on schizophrenia in families, Heston (1970) found that a child with one schizophrenic parent has almost a fifty-fifty chance of becoming either schizophrenic or "schizoid," a term used to describe mildly schizophrenic traits such as rigidity of thought, flatness of emotional response, and suspiciousness and severe anxiety in social situations. A child with two schizophrenic parents has an even better chance (roughly 66 percent) of being schizophrenic or schizoid. Note, however, that if schizophrenia were purely a matter of genetics, then 100 percent of the identical twins in the Kallman study and, in the Heston study, at least 75 percent of the children of two schizophrenic parents (the percentage that would be expected if schizophrenia resulted from a dominant gene) should have been schizophrenic.

Researchers and therapists have tried for years to identify other constitutional factors that may be involved in schizophrenia. One particularly attractive possibility was that there was some chemical or hormonal foundation for psychotic behavior. One of the most popular recent theories has attempted to trace schizophrenic behavior to the brain's improper

TABLE 2. Family Relationship and Schizophrenia

Relation to Schizophrenic	Percentage Who Develop Schizophrenia
Identical (one-egg) twins	86.2
Fraternal (two-egg) twins	14.5
Siblings	14.2
Half-siblings	7.1
General population	.85

Source: J.C. Coleman, *Abnormal Psychology and Modern Life* (Glenview, Ill.: Scott Foresman, 1964) p. 121.

utilization of serotonin, a hormone in the central nervous system. So far, attempts to isolate a hormonal-chemical basis for schizophrenia have yielded suggestive but inconclusive results; however, research is being actively pursued in the hope that some major breakthroughs are not many years away.

It may be that some people inherit a predisposition to schizophrenia so that, when they encounter certain conditions of psychological stress, the disorder develops. This possibility, which also cannot be ruled out as a factor in senile psychosis and some manic-depressive reactions, suggests that the standard classification of psychoses as either "organic" or "functional" may need reexamination. Certainly the just-mentioned Kallman and Heston studies reveal data that support this contention.

As the psychologist D. O. Hebb has pointed out, each of us is 100 percent heredity *and* 100 percent environment. Thus there is no need to regard the constitutional hypothesis as competing with the *social-learning hypothesis*. According to the latter, psychosis results from detrimental psychological and social experiences, especially during childhood.

A number of studies have found a relation between early family life and the incidence of schizophrenia, and particular attention has been paid to the way parents interact with their children. One severe handicap in this type of research is the relatively short time that the average family containing schizophrenic members stays together. One way researchers deal with this problem is to use families of upper-class schizophrenic patients. Families from this socioeconomic level are more likely to remain intact and available for lengthy observation and study.

DESCRIPTIVE EVIDENCE

Investigator: S. Fleck

Source, Date: "Family Dynamics and Origin of Schizophrenia," 1960

Location: Yale University School of Medicine

Subjects: 15 intact upper-class families of schizophrenics, generally consisting of parents and at least 1 sibling

Materials: Interviews; psychological tests

This long-term study of the family background of young upper-class schizophrenic patients was conducted by a research team consisting of psychiatrists, clinical psychologists, and social workers. Social

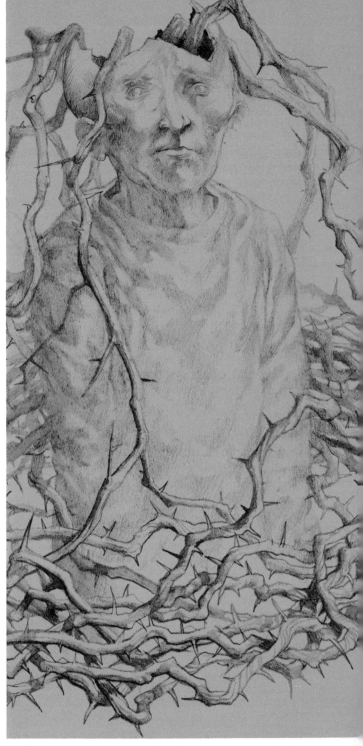

Figure 3. Artist's rendition of the subjective experience of schizophrenia, which often includes symptoms of hallucinations and delusions, inappropriate emotional reactions, withdrawal, thought disturbances, and disorientation.

workers conducted weekly interviews with family members. In addition, they periodically sought out and interviewed other relatives and friends. Psychologists administered psychological tests to assess the personality characteristics of all available members of the nuclear family. The psychiatrists acted as overall coordinators and consultants in the areas of interview and test interpretations and on the possibility of future therapeutic measures.

Data from this study indicate that mothers of schizophrenics suffer from a wide range of disturbances—no one personality type emerged as dominant, however. At least half the mothers of schizophrenic patients in the sample were considered to be psychotically disturbed. An even more significant factor than the disturbances of these "schizophrenic mothers," however, was the fact that these women were paired with husbands who would either constantly battle with and undermine an already anxious and insecure mother or who would acquiesce to their many irrational and bizarre notions. The author classifies these marriages as either "schismatic" (parental hostilities divide the family into opposing factions) or "skewed" (one spouse passively goes along with the aberrant ways and child-rearing practices of the more disturbed parent). Unlike other family pairs, no compensatory or ameliorative role is assumed by the more normal parent to balance the idiosyncratic deficiencies of the disturbed parent. Parents may communicate two contradictory messages to the child at the same time, placing him in an impossible position. Prolonged exposure to this kind of double-bind situation can have a serious effect on a child's personality. Suppose, for example, that a mother repeatedly approaches a young child with physical demonstrations of affection—and yet, just as she starts to hug him, her body tenses as if a feeling of revulsion has swept over her. In an extreme case, so the theory goes, the child may be so overwhelmed by contradictory messages like these that he loses touch with reality.

It is possible, however, that the search for a single type or trait, or even a consistent cluster of traits, that characterizes all parents of schizophrenic children is futile. Perhaps this approach is simply too narrow, doomed to failure in the same way as earlier studies that focused on what was "wrong" with the patient, neglecting the important role of parents. More significant findings may derive from examining the family dynamics that produce schizophrenia, from exploring the characteristics of the schizophrenic *family*, rather than those of schizophrenic patients, mothers, or fathers.

Before we leave the subject of psychoses, it should be pointed out that labeling someone "psychotic" is a serious matter. In the minds of many people the word "schizophrenic" is virtually synonymous with the word "hopeless"—and those people include not only the family, friends, and associates of the person in question but, all too often, his doctor and even himself. The word may be accurate enough when first applied to the person; the trouble is that the label, once stuck on, is hard to get off. A person who is hospitalized for schizophrenia may get so used to being thought of as schizophrenic and treated like a schizophrenic that he feels and acts more schizophrenic than he needs to and for a longer time. A vicious circle is set up—and the person may never escape. This is not to say that the words "schizophrenic" and "psychotic" should not be used (though some experts think they should not); it is merely to point out that we should be aware of their power to

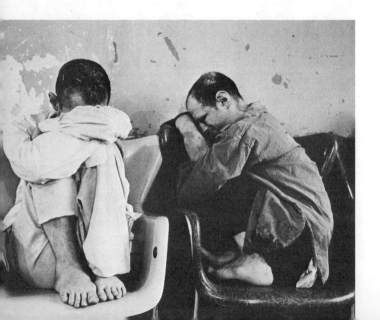

Figure 4. Are these psychotic patients merely not responding to their environment, or are they attending to inner visions that allow for no distractions?

TABLE 3.   Major Neuroses

Type	Dominant Symptoms
Anxiety reactions	Diffuse fears, persistent feelings of uneasiness to obsessive dread, palpitation of heart, cold sweat, sleeplessness, loss of appetite, inability to work
Dissociative reactions	Amnesia (loss of memory), multiple personality, sleepwalking
Conversion reactions	Hysterical reactions (physical disabilities without physical cause) such as paralysis, anesthesia, blindness, deafness, loss of voice
Phobic reactions	Irrational fears such as acrophobia (fear of high places), claustrophobia (fear of closed places), nyctophobia (fear of dark), zoophobia (fear of animals)
Obsessive-compulsive reactions	Recurrent thoughts and thought patterns (ranging from "I must get my work done" to "I think I'm going to kill someone"); cleanliness rituals, superstitious rites to ward off feared events, checking and rechecking locked doors and windows
Depressive reactions (or reactive depression)	Similar to psychotic depression but less severe and usually of shorter duration

Source: L. Fox, *Psychology as Philosophy, Science, and Art* (Pacific Palisades, Calif.: Goodyear Publishing Company, 1972), pp. 87–88.

become self-fulfilling prophecies (see Unit 2).

Neuroses are usually thought of as less severe disorders than psychoses—and, usually, they are. Society generally looks at the behavior manifestations of neurotics as more acceptable than those of psychotics and feels that the appropriate consequences of such abnormalities should be less austere. However, neurotics may have extreme dissociative reactions such as amnesia or multiple personality that result in behavior quite as bizarre as that of many psychotics.

Neurotic behavior encompasses a wide variety of psychological difficulties, as you can see by glancing down the list of major neuroses summarized in Table 3. Their common element is excessive anxiety. Although a severe neurosis can sometimes be as crippling as a psychosis, most neurotics are in much closer touch with reality than most psychotics. Sometimes it almost seems that the neurotic is *too* closely in touch with reality. A snub from a friend, a minor failure at work or school, an argument with husband or wife, or an even more routine incident that has symbolic significance for the person—these things can fling the neurotic into an acute anxiety attack, a depression that lasts for days or weeks, or an endless round of obsessional thoughts.

All of us sometimes feel anxious and act in ways that are called neurotic, just as all of us use defense mechanisms (see Unit 15) from time to time. The dividing line between neurosis and normality is not a sharp one. Usually, however, a person is considered neurotic when neurotic behavior patterns become the dominant ones in his life.

HYPOTHESES	SOCIAL LEARNING	PSYCHODYNAMIC
DESCRIPTIVE EVIDENCE	ASSESS: the conditioning of anxiety and its generalization	ASSESS: the relationship between unconscious motivation and anxiety
EXPERIMENTAL EVIDENCE		

2. WHAT CAUSES NEUROSES AND CHRONIC ANXIETY?

The ~~social-learning hypothesis~~ states that neurotic behavior is acquired in much the same manner as any other behavior pattern: through conditioning and modeling (imitation). Although most neurotic behavior, according to this hypothesis, is probably operantly conditioned (see Unit 27), an early experiment by Watson and Rayner (1920) showed that some phobias can be classically conditioned (see Unit 26). Watson and Rayner, working with an eleven-month-old child named Albert, conditioned a fear response to a variety of white furry objects (including a Santa Claus beard) by giving Albert a white rat to play with and then, just after presenting the rat, sounding a loud noise. The experiment described below was a similar attempt to condition a phobic reaction.

DESCRIPTIVE EVIDENCE

Investigator: K. Diven
Source, Date: "Certain Determinants in the Conditioning of Anxiety Reactions," 1937
Location: Harvard University
Subjects: 52 college students
Materials: GSR recording device; shock equipment; word lists

The subjects were told that they were participating in a study investigating muscle coordinations and that their bodies would be put in a circuit with the apparatus. The apparatus actually recorded changes in the activity of the autonomic nervous system. These were measured in terms of galvanic skin responses (GSR), which trace changes in the electrical conductivity of the skin. An increase in GSR occurs when, for example, the palms of the hands become sweaty; it is an indicator of emotional arousal.

Shock electrodes were attached to the subjects' feet, and they were asked for their verbal associations to a list of words. None of them showed any unusual GSRs in response to the words. Then the subjects were presented with a second list. The words "red" and "barn" occurred in it six times, and each time they were followed by shock. Completion of one presentation of the list ended the conditioning process.

Later, when they were asked to recall as many of the words on the list as possible but were given no shocks, the GSRs for all subjects indicated a strong reaction not only to "barn" and "red" but also to other words with rural connotations (such as "cow" and "pasture"). It was concluded that an emotional response similar to neurotic anxiety could be conditioned, and that the conditioned response tended to generalize to other, similar stimuli. To illustrate how this might happen outside the laboratory, suppose a child who has just learned to walk is slapped, told "No!" and put back in his playpen virtually every time he tries to explore his surroundings—when he pulls books off the bookshelf, when he tries to turn on the TV, when he gets fingerprints on the windowpanes, and so on. In time, he may come to associate punishment with all independent exploratory behavior and become a chronically anxious, passive "neurotic."

The effects of learning in real life are more complex and less controlled than they are in laboratory settings, however, so this kind of evidence should be interpreted with caution. Additional evidence is accumulating concerning other factors that may play a role in the genesis of neurotic behavior, such as imitation. For example, a child who develops an extreme fear of lightning may acquire it in imitation of his mother's response to electrical storms. Subtle interactions in the family and childhood environment contribute to the early "conditioning" of behavior, and it frequently is difficult to specify the exact stimuli that give rise to a response. The social learning approach to neurosis is nevertheless highly suggestive. Therapy in such cases actually amounts to an unlearning of inefficient response patterns, as described in Unit 20.

Although learning approaches are concerned with behavior as a function of external stimulation, the psychoanalytic approach stresses internal drives and childhood experiences as influencing behavior. The *psychodynamic hypothesis* states that the major determinants of neurotic behavior are intrapsychic events and unconscious motivations. Most psychodynamic notions of neurosis stemming from Freudian psychoanalysis are based on the idea that defense mechanisms are used to ward off anxiety. A distinguishing feature of this neurotic anxiety is that an alarm, a reaction that appears whenever there is a perceived threat, is frequently sounded in the absence of any apparently adequate cause: there is no consciously recognized source of danger. According to the psychodynamic view, the defenses have been inadequate to control or contain the anxiety.

DESCRIPTIVE EVIDENCE

Investigator: Sigmund Freud
Source, Date: "Complete Psychological Works of Sigmund
   Freud," 1909
Subject: 1 boy named Hans
Materials: Case study

The case of Little Hans, originally reported by Freud in 1909, should help bring the psychodynamic hypothesis into sharper focus. Hans' father had contacted Freud because the child suffered from a "nervous disorder," which basically meant that he was terrified by the prospect of being bitten by a horse. In those horse-and-buggy days, this phobia was quite damaging to his everyday functioning. According to Freud, the basis of Hans' phobic reaction was the Oedipus complex. Little Hans was assumed to be experiencing both love and hatred for his father as a result of the father's blocking Hans' imagined erotic advances toward the mother. In addition, Little Hans was presumably afraid that his father would retaliate against him for having incestuous impulses; this fear is experienced as castration anxiety. Thus, Little Hans is portrayed as being in conflict because of his ambivalence toward his father, his incestuous desire for his mother, and his fear of castration. Psychodynamic theorists maintain that this conflict was handled by Hans' ego through the repression of his ambivalent and incestuous impulses and through the defense mechanism of displacement; the fear of castration by the father was displaced to its symbolic representation—the fear of being bitten by a horse.

At the time, Freud indicated that the onset of the phobic reaction could be traced to a ride in a horse-drawn bus. Hans was with his mother and became very frightened when the horse fell down and was hurt. Freud interpreted this incident as merely the precipitating cause of Hans' phobia. He maintained that the real basis lay in the intrapsychic conflict that was evident in Little Hans during the Oedipal period.

In passing, it is interesting to note that the treatment of Hans was carried out by his father, a physician, who happened to be a student of Freud's at the time. Freud himself only saw the boy once during the entire treatment, although Hans' father kept him informed through written reports and periodic consultation. Critics have pointed out that in the dialogues between father and son the father asked leading questions, apparently colored by his expectations from his study of psychoanalytic theory. Thus, experimenter bias may have crept into the interpretation of the results (see Unit 2).

Both the learning hypothesis and the psychodynamic hypothesis, although emphasizing different things, contribute to our understanding of the neurotic individual. Alternate interpretations of the same data can be a healthy phenomenon, possibly leading to the assessment of multiple causation. Learning theorists, for example, see Hans' fear of horses as simply a conditioned anxiety response and feel that the incident on the bus is the cause of the entire disorder. They point out that Hans had previously had a number of unpleasant experiences with horses that probably oversensitized him. In other words, a fear response had been conditioned partially and the bus incident represented the final learning trial that established it. Once established through classical conditioning (see Unit 26), the phobic reaction was maintained by operant conditioning (see Unit 27): each time Hans successfully avoided a horse, his anxiety was reduced and his avoidance behavior reinforced.

Neurotic behavior patterns often interfere only slightly with an individual's relationship to society at large, but a third group of disorders is typified by what would ordinarily be considered "antisocial behavior." Persons displaying such characteristics (who may well be habitual criminals) are classified neither as psychotic nor as neurotic but as sociopaths, psychopaths, sexual deviants, and the like. In a sense, such labels are misleading, for they imply that a set of specific behaviors will identify the psychopathic personality. In reality, as Table 4 shows, the psychopath is recognized more by what he is not than by what he is. The common theme of the characteristics is a relatively flat and undifferentiated emotional life. It is as if the psychopath lives in a world devoid of any real feelings, conflicts, desires, or values. He differs strikingly from the neurotic in that he apparently feels no anxiety.

The protagonist of Camus' *The Stranger* voices such indifference when he notices that the prosecutor at his trial lays great stress on his intelligence—"It puzzled me rather why what would count as a good point in an ordinary person should be used against an accused man as an overwhelming proof of his guilt"—and then admits that he feels no remorse about the murder he has committed: "I really couldn't understand why he harped on this point so much. Of course, I had to own that he was right; I didn't feel much regret for what I'd done. Still, to my mind he overdid it, and I'd have liked to have a chance of explaining to him, in a quite friendly, almost affectionate way, that I have never been able really to regret anything in all my life. I've always been far too much absorbed in the present moment, or the immediate future, to think back."

TABLE 4. Characteristics of the Psychopath

Superficial charm
Intelligence
Absence of delusions and other signs of irrational thinking
Absence of anxiety and other neurotic symptoms
Unreliability; untruthfulness and insincerity
Lack of remorse, shame, or guilt
Inadequately motivated antisocial behavior (i.e., he may be
   suddenly aggressive or violent, for little reason at all)
Poor judgment (self destructively keeps making same mistakes)
Pathological egocentricity and incapacity for love; general
   poverty in major affective (emotional) reactions
Unresponsiveness in general interpersonal relationships
Sex life impersonal, trivial, and poorly integrated
Lack of insight into his own behavior; failure to devise or follow a life plan

Source: Adapted from H. Cleckley: *The Mask of Sanity* (St. Louis: C. V. Mosby, 1964).

HYPOTHESES	INDIFFERENCE TO PUNISHMENT	PARENTAL REJECTION
DESCRIPTIVE EVIDENCE	ASSESS: susceptibility to anxiety in primary and secondary psychopaths	ASSESS: relationship of parental treatment to psychopathic behaviors
EXPERIMENTAL EVIDENCE		

3. WHY DO SOME INDIVIDUALS DISPLAY ANTISOCIAL BEHAVIOR PATTERNS?

The sources of such a personality have not been identified. Indeed, it is doubtful that even a combination of the two most widely accepted theories, one of which focuses on the conditioning process and the other on parental behavior, can explain the origin and development of psychopathic behavior patterns.

Some researchers believe that the conditioned response of anxiety or fear that is acquired during childhood punishments may be the foundation of conscience (see Unit 5). Most "normal" individuals eventually abstain from antisocial behavior even when they are not threatened with direct reprisals. The *indifference-to-punishment hypothesis* states that it is because the conditioning process has broken down that the psychopath, though he can distinguish right from wrong, feels no guilt or remorse about antisocial behavior.

DESCRIPTIVE EVIDENCE

Investigator: D. A. Lykken
Source, Date: "A Study of Anxiety in the Sociopathic Personality," 1957
Subjects: 2 groups of institutionalized psychopaths, control group of normal subjects
Materials: Buzzer, shock, anxiety scale, physiograph, finger maze

It is possible to identify two basic types of psychopaths: *primary psychopaths* exhibit little or no anxiety and are much less likely to form emotional or close relationships than are *secondary psychopaths*, whose

disorder is more similar to a neurosis and probably related to underlying personality conflicts. Lykken tested subjects of both types along with a control group of normal subjects. All the subjects were required to learn a "mental maze" by being shocked whenever they made an incorrect turn. Then a buzzer was paired with the shock. The rate of learning in the maze, the conditioning of the fear response to the buzzer in terms of GSRs, and the scores on a test designed to measure chronic anxiety were recorded for each subject.

Primary psychopaths showed significantly less conditioned anxiety than the control subjects, and they also scored significantly lower than either the secondary psychopaths or the normal subjects on the anxiety scales. Finally, they did least well of the three groups in the learning task, with the "normals" doing best.

These results suggest that the primary psychopath and to some extent the secondary psychopath are deficient in their susceptibility to anxiety and that this may account for their tendency to engage in behavior customarily inhibited by anxiety or guilt.

The *parental-rejection hypothesis* is based on the assumption that a child who is rejected by his parents learns to hate instead of to love; consequently, he reacts to social standards and authority with violence and aggression. One survey by Bender (1942) of psychopathic children admitted to Bellevue Hospital, based on her own observations and clinical interviews with both the children and their parents, reported similar symptoms and relationships in all cases. Each child showed diffuse impulsiveness, an inability to feel guilt, a tendency to manipulate moral principles to his or her own ends, and an inability to relate emotionally to other people. Clinical evidence indicated that all the children had experienced some form of emotional deprivation, neglect, or discontinuous emotional experiences.

DESCRIPTIVE EVIDENCE

Investigators: R. L. Jenkins and L. Hewitt
Source, Date: "Types of Personality Structure in Child-Guidance Clinics," 1944
Location: Ann Arbor, Michigan
Subjects: 52 children
Materials: Background data on the children

Children from a child-guidance clinic who had been diagnosed as psychopathic on the basis of staff records were compared to 500 nonpsychopathic cases. Background information on all the children was obtained from the records of the clinic, and special emphasis was placed on the behavior and attitudes of the parents toward their children.

Many differences between the two groups were observed. Most notable, psychopathic children were raised by parents who indicated they hadn't wanted the child, who were in perpetual conflict with each other or had a history of repeated conflicts, and who frequently abused the child, probably as a result of their anger toward each other.

It was concluded from this and similar studies that the child who grows up in such an environment is likely to view himself in a very bad light, feel cheated, and be unresponsive to social norms. These children do not seem to develop guilt concerning misdeeds;

that is, they do not develop a "conscience."

The classic experiments in the laboratories of Harlow and his associates (see Unit 7) indicate that monkeys who are deprived of social relations and motherly affection in early infancy develop abnormal social behaviors when they become adults. Research by Siegman (1966) with human males shows a relationship between father absence during childhood and antisocial behavior later on.

Most psychologists agree that if there is some breakdown in the development of a child's positive emotional responses to his parents, the process of empathy or emotional identification with others may be disrupted or seriously distorted. The inability to engage in even remotely empathic behavior is certainly one of the primary characteristics of the psychopath.

An even more destructive form of disordered behavior, at least for the person involved, is suicide. During recent years the need for suicide-prevention centers, largely to serve people who have never before needed psychological treatment but are now prepared to take their own lives, has been increasingly recognized. Suicide can be treated in intellectual terms. At about the same time that he wrote *The Stranger* Camus claimed: "There is but one truly serious philosophical problem, and that is suicide. Judging whether life is or is not worth living amounts to answering the fundamental question of philosophy." But most psychologists adhere to the idea that suicide, rather than being a legitimate personal decision, is always or almost always a pathological act. Recent psychological investigations have concentrated on the alienation and depression that seem to characterize the suicidal personality.

QUESTION   4. WHY DO PEOPLE ATTEMPT SUICIDE?

HYPOTHESES	ALIENATION	DEPRESSION
DESCRIPTIVE EVIDENCE	ASSESS: interpersonal and home relationships of attempted suicides	ASSESS: records of emotional states of patients immediately preceding suicide
EXPERIMENTAL EVIDENCE		

4. WHY DO PEOPLE ATTEMPT SUICIDE?

The *alienation hypothesis* states that people who commit suicide (or try to) lack or have lost interpersonal relationships. They may have a long-standing inability to form strong ties, or the fault may lie in their particular situation at a given moment in time. The heroine of Sylvia Plath's *The Bell Jar* painstakingly describes the withdrawal from her mother, her friends, and her therapist that leads to a suicide attempt that "bared all the tatty wreckage of my life" before it "rushed me to sleep." She is almost as disturbed by her inability to communicate with a salesgirl about the difference between a water-repellent and water-proof raincoat as she is by the sight of her father's gravestone.

DESCRIPTIVE EVIDENCE

Investigators: J. T. Barter, D. O. Swaback, D. Todd
Source, Date: "Adolescent Suicide Attempts: Follow-up Study of Hospitalized Patients," 1968
Location: Colorado Psychiatric Hospital, Denver
Subjects: 45 adolescent psychiatric patients who had attempted suicide
Materials: Hospital charts, follow-up telephone interviews

This investigation was a follow-up study on forty-five adolescents who had attempted suicide, been hospitalized, and then been released. Through an analysis of the subjects' hospital records and through interviews with them after they had left the hospital, the investigators attempted to find out, first, whether there had been additional suicide attempts, and second, what factors distinguished those who had made later suicide attempts from those who had not.

The histories of the subjects before hospitalization showed that twenty-three of the forty-five patients had lost one or both parents through death, divorce, or separation. Of the remaining patients, half had parents who, though living together, had severe marital problems. Looking at the suicide attempts themselves, the investigators found that two-thirds of them had been precipitated by the actual or threatened loss of a parent or a boyfriend or girlfriend.

Through telephone interviews with the subjects after they had left the hospital, the investigators discovered that nineteen of them had made additional suicide attempts (none successful). This group showed significantly more alienation, both situational (as through the loss of a parent) and personal (as through a deficiency of social relationships), than did the twenty-six subjects who made no further suicide attempts. More than half (58 percent) of the attempted suicides did not live with their families, as compared with 16 percent of those who did not attempt suicide again; in addition, a higher proportion (63 percent) of the posthospitalization attempted-suicide group had lost a parent. Three-fourths of the group had made contact with a social agency (which the investigators interpret as a sign of poor social adjustment), and 68 percent reported minimal social life. By contrast, 88 percent of the others claimed to be leading active social lives (at least one date per week).

The alienation hypothesis emphasizes the aloneness of the potential suicide but does not explain its subjective correlate: severe depression. Plath's heroine powerfully expresses the desperation and grief that sometimes signal the onset of suicidal depression: "I couldn't understand why I was crying so hard. Then I remembered that I had never cried for my father's death. My mother hadn't cried either. She had just smiled and said what a merciful thing it was for him that he had died, because if he had lived he would have been crippled and an invalid for life, and he couldn't have stood that, he would rather have died than had that happen. I laid my face to the smooth face of the marble and howled my loss into the cold salt rain." Her next sentence is "I knew just how to go about it"—a statement that reflects the calm orderliness that often characterizes the suicide's psychological state. The *depression hypothesis* states that a relatively calm withdrawal behavior in an individual may mark the onset of suicidal depression.

DESCRIPTIVE EVIDENCE

Investigators: P. Keith-Spiegel and D. E. Spiegel
Source, Date: "Affective States of Patients Immediately Preceding Suicide," 1967
Location: Veterans Administration Center, Los Angeles
Subjects: 61 patients who had committed suicide
Materials: Suicide notes, hospital records

An analysis of the hospital records indicated that the terms used to describe patients just prior to suicide were less pejorative or hostile than those used to describe the other patients. The term "calm" was

FACTS AND FABLES ON SUICIDE

FABLE:	People who talk about suicide don't commit suicide.	**FACT:**	Of any ten persons who kill themselves, eight have given definite warnings of their suicidal intentions.
FABLE:	Suicide happens without warning.	**FACT:**	Studies reveal that the suicidal person gives many clues and warnings regarding his suicidal intentions.
FABLE:	Suicidal people are fully intent on dying.	**FACT:**	Most suicidal people are undecided about living or dying, and they "gamble with death," leaving it to others to save them. Almost no one commits suicide without letting others know how he is feeling.
FABLE:	Once a person is suicidal, he is suicidal forever.	**FACT:**	Individuals who wish to kill themselves are "suicidal" for only a limited period of time.
FABLE:	Improvement following a suicidal crisis means that the suicidal risk is over.	**FACT:**	Most suicides occur within about three months following the beginning of "improvement," when the individual has the energy to put his morbid thoughts and feelings into effect.
FABLE:	Suicide strikes much more often among the rich—or, conversely, it occurs almost exclusively among the poor.	**FACT:**	Suicide is neither the rich man's disease nor the poor man's curse. Suicide is very "democratic" and is represented proportionately among all levels of society.
FABLE:	Suicide is inherited or "runs in the family."	**FACT:**	Suicide does not run in families. It is an individual pattern.
FABLE:	All suicidal individuals are mentally ill, and suicide always is the act of a psychotic person.	**FACT:**	Studies of hundreds of genuine suicide notes indicate that although the suicidal person is extremely unhappy, he is not necessarily mentally ill.

Source: *Some Facts About Suicide* by E. S. Shneidman and N. L. Farberow, Washington D.C., PHS Publication No. 852, U.S. Government Printing Office, 1961.

Figure 5. Suicide is one of the 10 leading causes of death in the United States. No one has yet found a neat set of answers for why people want to die, but psychologists feel that attempts at or threats of suicide should be seriously regarded as cries for help.

applied more often to the suicidal patients than to the controls. Twenty-nine of the sixty-one suicide patients previously had been placed on the "suicide status" list because of threats, thoughts or impulses, and depression; twenty-seven of these were eventually removed from the list as "improved." The researchers concluded that a person with a background of suicidal threats and depression is a major suicide risk, even if he seems to have recovered. (Miss Plath's novel was autobiographical, and she successfully committed suicide a few years after writing it.)

Alienation and depression are not contradictory states, and the interplay between them may account for the suicide's situation. For example, personality difficulties may generate behavior that others respond negatively to, which increases alienation and deepens depression. That, in turn, leads to even more disturbed behavior, more rejection, more withdrawal. Suicide attempts are often regarded as "cries for help," but if they are not or cannot be answered, the attempts may continue and, sooner or later, succeed.

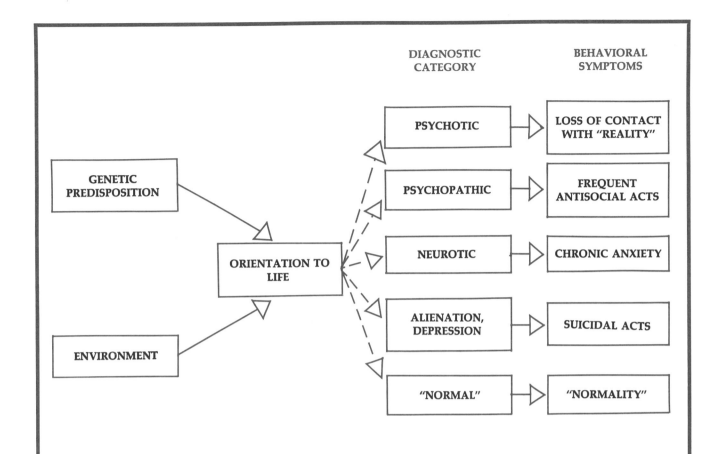

	DIAGNOSTIC CATEGORY		BEHAVIORAL SYMPTOMS
	PSYCHOTIC		LOSS OF CONTACT WITH "REALITY"
	PSYCHOPATHIC		FREQUENT ANTISOCIAL ACTS
GENETIC PREDISPOSITION → ORIENTATION TO LIFE ← ENVIRONMENT	NEUROTIC		CHRONIC ANXIETY
	ALIENATION, DEPRESSION		SUICIDAL ACTS
	"NORMAL"		"NORMALITY"

PUTTING IT TOGETHER: The Disordered Mind

Our conception of an individual's state of mental order or disorder involves our assessment of the adaptiveness of a life orientation to the culture in which one lives. One's *orientation to life* is a product of one's *genetic predisposition* as well as one's early and present *environment*. The origins of mental disorder may be in confused or rejecting relationships with parents during childhood and the resulting psychodynamic inner conflict, portions of which may not be available to conscious awareness.

Diagnostic categories are useful in communicating about individuals when prescribing treatment. However, they are not always clear-cut and should be exercised cautiously with respect to permanent labeling of individuals.

These categories are dependent upon social norms and accepted notions of "reality" and "normality." An individual is considered *psychotic* when his orientation to life generally involves a *loss of contact with reality*. One is considered to be *psychopathic* if one is indifferent to the rights of others and to social punishments and engages in *frequent antisocial acts*. A *neurotic* individual lives in a state of *chronic anxiety*. People whose life orientations are characterized by *alienation* from other people and who undergo severe depressions may engage in suicidal behavior which may involve abortive attempts at suicide or a completed suicidal act. If an individual's life orientation is generally adaptive we consider him to be "normal."

WHAT'S ACCEPTED AND WHAT'S DEBATED

1. WHAT'S ACCEPTED . . .

1. Individuals may inherit a constitutional or genetic *predisposition* to psychosis that may or may not emerge as a result of environmental forces.

2. Some neurotic and other disturbed behaviors can be simulated in experimental situations.

3. Neurotic behaviors can often be traced to early childhood learning experiences.

4. The development of antisocial and other sociopathic personality traits is associated with parental rejection.

5. Suicide is often related to depression and alienation; suicide threats and attempts should be taken seriously.

2. WHAT'S DEBATED . . .

1. Whether the primary determinants of the psychoses lie in genetic-biological anomalies or in the environment.

2. The relative contribution of social learning and psychodynamic interpretations to the genesis of neuroses.

3. The precise variables in the relation of parental rejection to the development of sociopathy.

4. The underlying processes in suicidal behaviors: whether these behaviors really should be classified with other *pathological* conditions.

ISSUE: IS MENTAL ILLNESS A MYTH?

As we have seen, psychologists still debate the origins of mental illness: is it determined by genetics, by the environment, or both? Recently, psychiatrist Thomas S. Szasz, whose criticisms of traditional approaches to mental disorders have generated widespread controversy, has made a surprising suggestion: mental illness is a myth. Szasz states flatly that psychiatry is a "pseudo-science," comparable to astrology and alchemy; the psychiatrist, he contends, is merely "impersonating" a medical role. Psychiatric diagnoses and terminology are just so much mumbojumbo, because mental illness does not exist at all.

Szasz readily concedes that there is a condition that we label "mental illness," but he claims that this condition is not an *illness.* It is, he claims, merely a deviation from socially acceptable modes of behavior, which society chooses to define as "mad." These definitions of "madness" vary from time to time and place to place. For example, if an American talks to spirits, we think this behavior very odd; but if someone living in a society that believes in spirits does so, then the behavior is perfectly normal and acceptable. There is, accordingly, a crucial difference between mental disorders and physical illness. The symptoms of measles, for instance, are the same everywhere in the world, and all doctors can agree on them. But the symptoms of mental disorders vary widely, depending on local social definitions.

Szasz believes that behavior labeled "mental illness" is really a "problem in living," a defective strategy that a person undertakes, usually involuntarily and unconsciously, in order to handle a difficult situation. Every society makes things easy for someone who occupies a "sick" role, and an individual who is under great stress may find it convenient to adopt the role of one who is mentally "sick" and thereby avoid responsibility for his or her actions. Mentally disordered behavior is, he feels, learned (environmentally determined) and is probably adopted because other forms of self-expression and interpersonal relationships have been ineffective. The psychiatrist, in effect, acts as an agent of society, defining the deviant as "mentally ill" in much the same way that clergymen once acted as agents of society and defined some deviants as "witches."

An even more radical critique of traditional psychiatry has been made by R.D. Laing, who regards mental disorders as simply an alternative form of consciousness, and possibly a better one than what passes for "sanity." Laing sardonically observes that "normal men have killed perhaps 100,000,000 of their fellow normal men in the course of this century" and contends that the statesmen of the world who boast they have doomsday weapons are more divorced from reality than the worst raving lunatic. Laing believes that people become mentally disordered as a result of previous stress, usually within the family context. The individual, he believes, feels his or her personality to be vulnerable, to consist of an outer, false self and an inner, true self. The boundary between the two threatens to collapse, driving the individual into the state termed mental illness. Laing insists that the behavior and speech of schizophrenics is not so random and disordered as it appears. If the observer takes the trouble to learn about the person's background, the supposedly disordered acts and statements become quite comprehensible.

To Laing, the experience of mental illness is in reality a "voyage into hypersanity," a journey into another form of consciousness. He sees this journey as part of a "natural healing process," a necessary experience which the psychiatrist merely disrupts by his attempts at "cure." Traditional cures are, Laing believes, simply a "degradation ceremony," a humiliation involving drugs, straitjackets, electric shocks, removal of civil rights, and incarceration. Instead, he feels, the psychiatrist should act as a "priest" who facilitates the voyage and thus hastens the healing process.

But Laing is not very much more enthusiastic about the experience that passes for "insanity" than that which passes for "sanity." Because hypersanity has its origins in our sanity, it is corrupted: "Our sanity is not 'true' sanity. Their madness is not 'true' madness. . . . The madness we encounter in 'patients' is a gross travesty, a mockery, a grotesque caricature of what the natural healing process . . . might be." Views such as these have excited intense interest. On some campuses, Laing has become a cult figure, while in some medical circles he is regarded as quite mad himself.

In 1973 a California psychiatrist, D.L. Rosenhan, published a study that attracted national attention. Rosenhan, who is also critical of traditional psychiatric labels, arranged for eight of his associates, all of whom were quite normal and had no history of psychiatric disorders, to present themselves individually at twelve different mental hospitals in five states. On arrival at the hospitals, they announced a single symptom: they could hear a voice uttering a single word, such as "thud." Apart from falsifying their names and jobs, they gave no other inaccurate information about themselves or their histories. In every case, they were admitted to the hospital and diagnosed as schizophrenics. They behaved perfectly normally inside the institutions, but were held for an average of nineteen days. The shortest stay was a week and the longest was fifty-two days. Ironically, many of the inmates approached these pseudopatients and charged that they were not really insane. They were thought to be journalists or researchers "checking up on the place." The staff, however, did not suspect the sanity of the pseudopatients in a single case. When the researchers were finally released they were termed "schizophrenics in remission." Rosenhan concluded from the study that "psychological categorization of mental illness is useless at best and downright harmful, misleading . . . at worst . . . How many are wrongly thought to be mentally ill?" Other psychiatrists, however, challenged his thesis and his methodology, suggesting that a better experiment would be to release eight mentally disordered people into the community and see if *they* were detected.

The views of Szasz, Laing and their supporters are rejected by most psychiatrists, but they are proving influential nonetheless. One important contribution they have made is to draw attention to the denial of civil rights to mental patients, and to urge more humane treatment of inmates in mental hospitals. A second contribution, which is likely to have long-term consequences, is to point out the limitations of a purely medical model of mental disorders and to emphasize the role of social definitions in determining who is "mad" and the role of social experiences in generating mental disorders.

The opinions of Laing, Szasz, Rosenhan may be—presently—radical statements. But they point us to serious problems about which most professionals and laypeople would agree: broad labelings such as "pathological" and "normal" *can* be dangerous, and "disorder" may be really a matter of degree rather than of kind.

Unit 14

Using Language

OVERVIEW

Some of the most important concepts and processes involved in the study of language as behavior are outlined. First, how children learn to speak the language of their culture in early childhood is discussed. Then some of the characteristics of language and its users that aid in understanding language are presented. Finally, what is known about the relationships between language and thinking is reviewed.

UNIT OUTLINE

DEFINITION AND BACKGROUND
1. *Definition:* using language is employing a grammatic combination of words to communicate meaning.
2. *Background:* Noam Chomsky (1928–   ).

QUESTIONS AND EVIDENCE
1. How does an infant develop the use of language?
Hypotheses:
   a. *Language-acquisition-device:* children are born with brain structures organized such that language will be developed in predetermined ways. **229**
   b. *Stages:* all infants pass through an invariant series of developmental stages as they acquire language. **231**
   c. *Rules:* the acquisition of new language develops by learning a set of grammatical rules. **232**
2. What helps us understand language?
   a. *Redundancy:* speech is highly predictable because the structure of language provides repeated clues about what is likely to come next. **234**
   b. *Familiarity:* the intelligibility of speech depends on the listener's ability to segment speech-as-sound into meaningful units. **234**
3. Are the rules of a language rules for thinking?
Hypotheses:
   a. *Cognitive-dependent:* a certain amount of cognitive or intellectual development must take place before language acquisition can proceed. **236**
   b. *Linguistic-relativity:* the characteristics of a particular language and its rules determine how its speakers think and even how they perceive reality. **238**
   c. *Equality:* any natural language or dialect is equivalent to any other in capacity for expression. **238**

IMPORTANT CONCEPTS

	page
grammar	228
instrumental learning	228
language	228
language acquisition	228
linguistics	229
object permanence	237
psycholinguistics	229
redundancy	234
reinforcement	232

The developing child's language environment is superimposed upon an innate capacity to use language.

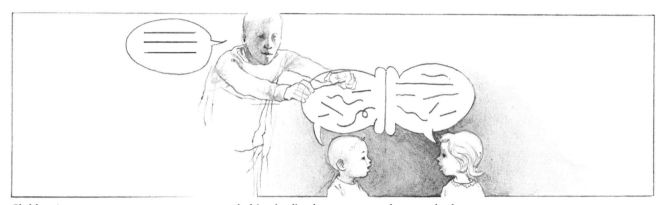

Children's attempts to communicate are aided by feedback concerning the use of rules.

The development of language competence enhances the ability to communicate.

DEFINITION AND BACKGROUND

Asked to name some languages, most people would probably embark on a world tour: English, French, Spanish, Russian, Chinese, Swahili, Urdu, Eskimo . . . After listing a dozen or more languages of this type, they might begin to think of others: the language of mathematics, for instance, or the gestural sign language of the deaf, or artificial languages such as FORTRAN, used with computers. Languages can be natural or artificial, spoken or gestural or written, verbal or numerical or pictorial. Their variety, like Cleopatra's, seems infinite.

Different as languages are from each other, linguists tell us that they have two things in common: they all include both semantic units (words, in most cases) and a set of rules for combining the units (grammar). More simply, a DEFINITION of using language is employing a grammatic combination of words to communicate meaning.

If you have ever visited a country where the language was totally unfamiliar to you, you are well aware that learning to understand and speak a new language is no simple matter. Yet ordinary children do it with apparent ease. By the age of four, a child has acquired most of the basics of his language, and he masters most of its subtleties by the time he is ten.

The process by which a child comes to know and use his native language, called language acquisition, is the main FOCUS of this unit. Also discussed are some characteristics of language that help people understand meaning, and the relation between language and thinking.

BACKGROUND: NOAM CHOMSKY (1928–   )

Until the 1950s, psychologists identified language behavior almost exclusively as an aspect of verbal learning and memory—a set of conditioned responses not significantly different from other learned behaviors. Psychologists thought of language as a collection of words, letters, and specific sounds, and they tried to see how these verbal bits and pieces became associated and remembered under specific conditions. Then, in 1957, B. F. Skinner of Harvard University published *Verbal Behavior,* in which he explained language acquisition in terms of instrumental learning: because children are rewarded for proper speech

Figure 1. The revolutionary linguistic theories of Noam Chomsky have caused many learning and developmental psychologists to reexamine their methods and assumptions.

and corrected when they make mistakes, so Skinner's argument went, they learn to talk in much the same way they learn to behave themselves (see Unit 27). Noam Chomsky, a linguist from MIT, took strenuous exception to Skinner's theory. Written just a few blocks away from Skinner's campus, Chomsky's 1959 review of *Verbal Behavior* emphasized that "the remarkable capacity of the child to generalize, hypothesize, and 'process information' in a variety of very special and apparently highly complex ways may be largely innate or may develop through some sort of learning or through maturation of the nervous system." Chomsky argued that the learning theories of psychology had failed completely to account for the grammatical structure of a language—that part of a language that linguists tend to regard as most important. How can a learning theory account for the native speaker's ability to produce and understand the many sentences he has never heard before?

Chomsky's powerful arguments landed explosively in the midst of the work of developmental psychology. If traditional learning theories could not explain language acquisition, what could? Where could research begin?

Language-oriented psychologists quickly proposed a number of controversial ideas. Chomsky himself, with some others, speculated that language acquisition may stem from an inborn "language-acquisition device" that helps an infant absorb his language. In one sense, this proposal did nothing but label a process that remained mysterious. However, it did give impetus to new research. Psychologists such as Roger Brown of Harvard began to consider the infant not merely a miniature adult speaker but a fluent speaker of an "exotic" language all his own. From this point of view, largely inspired by Piaget, a pioneer in the study of children's mental processes (see Unit 16), the psycholinguist's task is to discover what the rules for children's grammars are and to show how a child's language is gradually transformed into the language of his environment. In short Chomsky's proposal succeeded in turning psychologists away from an exclusive preoccupation with vocabulary and toward a concern for rules in language development and usage.

Many psychologists were also influenced by the distinction that Chomsky drew between language competence and language performance. Competence refers to a speaker's knowledge of a language. According to Chomsky, describing the nature of this knowledge is the primary task of linguistics. But psychologists are more interested in how a person actually uses his knowledge—that is, in language performance. Performance requires competence, but it also involves other factors, such as memory, attention, and fatigue.

The emergence of new ideas and controversies in the study of language development has continued, with many of the most basic issues still unresolved and debates over "the mechanism" of language acquisition still raging. Psychologists are just beginning to cope with the fact that language is a relatively complex ability that seems to be acquired by children in a relatively short time.

QUESTIONS AND EVIDENCE

1. How does an infant develop the use of language?
2. What helps us understand language?
3. Are the rules of a language rules for thinking?

1. HOW DOES AN INFANT DEVELOP THE USE OF LANGUAGE?

The *language-acquisition-device (LAD) hypothesis* states that children are born with brain structures organized such that language will be developed in predetermined ways. Although this idea, suggested in our time by Chomsky and others, remains controversial, it is not new. In fact, innate determinism was a dominant explanation in the nineteenth century. In the modern view, some innate mechanism or "pre-

QUESTION	1. HOW DOES AN INFANT DEVELOP THE USE OF LANGUAGE?		
HYPOTHESES	LANGUAGE-ACQUISITION DEVICE	STAGES	RULES
DESCRIPTIVE EVIDENCE		ASSESS: universality of developmental stages of language	ASSESS: 1. child's ability to apply rules of grammar to nonsense words 2. ability of chimpanzee to learn language
EXPERIMENTAL EVIDENCE	VARY: types of sounds presented MEASURE: ability to discriminate changes		

wiring" of the infant's brain would account for the great speed with which a child acquires language relative to other abilities.

Although this is a very difficult notion to test, the task of finding evidence to support the notion of innateness has not been beyond the scope of some investigators. They assume that if there is an innate LAD, infants might be able to perceive some differences in speech sounds very soon after birth.

EXPERIMENTAL EVIDENCE

Investigators: P. Eimas, E. R. Siqueland, P. Juscqyk, and J. Vigorito
Source, Date: "Speech Perception in Infants," 1971
Location: Brown University
Subjects: 36 one- and four-month-old infants
Materials: Special nipple, polygraph recorders, electronic speech synthesizer

One of the most vital discriminations a speaker must make is between voiced and unvoiced consonants. For example, in uttering the voiced consonant *b,* the vocal cords are used, as in "bun." The unvoiced consonant *p,* on the other hand, passes air through the lips only, as in "pun." The experimenters reasoned that if a very young infant could discriminate between the two, then it could be assumed that there is some language ability from birth and that the LAD may indeed exist.

Eimas and his colleagues devised a special dry nipple to capitalize on one of the few reliable motor skills of a one-month-old infant—sucking. The average sucking rate for each infant was obtained by hooking the nipple to a polygraph machine that recorded on a moving roll of paper (like an electrocardiogram) the frequency of sucking. Then an electronic voice synthesizer was hooked up to the nipple. The voice synthesizer simply presents completely uniform sounds, in this case either *b* or *p.* This machine was adjusted so that the rate of sucking influenced the volume of the voice synthesizer—the quicker the sucking, the louder the sounds.

As soon as an infant discovers that it can change the volume of *b*s pouring from the synthesizer by sucking faster, it will begin to exercise this skill, and the synthesizer booms out while the polygraph swings up to record the increase in sucking. Before long, however, the infant tires of this play, and the

sucking rate returns to its average rate—psychologists call this return *habituation* (see Unit 27). ~~The baby becomes habituated to the voice synthesizer and begins to suck at his normal pace again.~~

The experimenters knew from previous studies that after a baby was habituated to the nipple and voice synthesizer, any change in the sound perceptible to the baby would result in an increased sucking rate: the infant would explore the new sound much as it had the original sound, before habituation. They let the control group suck away happily after their initial habituation, with no change in the sound. The experimental group, on the other hand, was presented with *p*s instead of *b*s soon after habituation.

The results are presented in Figure 2. Apparently the experimental babies could perceive the difference between *b* and *p,* for their rate of sucking rose sharply after the synthesizer changed sounds, despite the fact that they certainly could not produce the sounds. Nor had they heard much speech. Nor, most importantly, were they rewarded for their accomplishment. While the experiment does not prove the existence of the

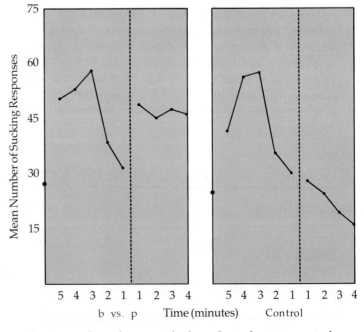

Figure 2. The sucking rate of infants changed in response to the change of sounds from *b* to *p* or *p* to *b,* indicating that infants can discriminate between some dimensions of language as speech relatively soon after birth. Adapted from Eimas, Siqueland, Juscqyk, and Vigorito (1971).

language acquisition device, it does show that some elements of speech ability are present at an age early enough to imply that at least part of language acquisition skills are innate.

The innate biological factors that influence language acquisition may not be present immediately after birth but may appear at later stages in the developmental process—as what psychologists call maturational events. The *stages hypothesis* states that all infants pass through an invariant series of developmental stages as they acquire language.

DESCRIPTIVE EVIDENCE

Investigators: D. I. Slobin and colleagues
Source, Date: "Universals of Grammatical Development in
    Children," 1970
Location: University of California, Berkeley
Subjects: Many children from several cultures
Materials: Tape recordings of speech samples

The Berkeley team has found that all American children go through similar stages of development in acquiring English grammar and is now examining the process in eight other languages: German, Russian, Finnish, Luo (Kenya), Samoan, Japanese, Serbian, and Bulgarian. The children's speech samples are analyzed as if they are languages in their own right rather than primitive versions of adult German, Russian, and so on.

The overall impression gained from the data so far is that children everywhere go through similar stages of development. Typically, there is a period of babbling, even in deaf children, that ends at approximately eighteen months. Overlapping this period is a stage of single-word utterances. Then, at about eighteen to twenty-four months, two-word phrases begin. The two-word utterances are very important, for they not only constitute a stage of development but also seem to follow particular patterns in all the languages being studied.

One general pattern is that each word of the two words can be put into one of two classes: a small class of "pivot" words that are used often, and a much larger "open" class of words that are always paired with the pivots (see Figure 3).

The pivot-open distinction emphasizes classification on the basis of structure. The content of the two-word utterances has also been classified accord-

Pivots	Opens
	Boy
Allgone	Sock
Byebye	Boat
Big	Fan
More	Milk
Pretty	Plane
My	Vitamins
See	Hot
Nightnight	Mommy
	Daddy

Figure 3. Sample pivot and open-class vocabulary from the speech of a two-year-old child. From McNeill (1966).

ing to use or function. The first six classes have to do with objects:

1. Object identification: "that car," "it ball"
2. Repetition or increase: "more milk"
3. Negation: "not shoe"
4. Nonexistence: "allgone cookie"
5. Possession: "my book"
6. Attribution: "pretty dress"

The last three have to do with *agents*.

7. Agent-action: "Adam do"
8. Agent-object: "Mommy shoe"
9. Action-object: "see hand"

These basic functional categories appear to be the earliest stage in the development of grammar—the rules that govern the production of meaningful sentences. Note that their meaning depends largely on context. "Mommy shoe" could denote possession—"Mommy's shoe"—or it could be a request—"Mommy, put on my shoe."

During the period when learning theories dominated psychology in the United States—roughly 1920 to 1950—the principal processes of language acquisition were thought to be imitation, conditioning, and reinforcement (reward). It was argued that whenever the child made languagelike sounds in imitation of adults, the adults rewarded such behavior with applause and encouragement. Thus, it was thought, the child acquired correct speech in order to avoid adult disapproval.

Psychologists generally accept that a child can learn the meaning of particular words by imitation and reinforcement, particularly such words as "Mama," "Papa," and "cookie." But the rules of grammar are seldom, if ever, presented to him directly. Few adults understand grammar well enough to teach it systematically, and the child could not understand such abstract instructions anyway. David McNeill (1966) recorded a conversation that illustrates the difficulties of using the imitation-and-reward theory for explaining how grammar is acquired:

Child: Nobody don't like me.
Mother: No, say "nobody likes me."
Child: Nobody don't like me.
Mother: No, say "nobody likes me."
Child: Nobody don't like me.
[Seven more repetitions . . .]
Mother: No, now listen carefully; say "nobody likes me."
Child: Oh! Nobody don't likes me!

One widely accepted idea in cognitive psychology is that children learn rules rather than a hodgepodge of single associations or ideas. This agrees very well with the linguists' conception of grammar, which itself is a collection of such rules about how to speak. The *rules hypothesis* states that the acquisition of new language develops by learning a set of grammatical rules.

Because the relation between an object and the sound that represents it is arbitrary, vocabulary words and their pronunciations must be learned one at a time. A child cannot speak a word he has never heard, for he has no way to predict what it might be. There is nothing about the fruit of an oak tree that suggests it should be called an acorn, and even representational words such as "bow-wow" and "quack" would be hard to come up with if one had never heard them before.

Sentences and other complex constructions, by contrast, need not be learned singly. The grammar of a language provides general rules for combining words in a meaningful fashion—rules that few of us can state but all of us, including young children, use with ease. A child's grammar guides him to say, "Put your coat on" but never "On coat your put." Once he can say "Put your coat on," he can also say "put your wig on" (assuming that he knows the word "wig"), even though he has never heard that particular sentence before. If a child really does learn rules, then he should be able to use nonsense words to produce grammatically meaningful sentences that he has never heard.

DESCRIPTIVE EVIDENCE

Investigator: J. Berko
Source, Date:"The Child's Learning of English Morphology,"
  1958
Location: Radcliffe College
Subjects: 94 children from ages four to seven
Materials: Sentences, nonsense words, and pictures

In individual interviews, each child was shown something in a picture and asked to complete a sentence using a nonsense word. For example:
"This is a wug. Now there is another one. There are two of them. There are two ——."
Most of the children verbally answered "wugs," with a "z" sound, indicating the application of rules to sounds they had never heard before.

Children were also asked to complete the following sentence: "This is a man who knows how to gling. He glings every day. Today he glings. Yesterday he ____." Most children replied "glinged."This was an especially interesting response, indicating the use of the child's own rules rather than imitation of adults, because most adults answer "glang" or "glung."

Until recently, it was thought most unlikely that lower animals could learn any grammatical rules. During the first half of this century, several experimenters made valiant efforts to teach chimpanzees to speak, raising them in their own homes and treating them like human children, but the chimps never managed to master more than a few rough approximations of word sounds. Then, in the late 1960s, a breakthrough occurred. The trouble with the earlier experiments, it seems, was not that chimps have no capacity for acquiring language but that they find spoken sounds an unsuitable medium.

DESCRIPTIVE EVIDENCE

Investigators: R. A. Gardner and B. T. Gardner
Source, Date: "Teaching Sign Language to a Chimpanzee,"
* 1969*
Location: University of Nevada
Subject: Washoe, a female chimpanzee
Materials: American Sign Language

A Dutch zoologist, Dr. Adriaan Kortlandt, noted in a 1967 paper published after one of several expeditions to Africa that chimpanzees use their hands extensively for signaling one another. "It is hardly possible to overestimate the importance of the hand in chimpanzee social life," Kortlandt wrote. "The hand is used to beg for food, to ask and give reassurance and encouragement and in various other kinds of contact." There are gestures for, among other things, "Come with me," "May I pass?" and "You're welcome."

Even as Kortlandt was reporting these observations, the Gardners had begun their experiments with a one-year-old chimp, Washoe. Washoe was given her own house trailer, and the experimenters agreed to converse with one another, as well as with the chimp, only in American Sign Language. (American Sign Language—ASL—is the system used by the deaf in the United States and Canada.) By the time Washoe was six years old, the Gardners had taught her a vocabulary of 150 signs. Their experiment has engaged the attention of linguists, psychologists, and zoologists all over the world.

Chimpanzees, the researchers have found, seem to enter into language training without necessarily expecting rewards. Although it is true that a reward system is used to teach vocabulary, combinations of words appear spontaneously. Washoe has not only learned word signs; she has also acquired an elementary grammar and can construct sentences.

In 1971 Washoe moved to the University of Oklahoma, where she joined a whole colony of chimpanzees and researchers, all of whom are in the process of learning ASL. A writer with a special interest in chimpanzees recently visited the community and recorded this moment with Washoe, who was standing in the middle of a pond on a small island given over wholly to the chimpanzees.

> She begged and begged Roger to come and fetch her. She kept signing, "Roger ride come gimme sweet eat please hurry hurry you come please gimme sweet you hurry you come ride Roger come give Washoe fruit drink hurry hurry fruit drink sweet please please." . . . But here is the unbelievable part. A plane flew over just then, and Washoe mentioned that, too. She signed, "You me ride in plane." She really did! [Hahn, *The New Yorker*, 1971.]

The community in Oklahoma is new, and researchers are watching its development closely. Will the chimpanzees, once they have learned enough signs, begin to speak to one another? When and if they have baby chimpanzees, will the parents teach the infants to sign?

Washoe's language, you may have noticed, is rather telegraphic. Where you or I might say, "Roger, would you please ride over here and give me a sweet to eat—and hurry!" Washoe says, "Roger ride come gimme sweet eat please hurry hurry." Yet both sentences are easy to understand, and both have roughly the same meaning. The reason we can readily understand both versions lies partly in the way languages themselves are structured and partly in our capacity to impose structures on them.

Figure 4. A conversation with the chimpanzee, Washoe, using American Sign Language. Washoe has learned word signs, acquired an elementary grammar, and she can construct sentences.

HYPOTHESES	REDUNDANCY	FAMILIARITY
DESCRIPTIVE EVIDENCE		
EXPERIMENTAL EVIDENCE	VARY: number of letters in written passage MEASURE: ease of predicting next letter	VARY: 1. placing of clicks in sentences 2. amount of violation of rules of grammar MEASURE: 1. subjective localization of clicks 2. how quickly passage can be memorized

2. WHAT HELPS US UNDERSTAND LANGUAGE?

It is possible that language is not quite as complex and variable as it seems to be. You must have noticed how you can sometimes know and respond to what another person is saying long before he finishes speaking. One explanation for this ability can be formulated as the *redundancy hypothesis,* which states that speech is highly predictable because the structure of language provides repeated clues about what is likely to come next.

EXPERIMENTAL EVIDENCE

Investigators: N. G. Burton and J. C. R. Licklider
Source, Date:"Long-Range Constraints in the Statistical Structure of Printed English," 1955
Location: Massachusetts Institute of Technology
Subjects: 10 college students
Materials: 100 passages from 10 paperback novels in English

The passages, chosen at random, were roughly equal in reading difficulty but varied in length. The first included no letters at all; the other nine were 1, 2, 4, 8, 16, 32, 64, 128 and 10,000 letters long. The subjects had to look at each passage and guess which letter of the alphabet would come nex (did you guess?). Spaces between words were counted as letters. The subjects had to continue guessing until they named the next letter correctly.

The results of this study appear in Figure 5, which depicts relative redundancy (the average percentage of guesses before a subject named the next letter correctly) as a function of the number of letters given to the subject. Up to thirty-two letters, the ease with which subjects guessed the next letter increased rapidly. After that point, additional letters did not seem to help.

Most printed passages in English are longer than thirty-two letters. The average redundancy for such passages in this experiment is between 66 and 80 percent; that is, any letter after the thirty-second is 66 to 80 percent determined by the preceding material.

In everyday speech, where we ordinarily deal with language from moment to moment, its predictability and interdependence help us greatly. No one would question that the intelligibility of speech also depends on the listener's knowledge of the language he is hearing. Less obvious, perhaps, is the idea that a speaker or listener actually imposes structure and form on a stream of speech. The *familiarity hypothesis* states that the intelligibility of speech depends on the listener's ability to segment speech-as-sound into meaningful units.

The speakers of a language with which we are unfamiliar often seem to be talking too fast, running all the words together into a jumble. Actually the objective, acoustical reality of speech-as-sound, this "jumble" is all our ears are ready to recognize. On the other hand, the speakers of our own language seem to

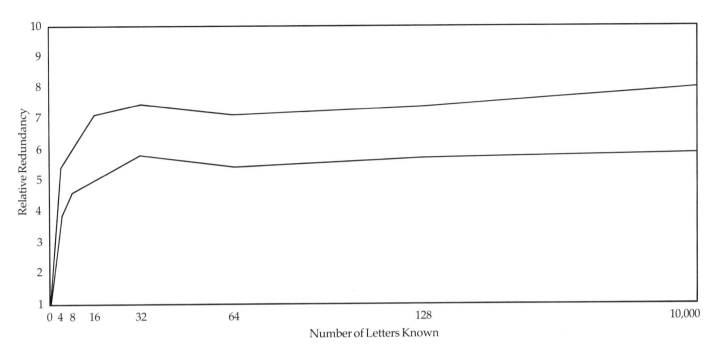

Figure 5. Relative redundancy as a function of the number of letters known by the subjects in the Burton-Licklider study (1955). Graph shows upper and lower limits as measured by the number of guesses required for each passage.

place tiny pauses between the separate words, and the demarcations between phrases and sentences can be clearly "heard."

Normal speech is largely a continuous flow, an "acoustic stream" of sound that rarely stops and constantly changes. Segmentation and structure are superimposed on this flow by the listener's perceptual processes and, ultimately, by his knowledge and experience with the grammar of the language.

EXPERIMENTAL EVIDENCE

Investigators: J. A. Fodor and T. G. Bever
Source, Date: "The Psychological Reality of Linguistic Segments," 1965
Location: Massachusetts Institute of Technology
Subjects: 36 right-handed college students
Materials: Recorded tapes of 25 sentences and tapes of click noises; earphones

The subjects were presented with normal English sentences eight to twenty-two words in length, such as "That he was happy was evident from the way he smiled." While receiving one of these sentences in one ear, they heard a click in the other ear. Each subject was instructed to write the entire sentence out and to indicate graphically where in the sentence the click had occurred.

The subjects did not always "hear" the click where it had actually occurred in the sentence. Instead, the clicks tended to be perceived near the major grammatical boundaries in the sentences—between what linguists call the constituents of a sentence. For example, in "That he was happy was evident from the way he smiled," the major constituent break occurs between "happy" and "was," and a click actually added before or after this point was reported as being heard nearer the break. The reported clicks "gravitated" toward the boundaries between constituents. When the click actually occurred at the boundary, subjects made very few errors in localizing it accurately. But when it occurred between boundaries or between a boundary and the end of the sentence, the average error rate rose to 80 percent.

If the perceptual units of language are determined by the speaker-listener's knowledge of, and familiarity with, his language and its grammar, then those are, to some degree, rules for perceiving. But they may also be rules for learning and remembering. If language and grammar do provide such rules, then a sentence like "'Twas brillig and the slithy toves did gire and gimble in the wabe" should be easier to memorize than "Gimble the in toves gire and the Brillig the did wabe 'twas slithy."

EXPERIMENTAL EVIDENCE

Investigator: W. Epstein
Source, Date: "The Influence of Syntactical Structure on Learning," 1961
Location: University of Kansas
Subjects: 192 introductory psychology students
Materials: Nonsense words and normal words

Six categories of word strings were used:

1. Nonsense words plus function endings ordered to look like a grammatically structured sentence—for example, "The yigs wur vumly rixing hum in jegest miv."
2. The same nonsense words without function endings—for example, "The yig wur vum rix hum in jeg miv."
3. The same nonsense words as in 1, but in random order—for example, "Yigs rixing wur miv hum vumly the in jegest."
4. The same nonsense words but with function endings randomized—for example, "The yigly wur vums rixest hum in jeging miv."
5. Semantically anomalous but grammatical sentences—for example, "Cruel tables sang falling circles to empty bitter pencils."
6. Same words as 5, but in random order—for example, "To falling sang pencils bitter circle empty table cruel."

The subjects were divided into six groups corresponding to the above categories, and each subject received just two sentences in the category. After viewing a string for seven seconds, the subject was given thirty seconds to write out the string word for word. This procedure was repeated until the response was a perfect repetition of the sentence. The rate of learning was measured by the number of seven-second trials it took the subject to reach one perfect repetition.

The grammatical sentence made up of real words and rules (5) was the easiest to learn. Nonsense words arranged according to grammatical rules (1) proved easier to learn than the same nonsense words arranged without rules (3).

On the level of learning and remembering, grammatical rules affect mental processes. But how, if at all, is the ability to remember even such nonsensical structures related to the ability to think, at least in English?

3. ARE THE RULES OF A LANGUAGE RULES FOR THINKING?

The *cognitive-dependent hypothesis* predicts that a certain amount of cognitive or intellectual development must take place before language acquisition can proceed. In other words, language development will,

QUESTION	3. ARE THE RULES OF A LANGUAGE RULES FOR THINKING?		
HYPOTHESES	**COGNITIVE DEPENDENT**	**LINGUISTIC RELATIVITY**	**EQUALITY**
DESCRIPTIVE EVIDENCE		ASSESS: relation of different language structures to qualities used to match various objects	ASSESS: ability of both black and white children to repeat black English and standard English sentences
EXPERIMENTAL EVIDENCE	VARY: naming of toys MEASURE: toy preferences according to stage of cognitive development		

to some extent, depend on intellectual development.

This hypothesis stems largely from the work of the psychologist Jean Piaget (see Unit 16). Though he does not argue that language acquisition occurs as a function of intellectual accomplishments alone, he does lead us to expect some direct correspondences between cognitive development and comparable language development.

EXPERIMENTAL EVIDENCE

Investigators: G. C. Roberts and K. N. Black
Source, Date: "The Effect of Naming and Object Permanence
on Toy Preferences," 1972
Location: Purdue University
Subjects: 40 children, eighteen to twenty-two months old
Materials: Toys and timers

The basis for the first part of this experiment was the general assumption that naming something goes a long way toward placing the use of that object for a child. When a child asks, "What dat?" he is seeking not only a name but also a function. The two are inseparable, for to know what something is called is to know what it is used for, though the function may not be discovered at the same time as the name.

Roberts and Black assumed that if a child knew the name of a toy, he would be more likely to feel he knew what to do with it. They therefore predicted that he would be more likely to choose to handle or look at a named toy than an unnamed one.

The experimenters presented each child with sixteen toys, one at a time, and allowed him to hold and play with each toy for one minute. The toys were divided into eight pairs: a plastic banana and a plastic pear, a rubber squeaky kitty and a rubber squeaky fish, and so on. One of each pair was named, the other unnamed. The experimenter might say, for example, "Here is the kitty. You can hold the kitty. The kitty squeaks. What is it called? That's right, a kitty." The name was used about ten times in one minute. But in presenting the squeaky fish, he would say only, "Here is the toy. You can play with it. The toy squeaks." Finally, the experimenter presented the toys as matched pairs, plastic orange with plastic apple, or stuffed dog with stuffed donkey, and recorded the amount of time the child spent handling or looking at each toy of the pair in one minute. As

predicted, the children generally spent more time with the named toy.

The second part of the experiment measured the children's *object permanence.* An idea originating with Piaget, object permanence refers to a stage in cognitive development when a child begins to conceive of objects as having an existence even when out of sight or touch and to conceive of space as extending beyond his own perception. Once the child has object permanence, a missing object might be found in a place not immediately perceptible to the child. This, Piaget says, is a symbolic function, the beginning of the child's ability to operate with factors beyond his immediate sensations.

The test itself consisted of hiding a small object, such as a toy car or doll, behind one of three "screens": a plain green cloth, a plain blue cloth, and a green pillow. The experimenter first hid the object in her closed hand, then hid her hand under each of the screens in succession, leaving the object under the last screen. A child got a low score—showed little object permanence—if he searched for the toy only in the experimenter's hand, and a high score if he immediately searched directly underneath the last screen.

The children who were more sophisticated in searching for the hidden toy turned out to be the ones who, in the first part of the experiment, had been more likely to follow the cue of specific names in choosing the toy. Roberts and Black concluded "that children do spend more time on tactual manipulation of named objects than unnamed objects if they have achieved the stage of object permanence where they can follow an object through a sequence of invisible displacements, and that this difference is greatest when they have acquired a complete concept of object permanence." This implies that naming, the use of language, does affect the child's perception and use of objects, but only after a certain stage in his cognitive development has been reached.

Although this experiment does not indicate precisely what the relationship between cognitive and linguistic development is, it does suggest that the relationship is profound and subtle. It may even be possible that the particular language one uses affects how one thinks and perceives the world. This idea was developed by the very influential linguist and anthropologist Benjamin Whorf (1956). On the basis of his own observations of American Indian languages, especially Navaho, Whorf became the chief advocate of the *linguistic-relativity hypothesis, which states that the characteristics of a particular language and its rules determine how its speakers think and even how they perceive reality.*

In his own lifetime, this hypothesis became so associated with Whorf's writings that it is often referred to as the Whorfian hypothesis. It is very difficult to test, however, and there is little evidence even of a descriptive and correlational sort for the hypothesis.

DESCRIPTIVE EVIDENCE

Investigators: J. B. Carroll and J. B. Casagrande
Source, Date: "The Functions of Language Classification in Behavior," 1958
Location: Southwest Project in Comparative Linguistics
Subjects: 59 Navaho-dominant Navahos, 43 English-dominant Navahos, and 47 white Americans—all children
Materials: 10 sets of 3 "objects" per set, specially constructed.

Each of the children in three groups—Navaho children whose native language was Navaho, Navaho children whose native language was English, and white American children from Boston—was presented with ten pairs of objects, one pair at a time. The objects in each pair varied in only two of three respects: color, shape, and size. For example, a yellow stick was presented with a blue rope (differing in color and shape, size the same) or a small red ball with a large green ball (color and size differing, shape the same). After each pair had been shown to him, the child was given a third object and asked which of the other two "went best" with it. The third object was always the same as one of the original objects in one respect and the same as the other in another. For example, with a yellow stick and a blue rope, the third object might be a yellow rope or a blue stick. With a small red ball and a large green ball, the third object might be a small green ball or a large red one.

On the basis of Navaho verb forms, it was possible to predict that the Navaho child might pair objects on the basis of shape. For example, he would be likely to choose the yellow stick (not a blue rope) to go with a blue stick. On the other hand, an English-speaking child would be just as likely to use color as shape for

matching. English grammar, unlike Navaho, does not specify shape. Similarly, when shape and size were the variables, the Navaho-speaking child was expected to choose on the basis of shape rather than size; the English-speaking child might do either. These predictions assumed that the different forms of the Navaho and English languages would influence thinking in this kind of task.

To a large extent, the predictions were verified. The Navaho-speaking children did tend to match the objects according to shape, and the English-speaking children were more likely to sort on the basis of color or size. So it is possible to argue that the Navaho verb forms, which specify shape, influence the way Navaho-speaking children interact with the objects, relative to English-speaking children.

It should be noted, however, that the data only demonstrate a relationship. They do not show that language structure caused the differences in performance. There is always the possibility, for example, that the parents of the Navaho-speaking children stressed shape in early childhood play, while English-speaking parents stressed the value of knowing color differences.

Languages that have many words for colors make it easier for the language user to remember and recognize subtle shadings. Similarly, Eskimos have several words for snow and presumably can distinguish, remember, and recognize differences in its quality better than most other people. Australian Aborigines have many words for "kangaroo" (and no one word for kangaroos in general). Americans and Europeans have many words for "different" kinds of cars. But this does not prove that the members of other cultures are unable to make the perceptual discriminations involved. They may simply have no reason to bother.

Cross-cultural studies have also laid to rest the idea that some languages or dialects are "better" than others. As far as linguists and anthropologists have been able to discern, any language is capable of saying anything that any other language can say (though in some languages new words may have been coined to handle specific subjects). The *equality hypothesis* states that any natural language or dialect is equivalent to any other in capacity for expression.

Regardless of direct teaching or parental reward, children all over the world learn their native language adequately. This knowledge has led to the rejection of

TABLE 1. Differences Between Standard English and Black English

Standard English (SE)	Black English (BE)
Grammatical	
He's always coming.	He be comin'.[1]
He's been coming.	
He is working.	He workin'.[2]
He said he was coming.	He say he comin'.[3]
I asked *if* he wanted to go.	I aks *did* he want to go.[4]
I don't have any.	I don't got none.[5]
John's cousin	John cousin[6]
Two dogs, three cats, 50 cents.	Two dog, tree cat, 50 cent[7]
Sound	
This, that, thin	Dis, dat, tin
Right, tight	Rat, tat
Word, hold, mend	Wor', hole', men'
Brother, mother	Bruvvah, muvvah
Six, box	Sick, bock
Ain't, don't	Ain', don'
Ask	Aks
Vocabulary	
Peanut	Goober
Turtle	Cooter
Carry	Tote

[1]BE uses forms of "be" to indicate habitual activity.

[2]The word "is" does not normally occur in BE.

[3]BE does not change grammar to indicate past tense, and the meaning is usually clear from the context.

[4]See Baratz (1969) in the text.

[5]In BE double and triple negatives are not "mistakes"—they're obligatory, and always interpreted as one negative would be in SE.

[6]Possessives are indicated by word order only in BE.

[7]Since plurality is indicated by the number, the SE "s" is not really necessary and does not normally occur in BE.

Source: Adapted from J. C. Baratz, *Child Development*, 40 (1969), 889–901; and D. Z. Seymour, "Black English," *Intellectual Digest*, 2 (1972), 78–80.

the old notion that black children in America are "poor in language ability" or that they use "poor" English. Rather, what they usually speak is black English (BE), a language that has much in common with standard English (SE) but differs from it in several important ways (see Table 1). Some black English words—such as "dig" and "rap"—are now common usage.

DESCRIPTIVE EVIDENCE

Investigator: J. C. Baratz
Source, Date: "A Bi-dialectal Task for Determining Language Proficiency in Economically Disadvantaged Negro Children," 1969
Location: Education Study Center, Washington, D.C.
Subjects: Third and fifth graders from an inner-city school (black children) and from a lower-middle-class suburban school (white children)
Materials: 15 standard English and 15 black English sentences

The same fifteen sentences were spoken on tape in both standard and black English by a white male fluent in both languages. Each child heard a sentence twice, then had to try to repeat it orally word for word. After each child had responded to all the sentences on the tape, he listened to two additional sentences, one in standard and the other in black English, and was asked to guess who the speaker was from among a group of pictures containing black, white, and Oriental men, women, boys, and girls.

Results showed that white children were better than black at repeating standard English sentences, but black children were better than white at repeating black English sentences. The kinds of "errors" each child made are also interesting. For example, one typical difference between black English and standard English is the "do-he" or "did-he" flip. The standard English sentence "I asked Tom *if* he wanted to go to the picture that was playing at the Howard" is expressed in black English as "I aks Tom *do* he wanna go ta the picture that be playin' at the Howard." The black children consistently switched the standard "if" to "do" or "did" on their responses, while white children consistently switched the black English "do" or "did" to "if" in their responses. Both black and white children judged the black English sentences to be spoken by a black man 83.3 percent of the time, and both judged the standard English sentences to be spoken by a white man an average of about 78.4 percent of the time.

Black English has an identifiable and well-ordered structure, with its own rules. Its use is a disadvantage in American school systems only because standard English is usually used as the sole criterion of correctness in speaking and writing.

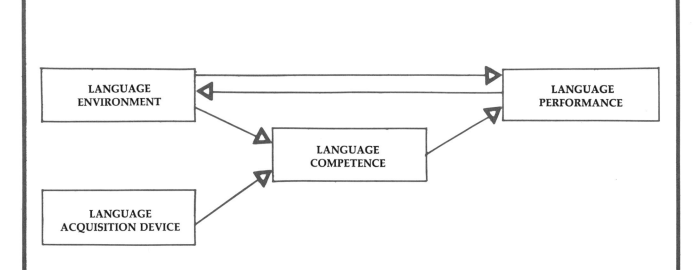

PUTTING IT TOGETHER: Using Language

Since the use of language involves communication, there is a constant relationship between *language performance* and the *language environment*. In learning how to use language to communicate, an infant babbles and discovers that certain sounds and voice inflections modify the environment. For example, a mother is likely to tell her baby "Go to papa," while handing the baby to one certain person. An important part of *language environment* is redundancy in meaning which allows for some predictability in anticipating appropriate responses. *Language environment* therefore provides immediate feedback and also helps develop long-range language competence.

Constant exposure to the language environment in conjunction with some sort of innate *language acquisition device* develops language competence. The LAD probably includes a predisposition to discover the grammatical rules of language, since some set of rules seems to be among the first properties of language an individual acquires. Competence includes the ability of the listener to segment continuous speech into meaningful units and this requires a special kind of familiarity with language. In general, the development of *language competence* seems to be dependent upon a sequence of stages in cognitive development.

It is reasonably clear that the way in which an individual uses language reflects how he or she thinks, but it is not so clear how restrictive or causal the relationship is between thinking processes and *language performance*. Evidence indicates that all languages and dialects are equally sophisticated in their capacity to communicate.

1. WHAT'S ACCEPTED . . .

1. There is some inborn basis for language acquisition.

2. The principles of imitation, learning, and reinforcement play some part in language development.

3. There are identifiable stages in the development of language, which hold true across cultural boundaries.

4. Redundancy or predictability in language helps a speaker-listener to anticipate and comprehend what he hears.

5. Much of a person's ability to interpret and use language depends on his familiarity with the sounds and grammar of the language.

6. Language, cognition, and memory are intimately related.

7. Any natural language or dialect is as capable as any other in expressing both precision and subtleties of meaning.

2. WHAT'S DEBATED . . .

1. Which aspects of language development can be attributed to an inborn language-acquisition device.

2. Whether such a device is specific to language abilities or shares general properties of cognitive structures.

3. The degree to which stages in language development are invariant in order, biologically determined, and may resist artificial acceleration.

4. Precisely what role social rewards and reinforcements play in language acquisition.

5. How language and cognition interact.

6. What methods should be used to help language-disadvantaged children to achieve competence in standard English in school.

The *linguistic-relativity hypothesis,* as we have seen, states that the characteristics of a language determine how its speakers think and even how they perceive reality. Benjamin Whorf raised the issue (also called the "Whorfian hypothesis"), and ever since psychologists and psycholinguists have been fascinated with this aspect of the relationship between language and thought.

It is difficult to judge the real effects of these linguistic differences. The Aztecs, for example, had only one word for snow, frost, cold, and ice. Does this mean that they perceived them all as one? We have only one word for "camel," while the Arabs have over a hundred. How does this influence their perception of camels as compared to ours? The French have only one word, *conscience,* for our two words, "conscience" and "consciousness." What exactly does their word mean to them? Can we truly understand their word *conscience*? Can they truly understand our two words, "conscience" and "consciousness"? The language of the Hopi Indians has no future tenses as we understand them. How does this affect the Hopi conception of time?

Some of these different usages seem to be of academic interest only, but some may have very real effects. Consider the example of the concept of "heat," which in all European languages appears as a noun—as though it were a thing or substance. In many other languages, however, the concept appears more accurately expressed as a verb ("heating")—as though it were a process, which in fact it is. Early scientific experiments, however, occurred almost exclusively in Europe. For centuries alchemists tried to discover "heat." They attempted to isolate "heat" in gas jars, to trap it in bottles, or to combine it with other chemicals—all, of course, to no avail. But if the concept of heat had been expressed in European languages as a verb (in the way that we speak of "boiling" but not of a substance called "boil"), would it even have occurred to the alchemists to look for it? If European languages had expressed the process of boiling as a noun, might the alchemists have looked for "boil" as well as for "heat"?

Social scientist Basil Bernstein has recently focused new interest on the linguistic-relativity hypothesis through an attempt to apply the concept to educational psychology. Bernstein believes that linguistic differences between middle-class and lower-class children are the main cause of the relatively poor academic achievement of the latter group.

Educational success, Bernstein points out, depends very much on linguistic skills. Through language, the child is able to organize his ideas and experiences, to think in terms of choices and possibilities, to manipulate and reorganize a problem mentally while attempting to solve it. Clearly, thinking cannot be more precise than the language it uses. The more the school requires abstract thought from the pupil, the more sophisticated the pupil's language has to be.

Bernstein believes that language can be classified into two quite distinct codes. One is available to both middle-class and lower-class children. But one is available to the middle class only.

The first code, which Bernstein terms the "restricted code" is the ungrammatical, colloquial speech that we all use most of the time. The speech has short, unfinished sentences, a small vocabulary, and a number of private, in-group phrases. Meaning is often implied by gestures, pauses, and facial expressions. We all use this code when talking to our close associates. A group of students, friends, prison convicts, or housewives all talk together in this private, restricted form of speech. But, Bernstein argues, this is the only form of speech that is available to the lower class child.

The second code, which Bernstein terms the "elaborated code" is the kind of formal language that we might use in writing, in giving a lecture, or in any other fairly formal situation. The language is highly individualized. Choice of words and phrases depends very much on the particular speaker. Sentences are longer, with wide vocabulary and extensive use of subordinate clauses. Grammar is accurate and meaning is made explicit by the use of very precise sentence structures. This code, Bernstein argues, is available only to middle-class children.

In school, the lower-class child is confronted by teachers who use an elaborated code. The child finds that his own language imprisons him in a restricted, concrete view of the world, and he cannot understand or use a great deal of the abstract speech that he hears around him. His early linguistic environment serves to channel him into the less academic tracks at school, and he becomes a chronic underachiever.

Research evidence has lent some support to Bernstein's theory. It has been found, for example, that deaf children suffer much more intellectual retardation than blind children, which suggests that access to language is basic to academic achievement. When the differences are analyzed, it is found that most of the difference occurs in the verbal rather than in other parts of the test. Poor verbal facility is the main reason for the apparently lower intelligence of lower class children.

There could, of course, be many other reasons for the poor academic achievement of lower-class children, such as the effects of poverty, overcrowding, and malnutrition, a lack of books and educational materials in the home, a fatalism on the part of parents who do not encourage academic success in their offspring, or even the negative response of middle-class teachers to "rough" lower class children with "bad manners." But Bernstein's theory is a valuable application of an old hypothesis to a new problem, and lends support to those educational psychologists who emphasize that preschool education should focus above all else on the development of language skills.

Unit 15

Personality

OVERVIEW

This unit looks at human personalities—those clusters of traits and behaviors uniquely combined in each individual. First, personality development is discussed in relation to physical and genetic constitution, Freudian theory, and early childhood experiences. Then some research on human personality traits and dimensions is summarized. The third part of the unit presents the three theoretical views of personality currently most prominent in psychology—more about Freudian theory, the personalistic-subjective view, and behavioral specificity (or "social learning") theory. Finally, the issue of the reliability of personality tests is discussed.

UNIT OUTLINE

DEFINITION AND BACKGROUND
1. *Definition:* the unique set of characteristics that describes how a person thinks, feels, and acts.
2. *Background:* Sigmund Freud (1856–1939).

QUESTIONS AND EVIDENCE
1. What are the origins of personality differences?
Hypotheses:
> a. *Temperament:* personal characteristics existing at birth remain unchanged throughout the growth and development of personality in the individual. **250**
> b. *Psychosexual-stages:* fixation at a certain psychosexual stage will result in personality characteristics that are specific to that stage. **251**
> c. *Early-experience:* experience early in childhood affects the subsequent development of personality. **253**

2. What are some dimensions that differentiate personalities?
Hypotheses:
> a. *Authoritarianism:* highly authoritarian people will exhibit a pattern of behavior consistent with their attitudes. **254**
> b. *Locus-of-control:* high internal or high external control will predict how a person performs on intellectual tasks and in other situations. **255**
> c. *Source-traits:* measurements on a small number of fundamental dimensions of personality can completely describe an individual's personality. **256**

3. How does an individual's personality affect his behavior?
Hypotheses:
> a. *Defense-mechanisms:* in order to avoid painful feelings of anxiety, people employ unconscious defense mechanisms that remove the anxiety-provoking thoughts and feelings from conscious awareness. **258**
> b. *Self-acceptance:* psychologically adjusted people are more self-accepting than less adjusted people. **261**
> c. *Behavioral-specificity:* a person's behavior is determined by an interaction between the characteristics of the present situation and what the person has learned from relevant past situations. **261**

IMPORTANT CONCEPTS

page

anxiety	258
authoritarian personality	254
defense mechanism	258
ego	246
Electra complex	246
factor analysis	256
hedonism	246
id	246
latency period	246
libido	246
locus of control	255
Oedipus complex	246
projective test	249
psychoanalysis	246
psychosexual stages	246
self-actualization	260
social learning	261
superego	246
unconscious	247

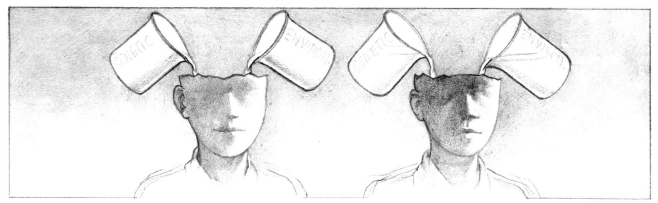

Each individual receives a unique mix of genetic endowment and environmental experiences.

The degree to which an individual is allowed to develop his uniqueness during childhood is one among many important determinants of personality.

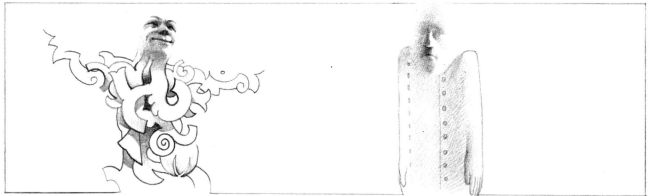

Variations in adult personality are governed by each individual's unique interaction between his genetic endowment and developmental experiences.

DEFINITION AND BACKGROUND

Personality is one of the oldest, most familiar, and at the same time most difficult concepts in psychology. All of us have a working knowledge of what personality is, and we often use it to predict and explain behavior: "If it's a big party, there's no sense asking Joe—he's not the sociable type"; "Sue didn't mean to be rude—she just always says what she thinks." Yet it is difficult to give a comprehensive explanation of what personality is.

Two key features of the study of personality are that it tries to make sense of the ways people characteristically differ from each other and that it emphasizes the relatively stable aspects of a person's behavior. Someone normally unsociable, like Joe, might act wildly outgoing on a particular occasion—after drinking a lot of champagne at a friend's wedding reception, say—but a student of personality would be more interested in explaining his consistent unsociability than the single aberration. The hallmarks of personality are its uniqueness and its relative permanence. Perhaps the best DEFINITION, then, is that personality is *the unique set of characteristics that describes how a person thinks, feels, and acts.*

This unit will FOCUS on factors that influence the developing personality, describing some of the major theories of personality development. It also discusses some dimensions of personality that psychologists use to describe distinctions among people and the tests and other measures used to assess personality.

BACKGROUND: SIGMUND FREUD (1856–1939)

A teacher of Freud's at medical school, noting his growing interest in neurology and laboratory techniques, once warned Freud that his dedication was misdirected: very few Austrian universities of the day had a place for a Jewish professor. Freud decided to go into the clinical practice of medicine. From his medical practice, he gradually evolved his theory of personality and the method for treating "nervous disorders" called psychoanalysis (see Unit 20).

Freud's theory of personality development revolutionized the study of personality and has had a lasting impact on our culture. His was the first truly dynamic theory of personality, an account both of its origins and of the processes of change that lead to individual differences.

According to Freud, personality development begins with the early experiences of childhood and moves through five stages, each associated with a particular source of gratification. The newborn infant is at the *oral* stage: most satisfactions and pleasures at this time come from the mouth, sucking, and feeding. Near the end of the first year, an *anal* phase begins: the infant experiences the gratifications of holding and letting go while learning bowel control. By age three, the child begins to associate pleasure with the manipulation of the genitals, masturbation. Here the *phallic* phase starts. At about this time, a crisis ensues: the Oedipus complex for boys, the Electra complex for girls (see Unit 6). The child gradually suppresses his sexual feelings toward the parent of the opposite sex, identifies with the parent of his own sex, and begins to turn his interest toward the outside world. The school-age child is in the period of sexual *latency,* which lasts until puberty. Then the final *genital* stage begins, leading into the kind of sexual relationships characteristic of mature adulthood.

Freud's theory can be used to explain abnormalities as well as personality differences. For example, too much frustration or gratification at a particular stage can produce *fixation,* in which the type of gratification characteristic of that stage remains a dominant force throughout one's lifetime. Oral fixation may lead to passivity and dependency later, perhaps symptomatized by overeating, alcoholism, or similar problems. Problems during the anal stage can yield two types of personality characteristics, "retentiveness" and "expulsiveness." The anal-retentive person can be thought of as being psychologically constipated—stingy and unwilling to give of himself; the expulsive person is messy, disorderly, perhaps destructive.

In the developing personality, Freud distinguished among three psychic structures, each with its own set of functions: the id, the ego, and the superego. The *id,* or "pleasure principle," is seen as the original psychic structure, present at birth—the animallike, instinctual basis for human behavior. The id is the storehouse of the psychosexual energy that Freud called the *libido,* and also of a primitive urge to fight, take, dominate, and, if necessary, destroy. The id urges the immediate gratification of its impulses and, left to itself, would be purely self-centered and pleasure-seeking (hedonistic).

The *ego,* or "reality principle," is responsible for

holding the id in check and aligning the individual's behavior with the realities of the physical and social world, to which the id is blind. Roughly corresponding to consciousness, the ego seeks delay of gratification and the channeling of the id's energies into safe and socially acceptable modes. The *superego* represents the internalized restrictions and ideals superimposed on the child's ego by his parents and culture. The superego corresponds roughly to what is called conscience. It places further restrictions on the id and is the watchdog of the ego. It may inflict guilt upon the ego for giving in too easily to demands of the id.

Freud's ideas were considered scandalous when they were first proposed. The attribution of sexuality to "innocent" children particularly outraged Victorian sensibilities, and Freud's insistence on the irrational, "animal" nature of the unconscious mind was profoundly distressing in an era that stressed rationality and control. His theories survived many years of virtually total public scorn—only to meet eventually with nearly as overwhelming a popular acceptance.

From the point of view of modern psychology, Freud's overall theory of personality almost defies verification. It is overladen with the mechanical, evolutionary, and biological metaphors common to the scientists of his time: energy, impulse, drive, growth, and so on. His theory of development is also criticized on the grounds that it was based on reports from adults, most of whom were "abnormal," about their memories of childhood experiences, rather than on direct observation of how ordinary children develop. Freud's theory is "slippery": it can easily be adjusted to account for almost any psychological state. Partly because experiments testing Freudian concepts are difficult to set up, few predictions about the course of behavior or its outcome have been firmly established in Freud's original terms. Yet any approach to the study of personality must start with Freud. His speculation about personality remains original and influential, and he has become, as W. H. Auden wrote, "a whole climate of opinion, under whom we conduct our differing lives."

Although the historical importance of Freud's ideas cannot be denied, contemporary psychologists who are interested in personality regard psychoanalytic theory as only one of many potentially explanatory theories. Modern psychologists are much more concerned with methodology and empirical research than previous generations were, and they are well aware of the enormous complexity of human behavior. As a consequence, many are reluctant to attempt to devise all-encompassing "global" theories of personality. At present, research is being directed toward processes, behaviors, and variables of all kinds and varieties, often without preconceptions about how people "should" behave or how personality "must" work. As you will see, contemporary approaches to personality are many and quite different from each other, but this eclectic approach leaves much room for optimism about our chances of finding out "what makes people tick."

QUESTIONS AND EVIDENCE

1. What are the origins of personality differences?
2. What are some dimensions that differentiate personalities?
3. How does an individual's personality affect his behavior?

Before we attack the first question, the methods psychologists use to get at personality dimensions and differences should be briefly described. Clinicians and psychiatrists often use *personal interviews* and *case histories.* These methods, though they tell a skilled interviewer a great deal, are not very objective; two interviewers of the same subject often come to quite different conclusions. Sometimes, too, a person resists revealing his innermost thoughts and feelings to someone who asks for such information directly. Therefore, a number of standardized, objective measures of personality attributes have been devised.

1. *Psychometric tests and inventories.* The subject is presented with a number of items or questions to which he must respond with a definite answer like "yes" or "no." One item by itself has little meaning, but groups of items can indicate a predisposition toward a specific personality characteristic. For example, checking "yes" to "I worry a great deal" and to similar items might indicate a personality obsessed with guilt and anxiety. Perhaps the most famous and most often used psychometric test is the Minnesota Multiphasic Personality Inventory (MMPI), briefly described in Unit 20. (See Figure 1.)

2. *Ratings.* Here trained judges "rate" or evaluate a subject on various personality dimensions or attributes, often using numerical scales. With Cattell's

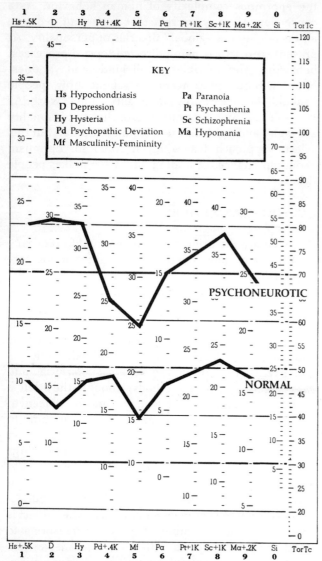

MMPI Profiles

KEY

Hs	Hypochondriasis	**Pa**	Paranoia
D	Depression	**Pt**	Psychasthenia
Hy	Hysteria	**Sc**	Schizophrenia
Pd	Psychopathic Deviation	**Ma**	Hypomania
Mf	Masculinity-Femininity		

PSYCHONEUROTIC

NORMAL

Figure 1. Samples of test materials used by psychologists to measure personality dimensions and differences. The Minnesota Multiphasic Personality Inventory (left) is a psychometric test in which the subject gives definite answers to many questions, and measurement of groups of these items can indicate a predisposition to a specific personality trait. The inkblot, similar to those used in the Rorschach Inkblot Test, is presented to a subject who is asked what it means to him, what it makes him think of, or what he sees in it. The Thematic Apperception Test (right), like the Rorschach, is a projective test in which the subject is asked to describe what is happening in an ambiguous picture that is presented to him. The interpretation of psychological tests is very complex and requires formal training.

list of personality dimensions, described later in this unit, for example, a subject might be rated on a scale from minus 10 to plus 10 for such traits as shrewdness versus naivete and activity versus inactivity.

3. *Projective Tests.* These are relatively unstructured tests in which a subject reveals ("projects") himself by, for example, interpreting a picture or telling a story. How can such a test be "scored"? In several ways, but most often by comparing the person's responses to average or typical responses given by a large number of people.

Probably the most famous projective test is the *Rorschach inkblot test,* in which a subject is presented with inkblots, as shown in Figure 1, and asked what he sees in the inkblot, what it means to him, or what it makes him think of. Interpretation of his answers requires training and is often quite complex. Another well-known projective test is the *Thematic Appercep-*

tion Test (TAT). The subject is asked to tell stories about characters in pictures—what they are doing, what will happen to them, and so on (See Figure 1.). This test is described more fully in Unit 21. Projective tests have often been criticized as having less reliability and validity (see Unit 12) than other psychological measures, but the clinicians who use them are the first to point out that they should be complemented by other data.

4. *Behavioral measures.* Here the subject's overt behavior is observed directly, usually in a contrived situation. For example, a child may be placed in a playroom with his mother, and an observer behind a one-way window might count the number of times child and mother interact, time each interaction, and note which person initiated it.

The uses of all four methods will be further illustrated in the research described below.

HYPOTHESES	TEMPERAMENT	PSYCHOSEXUAL STAGES	EARLY EXPERIENCE
DESCRIPTIVE EVIDENCE	ASSESS: temperament differences of young infants and relation to later behavior	ASSESS: relation of "orality" to behaviors predicted by Freudian theory	ASSESS: social behavior of infant monkeys following separation from mother
EXPERIMENTAL EVIDENCE			

1. WHAT ARE ORIGINS OF PERSONALITY DIFFERENCES?

Constitutional theories attribute variations in personality to differences in physiology and anatomy (and, finally, heredity). The oldest personality theory of any substance is Hippocrates' doctrine of the four humors, which assumed that there were four basic types of temperament (sanguine, phlegmatic, melancholic, choleric), determined by a predominance of different fluids in the body (blood, phlegm, black bile, yellow bile). This notion, quaint though it may seem today, dominated Western physiology and medical practice for almost 2,000 years.

In the early nineteenth century, the lively art of *phrenology* claimed that differences among people could be predicted from the bumps on their heads. Phrenology became tremendously popular; by 1840, there were some forty-five regional phrenological societies in the United States alone. Eventually recognized as simplistic and unreliable, phrenology did have some influence on thinking and research on localized functions of the brain.

The most famous constitutional theory of the twentieth century is the *somatotype* theory, formulated by William H. Sheldon (1940), a physician at Columbia University, and illustrated in Figure 2. As long as Sheldon's method of indexing variations in somatotypes is used only to describe physical differences among people, it cannot be argued with. However, Sheldon also claimed that somatotypes were related to personality differences: endomorphic individuals are "visceratonic" (good-natured and food-oriented); mesomorphs are "somatotonic" (aggressive and activity-oriented); and ectomorphs are "cerebrotonic" (sensitive and intellectual). At present, the question of whether these relationships really exist is unresolved and controversial.

So what can we really say about constitution, physiology, and temperament? Is it all just bunk? Most, probably yes; all, probably no.

The *temperament hypothesis* states that personal characteristics existing at birth remain unchanged throughout growth and development of personality in the individual. In the past few years, a concentrated research program by Thomas, Chess, and Birch has succeeded in showing—much to the surprise of some psychologists—that constitutional-temperamental differences among young infants cannot be ruled out as a possible origin of personality.

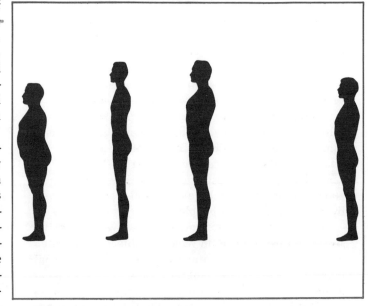

Figure 2. Profile view of Sheldon's somatotypes: from left to right, endomorphic, ectomorphic, and mesomorphic. Mr. Average Man is pictured to the far right.

DESCRIPTIVE EVIDENCE

Investigators: A. Thomas, S. Chess, and H. G. Birch
Source, Date: "The Origin of Personality," 1971
Location: New York University School of Medicine and
   Albert Einstein College of Medicine (Birch)
Subjects: 141 children from 85 families in higher socioeconomic class
Materials: Interviews, direct observation, psychometric tests

Extending over a period of years, this study attempted to identify consistent personality differences in very young infants and then to follow the behavior of the same infants as they grew older. Various measures were used. Initially, the most important ones were ratings of the two- and three-month-old infants' behavior. Each baby was scored on a three-point scale (high, medium, and low) for such things as overall activity level, acceptance of new experiences, and adaptability to changes in the environment. When all the data were analyzed and combined, it was found that the results could be summarized in terms of three "types" of infant temperament, which were called "easy," "slow to warm up," and "difficult." Some of the behaviors associated with each type are summarized in Table 1. Of the children studied, 65 percent could be categorized as having one of the three types of temperament, while the other 35 percent displayed a mixture of traits. These differences were apparent at two months of age.

The behavior of many of the children was also observed in the months and years following the original assessment. Later behavior cannot be attributed to any one set of factors, since temperamental and environmental factors (such as parental treatment) become inextricably intertwined. However, the researchers did note that "as a child grows his temperament tends to remain constant in quality: if he wriggles while his diaper is being changed at two months, his high activity level is likely to be expressed at one year through eager eating and a tendency 'to climb into everything.' A five-year-old child who behaved quietly in infancy may dress slowly and be able to sit quietly and happily during long automobile rides."

Seeking constitutional, physiologically based factors is only one approach to personality origins. Another approach is to look for the major stages or changes that occur in an individual during development. The most famous description of personality origins in terms of stages is Freud's psychosexual theory, described earlier in this unit. It has proved nearly impossible to test the theory as a whole in any conclusive fashion. However, it is possible to assess parts of it, if they can be clearly formulated for research purposes. For example, Freud's theory implies that "orality" and "anality" are meaningful dimensions of personality along which people will vary. The theory makes it explicit that traumatic or unusual experiences at any one stage may retard development or cause the individual to become "fixated" at that stage. Thus, a *psychosexual-stages hypothesis* can state that fixation at a certain psychosexual stage will result in personality characteristics that are specific to that stage. An oral fixation, for instance, will result in an "oral personality." Once an

TABLE 1. Behavior Associated With Infant Temperament Types

Type of Infant	Activity Level	Rhythmicity	Approach- Withdrawal	Adaptability	Intensity of Reaction	Quality of Mood
Easy	Varies	Very regular	Positive approach	Very adaptable	Low or mild	Positive
Slow to warm up	Low to moderate	Varies	Initial withdrawal	Slowly adaptable	Mild	Slightly negative
Difficult	Varies	Irregular	Withdrawal	Slowly adaptable	Intense	Negative

Source: A. Thomas, S. Chess, and H. G. Birch, "The Origin of Personality," *Contemporary Psychology: Readings From Scientific American* (San Francisco: W. H. Freeman and Co., 1971), 350–357.

appropriate measure of orality is found, then psychologists can see if it is related to the other kinds of behaviors that Freud predicted as products of an oral fixation.

DESCRIPTIVE EVIDENCE

Investigators: G. S. Blum and D. R. Miller

Source, Date: "Exploring the Psychoanalytic Theory of the 'Oral Character,' "1952

Location: University of Michigan

Subjects: 18 boys and girls in the third grade (about eight years old)

Materials: Time samples; teacher ratings; self-reports; simple tasks

This study assessed the relationship between orality in children and other aspects of their behavior. According to psychoanalytic theory, oral fixation should affect a person's behavior in several predictable ways: he will be dependent on outside sources ("receiving") for love and help, he will feel at a loss without support, he will have a great fondness for food and drink.

First, orality was measured by the number of non-purposive mouth movements exhibited by the children. Trained observers carefully noted all occurrences of mouth movements in each subject, during eight two-minute intervals over a three-week period. Would a child who displayed more of this kind of oral behavior also display the kind of behavior predicted by Freud's theory of oral character?

A number of behavioral measures were taken, but only the positive relationships will be reported here. Greater orality in the children was found to be associated with the characteristics summarized in Table 2. In the results, each of the predictions about oral character given in the table was borne out. Other predicted relationships were not borne out, but these and results from other studies lend some credence to parts of psychoanalytic theory, though the evidence is too weak to divide people into "types" on the basis of psychosexual stages.

A modern proponent of Freudian theory, Erik Erikson (1963), has added to and modified the theory of psychosexual development. He expanded Freud's stages to the following eight, each dominated by a particular "theme" in behavior: (1) infancy—sense of trust; (2) early childhood—sense of autonomy; (3) play age—sense of initiative; (4) school age—industry and competence; (5) adolescence—personal identity; (6) young adulthood—intimacy; (7) adulthood—productivity; and (8) mature age—integrity and acceptance. The theme of each stage represents both

TABLE 2. Characteristics Associated With Orality

Predicted Characteristics	Rationale for Prediction	How Behavior Was Assessed
Tendency to eat after a full meal	Orientation toward food and drink	Amount of ice cream eaten after a full meal
Need to be liked	Dependence on affection and attention from other people	Teachers' ratings
Concern over giving and receiving	Gifts and receiving are a form of "supplies"	Teachers' ratings
Social isolation	Passivity, demands for attention, hostility when demands are not met means he is not usually sought out by others	Subjects' self-reports
Intolerance for boredom	Lack of available supplies yields little tolerance for unrewarding activity	Persistence on a simple, boring task

Source: Adapted from G. S. Blum and D. R. Miller, "Exploring the Psychoanalytic Theory of the 'Oral Character,'" *Journal of Personality*, 20 (1952), 287–304.

the goal and the dominant force of the personality of an individual at that age.

Erikson has done much to extend the application of psychoanalytic theory to the adolescent period of development and to describe how biological and social factors interact during development. His description of the "identity crisis" is perhaps the most widely-accepted of his "stages of man." According to Erikson, during adolescence a person typically imitates a number of different people: parents, friends, perhaps a teacher. These different roles conflict, and an identity crisis ensues. The adolescent's ultimate goal is to find out "who he is," and he tries to do that by adopting various roles, then modifying some and discarding others. Erikson's ideas are important because, without denying the basic Freudian framework, they also emphasize social factors and the environment. Many of Erikson's ideas also have things in common with humanistic psychology, which is discussed later in this unit.

Perhaps the greatest contribution of Freud's theory was to draw the attention of psychologists to the importance of early childhood experiences in the development of personality. In working with his patients, Freud discovered that he could often trace the patient's problems back to an early experience—usually a traumatic emotional event. At present, psychologists are very skeptical about the damaging effects of single, isolated events in childhood, but they do not doubt that the character of a person's childhood experiences has a tremendous impact on his development, socially, intellectually, and personally.

The *early-experience hypothesis* states that experience early in childhood affects the subsequent development of personality. Freud's own theory emphasized the importance of oral and anal experiences, but certain social experiences are probably just as crucial. The next experiment describes what happened to the "personalities" of several young monkeys who were separated from their mothers.

DESCRIPTIVE EVIDENCE

Investigators: *C. Kaufman and L. Rosenblum*
Source, Date: *"Depression in Infant Monkeys Separated from Their Mothers," 1967*
Location: *Downstate Medical Center, Brooklyn, New York*

Subjects: *4 infant monkeys*
Materials: *Housing pen; one-way mirror*

Monkeys were separated from their mothers for a month at the age of five or six months. Interactions between the infant, his father, and another female were observed by the investigators through a one-way window several times per week. The reactions of the infants during separation fell into three phases: agitation, depression, and recovery. The agitation phase was characterized by erratic play, distress calls, and increased self-directed behavior. After twenty-four to thirty-six hours, depression began; the infants sat hunched over and rarely responded to social gestures. After five to six days, they began to recover a bit, assuming a more upright posture, exploring, and again interacting with the other monkeys. The depression continued, but at a less intense level.

When the mother was reunited with her infant, all the infants displayed a marked and prolonged intensification of the infant-mother relationship. Clinging by the infant, holding by the mother, and nipple contact all rose above preseparation levels. This closeness was particularly striking, because ordinarily, in infant monkeys of the age of those involved, these dependent behaviors diminish considerably. Thus, while normal infants were developing more independent behavior, those monkeys who were separated became depressed and later developed a higher dependence on their mothers.

There is little doubt that early social deprivation and other experiences can have drastic, long-term effects on personality (see Units 4, 7, and 29). Studies of the effects of similar experiences on humans require more subtle, nonexperimental methods, because one cannot subject human infants to severe deprivations. Even so, many correlational studies have shown that certain characteristics of adult personality, such as aggressiveness, dependency, and honesty, are related to early childhood experiences. Some of these studies are discussed in detail in Units 4, 5, and 6.

The discussion thus far has centered on three possible influences on personality development—innate constitution, psychosexual stages, and early experiences. Now we will turn from the developing to the developed personality and examine some personality traits and dimensions.

HYPOTHESES	AUTHORITARIANISM	LOCUS OF CONTROL	SOURCE TRAITS
DESCRIPTIVE EVIDENCE	ASSESS: child rearing practices of authoritarian mothers		ASSESS: dimensions that are needed to describe personality in its entirety
EXPERIMENTAL EVIDENCE		VARY: degree of preconceived control over electric shock MEASURE: errors on a memorization task	

2. WHAT ARE SOME DIMENSIONS THAT DIFFERENTIATE PERSONALITIES?

Identifying personality traits—aggressiveness, friendliness, and so on—is of little use if each is merely an isolated aspect of a person's behavior, with no relation to his behavior pattern as a whole. Of particular interest to psychologists, then, are personality traits which *predict consistent differences* in behavior. In earlier times, personalities were thought to come in *types*, with each type embodying a particular cluster of traits. The doctrine of the four humors exemplified this kind of thinking, which modern psychologists do not accept. Types or categories are too simple and restrictive to describe the variety and uniqueness of human personalities.

The more modern approach is to describe personality dimensions and how people vary in ways that are meaningfully related to overall behavioral differences.

In this part of the unit we will look briefly at two particular personality dimensions that interest psychologists because these dimensions do predict consistent differences in behavior among individuals. Then we will examine the attempt of one psychologist to tie together personality traits or dimensions into a "grand scheme" for describing personality variations.

The personality dimension of *authoritarianism* has been extensively investigated in the last twenty-five years, mainly by social psychologists. Their concern with authoritarianism started after World War II as an attempt to understand why so many people had been attracted to fascism. The main characteristics found to be associated with high authoritarianism are (1) extremely conventional opinions and attitudes, (2) sub-

mission to authority figures, (3) prudish sexual views, (4) a preoccupation with power and "law and order," (5) ethnocentrism (tending toward prejudiced attitudes—see Unit 8), (6) political and social conservatism, and (7) anti-Semitism.

For our purposes, the *authoritarianism hypothesis* states that highly authoritarian people will exhibit a pattern of behavior consistent with their attitudes. Many investigators believe that authoritarianism originates in the child-rearing practices of authoritarian parents. Support for this belief comes from studies like the following one.

DESCRIPTIVE EVIDENCE

Investigator: I. Hart
Source, Date: "Maternal Child-Rearing Practices and Authoritarian Ideology," 1957
Location: Duke University
Subjects: 126 mothers of children from 2 1/2 to 5 1/2 years old
Materials: Interviews; personality tests

The investigator spent about two hours with each mother, asking her about her attitudes toward child-rearing and discipline and her problems with her own child. In addition, the mothers took a psychometric test that measures authoritarianism. The goal of the study was to see if relatively authoritarian mothers raised their children in different ways than less authoritarian mothers.

Some consistent relationships emerged. Authoritarian mothers showed a tendency to select "non-love-oriented" punishments for their children, such as ridicule and physical punishment. In explaining punishment to the child, they focused on the importance of obeying rules. They were especially likely to use non-love-oriented punishments for independent and aggressive (as opposed to sexual and dependent) misbehavior. Less authoritarian mothers tended to use "love-oriented" punishments, such as denial or withdrawal of affection, for all misbehavior.

Figure 3. Authoritarianism tends to be passed on from one generation to another.

Other studies have shown that the children of authoritarian parents are likely to be authoritarian in their own attitudes and in the way they raise their own children: "If it was good enough for me, it's good enough for my kids." Authoritarians are more likely than other people to be influenced by statements attributed to authority figures (officials and the law), and to change their opinions when these are challenged by authority figures. They are generally more rigid and less creative problem solvers, more punitive to social inferiors than to superiors, and more pessimistic and cynical (but not more alienated) than other people. In short, the usefulness of the authoritarianism dimension of personality in predicting a consistent pattern of behaviors has been verified by a number of investigations.

A dimension of personality that has been identified more recently (Rotter, 1966) is *locus of control.* Locus of control refers to people's perceptions of where their rewards and punishments come from. People who attribute their rewards to fate, chance, and powerful other people are said to have "external locus of control," whereas people who attribute their rewards to their own efforts are said to have "internal locus of control." Locus of control (LC) is assessed by means of a psychometric test containing items like the following:

1. There is no justice in the world.
2. I am not noticed in proportion to my ability.
3. The only dependable rewards come from a higher being.
4. People respect me for my work.
5. One can get ahead by working hard.
6. People who are wealthy deserve their riches if they earned them.

A subject who answered the first three items True and the last three False would score high on external control; the reverse answers would indicate high internal control.

The *locus-of-control hypothesis* states that high internal or high external control will predict how a person performs on intellectual tasks and in other situations. The effects of locus of control on performance can be demonstrated in a number of ways, but they are most obvious when people are placed in situations where the rewards or punishments are very clear.

EXPERIMENTAL EVIDENCE

Investigators: D. Watson and E. Baumal
Source, Date: "Effects of Locus of Control and Expectation of
Future Control on Present Performance," 1967
Location: University of Toronto
Subjects: 60 female college students
Materials: LC scale; memory drum; dummy shock apparatus

Initially 565 women were given the Locus of Control Scale. From the 10 percent scoring highest on external control and the 10 percent scoring highest on internal control, two groups of 30 subjects each were chosen at random.

These two groups were asked to learn two lists of nonsense words, ostensibly as part of an experiment on learning-through-punishment. Half of each group was told that, during the test on the second list, they would receive an electric shock as punishment for making errors (they were led to believe shocks would be "controlled" by their own efforts). The other half of each group was told they would receive shocks during the second test on a random basis, when they erred but also when they were correct (thus they were led to believe the shocks would be beyond their control). In reality, no one was ever shocked, because the test on the second list was never given. The point was to see what effect the expectation of shock would have on the subjects' performance during the test of the first list.

It turned out that the subjects who scored high on internal control made more errors when they anticipated no control over the shocks. For subjects who scored high on external control, the reverse was true: they made more errors when they thought they *would* have control over the shocks. Apparently, the high internal control subject needed the knowledge that her performance would be instrumental in avoiding punishment, whereas the high external control subject preferred the idea of random punishment controlled by an outside agent. This is only one example of the behavior differences that locus of control can predict. Other differences are discussed in Units 2 and 10.

Authoritarianism and locus of control are two possible dimensions of personality. How many others are there? And can personality be completely described in terms of polar dimensions? In 1936 Gordon Allport and H. S. Odbert published a "psycholexicon," a collection of 17,953 English words describing personality. In response to this, an English psychologist living in America, Raymond B. Cattell, has conducted a long-term research program to reduce all possible descriptions of personality to a finite and manageable number of dimensions. Cattell began to reduce the Allport-Odbert list by combining synonyms and antonyms. Also, he eliminated many words in the psycholexicon because they referred to temporary states (such as "exultant"), were vague (for example, "puffy"), or for other reasons. Then Cattell added to the list some missing technical terms and traits that had been invented by psychologists. After much further work, he succeeded in combining related terms and their opposites into an assembly of 171

traits or dimensions, which he called the "personality sphere."

The task was not over yet. In fact, the most difficult steps were still to come. Cattell's goal was to further reduce the 171 traits by finding a smaller number of "source traits." He was seeking a smaller number of dimensions than 171 that would still embody all the meanings and implications in the sphere. This goal can be phrased as the *source-traits hypothesis,* which states that measurements on a small number of fundamental dimensions of personality can completely describe an individual's personality. The problem remained for Cattell to determine what the source traits were, a task for which he used a complex mathematical technique called factor analysis.

DESCRIPTIVE EVIDENCE

Investigators: R. B. Cattell and his associates
Sources, Dates: "Personality: A Systematic, Theoretical and Factual Study," 1950; "The Scientific Analysis of Personality," 1965
Subjects: Thousands of adults of both sexes
Materials: All varieties of psychometric tests and scales

Over a period of years psychological tests were devised and administered to thousands of people. All 171 of the dimensions of Cattell's personality sphere were represented in the tests. The scores on some of the tests turned out to be correlated; that is, a person who scored high on one tended also to score high on another. When test scores correlate in this manner, they can be viewed as measuring the same thing to some degree. What factor analysis does is describe the underlying "factor" or dimension that is responsible for correlations among tests. By using it, Cattell was able to reduce the 171 traits of the personality sphere to 19 factors or source traits. Variations on these dimensions encompass and "explain" variations in performance on all 171 traits. Note that factor analysis did not throw out dimensions until only 19 were left; rather, all the dimensions were collapsed or combined into only 19. Those 19 source traits, in essence, contained the same amount of information and embodied the same meanings as the original personality sphere.

The words used to label the 19 source traits were to some extent arbitrary choices. The final list appears in Table 3, where traits with strange names are described enough to give you an idea of what the dimension involves. Unlike the 171 traits of the sphere, these 19 factors are relatively independent of each other. That is, scoring near one end of one dimension does not predict one's score on some other dimension.

What does all this mean? In terms of a psycholexicon containing all possible descriptions of personality in English, Cattell's source traits represent a compendium—a compact but comprehensive summary of all the ways personality can vary, as measured by psychometric tests. Traits, however, are a static concept—they do not tell us how personality is formed, how it changes, how it "works," or how it affects behavior. Cattell's system is not dynamic but purely descriptive, and it suffers from the limitations of such systems. Some psychologists, in fact, are very critical of such work and view Cattell's research as largely a verbal exercise rather than as a legitimate psychological enterprise. However, Cattell's scheme is criticizable only if one tries to read into it more than is there. If one accepts the premise that it is desirable to describe the attributes of personality as completely as possible, then Cattell's source traits are as good a system as any available. Also, because 19 source traits embody a great many more and can be combined in many different ways, the system does succeed in attributing a credible degree of complexity to personality—enough to agree with intuition and provide possibilities for individual uniqueness.

TABLE 3. Personality Dimensions as Identified by Cattell Using Factor Analysis

Factor	Polar Ends of the Dimension
A	Cyclothymia (easygoing, frank, generous, warmhearted) vs. schizothymia (obstructive, indifferent, secretive, impassive)
B	Intelligence vs. unintelligence
C	Ego strength (mature, patient, stoic, unworried) vs. ego weakness (infantile, impatient, anxious, worrying)
D	Activity vs. inactivity
E	Domination vs. subordination (submissive)
F	Surgency (enthusiastic, talkative) vs. desurgency (silent, brooding)
G	Superego strength (conscientious, responsible, persevering) vs. superego weakness (unscrupulous, irresolute, undependable)
H	Parmia (carefree, brave) vs. threctia (careful, cowardly)
I	Premsia (sensitive, sentimental) vs. haria (insensitive, callous)
J	Coasthenia (self-oriented, independent) vs. zeppia (dependent, group-oriented)
K	Comention (cultured, elegant) vs. abcultion (crude, awkward, uncouth)
L	Protension (suspicious, wary) vs. security (trustful, gullible)
M	Autia (self-absorbed, abstract) vs. praxernia (earnest, practical, outward)
N	Shrewdness vs. naivete
O	Guilt proclivity (timid, depressed) vs. guilt rejection (self-confident)
Q(1)	Radicalism vs. conservatism
Q(2)	Self-sufficiency vs. group sufficiency (seeking social approval)
Q(3)	Controlled will vs. uncontrolled will (taking chances)
Q(4)	Id significance (frustrated, anxious) vs. id insignificance (relaxed, composed)

Source: R. B. Cattell, *The Scientific Analysis of Personality* (Baltimore: Penguin Books, 1965).

HYPOTHESES	DEFENSE MECHANISMS	SELF-ACCEPTANCE	BEHAVIORAL SPECIFICITY
DESCRIPTIVE EVIDENCE	ASSESS: relationships between conformity and overt and covert hostility	ASSESS: relation between adjustment and self-acceptance	
EXPERIMENTAL EVIDENCE			VARY: cooperation that is rewarded, and relationship between the participants MEASURE: cooperation and competitiveness in mutual responding in reward game

3. HOW DOES AN INDIVIDUAL'S PERSONALITY AFFECT HIS BEHAVIOR?

In this final section we will look at three current approaches to the study of personality. The first is derived from psychoanalytic theory; the second is the humanistic approach; and the third is based on social-learning theory. The three are very different and often seem to oppose each other, but one thing they have in common is that all are *dynamic*. Unlike Cattell's source traits, whose purpose is to describe the relatively static attributes of personality, these three approaches attempt to explain personality change, adaptation, and adjustment as reflected in ongoing behavior.

Psychoanalytic theory, which pictured the psyche as an active, fluid system of forces, was the first dynamic theory of personality. At the heart of the theory is the concept of *intrapsychic conflict*—the dynamic struggle that takes place between the psychic structures of id, ego, and superego. In the normal person these forces are thought of as stable, balanced, and even mutually cooperative: the ego succeeds in satisfying the instinctual demands of the id, the moral demands of the superego, and the everyday demands of reality. In a person with emotional problems, the ego somehow fails to cope with the intrapsychic forces; anxiety is generated, which pressures the ego to turn its attention to coping with the anxiety itself.

The ego tries to cope with anxiety by using various *defense mechanisms*. A list of common defense mechanisms is presented in Table 4. At one time or another everyone has used some of them. When more effective ways of dealing with guilt, anxiety, or internal hostility are not available, a defense mechanism can

be temporarily helpful. But some people adopt certain defense mechanisms as habitual ways of responding to threatening situations. According to psychoanalytic theory, when defense mechanisms dominate a personality or prevent the adoption of more effective solutions to a problem, they can lead to neuroses and other disorders (see Unit 13).

A central Freudian defense mechanism is *repression,* or motivated forgetting, which is used to avoid becoming aware of unpleasant feelings and associated experiences. Repression is a fairly extreme defense mechanism, but all of them are to some extent unconscious operations. The *defense-mechanisms hypothesis* states that, in order to avoid painful feelings of anxiety, people employ unconscious defense mechanisms that remove the anxiety-provoking thoughts and feelings from conscious awareness. Defense mechanisms, though their existence is commonly accepted, present formidable problems to a psychologist who wishes to test the hypothesis. How can one get at unconscious thoughts and feelings?

Assessing unconscious impulses is the main purpose for which projective tests were devised. In the following study, Louis Breger used the Thematic Apperception Test (TAT) to measure repressed feelings of hostility. Breger wanted to investigate the idea that conformity or yielding to group pressure is part of an ego-defense process that centers on the repression of hostility. According to this idea, people who conform under pressure do so because at some level of awareness they perceive opposition to the group as an act of defiance or aggression, which arouses anxiety. If that is correct, Breger reasoned, then conformers should (1) be less able than nonconformers to express

TABLE 4. Functioning of Defense Mechanisms

Defense Mechanism	Function	Example
Compensation	Anxiety about one area of behavior "compensated for" by accomplishment in another area	An ugly girl becomes an expert musician
Denial	Refusal to admit the truth	A possessive man believes his promiscuous wife has always been faithful
Displacement	Hostile energy directed toward an irrelevant recipient rather than the source of hostility	After parental scolding, a little boy takes it out on his little brother
Identification	Imitation of an admired person to avoid thinking about one's own inadequacies in some area	Anxious about popularity, a girl seeks a friend who is popular
Intellectualization	Feelings concealed from oneself by analyzing situations in an intellectual way	A woman becomes very interested in the different forms her teen-age daughter's hostility take
Introjection	Other people's attitudes adopted as one's own (opposite of projection)	Child adopts his parents' standards as a matter of self-protection
Projection	One's own behavior or characteristics attributed to other people	A man who dislikes his boss thinks he likes the boss fine, but the boss doesn't much like him
Rationalization	False but acceptable excuses created for one's unacceptable behavior	After failing to be accepted at law school, a young man decides he didn't really want to go anyway
Reaction formation	Exaggerated outward denial of one's real feelings	Person with homosexual tendencies becomes crusader against homosexuality
Regression	Reversion to earlier, infantile ways of dealing with frustration	Adult has a temper tantrum when he doesn't get his way
Repression	Motivated forgetting: anxiety-arousing thoughts are pushed into the unconscious	A woman cannot remember the details of the first time she had intercourse, though she remembers the date before that, when she said "no"

Handwritten annotations:

Projection: (HE CAN'T DEAL W/BOSS - HE SEES BOSS NOT liking Him.) ... (All the other people HAVE A problem - NOT ME)

Reaction formation: (usually in opposite DIRECTION)

Repression: — NOT CONSCIOUS. (BLANK IT OUT - SO ANXIETY PROVOKING) hostility directly and openly and (2) show more signs than nonconformers do of repressed or covert hostility.

DESCRIPTIVE EVIDENCE

Investigator: L. Breger
Source, Date: "Conformity as a Function of the Ability to Express Hostility," 1963
Location: Ohio State University
Subjects: 79 female college students
Materials: Asch conformity situation; Thematic Apperception Test (TAT); a behavioral measure

First it was necessary to distinguish high-conforming from less-conforming subjects. This was done by exposing subjects to a situation originally devised by Solomon Asch (1952), in which a subject is asked to judge which of three lines is the longest after he has heard other people make the same judgment. Though one line is somewhat obviously longer then the others, the other people—actually confederates of the experimenter—all choose another, shorter line. Will the subject conform to their judgment or state his independent opinion, defying the majority? In a series of such judgments, the high-conforming or yielding subject is the one who tends to agree with the other people, despite the evidence of his own perceptions. Based on their reactions to the Asch situation, the subjects were classified as high, medium, or low conformity.

Hostility was assessed in two ways. First, each subject told stories about ten pictures in the series that make up the Thematic Apperception Test (TAT), and the stories were scored for overt and covert hostility. Overt hostility was inferred from references to arguments, anger, fighting, revenge, and so on. Covert hostility was inferred from references to sickness, death, accidents, and so on. Second, a behavioral measure of hostility was used. The experimenter gave each subject some rather gruff instructions about a boring task—putting pegs into the holes in a pegboard—and then criticized her performance. Later, the subject was given a chance to express her feelings about the experimenter to a confederate of his who she thought was another subject. Overt hostility was inferred from such statements as "I'd like to slug him—I don't need this—"; covert hostility, from

statements like "I wish this experiment were over—it makes me so nervous—"

Breger's results turned out as psychoanalytic and defense-mechanism theory had predicted: the subjects who yielded most to social pressure expressed less overt hostility but more covert hostility than the subjects who behaved independently in the Asch situation. Both the TAT and the behavioral measure confirmed this relationship.

Most psychologists agree that defense mechanisms exist, that they occur in normal behavior, and that they can cause behavior problems. But there is considerable controversy and disagreement about their role in the way personality ordinarily functions. Though Freudians are inclined to assign them great importance, other psychologists place more emphasis on other dynamic aspects of personality, doubting that defense mechanisms are really basic to understanding personality and how it interacts with behavior.

One of the most popular recent alternatives to psychoanalytic theory has been the humanistic-personalistic approach to personality represented by such psychologists as Carl Rogers (see Unit 3), Abraham Maslow, and Rollo May. This movement has its roots in several convergent trends, including existentialism and phenomenology in philosophy and humanism in psychology. It is often associated with such terms as individual growth, free will, personal values, creativity, and self-realization. Unlike the strongly deterministic position of psychoanalysis, the humanistic approach assumes that the most important personality processes are conscious, self-determined, and not necessarily heavily influenced by past experiences. A basic concept underlying the humanistic view is Maslow's *self-actualization theory*, which describes self-actualization as the ultimate human motive, a process whereby a person develops his own individuality with all aspects of his personality in productive harmony.

Like psychoanalytic theory, humanistic views do not lend themselves to experimental verification, and investigators have had to settle for testing a small piece of the theory or one of its implications. Because the humanistic model regards the individual as unique and potentially more open to new experiences than determined by old ones, implying that comparisons among people are not very important or meaningful, studies usually involve an attempt to relate one aspect of a person's behavior to the person's subjective view of himself.

Humanistic growth or self theory assumes that the perceptions of a psychologically adjusted person will reflect the realities of the situation at hand. For example, the adjusted person has a realistic, accurate view of himself: he accepts himself as he really is, including the "bad" as well as the "good." For that reason, he is able to acknowledge uncomplimentary truths about himself rather than feeling threatened by them as a troubled person does. This idea can be formulated as the *self-acceptance hypothesis*, which states that psychologically adjusted people are more self-accepting than less adjusted people. Note that this hypothesis does not oppose the defense-mechanisms hypothesis; indeed, it could be regarded as a reformulation of it in positive terms. In general, the humanistic approach emphasizes the positive and the normal in personality functioning, whereas the psychoanalytic approach tends to pay more attention to how and why things go wrong.

DESCRIPTIVE EVIDENCE

Investigators: *C. Taylor and A. W. Combs*
Source, Date: *"Self-acceptance and Adjustment," 1952*
Location: *Syracuse University*
Subjects: *180 rural Pennsylvania sixth-grade children*
Materials: *California Test of Personality; Self-Acceptance Scale*

The California Test of Personality is a psychometric test much like the MMPI. On the basis of test scores, the subjects were divided into two equal-sized groups, the well-adjusted group and the less well-adjusted group. To test self-acceptance, the children were asked to agree or disagree with statements that are probably true of all children but at the same time are potentially damaging to the self. Some of the statements were the following:

1. I sometimes say bad words or swear.
2. I sometimes tell lies.
3. I sometimes tell dirty stories.
4. I sometimes talk back to my mother.
5. I sometimes am mean to animals.

Results showed that the better-adjusted children tended to accept as true more statements on the self-acceptance scale than did the less well-adjusted children, as predicted by the self-acceptance hypothesis.

Viewed as a "scientific theory," the humanistic approach to personality leaves much to be desired. It is hard to test, and its basic assumptions have never been woven into a single, comprehensive formulation; instead, they come from a variety of sources, and their cohesiveness and validity depend mainly on people's intuitive sense of "Yes, that's how it is." As a balance to psychoanalytic theory (and as a popular movement), though, the humanistic approach has much to recommend it. The Freudian emphasis on unconscious processes sometimes seems to imply that people are totally out of touch with their own personalities, and the humanists' attempt to "put the person back in personality" is a welcome one. Equally welcome is the refocusing of attention away from abnormal behavior and personality disorders and toward a person's ability to guide his own behavior (in Freudian terms, toward "ego" activity) and to determine his own destiny. An effort to synthesize the psychoanalytic and humanistic views into one theory is probably not very far off.

A third approach to personality, just as recent as the humanistic though very different in flavor and basic outlook, is the social-learning approach. According to this approach social behavior, like any other kind, is learned, and it is learned in two main ways: through conditioning (as described in Units 26 and 27) and through modeling (as described in Units 4 and 5). Social learning theorists do not look for traits or unconscious motives or other personal, internal, nonobservable structures or processes; instead, they assume that social behavior is under the control of environmental factors, both present and past.

For our purposes, this view can be summarized as the *behavioral-specificity hypothesis*, which states that a person's behavior is determined by an interaction between the characteristics of the present situation and what the person has learned from relevant past situations. Social-learning hypotheses, since they concern outward behavior rather than thoughts or feelings, are well suited to experimental testing. The following study, for example, shows that a person in a single situation can behave quite differently, depending on whom he is with and how he has interacted with them in the past.

EXPERIMENTAL EVIDENCE

Investigator: D. J. Cohen

Source, Date: "Justin and His Peers: An Experimental Analysis of a Child's Social World," 1962

Subjects: Justin, a normal 13-year-old boy and his brother (age 16), sister (age 14), close friend (age 13), mother, and a stranger (age 14)

Materials: Two adjacent rooms separated by a glass panel, each containing a plunger and a reward bin; pennies, candy

The main subject, Justin, was paired on different occasions with each of the other subjects in the experimental rooms. Minimal instructions were given: "You are going to play a game. You can keep all you get." When Justin and his partner "played the game" right (pushed their plungers in the correct order), both were rewarded with pennies or candy. The conditions were manipulated by the experimenter so that (1) sometimes Justin and his partner had to push their plungers almost simultaneously but in any order to be rewarded immediately; (2) sometimes Justin had to press first; (3) sometimes the partner had to press first; and (4) sometimes both had to press their plungers but only one was rewarded for a while, and then only the other was rewarded for a while. The point of these manipulations was simple enough: if behavior were only the product of one's personality traits and the situation, then Justin should behave much the same with any partner. On the other hand, if behavior is also the product of the specific relationship that one person has with another, then Justin might be expected to behave differently with different partners.

One result of this study was that each subject earned an average of $6.25 in money and candy during each experimental session, and most of the candy was eaten right away. Also, the way Justin interacted with each of his partners in the game varied considerably. Justin became the leader with the people with whom he had previous (nonexperimental) experience of leadership—his brother and his friend. With his mother and sister, things were very different: both became strong leaders during uncontrolled leadership (the first condition) and both exhibited resistance to following Justin's lead when they were not rewarded for leading (the fourth condition). With his friend, the stranger, and his mother the competitive potential of the situation was shortly converted into cooperation. But Justin and his sister always displayed strong competition against each other.

Justin's actions were influenced partly by the rewards available in the experimental situation and partly by the ways he had learned, in past situations, to behave with each of his partners. That is, according to the behavioral-specificity hypothesis, Justin demonstrated learned behavior that was appropriate to the particular situation in which he found himself—rather than, say, exhibiting one or more so-called personality traits.

The stress that social-learning theory puts on behavior can be regarded as its greatest strength or its greatest weakness, depending on one's point of view. Some people are delighted that the theory requires no "vague internal structures" like the ego or "pie-in-the-sky processes" like self-actualization; that it stresses the dynamics of development rather than static sets of already-acquired traits; and that it offers, at last, a way to study personality objectively and scientifically, in the laboratory. Others, probably including most psychologists who study personality, feel that learning theorists overestimate the importance both of behavior (as opposed to feelings and thoughts) and of the extent to which behavior is determined by external situations, whether present or past. They sometimes call the approach cold, mechanistic, and inhuman and say it tends to obliterate the very thing it set out to study—human personality.

Even these people, though, would agree that social-learning theory has made some valuable contributions. Like the humanistic approach, it has helped balance some of the excesses of the psychoanalytic view that historically has dominated the study of personality. It is simpler and considerably more concrete; it stresses normal behavior; and it makes more allowances for variations in individual development, because it assumes that the ways people develop are determined by their own particular experiences rather than unfolding in a predetermined set of stages, as in Freudian theory. Also like the humanistic approach, it is optimistic about the chances that a person's behavior can change for the better. And, as the advocates of the social-learning approach sometimes point out with justifiable pride, their claims about the malleability of human behavior and the power of conditioning techniques have been validated in many studies of behavior modification (as described in Unit 27).

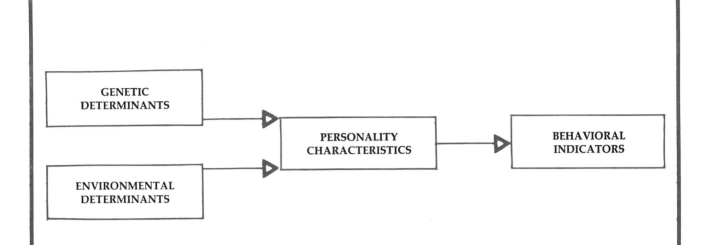

PUTTING IT TOGETHER: Personality

The development of personality has its origin in the interaction between *genetic and environmental determinants.* Each individual is born with some fairly stable characteristics of temperament which have a bearing on the social interactions with other people that form one's early experience. This interaction serves to direct personality development through a series of stages: psychosexual in Freudian terms, psychosocial in Erikson's terms. These stage theories are useful in predicting much about an individual's behavior.

Personality characteristics may be described in a number of ways. Many descriptive terms place an individual somewhere along a polarized dimension, such as internal-external control, or high-low authoritarianism. Cattell has reduced 171 personality traits down to 19 source traits, or dimensions, from which all the others flow.

Defense mechanisms may be employed by the individual to protect himself from the anxiety of having to deal consciously and directly with certain information about himself. But what we understand or predict about an individual can come only from *behavioral indicators.* Projective tests may be useful for understanding unconscious aspects. Self-reports, psychometric data, and behavioral measures are more widely used for most kinds of personality assessment.

In general, well-adjusted people are more self-accepting than poorly-adjusted people. In addition to the predictions that may be made about an individual from his enduring traits, much can be predicted about behavior in specific situations from knowledge about what an individual has learned from similar situations in the past.

WHAT'S ACCEPTED AND WHAT'S DEBATED

1. WHAT'S ACCEPTED . . .

1. Constitutional factors and experiences during infancy influence the subsequent course of personality development.
2. A variety of techniques of assessment can be used to examine both overt and unconscious aspects of personality.
3. Individuals differ reliably on many personality dimensions including locus of control and authoritarianism.
4. Individuals sometimes use unconscious defense mechanisms to ward off anxiety and avoid unpleasant thoughts.
5. Individuals are capable of self-directed behavior and defining their own goals.
6. The individual tends to respond to situational-contextual cues in his environment in ways consistent with past learning experiences.

2. WHAT'S DEBATED . . .

1. To what extent Freudian psychosexual stages or any stages are valid for the development of personality in general.
2. To what extent unconscious personality factors actually influence behavior.
3. To what extent identifiable personality dimensions have any practical use.
4. To what extent a personalistic-humanistic (subjective-oriented) approach to personality is amenable to rigorous testing and analysis.
5. How personality and behavior are related or interact—whether they're simply two sides of the same coin.
6. How much weight should be given to behavioral specificity versus trait consistency in the analysis of personality.

ISSUE: PERSONALITY TESTS

Personality tests such as those described in the unit are widely used in American society, and not only for clinical diagnostic purposes. Well over 80 percent of business firms now use psychological tests for employee selection, and of these tests about half focus on personality and temperament. The growing use of personality tests for such purposes has become so controversial that it has been the subject of congressional inquiry and criticism. Two main objections are made against the tests. The first is that they have limited reliability and may hurt individuals whose responses are misinterpreted. The second is that they may constitute an invasion of privacy.

Many psychologists doubt the validity of personality tests. Gordon W. Allport, former president of the American Psychological Association, suggested that if you want to know about a person, ask him or her directly. Other specialists in personality problems argue that observable reactions are more relevant than responses to a bunch of questions.

Accurate predictions are often difficult to achieve from both "objective" and "projective" tests. On objective tests, (such as the MMPI), the subject completes an inventory of questions. The answers are then scored by the tester to yield measures of various personality traits. A major problem, however, is that the subject may fake responses in order to create a better impression. Most tests have a built-in correction for faking, and incompetent fakers are easily detected. More skillful fakers, however, who do not claim improbable and inconsistent virtues for themselves may escape undetected. Ironically, how much a person lies on a test can be a better predictor of job success than a mass of honest answers. Many jobs, such as selling, may require the individual to appear poised, to seem confident, and to engage in deception. The more convincingly subjects can misrepresent themselves on the tests, the more effective they are likely to be on the job.

In the projective tests, (such as the TAT), the subject makes up a story in response to a word or a picture, or, as in the case of the well-known Rorschach Ink Blot test, interprets an apparently meaningless image. The trained psychologist then interprets the symbolic contents of the response in the hope of gaining insight into the subject's personality.

Problems arise, however, because the test is projective in two ways. The subject may be projecting inner hopes and fears, but the psychologist is also projecting personal assumptions and expectations when making an interpretation. Whenever the psychologist encounters some original projection by the subject, an item that the psychologist has not encountered before, the psychologist himself must make a new, highly personal interpretation. In consequence, different psychologists may interpret the same response in very different ways. About half the studies conducted on the validity of Rorschach tests have confirmed their value. But the other studies have come to the opposite conclusion. It is difficult to achieve objective interpretations of someone else's subjective symbolism.

Personality tests are of course very useful. They would not be so widely used if they were consistently unreliable. The Peace Corps, for example, was highly satisfied with its tests. The administrators had expected a 50 percent dropout rate from the Peace Corps, but after systematic screening of applicants with a battery of personality tests, they achieved a dropout rate of only 8 percent. The problem is not that the tests are generally unreliable, only that they can be highly unreliable in particular cases, with unfortunate effects for the individuals in question.

The argument that personality tests constitute an invasion of privacy has been heard increasingly in recent years. Professor Floyd Ruch contends that this attitude is part of a widespread anti-scientific feeling in modern society: "Medical research has developed truth serums and behavior-controlling drugs; advancing technology has brought infrared photography, the one-way mirror, the miniaturized tape recorder, the polygraph, and the directional microphone—plus the giant computer, with its almost limitless capacity for data storage and retrieval. These are appallingly efficient instruments to obtain information the individual might prefer to keep to himself." We live in an age when government agencies and private credit bureaus maintain millions of files on American citizens. Information is often fed into computers so that separate items can be formed into a full profile of the individual which is then available to anyone pressing a button at a computer output terminal.

Many job applicants resent being asked to answer such questions as "Do you like to attend parties frequently?"; "Are you satisfied with your sex life?"; "Do you cry easily?"; "Do odors of perspiration disgust you?"; or "Do you feel strongly against kissing a friend of your own age and sex?" All of these questions appear in the most commonly used personality tests. Many people consider these questions an invasion of privacy, and matters are not helped by the practice of many employers, particularly government agencies, of keeping a permanent record of the responses whether the applicant gets the job or not. The objection seems particularly well-founded when projective tests are used, because the very theory underlying these tests is that the subject has no conscious awareness of the personality traits he or she is revealing to the investigator. The study of personality is an old and legitimate interest of psychology. But the applications of such psychological research are highly controversial, and psychologists will have to confront this problem in the years ahead.

Unit 16

Children's Thinking

OVERVIEW

The concepts and research bearing on how children think, and how this thinking progresses toward adult modes of thought are discussed. Central to this study of cognitive development is Piaget's detailed description of the stages in children's thinking, and the wealth of evidence generated by Piaget's comprehensive theory. In contrast to Piaget's views, the more environmentally-oriented approaches of other psychologists are also described. The implications of Piaget's work for today's teachers is the focus of the final section.

UNIT OUTLINE

DEFINITION AND BACKGROUND
1. *Definition:* children's thinking is the process by which a child develops his understanding of the relationships between himself and objects in the world.
2. *Background:* Jean Piaget (1896–   ).

QUESTIONS AND EVIDENCE
1. What changes take place in the ways children think as they grow older?
Hypotheses:
    a. *Stages:* a child's thought processes develop in a series of identifiable stages. 270
    b. *Environmental:* a child's patterns of thought are determined more by his specific physical, social, and cultural surroundings than by the "ways of interacting with the world" that Piaget says typify various stages of development.
2. How can deficiencies in intellectual development be remedied?
Hypotheses:
    a. *Specific skills:* intensive education in one or two basic skills will promote general improvement in intellectual development. 276
    b. *Attitude:* children's intellectual development can be enhanced if they are taught to take responsibility for their performance on intellectual tasks. 277

IMPORTANT CONCEPTS

	page
animism	271
concrete-operational stage	272
conservation	272
developmental psychology	269
egocentrism	271
equilibration	270
formal operational stage	272
intelligence	270
language	271
object permanence	271
preoperational period	271
sensorimotor stage	271

Children's thinking develops out of early experiences with coordinating sensory and motor activities.

The individual's ability to think abstractly increases as he progresses through various stages of development.

With intellectual maturation individuals become capable of dealing with symbols and abstractions.

16. Children's Thinking 267

DEFINITION AND BACKGROUND

By the age of three the average child has already learned certain rudiments of organizing experience, symbolizing objects, and thinking. How did he get so far, and where does he go from here?

A workable DEFINITION of children's thinking is *the process by which a child develops his understanding of the relationships between himself and objects in the world.* This unit will FOCUS on the process of intellectual growth or cognitive development, as explained by the Swiss psychologist Jean Piaget. The unit discusses the four stages of children's thinking that Piaget described and the ways in which children's thinking differs from adult thinking. Particular environmental influences on children's thought and some possible ways of remedying deficiencies in intellectual development are also discussed.

BACKGROUND: JEAN PIAGET (1896–   )

Much of today's research on children's thinking has grown out of Piaget's observations of his own and other children. Born in Switzerland, Piaget had the intense curiosity and passion for knowledge that marks genius. One of his early hobbies was collecting and classifying species of mollusks from nearby lakes, and this work and the papers he published gave Piaget an international reputation in this field by the time he was fifteen.

An eclectic by inclination, Piaget has identified his eventual accomplishments with no one field or discipline, and he has carried on his writing, hobbies, pet studies, and wide-ranging interests throughout his life. First a degree in natural science from the Sorbonne, then training in clinical interviewing at a famous Swiss mental hospital, followed by work in measuring and testing intelligence in programs begun by Binet (see Unit 12) and Simon, and finally his own teaching and writing on the history and philosophy of science—all this prepared Piaget for his unique contribution to psychology.

One of the seeds of Piaget's interest in children's thinking was his work with intelligence tests. He became fascinated with why children "made mistakes" and began asking them to talk about their reasoning. From this work and from observing his own children, Piaget became convinced that a child's reasoning processes were quite different from the adult's conception of them. His first real chance to follow up his own insights came when he joined the staff of the Institute J. J. Rousseau in Geneva in 1921. There, working with an expanding group of students and co-workers, Piaget conducted many studies. At first they were basically observational or descriptive in nature, but later (about 1935) they became more vigorously experimental.

From his observations of how children of various ages solved problems, played games, and answered questions, Piaget developed an extensive theory that describes children's thinking in terms of four stages,

Figure 1.   Jean Piaget, a pioneer in the study of the cognitive development of children.

corresponding roughly to the ages birth to two years, two to seven, seven to eleven, and eleven to adulthood. In each stage the child develops a new type of thinking capacity until eventually he can use abstract adult logic.

For many years Piaget's work tended to be dismissed, especially in the United States, as an intriguing but untested theory. This neglect was to a great extent encouraged by the prominence of experimental learning theories in American psychology between 1920 and 1950. In the 1950s, however, as attention began to focus on improving learning in the schools, a number of Piaget's followers in the United States and elsewhere began to test his theories and ideas and to develop teaching practices based on his insights. To the surprise of some American researchers, controlled experiments yielded "hard" data that tended to verify many (though not all) of the ideas and conclusions that Piaget had formed from observational work and informal experimentation. At present Piaget's developmental stages and general theory form the basis of a great deal of the research conducted in child psychology. He no longer is—or can be—ignored. Other psychologists, building on Piaget's work, have contributed theories and research of their own. Especially notable is Lawrence Kohlberg's stage theory of moral development, described in Unit 5, and the work of

Jerome Bruner and his colleagues at Harvard on infant development. More and more researchers in developmental psychology are beginning to realize that children—even the tiniest infants—are not just passive responders and recipients of information. Rather, children actively organize and think about information, and their thinking is qualitatively as well as quantitatively different from adult thinking. Children are not just miniature but ignorant adults—they have their own qualitatively distinct systems for acquiring knowledge.

QUESTIONS AND EVIDENCE

1. What changes take place in the ways children think as they grow older?
2. How can deficiencies in intellectual development be remedied?

1. WHAT CHANGES TAKE PLACE IN THE WAYS CHILDREN THINK AS THEY GROW OLDER?

Before Piaget was "rediscovered" in the fifties, most psychologists believed that the basic differences between children's and adults' thinking were quantitative but not qualitative. That is, they thought that adults knew more than children, but they did not

QUESTION	1. WHAT CHANGES TAKE PLACE IN THE WAYS CHILDREN THINK AS THEY GROW OLDER?	
HYPOTHESES	**STAGES**	**ENVIRONMENTAL**
DESCRIPTIVE EVIDENCE	ASSESS: 1. characteristics of children's thought at various ages 2. egocentrism of children's thought during preoperational stage 3. abstractness of thought during formal operational stage 4. order in which different conservation abilities develop	ASSESS: relation between familiarity of event and animism of child's explanation
EXPERIMENTAL EVIDENCE		VARY: training in conservation of density task MEASURE: understanding of conservation of density

believe that children and adults organize experience in different ways. At present most child psychologists, following Piaget, believe that children's thinking develops through a sequence of stages, each characterized by a particular way of dealing with the world.

The *stages hypothesis* states that a child's thought processes develop in a series of identifiable stages. During each stage the child develops a particular mental framework of assumptions and techniques that he uses to organize incoming stimuli. As the child grows older, he develops new mental frameworks for organizing his experience. According to Piaget, the order or sequence in which these frameworks develop is identical and unchangeable for all children.

DESCRIPTIVE EVIDENCE

Investigator: J. Piaget
Source, Date: "The Child's Conception of Space," 1956
Location: Geneva, Switzerland
Subjects: Piaget's own three children, children in public schools and nurseries
Materials: Objects in the everyday world of the child

Piaget's observations of children led him to formulate some complicated but fascinating ideas about the development of intelligence. Piaget defines intelligence as the *construction of an understanding.* The word "construction" is important, because it awards the child an active role in his interactions with the environment. The child is not merely acted upon by outside stimuli that elicit responses; instead, responses are produced through an interaction between stimuli and the child's existing cognitive structures. (The character of the interaction will be described and illustrated below.) The word "understanding" is also important, because it distinguishes Piaget's view of intelligence from the view of intelligence that lies behind IQ tests (see Unit 12). IQ tests measure understanding to some extent, but they also rely heavily on acquired knowledge. For example, an item on one standard IQ test for children requires the child to put together the pieces of a puzzle to form a duck, which tests not only his understanding of spatial relationships but also his knowledge of ducks. To pick a more extreme example, some IQ tests include items like: "Which is farther from New York, Chicago or Los Angeles?"—a hard question for a child who has never heard of Los Angeles, no matter how well he understands the concept of distance. The point is that

Piaget, though he acknowledges the importance of information for solving some problems, believes that information without understanding is not real knowledge.

Piaget says that the child constructs his understanding of the world through a process called *equilibration,* which includes two steps: *assimilation* and *accommodation.* These words can best be explained by using an example. If you hand an infant a rattle, he will close his hand around it, perhaps shake it a bit, and probably put it into his mouth. If you then hand him a spoon, he will probably treat it the same way: the spoon can be *assimilated* into what Piaget would call the infant's existing "scheme" for grasping objects. Now suppose you hand the child an inflated plastic pillow, which is too large for him to get his fingers around. The child must *accommodate* his existing grasping scheme to the characteristics of the new object and will learn (sooner or later) to pick it up in both hands. Further accommodations take place later, as the child encounters things that cannot be grasped at all, such as an asphalt driveway and the smoke from a pile of burning leaves.

According to Piaget, equilibration—the interaction of assimilation and accommodation—is the general process by which knowing takes place. An adult, for example, would use the process to change his mind about the morality of any specific war; in fact, you are probably making an effort right now both to assimilate Piaget's ideas into your existing "schemes" and to accommodate your "schemes" to his ideas. Piaget observed, however, that infants and young children and older children and near-adults equilibrate in different ways; that is, human beings use different methods for interpreting their experience at each of four stages of development.

Piaget gave the following names to the four basic stages of intellectual development that he described: *sensorimotor, preoperational, concrete operational,* and *formal operational.* Although certain ages are associated with each stage, Piaget made it clear that the ages at which children enter and leave each stage vary. More important than age is the idea that all children move through the stages in the same order. No stage can be skipped, since later stages are built on the understanding gained during earlier ones, but all children do not necessarily reach the final stages. (Some adults are unable to carry out Piaget's formal-operational tasks.) Furthermore, the thought patterns that characterize early stages do not completely disappear when later stages are reached. For example, adults use sensorimotor knowledge when they swim, ride a bike, or feed themselves.

The **sensorimotor stage** begins at birth. As the label implies, most of the intelligent activity of the infant involves coordinating sensory experiences (such as looking and touching) with motor activities (such as sucking, reaching, and grasping). At this stage the infant knows the world in a primitive way that is based on overt action. He learns how to act in ways that will bring about certain effects (for example, he learns to pick up a rattle, then a spoon, then a plastic pillow) but he does not know what it is that he is doing. That is, he "knows" how to pick up a rattle in the sense that he can carry out the action, but he does not know that he is using a part of his body to pick up an external object. There is no distinction for him yet between objects and his actions upon them.

A young infant does not realize that objects continue to exist when he can't see them or touch them. Until he begins to develop *object permanency*, he will not search for a toy that is shown to him and then hidden under a pillow. Starting about eight months of age, the child will look under the pillow for a toy when he has seen someone hide it there; but if the toy is hidden first under one pillow and then, while the child

watches, rehidden under a second one, he still looks for it under the first pillow.

Not until the beginning of the **preoperational stage**, about age two, will the child show full object permanency. This he demonstrates through his ability to cope with "invisible displacements." For example, suppose you show a child a small block, then hide the block in a box and the box under a pillow while the child watches. Sneakily, while the child is not looking, you now take the block out of the box and put it in your pocket. Then you hand the empty box to the child. A child near the end of the sensorimotor period will look inside it for the block—and then give up. But a child who has entered the preoperational period and attained full object permanency will continue to search—under the pillow, in your hands, behind your back, maybe even in your pocket. Unlike the sensorimotor child, he is sure the block still exists, even though something has happened to it that he didn't see.

This understanding of object permanency paves the way for several major developments of the preoperational period, including *deferred imitation* and *language*. A child at this stage is able to imitate actions he has seen some time ago and to play make-believe games. Also, he begins to be able to think symbolically and thus to use language. He can understand, for example, that the word "dog" is a symbol that stands for certain four-legged objects.

Piaget has described the thinking of the preoperational child as *egocentric* and *animistic*. It is important not to confuse the word "egotism" which is sometimes used to describe a personality trait, with Piaget's concept of egocentrism. Egocentrism refers to the child's inability to understand that other people can perceive things differently and can have different viewpoints and different feelings from his own. As the study described next will show, a young child does not even understand that a three-dimensional object can be seen from different angles than the one from which he is viewing it. The animism that characterizes preoperational thinking shows up in children's tendencies to attribute life and will to inanimate objects. A young child riding in a car at night may believe that the moon is alive and following him. If the car window is open, he may remark that the wind is "mean" to be so cold or that the heater is "nice" because it warms up his feet.

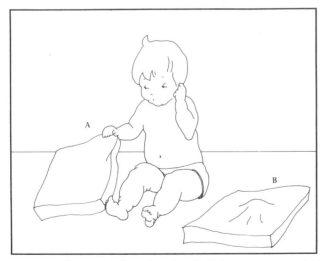

Figure 2. If a toy has been found under Pillow A, a young child who has not yet fully developed object permanency will look for it there again even though she has seen it placed under Pillow B.

The child's ability to symbolize increases dramatically during the concrete-operational stage, which runs from approximately seven to eleven years of age. Interpretations of experience are influenced more by logic and less by immediate perception and appearance. In particular, as indicated by the Elkind study described later, the child develops *conservation* abilities during this stage. For example, the understanding that a specific quantity of ice cream remains the same whether it is served in a high sundae glass or a wide dish does not develop in children's thinking until about the age of seven.

Another notable development of the concrete-operational period is *classification*. The child learns to add classes together to form larger classes; for example, he learns that dogs and cats and horses and cows, added together, form the larger class animals. He also learns to "multiply" classes. For example, suppose he is given cutouts of four dogs, four cats, four horses, and four cows; in each group, one animal is blue, one green, one red, and one yellow. The preoperational child, handed these cutouts and asked to put them in piles that "go together," might group them either by color (all the red cutouts, all the blue ones, and so on) or by shape (all the dogs, all the cows, and so on), or he might come up with these piles: all the dogs; the green cat, the green horse, and the green cow; the red and the yellow cats; and the red and the yellow horses. What he would not be able to do—and what the concrete-operational child can do—is coordinate the two characteristics of the cutouts, color and shape. A concrete-operational child can lay out the sixteen cutouts, arranging the rows by shape and the columns by color.

The ability to manipulate classes is a necessary preliminary to some of the developments of the formal operational stage. Near the start of adolescence, the child begins to be able to grasp scientific, religious, and political concepts and to deduce the consequences that they logically imply. The child who has reached this stage can reason hypothetically and carry out systematic experiments, considering all the possible causes of an event and gradually ruling out the ones that do not apply. A child at the concrete-operational stage can consider causal relationships between real events, but he has trouble working systematically with hypothetical ones until he reaches the formal operational stage.

DESCRIPTIVE EVIDENCE

Investigators: J. Piaget and B. Inhelder
Source, Date: "The Child's Conception of Space," 1956
Location: Switzerland
Subjects: Children four to eleven years old
Materials: Scale model of mountain range, table, chairs, dolls, photographs

The model of a mountain range was placed on a table that was surrounded by several chairs. Each child was asked to walk around the table and look at the model from all sides. He was then asked to depict by a variety of methods the views of the mountain range that would be seen from chairs other than his own. In one test, for example, a doll was placed in a chair and the child was asked to select from several photographs the one that showed the doll's view.

Younger children tended to pick the photograph that showed their own view of the mountain range. They were unable to understand that the doll would see things from a different angle. This inability to place oneself in the position of another person is one of several kinds of evidence Piaget presented to demonstrate the egocentricity of the growing child. (Unit 5 discussed Kohlberg's idea that the ability to role-play, which egocentrism does not permit, is essential to movement to higher stages of moral development.)

DESCRIPTIVE EVIDENCE

Investigators: J. Adelson and R. O'Neil
Source. Date: "Growth of Political Ideas in Adolescence: The Sense of Community," 1966
Location: University of Michigan
Subjects: 120 children from four grades: fifth, seventh, ninth, and twelfth; average ages of 10.9, 12.6, 14.7 and 17.7 years
Materials: Questionnaire concerning hypothetical political situations

The subjects were presented with the following hypothetical political situation: a thousand men and women, dissatisfied with the way things are going in their country, decide to purchase an island in the Pacific; once there, they must create a code of law and a mode of government. The subjects were asked several questions concerning how the island might be organized politically and legally.

Figure 3.   In a prepared environment of mixed ages, such as this Montessori classroom, children find materials to manipulate that will lead them from early concrete stages of development to later conceptual stages. The teacher as observer and helper responds to the needs of children individually, inviting them to explore materials that will enable them to progress with confidence from one stage to the next. The children are able to observe other children operating at levels that they themselves may not be ready for, but through their observations they are being indirectly prepared for later stages of development.

The study indicated that an abstract sense of community did indeed develop during adolescence. The responses of the younger children were very concrete, as illustrated by an eleven-year-old's answer to the question "What is the purpose of government?"

> Well . . . buildings, they would have to look over buildings that would be . . . um, that wouldn't be any use of the land if they had crops on it or something like that. And when they have highways the government could inspect it, certain details. I guess that's about all.

However, adolescents began answers to the same question from a perspective of community good and a need for social order, as shown in a thirteen-year-old's reply concerning the purpose of government:

> Well, I think it is to keep the country happy or to keep it going properly. If you didn't have it, then it would just be chaos with stealing and things like this. It runs the country better and more efficiently.

In another study of the ways children's political ideas develop, F. Rebelsky, C. Conover, and P. Chafetz (1969) found that young children (aged two to five) showed egocentrism in their political thought. Asked why they would like to be President, for example, these children answered things like to be tall, to have toys, to play drums, to "war my sister," and to run faster. When children from six to thirteen were asked the same question, over one-third answered that they wanted to stop the war in Vietnam. (And almost half the children between six and nine said they did *not* want to be President, because they didn't want to get shot.)

DESCRIPTIVE EVIDENCE

Investigator: D. Elkind
Source, Date: "Children's Discovery of the Conservation of Mass, Weight, and Volume: Piaget Replication Study II," 1961
Location: Beth Israel Hospital, Boston
Subjects: 175 school children in grades K through 6
Materials: Two clay balls

A young child does not understand conservation. Before the concrete-operational stage, which usually begins at about age seven, children think that a tall, thin beaker contains more liquid than a short, wide one, even though the amount is actually the same. They also think that a string of twenty beads pulled taut, in a straight line, "has more beads" than a twenty-bead string in the shape of a circle.

There are several different kinds of conservation ability, and according to Piaget's findings, they develop in a particular order. For example, conservation of mass develops before the conservation of weight, and conservation of weight develops before conservation of volume. (The usual ages are mass: seven or eight; weight, nine or ten; volume, eleven or twelve.)

In this study, Elkind used two balls of clay to assess the accuracy of that order. Each child was seated at a table and shown two clay balls of identical size. After the children had indicated that the two balls had the same amount of clay, the experimenter took one ball and flattened it out into a sausage shape. Then each child was asked which had more clay, the remaining ball or the sausage. Later, the same procedure was repeated except that the final questions were "Which weighs more?" and "Which takes up more space?"

The children's answers were in agreement with Piaget's theory. The older children showed conservation of mass, weight, and volume, answering in all cases that the ball and the sausage were the same. Slightly younger children showed conservation of mass and weight, but they still thought the sausage "took up more space" than the ball. The youngest children showed only conservation of mass.

Not all psychologists agree with Piaget's theory that cognitive development is basically a process of passing through the four stages that have been described. They may not dispute the various characteristics of children's thinking that Piaget and his followers have identified, such as animism and conservation, but they think that these characteristics are more likely related to particular experiences that the child has had than to the existence of universal stages of development. According to the *environmental hypothesis,* a child's patterns of thought are determined more by his specific physical, social, and cultural surroundings than by the "ways of interacting with the world" that Piaget says typify various stages of development.

Figure 4.   Until about age seven children have difficulty in applying logic to concrete ideas. This child witnessed the pouring of equal amounts of liquid into two vessels but insisted that the narrower vessel contained more. When one of two equal-sized balls of clay was rolled out to an elongated shape, the child asserted that the new shape contained more clay.

DESCRIPTIVE EVIDENCE

Investigator: M. Berzonsky
Source, Date: "The Role of Familiarity in Children's Explanation of Physical Causality," 1971
Location: University of Toronto
Subjects: 84 children between the ages of 3.5 and 4.5 years
Materials: Balance device, glass half full of water

Each child was asked to explain both familiar and unfamiliar events. Typical questions inquired about what makes a car move (familiar) and what makes clouds move (unfamiliar). If Piaget's developmental theory was universal, the investigator reasoned, each child should give either animistic or naturalistic explanations for both the familiar and the unfamiliar events, depending on his own stage of development. On the other hand, if the environmental notion applied, the children would be expected to give animistic explanations for unfamiliar events but naturalistic explanations for events with which they had had previous experience.

Consistent with the environmental hypothesis, the children gave many more animistic explanations for unfamiliar events: for example, they expressed the notion that "the clouds move themselves." Berzonsky then tested the hypothesis in a more controlled way. He showed the children a board balanced on a fulcrum by two equal weights placed on either end and asked what would happen when one of the weights was removed and why. The children's thoughts on why the board tilted were considered explanations of a familiar event. After five such trials, Berzonsky secretly placed a weight underneath one end of the board so that when he removed one of the weights, the board surprisingly tilted downward. The children's interpretations of this unexpected result were considered explanations of an unfamiliar event.

Once again, the children gave many more animistic explanations of the unfamiliar event than of the familiar event. This result is a significant caution against uncritical acceptance of the view that particular experiences, as exemplified by the variable of familiarity, plays only a minor role in children's thinking. The study suggests that whether or not animism characterizes children's thinking may depend more on the opportunities they have had to learn about specific events than on an invariant developmental sequence.

EXPERIMENTAL EVIDENCE

Investigators: C. J. Brainerd and T. W. Allen
Source, Date: "Training and Generalization of Density
Conservation: Effects of Feedback and Consecutive Simi-
lar Stimuli," 1971
Location: University of Windsor
Subjects: 40 children between the ages of ten and eleven
Materials: Clay balls, jar of water

According to Piaget, children do not develop conservation of density—the knowledge that an object will float or sink but not do both and that the shape of an object is irrelevant to whether it sinks or floats—until they are at least eleven and perhaps not until

Critics of studies of this type sometimes have found, in studies of their own, that children trained on specific Piagetian tasks learn specific answers to specific questions but do not understand why the answers are correct unless they were already on the verge of understanding the task before training began. However, Brainerd and Allen's study presents unusually strong evidence to support the notion that the children who received training did indeed understand the conservation of density, and their ages make it unlikely that they were on the point of doing so on their own. Nevertheless, training may lead to real understanding of only certain kinds of concepts, and not others.

QUESTION	2. HOW CAN DEFICIENCIES IN INTELLECTUAL DEVELOPMENT BE REMEDIED?	

HYPOTHESES	SPECIFIC SKILLS	ATTITUDES
DESCRIPTIVE EVIDENCE		
EXPERIMENTAL EVIDENCE	VARY: amount of language tutoring MEASURE: IQ scores and general behavior	VARY: attitude retraining vs. success only MEASURE: degree of disrupted performance following a failure

they are fifteen. These subjects, all between the ages of ten and eleven, first were shown that two clay balls floated in water. Then the experimenter flattened one of the balls into the shape of a raft, and the children were then asked whether the raft would float or sink. This procedure was repeated with several pairs of clay balls. After each trial, some of the children were told whether they were correct or incorrect (training, or "environmental feedback") and others were not.

Retested later, the children who had received training showed a greater grasp of the conservation of density concept than did the children who had not.

2. HOW CAN DEFICIENCIES IN INTELLECTUAL DEVELOPMENT BE REMEDIED?

Several recent studies have devoted particular attention to the importance of certain specific skills and general attitudes in the development of children's thinking abilities. Some children have a hard time at school because, for one reason or another, they lack a large number of the intellectual skills that the school wants them to have. It may not be necessary to provide such children with training in each deficient skill. The *specific skills hypothesis* proposes that intensive education in one or two basic skills will promote general improvement in intellectual development.

EXPERIMENTAL EVIDENCE

Investigators: M. Blank and F. Solomon
Source, Date: "A Tutorial Language Program to Develop Abstract Thinking in Socially Disadvantaged Preschool Children," 1968
Location: New York City
Subjects: 11 "disadvantaged" nursery-school children
Materials: Common objects such as paper, crayons, and blocks

The subjects, all between the ages of three and five, were divided into four groups matched for age, sex, and IQ. Two groups were tutored in language skills, one group three times a week and the other five times a week. Neither of the other two groups was tutored, but one of them received "attention": they participated in an unstructured play session every day of the week, supervised by the same teacher who did the tutoring. The actual tutoring (or play) sessions lasted for fifteen to twenty minutes per day and were conducted over a period of four months. Although the method of tutoring involved many detailed procedures, they all focused on eliciting and challenging explanations of everyday occurrences and provided instruction in a variety of basic concepts, such as "up" and "down."

Both the tutored groups gained from seven to fourteen points on the Stanford-Binet IQ test. Even more impressive was the reported general improvement in the tutored children's everyday behavior elsewhere in school and in play situations. In contrast to these results, the untutored groups continued to think and to behave in much the same way as they had prior to the study.

The fact that so-called disadvantaged children could make remarkable progress in a period of just a few months indicates that some tutoring programs may actually be effective, despite some discouraging evaluations of Project Head Start and other "enrichment" programs. However, there is still a great deal of controversy in this area, especially about how long the beneficial effects of tutoring last.

A different approach to a related issue relies on the *attitude hypothesis*, which states that children's intellectual development can be enhanced if they are taught to take responsibility for their performance on intellectual tasks.

The typical retarded child knows that, for as long as he can remember, he has never seemed to be able to do what other children can do. School is no different, and he may have come to believe that his own effort had very little to do with whether or not he succeeded or failed. As a result, his performance even in special classes may be far below what it could be. However, if such a child develops the belief that success or failure in school is a matter of effort, not luck, he may begin to realize his potential. (See Unit 2.)

EXPERIMENTAL EVIDENCE

Investigator: C. Dweck
Source, Date: "The Role of Expectations and Attributions in the Alleviation of Learned Helplessness in a Problem," 1972
Location: Yale University
Subjects: 12 retarded children between the ages eight and thirteen
Materials: Effort apparatus, toys

Prior to experimental training, the subjects' performance on arithmetic problems was observed to deteriorate rapidly after they answered a problem incorrectly. For example, when presented with some easy problems, then with a difficult problem, and then with the same easy problems, the children failed to complete accurately the very same easy problems they had already solved. After confronting the difficult problem, they seemed to give up and no longer knew what they were capable of doing.

The children were divided into two groups, labeled "success only" and "attitude retraining." The first group received fifteen daily trials that were arranged so that the children always answered correctly. The second group received identical training, except that two or three of the trials contained difficult problems that ensured failure. When this failure occurred, the child's performance was corrected in his presence and the experimenter attributed the failure to insufficient effort.

Children in the success-only group continued to evidence a severe deterioration in performance following any failure, whereas those in the attitude-retraining group gradually improved their perform-ance following failures. By the end of the study, failure on a previous trial no longer disrupted per-formance on subsequent trials, apparently because the children had acquired the belief that failure re-sulted from insufficient effort. They applied them-selves more to the problems given after failure and learned that they could answer them correctly. These results suggest one possible way to teach some chil-dren to reason more effectively.

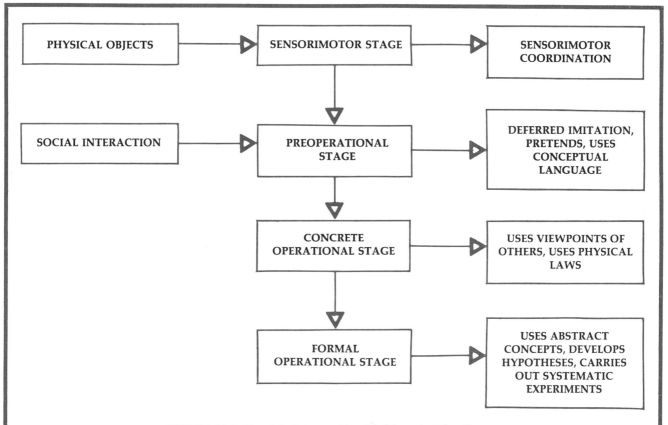

PUTTING IT TOGETHER: Children's Thinking

According to Piaget, the child constructs his understanding of the world through equilibration, the interaction between assimilation and accommodation. Assimilation is the incorporation of information into existing schema; accommodation is the adaptation of schema to information that cannot be assimilated.

Equilibration begins with the infant's exposure to *physical objects* in the environment. During the *sensorimotor* stage, up to about two years of age, the child learns about objects in space. Behavior corresponding with this stage of thinking involves *sensorimotor coordination*, sucking, reaching and grasping.

With *social interaction* the child progresses to the *preoperational stage* of thinking, from approximately two to seven years of age, learning object permanency and developing animistic and egocentric thought. Behavior includes *deferred imitation, pretending, and the use of conceptual language*.

The child then progresses to the *concrete operational stage*, which runs approximately from seven to eleven years of age. This stage of thinking is characterized by a comprehension of conservation of mass, weight, and volume and the addition and multiplication of classes. This can be observed in behavior involving *the use of others' viewpoints and the use of physical laws*.

After about eleven years of age, the child enters the *formal operational stage* of thinking, dealing with abstract thought and deductive reasoning. Behavior includes the *use of abstract concepts* in science, religion, and politics, *the development of hypotheses*, and *carrying out systematic experiments*.

There is evidence that progress may be facilitated through training in a few basic skills and through the enhancement of productive attitudes.

1. WHAT'S ACCEPTED . . .

1. Children proceed through a sequence of identifiable stages in the development of conceptual thinking.

2. WHAT'S DEBATED . . .

1. The importance of environmental factors, such as previous experience or familiarity, in cognitive development.

2. The unalterability of Piaget's description of the order in which children acquire various concepts.

3. The most efficient and practical method for teaching children to reason more effectively.

With the exception of Sigmund Freud, it is doubtful that any other psychologist has wrought such profound changes in our understanding of human psychology as Jean Piaget. The Swiss philosopher-psychologist—now in his eighties and still generating an enormous output of books and journal articles—has revolutionized our understanding of human intellectual development. His model of cognitive growth—complex, subtle, but fascinating—has given parents and teachers new insights into the minds of children by demonstrating how very different their thinking is from that of adults. The child, Piaget contends, is not simply an undeveloped adult, whose mental processes are merely quantitatively different from his elders'. Instead, Piaget argues, the child's thinking about his environment is qualitatively unlike that of adults.

Piaget's discoveries have had many important applications in the field of education. When teachers become familiar with his developmental system, they find that they never see children or children's thinking in quite the same light again. In the past, children were taught various concepts on the assumption that the child was merely a younger and more ignorant version of the adult. Piaget's experiments, however, have demonstrated that many of these concepts were taught to children at much too early an age. Before Piaget, few people suspected this. Because children seemed to be able to manipulate the concepts correctly, it was assumed that they understood them.

In fact, children may get their sums right but not have the slightest idea of what they are doing. The child may be able, for example, to convert pints to quarts with the greatest of ease—on paper. But as Piaget's experiments on the conservation of liquids have shown, the child has no comprehension of the meaning of the operation and no understanding of the concept of volume. The same is true of many other simple operations. Young children do not really understand the concept of speed as a time-distance relationship. If two toy cars are racing one another, the child will assert that the car in front is going "faster," even if the car behind is accelerating much more rapidly. And although young children may be able to count without difficulty, they have no real understanding of the concept of number. If a child is shown ten beads spaced out in a row and asked to put alongside the row an equal number of other beads, the child typically creates a row of equal length, without any regard to the number of beads in the new row. As a result of these and similar findings, teachers are now concentrating on the teaching of concepts, rather than on operations based on ideas that the child cannot understand. They are also delaying the teaching of some subjects until the child has reached the level of cognitive development that enables him or her to tackle the problem in a meaningful way.

The implications of Piaget's work are felt throughout elementary education. For example, Robert Karplus, an expert in physics and mathematics education, points out that most teachers use verbal propositions in teaching elementary schoolchildren. Much of this instruction is inevitably destined to go straight over the children's heads, even though they may understand the individual words that are being used. The teacher unknowingly uses the logic of formal operational thinking, although the child's thought, as we have seen in this unit, has not advanced beyond the preoperational level. Karplus and his associates are now developing programs to train teachers to instruct children in language that is appropriate to the preoperational level of intellectual development.

Psychologist David Elkind of the University of Rochester has also suggested that one of the reasons for the poor success rate of the New Math is its failure to take account of the differences between adult and childhood reasoning processes. When the New Math was first designed, a new "language" was developed in the belief that it would aid instruction in mathematical concepts. This new language, however, was geared to adult logical operations rather than to those of children, 'and so was doomed to failure. The New Math programs are now being revised so that physical rather than verbal models can be used to put across the concepts. The new programs will take into account the concrete rather than abstract nature of children's thought.

Piaget's work has also had great impact on the schools as a result of his belief that the developing individual is the active constructor of his environment and not simply a passive recipient of information. In the past, children were essentially *taught* by teachers. Today, they increasingly *learn* for themselves. By giving children structured opportunities to explore and understand their environment, teachers achieve far more success than they did under the old, passive-learning model.

At present about 40 percent of all preschool children in the United States are enrolled in some educational program. Few psychologists doubt the value of early education, but many are worried that the full implications of Piaget's work may not be taken into account, and that children may be taught material that they are not yet ready to absorb. Sheldon White of Harvard University feels that "middle class parents have been bullied, and it has gotten hysterical. We have some vague kind of alarm about the need to do something, God knows what, to kids before they are five." Elkind points out that "if you force a child to learn specific content before he is ready, he will develop a long-term attitude about school that may be negative." And Piaget himself has warned Americans against trying to teach children subjects without careful consideration of whether they are intellectually prepared to learn them. "If the aim is to accelerate the development of these operations," he insists, "it is idiotic."

Unit 17

Signs of Emotion

OVERVIEW

Some of the important data bearing on how humans identify their own emotions and the emotions of other people are briefly presented. These events involve both physiological processes such as arousal, and interpretations based on past experiences. Some external signs of emotion, such as facial expressions, appear to be unlearned or innate to some extent.

UNIT OUTLINE

DEFINITION AND BACKGROUND
1. *Definition:* signs of emotion are those overt and observable features of behavior that human beings associate with such states as joy, fear, awe, love, and hate.
2. *Background:* Charles Darwin (1809–1882).

QUESTIONS AND EVIDENCE
1. How do we identify the emotions we are feeling?
Hypotheses:
   a. *Labeling-of-arousal:* when a person is experiencing a generalized physiological arousal that cannot be readily explained, he will interpret his feelings in terms of the particular situation, from environmental and contextual cues. **286**
   b. *Cognitive-appraisal:* emotional arousal is not simply produced by some stimulus but rather by the manner in which the event is interpreted and appraised by the person. **287**
2. How do we identify the emotions others are feeling?
Hypotheses:
   a. *Facial-expression:* there are universal, unlearned facial expressions for certain basic emotions and people in all cultures associate the same expressions with the same emotions. **289**
   b. *Gesture:* a disposition to display specific emotions through certain types of gestures is culturally acquired. **291**

IMPORTANT CONCEPTS

	page
arousal	287
cognitive appraisal	287
hormones	286
labeling-of-arousal	286
nonverbal behaviors	288

In identifying emotions felt by ourselves and by others we appraise the circumstances as well as the signs of emotion.

The emotional labels we assign are dependent upon our interpretation of visceral states and past experience.

There is evidence that indicates that the facial signs of emotion are similar in all cultures and, in some cases, between humans and other animals.

DEFINITION AND BACKGROUND

We often can tell at a glance what emotion another person is experiencing—even if the person is a total stranger. A person's nonverbal behaviors—facial expressions, body movement, and posture and hand gestures—reveal a great deal. Considering the fleeting nature of these expressions and movements, it is remarkable how accurate our judgments can be and how rapidly they are made. Differences in emotional expression may be clearly perceived, and yet it may be impossible to state just what the differences are.

The DEFINITION of signs of emotion is *the overt and observable features of behavior that human beings associate with such states as joy, fear, awe, love, and hate.* This unit will FOCUS on how we identify the emotions we are experiencing and on how we recognize these emotions in others.

BACKGROUND: CHARLES DARWIN (1809–1882)

Few men in history match Darwin in their contribution to scientific knowledge. Born into a wealthy family, Darwin spent most of his life living in seclusion on his estate in England collecting data for a utopian book, a huge, definitive volume that would prove the reality of evolutionary change and the principle of natural selection. The *magnum opus* was never published; instead he hastily had to put together an abstract of his ideas because other scientists were beginning to think along the same lines. The abstract, titled *Origin of Species,* was published in 1859. The first edition sold out in a single day. Within ten years Darwin and his theory of evolution were known throughout the world.

Thirteen years later Darwin published a book, *The Expression of the Emotions in Man and Animals,* in which he applied his theory of evolution to the expression of emotions. He set out to show that not only physical structure but also the habits of all animals have been gradually evolved. He closely observed the expression of emotions in animals because, as he put it, they afforded "the safest basis for generalization on the causes, or origin, of the various movements of expression." He also studied expressions in infants, the blind, the mentally ill and aborigines who had little contact with Europeans. The study of emotional expression in aborigines was conducted by circulating a printed questionnaire to missionaries and officials in the far corners of the world. He insisted that actual observations and not memory be reported. These cross-cultural studies were deemed to be very important by Darwin, who wrote: "Whenever the same movements of the features or body express the same emotions in several distinct races of man, we may infer with much probability, that such expressions are true ones—that is, are innate or instinctive. Conventional expressions or gestures, acquired by the individual during early life, would probably have differed in the different races, in the same manner as do their languages."

Although his book on evolution had an enormous impact, the book on emotional expressions was largely ignored. Yet the interesting thing about the book is that many of Darwin's ideas are again very

Figure 1. Charles Darwin, father of evolutionary theory, who set out to show that not only physical structure, but also the habits and expressions of all animals have been gradually evolved.

Figure 2. Darwin applied his theory of evolution to expressions of emotion typical of various species of animals. (From Darwin, 1872.)

much part of modern research in psychology. Ethologists are continuing the study of animal behavior under natural conditions and use Darwin's ideas to explain the evolution and development of these behaviors (see Unit 30). And the results of Darwin's cross-cultural survey of emotional expressions in man—imperfect as it may have been—are being confirmed today by researchers who have at their disposal more sophisticated techniques.

QUESTIONS AND EVIDENCE

1. How do we identify the emotions we are feeling?
2. How do we identify the emotions others are feeling?

QUESTION	1. HOW DO WE IDENTIFY THE EMOTIONS WE ARE FEELING?	
HYPOTHESES	**LABELING OF AROUSAL**	**COGNITIVE APPRAISAL**
DESCRIPTIVE EVIDENCE		
EXPERIMENTAL EVIDENCE	VARY: expectation of the effect of a drug and social cues MEASURE: emotional responses	VARY: existence and content of sound tracks on film MEASURE: skin resistance and other emotional responses

1. HOW DO WE IDENTIFY THE EMOTIONS WE ARE FEELING?

Each of us knows what it feels like to be happy or unhappy. In the course of everyday conversation you may state that you are anxious, depressed, ecstatic, or angry. How are you aware of what your emotional state is? We say that we laugh because we are happy or cry because we are sad. But an early American psychologist, William James, proposed that the opposite happens. He claimed that stimuli in the environment set off physiological changes, and when the brain becomes aware of these changes it makes the proper emotional interpretation. In other words, we do not laugh because we are happy but are happy because we have laughed. James maintained that instead of saying "I felt afraid and my heart started pounding," we should say, "My heart was pounding, so I knew that I was afraid."

Basically what James proposed was that physiological components of the emotion come first and that feedback from body changes is perceived as the emotion. Since James' time, it has been determined that the brain is organized to provide generalized nonspecific arousal—an alerting signal—as well as specific information from situational cues (see Unit 21). It is conceivable that an individual identifies his own emotions through a situational labeling of generalized physiological arousal. In animals with well-developed cortex—upper brain—areas this labeling may originate in words or thought as well as in social situations.

The *labeling-of-arousal hypothesis* states that when a person is experiencing a generalized physiological arousal that cannot be readily explained, he will interpret his feelings in terms of the particular situation, from environmental and contextual cues.

EXPERIMENTAL EVIDENCE

Investigators: S. Schachter and J. E. Singer
Source, Date: "Cognitive, Social, and Physiological Determinants of Emotional States," 1962
Subjects: Male college students
Materials: Injected epinephrine (adrenalin) or saline solution; questionnaires

As each subject arrived he was taken into a private room and told that the experimenters were testing the effect of certain vitamin compounds on vision. He was asked if he would agree to receive an injection of a vitamin compound. A physician gave the injection. For some students the injected substance was actually epinephrine (adrenalin), a hormone in the body that causes increased blood pressure and heart rate, flushing, and occasionally tremors and palpitation. Other subjects received a saline solution, which has no side effects, as the injection.

Experimental conditions were manipulated by giving different explanations to subjects receiving epinephrine. Informed subjects were told what the side effects would be: that their hands would start to shake, their heart pound, and their face get warm and flushed. The effects lasted for fifteen or twenty minutes. Misinformed subjects were told that they would feel numb and itch. Ignorant subjects were not told anything about side effects. Students receiving the saline solution were treated in the same way as the ignorant subjects.

Each subject was asked to wait in another room in order to let the injected compound become absorbed into the bloodstream. In the room was a stooge, a member of the experimental team who was introduced as another subject. It was the stooge's task to create one of two situations. Either he acted in a playful, euphoric manner—flying paper airplanes, playing basketball with crumpled paper—or he behaved in an angry manner because of the insulting questionnaire the subjects were asked to fill out while waiting.

Subjects who received adrenalin and who had been told truthfully what to expect did not respond to the emotional cues provided by the stooges, even though they were experiencing physiological arousal. They could label their state of arousal as drug-induced and tended to ignore the situational cues. Subjects who received only the saline solution had a low level of physiological arousal and also exhibited a low level of response to the actions of the stooge. Misinformed and ignorant subjects picked up the mood of the stooges. In particular, the misinformed subjects joined into the euphoric activities. The ignorant subjects had lower activity than the misinformed subjects, and this was thought to be the result of self-information, that is, suspecting that the arousal was somehow connected with the injection.

Schachter and Singer concluded that a person who is in a state of physiological arousal that he cannot readily explain will turn to environmental and contextual cues for some explanation. They noted that a person who has no explanation for an aroused state can be manipulated to interpret his feelings as either euphoria or anger, depending upon the circumstances. If a person does have a completely satisfactory explanation, he will not label his arousal in terms of the situation and is relatively immune to manipulation. Also, the saline solution subjects showed that an individual reacts emotionally only to the extent that he experiences a state of physiological arousal.

The importance of cognitive factors in emotion can be seen in the results of Schachter and Singer's experiment. Given a state of arousal, we label in terms of our cognition or understanding of the situation. The cognition exerts a steering function—we feel arousal and try to find an appropriate label for it. Richard Lazarus argues that the labeling aspect of emotion has been overemphasized and that the initiating and steering functions of cognitive activity play a more important role than previously thought. The *cognitive-appraisal hypothesis* states that emotional arousal is not simply produced by some stimulus but rather by the manner in which the event is interpreted and appraised by the person. The appropriate physiological response follows this appraisal. In other words, the extent of arousal can be determined by intellectual, cognitive factors.

Figure 3. Subjects given injections to induce arousal experienced an emotion appropriate to what they thought was responsible for the arousal. Adapted from Mandler (1962).

Investigators: J. C. Speisman, R. S. Lazarus, A. Mordkoff, and L. Davison

Source, Date: "Experimental Reduction of Stress Based on Ego-Defense Theory,"1964

Location: University of California, Berkeley

Subjects: 56 male college students and 42 male airline executives

Materials: Anthropological film; personality questionnaires; skin resistance monitors

The subjects viewed a film of subincision puberty rites of a primitive Australian tribe. In the film adolescent males, thirteen or fourteen years old, were held down by three or four older men to prevent escape. The penis is grabbed, stretched, and cut on the underside from tip to scrotum with a piece of sharpened flint. The film was presented either without sound or with one of three soundtracks. One soundtrack played up the painful and threatening aspects of the operation; the second carried a commentary that intellectualized what was happening in a very detached way; the third carried denials that the operation was harmful or painful and stressed the social benefits of participation. Heart rate and skin resistance of the subjects were measured while they watched the film, and immediately after the film each subject completed a self-report on his feelings.

Emotional responses were the greatest when the soundtrack emphasizing the harmful and painful na-

ture of the operation was played, and the next greatest responses were to the silent version. With the denial and the intellectualization soundtracks, emotional responses were greatly decreased. Students had the lowest emotional response when they heard the intellectualizing commentary; the airline executives tended to have lower responses when they heard the denial soundtrack.

The results clearly show that cognitive appraisal of emotional situations can affect the physiological responses of the body. Specifically, cognitive activity can lower stress responses (see Unit 28).

Thus, it seems that both arousal and cognitive appraisal play important roles in determining how we identify the emotions we experience. If we become physiologically aroused for no apparent reason, we look to the context and the situation for explanations; if we are exposed to highly stressful or emotional situations, our body responses can be controlled to some extent by intellectual or cognitive appraisals of the situations.

2. HOW DO WE IDENTIFY THE EMOTIONS OTHERS ARE FEELING?

One way of communicating what emotions you feel is to tell other people that you are happy or angry or depressed. These verbal reports are based on how we interpret our various states of arousal. Yet it seems that a great deal of our awareness of other people's emotional states comes not from verbal reports but from the way they look. Nonverbal signs of emotion

QUESTION	2. HOW DO WE IDENTIFY THE EMOTIONS OTHERS ARE FEELING?	
HYPOTHESES	**FACIAL EXPRESSION**	**GESTURE**
DESCRIPTIVE EVIDENCE	ASSESS: if certain facial expressions have the same emotional meaning to all cultures	ASSESS: use of gestures by various cultural groups
EXPERIMENTAL EVIDENCE		

Figure 4. Bodily postures as well as facial expressions are signs of emotion.

are a definite part of the human communication system. Darwin wrote that the movements of expression in the face and body serve as the first means of communication between humans. He proposed that some facial expressions of emotion are inherited and are common to all races of man. The idea of inherited or innate behaviors is not popular with American psychologists; the mainstream point of view is that experience is the important factor that shapes behavior and emotion. However, some psychologists continue to explore the innate theory. Silvan Tompkins, for example, disputes the James theory that inner body physiological responses are the chief indicators of emotion. He asserts that emotions are identified primarily by feedback from facial behaviors and that the responses of the body are of secondary importance. In effect, he says that when we become aware of our facial responses, we are aware of our emotions. The facial responses are largely controlled by innately organized brain structures that control the muscles in the face. Although these innate responses can be transformed in various ways through learning, the basic response can always be elicited under appropriate conditions.

The *facial-expression hypothesis* states that there are universal, unlearned facial expressions for certain basic emotions and that people in all cultures associate the same expressions with the same emotions.

Figure 5. Facial expressions, gestures, and other body movements convey emotion, although psychologists debate whether they are innate or learned. Such feeling states as puzzlement, anger, and excitement are easily conveyed by nonverbal means.

DESCRIPTIVE EVIDENCE

Investigator: P. Ekman
Source, Date: "Universals and Cultural Differences in Facial
    Expressions of Emotion," 1971
Location: University of California, San Francisco
Subjects: 4 Western, 1 Eastern and 2 preliterate cultures
Materials: Photographs of facial expressions

Members of five literate cultures—United States, Brazil, Chile, Argentina, and Japan—were tested with photographs of facial expressions. The pictures were shown one at a time and the subjects had to state which of six emotions best fitted the expression in the photograph. The emotional categories were: happiness, anger, sadness, disgust, fear, and surprise. The results showed that in each culture persons associated the same facial expressions with the same emotions, indicating that they must have been familiar with experiences that would cause them to identify certain

facial expressions as indicative of specific emotions. Japanese and Americans had little trouble in identifying facial expressions that were meant to indicate happiness, surprise, or sadness even though their cultures and languages differed. But these results did not eliminate the possibility that contact among the cultures might be responsible for the similarity in perceiving facial expressions.

In order to find out if cross-cultural communication might have affected the recognition of facial expressions, subjects from remote, isolated and preliterate societies were tested. The first group studied was the Fore group in New Guinea, who until the late 1960s existed in the equivalent of a neolithic culture. Although some of the Fore group had been exposed to missionaries and other Westerners, only those who had virtually no contact were tested. The second preliterate group that was tested was the Dani, a tribe in the central highlands of New Guinea that had almost no contact with European or other cultures.

In both cases the subjects had little difficulty in distinguishing facial expressions for happiness, sadness, disgust, and surprise. The results provide strong evidence that facial expression of emotions is the same regardless of culture. The findings dispute the argument that visual contact among cultures is responsible for the similarity in facial emotional expression.

Ekman also recorded on videotape attempts by Fore natives to express emotions with their face. When the unedited videotapes were shown to American college students, they were able to accurately judge the intended emotion in four of the six cases. Only fear and surprise were incorrectly judged, often confused with each other. In general, the results indicate that regardless of language, culture, or degree of literacy, certain facial expressions have a universal meaning.

Ekman postulates a "neurocultural" theory of facial expression of emotion. The "neuro" refers to the innate response of facial muscles to certain emotions. The cultural aspect refers mostly to the events that elicit emotion. It is these elicitors that are in large part socially learned and culturally variable.

There is some evidence supporting Darwin's notion that facial expression of emotions is to a large extent universal. But what about other nonverbal behaviors, such as gestures? Are they also innate, or are they learned? The *gesture hypothesis* states that a disposition to display specific emotions through certain types of gestures is culturally acquired. The United States in the 1940s proved to be an excellent natural laboratory for testing this hypothesis because both traditional and assimilated ethnic groups could be studied simultaneously. If assimilated or "Americanized" individuals still retained gestures characteristic of their ethnic progenitor, this would not support the hypothesis that gestural behavior is culturally acquired.

DESCRIPTIVE EVIDENCE

Investigator: D. Efron
Source, Date: "Gesture, Race and Culture," 1972
Location: New York
Subjects: Jews and Italians in their natural communities
Materials: Films, sketches

The gestural behavior of traditional Jews in the Lower East Side of Manhattan and of traditional Italians in Little Italy was recorded in sketches of real-life situa-

Figure 6. Specific variations in emotional expression are learned through imitation.

tions by an artist, by direct observation and counting of gestures, and by secretly filming conversations on the street. Data on the behavior of assimilated Jews were collected at summer resorts in the Adirondack and Catskill mountains, at Columbia University, and at other schools. Data on assimilated Italians were collected at Columbia University, political gatherings, and homes. Objective measurement of gestures was done by projecting individual frames from films on graph paper and marking the positions of hands, wrists, elbows, and head. When sequential positions were joined, a precise representation of fluid movements was obtained.

Traditional Jews and traditional Italians differed greatly in the kind of gestures used. Jews used gestures to trace the logic and rhythm of the conversation; they rarely tried to depict the things being referred to. Each twist or turn in gestural movements corresponded to a change in the direction of thought. Traditional Italians, on the other hand, were inclined to illustrate the objects they were talking about with gestures. They drew pictures of the thing or action and used emphatic movements as exclamations at the end of statements.

Assimilated Jews and Italians lost most of the gestural behaviors that were characteristic of the traditional groups. The more assimilated the individual, the less Jewish or Italian gestural traits he was found to possess. The gestures of assimilated Jews and Italians resembled each other more than their respective traditional groups. The differences between traditional Jews and traditional Italians, and the lack of such differences between assimilated Jews and Italians, cannot be explained in terms of immigrant versus American born. It was found, for example, that American-born Jewish students studying to become rabbis exhibited the traditional gestures in their conversation.

Efron concludes that the results indicate that gestural behavior is conditioned by social and psychological factors. He also found a number of cases of "hybrid" gestures. Individuals exposed to two different cultural groups may adopt and combine certain gestural traits of both groups.

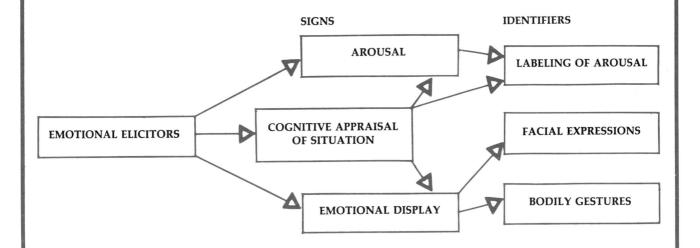

SIGNS   IDENTIFIERS

AROUSAL

LABELING OF AROUSAL

EMOTIONAL ELICITORS

COGNITIVE APPRAISAL OF SITUATION

FACIAL EXPRESSIONS

EMOTIONAL DISPLAY

BODILY GESTURES

PUTTING IT TOGETHER: Signs of Emotion

Emotional elicitors may include thoughts, memories or environmental events. The signs of emotion include a rather generalized *arousal* as well as a variety of *emotional displays*. *Cognitive appraisal of the situation* probably precedes arousal when the intensity is not great or the change too sudden.

We identify specific emotions in ourselves by *labeling the arousal*, and identify them in others through their *facial expressions* and *bodily gestures*. Cognitive appraisal of the situation probably plays some role whenever we identify emotions either in ourselves or in others.

The arousal of generalized emotion and most of the facial expressions we display seem to be consistent across all cultures, while the situations that elicit emotion and the bodily gestures people display are specific to each culture.

WHAT'S ACCEPTED AND WHAT'S DEBATED

1. WHAT'S ACCEPTED . . .

1. Emotions are associated with a state of physiological arousal.

2. The same state of physiological arousal can be interpreted as entirely different emotions depending upon the situation and the environmental cues that are provided.

3. Cognitive appraisal can modify the degree of physiological arousal to a stimulus.

4. Facial expressions, gestures, and other body movements convey emotional meaning.

2. WHAT'S DEBATED . . .

1. Whether arousal precedes cognitive appraisal or arousal is produced after the stimulus has been cognitively evaluated.

2. Whether facial expressions of emotion are innate or learned.

ISSUE: COMMUNICATING FEELINGS

Are there any universal signs of emotion in the human species? We know that in most other animals, nonverbal signs are the principal means of communication between individuals. And we know that these signs are expressed in rigid, innate patterns of behavior that any other member of the species can automatically interpret in only one way. The wagging of a dog's tail, the arching of a cat's back, the warning flap of an elephant's ears—their meaning is unmistakable to others of the same species. But what about the nonverbal signs that form such an important, if overlooked, element in human emotion? Are any of these signs innate, or are they all learned and subject to varying interpretations?

Most psychologists agree that the majority of our signs of emotion are learned through the process of socialization. We teach our children to wave good-bye or to shake hands. Later, they learn other, more subtle signs for themselves, such as the elaborate nonverbal rituals involved in a boy-meets-girl situation. These signals—like the prolonging, for a brief moment longer than necessary, of eye contact—form a repertory of communicative devices which are required through experience and which are often unconsciously used and interpreted.

The fact that so many of our signs of emotion have to be interpreted by others distinguishes most human nonverbal communication from that of other animals. Although our basic capacity to send these signals is biologically determined, the signals themselves are subject to a wide range of social interpretations. The shrug of the shoulders, for example, may mean different things in different cultures. In our own society, it implies indifference or ignorance, but there are parts of the South Pacific where the shrug means an emphatic "no." Approaching someone with an extended arm and an open hand is usually interpreted as a sign of friendship—except in some parts of the Far East, where it may signify an impending karate chop. In nearly every human society the nod of the head means "yes" and the shake of the head "no," but there are four small, isolated tribes that reverse this seemingly "natural" arrangement.

Even the smile needs interpretation. Shakespeare's

Hamlet, tricked and deceived by the friendly but wicked usurper King, observed wonderingly that "a man may smile, and smile, yet be a villain." The human smile and its various meanings has been the subject of a good deal of research in America. Professor Ray L. Birdwhistell of the University of Pennsylvania has subjected the American smile to a systematic examination and concludes that there are considerable regional variations in the frequency and meaning of the smile. The most unsmiling Americans of all, he discovered, live around the Great Lakes. Smiling is most frequent in the south and the midwest, while in New England people are very selective about whom they smile to. New Englanders are generous with their smiles to friends, but are much less inclined to bestow them on strangers. New Yorkers retain an unsmiling mask most of the time, probably because nonparticipation in the affairs of their many but anonymous fellow citizens is a norm in the city. Outside of the city, a New Yorker who smiles a great deal is viewed with some suspicion. He is considered to be "selling." Birdwhistell emphasizes, however, that the frequency of smiling is not necessarily an indication of friendliness. People may smile not only because they are happy and friendly, but also because they want to *appear* happy and friendly. A southerner may smile more than a New Englander not because he is more hospitable, but simply because he is more willing to remind people of his hospitality and friendliness. Even the circumstances of our smiling, then, are learned through socialization.

But there do appear to be some signs of emotion that—like those of other animals—are innate and universally subject to the same interpretation. The frown, for example, always means puzzlement or displeasure. Tears have the same meaning in every culture: the tearful person is emotionally overwrought or distressed. The extension of the lower lip into a pout always signifies sulking; and the disdainful curling of the lip can be interpreted in only one way. A submissive posture, too, is instantly recognizable in every culture. And there are many other innate signals that are so subtle that we are usually unaware of transmitting them. How many of us realize, for example, that we always raise our eyebrows slightly when we encounter somebody that we recognize?

Many of these innate signs of emotion are not normally under conscious control but derive instead from the workings of the autonomic nervous system. These signs, which include blushing, rapid pulse rate, trembling, or observable indications of tension stem from the release of the "fear and flight" hormone, adrenalin, into the body by the adrenal glands. In fact, the lie detector is based on our knowledge of these involuntary signs of emotion. The lie detector is simply a device to monitor and record various changes in the responses of the autonomic nervous system, such as heart rate and electrical discharges of the skin. The assumption behind the lie detector is that an individual who tells a lie experiences his lying as stressful, and responds with involuntary signs of emotion. The use of lie detectors is not usually acceptable as courtroom evidence, however. Many people are able to learn to control their autonomic responses (See Unit 35, Biofeedback), and other people may become so nervous when telling an important truth under these conditions that they may generate signs of emotion that can easily be misinterpreted.

We do share some innate signs of emotion with other species, then, but most of our signs are learned and have to be interpreted by others.

Unit 18

Problem Solving and Creativity

OVERVIEW

What we often call "thinking" includes both trying to find the specific answer to some questions (problem solving) and finding better solutions to open-ended problems (creativity). This unit discusses some of the most important factors affecting problem solving such as past experiences, language, and insight. Creativity is a difficult concept to analyze because it has implications for both abilities and personality traits. The unit also examines recent research involving the role of the hemispheres of the brain in thinking and problem solving.

UNIT OUTLINES

DEFINITION AND BACKGROUND
1. *Definition:* problem solving and creativity are self-directed activities in which an individual uses information to develop answers to problems, to generate new problems, and occasionally to transform the process itself by creating a unique new system.
2. *Background:* Wolfgang Köhler (1887–1967).

QUESTIONS AND EVIDENCE
1. What are some processes involved in solving problems?
Hypotheses:
   a. *Learning-sets:* problem-solving skills, including insight, are acquired primarily as learning sets gradually developed through experience. **300**
   b. *Functional-fixedness:* a knowledge of the customary functions of objects can make it difficult to solve a problem that requires using those objects in unusual ways. **302**
   c. *Language:* language can serve as a mediating process between the demands of a problem and its solution. **303**
   d. *Strategy:* problem solving can be represented as a mode of information processing—that is, as a series of manipulations of symbols and relationships. **304**
2. How does creative thinking differ from problem solving?
Hypotheses:
   a. *Creative-abilities:* creative thought is radically different from other kinds of problem solving and calls for separate talents and skills. **306**
   b. *Creative-personalities:* creative people differ from noncreative people not merely in certain abilities but in the basic structure of their character. **307**

IMPORTANT CONCEPTS

	page
cognitive psychology	299
computer simulation	305
convergent thinking	306
creativity	298
divergent thinking	306
Gestalt psychology	299
insight	298
intelligence	306
learning	300
problem solving	298
strategy	304

The information processing demands of a problem-solving task vary with the personal characteristics of individual problem solvers.

Individuals employ strategies that have been useful for them in the past.

Under some circumstances staying with old solutions may be a handicap. Creative people are relatively free of conventional restraints.

DEFINITION AND BACKGROUND

In this unit we shall use the DEFINITION of problem solving and creativity as *self-directed activities in which an individual uses information to develop answers to problems, to generate new problems, and occasionally to transform the process itself by creating a unique new system.* The critical distinction between problem solving and other cognitive processes such as remembering and paying attention, as well as daydreaming, is the extent to which the individual consciously and actively applies himself to the solution of problems. This does not mean, however, that the only way to solve intellectual problems is by directed thinking. Creative people in many fields have reported that solutions to problems they have been struggling with came to them while they were not consciously working on the problems at all. Daydreaming or undirected mental activity can contribute to the problem-solving process, as do memory, attention, and other cognitive processes.

Figure 1. The two-string problem is an insight problem requiring the solver to tie two hanging strings together although he cannot reach one while holding the other. Insight comes when he realizes that he can attach an object to one string and swing it like a pendulum.

The FOCUS of this unit is on the self-directed aspects of problem solving and creativity. It must be recognized, however, that other cognitive processes are also involved, as are social, emotional, and motivational forces.

BACKGROUND: WOLFGANG KOHLER (1887–1967)

Before and during World War I, Wolfgang Kohler, a German psychologist living on Tenerife, one of the Spanish Canary Islands, extensively studied the behavior of apes. Kohler placed the apes in problem situations where he could observe their behavior closely. For example, he hung bananas from the ceiling of an ape's cage, scattered boxes around in the cage, and then observed the ape's attempts to get the bananas. Kohler noted that after the ape vainly jumped at the bananas or tried to reach for them, it would then stop and sit, with little apparent activity. Then, all of a sudden, the ape would jump up, put a box under the bananas, place another box on top of it, and reach the bananas by standing on the two boxes.

Kohler observed similar kinds of sudden problem-solving behaviors with other animals in different situations. He put some fruit outside the cage of Sultan, his smartest chimpanzee, just a little too far away for him to reach with one of a set of sticks. Eventually, Sultan took the small stick that he had and pulled in from outside the cage a longer stick, which he used to pull the fruit into his cage. As Kohler (1926) described it, "he gazes about him (there are always in the course of these tests some long pauses during which the animals scrutinize the whole visible area). He suddenly picks up the little stick once more, goes up to the bars directly opposite to the long stick, scratches it toward him with the 'auxiliary,' seizes it, and goes with it to the point opposite the objective (the fruit), which he secures."

Again, Sultan's solution to his problem appeared suddenly, with little apparent preparation. Kohler gave the name *insight* to these sudden perceptions of useful or proper relations among objects necessary to solve the problem. The most interesting feature of insight was that it didn't seem to depend on prior learning or experience. And once an ape or chimp found a solution, it always responded correctly to later problems of the same type.

Kohler's observations were different from those of

Figure 2. Insightful problem-solving behavior in the chimpanzee. With no prior experience in box stacking, the chimp assesses the problem and develops a solution.

some previous researchers, notably E. L. Thorndike (see Unit 27). Thorndike's cats exhibited random exploratory behavior before they accidentally discovered the solutions to their problems. This led Thorndike to suggest that problem solving was primarily a matter of gradual trial-and-error learning rather than of sudden insight.

Kohler objected to this analysis on the grounds that Thorndike's puzzle box was "unfair" to the cats. The animals could not see the latch and so could discover the means of escape only by accident. But Kohler's apes, presented with all the information necessary to solve the problem, worked out solutions without recourse to trial and error. Kohler concluded that problem solving comes about through sudden perceptual reorganizations (insights) rather than "stamping in" of specific responses learned by trial and error.

The Thorndike-Kohler debate helped define certain central issues in the study of problem solving, and Kohler's work had a great influence on the thinking of the Gestalt psychologists (see Unit 23). What is now called cognitive psychology represents, in part, an attempt to combine the Gestalt tradition, which emphasized the internal organization of information, and

the behaviorist tradition, which emphasized the analysis of overt behavior and avoided speculations about internal processes.

QUESTIONS AND EVIDENCE

1. What are some processes involved in solving problems?

2. How does creative thinking differ from problem solving?

Work on problem solving has demonstrated fairly well that most problem solving involves both trial-and-error learning and insight. The basic issue now is to identify and examine the roles that experience plays in the acquisition of thinking skills. Some psychologists contend that problem-solving strategies arise entirely from experiences based on trial-and-error learning. Others emphasize the internal organization of previously learned rules that is made possible by language, for example. Still others attempt to identify thought processes by examining performance and studying the ways it is influenced by past experience.

HYPOTHESES	LEARNING SETS	FUNCTIONAL FIXEDNESS	LANGUAGE	STRATEGY
DESCRIPTIVE EVIDENCE	ASSESS: problem-solving speed during establishment of learning set			ASSESS: problem-solving strategies used by a computer
EXPERIMENTAL EVIDENCE		VARY: 1. manner in which common objects are presented 2. presence of labels on common objects MEASURE: problem solving ability	VARY: opportunity to use verbal mediation MEASURE: accuracy of recall by age of child	

1. WHAT ARE SOME PROCESSES INVOLVED IN SOLVING PROBLEMS?

A whole series of hypotheses has been formulated to answer this question. Each of these hypotheses offers different concepts for the interpretation of problem solving and gives its own emphasis to the roles and weights of prior experience and insight in the process of problem solving.

One of these hypotheses reflects the traditional approach to problem solving dating back to Thorndike's research. This *learning-sets hypothesis* states that problem-solving skills, including insight, are acquired primarily as learning sets gradually developed through experience. A learning set is a general ability to solve a whole group of similar problems in much the same way. For example, a person who has taken apart and repaired a transistor radio will probably have an easier time assembling a full-scale stereo system from scratch than will someone who approaches the larger job "cold." The person's earlier experience, including his mistakes, should help him not only interpret the instructions that come with the sound system—a formidable intellectual challenge in their own right—but cope with unforeseen problems, because they may resemble problems he coped with earlier. According to this hypothesis, insight only appears to be a sudden phenomenon: In fact, it is based on learned associations among related skills. The man who "suddenly" understood gravity when an apple fell on his head, remember, was neither a poet nor a shepherd but an experienced scientist.

In a celebrated series of experiments, Harry Harlow attempted to show that the theories advanced by Thorndike and Kohler were not necessarily incompatible. Insight into a particular type of problem does not occur in the absence of experience with the elements of the problem, but neither is there a set of accumulated associations that is sufficient in itself to account for insightful behavior. Learning sets are required. When an animal forms learning sets, Harlow says, it is *learning how to learn efficiently* in the situations that it frequently encounters. That is, a learning set is a general ability to solve a class of problems efficiently, and it is a joint function of previous experience and the skills that were used to organize that experience. Does the evidence of the following experiments tend to support the contention that a mechanism of learning sets is necessary in order to understand problem-solving behavior?

DESCRIPTIVE EVIDENCE

Investigator: H. F. Harlow
Source, Date: "The Formation of Learning Sets," 1949
Location: University of Wisconsin
Subjects: Monkeys
Materials: Discrimination learning apparatus

Specifically, Harlow proposed to find out whether a history of rewards for correct responses to a discrimination-learning problem (for example, choosing a triangle from a group of geometric figures) would transfer to a new but related problem.

Monkeys put in the apparatus pictured in Figure 3 were presented with two stimulus objects that covered food wells. Their task was simply to choose the object that covered the food—a triangle, say, rather than a circle or a square. The food underneath the object was the animal's reward.

Initially, the monkey made mistakes, but soon it learned to consistently pick the object of a certain color, shape, or size in order to get its reward. How fast the monkey learned was measured by the number of trials or picks it made before it began to make no mistakes at all: the sooner it made no mistakes, the faster it was learning and remembering which stimulus offered the reward. (Stimuli were randomized from left to right, so that right-left position preferences made no difference.) The evidence that indicates the existence of learning sets is this: once the monkey has performed in a particular situation many times, it will make few wrong choices, even when the problem is changed. For example, after the monkey has been trained with the triangle, the correct stimu-lus object is changed to the circle. In such a situation, the monkey learns to solve the new problem (picking the circle) much faster than it learned to solve the original problem (picking the triangle). Thus, through practice, the monkey learns how to approach and solve efficiently a whole class of problems of a similar type.

Although experience can certainly improve problem-solving skills, it is equally clear that there are limitations on the kinds of problems various species, and also individuals within those species, are capable of solving. After all, no one expects a monkey to be able to put together a stereo system.

Discrimination-learning problems of the type used by Harlow in his experiments seem to require only simple problem-solving behavior. However, such situations may not be typical of all those in which problem solving takes place. Another major hypothesis has been formulated to deal with quite different situations in which organization and insight seem to play more significant roles.

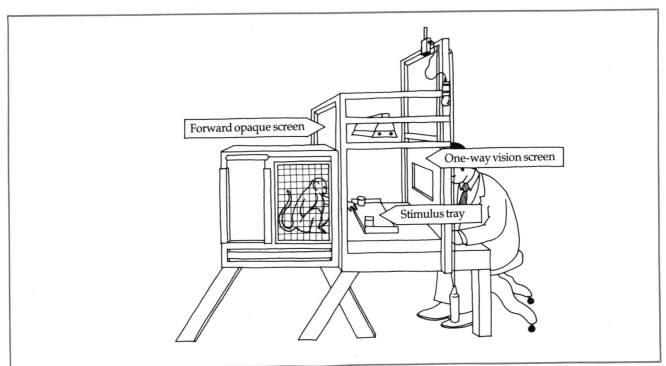

Figure 3. Wisconsin General Test Apparatus used for discrimination training with monkeys. The experimenter lowers the opaque screen before changing objects in the stimulus tray. He then watches the monkey through the one-way screen to record responses.

Working in the area of perceptual studies, Duncker (1945) coined the term "functional fixedness" to describe a certain property of problem situations requiring insight that seems particularly crucial in determining how fast they are usually solved. The *functional-fixedness hypothesis* states that a knowledge of the customary functions of objects can make it difficult to solve a problem that requires using those objects in unusual ways. Studies of functional fixedness suggest that an important factor in insight may be the ability to perceive the role each element plays in the whole: by understanding what it does (its function), one can see where it belongs, how it fits there, and what other function it might have.

Figure 4. An example of functional fixedness. The problem solver cannot assign an unusual function to an object, and he fails to see that the pliers can be used to complete the electric circuit.

EXPERIMENTAL EVIDENCE

Investigator: R. E. Adamson
Source, Date: "Functional Fixedness as Related to Problem Solving: A Repetition of Three Experiments," 1952
Location: Stanford University
Subjects: 57 college students
Materials: Ingredients of Duncker's (1945) "candle problem"

In Duncker's candle problem, each subject is provided with three candles, three small cardboard boxes, five thumbtacks, five matches, and a vertical soft wood screen. The task is to mount the candles on the vertical screen so that they will burn without going out. To solve the problem, it is necessary to melt the wax-end of the candle with a match, stick the candle in a box, and then attach the box to the screen with the tacks.

In the Adamson experiment the problem was presented in two ways: the experimental group received

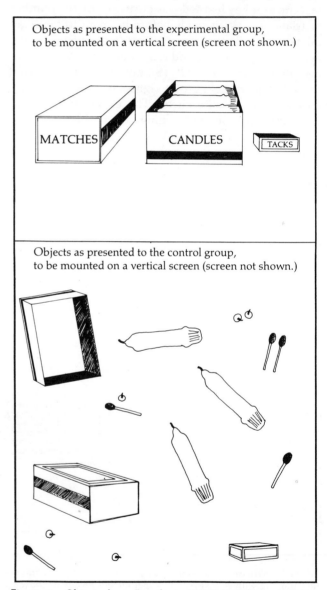

Figure 5. Objects from Duncker's (1945) "candle problem" as presented to the experimental group in Adamson's experiment (1952).

the tacks, matches, and candles sorted out into separate boxes, and the control group received all the objects scattered on the table. The problem was solved in less than twenty minutes by 86 percent of the second group but by only 41 percent of the first. According to Adamson, the subjects in the first group were hampered by functional fixedness. Because the boxes were presented to them as containers, these subjects found it more difficult to think of using the boxes as shelves for the candles than did the other subjects. That is, people have trouble seeing the other uses to which objects (boxes) might be put because they are accustomed to using them for a specific purpose (as containers).

Duncker's original conclusion involved precisely this concept of "preutilization" (customary use) of the functionally fixed objects. Sometimes the functional fixedness can be mediated through words rather than actual use, as in the following study.

EXPERIMENTAL EVIDENCE

Investigators: S. Glucksberg and R. W. Weisberg
Source, Date: "Verbal Behavior and Problem Solving: Some Effects of Labeling in a Functional Fixedness Problem," 1966
Location: Princeton University
Subjects: 24 college students
Materials: Objects of Duncker's (1945) "candle problem," now labeled

Three experimental groups were asked to solve Duncker's candle problem. Members of one group received the objects (tacks, matches, candles, boxes) clearly labeled with little signs. For the second group, only the tack box was labeled. For the third group, no labels were used.

More people in the first group solved the candle problem than in either of the other two groups. The results suggest that not only the possible functions of an object but the object itself can go unnoticed. That is, the subjects may have overlooked the possibility that the boxes might be used to solve the problem because the boxes seemed a less important piece of equipment than the other materials. Labeling all the objects encourages a subject to consider each of them in turn; in addition, labels may free new functions by categorizing each object in the subject's mind as a generic "thing."

Depending on the problem to be solved, functional fixedness (which may be considered a special form of set) can be a hindrance or a help. It tends to speed up problem solving when the problem requires using objects in usual ways but to slow it down when an unusual function is called for.

The labels on the objects in the Glucksberg-Weisberg experiment point toward other ways of explaining problem solving. Recall a recent experience in which you were faced with a fairly serious problem. When you thought about it, talked it through, or figured it out, didn't you use words or some similar kind of symbols in resolving the problem, by yourself or with others? Such common-sense observations raise the possibility that language or other symbols play a key role in problem solving.

Another hypothesis proposed to explain successful problem solving deals with the unique human ability to use language. The *language hypothesis* states that language can serve as a mediating process between the demands of a problem and its solution. Although the role that language plays in problem solving is by no means completely understood, it is well known that younger children do not seem to use language as a mediator, whereas children older than about six or seven do. Studies have been made to find out why younger children do not use language as a mediator and what skills are necessary in order for them to do so. The study described here was an attempt to clarify the difference between the ability to name objects (as three-, four-, and five-year-olds can) and the ability to use the names of objects in organizing one's thoughts during problem solving (as older children and adults can).

EXPERIMENTAL EVIDENCE

Investigators: J. H. Flavell, B. R. Beach, and J. M. Chinsky
Source, Date: "Spontaneous Verbal Rehearsal in a Memory Task as a Function of Age," 1966
Location: University of Rochester
Subjects: 60 boys and girls, kindergarten, second and fifth grades
Materials: Colored photographs of objects

The subjects were shown a set of seven pictures of common objects (such as an apple, a comb, a flag).

The experimenter pointed to three of the pictures. Then the pictures were taken away, rearranged in a different sequence, and shown to the subject again. The subject was asked to point to the three pictures that he had been told to remember, in the order that they had been indicated to him.

In order to distinguish the ability to name the objects from the ability to use the names to remember the objects, two experimental conditions were established. During one set of trials, subjects were asked to remember the objects immediately after they had been pointed out. In the other condition, a visor was placed before the subject's eyes for fifteen seconds, to allow time for verbal mediation to take place. Flavell predicted that the younger children would do equally poorly in the two conditions, whereas the older children would do better when allowed the fifteen-second period to use language as a mediator. All spontaneous verbalizations of the children were recorded. It was expected that kindergartners should not be using words at all; that second-graders would produce the most overt verbalizations; and that fifth-graders, who should already be internalizing the use of language, would think silently.

The results tended to confirm a lack of verbal mediation in younger children. The kindergarten subjects failed to use naming and rehearsal as a cognitive "trick" to help them recall the pictures in the proper order. They were able to name the objects easily when asked to do so in a separate task, so the problem was not one of inadequate vocabulary. The children simply did not know exactly when and how to use their vocabulary as an aid in completing the task.

Flavell and his colleagues also considered a second line of explanation for the younger children's failure to use verbal mediators. It seemed possible that a more general cognitive deficiency had prevented them from using the vocabulary words they knew. The deficiency may have had something to do with the ability to transform a visual sequence into verbal symbols and store them in a particular order. This possibility is consistent with Piaget's description of children in the preoperational stage of cognitive development (see Unit 16).

The use of language as mediator is a factor in a number of problem-solving procedures. Jerome Bruner and his colleagues at Harvard published their

Study of Thinking in 1956. This important work surveyed the different strategies people use to learn and handle concepts, discussed in detail in Unit 22. Four years later, in *Plans and the Structure of Behavior,* George Miller, Eugene Galanter, and Karl Pribram advanced a number of ideas that have much in common with Bruner's "strategies." They concluded, however, that associations and learning are simply inadequate to account for such complex processes as language use and problem solving. As an alternative, they proposed that thinking should be conceived as a step-by-step series of operations on information. This approach focuses on the basic nature of thought rather than on the way problem-solving abilities are acquired, and it treats the organism as an active processor of information rather than as a simple responder to stimuli.

With their books, Bruner, Miller, and their co-workers opened up an entirely new area of research by treating thinking as somewhat analogous to computer programming. Naturally enough, this fresh approach led to a new hypothesis about thinking.

The *strategy hypothesis* states that problem solving can be represented as a mode of information processing—that is, as a series of manipulations of symbols and relationships. Then problem solving can be simulated and studied by means of computer programs. If a computer can be programmed to solve problems in the same way that humans apparently solve them, the computer's program can be used as a theoretical outline of human thought. In the following investigation, a computer was programmed to look further into the complex processes by means of which logical theorems can be proved.

DESCRIPTIVE EVIDENCE

Investigators: A. Newell, H. A. Simon, and J. C. Shaw
Source, Date: "Elements of a Theory of Human Problem Solving," 1958
Location: Carnegie Mellon University
Subjects: Comparable machine and human behaviors
Materials: Proofs of theorems from Whitehead and Russell's Principia Mathematica

A general-purpose computer was programmed to discover proofs for theorems in elementary symbolic logic. The program designed for this purpose is called the Logic Theorist (LT). Next, a set of givens was stored in the computer's memory, and, finally, it was presented with a particular theorem and instructed to discover a proof for it. From this point on, the computer was the problem solver.

LT succeeded in proving thirty-eight of the fifty-three theorems given to it. About half the proofs were accomplished in less than a minute each; most of the others took from one to five minutes. In order to learn how the computer solved the problems, Newell and his co-workers instructed it to print out some of its intermediate results—"to work out its problems on paper" so to speak.

The LT program involved a set of rules of inference by which problems could be solved. The computer's use of these rules revealed many similarities to observed instances of both insight and trial-and-error among human and animal subjects. For example, LT sometimes reorganized available information, displaying a sudden grasp of the structure of the problem—the "aha!" reaction that is characteristic of insight. It also used trial-and-error strategies to reduce the number of possibilities under consideration. One of these, which human problem solvers also use, was to work backward from the goal through a range of possible solutions, but without actually working each solution through.

Newell and his colleagues, then, have developed a hypothesis about problem solving that favors insight as a primary component of human thinking.

If researchers can discover what operations a computer must be programmed to perform in order to prove theorems successfully, this may give them leads into the specific ways in which the human mind thinks, provided the analogy between computers and thought processes is a sound one. The uses the computer makes of the information it receives appear similar to processes of the human mind, and these uses can be specifically isolated and analyzed in the computer. For example, it "remembers" not only the theorems it has proved but also the various attempts at solution that proved unsuccessful. Both of these types of information can be used in approaching later problems.

The analogy between the computer's operations and human thought is not perfect, however. Though a mechanical product of the human mind, the computer differs from it in several important respects. For example, a computer cannot generate entirely new methods of dealing with problems, as the human mind can. The main advantage of computer simulation is that, in order to write a problem-solving program for the computer, one must specify very precisely the operations that characterize thinking behavior. Psychologists have quite properly been skeptical about the vague references to unspecified mental processes that have been used in most descriptions of thought.

QUESTION	2. HOW DOES CREATIVE THINKING DIFFER FROM PROBLEM SOLVING?	
HYPOTHESES	CREATIVE ABILITIES	CREATIVE PERSONALITIES
DESCRIPTIVE EVIDENCE	ASSESS: the relationship between IQ and divergent-thinking abilities	ASSESS: personality differences between creative and uncreative people
EXPERIMENTAL EVIDENCE		

2. HOW DOES CREATIVE THINKING DIFFER FROM PROBLEM SOLVING?

A major obstacle in the study of human thinking and reasoning processes has been the difficulty of analyzing operations that are, to a great extent, unobservable. Only the results or effects of thinking can be examined directly.

This problem is even more difficult when the thought to be examined is "creative." Here the thinker is usually not working toward one objectively correct solution. For example, think of how many solutions there are to the "problems" of designing parks for the year 2000 or writing a poem in memory of Martin Luther King. In such cases undirected thought can be at least as important as logical analysis.

Few topics in the literature of psychology have been studied more and understood less than creativity. Even those in the forefront of research on the subject cannot agree on a definition of creativity, and there is division over whether creative ability is possessed by all people to some degree or only by a few rare individuals. This confusion is mirrored in the two dominant traditions of research during the past twenty years. One series of studies has attempted to find a set of abilities, independent of intelligence, that can be legitimately described as creative abilities. The other line has concentrated on identifying the personality characteristics of people who are recognizably creative. Much of the investigation of creative thinking abilities has used children as subjects, whereas most of the personality studies have been concerned with adults. Both approaches have produced interesting new knowledge, but to date no real synthesis of the two points of view has taken place.

Identification and investigation of creative abilities distinct from intelligence have been guided by traditional psychological testing and measurement. The rationale goes like this: both intelligence and creativity are abilities, so perhaps they can be studied by similar methods.

The *creative-abilities hypothesis* states that creative thought is radically different from other kinds of problem solving and calls for separate talents and skills. Almost all the procedures used to measure such abilities stem from the research of J. P. Guilford of the University of Southern California. Guilford coined the term "divergent thinking" to describe the development of novel resolutions of a task or the generation of totally new ideas, two activities that characterize creativity. Convergent thinking, in contrast, is the kind that is used to solve problems that have only one correct answer. Tests used to measure divergent, or creative, thinking vary somewhat, but many of them rely on a similar set of activities. Usually, an index of "creative ability" is scored according to the number and uniqueness of the ideas a subject generates in various categories.

DESCRIPTIVE EVIDENCE

Investigators: M. A. Wallach and N. Kogan
Source, Date: "A New Look at the Creativity-Intelligence Distinction," 1965
Location: Duke University
Subjects: 151 fifth-grade children
Materials: Five procedures based on J. P. Guilford's divergent thinking tests

Five creativity measures, all administered in a game-like, informal atmosphere, were correlated with ten traditional general intelligence and achievement measures, including the Wechsler Intelligence Scale for Children and the Sequential Tests of Educational Progress. The creativity tasks were chosen because they were likely to stimulate quite different responses from the kind that IQ tests require. One type of test, for example, asked the child to name as many "round things" as he could think of. On that test, "Life Savers" was scored as a more creative response than "buttons," because it is a less common one.

Wallach and Kogan's creativity measures were highly correlated with each other but relatively uncorrelated with the intelligence scales. The average correlation (or association) among the creativity measures was about plus .40, the average correlation of the intelligence measures was about plus .50, but the average correlation between the intelligence and the creativity measures was only about plus .10.

Once they had established that divergent thinking and the thinking required by IQ tests do not call for identical abilities, Wallach and Kogan went on to investigate some psychological differences among the following groups: (1) children who scored high on both the creativity and the intelligence measures; (2) children who scored high on creativity but low on intelligence; (3) children who scored low on creativity but high on intelligence; and (4) children who scored low on both tests. To do this, they used ratings of the children's behavior at school over a two-week period and several measures of anxiety, conceptualizing styles, and other characteristics.

They found that the first group was high in self-confidence and self-esteem and low in defensiveness. These high-creativity, high-IQ children sought companionship with others and were also sought out by their classmates. They had a long attention span, but they also exhibited somewhat more disruptive behavior in the classroom than average. In contrast, the highly creative children who were low in IQ were the least confident, least self-assured, and least sought-out children. They exhibited more disruptive behavior in the classroom than any other group and seemed to be in angry conflict with themselves and with the school environment. Wallach and Kogan say these children appeared to be at a greater disadvantage in school than even the low-creativity, low-IQ group. Children of low creativity and high intelligence seemed to have a large investment in academic success. They were described by Wallach and Kogan as "addicted to school achievement." Socially, they tended to be reserved, though receptive to approaches from others. Finally, the subjects ranked low in both creativity and intelligence were described as friendly but anxious and "basically bewildered" at school. These children were observed engaging in behavior ranging from such useful adaptations as intensive social activity to defensive behavior including regression and passivity in stressful situations.

How does the creative-abilities hypothesis stand? Descriptive evidence from an investigation like Wallach and Kogan's does not strongly support a specific definition of the properties of creativity nor bear on its precise distinction from intelligence. It would be premature to conclude that the findings of Wallach and Kogan have established the differences between creative and uncreative individuals, but the results do suggest that various combinations of abilities present in children lead to different styles in dealing with academic and nonacademic situations.

However, this investigation and other studies like it give little indication of the extent to which high performance on any of the measures of divergent thinking predicts later creativity. Yet it would be very

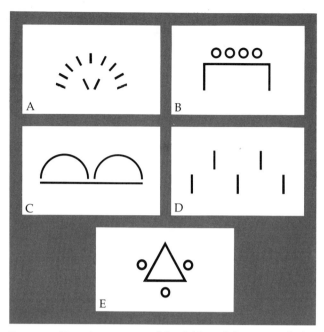

Figure 6. Test of creativity used for children. Subjects are asked to imagine what each pattern will be like when it is completed.

valuable to be able to predict creativity from tests given early in life. Before such predictions could be made reliably, much more work would have to be done.

The second line of research concentrates not on children but on adults who have already been recognized as highly creative. Studies in this area are based on the creative-personalities hypothesis, which states that creative people differ from noncreative people not merely in certain abilities but in the basic structure of their character. This hypothesis does not reject the creative-abilities hypothesis but goes beyond it to find the source or nucleus of such creative abilities in human character.

DESCRIPTIVE EVIDENCE

Investigator: D. W. MacKinnon
Source, Date: "The Nature and Nurture of Creative Talents," 1962
Location: University of California, Berkeley
Subjects: About 120 architects
Materials: Psychological tests measuring personality and IQ

Five university professors of architecture were asked to nominate the forty most creative architects in the United States. Invitations to a weekend of observation and interviews by psychologists were sent out to the eighty-six top architects named. Forty accepted. Two other groups of architects were also assembled: a group who had two years or more work experience with one of the forty "creative" architects and a group who had no work experience with any of the forty.

As measured by psychological tests, the three groups of architects did differ in personality. The forty creative architects were more flexible and open minded than the other groups. They also had a wider range of interests, had a greater preference for complexity, and were less interested in small details and in practical and concrete problems. They were described as more ambitious, dominant, and achievement-oriented, markedly more mature, emotionally and aesthetically sensitive, independent, individualistic, and enthusiastic. They seemed to accept themselves, to be more introspective, and to exhibit traits typically referred to as feminine. In social relations, they tended to be unconventional, rebellious, self-centered, and exhibitionistic. In fact, the creative architects seemed to be relatively free from conventional restraints and inhibitions, unconcerned with the impression they made on others. And above a certain minimum (about 120) IQ did not bear any relationship to creativity. In evaluating these descriptive data, it should be borne in mind that this sample of creative architects includes only volunteers among a larger sample of architects who had achieved recognition and success.

On a scale that measures values, the second and third groups of architects scored higher on economic gain than did the creative architects. The personality profile of the third group conveys the impression of the good citizen, responsible, productive, sensitive, and effective.

These descriptions convey the impression that creative individuals look for situations in which problems are not well defined and cannot be solved with single correct answers. Like Wallach and Kogan's fifth-graders who scored well on both creativity and IQ measures, the creative architects demonstrated greater flexibility, independence, and openness to experience. Their unconventional social relationships, though they contrast with the gregariousness of the high-creativity–high-IQ children, are somewhat reminiscent of those children's disruptive classroom behavior. One of the greatest difficulties encountered in studies of creative thinking has been the absence of a clearly defined vocabulary for talking about the subject. A needed first step toward the development of such a vocabulary is the recent conceptual analysis by Philip Jackson of the University of Chicago and Samuel Messick of Educational Testing Service. Their analysis begins by pointing out that intelligence is judged by criteria of correctness, whereas creativity is judged by criteria of "goodness." The four "goodness" criteria that they suggest for the judgment of creative products are unusualness, appropriateness, transformation, and condensation.

Unusualness refers to the infrequency of a given creative event or product as judged against ordinary behavior. Appropriateness relates both to the thinker's intentions (the internal context) and to the demands of the situation (the external context). For example, a new solution to a problem might be judged "about right," "just right," or "a perfect fit." The third criterion, transformation power, is described by Jackson and Messick as the ability to overcome the constraints on reality set by existing forms and to create new forms. It is judged in terms of the constraints that have been overcome. Finally, condensation is a measure of the "summary power" of the new solution compared with that which it has replaced. Einstein's theory of relativity is a good example: on the surface it appears very simple, but it encompasses the whole universe. Similarly, the childlike forms in the paintings of Paul Klee, the Swiss artist, convey much more meaning than the children's drawings they resemble. It is this interplay between simplicity and complexity that is the hallmark of creative condensation.

The typical "creativity" test, Jackson and Messick say, encompasses, at most, the first two criteria: unusualness and appropriateness. Transformation power and summary power have yet to be incorporated into creativity research, they find, although they assert that highly creative products must meet these criteria. Therefore, those people who score high on typical current creativity tests are not necessarily those likely to produce the most creative products.

Conceptual analyses and critical reviews of areas of research in psychology, like this report of Jackson and Messick, often produce creative results themselves in terms of both the summary and transformation power they exert on further research.

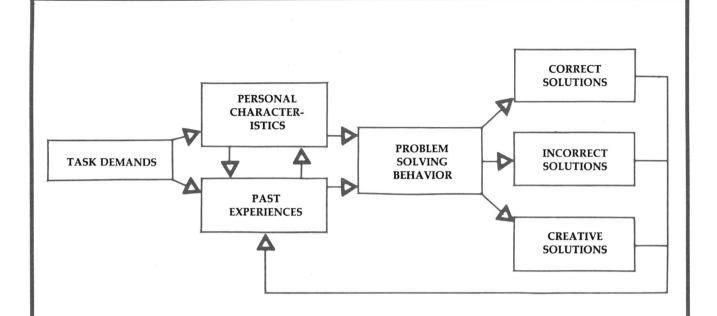

PUTTING IT TOGETHER: Problem Solving and Creativity

The type of problem-solving behavior a person engages in at any particular time is initially dependent upon the *demands of the task.*

In finding solutions there is continuous interaction between an individual's *personal characteristics* and *past experience.* Some people seem to have a predisposition toward seeking creative solutions to most problems. This predisposition is relatively independent of intelligence as currently defined by IQ tests. In drawing upon past experience for solutions to present problems, an individual may have developed a learning set for problem solving in general or for specific categories of problem solving.

Coping with ordinary life problems usually develops strategies for coping with new kinds of problems. Research with the problem-solving manipulations used by computers with known programs has been useful in providing insights into human problem-solving strategies. Our use of language helps us devise strategies out of the information stored in our memories. This problem-solving use of language apparently develops with age and experience. Past experience may occasionally produce functional fixedness, disrupting the kind of problem solving a specific task may demand.

These interactions between each individual's existing characteristics and past experiences produce a variety of *problem-solving behaviors.* When the problem demands only one possible correct answer, all answers can be divided into *correct solutions* and *incorrect solutions.* During the problem-solving process, the solver must compare the solutions he produces with "correctness" criteria from past experience so that he knows when the problem is solved. In carrying out this comparison process, the solver commonly assimilates the incorrect answers he produces in his experience and memory, so that he avoids repeating the same incorrect answers.

On the other hand, in creative problem solving, there is no one correct answer. To obtain *creative solutions,* the individual must compare possible answers to "goodness" criteria. Again, the solver usually remembers and records what he is doing, so that he can produce new solutions he hasn't tried to use before.

WHAT'S ACCEPTED AND WHAT'S DEBATED

1. WHAT'S ACCEPTED . . .

1. Learning sets and insights are reorganizations of past experience in reaction to the demands of a task.

2. Language serves as a powerful mediator of experience and helps organize problems so that they are more easily solved.

3. There are problems for which "correctness" is an inappropriate criterion for solution, and these problems probably require either different skills or different uses of skills, or both.

4. There is a set of creative abilities, usually called divergent thinking, independent of IQ.

5. Individuals identified as "creative" differ in certain personal characteristics from others not so identified.

2. WHAT'S DEBATED . . .

1. The interdependent relationships of associations, language, strategies, and reorganizations in different situations.

2. The order or sequence in which the above processes are used in solving different kinds of problems.

3. The extent to which the same or different skills are needed to solve problems for which correctness is the criterion of successful solution, versus those problems for which goodness is the criterion.

4. How well the divergent-thinking abilities actually predict adult creative behavior of a high order.

5. How much personal characteristics have to do with the people's selection and solution of different kinds of problems.

ISSUE: THE SPLIT BRAIN

The belief that problem solving and creative thinking are separate faculties of the mind is an ancient one. It has appeared in many forms as the contrast between reason and imagination, between logic and intuition. Today, we have new evidence that this old belief may be well-founded. These two forms of conscious thought appear to have two distinct physiological bases.

The human brain is divided into two hemispheres, connected by nerve tissues (see Unit 33). We have known for some time that each hemisphere controls one half of the body. The right hemisphere controls the left side, and the left hemisphere the right side. Recently, however, new evidence seems to indicate that these two hemispheres also specialize in particular modes of consciousness. The left hemisphere is primarily concerned with language, logical thought, and analytic ability. The right hemisphere is primarily concerned with spatial orientation, artistic ability, and intuitive thought. In short, the left hemisphere specializes in problem solving. The right specializes in creativity.

The two hemispheres do not operate independently. Their activities are coordinated by the connecting tissues of the corpus callosum. Nor are their functions rigidly predetermined from birth. In the infant, each hemisphere has the potential to develop either mode of thought. If the left hemisphere of a child is damaged, the child does not lose the capacity for language. Instead, the right hemisphere takes over. Adults, however, do not have the same flexibility. Damage to the "language center" in the left hemisphere may result in permanent speech defects or even total loss of speech. Similarly, damage to the right hemisphere of an adult may result in loss of spatial awareness, artistic creativity, or even the capacity to recognize others. The speech and thought processes remain unaffected, yet the person may be unable to recognize common objects, such as teacups or personal clothing.

The different functions of the two hemispheres can be studied by monitoring the brainwaves of people engaged in different mental tasks. Each hemisphere continuously gives off tiny electrical waves, but the frequency and intensity of the waves vary with the mental activity taking place at the time. When a person is engaged in a verbal task involving logical analysis, the electrical rhythms in the right hemisphere increase, but when the person is working on a spatial problem or creating some art form, the left hemisphere becomes more active.

Some of the most fascinating information concerning the functions of the two hemispheres has come from studies of people whose hemispheres have been surgically disconnected. This rather radical operation is sometimes performed on severe epileptics in order to reduce the frequency and intensity of epileptic seizures. Although it might be thought that the severing of the tissue between the hemispheres would have profound effects on the people concerned, in fact their behavior is fairly normal. Only in the controlled environment of the laboratory is it possible to discover the behavioral differences caused by the operation.

If, for example, a sexually arousing photograph is displayed only to the disconnected right hemisphere of the subject, an emotional response, such as increased heart rate or blushing is obtained. Yet the subject is unable to explain this physiological response, because the logical, verbal left hemisphere is unaware of what has happened. The subject can only guess what the cause of the emotional arousal might have been. In the same way, if the subject is asked to hold an object out of sight in his right hand, he can readily describe it. But if he holds it out of sight in his left hand, he can give no verbal description of it. The two hemispheres cannot communicate, and so the patient simply does not know what is in his left hand unless the information is made available to the right hemisphere through some external means, such as sight of the object. (See Unit 33, Brain Storage.)

People who have had split-brain operations also experience difficulty in some writing and drawing tasks. A right-handed person may still be able to produce handwriting as before, for this is a verbal, linguistic task. But the same person may be quite incapable of drawing objects and diagrams, for this is a spatial, relational task. If asked to copy a square, the subject might simply draw the corners, neatly stacked together. He is incapable of organizing the elements of the square in the proper relation. But if the subject uses his left hand, his abilities are reversed. He may be able to draw the square without difficulty, but finds it almost impossible to write a simple word.

Interestingly, split-brain individuals seem to be able to process more information than normal people. Their two hemispheres operate independently, so that neither depends on the other. In effect, they have two separate minds, each operating in its own sphere of consciousness, and each absorbing information in its own way. Normal people experience this phenomenon, but to a much lesser extent. One often faces problems for which the rational intellect suggests one answer but one's intuition and "heart" another. But because one of our hemispheres is usually dominant, it "subordinates" the other and assumes most of the load of gathering and sorting information.

One of the more challenging tasks of psychology in the years ahead will be to determine whether we function more efficiently if we have a dominant hemisphere, or whether, if we could develop both hemispheres equally, we would come closer to achieving our full human potential. It may be that the ancient division of intuition and reason, creativity and problem-solving, is an unnecessary one, and that ways can be found to develop both faculties of the mind to an equal degree.

Unit 19

Hypnosis

OVERVIEW

One of the real puzzles of human behavior is the hypnotic state. Two topics of primary interest are presented: what we know about how people vary in their susceptibility to hypnosis, and the ongoing controversy about the nature of the hypnotic state—whether it is an altered state of consciousness or simply an exaggeration of other kinds of normal human waking states.

UNIT OUTLINE

DEFINITION AND BACKGROUND
1. *Definition:* hypnosis is a trancelike state characterized by heightened suggestibility and a narrowing of attention.
2. *Background:* Friedrich Anton Mesmer (1734–1815).

QUESTIONS AND EVIDENCE
1. Are some people more susceptible to hypnosis than others?
Hypotheses:
- a. *Variability:* some people are consistently more susceptible to hypnotic induction than others. **316**
- b. *Personality:* people who are highly susceptible to hypnotic induction will have identifiable personality characteristics related to their susceptibility. **317**
2. Is hypnosis an "altered state of consciousness"?
Hypotheses:
- a. *Suggestibility:* the effects observed in a subject ostensibly "under hypnosis" are merely the product of the subject's high suggestibility combined with highly motivating instructions. **318**
- b. *Role-playing:* the effects observed in a hypnotized subject are produced by his deep personal involvement in playing the role of one who is hypnotized. **319**
- c. *Altered-state:* the hypnotic state is an identifiable psychological condition, as different from ordinary waking consciousness as meditation or dreaming. **319**

IMPORTANT CONCEPTS

	page
hypnosis	314
placebo	320
role playing	319
suggestibility	316

Among the characteristics related to variations in individual susceptibility to hypnosis is the extent to which an individual becomes involved in fantasy.

A variety of situations may induce a state resembling a hypnotic state.

Susceptibility to behavior control through hypnosis varies among individuals but is relatively stable in any specific adult.

DEFINITION AND BACKGROUND

Hypnosis is one of those "strange" phenomena that seems doomed to a never-ending struggle for full, unequivocal scientific respectability. Its status is less ambiguous than that of, say, extrasensory perception, but people still sometimes ask, as they do about ESP, whether one "believes in" hypnosis. Although some of its effects have been thoroughly documented, it retains an air of mystery. Some libraries persist in grouping even recent experimental studies on hypnosis with esoteric volumes on magic and other occult subjects.

Today, virtually all psychologists accept hypnosis as a valid field of scientific inquiry. Most—though not all—of them would classify it as an altered state of awareness, thus placing it in the same category as dreams (Unit 32), and some drug states (Unit 36).

One acceptable DEFINITION of hypnosis is *a trancelike state characterized by heightened suggestibility and a narrowing of attention.* It is as if one part of the hypnotized person's consciousness has become dissociated from the rest of his mind, in such a way that its content is partly controlled by the suggestions of the hypnotist. The Greek word *hypnos* means "sleep," but EEG recordings taken during hypnosis show brain waves characteristic of waking, not those of any of the four recognized stages of sleep (see Unit 32).

This unit will FOCUS on the factors that seem to differentiate people in terms of their susceptibility to hypnotic suggestion and on possible distinctions between the hypnotic state and normal waking consciousness.

BACKGROUND: FRIEDRICH ANTON MESMER (1734–1815)

According to the doctrine of animal magnetism, formulated by an astronomer during the sixteenth century, the "magnetism" originating in heavenly bodies could be directed by one man to another and used to promote human health. Mesmer, an Austrian physician, did considerable reading on animal magnetism as a young man and later witnessed several demonstrations of its power, one of them by a priest who convinced him that the human hand could be as strongly magnetic as metal plates.

Mesmer moved to Paris and began to use "mesmerism" to cure people of disease. His main technique was to have his patients sit around a tub filled with magnetized iron filings. Iron rods extended outward from the tub, and the magnetic influence was supposed to pass from the filings through the rods to the patients. Some of them experienced convulsive, orgasmic "fits" that were followed by a peaceful, trancelike state of passivity. Enough of them got well enough for mesmerism to become a fad.

The medical profession did not accept Mesmer's cures and branded him a quack. The King of France appointed a commission of French physicians to investigate his work—a commission chaired by Benjamin Franklin, gifted scientist and ambassador to France from the fledgling United States. The commission turned in a very negative report. It said that most of Mesmer's patients were not really ill—that many of them were wealthy Parisian women who came to Mesmer out of idleness or for amusement. Whatever cures did occur came about not because of the effectiveness of animal magnetism as a therapy but because of the power of Mesmer's patients' own imaginations. Franklin himself tested the imagination hypothesis by telling peasants that certain trees had been magnetized; when some of them stood under the trees and were cured, he considered the hypothesis confirmed.

Mesmer was forced to leave Paris, but his followers went on with their work. About 1820, shortly after his death, mesmerism again became a fad, this time not

Figure 1. Dr. Mesmer's patients sat around a tub filled with magnetized iron filings. The magnetic influence was supposed to pass to the patients, some of whom experienced convulsive fits followed by peaceful passivity.

just in Paris but also in Germany, England, and the United States. Another investigation was held, and another negative report turned in by medical men. There was a brief flurry of renewed interest in the 1840s, when reports reached England that a surgeon in Ceylon had performed some 3,000 operations, a number of them amputations, through the induction of a mesmeric trance. But these reports were quickly overshadowed by others arriving at the same time from the United States that told of the first successful operations using general anesthesia.

Meanwhile, a respected English surgeon named James Braid had coined the word "hypnotism." Braid became convinced, through his own experiments, that the phenomena induced by mesmerists were genuine but that they should be explained in physiological rather than in magnetic terms. Shortly after the middle of the nineteenth century, chiefly as the result of Braid's work, hypnosis began to attract the interest of the medical profession. Braid's own interest, however, began to shift away from the physiology of hypnotism and toward the role of psychological factors such as suggestion. Freud at first used hypnosis in psychotherapy, but he discarded the method when he found that not all patients could be hypnotized and that cures induced under hypnosis did not last very long.

In the years following World War I, dissatisfaction with the psychoanalytic definition of hypnosis stimulated a new, experimental approach to the subject. This approach stresses objective definitions of hypnotic phenomena. It has led to the development of objective scales to measure hypnotic susceptibility, the depth of hypnotic trance, and other hypnotic phenomena. Some of the findings from the use of the experimental approach are described in the balance of this unit.

QUESTIONS AND EVIDENCE

1. Are some people more susceptible to hypnosis than others?

2. Is hypnosis an "altered state of consciousness"?

There is little doubt about the effects of hypnosis. It is possible to make persons engage in and experience a variety of unusual behaviors when they are given suggestions under hypnosis. These include apparent hallucinations (seeing something that's not really there), negative hallucinations (not seeing something that is really there), hypnotic analgesia (feeling no

Items of the Stanford Hypnotic Susceptibility Scale, Form A (SHSS)	
Suggested Behavior	Criterion of passing (yielding score of +)
1. Postural sway	Falls without forcing
2. Eye closure	Closes eyes without forcing.
3. Hand lowering (left)	Lowers at least 6 in. by end of 10 secs.
4. Immobilization (right arm)	Arm rises less than 1 in. in 10 secs.
5. Finger lock	Incomplete separation of fingers at end of 10 secs.
6. Arm rigidity (left arm)	Less than 2 in. of arm bending in 10 secs.
7. Hands moving together	Hands at least as close as 6 in. after 10 secs.
8. Verbal inhibition (name)	Name unspoken in 10 secs.
9. Hallucination (fly)	Any movement, grimacing, acknowledgement of effect.
10. Eye catalepsy	Eyes remain closed at end of 10 secs.
11. Posthypnotic (changes chairs)	Any partial movement response.
12. Amnesia test	Three or fewer items recalled.

Figure 2. Stanford Hypnotic Susceptibility Scale. Adapted from Weitzenhoffer and Hilgard (1959).

pain), hypnotic amnesia (forgetting things), and hypnotic age regression (acting as when one was a child). The hypnotist always seems to be in control of the unusual responses.

Hypnotic susceptibility is not the same as a person's general suggestibility. *Suggestibility,* the broader term, refers to the extent to which a person responds to suggestions at any time, under any circumstances. *Hypnotic susceptibility,* on the other hand, refers specifically to the degree of suggestibility observed after an attempt to induce hypnosis has been made. Researchers have devised methods to measure both of these characteristics. One of the tests measuring suggestibility is the Barber Suggestibility Scale (BSS), shown in Figure 4. Each of the eight tasks is suggested to a subject, and the number of these suggestions he carries out determines his score.

One of the tests measuring hypnotic susceptibility is the Stanford Hypnotic Susceptibility Scale (SHSS), shown in Figure 2. After an attempt to induce hypnosis has been made, each of the twelve behaviors is suggested to the subject in turn; the number of these suggestions he follows determines his score.

DESCRIPTIVE EVIDENCE

Investigator: E. Hilgard
Source, Date: "Hypnotic Susceptibility," 1965
Location: Stanford University
Subjects: 533 college students
Materials: Stanford Hypnotic Susceptibility Scale

The distribution of scores in Figure 3 demonstrates that the subjects did vary considerably in measured susceptibility. Most of them were only moderately susceptible to hypnosis, but about one-quarter achieved a fairly deep hypnotic state, as demonstrated by such behavior as hallucinations and posthypnotic amnesia.

Many studies have also shown that hypnotic susceptibility is very stable in individuals over short periods of time. For groups of adults tested on two different occasions, test-retest correlations have been as high as .80 or above, even under different experimental conditions.

However, there are changes in long-term susceptibility. In another study at Stanford, Hilgard and

---

QUESTION	1. ARE SOME PEOPLE MORE SUSCEPTIBLE TO HYPNOSIS THAN OTHERS?	
HYPOTHESES	**VARIABILITY**	**PERSONALITY**
DESCRIPTIVE EVIDENCE	ASSESS: changes in individual susceptibility over time	ASSESS: relation of susceptibility to personality traits and past experiences
EXPERIMENTAL EVIDENCE		

---

1. ARE SOME PEOPLE MORE SUSCEPTIBLE TO HYPNOSIS THAN OTHERS?

The *variability hypothesis* states that some people are consistently more susceptible to hypnotic induction than others. Mesmerists in show business have always relied on these differences to explain defects in their "acts."

Morgan studied the relationships between age and hypnotic susceptibility. After testing 847 subjects of all ages, they found a steady, gradual increase in susceptibility to hypnosis to age ten and a decline thereafter. Reasons for these changes are not known, though one might guess that the increase to age ten is related to the greater distractibility of younger children.

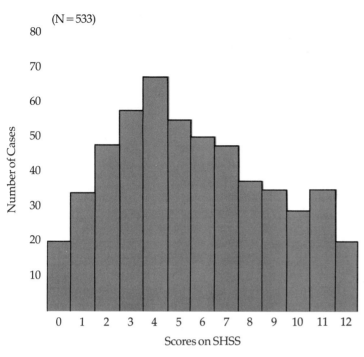

(N = 533)

Number of Cases

Scores on SHSS

Figure 3. Distribution of first-session scores among 533 Stanford University students on Stanford Hypnotic Susceptibility Scale. Adapted from Hilgard (1965).

The *personality hypothesis* predicts that people who are highly susceptible to hypnotic induction will have identifiable personality characteristics related to their susceptibility. This hypothesis has been surprisingly difficult to confirm, considering the consistency with which some people score high and others score low on hypnotic susceptibility tests. Some relationships between certain personality characteristics and hyp-notic susceptibility have been found, however; there are also data indicating that people who are susceptible to hypnosis tend to have in common certain past experiences, especially during childhood.

DESCRIPTIVE EVIDENCE

Investigator: J. Hilgard
Source, Date: "Personality and Hypnosis: A Study of Imaginative Involvement," 1970
Location: Stanford University
Subjects: 822 college students
Materials: SHSS and other measures; interviews

Data were collected both from interviews and from a variety of psychological tests. Then correlations were calculated between all possible pairings of the measures used. The highest correlation was for a factor referring to the degree to which a person can engross himself in an experience, shutting out both unrelated thoughts and the consciousness of unrelated, distracting external events.

Surprisingly, the next highest correlation was for severity of punishment during childhood. The greater the degree of childhood punishment reported by a subject, the greater his susceptibility to hypnosis. Some observers have explained this by pointing out that severe punishment may teach an immediate and unquestioning obedience to orders.

A third factor showing some positive relationship to susceptibility was fantasy involvement, the degree to which subjects were capable of involving themselves in imaginary events. This was measured by investi-

QUESTION	2. IS HYPNOSIS AN "ALTERED STATE OF CONSCIOUSNESS"?		
HYPOTHESES	**SUGGESTIBILITY**	**ROLE PLAYING**	**ALTERED STATE**
DESCRIPTIVE EVIDENCE		ASSESS: relation of susceptibility to acting ability	
EXPERIMENTAL EVIDENCE	VARY: suggestibility of instructions vs. hypnotic induction MEASURE: suggestibility scores		VARY: 1. hypnosis or placebo or nothing 2. kind of induction instructions MEASURE: 1. time working under pain 2. Galvanic Skin Response under pain

gating reading habits, religious experiences, creativity, imaginary playmates as a child, and the like.

Such correlational evidence can be used to predict with varying degrees of accuracy how a person will react to hypnosis. However, the wide range of individual differences in susceptibility must be kept in mind. Furthermore, a gradual decline in susceptibility does occur with age, on the average.

2. IS HYPNOSIS AN "ALTERED STATE OF CONSCIOUSNESS"?

When William James discussed hypnosis in his classic general psychology textbook of 1890, he wrote:

> The . . . trance can be induced in various ways, each operator having his pet method. The simplest one is to leave the subject seated by himself, telling him that if he will close his eyes and relax his muscles and, as far as possible, think of vacancy, in a few minutes he will "go off." . . . Braid used to make his subjects look at a bright button held near their forehead until their eyes spontaneously closed. The older mesmerists made "passes" in a downward direction over the face and body, but without contact. Stroking the skin of the head, face, arms and hands, especially that of the region round the brows and eyes, will have the same effect. Staring into the eyes of the subject until the latter droop; making him listen to watch's ticking; or simply making him close his eyes for a minute whilst you describe to him the feeling of falling into sleep, "talk sleep" to him, are equally efficacious methods in the hands of some operators; *whilst with trained subjects any method whatever from which they have been led by previous suggestion to expect results will be successful.* [Italics added.]

In this passage James implies, by talking about the many "pet methods" of different hypnotists and the susceptibility of trained subjects to "any method whatever" that "previous suggestion leads them to trust," that hypnotic states should be viewed with a certain skepticism.

The *suggestibility hypothesis* proposes that the effects observed in a subject ostensibly "under hypnosis" are merely the product of the subject's high suggestibility combined with highly motivating instructions. This hypothesis has been tested in an experiment run by T.X. Barber, a psychologist who is so skeptical about the existence of "hypnosis" as a special state, that he always puts the word between quotation marks.

EXPERIMENTAL EVIDENCE

Investigator: T. X. Barber
Source, Date: "Hypnosis: A Scientific Approach," 1969
Location: Medfield State Hospital, Medfield, Mass.
Subjects: 186 college students
Materials: Barber Suggestibility Scale (BSS)

The 186 subjects in this experiment were randomly assigned to three groups. Those in the first group received hypnotic induction. Those in the second group were given strongly worded "task-motivating" instructions. They were told that their imaginations were going to be tested, that the suggestions involved were easy ones that most people have no difficulty following, and that, if they really tried, they would experience the suggested feelings. The third group served as a control group; the subjects were told only that their imaginations were going to be tested. Then the subjects in all three groups took the Barber Suggestibility Scale (sample items are shown in Figure 4). The more BSS tasks they completed successfully, the higher their scores.

Out of a possible score of eight, the "hypnosis" group averaged 5.8 and the "motivated" group averaged 5.3. The average score in the control group was 3.0. The .5 difference between the scores of the first two groups is negligible—statistical tests show that it could easily have occurred by chance. Barber concluded that there was no meaningful difference between the "hypnotic" state and the state induced by strongly worded instructions.

Other conclusions can be drawn from the results, however. Perhaps the motivating instructions served to induce a hypnotic state in some subjects. Or perhaps hypnosis and highly motivating instructions can produce almost identical behavior. The fact that one can reach a destination by two routes does not negate the reality of either route.

Another skeptical position on hypnotic states, the

```
┌─────────────────────────────────────────────────────────────┐
│          Items of the Barber Susceptibility Scale (BSS)       │
├─────────────────────────────────────────────────────────────┤
│                                                               │
│  1. Arm lowering.              5. Verbal Inhibition.          │
│     Arm down: inches. _____       Said name before 5 secs. _____│
│                                   Said name after 5 secs.  _____│
│  2. Arm levitation.               Did not say name after      │
│     Arm up: inches.   _____       15 secs.                 _____│
│                                6. Body immobility.            │
│  3. Hand lock.                    Got up before 5 secs.    _____│
│     Hands opened before           Got up after 5 secs.    _____│
│     5 secs.           _____       Did not stand up after      │
│     Hands opened after            15 secs.                 _____│
│     5 secs.           _____    7. "Posthypnotic-like" response.│
│     Hands not opened              Did cough.               _____│
│     after 15 secs.    _____       Didn't cough.            _____│
│  4. Thirst "hallucination."    8. Selective amnesia.         │
│     Swallowed.        _____       Remembered amnesia task. _____│
│     Moved mouth.      _____       Didn't remember until       │
│     Licked lips.      _____       given permission.       _____│
│     Felt thirsty.     _____               Total Score.    _____│
│                                                               │
└─────────────────────────────────────────────────────────────┘
```

Figure 4. Barber Suggestibility Scale. Adapted from Barber (1969).

role-playing hypothesis, says that the effects observed in a hypnotized subject are produced by his deep personal involvement in playing the role of one who is hypnotized. Although this hypothesis should not be interpreted as meaning that the subject is "faking," it does cast doubt on the idea that a hypnotic state is qualitatively different from the ordinary waking one.

DESCRIPTIVE EVIDENCE

Investigators: T. R. Sarbin and D. T. Lim
Source, Date: "Some Evidence in Support of the Role-Taking Hypothesis in Hypnosis," 1963
Location: University of California at Berkeley
Subjects: 33 undergraduates
Materials: A hypnotic susceptibility scale (Friedlander-Sarbin scale)

Each subject was first tested on a hypnotic susceptibility scale. A week later he was asked to perform an improvisation of a given situation, in pantomime, before a panel of judges trained in the dramatic arts. A pantomime was used because it seemed to parallel more closely the items on the hypnotic susceptibility scale, which involve no verbal responses. A positive correlation was found between hypnotic susceptibility and role-playing ability. In fact, all the subjects whom the judges rated superior at role playing had scored above the mean on the hypnotic susceptibility scale. Sarbin has expressed the belief that all hypnosis may be just a form of role playing, in which the subject is so caught up in imagined reality that he loses awareness of himself and, without knowing it, acts out his expectations of hypnosis.

No causal relationship between role playing and hypnosis can be specified from this study, however, and other interpretations of Sarbin and Lim's data are certainly possible. For example, perhaps people who make good actors have personality characteristics that also allow them to fall more easily into a hypnotic state, possibly self-induced. It may even be that an actor who is fully involved in his role is, in fact, hypnotized.

The altered-state hypothesis asserts that the hypnotic state is an identifiable psychological condition, as different from ordinary waking consciousness as meditation or dreaming.

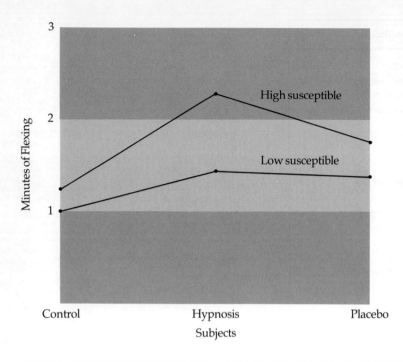

High susceptible

Low susceptible

Minutes of Flexing

3

2

1

Control   Hypnosis   Placebo

Subjects

Figure 5. Comparison of subjects with high and low susceptibility to hypnosis on a pain-tolerance task under three conditions. Adapted from McGlashlin, et al. (1969).

EXPERIMENTAL EVIDENCE

Investigators: T. H. McGlashlin, F. J. Evans, and M. T. Orne

Source, Date: "The Nature of Hypnotic Analgesic and Placebo Response to Experimental Pain," 1969

Location: Institute of the Pennsylvania Hospital and the University of Pennsylvania

Subjects: 24 male college students

Materials: Rubber bulb and flask apparatus; blood pressure cuff; metronome; two hypnotic susceptibility tests

The subjects had previously been given hypnotic susceptibility tests—they had been selected by the experimenters because their test scores indicated they were "high susceptible" or "low susceptible." To establish a base line, during the first session each subject was tested for tolerance to pain. A blood-pressure cuff was applied to his arm and he was then told to squeeze a bulb to pump water for as long as possible. The experimenters noted the number of minutes each subject was able to squeeze the bulb with his tourniqueted arm. (The pain felt when arterial blood flow is stopped in this way builds up rapidly and becomes excruciating but is not harmful in brief

doses.) In a second experimental session, the subjects were hypnotized and told they would feel no pain from the blood-pressure cuffs, which were then applied again.

At the third experimental session, all the subjects were told they were being given a drug that would reduce the pain they would feel. In fact, however, they received a harmless placebo. The cuffs were then applied to their arms and they were again instructed to squeeze the bulb for as long as possible.

The results are summarized in Figure 5, which shows how long the subjects were able to continue squeezing the bulb in the control, hypnosis, and placebo conditions. For subjects with low susceptibility to hypnosis, there was no significant difference between performances in the placebo and hypnotic conditions, though in both instances they were able to squeeze the bulb for a longer time than they had when they had received neither placebo nor hypnotic suggestion. The highly susceptible subjects, however, tolerated considerably more pain under hypnosis than they did in the control or placebo condition—and also considerably more than the low-susceptibility group. This difference suggests (though it does not prove) that the hypnotic state is different from the normal waking state. That is, the subjects who tolerated pain the longest may have reached a hypnotic condition with unique pain-killing capabilities.

Further evidence on the relation between hypnosis and pain was gathered in another experiment, in which reactions to pain were measured through physiological measurements rather than through performance.

EXPERIMENTAL EVIDENCE

Investigators: P. G. Zimbardo, C. Rapaport, and J. Baron
Source, Date: "Pain Control by Hypnotic Induction of Motivational States," 1969
Location: Stanford University
Subjects: 69 high-school seniors and college freshmen
Materials: GSR measures, shock apparatus

Prior to the establishment of the experimental conditions, the galvanic skin responses (GSRs) of each subject to a painful electric shock were recorded. Unlike pain toleration, the GSR is normally beyond people's conscious control.

One group of subjects underwent hypnotic induction and received an "anesthetic" posthypnotic suggestion: "The shock you will be given will not be painful." A second group also underwent hypnosis but received a posthypnotic suggestion unrelated to pain: while the shocks are administered, this group was told, "You should try hard to memorize this word list." A third group, the controls, did not undergo hypnotic induction and was instructed to role-play—to act "as if you don't feel any pain."

The group that received both hypnotic induction and the posthypnotic suggestion that the shock would

Figure 6. Psychologists still debate the degree to which role playing and strong motivating instructions are involved in observed behaviors following hypnotic induction.

not be painful did, in fact, show the greatest reduction in GSR. This result again suggests that something unique about the hypnotic state allows a subject more pain tolerance than he displays in the normal waking state.

Perhaps the last word on the question of whether hypnosis brings about an altered state of consciousness should be given to Ernest Hilgard, a psychologist who has done much work on hypnosis (some of it described in the first half of this unit). Hilgard is clearly a man who "believes in" hypnosis, but he also believes that the controversy over whether hypnosis is an altered state of consciousness involves such large theoretical issues that it is largely irrelevant for investigators at this point. "The state concept is a difficult one in any case," he says,

for it is hard to know even when a person is asleep (sleep is now known to be physiologically other than a single state), and it is hard to know when a person is intoxicated by alcohol, even if a blood sample is available. But I see no more reason to dismiss hypnosis as an interesting state (or set of states) than I do waking consciousness, sleep, or intoxication. I can get along without a state concept, if it proves too troublesome, still investigating the domain of hypnotic-like behaviors. [Hilgard, 1971].

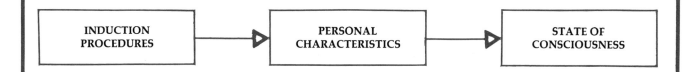

| INDUCTION PROCEDURES | → | PERSONAL CHARACTERISTICS | → | STATE OF CONSCIOUSNESS |

PUTTING IT TOGETHER: Hypnosis

In trying to understand what a hypnotic state is, it is useful to consider how a variety of induction procedures may produce in many people a state of consciousness characterized by heightened suggestibility and a narrowing of attention.

A large part of the mystery surrounding hypnosis stems from the observation that *induction procedures* may vary from staring intently into the eyes of a subject to giving the subject a highly motivating "sales pitch."

When susceptibility to hypnosis is measured in large populations of people, the evidence indicates that there are great variations in the depth to which individuals may be hypnotized but considerable stability in any specific adult. Among those *personal characteristics* specific to the most susceptible people are an ability to focus attention and shut out distractions, reports of a great deal of punishment during childhood, and a tendency to become highly involved in fantasies.

Most of the debate about hypnosis centers on the usefulness of considering the hypnotic state as a completely unique *state of consciousness* with characteristics unlike waking, dreaming or other known states of consciousness. While some theorists prefer to regard it as an altered state, others would rather consider hypnosis as the response of highly suggestible people to highly motivating instructions. Still others prefer to consider it as a special kind of role playing by people who are capable of deep personal involvement.

WHAT'S ACCEPTED AND WHAT'S DEBATED

1. WHAT'S ACCEPTED . . .

1. Individuals vary in their hypnotic susceptibility, but susceptibility tends to stay relatively the same in any adult individual.

2. Certain personality traits and past experiences are related to hypnotic susceptibility.

3. There are a number of ways to attain the so-called hypnotic state besides the formal induction procedures.

4. Hypnosis can be useful in minimizing the observable emotional and physiological responses to pain.

2. WHAT'S DEBATED . . .

1. That there is a "true" hypnotic state with unique capacities or properties that distinguish it from ordinary waking consciousness.

2. The degree to which strong motivating instructions to subjects can duplicate so-called hypnotic achievements.

3. The degree to which role playing is involved in observed behaviors following hypnotic induction.

ISSUE: HYPNOSIS, AN ALTERED STATE OF CONSCIOUSNESS?

The reputation of hypnotism has varied widely through the years in medical and psychological research. At times hypnosis has been taken quite seriously. Early in his career, Sigmund Freud believed it could be used to cure neuroses. At other times it has been dismissed as a fad or even the work of quacks. Even today, the medical and psychological respectability of hypnosis is shaky, perhaps because it is still used as staged entertainment as much as it is researched in clinical laboratories. As Ernest Hilgard laments, "Hypnosis can be both used and abused, and most often it's the abuses which occur to people first. Unfortunately, there's been a lack of professionalism among the practitioners themselves that has perpetuated the sideshow image associated with hypnosis in the popular mind. In our larger metropolitan areas there are all sorts of bizarre things in the yellow pages of the telephone directory. People ordinarily favorably disposed to hypnosis seek out some untrained, incompetent hypnotic magician listed in the directory—and leave disappointed. I don't blame them."

But a critical attitude toward hypnosis is not confined to the general public. Theodore X. Barber of the Medfield State Hospital in Massachusetts is convinced that there is no such thing as hypnosis. Barber argues forcefully that hypnosis is simply a form of suggestibility and ought not to be regarded as a separate phenomenon at all. "Thinking and imagining can have powerful effects," he claims. "It's a matter of becoming involved in thinking and imagining in such a way that we do not say to ourselves, 'I can't do it. It can't happen. I'm not going to do it. This is silly.' . . . Hypnotism has traditionally been associated with sleepwalking, trance states, special states of consciousness, and all sorts of mysterious things. However, it is actually closely related to the 'power of positive thinking,' 'mind control,' 'mind over matter,' and similar notions that popular writers like Dale Carnegie and Norman Vincent Peale have been talking about."

Barber believes that the subject's own prior conceptions about hypnosis are the source of the power of "hypnotic" suggestibility. People have stereotyped ideas about how hypnotized subjects are supposed to behave. They are expected, for example, to become glassy-eyed and immobile. When it is suggested to them that they have been hypnotized, they promptly behave as expected. Barber has shown that the results obtainable by hypnosis and ordinary suggestion are often indistinguishable. In one experiment, he subjected two groups of nurses to pain in the form of pressure on their fingers. One group was first hypnotized, then told to listen to a tape-recorded story as a means of ignoring the pain. The second group was not hypnotized, but was given the same instruction. The pain reduction was the same for both groups. Barber claims that mere suggestion could achieve similar results in any of the feats that are commonly believed to be achievable only under hypnosis. Even the well-known experiment in which a hypnotized individual can be directed to make his body so rigid that it can be placed like a plank between two chairs can be achieved by suggestibility. Barber claims: "Practically all normally awake persons can remain suspended between two chairs while supported only by the head and ankles."

Other researchers have certainly demonstrated that suggestion—stated or implied—can have the same effect as hypnosis. Hypnosis has often been hailed in the past as a miraculous cure for warts, but when New York school children had their warts painted with chemically inert dies that were identified as medication, the warts tended to disappear shortly thereafter. Mere suggestion can also be used to increase pulse rate, blood-glucose levels, and stomach-acid secretions. The use of the placebo, an inert tablet that the patient believes is a powerful drug, is widely used in medicine as an effective cure for psychosomatic disorders.

Philadelphia psychiatrist Martin Orne has conducted experiments which support Barber's contention that hypnotized subjects merely adopt the characteristics that they believe hypnotized subjects ought to have. Orne told one group of psychology students that whenever someone is hypnotized, the subject's dominant hand becomes immovable. There is no truth whatever in this statement, but when Orne later hypnotized some of his students he found that 55 percent of them were unable to move their dominant hand.

Other psychologists, however, are more skeptical of Barber's hypothesis. It may be true, they point out, that hypnosis and suggestion can yield identical results, but this does not mean that there are not two different ways of achieving those results. One could just as easily stand Barber's argument on its head—because hypnosis achieves the same results as suggestion, it could be argued that there is no such thing as suggestion.

At the moment, it looks as though the medical applications of hypnosis, whether the state really exists or not, are somewhat limited. Psychiatrists often find other methods such as word-association tests or long in-depth interviews a better means of gaining insight into their patients' anxieties than hypnosis. Medical practitioners are currently more interested in exploring the possibilities of biofeedback as a means of allowing patients to control bodily functions with their minds. Biofeedback has more commonly successful results, and also gives the patient much more sense of personal influence over his or her own body.

The main focus of interest in hypnosis in the future is more likely to be on its potential contribution to our understanding of altered states of consciousness. There are signs that college students, already interested in this field as a result of their experiments with psychedelic drugs, transcendental meditation or high-intensity encounter groups, are experimenting with hypnosis as a means of exploring the inner mysteries of the mind—a tendency that psychologists view with some alarm. The psychologists themselves recognize, however, that we are in a state of considerable ignorance about the various states that our mental awareness can take, and that experiments and research on hypnosis might contribute to a greater understanding of human consciousness.

Unit 20

Therapy for Individuals

OVERVIEW

Various forms of psychotherapy for treating mental disorders are discussed, and some of the evidence bearing on how well they work in practice is presented. The significant differences between psychoanalytic, client-centered, and behavior therapy are summarized, along with their different goals and the consequences these differences have for treatment.

UNIT OUTLINE

DEFINITION AND BACKGROUND
1. *Definition:* therapy for individuals is treatment sessions or interpersonal contacts between a trained healer and a sufferer through which the therapist, unaided by a group, attempts to produce beneficial changes in the patient's emotional state, attitudes, and behavior.
2. *Background:* Sigmund Freud (1856–1939).

QUESTIONS AND EVIDENCE
1. Do different types of therapy accomplish different results?
Hypotheses:
   a. *Client-centered-therapy:* if a therapist communicates empathic understanding of the client's point of view towards his problems, self-direction will be generated, and improvement in self-concept and adaptability will develop. **331**
   b. *Behavior-therapy:* the direct treatment of symptoms through learning principles can bring about the replacement of an individual's maladaptive habits with adaptive ones. **333**

2. Does therapy really help?
Hypotheses:
   a. *Improvement:* therapeutic techniques give relief to patients suffering from psychopathological disorders that would not otherwise come about through the patient's own improvement efforts or the mere passage of time. **335**
   b. *Status quo:* therapy is of little or no value because patients improve equally well when left to their own resources. **336**
3. Do personality factors affect the result of therapy?
Hypotheses:
   a. *Therapist-attributes:* therapists have identifiable characteristics and traits that affect the course and result of therapy. **337**
   b. *Patient-attributes:* patients with psychological disorders have identifiable characteristics and traits that affect the direction and outcome of treatment. **339**

IMPORTANT CONCEPTS

	page
action therapy	330
anxiety	333
behavior therapy	329
client-centered therapy	330
electroshock therapy	329
empathy	331
insight therapy	330
modeling	333
phobia	333
psychoanalysis	329
psychotherapy	328
self-actualization	331
systematic desensitization	333
unconscious	328

There is a large variety of therapeutic techniques for the relief of mental disorders.

The effectiveness of most therapeutic processes for individuals is dependent upon the nature of the relationship between patient and therapist.

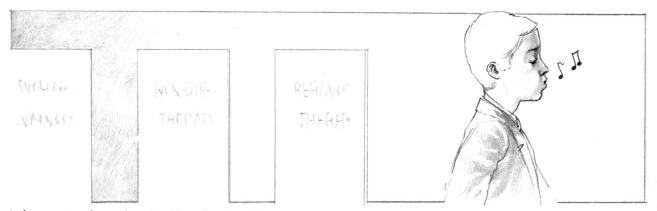

A therapeutic relationship should produce beneficial changes in the patient's emotional state, attitudes, and behavior.

DEFINITION AND BACKGROUND

Although therapy is the general term for any method used in treating an illness, there are many different types. Our concern is for therapy for the disordered mind (see Unit 13). Group therapies are discussed in Unit 11. Therapy for individuals usually involves a personal relationship between a healer (therapist) and a sufferer (patient or client) and its goal is the enhancement of the sufferer's overall feeling of well-being. Because practically all forms of personal influence may affect a person's sense of well-being, here the DEFINITION of therapy for individuals is: *treatment sessions or interpersonal contacts between a trained healer and a sufferer through which the therapist, unaided by a group, attempts to produce beneficial changes in the patient's emotional state, attitudes, and behavior.*

The variety of therapies for individuals is almost as great as the range of individuals who seek help. This unit will FOCUS on the similarities, differences, and effectiveness of a variety of therapeutic interactions.

BACKGROUND: SIGMUND FREUD (1856–1939)

The prevailing theory of insanity in medieval and well into modern times was that its victims suffered from "possession" by demons. Efforts at treatment were largely directed toward exorcising these demons through such rituals as prayer, weird brews and medicines, whipping, starvation, and torture. The emergence of modern day therapy as a distinctive

form of healing probably began with Anton Mesmer, whose work in the late eighteenth century is recognized as the precursor to hypnosis as a therapeutic technique (see Unit 19). Hypnosis originally prompted Sigmund Freud's interest in personality disorders and mental illness.

Sigmund Freud, a Viennese neurologist, became dismayed by the fact that all too frequently people of his profession could not effectively treat many types of symptoms, such as paralysis of the limbs and memory loss. In 1882 Freud joined Josef Breuer in neurological practice. Breuer had successfully treated such problems as hysteria by what he called catharsis (from the Greek word meaning "to vomit" or "to purge"). Breuer found that such hysterical symptoms as limb paralysis, disturbance in sight and speech, and inability to take food disappeared when the patient recalled in a hypnotic state the circumstances under which they had arisen. Freud, taking Breuer's lead in the use of hypnosis for producing states conducive to catharsis, felt that many symptoms of his patients seemed to be symbolic attempts to express and resolve chronic conflicts that had their roots in upsetting experiences during childhood. He also reasoned that this work with hypnosis underscored the power of the unconscious memories and suppressed emotions. This led Freud to develop a form of treatment based on detailed exploration of patients' personal histories, with emotional reliving of childhood experiences in the treatment setting. Freud soon realized that his personal relationships with his patients had far more therapeutic significance than the use of hypnosis and dropped it as a tool in his treatment sessions.

Unfortunately, Freud's theories, particularly his emphasis on childhood sexuality (see Unit 6), did not meet with approval in late Victorian and Edwardian Europe, where piano legs were draped for decency's sake and chicken breasts were first called "white meat" to avoid the anatomical allusion. He controverted traditional diagnostic theories by treating cases of male hysteria, which, as its name (from the Greek *hystera,* womb) indicates, was widely held to

Figure 1. Sigmund Freud, originator of psychoanalysis, in his study and consultation room.

be a purely female disease associated with the female organs. This general hostility may have led Freud to gather the small group of students who became the second generation of psychotherapists: Carl Jung, Alfred Adler, Ernest Jones (Freud's biographer), and others. The first public acceptance of Freud's ideas came not in Vienna or Europe but in America, when G. Stanley Hall invited Freud to speak at Clark University in 1909.

Although the dominance of psychoanalysis is now rivaled by more contemporary forms of psychotherapy such as client-centered and behavior therapy, Freud's influence as a psychological and philosophical thinker continues unabated. The notions of the mind's hidden layers and of humankind's profound sexuality originated with him, as did the belief in the importance of childhood experience to personality formation (see Unit 15). Many of the terms he and his disciples introduced—"Freudian slip," "complex," "repression"—are now part of our everyday language.

QUESTIONS AND EVIDENCE

1. Do different types of therapy accomplish different results?

2. Does therapy really help?

3. Do personality factors affect the result of therapy?

1. DO DIFFERENT TYPES OF THERAPY ACCOMPLISH DIFFERENT RESULTS?

The type of therapy used for treatment of the disordered mind depends upon the philosophy and training of the individual therapist and the diagnosis of the individual patient's disturbance (see Unit 13). Before discussing overall therapeutic effectiveness, a look into the similarities and differences, both in terms of technique and proposed accomplishments, among a few of the more contemporary and popular therapeutic strategies is an important initial step. Medical therapies, such as shock therapy and drug therapy (chemotherapy) are really in a separate category from the various forms of psychotherapy because they involve physical treatment and are used only by therapists with medical training. Thus they would not be used by the typical clinical psychologist. They are used for the treatment of mental disorders, however.

Drug therapy came onto the scene with a splash in the early 1950s with the advent of tranquilizers. The tranquilizing drugs have been shown to be particularly effective in the control of symptoms associated with schizophrenia. Drug therapies are discussed in Unit 36.

Electroshock therapy (EST) consists of about 110 to 150 volts of alternating current administered across the patient's temples for a period of eight-tenths of a second. As soon as the current is applied, the patient loses consciousness and undergoes a convulsion that

QUESTION	1. DO DIFFERENT TYPES OF THERAPY ACCOMPLISH DIFFERENT RESULTS?	
HYPOTHESES	CLIENT-CENTERED THERAPY	BEHAVIOR THERAPY
DESCRIPTIVE EVIDENCE		
EXPERIMENTAL EVIDENCE	VARY: presence or absence of client-centered therapy MEASURE: change in congruency between actual self and ideal self	VARY: 1. type of therapeutic treatment 2. type of therapeutic treatment MEASURE: 1. approach tendency to a feared object 2. anxiety aroused in public speaking

subsides within less than a minute. Upon regaining consciousness, the patient feels confused, but fully recovers within thirty minutes. The patient often temporarily loses memory of recent events. Usually, severe depressions are alleviated following shock therapy.

Although medical therapies are relatively harmless and painless (except psychosurgery, of course), most people seeking therapeutic aid tend to shy away from them in favor of more psychologically oriented therapies. In general, most psychotherapeutic techniques may be classified either as insight therapies or as action therapies. *Insight therapies* include psychoanalysis and client-centered therapy in which the therapist devotes most of his efforts to enhancing the self-awareness and understanding of the patient. Action therapies include actual manipulation of the pattern of the patient's acts (behavior therapy). In insight therapies the therapist seeks out particular motives that underlie the observed difficulty and, by exposing them, loosens their bond with the overt

disturbed behavior they supposedly produce. *Action therapists* tend to focus on the person's symptoms rather than on the underlying motivational states that may produce these symptoms. These behavior therapists view psychotherapy as a planned attack on symptoms of disorder and don't much care whether insight and self-understanding are later acquired.

Client-centered therapy (an insight therapy) emerged in 1942 when Carl Rogers presented a radical new kind of treatment. With its application of such concepts as repression and release, and its stress upon catharsis and insight, client-centered therapy has many roots in Freudian thinking and traditional psychoanalysis. However, there the similarity ends: Rogers rejects the psychoanalytic view that psychopathology develops because man is by nature irrational, self-defensive, and destructive; on the contrary, he asserts that man is basically good, ever moving toward self-fulfillment or self-actualization (see Unit 21). Unlike psychoanalysis, where the therapist is in definite control and is ready to guide through his

"*My mother doesn't understand me.*"

Figure 2.   A personal relationship with a sympathetic listener may have immediate therapeutic value for some kinds of problems.

interpretations at crucial points in the therapy, client-centered therapy leaves to the patient any initiative for progress. Meanwhile the client-centered therapist serves a catalytic function through his intense involvement in nurturing an empathic understanding of the client. In addition, Rogers sees psychotherapy as an exploratory experience where the goal is to facilitate the client's effort to gain an awareness of his own internal frame of reference, whereas Freud considered psychotherapy a technical, rational, and orderly procedure where the main objective was to make the unconscious conscious.

The major task of client-centered therapy is to establish an atmosphere conducive to greater openness to experience. The desired atmosphere is one that views the client as capable of achieving growth and self-development; this replaces the attitude of searching for a "cure." Above all, the therapist strives to maintain a relationship free of judgment and evaluation so as not to threaten the self-exploration process. The client-centered approach stresses the necessity of an accepting relationship developing between client and therapist so that the client will become less fearful of examining his own feelings and experiences. Optimally, the initial process of catharsis will be replaced by a phase in which insight becomes the most significant element, and this in turn by a phase marked by the increase in positive choice and action.

Instead of specifically interpreting what the patient is saying, the client-centered therapist uses reflection. That is, he restates what the patient has said in such a way that he exposes the feelings underlying the content of the patient's statement and communicates understanding and acceptance. The following excerpt from the concluding portion of the thirteenth interview with one client should illustrate the process:

[client:] I had really reached a low, and it seems maybe superficial to say that in three or four days I come back and I feel like a different person, but I think maybe I was reaching a certain emotional—setting myself for an emotional revelation, subconscious revelation which I didn't know but that it was just coming to the top like a boil.
[therapist:] Getting to the point where you had to do something about the whole business.
[client:] Yes, I realized the position, that I had to get it out, and I did, Tuesday night, and it wasn't

that I sat down and I said, "Well, Arnold, let's talk it out, leave us talk it out . . . " I didn't do that. My feeling of hatred towards him was so intense that I was weak already, really I was so weak—I said something and he misunderstood me. And then I misunderstood him and I said, "Arnold, we just don't meet at all, do we Arnold?" Then he said, "Well, let's talk" so we sat down and talked. So he took the initiative, and I started to talk to him for a whole hour and a half. Before it opened up I hated him, I couldn't talk, "Oh, he won't understand," "We don't meet on the same level." To myself, "Let's get away from each other. I can't stand to be with you, you irritate me . . . " Then all of a sudden, I said, "Arnold do you know that I feel sexually inferior to you," and that did it. The very fact that I could tell him that. Which was, I think that was the very thing, the whole thought to admit, not to admit to myself, because I knew that all the time, but to bring it up so that I could have admitted it to him, which I think was the whole turning point.
[therapist:] To be able to admit what you regarded as your deepest weakness.
[client:] Yes.
[therapist:] Just started the ball rolling.
[client:] This feeling of sexual inadequacy, but now that he knows it—it isn't important any more. It's like I carried a secret with me, and I wanted somebody to share it and Arnold of all people, and finally he knows about it so I feel better. So I don't feel inadequate.
[therapist:] The worst is known and accepted.
[Rogers, 1951]

The client-centered-therapy hypothesis states that if a therapist communicates empathic understanding of the client's point of view towards his problems, self-direction will be generated, and improvement in self-concept and adaptability will develop.

One of the major objectives of client-centered therapy is to help the patient release self-actualization—the inherent tendency of an individual to develop his capacities. The extent to which an individual's experiences can be fit into his self-concept and the degree of congruence between what he is and what he wants to be influences the extent to which self-actualization will be achieved.

EXPERIMENTAL EVIDENCE

Investigators: J. M. Butler and C. V. Haigh

Source, Date: "Changes in the Relation Between Self-Concepts and Ideal Concepts Consequent Upon Client-Centered Counseling," 1954

Location: University of Chicago

Subjects: 41 adults

Materials: Tests for actual and ideal self-concept (Q-Sort)

All forty-one subjects were tested first to determine the way they felt themselves to be in fact and then to determine how they would like to be ideally. The test itself consisted of simple declarative sentences such as: "I am a hard worker," "I am really disturbed," "I am afraid of a full-fledged disagreement with another person," and so on. The subjects were required to sort these into nine piles ranging from "like-me" to "un-like-me" and "like-ideal" to "unlike-ideal."

The subjects were divided into two groups. The first group consisted of twenty-five clients who actually showed up for therapy. Before this group started therapy, there was relatively little correspondence between their actual and ideal self-concepts. Thus,

the goal of client-centered therapy with these clients was to produce some significant relationship between these two self-concepts.

The second group of subjects consisted of sixteen matched controls who were *not* clients for therapy. These were matched with the first group in terms of sex, age, socioeconomic status, and student-nonstudent status. While the first group was receiving therapy, this second control group simply went about their usual daily activities for an equivalent length of time. It was expected that a comparison of the test scores of these two groups would indicate whether any change resulted from the passage of time or simply from the experience with the test.

To determine whether motivation for counseling rather than counseling itself produces congruence between actual and ideal self-concepts, fifteen of the original twenty-five from the therapy group underwent a sixty-day control period prior to counseling. Test scores over this sixty-day period should indicate whether test results of clients change as a result of motivation for therapy per se.

After the experimental group had been given treat-

Figure 3. Each of us has an ideal self-concept and an actual self-concept. A major objective of client-centered therapy is to help the client increase the similarity between them.

ment, all subjects again took the self-ideal tests. The first group, consisting of those who received therapy immediately and those who waited sixty days, showed a significant increase in congruence between the actual-self and ideal-self concepts. The control group showed no significant increase. This beneficial change continued to exist in follow-up tests six months to one year after the completion of therapy. These findings indicate that, as a consequence of client-centered therapy, a rise in clients' level of self-esteem and adjustment was brought about.

Whereas insight therapies like the client-centered approach may be more suited to disorders of meaning and feeling (for example, neuroses like obsession and diffuse anxiety states), behavior therapies may be better equipped to address disorders that can be defined by their symptoms, such as phobias. In addition, behavior therapies seem to have better success with some psychotics and patients afflicted with character disorders (see Unit 13). Behavior therapists firmly believe that psychopathology is learned and that, in this way, abnormal and normal behavior are similar. Just as Pavlovian conditioning (see Unit 26) and operant conditioning (see Unit 27) are functional in everyday learning experiences, so they may help patients who have behavior disorders to adapt more appropriate, socially acceptable responses. A behavior therapist does not scrutinize inner forces nor does he believe that symptoms are signs of deeper problems; the symptoms are present because they were learned and will disappear when they are unlearned. The behavior-therapy hypothesis states that the direct treatment of symptoms through learning principles can bring about the replacement of an individual's maladaptive habits with adaptive ones.

Because the behavior therapist does not require the patient to develop insight, the therapeutic strategy is more characterized by training than by depth interpretations or analysis of feelings. Training procedures used in behavior therapy may take a variety of forms.

One of the most widely used forms involves the use of reward—positive reinforcement—for appropriate behavior. Frequently, positive reinforcement is given to hospitalized patients for social behavior acceptable to other members of a group. Since the reinforcement is given in the form of tokens which can be cashed in for a variety of rewards, this procedure is referred to as a token economy. This is explained in more detail in

Unit 11, Therapy in Groups. However, similar procedures are sometimes used for hospitalized patients for behavior which is not necessarily applicable to groups and may, therefore, also be considered a therapy for individuals.

Because phobias—intense obsessive fears—are so often identified as resulting from a relatively simple learning experience, they are prime candidates for behavior therapy. In the following study, a common phobia is treated in several ways so that the effectiveness of various approaches may be compared. The two forms of behavior therapy are modeling and systematic desensitization. For our purposes we will describe modeling here and the process of systematic desensitization in the study that follows this one.

Modeling as a form of behavior therapy is based on the notion that some anxieties are learned from observing other people exhibit anxieties in specific situations. If this is the case, then it should follow that learned anxieties or fears may be unlearned by watching models exhibit fearlessness in the same situations. The procedure calls for the shaping of behavior (Unit 27) by asking the subject to imitate successive steps toward the goal-behavior.

EXPERIMENTAL EVIDENCE

Investigator: P. Carlson
Source, Date: "An Analysis of the Motor, Cognitive, and Physiological Components of Psychotherapeutically Induced Changes in Phobic Behavior," 1969
Location: University of Washington
Subjects: 20 college women who were fearful of snakes
Materials: Tame, nonpoisonous, 3-foot-long boa constrictor

Twenty college women, all of whom were intensely fearful of snakes, were assigned randomly to each of the following four treatment groups: (1) model observation, (2) desensitization sessions (another type of behavior therapy, discussed shortly), (3) lectures, and (4) no treatment (control group). The modeling group received the following orientation:

One of the ways we can tell that a person is afraid of something is by the way he behaves in its presence. For example, we infer that you are afraid of snakes because you have refused to handle one. If you could learn to handle snakes then we would no longer have a basis for saying that you were afraid of them. One of the best ways to learn a new behavior is to watch someone else perform it first and then try to imitate their performance. Psychologists have already used this technique successfully in a wide variety of situations. It is the technique that we will use here to teach you to handle snakes without fear.

What will happen is this: each time that we meet I will demonstrate a behavior with a snake, then you in turn will be asked to imitate my behavior. When you have successfully done so we will move on to another somewhat more difficult behavior. By the time we are finished you should be able to comfortably handle snakes [Carlson, 1969, p. 20].

The lecture group received a standard didactic presentation as follows:

People are afraid of things about which they know very little. This is largely because in the absence of knowledge people do not know what to expect and thus become uncertain and fearful. If you knew more about snakes and knew what to expect from them you would be much less fearful. Therefore, our five meetings will be used to teach you about snakes. This will happen in these ways: (1) each time we meet I will present a brief lecture on some aspect of snakes and their behavior and we will discuss what I present.(2) I will describe to you in detail how to handle a snake and what it feels like to do so. (3) You will discuss with each other the experiences you have had with snakes and the feelings that you have about them.

In this way you will gain considerable information that you do not have now. You will know better what to expect from a snake and thus will have much less reason to fear it. Do you have any questions before we continue? [Carlson, 1969, p. 21].

Each of the four groups was compared on whether subjects would look at, touch, or hold a three-foot boa constrictor. None of the subjects would go beyond simply looking at the snake on a pretest.   On the posttest immediately following the completion of all training procedures, the modeling group showed the strongest approach tendency. At the time of a six-week follow-up, the modeling and desensitization groups were superior in terms of adaptive behavior to the two other groups.

Like modeling, systematic desensitization aims at substituting nonanxious behavior for anxious behavior. The steps of the procedure are as follows: (1) information-gathering interviews to determine the exact nature of the symptoms, (2) information-giving interviews where the therapist informs the patient of the steps to be followed in therapy, (3) systematic desensitization training in which the therapist first trains the patient in deep muscle relaxation (some therapists use hypnosis to produce relaxation). Then he has the patient construct a list ranking stimuli causing anxiety in a specific situation. Next he uses the relaxation to reduce the patient's sensitivity to the anxiety-causing stimuli, and (4) desensitization sessions, in which the patient, who is in a state of deep muscle relaxation, is told to progressively visualize the items on his anxiety hierarchy starting with those that are least disturbing. The following case study involving a twenty-four-year-old student who experienced acute anxiety during examinations should provide some of the flavor of this popular behavior-therapy technique.

I am now going to ask you to imagine a number of scenes. You will imagine them clearly and they will generally interfere little, if at all, with your state of relaxation. If, however, at any time you feel disturbed or worried and want to attract my attention, you will be able to do so by raising your left index finger. First I want you to imagine that you are standing at a familiar street corner on a pleasant morning watching the traffic go by. You see cars, motorcycles, trucks, bicycles, people and traffic lights; and you can hear the sounds associated with all these things. (Pause of about 15 sec.) Now stop imagining that scene and give all your attention once again to relaxing. If the scene you imagine disturbed you even in the slightest degree I want you to raise your left index finger now. (Patient does not raise finger.) Now imagine that you are at home studying in the evening. It is the 20th of May, exactly a month before your examination. (Pause of 5 sec.) Now stop imagining the scene. Go on relaxing. (Pause of 10 sec.) Now imagine the same scene again—a month before your examination. (Pause of 5 sec.) Stop imagining the scene and just think of your muscles. Let go, and enjoy your state of calm. (Pause of 15 sec.) Now again imagine that you are studying at home a month before your examination. *(Pause of 5 sec.)* Stop the scene and now think of nothing but your own body. *(Pause of 5 sec.)* If you felt any disturbance whatsoever to the last scene raise your left index finger now. *(Patient raises finger.)* If the amount of disturbance decreased from the first presentation to the third do nothing, otherwise again raise your finger. *(Patient does not raise finger.)* Just keep on relaxing. *(Pause of 15 sec.)* Imagine that you are sitting on a bench at a bus stop and across the road are two strange men whose voices are raised in argument. *(Pause of 10 sec.)* Stop imagining the scene and just relax. *(Pause of 10 sec.)* Now again imagine the scene of these two men arguing across the road. *(Pause of 10 sec.)* Stop the scene and relax. Now I am going to count up to 5 and you will open your eyes, feeling very calm and refreshed. [Wolpe, 1966]

Desensitization procedures have been substantially confirmed as beneficial by many research studies.

EXPERIMENTAL EVIDENCE

Investigator: G. Paul

Source, Date: "Insight Versus Desensitization in Psychotherapy," 1966

Location: Stanford University

Subjects: 74 college students showing initial anxiety over public speaking

Materials: Self-report questionnaires, physiological measures (pulse rate and palm sweating)

Each of the subjects was assessed before and after completion of therapy on three separate measures—a self-report questionnaire, physiological measures, and a rating of their behavior in a real-life stress situation involving public speaking. Each of five therapists, using a variety of treatments including sys-

tematic desensitization, was allotted clients who showed anxiety over public speaking. After a relatively short period of treatment, subjects who had received desensitization treatment showed a significantly better response to treatment than any of the other groups of subjects as indicated by all three types of measurements. The superiority of the desensitized group was maintained during a six-week follow-up period. As the Carlson (1969) study dealing with women's fears of snakes indicated earlier, it is possible to bring about significant reductions in fear, even long-standing fears, by use of systematic desensitization. It should be pointed out, however, that Paul's 1966 study is best regarded as supporting the effectiveness of desensitization in its own right rather than indicating its superiority over other therapies because the brief period of treatment allotted in this study (at least five hours over six weeks) is insufficient for the complete execution of the longer-lasting insight therapies.

Now that you have some familiarity with the way various therapies for individuals are *supposed* to work, some investigation into whether they actually *do* work seems appropriate.

2. DOES THERAPY REALLY HELP?

The *improvement hypothesis* states that therapeutic techniques give relief to patients suffering from psychopathological disorders that would not otherwise come about through the patients' own improvement efforts or the mere passage of time. Although experimental proof of therapeutic effectiveness is difficult to come by, there is a good deal of anecdotal evidence that shows the therapeutic experience to be a very positive and beneficial one. The following statement by a former patient is one such example:

QUESTION	2. DOES THERAPY REALLY HELP?	
HYPOTHESES	**IMPROVEMENT**	**STATUS QUO**
DESCRIPTIVE EVIDENCE	ASSESS: effectiveness of desensitization on neurotic patients	ASSESS: improvement rate of both therapeutically treated and non-treated groups
EXPERIMENTAL EVIDENCE		

I have accepted "me." I know now everyone experiences anxiety and uses an individual mechanism to accommodate this. I understand my own particular pattern and can adjust accordingly . . .

I still have spells of incapacitating anxiety when confronted with large tasks, but have managed to face up to two major tasks successfully—Ph.D. orals and written exams. Perhaps I have found that I needn't be as good as I once thought I had to be in order to get by or to be accepted. Perhaps I have more faith and courage now than I had before. Also I am more willing to understand and to accept others (though still not very willing at times) . . .

The most important change, I think, has been letting go of my own fantasies and facing my situation and experiences for what they are. I had always been a suspicious person, looking for someone to hurt my feelings, and then dwelling on it . . . In many ways I'm an idealistic person and perhaps the most important change in me has been learning the difference between things as they are and things as I think they should be . . .

I have rid myself of the greatest inferiority complex possible. I feel I am now a fairly attractive, competent person, who can handle the necessary crises of life that I will encounter. My fear of people in crowds and my fear of being alone have both been overcome almost entirely. I thoroughly enjoy people, my life, and those about me . . .

I am a great deal more self-sufficient, so that my relationships are not based merely on need, but I can now be a part of a reciprocal situation. I can assume much more responsibility for my own actions and thus am better able to act rather than just react. My anger at my family has subsided, and I no longer feel that they are to blame for my unhappiness in any present sense. Most importantly, I am able to feel joy and pain, which even with the latter is good, because *I'm* living, and not just something parasitic. I can trust another person enough to care, and to risk the consequences of caring . . .

Here I must give an explanation. One of my problems before therapy was my inability to care about myself. It seems as though whenever I had someone else to care for or some responsibility to someone else, that I could handle problems okay.

When it came to caring for myself, I just did not. Since I left therapy I have married and my wife is expecting a child shortly. This gives me a responsibility that I know I must not fail in. Although problems still exist, I run no more. I find myself thinking back to my therapy sessions and trying to use what I learned there. I try to determine what is the best way to handle them. I do not let my problems pile up on me, I handle them as they come. I now realize that nothing is really as "earth shattering" as it may seem at the time, and after I have done all I can, I stand. [Strupp, Fox, and Lessler, 1969.]

There are few broad-based studies investigating the general effectiveness of therapy, but a number with limited scope are available. Because the overt changes brought about by behavior therapy are easier to operationalize, more recent published studies concentrate on this type of therapy than any other.

DESCRIPTIVE EVIDENCE
Investigator: J. Wolpe
Source, Date: "Systematic Desensitization Treatment of Neuroses," 1963
Subjects: 39 neurotic patients
Materials: 5-point rating scale

Thirty-nine neurotic patients took part in a total of 762 desensitization sessions. The average number of sessions was 11.2 for each anxiety hierarchy, and the actual desensitization procedure took up only part of each forty-five-minute session. Degree of change was rated on a five-point scale by each patient. Table 1 summarizes the data.

Although there were only thirty-nine patients, there were sixty-eight phobias and neurotic anxiety response habits because some cases were complex and warranted multiple hierarchies. The treatment was judged effective in thirty-five patients, and forty-five of the neurotic tendencies were either eliminated or markedly ameliorated.

However, even with therapeutic successes like those Wolpe experienced with his desensitization procedure, there is a good deal of support for the notion that therapy is not effective or, at least, has not been proven to be effective as a result of such problems as lack of experimental controls and methodological difficulties. Specifically, the *status quo hypothesis* states that therapy is of little or no value

TABLE 1. Results of Desensitization

Patients	39	
Number of patients responding to desensitization treatment	35	
Number of hierarchies	68	
Hierarchies overcome	45	91%
Hierarchies markedly improved	17	
Hierarchies unimproved	6	9%
Total number of desensitization sessions	762	
Mean session expenditure per hierarchy	11.2	
Mean session expenditure per successfully treated hierarchy	12.3	
Median number of sessions per patient	10.0	

Source: J. Wolpe, "The Systematic Desensitization Treatment of Neuroses," *The Journal of Nervous and Mental Disease*, 132 (1963), 189–203.

because patients improve equally well when left to their own resources.

Eysenck's 1952 study originally alerted people to the possibility that therapy might not facilitate recovery. It is a good example of research in this area because it vividly points out some of the methodological difficulties involved in examining therapeutic effectiveness.

DESCRIPTIVE EVIDENCE

Investigator: H. J. Eysenck
Source, Date: "The Effects of Psychotherapy: An Evaluation," 1952
Location: University of London
Subjects: 7,000 cases

Materials: 19 published studies in the psychological literature covering over 7,000 cases concerning the effectiveness of therapy

Eysenck's extensive analysis of nineteen published studies yielded the following data:

1. Patients treated by means of psychoanalysis improve to the extent of 44 percent.
2. Patients treated by a variety of other techniques improve to the extent of 64 percent.
3. Patients treated only custodially or by general practitioners improve to the extent of 72 percent.

From these and further analyses, he concluded that some therapists make their patients improve more than they would without therapy, some do nothing more than keep their conditions stable, and still others actually hinder the remedial process. What needs to be asked is not "Is therapy effective?" but a more specific question: "Is this type of treatment administered by this therapist effective with this type of patient?"

3. DO PERSONALITY FACTORS AFFECT THE RESULT OF THERAPY?

The *therapist-attributes hypothesis* states that therapists have identifiable characteristics and traits that affect the course and result of therapy. You know from your own experience that you are more likely to

QUESTION 3. DO PERSONALITY FACTORS AFFECT THE RESULT OF THERAPY?

HYPOTHESES	THERAPIST ATTRIBUTES	PATIENT ATTRIBUTES
DESCRIPTIVE EVIDENCE	ASSESS: 1. relationship between therapists' personality traits and therapeutic effectiveness. 2. characteristics of successful and unsuccessful therapists working with schizophrenics 3. similarities and differences between expert and nonexpert therapists	ASSESS: 1. relationship of personality structure to both duration and outcome of therapy MEASURE: Patients' self-disclosure in different A–B relationships
EXPERIMENTAL EVIDENCE		

bring your problems to some people than others. And there are some individuals you would never discuss your difficulties with. Therapists are well aware that some of their colleagues are more successful than others, and much research has gone into trying to discover exactly what it is that makes certain therapists stand above their peers.

DESCRIPTIVE EVIDENCE

Investigator: M. Wogan
Source, Date: "Effect of Therapist-Patient Personality Variables on Therapeutic Outcome," 1970
Location: University of North Carolina
Subjects: 82 hospitalized mental patients (55 men and 27 women), 12 psychiatric residents (10 men and 2 women)
Materials: Minnesota Multiphasic Personality Inventory, Patient Rating Scale, Therapist Rating Scale

In this study, the MMPI (Minnesota Multiphasic Personality Inventory) was first administered to both patients and therapists. The MMPI consists of a list of about 500 statements to which the subject may reply "true," "false," or "cannot say." Here are a few sample items: "I do not tire quickly." "I am worried about sex matters." "I believe I am being plotted against." "When I get bored I like to stir up some excitement."

After three weeks of therapy, the patients and therapists rated each other on several scales. For example, both patients and therapists rated each other on "mutual liking" and ability to communicate while the therapists rated the patients on their relative improvement at the end of the study. The results from these ratings were then compared with personality characteristics of the therapists and patients as originally determined by results from the MMPI.

Patients rated communicative ease higher when the therapist had higher scores on anxiety and lower scores on repression; they also tended to have greater liking for therapists who were more anxious. In addition, patients rated themselves as progressing more rapidly in therapy when the therapist had lower scores on the repression scale and higher scores on the subtlety scale. According to Wogan, these findings suggest that "patients both liked their therapist and showed more progress in therapy if the therapist was able to acknowledge some forms of unpleasant experience in himself (anxiety) and tended not to

deny symptoms in himself (repression)."

It should be noted that therapists' scores on the MMPI were all well within the limits of normality and that the range of scores among the therapists indicate personality patterns rather than abnormal deviations. Not only did the best liked *and* seemingly most effective therapists feel comfortable in acknowledging a certain amount of "pathological" concern on the MMPI, but these same therapists were considered the most outgoing and physically active and least bothered by feelings of depression.

An interesting phenomenon is that similarity between patient and therapist was considered detrimental to the relationship in two instances. Increasing similarity on the repression scale tended to detract from the patient's liking for the therapist, while increasing similarity on the subtlety scale tended to be accompanied by a lower patient rating of speed of progress. Wogan's conjecture was that this similarity in "defensive styles" might affect the therapist's ability to gain an objective understanding of the patient's problems. It could also possibly affect ease of communication because "if the patient and therapist both have similar ways of dealing with their psychological problems, then the therapist has nothing much to offer the patient that he does not already know, outside of theoretical knowledge."

It has been noted that certain therapists who are unsuccessful with one sort of patient may be extremely helpful with others. Psychiatrists Betz and Whitehorn sought to establish what therapist characteristics made a difference in the treatment of schizophrenic patients, a group that as a whole is particularly resistant to forming meaningful relationships with therapists.

DESCRIPTIVE EVIDENCE

Investigators: B. Betz and J. Whitehorn
Source, Date: "The Relationship of the Therapist to the Outcome of Therapy in Schizophrenia," 1956
Location: Henry Phipps Clinic of the Johns Hopkins Hospital
Subjects: 15 known successful therapists and 11 known unsuccessful therapists
Materials: Psychiatric records, Strong Vocational Interest Blank

After searching through past psychiatric records and using several criteria of success in psychotherapy, including discharge from the clinic because of improvement, two kinds of therapists emerged: one group achieved an improvement rate of 75 percent with schizophrenics (*A* therapists) while the other had a rate of only 25 percent improvement (*B* therapists). It was found that *A* therapists were more capable of grasping the meaning of the verbal communications of schizophrenics, tended toward helping them achieve adjustment in specific ways, and were expressive in their interactions. On the other hand, *B* therapists were more inclined to focus on symptoms and the nature of the pathology, and also tended to be formal in interactions with patients.

Once they had deduced these characteristics from a wide variety of measures, Betz and Whitehorn next tried to *predict* which therapists would be successful. In order to do this, they used the therapists' Vocational Interest test. It was found that the two groups differed with respect to four particular vocational groups: *A* therapists had interests similar to lawyers and certified public accountants; *B* therapists were much aligned with painters and math and science teachers.

Putting all this information together with the reliably observed phenomenon that much of the withdrawn attitude of schizophrenics can be attributed to the fear of being hurt and controlled by perceived authority figures, it is not difficult to discern why *A* therapists have a better success rate. *A* therapists appear to be more open and spontaneous and put greater stock in self-determination and individualism and are thus less threatening to schizophrenics than *B* therapists who value conforming and keeping a protective distance between themselves and patients.

Although a therapist's attitudes toward his patient have been shown to be important, his success rate should also be affected by his professional training and experience. If experts are, in fact, better than novices, it should be possible to demonstrate this generalization with an analysis of case studies.

DESCRIPTIVE EVIDENCE

Investigator: F. Fiedler
Source, Date: "A Comparison of Therapeutic Relations in Psychoanalysis, Nondirective and Adlerian Therapy," 1950
Location: University of Chicago
Subjects: 10 therapists of varying persuasions
Materials: Q-Sort

This study compared beginners with veterans in three major schools of psychotherapy—psychoanalysis, Adlerian psychotherapy (resembling psychoanalysis), and client-centered therapy—by submitting ten recorded sessions from different therapists to four judges. The judges saw only the records; they did not know the "school" each therapist came from. As in the study by J. M. Butler noted earlier, judges used the Q-Sort technique to rate patient-therapist communication, emotional distance, and the therapist's status "in the eyes" of the patient.

It was found that the relationships created by the experts (as defined by reputation), regardless of theoretical persuasion, more closely approximated the ideal therapeutic relationship than those created by therapists not considered to be experts. Judges also found that experts of all schools created therapeutic relationships that showed more similarity to each other than those created by experts and novices within the same school. On the whole, the greatest discrepancy between experts and novices was in patient-therapist communication—experts appeared superior in this ability. It appears that ability to understand and relate to the patient, at least in this study, is the most important criterion of expertness as a therapist.

Just as the attributes of the therapist can have an important effect on the course of therapy, so can the characteristics of the patient. The *patient-attributes hypothesis* states that patients with psychological disorders have identifiable characteristics and traits that affect the direction and outcome of treatment.

DESCRIPTIVE EVIDENCE

Investigators: W. L. Kirtner and D. S. Cartwright
Source, Date: "Success and Failure of Client-centered Therapy as a Function of Client Personality Variables," 1958
Location: University of Chicago
Subjects: 26 disturbed patients
Materials: Personality tests and ratings; interviews

The patients were divided into five groups, labeled "short success" or "short failure" (one to twelve therapy sessions), "intermediate" (thirteen to twenty-one sessions), and "long success" or "long failure" (more than twenty-one sessions). Their personalities were assessed by a number of standard psychological tests, and their improvement was rated by their therapists.

The most obvious discrepancies in personality were found between "short success" and "short failure" patients. The first group showed much more personality integration, better control of themselves, more openness in discussing their problems, and less confusion about their sex lives. For the other groups personality differences were not nearly as clearly demarcated.

This finding indicates two possibilities, but they are not mutually exclusive. It may be that the longer a patient is in therapy, the less his "normal" background personality really matters for the outcome of therapy. In other words, only on a relatively short-term basis does degree of personality integration make any real difference. On the other hand, it is also possible that it is simply difficult to differentiate normal personality traits from pathological ones: the rapidly improving patients may simply have been less disturbed in the first place than those who showed slower improvement.

The most fruitful research in the whole area of personal characteristics may well lie in the overall exploration of therapist-patient compatibility. The Betz and Whitehorn work cited earlier in this unit noted A therapists' success with schizophrenic patients. Later research has brought out the interesting finding that B therapists outperform A therapists with neurotic patients. This A-B variance could have broad relevance to therapist-patient interaction, and one way of assessing this would be to study patients generally regarded as relatively unpromising for therapy or "resistive." Patients with character disorders (see Unit 13) could be classified in this category.

EXPERIMENTAL EVIDENCE

Investigators: J. Berzins, W. Ross, and D. Cohen
Source, Date: "Relations of the A-B Distinction and Trust-Distrust Sets to Addict Patients' Self-Disclosures in Brief Interviews," 1970

Location: National Institute of Mental Health Clinical Research Center, Lexington, Kentucky
Subjects: 40 hospitalized narcotic addicts, 40 psychiatric aides
Materials: 20-minute interviews, rating scales

This multifaceted study, which used psychiatric aides as interviewers, investigated the effects of interviewers' A-B status, patients' A-B status, and whether the therapeutic environment was friendly or distrustful. This last variable was introduced by pre-interview instructions to the patient, which, in the distrust condition, stressed the manipulative personality of the prospective interviewer, while, in the friendly condition, the interviewer was described as trustworthy and warm. Following the twenty-minute interviews, participants filled out five-point rating scales dealing with reactions to their partners and their own behavior (for example, ease of communication, degree of trust, emotional involvement).

It was found that A therapists excelled in drawing out patients put in a distrustful situation, while B therapists obtained more self-disclosure from trustful patients. No support was evident, however, for the expectation that pairings involving dissimilar A-B status would outperform those whose members had the same status, a negative finding that suggests limitations on what the authors called the "complementarity hypothesis."

At this point it should be evident that the type of patient with the best prognosis varies from one therapeutic setting to another, depending to some extent on the biases and expectations of both the therapist and patient (see Unit 2), among other things. Each can markedly influence the other's behavior. The patient's initial *hope* for improvement, for example, has been found to be a contributing factor in the likelihood of it actually occurring. The interaction of a prospective patient with his social environment, which can markedly influence his feelings and expectation prior to therapy, can be both a blessing and a curse to the prospective therapist's chances for success.

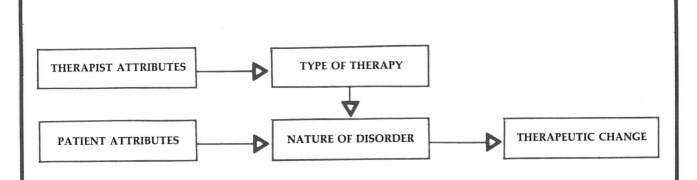

PUTTING IT TOGETHER: Therapy for Individuals

Individual psychotherapy for relief of mental disorder may be appropriately viewed as primarily a personal relationship between the patient and therapist. The outcome of this relationship depends in large measure on the *personal attributes of both therapist and patient.*

There is a variety of *types of therapy*, and the most efficient therapy may be dependent on the *nature of the disorder*. Insight therapies, such as client-centered therapy, focus on inner conflict. Behavior therapies, such as systematic desensitization, focus on feelings and behavior of which the patient is fully aware.

If the treatment is effective, the patient will undergo *therapeutic change* in emotions, attitudes and behavior.

1. WHAT'S ACCEPTED . . .

1. Both client-centered and behavior therapy provide useful treatment for specific types of disorder.

2. Different therapies and therapists are suited to different patients.

3. In most psychotherapies the interview situation and the relationship between patient and therapist that comes out of it are vitally important.

4. The personalities of both therapist and patient affect the course of treatment.

2. WHAT'S DEBATED . . .

1. Whether psychotherapy is the most effective form of treatment for mental disorders.

2. What relationship between patient and therapist is most effective for the various specific types of disorder.

3. Whether or not different types of therapy change different aspects of personality.

In recent years there have been many new methods of individual therapy. One careful count turned up at least 200 different schools of thought, most of them new, using a total of over 10,000 different therapeutic techniques.

How can the emergence of so many new forms of therapy be explained? Part of the reason is dissatisfaction with traditional psychoanalysis. Psychoanalytic methods are very expensive and very time-consuming. The Freudian theories on which they are based are also coming under critical scrutiny. Many of Freud's basic insights, perhaps meaningful in the 19th century Vienna in which they were developed, are considered irrelevant in the more liberal climate of modern America. Worse, traditional psychoanalytic methods do not yield the same high success rates that seem to be achieved by some other methods.

But dissatisfaction with psychoanalysis is not the only reason for the great number of new therapies. An important factor is the great increase in the number of Americans who feel the need to bare their souls to others and are seeking various ways of doing it. As Carl Rogers suggests, this widespread need is related to the affluent but anonymous nature of our society: "When a man is scrambling very hard to get his three meals a day, he doesn't have time to feel alienated from his fellow human beings. Now that we are an affluent society, we do have the time and we realize that we are lonely and alone, lacking deep contacts with others. We begin to say, 'I wish there was someone I could talk to.'"

One interesting new form of treatment is termed "reality therapy," and has been pioneered by Los Angeles psychiatrist William Glasser. His methods are almost a reversal of traditional Freudian psychoanalysis. Instead of searching for the origins of the problem, he dismisses them as irrelevant. Nothing, he says, can change the past and therefore therapy should be oriented to the future. Instead of maintaining a strictly neutral attitude and avoiding an intimate relationship with the patient, Glasser tries to develop as strong a personal bond as possible. Instead of refraining from any moral debate about his patients' views and acts, Glasser forces them to face up to their moral consequences. "If a patient says he's a thief and is willing to accept the consequences of being a thief, that's all right," says Glasser. "I don't judge it, but it's basic to reality therapy for him to judge it."

The assumption behind reality therapy is that those who seek treatment are "irresponsible." They fail to take responsibility for their own acts and lives, for adjusting to the demands of their fellows and the realities of the world around them. Glasser dismisses patients' tales of their unhappy childhoods, unsympathetic spouses and raw deals at work as "psychiatric garbage." His view is simply stated: "A lot of people are looking for excuses. Reality therapy says the hell with excuses; let's get on with the business of improving our lives."

One of the most common, successful, and yet controversial new therapies is behavior therapy. (See Unit 27.) Based on learning theories, this therapy rejects Freudian theory almost entirely. The therapists do not bother to discuss a patient's childhood or to probe the recesses of the mind and its dim memories of traumatic experiences. Instead, they assume that neurotic behavior is simply a bad habit, learned because it was reinforced in the past, and maintained because the patient still finds it in some way rewarding. The solution, then, is to make the behavior unrewarding, perhaps by delivering a sharp electric shock to the patient every time he engages in the habit or by rewarding another behavior that is counterproductive to the behavior to be eliminated. Attempts have been made, for example, to eliminate various forms of variant sexual behavior by this method. (A transvestite might be encouraged to put on female clothing, and then receive a painful shock.) If the treatment is repeated often enough, so the theory runs, the patient soon finds the habit highly unrewarding and ends it.

Humanistic psychologists have strongly attacked behavior modification of this nature on the grounds that it treats only symptoms, not underlying causes. They also charge that it treats man as a machine to be manipulated rather than a person to be understood. Behavior modification therapists are unimpressed by these arguments. Joseph Wolpe, a psychiatrist primarily responsible for the development of behavior therapy, retorts: "I think the essential thing is that if somebody comes to you with suffering, you have to use the best possible method to remove that suffering. Even if it's a mechanical method, if it works better than other methods, you should use it. How can there be any reasonable objection to that? It is the humanitarian thing to do."

The form of new therapy that employs the most diversified techniques is the encounter or sensitivity training group. Ernest Havemann characterizes the range of methods that the groups employ: "Groups of ordinarily staid businessmen work as if their lives depended on it to build play-houses of index cards; a college professor and an unemployed chorus girl sit back to back on the floor and try to 'communicate' with their shoulder muscles; a plump California housewife and an ascetic clergyman stand barefoot on a bed sheet, trying to tune their senses to the grass beneath; a man who earns $100,000 per year breaks down and weeps in front of a dozen strangers because nobody likes him; another group of strangers, men and women, shed their clothes and plunge naked into a swimming pool with a therapist who believes that nudity frees the emotions."

A listing of some of the other new forms of therapy provides a glimpse of the exotic, if formidable, array of new methods available. The troubled individual can choose from directive psychotherapy, orgonomy, rational-emotive therapy, transactional analysis, psychodrama, hypnotherapy, general semantics, existential therapy, Gestalt therapy, Horneyan psychology, experiential therapy, client-centered therapy, and interpersonal psychology, to name but a few. Many of the new therapies, of course, may be useless, and some may even be dangerous. But the new methods do offer the prospect of allowing us to end our exclusive reliance on one single form of therapy. In the future it may be possible to identify the particular form of therapy most suited to a particular individual and to direct the troubled person to the treatment that is most likely to be successful.

Part III
processes underlying behavior . . .
basic operations

21. Motivation

People are impelled by processes that energize and direct them toward certain goals and incentives. These basic processes are covered by the general term *Motivation*, a concept applied to behavior at several levels of understanding. At the physiological level are basic needs and drives of the organism such as hunger, thirst and sex which must be satisfied if the organism and its species are to survive. At the individual level, strivings for accomplishment and self-expression help determine how well the individual succeeds in adapting to the environment and achieving independence. At the social level, human beings are dependent on each other for the satisfaction and fulfillment of a variety of social needs and motives. Psychologists have devoted much time and energy to the study of motivation on all of these levels.

22. Concept Learning

One basic process involved in the development of human intellectual capacities is the individual's gradual acquisition of concepts, those attributes of the world that provide the critical cues for classifying objects, events and abstractions. *Concept Learning* is bound up with the development of both language skills and thinking abilities and has received a great deal of attention from developmental psychologists.

23. Perceiving

24. Paying Attention

25. Memory

At the very heart of psychology is the study of those basic processes involved in how individuals deal with their environment and the information they derive from it. *Perceiving* refers to how the individual organizes impressions of the world from all the available sensory data. How and what the individual perceives depend partly on the structure of the nervous system and partly on the individual's own past experiences. *Paying Attention* refers to the ability to select certain characteristics of events or objects and devote one's information-processing capacities to only those characteristics. In this way man's brain can deal efficiently with small amounts of data at one time rather than being overwhelmed by the variety and quantity of all that is available to the sense organs. Incoming information finally ends up in *Memory*, the storehouse of knowledge, impressions and associations accumulated by experience. In psychology the study of memory includes forgetting, recalling and visual and sensory memories as well as verbal information.

26. Pavlovian Conditioning

27. Operant Conditioning

One of the most significant contributions of psychology to the store of human knowledge has been its systematic study and description of the basic processes underlying learning. Traditionally the general subject of learning has been divided into two types: classical or *Pavlovian Conditioning* and instrumental or *Operant Conditioning*. One of the most important results of our knowledge about learning is that psychologists have been able to use learning principles to control and change behavior more effectively than ever before. The behavior-modification movement tries to apply learning principles to individual behavior problems, mental retardation and even the behavior of whole wards in mental hospitals, and these techniques show great promise.

Unit 21

Motivation

OVERVIEW

The variety of motives that direct or influence human behavior are surveyed. First, some important findings are presented on maintenance motives—those needs that have an obvious physiological basis, such as hunger and thirst. Secondly, research on that most important of human motives, the need for achievement and competence, is described. Finally, several of the many motives that influence people in their social interactions are discussed in conjunction with evidence that has tried to measure these motives in people.

UNIT OUTLINE

DEFINITION AND BACKGROUND
1. *Definition:* motivation of an organism refers to those factors that energize and regulate behavior directed toward achieving goals and satisfying needs.
2. *Background:* Clark Hull (1884–1951).

QUESTIONS AND EVIDENCE
1. How do basic needs of the organism affect behavior?
Hypotheses:
    a. *Central cues:* basic motive states are under the control of central brain mechanisms that regulate and initiate such behavior as eating or drinking.
    b. *Incentives:* individuals differ in their relative sensitivity to internal drives and external incentives. **352**
    c. *Arousal:* there is an optimal level of arousal for performance efficiency and arousal levels that are either too low or too high are detrimental for performance. **353**
    d. *Curiosity:* organisms are motivated by needs to explore, manipulate, and understand their environment. **355**
2. What factors influence whether a person will do his best?
Hypotheses:
    a. *Need-for-achievement:* people can be motivated by a need to succeed, excel, and accomplish something. **357**
    b. *Level-of-aspiration:* people are capable of using either internal (personal) or external (reference group) standards when they set performance goals for themselves in a competitive or achievement situation. **359**
3. What motives affect how people behave socially?
Hypotheses:
    a. *Need-for-affiliation:* people can be motivated by a need to be with other people. **360**
    b. *Need-for-approval:* people can be motivated by a need for approval, esteem, and status in the eyes of other people. **362**
    c. *Need-for-power:* people can be motivated by a need to dominate, influence, and control other people. **363**

IMPORTANT CONCEPTS

	page
anxiety	356
arousal	353
aspiration level	358
behaviorism	348
drive	348
effectance motive	359
functional autonomy	365
hypothalamus	352
incentive	348
motivation	348
self-actualization	365

The motivational bases of behavior derive from both biological and social needs.

Motivated behavior may be triggered by a variety of internal and external incentives.

People direct their behavior to fulfill their personal needs.

DEFINITION AND BACKGROUND

The DEFINITION of motivation of an organism *refers to those factors that energize and regulate behavior directed toward achieving goals and satisfying needs.* Even with its long and honorable history of theory and research, the concept of motivation is still one of the most comprehensive and controversial in psychology. In order to avoid confusion, three other concepts basic to the subject of motivation should be defined:

A *motive* is a particular goal-oriented disposition or state of an organism. Examples: hunger, wanting to "do well," wanting to be liked.

A *drive* is a state of arousal that has its origin in need or internal deficit. Examples: hunger pangs and feelings, need for achievement.

An *incentive* is a goal that provides stimuli toward which an organism may be motivated. Examples: food, high grades, friends and lovers.

The FOCUS of this unit is on some of the important psychological processes and factors involved in human motivations—from hunger, sex, and other drives to social motivations and the need to achieve or fulfill oneself. Emphasis will be placed on the variety of motivational states that direct or influence human behaviors.

BACKGROUND: CLARK HULL (1884–1951)

Clark Hull taught at Wisconsin for a time and then remained at Yale for the rest of his career. Building his own apparatus, running experiments, and tinkering around with new machines and ideas had far more appeal for Hull than any niceties of academic life in the 1930s. In fact, Hull seemed always to think of himself as a "hard" scientist, and he wanted to make psychology just that, a "real" science. Interested in logic and new directions in the philosophy of science, he undertook a long, involved series of experiments and observations that finally resulted in a "theory of behavior"—a grand scheme relating learning, motivation, and observable behavior. Precise description, rigorous logical deduction, and mathematical expression were the key points to his system. As an explanation of motivation and learning, Hull's theory was to have a broad impact on psychology, from elementary

Figure 1. Clark Hull, who spent his lifetime researching motivation, believed that behavior is the result of learning and internal drives.

learning processes to behavior in general.

Hull's theory, as summarized in *Principles of Behavior* (1943), was the product of a period of comprehensive theory building in psychology. The 1930s produced widely divergent strains of thought within psychology. Even behaviorism itself developed many differing points of view, though most behavioristic researchers still held to the tenet that overt, observable behavior, and not conscious or unconscious "mental states," should be the main concern of a truly scientific psychology. Hull worked within this tradition. But for him, overt behavior was not the result of only stimulus-response associations and temporal contiguity, as some of his fellow behaviorists proposed. Rather, behavior was the result of a combination of *learning* (stimulus-response connections or habits built up over time) and *drives* within the organism based primarily on biological needs—hunger, thirst, sex, and so on. Both habit and drive, then, produce behavior. In an experimental situation, for example, one rat deprived of food for a period of time will work harder and faster to find food at the end of a maze than another rat that had similarly learned the maze but had not been deprived of food.

Hull expressed this relationship between motivation and behavior in terms of a simple equation: Habit times drive equals behavior. Subsequent experimental work led Hull to modify his theory so that the equation became more complicated. However, his basic idea—that behavior and new learning depend on motivation as well as past habits—dominated psychological theory for many years. At the same time, Hull's conviction that behavior theory could and should be mathematized and rigorously deduced from basic "primitive" concepts and their relationships had a profound effect on his contemporaries.

In reaction to Hull's theory, an opposing view, originally stated by E. C. Tolman, proposed that motivation is based on something more than simple biological needs or drives. For example, curiosity and exploratory behaviors (observed in animals as well as man) are not easily explained in terms of physiological needs or deprivations. Some motivations also appear to be primarily "cognitive" rather than biological in origin. This sort of thinking led psychologists to reexamine the entire concept of motivation and to realize that the forces and goals that drive and direct an organism's behavior can be much more subtle and harder to define than needs and deprivations.

QUESTIONS AND EVIDENCE

1. How do basic needs of the organism affect behavior?
2. What factors influence whether or not a person will do his best?
3. What motives affect how people behave socially?

A motive is a complex disposition of an organism. This means we can't see a motive or point at it as a thing; all we ever see directly is the behavior of organisms. From this behavior we infer that certain dispositions, intentions, or "motivational states" exist in the organism at particular moments in time. Thus, from a series of a person's actions directed toward a goal, such as his entering a restaurant, sitting down at a table, and ordering food, we infer his hunger.

From this point of view, some motives have a less debatable status than others. For example, few would argue with the contention that all of us are motivated by physiological needs or *drives* such as hunger and thirst, a need to sleep regularly, and the need to avoid pain. On the other hand, potential motives such as the need for achievement or the need to be with other people or a need for "independence" seem much

QUESTION   1. HOW DO BASIC NEEDS OF THE ORGANISM AFFECT BEHAVIOR?

HYPOTHESES	CENTRAL CUES	INCENTIVES	AROUSAL	CURIOSITY
DESCRIPTIVE EVIDENCE		ASSESS: relationship between obesity and external cues for eating		
EXPERIMENTAL EVIDENCE	VARY: how food reaches stomach MEASURE: ability to regulate food intake; accuracy of food intake estimates		VARY: hours of food deprivation MEASURE: problem solving performance of chimps	VARY: 1. opportunity for food vs. novelty rewards 2. kinds of novel and familiar stimuli MEASURE: 1. number of visits to food or novelty goal box 2. stimulus preference

more questionable and harder to put your finger on.

In the first part of this unit the less debatable motives are discussed—the basic needs of the organism and how they affect behavior. The evidence drawn on will be mainly on two specific motives—hunger and curiosity. Other basic motives like thirst and sex are treated in more general terms, along with some comprehensive conclusions about motivation.

1. HOW DO BASIC NEEDS OF THE ORGANISM AFFECT BEHAVIOR?

Motives that are impelled by physiological needs such as hunger, thirst, and sex have the least controversial status: no one doubts their effects on behavior. On the other hand, even these motives differ considerably in how they work and in their consequences for the organism. Hunger and thirst, for example, are directly involved in the survival of the organism and must be regularly attended to. Survival of the individual organism does not depend on sex, and an animal can do without sexual gratification for his lifetime—although survival of the species does depend on sex. For this reason sexual behavior in animals is much more governed by opportunity and the presence of *incentives* (such as the presence of a member of the opposite sex) than are other drive states.

Motives impelled by drives such as hunger, thirst, sex, avoiding pain, and the need for sleep can be referred to as *maintenance* motives—needs that must be met and maintained if the organism and his kind are to survive and replenish themselves. Of these basic motives, hunger and thirst have traditionally received the greatest attention from psychologists and physiologists for the simple reason that these motives are the easiest to control and manipulate in the laboratory. Hunger or thirst can be operationally defined as "hours of deprivation" of food or water and measured accordingly.

The traditional question that researchers have asked about hunger is: How does an organism "know" when it should eat? What tells it that food is needed and that it should seek out a meal? The obvious, common-sense response to this question is hunger pangs in the stomach, feelings of emptiness, or, for thirst, a dry feeling in the mouth. This sort of idea—that hunger or thirst begins with cues from different parts of the body—is called the *peripheral*

hypothesis of hunger (or the "dry mouth" hypothesis of thirst). For many years this viewpoint was practically taken for granted as an explanation for why animals begin their eating and drinking behaviors. Along the same lines, it was thought that an animal would stop eating or drinking because of sensations of fullness coming from the stomach.

All of this is plausible enough, and data also support the application of the same notions for human beings. For example, a prominent physiologist, Walter Cannon (1934), conducted experiments in which human subjects swallowed a balloon that could be inflated until it was firm against the walls of the stomach. A small tube connected to the balloon enabled the experimenter to record every instance of stomach contraction. At the same time, the subject was given a telegraph key to press every time he experienced feelings of hunger. The data showed that a subject's

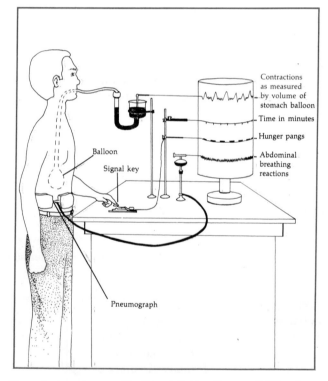

Figure 2. Apparatus used in Cannon's (1934) research. The subject swallowed a balloon that was inflated until it filled the stomach. A tube attached to the balloon allowed the experimenter to record stomach contractions. The subject pressed a telegraph key every time he experienced feelings of hunger. Results showed that the subject's pressing of the key occurred almost simultaneously with the stomach contractions.

pressing of the key occurred almost simultaneously with the contractions of the subject's stomach. Thus, it seems that the hunger drive can be identified as stimuli coming from the contracting stomach of a person, as the peripheral hypothesis would have it.

But like most scientific questions, the matter was by no means settled. Soon data began to emerge for which the peripheral hypothesis could not account. Rats whose stomachs were removed for experimental purposes still displayed hunger behavior like that of normal rats. Further experiments showed that, when the sensory nerves from the stomach to the brain are severed, a rat still exhibits normal hunger behavior.

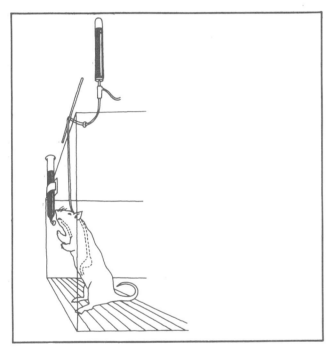

Figure 3. "Electronic esophagus" in rats. In order to compare mouth intake with stomach intake in regulating amount ingested, the apparatus delivers one substance to the mouth and another to the stomach. The rat's esophagus has been surgically arranged so that it will empty through the neck. Adapted from Mook (1963).

New evidence that appears to present exceptions to a hypothesis may still be found to fit under it satisfactorily, either after reinterpretation of the evidence or after slight extension, qualification, or revision of the hypothesis. But when even one solid piece of evidence flatly contradicts a hypothesis, alternatives must be sought. So the evidence countering the peripheral hypothesis led to its replacement.

The *central cues hypothesis* states that basic motive states are under the control of central brain mechanisms that regulate and initiate such behavior as eating or drinking. The idea here is that certain mechanisms in the brain somehow detect when the organism needs food or water. Then these energized mechanisms initiate and terminate feeding and drinking behaviors. For example, some mechanism might keep track of the blood-glucose level in the body, and when the amount of glucose in the blood becomes low enough, the mechanism would initiate feeding behavior. The mechanism might also initiate the hunger pangs that subjects experience as coming from their stomachs.

Do these central mechanisms exist? Investigation of the physiology of hunger in recent years has yielded affirmative evidence. One obvious difficulty in investigating hunger in humans is that information must be obtained without harming the individual or opening his brain. Eliot Stellar and his associates at the University of Pennsylvania devised ingenious ways to study human hunger and eating that sidestepped these difficulties.

EXPERIMENTAL EVIDENCE

Investigators: H. A. Jordan, S. P. Zebley, and E. Stellar
Source, Date: "A Comparison of Voluntary Oral and Intra-
  gastric Food Intake in Man," 1967
Location: University of Pennsylvania
Subjects: College students
Materials: Tube into the stomach; Metrecal

The student subjects regulated a button that, if pressed, would deliver a shot of food (Metrecal) either into the mouth through a straw (oral-intake condition), or directly into the stomach by means of a nasal tube (stomach-intake condition), or both at the same time. Throughout the course of the study, the subjects ate breakfast in this manner daily. The questions were: Would the subject be able to regulate his food intake under all three of these circumstances? How accurately would he be able to estimate his own food intake when he didn't know how fast the Metrecal was delivered to his stomach?

Although subjects could not identify the cues they were using to regulate (their estimates of how much

Metrecal they had taken in were not very accurate), it was found that they were able to control the amount they "ate" in the stomach-intake condition about as well as they did in the oral-intake condition. In other words, subjects were apparently able to control their intake of food even without the normal clues they might get from chewing, tasting, and swallowing the food. In the stomach-intake condition, on the first few days the subjects tended to take in somewhat less Metrecal than normal, but after that there were no differences between the groups. At the same time, the stomach-intake subjects were at a loss to identify either how they did it, or how much they had consumed.

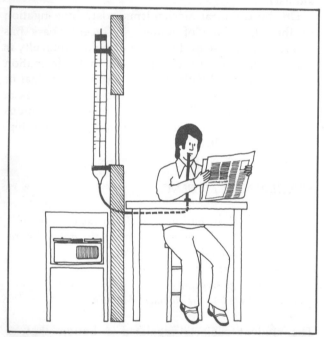

Figure 4. Apparatus that determined if humans could regulate liquid food intake when it was delivered directly to the stomach as well as when it was taken by mouth. Adapted from Stellar (1967).

These results point to "central" mechanisms in hunger. The specific brain mechanisms regulating eating and drinking behaviors in animals such as rats have been identified. The evidence indicates that the *lateral nucleus* of the hypothalamus produces the onset of hunger, while the *ventromedial nucleus* terminates eating. These areas of the brain are often referred to as the "feeding center" and the "satiety center," respectively, also discussed in Unit 34. The specific functions of these areas of the brain can be

demonstrated very dramatically by destroying them: When the satiety center is destroyed, an animal will continue to eat and overeat until it is grossly obese. (Overeating in this way is called "hyperphagia.") When both centers are destroyed, the animal stops eating for good—forever.

Don't get the idea from these results that taste and hunger pangs have no importance, normally. As Stellar says (1967), "hunger and thirst are under the control of a number of physiological factors, contributing to a central neural integrating mechanism that yields the physiological regulations, the motivational control, and perhaps also the subjective experience."

Normally an animal's internal, "central" brain mechanisms are involved in the regulation of its basic maintenance motives, including sex as well as hunger and thirst. The hypothalamus has been implicated in all these mechanisms. A study by Caggiula and Hoebel (1966), for example, showed that electrical stimulation of a certain area of the posterior hypothalamus was able to elicit copulation in male rats, over and over again, as long as the site was stimulated. Eliciting human sexual behavior depends much more on the presence of incentives and learned experiences, but human hypothalamic activity is probably involved in human sexual behaviors (sexual arousal), as it appears to be for other mammals.

Although purely physiological processes are perhaps primary for motivational processes in lower animals, the motivational states of humans might be more dependent on the totality of their learned experiences, associations, and expectations.

Imagine yourself at a friend's house, playing cards with a number of other people. You had a large supper before coming over, so you couldn't possibly need to eat anything more. Besides, you and the others have just devoured (almost unconsciously) a 69¢ bag of potato chips, and you've finished off 16 ounces of your favorite beverage. But when the host starts popping corn and the aroma hits your nose, you feel hungry again, and it also seems you could use a refill for your glass too. The *incentives hypothesis* states that individuals differ in their relative sensitivity to internal drives and external incentives.

As in your experience at a friend's house, the factors involved in eating for humans are very complex and subtle, depending on the interaction of external cues with internal factors. Stanley Schachter of Columbia University, with his associates, has proposed that the cues for the onset of eating may be related to whether people are relatively fat or not. Although normal-size people may be dependent primarily on internal cues ("feeling hungry") to tell them when to eat, obese persons may be more dependent on external environmental cues (smell, taste, seeing other people eat).

DESCRIPTIVE EVIDENCE

Investigators: R. Goldman, M. Jaffa, and S. Schachter
Source, Date: "Yom Kippur, Air France, Dormitory Food and the Eating Behavior of Obese and Normal Persons," 1968
Location: Columbia University
Subjects: 186 male freshman university students
Materials: Records of decisions and weight of students

Freshman students at the university could elect to eat in a dormitory dining hall and to join the dorm's prepay food plan at the beginning of the school year. At any time after November 1, students who so chose could cancel their food contract and receive the remainder of their food money back. Previous student surveys had reported widespread campus dissatisfaction with the quality of dormitory food and service. If this campus opinion was realistically based, according to this hypothesis the obese students, for whom external cues of taste or food quality are most important, should be most likely to drop out of the food plan.

The subjects were divided into obese and normal groups on the basis of university weight records. When the decisions of these groups to continue or drop out of the meal plan were totaled, some 87 percent of the fat freshmen had canceled their food contracts as compared with 67 percent of normal-weight students.

These data support the idea that obese persons tend to rely more on external cues or incentives for the onset of eating than normal-size persons, who rely more on internal cues. More generally, incentives and incentive-instigated motivation are much more relevant for human behaviors, normally, than for the behavior of lower animals. Human motives are adjusted and responsive to the particular situation and

frame of reference encountered by the individual. Further evidence for this generalization appears in other studies of a variety of human motives discussed later in this unit.

Although the motives of organisms depend on, and vary with, particular situations, behavior reveals another property of motivation in the general level of arousal or excitement of organisms. For example, you know there is a difference between the way you act when you are lethargic or half-asleep and the way you act when you are fully awake and alert. Motivation has varying intensity levels, then, regardless of the specific goals toward which behavior is directed. This motivational intensity is often called *arousal*.

At the physiological level, arousal can be measured by recording heart rate, rate of breathing, and perspiration. If arousal is regarded as a general property of motivation, then how is arousal related to behavior—especially to efficiency of learning and performance in various kinds of tasks?

The *arousal hypothesis* states that there is an optimal level of arousal for performance efficiency and that arousal levels that are either too low or too high are detrimental for performance.

Observations made in an experiment with food-deprived chimpanzees presented with a variety of problems requiring insight for solution give some support to this arousal hypothesis, provided that one accepts that short-term food deprivation of these animals corresponds to a low level of arousal and long-term deprivation to a high level.

EXPERIMENTAL EVIDENCE

Investigator: H. G. Birch
Source, Date: "The Role of Motivational Factors in Insightful Problem-Solving," 1945
Location: Yale University and Yerkes Laboratories
Subjects: Six chimpanzees
Materials: Cages; fruit, sticks, and strings

Chimps were deprived of food for periods of two, six, twelve, twenty-four, thirty-six, or forty-eight hours. Then each chimp was put in a cage where a piece of fruit could be seen outside the cage but beyond the chimp's immediate reach. However, the food could be reached with a stick or string. Ten problems were given each chimp by placing sticks in different places:

for example, near the fruit or in the cage but on the side opposite the fruit or out of the chimp's reach but tied to a string within reach.

When motivational arousal was low (two or twelve hours' food deprivation—the twelve hours included a night's sleep and was a normal cycle of no food), the chimps were easily distracted from their problems, and behavior tended to deteriorate into acts that were not directed toward the fruit as a goal. With intense motivation (thirty-six or forty-eight hours' deprivation), the chimps were so obsessed with the fruit that other features of the situation like the sticks, which were necessary for solution, were ignored. In the high-motivation situations, such behaviors as screaming and temper tantrums frequently hindered the animals in their problem solving efforts.

So, the chimps with *intermediate* levels of arousal (six or twenty-four hours of deprivation—the six hours involved skipping the noon meal and more activity, and therefore was more motivating than the twelve hours that included sleep) seemed to perform best on the problems. They were not easily distracted from their task, but at the same time their behavior was characterized by both direction and flexibility. Thus, as D. O. Hebb (1955) and others have proposed, usually an intermediate motivational arousal

level—neither too much nor too little—is optimal for performance on a task.

One of the reasons why arousal is an important concept for motivational theory is that it has a physiological basis quite distinct from specific drives and incentive systems. Starting with a study by Moruzzi and Magoun (1949), many investigators have shown that a particular system of nerve fibers called the *reticular formation* (leading from the spinal column, through the medulla, to the cortex of the brain) has the function of alerting and arousing the organism. These nerve tracts receive sensory input from all the senses, but they have only a general function of "lighting up the cortex." They make the organism more alert, aroused, and sensitive to further changes in the environment. (See Unit 36.)

The function of the reticular formation is now so well established that it is often referred to as the "reticular activating system" of the brain cortex. Its significance for behavior and motivation is that stimuli (such as incentives) have both a *specific* and a *general* effect on motivation. The general effect, which Hebb (1955) called "the vigilance function," is the arousal and activation of the organism. The specific effect, which Hebb called the "cue function," is the effectiveness with which stimuli guide behavior.

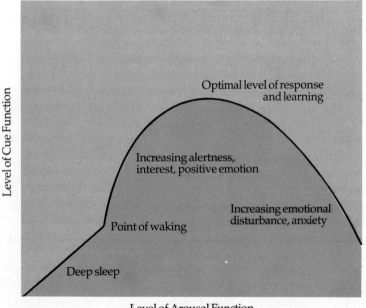

Figure 5. Motivated behavior is dependent upon arousal and regulated by the reticular formation of the brain. Each task has its own optimal level of arousal for efficient responding to the "cue function" of stimuli. Adapted from Hebb (1955).

An inverted U-curve of arousal and performance (Figure 5) portrays the dependence of the potential effect of the cue function of stimuli on the state of the vigilance function at a given moment in time.

The optimal level of arousal will be different for different people, for different tasks, and under different circumstances. The most effective degree of arousal for a football player will probably differ from the most efficient level for a chess player. But on any task or performance too much or too little arousal or alertness will lead to inefficiency. It will limit the degree to which the organism deals with stimuli effectively (the cue function).

You may be wondering if the only "basic motives" of organisms are physiologically oriented. This is not so. Some basic motives are more behavioral or psychological in nature, such as the needs to explore and manipulate the environment and the need for variation in stimulation. These motives can be gathered under the more general notion of curiosity. The *curiosity hypothesis* states that organisms are motivated by needs to explore, manipulate, and understand their environment.

A person entering a strange room will usually look all around himself. When people visit friends in a new city, they will want to explore it; anyway, their friends must show visitors the sights. After being "cooped up" in one place for a while, people crave a change in scene. All of these behaviors can be grouped, at least in part, under the curiosity motive. But how strong is this motive compared with some of the physiological drives? The following experiment with rats supports one answer to this question.

EXPERIMENTAL EVIDENCE

Investigators: B. T. Leckart and K. S. Bennett
Source, Date: "Reinforcement Effects of Food and Stimulus Novelty," 1968
Location: Ohio University
Subjects: 45 male rats from 90 to 120 days old
Materials: A wooden E-shaped maze painted gray with a start box, guillotine doors (so the rat cannot retrace his steps), two goal boxes; feeding dish with food pellets; "manipulable" objects (e.g., colored blocks, threads, whistles, marbles)

The rats were fed normally until seven days before the study began, when they were fed only every twenty-two hours, once a day. This schedule makes rats hungry. Rats were divided into three groups for testing in the E-maze apparatus. For one group, the food-and-novelty group (FN), for each test trial food pellets were available in one goal box of the maze and novel stimuli were available in the goal box at the other end of the maze. The novel stimuli consisted of changing the color and/or texture of the floor and walls of the novel goal box and placing manipulable objects in the box (but no food). For the food group (F), food was available in one goal box, and the other was empty. For the novelty group (N), novel stimuli were available in one goal box, and the other was empty.

In the experiment, the rats were each given thirty trials in the maze, one trial every twenty-four hours. Each rat was placed in the start box and allowed to go through the maze. When a rat entered a novel goal box, it was given ten seconds to explore and then removed. When a rat entered the food goal box, it was removed as soon as it finished eating. When it entered an empty goal box, it was removed after ten seconds.

The number of times each rat in the groups visited a specific kind of goal box was computed. The results showed that group F had a stronger preference for the food side of the maze than did group FN, and that group F's preference for the food side increased over trials (as the rat learned which side had the food), while group FN remained the same. A similar relationship occurred for group N as compared to FN: Rats in group N learned to go to the novelty box. There was no difference in the comparable performance of groups F and N.

These results indicate that learning occurred both when food and when novel stimuli were used as rewards. But food and novelty appear to be equally appealing to the rats, as indicated by the similarity in performance of food-rewarded and novelty-rewarded groups. This equality is even more evident in the finding for the FN group that no preference for either the food goal or the novelty side of the maze developed over the thirty trials—even when all rats in this group were hungry. Apparently, novelty can be as strong a "reward" as food, for hungry rats.

The kinds of new and unfamiliar objects and stimuli that people find novel or that arouse their curiosity vary in many ways. Some people find great novelty in what strikes others as dull. But perhaps human curiosity in its purest form occurs in children whose view of the world is fresh and for whom novelty still abounds. In the following study, the researchers found that children's preferences for novelty tend to be greater for some kinds of stimuli than for others.

EXPERIMENTAL EVIDENCE

Investigators: C. D. Smock and B. G. Holt

Source, Date: "Children's Reactions to Novelty—An Experimental Study of 'Curiosity Motivation,'" 1962

Location: Purdue University

Subjects: 44 pupils (22 of each sex) from the first grade of a rural elementary school

Materials: A mock TV set for presenting film strips, and a button and a lever for controlling presentation

In this study, individual children were given the chance to control what they would see on a TV screen. They were shown that, when they pushed the button, the same picture would reappear on the screen for a quarter of a second. The lever permitted the child to change the picture to a new one. Each child could press the button or lever in any order desired, depending on whether he wanted to see the same picture again or a new picture.

With this procedure, the investigators could measure the children's preferences for novel against familiar pictures, by giving the child choices between the two and noting which he preferred to see repeatedly. Several kinds of novel pictures were shown to the subjects (see Figure 6). For example, in one set of pictures the novel ones had more "ambiguous" or complex shapes than the familiar pictures. For example, an irregular shape (ambiguous) might be paired with a circle (unambiguous). In another set the stimuli varied in their "perceptual conflict." For example, a bird might be paired with an unfamiliar and "incongruous" creature that the child had not seen before. A third set named "conceptual conflict" allowed the subject to view figures in a "meaningful" (logical) sequence against a random sequence.

The children consistently pressed the repeat button for the novel stimuli more often than for the familiar ones. As many studies have found, novelty tended to increase "positive" approach behavior. At the same time, differences were also found between the varieties of novelty used. For example, stimulus

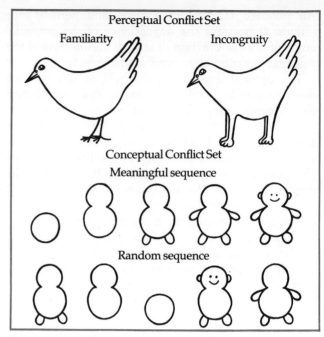

Figure 6. Stimuli used to determine children's preference for novelty. Children consistently preferred the novel and incongruous stimuli to those that were familiar. Adapted from Smock and Holt (1962).

ambiguity generally elicited less curiosity in the children than did the "perceptual conflict" of incongruous objects. Actually, the incongruous objects or creatures were especially preferred by the children. Also, consistent individual differences were displayed in these tasks, with some children considerably less drawn to the novel stimuli than others. Other aspects of children's preferences for novelty are discussed in Unit 24.

Most organisms tend to dislike too much novelty or complexity in the environment. Severe or dramatic changes in stimuli usually produce avoidance or flight responses in animals. These changes may even arouse another, antagonistic motive system—fear and anxiety. Why are stimulus novelty and complexity both approached and avoided by an organism? Speculatively, probably at any given moment some optimal stimulus change exists that the organism will find attractive in relation to its curiosity motivation. In much the same way that levels of arousal will affect performance on a task, levels of stimulus novelty and unfamiliarity can elicit approach or avoidance behavior from an animal. Tiny changes in stimulus level tend to be boring, large changes frightening, and only "intermediate" changes of level attract the animal.

When investigations have furnished evidence for a principle of this kind, it is tempting to apply it more broadly to other kinds of situations, even though solid evidence from the other situations is necessary before such applications can be anything more than mere speculation. The principle of approach or avoidance behavior for different levels of stimulus novelty might, for example, be extended to account for how artistic and aesthetic tastes of most people tend to change over time: Most people have to absorb newness and complexity in small or medium-size doses, and they will turn away from newness in large doses. Music composers, for example, may be too far "ahead of their time"; their contemporaries will reject their musical output as too jarring or complex. The music lover often seeks a new musical experience in what he hears—but not too unfamiliar, not full of things he doesn't understand.

On the other hand, when changes in stimuli are too slight and infrequent, people will be bored and will tend to welcome new elements in their environment. In fact, there is a very real need for stimulation or variation in stimulation. When all such variation is minimized or removed from a person's sensory input, the consequences can be serious. Some of these consequences—which resemble symptoms of true mental disorders—appear in sensory-deprivation studies, discussed in Unit 31.

2. WHAT FACTORS INFLUENCE WHETHER A PERSON WILL DO HIS BEST?

A classic study of motivation was reported in *The Achievement Motive* (1953) by David McClelland, John W. Atkinson, R. A. Clark, and E. L. Lowell. In addition to demonstrating the validity of the concept of achievement motivation, this book showed how human motives could be measured without depending exclusively on a subject's self-reports, what he says verbally about his motives.

The general approach taken by McClelland et al. was to analyze the fantasy behavior displayed by subjects when they were asked to write stories about ambiguous pictures. This approach is embodied in the Thematic Apperception Test (TAT), originally devised by Henry Murray and his associates (1938). Subjects are given a series of ambiguous pictures (involving people alone or in groups) one at a time. They are instructed to make up stories about what the characters in the pictures are doing or what will happen to them. Then the content of the subject's stories is analyzed for "imagery" related to specific motives—achievement, affiliation, power, or whatever.

The *need-for-achievement hypothesis* states that people can be motivated by a need to succeed, excel, and accomplish something.

In analyzing the stories of subjects for need for

QUESTION	2. WHAT FACTORS INFLUENCE WHETHER A PERSON WILL DO HIS BEST?	
HYPOTHESES	**NEED FOR ACHIEVEMENT**	**LEVEL OF ASPIRATION**
DESCRIPTIVE EVIDENCE	ASSESS: relationship of n–Ach scores to occupation some years later	
EXPERIMENTAL EVIDENCE		VARY: levels of expertise in outside reference groups; personal performance ratings MEASURE: level of aspiration

achievement (n-Ach), the researcher looks for themes and images of striving, competing, winning, and succeeding through one's own efforts. The achievement motive's importance is not simply that psychologists can measure it reliably but that these measures predict actual differences between people in behavior. Many investigations after those of McClelland et al. have demonstrated how n-Ach is related to behaviors and other personality dimensions. For example, college students who have a high n-Ach tend to be less conforming and more independent of authority figures, have experienced higher parental expectations, and tend to set more realistic goals than college students who have lower n-Ach scores.

Is a person's n-Ach a motive so basic that it will remain stable, allowing a researcher to use his n-Ach score to predict, on the average, what he does years after taking the test? The long-term experiments required to answer such questions are quite common in psychology. The following investigation of n-Ach scores, for example, was started in the late 1940s and completed in 1965.

DESCRIPTIVE EVIDENCE

Investigator: D. C. McClelland
Source, Date: "Need Achievement and Entrepreneurship: A Longitudinal Study," 1965
Location: Harvard University
Subjects: 55 graduates of Wesleyan University
Materials: N-Ach test scores and later occupation

Would tested n-Ach scores actually predict a person's probable occupation later? In this longitudinal study, McClelland assembled n-Ach scores for 55 college graduates, most of whom were tested within the 1947–1950 period, and graduated around 1950. These graduates' occupations approximately fourteen years after graduation were obtained from the alumni directory. These occupational entries were divided into two groups, business occupations and others. The business occupations were divided into entrepreneurial and nonentrepreneurial categories. An entrepreneurial occupation was operationally defined as one in which the individual has responsibility for initiating decisions, where objective feedback is available on the effects of his decisions, and where the job involves risk or challenge. Examples are selling, operating

one's own business, and being officer of a large company. Typical nonentrepreneurial occupations include data processors, credit and personnel managers, and appraisers.

When these occupational data were compared with the original n-Ach scores obtained fourteen years earlier, it was found that 83 percent of the individuals in entrepreneurial occupations had been high in n-Ach fourteen years earlier, as compared with only 21 percent of those in nonentrepreneurial positions. This, and similar evidence from other sources, led McClelland to conclude that, "at least in the United States and among white college students, males with high n-Ach tend to gravitate toward business occupations of an entrepreneurial nature where they can better satisfy their achievement aspirations." These findings lend credence to the conclusion that n-Ach scores on tests do have predictive validity, even over a period of years.

When people take tests or examinations, some try extra hard and persist in their efforts to do well on the test, whereas other people often get very anxious, or they simply don't try. These differences in behavior might appear to simply reflect differences in n-Ach, but Atkinson and Litwin (1960) were able to show that n-Ach is better viewed as a tendency to approach success, while test anxiety is independent of n-Ach—a motive to avoid failure rather than approach success. For example, people with high n-Ach tend to persist and try hard when taking a test, working throughout the time available. People with high test anxiety (fear of failure), on the other hand, usually get anxious and disturbed when taking a test. Then either their performance suffers or they are unable to continue taking the test and leave the testing situation to reduce their anxiety. Atkinson and Litwin were able to show that people who have high n-Ach and low test anxiety were more willing to take intermediate ("challenging") degrees of risk when competing in a game, compared to other subjects who tended to choose more of the extremes of risk (no risk or a great deal of risk).

A measure that has often been used to assess the level of the goal or achievement for which a person is striving is called the *level of aspiration.* In a typical test of aspiration, the person is given some practice on a task or problem. Then he is asked "what he hopes to attain" on his next performance. Note that "what he hopes to attain" does not mean the same as "what he would like to attain"—because everyone would like to do his best and "win," if given the chance. In other words, "hopes to do" is usually a somewhat more realistic appraisal than "would like." The comparison of a person's actual performance with his level of aspiration gives a "goal discrepancy" score—in other words, a measure of just how realistic the person's level of aspiration or "hopes" are.

The *level-of-aspiration hypothesis* states that people are capable of using either internal (personal) or external (reference group) standards when they set performance goals for themselves in a competitive or achievement situation.

In the following study, the investigators attempted to answer the question of whether people use their own or other people's standards when they estimate their own level of aspiration.

EXPERIMENTAL EVIDENCE

Investigators: D. W. Chapman and J. Volkmann
Source, Date: "A Social Determinant of the Level of Aspira-
tion," 1939
Location: Bennington College and Columbia University, re-
spectively
Subjects: 86 psychology students
Materials: 50-item multiple-choice test of "literary ac-
quaintance," Otis Self-Administering Tests of Mental
Ability—4 forms

Subjects were divided into four groups. One group was told that unskilled workers had reached a certain level of performance on the test (inferior reference group). A second group was told that authors and literary critics had attained the same level (superior reference group). The third group was told that some psychology students reached the same level (similar reference group). A fourth group, serving as a control, received no special instructions.

Results showed that the group that had been presented with literary critics' scores as a reference point had lower levels of aspiration than the group that received the unskilled workers' scores. This latter group also had higher levels of aspiration than did the group that had been given other students' levels of performance. The researchers concluded that the sug-

gested achievements of other groups can change the level of aspiration.

However, the study was not yet over. At this point, all subjects took an intelligence test described as a "test of the ability to solve problems" and then they were again asked to estimate their levels of aspiration for a subsequent test, using their own previous performance as a reference point. Finally, extraneous reference scores were again introduced. This time the levels of aspiration for all groups did not differ from each other. This finding implies that the frame of reference provided by the "other" group that each subject heard about only affected the subject's aspiration level when his own capabilities were largely unknown. But when a person has had some experience on the task or related tasks, he judges his future performance by his own standards and is less influenced by knowledge of how other groups performed.

This study implies that there are both internal and external standards of performance but that the standard that is used depends on the situation and its relationship to a person's past experiences.

Human achievements and advances need not all be attributed to need for achievement. A plausible theoretical discussion by R. W. White (1959) identified a striving for competence, or effectiveness, in dealing with the environment, which he called the "effectance" motive for much of man's adaptations to the world and for his scientific advances. White distinguished the effectance motive from the need for achievement because effectance depends primarily on feelings of satisfaction of the individual gained from having dealt effectively with the environment, but n-Ach is more dependent on results that meet the standards of others. Effectance motivation is closer to the curiosity motive than to the need for achievement or the striving for success.

Identification and discussion of general root motives like curiosity, the need for achievement, and the effectance motive are still highly speculative. Such discussion may be necessary, however, before we can begin to understand the motivation underlying such streams of human endeavor as science, business, medicine, and politics. And just the mention of these activities brings to mind their social motivation, a different set of motives from those that energize individuals.

HYPOTHESES	NEED FOR AFFILIATION	NEED FOR APPROVAL	NEED FOR POWER
DESCRIPTIVE EVIDENCE		ASSESS: relationship of n–App scores to approval-seeking behaviors and other personality dimensions	ASSESS: relationship of n–Power scores to power and control seeking behaviors
EXPERIMENTAL EVIDENCE	VARY: social context MEASURE: n–Aff test scores		

3. WHAT MOTIVES AFFECT HOW PEOPLE BEHAVE SOCIALLY?

Social motives are motivational states associated with how people interact with each other. All of us "need" other people, but the basic ways through which different individuals interact with other persons are diverse, as are their motives in these interactions. Perhaps the most basic social motive of all is what psychologists call the need for affiliation (n-Aff). The *need-for-affiliation hypothesis* states that people can be motivated by a need to be with other people.

Humans are gregarious creatures who need the company of their fellows. N-Aff may have its origin in the need for contact comfort, discussed in Unit 7. Regardless of its origin, in the 1950s psychologists developed ways to measure a person's n-Aff in much the same way as McClelland et al. (1953) developed effective measures for assessing n-Ach, by using the TAT pictures and analyzing stories of subjects for "affiliation" imagery (see Figure 7). Then researchers began to explore the behaviors and personality dimensions to which n-Aff might be related.

N-Aff and other human motives can be viewed in

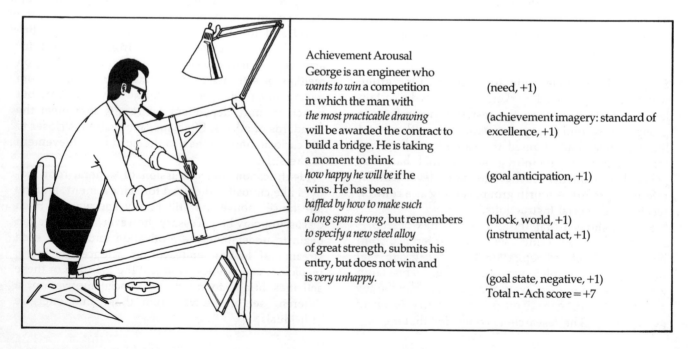

Achievement Arousal
George is an engineer who
wants to win a competition   (need, +1)
in which the man with
the most practicable drawing   (achievement imagery: standard of
will be awarded the contract to   excellence, +1)
build a bridge. He is taking
a moment to think
how happy he will be if he   (goal anticipation, +1)
wins. He has been
baffled by how to make such
a long span strong, but remembers   (block, world, +1)
to specify a new steel alloy   (instrumental act, +1)
of great strength, submits his
entry, but does not win and
is *very unhappy.*   (goal state, negative, +1)
                                                       Total n-Ach score = +7

Affiliation Arousal

George is an engineer who is
working late. He is
*worried that his wife will be
annoyed* with him for neglecting   (affiliation imagery, +1)
her.
She has been *objecting* that   (block, world, +1)
he cares more about his work
than his wife and family.
He seems *unable to satisfy*   (block, personal, +1)
both his boss and his wife,
but he *loves her* very much, and   (need, +1)
will do his best to *finish up*   (instrumental act, +1)
fast and get home to her.   Total n-Aff score = +6

Power Arousal

This is Georgiadis, a
famous architect, who   (prestige of actor, +1)
wants to win a competition   (need, +1)
which will establish who is
the best architect in the world.   (power imagery, +1)
His chief *rival*, Bulakovsky,   (block, world, +1)
has stolen his best ideas, and
he is dreadfully afraid of the
disgrace of losing. But he   (goal anticipation, negative, +1)
comes up with
a great new idea, which absolutely   (instrumental act, +1)
bowls the judges over, and wins!   (powerful effect, +1)
    Total n-Power score = +7

D. C. McClelland, *Assessing Human Motivation,* © 1971 General Learning Corporation. Reprinted by permission.

Figure 7. Typical responses to instructions to write a story about a picture of a man at a drawing board. The story was scored for motives such as achievement, affiliation, and power. Adapted from McClelland (1971).

two contrasting ways. One way to view n-Aff and other motives is as a motivational state that can be "aroused" or activated by the individual's situation. From this point of view, the goal of research is to find what kinds of experiences and circumstances will arouse the n-Aff motive. The second way is to consider n-Aff to be a sort of personality trait that varies among individuals but of which each individual has a normal, typical level. Then some individuals will have a greater n-Aff than others, and this trait is probably related to other discoverable dimensions of personality and experience, such as childhood learning and development. In a study taking the first approach, the investigators tried to show how n-Aff can be temporarily heightened by placing the individual in a specific, affiliation-arousing social context.

EXPERIMENTAL EVIDENCE

Investigators: J. W. Atkinson, R. W. Heyns, and J. Veroff
Source, Date: "The Effect of Experimental Arousal of the Affiliation Motive on Thematic Apperception," 1954
Location: University of Michigan
Subjects: 67 male undergraduates
Materials: 6 pictures as part of an n-Aff test

One group of thirty-one subjects gathered in the dining room of a fraternity house after dinner. For twenty minutes these subjects ranked lists of traits that would make a person likable, described themselves and classmates in terms of these traits, and chose at least three persons as most desirable close personal friends (all this was rationalized as a study in interpersonal relations and group performance). These procedures were designed to *arouse* the n-Aff motive in these subjects. After the twenty minutes, these subjects were tested for n-Aff by using standard pictures and story-writing procedures. The control group of thirty-six subjects were simply given, in a classroom setting, an anagram task (to make as many words out of "generation" as they could), followed by the n-Aff test. The anagram task was used only to reduce or at least minimize the chance of arousing n-Aff feelings.

As predicted, the aroused group obtained substantially greater n-Aff scores than the nonaroused group. More n-Aff themes or "imagery" occurred in the stories of the aroused group—descriptions of charac-

ters in terms of attempts to establish, maintain, or restore positive interpersonal relationships with other people. This kind of study illustrates why a motive such as n-Aff or n-Ach is not merely a personality dimension varying among individuals but is also a motivational state that any individual can experience to some degree, depending on the situation and its ability to arouse this motivational state.

Other studies taking the second approach have implicated n-Aff as an important personality variable that can discriminate between different people and their experiences. For example, Dember (1964) and others have shown that first-born persons tend to have a greater n-Aff than later-borns. How does this difference in n-Aff come about? Most likely it stems from differences in parental treatment of first-borns and later-borns. From this treatment, the first-borns acquire greater dependency—a greater need to be with other people. Being a first-born child means the child never has older siblings, while later-borns always have at least one older brother or sister. In what precise manner birth order can affect n-Aff has not yet been firmly established.

Another social motive that is very familiar to all of us is the need for approval (n-App). The *need-for-approval hypothesis* states that people can be motivated by a need for approval, esteem, and status in the eyes of other people. N-App, and especially the approval of "significant others" or "recognized authorities," probably lies at the basis of conformity. The need for approval from one's peer group—one's equals—is a powerful factor in forming and maintaining group cohesiveness and respect of the group for the individual.

The most concerted attempt to investigate the approval motive has been carried out by Douglas Crowne and David Marlowe and their associates.

DESCRIPTIVE EVIDENCE

Investigators: D. P. Crowne and D. Marlowe
Source, Date: "The Approval Motive," 1964
Location: University of Connecticut and Harvard University, respectively
Subjects: 57 male introductory psychology students
Materials: M-C Social Desirability Scale, simple spool-packing task, a rating questionnaire

As described in *The Approval Motive* (1964), Crowne and Marlowe opened their investigation of n-App with the development of a measure, the Marlowe-Crowne (M-C) Social Desirability Scale. This contains thirty-three items that a subject checks as true (T) or false (F), as applied to himself. Examples of items on the scale and subject responses are:

4. I have never intensely disliked anyone. (T)
7. I am always careful about my manner of dress. (T)
11. I like to gossip at times. (F)
30. I am sometimes irritated by people who ask favors of me. (F)

The rationale behind this scale is that, regardless of whether subjects tell "the truth" or not, those who have a high n-App would try to check the items in the socially approved direction (as indicated by the Ts and Fs above). For example, to item 11, a person with high n-App should answer F because "being gossipy" is not generally approved socially (by other people). If his n-App is really high, he should answer "F" to this item regardless of how gossipy he really is, because his motive is to seek approval, to behave in the socially accepted manner and to avoid disapproval. On the other hand, a person with low or little n-App would be more likely to answer the same item "honestly"—he should respond with what he knows about himself, because he doesn't care that much about whether his responses are socially desirable or not. In this way, according to Crowne and Marlowe's rationale, a relatively high score on the M-C scale ought to indicate high n-App, relative to other people.

To test this assumption, a number of studies were conducted to see if M-C scores could predict approval-oriented behaviors. In one study, for example, fifty-seven subjects took the M-C scale, then were asked to perform a boring, apparently senseless task for twenty-five minutes: they had to pack, unpack, and repack, one at a time, a box of twelve spools, using only one hand and going at their own speed. During this time the experimenter appeared to be taking notes and observing the subject. After this, subjects were asked to respond to a questionnaire that asked them to rate how much they enjoyed the study, whether they thought it might be measuring anything important, whether they would like to be in a similar study, and so on.

Would those individuals who scored relatively high in n-App on the M-C scale express more favorable attitudes toward spool packing than other subjects? The results tended to confirm this prediction. Presumably, some college students are likely to view professors and experimenters as sources of approval gratification, so these students "go out of their way" to please these sources of approval, whether explicitly or implicitly given. Less approval-dependent subjects gave a more realistic appraisal of the study. These and other results support the idea that responding in the "socially desirable direction" on the M-C scale is the expression of a more general need for approval.

In subsequent studies, Crowne and Marlowe showed how n-App is related to a number of behaviors and personality dimensions. Individuals who have high n-App (who score high on the M-C scale) are generally more conforming, cautious, persuadable, conventional, and self-protective than other people. Such traits as caution and self-protection have raised the question whether individuals high in n-App in these tests may not be basically defensive and seeking to avoid disapproval more than to attain approval. There is still room for speculation and further research on n-App. Further relationships between social desirability measures and self-acceptance or self-evaluation are discussed in Unit 15.

Of the many probable social motives, another important one is the need for power (n-Power). The *need-for-power hypothesis* states that people can be motivated by a need to dominate, influence, and control other people.

Obvious examples of historical candidates for high n-Power include Caesar, Genghis Khan, Napoleon, and Hitler. However, these were all highly exceptional people who combined considerable ability with high motivation. To what extent does a need for power motivate ordinary people? Or is it something only such exceptional people have?

One important post-Freudian psychoanalyst and writer, Alfred Adler, believed that the need for power is the basic one that drives human beings in their social interactions. Power is more basic even than Freud's concept of sexual instinct, according to Adler, once a disciple of Freud's. One important concept developed out of Adler's ideas—which is now even a cliché—is the "inferiority complex": feelings of inferiority and weakness that may goad an individual toward more than normal striving to satisfy his need for power.

Adler's hypothesis that the need for power is the most basic human motive has been questioned on several grounds. How could such a broad generalization be verified? Must a power-drive component be observed in every motive to prove his principle? There seem to be many distinct human motivational states, not one, and it is doubtful if power moves people in all of them. Or does Adler mean that other motives are secondary, actually directed toward power? Yet other motives seem to energize people for their own sakes, not for power. Because several interpretations of Adler's power hypothesis are possible, its validity in the broadest sense has been questioned.

On the other hand, there is little doubt that human beings can be motivated by a need for power and that some individuals are apparently more obsessed with satisfying this motive than others. If this is the case, the n-Power motive should be measurable and manifested in individual differences in human behavior.

DESCRIPTIVE EVIDENCE

Investigator: J. Veroff

Source, Date: "Development and Validation of a Projective Measure of Power Motivation," 1957

Location: University of Michigan

Subjects: 34 male campus political leaders and 34 other male undergraduates

Materials: 5 pictures, ratings by students of their own preferences, ratings of classroom behavior by the students' instructors

All subjects were asked to write stories about five pictures that contained scenes involving people, such as two men in a library, an instructor in a classroom, or a political scene. These stories were then scored for n-Power by identifying elements in the stories that were related to "power imagery"—indications that characters in the story were concerned with controlling or influencing other people. The more such indications, the higher a person's n-Power score (in much the same way that scores have been obtained for n-Ach and n-Aff).

The scoring system and use of this particular measure of n-Power was tested or validated in two different ways. First, it was hypothesized that n-Power scores, if they are valid, should be able to discriminate between the subjects who were campus leaders (who, by definition, are interested in influencing others) and those subjects who were students but not leaders. This prediction was confirmed, with the actual leaders scoring higher in n-Power than the other subjects.

The second way of validating the n-Power instrument or scoring system was to look to individual differences in behavior among the thirty-four non-leaders. If the n-Power scores are valid, measuring what they aim to measure, differences in scores should be related to the frequency of power-related behaviors in these students, as rated by other independent sources and (unknowingly) by the students themselves. Several such relationships were obtained in this study. Those students with higher n-Power scores were rated higher by their instructors on how frequently they argued in class and how frequently they tried to convince others of their points of view in the classroom. The students who had higher n-Power scores also showed, relative to the other students, a stronger interest in the "job satisfaction of being a leader," as opposed to greater satisfaction with other aspects of having a job.

These early findings helped validate n-Power as a measurable, useful motive and led to a number of other studies that demonstrated relationships between tested n-Power and behavior. For example, Veroff (1958) found that fathers who have high tested n-Power motive are more likely to treat their sons affectionately than fathers who have low tested n-Power motive. What does this relationship between high n-Power and affectionate behavior mean? It might mean that high n-Power fathers use their affection for their sons to try to influence them. Veroff also found that a mother's affection for her son is not related to n-Power but was related to n-Affiliation. In another study, Veroff, Atkinson, Feld, and Gurin (1960) found higher n-Power scores in groups that have been socially deprived, such as blacks and people with lower socioeconomic status. The need-for-power motive may develop more readily with severe deprivation.

When n-Power is carried to its extreme, more violent and coercive attempts at control and influence may be used by a person. Extreme n-Power might be called a "need for aggression," or n-Agg. Because this topic is so important for behavior and its consequences both for the high n-Agg person and his victims, aggression and related factors are treated in more depth in Unit 4.

Psychologists, then, are investigating many, presumably distinct human motives. It is natural to try to find some order in this diversity, an order relating all the motives to each other or fitting them together. Two theoretical ideas have attempted to tie together the whole range of human motives into some sort of understandable pattern or system.

One integrating idea, originally suggested by the social psychologist Gordon Allport, is called the "functional autonomy" of motives. When something is autonomous, it controls itself, without depending primarily on something else. "Functional autonomy" means that, after a motive has been repeatedly aroused and involved in behavior, the motive may develop autonomy and determine or influence behavior on its own, quite independently of the original causes for the arousal of the motivational state. Originally, for example, a person may be motivated to seek money as a means to gain food, shelter, and necessities. However, as money is acquired and used by a person, the incentive to acquire more of it may begin to operate on its own. The individual will begin to acquire more and more money "for its own sake."

Functional autonomy is one idea that can help explain how human beings can come to be dominated by particular kinds of incentives. This person has a passion for collecting stamps, that one is a gourmet, another is stirred by religious motives and concern for others. Incentive systems such as these may develop functional autonomy as the individual acquires habits and points of view that are centered around certain specific classes of incentives. These incentives act "autonomously" to influence behavior because they are no longer associated with the original causes for the specific motivational state.

Allport's concept of functional autonomy may also be useful in understanding why people who are fundamentally similar may react very differently to specific motivational incentives. The role of learned experiences in the development of functional autonomy cannot be denied.

The second integrating idea is that motives can be arranged in an ascending *hierarchy* from stronger or more basic kinds of needs to weaker, less frequent ones. Abraham Maslow, a humanistic psychologist, has made a statement of this idea (1954). A summary of his hierarchical arrangement of human needs and motives appears in Figure 8.

Data on "Hierarchy of Needs" from *Motivation and Personality* by A. H. Maslow (Harper and Row, 1954).

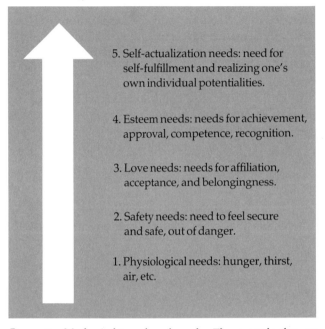

5. Self-actualization needs: need for self-fulfillment and realizing one's own individual potentialities.

4. Esteem needs: needs for achievement, approval, competence, recognition.

3. Love needs: needs for affiliation, acceptance, and belongingness.

2. Safety needs: need to feel secure and safe, out of danger.

1. Physiological needs: hunger, thirst, air, etc.

Figure 8. Maslow's hierarchy of needs. Those needs that are lower in the hierarchy must be fulfilled before higher needs become dominant as motivators.

In a difficult environment, the lower needs in this hierarchy will tend to dominate behavior and fill up a person's time. In other words, when food, safety, and love are difficult to achieve, the pursuit of these goals will be literally all a person has time for, and the remaining needs will not be very significant for the individual. As the satisfaction of the lower needs tends to become easier or even to be taken for granted, the higher-order needs on the hierarchy will then be more significant for behavior and for the individual's values.

A person's aesthetic needs and the need for self-actualization and fulfillment can thus best be served when his lower needs are no longer a problem. The invention and creativity that come with aesthetic, cognitive, and self-actualization needs require free time, when a person is not entirely devoted to the pursuit of food, safety, love, and esteem. As Aristotle said, the good life requires leisure.

As a theory, Maslow's scheme is not supported by much hard data. But it is a thought-provoking arrangement of motives that may help us understand the relationship between motives and the opportunities that the environmental conditions afford the motives. This kind of hierarchical arrangement of motives may also have practical implications for "real world" enterprise and activity, especially in the workaday world of labor and management. For instance, McGregor (1960) has noted that the hierarchy of motives—if it really exists—may indicate much about the kinds of working conditions for which labor and management should strive—a setting in which Maslow's higher-order motives can be activated to produce greater individual self-satisfactions, creativity, and production.

On the other hand, Maslow's scheme also paints a rather optimistic picture of human beings, with emphasis on "healthy" and normal motives that are acceptable to society. Where, one might ask, are the needs for power and aggression in Maslow's scheme? The frequency and importance of these needs for human behavior cannot be denied and should not be ignored. The conclusion that needs for violence, aggression, and power are somehow pathological and "sick" and that these needs ought to be regarded as exceptional and isolated events simply does not square with what we know about history and psychology. There is no reason to think that man is inherently "predatory" and aggressive. At the same time, predatory and aggressive motives of individual human beings occur with enough frequency and regularity to make it seem very optimistic indeed to regard them as exceptional or unimportant.

This survey of motivation has emphasized the variety and multiplicity of motives, especially motives that have distinct importance for human beings. This unit has attempted to show that the concept of motivation, which exists at all levels of psychological theory—physiological, psychological, individual, and social—presents many complicated, puzzling and worthwhile questions.

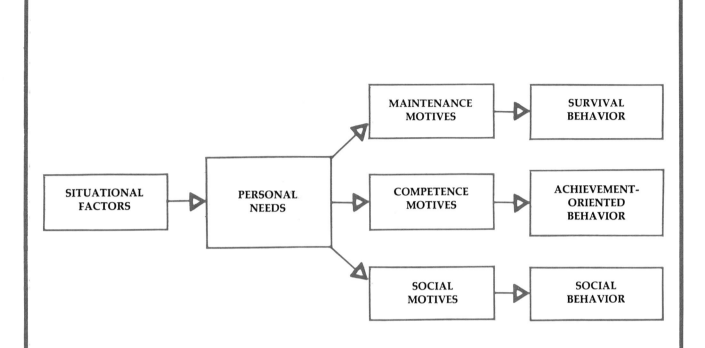

PUTTING IT TOGETHER: Motivation

The incentives for motivated behavior are usually provided by *situational factors.* Good food, high grades and nice people vary in their incentive value for motivating the behavior of different individuals according to their *personal needs.*

Each need, including that of satisfying curiosity, initiates a state of arousal which provides the drive for goal-oriented behavior. Each situation requires behavior for which there is an optimal amount of arousal. More or less than this optimal amount usually makes for poorer performance on the task.

There are apparently complex biological mechanisms which provide central cues through the central nervous system that initiate *maintenance motives,* such as hunger, thirst, sex, sleep, pain avoidance, and stimulation, all of which lead to basic *survival behavior.*

Competence motives stem from a need for achievement and vary according to each individual's level of aspiration, which may be determined from personal or from reference group standards. They lead to *achievement-oriented behavior.*

Social motives stem from needs for affiliation, approval, and power. They lead to such *social behavior* as seeking the company of others, seeking approval and respect, and attempts to influence and control others.

1. WHAT'S ACCEPTED . . .

1. Eating and drinking are primarily regulated by central brain mechanisms.
2. Basic maintenance motives depend on physiological mechanisms but are greatly modified by experience and learned preferences and incentives, especially in higher animals.
3. An optimal level of physiological arousal for performing a task exists, and levels that are too low or too high contribute to inefficiency of performance.
4. Curiosity is an important motive.
5. Need for achievement is a significant individual motive related to success and performance in many kinds of endeavors.
6. Level of aspiration can be influenced by both internal and external standards of performance.
7. Needs for affiliation, approval, and power can be aroused in people by the particular situations in which they become involved.

2. WHAT'S DEBATED . . .

1. How arousal and stimulus novelty and complexity are related.
2. How individual and social motives of different people are developed and strengthened during childhood.
3. To what extent such concepts as "functional autonomy" and Maslow's hierarchy of motives characterize behavior.

The material on hunger in this unit may be of particular interest to the many Americans who are overweight or dieting. We are, in fact, the most overweight society on earth, thanks both to our superabundance of food and our consumption of large quantities of carbohydrates and other fattening substances. Surveys have shown that at least one American in four is concerned about excess weight.

Surprisingly, there are some places in the world where obesity is highly valued. When missionaries first penetrated the jungle regions of central Africa, they reported finding tribal chiefs proudly married to wives who were so fat that they could hardly walk and had to be carried over distances of more than a few yards. Even today, female obesity is equated with beauty among some central African peoples. In parts of the Congo, for example, young girls are taken before puberty to "fatting houses"—special compounds where they are segregated from the rest of the tribe and systematically fed on the most fattening foods available. In due course, the plump maidens are produced for the acclaim and admiration of the young men, who compete with one another for the favors of the fattest girls.

The fact that obesity is valued in other cultures is of little consolation to the overweight person in the United States. Our social attitudes are not favorable to the obese, and fat people are usually considered less attractive than normal or even thin people. The objections to obesity are not merely cosmetic ones: they are based on health considerations as well. The overweight person runs a significant risk of heart disease—partly because of the excessive deposits of fat within the cardiovascular system, and partly because of the strain imposed on the heart, which must pump blood through a much greater body volume than normal.

How can obesity be controlled? Our growing knowledge of the physiological mechanisms involved in hunger offers one possibility, the development of a hunger "contraceptive," which might balance our system in favor of the ventromedial nucleus of the hypothalamus. Just as our knowledge of the menstrual cycle and hormonal changes involved in conception had made possible the birth control pill, so might our knowledge of the physiological basis for hunger lead to a pill that could influence the hypothalamus where feelings of hunger appear to originate and terminate.

Until such a pill is developed, the fat person will probably have to rely on motivation to cut down on excessive eating. Again, knowledge derived from psychological research can be useful in a diet program. We know, for example, that the hunger pangs that result from stomach contractions are learned, and should therefore be able to be unlearned. When we suddenly stop eating, intense hunger pangs continue for about three days. But thereafter they cease, even though we are in greater physical need of food than before. The body has simply learned that food is not available. A crash diet as drastic as this abrupt starvation is not recommended, as it can have serious side-effects. But a person wishing to cut down on food would be wise to concentrate on eating at irregular intervals, rather than simply reducing the amount of food taken at regular meals. If the body continues to expect regular meals, the hunger pangs will recur every mealtime. But if the body learns not to anticipate meals, the pangs of hunger tend to be less frequent and severe.

University of Michigan psychologist James V. McConnell has suggested several means by which a fat person may improve motivation to reduce food intake. Among the steps he recommends are these:

1. Begin by recording everything you eat for a period of a week. Note the circumstances that prompted the eating, and check to see who else is present at the time of eating and what their reactions are. Often, McConnell believes, the fat person may be encouraged to eat by friends or relatives. By analyzing the record of the week, the dieter can isolate particular events or people that stimulate eating behavior. This would be in keeping with Schachter's proposition that obese people are more dependent on external environmental influences than are normal size people.
2. Write down all the rewards and pleasures that would result from weight loss. A precise notion of these advantages serves as a better incentive than a hazy desire to lose weight.
3. Change your mealtimes to a very irregular schedule some weeks before the dieting starts.

This will greatly reduce your desire to eat.
4. When you start the diet program, make a large chart to record each aspect of daily routine, including exercise. Post the chart where others can see it, and arrange for them to give you regular rewards—a pat on the back or word of congratulation will do—every time you meet the daily goals you have set. The graph itself gives feedback that provides motivation, and the approval of others acts as further positive reinforcement, making relapse into overeating much less likely.
5. Don't expect too much too fast. Many dieters are too optimistic in the early stages of their programs, and failure to meet their impossible goals has a very negative effect on continued motivation.
6. It might be a good idea to discuss the problem of obesity with a psychologist as well as a medical practitioner. Many obese people are unconsciously motivated to remain fat because they find fatness rewarding for some reason, or because some person close to them unconsciously wishes them to remain fat.

The six point program above would also seem a reasonable way for smokers to cut down or stop the smoking habit.

In time, psychologists and medical researchers will probably discover simpler ways of reducing excess weight in obese people, perhaps by some appropriate influence on the hunger centers in the brain. Until then, however, the traditional method of dieting will remain in vogue—and the better the motivation, the greater the success will be.

Unit 22

Concept Learning

OVERVIEW

This unit presents a brief but modern view of a widely-studied area of human learning: the learning of concepts. The first part of the unit compares older and more recent views of the concept learning process. Then factors involved in the developmental changes in the concept learning of children are described. Finally, work with computers suggesting analogies for human concept learning is presented.

UNIT OUTLINE

DEFINITION AND BACKGROUND
1. *Definition:* concept learning is the process of classifying objects, events, or abstractions according to common attributes and the rules for applying these classifications correctly to the surrounding world.
2. *Background:* Jerome Bruner (1915–   ).

QUESTIONS AND EVIDENCE
1. How do people learn concepts?
Hypotheses:
   a. *Passive-learning:* concept learning takes place rather passively by means of simple discrimination learning reinforced by reward or knowledge of results. **375**
   b. *Active-testing:* concepts are learned by actively testing for some common attribute(s) of all the things to which each particular concept applies. **376**
2. What developmental changes take place in the learning of concepts?
Hypotheses:
   a. *Strategy-change:* as children grow older, they acquire new skills that change both the rate and the manner of concept learning. **378**
   b. *Linguistic-influence:* concept learning is influenced by the acquisition of language and by characteristics of a particular language. **380**

IMPORTANT CONCEPTS

	page
associationism	372
concept learning	372
conservative focusing	374
feedback	376
focus gambling	374
reinforcement	375
strategy	374
transposition	380

Concept learning begins with identification of specific attributes of the concept to be learned.

As we develop we test our understanding of concepts and receive feedback.

Learning the appropriate rules for concepts at higher levels of abstraction helps us to classify and understand order in the world about us.

DEFINITION AND BACKGROUND

During the span of years from infancy to adulthood the developing human being learns a great number of concepts. The DEFINITION of concept learning is *the process of classifying objects, events, or abstractions according to common attributes and the rules for applying these classifications correctly to the surrounding world.* Once we have acquired concepts, we take them for granted and use them habitually without any hesitation. Although the ability to use spoken language for naming concepts is considered to be uniquely human, lower animals can distinguish between such concepts as, for example, "triangle" and "square." Chimpanzees can learn to use irregularly shaped plastic chips as "words" to name such concepts as "fruit." A concept has great adaptive and communicative value for the organism because it is transituational—each classification can be used in many different places, at different times, sometimes for objects that seem superficially to have little in common. Through conceptualization, we bring order to our individual universe.

The FOCUS of this unit is on the processes by which such classifications and rules for their use are acquired. Some of the ways in which this process evolves as children grow into adulthood are also discussed. This process of learning concepts is intimately tied to such other topics in child development as language acquisition, children's thinking, and memory, which are discussed in more detail in other units (14, 16, and 25, respectively).

BACKGROUND: JEROME BRUNER (1915–   )

The modern psychological study of how concepts are learned has roots deep in the philosophical doctrine of *associationism.* The tradition began with the writings of the British philosopher John Locke in the seventeenth century. Arguing that the mind could be analyzed by analogy to chemical processes, Locke considered ideas or "elements of consciousness" and sensations to be the "atoms" of mental activity and claimed that these atoms combine (become "associated") to form larger units much like chemical compounds. Once two ideas were associated, when one of them came to mind it would tend to evoke the other. Other British philosophers, such as Berkeley, Hume, and John Stuart Mill, developed more detailed descriptions of what they believed this process must be like. Among the principles of associationism were *contiguity* (ideas that occur close together in time tend to become associated), *similarity* (ideas that are similar are more likely to be associated than dissimilar ones), and *repetition* (the more frequently ideas occur together, the more strongly they become associated).

Rejecting explanations based on innate ideas and biology, associationism emphasized the roles of experience and learning in mental activity. Locke pictured man's mind as a sort of *tabula rasa,* or "blank slate" on which experience writes itself. Consequently, associationism is primarily a doctrine of passive learning in which associations are determined entirely by one's environmental experiences, taking no account of conscious "forming" or "planning" as a part of learning. In America, the roles of experience and learning in the development of concepts were investigated by learning theorist Clark Hull in 1920.

This older, *passive* view of learning concepts has been supplemented in modern psychology by the view that such learning is a more *active* process of

Figure 1. Jerome Bruner, an innovative theorist in cognitive and child psychology, whose ideas on child development have influenced educators and psychologists.

searching for a rule defining the concept rather than simply associating similar stimuli with naming or labeling responses. The pioneer work in active learning is quite recent. The classic research was conducted by Bruner and his associates Jacqueline Goodnow and George Austin during a five-year cognition project in the Laboratory of Social Relations at Harvard University. Their summary of results from this project and of other new research was reported in *A Study of Thinking* (1956).

Bruner and his associates started with the observation that the ability to categorize, or place in categories or classes, is a crucial feature of human behavior. For example, it is known that about 7 million different colors can be discriminated by human beings. Yet if we were to respond to each subtle shading with a different label, we would be overwhelmed in characterizing our environment in just this small area alone. Categorizing greatly reduces the complexity of our responses to our surroundings. Instead of 7 million color names, most of us manage with a dozen or so.

Bruner and his associates conducted studies to probe the underlying psychological processes that occur as subjects learn to categorize stimuli. In one experiment, student subjects were presented with the array of stimuli shown in Figure 2. The eighty-one shapes in this figure can each be described as a combination of one value from each of four attributes: shape within the box (plus sign, circle, or square are "values"), color of the shape (green, red, or black), number of shapes on the box (one, two, or three), and number of lines in the border of the box (one, two, or three). The subjects were told that some of the boxes were examples of a concept and others were not. Their task was to learn a way of classifying the eighty-one shapes into these two groups.

The process began when each subject was presented with one of the shapes and told it was an example of the concept. The subject then chose one of the remaining shapes and asked the experimenter if it too was an example of the concept. The experimenter replied "yes" or "no" according to a rule known initially only to himself, much like the children's game of "20 Questions." The process continued until the subject had learned the rule.

Bruner, Goodnow, and Austin discovered that the subjects' choices showed evidence of consciously

Figure 2. To study strategies that humans use to classify information, Bruner and his associates used arrays of stimuli combining one of three values (plus sign, circle, or square) from each of four attributes (shape, color, number of shapes, and number of border lines). Adapted from Bruner et al (1956).

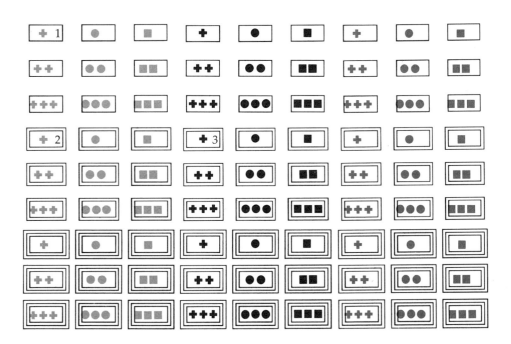

planned, highly organized strategies for obtaining the necessary information by means of the fewest possible questions. Different subjects used different approaches, but all of them seemed to rely on some strategy for learning the rule.

One strategy was called *conservative focusing.* As an example, suppose that the experimenter's rule is "plus signs are examples of the concept" and that he initially selects the pattern labeled 1 in Figure 2. A subject using conservative focusing will then select a pattern that differs in only *one* way from this example—say, pattern 2—and ask if this too is an example of the concept. Because it is, the subject now knows that the characteristic or attribute that changed—in this case the number of lines bordering the figure—cannot be a part of the rule defining the concept. The attribute that changed is simply irrelevant. If the second pattern had not been an example, then the subject would know that the feature he changed was in fact the basis of the rule and would have solved the problem.

On the second trial, the subject again selects a pattern that differs in only one way—say pattern 3—and is informed that this too is an example of the concept. Now he knows that neither color nor number of border lines is relevant. The process continues until the subject selects a different shape, at which point he will learn that the rule defining the concept is that "plus signs are instances." On each trial the subject has made a small step toward eliminating rules that are not applicable. He "focused" in on the relevant attribute. But his strategy was "conservative" because he changed only one attribute at a time.

Bruner, Goodnow, and Austin also found subjects who were willing to change more than one attribute at a time and termed this strategy *focus gambling.* If the selected pattern was an example of the concept, the lucky subjects eliminated two attributes in only one trial. If the pattern was not an example of the concept, the gamble failed, and they had to determine which of the two attributes that they had changed was in fact the critical one.

The discovery of these and other strategies suggested that at least some concept learning was an active process of searching for a rule defining the concept. Other concept learning might be simply a passive process of associating stimuli with naming responses, but this could not account for the use of strategies.

This identification of strategies for concept learning has had a great impact on the study of human learning and on the way in which psychologists view consciousness as a part of human behavior. The use of strategies strongly suggests that at least a part of learning may be qualitatively different from animal learning, not just more of the same. All human learning, or even all concept learning, need not depend on strategies.

Exploring the new areas for research opened by the pioneering work of Bruner, Goodnow, and Austin, cognitive psychologists have learned many more exciting things about human thought processes in the last twenty years than was learned during centuries of prescientific philosophizing. The study of human learning of concepts may hopefully someday lead to improved methods of teaching, problem solving, and other intellectual tasks.

QUESTIONS AND EVIDENCE

1. How do people learn concepts?
2. What developmental changes take place in the learning of concepts?

QUESTION	1. HOW DO PEOPLE LEARN CONCEPTS?	
HYPOTHESES	**PASSIVE LEARNING**	**ACTIVE TESTING**
DESCRIPTIVE EVIDENCE	ASSESS: ability to distinguish common features	
EXPERIMENTAL EVIDENCE		VARY: problem sequences and knowledge of results MEASURE: retention of subject's "hypothesis"

1. HOW DO PEOPLE LEARN CONCEPTS?

Any *concept* can be thought of as an attribute, or characteristic, of the object or event to be categorized that can be used to decide whether or not the object is an example of the concept. Concepts can embody any level of abstraction. Some concepts rest on extremely simple rules: "Any plane figure (or shape) with three sides is a triangle, but anything with a different number of sides is not." But most of them are more complicated: "Anything that has dry, scaly skin and a well-defined neck and that lays large, shelled eggs on land is a reptile; anything else is not." Sometimes the rule cannot be stated with any precision: Biologists, for example, are unable to agree on the exact rule for dividing living creatures into plants and animals because of the large number of organisms that have characteristics of both groups. The higher the level of abstraction, the less people can agree on classification rules. Thus there is little agreement in the case of concepts such as God, happiness, good. Nevertheless, it is generally accepted that some attribute or a relationship between several attributes can logically be used to define a rule for any concept.

Concepts are obviously crucial not only to verbal communication but also to thinking. The strategies studied by Bruner, Goodnow, and Austin are essentially techniques for developing appropriate concepts. Some psychologists have studied the more passive role of reinforcement in learning concepts; others have examined the more active process of strategy testing used in developing them, like the strategies used by the subjects in Bruner's experiment. The *passive-learning hypothesis* states that concept learning takes place rather passively by means of simple discrimination learning reinforced by reward or knowledge of results. The emphasis this hypothesis places on reinforcement may be useful in explaining the more concrete concept learning characteristic of some lower animals and of very young children. Rats can be taught to discriminate triangles from other symbols in order to find food, thereby learning the concept of triangularity. Monkeys will learn to choose the one odd object out of three when it is rewarding to do so (oddity concept). Concept learning can be achieved with lower animals if the level of abstraction is low enough and the rewards are worth it. However, many behavior psychologists believe, as Clark Hull did, that discrimination learning and reinforcement are largely responsible for concept learning in adult human beings, as well.

DESCRIPTIVE EVIDENCE

Investigator: C. L. Hull
Source, Date: "Quantitative Aspects of the Evolution of
    Concepts," 1920
Location: University of Wisconsin
Subjects: College students
Materials: Pseudo-Chinese characters

The subjects were shown twelve sets of pseudo-Chinese characters, each of which contained twelve different characters. Each character was given a unique nonsense name, and characters that had the same name had similar features in all the sets. Thus the word "li" was to be applied to all characters containing one particular basic feature (see Figure 3). Hull's subjects did not know Chinese, so he was certain that new concepts were being learned.

Feature	Set 1	Set 2	Set 3	Set 4	Set 5	Set 6
Li	力	的	勃	豺	帄	执 勢

Figure 3. Hull believed that common attributes could be discriminated even in unfamiliar figures through systematic reinforcement. Can you distinguish "li" in each character? Adapted from Hull (1920).

On each trial a subject was shown each of the twelve characters and asked to name them. His response was reinforced by his being told whether his naming was correct or incorrect but he was never given any information regarding the specific attribute that determined the correct name. Each set was practiced until the subject could give the correct names for all twelve characters in it. Then the next set was presented and the process repeated. The measure of concept learning was the percentage correct on the first trial of each new set.

This measure jumped from 8 to 27 percent on the average between the first set and the second, from 27 to 38 percent between the second and the third set, and so forth. By the sixth set, 56 percent of the first-trial responses were correct. As they went from set to set, subjects clearly showed a gradual improvement in their ability to apply the names consistently to characters having appropriate attributes.

At the end of the experiment, subjects were asked to sketch the component that defined each name. Many who had been able to apply a name correctly were unable to draw the basic attribute of the character. Hull introduced the term "functional concept" to describe a rule that is applied correctly even when it cannot be drawn or verbally expressed in general terms. His subjects had learned such functional concepts. In his view, the basic attribute became, by means of systematic reinforcement, a *discriminated stimulus* for the response of naming the character. This process, like conditioning, was assumed to involve no active or intentional effort on the part of the learner, having been absorbed passively and become, by reinforcement, nearly automatic.

Hull's interpretation implied that all concepts somehow "exist"—in a timeless world of ideal logical entities, perhaps—even when they cannot be verbalized.

Perhaps the conditions of Hull's experiment were such that conscious processes were not apparent or did not need to be involved. Thus, the common attributes of the very intricate pseudo-Chinese characters he used are difficult to sketch, to say nothing of the problems involved in describing them verbally, but his subjects could still discriminate them from each other and name them. In any event, Hull did not believe that active, conscious or verbal processes were necessary in establishing concepts for the particular

sets of stimuli in his experiment.

Conscious processes were the major concern of Bruner's studies, however, and these studies provided support for another hypothesis. This *active-testing hypothesis* states that concepts are learned by actively testing for some common attribute(s) of all the things to which each particular concept applies.

In Bruner's experiments, each guess the learner makes about what attributes define the concept is termed his "hypothesis." Learning proceeds by a process of testing a series of hypotheses. When the feedback from the environment is consistent with the hypothesis, it is retained; when the feedback contradicts a hypothesis, it is rejected, and a new one is explored. In this model of concept learning the learner is seen as consciously and actively solving a problem by trying out one hypothesis after another, rather than simply as being conditioned passively by attributes that the learner cannot sketch or describe in words.

Evidence for this kind of active hypothesis testing in the learning of concepts comes out clearly in an experiment in which the materials used were much simpler than those Hull had used. In scientific investigations, changes in some feature of the set-up of the experiment (in the materials, perhaps, or the instructions) will often yield quite different results that require making new hypotheses, as in the following case. Concept learning, like other topics, appears to have numerous facets that are gradually revealed by different kinds of investigations.

EXPERIMENTAL EVIDENCE

Investigator: M. Levine
Source, Date: "Hypothesis Behavior by Humans during Discrimination Learning," 1966
Location: New York State University, Stony Brook
Subjects: 80 introductory psychology students
Materials: Multidimensional stimuli

On each trial of the experiment, the subject was shown a card containing two letters, one of which was always an instance of the concept and the other was not. The letters differed in *color* (black or white), *shape* (X or T), *position* (left or right side of card), and *size* (large or small). These varying common attributes are easy to describe verbally, as opposed to the complex common attributes used by Hull. The subjects were instructed that the rule they had to learn was based on one of these attributes—for example, "Black letters are examples of the concept." Because there were four dimensions with two values each, there were eight possible hypotheses that might be "correct": black, white, X, T, left, right, large, or small (Figure 4).

On the first trial the experimenter informed the subject that his choice was "right" or "wrong" according to a prearranged schedule and regardless of the subject's actual response. Then four blank, or uninformed, trials were given. On each of these the subject had to choose which letter he thought was the instance of the concept but was not informed if his choice was "right." Following the blank trials, a single trial was given on which his choice was again reinforced, acknowledged as "right" or "wrong." Then four more blank trials were given, followed by one informed trial, and so on for sixteen trials.

The uninformed or blank-trial cards were selected so that for each of the eight possible hypotheses a different pattern of choices would be made. For example, if the subject began with the hypothesis "black," the pattern of choices would be X, T, t, x (see column headed "Black" in Figure 4); if the hypothesis was "right," then the pattern of choices would be t, T, X, x. Because each hypothesis generates a unique se-

quence of choices, the subject's pattern of responses during the blank trials could be used to determine which hypothesis he was using.

The data from the blank trials indicated that 92.4 percent of the subjects were testing hypotheses; that is, their response patterns during blocks of blank trials matched the pattern for one of the eight possible hypotheses. In 97.5 percent of the cases, the subjects' choice on the trial following a block of blank trials could be predicted from the inferred hypothesis.

Furthermore, a subject's hypothesis was maintained from one block of blank trials to the next if he was told "right" on the reinforced trial and his hypothesis was changed only if he was told "wrong." In 95 percent of the cases where a subject was informed he was "right" during an outcome trial, his hypothesis was maintained during subsequent trials, and in only 2 percent of the cases was a hypothesis maintained if the subject was informed that his hypothesis was "wrong."

This sort of patterning of responses is the natural form for the testing of a common feature. When the correct feature is finally tested, all responses based on it will be correct and that hypothesis will be reinforced and maintained indefinitely.

This active hypothesis testing model is now widely

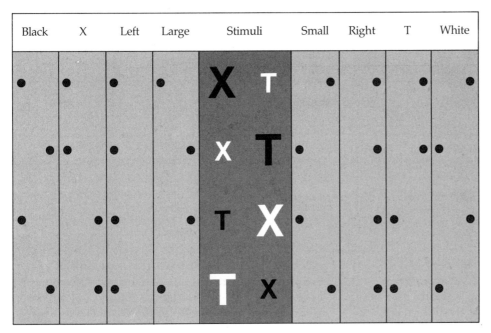

Black	X	Left	Large	Stimuli	Small	Right	T	White

Figure 4. The experimenter can predict which of eight concept "hypotheses" a subject is testing, by examining his sequence of dots. Adapted from Levine (1966).

accepted as an explanation of how concept learning occurs, but psychologists are still investigating the details of the process. For example, they are studying whether more than one hypothesis can be tested at once, how more complicated rules are learned, and what sorts of strategies subjects use to test hypotheses. None of this research is likely to overthrow the view of concept learning as an active process at least in adults.

But this technique is probably too sophisticated to explain all concept learning. Perhaps the passive learning model is sufficient to explain some concept development. It may be that most concept learning is more actively cognitive than Hull found, but still dependent on reinforcement, as Hull emphasized, during the process of selecting the correct hypothesis.

In concept learning by hypothesis testing a simple psychological process appears that seems to be analogous to scientific investigation. You are familiar with the ways in which all kinds of hypotheses are tested in terms of either descriptive or experimental evidence furnished by studies and investigations. The product or outcome of such testing is usually a supported or unsupported hypothesis. And hypotheses can be thought of as statements of complex concepts or statements of relations between concepts or variables. In these terms, the forming and testing of scientific hypotheses may be refined and elaborated processes of natural human concept learning.

change from childhood to adolescence and adulthood, with the development of new traits, abilities, and skills. Such changes are commonly recognized, for example, in discussions about when it is that people reach the "age of reason" and when they become "mature enough to vote." Ability to think abstractly, to reason logically, and to plan and guide one's activities accordingly seem to develop with age. It would not be surprising, then, to find that even the very simple ability to learn concepts, one element in the whole thought process, changes and develops with age.

The *strategy-change hypothesis* states that as children grow older, they acquire new skills that change both the rate and the manner of concept learning. The manner in which concept learning changes has been revealed by studies of reversal and nonreversal shifts.

DESCRIPTIVE EVIDENCE

Investigators: H. H. Kendler and T. S. Kendler
Source, Date: "Vertical and Horizontal Processes in Problem Solving," 1962
Subjects: Children between the ages of three and ten
Materials: Simple discrimination stimuli

The concept-learning task in this experiment involved discriminating among stimuli that varied in size and brightness (each with two values) though only one dimension was relevant at a time. At first large objects produced the correct response and small objects the

QUESTION   2. WHAT DEVELOPMENTAL CHANGES TAKE PLACE
                IN THE LEARNING OF CONCEPTS?

HYPOTHESES	STRATEGY CHANGE	LINGUISTIC INFLUENCE
DESCRIPTIVE EVIDENCE	ASSESS: relationship between age and ease of solving reversal and nonreversal shift problems	ASSESS: relation of language spoken to transposition learning and to reasons reported for making responses
EXPERIMENTAL EVIDENCE		

2. WHAT DEVELOPMENTAL CHANGES TAKE PLACE IN THE LEARNING OF CONCEPTS?

An important source of change in learning over time is the growth and development of the individual. You have seen some of the ways in which individuals

incorrect one. After the concept was learned, however, the problem was changed for the subject in one of two ways. A *reversal shift* consisted of retaining stimulus size as the relevant dimension, but reversed the responses, so that small objects would now be called positive (correct) and large ones negative (incorrect). In a *nonreversal shift,* brightness rather than size became the relevant dimension (see Figure 5).

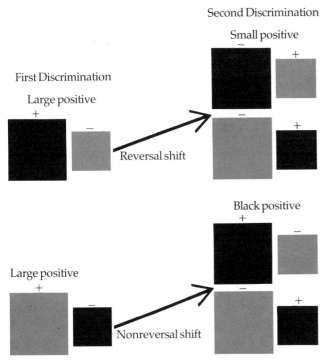

Figure 5. Reversal and nonreversal shifts. In the first discrimination, the subject learns that size is the relevant dimension. Ease with which shifts can be made in size or brightness as the relevant dimension is found to be related to developmental age. Adapted from Kendler and Kendler (1962).

The experimenters found that children over age six (and adults) find reversal shifts easier to execute than nonreversal shifts. However, for younger children (and, incidentally, also for lower organisms that do not use language, like rats) nonreversal shifts are easier. The finding that the relative difficulty of the two kinds of concept problems changes with the age of the child suggests that as children develop, the way in which they learn concepts changes.

Several possible reasons might account for the finding that reversal shifts are easier for older children and adults. The Kendlers themselves have favored an explanation involving "mediating responses" or *labels.* For example, if stimulus size is the relevant dimension for concept learning, the older child may think of the label "size" and then use it to help him get from "large positive" to "small positive" when the problem is reversed by the experimenter. Younger

children presumably have not yet developed this labeling ability.

However, it is also possible that the strategy change that occurs is bound up with developmental changes in attention: Greater attention may be required for the subject to keep responding to only one dimension of a stimulus when the reversal shift occurs. Thus, a reversal shift will be easier than a nonreversal shift for older, more attentive children because the relevant dimension remains the same, even though the responses may change.

A third possibility is that the strategy change in concept learning with age is merely one aspect of a more general change that occurs in normal children between the ages of five and seven. Such an overall change has been outlined by Sheldon White (1965, 1968) of Harvard University. After reviewing a wide variety of data concerning developmental changes in children's thinking, White suggested that all these changes may be reflecting a fundamental shift in the learning and thinking of children. Children younger than five to seven years employ a "juvenile logic" that is primarily associative and concrete in nature. The child learns to associate stimuli with responses, and these associations form the basis of the child's concept learning as well as most other thinking. The child's concept learning at this stage is thus in line with the passive-learning hypothesis. However, at about age seven, more advanced types of adult reasoning and thinking begin to appear, in which the child uses more complex kinds of cognitive operations, such as strategy testing, that are not stimulus-directed or stimulus-bound. This change occurs at about the same time that reversal shifts begin to predominate in concept learning, and about the same time that Piaget's "concrete operations" stage begins (see Unit 16). On the other hand, these changes also coincide with the onset of a child's participation in school, and the relationship of the changes to school is not clear. Does school cause the changes to occur, or do they merely occur at a time when the child is cognitively "ready" for school?

Words or other symbols are used in thinking and reasoning. Thoughts express concepts or assert or deny relations between concepts. Perhaps language, as a means of expressing concepts, is basic to the process of concept learning.

Research into the development of concept learning

in children is made more complex by the fact that language and labels are intimately bound up with how human beings learn concepts. This idea can be generalized in another major hypothesis about what changes take place in learning concepts. This *linguistic-influence hypothesis* states that concept learning is influenced by the acquisition of language and by characteristics of a particular language.

Before presenting evidence in support of this hypothesis, another aspect of concept learning, *transposition*, must be explained. Transposition is the ability of a subject to learn to respond to a *relationship* among stimuli, rather than to one characteristic of several stimuli. For example, transposition might involve a subject learning to select the larger of two stimuli to get a reward—no matter what pair of stimuli are presented. This kind of concept learning can be viewed as an advanced form, because the learner must examine the relationship between both stimuli before a choice decision can be made. As might be expected, the ability to learn transpositions increases with age. More interesting, however, is the finding that transposition learning also appears to be based on specific dimensions or characteristics of language.

DESCRIPTIVE EVIDENCE

Investigators: J. Glick, M. Cole, and J. Gay
Sources, Dates: "Cognitive Style Among the Kpelle of Liberia," 1968; "The New Mathematics and an Old Culture," 1967
Location: Yale University, University of California at Irvine, and Cuttington College, Liberia, respectively
Subjects: American children and children of the Kpelle tribe in Liberia
Materials: Transposition learning task; self-reports

In English one can say either "X is larger than Y" or "Y is smaller than X" and mean the same thing. In the Kpelle language of Liberia, however, comparisons of quantity are always made in only one direction. In Kpelle one can say "X is big past Y," but there is no way to say "Y is small past X." The question of this study was: Will this difference in language produce differences in transposition learning?

The subjects were repeatedly presented with pairs of different-sized objects, and subjects in one condition were always rewarded for choosing the smaller of the two objects (the "smaller-than" condition), while subjects in a second condition were rewarded for

choosing the larger of the two objects (the "larger-than" condition). The American children had no difficulty learning the transpositions. Given further pairs of objects differing in size, they learned to still choose the smaller (or larger) one, even when the larger (or smaller) was identical in size to the smaller (larger) object in the original pair of objects presented.

To the experimenters' surprise, nearly all the Kpelle children also learned the transpositions, and they learned "smaller than" transpositions as quickly as they learned "larger than" ones. However, differences between these two transpositions became apparent when the children were asked to give the *reasons* for their choice responses. These reasons could be classified as either size-relevant (that is, relevant to the transposition) or size-irrelevant. A size-relevant reason was something like "This one is smaller." Typical size-irrelevant reasons were responses like "It is beautiful" or "This is my choice."

The four- to five-year-old preschool Kpelle children gave 38 percent size-relevant responses in the "larger-than" condition, but only 3 percent in the "smaller-than" condition. Similarly, illiterate six- to eight-year-old Kpelle children gave 50 percent size-relevant reasons in the "larger-than" condition, but only 19 percent in the "smaller-than" condition. In contrast to these comparisons, the Kpelle children attending first grade in a school *where English is spoken* gave about the same percentage of size-relevant responses in both the "larger-than" and "smaller-than" conditions (55 percent against 44 percent). The American children at the same age as these Kpelle school children also gave equally relevant reasons in the two conditions.

This study demonstrates that the Kpelle children who speak only one language are influenced by the language in the style of their concept learning. Kpelle children who were in school and who had had some contact with English and its usages did not demonstrate this influence. Apparently the structures of the particular language can influence children's conceptual thinking. This study can be viewed as adding some support to the general contention that language influences thinking—a view sometimes known as the "Whorfian" hypothesis (after Whorf, 1956) or the linguistic-relativity hypothesis, which is discussed further in Unit 14.

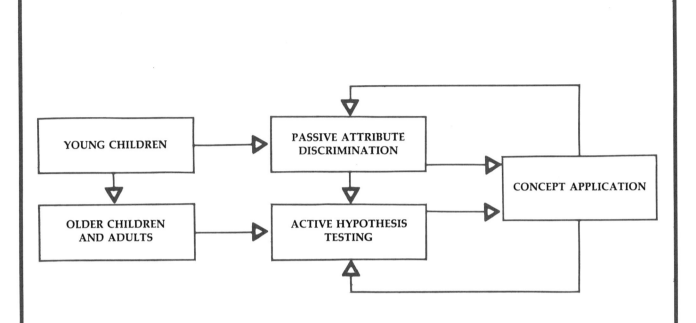

PUTTING IT TOGETHER: Concept Learning

Concept learning in very *young children* apparently involves mostly *passive attribute discrimination* as correct responses are associated with reward or knowledge of results. At this level there is probably little conscious effort to abstract rules for discriminating the appropriate attributes.

As *children grow older* and begin to make better use of language, they change their strategies for learning concepts. They begin to form and *actively test hypotheses* in classifying attributes. In this case the learner develops rules in the learning of specific concepts which are applicable in a variety of situations.

In either case, feedback from *application of the concept* determines when the process is complete and when the learner, making only correct responses, has learned the concept.

WHAT'S ACCEPTED AND WHAT'S DEBATED

1. WHAT'S ACCEPTED . . .

1. Young children may learn concepts through associations.

2. For adults, concept learning can proceed by testing hypotheses.

3. Some important changes in concept learning and thinking typically occur in children between the ages of five and seven.

4. Concept learning is influenced by the language one has acquired.

2. WHAT'S DEBATED . . .

1. The extent to which hypothesis testing is a conscious process.

2. The relationship of developmental changes in concept learning to more general changes in the development of thinking.

3. The nature of the relationship between language and concept learning.

ISSUE: ARTIFICIAL INTELLIGENCE

As this unit demonstrates, our ability to formulate concepts and to apply them to the process of problem-solving is a fundamental aspect of human intelligence. Indeed, our highly refined concept learning ability serves to distinguish us from all other members of the animal kingdom. But does it distinguish us from our own creations, the machines?

Until the advent of the electronic computer, the question of whether a machine can "think" and use concepts was a meaningless one. But modern computers are becoming steadily more complex and sophisticated, and can now perform many tasks much more quickly and efficiently than can human beings. Some computers are able to perform in a split second an operation that a skilled mathematician, using pencil and paper, might take many months to complete. But do computers actually use concepts or think?

Some psychologists contend that a computer can only be said to "think" if a human judge is unable to distinguish the responses of a computer from those of a human being. If the judge is able to put any questions he or she chooses to both a computer and another human, receives the answers via a typewritten printout, and cannot tell which answers are those of the human and which are those of the machine, then to all intents and purposes the machine has achieved a process indistinguishable from human thought.

There are already many similarities between the processes of computer thought and those of humans, for the simple reason that computers have been designed largely to duplicate these processes. Concept formation generally involves such activities as the processing of information, the abstracting of common features from a set of stimuli, and the combination or reorganization of the information in new ways according to certain rules. When a computer is programmed to solve particular problems, the programmer feeds into the machine a careful specification of the concepts that a human might use in a similar situation.

But there are crucial differences between computers and humans in their "thought" processes. The most important one is that the computer, unlike the human, cannot generate new concepts of its own accord. It can only perform the tasks that it has been programmed to do. Unlike the human brain, which can switch at will from the analysis of a musical score to the solving of an algebraic equation, the computer is restricted to those tasks and concepts that it has been programmed to handle.

Another major difference is that computers lack such uniquely human characteristics as intuition. This is one of the reasons why humans are still better than computers at the game of chess. Because they are much better than humans at sorting through a vast mass of information in a brief space of time, computers are very formidable chess players. The chess-playing computer runs through tens of thousands of possible moves before selecting one. But at the process of selecting and evaluating choices, humans are better. The skilled chess player often uses intuitions and sudden insights which are difficult even to identify or explain, let alone to program into computers. For this reason, chess-playing computers can still be outwitted by master chess experts—although the machines are more than a match for the rest of us.

The study of computer science has great relevance for psychologists. When computer experts first began to program computers, they had to draw on psychological findings about the nature of the information process in humans in order to replicate this process in the machines. But as the programming of computers becomes an ever more complex task, many of the findings of computer scientists are beginning to influence our understanding of concept formation in humans.

Why should computer programming provide "feedback" about human conceptual processes? The reason is that the computer scientist programs his machine in terms of a model based on a theory of human thought. The writing of the program requires a scrupulous attempt to replicate some of the thinking and information processing that human beings would use in handling a similar problem. But if, when the computer is programmed, it does not react like a human being, then clearly something was wrong with the original theory of human thought processes. In order to improve the program, the computer expert often has to refine his or her understanding of the basic concepts that a human uses. The attempt to achieve this understanding inevitably focuses attention on those very aspects of conceptual thought about which we are most ignorant. Work on computer models therefore has great potential for generating breakthroughs in our understanding of human thought processes.

Unit 23

Perceiving

OVERVIEW

Basic principles related to how people perceive the world that surrounds them are discussed. Perception involves the use of specific cues as well as relationships among stimulus information and past experience. Recent work in psychology has also indicated the importance of innate or unlearned capacities in certain kinds of perceiving, such as visual depth perception. Part of the unit deals with various ways in which our perceptions are affected by experience and learning. Research into extrasensory perception is presented in the Issue section.

UNIT OUTLINE

DEFINITION AND BACKGROUND
1. *Definition:* perceiving refers to the processes by which an organism interprets raw sense data as representing external objects and their relationships.
2. *Background:* Max Wertheimer (1880–1943).

QUESTIONS AND EVIDENCE
1. What properties of the physical environment are responsible for how we perceive objects?
Hypotheses:
   a. *Specific-cues:* accurate localization depends on the use of particular kinds of information abstracted from proximal stimuli—that is, on certain properties of sense organ activity. **389**
   b. *Relationships:* localization, size, and distance (depth) perception also depend on complex organizational systems or "higher-order variables" in the perceptual field. **391**
2. To what extent are perceptual capacities innate?
Hypotheses:
   a. *Depth:* space and depth perception are innate perceptual abilities. **394**
   b. *Sensory-unity:* perceiving and localizing are to some extent determined by innate sensory integrations. **396**
3. How are perceptual capacities learned?
Hypotheses:
   a. *Feedback:* the development of certain basic skills, such as the eye-hand coordination that permits a person to reach out and pick up an object, depends on simultaneous visual and kinesthetic feedback. **397**
   b. *Adaptation:* adjustments of perceptual processes in response to dramatic but consistent changes in the environment can be learned. **399**
   c. *Familiarity:* accurate perception depends largely on a person's previous acquaintance with the stimuli in the environment. **401**
   d. *Culture:* people reared in different societies, because of differences in their experiences, will differ in their susceptibility to optical illusions. **401**

IMPORTANT CONCEPTS

	page
adaptation	**399**
Ames room	**401**
autokinetic effect	**393**
distal stimuli	**386**
feedback	**397**
perception	**386**
proximal stimulus	**386**
retina	**399**
visual cliff	**394**

Environmental stimuli provide specific informational cues to a variety of receptor organs.

Capacities are innate for organizing some sensory information and learned for other sensory information.

Perceptual processes involve the individual organization and interpretation of environmental cues.

DEFINITION AND BACKGROUND

Physical energy strikes a sense organ, and information from the sense organ is conveyed to the central nervous system. Here something happens that we all take for granted: Sensations are combined, organized, and used to give us a picture of the world we live in. One DEFINITION of perceiving or perception is *the processes by which an organism interprets raw sense data as representing external objects and their relationships.*

Psychologists call physical events in the environment (optic arrays, acoustic vibrations, and so on) *distal* ("distant") *stimuli.* The activity at a sense organ itself they call a *proximal* ("near") *stimulus.* A basic problem in the study of perceiving is to determine how the organism "knows" what distal stimuli are like, since its only source of information is proximal stimuli. When you see objects, for example, you must infer their "real" characteristics on the basis of information provided by a pattern of stimulation on the inside surface of the eyeballs, the retina. This pattern (the proximal stimulus) is constantly changing—any movement of the eyes changes the proximal image, and the eyes vibrate constantly even when you stare at something—yet you see the world itself as stable, solid, and unchanging.

The study of perceiving is an old and very basic area of research, with a tradition spanning contributions from philosophers, physicists, artists, and physiologists as well as psychologists. This unit will FOCUS largely on the two most important modes of perceiving for humans—seeing and hearing—and on the interplay between innate ability and experience in the development of perceptual capacities.

BACKGROUND: MAX WERTHEIMER (1880–1943)

In 1910, at the University of Frankfurt, Max Wertheimer began a series of experiments that led to the publication of a landmark in psychological literature, "Experimental Studies of Apparent Movement" (1912). In this study, Wertheimer demonstrated that motion could be perceived even though none actually had occurred. In one experiment, for example, a line was briefly projected onto a screen by throwing light through a narrow vertical slit for a moment. Then, after varying intervals of time, the line was projected

Omikron

Figure 1. Max Wertheimer, whose research began in perceptual studies, was a founder of Gestalt psychology.

again, but this time the slit was inclined 20 or 30 degrees to the right. When the second line followed the first by a long interval, Wertheimer's subjects saw two successive lines. When the interval between the exposures was very short, the two lines were seen as appearing on the screen simultaneously. But between these extremes, the two lines appeared as a single line that moved from position A to position B, rather as if the second-hand on a clock was swinging rapidly from 12 to 1.

These effects were not unknown. Similar phenomena had been noted by earlier psychologists, and the stroboscope, a popular child's toy around the turn of the century, operated on the principle of apparent movement—as do modern neon signs, movies, and TV. But Wertheimer had devised methods for scientific observation of these phenomena—laboratory experiments that could be used to explore hearing as well as seeing and other modes of perceiving. Subsequently he proposed a theory to explain his findings. During the 1920s and 1930s, working closely with the brilliant students he attracted, he gradually elaborated the tenets that launched the Gestalt psychology movement.

This movement marked a genuine revolt within psychology, for the Gestaltists called into question the dominant theorists of the time. The introspectionists, for example, believed that an understanding of the separate elements of sensation would add up to an understanding of perception: that the whole (perception) was equal to the sum of its parts (the elements of sensation). The behaviorists, for another example, believed that perception could be explained in terms of discrimination learning. Gestalt psychologists objected to both points of view. They proposed that

perceptual wholes are not merely the sum of their parts—that perceiving should be considered an active, dynamic process that takes into account the whole pattern ("gestalt") of the perceptual field. If perception were merely a bundle of sensations and perceptual phenomena were based on trial-and-error learning, they asked, why would a person see movement when in fact none had occurred?

The Gestaltists went on to conduct many studies in perception and to describe a number of "laws" governing the organization of the perceptual field, especially in vision. Some of these laws of perceptual organization are summarized in Figure 3.

Though Wertheimer was always considered the Gestalt movement's foremost theorist, he was never much of a propagandist, even for his own point of view. He let others handle the internal quarrels that Gestalt theories briefly touched off in academic circles. His last major work, a book entitled *Productive Thinking,* became influential in educational psychology, but in many respects, his most important contribution to psychology was the new generation of Gestalt psychologists—Wolfgang Kohler, Kurt Koffka, Kurt Lewin, Karl Duncker, and others.

By 1940 the Gestalt approach had begun to blend with other general developments in psychology, and today the Gestalt school no longer exists as a separate movement. However, the Gestaltists' ingenuity in generating deceptively simple observations and studies, using the most elementary stimulus materials, has influenced many psychologists in widely different areas of research. Their emphasis on perceptual wholes has been felt outside the laboratory as well; Gestalt therapy, for example, stresses the wholeness of a person's here-and-now experience.

Figure 2. Motion can be perceived even though none actually has occurred. When viewed in rapid sequence, figures on the frames of this 1885 series from the Museum of Modern Art (New York), appear to move.

QUESTIONS AND EVIDENCE

1. What properties of the physical environment are responsible for how we perceive objects?

2. To what extent are perceptual capacities innate?

3. How are perceptual capacities learned?

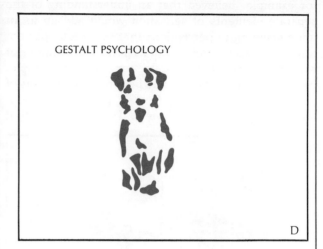

GESTALT PSYCHOLOGY

D

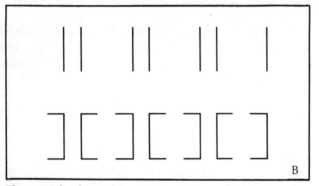

B

The principle of *proximity* causes us to group the lines into three pairs with an extra line to the right. The same lines, with extensions, pair oppositely under the principle of *closure*.

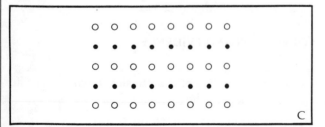

C

Spacing determines whether we see rows or columns *(proximity).* When all dots are equally spaced we group similar items together—rows of circles and rows of dots *(similarity).*

E

Figure 3. Perceived stimuli are grouped into ordered relationships described in the Gestalt laws of perceptual organization. A. *Common Fate:* Elements moving in a common direction. B. *Proximity:* Elements near each other. C. *Similarity:* Elements sharing common physical attributes. D. *Good Continuation:* Elements completing an established pattern. E. *Figure-Ground:* Elements standing out against a background.

HYPOTHESES	SPECIFIC CUES	RELATIONSHIPS
DESCRIPTIVE EVIDENCE	ASSESS: cues used in the localization of sound	ASSESS: perception of relative brightness of interesting regions
EXPERIMENTAL EVIDENCE		

1. WHAT PROPERTIES OF THE PHYSICAL ENVIRONMENT ARE RESPONSIBLE FOR HOW WE PERCEIVE OBJECTS?

When you turn your head in the direction of a particular sound, how do you know where it is coming from? Perhaps you already know where the source of the sound is (a doorbell, for example). But the interesting fact is that most people have little difficulty locating a sound even when they have no previous experience with it.

The *specific-cues hypothesis* states that accurate localization depends on the use of particular kinds of information abstracted from proximal stimuli—that is, on certain properties of sense organ activity. In the case of hearing, the two most familiar dimensions of sound stimuli (shown in Figure 6) are loudness (corresponding to sound-wave amplitude) and pitch (corresponding roughly to sound-wave frequency). Either loud and soft or high and low sounds can come from "off to the left." But research has shown that a combination of the two provides many of the cues for localization.

DESCRIPTIVE EVIDENCE

Investigators: S. S. Stevens and E. B. Newman
Source, Date: "The Localization of Actual Sources of Sound," 1936
Location: Harvard University
Subjects: 2 adults (the experimenters)
Materials: A tall swivel chair on top of a 9-foot ventilator on the roof of a building; a 12-foot movable arm

Stevens and Newman blindfolded themselves, then took turns sitting in the chair atop a tall building. Their task was to estimate the location of a loudspeaker from which various tones, hisses and clicks were broadcast. (The reason they sat on a roof was to minimize sound reflections from nearby objects.)

In scoring their estimates of location, they separated localization errors from so-called reversal errors. Reversal errors result from the normal difficulty of making back-front discriminations. A sound from straight in front of a listener seems to come from the same place as a sound from straight in back of him; to make a decision, a listener must turn his head slightly

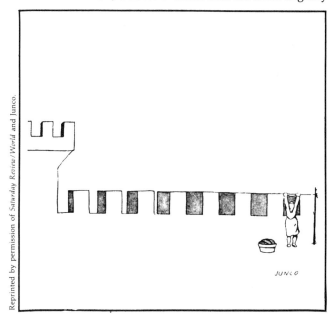

Figure 4. This optical illusion captures some insights of Gestalt psychology, including its ability to generate deceptively simply observations.

Reprinted by permission of *Saturday Review/World* and Junco.

Figure 5. We tend to organize complex stimuli into meaningful relationships. The ambiguous figure above is sometimes known as "my wife and mother-in-law." Which do you see?

1,100 feet per second), so that high-frequency sounds take as much time to get from one ear to the other as low-frequency sounds do, the phase differences in sound waves of frequencies above about 1,500 cycles are too small for a listener to detect.

Fortunately, amplitude (loudness) differences become increasingly helpful in localization as frequency increases. Especially at high frequencies, a listener can tell where a sound is coming from because of a detectable difference in loudness as the sound reaches each ear (the head is in the way).

Thus, localization errors are greatest at frequencies of about 3,000 cycles because phase differences have declined at that point, whereas loudness differences are not yet noticeable enough to offer much help. It is clear that human beings can localize sounds because of an interaction between their own physical characteristics (two ears, separated by six or seven inches of head) and the physical characteristics of sound waves (frequency and amplitude).

The specific cues for localizing objects visually (see Figure 8) are probably more familiar than those used for sound. They include:

in one direction or the other. A reversal error, then, is one in which a listener judges a sound coming from a few degrees to the right of straight-front to be coming from a few degrees to the right of straight-back. For the purposes of the Stevens-Newman experiment, such estimates were considered correct.

The results are shown in Figure 7. Note that errors reach a maximum at sound frequencies of about 3,000 cycles. (3,000 cycles per second is a medium-high sound: the highest note on a piano has a frequency of about 5,000 cycles per second; the lowest note, a frequency of about 30 cycles.) Above and below about 3,000 cycles, accuracy increased. The question was why errors peaked at that particular point instead of showing either a steady rise or a steady decline with increasing frequencies.

For sounds with frequencies below about 1,500 cycles per second, localization is accurate mainly because the sound waves reach the two ears at slightly different times, producing a binaural phase difference. Although all sound travels at the same speed (about

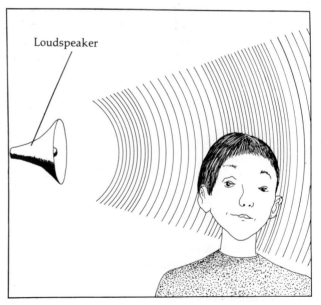

Figure 6. The sound wave arrives first at the ear closer to the loudspeaker, is stronger, and is in a different phase. The individual is therefore able to determine the direction from which the sound is coming.

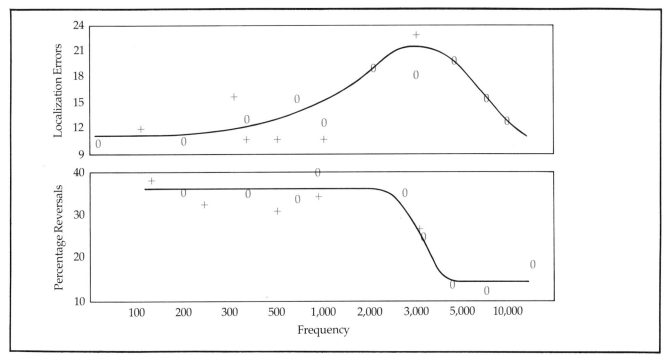

Figure 7. Errors in localizing sound sources at various frequencies. Upper graph shows average number of localization errors; lower graph indicates percentage number of errors in judgments of front or rear sources. Adapted from Stevens and Newman (1936).

1. *Familiar size.* Knowledge of the "real" size of a distant object helps to indicate how far away it is.

2. *Relative size.* An object known to be the same size as another appears smaller than the other to the extent that it is farther away.

3. *Interposition.* A nearby object covers up parts of farther-away objects behind it.

4. *Shadows.* Shadows can indicate depth or relief.

5. *Linear perspective.* Parallel lines going away from the observer tend to converge at the horizon.

6. *Convergence:* The eyes cross slightly when an observer looks at nearby objects.

Experiments have shown how each of these cues can be used to determine the size and distance of objects. In such experiments the cues are usually presented one at a time. Outside the laboratory, though, they occur together, in various combinations, and the perceiver tends to use mainly the information that is most obvious ("salient") or most reliable in a given situation.

The combining of specific cues into meaningful organizations and patterns is known as *perceptual organization,* a concept that covers both the relationships between elements and properties in the proximal stimulus and the ways those relationships are used by the individual perceiver. Some simple principles of perceptual organization in vision have already been illustrated by the Gestalt "laws" of figural perception shown in Figure 3. For hearing, perceptual organization can be illustrated by people's ability to recognize a familiar melody even when it is transposed from one key to another or up or down an octave, because the relationships between the notes stay the same despite the transposition.

The *relationships hypothesis* states that localization, size, and distance (depth) perception also depend on complex organizational systems or "higher-order variables" in the perceptual field. Clearly, our visual "knowledge" of location and depth is highly dependent on organizational relationships and patterns. Less obviously, so is our perception of brightness.

DESCRIPTIVE EVIDENCE

Investigator: H. Wallach
Source, Date: "Brightness Constancy and the Nature of Achromatic Colors," 1948
Subjects: Five human adults
Materials: Four slide projectors, white screen, dark room; circular and ring slides

Two circular areas were projected onto a screen, each with an outer, brighter ring surrounding a darker circle (see Figure 9). In the lefthand area the inner circle was set at 50 percent of the brightness of the outer ring (a ratio of 100 to 200 brightness units). In the righthand area, the outer ring was set at various brightness levels (50, 25, or 12.5) relative to the outer ring of the lefthand circle. The subjects' task was to adjust the intensity of the inner circle on the right so that it appeared to equal that of the inner circle on the left.

When the outer ring on the right was set at 50, 25, or 12.5, subjects adjusted the inner circle to 25, 12.5, or 6.25 respectively. In other words, the inner circles were seen as equal in brightness if they had the same relationship to their surrounding rings even when, in

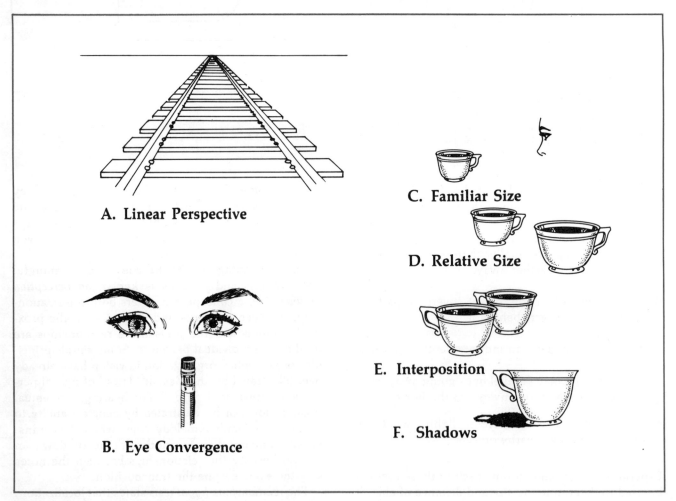

A. Linear Perspective

B. Eye Convergence

C. Familiar Size

D. Relative Size

E. Interposition

F. Shadows

Figure 8. Visual cues for localizing objects in space.

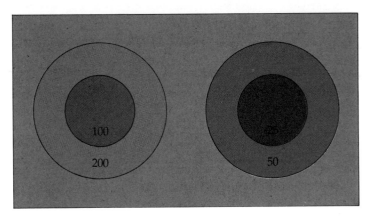

Figure 9. In Wallach's study (1948), the inner circles were seen as equal in brightness if they had the same relationship to their surrounding rings even when the inner circles were of different intensities.

fact, the inner circles were of different intensities. The intensity relationship of each inner circle to the surrounding ring was constant, and constant relationships produce constant perceived brightness.

As the Gestalt psychologists emphasized, an organism does not simply react to the sensory content of the visual field but perceives visual phenomena in terms of relationships within the field. Another important contribution to the understanding of visual relationships was made by James J. Gibson of Cornell University. He noted that the world is ordinarily seen as a number of surfaces slanting this way and that, at various angles in relation to each other. When the surfaces reflect light to the eyes, they take on a texture.

Gibson believes that the texture ("microstructure") of a surface extending away from the observer falls on the retina as a *gradient of density* that corresponds to increasing distances (see for example, Figure 10). This gradient provides the observer with a "scale" for object sizes or distances. And when the units in the texture are identical (as they are in Figure 10), then the gradient of density provides maximal information about objects or contrasting surfaces that might lie within it. When the perceiver relies on this kind of information to arrive at judgments, he is making full use of the possibilities of organization for the visual field.

The visual perception of motion or movement can also be accounted for by the relationships hypothesis—that is, by organizational principles. As Wertheimer's classic experiment demonstrated, it is not necessary for images to move across the retina for motion to be perceived. Further studies have identified the basic organizational property of movement perception: *in order for movement to be perceived meaningfully, an object must be observed to be changing position relative to its background or to a "stationary" object.* (The perception of one's own motion or acceleration is more dependent on muscular and kinesthetic perceptions than on visual cues.)

The dependence of perceived, meaningful movement on a background can be demonstrated by the *autokinetic effect,* where background cues are eliminated. If a room is completely darkened except for one point of light, so that background cues are eliminated, the point of light will appear to move about in a random fashion after an observer stares at it for a short time. Both the expectations of the observer and the movements of his eyes will affect how and how much the light is perceived to move—but the effect always occurs. The lack of a background or frame of

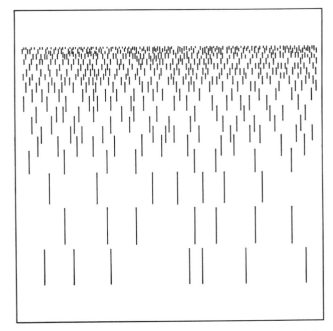

Figure 10. Gibson (1966) believes that the texture of a surface falls on the retina of the eye as a *gradient of density* that provides the observer with a scale for object sizes or distances.

reference in the autokinetic situation results in an unpredictable and "unjustified" wandering of the stimulus.

Perceptual organization is involved not only in vision but in all the sense modalities, and the variety of experiments and demonstrations conducted on perceptual phenomena is almost endless. During the past twenty years researchers have been more and more concerned with the extent to which various capacities for perceptual organization are innate.

difficulty can be minimized by keeping the infants isolated until the time of the study, but ethical considerations prevent the isolation of human infants. Very few parents would allow their babies to be confined in a dark room for six months, even for the sake of science.

These considerations should be borne in mind in evaluating the evidence supporting the *depth hypothesis,* which states that space and depth perception are innate perceptual abilities.

QUESTION	2. TO WHAT EXTENT ARE PERCEPTUAL CAPACITIES INNATE?	
HYPOTHESES	**DEPTH**	**SENSORY-UNITY**
DESCRIPTIVE EVIDENCE	ASSESS: ability of human infants to avoid visual cliff	
EXPERIMENTAL EVIDENCE	VARY: lightrearing conditions MEASURE: ability of animals to avoid visual cliff	VARY: presentation of real objects vs. virtual images MEASURE: behavioral indications that infant is disturbed, e.g., crying

2. TO WHAT EXTENT ARE PERCEPTUAL CAPACITIES INNATE?

Certain assumptions about innateness can be based on the observed behavior of animals. A wild gazelle can walk and even run minutes after birth, for example, so it can be concluded that this species is born with at least some capacity for visual perception and visual-motor coordination.

But human babies don't jump up and run like gazelles right after birth. Are they born with any capacity for, say, depth perception? This is a hard question to answer. Unless an infant is tested immediately after birth, no one can be fully confident that his performance is a result of innate abilities, for the abilities may have been acquired between birth and the time of the study. With lower animals, this

DESCRIPTIVE EVIDENCE

Investigators: E. J. Gibson and R. D. Walk
Source, Date: "The 'Visual Cliff,'" 1960
Location: Cornell University
Subjects: Human infants, six months to a year old
Materials: Visual-cliff apparatus, consisting of a horizontal sheet of glass raised from the floor, a checkerboard pattern attached to half of the glass sheet, with the same pattern on the floor under the other half

Infants who were just beginning to crawl (six months to a year old) were placed in the center of the apparatus shown in Figure 11. Observations and measurements were made of where they crawled. If an infant consistently avoided the "deep" side of the visual cliff, it was inferred that he was able to perceive depth.

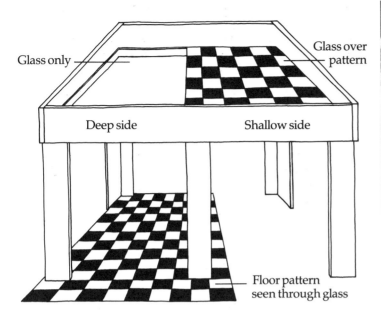

Glass only

Glass over pattern

Deep side

Shallow side

Floor pattern
seen through glass

Figure 11. Visual cliff used in studies of depth perception by Gibson and Walk (1960). The subject is placed on the narrow, glass-topped platform. To one side of the platform he can see, through the glass, a surface directly against the glass. Thus there is only *visually* a severe drop on one side. A child encouraged to cross over the visual cliff shows inborn caution.

Most infants consistently avoided the "deep" side of the table, refusing to crawl across it even when their mothers called to them. When called from the "deep" side, some infants crawled in the opposite direction; others cried but still refused to cross the apparent chasm.

This study indicates that most human infants can discriminate depth as soon as they can crawl. It does not prove that depth perception is innate in humans, however, because the infants already had a lot of visual experience. Stronger evidence in favor of the depth hypothesis is provided by experiments with nonhuman infants.

EXPERIMENTAL EVIDENCE

Investigators: R. D. Walk and E. J. Gibson
*Source, Date: "A Comparative and Analytical Study of
    Visual Depth Perception," 1961*
Subjects: Rats, baby and adult chickens, goats, turtles
Materials: Visual-cliff apparatus

With some variation from species to species, the same general procedure was followed for all animal sub-

jects. Each was placed on the center of the table, on the platform between the "deep" and "shallow" sides of the visual cliff. If the subject consistently avoided the deep side, it was considered capable of perceiving depth.

Some of the animals were reared from birth in darkness, while others had lived in light. However, all of them definitely tended to avoid the deep side of the cliff, including both light-reared and darkness-reared rats, and infant goats and chicks. There were some species differences: for example, turtles seemed to have less aversion to the apparent chasm than other animals. Taken together, the data strongly imply that depth perception is for the most part innate in many species.

Adult humans take such perceptual abilities for granted. They also take for granted their ability to integrate information from the various senses in a way that makes fuller understanding of the environment possible. They know, for example, that their sense of touch could be used to tell them that the visual cliff is really a flat piece of glass. Although the ability to use the senses to explore the environment is largely learned, the basic ability to integrate information from the various sense modalities may be another inborn characteristic. The *sensory-unity hypothesis* states that perceiving and localizing are to some extent determined by innate sensory integrations.

EXPERIMENTAL EVIDENCE

Investigator: T. G. R. Bower
Source, Date: "The Object in the World of the Infant,"
    1971
Location: Harvard University
Subjects: Over 40 human infants, less than two weeks old
Materials: Simple objects; polarized goggles, projectors

As an initial test of young infants' perceptive capacities, Bower wanted to discover whether they would hold their hands out for protection when something was moved toward their faces. He placed the two-week-old babies on their backs and moved a number of different-sized objects down toward them at different speeds. The infants didn't even blink—much less extend their arms. Then Bower learned that infants

Figure 12. Apparatus used by Bower (1971) to test infants' perception of objects. Newborns, wearing polarized goggles and watching an object projected on a screen (a "virtual image,") cried when they could see—but not feel—the object.

under two weeks old (who commonly sleep twenty hours a day) are hardly ever fully awake when they lie on their backs. He decided to try the same procedures again with the infants held in an almost upright position.

With this modification, the infants did show defensive responses to the approaching objects. They pulled back their heads, put their hands between their faces and the objects and cried in intense distress. In the second week of life, then, a baby already "expects" a seen object to have consequences for touch. There is good reason to believe that this perceptual ability is innate, for it is highly unlikely that the two-week-old infants had been previously hit in the face by approaching objects—that is, that their responses were learned.

To test this idea further, newborn infants were presented with real objects and with "virtual images" produced by the apparatus shown in Figure 12. The newborn infants touched and grasped real objects with no signs of disturbance. The "virtual images" caused the same infants to cry when their hands found nothing there. In other words, the infants became disturbed when their sense of touch contradicted what they saw. Given the very early age of the infants studied, the expectation that visual and tactile information should correspond is very probably innate. There are also some indications of primitive unity or innate perceptual capacities in the auditory system. Seizing an opportunity presented by his own new baby, Michael Wertheimer (1961) sounded a series of click noises near the infant, from a number of different locations and in random order. Her responses were noted by two observers, who agreed on most of their judgments.

Out of forty-five trials, the baby moved her eyes in response to twenty-two of the clicks, eighteen of those times toward the source of the noise. Although this study used only one subject, Wertheimer's conservative conclusion is certainly warranted: The infant was apparently able to make simple localization responses to sounds within the first ten minutes after birth. (Another suggestive experiment in auditory perception, conducted by Eimas, Siqueland, Juscqyk and Vigorito, is described in Unit 14. A related study performed by Fantz is reported in Unit 24.)

HYPOTHESES	FEEDBACK	ADAPTATION	FAMILIARITY	CULTURE
DESCRIPTIVE EVIDENCE		ASSESS: effects of wearing lenses which alter the retinal image		ASSESS: relationship between cultural experience and susceptibility to optical illusions
EXPERIMENTAL EVIDENCE	VARY: active vs. passive visual experiences MEASURE: responses to paw placement, visual cliff		VARY: real distance of familiar objects of unfamiliar size MEASURE: perceived distance	

3. HOW ARE PERCEPTUAL CAPACITIES LEARNED?

It seems clear that infants are born with some innate capacity for perceptual organization. The next question is, how is that capacity developed? The *feedback hypothesis* stipulates that the development of certain basic skills, such as the eye-hand coordination that permits a person to reach out and pick up an object, depends on simultaneous visual and kinesthetic feedback. The hypothesis further states that neither visual observation nor motor movement by itself is sufficient to develop visual-motor coordination. An interaction between these two systems is required: the organism must have an opportunity both to produce and to experience the consequences of its own movements.

EXPERIMENTAL EVIDENCE

Investigators: R. Held and A. Hein
Source, Date: "Movement Produced Stimulation in the
    Development of Visually-Guided Behavior," 1963
Location: Brandeis University
Subjects: Pairs of kittens
Materials: A large cylindrical apparatus; visual-cliff test

The kittens were raised in total darkness from birth to an age of about ten weeks. From then on each pair spent three hours a day using the gondola apparatus shown in Figure 13. The rest of the time, they were kept in the dark. The experimental apparatus, as the illustration shows, allowed both kittens to have the same view of the cylinder, but permitted only one of them—the "active" kitten—to push the gondola around. If visual experience alone were sufficient for visual-motor coordination, the experimenters reasoned, the "passive" kittens should do as well on coordination tests as their active partners. On the other hand, if both vision and feedback from self-produced movement are necessary, then the active kittens should perform better on the tests.

In the first test of visual-motor coordination, the experimenter held a kitten in his hands and moved the animal forward and down toward the edge of a table. A normal kitten extends its paws as it approaches the table edge, anticipating contact. In every pair of kittens in this experiment—they were tested after each three-hour session—the first kitten to respond normally was the active one.

When tested on the visual cliff, all the active kittens behaved normally, choosing the shallow side of the cliff every time they were tested. The passive kittens showed no indication that they could tell the two sides apart. These results confirm the importance of self-produced movement as well as visual experience for the development of coordinated behavior.

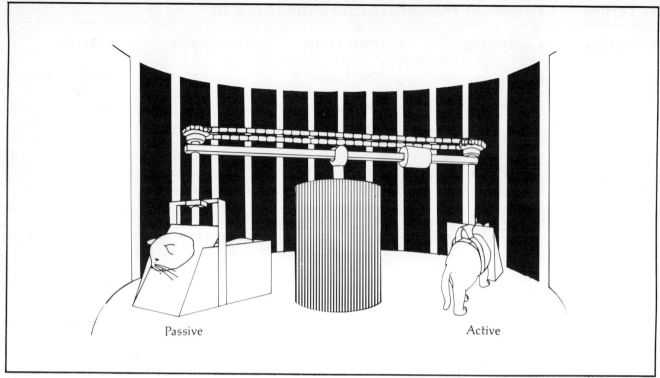

Figure 13. Apparatus used for studying visual-motor coordination. One kitten—the "active" kitten—can push the apparatus and control its movement, while the other, "passive" kitten cannot. The study showed the importance of self-produced movement as well as visual experience for the development of coordinated behavior. Adapted from Held and Hein (1963).

The Held-Hein finding may appear to contradict those obtained by Gibson and Walk (1960) on animals' innate capacity for depth perception, but the contradiction is only apparent. Presumably, the visual deprivation suffered by the Held-Hein kittens during their first ten weeks affected their innate abilities. The role of normal experience is to both encourage and modify adaptive perceptual capacities, however innate in origin these may be.

In a related study, Held and Bauer (1967) raised infant monkeys in an apparatus that prevented them from seeing their own limbs for the first thirty-five days of life. On the thirty-fifth day, when the monkeys were allowed to see their limbs for the first time, their ability to extend their arms, reach, and grasp was very poor compared to normal animals'. After twenty hours of normal experience, however, they had become noticeably skilled at reaching and grasping. After three months, their motor behavior was indistinguishable from that of normally raised monkeys. Held and Bauer concluded that the development of a visually directed reach appears to require specific experiences of viewing the moving hand.(These results appear to contradict those of Bower, 1971, previously discussed; again, the explanation is that extreme deprivation tends to obscure or override an animal's native abilities.)

What about the perceptual skills that are often said to distinguish "gifted" individuals? Most people believe that "perfect pitch"—the ability to identify a given musical tone as an E or an F sharp, for example—is an inborn endowment: one either has it or doesn't, like blond hair or dainty feet. But although perfect pitch cannot be taught, pitch discrimination can. In one study, performance was improved by 200 to 700 percent after intensive training (Lundin, 1969) with carefully controlled feedback.

Perceiving is marked by constant changes in response to the environment. A simple instance occurs when you enter a dark room from a brightly lit hallway. At first it is difficult to see and locate objects, but within a few moments the sensory mechanisms in the eyes adapt to the new level of illumination.

The *adaptation hypothesis* states that adjustments of perceptual processes in response to dramatic but consistent changes in the environment can be learned. Many experiments related to this hypothesis have altered the field of vision in some dramatic ways—by turning it upside down, reversing it from left to right, and so on. Here is an early one, conducted at the end of the last century.

DESCRIPTIVE EVIDENCE

Investigator: G. M. Stratton
Source, Date: "Vision without Inversion of the Retinal Image," 1897
Location: University of California
Subject: The experimenter
Materials: Special lenses that turn normally upside-down retinal images right-side up

Normally people see the world as right-side up, but their retinal images are upside down. Stratton is the first man known to have viewed the world with his retinal images consistently right-side up. For eighty-seven waking hours over a period of eight days (an average of almost eleven hours a day), he wore a special device that inverted the retinal images. The rest of the time he wore a blindfold.

On the first day, everything looked upside down. Also, Stratton did not always see the world as stable: the environment, as well as himself, seemed to be movin g. He reported his discomfort:

> Almost all movements performed under the direct guidance of sight were laborious and embarrassed. Inappropriate movements were constantly made . . . At table the simplest acts of serving myself had to be cautiously worked out. The wrong hand was constantly used to seize anything that lay to one side. . . . The unusual strain of attention in these cases, and the difficulty of finally getting a movement to its goal, made all but the simplest movements extremely fatiguing.

By the third day Stratton reported some improvement:

> I was now beginning to feel more at home in the new experience. . . . Walking through the narrow spaces between pieces of furniture required much less care than hitherto. . . . Head movements were still accompanied by a slight swinging of the scene, although in a markedly less degree than on the first day. The movement was referred more to the observer, so that it seemed to be more a moving survey of stationary objects.

By the fifth day:

> At breakfast, with the lenses on, the inappropriate hand was rarely used to pick up something to one side. . . . I usually took the right direction without reflecting and without the need any longer of constantly watching my feet.

Finally, on the eighth day, Stratton reported that "as long as the new localization of my body was vivid, the general experience was harmonious."

When Stratton took off the lenses on the ninth day, he had the same problems readjusting to normal vision that he had had adjusting to the lenses:

> I frequently either ran into things in the very effort to go around them, or else hesitated, for the moment, bewildered what I should do. I found myself more than once at a loss which hand I ought to use to grasp the door-handle at my side.

Years later, during the early 1960s, extensive investigations in visual distortion were conducted by Ivo Kohler. In some, the visual field was inverted as Stratton's had been, while in others the visual field was reversed from left to right and vice versa. Kohler reported that some elements of perception were altered immediately while other parts remained unchanged even after several days. Only after many weeks of wearing the lenses did subjects perceive "correctly" under the new circumstances. Thus the process of adaptation seems to occur bit by bit; a subject does not learn to reverse or invert the whole field "at once." And, as with Stratton's original work, when the special goggles were removed after a long period of reversal or inversion, the subjects needed to

Figure 14. The visual world in some cultures is considerably more angular than in others.

adjust all over again. The after-effects of distortion support the idea that, with adaptation over time, changes occur in the perceptual system that modify the individual's overall orientation to the world.

There is a mistaken tendency to conclude that, in such cases, the visual system adapts to the feedback from tactile and kinesthetic sensations. In fact, the process is just the reverse: changes in the felt position of the subject's arms, head, and eyes gradually occur to correspond with the new visual input. It is when a subject has finally readjusted his other senses to

"agree" with visual information that he experiences the world as "right," as stationary and with everything in its proper place. This conclusion has been verified more directly in a series of experiments by Irving Rock and his associates, who have indicated that, when visual information and tactile information are manipulated so that they conflict, the subject will interpret his tactile sensations to agree with his visual experiences.

Ordinary perceiving rarely, if ever, involves such dramatic adaptations. Indeed, the everyday perceptual world is taken for granted largely because so much in it has already been experienced.

The *familiarity hypothesis* states that accurate perception depends largely on a person's previous acquaintance with the stimuli in the environment. It has been tested by placing everyday things in artificial situations, so that familiarity can be pitted against other possible cues.

EXPERIMENTAL EVIDENCE

Investigator: W. H. Ittelson
Source, Date: "Size as a Cue to Distance: Static Location,"
  1951
Location: Princeton University
Subjects: 24 college students
Materials: 3 sizes of playing cards; L-shaped hall
  arrangement; movable stimuli

Each subject participated in a series of trials using what he believed were standard playing cards. Actually, some of the cards were twice normal size while others were half normal size. The subject was placed at the junction of an L-shaped room. Down one hall he could see a standard card placed at a distance of 7.5 feet. His task was to adjust the distance of other cards in the second hall so that they would appear to be the same distance away as the standard. (All cues other than the size of the cards were minimized: only one eye was used to view the adjustable stimuli, wall reflections were eliminated by darkness, the subject could not view both the standard and the test stimuli simultaneously, and so on.) In short, subjects expressed their distance judgments by adjusting a comparison target in a different alley.

Subjects consistently placed the double-size card twice as far away as the standard (15 feet), and the half-size card almost twice as close (4.6 feet). Familiar size, which depends on the past learning experiences, was used as a source of information about the distance of an object.

More dramatic demonstrations of the effects of familiarity on perception can be obtained with special rooms originally devised by Adelbert Ames. When viewed with one eye from a particular point, such a room appears to have the "normal" square corners and rectangular windows, though the setting is actu-

ally distorted in a highly controlled way this particular kind of distortion has some fascinating consequences. For example, a person walking across an Ames room from left to right appears to grow larger. What the Ames room shows is that the illusion of "normalness" provided by the "familiar" room is so powerful that it can outweigh other cues.

The Ames room is essentially an elaborate optical illusion. A great many psychological studies have investigated the effects and processes involved in such misperceptions of sensory information. Of particular interest is the influence of learned cultural standards on the organization of visual experience. The *culture hypothesis* predicts that people reared in different societies, because of differences in their experiences, will differ in their susceptibility to optical illusions.

DESCRIPTIVE EVIDENCE

Investigators: M. H. Segall, D. T. Campbell, and M. J.
  Herskovits
Source, Date: "Cultural Differences in the Perception of
  Geometric Illusions," 1963
Location: University of Iowa and Northwestern University
Subjects: 1,878 people from 14 non-Western groups, black
  South Africans and Filipinos, and 3 Western groups
  (44 white South Africans, 30 Northwestern under-
  graduates, and 208 residents of Evanston, Ill.)
Materials: 39 drawings of geometric illusions

Thirty-nine variations of the four basic figures shown in Figure 15 were used in the experiment. What varied was the lengths of the lines. For example, in one version of the Muller-Lyer illusion (Figure A), the line on the top was much longer than the line on the bottom; in another version the line on the top was only slightly longer than the line on the bottom; in still another version, the two lines were equal. In this way, the researchers were able to determine how much longer the top line had to be than the bottom one before a subject would see the two lines as equal. Each drawing was scored by the number of times subjects were deceived by the illusion, choosing as longer the line that most people overestimate.

In general, the Western groups were more susceptible to the acute- and obtuse-angle illusions (A and B). The non-Western groups were more susceptible to the right-angle illusions (C and D). The

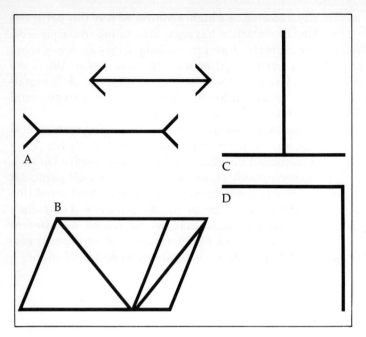

Figure 15. Optical illusions used in study of cultural differences in perception by Segall et al. A. Muller-Lyer illusion. Which horizontal line in the two figures is longer? B. Acute and obtuse angle illusion. Which internal diagonal line is longest? C. Right angle illusion I. Is the vertical or horizontal line longer? D. Right angle illusion II. Is the vertical or horizontal line longer? Subjects from Western cultures more often misjudged A and B. Subjects from non-Western cultures more often misjudged C and D.

researchers explained that since Western peoples—European and American—live in an environment including many rectangular objects, such as buildings, doorways, and windows, they tend to interpret acute and obtuse angles "as if" they represent rectangular objects in three-dimensional space, even when they are drawn two-dimensionally. Non-Western peoples, instead of inferring the true lengths of lines by means of traditional Western principles of perspective, habitually regard vertical lines as if they were extensions away from the observer on a horizontal plane. For example, C and D might be seen as the intersection of two paths on a flat plain, creating the impression that the vertical is longer than the horizontal line. These cross-cultural comparisons support the idea that size and depth cues are, to some extent, learned, and that differing ecological and visual environments may provide different cues.

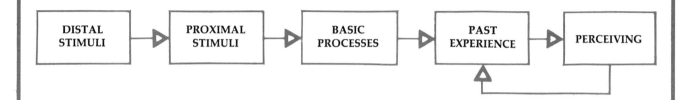

| DISTAL STIMULI | ▷ | PROXIMAL STIMULI | ▷ | BASIC PROCESSES | ▷ | PAST EXPERIENCE | ▷ | PERCEIVING |

PUTTING IT TOGETHER: Perceiving

Perceiving begins with *distal stimuli*—optic arrays, acoustic vibrations, and other changes in environmental energy received at the sense organs as *proximal stimuli.* These proximal stimuli embody the specific cues, relationships, gradients, and other higher-order variables that provide the information required to initiate the *basic processes* which apparently stem from the innate organization of the central nervous system. These include the abilities to perceive depth, sensory unity, and the organizational grouping of sensory information.

Further processing occurs through matching this input with *past experience* with similar and related inputs. Accumulated experiences may include general cultural training for specific organization of proximal stimuli, adaptation to persistent environmental changes, or familiarity with some environmental stimuli.

All of these components give rise to the final stage of *perceiving,* during which information may be reorganized momentarily through feedback from past experience, which may be thought of as a repository for information which is constantly being scanned and supplied with new information.

1. WHAT'S ACCEPTED . . .

1. Perceiving and localizing objects depend on the interpretation and use of specific cues contained in the proximal stimulus.

2. Perceptual organization makes use of relationships and higher-order variables embodied in the perceptual field.

3. To some extent, certain perceptual capacities (depth or sensory unity, for example) probably are present in organisms at birth.

4. The development of visual-motor coordination depends on feedback from self-produced movement.

5. Perceptual processes are able to adjust and adapt to dramatic but consistent changes in the perceptual field.

6. Ordinarily, the perception of objects and relationships is dependent on the individual's familiarity with those objects and relationships.

7. Past experiences, like one's cultural frame of reference, can persist into present perceptions.

2. WHAT'S DEBATED . . .

1. The manner in which perceivers "construct" their perceptual world out of the elements contained in the proximal stimuli.

2. The processes underlying perceptual organization, and whether some of these processes are primarily sensory or primarily central (in the brain).

3. To what extent perceptual capacities in man are actually innately determined.

4. Whether visual space should be regarded as "primarily learned" through early visual-motor feedback, or whether it is "primarily innate."

5. The processes underlying perceptual stability and adjustment.

ISSUE: E.S.P.

As this unit makes apparent, the majority of research that psychologists have conducted on perceiving focuses on our perception of everyday reality. But what of the phenomenon of extrasensory perception (ESP)?

ESP has attracted the attention of many key historical figures, including William James, Freud, Jung, Einstein, and Thomas Edison. These men and others have taken the view that our minds are frightfully closed. Physicist and author C. P. Snow says scornfully that "scientists regard it as a major intellectual virtue to know what not to think about." Novelist Arthur Koestler describes modern scientists as "Peeping Toms at the keyhole of eternity"—a keyhole blocked with traditional biases. Yet, as Koestler points out, many contemporary discoveries in the field of theoretical physics defy rational understanding—electromagnetic energy that sometimes acts as waves and sometimes as particles, but never both at the same time; neutrinos that have neither mass nor charge, particles that travel faster than light, or black holes in the universe. None of these is any more incredible than ESP. Why then, should we continue to deny the possibility that the phenomenon exists? Acupuncture was denied scientific credibility in the Western world for centuries. Only in the seventies is it being accorded respectability. (See Unit 31.) The claims of Eastern mystics about their abilities to control heart rate, body temperature or rate of urine formation were long dismissed as fakery. But our new knowledge of biofeedback proves that these abilities are indeed within the range of human capacities. (See Unit 35.) Might the same prove true of extrasensory perception?

Academic interest in ESP is unquestionably increasing. More than 100 U.S. colleges now offer courses in the subject. After many vain attempts, the American Parapsychological Association finally won admission to the prestigious American Association for the Advancement of Science in 1969, following an impassioned plea by anthropologist Margaret Mead: "The whole history of scientific advance is full of scientists investigating phenomena that the Establishment did not believe were there." The Pentagon is becoming interested in funding research in ESP, after reports that the Soviet Union is investing massive research efforts in the area. In England, the important journal *New Scientist* found that 70 percent of its readers, nearly all scientists and technicians, believe in the possibility of ESP.

The public, too, is becoming increasingly interested in the subject. Uri Geller, a young Israeli, has intrigued television audiences by apparently bending spoons with the power of his mind, reproducing drawings sealed in envelopes, deflecting magnetometers, disrupting nearby electronic equipment, and correctly calling the upper face of a die in a closed box eight times in succession. Apollo astronaut Edgar Mitchell claims to have conducted telepathy with friends on earth during his moon mission, and has founded an institute to study experiences that seem to defy rational explanation.

Others remain more skeptical. Daniel Cohen, former editor of *Science Digest,* observes caustically: "After decades of research and experiments the parapsychologists are not one step closer to acceptable scientific proof of psychic phenomena. Examining the slipshod work of the modern researchers, one begins to wonder if any proof exists." James Randi, America's leading stage magician, comments: "Scientists who fall for the paranormal go through the most devious reasoning. Fortunes are squandered annually in pursuit of mystical forces that are actually the result of clever deceits. The money would be better spent investigating the tooth fairy or Santa Claus. There is more evidence for their reality." The case for ESP, it is true, has certainly not been helped by the many fakes and quacks who are attracted to the field.

Researchers in the parapsychology of perception have categorized four basic types of ESP. These are *clairvoyance,* awareness of events lying beyond the reach of the five senses; *psychokinesis,* the ability to influence outside objects through the power of the mind; *precognition,* the capacity to anticipate events; and *out-of-body experience,* an apparent journey to a place distant from the physical self. A major problem in ESP research has been to achieve consistent results that might demonstrate the existence of any of these phenomena. Subjects who seem able to influence the fall of a die during one series of experiments may be unable to do so during another. Normal scientific procedure demands that experiments be replicable, a criterion that ESP experiments have conspicuously

failed to achieve. The inability of ESP advocates to postulate any physical process or medium through which ESP might operate has also hampered their efforts at achieving credibility for the phenomenon. ESP advocates retort, however, that ESP does not meet normal experimental criteria precisely because the phenomenon is paranormal, and that their inability to specify a physical process is merely a result of the infant state of their discipline.

The problem of the existence of ESP may never be resolved. After 25 years of studying ESP, William James commented, "I am theoretically no further than I was at the beginning, and I confess that at times I have been tempted to believe that the Creator has eternally intended this departure of nature to remain baffling." It seems certain, however, that ESP research will become more respectable in the future. Our traditional, Western scientific-rational view of the world is under more intense critical scrutiny than ever before, and psychologists of perception are likely to devote much more attention to ESP in the future.

Unit 24

Paying Attention

OVERVIEW

This unit focuses on the nature of attention, particularly its orienting and filtering characteristics, and discusses the ability of novel stimuli to command attention and the role of attention in learning. The evidence supports the importance of the orienting response, the filtering function of the perceptual system and effect of stimulus intensity, novelty, and complexity.

UNIT OUTLINE

DEFINITION AND BACKGROUND
1. *Definition:* attention is directing the senses to particular aspects of the environment and selecting certain stimuli for analysis, while ignoring or possibly storing for further analysis all other inputs.
2. *Background:* Wilhelm Wundt (1832–1920).

QUESTIONS AND EVIDENCE
1. What are some characteristics of paying attention?
Hypotheses:
   a. *Orienting-response:* whenever an organism is presented with a novel stimulus, it alerts itself so that it can deal with the possibilities that the stimulus may signal. **410**
   b. *Signal-detection:* detecting weak stimuli is a decision process where the problem is first to decide whether there is a stimulus in the environment worthy of attention and, second, to determine whether that stimulus is of any special significance. **411**
   c. *Selectivity:* the brain uses a "selective filter" to "tune in" certain messages and reject all others, thus reducing the processing load on the perceptual system.
2. What kinds of events command attention?
Hypotheses:
   a. *Novelty:* unfamiliar stimuli tend to command more attention than familiar ones. **414**
   b. *Complexity:* stimuli with many elements, such as a complicated pattern showing fine shadings of light and dark, command greater attention than simple stimuli. **415**
3. How is attention related to learning?
Hypotheses:
   a. *Learning-improvement:* ability to maintain attention under distracting circumstances enhances cognitive and intellectual performance. **417**
   b. *Subliminal-stimuli:* under certain circumstances behavior can be influenced by stimuli that are below sensory thresholds and hence receive no conscious notice. **418**

IMPORTANT CONCEPTS

	page
attention	**408**
orienting response	**410**
selectivity	**412**
subliminal stimuli	**418**

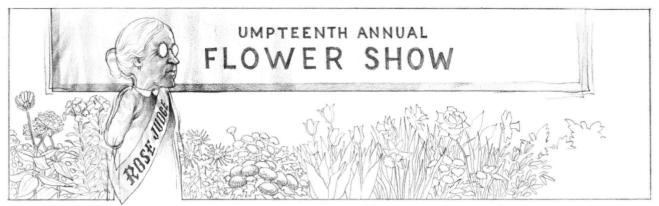

Environmental stimuli requiring attention may sometimes be imbedded in a complex array of irrelevant stimuli.

Becoming selectively attuned to specific environmental information is part of the process of paying attention.

Stimuli commanding the selective attention of an individual stand out as a signal against a background.

Any competent driver can carry on a conversation while guiding the car. He can also take note of problems like glare or a tremble in the steering wheel without interrupting his train of thought. That is, he can keep track of a variety of visual inputs and physical activities, plus at least two levels of conversation, all at once. This he manages by paying attention to certain stimuli, interpreting some of them, and disregarding others—an achievement that seems simple enough, until you ask yourself how it is done.

A DEFINITION of attention is *directing the senses to particular aspects of the environment and selecting certain stimuli for analysis, while ignoring or possibly storing for further analysis all other inputs.*

This unit will FOCUS on the nature of the attention process, particularly its orienting and filtering characteristics. It will also touch on the ability of novel or complex stimuli to command and maintain attention and on the role of attention in learning.

Figure 1. Wilhelm Wundt, who established the first experimental psychology laboratory, helped gain acceptance of psychology as a science through his extensive research on sensory experience.

Almost one hundred years ago, at the University of Leipzig, Germany, Wilhelm Wundt established the world's first experimental psychology laboratory. The year the laboratory was established, 1879, is also the one usually given as the birthdate of psychology as a science. By adapting the methods of natural scientists and physicists to the study of consciousness or "inner life," Wundt almost singlehandedly established psychology as a scientific discipline. As one historian of the field has put it, Wundt "succeeded so well in turning psychology into a laboratory-based science that since his time all other aspects of psychology have suffered from feelings of second-class citizenship" (Murphy and Kovach, *Historical Introduction to Modern Psychology*).

Wundt was interested in virtually every psychological issue of his day. At one time or another during his long life, he studied and tried to integrate such diverse fields as physiological psychology, child psychology, animal psychology, and folk psychology. His laboratory experiments concerned matters as different as the identification of just-noticeable differences in the intensity of a light or a tone and the study of word associations.

Wundt thought that psychological processes could and should be broken down into individual constituents for separate study—the same approach used by natural scientists and physicists in their study of the physical world. His chief research tool was the introspective method, in which subjects were asked to note and report their inner reactions to sensory stimuli. Wundt was perhaps his own most disciplined and talented subject: for example, after many sessions listening to the clicks of a metronome he reported that some tempos seemed more pleasant than others and that he experienced a feeling of tension just before each click and a feeling of relief after it.

Wundt's main contribution to the study of attention was his doctrine of "apperception," which stressed the distinction between focal and marginal events in an individual's experience. Although the word "apperception" is no longer used, many of its characteristics are studied today as aspects of attention. Wundt defined attention as a vivid perception of a narrow region of the content of consciousness and described the focus of attention as whatever is distinct from the rest of the perceptual field. His laboratory work showed that the range of attention and its fluctuations could be measured, though the results were difficult to interpret.

Trained in medicine and physiology and for a time a teacher of philosophy, Wundt was a sort of real-life version of the stereotyped German professor: gruff, precise, meticulous, and so demanding that he often seemed rude. He was, nevertheless, the most popular lecturer at the University of Leipzig, and his laboratory attracted students from all over the world. Two of his best-known American students were J. McK. Cattell, who did some important early work on span of attention, and E. B. Titchener. In 1892 Titchener established a laboratory at Cornell University modeled on Wundt's, where he and his colleagues did further research on the nature of attention and other questions Wundt had raised.

As psychology became increasingly "scientific," Wundt's introspective method came under strong attack. It had failed an important test of scientific measurement: the same experiment, run at different times, gave different results. Because introspection produces reports of people's subjective experiences, it does not yield findings that can be objectively verified. In addition, Wundt was criticized for his analytical approach—his desire to study separately each component of experience. William James, for example—who also played a central role in the study of attention—found Wundt's techniques not only unreliable but tedious and, worst of all, sterile. In James' opinion, the essential flavor of a psychological experience was lost when it was studied in fragments.

Today the writings of Wundt, James, and other early students of attention are being reread, not as quaint, "prescientific" classics but as collections of suggestive findings and acute observations that make excellent starting points for contemporary research.

QUESTIONS AND EVIDENCE

1. What are some characteristics of paying attention?
2. What kinds of events command attention?
3. How is attention related to learning?

Paying attention clearly involves two different levels of activity. First, it depends on the neurophysiological activities of the brain, the autonomic nervous system, and the sense receptors. Second, it depends on cognitive or intellectual activities; these are often described as concentration, thinking, or studying. While the first process is responsible for a general orienting response to the environment, the second selects certain elements or aspects of the environment for consideration. Along with the separation of certain signals from background noise, these two processes make up the major aspects of the state known as paying attention.

QUESTION	1. WHAT ARE SOME CHARACTERISTICS OF PAYING ATTENTION?		
HYPOTHESES	ORIENTING RESPONSE	SIGNAL DETECTION	SELECTIVITY
DESCRIPTIVE EVIDENCE			ASSESS: relationships among age, selective visual attention, and incidental learning
EXPERIMENTAL EVIDENCE	VARY: pairing of tone and shock MEASURE: habituation of the orienting response	VARY: stimulus intensity and frequency of presentation MEASURE: accuracy of bar pressing	VARY: listening conditions for pairs of words spoken by male and female voices MEASURE: accuracy of words reported according to age of child

1. WHAT ARE SOME CHARACTERISTICS OF PAYING ATTENTION?

The *orienting-response hypothesis* states that whenever an organism is presented with a novel stimulus, it alerts itself so that it can deal with the possibilities that the stimulus may signal. An animal, for example, orients by perking up its ears and looking in the direction of a stimulus. The orienting response (OR) is a universal reaction of great importance and is postulated to lie at the basis of all learning.

D. E. Berlyne, who has worked extensively in identifying the variables that affect attention, found in his review of the literature on the OR in 1960 that it has five essential components:

1. Changes in the sense organs. If a stimulus is visual, there will be an increase in sensitivity in the visual sense organs, with an accompanying decrease in the sensitivity of the other sense organs. If a stimulus excites more than one set of sense organs, both or all of them will show heightened sensitivity to incoming stimuli.

2. Changes in the skeletal muscles that direct the sense organs. When a hunting dog picks up the scent of a rabbit, there is a characteristic increase in the activity of the musculature of the nose—a behavior that is called sniffing. When a human being sees something interesting, his eyes open wide and are directed and fixated on the stimulus; the entire head may orient toward the source of the stimulation.

3. Changes in the general skeletal musculature. Ongoing actions are temporarily suspended, general muscle tension increases, and there is an increase in diffuse bodily movement.

4. Changes in the central nervous system. Brain waves (EEG) become irregular and fast (called alpha blocking), indicating increased cortical arousal. There is also increased activity in the reticular activating system and other subcortical brain areas.

5. Changes in the autonomic nervous system. The blood vessels contract, electrical conductivity of the skin (galvanic skin response) changes, and there are complex changes in heart rate and respiration.

The physiological changes that take place as an organism orients to a novel stimulus obviously play a central role in how it receives and deals with incoming stimuli. They focus attention first on the question "What is it?" and then on the question "What is to be done?"

The usual answer to the second question is "Nothing." Continuously bombarded with stimuli every day, we have to learn to ignore almost all of them. When a stimulus no longer elicits an OR from an organism, that stimulus is said to have become *habituated.* People who live in the city soon come to ignore much of the urban frenzy that surrounds them. (And a city dweller who retreats to a quieter environment—who spends a summer camped out in the mountains, say—may find that it takes days, even weeks, before he begins to respond to the less dramatic sights and sounds around him.)

On the other hand, a few of those millions of stimuli acquire significant meaning for the individual. A bird learns the importance of stimuli associated with the presence of a cat; a driver exceeding the speed limit becomes increasingly sensitive to the familiar markings of the police cruiser. To such stimuli, an organism develops a strong action-oriented response. This shift from the OR to a stronger level of response is called the *defensive reaction* (DR).

The DR is also a highly pervasive and generalized response. It can be distinguished from the OR both on the basis of the stimuli that elicit it and by the nature of the response itself. DRs are elicited by stimuli with extremely high intensity or with a painful quality. If sufficiently aversive or painful, they may not elicit an OR prior to eliciting a DR; most strong stimuli, however, will elicit an OR at least a few times before they begin to elicit an immediate DR. The clearest distinction between the two responses is probably physiological changes in the blood vessels of the head. During an OR, the blood vessels dilate (enlarge); during a DR, they become constricted.

EXPERIMENTAL EVIDENCE

Investigator: E. N. Sokolov
Source, Date: "Neuronal Models and the Orienting
Reflex" 1960
Location: USSR
Subjects: Human adult males
Materials: Electric shock, physiograph, tones

Each subject was presented with a tone and a shock separately. In both cases the stimuli were novel and resulted in ORs. After seventeen trials the OR habituated to the tone as an unimportant neutral stimulus.

Almost three times as many trials were required before the OR habituated to the meaningful stimulus, the shock. After forty-seven trials, the shock no longer elicited the OR, but it did elicit a strong DR: constriction of the blood vessels of the head.

The two stimuli were then paired, with the tone slightly preceding the shock. At first this novel combination of stimuli elicited the OR anew, but after thirty-five trials the tone itself elicited the DR because of its association with shock.

This experiment demonstrates the significance of the "what's to be done" function of the OR. When the tone was a meaningless event, the OR habituated, while the more important shock stimulus became associated with a defensive response. But when tone and shock were paired, so that the tone became a significant signal, over time it too came to elicit the DR.

The orienting response has for many years been assumed to be a prerequisite to attention and therefore to learning. In a series of experiments performed in 1963 the Russian investigator A. R. Luria demonstrated that retarded children frequently show no orienting response to stimuli of moderate strength and little habituation to very strong stimuli. There is little doubt that the OR is necessary for learning to occur. However, the exact relation between the OR and learning—whether the OR itself is an unlearned or a learned response—is still a topic of heated debate within experimental psychology.

When stimuli are strong enough to elicit an OR, the organism can then decide whether or not some more specific response is required. But even very weak stimuli, or those masked in a very noisy environment, can be of great potential importance. The *signal-detection hypothesis* states that detecting weak stimuli is a decision process where the problem is first to decide whether there is a stimulus in the environment worthy of attention and, second, to determine whether that stimulus is of any special significance.

It is a standard convention of the hard-boiled detective story that at some point the hero must thread his way through a menacing setting in which the signs of lurking danger are extremely faint. The ordinary citizen confronts a similar situation if, while walking alone down a dark city street, he begins to wonder whether he hears the footsteps of a mugger behind him. The basic difficulty here might be termed the ratio of signal to noise. Can those faint thuds, only one element in a vast array of impersonal sounds, accurately be interpreted as the threat of a mugging? Are those thuds a signal or just noise?

All the stimuli that might be interpreted as hostile footsteps are transmitted by the auditory system to that part of the brain that specializes in auditory perception. At this point the perceptual process initiates a decision-making sequence based on past experience. First a signal-to-noise ratio is estimated: how vivid was the potential signal (thuds) to the noise (background sounds)? If the ratio is too low (signal too small), no threatening interpretation will be made, and that is the end of that. If, on the other hand, the ratio is high enough (that is, an apparent signal is loud enough), the potential threat receives further consideration and the decision process continues.

It now draws upon the individual's accumulation of experiences and memories. These take the form of *expectations* about what is most likely to happen next—even newspaper stories about recent muggings can play a role here—and *motivations*, including the fear that may actually hinder the perception of strange sounds. Finally, there are *payoff incentives*, the possible consequences (benefits or losses) of an incorrect or correct response to the sound. The possible payoffs can be summarized in the form of a matrix (see Figure 2). Most individuals are more willing to be embarrassed than to be mugged, so they are more likely to "hear" the footsteps than not—even when the footsteps are not really there.

Footsteps Are	Response	
	Threat	No Threat
Real	Avoid mugger (correct)	Get mugged (incorrect)
Not Real	Be embarrassed (incorrect)	Nothing (correct)

Figure 2. When the signals (footsteps) stand out enough from background noise to arouse your attention, expectations and motivations help you consider the "payoff incentives" which accompany each possible response.

In the following experiment, rats were placed in a signal-detection situation. They were required to make a difficult perceptual decision in order to obtain water. The actual purpose of the experiment was to investigate the perceptual abilities of rats, but the experiment also serves as a good example of how a difficult-to-measure variable such as attention can be assessed experimentally in animals other than man.

EXPERIMENTAL EVIDENCE

Investigator: M. Hack
Source, Date: "Signal Detection in the Rat," 1963
Location: New York University School of Medicine
Subjects: 4 male albino rats
Materials: Auditory signals, training box with two levers,
    water reinforcement

In response to the soundings of a very weak tone, thirsty rats were supposed to press a bar in order to obtain water. Increasing the number of tones without increasing their loudness resulted in a higher number of "correct" bar presses; it also increased the number of "incorrect" bar presses. Basically, it increased the probability of some response, though not necessarily of the correct one. This result occurred partly because the ratio of the signal intensity to overall noise had not changed.

When he varied the intensity of the signal relative to the noise, Hack found that as the tone became louder, the animals' accuracy improved: the number of bar presses when the tone was present increased and the number of bar presses when the tone was absent decreased.

The task of attending to and making decisions about weak sensory information is very difficult and complex. The signal-detection paradigm is being used extensively in experimental psychology to observe the sensory sensitivity characteristics of various organisms, including man. It also serves as a model for testing various theories of decision making that involve the use of ambiguous or incomplete stimuli.

Moving beyond the basic orienting response and even beyond the more complex process of signal detection, the *selectivity hypothesis* states that the brain uses a "selective filter" to "tune in" certain messages and reject all others, thus reducing the processing load on the perceptual system.

If you hear your name called at a party, your auditory and visual sensitivity will increase as you scan the crowd, and you probably will find the person who is looking for you. Even amid the conversation and noise of the party, and even if your friend speaks softly, you will find you can follow what he is saying to you. The orienting response alone cannot account for this, since a heightened awareness of the entire auditory spectrum would hamper the ability to pick out specific relevant cues. The following experiment investigates the "selective listening" capacities of children of different ages.

EXPERIMENTAL EVIDENCE

Investigators: E. E. Maccoby and K. W. Konrad
Source, Date: "Age Trends in Selective Listening," 1966
Location: Stanford University
Subjects: 96 children between five and ten years old
Materials: Tape-recorded pairs of words, ear phones

All the children listened twice to a list of twenty-three pairs of words spoken simultaneously by two speakers, a man and a woman. On one run-through of the list, a child was asked to repeat the words spoken by the male voice; on the other, he was to repeat the words spoken by the female voice. Eleven pairs of words were monosyllabic; ten had two syllables; and three had three syllables. All were familiar to children the ages of those in the experiment.

The children were divided into two groups. In one group, called the "split" condition, the voice saying one word was fed into the right ear and the voice saying the other word, into the left ear. In the other group, called the "mixed" condition, the male voice speaking one word and the female voice speaking the other were heard simultaneously by both ears.

The task was quite difficult: all in all, the children reported correctly only about a third of the words they were instructed to listen to. The children in the "split" listening condition did better at repeating the words than those in the "mixed" condition. But in both conditions, performance clearly improved with age, with ten-year-olds getting about four more words correct than six-year-olds. In addition, older children made fewer "intrusive errors" (repeating the word spoken in the wrong voice) and used the language cues provided by multisyllabic words more effectively. The older the child, the more advantage he seemed to

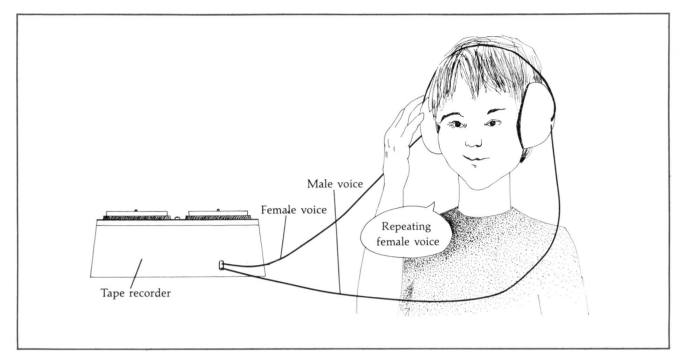

Figure 3. In the split condition of this experiment on the ability of children to listen selectively, a male voice speaks one word into one ear and a female voice speaks another into the other ear at the same time. In the mixed condition both voices are heard by both ears. Asked to repeat words spoken by only one of the speakers, children's performance in both conditions improved with age. Adapted from Maccoby and Konrad (1966).

derive from increased length of words. Thus, the filtering ability seems to be a learned process that develops as a child acquires experience, in this case with the complexities of language.

Impressive as the ability to select information from a welter of external stimuli may be, even more interesting is the ability to process and store information from more than one channel simultaneously, as the driver described at the start of this unit was doing. True, the driver's main concern shifted from moment to moment—from his driving to his conversation to the shimmy in the steering wheel—but he never became so absorbed in one thing that he lost track of the others. At a party, similarly, the conversation you are taking part in may have first claim to your attention, but you probably would not find it difficult to follow the drift of another (perhaps more interesting) one going on simultaneously a few feet away. The next study concerns the amount of information

people are able to retain from the nondominant channel, which seems to increase with age.

DESCRIPTIVE EVIDENCE

Investigators: A. W. Siegel and H. W. Stevenson
Source, Date: "Incidental Learning: A Developmental Study," 1966
Location: University of Minnesota
Subjects: 96 children seven to fourteen years old, and 24 adults
Materials: Slide projector, subject panel, pictures of common objects such as a truck, a frog, a fence

The nonessential or irrelevant information processed during a learning task is called "incidental learning." For example, if the primary task is discriminating pictures of circles from pictures of squares, learning that the circles used are pink and blue while the squares are green and yellow would be incidental. To the extent that the primary task is challenging a learner, incidental learning usually does not take place, since it reflects a dispersal of attention. A subject focusing only on relevant cues will not attend to extraneous details but will "filter out" or ignore them.

In this study, all the subjects (adults and children) were given three discrimination tasks. The first was simple: they were asked to discriminate between pictures of three common objects, such as a truck, a boat, and a plane, by pressing the correct one of three buttons in response to each picture. In the second task, they were asked to discriminate between three more complex pictures: one included the truck, one the boat, and one the plane, but each picture also included several other objects. In the third task, which was the test of incidental learning, pictures of each discriminative stimulus (the truck, boat, and plane) and pictures of each incidental object were presented separately. The measure of incidental learning was the number of times a subject responded to an incidental object as if it were the stimulus object with which it had appeared in the second task. For example, during the second task the correct response to a picture showing a truck, fish, rooster and star was to press the "truck" button; the correct response to a picture of a boat, frog, pig, and fence was to press the "boat" button. If, during the third task, a subject pushed the "truck" button when shown a picture of a fish and the "boat" button when shown a picture of a frog, then incidental learning had occurred.

The adults showed considerably more incidental learning than any of the children; for the children, incidental learning increased between the ages of seven and eleven, then fell off sharply (almost to the seven-year-old level) between the ages of twelve and fourteen. The experimenters concluded that the high level of incidental learning in adults probably occurred because the tasks were quite easy for them, whereas the decline for children between twelve and fourteen probably reflected the older children's increased "powers of concentration." They were better able than young children to disregard the irrelevant stimuli, but not yet as able as adults to keep track of a relevant stimulus without giving it their full attention.

These findings suggest that some kind of filtering mechanism does develop with age, but that it is not automatically applied. The requirements of the situation, and especially the difficulty of the primary task, will dictate how sharply attention is focused on that task.

2. WHAT KINDS OF EVENTS COMMAND ATTENTION?

The characteristics of the stimuli themselves often affect the kind and degree of attention they are given. Novel events (like a sudden gunshot) virtually demand to be noticed, and complex sets of stimuli (like the array of signs and intersections that confronts a driver negotiating a complicated cloverleaf) require very close examination.

The *novelty hypothesis* states that unfamiliar stimuli tend to command more attention than familiar ones. As the gunshot example suggests, attention to novelty is extremely functional. It is generally followed either by a defensive reaction, as when a deer runs away from the crack of a rifle, or, in less extreme cases, by exploratory behavior. In young children, for example, it has been found that events just different enough to be interesting will grip their attention—but only after a certain age.

QUESTION	2. WHAT KINDS OF EVENTS COMMAND ATTENTION?	
HYPOTHESES	NOVELTY	COMPLEXITY
DESCRIPTIVE EVIDENCE		
EXPERIMENTAL EVIDENCE	VARY: stimulus novelty MEASURE: duration of visual fixation by age of infant	VARY: stimulus complexity MEASURE: duration of visual fixation

EXPERIMENTAL EVIDENCE

Investigators: *F. Weizmann, L. B. Cohen, and R. J. Pratt*
Source, Date: *"Novelty, Familiarity, and the Development of Infant Attention," 1971*
Location: *University of Illinois, Urbana*
Subjects: *32 four-week-old infants*
Materials: *Stabiles (fixed visual stimuli)*

From the age of four weeks to the age of eight weeks, each infant was exposed to one of two stabiles (fixed visual patterns—the opposite of mobiles) suspended over his bassinet for thirty minutes a day. Half the infants spent this time becoming familiar with a stabile showing three yarn tassels (blue, green, and brown) suspended from a yellow disk; the other half saw a cluster of pink plastic flowers mounted on a red disk.

When the infants were six and eight weeks old, they underwent an eight-minute "test period." The familiar and the unfamiliar stabile were presented alternately for one minute each—first the yarn, then the flowers, then yarn again—and the amount of time each infant fixed its eyes on each stabile was recorded.

At age six weeks, as Table 1 shows, the infants preferred the familiar pattern, indicating less orienting to novel stimuli than to familiar ones. At eight weeks, however, the infants showed a marked increase in the attention paid to novel patterns. According to one theory, infants need time to develop an internal representation of the familiar before they are able to react to the novel; the findings in this experiment seem to confirm that theory.

TABLE 1. Mean Fixation Time in Seconds

Ages in Weeks	Novel Stabile	Familiar Stabile
6	62.5	93.1
8	90.9	72.2

Complexity, though probably less likely than novelty to serve as a spur to immediate action, resembles novelty in that it tends to stimulate exploratory behavior. The *complexity hypothesis* states that stimuli with many elements, such as a complicated pattern showing fine shadings of light and dark, command greater attention than simple stimuli. The following experiment is an attempt to answer the question, how old does an infant need to be before he shows a preference for complex patterns over simple stimuli?

EXPERIMENTAL EVIDENCE

Investigator: *R. L. Fantz*
Source, Date: *"Pattern Vision in Newborn Infants," 1963*
Location: *Western Reserve University*
Subjects: *Newborn infants*
Materials: *Six circular targets varying in complexity*

The infants, ranging from ten hours to five days old, were shown a set of six circular targets. Three of the circles were unpatterned—one yellow, one white, and one red; the other three were patterned—newsprint, concentric circles, and a schematic face. The set of targets was shown to the infants eight times, with targets in random order each time, and the amount of time an infant spent looking at each target was recorded.

The resulting order of preference was: face, circles, newsprint, white, yellow, and red. A similar order of preference is found in infants two to six months old. Apparently patterned stimuli can capture visual attention from birth on. This finding not only confirms that complex events tend to command more attention than simple ones but suggests that human infants have an innate capacity for pattern perception. The ability to perceive novelty, you will recall from the last experiment, seems not to develop before the age of about eight weeks.

Both novelty and complexity are relative matters: something that strikes one observer as novel and complex may strike another as oldhat and simple to the point of boredom. In addition, there is some evidence that a stimulus that is extremely novel or very complex may discourage attention instead of promoting it. A person who enjoys twentieth-century art, for example, may detect and appreciate the unfamiliar elements in a Picasso drawing he has never seen before but turn quickly away from a painting by a new artist who has radically violated standard conventions.

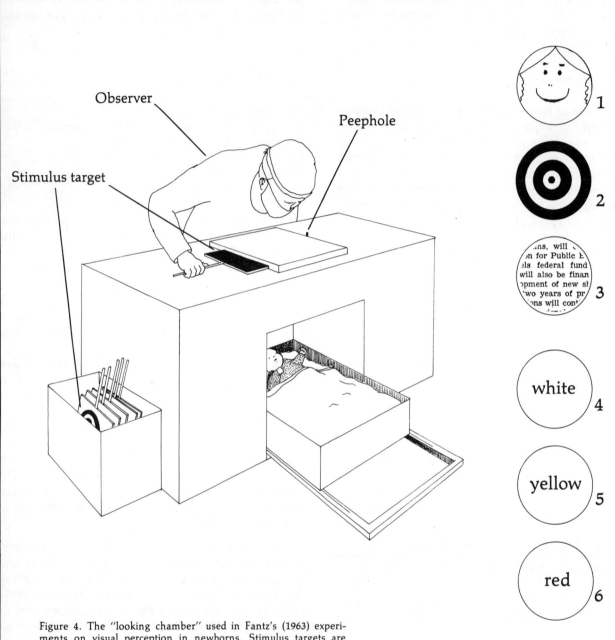

Figure 4. The "looking chamber" used in Fantz's (1963) experiments on visual perception in newborns. Stimulus targets are shown to the baby to determine types of (and preferences in) pattern vision. Right, stimulus targets in order of preference by newborn infants as measured by time spent looking at them.

HYPOTHESES	LEARNING IMPROVEMENT	SUBLIMINAL STIMULI
DESCRIPTIVE EVIDENCE	ASSESS: the relation of academic achievement to susceptibility of distraction	
EXPERIMENTAL EVIDENCE	VARY: training in attention to relevant attributes MEASURE: scores on conservation test	VARY: presentation of subliminal stimulation MEASURE: tests of stimulus effectiveness

3. HOW IS ATTENTION RELATED TO LEARNING?

Attention can be an important element in learning. The *learning-improvement hypothesis* states that ability to maintain attention under distracting circumstances enhances cognitive and intellectual performance.

DESCRIPTIVE EVIDENCE

Investigators: R. W. Baker and T. O. Madell
Source, Date: "Susceptibility to Distraction in Academically Underachieving and Achieving Male College Students," 1965
Location: Clark University
Subjects: 60 male college students
Materials: Various tape recordings, five-digit addition and subtraction problems

The subjects were divided into two groups: the "achievers," students whose percentile rank in class was at least two points above the rank predicted on the basis of their college entrance tests, and the "underachievers," whose actual rank was fifteen points below the predicted level. Their task was to solve a series of addition and subtraction problems while various background noises were played on a tape recorder. The distractions included a record of carpentry workshop noise, a Nichols and May comedy record, and someone reciting arithmetic computations like those on the test. The objective was to determine differences in the susceptibility of achievers and underachievers to distraction by the different background noises.

The only significant drop in performance occurred when the comedy record—clearly the most interesting one—was played. The computations were only slightly distracting, and the carpentry sounds did not damage performance at all. In general, the achievers worked faster than underachievers, suggesting that the underachievers were more susceptible to distraction.

EXPERIMENTAL EVIDENCE

Investigator: R. Gelman
Source, Date: "Conservation Acquisition: A Problem of Learning to Attend to Relevant Attributes," 1969
Location: Brown University
Subjects: 110 children, four to six years old
Materials: Colored plasticine balls, beakers filled with water; tall thin glass; short wide glass; 5 black checkers; 2 yellow sticks

Many young children fail to recognize such equivalencies as when water is poured from a tall glass to a short glass its quantity does not change. Such equivalencies of mass, volume, or length are referred to as *conservation*. Gelman reasoned that many young children fail to conserve because they attend to the wrong dimensions not because they genuinely lack understanding of the concept of conservation (see Unit 16). She therefore administered standard conservation tests of length, number, volume, and mass to kindergarten children and then gave special training to the sixty who failed all the tests.

The initial training, designed to teach the distinction between "same" and "different," involved two days of "oddity" problems. The child was shown three objects, two the same (for example, two toy lions) and one different (for example, a toy cup), and asked which of the three objects was the "odd" one. Next, the child was given a series of problems in which either length or number was the relevant concept. (For example, he was asked which had more, two rows containing five chips or one row containing three.) After each choice, the child was told whether he was correct or not and given a trinket when he was right. A control group received the same training but without feedback on the correctness of choice; a second control group was trained only with oddity problems, not with problems in length and number.

Following their training the children took the conservation tests again. The ones who had both kinds of training, with feedback, gave 94 percent correct answers. The control subjects were correct only 25 percent of the time. In addition, the trained subjects reached a level of 62 percent correct answers on tests of the conservation of mass and volume, in which they had no specific training, showing an ability to generalize what they had learned about length and number. The controls answered only 7 percent of the questions on mass and volume correctly. Retention tests after two weeks showed the same pattern, indicating stability of the training effects.

These results suggest that many estimates of cognitive competence in children may be too low and that, by structuring learning situations so that students are more likely to attend to crucial aspects of a task, teachers could make dramatic improvements the rule rather than the exception.

Attention is obviously not the sole factor in learning. Indeed, the *subliminal-stimuli hypothesis* has proposed that under certain circumstances behavior can be influenced by stimuli that are below sensory thresholds and hence receive no conscious notice. This idea aroused widespread public concern in the late 1950s, when there were reports that flashing commercial messages on movie screens for very brief exposure times might cause audiences to run out and buy the advertised products. Articles in the popular press expressed fear that subliminal messages could be used to control our behavior as if we were mindless robots.

EXPERIMENTAL EVIDENCE

Investigator: D. Byrne
Source, Date: "The Effect of a Subliminal Food Stimulus on Verbal Responses," 1959
Location: San Francisco State College
Subjects: A class of 108 college students
Materials: A film, completion test, word-association test, preference test, rating scale

An experimental group and a control group of subjects were shown the same film. For the experimental group the word "beef" was flashed on the screen every seven seconds for 1/200th of a second during the showing; for the control group no word was flashed. After seeing the film, the subjects took a sentence-completion test and a word-association test. In addition, they were asked to choose, from a menu listing five sandwiches, the kind they liked best, and to indicate on a rating scale how hungry they felt at the moment.

Because three subjects reported that they had seen a word flashed on the screen (two of them saw "beer" instead of "beef") the analyses were performed on only 105 of the 108. In neither the experimental nor the control groups was there any significant increase in the number of references to beef in the sentence-completion or word-association tests. Furthermore, the two groups did not differ in their preferences for roast-beef sandwiches. But the subjects in the experimental group *did indicate they were hungrier than did the control subjects.*

The fact that the subliminally delivered message influenced behavior in a very general way suggests that attention is not always necessary for influencing behavior. But a great deal more research needs to be done before any firm conclusions about this matter can be reached.

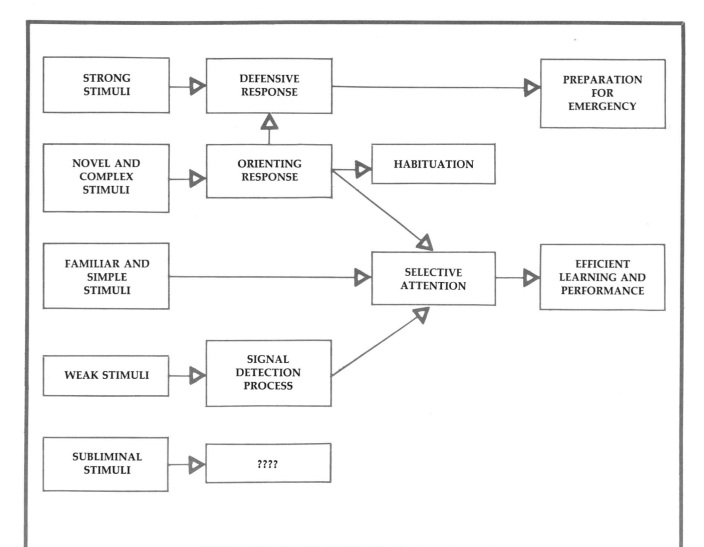

PUTTING IT TOGETHER: Paying Attention

Specific characteristics of environmental stimuli determine which aspects we will attend to and how we will respond. Very *strong stimuli* are probably immediate and direct in eliciting the *defensive response*, a physiological alerting reaction which initiates behavior in *preparation for responding to an emergency. Novel and complex stimuli* elicit the *orienting response*, a physiological alerting reaction similar to the defensive response. The orienting response facilitates the processing of enough information to determine the need for a defensive response, selective attention, or *habituation. Familiar and simple stimuli* may directly initiate a *selective attention* process that filters out information not relevant to the task at hand. This process, which apparently improves with age to an optimal level, promotes *efficiency in learning and performance. Weak stimuli* require rapid decision making, referred to as a *signal detection process,* before they are selectively attended. *Subliminal stimuli* apparently may have some effect on behavior without a person actually becoming aware of them, but how they affect behavior remains highly debatable.

1. WHAT'S ACCEPTED . . .

1. The OR prepares the organism to receive incoming information.

2. The OR habituates with repeated presentations of a stimulus.

3. Selective attention necessarily involves a filter of some type.

4. The ability to focus attention improves with age and training.

5. Stimulus variables such as intensity, novelty, and complexity affect attention.

2. WHAT'S DEBATED . . .

1. Whether the OR is a prerequisite to the DR, particularly with very strong stimuli.

2. Role of the OR in learning.

3. The nature of signal detection and its relationship to attention.

4. The exact nature of the filtering mechanism.

5. The chronological relationship between the OR and selective attention.

6. What effect subliminal stimulation has on behavior.

As we mentioned at the beginning of this chapter, it is possible, while driving, to perform various other tasks such as talking, thinking about something else, or listening for irregularities in the sound of the engine. The driver is able to pay attention to many different stimuli, focusing on some and disregarding others. But what if this process of paying attention is impaired, so that the driver can no longer discriminate between important and unimportant stimuli and focus on those that are crucial to his main task of driving?

The most common source of impairment to the attention-paying process in drivers is the use of drugs, particularly alcohol. And what about the effects of other drugs, including marijuana? More and more Americans are smoking marijuana, and increasing numbers are presumably driving while under the influence of the drug. An important area of research in psychology focuses on the effect of marijuana—and other drugs whose use has only recently become common—on the attention of drivers.

The United States has always been a nation of drug takers. When the pilgrims set sail for the New World, they took 14 tons of water—plus forty-two tons of beer and ten thousand barrels of wine. The use and abuse of psychoactive drugs has continued ever since. Every year we spend over a billion dollars on some 225 million prescriptions for psychoactive pills of all kinds: sedatives, tranquilizers, and stimulants. We drink over a billion gallons of spirits, wine, and beer each year. Nearly 8 million Americans have taken a psychedelic drug, such as LSD or mescaline. More than 26 million Americans, including 67 percent of college students, have smoked marijuana. Most of the interest that people have in these drugs centers on their effects on consciousness and interpersonal behavior, but their effects on attention can be vital—and fatal.

You probably already know about the effects of alcohol on the attention of drivers. Alcohol is very widely used in American society. About a quarter of all adults are classified as "heavy drinkers," and nearly 9 million of our citizens are compulsive alcoholics who are addicted to the drug. When people who have been drinking alcohol get behind the wheel of an automobile, the results can be disastrous. Research has shown that nearly three-quarters of drivers who are responsible for accidents have alcohol in their bloodstream, and 46 percent of them are highly intoxicated at the time of the accident. Some 60 percent of fatally injured drivers have been drinking, and the same is true of 74 percent of fatally injured pedestrians. The cost of property damage and medical expenses due to alcohol-related automobile accidents total over 1 billion dollars a year.

Alcohol contributes to road accidents in two main ways: slowed reaction time and impaired attention. Drivers who are intoxicated have great difficulty in focusing attention, in maintaining the focus, and in selecting the most important stimuli for their attention. But does marijuana have a similar effect?

The issue has been a controversial one for some time. Marijuana smokers often insist that the drug allows them to focus attention even better than they are able to do when not under the influence of the drug, and many claim that their driving capacity is not adversely affected in the least. The weight of psychological research findings, however, does not support this belief. Although it seems to be true that marijuana smokers can readily focus attention on simple ideas and tasks and exclude other irrelevant stimuli, this ability does not seem to extend to more complex tasks such as driving.

Simulated driving tests have demonstrated that marijuana has a substantial and adverse impact on driver performance. Like alcohol, the drug slows reaction time, blurs the focus of attention, and impairs judgment. Persons under the influence of the drug have been found to show particularly poor judgment on such tasks as overtaking. They consistently misjudge time-distance relationships and take unintentional risks.

Despite the criminal penalties attached to use of the drug, marijuana is becoming steadily more popular in the United States. It is likely that the laws against marijuana will tend to lapse into disuse or to be repealed in the future, so that even more citizens will be encouraged to experiment with the drug. Alcohol already causes some tens of thousands of traffic fatalities a year. Is marijuana usage likely to increase the deaths on our highways?

The National Commission on Marijuana and Drug Abuse recommended that the possession or sale of small quantities of marijuana be legalized, but firmly urged that driving under the influence of the drug carry strong criminal penalties, including imprisonment. Research is still needed to determine the level of dosage that impairs judgment and the precise nature of the impairment as compared to that caused by other drugs, but it is likely that the effects of marijuana on attention will compound the problem of road safety in America in the future.

Unit 25

Memory

OVERVIEW

Some of the most important findings of one of the most basic areas of psychology—the study of human learning and memory, are reported in this unit. The first matters discussed are factors affecting verbal learning and memory, and some theories of memory. Then the problem of determining how memory may be organized is briefly surveyed. Finally, different views on the several kinds of memory are presented, including the distinctions often made between short-term versus long-term, and verbal versus visual memories.

UNIT OUTLINE

DEFINITION AND BACKGROUND
1. *Definition:* memory is a general concept referring both to the information stored in the brain and the processes by which information is extracted.
2. *Background:* Hermann Ebbinghaus (1850–1909).

QUESTIONS AND EVIDENCE
1. What makes things easy or hard to learn?
Hypotheses:
   a. *Meaningfulness:* meaningful terms are easier to learn and remember than less meaningful ones. **425**
   b. *Imagery:* a word's ability to evoke imagery, like its meaningfulness, affects the ease of verbal learning. **427**
   c. *Serial-order:* the order in which verbal items are learned affects the ease with which they are remembered. **427**
   d. *Connectedness:* verbal material that forms a unified whole is easier to learn and remember than a collection of unrelated material.
2. Why do people (apparently) forget? **428**
Hypotheses:
   a. *Interference:* forgetting occurs because memories interfere with each other. **431**
   b. *Limited-retrieval:* forgetting occurs when the cues necessary to recall the data aren't supplied. **431**
   c. *Repression:* memories too unpleasant to remain in consciousness are forgotten.
3. How are memories organized?
Hypotheses:
   a. *Association:* the order in which material is recalled is determined by the strength of mental associations. **434**
   b. *Categorical-storage:* memory is systematically organized into hierarchical categories like those used by libraries. **434**
4. Is there more than one way to remember?
Hypotheses:
   a. *Iconic:* data to be remembered must pass through a very brief sensory or iconic stage that lasts less than a second. **436**
   b. *Two-stages:* data to be remembered must be rehearsed in an initial short-term memory (STM) stage to allow it to be coded and transferred to a more permanent long-term memory (LTM). **436**
   c. *Two-systems:* verbal information is subject to forgetting, while memorized sensory (iconic) images are relatively permanent. **437**

IMPORTANT CONCEPTS

	page
association	426
chunking	434
clustering	434
forgetting	431
iconic memory	436
learning	425
meaning	426
memory	424
mnemonic device	439
redundancy	428
rehearsal	436
semantic differential	426
serial position	427

Information is first stored in memory for a short term. Rehearsing the information holds it for brief periods.

Organizing the information aids in the shift from short-term to long-term memory.

The processes of remembering and forgetting involve retrieval as well as storage of information.

DEFINITION AND BACKGROUND

"I'll always remember what's-his-name!"

More than once, no doubt, you've had the maddening and mystifying experience of almost but not quite being able to remember a name, a fact, a face. It hovers at the edge of your brain and slithers across the tip of your tongue. Elusive as the mist, irritating as an itch—you know you know it, but *what is it*?

It can happen when you're relaxed—at a party when you see someone you know you've met, but can't quite place. It can happen when you're tense—during an exam, when you're searching your memory for the family name of one of the English kings: not Stuart, not Tudor, it begins with "P," not Windsor . . .

Why do we remember? How do we remember? What do we remember? And why, how, and what do we forget? These are questions that have fascinated philosophers for centuries. In recent years, they've fascinated psychologists, too. How memory works is one of the most intriguing—and potentially one of the most productive—areas that the psychologist can explore.

We will use this rather broad DEFINITION: *Memory is a general concept referring both to the information stored in the brain ("memories") and to the processes by which information is extracted.*

This unit will FOCUS on three memory processes: acquisition, retrieval, and forgetting. Acquisition and retrieval are the processes by which the brain "learns" and "remembers" data. The final aspect, *forgetting,* is not so easily defined. There is disagreement about whether forgotten material has actually disappeared from brain storage or is merely inaccessible for some reason. Most of the unit concerns verbal memories, but visual memories (images) will also be discussed.

BACKGROUND: HERMANN EBBINGHAUS (1850–1909)

The first major studies of learning and memory were performed by the German philosopher Hermann Ebbinghaus, who received his doctorate in philosophy in 1873. A few years later, while browsing in a secondhand bookshop in Paris, Ebbinghaus came across a copy of Gustav Fechner's *The Elements of Psychophysics* (1860). Fechner described experiments in which human sensory experiences were carefully

Figure 1. The scientific study of verbal learning and memory begins with Hermann Ebbinghaus, whose methods and principles are still used today.

measured. His demonstration that inner experience could be analyzed with precision came as a revelation to Ebbinghaus, who for years had been intrigued by the question of how memory works. Now, encouraged by Fechner's success, he resolved to find an objective way to get the answers.

In his own book, *Concerning Memory* (1885), Ebbinghaus first asked, "How [can] the probable course of inner processes be traced if almost entirely forgotten ideas return no more to consciousness?" and then answered, "By 'our method' of indirectly approaching the problem in a small and definitely limited sphere."

Ebbinghaus concentrated on the number of times it was necessary to repeat something before it was committed to memory, using this number as his principal unit of measurement. He performed all his experiments on himself—the sole subject as well as the experimenter. At first he attempted to memorize long lists of words, but he quickly discovered that the results were unreliable because the meanings he associated with some words made them easier to remember than others and interfered with his ability to observe the memory process in its "pure" form. So

HYPOTHESES	MEANINGFUL-NESS	IMAGERY	SERIAL ORDER	CONNECTED-NESS
DESCRIPTIVE EVIDENCE			ASSESS: relationship between serial position of word and rate of learning	ASSESS: relationship of verbal context to rate of learning
EXPERIMENTAL EVIDENCE	VARY: meaningfulness of items to learn MEASURE: rate of learning	VARY: power of items to evoke imagery MEASURE: rate of learning		

he devised the clever and practical idea of memorizing lists of "words" that made no sense at all. He concocted nonsense syllables like "ger," "zik," and "fap," which had no familiar meanings or associations to get in the way of the memory process. They were constructed so that no one syllable was apparently harder or easier to memorize than any other.

Ebbinghaus' procedure was first to memorize a list of nonsense syllables until he could repeat it perfectly. Then, periodically, he tested his ability to recall the syllables, keeping track of how many syllables he could recall from the list on each trial, whether his score improved or diminished with the passage of time, and whether there was any relationship between the order in which he remembered the syllables and the order in which he had originally memorized them. Later, he used nonsense syllables to measure more subtle and complex areas of memory, such as whether it made any difference if he learned a list all at one sitting or if he took breaks. It turned out that he remembered more when he did take breaks.

Ebbinghaus' book made a great impression on other investigators and was accepted as a breakthrough in the study of higher mental processes that can't be directly observed but must be inferred from performance. Although investigators are now carrying out more refined and sophisticated experiments, many of them still use procedures that Ebbinghaus introduced. It has been estimated that more experiments have been based on the research originally reported in Ebbinghaus' *Concerning Memory* than on any other single source in the history of psychology.

Recent memory research, using nonsense syllables and other techniques, explores some basic questions you may have asked yourself when your own memory has failed.

QUESTIONS AND EVIDENCE

1. What makes things easy or hard to learn?
2. Why do people (apparently) forget?
3. How are memories organized?
4. Is there more than one way to remember?

1. WHAT MAKES THINGS EASY OR HARD TO LEARN?

Ebbinghaus used nonsense syllables in his work because he wanted results that were "uncontaminated" by the influence of meaning on memory. Other researchers have brought meaning back into the picture.

The *meaningfulness hypothesis* states that meaningful terms are easier to learn and remember than less meaningful ones. That is, it states not only that familiar words—"pen," "table," "lamp"—are easier to memorize than nonsense syllables—"nep," "taleb," "malp"—but highly meaningful words are easier to learn and remember than those with less meaning.

In 1952 an American psychologist, C. E. Noble,

devised a procedure for measuring the meaningfulness of verbal items. After words are presented, a subject is given one minute to produce as many associations (other words that just "pop" into his head) as he can. The number of associations produced for each verbal item presented is averaged over many subjects to obtain a mean number, m, which indicates the item's meaningfulness, or m value.

Noble measured the m values of a great many words and nonsense syllables. Some examples of words with low meaningfulness are "matrix" (1.73) and "femur" (2.09). Words with medium meaningfulness include "yeoman" (4.60) and "fatigue" (5.33). Words such as "army" (9.43) and "kitchen" (9.61) are highly meaningful. Meaningfulness is not the same as the meaning of a word. Measures like Noble's m do not tell what a word means, but only the amount of meaning it possesses relative to other words. (Psychologists have also tried to devise ways to measure word meaning. An example is Osgood's semantic differential, where subjects are asked to rate specific words on different scales such as good-bad, passive-active, and hot-cold. The pattern of responses to these scales indicates something about the unique connotations of the word—its subjective meanings.)

EXPERIMENTAL EVIDENCE

Investigators: V. J. Cieutat, F. E. Stockwell, and C. E. Noble
Source, Date: "The Interaction of Ability and Amount of Practice with Stimulus and Response Meaningfulness (m, m¹) in Paired-Associate Learning," 1958
Location: Montana State University
Subjects: 170 college students
Materials: Memory drum; verbal items

Subjects were asked to learn a list of paired verbal items. Later, the first word in each pair was presented as a stimulus, and the subject was to respond by giving the second.

Different lists of ten pairs were used for each of four groups of student subjects. For one group (L-L) both the stimulus and response words in each pair were of low m. For another group (H-H) both the words were of high m. A third group (L-H) learned a list in which the stimulus words had low meaningfulness but the response words were of high m. The fourth group (H-L) had a list in which the stimulus words were of high m and the response items of low m.

On each trial (each run-through of the list) the percentage of correct responses to the stimulus words was recorded. The results (summarized in Figure 2)

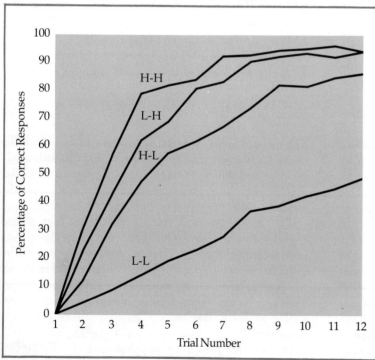

Figure 2. Results of paired associate learning when meaningfulness (m) of stimulus and response words are varied. H-H indicates both stimulus and response are high in m, L-H stands for low stimulus m and high response m, and so on. (Examples: H-H: envy-kitchen. L-H: matrix-kitchen. H-L: army-femur. L-L: matrix-femur). Adapted from Cieutat et al. (1958).

showed that meaningfulness exerted a profound effect on the rate of learning. (The relation between meaningfulness, as measured by the number of associations a word has, and memory suggests something about the mechanism by which words are learned. It is as if a word is easier to learn if it can be "hooked onto" a number of other words already stored in memory.)

Words have other associations besides verbal ones. Some, like "sunset," "car," and "alligator," immediately call up visual images in most people. Others, such as "shriek" and "grunt," are associated with nonverbal sounds, and still others, such as "sour" or "stench," with other sensory experiences. But a further group of words—"interim," "criterion," and "functional" are examples—rarely produce mental images of any sort. The *imagery hypothesis* states that a word's ability to evoke imagery, like its meaningfulness, affects the ease of verbal learning.

EXPERIMENTAL EVIDENCE

Investigators: A. Paivio, P. C. Smythe, and J. C. Yuille
Source, Date: "Imagery Versus Meaningfulness of Nouns in
*   Paired Associate Learning," 1968*
Location: University of Western Ontario
Subjects: 33 college students
Materials: Memory drum; nouns varying in imagery value

To set up this experiment, the imagery values *I* of 925 nouns were rated by students enrolled in introductory psychology courses. They were asked to locate each noun on a seven-point scale of imagery-evoking ability. When the means of the ratings were calculated, it was clear that the nouns differed greatly in this respect. The word "car" had one of the highest ratings in the sample: 6.87, very close to the maximum possible rating of 7.00. The word "surtax," on the other hand, had the lowest imagery rating of the entire sample: 1.63 (the minimum possible rating was 1.00).

Next, each of thirty-three students learned a sixteen-item list of paired words of four different types. In four pairs (L-L) both stimulus and response words were low in *I*. Four other pairs (H-H) coupled high-*I* stimulus words with high-*I* response words. In the two middle groups (L-H and H-L) either the stimulus word was high *I* and the response word low or the

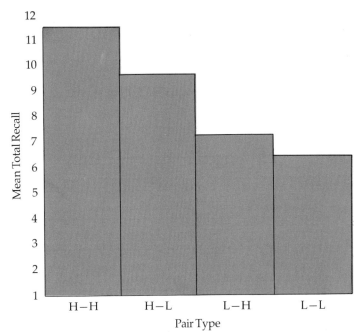

Figure 3. Results of paired associate learning when imagery-evoking power *I* of stimulus and response words are varied. H-H indicates high stimulus *I* and high response *I*, and so on. Adapted from Paivio et al. (1968).

stimulus word was low *I* and the response word high. The pairs in each category were randomly ordered in the list, and each subject went through the list four times. The measure was the total number of response items recalled during the four trials. The results (summarized in Figure 3) showed clearly that the ability of words to evoke imagery is an important factor in verbal learning.

Meaningfulness and imagery power, even when their effects are combined, do not fully account for variations in the ease of verbal learning. The *serial-order hypothesis* states that the order in which verbal items are learned affects the ease with which they are remembered. In an early experiment on this hypothesis, C. I. Hovland discovered the phenomenon called *serial-position effect.*

DESCRIPTIVE EVIDENCE

Investigator: C. I. Hovland
Source, Date: "Experimental Studies in Rote Learning
*   Theory," 1938*

Location: Yale University
Subjects: 32 college students
Materials: Serial lists of 12 items

Each subject was required to learn to repeat a list of items in a fixed order, so that each item served as the stimulus for recall of the next one. When the number of errors made on each item was plotted as a function of the item's position in the list, a bow-shaped curve resulted (see Figure 4). The first and last few items of the list were learned with the fewest errors, while the middle items were hardest to learn. This result is called the *serial-position effect.*

The superiority of the first few items is commonly referred to as the *primacy effect;* the superiority of the last few items is called the *recency effect.* Typically the primacy effect is found to be greater than the recency effect; that is, the items near the beginning of the list are learned with slightly fewer errors than the items near the end of the list. The serial-position effect has been obtained many times in studies, and serial position has been shown to affect tasks besides simple serial learning.

The serial-position effect suggests that a list of words is not actually learned in order, but that the beginning and the end are learned first, and then serve as anchors for the rest of the list. That is, the serial-position effect may result from the progressive learning of the list beginning at the ends and working toward the middle—as if the learner were digging a tunnel.

All lists are, by definition, serial. But some of them are unified as well, and this overall quality also affects learning. The *connectedness hypothesis* states that verbal material that forms a unified whole is easier to learn and remember than a collection of unrelated material. This commonsense notion—a line from a song is easier to learn than a grocery list—was confirmed by psychologists very early in the study of verbal learning and memory. In 1914 Lyon conducted an experiment that showed that it took only about ten minutes for the average subject to memorize a 200-word passage of poetry but about ninety-three minutes, or nearly ten times as long, to memorize a 200-item list of nonsense syllables.

Connected material is distinguished from unconnected material in several important ways. First, it forms a whole that has some *meaning* greater than the meanings of the individual items. Second, its coherence depends in part on *redundancy* (see Unit 14). As a technical term, redundancy can be defined as a measure of the predictability of later items from

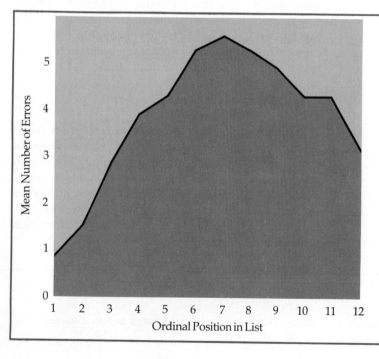

Figure 4. Mean number of errors made as a function of item's serial position in a list. Adapted from Hovland (1938).

earlier items. For example, the phrase "The dog" at the beginning of a sentence immediately sets up a restricted set of expectations about what will be said next. It is far more likely to be followed by a verb like "ran," "barked," or "chased" than by such words as "pencil," "flew," or "read." In contrast, the fact that a grocery list includes "eggs" does not indicate that it is likely to contain "milk" as well or that it is likely to contain "soap." Furthermore, connected material usually is *grammatical*—that is, it conforms to the rules of word usage for the given language—whereas unconnected material is not. Finally, some connected material, such as poetry and song, is also marked by *rhyming* and *rhythmic structures*. Unconnected material never possesses either of these features except by chance.

Each of these properties has been shown to be beneficial to verbal learning. Stated more strongly, the absence of one or more of the properties of connected material increases the difficulty of verbal learning and memory. In Lyon's experiment the poem had all four properties; the list of nonsense syllables had none.

DESCRIPTIVE EVIDENCE

Investigators: *G. A. Miller and J. A. Selfridge*
Source, Date: *"Verbal Context and the Recall of Meaningful Material," 1950*
Location: *Harvard University*
Subjects: *20 college students*
Materials: *Approximations to English*

An approximation to English is a string of words generated according to statistical properties of the language. Different orders of approximation take different numbers of words into account in biasing the selection of each word in the passage (see Figure 5). A zero-order approximation consists of words chosen at

Figure 5. Examples of approximations to English. A zero-order approximation consists of words chosen at random from a dictionary. As the order of approximation increases, the strings of words begin to make up units that have meaning. Adapted from Miller and Selfridge (1950).

Zero-Order Approximation
OUTFLOW FESTOON SHEAVES CANNOT LUMINOUS VELVET TRACTION DETESTABLE MUSLIN INTERPOLATION CENTAUR AMAZINGLY VICINITY WOBBLE PRECLUDE MISCHANCE

First-Order Approximation
THE THEN IS LAST LAKE THERE WHETHER INSURANCE BE THE IS INTO CLOSED WENT SIGHT HAD ORDER IN DUST COULD WHAT TERMS FRIENDS BOY A GOVERNMENT NIGHT

Second-Order Approximation
IS THIS IS THERE THEY WENT TO GO BACK HOME TO SEE THE DOG IS A BOY GOES THE PICTURE WAS IS GOING TO GO TO CLASS IS THAT IS THAT IS THAT WHICH ONE DAY IS

Third-Order Approximation
ARE SOMETIMES PROBLEMS OVERCOME ARE THE COLTS ARE A GROUP CAN DO ONLY WHAT IS THEY BOY MOUNTED HIS HORSE WAS A BOY JOE AND SAM CAME TOO WHICH IS

Fourth-Order Approximation
BELL WAS RINGING TOO LOUD THE NOISE DISTURBED THE MEN BECAUSE THEY HAVE NO LAWS IS NOT THE CORRECT METHOD TO DO THIS HE HAD LAST WORKED TUESDAY

Fifth-Order Approximation
GREAT PEOPLE ARE HUMBLE BECAUSE THEY HAVE NO ELECTRICITY BUT WE MADE IT IS TOO AND ALWAYS WILL BE IN HIS ROOM BY HIMSELF SO HE HAD A COLD BUT WENT

Sixth-Order Approximation
HOMES FOR PEOPLE ARE A NECESSITY CAN YOU DO THE JOB IF YOU ARE CAPABLE IS THE PHRASE SAID WHEN YOU WRITE ENCLOSE THREE DOLLARS BEFORE YOU REMIT THE

Eighth-Order Approximation
AN AUTOMOBILE WHEN THE VALVES GET STICKY NEEDS THE PROPER TREATMENT IS OUT OF THE SCOPE OF OUR IMAGINATION COME OUR NIGHTMARES WHICH ARE OFTEN

random from a dictionary. A first-order approximation is made up of words selected randomly but biased according to their frequencies of occurrence in the language. Thus, it is likely to contain such common words as "a," "the," and "is" and unlikely to include infrequent words like "fiduciary."

A second-order approximation can be constructed by presenting a word to someone and asking him to make up a sentence beginning with the word. Thus if the word is "is," he might say, "Is this the way to the library?" The first word following the stimulus word is then presented to another person, who generates a sentence beginning with it. In this case the sentence might be "This is my dog." This procedure is repeated until a string of words of the required length has been obtained: "Is this is there . . . "

Higher-order approximations are constructed in an analogous manner, except that longer and longer units are used in building strings. Notice that as the order of approximation increases, the strings begin to make up units that have meaning. A zero-order approximation seems totally incoherent, but an eighth-order approximation has a kind of stream-of-consciousness sense.

Miller and Selfridge asked subjects to listen to passages of various lengths and different orders of approximation and then to repeat them as accurately as possible. Plotting the percentage of words correctly recalled for the different orders of approximation, they found that for passages ranging in length from ten words to fifty words recall improved as the order of approximation became higher (see Figure 6). English text was recalled only slightly better than a seventh-order approximation, which indicates that most of the improvement in recall took place within the first few orders of approximation. Thus, connectedness helps learning and memory.

So much for the factors that affect the ease with which verbal material is memorized. What about the material one has learned and forgotten?

Figure 6. Percentage of words correctly recalled under conditions of varying lengths and orders of approximation to the statistical structure of English. Adapted from Miller and Selfridge (1950).

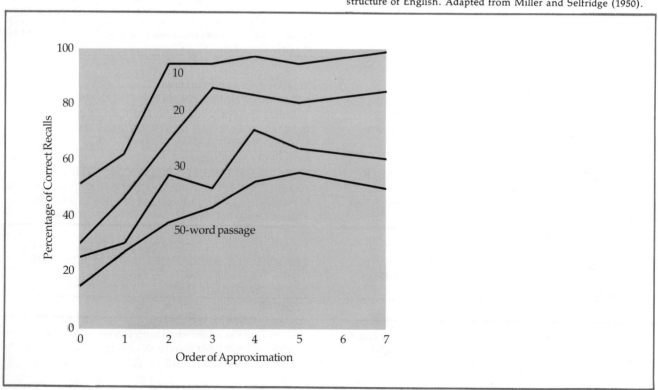

HYPOTHESES	INTERFERENCE	LIMITED RETRIEVAL	REPRESSION
DESCRIPTIVE EVIDENCE		ASSESS: characteristics of partially recalled memories	
EXPERIMENTAL EVIDENCE	VARY: amount of mental activity MEASURE: forgetting	VARY: methods for remembering MEASURE: amount remembered	VARY: pleasantness of memories MEASURE: forgetting

2. WHY DO PEOPLE (APPARENTLY) FORGET?

Before Ebbinghaus began to study memory processes systematically, the common explanation of forgetting was the leaky-bucket theory: memory is like a hole-riddled bucket from which information gradually and steadily flows into oblivion. The trouble with this theory is that it is not really an explanation—it merely describes the observation that memories seem to disappear as time goes on.

The *interference hypothesis* states that forgetting occurs because memories interfere with each other. For example, while visiting Spain, an American tourist who's conversant in French tries to master some basic Spanish phrases—it's a breeze. By afternoon he anticipates the Spanish social scene with confidence. That evening, he's in agony. Each time he tries to use his newly acquired Spanish, French phrases clutter his brain. He can't say *mi cara* when *ma cherie* interferes. On a later tour of France, the situation is reversed. When he reaches for the once familiar French, Spanish phrases interfere. This unfortunate tourist is suffering from both *retroactive interference*, in which new memories block out the old ones, and *proactive interference,* in which older knowledge gets in the way of the new.

EXPERIMENTAL EVIDENCE

Investigators: J. G. Jenkins and K. M. Dallenbach
Source, Date: "Oblivescence during Sleeping and Waking,"
    1924
Location: Cornell University
Subjects: 2 male college students
Materials: Memory drum, nonsense syllables

Both subjects were given lists of nonsense syllables to memorize. Then, to determine whether the number of syllables recalled was in any way dependent on the activity that took place after it was memorized, one subject was allowed to sleep for eight hours while the other stayed awake, going about his everyday activities. Both were then tested on how well they remembered the syllables. This procedure was repeated many times, with both subjects tested under both conditions.

After sleeping, the subjects tended to remember far more of the nonsense syllables than after being awake. This result suggested that the awake person's activities gave him new memories that interfered with the older ones—that is, with the list of nonsense words. According to this argument, the sleeping subjects did not accumulate new and "interfering" memories.

Interference is a vast improvement over the earlier, leaky-bucket notion, because the interference hypothesis at least suggests the mechanism responsible for the disappearance of memories. Also, it indicates that forgetting occurs during but not merely because of the passage of time. Still unsolved, however, is the question of whether the memory has permanently disappeared or is simply unretrievable at the moment recall is attempted.

The *limited-retrieval hypothesis* states that forgetting occurs when the cues necessary to recall the data aren't supplied. It implies that memories may be permanent but can't always be pulled out of storage. When a memory seems to be on the tip of your tongue but you can't remember it, you are experiencing the tip-of-the-tongue phenomenon—which, according to the limited-retrieval hypothesis, is a possible model of all forgetting.

DESCRIPTIVE EVIDENCE

Investigators: R. Brown and D. McNeill
Source, Date: "The 'Tip-of-the-Tongue' Phenomenon," 1966
Location: Harvard University
Subjects: 56 Harvard and Radcliffe students
Materials: Definitions of 49 uncommon words

To induce the tip-of-the-tongue (TOT) state, subjects were asked to identify words from definitions such as "a waxy substance from whales, used in perfumes," "an instrument used for measuring angular distances at sea," and "a person who collects postage stamps."

These phrases define English words that are neither very common nor very obscure, and many subjects reached the TOT state before they actually recalled "ambergris," "sextant," and "philatelist." The closer the subject came to successful recall, the more accurate the partial information he possessed. Among the typically remembered characteristics were the number of syllables in the word; some of the letters, most often the first or last; the most accented syllable; and the perceptual properties of the word (for example, where the "tall" letters were).

If a person's verbal memory is likened to a "dictionary in his head," then some features of the items stored in it may be easier to retrieve than others. For less common words the features easiest to recall may be the visual properties observed in the perception that is the first step in reading and identifying them.

The TOT situation, then, involves bits and pieces of memories as they were originally perceived. At other times, partial recall appears in different forms—as when, at a party, you can remember only the punchline of a story you wanted to tell. If the intensity and context of certain situations can trigger only parts of memories, the amount of information available to recall at any particular moment may vary according to the demands and cues that are present. This idea has been tested in an experimental situation through the use, again, of nonsense syllables.

EXPERIMENTAL EVIDENCE

Investigator: C. W. Luh
Source, Date: "The Conditions of Retention," 1922
Location: University of Chicago
Subjects: 20 college students
Materials: 90 series of nonsense syllables, 12 syllables in each series

This classic study tested the effects of five specific ways of remembering on the amount of material remembered.

1. *Recognition:* The subject had to pick out from a long list the syllables that he remembered from a list memorized earlier.
2. *Relearning:* The subject had to rememorize previously learned syllables until he could repeat them without error. What he remembered from his exposure, called "savings," was measured by subtracting the amount of time it took him to learn the list the second time from the amount of time he took originally.
3. *Free recall:* The subject had to recall all the syllables he could, in any order.
4. *Written reproduction:* The subject had to write the syllables on paper, trying to put them in the order in which he originally memorized them.
5. *Serial anticipation:* The subject had to recall each succeeding syllable in response to the last as a stimulus.

Periodic reexamination of the subjects during the next twenty-four hours showed (Figure 7) that recognition was the easiest of the five procedures: apparently, seeing the words themselves was the best cue for remembering them. Relearning was also more successful than the other measures, probably for the same reason.

If memory is limited by the circumstances in which the information is to be retrieved, is it possible that all experiences are permanently embedded in the brain? Some psychologists believe that, with the right cues present, information that has apparently been forgotten could easily be recalled.

But can forgetting continue even when all the appropriate cues are there? Perhaps. The *repression hypothesis* states that memories too unpleasant to remain in consciousness are forgotten.

EXPERIMENTAL EVIDENCE

Investigator: A. F. Zeller
Source, Date: "An Experimental Analogue of Repression," 1950
Location: Johns Hopkins University
Subjects: 20 male and female college students
Materials: Nonsense syllables, simple motor tasks

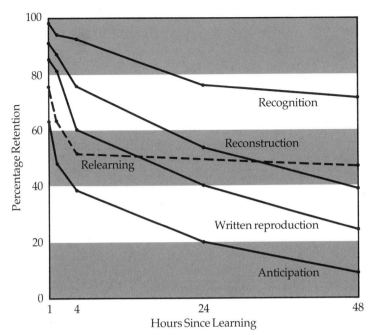

Figure 7. Comparison of effectiveness of five procedures for remembering nonsense syllables. Adapted from Luh (1922).

To explore whether the feeling of failure can repress memories, two groups of subjects were first asked to memorize a list of nonsense syllables. Their retention was then tested, and they were given a simple task involving manipulation of blocks. Members of the experimental group were given poor directions for the block manipulation and were constantly badgered by the experimenter, who told them that they were doing poorly. Members of the control group were given better directions and were constantly reassured by being told that they were doing well. Then everyone was directed to relearn the nonsense syllables and return in three days.

After three days they were tested for recall and again given the block manipulation task. This time the experimental group was permitted to be successful. Another test for recall of the nonsense syllables followed. Zeller summarized the results in this way: Induced failure at a task serves to reduce the ability to recall previously known material that has become associated with the failure task; induced success at the same associated task serves to increase the ability to recall the original material.

This study is considered a reasonable analogue of the repression concept of forgetting. However, the results could be explained equally well in terms of motivation, interest, or attitude, rather than as actual forgetting. Although repression does seem to account for some forgetting when unpleasantness is experienced, it cannot account for most ordinary forgetting.

QUESTION	3. HOW ARE MEMORIES ORGANIZED?	
HYPOTHESES	**ASSOCIATION**	**CATEGORICAL STORAGE**
DESCRIPTIVE EVIDENCE	ASSESS: clustering in free recall	ASSESS: relationship of category size to recognition time
EXPERIMENTAL EVIDENCE		VARY: degree of organization in materials memorized MEASURE: recall

3. HOW ARE MEMORIES ORGANIZED?

Our memories sometimes seem so tangled that it is almost impossible to see how we recall anything: "He never forgot anything but he never bothered to arrange his memories. Everything was thrown together like fishing tackle in the bottom of a rowboat, hooks and sinkers and line and lures and gaffs all snarled up" [John Steinbeck, *Cannery Row*].

On the other hand, evidence indicates that we do organize information so we can find our memories in a reasonably systematic way.

The *association hypothesis* states that the order in which material is recalled is determined by the strength of mental associations. Such associations have become very important in twentieth-century literature—all the way from the stream-of-consciousness novels of James Joyce and Virginia Woolf to the Beatles' lyrics. As Paul McCartney noted, "There's a lot of random in our songs—writing, thinking, letting others think of bits—then bang, you have the jigsaw puzzle." And patients in psychoanalysis are asked to "free-associate"—to speak aloud the first thought that comes into their minds, then to say what the thought suggests to them, then in turn what that thought suggests, until the random associations tend of themselves to zero in on a meaningful whole. The fact that the mind can produce memories in this way suggests that stream-of-consciousness may be the manner in which memory itself operates.

DESCRIPTIVE EVIDENCE

Investigator: W. A. Bousfield
Source, Date: "The Occurrence of Clustering in the Recall of Randomly Arranged Associates," 1953
Location: University of Connecticut
Subjects: 125 college students
Materials: English words of four categories

Individual subjects were given a list of sixty English words that could be classified into four different categories: animals, vegetables, professions, and first names of people. The subjects were not told of this classification, and after learning the words in random order, each was asked to recall them in any order he wished. Results showed a greater-than-chance tendency to recall the words in *clusters* containing words from the same category. A word like "rabbit," for example, would more naturally suggest "giraffe" or "toad" than "Arthur," "string bean," or "doctor." Thus, clustering involves storing new information in "categorical bins"—classification schemes based on past experience.

Another way of coding memories efficiently is to "chunk" together discrete bits of information so there are fewer individual items to store. "Head-of-lettuce," for example, is remembered as one chunk, not as individual words or letters or sounds. (It might further be remembered in the cluster "vegetable.") The telephone number 245-1350 can be stored as a chunk rather than as seven individual numbers. The chunking notion was suggested by George Miller of the Massachusetts Institute of Technology in 1956.

Considerations of clustering and chunking imply an even more comprehensive view of memory organization: maybe all memory storage is logically organized. The *categorical-storage hypothesis* states that memory is systematically organized into hierarchical categories like those used by libraries. If human memory is organized in this way, a person should be able to recall more data when he has been given category information.

EXPERIMENTAL EVIDENCE

Investigator: G. H. Bower
Source, Date: "Organizational Factors in Memory," 1970
Location: Stanford University
Subjects: College students
Materials: Hierarchical and randomized word lists

Words were presented to one group of subjects in random order and to another in a "hierarchical tree." Both groups were allowed the same amount of time to study and memorize the words. When tested for recall, the subjects who had studied the hierarchical tree easily outperformed those who had worked with randomized lists. The hierarchical-tree group recalled 65 percent of the words, while the random-order group could remember only 19 percent.

Another experiment that tested the categorical-storage hypothesis focused on the recognition of categories to which words belong.

DESCRIPTIVE EVIDENCE

Investigators: T. R. Landauer and J. L. Freedman
Source, Date: "Information Retrieval from Long-Term Memory: Category Size and Recognition Time," 1968
Location: Stanford University
Subjects: 72 undergraduates
Materials: Precategorized words; timers

Each subject was shown common English nouns ("cat," "banana," "copper") and was asked whether or not each belonged to a specified category ("animal," "fruit," "metal"). The experimenters recorded the "recognition time"—how long it took the subject to answer each question correctly. They were careful to cover a range of category sizes because some large categories include smaller ones. For example, "animals" includes dogs and cats, "dogs" includes collies and chihuahuas, and so on.

The average time required for the subject to place a noun in its correct category varied directly with the category size. Larger categories took longer. This result suggests that memory storage itself may be organized into categories, much like the hierarchical tree shown in Figure 8.

It is possible, however, that categorizing is a feature not of memory storage but of the retrieval process. Landauer and Freedman's experiment alone provides no way of deciding; in fact, psychologists have not yet found adequate tools for distinguishing where categorization takes place. There is much work still to be done on organization in memory, and the final answer will probably be nonexclusive: it seems likely that some organization takes place in memory storage and some in retrieval. The answer may also be partly determined by the answer to a fourth basic question.

Figure 8. Bower found that when words are organized into hierarchical categories they are easier to recall than when they are randomized. Adapted from Bower (1970).

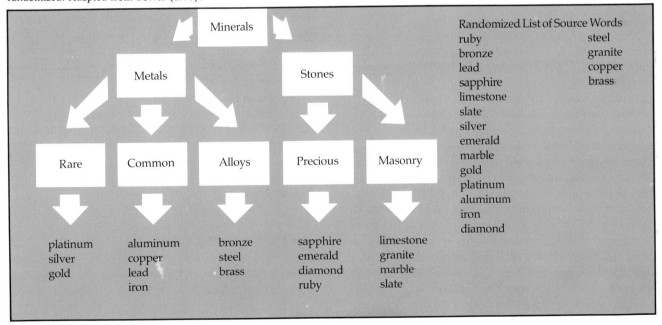

HYPOTHESES	ICONIC	TWO STAGES	TWO SYSTEMS
DESCRIPTIVE EVIDENCE	ASSESS: perceived duration of brief stimuli		ASSESS: 1. recognition memory for pictures 2. responses of subjects when surface of brain is stimulated electrically 3. effectiveness of using images to aid recall
EXPERIMENTAL EVIDENCE		VARY: time interval from stimulus presentation to recall without rehearsal MEASURE: recall	

4. IS THERE MORE THAN ONE WAY TO REMEMBER?

The only "access" we have to material to be memorized is through our senses—usually auditory or visual. Does the sensory processing of data play a mediating role in the memory process? According to the *iconic hypothesis,* data to be remembered must pass through a very brief sensory or iconic stage that lasts less than a second.

DESCRIPTIVE EVIDENCE

Investigators: R. N. Haber and L. G. Standing
Source, Date: "Direct Estimates of the Apparent Duration of a Flash," 1969
Location: University of Rochester
Subjects: Investigator (L. G. S.) and one naive subject
Materials: Tachistoscope, light flashes; click timer

Seated in front of an electronic tachistoscope—a device for controlling very brief presentations of visual stimuli—the subject was shown a brief flash of light at the same time (approximately) that he heard a clicking sound. By turning a dial, the subject was to adjust the click so that he heard it exactly when he saw the initial flash. Once the subject was satisfied that the click started when the flash did, he was asked to get the click to coincide with the end of the flash. By measuring how far apart the subject set the clicks, the experimenter was able to tell how long the subject thought the flash lasted.

Results showed that when the actual duration of the flash was 50 milliseconds, it seemed to the subject to last for 250 milliseconds. His visual processes had increased the effective length of the flash by at least 200 milliseconds. This stretching out of the sensory datum implies that we must experience stimulus energy for a minimum length of time before we can register it and store it in memory. Other experiments have shown that when brief visual stimuli are presented for longer than 200 milliseconds, subjective increases are minimized. So all sensory information passes through some such iconic lengthening process when stimuli are brief. What happens next?

The *two-stages hypothesis* proposes that data to be remembered must be rehearsed in an initial short-term memory (STM) stage to allow it to be coded and transferred to a more permanent long-term memory (LTM). You go through such a rehearsal when, for example, you repeat a friend's new telephone number to yourself in an effort to memorize it.

EXPERIMENTAL EVIDENCE

Investigators: L. E. and M. J. Peterson
Source, Date: "Short-Term Retention of Individual Verbal Items," 1959

Location: Indiana University
Subjects: 24 introductory psychology students
Materials: Nonsense syllables

The object of this experiment was to see whether preventing rehearsal would interfere with subjects' recall ability. The experimenter first spelled out a nonsense syllable and then spoke a three-digit number, from which the subject was told to count backward by threes or fours. For example, the experimenter might say "WOK, 694." The subject was to respond immediately, "691, 688, 685 . . . " The amount of time devoted to counting backward was varied from one to eighteen seconds.

The longer the counting backward continued, the less successful was the recall of the nonsense syllable. After nine seconds of counting, for example, only 30 percent of the subjects could recall the syllable, and after eighteen seconds fewer than 10 percent could recall it. These results provide support for the two-stages theory of memory, and for the idea that rehearsal in an initial STM is necessary before storage in LTM can be achieved.

In a similar experiment, B. B. Murdock (1961) showed that meaningful materials (words) weren't forgotten after eighteen seconds of preventing rehearsal. In fact, 80 percent of Murdock's subjects could remember the word he had spoken even when they were prevented from rehearsing it for the full eighteen seconds. If an STM does exist, its relation to LTM storage is not so simple as the rehearsal theory alone suggests. Meaningfulness (and probably other factors) has to be considered also.

Although many recent studies about memory have centered on the STM-LTM distinction, by no means all psychologists accept its existence. Many advocates of the *association hypothesis* discussed under Question 3, for example, believe that association principles combined with a modified version of the interference theory of forgetting may be able to account for all memory data, even apparent STM-LTM effects.

In addition to two stages of memory, it is also possible that there are several kinds of memory. The *two-systems hypothesis* states that verbal information is subject to forgetting, while memorized sensory (iconic) images are relatively permanent.

DESCRIPTIVE EVIDENCE

Investigators: L. Standing, J. Conezio, and R. N. Haber
Source, Date: "Perception and Memory for Pictures: Single-Trial Learning of 2500 Stimuli," 1970
Location: University of Rochester
Subjects: 21 college students
Materials: Slide projectors, photographic slides

To determine the long-term storage capacity of visual memory, subjects were presented with photographic slides—as many as 2,560 of them—in two sessions on succeeding days. Each slide appeared only once for ten seconds. An hour after he had seen the last of the slides, each subject was shown 280 pairs of slides, one member of each pair being a slide already shown and the other being one the subject had never seen. The subject's task was to identify the slide he had seen before.

The subjects were able to correctly identify an average of 85 to 95 percent of the slides seen earlier, even when those slides were presented (the second time around) as mirror-image reversals of those presented in the original batch.

Flashing images are sometimes used in television commercials, and the average viewer's response to them suggests that our capacity to remember visual images may be virtually unlimited. This perceptual (primary visual) and relatively permanent system of LTM storage can be distinguished from verbal-semantic memory, which depends mainly on STM for coding into LTM and seems less permanent. But is there any evidence that sensory impressions are in fact permanently stored and available for recall?

DESCRIPTIVE EVIDENCE

Investigator: W. Penfield
Source, Date: "The Excitable Cortex in Conscious Man," 1958
Location: Montreal Neurological Institute
Subjects: Patients suffering from epilepsy
Materials: Electrified needle or electrode

Perhaps the most dramatic demonstration of the notion that memories stay in our brains forever was provided by a brain surgeon who has performed

hundreds of operations to reduce the severity of epileptic seizures. Penfield's technique involves exposing the brain while the patient is under a local anesthetic, then probing certain brain areas with an electrified needle or electrode (tiny currents). Probing the temporal lobe of the patient frequently elicited what appeared to be old memories. Here is the actual verbal report of a patient at that point during such an operation: "There was a piano over there and someone playing. I could hear the song, you know . . . someone is speaking to another. He mentioned a name, but I could not understand it . . . It was like a dream . . . Yes. 'Oh Marie, Oh Marie!' Someone is singing it . . . Something brings back a memory. I can see Seven-Up Bottling Company—Harrison Bakery."

When the results of electric stimulation of the temporal lobe were first reported, speculation was rampant that all of a person's experiences might be stored forever in his brain. It should be pointed out, however, that dramatic "memories" are also dredged up by dreams, hypnosis, rumors, and excitement-hungry people, and frequently they have little to do with reality. It isn't clear that the experiences evoked by temporal lobe stimulation are valid memories or that the sensations evoked are samples of a complete lifetime record.

What about photographic memories? In 1968 a Russian psychologist, A. R. Luria, published a fascinating account of a Russian newspaper reporter who performed amazing feats of recall, relying almost totally on sensory images. This "mnemonist" (from the Greek word for memory) could look at a long list of random numbers; visualize, say, a 4 x 13 matrix containing the numbers, and reproduce its contents verbally—by rows, columns, or diagonals—fifteen years after he had seen it. Confronted with a more complex memory task, such as a long and complicated mathematical formula, he used more elaborate imagery techniques to patch together a sort of motion picture of visual images.

Figure 9. Bizarre images can be used as mnemonic devices for remembering word pairs.

That he remembered by visual images almost exclusively was supported by the fact that he did not, and apparently could not, use logical principles of organization and categorization to aid his memory. For example, when recalling a list of numbers that followed a simple pattern most people would see immediately, the mnemonist failed entirely to notice the pattern but continued to recall each number in the series by seeing the list in his mind. In his introduction to Luria's book, Jerome Bruner commented:

> Several notable things about the disorders of this mnemonist are especially fascinating from a psychological point of view. For one thing, the sheer persistence of ikonic memory [memory in visual images] is so great that one wonders whether there is some failure in the swift metabolism of short-term memory. His "immediate" images haunt him for hours, types of images that in much recent work on short-term memory are found to fade to a point where information retrieval from them is not possible after a second or so. Along with this trait there is also a non-selectivity about his memory, such that what remains behind is a kind of junk heap of impressions. Or perhaps this mnemonic disarray results from the evident failure to organize and "regularize" what is remembered . . . The gift of persistent, concrete memory appears to make for highly concrete thinking, a kind of thinking in images that is very reminiscent of young children . . .

The mnemonist's ability may actually be pathological. His view of the world is certainly very limited, and he may even have been genetically and biochemically different from other men. Whether observations about his ability are relevant to the memory processes of most people is a moot point.

As Bruner mentioned, however, many children seem to have highly developed visual memories that apparently are lost during development. The very young child may remember experience by coding it perceptually because he lacks the skill to code his experience in words. As verbal skill develops, however, he finds language more efficient and so codes more and more of his data in words. Eventually, so much of his experience is coded and remembered verbally that he simply gets out of the habit of using other kinds of memories.

Nevertheless, the capacity for remembering visual images can be very useful even for adults, as it is in making verbal associations.

DESCRIPTIVE EVIDENCE

Investigators: W. H. Wallace, S. H. Turner, and C. C. Perkins

Source, Date: "Preliminary Studies of Human Information Storage," 1957

Location: University of Pennsylvania

Subjects: Human adults

Materials: Word pairs

To evaluate the effectiveness of images in remembering, each subject was presented with pairs of words that were to be coupled in his memory. Each pair was presented only once for a number of seconds. The subject was specifically asked to form a "bizarre mental image" relating the two words. For example, to connect "cake" with "parachute," the subject might imagine a cake parachuting down to earth or a parachute shaped like a cake.

Later, on a recall test, each subject was given the first word of each pair he had seen and was asked to recall the second word. On the average, the subjects correctly recalled about 99 percent of all the items—even with lists as long as 500 word pairs presented only once to each subject. Recall only dropped to about 95 percent on lists of 700 pairs. Compared with normal paired-associate recall using no imagery, these are truly amazing performance levels.

Such strategies are called *mnemonic devices.* Their power is especially interesting in that they add information to the material that is to be remembered. One might think that it would be easier simply to memorize the number of days in each month than it would be to learn a mnemonic rhyme that incorporates that information, but no. It is easier to learn "thirty days hath September . . . "

The results of these experiments again strongly imply that there are at least two kinds of memory systems, one primarily visual and the other verbal-semantic, and that only meaning is remembered well in verbal-semantic memory.

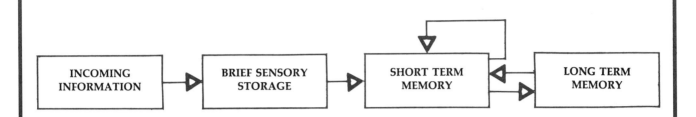

PUTTING IT TOGETHER: Memory

Incoming information to be stored for future use is first processed through the sensory organs and the central nervous system in a way that makes for *brief sensory storage*. That is, the information lasts a little longer iconically in the organisms than it does in the physical environment.

There is considerable evidence to suggest that there might be two qualitatively different systems for remembering information. One of these might be a sensory, or iconic, image which involves relatively permanent storage in its initially perceived form. The other system might involve verbal information which is subject to further processing. Apparently, verbal information goes through at least two stages: *short term memory* and *long term memory*.

The initial storage of information in short term memory involves principles of learning and is largely dependent upon certain characteristics of the information and the learner, capacity to evoke images, serial order of presentation, and the extent to which the learner perceives its connectedness.

Information to be transferred from short term memory to long term memory must be maintained in the first stage long enough to be coded for relatively permanent storage. This can be achieved by rehearsing information until transfer to long term memory takes place. This involves a feedback loop within short term memory.

In long term memory the information is apparently organized through associations with other information and in hierarchical categories. Conscious use of this information apparently requires recall into short term memory.

We call it forgetting when this process of retrieval permits only limited access, or when there is repression from conscious use, or when unwanted information interferes with the retrieval of desired information.

1. WHAT'S ACCEPTED . . .

1. Meaningful, imagery-evoking, and connected materials are easier to learn and remember than nonsense or randomly ordered materials.
2. LTM is very long-lasting in its storage.
3. Much apparent forgetting is a function of interference.
4. Information may be forgotten because of repression, but repression cannot explain ordinary forgetting.
5. Learning and recall are easier when items in memory can be clustered or chunked together according to an organizational principle.
6. There is a sensory (iconic) memory system that differs in many of its properties from verbal memory.
7. Mnemonic strategies, such as bizarre visual images, can be of great aid in remembering specific materials.

2. WHAT'S DEBATED . . .

1. Whether LTM storage is permanent.
2. Whether organization takes place in LTM storage or during retrieval.
3. Whether or not a distinct STM stage precedes LTM storage.
4. Whether it is more accurate to view memory retrieval as a reconstruction process or as a reappearance process.

You have learned in this unit about the main principles governing the workings of the human memory. But how can you apply these principles in practice—in memorizing information for examinations, for example? There are a number of methods that can be used, and all of them are based on the research findings presented earlier. Each of these methods should increase attention and provide the rehearsal necessary to encode the information from short term to long term memory. In addition, each provides practice in retrieving information from long term storage.

One useful technique is called "overlearning." It might seem to you that when you have learned a series of facts and can repeat them without making any mistakes, you have adequately memorized the subject matter. But you probably haven't—as you might discover if you try to repeat the series again a day or two later. One way of improving subsequent recall is to overlearn, to keep on practicing even when you think you have already memorized the material. Many experiments have shown that subjects who overlearn remember the material much better than subjects who stop work as soon as they feel they have learned it.

A second method is to review the material between the time it is learned and the time it must eventually be recalled. The first review after learning is often most valuable, because it serves to focus attention on many items that might not have been adequately learned on the first occasion. You will find that each subsequent review is much easier and takes much less time than the previous one. Many students make the mistake of leaving too long a period between learning and review, and of concentrating all their effort on one final review immediately before examinations. More regular and less frenzied reviewing could take less overall time and effort, and will certainly yield better results.

Reciting the material aloud is also a valuable way of improving your memory of learned material. Recitation is useful because it offers a way of tackling the memory problem which is complementary to the original learning process. Reading and memorizing the material is a relatively passive act, but reciting it is an active one which stresses recall as well as recognition. Recognizing the material you have learned is certainly important, but many examinations require you to recall information as well, and recitation helps develop this skill.

Another useful method is to have a friend quiz you. Again, this method emphasizes the recall rather than the recognition of material, and is a very good means of establishing the points at which your memory is weakest and where review is most necessary. If no friend is around or if your friends are too busy preparing for examinations themselves, you can test yourself with a closed book, although this may take more time.

Another method is to memorize material immediately before falling asleep. As we noted earlier in this unit, memory is often impaired by retroactive interference—that is, the material you have memorized may be "smudged" by material that you deliberately or inadvertently memorize immediately afterwards. By learning the material and then falling asleep, you minimize the possibility of any retroactive interference.

Another very important technique is that of "chunking" the material. The more you can organize the subject matter that you have to memorize into interconnected chunks, the more likely you will be to remember it. The reason is simply that you will have to remember only a single chunk, and not the many items of unrelated information that it may contain. In effect, it increases the meaningfulness of each set which should allow for easier retrieval from long term memory.

There are many different methods of "chunking" material. You can take the first letter of each item that is to be chunked and form them into a single word that is easily memorized or you can take items that seem to be logically connected and group them together. Often, a great many separate items can be remembered by setting up a hierarchy of chunks, a sort of intellectual pyramid in which the top chunk consists of a couple of lesser chunks, which in turn consist of other groups of chunks, and so on.

As Ebbinghaus himself discovered in his pioneering experiments, information is retained much more readily if it is meaningful. You will find it very difficult, for example, to memorize material you do not understand, and it is probably worth investing effort in understanding it rather than in attempting to memorize it. Chunks of information, too, are much more easily remembered if they are meaningful. A nonsense word containing the first letters of the items you wish to remember is less likely to be recalled than a meaningful word containing the same letters.

Finally, visual techniques for remembering material should not be overlooked. Few of us have the photographic memory of Luria's subject, but a great many people can retain a rough idea of the "shape" of a page of their own notes, and may sense that something is missing from their recall. Many items, too, can be linked to visual images to make them more memorable.

Unit 26

Pavlovian Conditioning

OVERVIEW

The basic conditions under which we learn to respond to events as signals for other events, and how these learned associations can be lost or extinguished are the focus of this unit. Some of these conditions, such as temporal contiguity of stimuli, generalization, and discrimination learning are basic to stimulus-response learning in almost all organisms.

UNIT OUTLINE

DEFINITION AND BACKGROUND
1. *Definition:* Pavlovian conditioning is a particular kind of learning in which a neutral, or ineffective, stimulus (CS) is presented repeatedly in a conjunction with an already established stimulus (UCS) until the neutral stimulus (CS) becomes a signal for the same response (CR) that the established stimulus (UCS) elicits (UCR).
2. *Background:* Ivan Petrovich Pavlov (1849–1936).

QUESTIONS AND EVIDENCE
1. What conditions are responsible for our learning to respond to some events as signals for other events?
Hypotheses:
   a. *Temporal-contiguity:* the length of the interstimulus interval is a strong determinant of efficiency in the acquisition of the classically conditioned response. **448**
   b. *Generalization:* after a conditioned response has been acquired, stimuli similar to the conditioned stimulus will have the effect of eliciting a similar conditioned response. **450**
   c. *Sensory-preconditioning:* stimuli that have never been paired with UCSs can elicit a conditioned response simply through prior association with a CS that is later paired with a UCS. **450**
   d. *Higher-order-conditioning:* stimuli that have been established as CSs can be used to establish conditioned responses to new stimuli. **451**
2. How can patterns of responses be eliminated?
Hypotheses:
   a. *Extinction:* the conditioned response will gradually decrease over time if the CS is no longer paired with the UCS. **453**
   b. *Discrimination:* stimuli that have come to elicit CRs through a process of generalization can be extinguished by preventing any further pairing of the stimulus with the UCS. **454**

IMPORTANT CONCEPTS

page

association	**448**
discrimination	**454**
generalization	**450**
interstimulus interval	**448**
Pavlovian conditioning	**446**
phobia	**450**

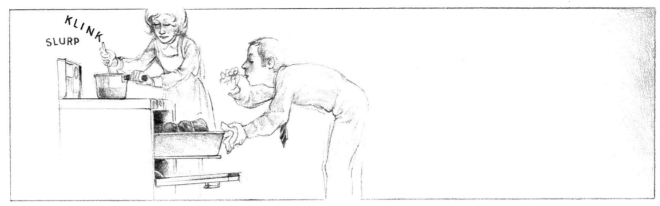

The basis of some nonvoluntary behavior is the association of neutral stimuli with response-eliciting stimuli.

A neutral stimulus previously associated with a response-eliciting stimulus may later be presented in isolation.

The previously neutral stimulus may then elicit the associated response, dependent upon the strength of the association.

DEFINITION AND BACKGROUND

Think for a moment of a food or drink of which you are especially fond. Then let your mind dwell on taking a mouthful of it and savoring it. What sort of response do you get? That's it—a flow of saliva. In the course of your previous experience you have been the subject of Pavlovian, or classical, conditioning. You have just illustrated one of your own conditioned responses.

In the example you have given, the flow of saliva in your mouth was a response of your salivary glands to stimulation. The previously established stimulus, such as food or drink in the mouth, is called the unconditioned stimulus (UCS) for the almost automatic or unconditioned response (UCR). The picture in a homemakers' magazine of a beautifully prepared roast, crisp salad, and rich chocolate cake is a stimulus that is neutral or ineffective to cause this response *until* you have actually tasted these things enough times so they become a signal of, or make you think of, their taste. Or perhaps the sounds of dishes and silverware clinking as dinner is being prepared can also start your mouth watering. Then the picture or dinnertime sounds become conditioned stimuli (CS) that bring about the conditioned response (CR). The conditioned response is usually identical, or nearly so, with the unconditioned response.

Thus, one reasonable DEFINITION of Pavlovian conditioning is *a particular kind of learning in which a neutral, or ineffective, stimulus (CS) is presented repeatedly in conjunction with an already established stimulus (UCS) until the neutral stimulus (CS) becomes a signal for the same response (CR) that the established stimulus (UCS) elicits (UCR).*

The FOCUS of this unit is first on how this conditioning is established and then on the ways by which it can be erased. This type of conditioning is called Pavlovian because a great deal of the initial work on it was done by a famous Russian scientist, Pavlov.

BACKGROUND: IVAN PETROVICH PAVLOV (1849–1936)

The son of a priest from a peasant background, Pavlov received an education that enabled him to enter the intelligentsia, which in Czarist Russia was a kind of intermediate class between the privileged aristocracy

Figure 1. Ivan Pavlov, Nobel-winning Russian neurophysiologist, studied digestive and nervous systems, and made important discoveries about reflexes and conditioning.

and the peasants. Too poor to aspire to an easy life of privilege, members of the Russian intelligentsia often used their education for academic or scientific careers or for government service.

Throughout his life Pavlov displayed an almost total dedication to his scientific work and seemed to care little about everyday things. Yet he retained much of a peasant's temperament and persistence. He sometimes threw tantrums over experimental mistakes and once scolded an assistant who had been delayed by street fighting during the Russian Revolution for showing up a few minutes late for an operation.

During a long career in science, unbroken by the ups and downs of Russian political life under both Czarist and Soviet regimes, Pavlov became famous for his uniquely controlled experiments in a number of fields. Primarily a physiologist with a knack for masterful surgery, acute laboratory observation, and precise experimental follow-through—his Nobel Prize in 1904 was for research on the digestive process—he is nevertheless best remembered for his contributions to experimental psychology. Many of his theories have been tested and applied with amazing success throughout the world. Pavlovian insights still dominate the discipline of psychology in the Soviet Union and for a time shaped one brand of psychology in the United States, especially among learning theorists.

It was his persistent attention to detail that led to Pavlov's discoveries in conditioning. While studying digestion in dogs, he noted that one dog showed minor irregularities in the process: the digestive glands began to function—that is, the dog began to salivate—before food was actually put in its mouth. Eventually, he showed food to the dog before each feeding, and it gradually became clear the dog began to salivate at the sight of food. But if the food was shown and then withheld repeatedly, the dog eventually would stop salivating even when shown the food.

Pavlov went on to conduct further experiments, pairing feeding with other seemingly unrelated stimuli, like a bell and a light. He demonstrated that under rigid laboratory controls a dog could be trained to salivate, twitch its hind leg, or perform similar reactions in response to merely the sound of a bell, the sight of a light, or other properly conditioned stimuli.

Out of these experiments grew the procedure of classical conditioning and its terminology. Pavlov's painstaking research has been put to a variety of uses, and much has been learned about the possible applications of conditioning, with research still in progress. Although Pavlov himself saw conditioning primarily as a tool in the study of the central nervous system, his work remains a major milestone for psychology.

QUESTIONS AND EVIDENCE

1. What conditions are responsible for our learning to respond to some events as signals for other events?
2. How can patterns of responses be eliminated?

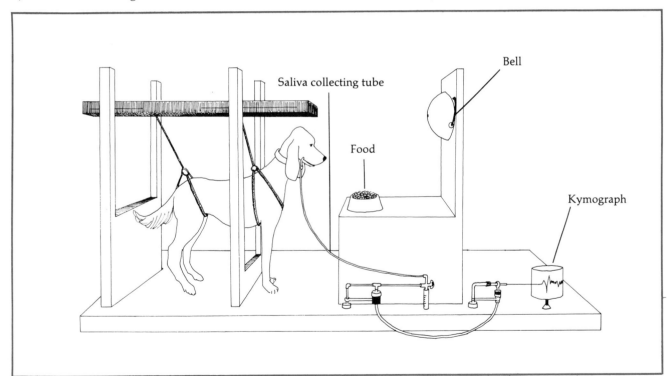

Figure 2. Apparatus similar to that used in Pavlov's famous early experiments on conditioning. The dog could be trained to salivate, twitch its leg, or perform other reactions in response to the sight of food or a light, the sound of a bell, or other stimuli.

HYPOTHESES	TEMPORAL CONTIGUITY	GENERALIZATION	SENSORY PRE-CONDITIONING	HIGHER-ORDER CONDITIONING
DESCRIPTIVE EVIDENCE		ASSESS: generalization of conditioned fear object		ASSESS: ease of establishing response with each higher order of presentation
EXPERIMENTAL EVIDENCE	VARY: temporal interval between the CS and the UCS MEASURE: frequency of closure of second eyelid		VARY: pairing of buzzer and light MEASURE: leg flexion response	

1. WHAT CONDITIONS ARE RESPONSIBLE FOR OUR LEARNING TO RESPOND TO SOME EVENTS AS SIGNALS FOR OTHER EVENTS?

The formation of conditioned responses makes up much of early-childhood learning. By means of conditioning, for example, a child learns very quickly and firmly that he must not touch stoves. The pain in his burned fingers (UCS) leads to immediate hand withdrawal (UCR), and probably on the first experience the sight of the stove (CS) is associated with burned fingers and hand withdrawal (CR) or at least with not touching the stove. Unless a mother is amazingly observant and unbelievably fast, she will find that a slap on the hand is a less effective way to warn her child not to touch the hot stove because it is usually not immediate.

Timing is an extremely important factor in the formation of conditioned responses, psychologists have found. There are three possibilities: In *forward conditioning* the CS (sight of stove) precedes the UCS (burn) that elicits the UCR (withdrawal); in *simultaneous conditioning* the CS onset coincides with the onset of the UCS that elicits the UCR; and in *backward conditioning* the onset of the CS occurs after the onset of the UCS and while the UCR is occurring.

The *interstimulus interval* is the time between the start of the conditioned stimulus (CS) and the start of the unconditioned stimulus (UCS), which can usually be measured very precisely (in milliseconds) by psychologists. The *temporal-contiguity hypothesis* states that the length of the interstimulus interval is a strong determinant of efficiency in the acquisition of the classically conditioned response.

Notice how much evidence was amassed in the following experiment to investigate the effects of the interstimulus interval on conditioning. A total of ninety-six rabbits was used in groups conditioned with different interstimulus intervals. The greater the total of evidence gathered in an experiment of this kind, the more solid the inferences from the evidence will be.

EXPERIMENTAL EVIDENCE

Investigators: M. C. Smith, S. R. Coleman, and I. Gormezano
Source, Date: "Classical Conditioning of the Rabbit's Nictitating Membrane Response at Backward, Simultaneous, and Forward CS-US Intervals," 1969
Location: University of Iowa
Subjects: 96 rabbits
Materials: Special apparatus for recording the second eyelid response, tone, and shock

The conditioned response (CR) used in this experiment was the closing of the second eyelid, which

Figure 3. An explosive noise is usually an *unconditioned stimulus* which elicits startle—or sudden tension—as an *unconditioned response.* If an overinflated balloon has come to signal an explosive noise, it has become a *conditioned stimulus,* eliciting tension as a *conditioned response.*

Figure 4. The time interval between the onset of the conditioned stimulus (CS) and that of the unconditioned stimulus (UCS) is an important variable in the formation of a conditioned response.

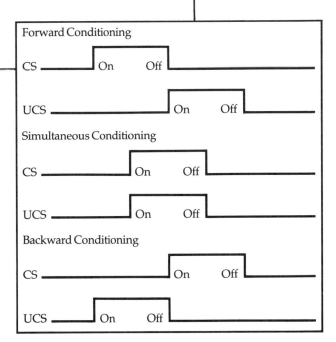

appears between the eye and the outside eyelid in the rabbit. Several groups of rabbits received paired presentations of a tone (CS) and a shock delivered near the right external eyelid (UCS). For forward-conditioning groups there were interstimulus intervals of .8, .4, .2, .1, and .05 second; in the simultaneous-conditioning group no interval (0 seconds) occurred between the CS and the UCS; for the backward-conditioning group the interval was minus .05 second (that is, the start of the UCS preceded the start of the CS). Conditioning was assessed against a control group in which the CS and the UCS were never paired.

Then the actual number of closures of the rabbit's second eyelid were measured. These results indicate that the groups conditioned at intervals of .05, 0, and minus .05 second showed no evidence of conditioning, whereas groups trained with intervals of .1 second or greater showed marked increases in the frequency of CRs over trials. Because the .05-second interval apparently was not long enough to result in conditioning, it would seem that the nervous system functions in such a way that the timing between the CS and the UCS must fall within a relatively limited range in order to produce the brain modifications basic to learning. Other experiments have indicated that presenting the CS about .5 second before the UCS usually results in the fastest conditioning.

The *generalization hypothesis* states that after a conditioned response has been acquired, stimuli similar to the conditioned stimulus will have the effect of eliciting a similar conditioned response. Generalization of conditioned stimuli gives us the capacity to react to new situations so far as they are similar to familiar situations in offering stimuli somewhat like the already conditioned stimuli.

Generalization was demonstrated in the following studies done by John B. Watson, who promoted Pavlovian conditioning among psychologists in America.

DESCRIPTIVE EVIDENCE

Investigators: J. B. Watson and R. Rayner
Source, Date: "Conditioned Emotional Reactions," 1920
Location: Harriet Lane Hospital
Subject: 1 eleven-month-old child
Materials: Furry objects, steel bar

Albert B., an eleven-month-old child, was presented with a white rat (CS) at the same time that a steel bar was struck behind him to make a loud noise (UCS). The UCR was a startle pattern and crying.

After five paired presentations of the rat and the noise, Albert cried when the rat was presented without the noise (CR). Five days later he still exhibited fear reactions to the sight of the rat. Other furry objects that had never been paired with the loud noise, such as a rabbit, a dog, a fur coat, and a Santa Claus mask with a furry white beard, also elicited fear in Albert. He had generalized the conditioned stimulus from the rat to the other similar furry objects (see Unit 20).

When such "phobic" responses are learned through the classical conditioning process, they may persist over time even though the UCS is not presented again after the original training period. Albert's fear of furry objects lasted with a certain loss in intensity for more than a month, at least. Modern psychologists are much more scrupulous about the ethics of performing this type of research with human subjects.

It has been suggested that many of the phobias of psychopathology (see Unit 20) are conditioned emotional responses learned either directly through past experience or indirectly through the process of generalization. The *sensory-preconditioning hypothesis* carries this idea one step further. It states that stimuli that have never been paired with UCSs can elicit a conditioned response simply through prior association with a CS that is later paired with a UCS. A boy may be perfectly happy with both his pet poodle and his German shepherd until the poodle bites him. Then, even if the German shepherd was away roaming the neighborhood at the time of the bite, the boy may be afraid of both of his former friends.

In the laboratory, preconditioning procedure involves three stages of training. Two neutral stimuli—for example, a light and a tone—are presented together over a number of trials. Next, a CR is learned to one of the stimuli, say the light. Then the second stimulus, the tone, is presented to determine whether the CR transfers to it.

EXPERIMENTAL EVIDENCE

Investigator: W. J. Brogden
Source, Date: "Sensory Preconditioning," 1939

Location: *Johns Hopkins School of Medicine*
Subjects: *16 dogs*
Materials: *Buzzer, light, shock*

Eight of the dogs received 200 pairings of a buzzer and a light presented simultaneously. Afterward, four of these dogs were trained with the tone CS paired with a shock UCS and the other four animals trained with the light CS until the animals eventually performed the CR (leg flexion) twenty times out of twenty trials. In stage three, the animals were repeatedly presented the other stimulus (that is the tone-trained dogs were presented the light, and vice versa). A control group of eight dogs received the same treatment except that the preconditioning phase was omitted.

The results measured as numbers of CR indicated that the control group made an aggregate of only four CRs to the test stimuli. Those in the experimental groups, however, gave an aggregate of seventy-eight CRs to the test stimuli, showing that prior association with the CS that was later paired with the UCS was sufficient to elicit the same response.

Because this investigation provided such a good supply of evidence and demonstrated such clear effects, the experimenter felt that he could generalize his inferences on sensory preconditioning very broadly:

It is a basic principle of psychology that organisms are capable of making responses in the light of past experience. Much of this modification in behavior takes place under circumstances which fit the principles of conditioning. It is likely that in the commonplace environment of any organism, the conditions of the experiment on dogs herein reported will be fulfilled in nature. The experience of two contiguous sensory stimuli completely divorced from any phasic reflex activity is frequent to any organism. If one of these stimuli becomes the signal for the response of a given reaction-pattern, the other will then elicit a similar response.

A child whose dinner is always served at 6:00 will eventually develop certain physiological responses to the events that usually occur at that time of day, such as his father's arriving home from work (CS). These responses (CR) may then occur as soon as he hears his mother's call (CS), even if it is only 5:30. And if she decides to use a bell (another CS) in order to save her voice, he may well respond to that sound in the same manner.

The *higher-order conditioning hypothesis* states that stimuli that have been established as CSs can be used to establish conditioned responses to new stimuli.

In the example of a child's conditioning, the father's arrival is a first-order conditioned stimulus (CS), the mother's call a second order CS, and her ringing a bell a third-order CS. Higher-order conditioning can become very elaborate in this manner. The following experiment provides a good example.

DESCRIPTIVE EVIDENCE

Investigators: *W. J. Brogden and E. Culler*
Source, Date: *"Experimental Extinction of Higher-Order Responses," 1935*
Location: *Johns Hopkins School of Medicine*
Subjects: *Dogs*
Materials: *Shock, tone, light, bell, electric fan*

To establish fourth-order conditioning, using foreleg flexion as the response (UCR) and shock as the UCS, the researchers first established a conditioned response (CR) to a tone (CS). A light was then used as a second order CS and the tone as the first order CS to elicit leg flexion. The four orders established using this procedure are shown in Figure 5.

The researchers report that occasionally it was necessary to go back to first-order conditioning for a few trials but that it became easier to establish the response as the order became higher. Whereas first-order conditioning took twenty-eight days of twenty-five trials per day for one animal, the second-order response was learned in eighteen days, the third-order in five days, and the fourth-order in three days.

Such complex patterns of conditioned responses can be and are set up in man as well as other animals. But obviously not all of these are beneficial, and a great deal of research has studied how such responses can be eliminated.

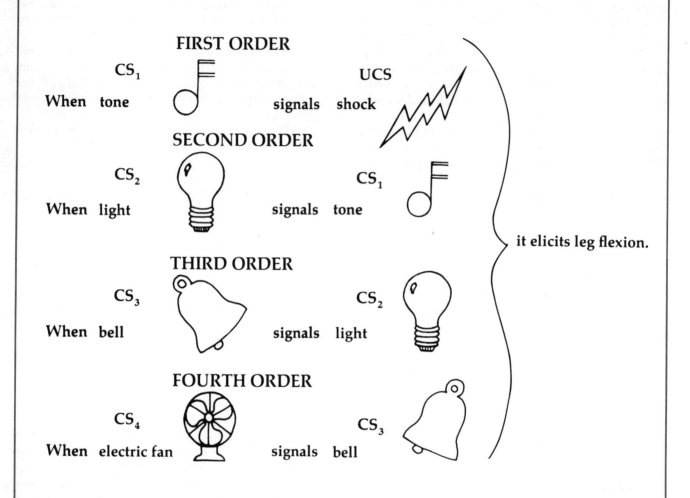

Figure 5. Four orders of conditioning established in dogs by Brogden and Culler (1935).

HYPOTHESES	EXTINCTION	DISCRIMINATION
DESCRIPTIVE EVIDENCE		
EXPERIMENTAL EVIDENCE	VARY: temporal interval between CS and UCS MEASURE: percentage of CRs	VARY: reinforced and unreinforced stimulus MEASURE: probability of conditioned eye-blink response

2. HOW CAN PATTERNS OF RESPONSES BE ELIMINATED?

People who are trying to quit smoking are often encouraged to extinguish the eliciting stimuli one by one. First cigarettes are eliminated while watching TV (CS), then with cups of coffee (CS), then when reading, then at the typewriter, and so on until no stimuli occasions for smoking remain. Whether or not this is an effective approach for most smokers who wish to give up cigarettes, it does lead us to the first hypothesis dealing with the elimination of conditioned responses.

The *extinction hypothesis* states that the conditioned response will gradually decrease over time if the CS is no longer paired with the UCS. Pavlov's dogs eventually stopped salivating to the bell when the food was never again paired with it. Somehow the bell was no longer linked with forthcoming food, so the conditioned response disappeared.

EXPERIMENTAL EVIDENCE

Investigators: K. W. Spence, M. J. Homzie, and E. F. Rutledge

Source, Date: "Extinction of the Human Eyelid CR as a Function of the Discriminability of the Change from Acquisition to Extinction," 1964

Location: University of Iowa

Subjects: 105 college students

Materials: Air-puff apparatus, tone

Having been told that this experiment concerned attention and fatigue, each subject was instructed to look steadily at a small milk glass disc directly in front of him. During this fixation period, he was conditioned to a tone (CS). The tone preceded by .5 second an air puff (UCS) directed to his right eye, which elicited an eye blink (UCR). After forty-nine acquisition trials during which the subject was conditioned to blink to the tone (CR), various methods of extinguishing that conditioned response were studied. In the first group the air puff (UCS) was simply discontinued altogether, while the tone (CS) continued. In the other two groups the time intervals between the presentation of the tone and the air puff were extended from the original .5 second to 1.5 seconds and 2.5 seconds.

The group in which the UCS was discontinued extinguished very rapidly. The other two groups also began to extinguish, though more slowly. The group in which the time interval was greater (2.5 seconds) extinguished more rapidly than the group with a 1.5-second interval between the air puff and the tone.

Although extinction has traditionally been accomplished by repeated presentation of the CS without the UCS, this experiment also demonstrates that the same end can be accomplished by lengthening the interval of time between the CS and the UCS. The link between them eventually becomes too remote to constitute a pairing.

The *discrimination hypothesis* states that stimuli that have come to elicit CRs through a process of generalization can be extinguished by preventing any further pairing of the stimulus with the UCS. For example, a child who has a generalized fear of playgrounds because he has been bullied by older children can be taken to playgrounds where he will be left alone. Eventually he will come to discriminate between being wary of bullies and being afraid of playgrounds, and his generalized conditioned response will decrease.

EXPERIMENTAL EVIDENCE

Investigator: M. D. Gynther
Source, Date: "Differential Eyelid Conditioning as a Function of Stimulus Similarity and Strength Response to the CS," 1957
Location: Duke University
Subjects: 100 undergraduates
Materials: Chin rest, booth, white light, air puff apparatus, device for measuring eye blinks

The subjects sat before a table, resting their heads on an apparatus that directed their vision into a booth that excluded extraneous stimuli and presented fairly constant conditions of general illumination. On the back wall of the booth was a small box with two quarter-inch holes spaced two inches apart. When a light came on behind the right-hand (CS plus) hole, an air puff (UCS) was delivered to one eye. When the other light came on (CS minus), no air puff was delivered. Measurements were made of the probability of an eye blink (CR) after the onset of the CS but before the onset of the air puff (or at the time when the air puff would have come) on both reinforced (CS plus) and unreinforced (CS minus) trials.

With extended training, subjects reliably blinked during the CS-UCS interval to the reinforced cue (light behind the right-hand hole) but not to the unreinforced cue (light behind the left-hand hole.) They had learned to discriminate between two similar but perceptibly different stimuli. Organisms, including humans, come to learn associations between events and, as the evidence presented above indicates, can also learn to recognize that past associations between events no longer hold.

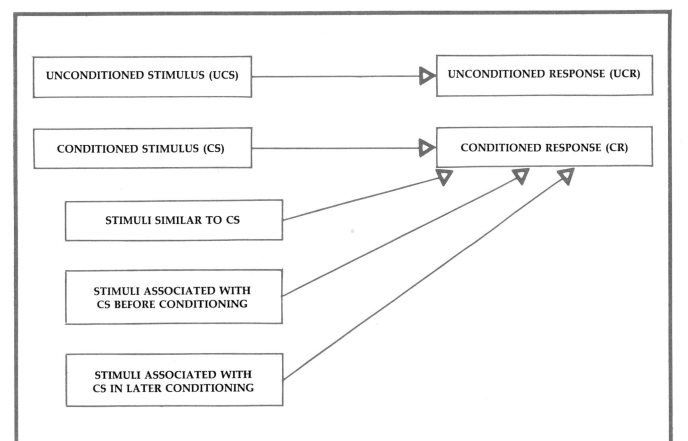

UNCONDITIONED STIMULUS (UCS)	→	UNCONDITIONED RESPONSE (UCR)
CONDITIONED STIMULUS (CS)	→	CONDITIONED RESPONSE (CR)
STIMULI SIMILAR TO CS		
STIMULI ASSOCIATED WITH CS BEFORE CONDITIONING		
STIMULI ASSOCIATED WITH CS IN LATER CONDITIONING		

PUTTING IT TOGETHER: Pavlovian Conditioning

The process of an organism acquiring new specific responses to some stimuli begins with a natural and automatic relationship between other stimuli and the same responses. Food in the mouth, for example, naturally and automatically elicits salivation. Food, the *unconditioned stimulus*, automatically elicits salivation, the *unconditioned response*. When new stimuli are associated with the unconditioned stimulus through temporal contiguity, they will also elicit responses which, in many respects, are the same as the original unconditioned response. Since this requires a conditioning process, the components of this new relationship are called the *conditioned stimulus* and the *conditioned response*.

Once this relationship has been established still other stimuli may elicit the same conditioned response: Through generalization, *stimuli similar to the* original *conditioned stimulus* may elicit the conditioned response. Through sensory preconditioning, *stimuli associated with the conditioned stimulus before conditioning took place* may elicit the conditioned response. Through higher order conditioning, a number of *stimuli associated with the conditioned stimulus in later conditioning* may elicit the conditioned response.

These processes may also be reversed: When the conditioned stimulus becomes dissociated from the conditioned response, extinction takes place. When extinction takes place only to generalized stimuli, it is referred to as discrimination.

WHAT'S ACCEPTED AND WHAT'S DEBATED

1. WHAT'S ACCEPTED . . .

1. Temporal contiguity is a critical variable in the acquisition of classically conditioned responses.

2. CRs will generalize to stimuli that are similar to the original CS or that are in close temporal relationship with the UCS in training.

3. Stimuli can be conditioned without prior pairing with a UCS through the process of sensory preconditioning.

4. Pairing neutral stimuli with established CSs will result in higher-order conditioning of the new stimuli.

5. Overgeneralized CRs can be eliminated through the process of extinction, preventing the UCS from being paired with any stimuli except the specific CS to be maintained.

6. Discontinuation of pairings of the UCS with the CS will result in extinction; that is, that the CS will no longer elicit the CR if the UCS is permanently removed.

2. WHAT'S DEBATED . . .

1. Whether backward or simultaneous conditioning does occur.

2. The importance of changing the CR in altering anxiety or fear reactions.

3. Whether classical conditioning is adequate to explain highly complex human behavior.

4. Whether extinction and discrimination have any practical value in eliminating CRs given the complexity of the conditioning environment.

ISSUE: THE SAUCE BEARNAISE SYNDROME

The principles of Pavlovian conditioning outlined in this unit have been of fundamental importance to psychology and to our understanding of learning in animals and humans. One of the most influential schools of modern psychology, behaviorism, derives its original inspiration from Pavlov's work. Even today, more than seventy years after his famous experiments, researchers are still refining our knowledge of the conditioning process that the Russian physiologist first brought to the attention of the scientific world.

One contemporary researcher who has further developed Pavlov's work is Martin Seligman of the University of Pennsylvania. A case of severe indigestion was the improbable starting point for his important criticisms of traditional Pavlovian principles.

Some years ago, Seligman attended an excellent dinner. The star attraction on the menu was a *filet mignon,* served with a very palatable *sauce Bearnaise.* Seligman enjoyed the meal—but a few hours later he became violently ill and spent the better part of the night throwing up. Later, he found that he had acquired a strong dislike for the taste of *sauce Bearnaise:* the mere thought of it nauseated him. At first sight, this incident seems to be an example of simple Pavlovian conditioning. The sauce (CS) was paired with the illness (UCS), eliciting the throwing up (UCR) so that subsequent experience with the sauce elicited nausea (CR).

In fact, however, the sauce Bearnaise episode violated several fundamental principles of Pavlovian conditioning as detailed in this unit. First, the interval between consuming the sauce and throwing up was about six hours. In the laboratory, however, the longest interval between two events that produces learning is about 30 seconds. Second, Seligman learned the association between sauce and throwing up in a single trial. In the laboratory, it invariably takes more than one trial for an association to be learned. Third, it was only the sauce that became distasteful to Seligman, and not the restaurant, nor his dining companion, nor the *filet mignon.* But in the laboratory, all associated stimuli would be expected to become distasteful. Fourth, Seligman subsequently discovered that the sauce had not in fact been the cause of his illness, yet he still retained his aversion to it. In the laboratory, the expectation of recurrence is thought to be the basis of avoidance behavior. Finally, Seligman continued to loathe the sauce for five years. But in the laboratory, conditioned responses usually die out within a dozen trials.

These observations led Seligman to challenge a basic Pavlovian assumption that *what* an animal learns is unimportant, that any stimuli or responses can be paired equally well. According to this traditional assumption, there should be no difference between teaching a pigeon to avoid a shock and teaching a professor to avoid a sauce. Why, then, did the professor learn his lesson so much faster and adhere to it so doggedly?

The reason, Seligman contends, is that the activities we teach animals in the laboratory do not occur in the real world. He asks, "When do rats normally have to press levers in order to get flour pellets? When do dogs come across little metronomes that signal meat?" The biology and evolutionary history of the animal in question, Seligman continues, makes a major difference in each learning situation. Pavlov's laws must be modified, he feels, to take account of different capacities of particular species to learn specific behaviors. Evolution does not prepare dogs to associate clicks with food, and so they are relatively slow to learn the association. On the other hand, evolution does prepare men for the *sauce Bearnaise* phenomenon. Any man who ate some poisonous substance, fell ill, made the association later, and lived to tell the tale, would have a distinct selective survival advantage over a man who failed to make the association and continued to eat the substance. Evolutionary

selection would favor those individuals who could stay away from the taste in the future, learn the lesson in one trial, avoid being misled by other surrounding stimuli, and retain the association for years after.

Seligman proposes that the laws of learning vary depending on the "preparedness" of the animal to learn the association in question. He distinguished between three states of preparedness. By *prepared,* he means that the biology and genetics of the animal contribute to its ability to make the association. It will learn the lesson quickly and easily. By *unprepared,* he means that nothing in the animal's evolutionary history contribute to learning the association, and so it is learned slowly after many trials. By *counterprepared,* he means that the animal is not at all suited to make the association. Dogs, for example, are counterprepared for yawning in order to get fed. No matter how easy we make the task, a dog will never learn to perform it.

It seems likely that human phobias—irrational fears of specific objects or experiences, such as mice, heights, or enclosed spaces—are a further example of the *sauce Bearnaise* phenomenon. Phobias are also *selective*: we fear heights, the dark, or insects; but not trees, pillows, or shoes. (Although fear of even these may accompany traumatic events.) Phobias are highly *resistant to extinction.* Like taste aversions, they are not affected by the individual's understanding that the response is an irrational one. In the past, phobias have usually been interpreted and treated in strictly psychoanalytic terms. Now it seems that they can be relevantly analyzed in terms of our deepening understanding of classical conditioning processes.

Unit 27

Operant Conditioning

OVERVIEW

How are new responses learned, maintained, and lost through the principles of operant conditioning? These principles are discussed in the context of human "behavior modification" research, rather than animal studies, even though most of the principles involved were originally derived from animal research. The controversy between behavior modification and humanism is presented.

UNIT OUTLINE

DEFINITION AND BACKGROUND
1. *Definition:* operant conditioning is a learning process through which behavior is acquired, maintained, or eliminated by the consequences of that behavior.
2. *Background:* E. L. Thorndike (1874–1949).

QUESTIONS AND EVIDENCE
1. How may behavior be acquired through reinforcement in operant conditioning?
Hypotheses:
   a. *Token-economy:* tokens for reinforcement can be used effectively in groups to replace negative, disruptive behavior with acceptable behavior. **465**
   b. *Shaping:* behavior can be acquired through the reinforcement of successive approximations to the desired behavior. **465**
   c. *Chaining:* complex patterns are built up by stringing together a number of simpler responses (or links) that are already in an animal's repertoire or can be added to it through shaping and other techniques. **467**
2. How may behavior be maintained through operant conditioning?
Hypotheses:
   a. *Control:* behavior that has been acquired may be maintained through either positive or negative reinforcement occurring continuously or intermittently.
   b. *Schedule-of-reinforcement:* the strength and frequency of a response will vary according to the pattern and frequency of reinforcements. **471**
3. How may behavior be eliminated through operant conditioning?
Hypotheses:
   a. *Extinction:* because reinforcement is necessary to maintain behavior, the removal of that reinforcement will eliminate it. **473**
   b. *Punishment:* an effective way to eliminate unwanted behavior is to provide brief aversive stimulation immediately upon the emission of the response.
   c. *Discrimination:* certain responses can be eliminated in some situations and retained in others through a combination of several conditioning procedures.

IMPORTANT CONCEPTS

	page
behaviorism	**461**
behavior therapy	**463**
chaining	**467**
discrimination	**475**
instrumental learning	**461**
learning	**461**
operant conditioning	**460**
reinforcement	**463**
shaping	**465**
Skinner box	**462**
successive approximations	**465**
token economy	**464**

The basis of some voluntary behavior is the association of specific acts with the consequences that follow.

The occasion may later be presented that signals the likelihood that the act will be followed by the same consequences.

The probability of the act recurring is then dependent upon the strength of its association with the consequence.

DEFINITION AND BACKGROUND

One DEFINITION of operant conditioning describes it as *a learning process through which behavior is acquired, maintained, or eliminated by the consequences of that behavior.* Operant conditioning follows many of the principles of Pavlovian conditioning, described in Unit 26, but there are some important differences. One of the most important is that the two kinds of conditioning involve different kinds of behavior. Pavlovian conditioning begins with a *reflex,* that is, with a behavior that a particular stimulus automatically *elicits* from an organism, such as the salivation reflex that food elicits in dogs. Operant conditioning, on the other hand, concerns *voluntary behavior* that an organism *emits,* as when a rat explores a strange cage or a baby just learning to crawl explores his playpen.

During operant conditioning, the frequency with which a particular behavior is emitted by an organism can be increased if the behavior is *reinforced* (rewarded) whenever it occurs. Reinforcement also has a second effect: in addition to increasing the frequency of a behavior, it brings the behavior under *stimulus control.* That is, the behavior will tend to occur whenever the organism finds itself in a situation similar to the one in which, on earlier occasions, the behavior has been reinforced.

In real life, these operant processes often occur naturally, in the ordinary course of events, without the deliberate intervention of anyone serving as an "experimenter." However, these processes can also be made to happen. For example, if you put a bottle of milk into a playpen with a hungry baby, the child will stop what he is doing and crawl toward the bottle. If you wanted to, you could construct a simple maze so that the baby would have to crawl through it to reach the bottle. Drinking the milk would reinforce the child's maze-crawling activity, which would probably become faster with practice. In addition, after a few trials, the hungry child would probably start down the maze whenever he was put into the playpen, illustrating stimulus control.

Operant conditioning can account for a wide variety of complex behaviors as well as for simple responses. Some psychologists believe that all behavior, including human behavior, is learned through conditioning.

Many others believe, however, that cognitive processes play a crucial role, particularly in the learning of complex human behavior. The cognitive approach to learning is described in Units 14, 16, and 22, and the effect of motives of many kinds on behavior is discussed in Unit 21. These approaches add other dimensions to the explanation of human behavior in particular, which may eventually need to be balanced against, or integrated with, the approach of operant conditioning.

The FOCUS of this unit is on the ways behavior can be acquired, maintained, and eliminated through operant conditioning techniques such as simple reinforcement, shaping, chaining, different reinforcement schedules, extinction, and punishment.

BACKGROUND: E. L. THORNDIKE (1874–1949)

At about the same time that Pavlov was conducting his famous experiments with the reflexive behavior of dogs, E. L. Thorndike was investigating the operant

Figure 1. American psychologist-educator Edward Lee Thorndike's findings on how lab animals select appropriate responses to given stimuli by trial and error became a keystone of subsequent learning theory.

behavior (he called it trial-and-error learning) of cats. In 1898 Thorndike published a report of a series of experiments in which hungry cats were put into various "puzzle boxes," which could be opened by pulling strings or by manipulating latches or knobs. Outside the boxes, in view of the cats, was food.

At first, the animals moved about excitedly but not purposefully; they would claw at the cage and push against it with their paws and head, apparently motivated simply by an intense desire to escape confinement. Eventually, by accident, a cat would release itself from the puzzle box by catching its claws in the proper string or pushing the proper knob. On later trials, the cat would take a smaller number of seconds to escape the box and obtain the food. The escape times recorded for one cat, for example, were 160, 30, 90, 60, 15, 28, and 20 seconds; by the twenty-fourth trial, the cat could escape in only 7 seconds.

likely than ever before to recur also. Conversely, any act which in a given situation produces discomfort becomes disassociated from that situation, so that when the situation recurs, the act is less likely than before to recur [1905, p. 202].

Thorndike's discovery of "trial and error" learning stimulated a great deal of interest in what was later called operant conditioning (or instrumental learning). His hypothesis of gradual problem solving was challenged by some who believed that the process was one of "insight" that occurred suddenly, in an all-or-nothing fashion. That controversy has yet to be resolved (see Unit 18). The law of effect, however, was the forerunner of present reinforcement hypotheses and introduced the explanation of learning in terms of environmental consequences rather than in terms of instinct.

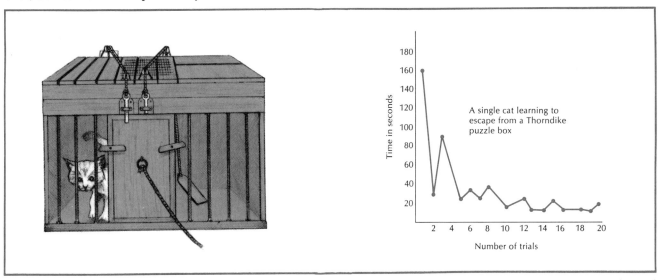

Figure 2. A single cat learning to escape from a Thorndike puzzle box.

The graph shows that with successive trials the cat requires less and less time to escape from the puzzle box.

Thorndike's observations, based on experiments not only with cats but with fish, dogs, monkeys, and children, led him to postulate the importance of reinforcement, or reward, in increasing the probability that a given behavior would occur. He formulated *Thorndike's law of effect,* which he stated as follows:

Any act which in a given situation produces satisfaction becomes associated with that situation, so that when the situation recurs, the act is more

B. F. Skinner, the well-known behaviorist, has been investigating operant conditioning extensively since the late 1920s. Skinner believed that operant conditioning applied to the learning of complex behaviors as well as to the learning of simple actions. One day, in a laboratory on the top floor of a flour mill in Minneapolis, Skinner and his associates accidentally discovered "shaping," which is one of the ways complex behavior is learned. They had snared one of the many pigeons that flocked around the window

Figure 3. Behavioral psychologist B. F. Skinner has concentrated on the role of reinforcement in conditioning.

sills and decided to use reinforcement to teach the bird to bowl. After waiting endlessly for the pigeon to swipe a small ball with its beak so that they could deliver a reinforcer, they hit on the idea of feeding the pigeon for any response that even approximated a swipe and then working the animal up to the final response. Within a very short time, the pigeon had been taught to bowl.

Since that time, Skinner has done a variety of experiments on the shaping of behavior and on the effects of different reinforcement schedules on performance. He has also reared a daughter in the "controlled environment" of a glass-enclosed crib, invented a popular piece of laboratory equipment called the Skinner box, and written a utopian novel called *Walden II.*

In his most recent book, *Beyond Freedom and Dignity* (1971), Skinner stresses the personal and social implications of operant conditioning as a means of behavioral engineering. Instead of describing an individual's state in terms of "crises," "alienation," "anxiety," or "low ego strength," Skinner argues, we should focus on the behavior that characterizes such states. Once the behavior has been identified, it

becomes possible to manipulate the contingencies that maintain it. Behavior description, Skinner suggests,

> will provide us with . . . an alternative account, which . . . suggests effective action. What he (the individual) tells us about his feelings may permit us to make some informed guesses about what is wrong with the contingencies (in his environment), but we must go directly to the contingencies if we want to be sure and it is the contingencies which must be changed if his behavior is to be changed.

Some people feel that Skinner's treatment of people and societies in *Beyond Freedom and Dignity* does not recognize those qualities which distinguish humans from machines. Although these ideas are controversial, there is no doubt that the basic principles of operant conditioning, as discovered and described by Skinner and other behaviorists, have provided a rich supply of techniques that aid the prediction and control of behavior.

Operant conditioning changes, or modifies, voluntary behavior through the consequences or effects of that behavior itself. Consider eating, for example. Within certain personal and social restrictions, what people eat, how much they eat, and when and where

Figure 4. Students using a Skinner box in a school laboratory.

they eat are voluntary behavior, dependent to some extent on their own choices or decisions.

Eating, then, must be open to operant conditioning. Suppose a person eats a dish of steamed clams for the first time and quickly becomes nauseated and sick. Probably these consequences will *eliminate* his choosing clams from the menu for a long time to come. Suppose, to the contrary, that he savors the rich smell and the salty taste of the clams, dipped in melted butter and washed down with hot clam bisque, and feels comfortably filled. His clam-eating behavior is, then, reinforced by its own positive effects, and he is more than likely to order clams the next time he sees them on a menu. He has *acquired* a "taste for steamed clams," as we say, and perhaps even, by stimulus generalization, a taste for clams in any form as well as for other shellfish. This taste may be *maintained* by repeated positive reinforcements, as he seeks out restaurants that offer "shore dinners," and his wife or mother adds "steamers" to his list of favorite dishes.

The acquiring, maintaining, and eliminating of any kind of voluntary behavior in this manner can also be called behavior modification ("behavior mod" for short). Many conditions in a person's internal or external environment may reinforce responses that lead to behavior modifications. The effects of these reinforcers determine the changes that take place in behavior. Knowledge of which reinforcers are most effective yields power to modify behavior.

Behavior therapy, on which a great deal of work is now being done by psychologists, is the application of the principles of operant conditioning to the modification of behavior of clients, including neurotic, severely retarded, and even psychotic individuals. Behavior therapy relies on using principles of learning through operant conditioning to change the behavior of such clients rather than developing their insight or resolving their unconscious conflicts by the techniques of traditional psychotherapy (see Unit 20).

The principles of behavior modification and therapy are based on the understanding of operant conditioning derived from many investigations of how this kind of learning takes place.

QUESTIONS AND EVIDENCE

1. How may behavior be acquired through reinforcement in operant conditioning?
2. How may behavior be maintained through operant conditioning?
3. How may behavior be eliminated through operant conditioning?

You will find your way much more easily through these questions if we concentrate for a moment on the meaning of that word "reinforcement" in question 1. Reinforcement is the key process by which behaviors are acquired in operant conditioning. Any response that is *reinforced* is one that is more likely to occur again than not. Almost anything that is important to an organism can act as a reinforcer. Some examples are shown in Table 1.

TABLE 1. Common Reinforcers

	Primary	Secondary
Positive	Food	Money
	Water	Tokens
	Sex	Esteem
	Elimination	Points
	Sleep	Grades
	Sensory stimulation	Status
		Approval
Negative	Shock	Low esteem
	Pain	Ridicule
	Extreme temperatures	Exclusion
	Loud noises	Violation of personal space
	Physical pressure	

Reinforcers can be *primary,* satisfying basic physiological needs such as the needs for food and water, or *secondary,* having learned, indirect values, as money does for most people. In addition, reinforcers may be grouped as *positive* or *negative.* A positively reinforced response is one that is more likely to occur again than not because the consequences are pleasant. For exam-

When a mother picks up a crying baby and feeds him, she is providing both primary and secondary positive reinforcement (food and attention). The baby, in turn, reinforces the mother's behavior by stopping his crying. The result is that the baby continues to cry when he is hungry and the mother continues to pick him up and feed him when he cries.

QUESTION	1. HOW MAY BEHAVIOR BE ACQUIRED THROUGH REINFORCEMENT IN OPERANT CONDITIONING?		
HYPOTHESES	**TOKEN ECONOMY**	**SHAPING**	**CHAINING**
DESCRIPTIVE EVIDENCE		ASSESS: use of shaping to improve verbal behavior	ASSESS: use of chaining to train retarded to dress themselves
EXPERIMENTAL EVIDENCE	VARY: use of tokens as reinforcement MEASURE: occurrences of disruptive behavior		

ple, food is a positive reinforcer that can be used to increase the probability that a rat will run a maze quickly and correctly. Electric shock can be a negative reinforcer that can be used for the same purpose. A negatively reinforced response is one that is more likely to occur again than not because it allows the organism to avoid an unpleasant consequence. An animal will run a maze either to get food or to get away from shock. In Thorndike's puzzle-box experiment, the cat's escape from confinement was a negative reinforcer and food was a positive reinforcer.

Shock and other negative, or aversive, stimuli can also be used as punishers, as opposed to negative reinforcers. Punishment *decreases* the probability that a given behavior will occur again. If an electric shock is given to a rat in the start box of a maze, the shock is being used as a negative reinforcer, for it will increase the probability that maze running will occur the next time the rat is placed in the start box. But if the shock is given at the end of the maze in the goal box, then it is being used as a punisher. It will decrease the probability that the rat will run to the goal box the next time it is given a chance.

1. HOW MAY BEHAVIOR BE ACQUIRED THROUGH REINFORCEMENT IN OPERANT CONDITIONING?

In behavior-modification experiments a great variety of positive and negative reinforcers of either primary or secondary character has been tested. These reinforcers may be put together in various combinations to produce effective behavior acquisition.

In many classrooms for both exceptional and normal children, one practical method of reinforcement in large groups uses a "token economy," which consists of giving tokens or secondary reinforcers as rewards for desirable behavior. The students can later choose to exchange their tokens (like money) for some edible (candy), manipulatable (toys), or social (games) reinforcement. When the goal of a teacher or parent is to reduce the occurrence of negative behavior, it is often most effective to accentuate the positive; that is, to provide reinforcement for behavior one wishes to *accelerate* and to *decelerate* negative behavior by ignoring it, if possible. It is important to realize that even a scolding can be rewarding to some children who are hungry for any kind of attention.

The *token-economy hypothesis* states that tokens for reinforcement can be used effectively in groups to replace negative, disruptive behavior with acceptable behavior. Token-economy reinforcement was the principal technique used for operant conditioning in the following experiment, in which the behavior-reinforcer program was the independent variable and disruptive behavior the dependent variable, measured by percentage of total behavior.

EXPERIMENTAL EVIDENCE

Investigators: J. G. Baker, B. Stanish, and B. Fraser
Source, Date: "Comparative Effects of a Token Economy in Nursery School," 1972
Location: Mental Retardation Center, Toronto, Ontario, Canada
Subjects: 19 retarded children (9 experimental and 10 controls) ages four to eight, average IQs of 32 and 37, respectively
Materials: Tokens (poker chips) for candy rewards

In one nursery school teachers selected an experimental group of nine retarded children who displayed disruptive or negative behavior. The ten control-group children (who also exhibited negative behavior) were chosen from five other nursery schools in order to randomize the effects of schools and teachers. Baseline ratings on negative behavior of the children were collected for five weeks before a behavior-modification program of eight weeks was started (there was a one-week break near the end of the program). Lay-volunteer teachers were trained during the baseline period in the modification techniques.

During predetermined segments of the daily program positive reinforcement was provided for appropriate behavior by giving a child tokens to be "cashed in" for candy and other goodies at a "store" just before going home. An attempt was made to ignore inappropriate behavior entirely. Punishment by "time-out" periods of five minutes of isolation in booths away from the nursery area was used only rarely for extremely disruptive behavior.

During the baseline rating period, the experimental-group children had showed consistently poorer behavior than children in the control group; mean percentages of negative behavior were 59 percent and 48 percent, respectively. The experimental-group mean negative behavior was reduced below that of the control group even in the first week of the token-economy program. By the end of the total program, reduction in negative behavior of the experimental group was 28 percent against 5 percent in the control group.

The investigators concluded that "The results should leave little doubt as to the effectiveness of a simple token economy in the teaching and behavioral control of trainable retardates in a nursery school setting." They also suggested that "in behavioral modification there lies a powerful professional technique which can be taught to relatively inexperienced para-professional behavioral technicians and administered by them under careful supervision."

A behavior that an organism emits without training, like the babbling of an infant or the running of a rat in a cage, can be increased in frequency simply by reinforcing it when it occurs. But some behavior, like the bowling that Skinner and colleagues taught their pigeons, does not occur without training and must therefore be developed gradually, or shaped. The *shaping hypothesis* states that behavior can be acquired through the reinforcement of successive approximations to the desired behavior.

Shaping can be used either to train an animal to display a behavior that, without shaping, it would never display at all, or it can be used to speed up the acquisition of behavior that, if an experimenter waited long enough, would occur anyway. For example, suppose that you wanted to run an experiment concerning the effects of different reinforcement schedules on the bar-pressing behavior of a rat. If you deprive the rat of food, put him into a Skinner box the rat then, and wait, he will eventually press the bar; once he has learned that pressing the bar yields food, you can begin your experiment. But if you do not want to wait for him to learn on his own, you can hasten the process by using shaping. To do that, you would reinforce the following basic responses: (1) being near the bar: (2) looking and turning toward the bar; (3) touching the bar with any part of the body; (4) placing a paw on the bar; (5) exerting a slight downward pressure on the bar; (6) a full pressing of the bar. As soon as each response has been acquired, you would withhold reinforcement until the animal performed the next response on the list, forcing it gradually along the sequence toward the behavior desired in the end.

In the early 1950s, K. and M. Breland, students of Skinnerian psychology, used shaping and other operant-conditioning techniques to create a commercial animal-training enterprise. They taught chickens a number of complex responses, including playing on a toy piano and tap dancing in costume and shoes. As they described their procedure: "The basic operation in all of these acts was reinforcement at the proper moment in the behavior sequence, by presenting the chicken with a small amount of scratch grain from the hopper. During the training period, successive approximations to the desired behavior, and component parts of the final act were reinforced." The power of shaping is shown both in the extraordinary number and variety of responses the animals learned to make and in the enduring strength of the acquired response patterns. The birds played thousands of performances without failure before audiences of up to 5,000 people per day. The Brelands' Animal Behavior Enterprises is still a success and their exhibits are in wide circulation.

You may as a child have played the game of finding some hidden thing or person by moving at random (and perhaps blindfolded) and following the cues given by your playmates—"getting warmer," "colder now," "freezing," "warmer again," "hot," and "hot-

Distributed by the authors, 12 Johnson Avenue, Binghamton, New York, 13905.

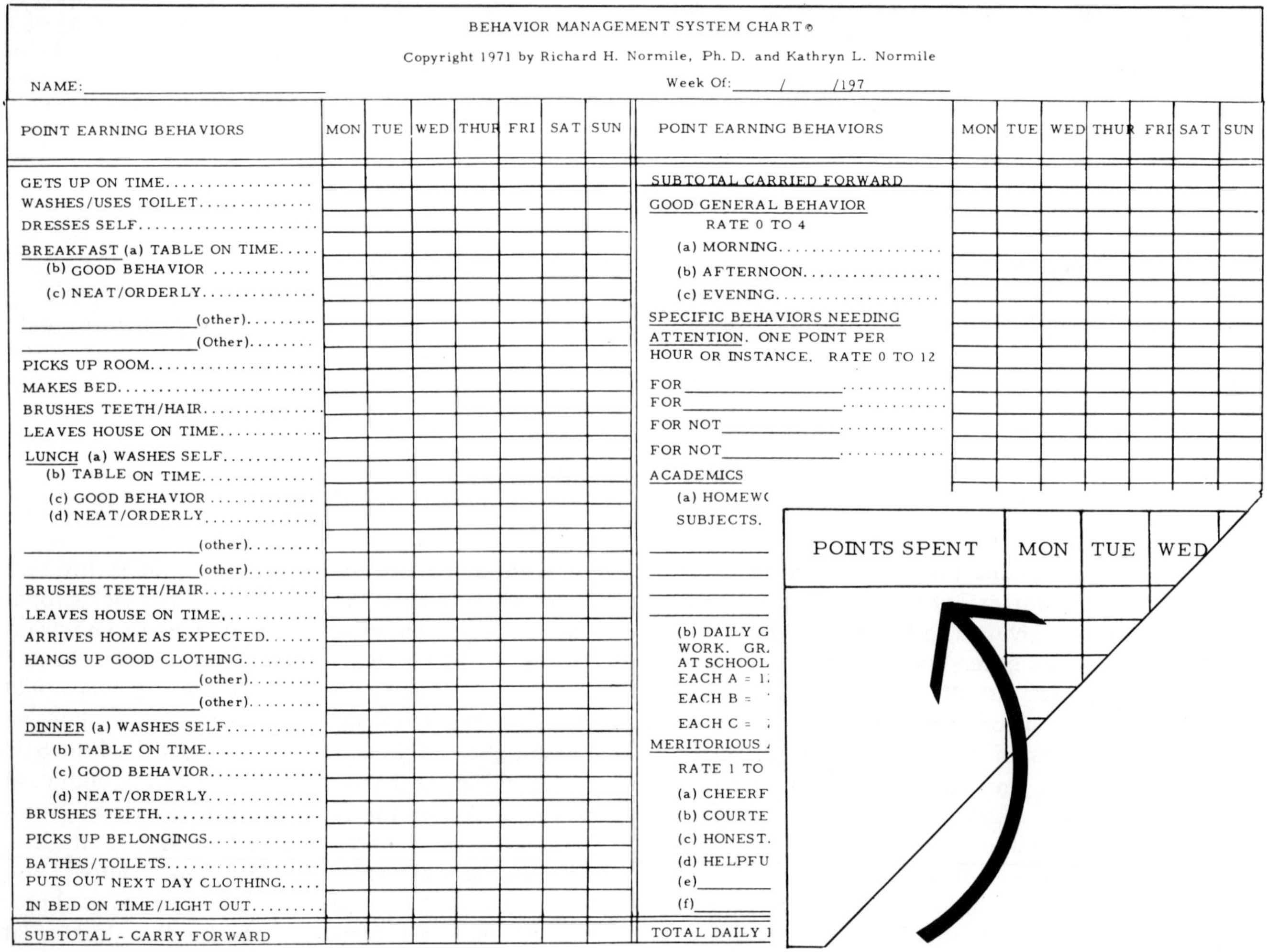

BEHAVIOR MANAGEMENT SYSTEM CHART®

Copyright 1971 by Richard H. Normile, Ph. D. and Kathryn L. Normile

NAME:________ Week Of: ___/___/197__

POINT EARNING BEHAVIORS	MON	TUE	WED	THUR	FRI	SAT	SUN
GETS UP ON TIME							
WASHES/USES TOILET							
DRESSES SELF							
BREAKFAST (a) TABLE ON TIME							
(b) GOOD BEHAVIOR							
(c) NEAT/ORDERLY							
________(other)							
________(Other)							
PICKS UP ROOM							
MAKES BED							
BRUSHES TEETH/HAIR							
LEAVES HOUSE ON TIME							
LUNCH (a) WASHES SELF							
(b) TABLE ON TIME							
(c) GOOD BEHAVIOR							
(d) NEAT/ORDERLY							
________(other)							
________(other)							
BRUSHES TEETH/HAIR							
LEAVES HOUSE ON TIME							
ARRIVES HOME AS EXPECTED							
HANGS UP GOOD CLOTHING							
________(other)							
________(other)							
DINNER (a) WASHES SELF							
(b) TABLE ON TIME							
(c) GOOD BEHAVIOR							
(d) NEAT/ORDERLY							
BRUSHES TEETH							
PICKS UP BELONGINGS							
BATHES/TOILETS							
PUTS OUT NEXT DAY CLOTHING							
IN BED ON TIME/LIGHT OUT							
SUBTOTAL - CARRY FORWARD							

POINT EARNING BEHAVIORS	MON	TUE	WED	THUR	FRI	SAT	SUN
SUBTOTAL CARRIED FORWARD							
GOOD GENERAL BEHAVIOR RATE 0 TO 4							
(a) MORNING							
(b) AFTERNOON							
(c) EVENING							
SPECIFIC BEHAVIORS NEEDING ATTENTION. ONE POINT PER HOUR OR INSTANCE. RATE 0 TO 12							
FOR________							
FOR________							
FOR NOT________							
FOR NOT________							
ACADEMICS							
(a) HOMEW(							
SUBJECTS.							
(b) DAILY G WORK. GR. AT SCHOOL							
EACH A = 1:							
EACH B =							
EACH C =							
MERITORIOUS RATE 1 TO							
(a) CHEERF							
(b) COURTE							
(c) HONEST.							
(d) HELPFU							
(e)____							
(f)____							
TOTAL DAILY I							

POINTS SPENT	MON	TUE	WED

Figure 6. This tally sheet used in behavior modification procedures illustrates one of the many practical applications of operant conditioning.

ter!'' These phrases and words were the reinforcers directing you by approximations toward the hidden object.

Similarly, in an entirely natural and habitual manner, a child learning to speak his first few words usually has his behavior shaped by social reinforcers from his parents. He will be rewarded at first with smiles and attention for almost any vocalized sounds. But as time goes on, the parents get used to hearing ''da'' and begin to act delighted only with ''DaDa'' and later with ''Daddy.'' We all naturally use the process, but we use it inefficiently because we do not completely understand it.

Now that the shaping process in operant conditioning has been clearly formulated, it can be more effectively used in behavior modification. In the following study, a procedure like that by which parents shape a child's learning to talk was used to increase and improve the speech production of two emotionally disturbed three-year-olds.

DESCRIPTIVE EVIDENCE

Investigators: K. Salzinger, R. S. Feldman, J. E. Cowan, and S. Salzinger
Source, Date: "Operant Conditioning of Verbal Behavior of Two Young Speech-Deficient Boys," 1965
Location: New York State Psychiatric Institute
Subjects: 2 speech-deficient boys, aged three years seven months and three years ten months
Materials: Food reinforcers

Before operant conditioning began, the vocal behavior of one child consisted of whines, grunts, and various babbling sounds, but no words; the other child would say only ''no'' and a few other words, many of them poorly articulated.

For both children the unit of measurement of vocal or verbal behavior was the number of seconds of vocalization per minute of clock time. Verbalization was reinforced with both primary (candy, peanuts, soda) and secondary (praise) reinforcers. In 195 forty- to sixty-minute sessions, the children went through several major steps, different for each child. For one child the six identifiable steps in the shaping process

were: Reinforcement of (1) discrete sounds—not yelling, screaming, or babbling; (2) close approximations to word sounds; (3) exact or very close word sounds; (4) matching words to objects; (5) spontaneous emission of words; and (6) obeying verbal commands such as ''bring me the ball.''

Relatively high, steady vocalization rates were achieved by both boys. After a twenty-month speech-shaping program, one boy was speaking almost entirely in sentences and employing a variety of grammatical structures. The experimenters also noted a marked improvement in his social development paralleling his acquisition of speech.

The process of reinforcing successive approximations for specific and/or specialized behavior accounts for a large percentage of our normal behavior patterns. As the athlete, the musician, and the high-school student learning to drive acquire their skills, their behavior is being shaped by coaches or teachers into closer and closer approximations of expert performance. However, all of these patterns involve learning not merely through successive steps but also through longer and more highly organized sequences of behaviors. The *chaining hypothesis* states that complex patterns are built up by stringing together a number of simpler responses (or links) that are already in an animal's repertoire or can be added to it through shaping and other techniques. After the ''chain'' has been established, reinforcement of each response is no longer necessary. The completion of each step or link in the chain now serves as the reinforcer, as well as the cue for the next step, until the whole complex pattern is completed.

In 1938 Skinner published a detailed account of a famous experiment demonstrating the use of chaining in the acquisition of novel response patterns. By means of a carefully pieced together set of response sequences, a rat was trained to pull on a string to get a marble from a rack, pick up the marble with its forepaws, carry it across a cage to a vertical tube rising two inches from the floor, lift the marble, and drop it into the tube.

The procedure of chaining obviously requires extended time periods and a large number of trials, but the results can be spectacular. Pigeons have been taught to play Ping-Pong and bowl, and dogs to ride bicycles. A pig even learned to earn a chip that it then places in a large piggy bank (as a promotion stunt for

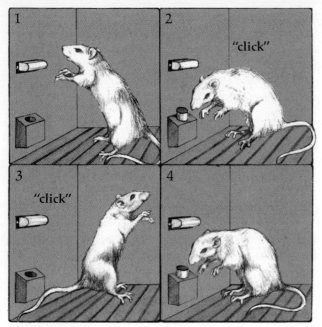

Figure 7. **Reinforcement.** The thirsty rat is taught to associate a loud click with the delivery of water from a dispenser. Eventually the click itself is sufficient to get the rat to approach the dispenser; it is a conditioned reinforcer.

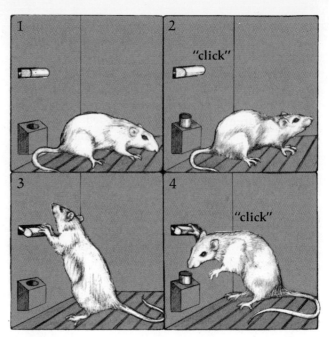

Shaping. Reinforcement is used to strengthen some of the animal's natural behaviors in order to teach him to press a bar. By selectively reinforcing closer and closer approximations to the desired activity—rising on its hind legs, bending forward, and so on—we can shape a bar press.

Chaining. After shaping each of the components of the routine, each component is linked with others in longer and longer sequences—the completion of each link in the chain serving as the cue for the next step.

Because behavior that is reinforced tends to be repeated, the skillful trainer can modify an animal's behavior to his own ends. The goal here is to teach a rat to push a cart to the base of a tower, climb the tower, then ascend a ramp to receive its reward.

a bank). Many human tasks, like typing or driving, involve chaining. Think for a moment of the number of responses you must emit before leaving the driveway: opening the car door, getting in, closing the door, fastening seat belt, inserting the key in the ignition, and so forth.

The whole chained series of behavior steps involved in getting into a car and driving off is one of the many patterns of our everyday, normal behavior. What about abnormal or impaired behavior? Shaping and chaining are proving to be highly successful techniques for teaching relatively complex behavior patterns or skills to severely handicapped people. Furthermore, operant conditioning can readily be practiced by aides and technicians, once they have received training in its principles and in the specific behavior with which they are trying to cope. Thus, reinforcement procedures can be used in a great variety of clinical situations. The following experiment provides one example.

DESCRIPTIVE EVIDENCE

Investigators: G. L. Martin, B. Kehoe, E. Bird, V. Jensen, and M. Darbyshire
Source, Date: "Operant Conditioning in Dressing Behavior of Severely Retarded Girls," 1971
Location: Manitoba Training School and University of Manitoba, Canada
Subjects: 11 autistic and severely retarded girls, ages seven to twenty, IQs of 40 to untestable, with cerebral dysfunctions
Materials: Sweaters, socks, shoes, bras, underpants, undershirts; food reinforcers

All eleven subjects entering this operant-conditioning experiment could follow only a few simple commands. Eight could say a few words and partially dress themselves. Full self-dressing became the immediate goal of the step-by-step chain-training procedure.

Psychiatric nurses and nurses' aides were trained in the chaining principles to teach the girls, one step at a time, the dressing procedure for each garment. First they had to shape an adequate attention span for each girl, which took an average of over three hours of sessions. Correct responses for each dressing step were reinforced with verbal praise and food, and later with tokens. Incorrect responses were followed by a sharp "no" and a time-out of ten seconds. The girls were neither reprimanded nor interacted with by the experimenter when they displayed inattentiveness. As a girl passed through the steps of each stage, she was required to perform all previously learned steps on each trial for a single reinforcer and then trained on the new step.

Training sessions with individual subjects lasted from fifteen to thirty minutes. The number of sessions required to learn to put on each garment ranged from three for undershirts to thirty-six for lacing and tying shoes. The average initial dressing time was reduced by half with the operant-conditioning program. Reinforcement was subsequently given by token economy in the wards for dressing in the morning as well as in training sessions, with many instances of response generalization to other ward situations. More independent functioning of the subjects, like self-dressing, gave the staff extra time to spend on more severe problems.

Later research on chaining has demonstrated that the middle responses in a chain are the hardest to acquire and that chained responses tend to occur as units. Recently investigators have been attempting to develop a more sophisticated definition of the variables affecting the acquisition of long chains of responses.

However, even a more complete description of chaining cannot explain how the responses that have been acquired are "kept alive" after the initial conditioning has taken place. A child's parents may shape his acquisition of the word "Daddy," but why does the child keep using the word when his parents have stopped smiling and nodding whenever he utters it? Much behavior originally acquired through reinforcement persists long after the time when reinforcers are systematically delivered. Sometimes, in fact, it is difficult to see that any reinforcement is following the behavior at all. How, then, is this behavior maintained?

HYPOTHESES	CONTROL	SCHEDULE OF REINFORCEMENT
DESCRIPTIVE EVIDENCE	ASSESS: withholding attention to control psychotic verbal behavior	ASSESS: use of reinforcement schedules for reading improvement and maintenance
EXPERIMENTAL EVIDENCE		

2. HOW MAY BEHAVIOR BE MAINTAINED THROUGH OPERANT CONDITIONING?

A clue to uncovering one answer to this question is offered by a finding from Baker's experiment (described earlier) on operant conditioning of disruptive nursery-school children. When the continuous reinforcement by tokens was entirely stopped for a week near the end of the experiment, the negative behavior of the experimental-group subjects went up, although the level was not as high as the level before the reinforcement started. Return to the token economy the following week did not immediately reduce the negative behavior to its previous low level. However, ratings of the children remaining on reinforcement for the following term indicated a return to the low levels. This finding implies that maintenance of acquired behavior requires at least some reinforcement.

The *control hypothesis* states that behavior that has been acquired may be maintained through either positive or negative reinforcement occurring continuously or intermittently.

Positive control maintains behavior through ongoing, positive reinforcers. Such polite behavior as saying "Please" and "Thank you," for example, which is initially acquired through careful and specific reinforcement by the parents, is maintained by social reinforcement from other people throughout an individual's life. Standards of dress, speech, and hair style may change over time, but even those changes are reinforced by the peer group on a more or less continual basis. A driver's behavior is maintained by

the fact that the car does what it is supposed to do. Note, also, that some responses in a chain may be reinforced less than others and may therefore weaken or drop out entirely. For example, a driver may stop pushing the clutch pedal all the way to the floor if doing so yields no smoother a gearshift than pushing it halfway down.

Negative control refers to the fact that behavior will be maintained when it continues to result in the avoidance or termination of aversive stimuli—that is, when it continues to be negatively reinforced. The new bridegroom may find that buying flowers for his upset wife eliminates her pouting and crying but has given her a means of negative control: "Why don't you bring flowers anymore?" The importance of the speed limit may be established by the criticism of the driving instructor, but it is maintained by the more general threat of being arrested for speeding.

Such subtle reinforcements in the nonstructured environment of a mental hospital ward may inadvertently help to maintain the unusual psychotic behavior of its patients. Some evidence for this contention was furnished in the following investigation.

DESCRIPTIVE EVIDENCE

Investigators: T. Ayllon and E. Haughton
Source, Date: "Modification of Symptomatic Verbal Behavior of Mental Patients," 1964
Location: Saskatchewan Hospital, Weyburn, Saskatchewan

Subjects: 3 psychotic females
Materials: Ward staff, attention, cigarettes

In the first phase of this research, psychotic statements, such as "I'm the Queen. Why don't you give things to the Queen? The Queen wants to smoke . . . How's King George, have you seen him?" were rewarded with attention and cigarettes and other small items from the ward staff and the psychologists. In the second phase, all reinforcement for such behavior was stopped—and the behavior declined dramatically. The results indicate that the diffuse reinforcements available in the usual hospital environment can maintain psychotic behavior. In one case psychotic talk nearly doubled when it was deliberately reinforced with attention and dropped to less than half of its original rate when the attention was withdrawn. Similar results were reported for the other subjects.

The regularity with which reinforcers are received in the course of operant conditioning has been found to be very significantly related to the maintenance as well as the acquisition of the behavior. If you are not quite sure whether or not you will be rewarded every time you try, you will probably keep trying longer. This principle is very effectively used in gambling. Jackpot machines are programmed to maintain coin-depositing behavior over long stretches of time by paying off irregularly.

The *schedule-of-reinforcement hypothesis* states that the strength and frequency of a response will vary according to the pattern and frequency of reinforcements.

Five types of reinforcement schedules are most commonly used in behavioral research, and each has a different effect on the animal's behavior. First and simplest is the *continuous reinforcement schedule,* in which a reinforcer is delivered for each correct response. This schedule is the most productive in establishing a new behavior. It also maintains behavior at a high rate, but the behavior will drop off abruptly if reinforcement is stopped. A pigeon will peck a key at a high, steady rate, for example, if it is rewarded with grain for each accurate peck, but it will quickly stop pecking if the grain stops appearing.

The best schedules for maintaining a response once it has been acquired are *intermittent-reinforcement schedules,* of which there are four main types: fixed interval, variable interval, fixed ratio, and variable ratio. "Interval" refers to the length of time between reinforcements; "ratio" refers to the number of correct responses between reinforcements. Some examples will clarify the possibilities:

1. *Fixed-interval schedule.* A pigeon is reinforced for pecking a key every thirty seconds. That is, a piece of grain will appear in the hopper the first time the pigeon pecks the key thirty seconds or more after the delivery of the last piece of grain. On this schedule, the pigeon usually pecks rather unenthusiastically just after a piece of grain has been delivered but delivers a fast burst of pecks just before the allotted time is up.

2. *Variable-interval schedule.* The pigeon is reinforced on the average of every thirty seconds, but the actual interval varies. Sometimes the first peck after the five-second mark is reinforced; sometimes the first peck after twenty-five seconds; sometimes the first peck after forty-five seconds; and so on. A variable-interval schedule results in a high pecking rate, and the behavior will persist for a long time even in the absence of any reinforcement.

3. *Fixed-ratio schedule.* Here the pigeon receives grain for, say, every tenth key-peck, regardless of time elapsed since the last reinforcer. This is comparable to paying a factory worker for every ten cartons of rubber ducks that he packs. The schedule tends to maintain behavior at a high, steady rate; if reinforcement is terminated, the behavior continues for a little while beyond the first "missed payment."

4. *Variable-ratio schedule.* The pigeon is rewarded for his sixth key-peck, then his fifteenth, then every other one for a while, then not until his thirty-second peck; on the average, the ratio of rewards to correct responses is one to ten. This is the schedule that slot machines follow; as any gambler knows, it leads to a high rate of responding and very durable behavior.

The responses emitted under each of these schedules during laboratory experiments are usually kept track of automatically, by means of cumulative records, as shown in Figure 8. Because each schedule leads to a different pattern of responding, an experienced psychologist can tell by looking at a cumulative record which schedule is being used to maintain an animal's behavior.

You can see in the following investigation how reinforcement schedules can be used and varied for maintaining behavior.

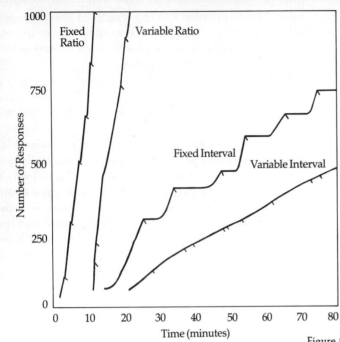

Figure 8. Typical rates of responding under different reinforcement schedules. "Ratio" refers to number of responses before reinforcement occurs; "interval" refers to time periods before reinforcement occurs. Short diagonal lines indicate occurrence of reinforcement.

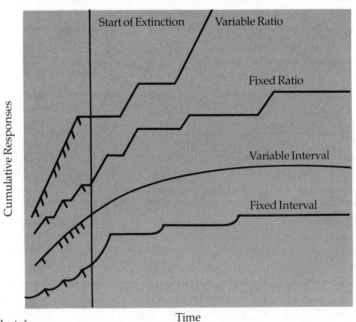

Figure 9. Extinction. Typical rates of responding when all reinforcement has ceased for behavior acquired under various reinforcement schedules. Adapted from Reynolds (1968).

DESCRIPTIVE EVIDENCE

Investigators: A. W. Staats and W. H. Butterfield
*Source, Date: "Treatment of Nonreading in a Culturally
Deprived Juvenile Delinquent: An Application of Rein-
forcement Schedules," 1965*
Location: University of California
Subject: A fourteen-year-old boy
*Materials: Science Research Associates reading materials,
tokens (secondary reinforcers)*

The subject was a delinquent child whose disruptive
behavior and lack of skills had made him very unpopular with teachers. He was trained in reading skills
during forty one-hour sessions over four-and-a-half
months. At first, correct verbal responses to word-
stimulus cards were reinforced on a continuous reinforcement schedule, using tokens (secondary reinforcers) of varying values. As the training progressed,
the experimenters decreased the value of the tokens.
The child was trained to read paragraphs silently, and
the reinforcement schedule was changed to a fifteen-
second variable-interval schedule. Then the child was
rewarded only for finishing each story in a graded set,
so that he had to read longer, more difficult material
for each token. This variable-interval schedule produced a high, steady level of responding. By the end
of the program, the boy's reading level had risen from
a 2.0 grade level to a 4.3 grade level. In response to the
word-stimulus cards, he had emitted 64,307 responses
worth a total of $20.31 in tokens!

3. HOW MAY BEHAVIOR BE ELIMINATED THROUGH OPERANT CONDITIONING?

If the reinforcements that are maintaining a behavior
can be identified, it would seem simple enough to
eliminate unwanted responses by removing those
reinforcers. Often this can be done. But under some
circumstances, when self-destructive behavior must
be eliminated quickly, for example, or when only one
type of behavior within a general behavior class needs
to be eliminated, other measures must be worked out.

The *extinction hypothesis* states that because reinforcement is necessary to maintain behavior, the
removal of that reinforcement will eliminate it. Because many behaviors are maintained by a multitude
of reinforcers—both primary and secondary—it is
sometimes difficult to recognize, let alone eliminate,
all of them. Nevertheless, researchers have had notable success in using extinction to eliminate a wide
variety of unwanted behavior patterns.

Outside the laboratory, extinction has probably
been used most fruitfully in classroom settings, where
disruptive behavior can be a major problem for teachers. Assuming that disruptive actions are reinforced
mainly by attention, even punishing such behavior
can be reinforcing, because it constitutes attention
from the teacher and usually gets the child attention
from his peer group as well. A more useful technique
is to withdraw attention, perhaps by using a "time-
out" room. This is simply a small empty room or
office (or even a corner of the classroom) where the

QUESTION	3. HOW MAY BEHAVIOR BE ELIMINATED THROUGH OPERANT CONDITIONING?		
HYPOTHESES	**EXTINCTION**	**PUNISHMENT**	**DISCRIMINATION**
DESCRIPTIVE EVIDENCE	ASSESS: extinction of tantrum behavior	ASSESS: effectiveness of shock in suppression of pathological behavior	ASSESS: treatment of homosexual behavior through discriminative control
EXPERIMENTAL EVIDENCE			

disruptive child can be taken. Aside from the very brief period of minimal attention while the child is escorted to the timeout room, there is no reinforcement for any behavior once he or she is there. Time out has been interpreted as a mild form of punishment, as well as a removal of reinforcers, in some situations and for some subjects. This procedure has been used in some classrooms with impressive results. A similar extinction procedure can be used by parents, as the following study indicates.

DESCRIPTIVE EVIDENCE

Investigator: C. D. Williams
Source, Date: "Case Study: The Elimination of Tantrum Behavior by Extinction Procedures," 1959
Location: University of Miami
Subject: Twenty-one-month-old boy
Materials: Crib, bedroom, removal of attention

This classic research eliminated the bedtime tantrums of a twenty-one-month-old child. The parents were instructed to put the child to bed at the regular time but to ignore completely the ensuing tantrum. On the first day of extinction the child cried forty-five minutes. On the third day the crying had been reduced to ten minutes, and by the seventh day it had completely stopped. No unfortunate side-effects or after-effects were observed.

The important element in extinction is that the process of removing all reinforcement for the behavior must be uniform and complete. Extinction with intermittent, even accidental, reinforcement is in reality a partial-reinforcement schedule, which will maintain rather than eliminate behavior. When an aunt inadvertently reinforced one tantrum of the boy in the Williams research by going into his room and staying with him until he fell asleep, the rate of crying returned to fifty-five minutes and the extinction procedure had to be gone through all over again.

When the reinforcers of a behavior or behavior pattern are highly diffuse, simple extinction may not be possible. Furthermore, the unwanted behavior

often increases at the start of extinction; and with seriously self-destructive behavior, extinction may be too slow a process.

The *punishment hypothesis* states that an effective way to eliminate unwanted behavior is to provide brief aversive stimulation immediately upon the emission of the response. Although punishment probably will not eliminate a behavior permanently, it will suppress it, thereby providing an opportunity for reinforcing a more desirable behavior that is incompatible with the undesirable one.

If a young child is playing in a busy street, for example, his mother cannot reasonably be expected to ignore his behavior. One way to eliminate it is to say "No!" firmly when the child goes into the street, take him back to the yard, and praise him as he starts to play there. Future incidents of playing in the street should continue to be punished, with further positive reinforcement for playing in the yard.

DESCRIPTIVE EVIDENCE

Investigators: O. I. Lovaas, B. Schaeffer, and J. Q. Simmons
Source, Date: "Building Social Behavior in Autistic Children by Use of Electric Shock," 1965
Location: University of California, Los Angeles
Subjects: Two five-year-old autistic twin-boys
Materials: One-way mirror, experimental room with grid floor for shock

Lovaas and his colleagues have provided a wealth of data on the usefulness of punishment in quickly eliminating dangerous and undesirable behavior. In this research, electric shock was used with psychotic children to eliminate severe tantrums and self-stimulatory behavior such as rocking and fondling themselves. Lovaas has also demonstrated that punishment can increase children's affectionate and social responses to adults when those adults are associated with shock termination. For these results, shock is administered whenever a tantrum or self-stimulation begins and stopped whenever the child approaches the experimenter.

The record of the proportion of time spent in

pathological and in social behavior by two identical twins before and after shock is shown in Table 2.

Although shock was applied for only three consecutive days, it was effective in suppressing pathological behavior and in promoting social behavior for between ten and eleven months. During such an interval of suppression, the child may acquire a large repertoire of reinforced positive responses that, in turn, may prevent the reoccurrence of psychotic behavior.

TABLE 2. Effect of Shock on Pathological Behavior

	Pathological Behavior (Percentage)	Social Behavior (Percentage)
Preshock	65–85	0
Postshock	0	85

Source: O. I. Lovaas, B. Schaeffer, and J. Q. Simmons, "Building Social Behavior in Autistic Children by Use of Electric Shock," *Journal of Experimental Research in Personality*, 1 (1965), 99–109.

The use of painful shock with children is an extreme method, as Lovaas and his colleagues are well aware, and shock is used only in extreme cases. The autistic children in the experiment just described, for example, had been intensively treated in a residential setting by conventional psychiatric techniques for a year without any observable change in their behavior. If the situation had continued, their future was certain institutionalization. Other research indicates that autistic and other severely schizophrenic children like these boys, who do not use language or play appropriately with toys by the age of five, do not improve despite psychiatric treatment or psychotherapy for child and family.

Furthermore, Lovaas and his associates noted that the children seemed frightened by the shock only at the very beginning of training. Once they had been trained to avoid shock, the children often smiled, laughed, and gave other signs of pleasure. The experimenters suggest that the avoidance of pain may have generated contentment.

Clinical reports like these raise a serious question: When, if ever, is the use of painful punishment such as electric shock justifiable as a behavior-modification procedure? Clearly, pain is an aversive, noxious stimulus to be diminished or avoided by anyone as far as possible. Can adding the pain of shock to that caused by self-injury or self-destruction ever be justified?

In a review of recent research on the modification of self-injurious behavior with operant techniques, S. R. Smolev (1971) adheres to the principle that the procedure should be chosen that causes the least possible pain to the subject consistent with the probable elimination of the behaviors through positive reinforcement first, then extinction as the next best procedure, followed by the use of time out. However, none of these may work under the circumstances or may not be quick enough to forestall serious self-damage while they are being attempted.

Provided that such operant procedures have not worked, or could not feasibly be used, Smolev considers aversive punishment to be an alternative. She points out that shock, for example, usually has fairly immediate effects, so a great deal of shocking need not be used. Also, the suppression of self-destructive behavior often clears the way for other operant procedures to be used effectively and for generalization of the new responses outside the experimental setting. Finally, shock is probably less stunting for patients' psychological, and even physical, growth than physical restraint, and suppression of self-injury facilitates the acquisition of desirable behavior.

At this stage in the development of operant research, then, the conclusion seems to be that electric shock has a justifiable, but severely restricted, function.

In certain complex patterns of behavior, the distinctions between wanted and unwanted components may be too subtle for the effective use of extinction or punishment alone. The *discrimination hypothesis* states that certain responses can be eliminated in some situations and retained in others through a combination of several conditioning procedures. Perhaps a particular response must be shaped and reinforced under certain circumstances, but extinguished or punished under others. The following treatment illustrates how this kind of fine discrimination can be achieved by operant procedures.

DESCRIPTIVE EVIDENCE

Investigators: M. P. Feldman and M. B. MacCulloch
Source, Date: "A Systematic Approach to the Treatment of Homosexuality by Conditioned Aversion: Preliminary Report," 1964
Location: Crumpsall Hospital, Manchester
Subject: Homosexual hospital patient
Materials: Slides of males and females, subject switch, shock source

The patient stated that he wished to be "normal and have children" and establish a normal heterosexual relationship with his girl friend. The task of the therapist was to design a therapy program that would maintain the patient's sexual arousal with females but eliminate it with males. The therapy consisted of administering a severe shock to the patient when he was presented with homoerotic stimuli (slides of males). Termination of shock was associated with presentation of erotic stimuli (slides of females). Thus homosexual stimuli became associated with aversive punishment, while heterosexual stimuli became associated with termination of shock (negative reinforcement).

The results show that the patient was successful in his attempt to get sexual arousal under the discriminative control of heterosexual stimuli. His homosexual activities and fantasies decreased and his attraction to other males was minimized. He was able to establish and maintain an adequate heterosexual life. The patient concluded, in his own words, "I feel I can now look forward to living normally and having a home life and children. A year ago this seemed less and less likely. I feel that progress is being more than maintained."

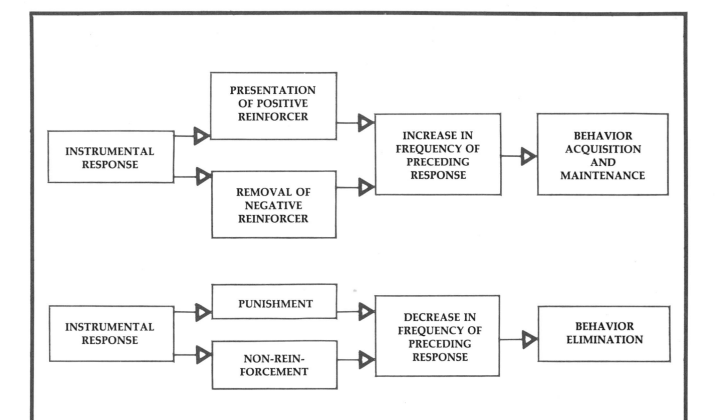

PUTTING IT TOGETHER: Operant Conditioning

The basis of operant conditioning lies in behavioral responses which are instrumental in producing specific consequences. When the *instrumental response produces a positive reinforcer* or *removes a negative reinforcer*, there is an *increase in the frequency of that response*. Just about any response available within an organism's repertoire may be brought under control by shaping, or reinforcing successive approximations to the desired response. Complex behaviors may be brought under control by using chaining procedures. After an increase in the frequency of the *behavior has been acquired*, the behavior *may be maintained* by using an appropriate schedule of reinforcement.

Responses may also be instrumental in producing *punishment,* which serves to temporarily suppress the response; or if the response was acquired by reinforcement, it may be extinguished by *non-reinforcement.*

Both punishment and extinction may be responsible for a *decrease in the frequency of the instrumental response* and thus are useful for the *elimination of behavior*. When these procedures are used to eliminate behavior only under specific conditions, it is referred to as discrimination.

These techniques may be especially useful with groups for replacing the undesirable behavior of group members with desirable behavior by using tokens for reinforcement. This method of group control of behavior is known as a token economy.

WHAT'S ACCEPTED AND WHAT'S DEBATED

1. WHAT'S ACCEPTED . . .

1. Consequences affect the probability of preceding behaviors.

2. Presenting a positive event or removing a negative event will increase the probability of a preceding behavior.

3. Presenting an aversive event or removing a positive event will decrease the probability of a preceding behavior.

4. Reinforcing successive approximations to a desired response as in shaping will lead to the acquisition of new behavior.

5. Reinforcing sequences of responses as in chaining will lead to the acquisition of complex responses.

6. Thinning out reinforcement through different partial reinforcement schedules will increase the durability of behavior.

7. Reinforcing particular behaviors in the presence of discriminative stimuli will bring those behaviors under environmental control.

2. WHAT'S DEBATED . . .

1. Whether cognitive processes themselves can be reduced to an operant-conditioning paradigm.

2. Whether operant conditioning is useful only for application to animal research and simple human behavior.

3. Whether observational learning, or modeling, rather than shaping or chaining is typically the normal process in the acquisition of novel responses in humans.

ISSUE: BEHAVIOR MODIFICATION PROS AND CONS

To B. F. Skinner and to many advocates of behavior modification the potential of operant conditioning techniques goes far beyond the laboratory. It offers unlimited hope for the future. All behavior, Skinner proposes, can be controlled by a system of carefully calculated rewards and punishments. This system, he states, can be used to create a controlled human environment, a society in which men and women can live, learn, work and love in security, equality and peace. Skinner fictionalized in his book *Walden II* and argues in his recent best seller *Beyond Freedom and Dignity* that freedom is an illusion; we are already shaped and controlled by our environment, but in a random, haphazard way. Instead, Skinner believes we should control ourselves in an ordered manner through a new "behavioral technology"—changing people by changing their environment, thus eliminating socially undesirable behavior. We should be no less free than we are now, but our society could be utopian.

Skinner's critics contend that this proposition reduces man to a mere machine, and that the methods of behavior modification have menacing and totalitarian implications. One of his sternest critics, novelist Arthur Koestler, describes behaviorism as "a monumental triviality that has sent psychology into a modern version of the Dark Ages." To theologian Richard Rubenstein, Skinner's proposal is "less likely to be a blueprint for the Golden Age than for the theory and practice of hell." At its roots, this debate is an old chestnut of philosophy: free will versus determinism. Is man in control of his destiny, or is he a mere plaything of circumstance? Skinner takes the latter view. He believes that the notion of some inner autonomous "person" in each of us is a myth, a lingering superstition from the past that has been exploded in this century by behaviorism. The attitudes, values, choices and acts of an individual, he believes, are products of the outer environment rather than some hypothetical inner personality. To Skinner's opponents, these views are deeply antihumanist, demeaning of all that is noblest in man. They charge that Skinner neglects consciousness and will, mind and purpose, imagination and feeling. M.I.T. Professor Noam Chomsky charges that Skinner's ideas are "vacuous," and dismisses him as someone who "cannot tell a pigeon from a poet."

These are heady philosophical issues. Yet they recur at the practical level in the real world. The technical effectiveness of behavior modification methods is little doubted, but many psychologists hesitate to use them, especially when punishment must be used to eliminate undesirable behavior. As Professor Donald Baer of the University of Kansas notes: "We can see that pain is a good teacher as long as it is inflicted by inanimate objects—hard floors, hot radiators, sharp knives. But somehow, pain inflicted by a human being seems different—barbaric and repellent." Baer argues, however, that the moral position that pain should be avoided becomes itself immoral when it prevents us from helping persons who have learned maladaptive behavior that puts them in even greater pain. A small number of brief, painful experiences is preferable, he believes, to the interminable pain of lifelong maladjustment.

To illustrate this view, Baer quotes the case of Jimmy, a retarded boy of seven. Jimmy would repeatedly bite his hands until they were swollen, bleeding and infected. The only way the behavior could be prevented, it seemed, was for nurses to hold his hands and keep them from his mouth. Jimmy's behavior was probably an attention-getting device: the nurses could ignore him at other times, but not when he was literally tearing the flesh from his hands. When a behaviorist consultant suggested that the nurses should reverse their behavior, rewarding the boy by attending to him when he did not bite his hands but neglecting him when he did, the nurses hesitated to carry out the plan on the grounds that it was cruel and inhumane. Eventually a compromise was reached. Jimmy was fitted with a device that would give him a very sharp electric shock every time he lifted his hands to his mouth. After two sessions of less than an hour each, Jimmy stopped biting his hands and the problem was eliminated.

In another case quoted by Baer, a 17-year-old girl named June could not stop sneezing. She sneezed at least once every 40 seconds throughout the day. June had consulted neurologists, endocrinologists, allergists, urologists, psychiatrists, and even hypnotists, but all to no avail. Finally, behavior modification was attempted. A microphone was placed around June's neck and connected to a voice key and an electric shock source. Whenever she sneezed, the sound relay triggered a sharp and painful electric shock. June stopped sneezing after she had worn the apparatus for four and a half hours.

Advocates of behavior modification claim that they are not really imposing a strait-jacket on human behavior by the use of such methods. Rather, they are replacing random influences with carefully controlled ones. To many others the question is not whether man should be controlled, but rather how. This view is strongly challenged by other psychologists who take a humanistic perspective. Social psychologist Herbert C. Kelman maintains:

"For those of us who hold the enhancement of man's freedom of choice as a fundamental value, any manipulation of the behavior of others constitutes a violation of their essential humanity, regardless of the 'goodness' of the causes that this manipulation is designed to serve." Kelman takes the view that human dignity is incompatible with a controlled environment that would in essence reduce people to robots.

All indications are that behavior modification will become a more frequently used therapeutic tool in the future. Whether it will also be used for the purposes of large-scale social engineering only time will tell.

Part IV
biology and
behavior . . .
basic relationships

28. Stress and Anxiety

Underlying many physical and psychological diseases and problems are *Stress and Anxiety*. Stress generally refers to the wear and tear that life imposes on the organism. The effects of stress range from hypertension and high blood pressure to ulcers and other illnesses. All of us experience anxiety at times in our daily lives, but chronic, uncontrollable anxiety can lead to stress, psychosomatic illness and a host of mental problems. The ability to cope with stress and anxiety becomes increasingly important as society grows more complex and each individual is called upon to deal with more new problems.

29. Genes and Their Nurture

30. Built-in Behavior

The growth and development of organisms depend on an interaction between their genetic makeup and their experiences. Investigating *Genes and Their Nurture* usually requires experiments employing lower animals as subjects since we cannot ethically manipulate the genetic makeup of human beings. Genes are also involved with the various kinds of *Built-in Behavior* that many species of animals display in their normal adaptations to the environment. Behavior is considered to be built-in when it is typical of the species for a given situation and is highly dependent on innately organized structures. The study of such behaviors is important for sorting out the different kinds of processes involved in the development of organisms in general.

31. The Senses

32. Sleep and Dreams

33. Brain Storage

One of the ultimate goals of all of psychology is to understand how the brain works, how it processes data from its own memories and from the external world. Today a number of psychologists are working on problems closely tied to brain physiology. For example, discovering how *The Senses* operate and relay their information to the brain will likely provide much of the basis for the psychology of perceiving. Only in the last twenty years has most of the important knowledge about *Sleep and Dreams* come to light. There are indications that physiological processes during sleep are involved in processing and sorting information stored in the brain. Despite some powerful clues, the basic question of *Brain Storage,* how and where memories are registered in the brain, is still largely a mystery. Research in the 1960s produced several promising leads in the biochemistry of memory that require much further testing before any firm conclusions can be reached.

34. Brain Stimulation

35. Biofeedback

36. Psychoactive Drugs

The control of behavior can be achieved by influencing or manipulating the physiological processes within an individual. *Brain Stimulation* is the attempt to influence behavior by directly stimulating the brain. Psychologists have demonstrated that specific behavior patterns as well as emotional states can be evoked with brain stimulation. *Biofeedback* refers to the fact that organisms can learn to control many processes formerly considered inaccessible to voluntary control. *Psychoactive Drugs* have been with us for quite a while and also can be used to control behavior. This control can be undesirable and destructive, as with narcotic dependencies and alcoholism, or it can be beneficial, as in the treatment of certain diseases and mental disorders.

Unit 28

Stress and Anxiety

OVERVIEW

Some of the typical physiological and psychological factors involved in stress and anxiety reactions are summarized. Both human and animal studies are presented, indicating the circumstances under which stressors create problems for the organism, or are succesfully coped with by the organism. Especially relevant are the predictability of stressful experiences and the past history of the individual organism. The last section focuses on the concept of continual stress in highly technological societies.

UNIT OUTLINE

DEFINITION AND BACKGROUND
1. *Definition:* stress is pressure from an adverse force or influence that imposes unusual demands on an organism; anxiety is a state of apprehension or uneasiness concerning some uncertain event.
2. *Background:* Hans Selye (1907–   ).

QUESTIONS AND EVIDENCE
1. Why do individual organisms respond differently to similar stresses?
Hypotheses:
    a. *Early exposure:* experiences during development influence the way an adult reacts to stress. **486**
    b. *Genes:* an individual's genetic heritage helps determine adult stress reactions.
    c. *Learned-helplessness:* living in an uncontrollable stressful environment diminishes an animal's ability to cope with future stress that is controllable. **489**
2. What conditions alter the severity of stress responses?
Hypotheses:
    a. *Predictability:* the expectation of stress affects the anticipatory response to it, with familiar and expected stressors usually producing less extreme anxiety and physiological mobilization than unfamiliar and unexpected stressors. **490**
    b. *Experience-with-coping:* the symptoms of anxiety may be caused by a person's fear that he or she will be unable to cope with an anticipated stress. **492**

IMPORTANT CONCEPTS

	page
anxiety	484
autonomic nervous system	491
general adaptation syndrome (GAS)	485
genotype	488
homeostasis	484
hormones	484
hypothalamus	491
learned helplessness	489
pituitary gland	487
psychosomatic disorders	484
stress	484

An individual's response to stressors is related to his biological makeup as well as his past experience in coping with stressors.

Stress and anxiety responses include activity in the hypothalamic-pituitary-adrenal cortex system.

Evidence indicates that appropriate coping behavior diminishes glandular stress and anxiety responses.

DEFINITION AND BACKGROUND

A DEFINITION of stress is *pressure from an adverse force or influence that imposes unusual demands on an organism.* The stimuli that cause stress are called *stressor stimuli*; they include emotional crises, physical trauma (as when a person is injured in a car accident or a mouse is pounced on by a cat), infection, physical restraint, and cold. An organism's physiological response to stress is called the *stress reaction.* It is typified by a disturbance of body homeostasis in which the hypothalamus-pituitary-adrenal system is activated. The pituitary gland secretes an increased amount of adrenocorticotropic hormone (ACTH), which stimulates the adrenal system to release adrenal corticoids to the body. This physiological stress reaction is usually followed by behavioral attempts to deal with the stressor (the mouse runs away from the cat) or with the stress reaction itself (the person injured in the car accident tries to relax while he waits for the doctor).

One DEFINITION of anxiety is *a state of apprehension or uneasiness concerning some uncertain event.* As a subjective sensation anxiety is similar to fear, but it tends to be less sharply focused. A person may fear a large, unfriendly looking dog running toward him, or he may be anxious about his physical safety whenever he ventures onto the street. Anxiety plays an important part in neuroses, as explained in Unit 13. Often, a chronically anxious person is one with a history of stressful experiences that he has not been able to predict or control.

Stress and anxiety have received a great deal of attention in medicine, psychology, industry, studies of family and social relations, and education. They have been held responsible for mental illness, psychosomatic disorders, breakdowns in industrial productivity, divorce and substandard school performance, to name but a few of the suspected consequences. This unit will FOCUS on the physiological and behavioral effects of stress, with particular attention on conditions that influence the strength of stress reaction.

BACKGROUND: HANS SELYE (1907–)

Although Hans Selye succeeded in establishing stress as a meaningful physiological and psychological con-

Figure 1. Canadian scientist Hans Selye's General Adaptation Syndrome outlines the physiological reaction to stress.

cept, the essential groundwork for the study of stress was laid by a scientist from the generation before Selye's, Walter B. Cannon (1871–1945) of the Harvard Medical School. Cannon's book *Bodily Changes in Pain, Hunger, Fear and Rage* (1929) implicated the autonomic nervous system and especially the adrenal glands in fear and rage. His work helped convince psychologists and physiologists that important physiological changes are involved in emotional states and that these changes could be investigated in the laboratory, with human beings as well as with lower animals.

Selye was born in Vienna and received his medical training in Europe, but he has done most of his scientific research in Canada. As a medical student, he became interested in illness, in "the syndrome of just being sick." Patients with completely different kinds of disease, he noted, nevertheless showed many common symptoms: intestinal disorders, poor appetite, weight loss, aches and pains in joints and muscles, loss of ambition, and fatigue. At that time, however, medical training and practice were directed toward identifying the specific causes of particular diseases, so the study of broader effects would have thrown Selye's professional career off course. Attributing his interest to aimless, youthful dreaming, he decided to follow a more traditional path and spent some ten years in endocrinology and biochemical research.

But questions about the apparently common features of illnesses haunted him, and he soon resolved to devote himself to study of the problem. The result, published in 1956, was a theory and a revolutionary conception of stress that attempted to explain its chemical and physical effects on the body.

What persuaded Selye to return to his earlier insight was a failure in another line of research. Attempting to isolate a new sex hormone, he was injecting rats with a hormone extract. The rats all reacted the same way: the adrenal cortex enlarged, lymphatic structures shrank, and ulcers appeared in the stomach and part of the gut. In each instance the same threefold reaction occurred and appeared to form a definite syndrome—later dubbed the general adaptation syndrome (GAS). When the injections were increased, the reaction became stronger. When Selye used other kinds of extracts, he got the same responses from his animals. He even injected them with foreign toxic substances and obtained the same results, in more pronounced forms. Because practically any substance appeared to bring the reaction about, it was entirely nonspecific. Selye could not help concluding that his efforts to discover a new hormone had failed.

As he was reviewing the apparent failure of the experiments, it occurred to Selye that there might be a general, nonspecific reaction to bodily damage of any sort. Otherwise, why had the rats shown the same reactions, no matter what agent they were injected with? Selye resolved to track down these nonspecific effects, even though the tradition of research at the time demanded that specific agents be tied to specific reactions. Working against considerable criticism, and at first with little encouragement from others, Selye devoted the rest of his career to the study of how stressful events, both acute and chronic, affect physiology. His findings have done much to clarify the effects of traumatic physical injury, disease, and psychosomatic illnesses (physiological disorders with psychological causes).

Through a series of complicated biochemical and surgical experiments that continued through the 1940s and 1950s, Selye gave a precise physiological meaning to the concept of stress. Some stress is an inevitable part of life, and most organisms cope with it successfully. But excessive stress, Selye found, causes reactions in the body, primarily in the adrenal and nervous systems, that can be harmful. He called these systemic responses to continuous nonspecific, noxious stimuli the *general adaptation syndrome* (GAS). The GAS occurs in three stages. Stage 1 is an alarm reaction in which symptoms of vascular and nervous depression are followed by ACTH release. During stage 2 the animal shows increased resistance to the specific stressor and decreased resistance to other stressors. Stage 3 is characterized by exhaustion; the acquired adaptation is no longer maintained. If strong stress continues long enough, the animal may develop a "disease of adaptation" or even die.

Recent research based on Selye's work has added new knowledge about stress and physiological processes it involves. The effects of the stress of everyday

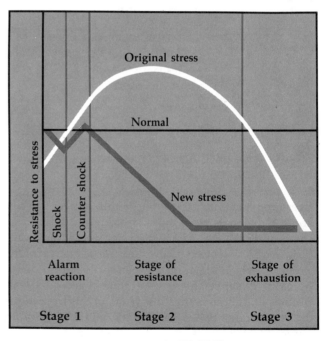

From INTRODUCTION TO PSYCHOLOGY by Clifford T. Morgan and Richard A. King. Copyright © 1971 by McGraw-Hill, Inc. Used with permission of McGraw-Hill Book Company.

Figure 2. In the general adaptation syndrome (GAS), as described by Selye, an organism has a three-stage response to stress. Stage 1 is an alarm reaction. During stage 2 the animal shows increased resistance to the original stressor. Stage 3 brings exhaustion. If stress is prolonged, the animal may die. White line shows resistance to original stress, brown line resistance to new stress imposed at different stages of the GAS.

living, of illness apart from specific disease factors, and of disorders with psychosomatic aspects, such as arthritis, ulcers, and hypertension, are appreciated now in large part because of Selye.

QUESTIONS AND EVIDENCE

1. Why do individual organisms respond differently to similar stresses?

2. What conditions alter the severity of stress responses?

indicated poor stress-coping capacities in the "sickest" women. What would these two groups have to say about their childhood experiences? The survey revealed that women in the "sick" group perceived their childhood environments as including more stringent demands and more conflicts and degradations than did the women in the "healthy" group. Similarly, the "sick" women saw their adult environments as more demanding and their occupations as less satisfying. There were no significant differences

---

QUESTION   1. WHY DO INDIVIDUAL ORGANISMS RESPOND DIFFERENTLY TO SIMILAR STRESSES?

HYPOTHESES	EARLY EXPOSURE	GENES	LEARNED HELPLESSNESS
DESCRIPTIVE EVIDENCE			
EXPERIMENTAL EVIDENCE	VARY: cage confinement of rats during the first three weeks of life MEASURE: plasma corticosterone levels in response to novel environment	VARY: genetic strains of mice MEASURE: plasma corticosterone levels in response to shock	VARY: exposure to unavoidable shock MEASURE: subsequent effectiveness in learning to avoid shock

---

1. WHY DO INDIVIDUAL ORGANISMS RESPOND DIFFERENTLY TO SIMILAR STRESSES?

Everyone reacts to stress, but within a given species some individuals react more strongly, or differently, than others. One explanation for these individual differences is offered by the *early-exposure hypothesis*, which states that experiences during development influence the way an adult reacts to stress. Studies of human beings that relate to this hypothesis are scarce. In 1957 L. E. Hinkle and H. G. Wolff surveyed 20 of the "sickest" and 20 of the "healthiest" in a group of 336 working American women. They assumed that a high incidence of physical illness

between the groups on exposure to infection, constitutional factors, or economic and cultural backgrounds. These data tend to support the general notion that early difficulties with stress are reflected in later susceptibility to illness, though the data are hardly conclusive

Partly because it is difficult to get reliable data from people about their early childhood experiences, most research on the early-exposure hypothesis has been done with animals. In the animal laboratory an experimenter can control the early experiences of the animals himself and then see what differences his experimental manipulations make for the later behavior of the animals.

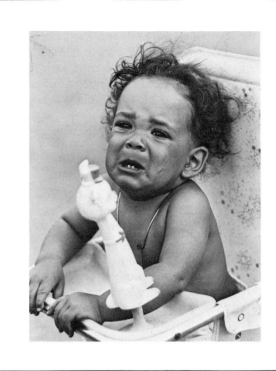

Figure 3. Occasional mild stress in childhood may lead to adaptive responses to stress in adulthood. Chronic severe stress in childhood may increase adult susceptibility to illness.

EXPERIMENTAL EVIDENCE

Investigators: J. L. Hess, V. H. Denenberg, M. X. Zarrow, and W. Pfeifer
Source, Date: "Modification of the Plasma Corticosterone Response Curve as a Function of Stimulation in Infancy," 1969
Location: Purdue University
Subjects: Albino Wistar rats
Materials: Rearing cages and waiting cages; novel environment called an "open field"

Four groups of rats were provided with different infantile experiences. Those in the first group were left undisturbed with their mothers from birth through three weeks of age (the time of weaning). This was the "no early stress" group. Rats in the second group were removed from their mothers' cages for three minutes on each of the first five days of life and placed in individual cans containing wood

shavings. Then they were returned to their mothers. This was the "some stress" group. Rats in the third ("more stress") group were treated the same as those in the second but throughout the entire three-week preweaning period instead of only for five days. The fourth ("less stress") group, like the second, underwent stress for only five days, but the rats were placed collectively rather than individually in an artificial nest maintained at the mothers' body temperature. This condition was assumed to be a milder departure from normal rearing than that of the second or third group.

At weaning the rats, in pairs, were placed in waiting cages and left there for two weeks. Then they were exposed to a novel environment, which commonly produces stress reactions in inexperienced animals. At the time of testing, each rat was put alone into the novel environment for three minutes. Then it was returned to the waiting cage. After intervals of fifteen, thirty, and sixty minutes, blood samples were taken and analyzed for corticosterone, one indicator of stress reactions in the rat.

In mammals, the brain regulates the pituitary gland by regulating the flow of hormones. During stress, the brain causes the pituitary gland to release hormones in greater than normal quantities. One of the pituitary hormones is ACTH, which stimulates the adrenal cortex to increase its secretion of cortisone-type hormones such as corticosterone. Because this sequence of events occurs each time an animal is stressed, the increase in the amount of corticosterone found in the blood plasma after stress can be used as a measure of reaction to stress.

It was found that the rats in the first, undisturbed group had the greatest stress reactions (in terms of increased secretion of corticosterone). The other three groups showed less extreme stress reactions to the new environment. Behaviorally, the stress typically produced "freezing" in the group 1 animals, whereas those that had been removed from their cages for three minutes a day during the first three weeks of life tended to explore the novel environment freely.

As important as early experiences are, they probably are not solely responsible for individual differences in stress reactions. Another source of variability may be the genetic constitutions of the individual animals. The *genes hypothesis* states that an individual's genetic heritage helps determine his adult stress reactions. For example, there are genetic differences in the ability of different breeds of dogs to cope with young children. The docile bassett hound—in contrast to, for instance, the miniature poodle—seems able to tolerate almost any amount of abuse from a toddler.

Application of the genes hypothesis to human beings involves difficulties. There are some studies of identical twins, but, again, animal studies are more conclusive because the genetic make-up of animals is easier to control and manipulate.

EXPERIMENTAL EVIDENCE

Investigators: S. Levine and D. M. Treiman
Source, Date: "Differential Plasma Corticosterone Response
    to Stress in Four Inbred Strains of Mice," 1964
Location: Stanford University
Subjects: Four inbred strains of mice
Materials: Shock chambers for inducing stress reactions

Through inbreeding, four strains of mice were obtained. The individuals of all four strains were raised in identical environments. During the two weeks before testing, the animals were housed in groups of five, without mixing strains. Blood was sampled from one animal in each cage and a base level of corticosterone obtained. Another animal from each cage was placed in a shock chamber for fifteen minutes but given no shock; then a blood sample was taken and analyzed for corticosterone. Thus two of the five animals from each cage served as controls.

The remaining animals were placed in the shock chamber and stressed—given two thirty-second shocks, with a ten-second interval between. Immediately following the shocks, the animals were transferred to holding cages for periods ranging from thirty seconds to an hour. Then blood was collected for analysis from each animal.

Figure 4 shows the elevations in corticosterone that were obtained under the various conditions for the four inbred strains of mice. As the graph indicates, the animals with different genotypes (genetic constitutions) reacted differently to the experimental conditions. The smaller increases in corticosterone for two of the strains reflect the milder stress reactions than were present in the other two strains of mice.

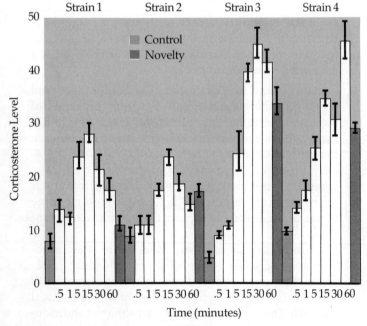

Figure 4. Average corticosterone levels in four strains of mice following exposure to stress. Brown column represents response to electric shock at different time intervals. Gray column represents animals placed in a shock chamber but not shocked. Horizontal lines on each column indicate standard error of the mean, a measure of variability. Time refers to period elapsed between exposure to shock and slaughter. Adapted from Levine and Treiman (1964).

Usually, when an animal experiences stress it responds with behavior that is designed to alleviate the stress. This is not always true, however: sometimes the animal seems to be so overwhelmed by the stress that it gives up. A dramatic demonstration of this phenomenon in human beings is voodoo death, in which death is brought about by casting a ritual spell. R. Herbert Basedow, in his book *The Australian Aboriginal,* describes voodoo death as follows:

> The man who discovers that he is being boned by an enemy is, indeed, a pitiable sight. He stands aghast with his eyes staring at the treacherous pointer, and with his hands lifted to ward off the lethal medium, which he imagines is pouring into his body. His cheeks blanch, and his eyes become glassy, and the expression of his face becomes horribly distorted. He attempts to shriek but usually the sound chokes in his throat, and all that one might see is froth at his mouth. His body begins to tremble and his muscles twitch involuntarily. He sways backward and falls to the ground, and after a short time appears to be in a swoon. He finally composes himself, goes to his hut and there frets to death.

Walter Cannon, the physiologist mentioned at the start of the background section of this unit, described the process of voodoo death as one in which the victim seems to lose all ability to cope with stress. Physiologically, the result of the curse is an enormous outpouring of adrenalin, which, in Cannon's words, "fully mobilizes the bodily forces for action. If this state of extreme perturbation continues . . . for any considerable period without the occurrence of action, dire results may ensue." That is, it is the cursed person's failure to respond actively to stress that leads eventually to death.

A "giving-up reaction" accounts sometimes for death in our culture as well. This reaction is recognized by physicians as a persistent danger during serious illness. The kind of hopelessness that can prevent a patient from ever getting well is sometimes signaled by such statements as, "it's too much," "it's no use," and "I can't take it anymore." Perceptions of the self become negative, and memories of and feelings about the past become unpleasant and distant. Medical research is being done on the problem of giving-up reactions, and physicians are trying to devise therapy techniques that will enable people to respond actively and positively to the stress of illness.

Repeated experiences with relatively moderate stresses over which the organism has no control can be nearly as paralyzing as the overwhelming stress of a voodoo spell or a serious illness. Some investigators have suggested that such experiences may lead to "learned helplessness" on the part of the organism. The *learned-helplessness hypothesis* states that living in an uncontrollable stressful environment diminishes an animal's ability to cope with future stress that *is* controllable. The study that follows was an attempt to produce learned helplessness in the laboratory, using dogs as subjects.

EXPERIMENTAL EVIDENCE

Investigators: J. B. Overmeier and M. E. P. Seligman
Source, Date: "Effects of Inescapable Shock upon
    Subsequent Escape and Avoidance Responding," 1967
Location: University of Pennsylvania
Subjects: 32 mongrel dogs
Materials: Two separate shock units

The dogs were divided into four groups. Three groups were exposed to inescapable shock, and the fourth was not. The three shock groups differed in the number of shocks received, the average interval between shocks, and the duration of the shocks. The four groups were then given a training task in which shocks were administered when errors were made. Performance was measured by successful avoidance of the shocks.

The group with no prior experience of inescapable shock most successfully avoided the shocks. The three groups previously subjected to inescapable shocks did poorly. Interestingly, although the frequency, duration, and number of shocks varied considerably for the three shock groups, the variations did not appear to influence performance. Inescapable shock, whether mild or severe, had debilitating effects.

These results suggest that animals can learn it is futile to try to avoid a stressor and that an individual who is unable to cope with stress may be a product of past experiences in which his attempts to avoid stress were unsuccessful. However, some researchers have questioned this interpretation of the Overmeier-

Seligman data, pointing out that the dogs may possibly have undergone biochemical changes as a consequence of the persistent, inescapable shock. These changes could cause a temporary lack of response to any stimulation. If so, then the dogs' helplessness may have been more muscular than cognitive.

Subjects participated in a shock anticipation experiment designed to assess how the predictability of a stressor affects the anticipation of that stressor. Shock was used as a stressor because it is safe, easy to use, and relatively unfamiliar to most people.

Heart rate was used as the primary index of the

QUESTION   2. WHAT CONDITIONS ALTER THE SEVERITY OF
                STRESS RESPONSES?

HYPOTHESES	PREDICTABILITY	EXPERIENCE WITH COPING
DESCRIPTIVE EVIDENCE		ASSESS: coping responses in astronauts
EXPERIMENTAL EVIDENCE	VARY: 1. shock occurrence on the first trial 2. predictability of an electric shock MEASURE: 1. heart rate changes 2. ulceration	VARY: opportunity to avoid or escape shock MEASURE: weight loss

2. WHAT CONDITIONS ALTER THE SEVERITY OF STRESS RESPONSES?

A number of subjective factors can influence the severity of a stress reaction. Whether the individual has been alerted to expect stress is one consideration; another is his previous experience in coping, which provides (or fails to provide) confidence. Both these factors have been studied by psychologists.

If a person is sure that an anticipated situation will indeed arise, he may experience fear and signs of physiological stress. If he is uncertain about its occurrence, he may experience anxiety. The *predictability hypothesis* states that the expectation of stress affects the anticipatory response to it, with familiar and expected stressors usually producing less extreme anxiety and physiological mobilization than unfamiliar and unexpected stressors.

EXPERIMENTAL EVIDENCE

Investigator: C. P. Bankart
Source, Date: "Heart Rate and Skin Conductance in Anticipation of Painful Electric Shock," 1971
Location: Dartmouth College
Subjects: 80 male undergraduate students
Materials: Shock generator, recorder, heart-rate machine

strength of the anticipatory response.   The average heart rate of the subjects in anticipation of the first shock was around ninety-eight beats per minute, almost thirty beats higher than normal. On subsequent trials, the anticipatory increase was smaller and smaller, suggesting that the shock caused less anxiety as it became a more familiar sensation.

For one group of subjects, no shock was administered on the first trial, but the subjects did not know this would be the case. They showed the same heart-rate acceleration that the other groups did. After the first trial, the average heart rate in the unshocked group did not diminish; it remained high until shock was administered on the second trial. Stressful experiences can have a dramatic effect on the autonomic nervous system and, through it, on the gastrointestinal tract. It is well known that people in circumstances they find extremely stressful may develop ulcers, and almost everyone has experienced a loss of appetite before or after a stressful event. A number of experiments have been conducted to measure the gastrointestinal effects of stress. The following study concerns the relation between the predictability of stress and ulcers in rats.

AUTONOMIC NERVOUS SYSTEM

(Black = sympathetic system; brown = parasympathetic system)

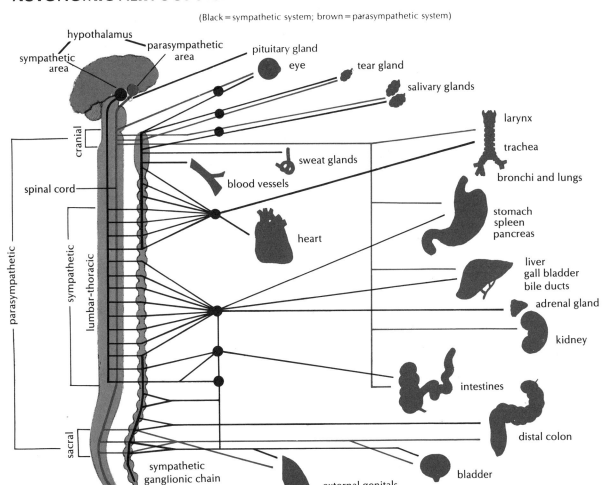

Figure 5. A schematic representation of the autonomic nervous system showing both the sympathetic and parasympathetic divisions. As indicated, the ANS is involved in the regulation of the visceral organs and their secretions and in the control of smooth muscles. Generally, the two divisions of the ANS act in opposition to one another. The parasympathetic division predominates during quiet, restful periods and is involved in the normal regulation of organ systems. The sympathetic division is primarily active during periods of stress and emergency. Both the sympathetic and parasympathetic divisions are represented in the *hypothalamus.* This lower brain structure is believed to have a regulatory function for both neural and hormonal pathways. The posterior portion of the hypothalamus (in which is represented the sympathetic division of the ANS) activates the pituitary gland to release adrenocorticotropic hormone (ACTH) which in turn activates the release of adrenal corticoids from the cortex of the adrenal glands (located at the top of each kidney). In a short-term emergency, the sympathetic division of the ANS directly activates the release of adrenalin from the medulla of the adrenal glands.

EXPERIMENTAL EVIDENCE

Investigator: J. M. Weiss
Source, Date: "Psychological Factors in Stress and
  Disease," 1972
Location: Rockefeller University
Subjects: Albino rats
Materials: Shock chambers with signals

Weiss attached electrodes to the rats' tails in order to be sure that each animal would receive the prescribed number and intensity of shocks. If shock had been delivered through a grid floor, as is usual in experiments using shock, the animals could have lessened their discomfort by jumping, crouching, or shifting position.

Shocks were delivered to two rats at a time within the experimental groups. For one, a beeping tone was sounded ten seconds before each shock; for the other the tone was sounded at random intervals, and bore no relation to the timing of the shocks. The two rats received the same number of shocks. A rat from a third group served as a control. It was placed in a similar chamber and had electrodes attached to its tail, but received no shock.

The control rat developed very little gastric ulceration. The rat able to predict when the shocks would occur also showed little ulceration. But the rat that was shocked unpredictably showed a considerable amount of ulceration.

This study supports the predictability hypothesis, since the animal with no forewarning of the unpleasant events (shock) developed more gastric ulceration as a consequence of the stress reaction than the animal given prior warning of the same events. An important factor in the experiment may have been that the rat in the predictable situation could relax until it heard the tone that preceded shock. The rat in the unpredictable situation presumably had to endure a state of constant heightened alertness because it had no way of knowing when shock would occur.

A human being in the situation of the rat that developed ulcers would probably have experienced acute anxiety. (It is not known as yet whether subhuman animals experience anxiety or not.) The sensations he might have felt include a knot in the stomach, hot flashes and a feeling of warmth throughout the body, a tightening of the muscles, a lump in the throat, sweating palms, and perhaps nausea and spots before the eyes.

Acute anxiety is not a pleasant feeling. According to the *experience-with-coping hypothesis,* the symptoms of anxiety may be caused by a person's fear that he or she will be unable to cope with an anticipated stress. The hypothesis states that coping successfully with a stressful situation will reduce the severity of a person's anxiety symptoms when he must face similar situations in the future.

Studies comparing novice and experienced skydivers on subjective sensations of anxiety and on physiological measures of fear show that both decrease as competence in parachuting is gained. But if an experienced skydiver's self-confidence is disturbed, as when an emergency in the air makes it necessary for him to jump before he had planned to, anxiety occurs at a high level again. This supports the coping hypothesis, because it suggests that the experienced diver's confidence in his ability to respond well to a particular situation is the crucial factor in reducing his anxiety. The relation between experience, self-confidence, and reduced anxiety during the performance of dangerous, skilled tasks is also demonstrated by the following study of Mercury astronauts.

DESCRIPTIVE EVIDENCE

Investigators: G. E. Ruff and S. J. Korchin
Source, Date: "Adaptive Distress Behavior," 1962
Location: Cape Kennedy
Subjects: 7 Mercury astronauts
Materials: Personality tests, test of flight competence,
  stress-sensitive psychological tests

Throughout this study, which followed the subjects through their astronaut training, their behavior was observed under various potentially disturbing conditions. In most cases anxiety seemed to be more closely related to an intense concern with the success of the mission than to fear of injury, death, or personal failure. The usual response was to call upon technical skill in overcoming fear. As one man put it, "Whenever I think of something that may go wrong, I think of a plan to master it."

The most striking finding of the study was the effectiveness of adaptive responses based on past experience and professional competence. In this group of men, who had repeatedly succeeded in accomplishing hazardous duties and then received additional training, the resulting behavior patterns were highly organized, efficient, and surprisingly free of signs of disruptive stress.

In another experiment, performed by the same investigator who studied the relation between the predictability of shock and ulceration in rats, an animal was prevented from gaining experience in coping with stress by experimentally contrived helplessness. The result was an increase in the severity of the animal's stress reaction.

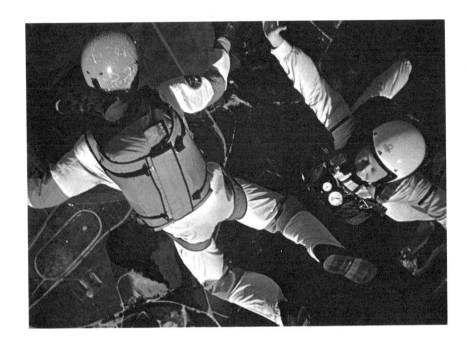

Figure 6. Two people in the same situation may show very different stress responses.

Investigator: J. M. Weiss

Source, Date: "Psychology Factors in Stress and Disease,"
    1972

Location: Rockefeller University

Subjects: Albino rats

Materials: Shock chambers with signals and platforms

In this experiment, rats from each of two groups received the same number of shocks and were provided with a signal when shock was about to occur. Rats from only one group, however, were allowed to control the shock. If they jumped onto a platform during the warning signal, the signal was turned off and the shock was not administered; if they jumped after shock had begun, the stimulus was immediately stopped. When these animals prevented or terminated a shock, they did so for both themselves and their partners. The partners were powerless to control the shock no matter when or where they jumped. As in the Weiss experiment described earlier, animals from a third group served as controls and received no shock.

The intensity of the animals' stress reactions was measured by weight loss (presumably from a diminished appetite). The rats without control of the shock showed an 80 percent reduction in normal weight gain over the series of testing sessions, while the rats given the opportunity to cope showed only a 30 percent reduction.

Later, the same basic experiment was repeated, except that this time the rats had to touch a panel mounted just outside the cage in order to avoid or escape shock for their partners and themselves, and ulceration instead of weight loss was used as a measure of stress. Again, the rats capable of preventing or terminating the shock were the least victimized by stress. They showed only a third as much ulceration as their helpless partners.

In explaining his results, Weiss suggested that a crucial aspect of the situation was that the coping rats' responses not only prevented the shock but terminated either shock or warning signal, whichever was occurring at the time of the response. In other words, the response had an immediate observable consequence. The helpless animals may have made a large number of attempts to prevent or avoid shocks, but their behavior had no observable consequence. The complete lack of feedback may help account for the severity of the powerless rats' stress reactions.

Weiss' experiments indicate that the severity of stress can be considerably reduced if an organism is able to distinguish between situations where it will occur and those where it will not (the predictability condition) and if the organism can cope with it and gain some degree of control over its occurrence. Conversely, stress is most severe where the situation is unpredictable and cannot be coped with.

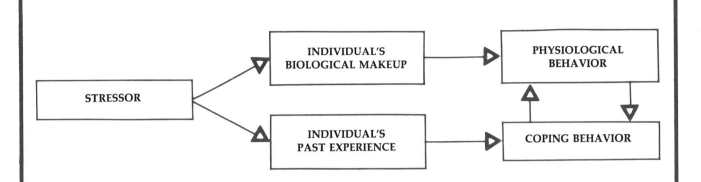

PUTTING IT TOGETHER: Stress and Anxiety

In discussing stress and anxiety we differentiate them in terms of their origins and the time during which they affect an individual. If the bodily demands are relatively temporary and are attributable to a specific cause or event, we call it stress. If demands are relatively long-lasting and cannot be attributed to specific causes or events, we call it anxiety.

Both stress and anxiety result in the same or similar responses from the adrenal medulla and the adrenal cortex. The long-lasting effects of anxiety, however, may be more disruptive in that they use up more bodily resources and go into a later phase of the General Adaptation Syndrome.

How an individual responds to a *stressor* depends upon his *biological makeup* and his *past experience* with the same stressor and with stressors in general. Biological makeup is a function not only of heredity but also of exposure to stressors early in life.

Learned helplessness, past experience with successful coping behavior and being able to predict when a stressor will occur all affect the severity of an individual's total response to stressors and the general amount of anxiety an individual feels. Thus the concepts of stress and anxiety are helpful in understanding psychosomatic disorders and the nature of the disordered mind.

The individual's biological makeup may be responsible for the *physiological behavior* in response to stressors, and the effectiveness of *coping behavior* may be a function of past experience, but there is a continuous feedback relationship between these two classes of behavior.

WHAT'S ACCEPTED AND WHAT'S DEBATED

1. WHAT'S ACCEPTED . . .

1. Prior experience influences the way an individual organism deals with stress.

2. Genetic differences between species and strains affect responses to stress and help define what will be stressful to a particular organism.

3. Predictability of the occurrence of a stressor can affect the way individuals respond to stress.

4. Successful experience in coping with a stressor reduces its stressful quality.

2. WHAT'S DEBATED . . .

1. That laboratory studies of learned helplessness are analogous to human experiences of learned helplessness.

ISSUE: HEART DISEASE

Until this century heart disease was almost unknown. There are no descriptions of cardiovascular diseases in medical records until late in the 19th century, and the problem was insignificant in the United States as recently as the twenties. Today, heart disease is the largest single killer in the U.S., taking well over 700,000 lives a year—more than a third of them from people under 65 years of age. Cardiovascular disease is still relatively rare in the developing nations, but among the large industrial societies it has become a critical medical and social problem.

For some decades, medical scientists have believed that the factors responsible for heart disease are lack of exercise, smoking, and a diet high in saturated fats and cholesterol. Today, that view is being challenged and a new culprit identified—stress. As Professor John R. P. French Jr. has pointed out, the known risk factors cannot provide a full explanation for the rising rate of heart disease. He states: "If you could perfectly control cholesterol, blood pressure, smoking, glucose level, serum uric acid, and so on, you would have controlled only about one-fourth of coronary heart disease." But how can stress be a factor in shortening lives?

An important difference between ourselves and our ancestors is that they were typically subjected to *occasional physical stress,* perhaps in time of battle, or under sudden threat of attack from a wild animal. We however, are typically under *long-term psychological stress,* especially in the urban environment in which most of us live. There are the stresses of competition at school and work. There are anxieties about grades and deadlines, about trains to catch, about corporate intrigues, about unpaid bills. There is the fear of being mugged in the street, even of the stranger's knock on the door. There is the stress induced by crowded anonymous conditions. We experience a crowded rush-hour subway car as stressful, even if it does not make us physically uncomfortable. We are barraged by the countless stimuli and demands of the most complex fast-paced society in history. We already know that stressful conditions can lead to psychosomatic illness, such as backaches and headaches, and even to physical disorders such as ulcers and asthma. Now there is strong evidence that stress may lead to heart disease as well.

When we are subjected to stress, the body responds immediately. Adrenalin pours into the system, summoning energy for the muscles and the brain, stimulating the pulse, increasing respiration, and raising blood pressure. Blood circulation rate steps up to increase oxygen intake and eliminate the carbon dioxide produced by physical exertion. Digestive processes stop, so that no energy is wasted that could be used elsewhere. Blood chemistry alters to ensure quick clotting in the case of a wound. When the stressful stimulus recedes, the body returns to normal. But what if the stress is essentially permanent and psychological in origin? The result, according to Hans Selye is that a prolonged deterioration of the body's defenses sets in. We react much as we would if permanently confronted by a physical danger, and we are gradually "worn down." Dr. Selye suggests that "there are two ages, one which is chronological and absolute, and the other which is biologic and is your effective age. It is astonishing how the two can differ."

Evidence is steadily mounting to indicate that jobs involving high responsibility or competitiveness represent a greatly increased danger of cardiovascular disease. We know, for example, that the rate of heart disease among men is much higher than among women. Women are usually assigned less stressful job roles. Of the young and middle-aged people who die of heart disease in America each year, some seventy percent are male. Research conducted for NASA has shown that the rise of serum cholesterol, blood sugar and blood pressure in ground managers is much greater during manned space flights than during unmanned flights. The managers, who must take responsibility for major life and death decisions, suffer three times as many heart attacks as the scientists and engineers involved in the programs. In 1972, a Federal report, *Work in America,* found widespread anxiety and alienation in the nation's labor force, and spoke of extensive "blue collar blues" and "white collar woes." The report found that job satisfaction is the single most important predictor of longevity, a better predictor, even, than such measures as use of tobacco or a prognosis by an examining physician.

It may be possible in the future to determine which people are particularly prone to heart disease resulting from stress. Two California scientists, Meyer Friedman and Ray H. Rosenman, believe that people can be roughly divided into two personality types. *Type A* has intense drive, ambition, aggressiveness, and confidence. *Type B* is easygoing, patient, uncompetitive, and contented. Research shows that Type A is two to three times more likely to suffer heart disease in middle age.

Our increasing knowledge of the possible effects of stress on the body already has several practical implications. Courts of law, for example, are beginning to recognize that working conditions can contribute to heart disease. Many courts have shown themselves willing to award damages and compensation to workers on these grounds. Psychologists are attempting to refine our techniques for predicting which people might be vulnerable to stress-induced disease, so they can be steered away from occupations or activities that might increase their chances of an early death. And the Federal report, *Work in America,* made considerable impact with its recommendation that work in the United States be fundamentally redesigned in order to give employees more sense of control over their destinies and less alienating and psychologically stressful working conditions.

Unit 29

Genes and Their Nurture

OVERVIEW

How can prenatal factors and experiences in early infancy affect the development of the individual? Prenatal factors include genetic potential, intrauterine factors, and the experiences of the mother during pregnancy. Experiences crucial for the developing organism are the amount of stimulation it receives, the mother's behavior, and the quality of the surrounding environment. Recent discoveries in the field of genetics, particularly the process of "cloning" are presented in the final part of the unit.

UNIT OUTLINE

DEFINITION AND BACKGROUND
1. *Definition:* genes and their nurture refer to the fact that after conception how the organism develops is the result of the interaction between the genotype and the environment.
2. *Background:* R. C. Tryon (1901–1967).

QUESTIONS AND EVIDENCE
1. What prenatal factors can affect postnatal development of behavior?
Hypotheses:
   a. *Genetic:* some behaviors are inherited in the same way that eye color and hair color are. **503**
   b. *Uterine:* the environment in the uterus can affect not only the physical development of the organism but also its behavior after birth. **505**
   c. *Maternal-stress-and-anxiety:* a mother's experiences with stressful and anxiety-producing situations can have an effect on the emotionality of the developing fetus. **507**
2. What are some early experiences that affect later behavior?
Hypotheses:
   a. *Infantile-stimulation:* emotional stimulation in infancy is necessary for development of adaptive responses to unpleasant situations. **509**
   b. *Maternal-behavior:* the behavioral interaction of a mother and her infant offspring will affect the behavior of the offspring in adulthood. **511**
   c. *Enriched-environment:* a stimulating environment can produce changes in a developing brain. **511**

IMPORTANT CONCEPTS

    page

ACTH (adrenocorticotropic hormone)	**511**
anxiety	**507**
gene	**500**
genetics	**503**
genotype	**500**
intra-uterine environment	**505**
RNA	**500**
stress	**507**

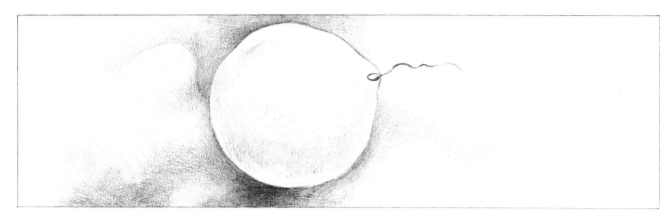

At the moment of conception there is a unique combination of genes in a unique environment.

The uterine environment is responsive to external events through maternal hormonal changes.

Evidence indicates that individual differences in behavior are influenced by prenatal as well as postnatal environments.

29. Genes and Their Nurture   **499**

The laws of heredity were discovered by biologists who studied the transmission of certain physical characteristics from one generation to the next. Easily distinguishable markers like eye color in fruit flies and albinoism in animals were used to determine what the results of interbreeding were. The unit of heredity that determined a particular characteristic was called a gene. The chemical and physical nature of the gene was not known by early geneticists. It was not until the late 1940s and the 1950s that experiments with bacteria and viruses showed that deoxyribonucleic acid (DNA) is the genetic material (in certain plant viruses it is ribonucleic acid, RNA). DNA is found principally in the nucleus of living cells. Within the nucleus it is concentrated in threadlike structures

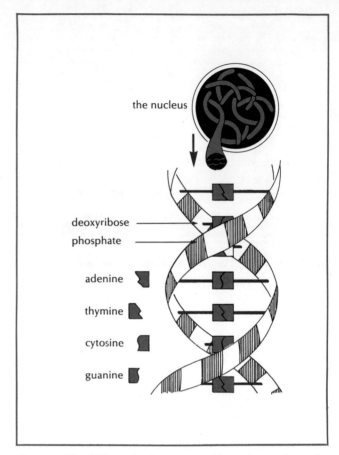

Figure 2. The DNA molecule consists of long chains of complex molecules constituting a genetic code.

called *chromosomes.* Within the chromosomes each DNA molecule is organized into functional units that carry the genetic information necessary for the development of a specific trait. These units are the *genes.* Each gene is a part of a molecule of DNA. A gene has the ability to reproduce itself exactly, and this is how the code of life is transferred from generation to generation.

The sum total of the genes that are inherited by an organism from its parents constitutes its *genotype.* The genotype is the organism's genetic potential. It determines whether the organism will be a sweet pea, a fly, a snake, or a man. But to replicate themselves and to initiate the growth of structural features in the organism, genes must enter into some sort of reaction with the materials in their surroundings. Looked at in this way, the transmission of the genotype from one generation to the next is virtually completed at the

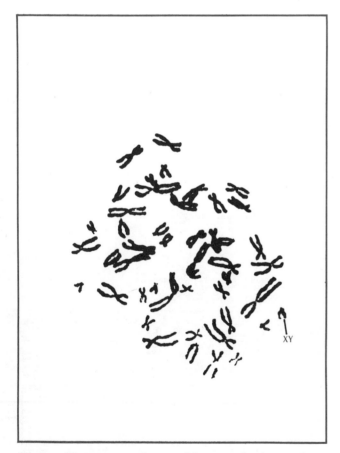

Figure 1. Chromosomes of a normal human male, showing the 23 pairs, including the XY pair of sex chromosomes.

moment of conception. Our DEFINITION of genes and their nurture refers to the fact that *after conception how the organism develops is the result of the interaction between the genotype and the environment.* When the same genes encounter different materials and different environments, they lead to the development of different traits or characteristics. We are not saying the environmental differences change the structure of the gene; rather what we mean is that after conception the environment plays an intimate role in determining how the genetic potential is developed (the development of genetic potential is sometimes called gene expression).

The physical features or the characteristic behavior patterns by which we recognize an organism constitute its *phenotype,* which is the result of interaction between the genotype and the environment. "All bodily structures and functions, without exception, are products of heredity realized in some sequence of environments," says the eminent American geneticist Theodosius Dobzhansky (1972). "So also are all forms of behavior, without exception." He goes on, however, to remind us that "nothing can arise in any organism unless its potentiality is within the realm of possibilities of the genetic endowment. . . . lest I sound to you an extreme hereditarian, I hasten to add that potentialities that are realized in a given sequence of environments are, especially in man, only a tiny fraction of the individual's total potentialities. Surely, almost everyone has an intuitive certainty that he or she would be a different person in more favorable or in more adverse circumstances."

The mother's emotional state, as we shall see, can influence the development of the offspring in her womb. From the moment of fertilization to the time the individual enters the world as a newborn, the mother's body systems and placenta serve as the total environment for the developing fetus. The mother's physical, emotional, and nutritional state all contribute to the development of the infant growing within her.

A working classification of the factors involved in behavioral development has been proposed by D. O. Hebb, who feels that in the whole field of biological investigation the heredity-environment issue has been oversimplified. (See Table 1.) Hebb classes only the initial factor as genetic, and even that classification is qualified because the ovum or egg often consists of genetic material plus nutritive matter, as birds' eggs do. No innate behavior can be produced by the genetic factor alone, he says, because the fertilized ovum requires a nutritive environment to produce something that can manifest behavior.

This unit will FOCUS on the *interaction* of genetic and environmental factors, particularly in the prenatal and the early neonatal stages of development.

TABLE 1. Classes of Factors in Behavioral Development

No.	Class	Source, Mode of Action
I	Genetic	Physiological properties of the fertilized ovum
II	Chemical, prenatal	Nutritive or toxic influence in the uterine environment
III	Chemical, postnatal	Nutritive or toxic influence: food, water, oxygen, drugs, etc.
IV	Sensory, constant	Pre- and postnatal experience normally inevitable for all members of the species
V	Sensory, variable	Experience that varies from one member of the species to another
VI	Traumatic	Physical events tending to destroy cells: an "abnormal" class of events to which an animal might conceivably never be exposed, unlike Factors I to V

Source: D. O. Hebb, *A Textbook of Psychology* (Philadelphia: W. B. Saunders Company, 1966), p. 157.

BACKGROUND: R. C. TRYON (1901–1967)

The seminal work in the field of behavior genetics was that of R. C. Tryon, a psychologist at the University of California at Berkeley. He tested a large number of laboratory rats for their ability to get through a complicated maze. Then he mated the "maze-bright" males with the "maze-bright" females and the "maze-dull" males with the "maze-dull" females. His classic experiments were simple. He tested the offspring in the same maze, and for several consecutive generations he selected the rats that learned to run the maze the fastest and also the rats that ran the maze the slowest. He bred the fast learners together and the slow learners together. By the eighth generation there was little overlap in the maze-running scores of the bright and the dull groups. These experiments were made at a time when there was the general belief among psychologists that behavior could not be inherited. The results seemed to show that the ability to get through a maze is dependent on heredity.

Tryon continued the selective breeding of the rats for eighteen generations. After the eighth generation, however, the selective breeding did not produce any further differences in the abilities of the two groups. The maze-bright rats did not continue to get brighter. Furthermore, only a few of the offspring of the maze-bright rats ever surpassed the performance of the brightest members of the original group of rats. When the descendants of each group of rats were tested about thirty years later, the maze-bright descendants were still more successful in getting through the maze than the descendants of the maze-dull rats.

Tryon's pioneering work prompted other behavioral scientists to investigate the phenomenon of inherited behavior. They soon found that environmental and genetic factors are intertwined and both play a role. What will be explored here is how heredity and environment interact to produce variations in individuals.

QUESTIONS AND EVIDENCE

1. What prenatal factors can affect postnatal development of behavior?

2. What are some early experiences that affect later behavior?

R. C. Tryon, whose pioneering work with "maze-bright" and "maze-dull" rats prompted other behavioral scientists to investigate the phenomenon of inherited behavior.

1. WHAT PRENATAL FACTORS CAN AFFECT POSTNATAL DEVELOPMENT OF BEHAVIOR?

HYPOTHESES	GENETIC	UTERINE	MATERNAL STRESS AND ANXIETY
DESCRIPTIVE EVIDENCE			ASSESS: relationship between pregnant mother's anxiety and infant crying after birth
EXPERIMENTAL EVIDENCE	VARY: breeding strains of mice	VARY: pre- and postnatal environments	VARY: emotional stress of pregnant rats
	MEASURE: amount of food hoarded	MEASURE: susceptibility to fatal seizures; aggressiveness	MEASURE: activity level of offspring in open field, time taken to leave cage.

1. WHAT PRENATAL FACTORS CAN AFFECT POSTNATAL DEVELOPMENT OF BEHAVIOR?

The *genetic hypothesis* states that some behaviors are inherited in the same way that eye color and hair color are. To isolate the effects of genetic factors, geneticists have developed a standard breeding plan. For example, when geneticists find some mice with the characteristics they wish to study, they will develop an inbred strain by mating brothers and sisters. When brothers and sisters are mated for about twenty successive generations, the amount of genetic variation in individual animals becomes negligible. In other words, all the mice of an inbred strain have virtually the same genotype.

Many inbred strains of mice and rats have been created for laboratory experimentation and maintained for dozens of generations. A researcher can select from existing strains animals with characteristics he wishes to study.

One way to study the effects of genetic factors on behavior is to study a specific behavior of different strains of the animal in identical environmental conditions. If some strains of mice exhibit less food-hoarding behavior than other strains under identical conditions, then we can conclude that genetic factors play a role. But we would not know how big a role. To find out more about the genetic factors, two strains of mice—high hoarders and low hoarders, for example—could be cross-bred according to the standard breeding plan, which consists of first cross-breeding the two parent strains, then mating brothers and sisters of the first generation and also backcrossing some of the first generation with each of the parents.

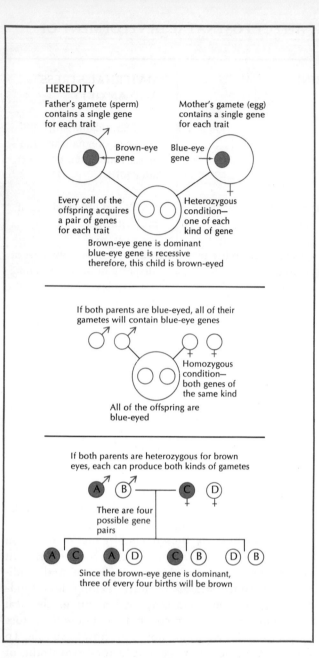

HEREDITY

Father's gamete (sperm) contains a single gene for each trait

Mother's gamete (egg) contains a single gene for each trait

Brown-eye gene

Blue-eye gene

Every cell of the offspring acquires a pair of genes for each trait

Heterozygous condition— one of each kind of gene

Brown-eye gene is dominant blue-eye gene is recessive therefore, this child is brown-eyed

If both parents are blue-eyed, all of their gametes will contain blue-eye genes

Homozygous condition— both genes of the same kind

All of the offspring are blue-eyed

If both parents are heterozygous for brown eyes, each can produce both kinds of gametes

There are four possible gene pairs

Since the brown-eye gene is dominant, three of every four births will be brown

Figure 3.

EXPERIMENTAL EVIDENCE

Investigator: M. Manosevitz
Source, Date: "Hoarding—An Exercise in Behavioral Genetics," 1970
Location: University of Texas
Subjects: Two strains of inbred mice
Materials: Testing apparatus for hoarding

Two strains of mice with a large difference in hoarding behavior were selected as the parental groups. To make it easy to determine the results of cross-breeding, the strains selected also had different coat colors: the high hoarders had pink coats and the low hoarders had black coats. Both the frequency of coat color and hoarding behavior in the offspring of various interbreedings were calculated according to a simple polygenetic inheritance principle, in which it was assumed that many genes influence hoarding and each gene contributes an equal but small part.

The hoarding test consisted of counting the number of food pellets a mouse would bring to its home cage from a bin at the far end of a runway. In most tests the mouse was given thirty minutes to hoard and usually was tested once a day for ten days. Pink-coated mice were mated and the hoarding score of their offspring was measured. The same was done for the offspring of the black-coated mice. Then some pink-coated and black-coated mice were mated. The hoarding score of the cross-breeds was between the scores of their parents, as would be expected if genes from each parent contributed an equal amount to hoarding performance. Brothers and sisters in the cross-bred offspring were mated, and again the hoarding went down. But when cross-breeds were mated with the original parental groups, the hoarding scores went up for the backcrosses with pink-coated parents and went down for backcrosses with the black-coated parental group.

Thus the inherited genes apparently form a part of the prenatal factors that affect postnatal behavior. Hypotheses can be formulated about other factors. The fetus is subject to its immediate environment in the uterus, for example, as well as to its genes. The hypothesis that changes in the uterine environment might have lasting effects is therefore a worthwhile one to explore.

TABLE 2. Effects of Genetic Factors on Hoarding

Generation	Mating	Observed Phenotypic Coat Colors	Mean Hoarding Scores for Each Strain	
			Observed	Expected
Parental (P_1)	$P_1 \times P_1$	pink	114.8	—
Parental (P_2)	$P_2 \times P_2$	black	40.9	—
First filial (F_1)	$P_1 \times P_2$	black	94.9	77.8[1]
Second filial (F_2)	$F_1 \times F_1$	black, brown, gray, pink	78.6	77.8[1]
Backcross (B_1)	$P_1 \times F_1$	black, brown, gray, pink	101.7	104.8[2]
Backcross (B_2)	$P_2 \times F_1$	black	65.5	67.9[3]

[1]Expected value = $(P_1 + P_2)/2$.
[2]Expected value = $(P_1 + F_1)/2$.
[3]Expected value = $(P_2 + F_1)/2$.
Source: M. Manosevitz, "Hoarding—an Exercise in Behavioral Genetics," *Psychology Today* (August 1970), p. 58.

The *uterine hypothesis* states that the environment in the uterus can affect not only the physical development of the organism but also its behavior after birth. Lack of certain nutrients, such as vitamins or proteins, can produce effects that have behavioral consequences. Injection of a male sex hormone into a mother at a critical period during uterine development will cause a female mouse to have a "male" brain. The most dramatic demonstration that the uterine environment interacts with the development of genetic potential comes from transplanting fertilized ova from one strain of mice into the wombs of females of another strain. The results observed should be a good test of the uterine hypothesis, for it is the wombs that have changed, not the genetic factors already given the embryos that are transplanted.

EXPERIMENTAL EVIDENCE

Investigators: B. E. Ginsburg and R. B. Hovda
Source, Date: "Intra-uterine Effects on Behavioral Capacities in Mice," by B. Ginsburg, 1969

Location: Jackson Laboratory, Bar Harbor, Maine
Subjects: Seizure-sensitive mice
Materials: Tools for ova transplants, testing apparatus for seizures and aggression

While working one summer at the Jackson Laboratory Ginsburg and some students noticed that a particular strain of mice had unusual variability in sensitivity to convulsive seizures when exposed to a loud sound. Most of the mice of that particular strain would stop breathing during a convulsion and die unless revived by artificial respiration. About 10 percent, however, recovered spontaneously after convulsion. Looking into the matter, the researchers found that the mice indeed did come from the same forebears but that there was a difference in their histories. Most of the animals were descendants of the standard strain, but some were descendants of the standard strain mice who had been transplanted as fertilized ova into the wombs of females of another strain. The transplanted ova developed in the uterus of the pseudomother and after birth were nursed and reared by the female that bore them. Descendants of the transplanted mice, even generations later, exhibited less fatal respiratory arrest during convulsions than did the standard animals.

Ginsburg repeated the transplant experiment with the same strains of mice that were used in the original experiment. He transplanted fertilized ova of the more sensitive mice (strain 1) into the wombs of the less sensitive (strain 2). He also provided for controls by transplanting strain 2 ova into the wombs of strain 1 females and also ova from one strain 1 female to another and from one strain 2 female to another. He found that when the more susceptible strain 1 mice developed in the prenatal environment of strain 2 females their recovery from seizures was improved and that their descendants also showed a lower proportion of fatal respiratory arrests. To find out if postnatal experiences like nursing were involved, he divided both pure strain and transplant offspring into various groups: some were reared by the female that gave birth to them, some were reared by a foster mother from strain 1, and some reared by a foster mother from strain 2. In the strain 1 males the susceptibility to fatal seizures was closely associated with aggressiveness, and both kinds of behavior were tested in the various offspring.

Foster nursing had no effect on the aggressiveness of the strain 1 males but did have an effect on strain 2 males, who showed an increase in aggression when fostered by a mother other than their own.

From his results Ginsburg concluded that the uterine environment interacts with the genetic potential in some instances and that some of the effects may last for more than a single generation. He suggests that the behavioral changes are the result of the activation or repression of particular genes during sensitive periods of intrauterine development.

It was believed not too long ago that the placenta provided an impenetrable barrier to almost everything in the mother's bloodstream except the nutritive elements required by the embryo. We know now that this is not so. The German measles virus can pass through the placenta and, depending upon the stage of development in human embryos, can produce multiple defects, including heart disease, blindness, and mental retardation. Thalidomide, a supposedly "safe" tranquilizer, produced gross malformation of

TABLE 3. Experimental Design and Results of Ginsburg and Hovda Studies

	Natural Mothers	Strain 1 Uterus	Strain 2 Uterus	
Strain 1 Ova	seizure prone	seizure prone	improved recovery from seizures; descendents: fewer fatal respiratory arrests	Prenatal Environment
Strain 2 Ova	non-seizure prone	non-seizure prone	non-seizure prone	

	Natural Mothers	Foster Mother Strain 1	Foster Mother Strain 2	
Strain 1 Males	aggressive	aggressive	aggressive	Postnatal Environment
Strain 2 Males	non-aggressive	increased aggressiveness	non-aggressive	

Source: Adapted from B. E. Ginsburg and R. B. Hovda, "Intra-uterine Effects on Behavioral Capacities in Mice," Paper presented at the Symposium on the Effects of Intra-Uterine Experience, 14th International Congress of Psychology, July 28, 1969; London, England. (Colored areas indicate effects of experimental manipulations.)

limbs. This tragic example made physicians aware that they must be alert to the consequences of the drugs they prescribe for pregnant women.

What kind of changes in the mother beyond the immediate uterine environment could so affect the embryo prenatally as to result in changes in its postnatal development? Could any psychological maternal factors as well as physiological changes be so involved?

Hormones that circulate in the mother's bloodstream can affect the prenatal infant. When stressful situations are encountered by the mother, one of the results is an increase in the amount of the hormone adrenaline in her bloodstream. The *maternal stress-and-anxiety hypothesis* states that a mother's experiences with stressful and anxiety-producing situations can have an effect on the emotionality of the developing fetus.

EXPERIMENTAL EVIDENCE

Investigator: W. R. Thompson
Source, Date: "Influence of Prenatal Maternal Anxiety on Emotionality in Young Rats," 1957

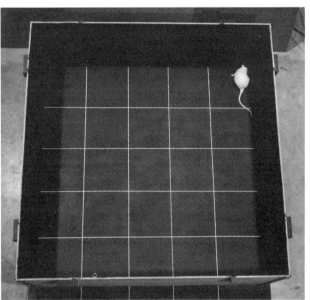

Figure 4. The emotional behavior of rats can be measured in the "open field," an area four feet square divided up into smaller squares. Normal rats usually run around and explore the strange environment. Emotionally disturbed rats huddle in a corner and defecate.

Location: Wesleyan University, Middletown, Connecticut
Subjects: Hooded rats
Materials: Shuttlebox with electric shock and buzzer

Previous research had shown that hormones such as adrenaline, when injected into the bloodstream of a pregnant female, had noticeable effects on the fetus. Because strong emotion could release such a hormone into the mother's bloodstream, Thompson suspected that the emotional experience of pregnant females could have an important influence on fetal development. To test his idea he created a situation that would arouse strong emotional anxiety without any actual physical stress. Hooded female rats were put into a double compartment shuttlebox that had a door between the compartments. Just before a strong shock was delivered through the floor of one compartment, a buzzer sounded. The female rat could escape the shock by running through the door to the other compartment when the buzzer sounded or after the shock had started. When the rats had learned to avoid the shock by escaping when the buzzer sounded, they were mated. While pregnant they were placed in the shock compartment and exposed to the buzzer three times per day. The shock was turned off and the door was locked so they could not escape to the other compartment. All of the pregnant rats showed signs of anxiety when they heard the buzzer and could not escape. The anxiety-producing treatment ended when the females gave birth to their young. Control mothers were pregnant hooded rat females that had not received any avoidance training or stressful experiences prior to mating.

To determine if postnatal influences affected the results, the offspring were cross-fostered with control mothers in such a way that the prenatal and postnatal experiences could be distinguished. All the offspring were tested at 30–40 days of age and again at 130–140 days of age. In the first test the activity of the rat in an open field was measured. In the second test the time it took a rat to leave its cage to get food at the end of an alley was the measure. Both tests had previously been shown to be appropriate measures of emotionality in rats. In both cases the offspring of mothers who had experienced stress during their pregnancy exhibited significantly lower activity than the controls. Thompson concluded that there are some grounds for supposing that prenatal maternal anxiety does actually increase the emotionality of offspring.

Evidence for the maternal stress-and-anxiety hypothesis can be obtained experimentally with female hooded rats and their offspring. No one would judge it right, however, to propose similar experiments on human mothers and their babies. Further evidence for the generalization of this hypothesis to humans has to be obtained descriptively. Rather than creating anxiety, as in the maternal rats, the investigators in the next study simply tested and grouped human mothers for their given levels of anxiety.

DESCRIPTIVE EVIDENCE

Investigators: D. R. Ottinger and J. E. Simmons
Source, Date: "Behavior of Human Neonates and Prenatal Maternal Anxiety," 1964
Location: Purdue University and Departments of Obstetrics and Nursing, Indiana University
Subjects: 19 mothers and their babies
Materials: Anxiety-level psychological test, microphone and infant moving measuring device

The researchers gave the anxiety test to a large number of pregnant women. They chose those who ranked exceptionally high and very low in anxiety. When the baby was born he or she was put into a special bassinet that had a microphone to record crying and a device for measuring the number of movements made by the infant.

The babies of high- and low-anxiety mothers did not differ in average weight at birth or during the first four days. Nor was there much difference in body-movement scores. However, the babies of the high-anxiety mothers cried more before feeding than those of low-anxiety mothers.

The increase in crying could be due to the emotional state of the mothers during pregnancy. The alternative hypothesis, also reasonable, is that genetic factors are responsible for both the mother's anxiety and the baby's crying. In either case, the results show that there is a positive relation between a mother's anxiety level and the amount of her infant's crying.

HYPOTHESES	INFANTILE STIMULATION	MATERNAL BEHAVIOR	ENRICHED ENVIRONMENT
DESCRIPTIVE EVIDENCE			
EXPERIMENTAL EVIDENCE	VARY: amount of stimulation in infancy	VARY: foster rat mothers and natural mouse mothers	VARY: environment of young rats
	MEASURE: adult avoidance learning behavior	MEASURE: aggressiveness and exploratory activity after weaning	MEASURE: changes in brain anatomy and chemistry

2. WHAT ARE SOME EARLY EXPERIENCES THAT AFFECT LATER BEHAVIOR?

Many behavioral traits, such as hoarding and aggressiveness, can be manipulated by breeding, but it is the environment after birth that determines the degree to which a behavior is expressed. The *infantile-stimulation hypothesis* states that emotional stimulation in infancy is necessary for development of adaptive responses to unpleasant situations.

EXPERIMENTAL EVIDENCE

Investigators: S. Levine, J. A. Chevalier, and S. J. Korchin
Source, Date: "The Effects of Shock and Handling in
    Infancy on Later Avoidance Learning," 1956
Location: Ohio State University
Subjects: Infant rats
Materials: Shock cage

To find out if painful or traumatic experiences in infancy would cause emotional disorder in adulthood, the researchers subjected a group of infant rats to mild electric shocks at the same time each day for a number of days. For control purposes they routinely placed another group of infant rats in the shock cage for the same length of time each day but did not give them shocks. A third group of infant rats were left in their standard laboratory cages and were not handled at all.

Answer the following question before reading on: How would you predict these three groups of rats would rank in terms of their extent of adult emotional disorder, if any, resulting from their treatment as infants?

Depending on your answer, you may be as surprised as the investigators. When the rats reached adulthood it was the control group, the rats that had not been handled at all, that were least able to learn to avoid a noxious stimulus. In addition the nonhandled animals were considered to be "emotionally unstable" as defined by greater defecation and cowering in a novel situation. The behavior of the rats that had been shocked was no different from the behavior of the rats that had only been handled. It appeared that the mild stimulation provided by handling produced the same effects on avoidance learning as did the traumatic experience of shock and that it was a lack of stimulation that produced maladaptive behavior.

Often investigations that disprove the hypothesis they are designed to test are more fruitful than those that simply verify the hypothesis. These unexpected results prompted Levine and his associates to repeat the experiment many times, subjecting infant animals to a variety of stimulations or stresses. In all cases, it was the animals provided with no additional stimula-

Figure 5. Denenberg et al. (1966) tested the effects of raising infant mice with rat mothers. Rats and mice have different maternal behaviors. Tests showed that the mice's early exposure to the rat did affect their adult behaviors.

tion—either shock or handling—that exhibited deviations in behavior. Other investigators had found that stressful situations release ACTH (adrenal-corticotrophic hormone) from the pituitary gland, which in turn causes the adrenal gland to release a hormone (corticosterone in rats) that affects heart rate, blood pressure, and muscle tension (see Unit 28). Levine came to the conclusion that some degree of stressful experience in infancy may be necessary for successful adaptation to the environments encountered later in life.

The *maternal-behavior hypothesis* states that the behavioral interaction of a mother and her infant offspring will affect the behavior of the offspring in adulthood. But is maternal influence strong enough to counter strongly inherited tendencies for behaviors such as aggression and fighting? Motherhood involves many postnatal activities of the mother in caring for her young. How strongly, if at all, do these activities in the external environment of the young affect the expression of the potential behaviors that these infants have inherited?

EXPERIMENTAL EVIDENCE

*Investigators: V. H. Denenberg, G. A. Hudgens, and
 M. X. Zarrow*
*Source, Date: "Mice Reared with Rats: Effects of Mother on
 Adult Behavior Patterns," 1966*
Location: Purdue University
Subjects: 36 litters of infant mice and rat mothers
Materials: Fighting box, activity measurement box

Four-day-old mice from an inbred strain were given to a lactating female rat. Control litters were left with the mouse mother. Although both the mouse and the rat are rodents, their maternal behaviors are different, and fostering mice to rat mothers provided a means of separating genetic and postnatal contributions to behavior. The rat mother engaged in all the appropriate maternal behaviors with respect to the mouse pups, including grooming, nursing, and retrieving them when they wandered from the nest. When the mice were forty to forty-three days old they were tested for exploratory activity and at fifty days for aggressive-

ness. Exploratory behavior was determined by placing a single mouse in a large open box whose floor was marked into four-inch squares. The number of squares that the mouse entered in a three-minute period was recorded as the measure of activity. Fighting behavior was measured by placing two male mice in a fighting box, which had two compartments separated by a sliding door. When the door was opened, normally reared adult male mice of the inbred strain used would fight in a large percentage of the cases. The fighting began spontaneously and could become so vicious that the fighters could be severely injured or killed unless they were separated.

The open field activity of the rat-reared mice was significantly less than the mouse-reared controls. The most important finding was that rat-reared mice would not fight when placed in the standard fighting-box situation. Whereas ten out of thirteen pairs of the mouse-reared controls fought, only one of eleven pairs of the rat-reared mice fought each other.

If amount and type of early experience can result in long-lasting differences in behavior, what might be the effects on the central nervous system? The *enriched-environment hypothesis* states that a stimulating environment can produce changes in a developing brain. This idea is quite the opposite of the view that brain size and complexity are exclusively determined by genetic factors.

EXPERIMENTAL EVIDENCE

*Investigators: M. R. Rosenzweig, E. L. Bennett, and M. C.
 Diamond*
*Source, Date: "Brain Changes in Response to Experience,"
 1972*
Location: University of California, Berkeley
Subjects: Inbred strain of male rats
Materials: Enriched environment cages, isolation cages

At weaning, three male rats were taken from each of a dozen litters. One rat was put in a standard laboratory cage, where he lived with two or three other rats. Another rat was placed in a large cage with a variety of play objects. Usually a dozen rats lived together in the enriched-environment cage. The third littermate lived alone in an isolated cage, an impoverished environment except for freely available food and water. After thirty days all the rats were sacrificed and various measurements of their brains were made. It was found that rats from the enriched environment had greater weight of the cerebral cortex and a greater thickness of the cortex. Analysis of electron-micrograph enlargements of brain sections showed that rats from the enriched environment had more connections between nerve cells in the brain.

When the inbred laboratory rats were placed outdoors in thirty-foot by thirty-foot enclosures with a screen over the top, they quickly began to make burrows, something that their ancestors in the laboratory had not done for more than one-hundred generations. Rats kept for one month in the outdoor setting showed a greater brain development than even the rats from the laboratory enriched environment. This finding suggests that compared with the natural environment the artificially enriched laboratory environments are considerably less rich in the variety and intensity of experience they provide.

What implications do findings from the enriched-environment experiments have for man? Obviously one cannot extrapolate directly from rat brains to human brains, but the findings do raise some interesting speculations. Further, one cannot deliberately create impoverished environments for infants in order to investigate the differential effects of such environments compared with enriched environments.

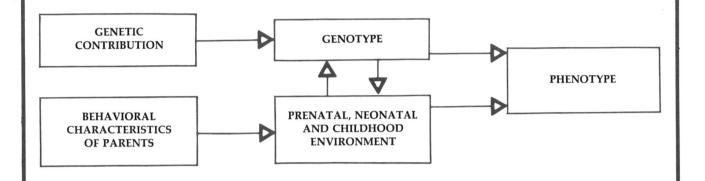

PUTTING IT TOGETHER: Genes and Their Nurture

Parents influence the uniqueness of each individual both through their *genetic contribution* and their behavioral characteristics. The *genotype*, or inherited potential of the organism, is encoded in the genes at the moment of conception. The *behavioral characteristics of the parents* also influence the individual through the *environment* they provide.

There is a continuing interaction between the genotype and the environment inasmuch as the genotypic temperament influences in some measure the nature of the environment acting upon the organism. The uterus provides the *prenatal environment* which, among other things, can influence the individual's general emotionality through maternal stress and anxiety. The amount of infantile stimulation during the *neonatal* period, as well as maternal behavior and richness of the environment during the *childhood* years are important environmental variables.

This interaction between the genotype and the environment produce the *phenotype*, or functioning individual.

WHAT'S ACCEPTED AND WHAT'S DEBATED

1. WHAT'S ACCEPTED . . .

1. The physical and the behavioral characteristics of an organism are the result of interactions between environmental factors and genetic factors.

2. Early experiences during periods of rapid growth or change, such as in the womb or just after birth, can produce long-lasting effects on behavior.

2. WHAT'S DEBATED . . .

1. Whether it is possible to separate and evaluate exactly how much genetic factors and how much environmental factors are each responsible for a behavioral characteristic of the phenotype.

2. What the limits of environmental manipulations are that can affect gene expression.

ISSUE: GENETIC ENGINEERING

The recent discoveries in the field of genetics that are described in this unit may prove to be of great importance for the future of mankind. For the first time in the history of our planet, a species has developed the capacity to control its own evolutionary future. The implications are awesome. If we wish, we can be released from the random processes of nature that determine the evolution of all life forms, but we would have to assume the disturbing responsibility for directing our own evolutionary future.

The technology for genetic engineering of the human species has not yet been developed. But we know how to perform this engineering in principle and have already applied it to other species. The idea of one human fashioning another to order is no longer science fiction. Robert Sinsheimer, a leading biologist at the California Institute of Technology, considers that it will be possible to produce human organisms by artificial means within ten to twenty years.

The process involved is called *cloning*, and results in the production of an organism—or countless organisms—genetically identical to the donor organism. The technique of cloning was pioneered in the sixties by Professor F. C. Steward at Cornell University. Working with single carrot cells which he placed in different nutrient environments, he succeeded in getting them to divide, grow, and differentiate into specialized carrot cells. Eventually he carried one individual cell to the ultimate stage of a complete carrot plant, a genetic duplicate of the plant from which the original cell had been taken.

If the vegetable could be cloned then so, in principle, could an animal. John Gurdon, a biologist at Oxford University, set about the task of cloning a frog. Using sophisticated techniques involving radiation and microsurgery, he was able to destroy the unfertilized nucleus of a frog egg cell while retaining the body of the egg intact. He then extracted the nucleus from another frog cell (this time from the intestine) and implanted it in the emptied egg cell. Since the cell from the intestine had its full complement of chromosomes, the newly constructed egg was equivalent to a fertilized egg cell, and ought to begin to divide, differentiate, and develop into a frog.

This is precisely what happened. Gurdon was able to raise a number of cloned frogs, all of them genetically identical to one another and to the donor frog. In theory, similar techniques can be used to clone replicas of any other animal.

Cloning animals in this way could have many practical uses. Endangered species might be saved by fabricating additional specimens. Fine racehorses or superior breeds of cattle could be reproduced without the tiresome necessity of submitting the breeding process to the random combinations of genes that are part of natural reproduction. But this intervention in the breeding process would have its cost: evolutionary development would cease. And evolutionary development, through its chance mutations, is the source of genetic improvements as well as genetic flaws in every species.

What of the prospects for cloning humans, for producing one, ten, a thousand genetic copies of any single individual? The technical problems are severe, partly because the human egg is microscopic in size and much smaller than that of the frog. (The human egg is implanted in the wall of the uterus soon after fertilization, and feeds directly from the mother through the placenta. Consequently, there is no necessity for the egg to be large.) New techniques for microsurgery would have to be developed before the cloning of humans could become a reality.

The greatest problem, however, would be ethical. Do we really want to create genetic copies of ourselves, or perhaps of those artists and statesmen we most admire? Dr. Willard Gaylin, a professor of psychiatry and law at Columbia University, points to some of the ethical problems involved: "If we do attempt human cloning, what will we do with the debris, the discarded messes along the line? What will we do with those pieces and parts, near-successes and almost-persons? What will we call the debris? At what arbitrary point will the damaged goods become damaged children, requiring nurture rather than disposal? The more successful one became at this kind of experimentation, the more horrifyingly close to human would be the failures. The whole thing seems beyond contemplation for ethical and esthetic, as well as scientific reasons."

One misconception about cloning is that an individual would be able to serve as donor for *exact* copies of him or herself. The cloned human would be a replica of the donor, but only a genetic replica. As we have seen in this unit, the development of any individual depends on a complex interplay of genetic and environmental factors. As a result, a cloned human could never be an exact copy of the donor in such matters as personality attributes, or even in height and weight. The genetic makeup would be identical, and appearance very similar, but there would not necessarily be any further resemblance. A donor and his clone would be replicas in the sense that identical twins are similar. And identical twins may have very different personalities, especially if they are reared separately.

Cloning is only one of several possibilities already opening to us in the field of genetic engineering. As Gaylin suggests, these new possibilities raise profound questions about what man can do, what he will do, and what he should do.

Unit 30

Built-in Behavior

OVERVIEW

This unit discusses behaviors often referred to as "species-typical"—behaviors whose appearance is controlled primarily by genetic and physiological mechanisms. Much of the behavior of lower animals is genetically predetermined in this fashion, including courtship behavior in birds, reactions to light and gravity in fish, and nest-building in many species. The status of man with respect to "built-in" behavior is much more controversial and difficult to investigate.

UNIT OUTLINE

DEFINITION AND BACKGROUND
1. *Definition:* built-in behavior refers to behavioral patterns that are highly predictable for specific environmental conditions and typical of all members of a given species.
2. *Background:* Konrad Lorenz (1903–   ).

QUESTIONS AND EVIDENCE
1. Why do members of a species exhibit similar behavior in certain situations?
Hypotheses:
    a. *Inherited-characteristics:* each animal species inherits some patterns of behavior. 521
    b. *Early-experience:* some behaviors typical of a species are shaped by exposure to the behavior of others of the same species. 523
2. What post-natal events effect the built-in behavior of members of a species?
Hypotheses:
    a. *Maturation:* certain forms of behavior after birth are the result of maturation of physical and neural systems, first appearing at an appropriate stage of development. 524

    b. *Critical-periods:* the acquisition of some species–typical behavior requires stimulation during specific stages of the animal's development. 525
    c. *Key stimuli:* innate releasing mechanisms for some behavior patterns are triggered by certain environmental cues called key stimuli. 527

IMPORTANT CONCEPTS

	page
adaptation	**518**
critical period	**525**
ethology	**519**
fixed-action pattern	**518**
imprinting	**519**
instinct	**518**
key stimuli	**518**
orienting response	**518**
species-typical behavior	**518**
taxis	**518**

Each species of animal is sensitive to specific characteristics of the environment which become key stimuli.

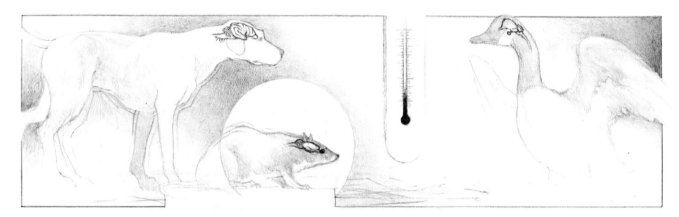

Key stimuli trigger innate releasing mechanisms for fixed action patterns.

Some species-typical patterns of behavior are present at birth. Others occur late in maturational development.

DEFINITION AND BACKGROUND

If you watch dogs or cats playing or pigeons feeding, you will quickly notice that animals of the same species do many things in almost an identical manner. Like the physical features that distinguish members of a species, many components of their behavior are inherited. These innate behavior patterns may be fully functional at birth or may develop gradually as an animal grows older. Such patterns develop even if the animal is raised in isolation, so they are not necessarily learned by observing and imitating. The DEFINITION of built-in behavior is *behavioral patterns that are highly predictable for specific environmental conditions and typical of all members of a given species.* Form-constant movements that are characteristic of a species and that do not have to be learned are called *fixed action patterns.* They are complicated and often elaborate motor patterns whose coordination is presumed to be blueprinted genetically (the original German term is *Erbkoordination*—inherited coordination). The pattern may be functional at birth, as with the newly hatched chick that can immediately peck at seeds and scratch the ground, or it may develop automatically with maturity, as with the duck that will perform the courtship ritual typical of its species even if it is raised in isolation from other ducks.

Fixed action patterns normally occur with orienting movements superimposed on them. Orienting movements in response to particular environmental stimuli are called *taxes.* An example of *taxis* is the way a frog will always turn its body so that its snout points directly toward its prey before it flicks its tongue out. The orienting movement is the taxis; the tongue flick is the fixed action pattern. Many fishes orient simultaneously to gravity and to light. When light comes horizontally from the side, the fish will rotate 90 degrees so that the light falls on its back. If the gravity receptors in the inner ear are destroyed, the fish will swim upside down when the light comes from below. Taxis requires continuous directing stimuli for the behavior to continue. In contrast, once a fixed action pattern has started, in general the stimulus is no longer necessary for the behavior to run its course.

The unity or combination of taxis and fixed action pattern is the basis of instinctive activity. A good example is the egg-rolling behavior of the greylag goose. If an egg gets outside the nest, the female greylag reaches over the egg and places her bill on the ground beyond it. She carefully pulls the egg back to the nest with the underside of her bill, balancing the rolling egg by moving her bill from side to side. If the egg is removed after the rolling movement has started, the fixed action pattern will continue and the goose will pull its neck back to the nest in a straight line. The lateral balancing movements, which are the taxis component of the activity, cease when the stimulus (egg) is absent.

Many highly specific behaviors are triggered by very specific stimuli or configurations of stimuli in the environment. These *key stimuli* can elicit appropriate actions even though the animal has never experienced them before. For example, the courtship behaviors of many birds are triggered by key stimuli. In the same way that a key opens a lock, the key stimuli act upon an assumed *innate releasing mechanism.* This mechanism is a stimulus filter; it allows the nerve impulses for a certain behavior to reach the muscles only when the key stimuli are encountered.

This unit will FOCUS on the development of built-in behavior and on the factors that influence it. It will discuss the role of genetic makeup in and the influence of environmental factors, maturation, experience, and critical periods on adaptive behavior.

Although we may use the terms "innate," "inherited," and "instinctive" behavior, we do not mean that the behavior itself is inherited. What is inherited is the potential for performing various activities. Not all potentials are developed, and those that are can be influenced by the environment to a certain degree. Each species-typical behavior pattern is the result of adaptive changes that have been subjected to natural selection. Thus, when we say innate or instinctive behavior, we are referring to phylogenetic adapted behavior, that is, those behaviors that a species has evolved through genetic variation and natural selection in the same way that physical changes in a species occur through genetic variation (mutations) and natural selection.

BACKGROUND: KONRAD LORENZ (1903–   )

In many ways the systematic study and comparison of animal behaviors is a direct outgrowth of Darwin's theory of evolution. Darwin not only sought to explain the evolutionary development of plant and ani-

Figure 1. The noted ethologist Konrad Lorenz imprinted young geese on himself. They treat him as their mother, to the complete exclusion of their natural mother.

mal species but also described how species came to differ in their physical characteristics and behavior because of the interaction of genetic variation and natural selection.

Konrad Lorenz is widely regarded as the father of ethology—the comparative study of animal behavior patterns. Lorenz, an Austrian, has made an immense contribution to the biological approach to the behavioral sciences. In the 1930s his descriptions of innate, unlearned patterns of behavior in geese, ducks, goats, and other animals inspired others to take seriously innate patterns of behavior. About the same time, Niko Tinbergen of Holland was establishing a reputation with his ethological approach to the study of animal behavior. In 1936 Lorenz invited Tinbergen to spend a couple of months with him in his outdoor laboratory at an estate in Austria. Of his relationship with Lorenz, Tinbergen says: "We supplemented each other. I was more a verifier, an experimenter whereas he had a ray of light at first sight."

Lorenz spent many years observing his animals. One of his most intriguing and widely known findings is the phenomenon of *imprinting*. This is the rapid and permanent acquisition of a strong attachment to an object, which, in nature, is usually the parent. He noted that newly hatched goslings will follow the first moving object that they see. In his classic experiment he divided a clutch of eggs laid by a greylag goose into two groups. One group of eggs was hatched in an incubator; the other, by the mother goose. The naturally hatched goslings followed their mother around the estate after they left the nest. The first moving thing that the incubator-hatched goslings saw was Lorenz, and they followed him wherever he went. To find out if goslings have an innate preference for members of their own species, Lorenz put distinguishing marks on the two groups and then placed them under a large box. He and the mother goose stood by when the box was lifted. Each group of goslings approached their respective "mothers." Lorenz called the process of rapid and permanent acquisition of a strong attachment to the parent or parent-substitute *Pragung,* a German term for "stamping" or "coinage." The term has been translated into English as "imprinting." Subsequent studies have found that imprinting occurs in animals that are able to move shortly after birth. Most imprinting studies have been with birds—ducks, chickens, quail—but imprinting in sheep, goats, deer, buffalo, insects, and fish has also been described.

The European ethologists (of whom Lorenz is the most widely known) explain spontaneous, unlearned behavior in terms of innate or inherited "blueprints" or "programs," and advocate the observation of animal behavior in natural habitats. In recent years, their approach and findings have been in conflict with those of the "behaviorists" of the American school. The behaviorists, who contend that specific behaviors must be studied under controlled conditions in the laboratory, try to explain animal behavior in terms of stimulus and response.

To some extent a synthesis of these two views is now occurring. European scientists are calling ethology the *comparative* study of behavior and American researchers have started to take their laboratory equipment into the field to record animal behavior as it actually happens in nature. Ethologists see their field as a branch of biology that has borrowed some of the analytic methods of behaviorists for causal analysis. Some behaviorists are shaking off their former reliance on highly controlled experiments—many of which simply deprived the animal of the stimuli necessary for normal development—and are beginning to study "natural" development.

QUESTIONS AND EVIDENCE

1. Why do all members of a species exhibit similar behavior in certain situations?
2. What postnatal events affect the built-in behavior of members of a species?

1. WHY DO ALL MEMBERS OF A SPECIES EXHIBIT SIMILAR BEHAVIOR IN CERTAIN SITUATIONS?

Members of the same species not only have similar physical characteristics but also exhibit similar behavior patterns. In contrast to the physical features, the behavioral sequences are not always readily visible. However, behavioral patterns can be recorded on film and sound tapes, and such records can then be used for comparative analysis.

QUESTION	1. WHY DO ALL MEMBERS OF A SPECIES EXHIBIT SIMILAR BEHAVIOR IN CERTAIN SITUATIONS?	
HYPOTHESES	INHERITED CHARACTERISTICS	EARLY EXPERIENCE
DESCRIPTIVE EVIDENCE		
EXPERIMENTAL EVIDENCE	VARY: genetic factors by cross-breeding birds with different nest-building patterns	VARY: exposure of young birds to parents' song patterns
	MEASURE: nest-building patterns of offspring	MEASURE: similarity of offspring and parent song patterns

The behavior patterns common to members of a species are called *species-typical* behaviors. In lower species, such as birds, extremely complex patterns of behavior involving nest building, courtship, food gathering, and song patterns are virtually identical among members of the same species. Many species can be identified solely on the basis of their characteristic behavior patterns.

Ethologists like Lorenz explain species-typical behavior primarily by the *inherited-characteristics hypothesis,* which states that each animal species inherits some patterns of behavior. Experiments have lent support to this hypothesis in that animals reared in isolation nevertheless display certain characteristic patterns of behavior.

The following experiment provides a test of the inherited-characteristics hypothesis, but it also raises an important question. Take two species of a genus that have been demonstrated to have different species-typical behavior in the same activity. When you cross-breed members of these species, what species-typical behavior will the offspring have, and why?

EXPERIMENTAL EVIDENCE

Investigator: W. C. Dilger
Source, Date: "The Behavior of Lovebirds," 1962
Location: Laboratory of Ornithology, Cornell University
Subjects: Two forms of lovebirds and their hybrid offspring
Materials: Simulated natural setting for lovebirds

In nest building, both the peach-faced lovebird and Fischer's lovebird cut strips from paper, bark, and leaves with their bills. The Fischer's lovebird carries strips one at a time in its bill, as do most birds. The peach-faced lovebird, however, on only about 3 percent of its trips carries material in its bill. The rest of the time it tucks several strips of nesting material in its rump feathers, which have small hooks that hold the strips in place; it loses about half of the strips before it gets to its nest site.

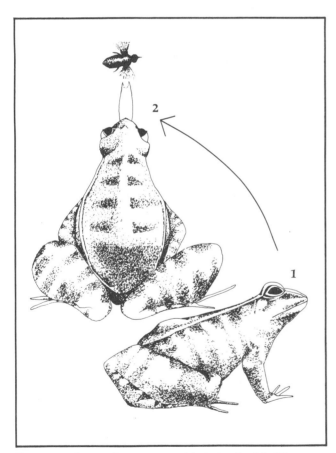

Figure 2. A frog catching its prey: (1) aiming (*taxis*); (2) tongue-flick (*fixed action pattern*).
  The egg-rolling movement—an instinctive activity—of the grey-lag goose.
[Source: I. Eibl-Eibesfeldt, *Ethology, the Biology of Behavior* (New York: Holt, Rinehart, & Winston), 1970.]

Liz Forrestal – N.A.W.D.F.

Figure 3. As a pup, this wolf serves as a key stimulus to trigger the innate releasing mechanism for pup retrieval behavior in the adult female coyote. The behavior is so compelling that the coyote persists even though the wolf pup is much larger than she can handle.

When the peach-faced and Fischer's lovebirds were mated, the offspring displayed both patterns of carrying nest-building material. They cut material with no difficulty but seemed to be completely confused about whether to carry the strips in their tail feathers or in their bills. Initially they got material to the nest site only when they carried it in their bills, which they did about 6 percent of the time. The hybrids repeatedly attempted to tuck material into their tail feathers, but even if they were successful the material fell out before they reached the nest site.

Two months later the hybrids became more experienced and carried almost half of the material in their bills. However, when collecting the material they still made tucking movements. It took two years for them to learn to diminish the tucking activity, and even then they continued to perform some of the movements associated with tucking. Eventually they did learn to carry nesting material only in their bills like the Fischer's lovebird. Thus, although the hybrids inherited both sets of parental behavior, experience eventually modified their behavior so that one genetically determined pattern virtually disappeared and the other became dominant.

Figure 4. Behavior of peach-faced lovebird. Nest-building is done by tucking several strips of material in its hooked rump feathers.
Behavior of Fischer's lovebird. Nest-building materials are carried in the bill.
The graph shows the conflicting patterns of carrying nest-building materials inherited by hybrid lovebirds, produced by mating peach-faced with Fischer's lovebirds. The hybrid eventually learns to carry the materials in its beak, like the Fischer's lovebird does, and the number of irrelevant movements and inappropriate activities decreases.

PEACH-FACED LOVEBIRD

FISCHER'S LOVEBIRD

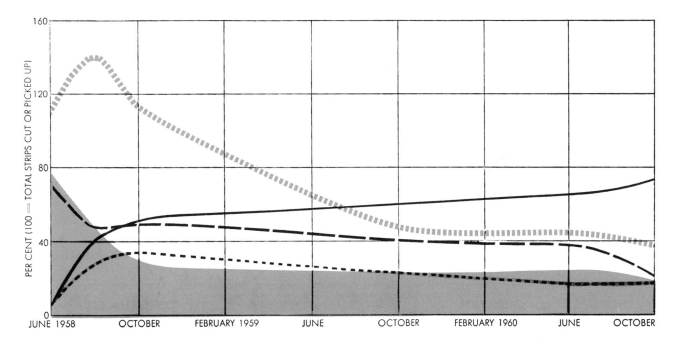

160

120

PER CENT (100 = TOTAL STRIPS CUT OR PICKED UP)

80

40

0

JUNE 1958   OCTOBER   FEBRUARY 1959   JUNE   OCTOBER   FEBRUARY 1960   JUNE   OCTOBER

In this experiment, the experience of the individual hybrid offspring eventually led to the dominance of one species-typical pattern as opposed to another. Does experience play any cultural role? In other words, does the species-typical behavior of older members of a species affect the behavior of the young? The *early-experience hypothesis* holds that some behaviors typical of a species are shaped by exposure to the behavior of others of the same species.

EXPERIMENTAL EVIDENCE

Investigators: P. Marler and M. Tamura
Source, Date: "Culturally Transmitted Patterns of Vocal
*   Behavior in Sparrows," 1964*
Location: University of California, Berkeley
Subjects: Male white-crowned sparrows
Materials: Acoustical chambers

Although the basic sound characteristics of songs of male white-crowned sparrows is species-typical,

males in different areas develop noticeable dialects: all the males from the same neighborhood have the same dialect. In nature the young male white-crown hears the song of its father and neighboring males for about the first hundred days after it is hatched. During their summer molt the male adults stop singing. When singing is resumed in late winter or early spring, the young males participate and exhibit the characteristic dialect.

Young male white-crowns between thirty and one-hundred days of age were captured in various areas and raised in pairs in acoustical chambers. The following spring they began to sing, and their song patterns matched the dialect of their home area. Males taken at ages three to fourteen days and raised as a group in a soundproof room developed song patterns that lacked the characteristics of the home dialect, and birds from different areas had strikingly similar song patterns. Males aged three to fourteen days who were individually isolated also developed songs that lacked the characteristics of their home dialect. The songs developed by males captured at a young age, however, did exhibit species-typical characteristics regardless of whether the males were raised in a group or in isolation.

The conclusion was that cultural transmission does play a role in the development of the song of the male white-crowned sparrow and that the dialect is acquired in the first hundred days of life by learning from older males. When songs of related sparrows were played to isolated young males, there was no effect. When songs of a bird of a different species and of white-crowned sparrows were alternated, the males developed fair copies of the white-crowned sparrow song. This indicates that there may be a predisposition in white-crowned sparrows to learn the species-typical sound rather than the song of other species.

pendent on learning, what events could be responsible for their late appearance?

The *maturation hypothesis* states that certain forms of behavior after birth are the result of maturation of physical and neural systems, first appearing at an appropriate stage of development.

EXPERIMENTAL EVIDENCE

Investigator: *L. Carmichael*
Source, Date: *"A Further Study of the Development of Behavior in Vertebrates Experimentally Removed from the Influence of External Stimulation," 1927*
Location: *Princeton University*
Subjects: *Salamander embryos*
Materials: *Chloretone anesthetic*

QUESTION   2. WHAT POSTNATAL EVENTS AFFECT THE BUILT-IN BEHAVIOR OF MEMBERS OF A SPECIES?

HYPOTHESES	MATURATION	CRITICAL PERIODS	KEY STIMULI
DESCRIPTIVE EVIDENCE			ASSESS: nest-building in naive rats
EXPERIMENTAL EVIDENCE	VARY: age at which salamanders are allowed to swim MEASURE: ability to swim	VARY: age of exposure to moving decoy MEASURE: strength of attachment	

---

2. WHAT POSTNATAL EVENTS AFFECT THE BUILT-IN BEHAVIOR OF MEMBERS OF A SPECIES?

Many species-typical behaviors do not appear until certain stages during an animal's development. Birds do not fly or babies walk until some time after birth. Other well-patterned behaviors such as nest building and caring for the young first appear when the animal is mature.

If these behaviors are indeed built-in and not de-

Salamander eggs were divided into two groups. One set, the control group, was placed in plain water while the other, the experimental group, was placed in an anesthetic solution made up of 4 parts of chloretone in 10,000 parts of water. The eggs were at a point of development well before any apparent movement occurs. The larvae in the plain water became free swimmers. The drugged embryos, although they continued to develop, exhibited no swimming motions and showed absolutely no response when touched with a blunt rod. When the drugged larvae had developed well beyond the point required for them to become good swimmers, they were placed in fresh water. It took several minutes for the anesthetic to wear off, and when it did they began swimming normally. As a check some of the control larvae raised to the free-swimming stage in fresh water were anesthetized and then returned to fresh water. Again it took several minutes before they began swimming normally, indicating that the delay before swimming was not a period of learning but rather the interval required for the elimination of the effect of the anesthetic.

Carmichael's classic study frequently is interpreted as confirming the hypothesis that the neuromuscular mechanisms upon which some behavior depends is developed by a mere maturation of innate determiners. Subsequent similar studies with other animals have provided additional confirmation. Apparently, even walking in humans is less dependent upon learning than it sometimes appears to be.

Closely related to the concept of maturational readiness is the *critical-periods hypothesis,* which states that the acquisition of some species-typical behavior requires stimulation during specific stages of the animal's development. A critical period is usually a short amount of time in which a relatively small amount of exposure or effort produces a lasting effect on the animal's behavior. Critical periods almost always occur during times of rapid change or growth. As an animal grows it may go through a series of critical periods, each for different behaviors.

Domestic dogs have a critical period in which they will form a strong attachment to people. This period extends approximately from six weeks to twelve weeks after birth. In the early part of the critical period a puppy can form a strong attachment to a new object within twenty-four hours and will whimper when separated from the object. If exposure to human beings is postponed until after the critical period, a dog will prefer to consort with other dogs instead of human beings whenever given the chance.

Following the publication of Konrad Lorenz's accounts of imprinting in geese, ducks, and jackdaws, this phenomenon received a great deal of attention. Imprinting in precocial birds usually occurs most strongly within the first twenty-four hours after hatching. With animals, the critical period may be immediately after birth or it may not be until several days later.

EXPERIMENTAL EVIDENCE

Investigator: E. H. Hess
Source, Date: "Imprinting," 1959
Location: University of Chicago
Subjects: Mallard ducklings
Materials: Incubator, duck decoys, recording equipment

E. H. Hess investigated the critical age for imprinting, the period during which a strong attachment to the parent or parent substitute is rapidly and permanently formed. Mallard eggs were placed in a quiet dark incubator under strict laboratory conditions and after the young birds hatched they were transferred in the dark to individual small cardboard boxes. The boxes were placed in a brooder. Ducklings of various ages, ranging from one hour to thirty-two hours, were tested by exposing them to a model of a male mallard that contained a loudspeaker. The decoy, which could be moved, repeated the sound of a human voice saying gock, gock, gock, gock. After the ducklings were exposed to the decoy, they were returned to their boxes by means of a trap door. At no time did they see the experimenter or were they handled by him.

When the ducklings were tested later, it was found that those who had been exposed to the decoy between thirteen and sixteen hours after hatching were the most strongly imprinted, although some imprinting occurred in ducklings exposed during the first twelve hours after hatching (see Figure 5). Imprinting was almost nonexistent when the ducklings were exposed to the decoy thirty-two hours after hatching.

An interesting follow-through from Hess' laboratory studies is his recent concern with differences between findings from the laboratory and from nature. Whereas laboratory imprinting of ducklings to human beings is often reversible, natural imprinting to their natural mothers is not. Even though much of Hess' own research during the past twenty years was conducted on birds in artificial laboratory conditions, he now says that "the usual laboratory imprinting has only a limited resemblance to natural imprinting" (1972).

Figure 5. Apparatus used in studying imprinting under laboratory conditions. The duckling follows the decoy duck around the runway. Controls of the apparatus are in the foreground. Adapted from Hess (1959).

Figure 6. Hess (1973) is studying imprinting under natural conditions. The nest boxes in which the female mallard incubates her eggs are located 300 to 700 feet from the recording apparatus.

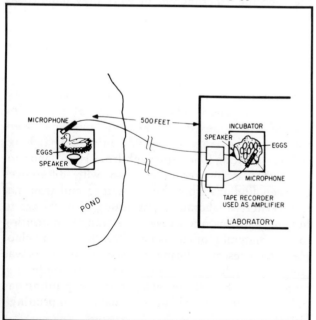

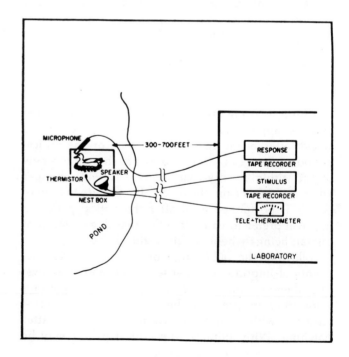

So Hess has taken his sophisticated laboratory recording equipment into the field. He has photographed the behavior of the female mallard and the ducklings and recorded all sounds from the nest before as well as after hatching. For one experiment he transmitted sounds from a brooding mallard on an outside nest to mallard eggs in an incubator. Another variation was to play a tape recording of prehatching sounds from mallard eggs to a wild mallard who was sitting on her own eggs. Hess was able to show that there is a considerable amount of vocal interaction between the mother mallard and the ducklings even before hatching and that these interactions may be important factors in natural imprinting.

The *key stimuli hypothesis* states that innate releasing mechanisms for some behavior patterns are triggered by certain environmental cues called *key stimuli.* These innate releasing mechanisms can cause an animal to respond unselectively to simple key stimuli, but usually the animal becomes more selective through individual experience. For example, a toad will snap unselectively at any moving object about the size of an insect, but it quickly learns to avoid bad-tasting or stinging insects.

Lorenz describes how a human-reared raven that has never sought prey will suddenly swoop toward the one sick jackdaw among dozens of healthy ones and kill it with a skillful blow on the back of the skull. One might think that somehow the raven "knows" not to prey on healthy jackdaws and is capable of recognizing symptoms of illness. But this would be overassessing the raven's intellectual capabilities. Its behavior can be explained more simply. Like many birds and animals of prey, the raven possesses an innate releasing mechanism that triggers the fixed action patterns of prey catching when a key stimulus is perceived. A slight stumbling or an irregular wing beat may be such a key stimulus. Such apparently trivial irregularities will elicit a predatory attack with the predictability of a reflex, as trainers of lions, leopards, and tigers have learned to their cost.

It has long been thought that the silhouette of a hawk overhead triggers an innate releaser of fear in birds. Lorenz and Tinbergen found that a moving model that looked like a hawk with a short neck and a long tail frightened young turkeys and geese. When the model was reversed so that it looked like a long-necked goose, the young birds showed no fear response. More recent experiments have shown that turkeys show less fear as they become accustomed to a moving shape. However, they appear to get used to some shapes more than to others. Thus, the original findings that the shape of a hawk releases a fear response may now be explained in terms of whether the potential prey perceives objects in the sky as more or less familiar.

The sparrow hawk is a natural predator of quail, yet newly hatched young quail have been successfully imprinted to hawks. In one case, the quail customarily followed within one foot of the hawk. However, on one occasion the hawk accidentally had not been fed before the experiment. It immediately attacked the imprinted quail, but the researchers rescued the quail before it was hurt. A few hours later the quail was tested again, and to everyone's surprise it moved to within a foot of its imprinted "mother," apparently completely unaware of its adopted mother's previous intentions.

Other behaviors that appear to involve releasing mechanisms that are triggered by key stimuli are courtship and mating rituals, nest building, and feeding offspring.

DESCRIPTIVE EVIDENCE

Investigators: B. F. Riess and I. Eibl-Eibesfeldt
Source, Date: "Ethology: The Biology of Behavior" by Eibl-Eibesfeldt, 1970
Subjects: White rats
Materials: Cages and nest-building materials

Most textbooks state that nest building in rats is innate and does not have to be learned. However, in 1954 B. F. Riess raised isolated rats in wire cages and fed them only powdered food. After the females matured and were mated, he placed them in a wooden box with strips of paper hanging from the wall. The naive rats pulled paper from the wall but failed to build nests even when they bore offspring. Riess concluded that nest building must be learned as a result of handling solid objects even if these objects are only food. Analyzing the situation Eibl-Eibesfeldt decided that what had been lacking were the relevant key stimuli rather than lack of learning. Even rats experienced in nest building will not build a nest in a strange environment at first but will explore instead. When tested in their home cages, rats raised according to Riess' method built nests in their sleeping corners. Other experiments show that the impoverished environment of a cage can interfere with nesting. Simply placing a vertical screen in one corner will trigger nest building even in virgin rats. It was concluded that key stimuli for nest building in rats are a familiar or naturally suitable nesting place with good cover and the presence of nest-building materials. The latter stimuli release certain motor patterns like

A.

B.

C.

D.

Figure 7. Naive female rats (raised in isolation in wire cages) who had not learned nest-building built nests in the sleeping corners of their home cages. A. Rat pulling the crepe paper from the holder. B. Pulling the crepe paper in during nest building. C. Sleeping nest made from split straw. D. Sleeping nest made from crepe paper strips. From Riess-Eibl-Eibesfeldt (1970).

Figure 8. Lorenz believes that certain characteristics of young animals are generally considered "cute" and activate the drive in adults to care for the young. Adult proportions (right) do not activate the drive.

nibbling and carrying paper. But only when the animal has a nest site will the rat's activity lead to the building of a nest. Naive rats that built nests appeared to have no idea what the result of their behavior would be. They would carry material to the site, drop it, make brief pushing and scratching motions, and then start back for more material. In all cases the end result was a nest.

Some have argued that the human infant is equipped with fixed action patterns and innate releasing mechanisms. The rhythmic searching movements of a newborn—a turning of the head back and forth—ends when the infant gets a nipple into the mouth.

The rhythmic seeking occurs only in the first days after birth; it soon is replaced with an oriented search for the breast. Crying and smiling in newborn infants seem to release certain appropriate behaviors in the mother.

Lorenz postulated that certain characteristics of the human child release emotional responses in adults, specifically: (1) large head and a small rounded body; (2) protruding forehead; (3) large eyes; (4) short, thick extremities; (5) soft body surfaces; (6) round, protruding cheeks. Examination of Walt Disney's "lovable" and "cute" creatures shows how he takes advantage of these characteristics.

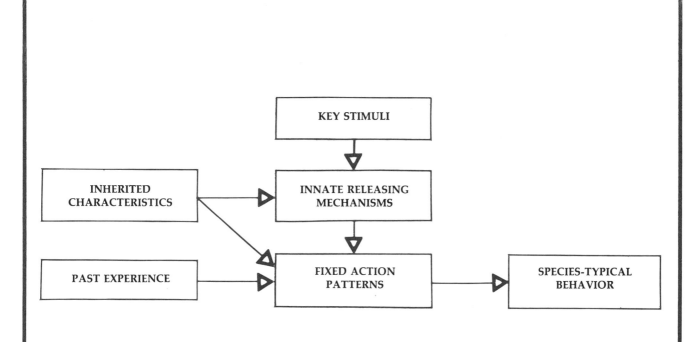

PUTTING IT TOGETHER: Built-in Behavior

Each species of animal engages in behavior in specific environmental conditions which is typical of that species. This is a function of the characteristics inherited by the species as well as the history of experiences unique to that species. *Inherited characteristics* include the structures responsible for innate releasing mechanisms and fixed action patterns. Some fixed action patterns occur only during certain periods of life, many not appearing until after the organism has reached full maturity. *Past experiences* may modify the nature of fixed action patterns, especially if those experiences occur during critical periods in the early life of the organism. The best known example is imprinting to unusual objects in many young birds.

Specific *species-typical behavior* is initiated by environmental releasers, or *key stimuli*, which trigger *innate releasing mechanisms* to set into motion *fixed action patterns*.

WHAT'S ACCEPTED AND WHAT'S DEBATED

1. WHAT'S ACCEPTED . . .

1. Certain species-typical behaviors are inherited but can be modified by experience.
2. Some species-typical behaviors are present at birth, but others occur later in maturational development.
3. Certain key stimuli trigger specific patterns of behavior, some of which can be quite complex.

2. WHAT'S DEBATED . . .

1. The specific physiological mechanism involved in built-in behavior.
2. The "learned" component of behavior patterns. To what extent specific fixed action patterns have learned components.
3. Whether any of man's behavior is "built-in."

ISSUE: TERRITORIALITY

As we have seen, this unit has focused on the development of built-in behavior and those factors which influence it. One of the more intriguing issues researched by ethologists is *territoriality,* the drive to mark out and protect an area as one's own.

Ethological research has shown beyond doubt that there is a built-in tendency in individuals of many species for individuals to possess territory and to defend it against intruders of the same species. Konrad Lorenz, who first systematically studied this behavior, believes that it is vital for the preservation of a species, since it spaces out the population and ensures an adequate food supply. In some species, such as wolves, the territory is socially defended by an entire group of animals, while in other species, such as shrews, an individual animal possesses and defends a patch of land. Territoriality in many animals seems to be intimately linked to aggression. When a bird sings its sweet song it is not serenading its mate, as poets have romantically imagined. It is declaring itself the owner of the surrounding area and warning other males to stay away. Lorenz has found one universal feature in battles over territory, whether they occur in fish, birds or mammals: the closer the battle is to the center of the territory of the possessor, the more likely it is that the possessor will win, irrespective of the relative strengths of the antagonists. Lorenz suggests that the same is true of humans, and argues that territoriality and associated aggression are built into human beings as well. Other popular writers, including Desmond Morris and Robert Ardrey, have spread these views in a somewhat simplified and distorted form to a wide reading public. Millions of laymen are now under the impression that it has been proven that man is innately territorial and aggressive.

Nobody disputes that humans often behave in territorial ways. We resent intruders in the home. We go to great lengths to personalize our domestic surroundings, with decorations or private possessions. We do this in much the same way, suggests Lorenz, as a dog urinates on lampposts to personalize its neighborhood. Humans are often prepared to die in battle for some wretched and distant patch of desert, for no other reason than that they feel it is their own, the property of the group to which they belong. We are also defensive about our *personal space.* When we occupy a train seat or park bench we may spread newspapers about to discourage others from sitting beside us. We usually require a certain distance between ourselves and other people. This is particularly true of Americans, who demand more distance between one another than the inhabitants of most societies.

But if there is agreement on the fact that human territoriality exists, there is little on its origins. Many ethologists, noting that parallel behavior is innate in other animals, take the view that it is genetically determined in man as well, an inherited residue from his animal past. Many psychologists vigorously reject this view and insist that territorial behavior is learned and that the parallel between ourselves and other animals is merely coincidental. Man, they believe, has few if any "instincts," and virtually all his behavior is learned.

The debate is further complicated by political ideology. Liberals and humanists are reluctant to concede that man might be the prisoner of his genetic endowment, especially in such matters as territorial possessiveness and aggression. Conservatives are more likely to accept that man is born with some undesirable attributes that must be constantly checked by social discipline and self-control. The issue is difficult to resolve, because it is not subject to controlled experiment. There is no human being who has not been born and raised in a place or territory into which he has been socialized.

But if the issue of the origins of territoriality remains unresolved, the debate has at least stimulated new interest in the psychological implications of the behavior. Architect Oscar Newman believes that the high rate of crime in high-rise apartments is related to the inability of the tenants to form strong territorial feelings in their anonymous surroundings. Newman points out that the stairwells of tall buildings are now a favorite haunt for criminals who might once have lurked instead in back alleys, and he cites evidence to show that the rate of crime increases proportionately to the height of a building. Because the tenants do not have highly developed territorial attitudes—such as those a suburban householder might display to an intruder on his lawn—the trespasser encounters no suspicious looks or questioning glances, and so feels safe and secure in the impersonal surroundings. Newman recommends that new housing estates be constructed in accordance with his notion of "defensible space." There should be a larger number of smaller buildings, carefully planned to encourage tenant feelings of territoriality and identity with the surroundings.

Unit 31

The Senses

OVERVIEW

How do our sense organs work, and what are some of the processes involved in how organisms interpret sensory input? The visual system and color vision are described first, since probably more is known about vision than any other sense modality. Next, theories of hearing and the other senses are presented. Finally, the unit briefly discusses the gate-control theory of pain as one possible explanation of acupuncture.

UNIT OUTLINE

DEFINITION AND BACKGROUND
1. *Definition:* the senses are an organism's physiological means for receiving and detecting physical changes that occur in the environment.
2. *Background:* Johannes Müller (1801–1858).

QUESTIONS AND EVIDENCE
1. How are sensory qualities coded and used in vision?
Hypotheses:
 a. *Quality-coding:* opponent-color coding processes take place in the eye and the brain after the original component-color information has been received by the cones in the retina. **538**
 b. *Form-analysis:* receptor mechanisms at the cortical level are responsive to specific shape and orientation characteristics of visual stimuli. **540**
 c. *Interpretation:* what people perceive visually depends not only on the sensory input being received but also on how the perceiver interprets that input. **542**
2. How are sensory qualities coded in sense modalities other than vision?
Hypotheses:
 a. *Traveling-wave:* sound frequency is coded at the place on the basilar membrane that vibrates most when the membrane is set in motion by a sound.
 b. *Pattern-coding:* the transmission of sensory information in the gustatory (taste) sense takes place through patterns of cell activity, not just through the firing of single nerve fibers. **546**

IMPORTANT CONCEPTS

	page
afterimage	538
cutaneous sensitivity	548
fading	543
gustation	546
hallucination	543
olfaction	548
perception	536
retina	538
rod	538
senses	536
sensory deprivation	543

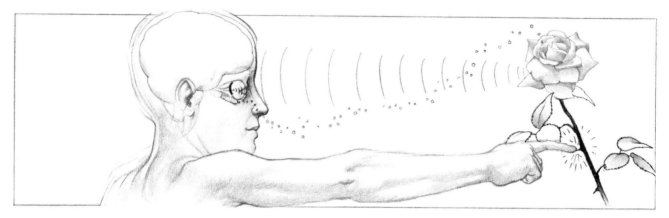

The processing of information from sensory stimuli is initiated by the activation of receptors that transform the original energy into neural energy.

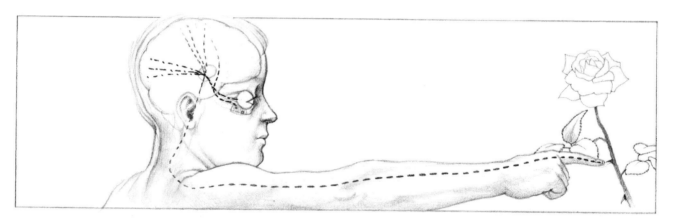

Each characteristic of sensory information has its own specific code that is transmitted to various parts of the brain.

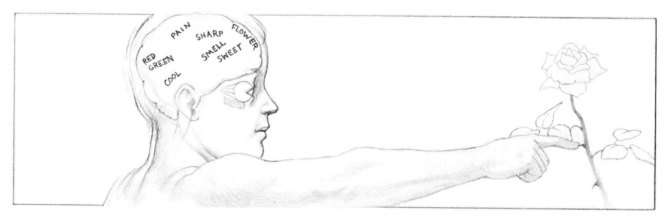

The decoding of various sensory attributes takes place in the brain.

DEFINITION AND BACKGROUND

A basic DEFINITION of the senses is simple enough. They are *an organism's physiological means of receiving and detecting physical changes that occur in the environment.* The senses are our links with the outside world.

This unit will FOCUS on the reception and processing (for transmission to the brain) of sensory information, particularly visual and auditory information. Some attention is also given to the operation of the other senses, to the relation between immediate sensory stimuli and past experience in perception, and to the abnormal functioning that results when people are deprived of variations in sensory stimuli.

BACKGROUND: JOHANNES MULLER (1801–1858)

In 1826 Müller, a German physiologist, formulated the "doctrine of specific nerve energies." Based on some earlier hypotheses of Charles Bell, this theory represented a radical departure from earlier views of the way the senses operate and gave scientists and philosophers for the first time a basis for developing a scientific method for studying sensation.

Figure 1. Johannes Müller's work on senses and sensation laid the groundwork for perception research.

Before Müller's time it was believed that the sensory processes operated by reproducing images of the world inside the head. For example, the ancient Greeks believed that hearing took place when sounds in the outside world rang a gong or bell inside the ear and that sight occurred when lights in the outside world lit a lantern inside the eye. But Müller asserted that sensation is not an awareness of the real world directly, but only an awareness of the state of neural pathways. According to Müller, the world is perceived through coded messages traveling along sensory nerves.

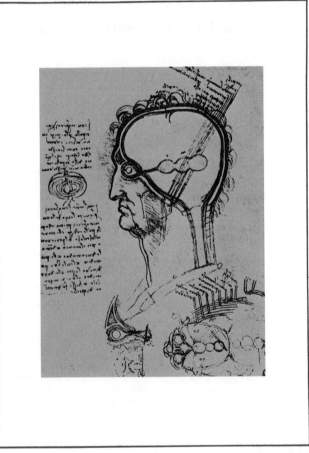

Figure 2. Leonardo da Vinci sketch of anatomical relationships between the eye and the brain.

Müller's doctrine of specific nerve energies contained several other important postulates. One idea was that no matter how a sensory nerve is stimulated, the sensation will always be the same. For example, whether the optic nerve is stimulated by light, by chemicals, or by electricity, a visual sensation is always produced. Conversely, the same kind of stimulation to different sensory nerves can produce different sensations. For example, electricity applied to the auditory nerve produces a sound sensation; applied to the skin it produces a feeling of heat. These basic ideas have been verified in many experiments.

Müller's ideas were developed at just the time that physicists were trying to understand how colors were produced and how different sounds combined. Between 1840 and 1870 Hermann von Helmholtz—a physicist, physiologist, and psychologist—based many elegant theories of sensation on physical models that probably would not have been developed without Müller's ideas.

As important as it still is, the doctrine of specific nerve energies in its original form is only rarely relevant today. Today psychologists and physiologists are more interested in detailing the way sensory information is coded than in exploring the philosophical problem of the relation between sensations and physical reality. Modern researchers now analyze sensing in terms of three basic factors. First is the *reception* of the physical stimulus by specialized nerve cells located in the peripheral sense organs such as the eye and ear. Second is the process of *transduction*. Transduction involves converting the energy of a physical stimulus, such as light that falls on the retina, into neural energy—nerve impulses that the brain can interpret. The third is the *transmission* of those nerve impulses from the sensory organ to the part of the brain that can interpret the information they carry.

QUESTIONS AND EVIDENCE

1. How are sensory qualities coded and used in vision?

2. How are sensory qualities coded in sense modalities other than vision?

	Sense	Stimulus	Sense organ	Receptor	Sensation
The stimuli and receptors of the human senses	Sight	Light waves	Eye	Rods and cones retina	Colors, patterns, textures, etc.
	Hearing	Sound waves	Ear	Hair cells of organ of Corti	Noises, tones
	Skin sensations	Skin	Skin	Nerve endings in skin	Touch, pain, warmth, cold
	Smell	Volatile substances	Nose	Hair cells of olfactory epithelium	Odors (musky, flowery, burnt, minty, etc.)
	Taste	Soluble substances	Tongue	Taste buds of tongue	Flavors (sweet, sour, salty, bitter)
	Body movement	Mechanical energy	Muscles, joints, tendons	Nerve endings	Position, movement, pressure, pain
	Equilibrium	Mechanical and gravitational forces	Inner ear	Hair cells of semi-circular canals and vestibule	Spatial movement, gravitational pull
	Organic sensitivity	Mechanical energy	Portions of digestive tract	Nerve endings	Pressure, pain

Figure 3. The senses—vision, hearing, equilibrium, and others—provide organisms with critical information about events outside and within their bodies. The study of sensation is a search for the lawful and consistent correlations between physical events acting as stimuli on living organisms and the behavior or experiences that they evoke. It also tests the physiological capacity of an organism, for sensation only occurs when a stimulus is appropriate and intense enough to activate a receptor.

HYPOTHESES	QUALITY CODING	FORM ANALYSIS	INTERPRETATION
DESCRIPTIVE EVIDENCE			ASSESS: subjective perceptual reports on stabilized retinal images
EXPERIMENTAL EVIDENCE	VARY: colors presented to monkeys	VARY: positions of form stimuli presented to cats	
	MEASURE: nerve cell activity in parts of brain	MEASURE: nerve cell activity in areas of cortex	

1. HOW ARE SENSORY QUALITIES CODED AND USED IN VISION?

Perhaps the most vivid and immediately obvious aspect of the average person's sensory world is color. The perception of color differences corresponds to differences in the lengths of waves of light. (Light is the visible portion of the electromagnetic spectrum of energy.) On the retinal surface (inside coating) of the eyeballs are two kinds of sense-receptor cells that react to light. One kind, called *rods* (because they are shaped like rods), are sensitive only to light intensity at low levels of illumination. Thus, the rods are most sensitive to light when the surrounding illumination is relatively dark. At higher levels of illumination—in broad daylight or with good artificial lighting—the cells responsible both for visual acuity and for color reception are the *cones*. These are heavily clustered in the center of the retina, which is called the *fovea*. Therefore, information from the central part of the visual field is better for form and color than information from edges of the visual field (see Figure 4).

During the 1960s several researchers discovered independently that there are actually three kinds of cone cells in the retina, each containing different chemical substances. These cells respond preferentially to one part of the visible spectrum, such as red, green, or blue.

Interestingly enough, an English physicist and physician, Thomas Young, predicted more than 160 years ago that exactly three such substances would be found in the eye. In the mid-nineteenth century, Helmholtz adapted Young's ideas and developed the Young-Helmholtz "trichromatic" or *three-component theory* of color vision. The theory stated that all phenomena in color vision might be explained by the existence of three primary-color receptors in the eye. It was an exciting idea, for it could easily account for the more common types of color blindness (by saying that one kind of receptor was missing) as well as other color phenomena. The physiological work in the 1960s tended to confirm the component viewpoint, at least as far as the retina itself is concerned.

But the retina is not the sole source of color vision. The component theory has trouble explaining certain color phenomena, such as the greenish afterimage that you see when a red light is turned off. This effect is better explained by the *opponent theory*, which was originally proposed by Ewald Hering. The opponent theory postulates three independent color systems composed of "opposite" colors: red versus green, blue versus yellow, and white versus black. Each member of a pair is antagonistic to the other, so that a build-up of red is also a lack of green, and vice versa. Thus, green afterimages emerge when the red receptor has been "tired out."

The fact that three kinds of primary-color cones have been discovered in the retina does not invalidate this idea. The *quality-coding hypothesis* states that opponent-color coding processes take place in the eye and the brain after the original component-color information has been received by the cones in the retina.

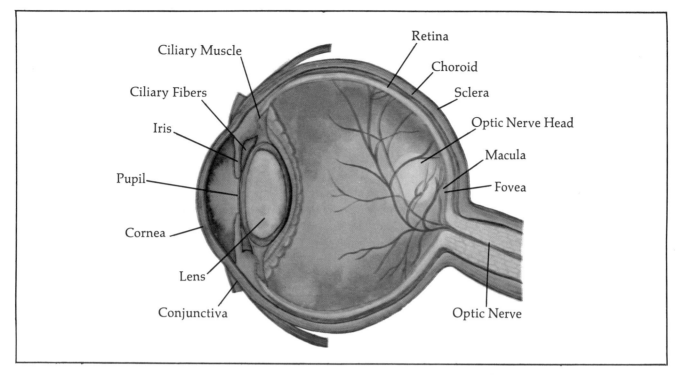

Figure 4. The opaque outside covering of the eyeball, the "white of the eye," is the *Sclera.* Behind this is the *Choroid,* a dark layer of pigmented tissue absorbing stray light inside the eye. The *Conjunctiva* is a protective membrane covering the front of the eye and extending to the inside of the eyelid. Light enters the membrane. It then passes through the *Pupil,* a hole in the circular curtain called the *Iris,* which regulates the size of the pupil according to the amount of light present. The *Lens,* whose shape is adjusted by the *Ciliary Fibers* and the *Ciliary Muscle,* focuses the light on the *Retina* containing the visual receptors as discussed in Figure 5. Whenever the eye fixates on a portion of the visual field, the image is centered on the *Macula,* surrounding the *Fovea:* a pinhead-size portion of the retina with tightly packed cones providing maximal resolution of the image. Visual information from the entire retina is encoded and transmitted through the *Optic Nerve.*

EXPERIMENTAL EVIDENCE

Investigator: R. L. DeValois
Study, Date: "Analysis and Coding of Color Vision in the Primate Visual System," 1965
Location: Indiana University
Subjects: Monkeys
Materials: Electronic equipment; surgical preparations

The color vision of some monkeys and other higher primates is practically the same as man's. In his studies DeValois inserted tiny microelectrodes in specific cells in certain areas of monkeys' brains and then, while the monkeys viewed reflected light of different colors, recorded the electrical activity of the cells. Of particular interest was a certain area in the thalamus of the brain known as the lateral geniculate nucleus, or LGN. The LGN, which is composed of groups of cells involved in different color processes, is a sort of "color switchboard" for the rest of the brain. DeValois was able to record the electrical activity of specific nerve cells within each layer.

Both the Young-Helmholtz theory (the component theory) and Hering's explanation of color vision (the opponent theory) were partially confirmed by the results. When common or primary colors (red, green, yellow, blue) were viewed by the monkeys, distinctive cell activity was found.

Some cells fired both when a red light was turned on and when a green light was turned off: "red-on, green-off" cells. Other cells fired when a yellow light was turned on or a blue one turned off: "yellow-on, blue-off" cells. "Red-off, green-on" and "yellow-off, blue-on" cells were also discovered.

But simple color cells were also discovered. Some of these responded only to the turning on of red, or green, or blue, or yellow lights; others responded only to turning the lights off.

Thus, modern research has shown—as it so often does—that the older theories were basically true but too simple, and that apparently conflicting theories are not as contradictory as they seemed. The current picture of color vision is extremely complex, with certain brain areas like the LGN acting as way stations between sense receptors, cortical projection areas, and the even more complex cortical centers where perception ultimately occurs.

Visual perception involves more than color, of course. Shapes, sizes, distances, objects, and movement are all extremely important. In 1959 J. Y. Lettvin and several colleagues at MIT published an imaginative physiological analysis of the frog's vision that identified in the frog's eye four very specific kinds of "detectors" of form or patterns, such as edges, moving edges, and sudden dimming. The most fascinating of these were the so-called bug detectors, nerve cells that responded only to small, dark objects passing across the visual field. This discovery indicates that the eye sends to the brain messages that are already highly organized, with specific meanings, instead of submitting a relatively simple "copy" of the visual field.

For the frog, as for many other lower animals, much interpretation of stimuli takes place at peripheral sites. In other words, the frog's retina is a highly complex nervous structure, though its brain is much more primitive than ours. The frog's bug-detector system has great functional value, since insects are its prime food. A complex interaction between the eye and the tongue also aids the frog in its search for food.

In higher mammals and man, some detectors for form and relationships within the visual field are in peripheral sense organs, just as they are in the frog, but only the first step in the processing of this information takes place in the retina. The highest forms of processing occur in the brain itself. Of particular interest are certain areas on the brain surface, or cortex: the cortical projection areas for vision (see Figure 5). The *form-analysis hypothesis* states that receptor mechanisms at the cortical level are responsive to specific shape and orientation characteristics of visual stimuli.

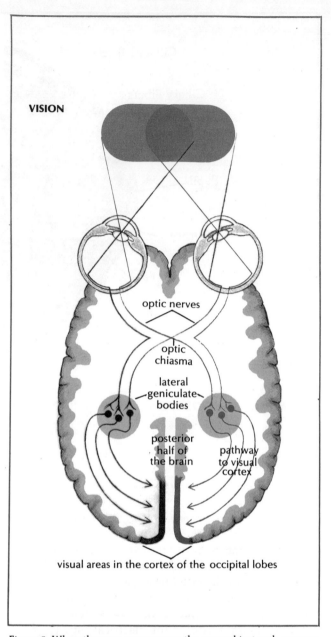

VISION

optic nerves

optic chiasma

lateral geniculate bodies

posterior half of the brain

pathway to visual cortex

visual areas in the cortex of the occipital lobes

Figure 5. When the eyes converge on the same object each eye sees a slightly different image. Light from a point on the right side of the visual field falls on the left side of both retinas. The path of the optic nerve is such (note the crossing over at the optic chiasma) that impulses from the left side of both retinas activate areas only in the left visual cortex at the back of the brain. The pathway is mirrored for the right side of the retinas. Each side of the brain, therefore, receives slightly different signals from the same half of the visual field, but somehow we are able to assemble a meaningful image.

The Young-Helmholtz Theory

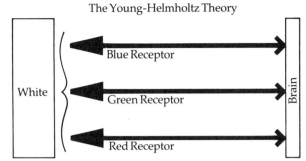

The Sensation of White

According to the Young-Helmholtz theory, there are three types of color receptors in the retina. These absorb varying amounts of red, green and blue, relaying signals directly to the brain where they are mixed to yield the different color sensations. In this example, the brain senses white by receiving signals from all three receptors.

The Hering Theory

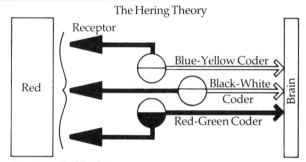

Sensing a Red Light

Hering argued that all three types of color coders receive light from undiscriminating receptors. When red light is viewed, only the red portion of the red-green coder is stimulated. The green portion shuts down and does not send a green signal to the brain.

A Composite Theory

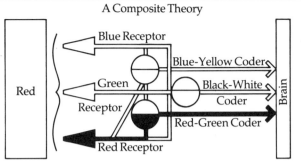

A Red Signal

A combination of the Young-Helmholtz and Hering theories might work like this: A color-sensitive receptor detects red light and sends an impulse to a red-green coder, which absorbs and deciphers it before transmitting the proper signal to the brain's visual center.

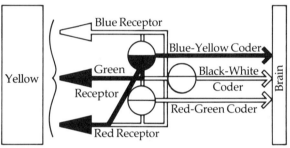

A Yellow Signal

Yellow, in the composite theory, draws responses from both red and green receptors. They feed impulses to the blue-yellow coder, which combines them into a yellow signal to the brain. If other coders are also signaling red, an orange color will be perceived.

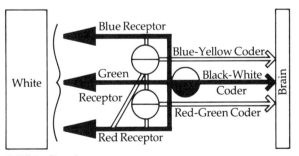

A White Signal

All three types of receptors react to white by transmitting equally strong signals from their thirds of the spectrum. The combined impulses activate the white part of the black-white coder, which then relays an all-color signal that the brain interprets as white.

Figure 6. Copyright Time Inc. from the Life Science Library, *Light and Vision.*

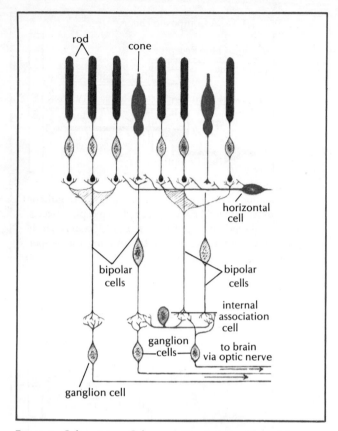

Figure 7. Color vision. Color reception is a function of the cone cells, which operate during periods of relatively high illumination. The cones of the fovea, the area of greatest visual sensitivity, have their own direct paths through bipolar cells with single endings. Outside the fovea larger bipolar cells with multiple endings collect signals from a number of sensors. Note how the rods, cones, and bipolar cells of the retina are also interconnected by internal association cells and horizontal cells.

EXPERIMENTAL EVIDENCE

Investigators: D. H. Hubel and T. N. Wiesel
Studies, Dates: "Receptive Fields, Binocular Interaction and
*   Functional Architecture in the Cat's Visual Cortex,"*
*   1962; "Shape and Arrangement of Columns in Cat's*
*   Striate Cortex," 1963*
Location: Harvard University Medical School
Subjects: Cats
Materials: Electronic equipment; surgical preparations

Tiny microelectrodes (about 1/100 of the diameter of a human hair) were inserted into single cortical cells in the visual cortex of cats. With electronic equipment, records were taken of the frequency with which these cells fired in response to different visual stimuli. Projected on a screen in front of the cat were certain simple relationships, such as a dark bar moving vertically, horizontally, or at various angles against a light background.

It was found that specific kinds of cells were activated by specific kinds of stimulus relationships. Some fired only when the cat saw horizontal bars moved up or down; some only when it saw vertical bars moved sideways and some only when the animal saw the bar angled across the visual field. These findings indicate that form perception is composed, at least in part, of sensations of lines, angles, and the like that are set up in the cortex in terms of a general relationship to the light patterns falling on the retina. Similar mechanisms may help account for the highly stereotyped responses of cats and other lower animals that are called "species-typical" or even "instinctive" (see Unit 30).

Human perception often goes beyond the simple givens of a visual stimulus. Much of our visual experience is determined not so much by activity at the retina as by higher brain processes that depend on past experience. The *interpretation hypothesis* states that what people perceive visually depends not only on the sensory input being received but also on how the perceiver interprets that input.

One of the most interesting approaches to this hypothesis—and, indeed, to the study of human visual processes—is found in experiments where an attempt is made to fix or stabilize a visual image on the retina. Under ordinary circumstances, the human eye is in constant motion—even when the observer stares at a stationary point, tiny involuntary movements of the eyeball keep it moving. These vibrations are essential to vision and cannot be stopped without endangering the eye.

DESCRIPTIVE EVIDENCE

Investigators: R. M. Pritchard, W. Heron, and D. O. Hebb
Study, Date: "Visual Perception Approached by the
*   Method of Stabilized Images," 1960*
Location: McGill University, Montreal, Canada
Subjects: Human adults
Materials: A tiny optical slide projector, mounted on a
*   tight-fitting contact lens*

Tiny projectors were used to attach a viewing target to the eyeball itself, so that the entire device moved with the eyeball's motions. (Mounting such a device on the eyeball is completely painless and causes no discomfort.) As a result, the image of the target was stabilized—it fell constantly on the same part of the retina. Each subject, while attending to the target's image, reported his perceptual experiences to the experimenter.

Subjects reported that the image stabilized on the retina soon faded and disappeared, leaving a structureless gray field of light it its place. They also observed, however, that the image or parts of it reappeared a short time later. Over prolonged periods of time, it alternately faded and reappeared. Of particular interest to a psychologist is the finding that the form of the image or part-image that reappeared was apparently related to the shape and meaning of the original image. For example, simple images such as lines usually faded and reappeared in their entirety (rather than, say, reappearing in shorter segments). But the figure of a human face or profile tended to fade and reappear in clusters of features. Features on the front of the face, or the back of the head, tended to fade and reappear together, not separately. Other consistent effects were also obtained in these studies.

These findings indicate that for stabilized images, with which the actual light stimulation that reaches the retina is constant, it is the subject's perceptions that change, not the stimulation. Fading occurs because the receptor cells in the retina (and perhaps also higher in the brain) become fatigued by the constant stimulation. Images and their parts reappear to the subject as meaningful units, not in random glimpses, because the organized, recognizable, or meaningful parts of the image are the perceptual elements most familiar to him. What he experiences when images are stabilized is not purely his sense organ activity at the retina but also his perceptual interpretations of sensations as they vary, fade, and reappear over time. The sensations fade, but the structure of the reappearing images and part-images is given form and meaning by perceptual processes at higher levels in the brain.

Even more drastic sensory-perceptual "interpretations" occur when people are deprived of sensory stimulation. A number of sensory deprivation studies have been conducted by Woodburn Heron and his associates, also at McGill University. The subjects (volunteers) are not deprived of sensation itself but of changes in stimulation. They are placed in a room where the stimulation of each sense is minimized: translucent glasses provide a structureless field of light, cotton gloves restrict touch, an air conditioner creates a constant temperature and produces a low, unceasing hum, and so on. Brain wave recordings are taken, and the subject can also communicate with the experimenter by means of microphone. Subjects leave the cubicle only for meals and to use the bathroom.

Many subjects at first go to sleep. When they awaken, their minds eventually begin to drift. After only a few hours, they begin to report simple visual hallucinations, such as simple dots of light and patterns. Abstract patterns and recognizable figures follow, and then more integrated scenes—animals and cartoonlike sequences. At this point the subjects may enjoy hallucinating. But soon the images become more vivid, then disturbing and even frightening, interfering with normal sleep. Subjects report that they have almost no control over the content of the hallucinations. Some see the same scenes or images over and over again—dogs, or eyeglasses, or babies. Nonvisual sensations are also reported; hearing music, for example, or feeling a touch and the like.

When a subject leaves the cubicle, he experiences afterimages and feels disoriented. His brain waves may be disturbed, or slower than usual. He may feel that the room is out of proportion, curved, or in motion. Some subjects even report "paranoid" ideas (the experimenter is "against" them).

Outside the laboratory, extreme sensory deprivation is rare, but patients confined in iron lungs for long periods of time have reported some experiences similar to those of Heron's subjects. For the normal operation of an organism's sensory-perceptual processes, variation in stimulation seems to be needed. When it is not provided, perceptual processes in the brain "create" experiences, many of them visual. If there were a simple one-to-one "isomorphic" relationship between sensation and perception, then the subjects in sensory deprivation experiments should report experiencing almost nothing.

This brief survey has emphasized a few basic problems and some of the most important or interesting findings concerning visual sensations. To sum up, in lower animals, such as the frog, visual processes tend to occur near the peripheral sense organ as well as in the brain. Higher up the phylogenetic scale, cats depend on special processing cells that are located in the cortex or surface area of the brain. Finally, in the higher nonhuman primates and man, visual-perceptual processes become highly sophisticated, and the perceptual world is less directly associated with or dependent on sensory information alone.

higher sound frequencies produce faster-firing nerve cells. But this theory by itself cannot account for the coding of pitch, because it has been found that nerve cells cannot fire faster than about 1,000 times per second. In contrast, the *place theory* has assumed that the brain gets its cues not from the frequency of neural firing but from the location in the inner ear of responses to different frequencies. The prime candi-

QUESTION   2. HOW ARE SENSORY QUALITIES CODED IN SENSE MODALITIES OTHER THAN VISION?

HYPOTHESES	TRAVELING WAVE	PATTERN CODING
DESCRIPTIVE EVIDENCE		
EXPERIMENTAL EVIDENCE	VARY: frequency of sound waves	VARY: taste stimuli placed on the tongue
	MEASURE: movements of the basilar membrane in the inner ear	MEASURE: nerve cell activity in layers of the gustatory nerve

2. HOW ARE SENSORY QUALITIES CODED IN SENSE MODALITIES OTHER THAN VISION?

Hearing also presents fascinating problems to sensory psychologists and physiologists. Accounting for loudness of sounds is not particularly difficult: one need only postulate that the louder the sound, the more nerve fibers that fire (and the more nerve impulses per second in each fiber). Research has tended to verify this conclusion. The major questions arise in regard to pitch. Humans can hear an extremely wide range of sound frequencies, from as low as 12 to 20 cycles per second to as high as 15,000 or 20,000 cycles per second. How are these frequencies coded in the inner ear and transmitted to the brain?

Early theories on that question can be divided into two broad categories. *Telephone theories* simply assumed that the auditory nerve carries nerve impulses that fire at the same frequency as a sound itself:

date of place theorists has been the hair cells along the basilar membrane (see Figure 8), which were thought to resonate at different frequencies, thus transmitting their message about pitch to the brain. But this theory (which Helmholtz thought was correct) also cannot hold, because the fibers along the basilar membrane do not differ enough in size or mass to be significantly affected by different frequencies.

At the turn of the century, a special form of the place theory arose. The *traveling-wave hypothesis* states that sound frequency is coded at the place on the basilar membrane that vibrates most when the membrane is set in motion by a sound. A wave that travels from one end of the basilar membrane to the other is easy enough to imagine if you have ever snapped one end of a rope or a whip. A more detailed description of this process was provided by the ingenious research of Georg von Bekesy, who received the Nobel Prize in 1961 for his work on hearing.

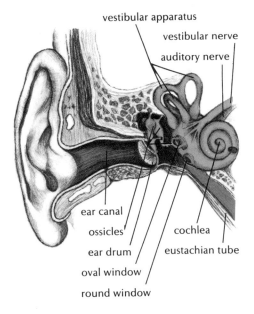

vestibular apparatus
vestibular nerve
auditory nerve

ear canal
ossicles
ear drum
oval window
round window

cochlea
eustachian tube

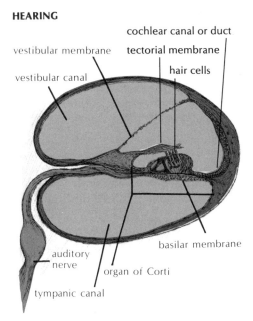

cochlear canal or duct
vestibular membrane
tectorial membrane
vestibular canal
hair cells

auditory nerve
organ of Corti
tympanic canal
basilar membrane

Figure 8. Cross-section of outer, middle, and inner ear (left) with a detail drawing (middle) of the cross-section of the cochlea.

The human ear is able to sense frequencies in the range of 20 to 20,000 cycles per second. Note, however, how the volume must be increased to be audible to the older ear. Zero decibels represents a barely audible sound. Sounds above 100 decibels can be deafening.

Cross Section of the Cochlea. There are three chambers within the cochlea: the *Vestibular Canal,* the *Cochlear Duct,* and the *Tympanic Canal.* In the cochlear duct, resting on the *basilar membrane* are the hearing receptors. Pressure waves initiated by the movements of the three-bone lever are set up in the cochlear fluid and the basilar membrane. These movements brush the hair cells against the overhanging *Tectorial Membrane,* producing the potentials that are transmitted from the hair cells by the auditory nerve.

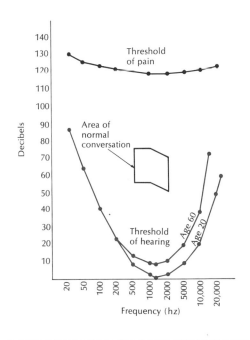

Decibels

Threshold of pain

Area of normal conversation

Threshold of hearing

Age 60
Age 20

Frequency (hz)

Investigator: G. von Békésy
Source, Date: "Current Status of Theories of Hearing," 1956
Subjects: Animals and human cadavers
Materials: Surgical preparations; artificial models of
hearing structures

One of Békésy's procedures was to build models of the hearing structures that duplicated the physical properties of real ones. By observing the action of these models, he was able to make inferences about how the actual basilar membrane works and how sound frequency is coded or transduced for the nervous system.

What Békésy discovered was that the basilar membrane varies in elasticity along its length. In fact, the membrane is about one hundred times stiffer near the base than at its apex. As a consequence of this gradual change in stiffness, different frequencies of sound produce the most vibratory activity (the "highest" wave) at different points along the membrane. High frequencies cause the strongest wave to appear at one place, while low frequencies produce the largest wave at another spot along the membrane.

Békésy's theory begins, logically enough, with sound entering the ear as a change in air pressure, which makes the eardrum vibrate. The eardrum passes the vibratory activity through the inner ear bones to the stirrup, which pushes in and out at the oval window. This window vibrates the inner ear fluid in the cochlea. The fluid vibrates the basal end of the basilar membrane and starts a traveling wave down its length. At the precise place of greatest vibration of the membrane, the membrane's hair cells send out an electrical pattern. This pattern sets off the nerve fibers that transmit the message to the brain, and the message concerns which part of the basilar membrane has been stimulated.

Even Békésy's revised place theory cannot account for sounds at the lowest frequencies we are able to hear. For these, theorists are still inclined to apply the telephone concept: they think very low frequencies are directly encoded by the frequency of nerve-cell discharges. Thus, the most recent theory of hearing again encompasses two older explanations, both of which were at least partly correct.

Several major questions about hearing remain unanswered. For example, it is still not fully understood how we can tell the difference between tones only a few cycles per second apart in frequency (say 1000 hz. versus 1003 hz.). Neither has the ability to distinguish complex sounds and noises from simple tones yet been explained satisfactorily.

Before we end our discussion of the ear, mention should be made of the cochlea's close neighbor, the *vestibular apparatus* (see Figure 8), which senses changes in balance and body orientation. This is one of the least understood sensory mechanisms, chiefly because it is hard to study an organ buried so deeply inside the head. There is little doubt, however, that the vestibular apparatus is extremely important, as the comments of one team of researchers show:

> One of the best demonstrations of the beautiful functioning of this system is something you may have tried with one of your neighbor's cats. A cat, suspended upside down by its feet and then released will manage to right itself and land on its feet. . . . It is clearly the vestibular system alone that performs this bodily orientation in mid-air. A cat whose vestibular organs have been destroyed lands in a heap when it is dropped. But a normal cat, dropped even in the dark, lands on its feet. [Alpern, Lawrence, and Wolsk, *Sensory Processes*]

Given the formidable complexity of vision and hearing, the other sensory systems (taste, touch, smell) seem easier to understand. At least the receptor mechanisms work more simply. On the other hand, the way these other systems transmit their messages to the brain is by no means simple. To illustrate, the *pattern-coding hypothesis* states that the transmission of sensory information in the gustatory (taste) sense takes place through patterns of cell activity, not just through the firing of single nerve fibers.

EXPERIMENTAL EVIDENCE

Investigator: C. Pfaffmann
Source, Date: "The Afferent Code for Sensory Quality,"
1959
Location: Brown University
Subjects: Rats
Materials: Electronic equipment; surgical preparations

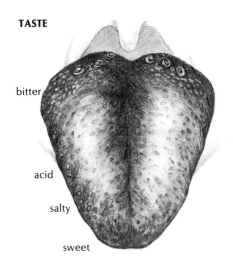

TASTE

bitter

acid

salty

sweet

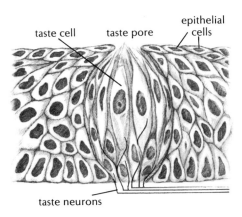

taste cell   taste pore   epithelial cells

taste neurons

Figure 9. Taste is the detection of certain chemical substances, in solution, by the receptors on the tongue, larynx, and pharynx. Experiments have shown that taste is a mixture of four specific responses: to salt, to sweet, to sour, and to bitter. The different parts of the tongue are primarily sensitive to one of the four different sensations: the front of the tongue to salt, the middle-front to sweet, the back to bitter, and the sides to sour. Because the taste buds are replenished every seven days, a burned tongue is only a temporary problem.

Man's tongue contains approximately 10,000 taste buds, with ten to fifteen sensory cells within each bud. These cells send out hairlike projections, through pores, to the tongue's surface. Around the sensory cells are wrapped endings of sensory nerves, which carry information from the sensory cell to the brain. Different parts of the tongue are primarily sensitive to different sensations: sweet, salty, bitter, and sour, or acid.

A single taste bud consists of a cluster of ten to fifteen sensory taste cells embedded in the epithelium of the tongue. Sensory nerve endings wrapped around the taste cells carry information to the brain.

In mammals the main nerve that conducts taste information away from the tongue to the brain is the afferent nerve called the *chorda tympani*. Pfaffmann inserted tiny microelectrodes in this nerve in rats and then placed specific taste stimuli on the animals' tongues. Sensitive electronic equipment amplified the electrical activity that took place in different fibers of the gustatory nerve as the tongue was stimulated by the different substances.

Pfaffmann studied nine different sensory nerve fibers in the rats' system and again found that different patterns of response arose when different substances were placed on the tongue. For example, a low concentration of salt might discharge only fiber A, while higher concentrations of salt might discharge fiber B as well as A, though nerve activity in A will remain higher than in B. At the same place on the tongue, low concentrations of sugar might activate B and higher concentrations both B and A, but B will fire more frequently than A. Either A or B can be zero. What is important is the relative amount of activity in parallel fibers.

These findings have forced a modification of Muller's older doctrine of the specific energies of nerves.

SKIN SENSES

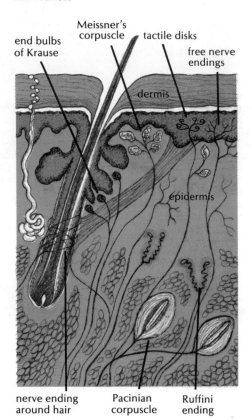

Figure 10. A graphic representation of a section of skin showing the various structures associated with the skin senses. Although several different types of receptors are found in the epidermis of the skin, no clear correlation between a specific sensation (pain, cold, warmth, touch) and a particular type of receptor has been found. Most recent research tends to indicate that the different skin sensations are due to stimulation of receptive sites whose nerve fibers vary in diameter and terminate in different parts of the central nervous system. The receptors for the skin senses are *Free Nerve Endings* and *Nerve Endings around Hair,* and *Meissner's and Pacinian Corpuscles.*

It appears that differential sensitivity of nerves rather than absolute sensitivity is the rule. In other words, taste is coded in terms of relative activity between nerve fibers rather than by fibers tuned exclusively to sense quality. Nevertheless, the basic idea of Muller still stands: The sensory system produces specific spatial patterns that correspond to the qualities of taste.

In the late 1800s a German physiologist, Max von Frey (1852–1932), made some important early studies on the skin senses. From his examination of receptiv-ity at different spots on the body, he concluded that there were four dimensions of cutaneous sensitivity: touch, pressure, temperature, and pain. However, modern researchers have shown—again—that this early theory is too simple. Most individual skin receptors respond to all forms of cutaneous stimulation, though some respond in different ways, have different thresholds, and use different pathways for transmitting their message to the brain. Findings on this subject suggest that the pattern-coding hypothesis is probably as relevant for cutaneous sensitivity as it is for taste.

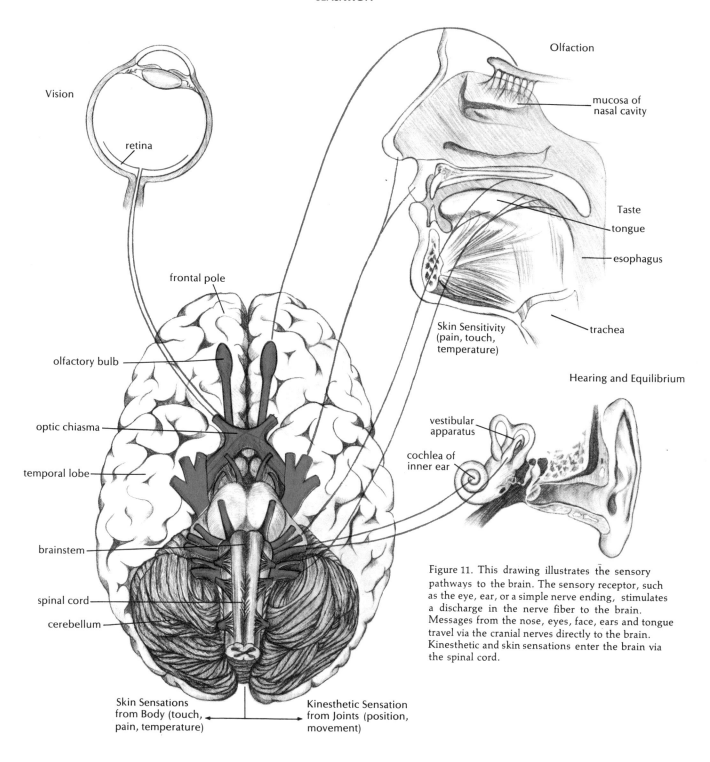

Vision

retina

Olfaction

mucosa of
nasal cavity

Taste

tongue

esophagus

frontal pole

Skin Sensitivity
(pain, touch,
temperature)

trachea

olfactory bulb

Hearing and Equilibrium

optic chiasma

vestibular
apparatus

temporal lobe

cochlea of
inner ear

brainstem

spinal cord

cerebellum

Skin Sensations
from Body (touch,
pain, temperature)

Kinesthetic Sensation
from Joints (position,
movement)

Figure 11. This drawing illustrates the sensory
pathways to the brain. The sensory receptor, such
as the eye, ear, or a simple nerve ending, stimulates
a discharge in the nerve fiber to the brain.
Messages from the nose, eyes, face, ears and tongue
travel via the cranial nerves directly to the brain.
Kinesthetic and skin sensations enter the brain via
the spinal cord.

SMELL

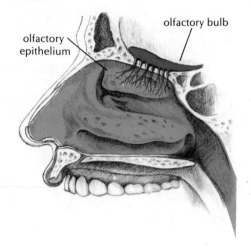

olfactory epithelium

olfactory bulb

Figure 12. Impulses conveying the sense of smell arise from nerve cells embedded in the olfactory epithelium at the top of the nasal passage and travel only a very short distance to the olfactory bulb of the brain.

Smell, the sense that so much of the animal kingdom depends on, still presents great mysteries. Although there is at least some agreement among experts about the major dimensions of each of the other senses, there is as yet no consensus on even the basic characteristics of smells. Several classification systems have been proposed, but none is generally accepted.

One of the more interesting research efforts on smell was carried out in the 1960s by John Amoore and his associates, who postulated that the crucial cue for differences in smell are the sizes and shapes of the molecules of the substance that is smelled. Their results provided some support for the hypothesis.

It is also known that the brain processes involved in smell are located in a different and, in evolutionary terms, much older part of the brain (specifically, in the *telencephalic nuclei*) than those associated with the other senses. However, the actual workings of the olfactory sense and the relationships among the myriad different smells at the level of process have yet to be determined.

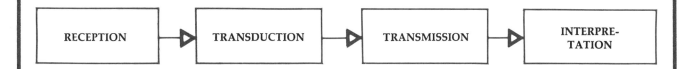

| RECEPTION | ▷ | TRANSDUCTION | ▷ | TRANSMISSION | ▷ | INTERPRE-TATION |

PUTTING IT TOGETHER: The Senses

Using sensory information about the environment is a process in which the physical stimuli impinge upon bodily receptors which decode the energy into neural impulses, transmitting the information to the brain where it may be further analyzed and interpreted.

Reception occurs at specific receptor organs, such as the eyes, ears, tongue and nose. Each receptor organ transduces the physical energy into neural energy through specialized receptor components such as the rods and cones in the retina of the eye, the Organ of Corti in the inner ear, the taste buds on the tongue and the olfactory epithelium in the nose.

In the process of *transduction*, some encoding of information takes place. For example, there is some quality coding for color characteristics in the rods and cones of the eye.

The next step is *transmission* of the transduced energy to sensory projection areas in the cortex of the brain. For example, visual information is transmitted via the optic nerve to the visual cortex and auditory information is transmitted via the auditory nerve to the auditory cortex.

Auditory information is probably coded by means of a traveling wave on the basilar membrane to send information about physical frequency over appropriate parts of the auditory nerve. Varieties in the quality of taste are encoded through patterns of firing in the chorda tympani.

Once information has arrived at the appropriate cortical sensory projection areas, it is integrated and *interpreted* meaningfully in terms of information which has previously been stored in the brain.

WHAT'S ACCEPTED AND WHAT'S DEBATED

1. WHAT'S ACCEPTED . . .

1. Color vision involves both component and opponent sensory coding processes.

2. Specific cortical cells interpret specific form and pattern dimensions of sensory stimuli, at least in some species.

3. There is no one-to-one (isomorphic) relationship between sense-receptor activity and what is perceived.

4. Variation in stimulation is a psychological and physiological need; sensory deprivation leads to mental disturbance and dysfunction.

5. The traveling-wave theory, combined with the telephone theory for low frequencies, can account for the basic facts about how pitch is heard.

6. The transmission of sensory information in several modalities takes place through patterns of nerve-cell activity, not through the activity of single nerve cells.

2. WHAT'S DEBATED . . .

1. How fine differences in sound frequencies are discriminated, and how complex sounds are coded neurally.

2. How cutaneous sense qualities are coded and transmitted to the brain.

3. How smelling works, and even the basic dimensions and qualities of the possible odors.

ISSUE: ACUPUNCTURE

Our understanding of the workings of our senses is already highly developed, as this unit shows. But recently psychologists working in this field have been presented with a new challenge: how to explain *acupuncture.*

Acupuncture has been used in Chinese medicine for over 2000 years. Physicians there are able to cure symptoms and ease pain by the insertion of thin needles at very precise points in a patient's body. The needles may range from half an inch to several inches in length. The treatment is accomplished both by the manner in which the needles are twirled and vibrated and by the depth to which the needles are penetrated. Major operations have been performed on a fully conscious subject after the insertion of a few needles at appropriate points in the body. Usually these insertion points seem entirely unrelated to the part of the body that is being operated on.

The western world has long scoffed at acupuncture, regarding it as a form of hypnosis at best and trickery at worst. Western medicine derives from the systematic, rational study of physiology, biochemistry, and physics. Traditional Chinese medicine, on the other hand, derives from philosophy and religion. The Chinese explanation of how acupuncture works seems to Westerners more a matter of obscure theology than science. In the Chinese theory, a life energy called *Ch'i* flows through the body. This life force is controlled by *yin* (the spirits) and *yang* (the blood), two universal opposites. *Yin* represents negative forces and *yang* positive forces. All organs of the body are divided between *yin* and *yang,* and the life energy flows from organ to organ through a network of meridians (channels) beneath the skin. Arrayed along these meridians are about 365 specific points that the acupuncturist may pierce to correct imbalances in the flow of energy, bringing *yin* and *yang* into harmony again. In treating a stomach ulcer, for example, he inserts the needle at a point situated above the division between the second and third toe. Since Western science knows of no possible basis for these supposed energy flows or meridians, it is hardly surprising that acupuncture has traditionally been discounted in our medicine.

But acupuncture works. Americans were rapidly made aware of this when U.S.-Chinese relationships improved in the seventies and scientists and journalists were allowed to visit China. One of them, James Reston of *The New York Times,* suffered an acute appendicitis on arrival, and was treated with acupuncture. So successful was the procedure that he wrote glowing accounts of the method for his newspaper. Teams of American physicians visited China soon afterward, and reported astounding achievements for acupuncture. In one case they witnessed the removal of a lung in which acupuncture was used as an anaesthetic. The acupuncturist merely inserted a single needle in the patient's left forearm and vibrated it to and fro for some twenty minutes. The surgeon then made a fourteen-inch incision across the patient's breastbone, cut through several ribs, and inserted a chest retractor to spread open the rib cage and expose the lung. The patient, anaesthetized by nothing more than a single needle in his arm, kept up a steady banter with the surgeon and even paused to eat some fruit during the operation.

The American physicians witnessed many similar operations. In most cases, however, they noted that the patient was also equipped with a volume of the thoughts of Chairman Mao. Might the patient's belief in Mao exercise an autohypnotic effect, they wondered? Apparently not: the Chinese host commented that "We have been producing the same effect in the rabbit and the cat, and as far as we know, they have not been influenced by the thoughts of Chairman Mao."

The Chinese use acupuncture not only for the relief of pain, but also to cure or relieve the symptoms of a variety of other diseases ranging from malaria to hypertension. Although the claims have not been verified by Western observers, the Chinese have recorded success in curing polio with acupuncture, and even claim to have restored sight to 11 persons who had been blind for up to 40 years.

How does acupuncture work? Psychologists and physiologists are still baffled. However, the most popular explanation centers around the *gate-control theory* of pain proposed in 1965 by McGill University psychologist Ronald Melzack and London physiologist Patrick Wall. In contrast to the more traditional, *specificity theory* of pain which postulated specific pain receptors in the body as sending pain signals directly to a pain center in the brain (much like a telephone switchboard), the gate-control theory proposes that the pain signals are sent from the body to the spinal cord and brain through a dynamic and changing process. This process is controlled by a series of gate-like mechanisms in the body's pain-signaling system.

A closed gate prevents any pain signals from reaching the brain. Nerve impulses in the large and small fibers of each sensory nerve can open or close gates to varying degrees. Large-diameter fibers tend to close gates and reduce pain, small-diameter fibers to open them and increase pain. Fibers descending from the reticular formation of the brain stem as well as fibers from the brain cortex are also capable of controlling gates.

Acupuncture may change pain signals in several ways. The small electric current passed from the needles to the skin and tissues beneath it tends to activate more large fibers—which close gates and reduce pain—than small fibers. This may explain the decrease in pain at the place where the needles are inserted.

Acupuncture may lessen pain at sites of the body far from the needles. It is generally known that nerve cells in the reticular formation receive signals from wide areas of the body, and when certain points in the reticular formation of the brain stem are electrically stimulated, pain may be decreased over a large area of the body.

Fear and anxiety are known to increase perception of pain. Nerve fibers that descend from the cortex of the brain, which controls anxiety, memory, attention, etc. can block pain signals. If pain can be increased by anxiety, it can be reduced by diminishing the anxiety, both by physiological means (the insertion of a needle) or by psychological means (the patient's expectation plus the acupuncturist's suggestions that the procedure will work).

Although the gate-control theory may explain how acupuncture can abolish pain at the site of insertions, over a large area of the body, and diminish anxiety, scientists still do not understand how major surgery, such as the removal of organs, can be performed with acupuncture as the sole anaesthetic.

At present, we have no final answers. But as psychologists and physiologists unravel the mystery, they may find that we have enhanced our understanding of the senses. As happens so often in the development of a science, we have reached a point at which our existing theories cannot accommodate new facts—facts so contrary to our preconceived notions that we rejected them for centuries.

Unit 32

Sleep and Dreams

OVERVIEW

Data obtained from one of the more recently developed research areas in psychology and physiology is discussed. The EEG machine, and the discovery some twenty years ago that dreaming has reliable physiological correlates, have opened up whole new vistas of knowledge about the nature of sleep and dreams. Despite these new discoveries, the basic functions of sleep and dreaming remain largely fascinating mysteries.

UNIT OUTLINE

DEFINITION AND BACKGROUND
1. *Definition:* sleep is a natural, temporary, periodic lessening of physical activity, feeling, and thought that results in a cessation of consciousness; dreams are the thoughts, images, and emotions that occur during sleep.
2. *Background:* Nathaniel Kleitman (1895–   ) and Eugene Aserinsky (1921–   ).

QUESTIONS AND EVIDENCE
1. What happens to the body during sleep?
Hypotheses:
    a. *Stages:* sleep occurs in different stages. **557**
    b. *Need:* depriving a person of sleep or dreams will affect his physiological and psychological functioning. **558**
2. What do people dream about?
Hypotheses:
    a. *Recent-experience:* the content of dreams is determined mainly by the daily experiences and concerns of the dreamer. **562**
    b. *Nightmare:* true nightmares are qualitatively different from ordinary dreams and occur during a different stage of sleep. **562**
3. Can we retain information received while we're asleep?
Hypotheses:
    a. *State-specific:* suggestions heard during sleep may be obeyed during the state of sleep, and even during later sleeping sessions—though the subject will remember nothing of these experiences when awake. **563**

IMPORTANT CONCEPTS

	page
brain waves	**556**
dreams	**556**
sleep	**556**

Patterns for sleep and dreams differ among individuals. Age is one of the variables associated with these differences.

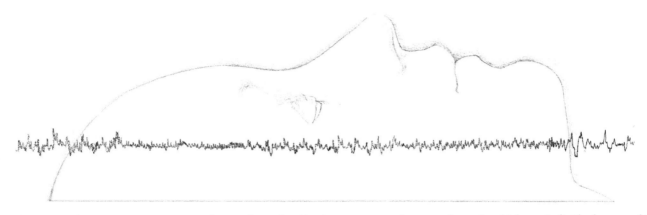

Changes in brain-wave patterns can be used to identify the sequence of stages through which an individual goes while sleeping.

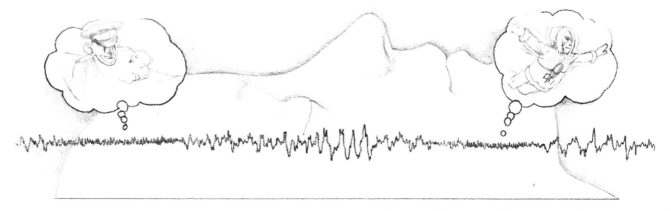

Evidence indicates that most dreaming occurs during a stage of sleep that is easily monitored by patterns of brain waves and eye movements.

32. Sleep and Dreams   555

DEFINITION AND BACKGROUND

A DEFINITION of sleep is *a natural, temporary, periodic lessening of physical activity, feeling, and thought that results in a cessation of consciousness.* Dreams are *the thoughts, images, and emotions that occur during sleep.* Unfortunately, these objective definitions fail to convey the subjective flavor of sleep and dreams—the fondness with which most of us look forward to or back on a good night's sleep, for instance, and the intriguing nature of dreams. Perhaps not everyone is intrigued by dreams in general, but have you ever met a person who wasn't fascinated by his own?

In the last twenty years or so, a number of new techniques have been discovered for the scientific study of sleep and dreaming. Interpreting the content of dreams, however, is still at least as much an art as a science. This unit will FOCUS on the physiological and psychological functions of sleep and dreams, treating interpretations of dream content only peripherally.

BACKGROUND: NATHANIEL KLEITMAN (1895–) AND EUGENE ASERINSKY (1921–)

In 1953 Nathaniel Kleitman, a well-known sleep researcher, and Eugene Aserinsky, a fellow in physiology, reported a series of experiments at the University of Chicago that led to their discovery of a way to determine when someone is dreaming. They used the electroencephalograph (EEG), which had been developed by Hans Berger in 1929 to measure electrical activity at the surface of the brain. With this device, electrical impulses from electrodes attached to certain points on the scalp are transmitted to a machine that amplifies and reproduces them as a series of waves. The result is a printed record.

Kleitman and Aserinsky were investigating the sleep of infants when a question occurred to them: What do the eyes do while the eyelids are closed in sleep? Aserinsky began to watch the movements of the infants' eyes and discovered that eye movements continued after body movements had almost completely ceased. To determine whether eye movement was related to depth of sleep, Kleitman and Aserinsky made EEG recordings of sleeping adults.

Kleitman and Aserinsky placed electrodes near the eye in such a way that a graph of the eye movements was observable on the moving paper along with the EEG. They found there were periods of very rapid eye movements (REMs, for short). When they awakened an adult during periods of REM, he usually reported having a dream: during periods with no REM the subjects reported very few dreams. Dreams were reported in 74 percent of the awakenings during REM sleep, but in only 7 percent of the non-REM awakenings.

Kleitman and Aserinsky determined that a person averages four dreams a night. Furthermore, contrary to the popular notion that dreams were a kind of millisecond adventure, Kleitman and W. C. Dement inferred from their research several years later that dreams occur in real time: in other words, a dream that seems to take eight to ten minutes probably does last that long.

Figure 1. Physiologist Nathaniel Kleitman conducted landmark research on sleep/wake patterns.

HYPOTHESES	STAGES	NEED
DESCRIPTIVE EVIDENCE	ASSESS: EEG and REM activity of sleeping subjects	ASSESS: 1. behavior follow-ing sleep deprivation 2. behavioral and physiologi-cal measures following REM sleep (dream) deprivation
EXPERIMENTAL EVIDENCE		

As important as the specific findings was the dis-covery of a method for studying dreams experimental-ly. The new techniques opened fresh possibilities for research in the psychology of sleep and dreams and gave hope for answers to some age-old questions.

QUESTIONS AND EVIDENCE

1. What happens to the body during sleep?

2. What do people dream about?

3. Can we retain information received while we're asleep?

1. WHAT HAPPENS TO THE BODY DURING SLEEP?

The *stages hypothesis* states that sleep occurs in different stages. We speak of being awake or being asleep as if these two words implied two separate states of existence, but sleep is a matter of degree. It seems reasonable to suppose that there is a con-tinuum running from full wakefulness to deep sleep. In 1957 an EEG investigation of sleep led to a four-stage classification of sleep levels that was quickly accepted and, with little modification, is still used today.

DESCRIPTIVE EVIDENCE

Investigators: W. C. Dement and N. Kleitman
Source, Date: "The Relation of Eye Movements During Sleep
to Dream Activity: An Objective Method for the Study of
Dreaming," 1957
Location: University of Chicago
Subjects: 26 male and 7 female adults
Materials: EEG and body-movement recorders

The EEG was used to determine the frequency and quantity of REMs and body movements throughout sleep. REM was used as an objective measure of dream activity. The EEG pattern of brain waves fell into four categories as shown in Figure 4. Stage 1 was characterized by brain waves with low voltage and high frequency; there were no spindle bursts (groups of high voltage, high frequency waves). Stage 2 waves showed spindle activity against a low voltage back-ground. Stage 3 waves were between stages 2 and 4, having high voltage, slow waves, and some spindling. Stage 4 waves were slow, with high voltage.

Each subject showed periods of REM with the eyes synchronized and moving in all directions. Eye-movement periods usually were longer late in the night. REM periods occurred in cycles with about one-half-hour to one-hour intervals between the end of one period and the beginning of the next.

REM occurred only during stage 1 sleep, never during stages 2, 3, or 4. However, stage 1 sleep sometimes occurred without REM. For example, the first REM period did not begin until about an hour after the subjects had gone to sleep. During the early part of that hour, there were no rapid eye movements even though the subjects' EEGs showed the brain waves of stage 1 sleep. If the subjects were awakened at that time, they reported reveries, not dreams, and said that they were not really asleep.

After the onset of stage 1 sleep, the subjects progressed rapidly to stage 4. Soon the EEGs showed an

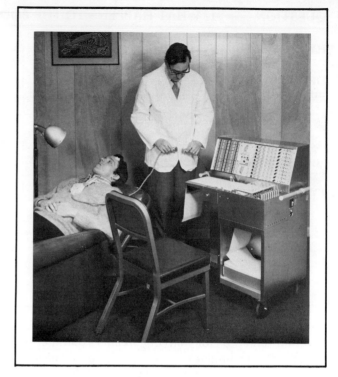

Figure 3. The electroencephalograph (EEG) records electrical activity in the brain through electrodes attached to the scalp. Specific patterns can be used to identify dreaming and the various stages of sleep.

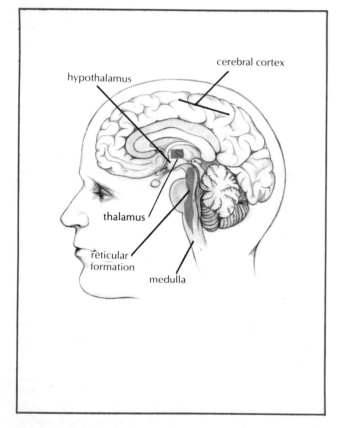

Figure 2. Brain structures involved in sleep and dreams. The upper portion of the reticular formation and portions of the hypothalamus activate the cortex, maintaining the organism in a waking state. Another portion of the reticular formation with associated areas of the thalamus and hypothalamus are involved in nonREM sleep. The area of the reticular formation in the medulla may be involved in REM sleep.

abrupt return to stage 2 or 3, then to stage 1 with REM. After this first REM period stage 3 or 4 was reached through stage 2, again followed by an abrupt progression to the second incident of stage 1 with an REM period. The cycle recurred throughout the night.

Body movements also underwent cyclic variations. Gross body movements occurred during stages 2, 3, and 4 but ceased abruptly when REM began and resumed when REM stopped. During REM only very slight movements of the limbs and fingers occurred.

We spend more time dreaming than was previously recognized. Apparently, people dream several times every night, for periods ranging from a few minutes to a couple of hours. See Figure 5.

Clearly, sleep is a basic human need. The *need hypothesis* states that depriving a person of sleep or dreams will affect his physiological and psychological functioning. Although all studies of sleep deprivation

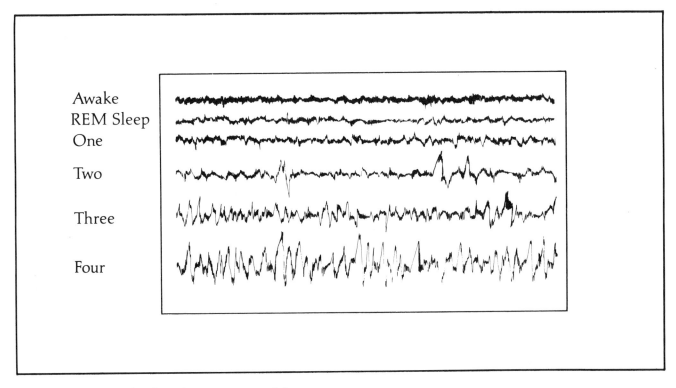

Figure 4. EEG patterns identifying the various stages of sleep.

tend to confirm the hypothesis, the effects noted vary from one investigation to the next. For example, some studies suggest that long periods without sleep lead to major psychological disorganization, but the subject in the study described below, who underwent one of the longest sleep deprivations on record, showed no delusions, hallucinations, or delirium.

DESCRIPTIVE EVIDENCE

Investigators: L. C. Johnson, E. S. Slye, W. Dement, and G. Gulevich
Source, Date: "Psychiatric and EEG Observations on a Case of Prolonged (264 Hours) Wakefulness," 1966
Subject: Seventeen-year-old male high-school student
Materials: EEG, recorder for heart rate, skin temperature, skin resistance, and respiration, and EMG (electromyogram, which measures muscular activity)

Randy Gardner, the subject, deprived himself of sleep for 264 hours as a research project for a science fair. Every six hours, two friends who were constantly with him administered tests to determine his general performance and his ability to respond to stimuli. Systematic physiological data were obtained only at 236 hours and 249 hours of deprivation. After deprivation, during recovery, many measurements were taken.

At 236 and 249 hours Randy's heart rate was fast and his temperature and skin resistance were low, suggesting autonomic activation. Autonomic response to sounds was depressed during deprivation. After the onset of the first recovery sleep there was a rapid rise in skin temperature and a decrease in heart rate.

On the first three recovery nights Randy showed more slow-wave sleep (especially stage 4) and REM sleep than he did after full recovery from the deprivation. On the first and second recovery nights the REM sleep was often interrupted by stage 2 sleep. The EMG recorded no muscular activity on the first recovery sleep night, but after that the usual pattern occurred—muscle activity during slow-wave sleep and not during REM sleep.

Comparisons of these results with earlier ones following shorter deprivations suggests that unresponsiveness to stimuli increases as deprivation is extended. The physiological effects of sleep deprivation appear early, with the final effects being autonomic arousal and depression of the central nervous system.

Randy became noticeably irritable on the fourth and fifth days of wakefulness, and the irritability continued to increase as deprivation went on. He

Figure 5. REM sleep, about 50 percent of the newborn's sleep, stabilizes at about 25 percent by the age of ten.

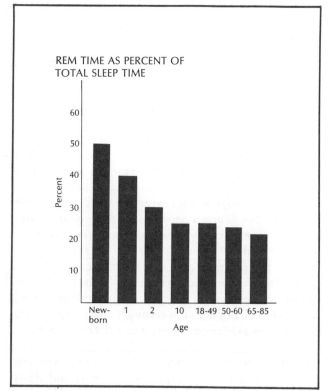

REM TIME AS PERCENT OF
TOTAL SLEEP TIME

showed considerable resentment at the constant questions about his wakefulness. After a psychiatric interview at 262 hours of wakefulness, the investigators reported: "Throughout the vigil and particularly toward the end, lack of movement and stimulation brought on extreme drowsiness with a concomitant deterioration in performance, while movement, stimulation, and novel experiences, on the other hand, were almost always associated with a return of virtually normal function." Some of the minor neurological signs that developed were finger tremor, hyperactive reflexes, and drooping eyelids; these were completely reversed a week after the first recovery night.

Previous investigators had suggested that a sleep-deprivation psychosis exists. But Randy Gardner was able to cope with the ego-disorganizing effects of sleep deprivation very successfully. At no time was there evidence of delusions, hallucinations, or delirium. Randy was young, healthy, and had the total support of his family and of the social and scientific community.

Dream deprivation as an experimental procedure has been possible only since the discovery of the relation between dreaming and rapid eye movement (REM) sleep. On the average most people experience stage 1 REM sleep for about ninety minutes total each night. This holds even for persons who claim never to dream at all; they simply don't recall dreaming. When such people are awakened during REM sleep periods, they almost invariably report dreams.

Are there serious after-effects if dreaming is prevented? Is dreaming an important manifestation of brain functioning, or is it a by-product of recovery activity going on during sleep? Many investigators have attempted to deprive subjects of REM sleep in order to deprive them of dreaming.

Physiological effects of REM deprivation include an increase in the number of required awakenings during successive nights of deprivation and, usually, an increase in REM time on nights following deprivation. Psychological effects vary, however, and the precise effects have been controversial. In an effort to get more clear-cut results, some investigators have used as subjects psychotic patients, who are already psychologically vulnerable.

DESCRIPTIVE EVIDENCE

Investigators: G. W. Vogel and A. C. Traub; P. Ben-Horen and G. M. Meyers

Source, Date: "REM Deprivation: I. The Effect on Schizophrenic Patients; II. The Effect on Depressed Patients," 1968

Location: University of Chicago, Michael Reese Hospital

Subjects: Chronic schizophrenics, 4 men and 1 woman, ages thirty-one to thirty-seven; psychotically depressed patients, 4 women and 1 man, ages forty-nine to sixty-two

Materials: EEG, battery of psychological tests, standardized interviews, and behavior-rating schedule

The schizophrenic subjects were observed for two to three base-line nights, seven REM deprivation nights, and five recovery nights. Like normal subjects in previous investigations, these people showed a clear tendency in successive REM deprivation nights to require more awakenings, indicating that more REM periods were begun each night. Also, after deprivation the percentage of the night spent in REM sleep was higher than usual for several recovery nights. As deprivation continued, the subjects were harder to wake both at the beginning of an REM period and in the morning at their usual time of awakening. There were no meaningful psychological changes during or after dream deprivation, according to the researchers.

The depressed patients were treated the same way as the schizophrenics. REM deprivation had no adverse effects on them. Two subjects, both of whom showed considerable REM rebound on postdeprivation nights, even improved clinically to the point of being discharged from the hospital. Three subjects who did not show REM rebound made no significant clinical gains.

Because of the small samples and the variables inherent in such experiments, these results are only suggestive, not conclusive. But it was clear that none of these patients showed adverse psychological effects or, indeed, any clear-cut effects that could be ascribed confidently to lack of REM sleep.

Because deprivation causes the physiological mechanisms of the brain to increase their dream attempts, however, it does seem that dreaming is both physiologically and psychologically important. Some investigators have suggested that dreams may reorganize memories, especially those with emotional content—that is, dreams may serve a kind of housekeeping function. The best guess at this time is that stage 1 REM sleep may have primarily psychological functions, while stage 4 deep sleep restores the biochemical balance necessary for physiological well-being.

2. WHAT DO PEOPLE DREAM ABOUT?

Whatever function dreams may have, it is evident that they are not empty. An outsider may record REMs, but for the sleeper himself it is the perceived content that distinguishes dreaming from the other stages of sleep.

Freud believed that the most important contents of dreams are the symbols released by repressed sexual impulses. There is no denying that dreams can be

QUESTION	2. WHAT DO PEOPLE DREAM ABOUT?	
HYPOTHESES	**RECENT EXPERIENCES**	**NIGHTMARES**
DESCRIPTIVE EVIDENCE	ASSESS: content of large number of dreams	ASSESS: relationship of nightmares to stages of sleep
EXPERIMENTAL EVIDENCE		

highly emotional, sexual, and symbolic. But Freud's conclusions were based mainly on dreams obtained from disturbed individuals, and there are no well-defined rules for psychoanalytic interpretation of a dream. Any convex (pointed) surface may be interpreted as a male sexual symbol, any concave (hollowed out) surface as a female sexual symbol. Perhaps the greatest myth to develop out of Freudian dream interpretations was the incorrect notion that the contents of a dream can be interpreted independently of the dreamer and his experiences.

The *recent-experiences hypothesis* states that the content of dreams is determined mainly by the daily experiences and concerns of the dreamer. Although the hypothesis implies that people usually dream about commonplace sorts of things (rather than about deep intrapsychic conflicts), it does not deny that dreams can be emotional, exciting, and meaningful. The study described below summarizes the contents of thousands of dreams.

DESCRIPTIVE EVIDENCE

Investigator: C. S. Hall
Source, Date: "What People Dream About," 1951
Location: Western Reserve University
Subjects: Educated adults
Materials: Questionnaires describing 10,000 dreams

Hall classified the reported dreams according to setting, cast of characters, plot, emotions, and color. The settings tended to be common, with play or recreational surroundings occurring more often than those associated with work or school.

In 15 percent of the dreams the dreamer was by himself. In the remaining dreams, 43 percent of the persons other than the dreamer were strangers to the dreamer, 37 percent were friends or acquaintances, and 19 percent were relatives. Only 1 percent of the people in the dreams were public figures. Young people tended to dream about their peers, whereas older people dreamed more about their families. As a rule, children dreamed about their parents and parents about their children. Wives dreamed about their husbands, husbands about their wives.

Plots varied considerably, but there were tendencies

toward more play than work, more traveling than staying in the same place, more aggressive acts than friendly ones. Many of the dreams appeared to concern gratification, particularly of sexual and aggressive impulses. These findings harmonize with Freudian theory.

Apprehension was the dominant emotion in 40 percent of the reported dreams. Anger, excitement, and happiness each occurred in 18 percent of the dreams. Color was reported in 29 percent of the 3,000 dreams for which this question was asked. Color seemed to be unpredictably random in dreams, though apparently some people always dream in color and others never do so.

These reported dreams of common things from dreamers' recent experiences may or may not be typical. Most dreaming is forgotten, and it is possible that the characteristics of forgotten dreams are quite different from those of remembered ones.

What about the dreams that are called nightmares? The *nightmare hypothesis* states that true nightmares are qualitatively different from ordinary dreams and occur during a different stage of sleep.

DESCRIPTIVE EVIDENCE

Investigators: C. Fisher, J. V. Byrne, A. Edwards, and
*   E. Kahn*
Source, Date: "REM and NREM Nightmares," 1970
Location: Mount Sinai Hospital, New York
Subjects: 23 female and 14 male subjects with histories of
*   nightmares*
Materials: Equipment to measure EEG waves, REMs, heart
*   rate, and respiration rate and to record voices*

The subjects were selected from those who answered a newspaper ad soliciting people who frequently had nightmares. They came to the lab on certain nights, were wired for physiological measures, and then slept. The experimenters did not wake them, but when a subject spontaneously had a nightmare and woke up, he or she was immediately questioned about the nightmare. The information in the answers was then compared with the record of the subject's reactions during the nightmare.

In 150 nights of observation, two kinds of experiences emerged. Eleven subjects awoke during stage 1 REM experiences a total of twenty-two times; six subjects awoke during stage 4 experiences fifty times. The stage 1 REM experiences were vivid and sometimes unpleasant dreams but comparatively mild; during them, the subjects' physiological measures stayed relatively normal. The stage 4 experiences, however, were true nightmares with great emotional arousal in both feelings and physiological measures. Several times subjects sat straight up in bed and let out bloodcurdling screams, then awakened in panic. These experiences were short, with no warning on the EEG monitor or any other indicator. On awakening in considerable panic or discomfort, subjects usually did not report in detail the visual content or events of the dream but rather spoke of a single terrifying scene that was neither vivid nor clear. The longer a subject had been in stage 4 sleep, the more intense the nightmare.

when a subject is really asleep. Still, subjective experience keeps alive the hope that we can retain information received while we're asleep.

The *state-specific hypothesis* says that suggestions heard during sleep may be obeyed during the state of sleep, and even during later sleeping sessions—though the subject will remember nothing of these experiences when awake.

DESCRIPTIVE EVIDENCE

Investigators: F. J. Evans, L. Gustafson, D. O'Connell, M. Orne, and R. Shor
Source, Date: "Verbally Induced Behavioral Responses During Sleep," 1970
Location: University of Pennsylvania
Subjects: 19 male student nurses
Materials: EEG and other equipment

QUESTION	3. CAN WE RETAIN INFORMATION RECEIVED WHILE WE'RE ASLEEP?
HYPOTHESES	STATE-SPECIFIC
DESCRIPTIVE EVIDENCE	ASSESS: subject's responsiveness while asleep or awake to suggestions given during stage 1 sleep
EXPERIMENTAL EVIDENCE	

3. CAN WE RETAIN INFORMATION RECEIVED WHILE WE'RE ASLEEP?

In the early 1950s the idea of learning while asleep became very popular, probably as a result of reports of effective sleep learning from the Soviet Union. Although some commercial establishments sold tape machines designed to provide time-saving, passive sleep learning, American research laboratories could provide no confirmation for the phenomenon. A study conducted in 1956 by Emmons and Simon produced evidence that the closer to actual sleep a subject is when information is presented, the less he will recall, and that learning does not occur at all

The subjects were told they were participating in a study of sleep cycles and received no indication that they were to be given suggestions while asleep. They were asked to sleep only about four hours the night before the study, so that they would readily fall asleep in the laboratory. As each subject slept, his EEGs were monitored, and suggestions were given to him only during emergent stage 1 sleep (that is, while he was coming out of stage 2 or 3). Great care was exercised to ensure that the suggestions were not given when alpha waves (a possible sign of awakening) were present. A typical suggestion was, "Whenever I say the word 'itch,' your nose will feel itchy until you scratch it." The cue word ("itch") was repeated during each stage 1 period that occurred after the suggestion had been made. Two new suggestions, in separate sleeping periods, were given to the subject on each of two nights.

Sixteen of the nineteen subjects responded in some way to the cue words, even though they were asleep both at the time of the suggestion and at the time of the response. On the average, a clear and appropriate response was observed to one out of five cues. When the researchers presented the cue words to the sub-jects the next day, while they were awake, they did not respond in the prescribed manner. Nor did they have any recollection of the suggestions or cues when they were asked about them at the end of the study. However, the subjects did respond to the first-night cues while asleep on the second night without being given the suggestion again—in fact, they still responded to the same cues five months later! The waking amnesia for sleep-acquired material seems very similar to the amnesia that follows hypnosis.

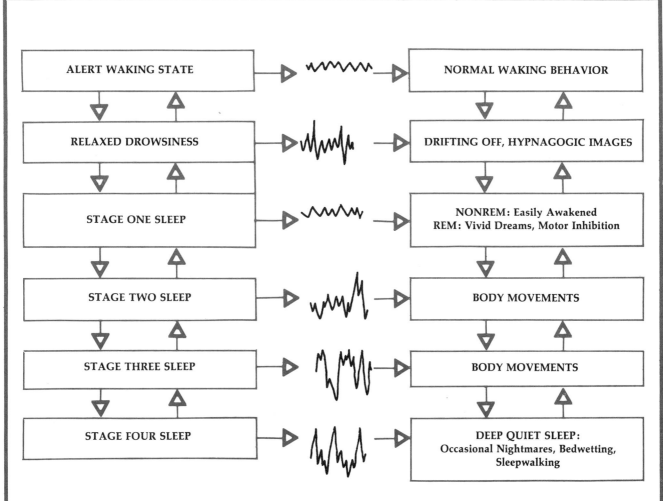

ALERT WAKING STATE		NORMAL WAKING BEHAVIOR
RELAXED DROWSINESS		DRIFTING OFF, HYPNAGOGIC IMAGES
STAGE ONE SLEEP		NONREM: Easily Awakened REM: Vivid Dreams, Motor Inhibition
STAGE TWO SLEEP		BODY MOVEMENTS
STAGE THREE SLEEP		BODY MOVEMENTS
STAGE FOUR SLEEP		DEEP QUIET SLEEP: Occasional Nightmares, Bedwetting, Sleepwalking

PUTTING IT TOGETHER: Sleep and Dreams

At least *four different stages of sleep* are identifiable by their *EEG patterns*, with dreaming identified by the combination of stage one EEG and rapid eye movements. Dreaming does not usually occur during the onset of sleep. Rather, it follows the first complete cycle through the various stages with a return to stage one. There seems to be a general need for sleep and especially that state during which dreams occur, but it remains unclear what their functions are.

In general most dreams seem to derive from recent experiences. Nightmares are physiologically different from ordinary dreams and occur during stage four sleep.

Whatever learning may occur during sleep appears to be state-specific. Some information can apparently be learned while drowsy, but the procedure may prevent sleep and is therefore inefficient. Some information heard during stage one sleep may be retrieved later while in stage one sleep but is not available to consciousness while awake.

WHAT'S ACCEPTED AND WHAT'S DEBATED

1. WHAT'S ACCEPTED . . .

1. EEG activity shows the relative depth of sleep, and REMs usually indicate when a person is dreaming.
2. The average amount of sleep people need varies with age and among individuals.
3. The contents of dreams vary greatly but are predominantly recent past experiences and emotions of the individual.
4. True nightmares are different in most respects from ordinary dreams.

2. WHAT'S DEBATED . . .

1. What the specific functions of the different stages of sleep are.
2. The function of dreaming (if it has one).
3. The quantity and quality of NREM sleep.
4. How dream content is related to emotional and sexual matters, and to repression.
5. Whether sleep-learning is possible for waking use.

ISSUE: SLEEPWALKING, NIGHTMARES AND BIOLOGICAL CLOCKS

The systematic study of sleep has been a major focus of psychological research for little over a decade, but we have already learned a great deal about the subject. The various discoveries recounted in this unit—from the detection of EEG rhythms marking stages of sleep to the finding that nightmares and dreams are very different phenomena—are fascinating to scientists and laymen alike. It is true that our understanding of sleep and dreams is still quite incomplete. But modern research techniques have given us new insights into the nature of this subject which, though a part of each of our lives, has long proved so mysterious and inaccessible to investigation. New and exciting findings are being reported every year by sleep researchers.

One interesting finding is that sleepwalking, like nightmares and bedwetting, seems to occur in the very deepest stages of sleep, often immediately before the sleeper passes back into the REM stage. Like the trauma of the nightmare, the strange behavior of sleepwalking happens only when the individual is "switched off" into a profoundly unconscious state. The sleepwalker typically moves about with his or her eyes wide open, avoiding obstacles yet apparently not recognizing objects or people. After the experience, the sleepwalker usually remembers nothing of the event. The habit can be a dangerous one, of course, because the sleepwalker may, and sometimes does, climb through upper story windows or march onto a highway. Research indicates that sleepwalking starts in deep sleep, but EEG patterns thereafter show a shift to the REM stage, where the sleeper remains until either awakening or returning to bed.

Psychologists are also giving new attention to nightmares. A nightmare is not only frightening—some observers have described it as the most terrifying psychic experience known to man—but it may also contribute to insomnia in nightmare-prone people who are afraid to sleep. So far only one effective way of reducing the number of nightmares suffered by a sleeper has been found: to administer drugs that interfere with the normal sleep cycle by restricting the amount of time spent in deep sleep. It is not yet clear if there are any adverse side-effects from the deprivation of deep sleep, but persons treated in this way report a general increase in feelings of well-being. Some physicians remain reluctant to prescribe these drugs, however, and are hoping that research will shed light on the actual causes, physiological or psychological, of nightmares.

Another interesting research finding is that young children and particularly infants spend a great deal more time in REM sleep than adults. In fact, newborn babies spend about half of their daily sleep in the REM period, compared to the 25 percent spent by adults. It has been hypothesized that REM sleep in infants provides excitation and stimulation of the higher brain centers, and so serves the important function of promoting development of the sensory and motor areas of the central nervous system. The child is thus prepared for the subsequent task of processing stimuli from the environment.

Earlier in this unit we mentioned sleep research on schizophrenics. More recent research has indicated that chronic schizophrenics fail to show the usual "REM rebound" effect when they have been deprived of REM sleep. Unlike other people, they seem to have no need to spend long periods in REM sleep to compensate for the loss. Could it be that schizophrenic behavior represents the discharge of activities that would normally be discharged as dreams? Much more research is needed in this area, but a useful hypothesis would be that some part of the central nervous system is responsible for these discharges, and if it is for some reason prevented from performing this function in sleep, uncontrolled discharges of REM activity may occur in the waking state.

Another interesting area of research aims at establishing the connection between sleep and the various biological cycles of the human body. Some of these cycles, such as menstruation and sleeping-wakefulness, are well known, but others have only recently been identified. Many psychologists believe, for example, that people may have "mood cycles," in which feelings of depression and elation alternate regularly. One of the most important of all cycles is the *circadian cycle* (the term derives from the Latin *circa die,* "about a day"). This cycle, which lasts 24 hours, seems to be genetically inherited and closely related to changes in body chemistry and hormonal balance. At the high point of the cycle, which normally occurs during the day time, many physical functions such as pulse rate, the formation of white blood cells, and body temperature are at the peak. People tend to feel at their best at this point. The differences in the cycle of body temperature tend to divide people into "morning people" (temperature peaks in the A.M.) and "evening people" (temperature peaks in the P.M.). The low point usually occurs at night, during sleep, when body temperature and heart rate fall to a low level. Scientists have found that the ability to withstand stress is weakest during these low periods. Most terminally ill patients die at night, and more babies are born in the early hours of the morning than in the afternoon.

It may be that one of the reasons why sleep deprivation has such a traumatic effect is that it represents a break in these natural rhythms. Any air traveler who crosses international time zones knows how exhausting a disruption of the natural cycles can be. Indeed, psychologists have drawn attention to the undesirability of globe-trotting statesmen immediately attending summit conferences after many hours in flight. If their *biological clocks* are out of time with their wristwatches, their negotiating powers may be severely impaired.

Unit 33

Brain Storage

OVERVIEW

Some of the significant research devoted to discovering how information is physiologically stored in the brain is briefly surveyed in this unit. Though little is actually known for sure about such brain processes, there are several clues about some brain locations and brain processes which may be involved in learning and memory. The question of memory transfer is treated in the final section.

UNIT OUTLINE

DEFINITION AND BACKGROUND
1. *Definition:* brain storage refers to those persistent changes in the brain that retain information from past events.
2. *Background:* Karl Spencer Lashley (1890–1958).

QUESTIONS AND EVIDENCE
1. Where is information stored in the brain?
Hypotheses:
    a. *Dominant-hemisphere:* certain learning and memory functions, such as language production, are located only in one cerebral hemisphere, the "dominant" one. **571**
    b. *Hippocampus:* important memory functions are handled in the brain by the hippocampus, located in the temporal lobe. **574**
    c. *Frontal-lobes:* memory is handled in part by the brain's frontal lobes. **576**
2. How is information stored in the brain?
Hypotheses:
    a. *Consolidation:* new memories require time before they "consolidate" or become stable and permanent. **577**
    b. *Macromolecules:* learning and memory are reflected at the biochemical level of brain activity by changes in certain complex chemicals, or macromolecules. **579**

IMPORTANT CONCEPTS

	page
cerebral cortex	**570**
corpus callosum	**571**
DNA	**579**
glia	**579**
hippocampus	**571**
neuron	**570**
RNA	**579**
synapse	**579**

Information to be memorized requires some form of brain storage.

In processes like the rehearsal of information a transition is made from short-term to long-term memory.

Consolidation in permanent brain storage probably involves biochemical changes.

DEFINITION AND BACKGROUND

Less than 10 percent of the human brain's neurons are devoted to sensation and movement. In simple animals such behavior is largely controlled by stimulus-response networks. In man most of the brain analyzes data and information received through the senses and explores alternatives.

Storage of information is called memory, which is the human brain's most essential function. Without memory we could deal only with the sensations of the moment. Memory is the mysterious power by which we order, store, and recall what we perceive. The brain handles this information in at least two ways, as short-term and as long-term memory (see Unit 25).

Long-term memory is our lifetime supply of information. Learning would not occur without long-term memory. The mechanism of such information storage depends on enduring changes in the nervous system. The DEFINITION of brain storage refers to *those persistent changes in the brain that retain information from past events.*

This unit will FOCUS on what psychologists and physiologists have been able to find out about where and how n.emories are stored in the brain.

BACKGROUND: K. S. LASHLEY (1890–1958)

At the University of his native West Virginia in 1905, Karl Spencer Lashley thought he might major in Latin or English until an accidental encounter with a neurologist got him interested in the way the brains of frogs worked. In 1914 Lashley obtained a Ph.D. in zoology

from the Johns Hopkins University. Early in his career he was influenced by two very important figures in psychology and physifflology. Around 1915 Lashley worked with John B. Watson, the founder of behaviorism in America, and became a believer in Watson's nonmentalistic approach. During the same period Lashley also became a pupil of the prominent physiologist S. I. Franz, at St. Elizabeth Hospital in Washington, D.C. Franz encouraged Lashley to investigate the effects removing parts of the cerebral cortex had on learning.

Lashley studied the role of the rat's cortex in maze learning. The larger the area of cortex he destroyed, the less the rat learned, and the less the rat remembered of the maze it had learned before the operation. This result occurred regardless of which particular part of the cortex was destroyed. The larger the lesion was, the greater the impairment. In 1917 Lashley and Franz published results of their research.

Lashley's discoveries were revolutionary because they demonstrated the equipotentiality of much brain tissue in the process of learning, thus showing incorrectness of the previous view that every psychological function necessarily had a specific, irreplaceable location in the cortex. In 1929 Lashley was elected president of the American Psychological Association, and in the same year he published *Brain Mechanisms and Intelligence,* one of the classics of psychology. This book presented the methods, stated the questions, and set down the criteria and standards for evaluation that would guide and influence subsequent studies using operations to study the brain.

This work has led many scientists to the hypothesis that memories are stored in vast patterns of interconnections called "engrams" by Lashley, or millions of neurons. Each neuron would be part of many engrams; each could be reached through many different inputs. In his search for the engram (the physiological basis of an item in memory or a learned experience), Lashley once remarked, "I sometimes feel, in reviewing the evidence on the localization of the memory

Fabian Bachrach.

Figure 1. Karl Lashley's studies of brain function established procedures and conditions for later psychologists.

trace, that the necessary conclusion is that learning is just not possible" (1950).

If memories *are* stored in many neural nets in many places, it would answer one of the oldest questions: where is the "place" for memories? Many researchers have elaborated on the question of where the memory trace or learned experiences are stored, by investigating the effect of removal of major parts of the brain, and on the question of how memory is stored by studying in detail the characteristics of memory and its relation to learning. More than any other single influence, the work of Lashley has stimulated modern researchers to attack these problems.

QUESTIONS AND EVIDENCE

1. Where is information stored in the brain?

2. How is information stored in the brain?

brain are presented in the units on brain stimulation (34), and the senses (31).

1. WHERE IS INFORMATION STORED IN THE BRAIN?

The *dominant-hemisphere hypothesis* states that certain learning and memory functions, such as language production, are located only in one cerebral hemisphere, the "dominant" one.

The human brain has a right and left half (hemisphere). These halves are connected mainly by a sheet of nerve fibers called the *corpus callosum.* When the corpus callosum is severed, the separated halves of the brain continue to function. For some years, a group of researchers at the California Institute of Technology have been studying the behavioral and psychological effects of separating or "splitting" the

QUESTION	1. WHERE IS INFORMATION STORED IN THE BRAIN?		
HYPOTHESES	**DOMINANT HEMISPHERE**	**HIPPOCAMPUS**	**FRONTAL LOBES**
DESCRIPTIVE EVIDENCE	ASSESS: use of brain-stored information following callosal surgery	ASSESS: retention of new memories following hippocampal surgery	
EXPERIMENTAL EVIDENCE			VARY: intactness of frontal lobes of monkeys
			MEASURE: test performance and memory factors

The overall topography of the human brain is pictured from one side in Figure 2. The *cerebrum* is symmetrical and includes a thick layer called the *cortex,* which consists of four *lobes* on each side, or *hemisphere.* The four lobes are the *frontal, temporal, parietal,* and *occipital;* some of their very general functions are indicated in the figure. On the medial side of the temporal lobe is a region called the *hippocampus.* The *cerebellum* is responsible for coordination of muscles and movement. Other views of other parts of the

brain in two. In the 1950s, this work was done on lower animals, but more recently interesting work has been performed on human epileptic patients. Severing the corpus callosum has been found to alleviate otherwise hopeless behavioral problems (for example, severe, dangerous convulsive seizures). In general, all or a substantial part of the epileptic patients' symptoms disappear as a result of these operations, and the patients are able to resume normal living. What did the cerebral deconnecting itself do to behavior?

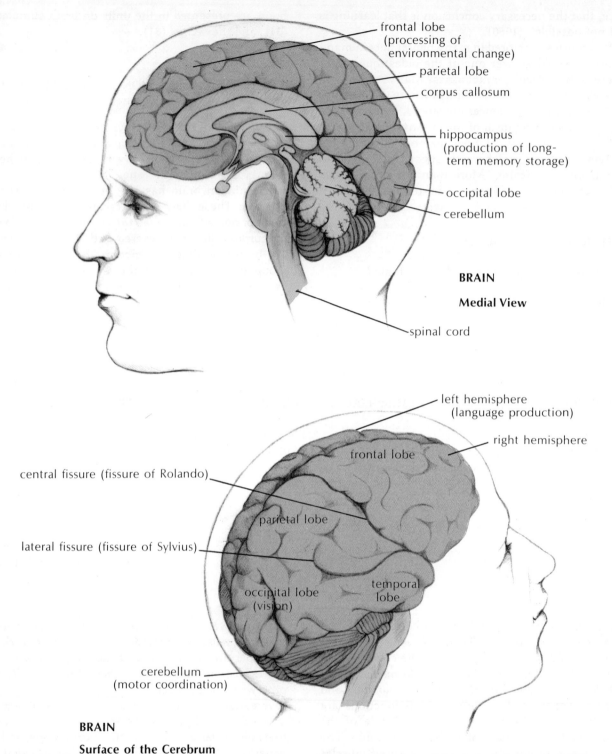

frontal lobe
(processing of
environmental change)

parietal lobe

corpus callosum

hippocampus
(production of long-
term memory storage)

occipital lobe

cerebellum

BRAIN

Medial View

spinal cord

left hemisphere
(language production)

right hemisphere

frontal lobe

central fissure (fissure of Rolando)

parietal lobe

lateral fissure (fissure of Sylvius)

occipital lobe
(vision)

temporal
lobe

cerebellum
(motor coordination)

BRAIN

Surface of the Cerebrum

Figure 2. Two views of the brain indicating certain important divisions and some localized functions.

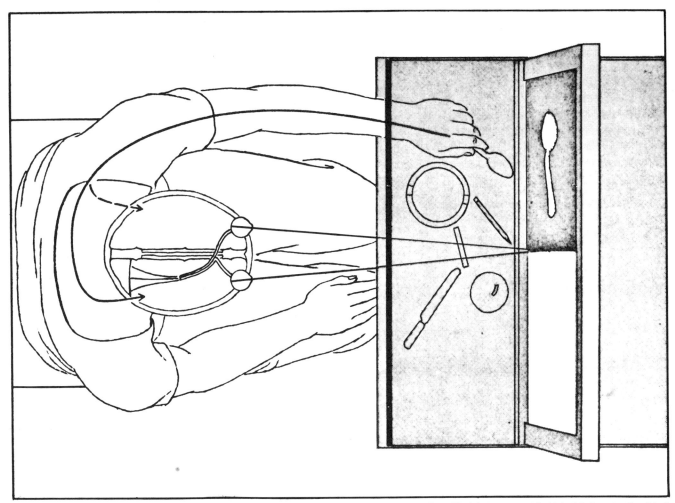

Figure 3. Visual-tactile association is performed by a split-brain patient. A picture of a spoon is flashed to the right hemisphere; with the left hand he gets a spoon from behind the screen. The touch information from the left hand projects mainly to the right hemisphere. This is usually not enough to enable him to say (speech uses the left hemisphere) what he has picked up. Adapted from Sperry and Gazzaniga (1968).

DESCRIPTIVE EVIDENCE

Investigators: R. W. Sperry and M. S. Gazzaniga
Source, Date: "Hemisphere Deconnection and Unity in Conscious Awareness," 1968
Location: California Institute of Technology
Subjects: 11 serious epileptic patients, after cerebral deconnection
Materials: Testing apparatus consisting of two horizontal screens, side by side, in front of a subject

The effects of separating the hemispheres are not obvious, and ordinary behavior appears to be unaffected. However, appropriate tests can demonstrate important changes, especially in vision. By controlling visual input in such a way that only one hemisphere received information, the memory and information-processing capacities of each brain half can be investigated. This method is made possible by the fact that each half of the visual field of each eye is connected to only one hemisphere. Facing forward with the viewer, the right side of the visual field is received on the left side of each eyeball, connected to the left hemisphere. Similarly, the left side of the visual field is received on the right side of each eyeball, connected to the right hemisphere of the brain (see Figure 4).

To control visual input, the subject is placed in front of two screens and is asked to fixate his vision on a point midway between the screens. When he does this, visual information on the right screen reaches the left hemisphere only, while stimuli on the left reach the right hemisphere only.

Under these circumstances, right-handed deconnected subjects will respond normally to any object in their right visual field (or right hand): shown a pencil or handed a pencil in his right hand, a subject will say, "That is a pencil." But the same object, when presented to the left visual field (or left hand), will elicit different answers: the subject will say he only saw a flash of light with no details or that his left hand feels numb. What is happening here is that the subject's *language-production* capacities are located only in the left hemisphere. Consequently, when the subject answers a question verbally, only his left hemisphere is speaking—and the left hemisphere doesn't know what is happening in the left visual field or the left hand.

Does this mean the right hemisphere is "inferior" to the left? The right hemisphere does lack language-production capacities, but further tests showed that the right hemisphere can understand verbal instructions, and, when objects are placed in the left hand, the right hemisphere can identify them by pointing with the left hand at pictures on the left screen. other words, though the right hemisphere cannot verbally name or describe an object, it can identify the object by using gestures, or it can even draw with the left hand what it sees in the left visual field. Sperry (1968) also showed that, if the word "key" appears in the left visual field and "case" in the right, the subject will say he doesn't know what he saw on the left, but he still can search with the left hand and find a key. But when he is asked what he holds in his left hand, the subject says it's a case of some sort.

These simple but dramatic demonstrations show that two independent, conscious brains are produced by cerebral deconnection, two brains that can no longer communicate with each other directly. As the cliché goes, the left hand doesn't know what the right hand is doing. Because only the left hemisphere can

produce language, the right half is "speechless" but nevertheless functional and capable of understanding and intellectual performance. The left hand, controlled by the speechless right hemisphere, cannot write language either. The simple functional differences between the hemispheres are summarized in Figure 4, where "stereognosis" refers to touching and feeling.

Normally the brain halves can communicate with each other and exchange information originally detected only by one half. But with cerebral bisection, the hemispheres function independently. The fact that each independent half receives only part of the perceptual information is not a serious handicap for the former epileptic patients in their daily lives, where their behavior is indistinguishable from other people's. It's not a handicap because most of the time both hemispheres receive that same perceptual information anyway, and all verbalization is controlled by the "dominant" hemisphere which is almost always the left one. It is interesting that Sperry (1968) also notes that the right, nonspeaking hemisphere appears to be superior to the left (dominant) in understanding spatial and geometric relationships. For example, when duplicating a pattern of blocks, the right hemisphere (left hand) does it quickly and smoothly, while the left hemisphere (right hand) must go slowly, a step at a time.

The *hippocampus hypothesis* states that important memory functions are handled in the brain by the hippocampus, located in the temporal lobe.

DESCRIPTIVE EVIDENCE

Investigators: W. B. Scoville and B. Milner
Source, Date: "Loss of Recent Memory after Bilateral Hippo-
campal Lesions," 1957
Location: Hartford Hospital, McGill University, and the
Montreal Neurological Institute, Canada
Subjects: 1 severely afflicted epileptic patient and 9 psychotic
patients
Materials: Surgical extirpations, memory and intelligence
tests

Each patient was operated on to bilaterally remove the medial temporal lobes. The operations were without significant therapeutic effect in psychosis, although slight improvements were noted in a few patients. Unexpectedly, there was a grave loss of recent memory in those cases that involved bilaterally removing the hippocampal complex of the temporal lobes. These patients' intelligence, reasoning abilities, vocabulary, and distant memory were normal. Yet after the operation those most severely affected appeared "to forget the incidents of their daily life as fast as they occur." After these results were published, many animal studies were conducted in which hippocampus brain regions were removed and behavioral effects observed. The results from these studies are controversial.

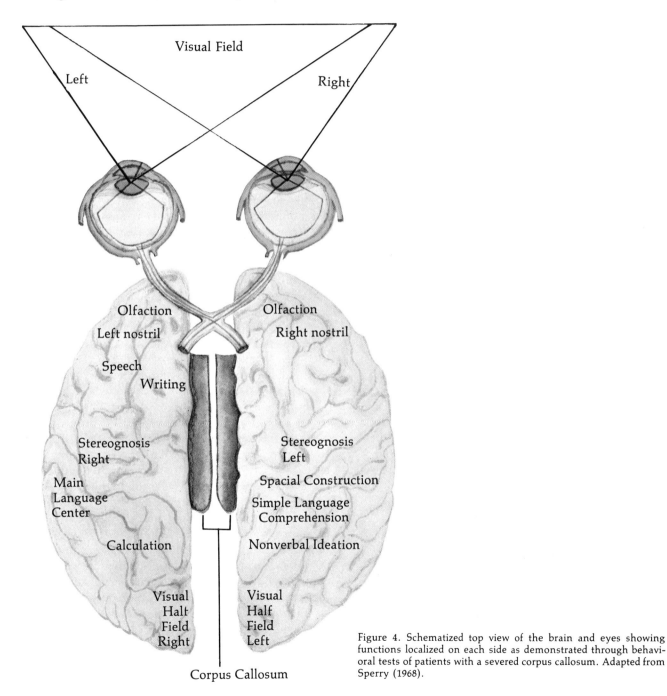

Figure 4. Schematized top view of the brain and eyes showing functions localized on each side as demonstrated through behavioral tests of patients with a severed corpus callosum. Adapted from Sperry (1968).

Some difficulties in defining cortical function may derive from exclusively using the method of experimentally damaging cortical tissue. Another approach to locating brain function has been to stimulate the surface of the brain with electrical probes. A noted physician and researcher who has made use of this method is Wilder Penfield (1958). Penfield studied the temporal lobe of epileptic patients whose brains were exposed for surgery in order to locate the epileptic focus and remove it. The "open brain" operations are performed under local anesthesia. The operation is painless, and the patient is completely awake and conscious. Penfield found that stimulations in the temporal lobe region often evoked memory sequences that were old and completely forgotten. (See Unit 25.) The subjects reported these memories were very vivid and almost perfect. When the temporal lobes are damaged in man, patients may be able to recall their past life very well but be unable to remember things that happened a few hours earlier. They remember if they are tested within fifteen minutes, but after that the memory disappears.

These results suggest that temporal-lobe damage separates two memory processes, a temporary memory process of short retention that the lesion spares and a more permanent memory process that the lesion impairs.

The *frontal-lobes hypothesis* states that memory is handled in part by the brain's frontal lobes.

For some years a concentrated research attack on the frontal lobes has been conducted by Karl Pribram and his associates, who have tentatively concluded, from evidence like the following, that the frontal lobes provide some of the ongoing working memory and "fine tuning" that human beings rely on when they are engaged in intellectual tasks that depend on attentional and sequential processing of inputs.

EXPERIMENTAL EVIDENCE

Investigators: K. H. Pribram and W. E. Tubbs
Sources, Dates: "A Further Experimental Analysis of the Behavioral Deficit That Follows Injury to the Primate Frontal Cortex," 1961; "Short-Term Memory, Parsing, and the Primate Frontal Cortex," 1967
Location: Stanford University
Subjects: Monkeys
Materials: Surgical preparations; Wisconsin General Testing Apparatus

Many studies were conducted to ascertain the effects of removing portions of the frontal cortex on performance and behavior. In one important study by Pribram (1961), three groups of monkeys were presented with a task where, on each trial, a monkey had to choose between two objects in front of him. The two objects were a tobacco tin and a flat ashtray, each of which covered a hole that might contain a food reward (peanut). Initially, all subjects were rewarded only when they chose the tobacco tin, and thus, with repeated trials, each monkey learned to pick up the tobacco tin in order to get a peanut. There were three groups of monkeys: one had the frontal lobes removed, a second group of controls was operated on but had had no frontal lobe surgery (temporal lobe lesions were made), and a third group of monkeys were unoperated controls.

The performance of all monkeys on the initial task did not differ; all three groups learned where the peanut was equally fast. How would each group of monkeys adapt to a change (reversal) in the situation? When each monkey chose the tobacco tin correctly ten times in a row, the peanut was switched and placed under the ashtray until ten consecutive responses were obtained again. As the trials were repeated, eventually the position of the peanut was reversed when the animal made five correct responses in a row, then four in a row, then three; and finally only two in a row. How would the experimental animals adapt to this situation?

Both control groups of animals were able to adapt to these changes, so that they showed progressively fewer initial errors once they encountered a reversal, that is, they learned to "switch" their answer as soon as they encountered a mistake (in the manner of Harlow's learning sets, discussed in Unit 18). But the monkeys with frontal lesions had trouble with these reversals, and they showed no improvement in performance throughout the experiment. Thus, in an ordinary choice-learning task, frontally lobotomized monkeys learned a simple, well-defined task as fast as controls. But when an incorrect response signaled that a reversal had been made, monkeys with frontal lesions did not make nearly as good use of this signal as did the controls.

This was only one result from a number of similar, related experiments. The results suggest that the function of the frontal lobes may be (1) to help maintain continuous attention on a task and (2) to help store and process ongoing changes in the situation. Pribram concluded that "frontal lesions interfered with some organization process that takes place in a relatively unreliable situation in the presence of stimulus events that must serve subsequently as guides to action" (1961). Thus, the best evidence we have at this time suggests that the frontal lobes perform complex mediating functions between stored information and changes in stimulus inputs. These results are by no means final, and, to a large degree, a really complete picture of frontal-lobe functioning is yet to come.

In this unit, so far, our discussion has centered on a few of the indications from research about what *places* in the brain may be most important for brain storage and memory processes. In fact, no one place in the brain is indisputably implicated in brain storage, though some locations are clearly involved in certain aspects of behavior, such as language or visual perception.

remember to make the same response? If there is a consolidation process, then the electroconvulsive shock may succeed in disrupting the consolidation process and make the animal forget what it learned. Some years ago, Duncan (1948) performed the first experiment of this kind, and his results tended to show that the shock could disrupt consolidation and "erase" what the animal had learned. Because there were interpretive problems with Duncan's early procedure, more recent investigators have sought ways to define more clearly just what is involved and just how long the supposed consolidation process must take before the animal has a "permanent," nonerasable memory. One of these studies is described below.

EXPERIMENTAL EVIDENCE

Investigators: R. Kopp, Z. Bohdanecky, and M. E. Jarvik
Source, Date: "Long Temporal Gradient of Retrograde
Amnesia for a Well-Discriminated Stimulus," 1966

QUESTION 2. HOW IS INFORMATION STORED IN THE BRAIN?

HYPOTHESES	CONSOLIDATION	MACROMOLECULES
DESCRIPTIVE EVIDENCE		
EXPERIMENTAL EVIDENCE	VARY: interval between avoidance learning and electroconvulsive shock; presence or absence of shock or punishment	VARY: learning tasks
		MEASURE: chemical brain changes
	MEASURE: recall of avoidance response	

2. HOW IS INFORMATION STORED IN THE BRAIN?

The *consolidation hypothesis* states that new memories require time before they "consolidate" or become stable and permanent.

One of the most popular methods for testing and measuring consolidation processes in the brain has been the use of *electroconvulsive shock* (ECS). In this method, an animal learns some simple response to a stimulus, and then a strong electrical current is passed through its brain. When the animal is placed in the same learning situation as before, will it be able to

Location: Albert Einstein College of Medicine, Bronx, N.Y.
Subjects: 150 female mice, approximately 60 days old
Materials: Two-chamber box with one side brightly lit,
and other side darkened; shock equipment

Mice were assigned to one of three general conditions. All mice were placed in the brighter of two connected boxes. Under these circumstances, a mouse will soon approach the darker box and enter it. The animals in the experimental condition received a severe, punishing shock (not electroconvulsive) to their feet as they stepped through the opening. Ordinarily, this one experience is enough to make a mouse totally reluctant ever to step through into darkness again; thus this mouse has learned to avoid the dark box. Could it be made to forget what it learned?

After this one learning trial, the animals in the experimental group received electroconvulsive shock at different intervals of time, one interval per mouse: 5, 20, 80, 320 seconds, one hour, or six hours after learning. One control group received the same learning trial (foot shock), but no subsequent electroconvulsive shock. A second control group received no punishing shock, but did receive the electroconvulsive shock ten seconds after stepping through.

All mice were given a retention test twenty-four hours after learning, by placing them again in the two-chamber box. The experimenter then recorded how much time passed before a mouse entered the darker box. The results are summarized in Table 1. As can be seen in the table, the mice in the main control group (no ECS) only rarely returned to the darkened box: they remembered to avoid it. For the experimental mice, the sooner they had received electroconvulsive shock after learning, the more likely they were to forget, and therefore step through sooner. The second control group, having received no punishment, quickly went to the darkened box in an average time of five seconds.

The sooner ECS occurs after the original learning experience, the more likely it is that the experience will be forgotten. Evidently memory processes are *time-dependent.* Other studies have shown that, after eight hours, administration of ECS will no longer affect long-term memory, and the animal will always avoid punishment just as nonshocked animals do.

Consolidation experiments indicate that some process occurs that takes time, before a memory becomes relatively permanent. Similar results are usually found in cases of traumatic amnesia with humans, when people have received violent concussive injuries to their heads. The most common result of these concussions is *retrograde amnesia,* where the individual forgets the experiences that occurred immediately prior to his accident. In general, the more serious the concussion, the further back the individual is unable to remember his life.

Consolidation studies lend support to the idea that there are at least two kinds of memory, one short-term and temporary, the other long-term and possibly permanent. They suggest that one kind of initial brain process takes time while it lays down a more permanent memory trace of another sort. The conclusion from these studies is that memories are retained first by a reversible process, but after some time more permanent changes occur in the brain.

The first process, temporary and reversible, may be

TABLE 1. Consolidation Study

Electroconvulsive Shock Administered After Learning	Typical Retest Time (median seconds)
5 seconds	9.3 seconds
20 seconds	27.8 seconds
80 seconds	50.3 seconds
320 seconds	82.8 seconds
1 hour	127.7 seconds
6 hours	195.0 seconds
Control: No ECS	300.0 seconds +
Control: ECS 10 seconds After stepping through (No punishment)	5.0 seconds

Source: R. Kopp, Z. Bohdanecky, and M. E. Jarvik, "Long Temporal Gradient of Retrograde Amnesia for a Well-Discriminated Stimulus," *Science,* 153, (1966), 1547–1549.

an electrical or chemical change at a synapse, where neurons come together, or group of synapses. The second more permanent process may be a swelling of nerve terminals or outgrowths of nerve terminals or even a change in the chemical structure of protein molecules in the neurons.

One of the most influential books in modern psychology has been *The Organization of Behavior* (1949) by D. O. Hebb, a Canadian psychologist. Among other things, the book developed the role that reverberating circuits might play in memory consolidation. A reverberating circuit is a closed loop of nerve cells that, once stimulated, tends to perpetuate its own activity. Consolidation may involve activity of nerve cells in reverberating circuits that manufacture in some way the more permanent long-term memory trace.

The possible biochemical bases of long-term memory are also highly speculative but provocative. The *macromolecules hypothesis* states that learning and memory are reflected at the biochemical level of brain activity by changes in certain complex chemicals, or macromolecules.

Interest in biochemical changes as a basis for memory storage dates back to 1950, when Katz and Halstead proposed that memory is stored in the brain by means of ribose-nucleic acid (RNA) molecules and protein. This initial work was virtually ignored for ten years. However, during that time the importance of deoxy-ribose-nucleic acid (DNA) and RNA for genes and heredity became apparent. As a result, a great deal of interest has been generated in the possibility that brain storage may involve changes in large protein molecules, and especially in RNA.

Some of the most important (and most ingenious) studies on the biochemical basis for memory and learning have come from the laboratory of Holger Hydén in Sweden. Many studies have been done there, but only two will be described here.

EXPERIMENTAL EVIDENCE

Investigator: H. Hydén
Source, Date: "The Question of a Molecular Basis for the Memory Trace," 1970
Location: Institute of Neurobiology, University of Göteborg, Sweden
Subjects: Rats
Materials: Narrow glass tube; 45 degree tightwire

Like people, rats are usually right-handed or left-handed; when they use their paws in complex movements, they prefer to use one paw or the other. In one experiment, right-handed rats were trained to use the left paw to retrieve food from far down a narrow glass tube. Training took place over a period of days, with each rat receiving two training sessions of twenty-five minutes each per day. After five or six days, the rat could readily retrieve the food from the glass, quickly and smoothly, with its initially "nonpreferred" left paw.

At this point, the rats were killed, and their brains analyzed for chemical changes. It was found that there were increases in the amount of RNA per cell on the learning (right) side of the brain cortex surface that corresponds to the left hand. This increase was relative to the amount of RNA present in control rats whose brain cells were analyzed on the first or second day of training, before the response had been learned well. The increase was also relative to the same rats' cells on the other side of the brain, which had not received training.

In the second study, Hydén trained animals to walk up a tightwire placed at an angle of 45 degrees to the floor in order to obtain food. When the animals had learned to perform the task well, they were killed and cells of the brainstem vestibular nuclei were analyzed for amount of RNA present. The vestibular nuclei are brain cells involved in gravity perception and balance, those abilities that had to be trained in the animals who learned to walk the tightwire. An increase in the amount of RNA in the cells of the vestibular nuclei occurred after training.

An important contribution made by Hydén and his colleagues was to point out the potential importance that *glial cells* may have for brain storage. In addition to neurons in the central nervous system, there are glial cells, which are ten times more numerous. The glia structurally support the neurons and provide them with nourishment. Unlike the rest of the cells in the body, nerve cells are not fed directly from blood vessels. The glial cells regulate the chemical environment of the nerve cells. The glia make up almost half the brain's weight in mass, but before 1960 it never occurred to anyone that the glia might be involved in brain storage. Hydén showed that the glia are a repository for RNA and that changes in glial biochemical composition may accompany learning.

While these studies tend to indicate that macromolecules play some role in storing information in the brain, it remains to be seen whether the macromolecule actually constitutes the stored information in the brain.

Other experiments have attempted to find a transfer of learning when chemicals extracted from an animal that has recently learned a task are injected into a naive animal. Such experiments are exceedingly difficult and highly controversial.

In summary, the most important discoveries in the physiological-psychological study of brain storage are yet to come. There are promising leads and several significant clues but as yet very few well-established conclusions. Most researchers in brain storage believe that learning and memory have a biochemical, macromolecular basis, but precisely what the basis is and how it works in memory storage and retrieval are still open questions.

Figure 5. Glial cells. Surrounding the nerve cells of the brain, they may be involved in the storage of information.

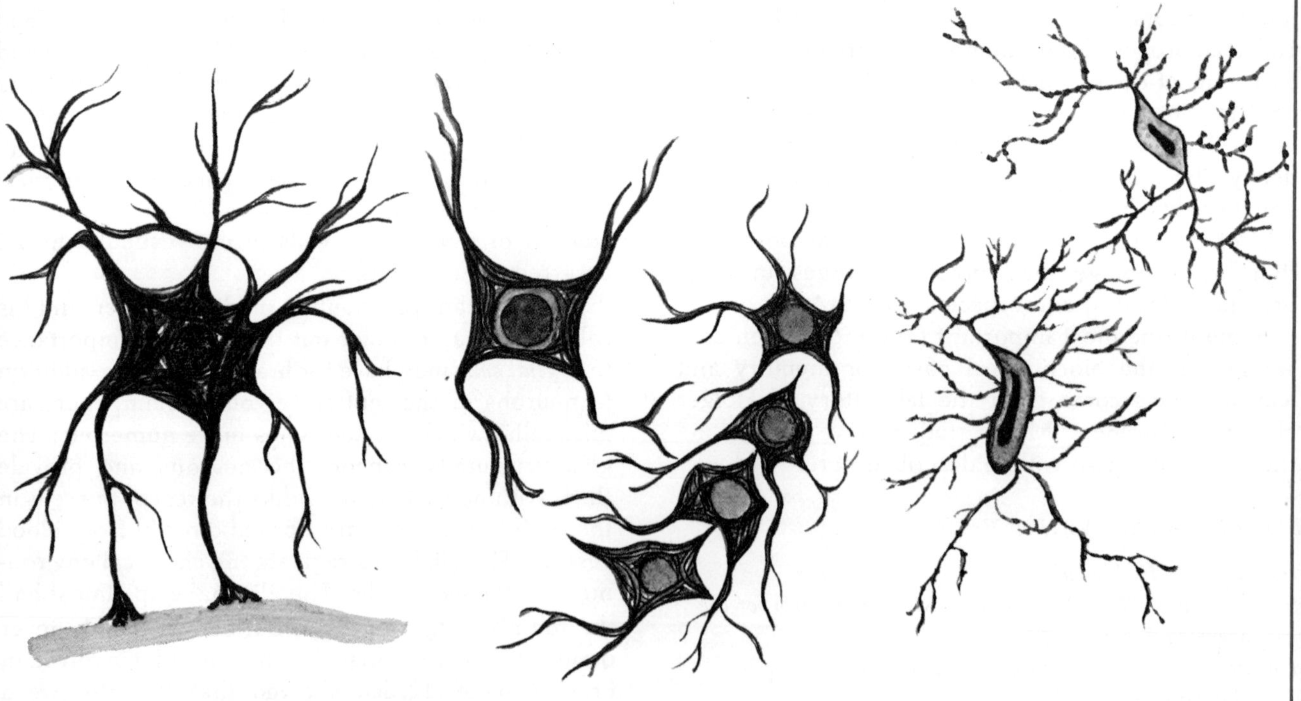

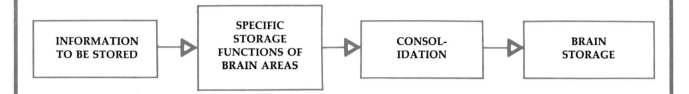

| INFORMATION TO BE STORED | | SPECIFIC STORAGE FUNCTIONS OF BRAIN AREAS | | CONSOL-IDATION | | BRAIN STORAGE |

PUTTING IT TOGETHER: Brain Storage

Although research has provided us with a great deal of information that is involved in the process of storing information in the brain, the essential components and the sequence of events remain highly speculative.

Apparently, *various brain areas have specific functions* which must be performed for storage to occur. When information is received by the organism, it probably is monitored to determine whether it includes new information or is identical with information already stored. Some experimental evidence from research with monkeys indicates that the frontal lobes of the brain may be involved in this function of mediating between stored information and changes in sensory input. Research with people whose brain hemispheres have been surgically deconnected indicates that communication of sensory input seems to be stored in verbal terms. The hippocampus is apparently involved in the process of transferring new information from short term to long term memory.

The final stage of the storage process is apparently some sort of *consolidation* transferring the information from neuronal activity, such as reverberating circuits, to structure, such as macromolecules within the individual neurons of glial cells.

Whatever the chain of events may be, it is clear that much *information stored in the brain* is available in portions of the temporal lobe and may be dramatically and vividly retrieved by electrical stimulation.

WHAT'S ACCEPTED AND WHAT'S DEBATED

1. WHAT'S ACCEPTED . . .

1. The cerebral hemispheres differ in their functional assignments, and separating them will result in independent hemispheric brain storage and operations.

2. There are at least two distinct processes involved in brain storage, one short-term and one long-term.

3. In the transition between short-term and long-term storage, there is a consolidation period when memory is very labile and easily disrupted.

4. There is a macromolecular basis for long-term memory storage that may involve RNA.

2. WHAT'S DEBATED . . .

1. Whether brain storage involves changes in single neurons, changes in relationships among neurons, or assignment of specific neurons to specific functions.

2. The specific roles of the hippocampus, temporal lobes, and frontal lobes in brain storage and recall processes.

3. The total memory or brain storage capacity of the human brain.

ISSUE: MEMORY TRANSFER

Science fiction writers make good use of the psychologist's finding that memory may be stored in the brain in chemical form. A recurrent theme in descriptions of the education process of the next century is the "information pill," a pill that a student could ingest as a substitute for the tiresome traditional learning process. Writers have given optimistic accounts of a society in which a student would swallow a number of complex molecules, digest them, and then begin to speak fluent French or tackle a difficult mathematical problem.

These ideas seem far-fetched. But some hotly debated experiments conducted by James V. McConnell of the University of Michigan have suggested that, at least among one lower form of life, the transfer of simple, chemically-encoded memory between one organism and another may be possible.

For his experiments McConnell selected the planarian (flatworm), an inch-long creature that crawls about the bottoms of ponds in many parts of the world. The planarian is an unusual creature. It is the simplest animal to possess a true brain. Its brain structure is extremely basic, consisting of a small clump of neurons and synapses. The flatworm also has unusual reproduction abilities. It can reproduce by mating with another planarian, by mating with itself, or simply by dividing in two. If a planarian is cut in half, the tail grows a head and the head grows a tail, and in a matter of a few weeks two complete new planaria take the place of the one severed creature. In fact, the worm is able to regenerate even if it is cut into as many as six separate pieces. Each segment eventually grows into a full worm again.

McConnell began his work by trying to demonstrate that these very lowly worms could be conditioned through standard techniques despite their primitive nervous system. His system was to flash an electric light on the worms and immediately follow with an electric shock. When shocked, the creatures responded by contracting violently. After numerous trials, McConnell was able to condition the worms to contract to the flashing of the light alone. This process of conditioning took much longer than it would with higher animal forms. Rats, for instance, will normally learn the association of light and shock within about three trials. There, however, seemed no doubt that the lowly worm could learn and remember. But what would happen if the worms were cut in half and allowed to regenerate their bodies? Is memory in these creatures stored only in the head or is it in the whole body?

McConnell expected that the worm growing from the original head and brain might remember that a light preceded a shock and respond to the light only by contracting, whereas the worm regenerating from the original tail would show no evidence of learning. In fact, he found that the worms that had grown new heads learned the task just as fast as those that had kept their original heads and regenerated new tails. Furthermore both groups learned the task just as fast as a control group of conditioned planaria which had not been sectioned. However the memory was stored, the location of the information did not seem restricted to the brain area. By cutting up worms into more than two pieces and regenerating a series of new worms, McConnell went on to demonstrate that the memory was probably stored throughout the entire body: each piece remembered what the original body had learned.

The next question was even bolder: McConnell asked what would happen if conditioned flatworms were fed to unconditioned flatworms. He hypothesized that it might be possible to transfer the chemical responsible for the memory (altered RNA) from a conditioned to an unconditioned worm, and that the unconditioned worm would then react to the light by contracting its body. The planarian worm, among its other peculiarities, has no stomach. When it eats, particles of food circulate inside the animal and each cell draws off whatever nutrient it needs. McConnell simply chopped up some conditioned worms and fed them to unconditioned worms. After digestion had taken place, he tested the cannibal worms. He found they responded to the light in significantly fewer trials than untrained noncannibals. Memory, he inferred, had been chemically transferred from one animal to another.

Inspired by McConnell's work, Georges Ungar of Houston attempted a similar memory transfer with rats. Like many other rodents, rats are largely nocturnal and instinctively seek the dark, particularly if placed in a strange environment during the daytime. Ungar placed rats in an open box containing dark chambers. The animals automatically entered the chambers where they received an electric shock which promptly drove them out again. The rats soon learned to avoid the dark areas and would react with squeaks, biting, and defecation even if pushed in the direction of the chambers. Next, Ungar killed the conditioned rats and injected chemicals extracted from their brains into the brains of untrained rats. When these rats were placed in the box for the first time, his findings indicated that they tended to avoid the dark chamber.

Ungar trained a further 4000 rats to avoid the dark, killed them, and then analyzed the chemical constituents of their brains. He found a protein in the brains of the trained rats which was not present in the brains of untrained rats. He concluded that this chemical was the basis for the memory of the unpleasant shocks associated with the dark chamber. Next, Ungar synthesized quantities of the compound and injected the substance into the brains of untrained rats. These rats proceeded to avoid the dark exactly as if they had been trained themselves.

These experiments conducted by McConnell and by Ungar are technically complex and difficult to replicate. Some researchers claim to have repeated the experiment with similar results, while others claim negative results. It has been suggested that there were faults in the design or in the interpretation of the original experiments. The controversy continues, but if the memory transfer findings can be ultimately confirmed, exciting possibilities for research will abound. It is a big leap, however, from the lowly planarian brain to the vastly complex human one, and for the time being at least, the human "information pill" will have to remain in the realm of science fiction.

Unit 34

Brain Stimulation

OVERVIEW

Research on the behavioral effects of directly stimulating the brain cells of organisms with electricity or chemicals is discussed. A variety of studies demonstrate that direct brain stimulation can repeatedly evoke behaviors as simple as a muscle twitch and as complex as a whole sequence of gross behavioral acts. Both animal and human subjects appear to find stimulation of some brain sites pleasurable. There is also a great potential for brain stimulation as a form of treatment for certain neurological and behavior problems, such as epilepsy.

UNIT OUTLINE

DEFINITION AND BACKGROUND
1. *Definition:* brain stimulation is any direct physical procedure, usually electrical or chemical, by which brain activity, and consequently behavior, is altered.
2. *Background:* Walter R. Hess (1881–   ).

QUESTIONS AND EVIDENCE
1. What kinds of behavior does brain stimulation induce?
Hypotheses:
    a. *No-fatigue:* certain brain locations can be stimulated to produce motor responses repeatedly, and indefinitely. **590**
    b. *Emotion:* emotional behavior can be elicited by electrical stimulation of the brain. **591**
    c. *Pattern:* stimulation can be used to evoke complex, sequential patterns of responses. **593**
2. How does brain stimulation affect motivated behavior?
Hypotheses:
    a. *Reward:* organisms will work to obtain ESB in certain areas. **594**
    b. *Trigger:* stimulation can activate brain mechanisms that produce such motivated behavior as feeding, sexual activity, and maternal responses. **594**
3. Can brain stimulation direct social behavior?
Hypotheses:
    a. *Aggression:* brain stimulation can be used to make an animal more aggressive and socially dominant. **595**
4. Can brain stimulation be useful clinically with human patients?
Hypotheses:
    a. *Self-control:* medical patients can learn to use self-initiated brain stimulation to help control or alleviate their problems. **597**

IMPORTANT CONCEPTS

                            page

affective defense reaction	**592**
brain stimulation	**586**
cerebellum	**589**
cerebral cortex	**586**
hypothalamus	**587**
neuron	**589**
pleasure center	**594**
Skinner box	**594**
synapse	**589**

Electrodes may be surgically implanted without damage in any location in the brain of an organism.

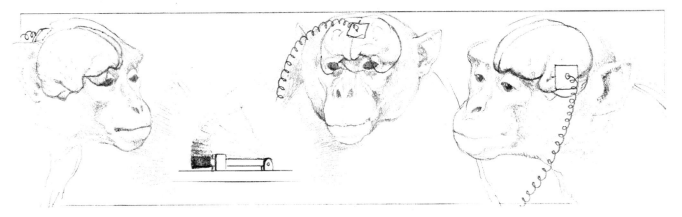

Electrical stimulation may be painlessly provided through these implanted electrodes.

A wide variety of behaviors may be controlled through brain stimulation.

DEFINITION AND BACKGROUND

The DEFINITION of brain stimulation is *any direct physical procedure, usually electrical or chemical, by which brain activity, and consequently behavior, is altered.* In electrical stimulation, electrodes—fine electrical wires that are insulated except at the tips—are implanted in particular parts of the brain and an electrical current passed through them. In chemical stimulation, a tiny tube called a cannula is inserted in the brain and a chemical passed through it. Using stimulation techniques, the functions of some parts of the brain have been identified with considerable precision. For example, electrical stimulation of certain parts of the hypothalamus will cause a satiated animal to continue eating until it becomes grossly overweight; stimulation of other parts of the brain causes animals to attack, or to become submissive, and so on.

This unit will FOCUS on the brain-behavior relationships that have been identified or suggested by experimental work on brain stimulation to date. Most research in this area uses subhuman animals as subjects, but the unit also describes some therapeutic applications of brain stimulation in treating epileptics and other human medical patients.

BACKGROUND: WALTER RUDOLF HESS (1881–   )

At the age of thirty-one, Hess, a Swiss, made a personal decision that led to his becoming a major contributor to our understanding of the brain: He quit a lucrative practice as an ophthalmologist to devote his time to basic research in physiology. After a year as an assistant professor at the University of Bonn, he accepted a professorship at the University of Zurich. Twelve years later, he was perfecting a new technique of brain mapping that offered scientists a revolutionary approach to the study of the nervous system.

Whereas previous exploration had been limited to the cortex, or surface, of the brain, Hess was interested in probing the depths of the organ. He particularly wanted to investigate the region of the brain that communicates directly with the spinal cord—the *brainstem,* which lies under the two *cerebral hemispheres.* As his work progressed, Hess came to concentrate on the uppermost section of this area, the *diencephalon.*

Figure 1. Walter Rudolf Hess discovered control centers in the brain for certain basic functions such as blood pressure and breathing. He received a Nobel Prize in 1949 for his research.

His technique was to implant fine electrodes at precisely selected points in the diencephalons of anesthetized animals (cats, in most of his experiments) through tiny holes in their skulls. After the anesthesia wore off, the animals resumed a nearly normal existence, apparently unbothered by the wires connected to their brain and projecting from their heads. Hess then stimulated the deep brain areas with small amounts of electrical current and observed the animals' behavior. Later, he used stronger current to damage tissue around the tip of the electrodes and then studied the animals' behavior to assess the functional loss caused by the damage. Upon completion of these tests, he sacrificed the animals so that he could pinpoint the location of the electrodes. These steps allowed him to study the relation between function and structure in the brain.

These careful investigations led Hess to postulate the existence of control centers for some of life's most fundamental functions, such as respiration and blood pressure. Even more important, though, was his discovery that these control centers are not discrete regions, each with its own particular function. Instead, each function seemed to be carried out through a complex interrelationship of structures, and each structure seemed to be involved in a number of functions. For example, stimulation of one small area of the brain that seemed to control only one internal organ could also initiate a complex set of reactions, ranging from friendly submission to vicious rage and attack.

As Hess sorted out the responses evoked by electrical stimulation of the brain, it became evident that an important coordinating center exists in the *hypothalamus*. This center seemed to integrate the activities of the involuntary nervous system, which innervates smooth muscle, cardiac muscle, and glands. The *sympathetic* component of these activities accelerates activity and prepares the organism for action, for example, by speeding up the heartbeat and dilating the pupils of the eyes. The *parasympathetic* component decelerates activity and prepares the animal for inactivity, for example, by slowing the heartbeat and contracting the pupils. The hypothalamus can activate either system, depending upon the needs of the organism. Thus the two complementary systems are integrated by this region of the brain.

Hess' major work was published in 1932, and in 1949 he was awarded the Nobel Prize in physiology and medicine for his research on the brain. The work of later researchers, much of it based on questions raised by Hess' studies, will be discussed here.

QUESTIONS AND EVIDENCE

1. What kinds of behavior does brain stimulation induce?

2. How does brain stimulation affect motivated behavior?

3. Can brain stimulation direct social behavior?

4. Can brain stimulation be useful clinically, with human patients?

Before surveying the evidence on these questions, a few important structures and functions of the brain

Figure 2. Dr. Jose Delgado stopped this charging bull by transmitting a radio-controlled signal to an electrode he had implanted in the bull's brain.

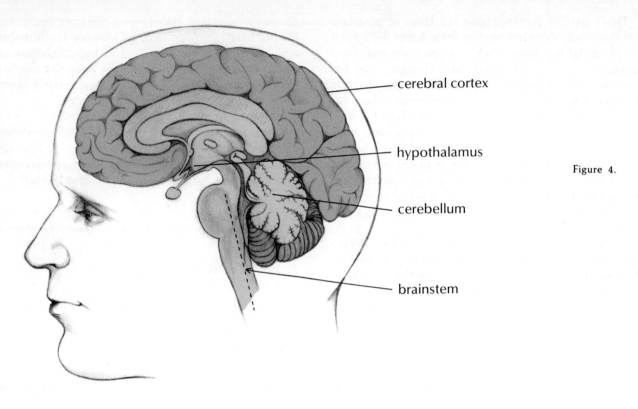

cerebral cortex

hypothalamus

cerebellum

brainstem

Figure 4.

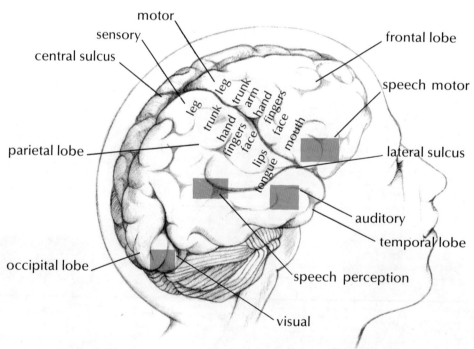

motor

sensory

central sulcus

frontal lobe

speech motor

leg
leg
trunk
trunk
arm
hand
hand
fingers
trunk
fingers
hand
face
fingers
face
face
mouth
lips
tongue

lateral sulcus

parietal lobe

auditory

temporal lobe

occipital lobe

speech perception

visual

Figure 5.

CEREBRAL CORTEX

588 IV. Biology and Behavior

Figure 4. Medial view of the human brain. The *cerebral cortex* is involved in the control of motor and sensory functions, as well as abstract thinking. The *hypothalamus* controls a large number of functions, including the coordination of the sympathetic and parasympathetic divisions of the autonomic nervous system (See Unit 35, Biofeedback) and the ingestion of food. The *cerebellum* coordinates motor functions.

should be reviewed. Although Hess discovered that some structures and functions are interrelated in complex ways, it is still possible to consider certain brain centers as performing certain primary tasks (see Figure 4). For example, the *cerebellum* controls certain motor coordinations; the *hypothalamus* controls visceral coordinations; and the *cerebral cortex* is responsible for abstract thinking.

There are some 10 billion *neurons (nerve cells)* in the brain (see Figure 6). Most neurons in the brain and spinal cord look like a tree with many branches and roots. They interact with one another across *synapses,* the regions of contact between neurons. Obviously, a great many neurons must interact to effect any one brain function.

The transmission of information from neuron to neuron in the brain is biochemical as well as electrical. An electrical impulse travels the length of a neuron and causes a chemical substance—acetylcholine (ACh)—to be released at the synaptic endings. ACh acts as a transmitter between neurons, enabling the impulse to move across the synapse to the next neuron.

The strength of the electrical signals transmitted by any one neuron is always the same. The nerve cell either fires all of its charge or it doesn't fire at all; it does not fire strongly on one occasion and weakly on another. This is known as the *all-or-none law.* The strength of the incoming signal received by the brain therefore depends on the rate at which the neurons fire, not on the intensity of the transmitted impulses, which is constant.

Figure 5. Side view of the human brain. The lobes of the cerebral cortex are: *frontal, parietal, occipital* and *temporal.* The depressions are called sulci. Major sulci are the *central sulcus* which separates the frontal lobe from the parietal lobe, and the *lateral sulcus,* below which lies the temporal lobe. The area in front of the central sulcus controls behavior as marked, while the area behind the central sulcus receives sensory information about the same bodily areas. Other functions of the brain have some localized controlling influences as marked.

Sensory receptors are special nerve cells that transform information about the environment into activations or deactivations of neural energy, as explained in Unit 31. Neurons in the central nervous system are sensitive both to excitatory and to inhibitory inputs from sensory receptors (as well as from other neurons within the nervous system itself). When excitatory inputs outweigh inhibitory inputs, a neuron sends signals to other neurons at a high frequency. Sometimes the firing rate is as high as one hundred times per second. When inhibitory inputs are stronger, a neuron may not fire at all.

These "basic facts about the brain" should be kept in mind as you consider the research described below. The first group of experiments concerns the effects of brain stimulation on motor behavior, on emotional behavior, and on larger, more complex patterns of response.

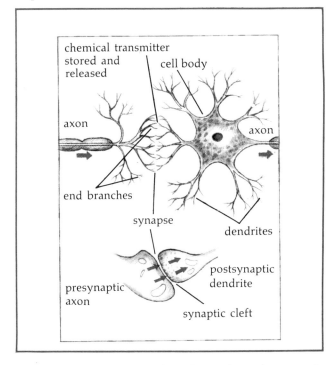

Figure 6. Schematic diagram of simple spinal neural circuit. The receivers of stimulation are the *Dendrites.* Excitation is transferred between neurons through the *Release of a Chemical Transmitter* across the Synapse—the area of junction between neurons. The upper drawing shows the cell body, axon and dendrites of a typical neuron. Below it is shown the synapse, the junction between the axon of one neuron and the dendrite of another.

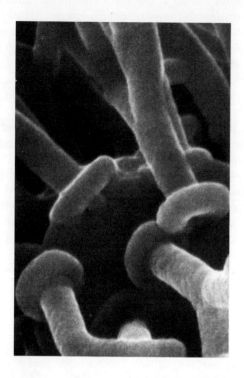

Photo made with the scanning electron microscope shows the ends of many axons, called synaptic knobs (a millionth of a millimeter in diameter), synapsing on a cell body.

HYPOTHESES	NO FATIGUE	EMOTION	PATTERN
DESCRIPTIVE EVIDENCE			
EXPERIMENTAL EVIDENCE	VARY: amount of stimulation and placement of electrode	VARY: amount of stimulation and placement of electrodes	VARY: placement of electrodes
			MEASURE: kinds of behavior patterns elicited
	MEASURE: persistence of response	MEASURE: kinds of emotional behaviors elicited	

1. WHAT KINDS OF BEHAVIOR DOES BRAIN STIMULATION INDUCE?

Some motor responses, such as yawning, arm lifting, hand clenching, leg shaking, and head turning, can be elicited by electrical stimulation of certain brain areas but become slower and weaker with repeated stimulations. Other areas of the brain do not tire in this fashion. The *no-fatigue hypothesis* states that certain brain locations can be stimulated to produce motor responses repeatedly, and indefinitely.

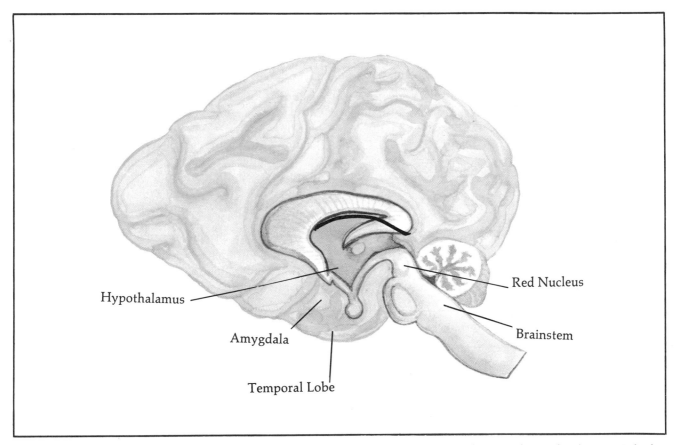

Hypothalamus

Amygdala

Temporal Lobe

Red Nucleus

Brainstem

Figure 7. Sites of stimulation in the monkey brain in Delgado's studies. When the *Amygdala* region of the *Temporal Lobe* was stimulated for long periods of time, there was no fatigue in the elicited facial response. When the *Red Nucleus* of the *Brainstem* was stimulated, the response was a long sequence of behavior.

EXPERIMENTAL EVIDENCE

Investigators: J. Delgado, M. Rivera, and D. Mir
Source, Date: "Repeated Stimulation of Amygdala in
  Awake Monkeys," 1971
Location: Yale University
Subjects: Rhesus monkeys
Materials: Implanted electrodes and stimulator

After repeated probes into the brain, the investigators found a site in the *amygdala* region of the temporal lobes (see Figure 7) that, when stimulated, caused a monkey to open its lips slightly and to retract one corner of its mouth, yielding a facial expression similar to a lopsided smile. The amygdala was stimulated for a second and a half every fifteen seconds, day and night, for forty-three days. Although that amounted to a total of 408,960 stimulations, the response remained constant.

After the experimental period was over, the animal displayed normal spontaneous activity, vision, and exploratory behavior. There was more muscular de-velopment on the side of the face that had been stimulated than on the other, but the muscularity disappeared after two months without stimulation.

Thus, it appears that some subcortical structures can be stimulated to produce a uniform response indefinitely, with no fatigue. Such stimulation apparently has no harmful effects on the animal's behavior later on.

Motor behavior is not the only kind of behavior that brain stimulation can induce. The *emotion hypothesis* states that emotional behavior can also be elicited by electrical stimulation of the brain.

Hess had noted in his cats behavior that is usually correlated with emotion—spitting, hissing, snorting, and the like—when certain areas of the brain were stimulated. But he felt that the responses were individual reflexes rather than behavioral sequences, and he questioned whether the animals' "psyches" were really involved in such states of "emotion." More recent investigations have shown that the sequences of emotional behavior evoked by electrical stimulation of the brain (ESB) are indistinguishable from the normal reactions of cats to stressful situations.

EXPERIMENTAL EVIDENCE

Investigators: R. W. Hunsperger and V. M. Bucher
Source, Date: "Affective Behavior Produced by Electrical Stimulation in the Forebrain and Brainstem of the Cat," 1967
Location: University of Zurich

Subjects: 134 cats
Materials: Implanted electrodes at 840 points; stimulator

Electrodes implanted in the cats' brainstems permitted study of the threat pattern, or "affective defense reaction"—a behavioral sequence that includes lowering the head, laying back the ears, hunching the back, growling and hissing, pupillary dilation, and other reactions of the sort cats display when they confront, say, a strange dog. The experimenters found that prolonged stimulation added an element of attack to the behavior: the cat raised a forepaw, ready to strike. The investigators demonstrated that the full threat pattern could be regularly evoked with ESB—although sometimes, after a fierce threat display, the cat resorted to flight instead of actually attacking.

Other researchers have used ESB to elicit a peculiarly menacing, "quiet" kind of attack in which a cat

The cat's threat pattern is produced by electronic stimulation of its brainstem.

stalks and kills a rat. (It is no mean feat to get a well-fed laboratory cat to attack a rat.) Such studies have led to general acceptance of the idea that emotional responses and sequences can be elicited by excitation of a variety of brain areas.

The ability of ESB to elicit emotional behavior can be viewed as part of a larger, more comprehensive idea, the *pattern hypothesis*. This hypothesis states that stimulation can be used to evoke complex, sequential patterns of responses.

EXPERIMENTAL EVIDENCE

Investigator: J. Delgado
Source, Date: "Sequential Behavior Induced Repeatedly by
  Stimulation of the Red Nucleus in Free Monkeys,"
  1965
Location: Yale University
Subjects: Rhesus monkeys
Materials: Implanted electrodes, stimulators

Stimulations applied to a point in the so-called red nucleus (see Figure 7) of the diencephalon produced an entire sequence of events. Delgado elicited the pattern in a female monkey named Ludi for fourteen days and, also in four other monkeys for shorter periods. The animals were stimulated (using radio-activated stimulators) while they were completely free moving.

The behavioral sequence began with the interruption of whatever the animal was doing. Next, the animal changed its facial expression, turned its head to the right, stood up on two feet, climbed a pole in the cage, and descended back to the floor. It uttered a low sound, threatened the other monkeys, and finally adopted a peaceful attitude and resumed its normal activities. After two weeks and more than 20,000 stimulations, Ludi—who was the dominant animal in a five-monkey colony—still repeated the pattern step-by-step, giving no indication that the experiment could not continue indefinitely.

In behavioral sequences that have been observed thus far, both fragmented and whole patterns of responses to ESB have been seen. By varying the site of the electrical stimulation, it is possible to elicit either isolated fragments, which have no apparent purpose for the organism and seem unrelated to the social situation, or well-organized and apparently meaningful sequences of actions.

Some ESB-electrically evoked behavior patterns may be "motivated" responses on the part of the organism. Researchers have directed considerable attention to the pleasure sometimes produced by stimulation as well as to the precise behavior elicited.

QUESTION	2. HOW DOES BRAIN STIMULATION AFFECT MOTIVATED BEHAVIOR?	
HYPOTHESES	**REWARD**	**TRIGGER**
DESCRIPTIVE EVIDENCE		
EXPERIMENTAL EVIDENCE	VARY: placement of electrodes	VARY: placement of electrodes
	MEASURE: rate and persistence of self-stimulation with ESB	MEASURE: amount of food eaten

2. HOW DOES BRAIN STIMULATION AFFECT MOTIVATED BEHAVIOR?

The *reward hypothesis* states that organisms will work to obtain ESB in certain areas. Because the responses are just like those of hungry laboratory animals who work to obtain food, it has been proposed that certain types of ESB might be used as reinforcers during operant conditioning (see Unit 27).

EXPERIMENTAL EVIDENCE

Investigators: J. Olds and P. Milner
Source, Date: "Positive Reinforcement Produced by
    Electrical Stimulation of Septal Area and Other
    Regions of Rat Brain," 1954
Location: McGill University
Subjects: Rats
Materials: Implanted electrodes, stimulator

Upon stimulating the septal region of a rat's brain the investigators first thought they had discovered a "curiosity" center because the animals kept returning to the spot in their cages where they had received the stimulation. But as testing continued, Olds and Milner began to suspect that their electrode was placed in a "pleasure center" of the brain and that the animals went to a particular spot because they had enjoyed the ESB.

Further experiments were carried out by placing rats in a Skinner box where they could deliver ESB to themselves by pressing a bar. A fast rate of bar-pressing was taken to mean that the animal enjoyed the ESB. Using this technique, Olds and Milner identified certain areas in the hypothalamus as "pleasure centers"—and perhaps as the most powerful centers of reinforcement. An animal with an electrode in one of these areas might stimulate itself as many as 5,000 times in an hour. Some rats would press the bar more than 2,000 times an hour for twenty-four consecutive hours.

The powerful drive to obtain the "pleasure" of ESB has also been demonstrated in other ways. For example, rats on a runway will run much faster to receive electrical stimulation of a reward area than to obtain food, even when they are hungry. Rats trained to cross an electric grid in order to receive either food or stimulation of a reward area will endure greater shock if rewarded with ESB than if rewarded with food.

Motivating such behavior, apparently, is a "drive" for the electrical stimulation of reward areas itself. But other types of motivated behavior can also be controlled by ESB. The *trigger hypothesis* states that stimulation can activate brain mechanisms that produce such motivated behavior as feeding, sexual activity, and maternal responses.

Feeding is partly under the control of a dual brain mechanism. In the lateral area of the hypothalamus, electrical or chemical stimulation induces feeding, and destruction of this region depresses feeding. In the ventromedial nucleus this situation is reversed: stimulation suppresses feeding, while destruction augments it.

EXPERIMENTAL EVIDENCE

Investigators: B. Hoebel and P. Teitelbaum
Source, Date: "Hypothalamic Control of Feedings and
    Self-Stimulation," 1962
Location: University of Pennsylvania
Subjects: Rats
Materials: Implanted electrodes and stimulator

The investigators implanted electrodes in the region of the hypothalamus where electrical stimulation caused the rats to eat. Starting the day after implantation, feeding behavior was elicited reliably each time the hypothalamus was stimulated. Even rats that were already full of food began to eat within ten seconds of the onset of stimulation and continued eating for a few seconds after the stimulus was turned off.

In another experiment, conducted by Neal Miller (1967), rats were trained to get water from a spout and to obtain food by pushing aside a little hinged door. Then ESB was administered in the feeding center of thirsty rats at the water spout. The thirsty rats promptly went to the food door and opened it. The fact that the stimulation elicited this learned response shows that it has at least some of the motivating properties of normal hunger.

If electrodes are implanted in the feeding centers of rats and the rats are allowed to control ESB themselves, they stimulate the feeding center at a much higher rate when they are hungry than when they are satiated. This finding suggests that the mechanism triggered by ESB in this particular area is probably involved in the control of feeding behavior under natural conditions. The same feeding centers can be controlled by chemical brain stimulation.

In similar experiments exploring sexual responses, Fisher (1964) injected a small amount of the male sex hormone, testosterone, into part of a male rat's brain to see if it would trigger male sexual behavior. But instead of trying to mount a female, the male grabbed her by the tail and pulled her across the cage. When newborn rat pups were placed in the cage, the male picked them up and carried them to a corner, built a nest with strips of paper, and started behaving like a mother rat. Though the effect soon wore off, when testosterone was injected into the same site again, the male repeated the maternal behavior. The meaning of Fisher's results is not thoroughly understood.

Other experiments have shown that ESB can trigger aggressive behavior and escape behavior. It can also affect behavior related to the balance of water and salt in the body and bring about physiological changes related to body heat.

3. CAN BRAIN STIMULATION DIRECT SOCIAL BEHAVIOR?

The question of whether ESB can control social behavior is still open to debate. Are the "social responses" evoked by ESB merely isolated reactions to the stimulation or do they occur within the context of past social experiences and lead to relatively permanent changes in an animal's behavior? The question is hard to answer, partly because social behavior is so complex.

One fruitful line of research has focused on aggressive behavior in monkey colonies. A colony of rhesus monkeys usually has a well-defined dominance hierarchy. The largest and most aggressive animals have their choice of food, space, and mates; the others must take the leftovers. Aggressive behavior is instrumental in the formation of the hierarchy, in its maintenance, and in status changes among group members. Before a hierarchy has been established, aggressive encounters make up some 80 percent of all social activity in the group. Later, attack behavior is largely replaced by less disruptive forms of aggression such as threatening displays. The few attacks that do occur are almost always directed at subordinate animals by dominant ones. Only rarely do dominance hierarchies change.

Thus the dominance hierarchies in a monkey colony can be used to assess the changes in social behavior brought about by ESB. The *aggression hypothesis* states that brain stimulation can be used to make an animal more aggressive and socially dominant.

QUESTION	3. CAN BRAIN STIMULATION DIRECT SOCIAL BEHAVIOR?
HYPOTHESIS	AGGRESSION
DESCRIPTIVE EVIDENCE	
EXPERIMENTAL EVIDENCE	VARY: 1. position in dominance hierarchy 2. administration of ESB MEASURE: 1. aggressive behaviors in response to ESB 2. changes in dominance hierarchy

Investigator: J. Delgado
Source, Date: "Social Rank and Radio-Stimulated
    Aggressiveness in Monkeys," 1967
Location: Yale University
Subjects: Rhesus monkeys
Materials: Electrodes, radio stimulators

Four to six monkeys with electrodes implanted in their brains were housed together in large cages. Electrical stimulation, which was controlled by radio signals so that the animals would be completely free to move about, evoked offensive and aggressive behavior.

Delgado found that the expression of aggression in response to ESB varied from one animal to another, depending on the monkey's position in the dominance hierarchy. With stimulation, the dominant monkey in a cage would launch systematic attacks against the subordinate animals, chasing them around the cage and often striking and biting them. But a female who was at the bottom of the dominance hierarchy in her cage initiated only a small number of attacks in response to ESB. When the members of the colony were changed so that she could assume a more dominant position, her aggressive reactions to ESB increased. It would seem, therefore, that the social behavior evoked by ESB is greatly influenced by the context in which it occurs.

EXPERIMENTAL EVIDENCE

Investigators: B. W. Robinson, M. Alexander, and G. Bowne
Source, Date: "Dominance Reversal Resulting from Aggressive Responses Evoked by Brain Telestimulation," 1969
Location: Emory University
Subjects: Rhesus monkeys
Materials: Implanted electrodes, radio stimulators

Each of two implanted males was placed with a larger, dominant male and his female consort. At first, the experimental animal made every effort to avoid the larger male, grimacing and crouching at his approach, and ignored all sexual presentations by the female. But in response to ESB, the subordinate male attacked the dominant male, who fought back vigorously. The fights were intense and vicious. Initially the subordinate experimental animal lost most of the battles and, between stimulations, continued to behave submissively. Later on, after repeated attacks by the stimulated male, the dominant animal began to fight less effectively, and a reversal of power began. Eventually, the newly dominant male was able to pace freely about the cage and to keep his opponent in check easily. He also mounted the female and eventually was groomed by her.

Before the shift in dominance occurred, the female regularly joined her dominant partner in retaliation against the subordinate. As the turning point approached she stayed out of all fights. Right after the reversal, she would approach the defeated male, groom him, and assume a sexual position, but he would consistently avoid her. Finally, she turned her attention to the other, now-dominant male.

The change in status remained stable for some time after ESB was terminated. This fact, as well as the fact that the stimulated male's attacks were always directed toward the dominant male (never toward the female), suggests that the social behavior evoked by ESB was not a mechanical "reflex response" but had much in common with the social behavior that occurs under ordinary conditions.

QUESTION 4. CAN BRAIN STIMULATION BE USEFUL CLINICALLY WITH HUMAN PATIENTS?

HYPOTHESIS	SELF-CONTROL
DESCRIPTIVE EVIDENCE	ASSESS: effects of ESB self-control on behavior of an epileptic patient
EXPERIMENTAL EVIDENCE	

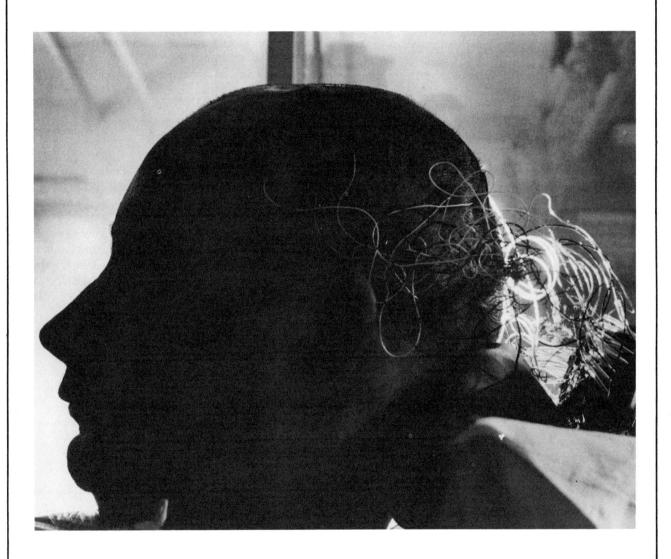

Figure 8. Brain stimulation in humans has been used successfully to relieve unpleasant symptoms.

4. CAN BRAIN STIMULATION BE USEFUL CLINICALLY WITH HUMAN PATIENTS?

Experimental work with primates has suggested to some scientists that ESB might be used to diagnose and treat human medical problems. Epilepsy is an example; the neurosurgeon Wilder Penfield has reported a number of cases in which stimulation of the cortex of the brain indicated the site of disease, enabling him to relieve the patient's major symptoms through surgery.

The *self-control hypothesis* states that medical patients can learn to use self-initiated brain stimulation to help control or alleviate their problems. Because this area is still highly experimental, ESB has usually been tried only when conventional methods of treatment have failed.

DESCRIPTIVE EVIDENCE

Investigator: R. Heath
Source, Date: "Electrical Self-Stimulation of the Brain in Man," 1963
Location: Tulane University

Subject: A male epileptic patient
Materials: Implanted electrodes, self-stimulator

The patient suffered from narcolepsy, which caused him to fall asleep without warning, even while walking, driving, or eating. Heath implanted two electrodes in the patient's brain, one in a "reward" center and the other at a spot in the brainstem that, when activated, alerted or woke him. The patient controlled the stimulation by using an apparatus attached to his belt. He reported that stimulation of the reward center made him "feel good," almost as if he were approaching sexual orgasm (though even repeated, rapid stimulation failed to produce actual sexual orgasm). When the patient felt that he might fall asleep, he could stimulate himself by activating the other electrode and feel wide awake again. If he fell asleep too quickly to stimulate himself, another person could awaken him by pushing the correct button on his stimulator.

Heath also worked with an epileptic whose seizures resulted in agitated and violent "psychotic" behavior. After an electrode had been implanted in his reward center, the patient could counter his rage and disorganization by stimulation, which changed his mood abruptly to happiness and mild euphoria.

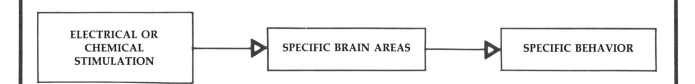

| ELECTRICAL OR CHEMICAL STIMULATION | → | SPECIFIC BRAIN AREAS | → | SPECIFIC BEHAVIOR |

PUTTING IT TOGETHER: Brain Stimulation

Electrical stimulation of the brain may be initiated through electrodes, and *chemical stimulation* through cannulae inserted into the brain. Depending upon which *area of the brain* is stimulated, a wide variety of *specific behavior* may be elicited.

One unusual property of direct brain stimulation is that some behaviors appear to persist without fatigue. The stimulation of some brain areas results in an invariably sequential complex pattern of behavior, while still other areas trigger whatever behavior will satisfy specific motives. Stimulation of some areas lead to persistent self-stimulation which is apparently rewarding. Emotional and aggressive behavior may also be elicited and, depending upon the area stimulated, be without direction, or directed towards a specific social target.

In humans with certain brain disorders, brain stimulation is occasionally clinically useful to permit the patient normally unavailable self-control.

WHAT'S ACCEPTED AND WHAT'S DEBATED

1. WHAT'S ACCEPTED . . .

1. ESB can produce either fragmented responses or complex behavioral patterns.

2. Electrical and chemical stimulation can elicit motivated behavior such as feeding.

3. ESB can be experienced as very rewarding or very punishing.

4. ESB can alter social organization in groups of nonhuman animals.

5. ESB is a useful diagnostic and surgical tool for brain surgery and, as a therapeutic method, has potential for helping to alleviate medical problems.

2. WHAT'S DEBATED . . .

1. Whether artificial, prolonged brain stimulation harms the brain.

2. Whether brain stimulation can produce only responses that are already in an animal's behavioral repertoire.

3. The eventual social consequences of control through brain stimulation.

ISSUE: ELECTROLIGARCHY

Few areas of psychological research have stimulated as much popular attention as brain stimulation. Countless magazine articles have been devoted to the subject, many of them dealing speculatively (and unenthusiastically) about the prospects of a future totalitarian society in which the people would be controlled by remote radio signals directed to electrodes implanted in every brain.

Esquire magazine, for example, wrote about a possible "electroligarchy," ruled by a small minority whose brains would be untouched, but would have a computer-based control over the minds of everyone beneath them. The second rank in society would be the "Electrons," a group with a few implanted electrodes to keep them contented and creative. The third rank would be the "Positrons," a white-collar group with more electrodes, who would be in charge of administrative tasks. The lowest and largest group would be "Neutrons," completely robotized workers who would "dig ditches all day and love every minute of it."

These speculations are of course fanciful, and belong more to the realm of science fiction than to our likely future reality. People are sometimes disturbed, however, by the thought that an electrical stimulus can govern their behavior. When Dr. Jose Delgado administered a stimulus to one man to make him close his fist, the man found that his conscious attempts to open it were useless. "I guess, Doctor, that your electricity is stronger than my will," he complained. Delgado has lent some force to the fears of a future "electroligarchy" by his advocacy of what he calls "psychocivilization"—the use of all relevant physiological, pyschological and psychiatric knowledge to help form the mind of the child. "Truly," he contends, "heaven and hell are within the brain," and he believes that we can and should work toward enhancing the "heaven" component. (One of the most interesting discoveries in the brain stimulation of rats is that the animals appear to find stimulation of 60 percent of the area of the brain pleasurable, 35 percent neutral, and only 5 percent unpleasant.)

Delgado's hopes certainly seem over-ambitious in the present state of our knowledge of brain stimulation. The most likely applications of our growing knowledge of the field will be in the area of medicine. Already, Dr. Robert Heath of Tulane University has prevented epileptic seizures by implanting electrodes in the brain. He has also managed to relieve the excruciating pain felt by some terminal cancer patients—whose pain often cannot be alleviated by drugs—through the use of brain stimulation, although as many as 125 separate electrodes may be needed.

Other researchers, such as neurosurgeon Vernon Mark of the Boston City Hospital, have used brain stimulation to eliminate outbursts of rage in persons suffering from epilepsy in the temporal lobe of the brain. Electrodes are implanted in the brain to locate the area responsible for the attacks, and the area is then burned out with a stronger burst of current.

Among the more exciting new areas of research are tentative steps to create a mechanical substitute for the brain itself. Dr. Lawrence Pinneo and his associates at the Stanford Research Institute are not attempting to duplicate the complexity of the reasoning powers of the brain, but they are hoping to replicate some of the brain's natural motor functions involving the purposeful movement of legs and arms. Their intention is to help millions of persons whose limbs have been paralyzed through brain damage caused by strokes.

Bodily movement is directed by the motor areas of the cerebral cortex and is integrated in the brain stem. When a person suffers a stroke, the blood supply to the cortex is disrupted and cells in the motor areas are destroyed, causing paralysis in the limbs that these areas govern. Pinneo and his associates determined to find out whether the brain stem, which is not usually affected by strokes, can be electrically stimulated to assume the functions of the damaged cortex motor areas. In experiments on monkeys, they discovered some 200 different sites in the brain stem that when electrically stimulated produced movements in supposedly paralyzed limbs. In fact, the movements were even more precise than they would have been if the cerebral cortex itself had been stimulated.

Next, the researchers programmed a computer to fire electrodes in sequence to bring about purposeful motion in the paralyzed limbs of a monkey. One program, for example, enabled the monkey to extend its arm, pick up food, and place the food in its mouth. Another allowed the monkey to scratch its back, and a third enabled it to use a paralyzed arm for climbing. The monkey was presented with a set of switches controlling the computer, and was able to pick a program to control its own bodily movements.

Pinneo and his associates believe that it will be possible to extend the same capacities to humans who have been partially paralyzed by strokes. More research will be needed to work out the maximum possible number of combinations and permutations so as to allow for the widest range of motor movements, and the computer equipment itself will have to be miniaturized for everyday use. The uses of the method may even extend beyond the treatment of stroke victims. Pinneo believes that it may be possible to restore vision in some forms of blindness.

Brain stimulation also offers us new prospects for understanding what is perhaps the most mysterious object in the known universe: our own minds. Shielded for centuries behind a thick skull and a wall of superstition, this 3-pound mass of pinkish grey jelly has long defied our attempts to understand its workings. We are now on the brink of what may be the greatest "breakthrough" in all psychology—the capacity of the human mind to comprehend itself.

Unit 35

Biofeedback

OVERVIEW

This unit presents data from an area of psychology that has emerged only in the last 15 years—how people can learn to control their "involuntary" body functions by means of biofeedback. In the first part of the unit, examples are presented demonstrating how animals and humans can learn to control autonomic activity, fine muscle activity, and brain wave patterns. The remainder of the unit examines recent evidence on how these abilities might be applied to the betterment of man.

UNIT OUTLINE

DEFINITION AND BACKGROUND
1. *Definition:* biofeedback is the reception of information by an individual about ongoing changes in his own body, through sensitive electronic instruments that sense these changes and display them to the subject in the form of some easily observable stimulus (usually a light or sound).
2. *Background:* Neal Miller (1909–   ).

QUESTIONS AND EVIDENCE
1. What physiological processes usually thought of as involuntary can we learn to control?
Hypotheses:
    a. *Autonomic-activity:* an individual can learn to control autonomic functions if he is given information or feedback about the ongoing changes that occur. **606**
    b. *Individual-motor-units:* individual motor units can be singled out and voluntarily controlled through the use of biofeedback. **608**
    c. *Brain-waves:* using biofeedback, an individual can learn to enhance or suppress specific components (rhythms) of his own brain waves at will. **609**
2. How can biofeedback techniques be used for therapeutic purposes?
Hypotheses:
    a. *Relaxation:* by means of biofeedback, individuals can achieve states of profound relaxation. **611**
    b. *Migraine-relief:* the symptoms of migraine headache can be reduced by teaching an individual, through biofeedback, to simultaneously warm his hands and cool his forehead. **611**
    c. *Muscular-rehabilitation:* individuals can learn, using biofeedback, to activate and control nerve pathways to their muscles and thus to regain some use of muscles and limbs formerly useless. **612**
3. How might biofeedback be used to enhance self-awareness?
Hypotheses:
    a. *Hypnagogic-imagery:* if the images appearing in a twilight state of consciousness are made accessible to conscious thought, the individual involved will gain enhanced self-awareness and productivity. **614**

IMPORTANT CONCEPTS

                                page

autonomic nervous system **604**
biofeedback **604**
brain waves **609**
feedback **605**
hypnagogic imagery **614**
motor unit **608**
operant conditioning **604**
psychosomatic disorders **611**
shaping **605**
successive approximations **605**

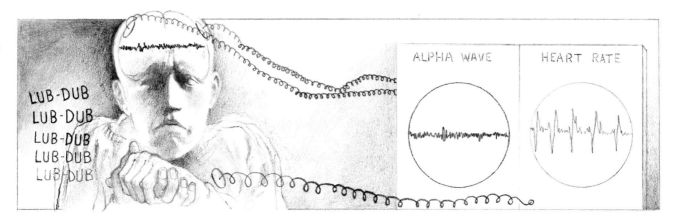

Biological states about which we are normally unaware may be monitored and displayed by electronic instruments.

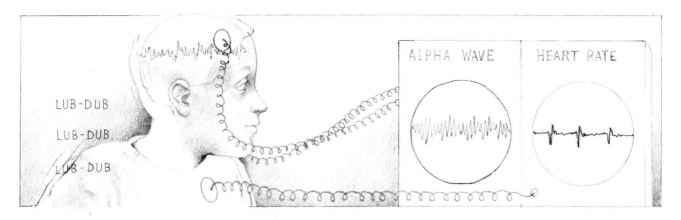

This display can provide feedback for people about the biological difference between desired and undesired states.

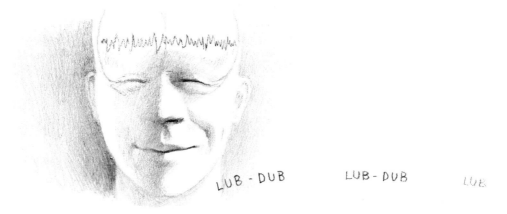

With the use of biofeedback some people can learn to control desirable states not normally under voluntary control.

DEFINITION AND BACKGROUND

In recent years psychologists and physiologists have been exploring the possibility that certain people can and do control their own bodily processes in ways usually thought of as impossible in our culture. Out of this research has emerged a new technique that may have significant consequences for the understanding of human behavior.

A working DEFINITION of biofeedback is *the reception of information by an individual about ongoing changes in his own body, through sensitive electronic instruments that sense these changes and display them to the subject in the form of some easily observable stimulus* (usually a light or sound).

By perceiving the changes that are occurring inside his own body, the individual acquires the potential means for learning to control those bodily functions consciously. A person who is made aware of changes in his or her pulse rate, blood pressure, or skin temperature, for example, may gradually attain conscious control of these autonomic or involuntary functions.

Many older, traditional notions about the nature of voluntary control of the body are being challenged by biofeedback research. This unit will FOCUS on the practical implications of the possibility that bodily functions can be controlled through biofeedback training.

Figure 1. Neal Miller, whose research showed that processes of the autonomic nervous system can be controlled through biofeedback.

BACKGROUND: NEAL E. MILLER (1909–   )

By the 1950s Neal Miller had established himself as one of the leading experimental psychologists and theorists in the study of learning. At that time, Miller was bothered by a basic assumption of traditional psychology: the notion that there are two distinct kinds of learning. According to traditional psychologists, one type of learning is expressed through the skeletal muscles regulated by the central nervous system (CNS) and the other is expressed through visceral and glandular responses (such as blood pressure, skin temperature, and stomach contractions) regulated by the autonomic nervous system (ANS). These two kinds of learning are referred to as operant conditioning (see Unit 27) and Pavlovian conditioning (Unit 26).

It was known that, through the CNS, the move-ments of skeletal muscles could be conditioned by means of trial-and-error or operant conditioning. When an animal discovers an activity that results in a reward, it tends to repeat the responses that it made when it got the reward. On the other hand, the ANS had received its name because it was believed to be autonomous or independent of the organism's will. Because, for example, the heart speeds up according to the needs of the body, not as a result of volition, it was believed that such responses could not be altered or affected through operant conditioning. Instead, they were thought to require Pavlovian or classical conditioning.

Miller set out to show that the autonomic responses *could* be operantly conditioned. One important difficulty had to be surmounted: in order to ensure that the results were not contaminated by the activity of the skeletal system, the movements of the skeletal system had to be eliminated from the experiments entirely. The solution was to inject an animal with a drug (like curare) that would paralyze the skeletal system totally, leaving the ANS relatively intact and functioning. In one experiment paralyzed rats were divided into two groups. One group was rewarded with electrical stimulation of the brain (see Unit 34) for increasing its heart rate, and the other was rewarded for slowing down its heart rate. At first, members of the "up" group were rewarded whenever their heart rate was even a tiny bit above average, and the "down" group whenever their heart rate was a tiny bit below average. As the experiment progressed, these small changes were no longer rewarded, and the animals had to produce ever larger changes to get a reward. This technique of gradually rewarding successive approximations toward the desired response is known as "shaping." By the end of ninety minutes of training, the difference in heart rate between the two groups was so great that no doubts were left: rats could learn to control their heart rate to get rewards. These results were published by Miller and DiCara in 1967.

Other researchers have since confirmed these results and extended them to other visceral and glandular responses, including the secretion of gastric juice in the stomach, the output of bile from the liver, and the rate of urine formation. All these processes could be conditioned by means of operant procedures.

All operant conditioning has certain requirements. The following are applicable to training of internal functions:

1. *The physiological function must be labile and capable of being monitored.* Your heart rate, blood pressure, and brain waves all change from time to time and are therefore labile functions. But there must also be equipment sensitive enough to detect the changes, which may often involve less than a millionth of a volt of electricity.

2. *The physiological changes must be reflected back to the subject as feedback.* With lower animals, feedback information can be given in the form of rewards; with humans, it can be presented directly as readings on an instrument.

3. *The subject must be motivated to learn.* This is a universal principle, no different for biofeedback than for any other type of learning.

In 1958 at the University of Chicago, Joe Kamiya

showed that people could be trained to distinguish among their own brain wave patterns. Mulholland, at the Bedford, Massachusetts Veterans Administration Hospital had started to work with the processes involved in paying attention. Certain brain-wave patterns appeared to be associated with paying attention and others with unfocused attention.

Fifty years earlier, Johannes Schultz, a German physician, was the originator of a type of medical practice called autogenic training. Schultz taught his patients how to will their hands warm, their forehead cool, and their heart and respiration to slow down, all supposedly involuntary or autonomic functions.

Schultz's American counterpart was E. Jacobson, who developed a process called progressive relaxation. This process is widely used in behavior therapy and in biofeedback training.

Figure 2. Electronic recorders monitor various bodily states to inform this man of his progress in learning to control them.

It is only within the last few years that these disparate but parallel traditions have come together. The cross fertilization of ideas from animal research, human research, and the medical clinic shows promise for interesting results in the future.

QUESTIONS AND EVIDENCE

1. What physiological processes usually thought of as involuntary can we learn to control?

2. How can biofeedback techniques be used for therapeutic purposes?

3. How might biofeedback be used to enhance self-awareness?

equilibrium under varying environmental circumstances.

The *autonomic-activity hypothesis* states that an individual can learn to control autonomic functions if he is given information or feedback about the ongoing changes that occur.

EXPERIMENTAL EVIDENCE

Investigators: J. Brener and R. A. Kleinman
Source, Date: "Learned Control of Decreases in Systolic Blood Pressure," 1968
Location: University of Tennessee
Subjects: 10 college students

QUESTION — 1. WHAT PHYSIOLOGICAL PROCESSES USUALLY THOUGHT OF AS INVOLUNTARY CAN WE LEARN TO CONTROL?

HYPOTHESES	AUTONOMIC ACTIVITY	INDIVIDUAL MOTOR UNITS	BRAIN WAVES
DESCRIPTIVE EVIDENCE		ASSESS: ability of subjects to control single motor units when biofeedback is given	ASSESS: ability of subjects to discriminate and control brain wave patterns when biofeedback is given
EXPERIMENTAL EVIDENCE	VARY: instruction to use feedback MEASURE: change in blood pressure		

1. WHAT PHYSIOLOGICAL PROCESSES USUALLY THOUGHT OF AS INVOLUNTARY CAN WE LEARN TO CONTROL?

Perhaps biofeedback's greatest challenge to traditional points of view in our culture is the notion that the autonomic nervous system can be brought under voluntary control.

Autonomic activities of the body regulate blood pressure, heart rate, skin temperature, and the other internal processes that are required to maintain bodily

Materials: Manometer to measure blood pressure, counter to accumulate pressure readings during each trial

Five experimental and five control subjects were exposed to identical conditions except for the instructions given them. The control subjects were told that the procedure was an investigation of cardiovascular processes and that they should merely watch the visual displays. The experimental subjects were told that their systolic blood pressure was being monitored and that they should make a deliberate effort to keep

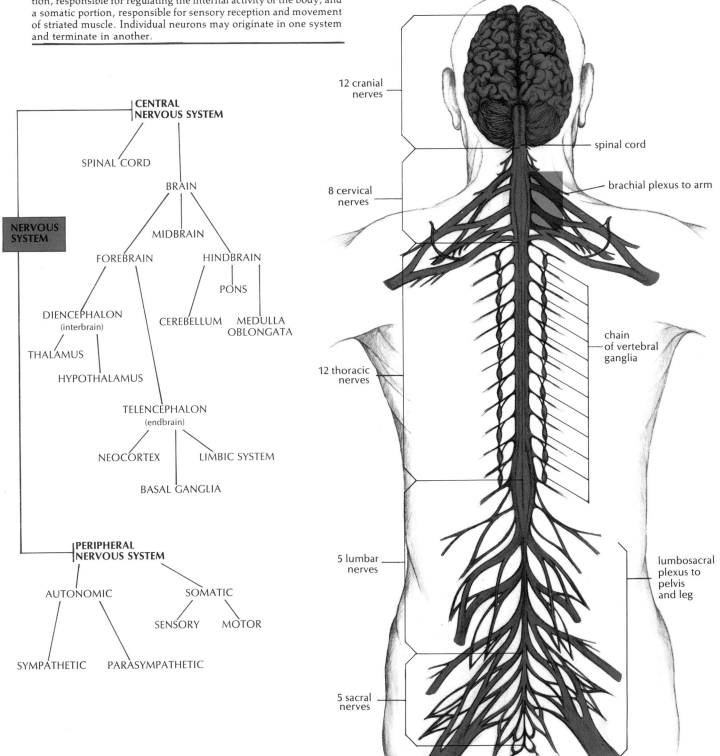

Figure 3. Schematic diagram of the major divisions of the nervous system. The central nervous system consists of the brain and spinal cord. The peripheral nervous system includes an autonomic portion, responsible for regulating the internal activity of the body, and a somatic portion, responsible for sensory reception and movement of striated muscle. Individual neurons may originate in one system and terminate in another.

NERVOUS SYSTEM

CENTRAL NERVOUS SYSTEM
- SPINAL CORD
- BRAIN
  - MIDBRAIN
  - FOREBRAIN
    - DIENCEPHALON (interbrain)
      - THALAMUS
      - HYPOTHALAMUS
    - TELENCEPHALON (endbrain)
      - NEOCORTEX
      - BASAL GANGLIA
      - LIMBIC SYSTEM
  - HINDBRAIN
    - PONS
    - CEREBELLUM
    - MEDULLA OBLONGATA

PERIPHERAL NERVOUS SYSTEM
- AUTONOMIC
  - SYMPATHETIC
  - PARASYMPATHETIC
- SOMATIC
  - SENSORY
  - MOTOR

12 cranial nerves
8 cervical nerves
12 thoracic nerves
5 lumbar nerves
5 sacral nerves

spinal cord
brachial plexus to arm
chain of vertebral ganglia
lumbosacral plexus to pelvis and leg

both the manometer readings and the counter readings as low as possible. One session consisted of a series of twenty trials of fifty seconds each, with a half-minute rest in between. Each subject participated in two such sessions.

Relative to the control group, the experimental subjects were able to decrease their mean blood pressure readings over the twenty trials of a single session (about 12 percent on the average). These results showed that the degree of control over blood pressure is larger than previously thought possible, a finding with therapeutic potential for patients with chronic high blood pressure.

Another process traditionally thought to be involuntary is the contraction of individual motor units. Skeletal muscle contraction is the result of summed contractions of individual motor units. A motor unit consists of one spinal motoneuron and the muscle fibers it innervates. Normal contractions are varied in strength and speed both by the addition of motor units and by the increased frequency of discharge of individual motoneurons. One normally is not aware of this process, but only of the final result—the contraction of the muscle.

The *individual-motor-units hypothesis* states that

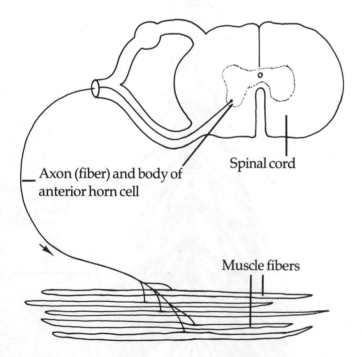

Axon (fiber) and body of anterior horn cell

Spinal cord

Muscle fibers

individual motor units can be singled out and voluntarily controlled through the use of biofeedback.

DESCRIPTIVE EVIDENCE

Investigator: J. V. Basmajian
Source, Date: "Control and Training of Individual Motor Units," 1963
Location: Queen's University, Kingston, Ontario
Subjects: 16 individuals ranging from twenty to fifty-five years of age
Materials: Electromyograph (EMG) with loudspeaker and oscilloscope outputs

Each subject had a pair of fine wire electrodes inserted in a muscle of the thumb. Whenever a contraction occurred in the vicinity of the electrode, a small pulse of electricity was produced, which the electrode carried to the electromyograph (EMG), where the signal was amplified and displayed both on an oscilloscope and through a loudspeaker. Each motor unit generated a slightly different sound from the others in the thumb, so the subject could readily identify the one unit that he was to try to control.

Within fifteen to thirty minutes of seeing and hearing feedback from their thumbs' muscle activity, subjects learned how to relax the muscles in the thumb completely, then to recruit the activity of a single motor unit among the hundred or so in the vicinity of the electrode. Then subjects were instructed to try to shut off the first motor unit, pick another, and keep it active while the rest of the muscle relaxed. All the subjects were able to do this, and over half were able to isolate and control still a third such motor unit.

Most interesting were the achievements of the eleven subjects with the finest control when they were asked to reduce and increase the firing rate of a single motor unit. Most of them could do this at will; some even produced drum beating sounds, galloping rhythms, and so on.

Apparently, with the proper feedback an individual can pick out one of the motor units in his body and

Figure 4. Schematic drawing of a single motor unit controlled through biofeedback. Adapted from Basmajian (1963).

make it work faster or slower or even rhythmically. Musicians working with Basmajian are attempting to use these EMG feedback techniques to show students what they are doing wrong, since there are measurable differences between the kinds of muscle activity that the beginning musician exhibits as compared to that of an advanced performer. One can speculate about possible uses of this ability for therapeutic purposes. For example, would it be possible for amputated individuals to learn to control and drive an artificial limb precisely?

When we think of voluntary control, we tend to think in terms of higher levels of the brain. Yet there are specific states of the brain measured by brain waves that most of us never think of controlling simply because we don't know about them. Brain waves are tiny electrical charges generated by the brain and detectable at the scalp. The *brain-waves hypothesis* states that, using biofeedback, an individual can learn to enhance or suppress specific components (rhythms) of his own brain waves at will.

With electrodes pasted to the scalp, brain waves are measured by an electroencephalograph (EEG) (see Unit 32). Many types of rhythms are detectable, and the rhythms normally vary with the time of day and a person's age and state of arousal—for example, whether he is daydreaming or consciously analyzing. Two of the most common EEG patterns during waking are the alpha rhythm (slower, larger waves) and the beta rhythm (faster, smaller). The beta rhythm is typical of active waking behavior, while the alpha is typical of more inner-directed, more relaxed wakefulness. In the normal EEG output from a subject who is awake, alpha waves make up about 20 to 80 percent of the brain wave activity over time.

As with blood pressure and single motor units, brain waves are internal, normally involuntary events. Is it possible to consciously discriminate the rhythms of one's own electroencephalogram? The study by Joe Kamiya reported here was actually first conducted as early as 1958.

DESCRIPTIVE EVIDENCE

Investigator: J. Kamiya
Source, Date: "Operant Control of the EEG Alpha Rhythm and Some of Its Reported Effects on Consciousness," 1969

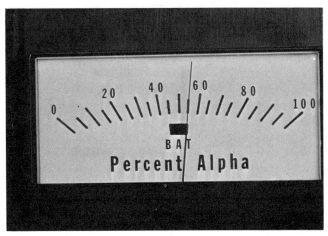

Figure 5. Subjects can learn to produce alpha brain waves through biofeedback techniques. The alpha rhythm is associated with relaxed wakefulness.

Location: University of Chicago
Subjects: 6 college students
Materials: EEG; bell

While each subject was lying comfortably with electrodes pasted to his scalp, the investigator watched his EEG output to determine whether or not at any given moment he was producing alpha- or nonalpha-wave pattern. The investigator rang a bell about five times a minute, scheduling the rings so that they occurred half the time when alpha was present and half the time when it was absent. The subject's task was to guess, at each ring of the bell, whether he was in state A (alpha) or B (nonalpha), and he was informed immediately of whether his guess was correct or not.

By the third hour in these conditions, many subjects were correct in 75 to 80 percent of their guesses. The initial success rate had been 50 percent (chance). Some subjects learned to identify their brain wave states correctly 100 percent of the time.

In subsequent investigations in dozens of labs throughout the country it was demonstrated that once they have been trained to discriminate components of their own EEG, subjects are also able to control them.

To suppress the alpha rhythms, for example, researcher Thomas Mulholland found that paying visual attention was a significant factor. Alpha and visual attention seemed to be mutually exclusive states. Researcher Barbara Brown showed that there was significant agreement among subjects as to the subjective states associated with alpha. After allowing subjects to see their different brain wave patterns displayed—alpha, beta, and theta—through three different lights, they were asked to give their subjective associations to each of the lights (they did not know ahead of time which light represented which brain-wave pattern). The subjects' brief written descriptions are remarkably alike: fourteen used such words as "pleasant feeling," "well-being," "pleasure," "tranquility," "relaxation"; seven used such words as "increased awareness of thoughts and feelings"; and three reported no special feelings. Thus, although subjects could not verbalize how they produced one or another brain-wave state, they were in close agreement as to the feelings associated.

An experiment by Wyrwicka and Sterman (1968) suggests one application of brain-wave control. They recorded the local slow-wave activity from the sensorimotor cortex of the freely moving awake cat. This slow-wave activity was reinforced by offering milk to the cats whenever it appeared. The cats subsequently produced much more of the local slow-wave activity as long as its appearance was followed by milk. The response was extinguished when milk was no longer offered.

These slow waves were always preceded by substantial inhibition of movement by the cats. Later, some of the animals were accidentally exposed to a poison that causes epilepticlike seizure and usually results in death. Those cats that earlier had learned to produce the brain-wave response became sick, but none of them died. Had the seizures been controlled in some way by their ability to produce the slow-wave activity?

Perhaps human beings might be able to use biofeedback to suppress the seizures and abnormal brain activity of true epilepsy. At present Sterman is conducting further studies to investigate this possibility in epileptic patients, and his preliminary results have been very encouraging. For example, one patient who was having twelve to fifteen severe epileptic seizures per month showed a gradual decline of seizures with three months of biofeedback training, by which time all seizures had stopped. The possibilities of brain-wave control are enormous, but conclusions about its use must wait for more evidence.

QUESTION	2. HOW CAN BIOFEEDBACK TECHNIQUES BE USED FOR THERAPEUTIC PURPOSES?		
HYPOTHESES	RELAXATION	MIGRAINE RELIEF	MUSCULAR REHABILITATION
DESCRIPTIVE EVIDENCE		ASSESS: relationships between temperature control by biofeedfack and migraine relief	ASSESS: use of EMG feedback training on muscular rehabilitation
EXPERIMENTAL EVIDENCE	VARY: EMG feedback from forehead muscles MEASURE: forehead EMG level decreases (i.e., relaxation)		

2. HOW CAN BIOFEEDBACK TECHNIQUES BE USED FOR THERAPEUTIC PURPOSES?

It is known that stress and anxiety play a role in the genesis of many psychosomatic illnesses such as ulcers (see Unit 28). It is probable that such tensions are the products of the habits and behavior patterns an individual has learned in his interactions with the environment and other people. Thus, learning to relax and eliminate feelings of stress and tension might benefit one's health.

This general assumption is embodied in a traditional practice called *autogenic training,* in which an individual is trained to be able to enter a state of complete, profound relaxation at will. Widely practiced in Europe, the training consists of a series of six exercises to be learned in order. As an example, the first two exercises of autogenic training focus on cultivating sensations of heaviness and warmth in the limbs, sensations that have been long associated with muscular relaxation and increased blood flow to the area or limb involved. The profoundly relaxed state of a fully trained individual is called *trophotropic relaxation* to distinguish it from the ordinary levels of relaxation that we all experience in our daily lives. Trophotropic relaxation is characterized by less electrical activity in muscles and lower heart rate.

Recent research has focused on the question of whether biofeedback techniques might enable a person to learn to achieve trophotropic relaxation much faster than autogenic training permits.

The *relaxation hypothesis* states that, by means of biofeedback, individuals can achieve states of profound relaxation. It has been tested by experiments that concentrate on one of the most sensitive registers of anxiety tension in the human body, the band of muscle fibers in the forehead called the frontalis muscle.

EXPERIMENTAL EVIDENCE

Investigators: T. H. Budzynski, J. M. Stoyva, and C. Adler
Source, Date: "Feedback-induced Muscle Relaxation:
    Application to Tension Headache," 1970
Location: University of Colorado Medical Center
Subjects: 15 paid adult volunteers

Materials: Electromyograph (EMG); audio feedback signal; dimly lit, quiet room

Three groups of subjects were instructed to relax as much as possible, particularly concentrating their efforts on their foreheads, as they sat in a dimly lit, quiet room with frontalis muscle tension being recorded on an electromyograph (EMG). The experimental group received feedback from their frontalis muscle in the form of a tone that rose in pitch as tension increased and fell in pitch as tension decreased. One control group received no such feedback, while a second control group received irrelevant feedback (a steady low tone). In this way, the relaxing effects of the direct muscle feedback could be compared with the depth of relaxation achieved by subjects who simply tried to relax without feedback.

In three sessions, the experimental group had lowered frontalis EMG levels 50 percent, compared with 24 percent for the no feedback group, and a 28 percent rise for the irrelevant feedback subjects. The conclusion drawn from this study was that people can relax without any feedback but that the amount of relaxation can be greatly increased with the aid of tension feedback.

This evidence suggests that a new and promising area of research might be the application and use of relaxation training by means of EMG feedback for pathological conditions: for example, asthma, essential hypertension, insomnia, lower back pains, tension headache, and anxiety.

The second exercise in autogenic training involves trying to cultivate a sense of warmth in the hands and feet (by encouraging greater blood flow to the limbs). In 1969 Elmer Green and his associates at the Menninger Foundation achieved some success in teaching subjects, with biofeedback, to raise the temperature in their hands. During this research one volunteer subject who suffered from chronic migraine headaches reported that she experienced dramatic relief from a headache during one session in which her hand temperature had risen dramatically. The *migraine-relief hypothesis* states that the symptoms of migraine headache can be reduced by teaching an individual, through biofeedback, to simultaneously warm his hands and cool his forehead.

DESCRIPTIVE EVIDENCE

Investigators: J. D. Sargent, E. E. Green, and E. D. Walters
Source, Date: "Preliminary Report on the Use of Autogenic
  Feedback Techniques in the Treatment of Migraine and
  Tension Headaches," 1971
Location: Menninger Foundation
Subjects: 28 migraine sufferers (in the original study)
Materials: Portable thermal-feedback instruments

Migraine, without known organic basis, is one of several different types of headaches. The researchers made certain that the subjects' problems were not organic in origin.

Each subject was trained with the aid of a heat-sensitive instrument that continuously monitored hand temperature changes and displayed fluctuations as small as 0.1 degree F on a meter. This feedback made the patients aware of minute temperature increases (normally below the threshold of awareness) so that they could try to prolong or intensify the state of mind during which they were occurring. During a three-month period patients practiced at the clinic and at home with portable feedback units.

Successful trainees produced temperature differentials (finger relative to forehead) of 3 to 15 degrees. More importantly, the records of sixty-seven patients have been evaluated, and 74 percent of them are rated as improved on the basis of decline in the frequency, intensity, and duration of reported headache symptoms.

This recent research needs verification, but learning warmth control for migraine patients appears to be very useful. There is optimistic speculation about the use of biofeedback for other diseases that involve defects in blood circulation.

Biofeedback can also be used to encourage muscle activity in people who have become partially or completely paralyzed as a result of polio, stroke, or other types of nerve damage. By the time the restorative processes of the body have succeeded in repairing damaged nerve fibers, patients frequently have lost the ability to use their muscles. They try to contract certain muscles but nothing happens, even though the nerve and muscle tissues are healthy.

The *muscular-rehabilitation hypothesis* states that individuals can learn, using biofeedback, to activate

Figure 6. Through biofeedback training many bodily functions can be brought under conscious control. Upper left: Somatic pathways include *Sensory Nerve Cells* which bring information about tension from Muscle Fibers into the central nervous system by transmitting neural impulses to *Spinal Nerve Cells.* Upper right: The central nervous system receives information in the *Spinal Cord* by way of *Sensory Roots,* in which cell bodies collect at the *Ganglion.* Muscle control requires excitation in *Motor Roots.* Lower left: The autonomic nervous system controls internal organs and the circulatory system. The sympathetic division diffusely activates through a vertical chain of sympathetic ganglia called the *Sympathetic Trunk.* Lower right: *Sympathetic Fibers* are imbedded in *Gland Cells* for activation. With high sympathetic arousal there is constriction in the *Circulatory System,* with elevated blood pressure and stomach tightening.

and control nerve pathways to their muscles and thus to regain some use of muscles and limbs formerly useless.

DESCRIPTIVE EVIDENCE

Investigators: H. Johnson, and W. H. Garton
Source, Date: "A Practical Method of Neuro-muscular
  Rehabilitation in Hemiplegics Using EMG," 1971
Location: Casa Colina Hospital, Pomona, California
Subjects: 20 stroke patients
Materials: Portable EMG feedback units

Building on the groundwork laid by Basmajian and others, Herbert Johnson, a neurologist at the Casa Colina Hospital in California, decided to assess the utility of home training procedures for hemiplegia (stroke) victims.

EMG electrodes, which were pasted to the leg, conducted electrical impulses from a muscle to an electromyograph, which amplified them and fed them back to the patient as noise which became louder as the muscle became more efficient. Most of the patients were completely paralyzed in the muscle group that was being retrained, but they could walk with the aid of a leg brace.

Patients were afforded massive practice time, because with their own home unit, they, and not the doctor, were responsible for their own recovery. They practiced as much as they wanted and were not limited to certain hours at the hospital. This treatment program was valuable to Dr. Johnson as well, because it freed him to treat many more patients than if he had been forced to rely upon the hospital's diagnostic electromyograph.

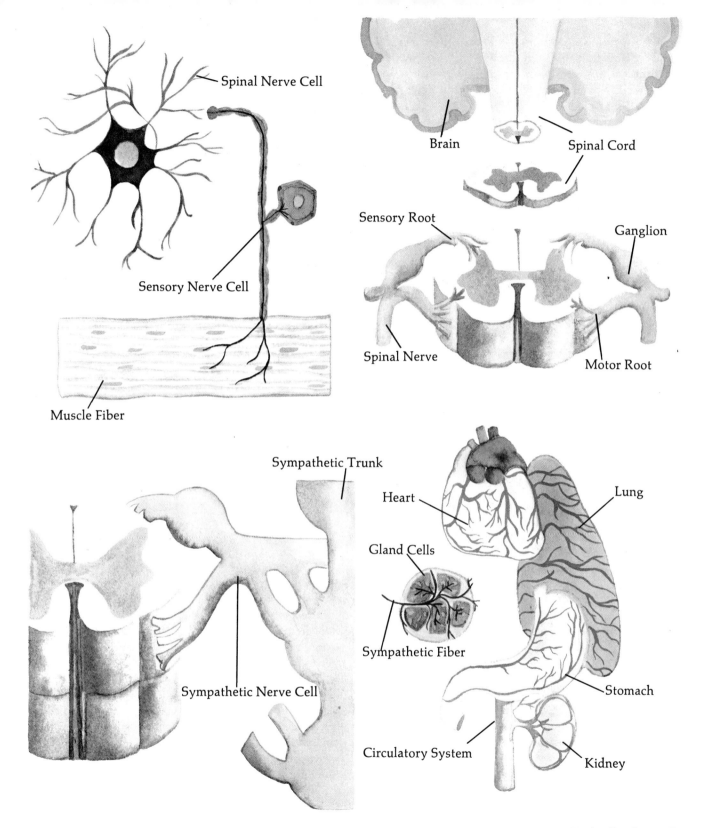

Spinal Nerve Cell

Sensory Nerve Cell

Muscle Fiber

Brain

Spinal Cord

Sensory Root

Ganglion

Spinal Nerve

Motor Root

Sympathetic Trunk

Heart

Lung

Gland Cells

Sympathetic Fiber

Stomach

Sympathetic Nerve Cell

Circulatory System

Kidney

Of the ten subjects in the study, three regained enough function to enable them to do away with the leg brace entirely. Less impressive results were achieved with the other patients, but all showed definite improvement.

One hopes that in the future, anyone who is paralyzed from an accident or stroke will not be allowed to lie in a hospital bed for weeks, doing nothing while his muscles atrophy. Initially, EMG electrodes may be placed all over the patient's body to help him detect any latent muscle activity. With such biofeedback, even if to the eye a muscle appears totally paralyzed, neuromuscular retraining can be attempted. In this way all the motor units that are functioning can be constantly exercised.

the happy position of not having to pay volunteer subjects, for word about something called the "alpha high" soon got around. People began to refer to alpha-theta brain-wave control as "electronic yoga," "a short cut to nirvana," or "the magical mystery tour."

As already mentioned, alpha is the name for a particular brain-wave pattern in which the waves occur anywhere between eight and thirteen times per second (relatively slow). This pattern is typical of a normal person who is awake, with his eyes closed, and not paying too close attention to anything. Another pattern, called theta, also has large and regular waves, but is somewhat slower than alpha— only four to eight waves per second. This whole range

QUESTION	3. HOW MIGHT BIOFEEDBACK BE USED TO ENHANCE SELF-AWARENESS?
HYPOTHESIS	HYPNAGOGIC IMAGERY
DESCRIPTIVE EVIDENCE	ASSESS: existence and type of imagery associated with various brain rhythms
EXPERIMENTAL EVIDENCE	

3. HOW MIGHT BIOFEEDBACK BE USED TO EN-HANCE SELF-AWARENESS?

When asked how they feel after an experience with biofeedback, most people report that learning to control their own physiology is a pleasurable experience. Much investigation of this question has centered around control of the brain waves, although muscular and visceral biofeedback therapy also have their altered consciousness aspects. When people are trained to stabilize their EEG so as to maintain certain rhythms, their self-awareness is often increased and their responsiveness to some external stimuli may sometimes be decreased.

In his research during the 1960s at the Langley Porter Neurological Institute Kamiya found himself in

from four to thirteen cycles per second is called the alpha-theta range. Apparently people can learn to control their mental state, so that the brain-wave activity is mostly alpha, or mixed alpha and theta. Producing theta by itself, a promising part of the research in this area, is only just beginning. What consequences might control over either of these patterns have for the person's experience?

The *hypnagogic-imagery hypothesis* states that if the images appearing in a twilight state of consciousness are made accessible to conscious thought, the individual involved will gain enhanced self-awareness and productivity.

Robert Holt (1964) has suggested that "imagery may furnish the key to the fabulous storehouse of memory, if we can learn how to make use of this

Typical Trace Measured on Subject's Scalp

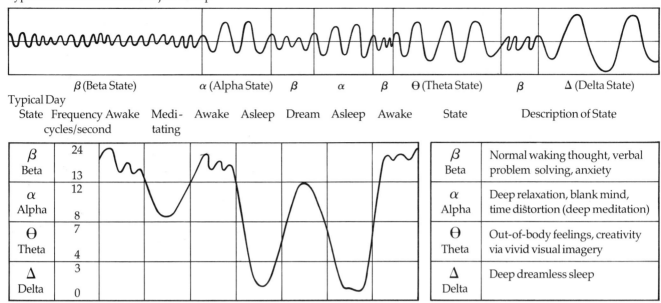

Figure 7. Brain wave patterns seen under a variety of mental states: wakefulness, meditation, sleep, dreaming. The state associated with each wave pattern is described at lower right.

neglected capacity." Dr. Elmer Green and his associates at the Menninger Foundation who have been investigating the experiences people have when they develop alpha-theta control felt that the presence of alpha rhythm might indicate a state of consciousness in which there is ready access to some memory processes.

DESCRIPTIVE EVIDENCE

Investigators: E. E. Green, A. M. Green, and E. D. Walters
Source, Date: "Voluntary Control of Internal States: Psychological and Physiological," 1970
Location: Menninger Foundation, Topeka, Kansas
Subjects: 12 volunteers
Materials: Electroencephalograph (EEG), button on which subject's finger rests

The EEG equipment was arranged so that whenever subjects generated certain brain waves, a button bumped their fingers. Each subject was instructed to report on the focus of his attention when the button bumped his finger by classifying his subjective experiences into one of the following four categories: (1) internally focused on hypnagogic imagery; (2) internally focused on thinking; (3) externally focused on the environment; or (4) externally focused on the finger. "Hypnagogic imagery" was a term the subjects were to use if their consciousness at the moment involved pictures or words that they did not consciously generate or manipulate, but which sprang into the mind "full blown."

It turned out that hypnagogic imagery was frequently associated with drowsiness and the presence of theta waves. When the subjects' finger was bumped the images appeared in conscious awareness with a burst of alpha waves on the EEG. Reports of concrete images or external objects usually accompanied beta waves.

Of special interest for the implications of the use of biofeedback to enhance self-awareness is the account of one subject who reported "that the stimulus caused him to suddenly become aware of 'little pictures' in his mind that he did not know were there. He described a 'void' into which the pictures 'popped' when the stimulus was given. Without the stimulus, he said, he would not have been able to remember what was in his mind."

These results suggested to the experimenters that material from the drowsy, twilight state could be recovered, if subjects were given a stimulus at appropriate moments. It was as if they were saying to the subjects: "you are very internally focused. Don't fall asleep and forget the creative material you are producing. Come back to the external world for a moment and report on your experience."

Alpha-theta waves tend to occur during a state in which the individual is so unresponsive to *external* stimuli that *internal* events, perhaps from some "deeper" level of consciousness, may "pop" into the mind. In the relaxed and open "twilight" between sleep and wakefulness the individual is often not trying to think or do anything in particular. According to Green, if this twilight state is made more ac-

cessible, then individuals may be able to gain greater self-awareness.

The "let it happen" state of mind (as contrasted with the "make it happen" approach) also has much in common with certain philosophical and religious practices of Eastern wisdom. Studies of Zen masters have shown that the best way to attain the state of enlightenment may be to stop seeking it. Similar parallels exist with certain physiological abilities of Eastern Yogis and other specialized individuals. Their rather remarkable feats have been relatively unexplored by Western science but a few studies have shown that when Yogis are meditating, their EEG patterns display large amounts of alpha activity.

Such studies have led to considerable speculation about the possibility of developing extrasensory perception through biofeedback. Although some commercial organizations have cashed in on these speculations by promising to develop extrasensory powers through biofeedback, there has been no confirmation from reputable laboratories as yet.

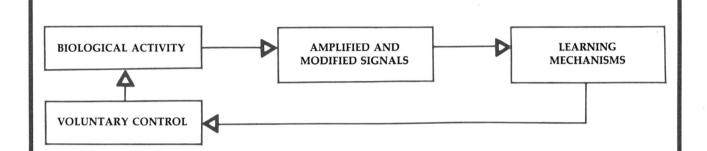

BIOLOGICAL ACTIVITY

VOLUNTARY CONTROL

AMPLIFIED AND
MODIFIED SIGNALS

LEARNING
MECHANISMS

PUTTING IT TOGETHER: Biofeedback

Most of the time we are not aware of much of our *biological activity,* including that of the autonomic nervous system, highly specialized motor units, and the production of a variety of brain wave patterns. Many of these activities can be *amplified* through sensitive electronic instruments and *modified into signals* fed back to people in some form that is easily received, such as patterns on an oscilloscope, flashing lights, or sounds.

With continued feedback through the *learning mechanisms* of the central nervous system an individual may learn, through practice, to exert highly refined *voluntary control* over these biological functions. Some of the possible results of biofeedback training may be highly efficient relaxation procedures, relief from migraine headaches, muscular rehabilitation for handicapped people, and production of creative states.

WHAT'S ACCEPTED AND WHAT'S DEBATED

1. WHAT'S ACCEPTED . . .

1. People and animals can learn to control some normally involuntary responses through biofeedback training.

2. Biofeedback training techniques have potential for practical use in psychosomatic and psychiatric medicine.

3. Some people can learn to control their state of mind so that particular patterns of brain-wave activity predominate.

2. WHAT'S DEBATED . . .

1. The mechanism by which internal control of involuntary physiological responses is achieved.

2. Whether EEG biofeedback and alpha-wave training and control may be used to generate unusual states of consciousness.

ISSUE: BIOFEEDBACK APPLICATIONS IN MEDICINE

As we have seen in this unit, biofeedback has many different applications. Perhaps the most important are likely to be in the field of medicine, where some striking successes have already been achieved, often in cases where traditional modes of treatment have failed.

Biofeedback has been used, as we have seen, to prevent migraine headaches. Some forms of migraine seem to be caused by the enlargement of the blood vessels in the brain. These vessels expand so much that they transmit to the surrounding tissues a magnified pulse beat, so that the well-known "throbbing headache" results. By controlling the temperature and flow of blood in their foreheads, patients have learned to prevent the migraines that even drugs could not combat effectively.

Patients suffering from potentially lethal, irregular heart rates have also learned to control the beating of their hearts, initially while wired to biofeedback electronic equipment, but later simply on command. They were trained in a quiet laboratory where their heart beats were recorded as electrical signals and then projected as colored lights at the foot of their beds. The patients were instructed to "drive" their hearts as they would a car. A red light meant to slow down, green to speed up. Their goal was to keep their heartbeats in the safe, yellow zone. After practice, patients were able to "feel" how to adjust their heart rates without the aid of the electronic equipment.

Biofeedback has also been used to treat insomnia, which is usually a habit that evolves from tension. Volunteers lie down on a bed in the laboratory, wearing earphones and with electrodes on their foreheads. When the forehead muscle contracts—a sign of tension—the tone in the earphones is high-pitched. When the muscle relaxes, the tone lowers. The volunteers were instructed to keep the tone low, and in minutes they had reduced their muscle tension by half. They reported learning merely to "let go."

Other habits of tension that may evolve into disease have also been controlled and even eliminated. The capacity to perform such an apparently simple task as relaxing the muscles of the forehead can cure neck and back aches. If the forehead is relaxed, the upper half of the body tends to relax as well. In one case, a 22-year-old woman was freed from a large number of phobias:

> including panic attacks, fear of heights, fear of crowds, fear of riding in cars, and claustrophobia. When systematically confronted with the feared images in a relaxed state, she gradually lost her intense feelings about them. It is almost impossible to remain highly anxious when deeply relaxed. [Luce and Peper, "Biofeedback: Mind over Body, Mind over Mind," *The New York Times Magazine,* Sept. 12, 1971, p. 132.]

Hypertension, a form of high blood pressure which is probably psychological in origin and which can lead to strokes and heart attacks, can be controlled through biofeedback methods that enable the patient to lower his or her blood pressure at will. Even patients who have lost the use of their limbs as a result of strokes have learned to walk again. Normally, these patients are left in bed, and any limb muscles unaffected by the stroke slowly atrophy into uselessness. The use of biofeedback makes it possible to identify these remaining functional muscles, which can then be exercised until the person regains at least partial control of the limb.

Biofeedback is not a panacea, however. It cannot cure medical problems that result from permanent tissue damage. Nor is everyone equally adept at controlling the autonomic nervous system through biofeedback. For reasons that are not fully understood, some people achieve control of their responses much more readily than others. And biofeedback training can often be very costly, in terms of time as well as money. It may take many weeks or months of constant training before any success is apparent, and some people are unable to sustain motivation over a prolonged period.

An important result of biofeedback research has been to upset many of our old assumptions about man and his body. The traditional distinction between those bodily functions that are subject to voluntary control and those that are involuntary has become increasingly shaky. The belief that we are at the mercy of our autonomic nervous system has profoundly influenced western man's conception of himself and shaped the self-image that we all have. But patients who have been helped by biofeedback and experimental subjects who have discovered unsuspected power in their minds are exultant: "I did it!"

Unit 36

Psychoactive Drugs

OVERVIEW

Relationships between drugs, psychological factors, and their mutual effects on behavior are surveyed in this unit. These effects range from valuable therapeutic aids in psychiatric medicine to the unfortunate addictions and psychological dependencies that can destroy people's lives. The reputation of some drugs as "mind expanders" is also discussed.

UNIT OUTLINE

DEFINITION AND BACKGROUND
1. *Definition:* a psychoactive drug is any natural or synthetic substance that affects mental activities, perceptions, consciousness, or mood.
2. *Background:* Henri Laborit (1914–   ).

QUESTIONS AND EVIDENCE
1. How do psychoactive drugs affect mental disorders?
Hypotheses:
    a. *Expectation:* the belief that an ingested drug will have a specific effect may serve to produce the expected effect. **624**
    b. *Biochemical:* the chemical actions of a psychoactive drug produce specific effects on the nervous system that, in turn, produce changes in mental activity and behavior. **625**
2. What kinds of mental experiences can be induced by drugs?
Hypotheses:
    a. *Mind-expansion:* hallucinogenic or psychedelic drugs can result in insights into the nature of one's own mind and enhance one's perception of other people and the physical environment. **627**
3. What factors lead to drug dependence and drug abuse?
Hypotheses:
    a. *Physical-addiction:* drug dependence can arise from changes in the body's biochemistry that are induced by the drug. **629**
    b. *Relief:* the regular use of an addicting drug, once established, is maintained by the relief it provides from withdrawal symptoms. **632**
    c. *Peer-group:* the attitudes and values of other people may justify a person's initial decision to try a drug. **632**

IMPORTANT CONCEPTS

	page
addiction	628
amphetamine	626
barbiturates	624
drug dependence	628
hallucinogen	627
narcotic	629
psychoactive drug	622
tranquilizers	632

Drug dosage, the way drugs are taken, and user expectations are among the variables influencing the effects of psychoactive drugs.

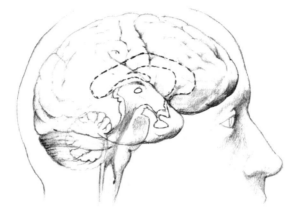

The biological effects of psychoactive drugs involve changes in brain activity.

Individual reaction to psychoactive drugs is related to a combination of variables.

36. Psychoactive Drugs   **621**

DEFINITION AND BACKGROUND

Our normal waking consciousness, rational consciousness as we call it, is but one special type of consciousness, whilst all about it, parted from it by the filmiest of screens, there lie potential forms of consciousness entirely different. [William James, after inhaling nitrous oxide—"laughing gas"]

Throughout recorded history man has been intrigued with substances that could alter mental functions and perceptions. In the Western world alcohol has long been used as both a euphoriant and a tranquilizer. Today marijuana, LSD, mescaline, and a host of as yet unevaluated hallucinogens are being experimented with by professionals and amateurs, the latter performing the experiments on themselves.

The "amateur" use of hallucinogens (psychedelics) and narcotics has received so much attention in recent years that one might almost be misled into thinking they are the only psychoactive drugs. But this is by no means true.

A broad DEFINITION of a psychoactive drug is *any natural or synthetic substance that affects mental activities, perceptions, consciousness, or mood.* Table 1 shows the major categories of psychoactive drugs. As you can see, their effects and major medical uses vary widely—as do their legality and availability.

This unit will FOCUS on the behavioral and psychological effects of some of these drugs, including those used to treat mental disorders and those used for "mind expansion," and on factors that lead to drug abuse.

BACKGROUND: HENRI LABORIT (1914–   )

During World War II Henri Laborit, a French surgeon, became interested in the adverse effects of postoperative anxiety. Patients with high anxiety would sometimes go into a state called surgical shock and were treated with morphine, which would alleviate pain but not the anxiety. After the war Laborit learned that antihistamines had the side-effect of reducing anxiety. In 1949 he used them experimentally to treat some surgical patients. The results were encouraging, so Laborit began to search for antihistamines with greater anxiety-reducing effects. He found what he was looking for in chlorpromazine, a

Figure 1. Henri Laborit was the first systematically to treat psychotic anxiety with chlorpromazine, initiating the widespread use of tranquilizing drugs.

drug that is chemically related to antihistamines and reduces anxiety but lacks significant antihistamine action. Chlorpromazine was first synthesized by a French chemist in 1950. Within a few years researchers had identified such a large number of actions of the drug on the nervous system some of them renamed it Largactil.

When Laborit noted that chlorpromazine had a marked quieting effect on excited, overactive patients, he arranged to use it in the treatment of psychiatric patients. The first study showed that the drug not only reduced anxiety but appeared to act on the psychotic process itself. News of Laborit's success in treating psychotic anxiety with chlorpromazine spread rapidly; by 1956 mental hospitals throughout the world were using the new drug, which came to be called a "tranquilizer." (The term "tranquilizer" had been coined 150 years earlier by Benjamin Rush, a signer of the Declaration of Independence and a physician interested in the treatment of the mentally ill. One of his techniques was to strap violent patients into a wooden chair until they calmed down. He called the chair a tranquilizer.)

Before Laborit's discovery of chlorpromazine psychiatrists tended to believe that the only effective physical method of treating schizophrenia was some form of shock treatment. Insulin shock treatment, in which an injection of insulin causes a rapid drop in the glucose level of the blood, leaving the patient in a coma, seemed to be only temporarily effective: the relapse rate was high. Then it was proposed that convulsions induced by drugs might eliminate the symptoms of schizophrenia. Drug-induced convulsions had undesirable side-effects, however, and electroconvulsive shock therapy came into vogue. Initially, the electric shock was administered through electrodes placed in the patient's mouth and rectum, but placement of the electrodes on the scalp was found to be safer and more effective. Today electroconvulsive therapy is seldom used with schizophrenics; however, it still is used to good effect with patients who are suffering from severe depression.

The introduction of chlorpromazine as a therapeutic agent for the treatment of schizophrenics and other psychotics led to a decline in the number of patients residing in mental hospitals in the United States. Until 1955 the number of patients had increased each year, reaching a peak of 560,000. But by 1970 the number of patients in mental hospitals had dropped to 340,000, despite a steadily growing population in the United States. Following the success of chlorpromazine, other drugs for treating specific mental illnesses were discovered and used.

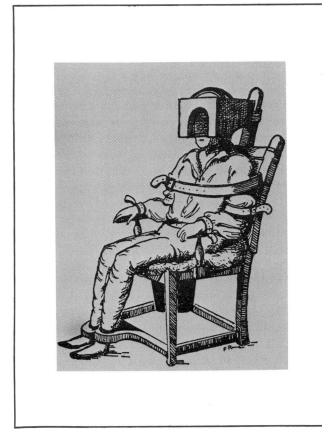

Figure 2. In the 1700s violent patients were strapped to a chair called a tranquilizer.

QUESTIONS AND EVIDENCE

1. How do psychoactive drugs affect mental disorders?

2. What kinds of mental experiences can be induced by drugs?

3. What factors lead to drug dependence and drug abuse?

1. HOW DO PSYCHOACTIVE DRUGS AFFECT MENTAL DISORDERS?

HYPOTHESES	EXPECTATION	BIOCHEMICAL
DESCRIPTIVE EVIDENCE		
EXPERIMENTAL EVIDENCE	VARY: administration of tranquilizer or placebo MEASURE: reduction of anxiety as related to acquiescence	VARY: 1. administration of stimulant or placebo 2. amount of drug MEASURE: 1. reduction of hyperactivity 2. sensory responsiveness according to type of mental disorder

1. HOW DO PSYCHOACTIVE DRUGS AFFECT MENTAL DISORDERS?

When chlorpromazine and related drugs appeared, some psychiatrists became so enthusiastic about their potential that they stated publicly that the new drugs would stop the symptoms of psychosis just as insulin stops the symptoms of diabetes. On the surface this appeared to be true, for the new tranquilizing drugs calmed psychotic patients without putting them to sleep, as barbiturates did, and produced a marked quieting of motor activity. Hyperactive patients would calm down, stop being loud and profane, and sit still at least long enough to eat. But conflicting reports on the efficacy of tranquilizers soon began to appear. In many cases, patients given placebos (inert substances that have no physiological effects) showed just as much improvement as did patients given tranquilizers.

The *physiological effects* of a drug—alteration in the activity of nerve cells, increasing or decreasing heart rate, dilation of pupils, and so on—depend on biochemistry. Chlorpromazine, for example, has a depressant effect because it reduces the sensory input to the reticular system (see Figure 3), lowering the activity of that system (which controls the arousal level of the brain). The depressant action of antianxiety drugs is primarily on the limbic system, which links the hypothalamus (see Figure 3) and the cerebral cortex, both of which are involved in emotion. Depressing the information exchange between hypothalamus and cortex results in a decrease in anxiety. These physiological effects will occur whether or not a person knows he is receiving a drug and whether or not he believes in the drug's effects.

The effect of psychoactive drugs on behavior and mental activities, however, also depends on the background of the individual, his psychological state, and environmental factors such as the setting in which the drug is taken. The *expectation hypothesis* states that the belief that an ingested drug will have a specific effect may serve to produce the expected effect (see Unit 2). Since even the expectations of the person administering the drug can influence the effect that is experienced by the recipient, most drug research is conducted under *double-blind* conditions, in which neither the researcher nor the subject knows whether a substance ingested by each subject is the drug being investigated or a biochemically inactive preparation called a *placebo*. After the results are noted, the records are decoded to determine which substance each subject ingested.

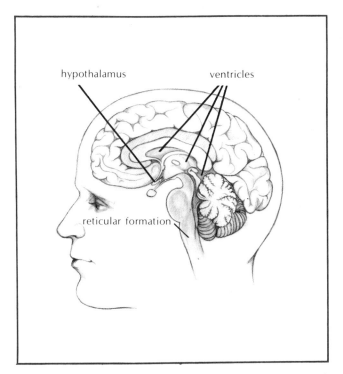

Figure 3. The depressant effects of some drugs are due to decreased activity in the *reticular* system. Some drugs decrease anxiety by reducing cortical input from the *hypothalamus*. The *ventricles* contain cerebrospinal fluid which may serve to localize the activity of some drugs.

EXPERIMENTAL EVIDENCE

Investigators: D. M. McNair, R. J. Kahn, L. F.
Doppleman, and S. Fisher
Source, Date: "Patient Acquiescence and Drug Effects,"
1968
Location: Boston University Medical Center
Subjects: 40 female and 20 male outpatients
Materials: Valium (diazepam); Bass Scale of Acquiescence

Within ten days after being accepted for treatment, each patient was given a psychiatric interview and took the Bass test, which measures a person's tendency to accept authoritative statements and may indicate a need to please other people. The person being tested is asked to indicate whether or not he agrees with such statements as "They never fail who die in a great cause," "Wild colts make good horses," and "You can't teach an old dog new tricks." Then the subjects were randomly assigned to two groups. One group received Valium, a mild tranquilizer, and the other group received only placebos.

Patients with high scores on the Bass scale—that is, those who were more acquiescent—showed a greater reduction of anxiety when given the placebo than when given the tranquilizer. Patients who were not acquiescent had a greater reduction of anxiety in response to the drug than to the placebo. The results suggest that the personality characteristics of the patient play a role in his response to drugs (and placebos). The personality traits of the patient and environmental factors may be particularly important in determining the effects of drugs on mental disorders that have a nonorganic basis.

The *biochemical hypothesis* states that the chemical actions of a psychoactive drug produce specific effects on the nervous system that, in turn, produce changes in mental activity and behavior. Exactly how some drugs affect the nervous system is not fully known but studies have been conducted on the ways in which psychoactive drugs alter behavior or responses to sensory stimuli.

EXPERIMENTAL EVIDENCE

Investigators: C. K. Conners and L. Eisenberg
Source, Date: "The Effects of Methylphenidate on
Symptomatology and Learning in Disturbed Children,"
1963
Location: Johns Hopkins University
Subjects: 81 hyperactive and emotionally disturbed children
Materials: Ritalin (methylphenidate)

The study was designed to test the validity of clinical reports that Ritalin, a mild stimulant, has the paradoxical effect of reducing hyperactivity in children. Hyperactivity affects boys more commonly than girls. Symptoms are restlessness, short attention spans, and impulsiveness. A double-blind procedure was used: half of the children in the study received Ritalin and half received a placebo, but neither the staff members who evaluated hyperactive symptoms nor the children knew who received what. The results supported the clinical observations that Ritalin significantly reduces hyperactive symptoms.

Amphetamine, another stimulant, also is effective in reducing hyperactivity in children, but individuals vary greatly in their reaction to the drug. Why a stimulant should reduce activity is not known. The effects seem to result from specific biochemical action on some as yet unidentified part of the nervous system.

Further evidence that supports the biochemical hypothesis comes from recent studies of the effects of tranquilizers on paranoid schizophrenics, nonparanoid schizophrenics, and normal subjects.

EXPERIMENTAL EVIDENCE

Investigators: M. Rappaport, J. Silverman, H. K. Hopkins, and K. Hall
Source, Date: "Phenothiazine Effects on Auditory Signal Detection in Paranoid and Nonparanoid Schizophrenics," 1971
Location: Agnews State Hospital, San Jose, California
Subjects: 22 paranoid schizophrenics, 24 nonparanoid schizophrenics, 16 normal people, all adults
Materials: Phenothiazine tranquilizers; earphones, sound equipment

Paranoid schizophrenics respond to many irrelevant stimuli in the environment and have difficulty focusing their attention. They appear to be "wide open" to sensory stimuli. Nonparanoid schizophrenics tend to cut themselves off from strong stimuli, but they have a peculiar hypersensitivity to stimuli of low intensity. The tranquilizers commonly used to treat both types of schizophrenia are the phenothiazines—chlorpromazine and its derivatives.

Rappaport and his colleagues hypothesized that the tranquilizers would produce opposite changes in the sensory responsiveness of the two types of schizophrenics. The patients were tested under three conditions: no medication, moderate medication, and moderately heavy medication. The normal subjects were tested under two conditions: no medication and moderate medication. Each subject was asked to try to detect signal tones of various intensities, each tone presented against a background of white noise. The tests were made in a soundproof room, with the signals and white noise delivered through earphones.

With increasing doses of the tranquilizer, the paranoid schizophrenics' ability to detect the signal improved, presumably because they were better able to focus their attention. In the no-medication condition, nonparanoid schizophrenics detected weak signals almost as well as normal subjects, but with increasing doses of the tranquilizer their ability to detect both weak and strong signals decreased. Normal subjects also performed less efficiently under the drug. Thus, although the tranquilizer's effect is to reduce sensory sensitivity in all cases, its behavioral effects can be quite different. The researchers conclude that the differential effects of phenothiazine tranquilizers should be taken into account in any treatment of schizophrenic patients: their findings and those of other researchers show that the tranquilizers are more likely to reduce thought disorder and improve attention in paranoid schizophrenics than in nonparanoid schizophrenics.

Although the effects of psychoactive drugs are tempered by psychological and environmental factors, it should not be forgotten that they produce specific biochemical actions that allow changes in mood and thinking to occur. Not surprisingly, their effects on normal people can be just as dramatic as their effects on people with mental disorders.

QUESTION	2. WHAT KINDS OF MENTAL EXPERIENCES CAN BE INDUCED BY DRUGS?

HYPOTHESIS	MIND EXPANSION
DESCRIPTIVE EVIDENCE	ASSESS: individual responses to marijuana
EXPERIMENTAL EVIDENCE	

2. WHAT KINDS OF MENTAL EXPERIENCES CAN BE INDUCED BY DRUGS?

In the eighteenth century Humphry Davy investigated the effects of nitrous oxide upon himself, and he also convinced a number of his contemporaries, including Samuel Taylor Coleridge, the poet, and Peter Roget, a young physician later known for his thesaurus, to breathe some of his "laughing gas." In fact, breathing bags of nitrous oxide became a fashionable parlor pastime during that period. Davy noted that the effects of the gas varied from individual to individual and that in himself it could alleviate anxiety. Roget wrote: "My ideas succeeded one another with extreme rapidity, thoughts rushed like a torrent through my mind, as if their velocity had been suddenly accelerated by the bursting of a barrier which had before retained them in their natural and equable course."

The *mind-expansion hypothesis* states that hallucinogenic or psychedelic drugs can result in insights into the nature of one's own mind and enhance one's perception of other people and the physical environment.

In this century, the idea that drugs can throw light on hitherto unknown regions of one's mind has perhaps been most effectively propagandized by Aldous Huxley, in particular through his vivid description of a mescaline trip in *The Doors of Perception,* published in 1954. Huxley's experiences—and his genius with words—helped lay the groundwork for the later popularity of experimentation with hallucinogenic drugs.

Huxley, accompanied by a professional researcher who remained on hand at all times, took four-tenths of a gram of mescaline in a half a glass of water. He was eager to try the drug, for he hoped it would admit him to the kind of visual inner world described by William Blake.

Here is an excerpt from his description of that experience:

> The legs . . . of that chair—how miraculous their tubularity, how supernatural their polished smoothness! I spent several minutes—or was it several centuries?—not merely gazing at those bamboo legs, but actually *being* them—or rather being myself in them; or, to be still more accurate (for "I" was not involved in the case, nor in a certain sense were "they") being my Not-self in the Not-self which was the chair.
>
> Compelled by the investigator to analyze and report on what I was doing (and how I longed to be left alone with Eternity in a flower, Infinity in four chair legs, and the Absolute in the folds of a pair of flannel trousers!) . . .

But, as Huxley was well aware, the experiences induced by drugs are not always pleasant and wondrous. Mind-expansion can go the other way into nightmarish experiences of blackness, gloom, and desolation. A hallucinogen like LSD may release a flood of experiences and feelings that are too much for an individual to integrate. The result may be a panic reaction or, if LSD is taken repeatedly, a psychosis in which hallucinations may force their way into consciousness even when the drug has not been taken for months. Reports of adverse reactions to LSD are not uncommon in medical journals.

The following is a case study reported by W. A. Frosch, E. S. Robbins and M. Stern (1965): A twenty-one-year-old woman was admitted to the hospital after she had taken about 200 milligrams of LSD provided by her lover, who had taken the drug several times before. Half an hour after taking the LSD, she noticed that the bricks in the wall went in and out and that light had a strange effect on her. When she realized that she could not distinguish her body from the chair she was sitting on, she became frightened. Her fear turned to panic when she began thinking that she would not be able to get back to her previous self. She became hyperactive, laughed at odd times, and talked illogically. Although the reactions ceased in two days, the fear of the drug and her experiences remained.

It is well-established now, both from case histories such as this and from LSD experiments under controlled conditions, that a person's reaction to hallucinogens depends upon his psychological make-up, his mood and expectations, his feelings about the person administering the drug, and the physical setting. Even a healthy normal individual apparently can have a bad trip and postdrug flashbacks; on the other hand, many somewhat unstable people report that they have had unequivocally positive hallucinogenic experiences.

What about the mental effects of milder psychoactive drugs, such as marijuana? Because the standard laboratory situation hardly allows for the study of subjective sensations, one researcher, supported in part by a government grant, had experienced users of marijuana answer a 206-item questionnaire.

DESCRIPTIVE EVIDENCE

Investigator: C. T. Tart
Source, Date: Marijuana Intoxication: Common
    Experiences," 1970
Location: University of California, Davis
Subjects: 153 experienced marijuana users
Materials: Questionnaires

To explore the effects of marijuana under conditions of ordinary use, Tart distributed through informal channels a questionnaire that included 206 descriptions of possible effects. He asked that only people who had used marijuana at least a dozen times fill in the questionnaire, and he received 153 replies. Tart categorized an effect as "characteristic" if at least half the respondents rated it as occurring very often or usually. If at least half the respondents rated an effect as occurring sometimes, very often, or usually, Tart classified it as "common." Here are some examples of characteristic and common effects of marijuana.

Characteristic: "I can see patterns, forms, figures, meaningful designs in visual material that does not have any particular form when I'm straight."

Common: "My visual perception of space around me is changed so that what I'm looking at is very real and clear but everything else I'm not focusing on visually seems farther away or otherwise less real or clear."

Characteristic: "Time passes very slowly."

Common: "I am much more aware of the beating of my heart."

Characteristic: "Commonplace sayings or conversations seem to have new meanings, more significance."

Common: "I can continue to carry on an intelligent conversation even when my memory span is so short

that I forget the beginnings of what I started to say; for example, I may logically complete a sentence even as I realize I've forgotten how it started."

Characteristic: "I often forget to finish some task I've started, or get sidetracked more frequently than when straight."

Common: "I get somewhat paranoid about the people with me; I am suspicious about what they're doing."

The evidence suggests that marijuana enhances some mental experiences, such as visual perception, but that mental disorganization can also occur. At present, it is impossible to predict just who will have exactly what kind of experience, though it appears that the risks are greater for people with preexisting personality disorders, especially if the drug is taken under stressful conditions.

With marijuana, as with alcohol, certain personality characteristics appear to be associated with chronic use of the drug. Personality descriptions of drug-dependent individuals, however, at best represent very general patterns and tendencies. It is impossible to discern at present whether the implicated personality characteristics are the cause of chronic drug use, the effects of it, or neither. (Both could be the result of some third factor.)

3. WHAT FACTORS LEAD TO DRUG DEPENDENCE AND DRUG ABUSE?

The repeated administration of a psychoactive drug may lead to drug dependence, a state of mental or physical dependence, or both, on a drug. Though not all psychoactive drugs are physically addicting, all of them do appear to be capable of creating psychological dependence. In this state there is a feeling of relief when the drug is taken and a feeling of anxiety when the drug cannot be obtained. Physical dependence or addiction occurs when the drug induces changes in the body's biochemistry in such a way that, when drug use is discontinued, uncomfortable and painful withdrawal symptoms develop (craving for the drug, anxiety, perspiration, goose bumps, muscle twitches, vomiting, diarrhea, and intense discomfort). Two other features characterize drug addiction: increasing tolerance for the drug, which means increasingly

HYPOTHESES	PHYSICAL ADDICTION	RELIEF	PEER GROUP
DESCRIPTIVE EVIDENCE			ASSESS: prestige as factor in drug use
EXPERIMENTAL EVIDENCE	VARY: substances injected into cerebral ventricular system of monkeys MEASURE: morphine tolerance and dependence	VARY: presence of withdrawal symptoms MEASURE: drug-seeking behavior	

larger doses must be taken in order to maintain the original intensity of effects, and an intense desire to continue taking the drug that displaces all other drives.

Consider the following case. One particular drug in low and moderate doses first acts as a stimulant then as a depressant. In high doses it causes tremors that can develop into convulsions, frequently terminated by death. The cause of death is suffocation: the drug paralyzes the muscles required for breathing.

There are a number of drugs that could account for some of the symptoms described, but the drug in this case was nicotine. Although psychological factors—habits—play a large role in cigarette smoking, there is some evidence that nicotine is physically addicting.

The *physical-addiction hypothesis* states that drug dependence can arise from changes in the body's biochemistry that are induced by the drug. Alcohol, barbiturates, antianxiety agents, and narcotics are said to be physically addictive because, when the heavy, regular use of these drugs is discontinued, withdrawal symptoms occur.

In addition, tolerance develops with regular use of these drugs. (It should be mentioned that some drugs produce tolerance but not withdrawal symptoms; these drugs are not regarded as physically addicting.) The following experiment shows that morphine, per-haps the best pain-killing drug known to medicine and also the prototype narcotic, can produce both tolerance and withdrawal symptoms when it is injected directly into the brain.

EXPERIMENTAL EVIDENCE

Investigators: E. Eidelberg and C. A. Barstow
Source, Date: "Morphine Tolerance and Dependence
    Induced by Intraventricular Injection," 1971
Location: St. Joseph's Hospital, Phoenix, Arizona
Subjects: Six young stump-tailed macaques (monkeys)
Materials: Morphine, tube implanted into openings in
    the brain

The researchers sought to find an efficient method for conveying morphine directly to the brain without having it first pass through other body tissues. After training the monkeys to press a button for food at a stable rate, the experimenters injected morphine into the fluid surrounding the monkeys' brains through tubes implanted into the ventricular system. (See Figure 3.) Under control conditions they injected saline solution. The effect of the drug was measured by the amount it decreased the learned button-

TABLE 1. Facts About Drugs (Question marks indicate conflict of opinion. It should be noted that illicit drugs are frequently adulterated and thus pose unknown hazards to the user.)

Name	Slang Name	Chemical or Trade Name	Source	Classification	Medical Use	How Taken
Heroin	H., Horse, Scat, Junk, Smack, Scag, Stuff, Harry	Diacetylmorphine	Semi-synthetic (from morphine)	Narcotic	Pain relief	Injected or sniffed
Morphine	White Stuff, M.	Morphine Sulphate	Natural (from opium)	Narcotic	Pain relief	Swallowed or injected
Codeine	Schoolboy	Methylmorphine	Natural (from opium), Semi-synthetic (from morphine)	Narcotic	Ease pain and coughing	Swallowed
Methadone	Dolly	Dolophine Amidone	Synthetic	Narcotic	Pain relief	Swallowed or injected
Cocaine	Corrine, Gold Dust, Coke, Bernice, Flake, Star Dust, Snow	Methylester of Benzoylecgonine	Natural (from coca, NOT cacao)	Stimulant, local anesthesia	Local anesthesia	Sniffed, injected, or swallowed
Marijuana	Pot, Grass, Hashish, Tea, Gage, Reefers	Cannabis Sativa	Natural	Relaxant, euphoriant; in high doses, hallucinogen	None in U.S.	Smoked, swallowed, or sniffed
Barbiturates	Barbs, Blue Devils, Candy, Yellow Jackets, Phennies, Peanuts, Blue Heavens	Phenobarbital Nembutal, Seconal, Amytal	Synthetic	Sedative-hypnotic	Sedation, relief of high blood pressure, epilepsy, hyperthyroidism	Swallowed or injected
Amphetamines	Bennies, Dexies, Speed, Wake-Ups, Lid Proppers, Hearts, Pep Pills	Benzedrine, Dexedrine, Desoxyn, Meth-amphetamine, Methedrine	Synthetic	Sympatho-mimetic	Relief of mild depression, control of appetite and narcolepsy	Swallowed or injected
LSD	Acid, Sugar, Big D, Cubes, Trips	D-lysergic Acid Diethylamide	Semi-synthetic (from ergot alkaloids)	Hallucinogen	Experimental study of mental function, alcoholism	Swallowed
DMT	AMT, Business-man's High	Dimethyl-triptamine	Synthetic	Hallucinogen	None	Injected
Mescaline	Mesc.	3,4,5-trimethoxy-phenethylamine	Natural (from peyote)	Hallucinogen	None	Swallowed
Psilocybin		3 (2-dimethyl-amino) Ethylin-dol-4-oldihydro-gen Phosphate	Natural (from psilocybe)	Hallucinogen	None	Swallowed
Alcohol	Booze, Juice, etc.	Ethanol Ethyl Alcohol	Natural (from grapes, grains, etc. via fermentation)	Sedative-hypnotic	Solvent, antiseptic	Swallowed
Tobacco	Fag, Coffin Nail, etc.	Nicotiana Tabacum	Natural	Stimulant-sedative	Sedative, emetic (nicotine)	Smoked, sniffed, chewed

Source: *Resource Book for Drug Abuse Education.* Developed as a part of the Drug Abuse Education Project of the American Association for Health, Physical Education, and Recreation and the National Science Teachers Association (NEA). 1969, 117 pp. $1.25. Quantity discounts. Order from NEA Publications-Sales. Additional information is available from AAHPER, NEA Center.

From *Today's Education: NEA Journal,* February 1971.

Usual Dose	Duration of Effect	Effects Sought	Long-Term Symptoms	Physical Dependence Potential	Mental Dependence Potential	Organic Damage Potential
Varies	4 hrs.	Euphoria, prevent withdrawal discomfort	Addiction, constipation, loss of appetite	Yes	Yes	No*
15 Mild grams	6 hrs.	Euphoria, prevent withdrawal discomfort	Addiction, constipation, loss of appetite	Yes	Yes	No*
30 Milligrams	4 hrs.	Euphoria, prevent withdrawal discomfort	Addiction, constipation, loss of appetite	Yes	Yes	No
10 Milligrams	4-6 hrs.	Prevent withdrawal discomfort	Addiction, constipation, loss of appetite	Yes	Yes	No
Varies	Varied, brief periods	Excitation, talkativeness	Depression, convulsions	No	Yes	Yes?
1-2 Cigarettes	4 hrs.	Relaxation; increased euphoria, perceptions, sociability	Usually none	No	Yes?	No
50-100 Milligrams	4 hrs.	Anxiety reduction, euphoria	Addiction with severe withdrawal symptoms, possible convulsions, toxic psychosis	Yes	Yes	Yes
2.5-5 Milligrams	4 hrs.	Alertness, activeness	Loss of appetite, delusions, hallucinations, toxic psychosis	No?	Yes	Yes?
100-500 Micrograms	10 hrs.	Insightful experiences, exhilaration, distortion of senses	May intensify existing psychosis, panic reactions	No	No?	No?
1-3 Milligram	Less than 1 hr.	Insightful experiences, exhilaration, distortion of senses	?	No	No?	No?
350 Micrograms	12 hrs.	Insightful experiences, exhilaration, distortion of senses	?	No	No?	No?
25 Milligrams	6-8 hrs.	Insightful experiences, exhilaration, distortion of senses	?	No	No?	No?
Varies	1-4 hrs.	Sense alteration, anxiety reduction, sociability	Cirrhosis, toxic psychosis, neurologic damage, addiction	Yes	Yes	Yes
Varies	Varies	Calmness, sociability	Emphysema, lung cancer, mouth and throat cancer, cardiovascular damage, loss of appetite	Yes?	Yes	Yes

*Persons who inject drugs under nonsterile conditions run a high risk of contracting hepatitis, abscesses, or circulatory disorders.

pressing behavior. There was a progressive increase as time passed in the amount of morphine required to eliminate the button-pressing, showing that the animals had developed a tolerance for the drug.

Morphine dependence was tested by terminating injection of the drug. Since morphine withdrawal symptoms in stump-tailed macaques are known to be rather mild, however, the experimenters not only stopped the morphine injections but used a morphine antagonist, nalorphine (which can precipitate more intense morphine withdrawal symptoms), as well. When the morphine antagonist was injected, definite withdrawal symptoms occurred, including hyperactivity, drooling, vomiting, and body contortions. The symptoms were readily terminated by readministering morphine. (The severity of the withdrawal symptoms varied among individual monkeys, as did the rate of development of tolerance.)

Although it had previously been suspected that physical withdrawal symptoms developed because of a drug's action on parts of the brain, there was no direct evidence to support the idea. The reason for this is that most investigators usually administer narcotics orally or by injection into muscle tissues or bloodstream, which makes entrance of the drug into the brain contingent upon its uptake in other tissues and fluids first. The findings in this study indicate that the major sites of morphine action are parts of the brain in contact with the fluid that surrounds the brain.

The *relief hypothesis* complements the physical-addiction hypothesis. It states that the regular use of an addicting drug, once established, is maintained by the relief it provides from withdrawal symptoms. Although drug dependence in humans may begin because of the pleasure or reduction in anxiety that the drug provides, the drug user quickly develops additional motivation for continual use of the drug. Drug-taking behavior becomes closely tied to relief or prevention of withdrawal symptoms.

EXPERIMENTAL EVIDENCE

Investigator: John R. Nichols
Source, Date: "How Opiates Change Behavior," 1965
Location: Southeastern Louisiana College

Subjects: Morphine-addicted rats
Materials: Morphine, cages with two drinking tubes

Rats in cages containing two drinking tubes, one supplying water and the other a morphine solution, will not voluntarily drink the morphine solution because of its bitterness. Two groups of rats were given daily injection of morphine for twenty-five days. When the injections were stopped the rats developed withdrawal symptoms. One group of rats was given injections of morphine at six-hour intervals to prevent most of the withdrawal symptoms (a few symptoms did arise toward the end of the six-hour interval). The second group of rats received no injections. Both groups were tested in cages that contained water and a morphine solution. The continuously injected rats drank water freely but did not drink much of the morphine solution. The uninjected rats drank large amounts of the morphine solution. The researcher concluded that when the development of withdrawal symptoms is suppressed, behavior directed toward obtaining the drug also is suppressed.

One obvious step in the development of drug dependency and abuse in humans is the initial acceptance of an opportunity to take a drug. The *peer-group hypothesis* states that the attitudes and values of other people may justify a person's initial decision to try a drug.

DESCRIPTIVE EVIDENCE

Investigator: H. Feldman
Source, Date: "Ideological Supports to Becoming and Remaining a Heroin Addict," 1968
Location: New York City
Subjects: Youths in a "slum" environment
Materials: Interviews

In observing the behavior of youth groups and in interviewing drug-dependent youths, Feldman stressed the importance of the conscious considerations that lead them to take drugs. He found that when heroin was introduced into the particular neighborhood studied, the prestigious members of youth groups were the first to experiment with it. This decision was largely the result of the social value placed on daring

Figure 4. The messages of these two drug advertisements are contradictory. Only recently has the public been alerted to the addictive property of certain psychoactive drugs.

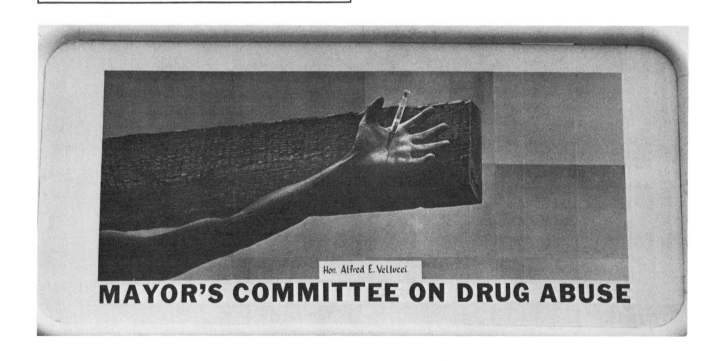

and "tough" behavior. The younger and less prestigious members of the groups were eventually influenced toward drug use by their desire to emulate the leaders.

His own observations as a social worker, Feldman reports, were the same as those reported by Claude Brown in *Manchild in the Promised Land* (1965):

> When I came home, Kid and Butch and Danny weren't smoking reefers anymore. I'd have a smoke, but they were doing other things. And the first thing that Danny told me was that they were using something they called "horse." . . . It seemed that they were saying this was something I wasn't old enough for. But I wanted to do the same things they were doing . . . All the older cats were using horse. The younger cats were still smoking reefers, drinking wine, and stuff like that. But I didn't want to be young. I wanted to be old. And the first time Danny spoke to me about it, I knew I was going to get some horse somehow, somewhere—soon.
>
> Horse was a new thing, not only in our neighborhood but in Brooklyn, the Bronx, and every place I went, uptown and downtown . . . The only way to take up where I had left off and be the same hip guy I was before I went to Wiltwyck was to get in on the hippest thing, and the hippest thing was horse.

On the basis of his analysis of peer-group interaction Feldman concluded that heavy drug use can result from an individual's desire to obtain prestige within his peer group rather than from unconscious, dynamic processes. This sociological approach to the problem of drug abuse is generally regarded as a complement to the physical dependence and the psychological approaches.

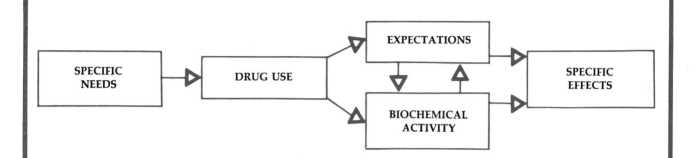

PUTTING IT TOGETHER: Psychoactive Drugs

The use of psychoactive drugs is initiated by a variety of *specific needs,* which may include maintaining or gaining prestige among peers, or relief from hyperactivity, anxiety, depression, or psychotic symptoms. Satisfaction of these needs may be instigated by a variety of social situations or by a physician's prescription.

Drug use may include sedatives, (such as alcohol,) narcotics, hallucinogens, stimulants, depressants and tranquilizers.

The use of any drug will initiate specific expectations with respect to its effects as well as biochemical activity specific to the drug and dependent upon dosage, manner of taking the drug, and the user's individual physiology. The effects may result from interaction between the user's *expectations* and the *biochemical activity* of the drug.

Possible *specific effects* include euphoria, excitation, relaxation, anxiety reduction, sensory distortion, sociability, psychological dependence, and addiction.

1. WHAT'S ACCEPTED . . .

1. The chemical effects of drugs are modified by psychological and social factors.

2. Drug dependence can be physical or psychological or both.

2. WHAT'S DEBATED . . .

1. Exactly how and where in the nervous system many drugs have their effect.

2. Whether hallucinogens such as LSD are "safe."

Earlier in this unit mention was made of William James's belief in the existence of many varied forms of human consciousness. To James, as to many other writers and scholars of his age, the exploration of these forms of consciousness was an urgent task for the emerging discipline of psychology. But somehow psychologists never met the challenge. The reasons were many, but two were of prime importance. First, many of the psychoactive drugs that were freely available early in the century—such as hashish, opium, and cocaine—were soon made illegal. These drugs had once been used by poets, artists, and respected members of the community. Now they became the drugs of outlaws and unprivileged minority groups, and the altered states of consciousness the drugs induced were considered unfit for study. Second, most American psychologists came under the influence of the behaviorist school, whose pragmatic approach emphasized the study of observable behavior, not internal states of consciousness, as the appropriate subject matter of the human sciences.

Accordingly, psychologists in America were ill-prepared for the explosion in drug use among young people during the last decade. Even hypnotism, meditation, and other trance-like states had been poorly researched, and the altered forms of consciousness induced by psychedelic drugs were a mystery to most psychologists. Research on drugs and drug users in the early sixties reflects the uncomprehending attitude and behaviorist bias of the researchers. Accounts of the effects of marijuana, for example, ignored the subjective experience of the users and concentrated instead on the behavioral consequences—increased pulse rate, degree of talkativeness, pupil dilation, and so on—as though these features captured the essence of the drug experience.

But the situation has changed rapidly. The widespread challenge to the traditional, rational-scientific Western world view, which has always denied the validity and sometimes even the existence of altered states of consciousness, has had a marked effect on contemporary American psychology. A much more humanistic tone is detectable, and psychologists are beginning to explore the many forms that human consciousness can take.

All of us have experienced at least some form of

altered consciousness. Among the most common are daydreaming, dreaming, nightmares, delirium, psychedelic states, meditation, mystical rapture, hypnosis, psychosis, trance, anesthesia, or hallucinations induced by sensory overload or sensory deprivation. Apart from the various forms of normal waking or sleeping consciousness, the forms most commonly experienced in America today are those induced by psychoactive drugs.

Why do people take psychoactive drugs, particularly those that bring about radically altered states of consciousness? Many theories have been offered: adolescent rebellion, sheer perversity, desire for "kicks," victimization by pushers, or pressure from peer groups. But Dr. Andrew Weil, an expert in drug abuse and drug education, offers a new explanation that has attracted a good deal of attention: "The desire to alter consciousness is an innate psychological drive arising out of the neurological structure of the human brain." Weil compares the urge to experience new forms of consciousness with such basic drives as those for hunger and for sex—perhaps not as strong, but a basic drive nonetheless.

Weil points out that every society in history has made use of chemicals to alter consciousness (except the Eskimos, whose land was so bleak that they could not grow anything). The reason for this cultural universal, Weil suggests, is that the search for altered consciousness is innate: these mental states are doorways to the next stages of evolutionary development of the human nervous system. Many of the most artistic, noble, and creative human achievements are intimately linked to altered states of consciousness, Weil argues, and our capacity to achieve these states is an important characteristic distinguishing us from lower animals.

But Weil is not an advocate of the use of psychoactive drugs, particularly in a context in which social factors create an unproductive setting for the drug user. Many young people experimenting with drugs are drawn into the negative aspects of drug use rather than the positive opportunity for the exploration of human potential that the drugs might have offered. Moreover, Weil contends, the drugged state is only a substitute for higher forms of consciousness: "A great many experienced drug takers give up drugs for meditation, but no meditators switch to drugs. . . The point is not to deny people the experience of

chemically altered consciousness but to show them how to have it in forms that are not harmful to themselves or to society. And the way to do that is to recognize the simple truth that the experience comes from the mind, not from the drug. Once you have learned from a drug what being high really is, you can begin to reproduce it without the drug; all persons who accomplish this feat testify that the nonpharmacological [non-chemical] high is superior."

An important concern of psychologists in the future will be the understanding of our various potential states of consciousness. We need to know about their physiological correlates in the electrochemistry of the brain. We need to know about their relationship to one another. Is there some kind of "hierarchy" of forms of consciousness? And what factors determine whether an experience will be "good" (a pleasant dream, a good trip, an ecstatic episode) or "bad" (a nightmare, a bad trip, a psychotic episode)? Finally, we need to know why our brains have this built-in capacity to transcend ordinary reality. The ability seems to offer no particular survival advantages to the species—a hallucinating caveman would be no match for a beast of prey—so what evolutionary function does this extraordinary capacity fulfill? The drug explosion of recent years seems likely to alter the course of much psychological research as investigators pursue an important but neglected aspect of human experience.

bibliography

1. The Study of Psychology

A career in psychology. Washington, D.C.: American Psychological Association, undated.

Dennis, W. (Ed.) *Readings in the history of psychology.* New York: Appleton Century Croft, 1948, pp. 457–471.

Feynman, R. P. The relation of science and religion. In E. Hutchings, Jr., Ed., *Frontiers in science.* New York: Basic Books, 1958, pp. 307–317.

Matsun, F. W. Humanistic theory: the third revolution in psychology. *The Humanist,* March/April 1971.

Miller, G. A. *Psychology: the science of mental life.* New York: Harper and Row, 1962.

Psychology encyclopedia. Guilford, Conn.: The Dushkin lishing Group, 1973.

Sanford, F. H. *Psychology: a scientific study of man.* Belmont, California: Wadsworth, 1965, p. 40.

2. Self-Fulfilling Prophecy

Barber, T. X., & Silver, M. J. Fact, fiction and the experimenter bias effect. *Psychological Bulletin Monographs,* 1968, 70, 1–29.

Coleman, J. S. *Equality of educational opportunity.* Washington, D.C.: U. S. Government Printing Office, 1966.

Jones, L. V., & Panitch, D. The self-fulfilling prophecy and interpersonal attraction. *Journal of Experimental Social Psychology,* 1971, 7, 356–366.

Laing, R. D., & Esterson, A. *Sanity, madness and the family.* London: Tavistock Press, 1964.

McGhee, P. E., & Crandall, V. C. Beliefs in internal-external control of reinforcements and academic performance. *Child Development,* 1968, 39, 91–102.

Merton, R. K. *Social theory and social structure.* New York: Free Press, 1957.

Orne, M. T. On the social psychology of the psychological experiment: with particular reference to demand characteristics and their implications. *American Psychologist,* 1962, 17, 776–783.

Pierce, A. H. The subconscious again. *Journal of Philosophy and Psychology Scientific Methods,* 1908, 5, 264–271.

Rosenthal, R. Clever Hans: a case study of scientific method. In Gazzaniga, M. S., & Lovejoy, E. P. (Eds.), *Good reading in psychology,* Englewood Cliffs, New Jersey: Prentice-Hall, 1971. Pp. 498–518.

Rosenthal, R., & Fode, K. L. The effect of experimenter bias on the performance of the albino rat. *Behavioral Science,* 1963, 8, 183–189.

Rosenthal, R., & Fode, K. L. Three experiments in experimenter bias. *Psychological Reports,* 1963, 12, 491–511.

Rosenthal, R., & Jacobson, L. F. *Pygmalion in the classroom: teachers' expectations and pupils' intellectual development.* New York: Holt, Rinehart & Winston, 1968.

Szasz, T. S. The myth of mental illness. *American Psychologist,* 1960, 15, 113–118.

Thomas, W. I., & Znaniecki, F. *The Polish peasant in Europe and America,* (5 vols.). Boston: Badger, 1918–1920.

●

Becker, H. *Outsiders.* New York: Free Press, 1964.

Scheff, T. *Being mentally ill.* Chicago: Aldine-Atherton, 1966.

3. Helping Others

Aderman, D., & Berkowitz, L. Observational set, empathy, and helping. *Journal of Personality and Social Psychology,* 1970, 14, 141–148.

Baldwin, A. L., Kalhorn, J. & Breese, F. H. Patterns of parent behavior. *Psychological Monographs,* 1945, 58, 1–75.

Berkowitz, L., & Connor, W. H. Success, failure and social responsibility. *Journal of Personality and Social Psychology,* 1966, 4, 664–669.

Betz, B. J., & Whitehorn, J. C. The relationship of the therapist to the outcome of therapy in schizophrenia. *Psychiatric Research Reports No. 5. Research techniques in schizophrenia.* Washington, D.C., American Psychiatric Association, 1956, 89–117.

Brandt, R. (Ed.). *Value and obligation: systematic readings in ethics.* New York: Harcourt, Brace & World, 1961.

Bryan, J. H., & Test, M. A. Models and helping: naturalistic studies in aiding behavior. *Journal of Personality and Social Psychology,* 1967, 6, 400–407.

Carlsmith, J. M., & Gross, A. E. Some effects of guilt on compliance. *Journal of Personality and Social Psychology,* 1969, 11, 232–240.

Darlington, R. B., & Macker, C. E. Displacement of guilt-produced altruistic behavior. *Journal of Personality and Social Psychology*, 1966, 4, 442–443.

Freedman, J. L., Wallington, S. A., & Bliss, E. Compliance without pressure: the effect of guilt. *Journal of Personality and Social Psychology*, 1967, 7, 117–124.

Freud, S. *Civilization and its discontents*. London: Hogarth, 1930.

Gore, P. M., & Rotter, J. B. A personality correlate of social action. *Journal of Personality*, 1963, 31, 58–64.

Heine, R. W. A comparison of patients' reports on the psychotherapeutic experience with psychoanalytic, nondirective, and Adlerian therapists. Unpublished Doctoral Dissertation, University of Chicago, 1950.

Hogan, R. Development of an empathy scale. *Journal of Consulting and Clinical Psychology*, 1969, 33, 307–316.

Krebs, D. The effect of prior experience on generosity—role taking or modeling. Preparation for publication, 1972.

Latané, B., & Darley, J. Group inhibition of bystander intervention in emergencies. *Journal of Personality and Social Psychology*, 1968, 10, 215–221.

Rogers, C. R. *On becoming a person*. Boston: Houghton-Mifflin, 1961.

Rutherford, E., & Mussen, P. Generosity in nursery school boys. *Child Development*, 1968, 39, 755–765.

Shilkret, J. P. (Ed.). *Dynamic readings for an introduction to psychology*. Berkeley, Calif.: McCutchan, 1970.

Whitehorn, J. C., & Betz, B. J. A study of psychotherapeutic relationships between physicians and schizophrenic patients. *American Journal of Psychiatry*, 1954, 111, 321–331.

•

Zimbardo, P. G. The human choice: individuation, reason and order vs. deindividuation, impulse, and chaos. In *Nebraska Symposium on Motivation*, 1969, Vol. 17. Lincoln, Nebraska: University of Nebraska Press, 1970, 237–307.

4. Hurting Others

Ardrey, R. The violent way. *Life,* Sept. 11, 1970.

Bandura, A., Ross, D., & Ross, S. A. Imitation of film-mediated aggressive models. *Journal of Abnormal and Social Psychology*, 1963, 66, 3–11.

Berkowitz, L. Some aspects of observed aggression. *Journal of Personality and Social Psychology*, 1965, 2, 359–369.

Calhoun, J. B. Population density and social pathology. *Scientific American,* 1962, 206, 139–148.

Campbell, O. J., VanGundy, J., & Shrodes, C. (Eds.). An exchange of letters between Sigmund Freud and Albert Einstein. In *Patterns for Living*, 3rd edit. New York: MacMillan, 1949.

Eron, L. D., Lefkowitz, M. M., Huesmann, L. R., & Walder, L. O. Does television cause aggression? *American Psychologist,* 1972, 27, 253–263.

James, W. The moral equivalent of war. In *Memories and Studies*. New York: Longmans, Green, 1911.

Milgram, S. Some conditions of obedience and disobedience to authority. *Human Relations,* 1965, 18, 57–75.

Milgram, S. The experience of living in cities. *Science,* 1970, 1967, 1461–1468.

Seay, B., Alexander, B. K., & Harlow, H. F. Maternal behavior of socially deprived rhesus monkeys. *Journal of Abnormal and Social Psychology*, 1964, 69, 345–354.

Steele, B. F., & Pollock, C. B. A psychiatric study of parents who abuse infants and small children. In Helfer, R. E., & Kempe, C. H. (Eds.), *The battered child.* Chicago: University of Chicago Press, 1968. Pp. 103–147.

Weisz, A. E., & Taylor, R. L. American presidential assassination. *Diseases of the Nervous System,* 1969, 30, 659–668.

Zimbardo, P. G. The human choice: individuation, reason and order vs. deindividuation, impulse, and chaos. In *Nebraska Symposium on Motivation*, 1969, Vol. 17. Lincoln, Nebraska: University of Nebraska Press, 1970. Pp. 237–307.

•

Benedict, R. *Patterns of culture*. New York and Boston: Houghton Mifflin, 1934.

Jacobs, J. *The death and life of great American cities*. New York: Random House, 1961.

Zimbardo, P. G. Pathology of imprisonment. *Society,* 1972, 9.

5. Morality

Aronfreed, J. The effects of experimental socialization paradigms upon two moral responses to transgression. *Journal of Abnormal and Social Psychology*, 1963, 66, 436–448.

Bandura, A., & McDonald, F. J. Influence of social reinforcement and the behavior of models in shaping children's moral judgments. *Journal of Abnormal and Social Psychology*, 1963, 67, 274–281.

Cowan, P. A., Langer, J., Heavenrich, J., & Nathanson, M. Social learning and Piaget's cognitive theory of moral development. *Journal of Personality and Social Psychology*, 1969, 11, 261–274.

Hartshorne, H., & May, M. A. *Studies in the nature of character,* (3 vols.). New York: Macmillan, 1928, 1929, 1930.

Hoffman, M. L., & Saltzstein, H. D. Parent discipline and the child's moral development. *Journal of Personality and Social Psychology,* 1967, 45–57.

Kohlberg, L. Development of character and moral ideology. In Hoffman, M. L., & Hoffman, L. W. (Eds.), *Review of Child Development Research,* Vol. I. New York: Russell Sage Foundation, 1964. Pp. 383–431.

Kohlberg, L. The child as a moral philosopher. In *Readings in Developmental Psychology Today.* Del Mar, Calif.: CRM Books, 1970. Pp. 109–115.

Kohlberg, L. Stage and sequence: The cognitive developmental approach to socialization. In Goslin, D. (Ed.), *Handbook of socialization theory and research.* Chicago: Rand McNally, 1969.

Krebs, R. L. Some relationships between moral judgment, attention and resistance to temptation. Unpublished Ph.D. dissertation, 1967.

Lasson, K. *The workers.* New York: Bantam Books, 1972. Pp. 118–119.

Vitro, F. The relationship of classroom dishonesty to perceived parental discipline. *Journal of College Student Personnel,* 1971, 12, 427–429.

●

Fishkin, J., Keniston, K., & Mackinnon, C. Moral reasoning and political ideology. *Journal of Personality and Social Psychology,* 1973, 27, 109–119.

Haan, N., Brewster Smith, M., & Block, J. H. Moral reasoning of young adults. *Journal of Personality and Social Psychology,* 1968, 10, 183–201.

Hampden-Turner, C., & Whitten, P. Morals left and right. *Psychology Today,* April 1971.

Kohlberg, L., & Kramer, R. Continuities and discontinuities in childhood and adult moral development. *Human Development,* 1969, 12, 93–120.

Piaget, J. *The moral judgment of the child.* London: K. Paul, Trench, Trubner and Co., Ltd., 1932.

Cleaver, E. The allegory of the black eunuchs, *Soul on Ice.* New York: McGraw-Hill. P. 162.

Deaux, K., & Taynor, J. Evaluation of male and female ability: bias works two ways. Unpublished paper, Department of Psychology, Purdue University, 1971.

Freeman, J. The social construction of the second sex. In M. Garskof (Ed.), *Roles women play: readings toward women's liberation.* Belmont, Calif.: Brooks/Cole, 1971, p. 136.

Freud, S. *Three essays on the theory of sexuality.* Edited, translated by J. Strachey. New York: Basic Books, 1963.

Greer, G. *The female eunuch.* New York: Bantam Books, 1972. P. 5.

Horner, M. S. Fail: bright women. *Psychology Today,* 1969, 3, 36–38, 62.

Kagan, J., & Moss, H. A. The stability of passive and dependent behavior from childhood through adulthood. *Child Development,* 1960, 31, 577–591.

Lewis, M. Culture and gender roles: There's no unisex in the nursery. *Psychology Today,* 1972, 5, 54–57.

Mead, M. *Male and Female.* New York: William Morrow and Co., 1949, 1970.

Parker, D. "Indian Summer" by Dorothy Parker, from *The Portable Dorothy Parker,* copyright 1926, 1954 by Dorothy Parker. All rights reserved. Reprinted by permission of the Viking Press, Inc.

●

Bowers, F. Homosex: living the life. *Saturday Review,* February 12, 1972.

Davis, K. Sexual behavior. In R. Merton and R. Nisbet (Eds.), *Contemporary Social Problems.* New York: Harcourt Brace Jovanovich, 1971.

Ford, C. S. & Beach, F. A. *Patterns of sexual behavior.* New York: Harper & Row, 1951.

Hoffman, M. Homosexuality. *Today's Education,* November 1970.

Kinsey, A. C. *Sexual behavior in the human male.* Philadelphia: W. B. Saunders, 1948.

Kinsey, A. C. *Sexual behavior in the human female.* Philadelphia: W. B. Saunders, 1953.

6. Sexuality

Bardwick, J. M. *Psychology of Women.* New York: Harper and Row, 1971.

Bardwick, J. M. Her body, the battleground. *Psychology Today,* 1972, 6, 50–54, 76, 82.

Brown, D. G. Masculinity-femininity development in children. *Journal of Consulting Psychology,* 1957, 21, 197–202.

7. Love

Aronson, E., & Linder, D. Gain and loss of esteem as determinants of interpersonal attractiveness. *Journal of Experimental Social Psychology,* 1965, 1, 156–171.

Byrne, D. Interpersonal attraction and attitude similarity. *Journal of Abnormal and Social Psychology,* 1961, 62, 713–715.

Chamove, A., Harlow, H. F., & Mitchell, G. Sex differences in the infant-directed behavior of preadolescent rhesus monkeys. *Child Development*, 1967, 38, 329–335.

Fromm, E. *The art of loving.* New York: Harper & Row, 1956.

Harlow, H. F. The nature of love. *American Psychologist,* 1958, 13, 673–685.

Harlow, H. F. *Learning to Love.* San Francisco: Albion, 1971.

Harlow, H. F., Joslyn, W. D., Senko, M. G., & Dopp, A. Behavioral aspects of reproduction in primates. *Journal of Animal Science,* 1966, 25, 49–67.

Maslow, A. H. A philosophy of psychology: the need for a mature science of human nature. *Main currents in modern thought,* 1957, 13, 27–32.

Meerloo, J. A. M. *Conversation and communication.* New York: International Universities Press, 1952.

Murstein, B. I. Self-ideal-self-discrepancy and choice of marital partner. *Journal of Consulting and Clinical Psychology,* 1971, 37, 47–52.

Valins, S. Cognitive effects of false heart-rate feedback. *Journal of Personality and Social Psychology,* 1966, 4, 400–408.

Walster, E. The effect of self-esteem on romantic liking. *Journal of Experimental Social Psychology,* 1965, 1, 184–197.

Walster, E., Aronson, V., Abrahams, D., & Rottmann, L. Importance of physical attractiveness in dating behavior. *Journal of Personality and Social Psychology,* 1966, 4, 508–516.

●

Rutter, M. *Maternal deprivation reassessed.* London: Penguin, 1972.

Zigler, E. On growing up, learning and loving. *Human Behavior,* March 1973.

8. Prejudice

Adorno, T. W., Frenkel-Brunswik, E., Levinson, D. J., & Sanford, R. N. *The authoritarian personality.* New York: Harper and Row, 1950.

Allport, G. W. Attitudes. In Murchison, C. M. (Ed.), *Handbook of social psychology.* Worcester, Mass.: Clark Univ. Press, 1935. Pp. 798–844.

Bettelheim, B., & Janowitz, M. *Dynamics of Prejudice.* New York: Harper, 1950.

Deutsch, M., & Collins, M. E. *Interracial housing.* Minneapolis: The University of Minnesota Press, 1951.

Dienstbier, R. A. A modified belief theory of prejudice emphasizing the mutual causality of racial prejudice and anticipated belief differences. *Psychological Review,* 1972, 79, 146–160.

Frenkel-Brunswik, E. Prejudice in children. *Human Relations,* 1948, 1, 295–306.

Frenkel-Brunswik, E., & Sanford, R. N. Some personality factors in anti-semitism. *Journal of Psychology,* 1945, 20, 271–292.

Greer, G. *The female eunuch.* New York: Bantam Books, 1972. P. 30.

Hovland, C., & Sears, R. Minor studies in aggression: VI. Correlation of lynchings with economic indices. *Journal of Psychology,* 1940, 9, 301–310.

Katz, D., & Braly, K. W. Racial stereotypes of one hundred college students. *Journal of Abnormal and Social Psychology,* 1933, 28, 280–290.

Miller, N. E., & Bugelski, R. Minor studies of aggression: II. The influence of frustrations imposed by the in-group on attitudes expressed toward out-groups. *Journal of Psychology,* 1948, 25, 437–442.

Rokeach, M. *The open and closed mind.* New York: Basic Books, 1960.

Rokeach, M. Long-range experimental modification of values, attitudes and behavior. *American Psychologist,* 1971, 26, 453–459.

Stein, D. D., Hardwyck, J. A., & Smith, M. B. Race and belief: an open and shut case. *Journal of Personality and Social Psychology,* 1965, 1, 281–289.

Tajfel, H., & Wilkes, A. L. Classification and quantitative judgment. *British Journal of Psychology,* 1963, 54, 101–114.

Young, R. K. Student attitudes towards the Negro. In Deloach, J., & Miller, J. (Eds.), *Contemporary explorations in behavior.* Berkeley, Calif.: McCutchan, 1970. Pp. 138–147.

●

Allport, G. W. *The nature of prejudice.* Garden City, New York: Doubleday, 1958.

Jahoda, N. M. X-ray of the racist mind. *UNESCO Courier,* October 1960.

The Study of Society. Guilford, Connecticut: Dushkin Publishing Group, 1974.

9. Groups and Leaders

Asch, S. E. Opinions and social pressure. *Scientific American,* 1955, 193, 31–35.

Bales, R. F. *Interaction process analysis: a method for the study of small groups.* Cambridge: Addison-Wesley, 1950.

Burke, R. L., & Bennis, W. G. Changes in perception of self and others during human relations training. *Human Relations, 1961,* 14, 165–182.

Carter, J. H. Military Leadership. *Military Review, 1952, 32,* 14–18.

Fiedler, F. E. Validation and extension of the contingency model of leadership effectiveness: a review of empirical findings. *Psychological Bulletin, 1971, 76,* 128–148.

Gibb, C. A. Leadership. In Lindzey, G., & Aronson, E. (Eds.), *The Handbook of social psychology* (2nd edit.), Vol. IV. Reading, Mass.: Addison-Wesley Publishing Co., 1969. Pp. 205–282.

Halpin, A. W., & Winer, B. J. The leadership behavior of the airplane commander. Columbus, Ohio: Ohio State University Research Foundation, 1952.

Janis, I. L. *Victims of groupthink: a psychological analysis of historical decisions and fiascos.* Boston: Houghton Mifflin, 1973.

Lewin, K., Lippitt, R., & White, R. K. Patterns of aggressive behavior in experimentally created "social climates," *Journal of Social Psychology,* 10, 271–299.

Merei, F. Group leadership and institutionalization. *Human Relations,* 1949, 2, 23–39.

Sherif, M. *The psychology of social norms.* New York: Harper & Brothers, 1936.

Stoner, J. A. F. A comparison of individual and group decisions involving risk. Unpublished Master's Thesis, M.I.T., School of Industrial Management, 1961.

Stoner, J. A. F. Risky and cautious shifts in group decision: the influence of widely held values. *Journal of Experimental Social Psychology,* 1968, 4, 442–459.

Wallach, M. A., Kogan, N., & Bem, D. J. Diffusion of responsibility and level of risk taking in groups. *Journal of Abnormal and Social Psychology,* 1964, 68, 263–274.

●

Janis, I. L. Groupthink. *Yale Alumni Magazine.* January 1973.

Townsend, R. *Up the organization.* New York: Knopf, 1970.

Biondo, J., & MacDonald, A. P., Jr. Internal-external locus of control and response to influence attempts. *Journal of Personality,* 1971, 407–419.

Brehm, J. W. Attitudinal consequences of commitment to unpleasant behavior. *Journal of Abnormal and Social Psychology,* 1960, 60, 379–383.

Festinger, L. *A theory of cognitive dissonance.* Evanston, Ill.: Row-Peterson, 1957.

Hovland, C. I., Lumsdaine, A. A., & Sheffield, F. D. *Experiments on mass communication.* Princeton, N. J.: Princeton University Press, 1949.

Kelman, H. C., & Hovland, C. I. "Reinstatement" of the communicator in delayed measurement of opinion change. *Journal of Abnormal and Social Psychology,* 1953, 48, 327–335.

Litt, E. Civic education, community norms and political indoctrination. *American Sociological Review,* 1963, 28, 69–75.

Lumsdaine, A. A., & Janis, I. L. Resistance to "counterpropaganda" produced by one-sided and two-sided "propaganda" presentations. *Public Opinion Quarterly,* 1953, 17, 310–318.

Newcomb, T. M. *Personality and social change.* New York: Dryden Press, 1943.

Newcomb, T. M. Persistence and regression of changed attitudes: long-range studies. *Journal of Social Issues,* 1963, 19, 3–14.

Zimbardo, P., & Ebbesen, E. B. *Influencing attitudes and changing behavior.* Reading, Mass.: Addison-Wesley, 1969.

●

Kretch, D. & Krutchfield, R. Perceiving the world. In Wilbur Schramm and Donald Roberts (Eds.), *The process and effects of mass communications.* Urbana, Illinois: University of Illinois Press, 1971, 116–137.

McGinniss, J. *The selling of the president, 1968.* New York: Trident, 1969.

Nader, R. The great American gyp. *New York Review of Books,* November 21, 1968.

Robertson, I. & McKee, M. *Social problems.* New York: Random House, 1975.

Schramm, W. *Television in the lives of our children.* Stanford: Stanford University Press, 1961.

10. Social Influence

Allport, G. W., & Postman, L. J. The basic psychology of rumor. *Transactions of the New York Academy of Sciences,* 1945, 8, 61–81.

Allyn, J., & Festinger, L. The effectiveness of unanticipated persuasive communications. *Journal of Abnormal and Social Psychology,* 1961, 62, 35–40.

11. Therapy in Groups

Atthowe, J. M., Jr., & Krasner, L. The systematic application of contingent reinforcement procedures (token economies) in a large social setting: a psychiatric ward. Paper presented at the Annual Meeting of the American Psychological Association, Chicago, 1965.

Ayllon, T., & Michael, J. The psychiatric nurse as behavioral engineer. *Journal of the Experimental Analysis of Behavior,* 1959, 2, 323–324.

Coons, W. H., & Peacock, E. P. Interpersonal interaction and personality change in group psychotherapy. *Canadian Psychiatric Association Journal,* 1970, 15, 347–355.

Fairweather, G. W. (Ed.). *Social psychology in treating mental illness.* New York: Wiley, 1964.

Fairweather, G. W., Sanders, D. H., Maynard, R. F., & Cressler, D. L. *Community life for the mentally ill: alternative to institutional care.* Chicago: Aldine, 1969.

Frank, J. D. *Persuasion and healing.* New York: Schoken Books, 1965.

Goldenson, R. M. *Encyclopedia of human behavior.* 1, 524; 2, 1235–1236. New York: Doubleday & Co., Inc., 1970.

Janis, I., & Mann, L. Effectiveness of emotional role playing in modifying smoking habits and attitudes. *Journal of Experimental Research in Personality,* 1965, 1, 84–90.

Miles, A. Changes in the attitudes to authority of patients with behavior disorders in a therapeutic community. *British Journal of Psychiatry,* 1969, 115, 1049–1057.

Mone, L. C. Short-term psychotherapy with postcardiac patients. *International Journal of Group Psychotherapy,* 1970, 20, 99–108.

Moreno, J. L. *Psychodrama.* New York: Beacon House, 1946.

Solomon, M. L., & Solomon, C. K. Psychodrama as an ancillary therapy on a psychiatric ward. *Canadian Psychiatric Association Journal,* 1970, 15, 365–373.

Thomson, R. *The pelican history of psychology.* Baltimore: Penguin Books, 1968.

•

Back, K. W. The way of love and trust: the sensitivity/encounter movement. *Society,* June 1972.

Lieberman, M., Yalon, I. & Miles, M. Encounter: the leader makes the difference. *Psychology Today,* March 1973.

12. Intelligence

Bayley, N. Learning in adulthood: the role of intelligence. In Klausmeier, H. J., & Harris, C. W. (Eds.), *Analyses of concept learning.* New York: Wiley, 1966. Pp. 117–138.

Bayley, N. Behavioral correlates of mental growth: birth to 36 years. *American Psychologist,* 1968, 23, 1–17.

Bodmer, W. F., & Cavalli-Sforza, L. L. Intelligence and race. In *Contemporary Psychology: Readings from Scientific American.* San Francisco: W. Freeman and Co., 1971. Pp. 437–447.

Cicirelli, V G. *et al. The impact of Head Start. An evaluation of the effects of Head Start on children's cognitive and affective development.* Washington, D.C.: Clearinghouse Fed. Sci. Tech. Inform., U.S. Department of Commerce, National Bureau of Standards. Institute of Applied Tech. Pp. 184–328.

Coleman, J. S. *Equality of educational opportunity.* Washington, D.C.: U.S. Government Printing Office, 1966.

Cooper, R. M., & Zubek, J. P. Effects of enriched and restricted early environments on the learning ability of bright and dull rats. *Canadian Journal of Psychology,* 1958, 12, 159–164.

Erlenmeyer-Kimling, L., & Jarvik, L. F. Genetics and intelligence: A review. *Science,* 1963, 142, 1477–1479.

Goldenson, R. M. *The encyclopedia of human behavior: psychology, psychiatry, and mental health.* New York: Doubleday & Co., Inc., 1970.

Goldsby, R. A. *Race and races.* New York: Macmillan, 1971.

Guilford, J. P. *The nature of human intelligence.* New York: McGraw-Hill, 1967.

Jensen, A. R. How much can we boost IQ and scholastic achievement? *Harvard Educational Review,* 1969, 39, 1–123.

Karnes, M. B. Research and development program on preschool disadvantaged children. Final Report, Vol. 1, University of Illinois, Contract No. OE–6–10–235, U.S. Office of Education, 1969.

Kennedy, W. A. A follow-up normative study of Negro intelligence and achievement. *Monograph of the Society for Research in Child Development,* 1969, 34, 1–40.

Lesser, G. S., Fifer, G., & Clark, D. H. Mental abilities of children from different social class and cultural groups. *Monograph of the Society for Research in Child Development,* 1965, 30, No. 4.

Spearman, C. *The abilities of man.* New York: Macmillan, 1927.

Spicker, H. H. Intellectual development through early childhood education. *Exceptional Children,* 1971, 37, 629–640.

Thurstone, L. L. *Primary mental abilities.* Chicago: University of Chicago Press, 1938.

Watson, R. I. *The Great Psychologists, Aristotle to Freud.* Philadelphia and New York: J. B. Lippincott Co., 1963.

Wechsler, D. *The Wechsler Adult Intelligence Scale.* New York: The Psychological Corporation, 1955.

•

Shaffer, R. A. Probing the mind: brain wave monitor seen as improved way to gauge intelligence. *Wall Street Journal,* July 1, 1971.

Shuey, A. M. *The testing of negro intelligence.* New York: Social Science Press, 1966.

Taking the chitling test. *Newsweek,* July 15, 1968.

Whimbey, A. Something better than Binet. *Saturday Review/World,* June 1, 1974.

13. The Disordered Mind

Barter, J. T., Todd, D., & Swaback, D. C. Adolescent suicide attempts: follow-up study of hospitalized patients. *Archives of General Psychiatry*, 1968, 19, 523–527.

Camus, A. *The stranger.* New York: Vintage Books, 1954. Pp. 126–127.

Coleman, J. C. *Abnormal psychology and modern life.* Glenview, Ill.: Scott, Foresman and Co., 1964. P. 121.

Diagnostic and statistical manual of mental disorders. Washington: American Psychiatric Association, 1968. (2nd edition)

Diven, K. Certain determinants in the conditioning of anxiety reactions. *Journal of Psychology*, 1937, 33, 291–308.

Farina, A., & Holzberg, J. D. Attitudes and behaviors of fathers and mothers of male schizophrenic patients. *Journal of Abnormal Psychology*, 1967, 72, 381–387.

Fleck, S. Family dynamics and origin of schizophrenia. *Psychosomatic Medicine*, 1960, 22, 333–343.

Fox, L. *Psychology as philosophy, science, and art.* Pacific Palisades, Calif.: Goodyear Publishing Co., 1972.

Freud, S. *The standard edition of the complete psychological works of Sigmund Freud.* Translated by James Strachey. Vol. 1. London: Hogarth, 1909.

Hebb, D. O. *A textbook of psychology.* Philadelphia: W. B. Saunders Co., 1966.

Heston, L. The genetics of schizophrenia and schizoid disease. *Science*, 1970, 167, 249–256.

Jenkins, R. L., & Hewitt, L. Types of personality structure in child guidance clinics. *American Journal of Orthopsychiatry*, 1944, 14, 84–94.

Kallman, F. J. *The genetics of schizophrenia.* New York: Augustin, 1938.

Keith-Spiegel, P., & Spiegel, D. Affective states of patients immediately preceding suicide. *Journal of Psychiatric Research*, 1967, 5, 89–93.

Kraepelin, E. *Psychiatry.* Leipzig: Barth, 1915.

Lykken, D. A. A study of anxiety in the sociopathic personality. *Journal of Abnormal and Social Psychology*, 1957, 55.

Plath, S. *The bell jar.* New York: Harper & Row, 1971.

Schiele, B. C., & Brozek, J. "Experimental neurosis" resulting from semi-starvation in man. *Psychosomatic Medicine*, 1948, 10, 31–50.

Siegman, A. W. Father absence during early childhood and antisocial behavior. *Journal of Abnormal Psychology*, 1966, 71, 71–74.

Stevenson, R. L. *Dr. Jekyll and Mr. Hyde and other famous tales.* New York: Dell, 1966.

Thigpen, C. H., & Cleckley, H. *The three faces of Eve.* New York: McGraw-Hill, 1957.

Watson, J. B., & Rayner, B. Conditioned emotional reactions. *Journal of Experimental Psychology*, 1920, 3, 1–14.

Wolpe, J., & Rachman, S. Psychoanalytic "evidence": a critique based on Freud's case of Little Hans. *Journal of Nervous and Mental Disease*, 1960, 131, 135–148.

•

Laing, R. D. *The divided self.* New York: Pantheon, 1969.

Laing, R. D. *The politics of experience.* New York: Pantheon, 1967.

Rosenhan, D. L. On being sane in insane places. *Science*, 1973, 179, 250–258.

Szasz, T. *The myth of mental illness.* New York: Harper & Row, 1961.

14. Using Language

Baratz, J. C. A bi-dialectal task for determining language proficiency in economically disadvantaged Negro children. *Child Development*, 1969, 40(3), 889–901.

Berko, J. The child's learning of English morphology. *Word*, 1958, 14, 150–177.

Burton, N. G., & Licklider, J. C. R. Long-range constraints in the statistical structure of printed English. *American Journal of Psychology*, 1955, 68, 650–653.

Carroll, J. B., & Casagrande, J. B. The functions of language classification in behavior. In Maccoby, E. E., Newcomb, T. M., & Hartley, E. L. (Eds.), *Readings in social psychology* (3rd Edit.). New York: Holt, Rinehart & Winston, 1958, Pp. 18–31.

Chomsky, N. A review of *Verbal Behavior* by B. F. Skinner. *Language*, 35, 26–58 .

Eimas, P., Siqueland, E. R., Juscqyk, P., & Vigorito, J. Speech perception in infants. *Science*, 1971, 171, 303–306.

Epstein, W. The influence of syntactical structure on learning. *American Journal of Psychology*, 1961, 74, 80-85.

Fodor, J. A., & Bever, T. G. The psychological reality of linguistic segments. *Journal of Verbal Learning and Verbal Behavior*, 1965, 4, 414–420.

Gardner, R. A., & Gardner, B. T. Teaching sign language to a chimpanzee. *Science*, 1969, 165, 664–672.

Hahn, E. Washoese. *The New Yorker*, 1971, 4, (17, 46–97), (24, 46–91).

McNeill, D. Developmental psycholinguistics. In Smith, F., & Miller, G. A., (Eds.), *The genesis of language.* Cambridge, Mass.: M.I.T. Press, 1966. Pp. 15–84.

Roberts, G. C., & Black, K. N. The effect of naming and object permanence on toy preferences. *Child Development*, Sept. 1972, in press.

Seymour, D. Z. Black English. *Intellectual Digest,* 1972, 2(6), 78–80.

Skinner, B. F. *Verbal Behavior.* New York: Appleton, 1957.

Slobin, D. I. Universals of grammatical development in children. In D'Arcais, F., & Levelt, J. M. (Eds.), *Advances in psycholinguistics.* Amsterdam, Netherlands: North-Holland Publishing Co., 1970. Pp. 174–186.

Slobin, D. I. *Psycholinguistics.* Glenview, Ill.: Scott, Foresman and Co., 1971.

Whorf, B. L. *Language, Thought and Reality.* New York: Wiley, 1956.

•

Bernstein, B. B. *Class, codes and control.* London: Routledge & Kegan Paul, Vol. 1, 1971.

15. Personality

Allport, G. W., & Odbert, H. S. Trait-names: a psycho-lexical study. *Psychological Monographs,* 1936, 47, 1–171.

Asch, S. E. *Social psychology.* Englewood Cliffs, N. J.: Prentice-Hall, 1952.

Auden, W. H. *The Collected Poetry of W. H. Auden.* New York: Random House, 1945. Pp. 163–167.

Blum, G. S., & Miller, D. R. Exploring the psychoanalytic theory of the "oral character." *Journal of Personality,* 1952, 20, 287–304.

Breger, L. Conformity as a function of the ability to express hostility. *Journal of Personality,* 1963, 31, 247–257.

Cattell, R. B. *Personality: a systematic, theoretical and factual study.* New York: McGraw-Hill, 1950.

Cattell, R. B. *The scientific analysis of personality.* Baltimore: Penguin Books, 1965.

Cohen, D. J. Justin and his peers: an experimental analysis of a child's social world. *Child Development,* 1962, 33, 697–717.

Erikson, E. H. *Childhood and society.* New York: W. W. Norton, 1963.

Freud, S. *The basic writings of Sigmund Freud.* New York: Modern Library, 1938.

Hart, I. Maternal child-rearing practices and authoritarian ideology. *Journal of Abnormal and Social Psychology,* 1957, 55, 232–237.

Kaufman, C., & Rosenblum, L. Depression in infant monkeys separated from their mothers. *Science,* 1967, 155, 1030–1031.

Sheldon, W. H. (with S. S. Stevens and W. B. Tucker). *The varieties of human physique: an introduction to constitutional psychology.* New York: Harper & Row, 1940.

Taylor, C., & Combs, A. W. Self-acceptance and adjustment. *Journal of Consulting Psychology,* 1952, 16, 89–91.

Thomas, A., Chess, S., & Birch, H. G. The origin of personality. In *Contemporary psychology: readings from Scientific American.* San Francisco: W. H. Freeman and Company, 1971. Pp. 350–357.

Watson, D., & Baumal, E. Effects of locus of control and expectation of future control upon present performance. *Journal of Personality and Social Psychology,* 1967, 6, 212–215.

•

Maslow, A. *Motivation and personality.* New York: Harper and Brothers, 1954.

McMahon, F. B., Jr. Personality testing: a smoke screen against logic. *Readings in Psychology Today.* Del Mar, California: CRM Books, 1974, 245–248.

Rotter, J. Generalized expectancies for internal versus external control of reinforcement. *Psychological Monographs: General and Applied,* 1966, 80 (1), 1–28.

Ruch, F. L. Personality: public or private. *Readings in Psychology Today.* Del Mar, California: CRM Books, 1974, 241–244.

16. Children's Thinking

Adelson, J., & O'Neill, R. P. Growth of political ideas in adolescence: the sense of community. *Journal of Personality and Social Psychology,* 1966, 4, 295–306.

Berzonsky, M. D. The role of familiarity in children's explanations of physical causality. *Child Development,* 1971, 42, 705–717.

Brainerd, C. J., & Allen, T. W. Training and generalization of density conservation: effects of feedback and consecutive similar stimuli. *Child Development,* 1971, 42, 643–705.

Bruner, J. S., Goodnow, J. J., & Austin, G. A. *A study of thinking.* New York: Wiley, 1956.

Dweck, C. *The role of expectations and attributions in the alleviation of learned helplessness in a problem-solving situation.* Unpublished Doctoral Dissertation, Yale University, 1972.

Elkind, D. Children's discovery of the conservation of mass, weight, and volume: Piaget Replication Study II. *Journal of Genetic Psychology,* 1961, 98, 219–227.

Piaget, J. The stages of the intellectual development of the child. *Bulletin of the Menninger Clinic,* 1962, 26, 120–145.

Piaget, J., & Inhelder, B. *The child's conception of space* (translated by F. J. Langdon & J. L. Lunzer). London: Routledge & Kegan Paul Ltd., 1956. (Original French edition, 1948).

Rebelsky, F., Conover, C., & Chafetz, P. The development of political attitudes in young children. *The Journal of Psychology,* 1969.

Ames, L. B. Don't push your preschooler. *Family Circle,* December 1971.

Elkind, D. Giant in the nursery—Jean Piaget. *The New York Times Magazine,* May 26, 1969.

Elkind, D. Misunderstandings about how children learn. *Today's Education,* March 1972.

Moore, R. S., & Moore, D. R. The dangers of early schooling. *Harper's,* July 1972.

17. Signs of Emotion

Darwin, C. *The expression of the emotions in man and animals.* London: John Murray, Albemarle Street, 1872.

Darwin, C. *Origin of species.* New York: Modern Library, 1949.

Efron, D. *Gesture, race and culture.* Mouton, 1972.

Ekman, P. Universals and cultural differences in facial expressions of emotion. *Nebraska Symposium on Motivation,* J. K. Cole (Ed.), 1971.

Fulcher, J. S. "Voluntary" facial expression in blind and seeing children. *Archives of Psychology,* 1942, 272, 5–49.

Gitin, S. R. A dimensional analysis of manual expression. *Journal of Personality and Social Psychology,* 1970, 15, 271–277.

James, W. *Psychology.* New York: Henry Holt & Co., 1910.

Schachter, S., & Singer, J. E. Cognitive, social, and physiological determinants of emotional state. *Psychological Review,* 1962, 69, 379–399.

Speisman, J. C., Lazarus, R. S., Mordkoff, A. M., & Davison, L. A. Experimental reduction of stress based on ego-defense theory. *Journal of Abnormal and Social Psychology,* 1964, 68, 367–380.

Tomkins, S. S., & McCarter, R. What and where are the primary affects? Some evidence for a theory. *Perceptual and Motor Skills,* 18, 119–158. Southern Universities Press, 1964.

•

Shenker, I. What's in a smile? It depends on where you're from. *The New York Times,* July 13, 1972.

18. Problem-Solving and Creativity

Adamson, R. E. Functional fixedness as related to problem solving: a repetition of three experiments. *Journal of Experimental Psychology,* 1952, 44, 288–291.

Bruner, J. S., Goodnow, J. J., & Austin, G. A. *A study of thinking.* New York: Wiley, 1956.

Duncker, K. On problem solving. *Psychological Monographs,* 1945, No. 270.

Flavell, J. H., Beach, D., & Chinsky, J. M. Spontaneous verbal rehearsal in a memory task as a function of age. *Child Development,* 1966, 37, 2, 283–289.

Glucksberg, S., & Weisberg, R. W. Verbal behavior and problem solving: some effects of labeling in a functional fixedness problem. *Journal of Experimental Psychology,* 1966, 71, 659–664.

Guilford, J. P. *The nature of human intelligence.* New York: McGraw-Hill, 1967.

Harlow, H. F. The formation of learning sets. *Psychological Review,* 1949, 56, 51–65.

Jackson, P. W., & Messick, S. The person, the product, and the response: conceptual problems in the assessment of creativity. *Journal of Personality,* 1965, 33, 309–329.

Kohler, W. *The mentality of apes.* New York: Harcourt, 1926.

MacKinnon, D. W. The nature and nurture of creative talent. *American Psychologist,* 1962, 17, 484–495.

Miller, G. A., Galanter, E., & Pribram, K. *Plans and the structure of behavior.* New York: Holt, Rinehart and Winston, 1960.

Newell, A., Shaw, J. C., & Simon, H. A. Elements of a theory of human problem solving. *Psychological Review,* 1958, 65, 151–166.

Thorndike, E. L. The law of effect. In *Selected writings from a connectionist's psychology.* New York: Appleton-Century-Crofts, 1949.

Wallach, M. A., & Kogan, N. A new look at the creativity-intelligence distinction. *Journal of Personality,* 1965, 33, 348–369.

•

Ornstein, R. Right and left thinking. *Psychology Today,* May 1973.

19. Hypnosis

Bailly, J. S. *et. al.* Secret report on mesmerism, or animal magnetism. In Shor, R. E., & Orne, M. T., *The nature of hypnosis: selected basic readings.* New York: Holt, Rinehart and Winston, 1965. Pp. 3–7.

Barber, T. X. *Hypnosis: a scientific approach.* New York: Van Nostrand Reinhold, 1969.

Braid, J. *Neurypnology: or the rationale of nervous sleep considered in relation to animal magnetism.* London: Churchill, 1843.

Hilgard, E. Hypnotic phenomena: The struggle for scientific acceptance. *American Scientist,* 1971, 59, 567–577.

Hilgard, E. *Hypnotic susceptibility.* New York: Harcourt, Brace & World, 1965.

Hilgard, J. R. *Personality and hypnosis: a study of imaginative involvement.* Chicago: University of Chicago Press, 1970.

James, W. *Principles of psychology.* New York: Dover, 1890. Pp. 593–616.

McGlashlin, T. H., Evans, F. J., & Orne, M. T. The nature of hypnotic analgesic and placebo response to experimental pain. *Psychosomatic Medicine,* 1969, 31, 227–246.

Mesmer, F. A. Animal magnetism. In Dennis, W. (Ed.), *Readings in the history of psychology.* New York: Appleton-Century-Crofts, 1948. Pp. 93–95.

Sarbin, T. R., & Lim, D. T. Some evidence in support of the role-taking hypothesis in hypnosis. *International Journal of Clinical Hypnosis,* 1963, 11, 98–103.

Weitzenhoffer, A. M., & Hilgard, E. R. *Stanford Susceptibility Scale Form A and B.* Palo Alto, Calif.: Consulting Psychologists Press, 1962.

Zimbardo, P. G., Rapaport, C., & Baron, J. Pain control by hypnotic induction of motivational states. In Zimbardo, P. (Ed.), *The cognitive control of motivation.* Glenview, Ill.: Scott-Foresman, 1969. Pp. 136–152.

•

Questioning hypnosis. *Time,* July 13, 1970.

20. Therapy for Individuals

Berzins, J. I., Ross, W. F., & Cohen, D. L. Relations of the A-B distinction and trust-distrust sets to addict patients' self-disclosures in brief interviews. *Journal of Consulting & Clinical Psychology,* 1970, 34, 289–296.

Betz, B. J., & Whitehorn, J. C. The relationship of the therapist to the outcome of therapy in schizophrenia. In Kline, N. S. (Ed.), *Psychiatric Research Reports* No. 5 Washington: American Psychiatric Association, 1956. Pp. 89–105.

Butler, J. M., & Haigh, C. V. Changes in the relation between self-concepts and ideal concepts consequent upon client-centered counseling. In Rogers, C. R., & Dymond, R. F. (Eds.), *Psychotherapy and personality change.* Chicago: University of Chicago Press, 1954. Pp. 55–75.

Carlson, P. M. An analysis of the motor, cognitive, and physiological components of psychotherapeutically induced changes in phobic behavior. Unpublished Doctoral Dissertation, University of Washington, 1969.

Cerletti, U. Electroshock Therapy. In Marti-Ibanex, F., Sackler, A., and Sackler, R. (Eds.), *The Great Physiodynamic Therapies in Psychiatry.* New York: Hoeber, 1956.

Eysenck, H. J. The effects of psychotherapy: an evaluation. *Journal of Consulting Psychology,* 1952, 16, 319–324.

Fiedler, F. E. A comparison of therapeutic relations in psychoanalysis, nondirective and Adlerian therapy. *Journal of Consulting Psychology,* 1950, 14, 436–445.

Frank, J. D. *Healing and Persuasion.* Baltimore: Johns Hopkins Press, 1961.

Freud, S. *Der Traumdeutung* (Interpretation of Dreams). (Translated by A. A. Brill.) New York: Macmillan, 1900.

Kirtner, W. L., & Cartwright, D. S. Success and failure in client-centered therapy as a function of client personality variables. *Journal of Consulting Psychology,* 1958, 22, 259–264.

Klerman, G., Davidson, E., & Kayce, M. Factors influencing the clinical responses of schizophrenic patients to phenothiazine drugs and to placebo. In Solomon, P., & Glueck, B. (Eds.), *Recent Research on Schizophrenia,* Washington, D.C.: American Psychiatric Association, 1964.

Paul, G. L. *Insight versus desensitization in psychotherapy.* Palo Alto, Calif.: Stanford University Press, 1966.

Raymond, M J. Case of fetishism treated by aversion therapy. *British Medical Journal,* 1956, 2, 854–857.

Rogers, C. R. *Client-Centered therapy.* Cambridge, Mass.: The Riverside Press, 1951.

Rogers, C. R. *Counseling and psychotherapy.* Boston: Houghton Mifflin, 1942.

Strupp, H. H., Fox, R. E., & Lessler, K. *Patients View Their Psychotherapy.* Baltimore: Johns Hopkins Press, 1969.

Wogan, M. Effect of therapist-patient personality variables on therapeutic outcome. *Journal of Consulting and Clinical Psychology,* 1970, 35, 356–361.

Wolpe, J. *The Practice of Behavior Therapy.* New York: Pergamon Press, 1966.

Wolpe, J. The systematic desensitization treatment of neuroses. *The Journal of Nervous and Mental Disease,* 1963, 132, 189–203.

•

Havemann, E. Alternatives to analysis. *Playboy,* November 1969.

21. Motivation

Atkinson, J. W., Heyns, R. W., & Veroff, J. The effect of experimental arousal of the affiliation motive on thematic apperception. *Journal of Abnormal and Social Psychology,* 1954, 49, 405–410.

Atkinson, J. W., & Litwin, G. H. Achievement motive and text anxiety conceived of as motive to approach success and motive to avoid failure. *Journal of Abnormal and Social Psychology,* 1960, 60, 52–63.

Birch, H. G. The role of motivational factors in insightful problem-solving. *Journal of Comparative Psychology,* 1945, 38, 295–317.

Caggiula, A., & Hoebel, B. "Copulation-reward site" in the posterior hypothalamus. *Science,* 1966, 153, 1284–1285.

Cannon, W. B. Hunger and thirst. In Murchison, C. (Ed.), *Handbook of general experimental psychology.* Worcester, Mass.: Clark Univ. Press, 1934. Pp. 247–263.

Chapman, D. W., & Volkmann, J. A social determinant of the level of aspiration. *Journal of Abnormal and Social Psychology,* 1939, 34, 225–238.

Crowne, D. P., & Marlowe, D. *The approval motive.* New York: Wiley, 1964.

Dember, W. N. Birth order and need affiliation. *Journal of Abnormal and Social Psychology,* 1964, 68, 555–557.

Goldman, R., Jaffa, M., & Schachter, S. Yom Kippur, Air France, dormitory food, and the eating behavior of obese and normal persons. *Journal of Personality and Social Psychology,* 1968, 10, 117–123.

Hebb, D. O. Drives and the CNS (Conceptual Nervous System). *Psychological Review,* 1955, 62, 243–254.

Hull, C. L. *Principles of behavior.* New York: Appleton-Century-Crofts, 1943.

Jordan, H. A., Zebley, S. P., & Stellar, E. A comparison of voluntary oral and intragastric food intake in man. Paper read at Eastern Psychological Association Annual Meeting, Boston, 1967.

Leckart, B. T., & Bennett, K. S. Reinforcement effects of food and stimulus novelty. *Psychological Record,* 1968, 18, 253–260.

Maslow, A. *Motivation and personality.* New York: Harper and Row, 1954.

McClelland, D. C. Need achievement and entrepreneurship: a longitudinal study. *Journal of Personality and Social Psychology,* 1965, 1, 389–392.

McClelland, D. C. *Assessing human motivation.* New York: General Learning Press, 1971.

McClelland, D. C., Atkinson, J. W., Clark, R. A., & Lowell, E. L. *The achievement motive.* New York: Appleton-Century-Crofts, 1953.

McGregor, D. *The human side of the enterprise.* New York: McGraw-Hill, 1960.

Mook, D. Oral and postingestional determinants of the intake of various solutions in rats with esophageal fistulas. *Journal of Comparative and Physiological Psychology,* 1963, 56, 645–659.

Moruzzi, G., & Magoun, H. W. Brain stem reticular formation and activation of the EEG. *Electroencephalography and Clinical Neurophysiology,* 1949, 1, 455–473.

Murray, H. A. *Explorations in personality.* New York: Oxford University Press, 1938.

Smock, C. D., & Holt, B. G. Children's reactions to novelty: an experimental study of "curiosity motivation." *Child Development,* 1962, 33, 631–642.

Stellar, E. Hunger in man: comparative and physiological studies. *American Psychologist,* 1967, 22, 105–117.

Veroff, J. Development and validation of a projective measure of power motivation. *Journal of Abnormal and Social Psychology,* 1957, 54, 1–8.

Veroff, J. An exploratory study of parental motives, parental attitudes and social behavior of children. Unpublished Doctoral Dissertation, University of Michigan, 1958.

Veroff, J., Atkinson, J. W., Feld, S., & Gurin, G. The use of thematic apperception to assess motivation in a nationwide interview study. *Psychological Monographs* No. 74, 1960, (Whole No. 499).

White, R. W. Motivation reconsidered: the concept of competence. *Psychological Review,* 1959, 66, 297–333.

•

Allport, G. *Personality, a psychological interpretation.* New York: Henry Holt and Co., 1937.

McConnell, J. V. *Understanding human behavior.* New York: Holt, Rinehart, & Winston, 1974.

Tolman, E. *Purposive behavior in animals.* New York: Appleton Century Croft, 1932.

22. Concept Learning

Bruner, J. S., Goodnow, J. J., & Austin, G. A. *A study of thinking.* New York: Wiley, 1956.

Gay, J., & Cole, M. *The new mathematics and an old culture.* New York: Holt, Rinehart and Winston, 1967.

Glick, J. Cognitive style among the Kpelle of Liberia. Paper presented at the American Educational Research Association convention, Chicago, February, 1968.

Hull, C. L. Quantitative aspects of the evolution of concepts. *Psychological Monographs,* 1920, 28, (Whole No. 123).

Kendler, H. H., & Kendler, T. S. Vertical and horizontal processes in problem solving. *Psychological Review,* 1962, 69, 1–16.

Levine, M. Hypothesis behavior by humans during discrimination learning. *Journal of Experimental Psychology,* 1966, 71, 331–338.

White, S. H. Evidence for a hierarchical arrangement of learning processes. In Lipsitt, L. P., & Spiker, C. C. (Eds.), *Advances in child development and behavior,* Vol. II. New York: Academic Press, 1956. Pp. 187–220.

White, S. H. Changes in learning processes in the late preschool years. Paper presented at the Early Learning symposium, American Educational Research Association Convention, Chicago, 1968.

Whorf, B. *Language, thought and reality.* New York: Wiley, 1956.

23. Perceiving

Bower, T. G. R. The object in the world of the infant. *Scientific American,* 1971, 225, 30–38.

Gibson, E. J., & Walk, R. D. The "visual cliff." *Scientific American,* 1960, 202, 64–71.

Gibson, J. J. *The senses considered as perceptual systems.* Boston: Houghton Mifflin, 1966.

Held, R., & Bauer, J. A. Visually guided reaching in infant monkeys after restricted rearing. *Science,* 1967, 155, 718–720.

Held, R., & Hein, A. Movement produced stimulation in the development of visually-guided behavior. *Journal of Comparative and Physiological Psychology,* 1968, 56, 872–876.

Ittelson, W. H. Size as a cue to distance: static location. *American Journal of Psychology,* 1951, 64, 54–67.

Kohler, I. The formation and transformatton of the perceptual world. Translated by H. Fiss. *Psychological Issues,* 1964, 3, 1–173.

Rock, I., & Victor, J. Vision and touch: an experimentally created conflict between the two senses. *Science,* 1964, 143, 594–596.

Segall, M. H., Campbell, D. T., & Herskovits, M. J. Cultural differences in the perception of geometric illusions. *Science,* 1963, 139, 769–771.

Stevens, S. S., & Newman, E. B. The localization of actual sources of sound. *American Journal of Psychology,* 1936, 48, 297–306.

Stratton, G. M. Vision without inversion of the retinal image. *Psychological Review,* 1897, 4, 341–360; 463–481.

Walk, R. D., & Gibson, E. J. A comparative and analytical study of visual depth perception. *Psychological Monographs,* 1961. 75, Whole No. 519.

Wallach, H. Brightness constancy and the nature of achromatic colors. *Journal of Experimental Psychology,* 1948, 38, 310–324.

Wertheimer, M. Experimental studies of apparent movement. *Zeitschrift fur Psychologie,* 1912, 61, 161–165.

Wertheimer, M. *Productive thinking.* New York: Harper, 1945.

Wertheimer, M. Psychomotor coordination of auditory and visual space at birth. *Science,* 1961, 34, 1692.

Boom times on the psychic frontier. *Time,* March 4, 1974.

Koestler, A. *The roots of coincidence.* New York: Vintage, 1973.

Lundin, R. *Personality: a behavioral analysis.* New York: Macmillan, 1969.

24. Paying Attention

Baker, R. W., & Madell, T. O. Susceptibility to distraction in academically underachieving and achieving male college students. *Journal of Consulting Psychology,* 1965, 29, 173–177.

Berlyne, D. E. *Conflict, arousal and curiosity.* New York: McGraw-Hill, 1960.

Byrne, D. The effect of a subliminal food stimulus on verbal responses. *Journal of Applied Psychology,* 1959, 43, 249.

Fantz, R. L. Pattern vision in newborn infants. *Science,* 1963, 140, 296–297.

Gelman, R. Conservation acquisition: a problem of learning to attend to relevant attributes. *Journal of Experimental Child Psychology,* 1969, 7, 167–187.

Hack, M. Signal detection in the rat. *Science,* 1963, 136, 758–759.

James, W. *Principles of psychology.* New York: Henry Holt & Co., 1890.

Luria, A. R. *The mentally retarded child.* Oxford: Pergamon Press, 1963.

Maccoby, E. E., & Conrad, K. W. Age trends in selective listening. *Journal of Experimental Child Psychology,* 1966, 3, 113–122.

Miller, G. A. *Psychology: the science of mental life.* New York: Harper & Row, 1962.

Murphy, G., & Kovach, J. K. *Historical introduction to modern psychology,* 3rd. edit., Harcourt Brace Jovanovich, 1972.

Siegel, A. W., & Stevenson, H. W. Incidental learning: a developmental study. *Child Development,* 1966, 37, 811–817.

Sokolov, E. N. Neuronal models and the orienting reflex. In Brazier, M. A. B. (Ed.), *The central nervous system and behavior* (3rd Conference). Madison, Wisc.: Madison Printing Co., 1960. Pp. 187–276.

Weizmann, F., Cohen, L. B., & Pratt, R. J. Novelty, familiarity, and the development of infant attention. *Developmental Psychology,* 1971, 4, 149–154.

Drug use in America: problem in perspective. Second Report of the National Commission on Marijuana and Drug Abuse. Washington, D.C.: U.S. Government Printing Office, 1973.

25. Memory

Bousfield, W. A. The occurrence of clustering in the recall of randomly arranged associates. *Journal of General Psychology,* 1953, 49, 229–240.

Bower, G. H. Organizational factors in memory. *Journal of Cognitive Psychology,* 1970, 1, 18–46.

Brown, R. W., & McNeill, D. The "tip-of-the-tongue" phenomenon. *Journal of Verbal Learning and Verbal Behavior,* 1966, 5, 325–337.

Cieutat, V. J., Stockwell, F. E., & Noble, C. E. The interaction of ability and amount of practice with stimulus and response meaningfulness (m, m) in paired-associate learning. *Journal of Experimental Psychology,* 1958, 56, 193–202.

Ebbinghaus, H. *Uber das Gedachtnis* (Concerning Memory). Liepzig: Duncker, 1885; New York: Teachers College, 1913.

Fechner, G. T. *Elemente der Psychophysik.* Leipzig: Breitkopf and Hartel, 1860.

Haber, R. N., & Standing, L. G. Direct estimates of the apparent duration of a flash. *Canadian Journal of Psychology,* 1970, 24, 216–229.

Hovland, C. I. Experimental studies in rote learning theory. III. Distribution of practice with varying speeds of syllable presentation. *Journal of Experimental Psychology,* 1938, 23, 172–190.

Jenkins, J. G., & Dallenbach, K. M. Oblivescence during sleep and waking. *American Journal of Psychology,* 1924, 35, 605–612.

Landauer, T. K., & Freedman, J. L. Information retrieval from long-term memory: category size and recognition time. *Journal of Verbal Learning & Verbal Behavior,* 1968, 7, 291–295.

Luh, C. W. The conditions of retention. *Psychological Monographs,* 1922, 31, No. 142.

Luria, A. R. *The mind of a mnemonist.* New York: Basic Books, 1968.

Lyon, D. O. The relation of length of material to time taken for learning and the optimum distribution of time. Part II. *Journal of Educational Psychology,* 1914, 5, 85–91.

McCartney, P. *The Beatles' illustrated lyrics.* New York: Delacorte Press, 1969, P. 13.

Miller, G. A., & Selfridge, J. A. Verbal context and the recall of meaningful material. *American Journal of Psychology,* 1956, 63, 176–185.

Murdock, B. B., Jr. The retention of individual items. *Journal of Experimental Psychology,* 1961, 62, 618–625.

Noble, C. E. An analysis of meaning. *Psychological Review,* 1952, 59, 421–430.

Paivio, A., Smythe, P. C., & Yuille, J. C. Imagery versus meaningfulness of nouns in paired associate learning. *Canadian Journal of Psychology,* 1968, 22, 427–441.

Paivio, A., Yuille, J. C., & Madigan, S. A. Concreteness, imagery, and meaningfulness values for 925 nouns. *Journal of Experimental Psychology,* 1968, 76, Monograph Supplement No. 1, Pt. 2, 1–25.

Penfield, W. *The excitable cortex in conscious man.* Springfield, Ill.: Charles C Thomas, 1958.

Penfield, W. The interpretive cortex. *Science,* 1959, 129, 1719–1725.

Peterson, L. E., & Peterson, M. J. Short-term retention of individual verbal items. *Journal of Experimental Psychology,* 1959, 58, 193–198.

Schachtel, E. G. On memory and childhood amnesia. In Mullahy, F. (Ed.), *A study of interpersonal relations.* New York: Grove Press, 1949. Pp. 3–49.

Standing, L., Conezio, J., & Haber, R. N. Perception and memory for pictures: single-trial learning of 2500 stimuli. *Psychonomic Science,* 1970, 19, 73–74.

Steinbeck, J. *Cannery row.* New York: Viking Press, 1945.

Wallace, W. H., Turner, S. H., & Perkins, C. C. *Preliminary studies of human information storage.* Signal Corps Project No. 132C, Institute for Cooperative Research, University of Pennsylvania, Dec., 1957.

Zeller, A. F. An experimental analogue of repression. II. The effect of individual failure and success on memory measured by relearning. *Journal of Experimental Psychology,* 1950, 40, 411–422.

●

Osgood, C. & Snider, J. (Eds.) *Semantic differential technique: a sourcebook.* Chicago: Aldine-Atherton, 1969.

Ruch, F., & Zimbardo, P. *Psychology and life.* 8th edition. Glenview, Illinois: Scott, Foresman & Co., 1971.

Zippel, H. P. (Ed.) *Memory and transfer of information.* New York: Plenum, 1973.

26. Pavlovian Conditioning

Brogden, W. J. Sensory preconditioning. *Journal of Experimental Psychology,* 1939, 25, 323–332.

Brogden, W. J., & Culler, E. Experimental extinction of higher-order responses. *American Journal of Psychology,* 1935, 47, 663–669.

Gynther, M. D. Differential eyelid conditioning as a function of stimulus similarity and strength of response to the CS. *Journal of Experimental Psychology,* 1957, 53, 408–416.

Pavlov, I. P. Conditional reflexes: an investigation of the physiological activity of the cerebral cortex. (Translated and edited by G. V. Anrep.) London: Oxford University Press, 1927.

Smith, M. C., Coleman, S. R., & Gormezano, I. Classical conditioning of the rabbit's nictitating membrane response at backward, simultaneous, and forward CS-US intervals. *Journal of Comparative & Physiological Psychology*, 1969, 69, 226–231.

Spence, K. W., Homzie, M. J., & Rutledge, E. F. Extinction of the human eyelid CR as a function of the discriminability of the change from acquisition to extinction. *Journal of Experimental Psychology*, 1964, 67, 545–552.

Watson, J. B., & Rayner, R. Conditioned emotional reactions. *Journal of Experimental Psychology*, 1920, 3, 1–14.

•

Seligman, M. E. P. For helplessness: can we immunize the weak? *Readings in Psychology Today.* Del Mar, California: CRM Books, 1974, 126–128.

Seligman, M. E. P. & Hager, J. L. Biological boundaries of learning: the sauce-bearnaise syndrome. *Readings in Psychology Today.* Del Mar, California: CRM Books, 1974, 122–126.

27. Operant Conditioning

Ayllon, T., & Haughton, E. Modification of symptomatic verbal behavior of mental patients. *Behavior Research and Therapy*, 1964, 2, 87–97.

Baker, J. G., Stanish, B., & Fraser, B. Comparative effects of a token economy in nursery school. *Mental Retardation*, 1972, 10, 16–19.

Bandura, A., & Walters, R. H. *Adolescent aggression.* New York: Ronald Press, 1959.

Breland, K., & Breland, H. A field of applied animal psychology. *American Psychologist*, 1951, 6, 202–204.

Bryan, W. L., & Harter, N. Studies in the physiology and psychology of the telegraphic language. *Psychological Review*, 1897, 4, 27–53.

Feldman, M. P., & MacCulloch, M. B. A systematic approach to the treatment of homosexuality by conditioned aversion: preliminary report. *American Journal of Psychiatry*, 1964, 121, 167–171.

Lovaas, O. I., Schaeffer, B., & Simmons, J. Q. Building social behavior in autistic children by use of electric shock. *Journal of Experimental Research in Personality*, 1965, 1, 99–109.

Martin, G. L., Kehoe, B., Bird, E., Jensen, V., & Darbyshire, M. Operant conditioning in dressing behavior of severely retarded girls. *Mental Retardation*, 1971, 9, 27–31.

Salzinger, K., Feldman, R. S., Cowan, J. E., & Salzinger, S. Operant conditioning of verbal behavior of two young speech-deficient boys. In Krasner, L., & Ullman, L. P. (Eds.), *Research in behavior modification.* New York: Holt, Rinehart & Winston, 1965. Pp. 82–105.

Skinner, B. F. *The behavior of organisms.* New York: Appleton-Century-Crofts, 1938.

Skinner, B. F. *Beyond freedom and dignity.* New York: Alfred A. Knopf, 1971.

Skinner, B. F. *Walden II.* New York: Macmillan, 1948.

Smolev, S. R. Use of operant techniques for the modification of self-injurious behavior. *American Journal of Mental Deficiency*, 1971, 76, 295–305.

Staats, A. W., & Butterfield, W. H. Treatment of nonreading in a culturally deprived juvenile delinquent: an application of reinforcement schedules. *Child Development*, 1965, 36, 925–942.

Thorndike, E. L. Animal Intelligence. *Psychological Review Monograph Supplements*, 1898, 2, (Whole No. 8).

Williams, C. D. Case report: the elimination of tantrum behavior by extinction procedures. *Journal of Abnormal and Social Psychology*, 1959, 59, 269.

•

Baer, D. M. Let's take another look at punishment. *Psychology Today*, October 1971.

Normile, R. H. *The behavior management system.* Binghamton, N.Y.: privately published by author, 1971.

Skinner's utopia: panacea, or path to hell? *Time*, September 20, 1970.

28. Stress and Anxiety

Bankart, C. P. Heart rate and skin conductance in anticipation of painful electric shock. Unpublished Doctoral Dissertation, Dartmouth College, 1971.

Basedow, H. R. *The Australian aboriginal.* Adelaide, Australia: 1925.

Cannon, W. B. *Bodily changes in pain, hunger, fear and rage.* New York: Appleton-Century-Crofts, 1929.

Cannon, W. B. "Voodoo" death. *American Anthropologist*, 1942, 44, 169.

Hess, J. L., Denenberg, V. H., Zarrow, M. X., & Pfeifer, W. D. Modification of the plasma corticosterone response curve as a function of stimulation in infancy. *Physiology and Behavior*, 1969, 4, 109–111.

Hinckle, L. E., & Wolff, H. G. *A. M. A. Archives of International Medicine*, 1957, 99, 442.

Levine, S., & Treiman, D. M. Differential plasma corticosterone response to stress in four inbred strains of mice. *Endocrinology*, 1964, 75, 642–644.

Masuda, M., & Holmes, T. H. Magnitude estimations of social readjustments. *Journal of Psychosomatic Research*, 1967, 11, 219–225.

Overmeier, J. B., & Seligman, M. E. P. Effects of inescapable shock upon subsequent escape and avoidance responding. *Journal of Comparative and Physiological Psychology,* 1967, 63, 28–33.

Ruff, G. E., & Korchin, S. J. Adaptive distress behavior. In Applye, M. H., & Trumbull, R. (Eds.), *Psychological Stress.* New York: Appleton-Century-Crofts, 1962. Pp. 205–221.

Selye, H. *The stress of life.* New York: McGraw-Hill, 1956.

Weiss, J. M. Psychological factors in stress and disease. *Scientific American,* 1972, 226, 104–113.

•

McQuade, W. What stress can do to you. *Fortune,* January 1972.

Work in America: report of a special task force to the Secretary of Health, Education, and Welfare. Cambridge, Mass.: MIT Press, 1973.

29. Genes and Their Nurture

Denenberg, V. H., Hudgens, G. A., and Zarrow, M. X. Mice reared with rats: effects of mother on adult behavior patterns. *Psychological Reports,* 1966, 18, 451–456.

Dobzhansky, T. Genetics and the diversity of behavior. *American Psychologist,* 1972, 27, 523–530.

Ginsburg, B. E. Intra-uterine effects on behavioral capacities in mice. Paper presented at the Symposium on the Effects of Intra-Uterine Experience, 14th International Congress of Psychology, July 28, 1969; London, England.

Ginsburg, B. E., & Hovda, R. B. On the physiology of gene controlled audiogenic seizures in mice. *Anatomical Record,* 1947, 99, 621.

Hebb, D. O. *A textbook of psychology.* Philadelphia: W. B. Saunders Co., 1966.

Levine, S., Chevalier, J. A., & Korchin, S. J. The effects of shock and handling in infancy on later avoidance learning. *Journal of Personality,* 1956, 25, 475–493.

Manosevitz, M. Hoarding—an exercise in behavioral genetics. *Psychology Today,* August, 1970.

Ottinger, D. R., & Simmons, J. E. Behavior of human neonates and prenatal maternal anxiety. *Psychological Reports,* 1964, 14, 391–394.

Rosenzweig, M. R., Bennet, E. L., & Diamond, M. C. Brain changes in response to experience. *Scientific American,* February, 1972.

Thompson, W. R. Influence of prenatal maternal anxiety on emotionality in young rats. *Science,* 1965, 150, 1844–1845.

Tryon, R. C. Genetic differences in maze learning in rats. *39th Yearbook of the National Society for the Study of Education,* 1940. Bloomington, Ill.: Public School Publishing Co., 1940. Pp. 111–119.

•

Gaylin, W. We have the awful knowledge to make exact copies of human beings. *The New York Times Magazine,* March 5, 1972.

30. Built-in Behavior

Carmichael, L. A further study of the development of behavior in vertebrates experimentally removed from the influence of external stimulation. *Psychological Review,* 1927, 34, 34–47.

Cruze, W. W. Maturation and learning in chicks. *Comparative Psychology,* 1935, 19, 371–409.

Dilger, W. C. The behavior of lovebirds. *Scientific American,* 1962, 206, 88–98.

Eibl-Eibesfeldt, I. *Ethology, the biology of behavior.* New York: Holt, Rinehart, & Winston, 1970.

Hess, E. H. Imprinting. *Science,* 1959, 130, 133–141.

Lott, D., Scholz, S. D., & Lehrman, D. S. Environmental stimulation of the reproductive system of the female ring dove. In Kagan, J., Haith, M. M., & Caldwell, C. (Eds.), *Psychology: adapted readings.* New York: Harcourt Brace Jovanovich, 1971. Pp. 191–193.

Marler, P., & Tamura, M. Culturally transmitted patterns of vocal behavior in sparrows. *Science,* 1964, 146, 1483–1486.

Melvin, K. B., Cloar, F. T., & Messengill, L. S. Imprinting of bobwhite quail to a hawk. *Psychological Record,* 1967, 17, 235–238.

Riess, B. F. The effect of altered environment and of age on the mother-young relationships among animals. *Annals of the New York Academy of Science,* 1954, 57, 606–610.

Spalding, D. A. Instinct, with original observations on young animals. *Macmillan's Magazine,* 1873, 27, 282–293.

•

Hess, E. H. "Imprinting" in a natural laboratory. *Scientific American,* 1972, 227, 2.

Lorenz, K. *On aggression.* New York: Harcourt, Brace, Jovanovich, 1966.

Montagu, A. (Ed.) *Man and aggression.* New York: Oxford University Press, 1973.

Newman, O. A theory of defensible space. *Intellectual Digest,* March 1973.

31. The Senses

Alpern, M., Lawrence, M., & Wolsk, D. *Sensory processes.* Belmont, Calif.: Brooks/Cole, 1967.

Amoore, J. Current status of the steric theory of odor. *Annals of the New York Academy of Science,* 1964, 116, 457–476.

Békésy, G. von. Zur Theorie des Hörens. Die Schwingungsform der Basilarmembran. *Physikalische Zeitschrift,* 1928, 29, 739–810.

Békésy, G. von. *Experiments in hearing.* New York: McGraw-Hill, 1960.

Boring, E. G. *Sensation and perception in the history of experimental psychology.* New York: Appleton-Century-Crofts, 1942.

DeValois, R. L. Analysis and coding of color vision in the primate visual system. *Cold Harbor Spring Symposia,* 1965, 30, 567–579.

Hering, E. *Outlines of a theory of the light sense.* Cambridge: Harvard University Press, 1964.

Hubel, D. H., & Wiesel, T. N. Receptive fields, binocular interaction and functional architecture in the cat's visual cortex. *Journal of Physiology,* 1962, 160, 106–154.

Hubel, D. H., & Wiesel, T. N. Shape and arrangement of columns in cat's striate cortex. *Journal of Physiology,* 1963, 165, 559–568.

Lettvin, J. W., Maturana, H. R., McCulloch, W. S., & Pitts, W. H. What the frog's eye tells the frog's brain. *Proceedings of the Institute of Radio Engineers,* 1959, 47, 1940–1951.

Pfaffmann, C. The afferent code for sensory quality. *American Psychologist,* 1959, 14, 226–232.

Pritchard, R. M., Heron, W., & Hebb, D. O. Visual perception approached by the method of stabilized images. *Canadian Journal of Psychology,* 1960, 4, 67–77.

Watson, R. I. *The great psychologists from Aristotle to Freud.* Philadelphia: Lippincott, 1936.

●

Acupuncture: myth or miracle? *Newsweek,* August 14, 1972.

Intellectual Digest. The theory of acupuncture: an interview with J. Robert Moskin. September 1973.

Melzack, R. Shutting the gate on pain. *Science Year, 1975.* Chicago: Field Enterprises Educational Corporation, 1974, pp. 65–67.

32. Sleep and Dreams

Aserinsky, E., & Kleitman, N. Regularly occurring periods of eye mobility and concomitant phenomena during sleep. *Science,* 1953, 118, 273–274.

Dement, W. C., & Kleitman, N. The relation of eye movements during sleep to dream activity: an objective method for the study of dreaming. *Journal of Experimental Psychology,* 1957, 53, 339–346.

Evans, F. J., Gustafson, L. A., O'Connell, D. N., Orne, M. T., & Shor, R. E. Verbally induced behavioral responses during sleep. *Journal of Nervous & Mental Disease,* 1970, 150, 171–187.

Fisher, C., Byrne, J. V., Edwards, A., & Kahn, E. REM and NREM nightmares. In Hartman, E. (Ed.), *Sleep and dreaming.* New York: International Psychiatry Clinics, Vol. 7, No. 2, 1970.

Fisher, C. & Dement, W. C. Studies on the psychopathology of sleep and dreams. *American Journal of Psychiatry,* 1963, 119, 1160–1168.

Hall, C. S. What people dream about. *Scientific American,* 1951, 184, 60–63.

Gulevich, G., Dement, W., & Johnson, L. Psychiatric and EEG observations on a case of prolonged (264 hours) wakefulness. *Archives of General Psychiatry,* 1966, 15, 29–35.

Johnson, L. C., Slye, E. E., & Dement, W. Electroencephalographic and autonomic activity during and after prolonged sleep deprivation. *Psychosomatic Medicine,* 1965, 27, 415–423.

Kleitman, N. Patterns of dreaming. *Scientific American,* 1960, 203, 81–88.

Vogel, G. W., & Traub, A. C. REM deprivation: I. The effect on schizophrenic patients; II. The effects on depressed patients. *Archives of General Psychiatry,* 1968, 18, 287–311.

●

Allison, T., & Van Twyver, H. The evolution of sleep. *Natural History,* February 1970.

Diamond, E. The most terrifying psychic experience known to man. *The New York Times Magazine,* December 7, 1969.

Emmons, W. & Simon, C. The non-recall of material presented during sleep. *American Journal of Psychology,* 1957, 69, 76–81.

Johnson, L. G. Are the stages of sleep related to waking behavior? *American Scientist,* 61, 326–338.

33. Brain Storage

Duncan, C. P. Habit reversal induced by electroshock in the rat. *Journal of Comparative and Physiological Psychology,* 1948, 41, 11–16.

Gazzaniga, M. S. *The bisected brain.* New York: Appleton-Century-Crofts, 1970.

Hebb, D. O. *The organization of behavior.* New York: Wiley, 1949.

Hydén, H. The question of a molecular basis for the memory trace. In Pribram, K. H., & Broadbent, D. E. (Eds.), *Biology of memory.* New York: Academic Press, 1970. Pp. 101–119.

Katz, J. J., & Halstead, W. C. Protein organization and mental function. Comparative Psychology Monographs, 1950, 20, 1–38.

Kopp, R., Bohdanecky, Z., & Jarvik, M. E. Long temporal gradient of retrograde amnesia for a well-discriminated stimulus. *Science,* 1966, 153, 1547–1549.

Lashley, K. S. *Brain mechanisms and intelligence.* Chicago: University of Chicago Press, 1929. Reprinted by Dover Press, 1963.

Lashley, K. S. In search of the engram. *Symposium of the Society of Experimental Biology,* 1950, 4, 454–482.

Penfield, W. *The excitable cortex in conscious man.* Springfield, Ill.: Charles C Thomas, 1958.

Pribram, K. H. A further experimental analysis of the behavioral deficit that follows injury to the primate frontal cortex. *Experimental Neurology,* 1961, 3, 432–466.

Pribram, K. H., & Tubbs, W. E. Short-term memory, parsing, and the primate frontal cortex. *Science,* 1967, 156, 1765–1767.

Scoville, W. B., & Milner, B. Loss of recent memory after bilateral hippocampal lesions. *Journal of Neurology, Neurosurgery, and Psychiatry,* 1957, 20, 11–21.

Sperry, R. W. Hemisphere deconnection and unity in conscious awareness. *American Psychologist,* 1968, 23, 723–733.

•

McConnell, J. V. *Understanding human behavior.* New York: Holt, Rinehart, & Winston, 1974.

Hoebel, B. G., & Teitelbaum, P. Hypothalamic control of feedings and self-stimulation. *Science,* 1962, 135, 375–377.

Hunsperger, R. W., & Bucher, V. M. Affective behavior produced by electrical stimulation in the forebrain and brainstem of the cat. In Adey, W. R., & Tokizane, T. (Eds.), *Structure and function of the limbic system.* New York: Elsevier, 1967.

Olds, J., & Milner, P. Positive reinforcement produced by electrical stimulation of septal area and other regions of rat brain. *Journal of Comparative and Physiological Psychology,* 1954, 47, 419–427.

Penfield, W. *The excitable cortex in conscious man.* Springfield, Ill.: Charles C Thomas, 1958.

Robinson, B. W., Alexander, M., & Bowne, G. Dominance reversal resulting from aggressive responses evoked by brain telestimulation. *Physiology and Behavior,* 1969, 4, 749–752.

•

Blakeslee, S. "Artificial brain" lets paralyzed monkeys move. *The New York Times,* February 10, 1972.

The electric brain. *Newsweek,* February 21, 1972.

Hess, W. R. *The method of localized stimulation and the elimination of sub-cortical extirpation.* Leipzig: Thieme, 1932.

Miller, N. E., & DiCara, L. Instrumental learning of heart rate changes in curarized rats: shaping and specificity to discriminative stimulus. *Journal of Comparative and Physiological Psychology,* 1967, 33 (1), 12–19.

Probing the brain. *Newsweek,* June 21, 1971.

Waggoner, K. Psychocivilization or electroligarchy: Dr. Delgado's amazing world of ESB. *Yale Alumni Magazine,* January 1970.

34. Brain Stimulation

Delgado, J. M. R. Sequential behavior induced repeatedly by stimulation of the red nucleus in free monkeys. *Science,* 1965, 148, 1361–1363.

Delgado, J. M. R. Social rank and radio-stimulated aggressiveness in monkeys. *Journal of Nervous and Mental Disease,* 1967, 144, 383–390.

Delgado, J. M. R., Rivera, M. L., & Mir, D. Repeated stimulation of amygdala in awake monkeys. *Brain Research,* 1971, 27, 111–131.

Fisher, A. E. Chemical stimulation of the brain. *Scientific American,* 1964.

Heath, R. G. Electrical self-stimulation of the brain in man. *The American Journal of Psychiatry,* 1963, 120, 571–577.

Hess, W. R. *The Diencephalon.* New York: Grune and Stratton, 1954.

35. Biofeedback

Anand, B. K., China, G. S., & Singh, B. Some aspects of electroencephalographic studies in yogis. *Electroencephalography and Clinical Neurophysiology,* 1961, 13, 452–456.

Basmajian, J. V. Control and training of individual motor units. *Science,* 1963, 141, 440–441.

Brener, J., & Kleinman, R. A. Learned control of decreases in systolic blood pressure. *Journal of Comparative and Physiological Psychology,* 1968, 65, 812.

Brown, B. B. Recognition of aspects of consciousness through association with EEG alpha activity represented by a light signal. *Psychophysiology,* 1970, 6, 442–452.

Budzynski, T. Some applications of biofeedback-produced twilight states. Paper presented at the American Psychological Association Convention, Washington, D.C., 1971.

Budzynski, T., Stoyva, J., & Adler, C. Feedback-induced muscle relaxation: application to tension headache. *Journal of Behavioural, Therapeutic, and Experimental Psychiatry,* 1970, 1, 205–211.

Green, E. E., Green, A. M., & Walters, E. D. Voluntary control of internal states: psychological and physiological. *Journal of Transpersonal Psychology,* 1970, 2, 1–26.

Green, E. E., Walters, E. D., Green, A. M., & Murphy, G. Feedback technique for deep relaxation. *Psychophysiology,* 1969, 6, 371–377.

Harrison, V. F., & Mortensen, O. A. Identification and voluntary control of single motor unit activity in the tibialis anterior muscle. *Anatomical Record,* 1962, 144, 109–116.

Holt, R. R. Imagery: the return of the ostracized. *American Psychologist,* 1964, 19, 254–264.

Jacobson, E. *Progressive relaxation.* Chicago: University of Chicago Press, 1938.

Johnson, H., & Garton, W. H. A practical method of neuromuscular rehabilitation in hemiplegics using EMG. Presented at the American Congress of Rehabilitated Medicine, 1971.

Kamiya, J. Conditioned discrimination of the EEG alpha rhythm in humans. Paper presented at the Western Psychological Association Meeting, San Francisco, 1962.

Kamiya, J. Operant control of the EEG alpha rhythm and some of its reported effects on consciousness. In Charles T. Tart (Ed.), *Altered states of consciousness.* New York: Wiley, 1969.

Marinacci, A. A., & Horande, M.: Electromyogram in neuromuscular reeducation. *Bulletin Los Angeles Neurological Society,* 1960, 25, 57–71.

Miller, N. E., & DiCara, L. V. Instrumental learning of heart rate changes in curarized rats: shaping, and specificity to discriminative stimulus. *Journal of Comparative and Physiological Psychology,* 1967, 63, 12–19.

Mulholland, T., & Runnals, S. The effect of voluntarily directed attention on successive cortical activation responses. *Journal of Psychology,* 1963, 55, 427–436.

Sargent, J. D., Green, E., & Walters, E. D. Preliminary report on the use of autogenic feedback techniques in the treatment of migraine and tension headaches. Menninger Foundation, 1971. Unpublished paper.

Schultz, J. H., & Luthe, W. *Autogenic training: a physiologic approach in psychotherapy.* New York: Grune and Stratton, 1959.

Wyrwicka, W., & Sterman, M. B. Instrumental conditioning of sensorimotor cortex EEG spindles in the waking cat. *Physiology and Behavior,* Vol. III. Elmsford, N. Y.: Pergamon Press, 1968.

•

Karlins, M., & Andrews, L. M. *Psychology: what's in it for us?* New York: Random House, 1973.

Luce, G., & Peper, E. Mind over body, mind over mind. *The New York Times Magazine,* September 12, 1971.

Weiss, T., & Engle, B. Operant conditioning of heart rate in patients with premature ventricular contractions. *Psychosomatic Medicine,* 1971, 33, 301–321.

36. Psychoactive Drugs

Brown, D. *Manchild in the promised land.* New York: Macmillan, 1965. Pp. 263–264.

Caldwell, A. E. Origins of Psychopharmacology: from CPZ to LSD. Springfield, Ill.: Charles C Thomas, 1970.

Connors, C. K., & Eisenberg, L. The effects of methylphenidate on symptomatology and learning in disturbed children. *American Journal of Psychiatry,* 1963, 120, 458–465.

Eidelberg, E., & Barstow, C. A. Morphine tolerance and dependence induced by intraventricular injection. *Science,* 1971, 174, 74–76.

Feldman, H. W. Ideological supports to becoming and remaining a heroin addict. *Journal of Health and Social Behavior,* 1968, 9, 131–139.

Freedman, L. Z. "Truth" drugs. *Scientific American,* 1960, 202, 145–154.

Frosch, W. A., Robbins, E. S., & Stern, M. Untoward reactions to lysergic acid diethylamide (LSD) resulting in hospitalization. *The New England Journal of Medicine,* 1965, 273, 1236.

Goodman, L., & Gilman, A. (Eds.). *The pharmacological basis of therapeutics.* 2nd Edition. New York: Macmillan, 1960.

Huxley, A. *The doors of perception.* Baltimore: Penguin, 1954.

McNair, D. M., Kahn, J., Droppleman, L. F., & Fisher, S. Patient acquiescence and drug effects. In Rickels, K. (Ed.), *Non-specific factors in drug therapy.* Springfield, Ill.: Charles C Thomas, 1968.

Nichols, J. R. How opiates change behavior. *Scientific American,* 1965, 212, 80–88.

Rappaport, M., Silverman, J., Hopkins, H. K., & Hall, K. Phenothiazine effects on auditory signal detection in paranoid and nonparanoid schizophrenics. *Science,* 1971, 174, 723–725.

Ray, O. S. *Drugs, society and human behavior.* St. Louis: C. V. Mosby, 1972.

Tart, C. T. Marijuana intoxication: common experiences. *Nature,* 1970, 226, 701–704.

•

Weil, A. Man's innate need: getting high. *Intellectual Digest,* August 1972.

glossary

A

abnormal: irregular, deviating from the norm or average. Abnormal implies the presence of a mental disorder that leads to behavior that society labels as deviant. There is a continuum between normal (see) and abnormal. These are relative terms in that they imply a social judgment.

achievement drive: the need to attain self-esteem, success, or status. Society's expectations strongly influence the achievement motive.

ACTH (adrenocorticotropic hormone): The part of the brain called the hypothalamus activates the release of the hormone ACTH from the pituitary gland when a stressful condition exists. ACTH in turn activates the release of adrenal corticoids from the cortex of the adrenal gland.

action therapy: a general classification of therapy (as opposed to insight therapy, see) in which the therapist focuses on symptoms rather than on underlying emotional states. Treatment aims at teaching new behavioral patterns rather than at self-understanding.

acupuncture: the technique for curing certain diseases and anesthetizing by inserting needles at certain points of the body, developed in China and now being studied and applied in the West.

adaptation: the process of responding to changes in the environment by altering one's responses to keep one's behavior appropriate to environmental demands.

adaptation, sensory: the reduction in sensitivity as stimulation persists, usually because of a decreased output of sensory receptors.

addiction: physical dependence on a drug. When a drug causes biochemical changes that are uncomfortable when the drug is discontinued, when one must take ever larger doses to maintain the intensity of the drug's effects, and when desire to continue the drug is strong, one is said to be addicted.

affective defense reaction: a sequence of behavior including lowering the head, growling, hissing, etc. that electronic brain stimulation (see) produces in cats.

affective disorder: Affect means feeling or emotion. An affective disorder is mental illness marked by a disturbance of mood (e.g. manic depression.)

afterimage: a visual impression that lasts longer than the stimulation that produced it.

aggression: any act that causes pain or suffering to another. Some psychologists believe that aggressive behavior is instinctual to all species, including man, while others believe that it is learned through the processes of observation and imitation.

alienation: indifference to or loss of personal relationships. An individual may feel estranged from family members or, on a broader scale, from society.

altruism: behavior motivated by a desire to benefit another person. Altruistic behavior is aided by empathy (see) and is usually motivated internally, not by observable threats or rewards.

Ames room: a room designed by Adelbert Ames that produces a particular optical illusion. For example, a person walking from left to right seems to grow larger. These rooms have been used in many studies of perception (see.)

amphetamine: a psychoactive drug (see) that is a stimulant. Although used in treating mild depressions or, in children, hyperactivity, its medical uses are doubtful, and amphetamines are often abused.

animism: the quality of believing life exists in inanimate objects. According to Piaget, animism is characteristic of children's thinking until about age two.

anonymity: refers to the conditions that occur when people cannot be recognized individually.

anxiety: an important term that has different meanings for different theories (psychoanalysis, behavior theory); a feeling state of apprehension, dread, or uneasiness. The state may be aroused by an objectively dangerous situation or by a situation that is not objectively dangerous. It may be mild or severe.

arousal: a measure of responsiveness or activity; a state of excitement or wakefulness ranging from deepest coma to intense excitement. Arousal can be measured physiologically or assessed behaviorally and may be produced by emotional, intellectual, or physical stimuli.

aspiration level: the level of achievement a person strives for. Studies suggest that people can use internal or external standards of performance.

assimilation: See equilibration.

association: has separate meanings for different branches of psychology. Theory in cognitive psychology (see) suggests that we organize information so that we can find our memories systematically, that one idea will bring another to mind. In psychoanalysis (see), the patient is asked to free associate (speak aloud all consecutive thoughts until random associations tend of themselves to form a meaningful whole).

associationism: a theory of learning suggesting that once two stimuli are presented together, one of them will remind a person of the other. Ideas are learned by association with sensory experiences and are not innate. Among the principles of associationism are contiguity (stimuli that occur close together are more likely to be associated than stimuli far apart), and repetition (the more frequently stimuli occur together, the more strongly they become associated.)

attention: the tendency to focus activity in a particular direction and to select certain stimuli for further analysis while ignoring or possibly storing for further analysis all other inputs. Not all stimuli are processed (selectivity), and factors such as the complexity and novelty of a stimulus will affect the amount of attention it will receive.

attitude: an overall tendency to respond positively or negatively to particular people or objects in a way that is learned through experience and that is made up of feelings (affects,) thoughts (evaluations,) and actions (conation.) Attitudes are dynamic rather than unchanging.

authoritarian leader: a type of group leader who is dictatorial and aloof and does not participate in group projects.

authoritarian personality: a personality pattern marked by a desire for obedience from anyone considered lower in power or influence.

autokinetic effect: When a dot of light is projected in a totally dark room, it seems to move by itself.

autonomic nervous system: the part of the nervous system (The other part is the central nervous system.) that is for emergency functions and release of large amounts of energy (sympathetic division) and regulating functions such as digestion and sleep (parasympathetic division.) Biofeedback (see) can lead to voluntary control of autonomic processes.

B

barbiturates: sedative-hypnotic, psychoactive drugs *(see)* widely used to induce sleep and to reduce tension. Overuse can lead to addiction *(see.)*

behavior: any observable activity of an organism, including mental processes.

behaviorism: a school of psychology stressing an objective approach to psychological questions, proposing that psychology be limited to observable behavior and that the subjectiveness of consciousness places it beyond the limits of scientific psychology.

behavior therapy: the use of conditioning processes to treat mental disorders. Various techniques may be used, including positive reinforcement in which rewards (verbal or tangible) are given to the patient for appropriate behavior, modeling in which patients unlearn fears by watching models exhibit fearlessness, and systematic desensitization *(see)* in which the patient is taught to relax and visualize anxiety-producing items at the same time. *See* insight therapy.

biofeedback: the voluntary control of physiological processes by receiving information about those processes as they occur, through instruments that pick up these changes and display them to the subject in the form of a signal. Blood pressure, skin temperature, etc. can be controlled.

brain stimulation: the introduction of chemical or electrical stimuli directly into the brain by which brain activity, and thus behavior, is altered. The brain is stimulated through either chemical (CSB) or electrical (ESB) means. Stimulation of different parts of the brain produces different behaviors, emotional and motivated as well as motor.

brain waves: electrical responses produced by brain activity that can be recorded directly from any portion of the brain or from the scalp with special electrodes. Brain waves are measured by an electroencephalograph (EEG.) Alpha waves occur during relaxed wakefulness and beta waves during active behavior. Theta waves are associated with drowsiness and vivid visual imagery, delta waves with deep sleep.

C

cautious shift: Research suggests that the decisions of a group will be more conservative than that of the average individual member when dealing with areas for which there are widely held values favoring caution (e.g. physical danger or family responsibility.) *See* risky shift.

cerebellum: the part of the brain responsible for muscle and movement control and coordination of eye-body movement.

cerebral cortex: the part of the brain consisting of the outer layer of cerebral cells. The cortex can be divided into specific regions: sensory, motor, and associative.

chaining: Behavior theory suggests that behavior patterns are built up of component parts by stringing together a number of simpler responses.

character disorder (or personality disorder): a classification of psychological disorders (as distinguised from neurosis or psychosis.) The disorder has become part of the individual's personality and does not cause him discomfort, making that disorder more difficult to treat psychotherapeutically.

chromosome: *See* gene.

chronological age: age since birth. (Contrasted with mental age, *see.*)

chunking: the tendency to code memories so that there are fewer bits to store. We tend to remember telephone numbers, for example, as chunks rather than as seven separate numbers.

circadian cycle: the genetically inherited daily rhythm of the body, including changes in body temperature, blood chemistry, hormonal balance and mood.

client-centered therapy: a nondirective form of psychotherapy developed by Carl Rogers in which the counselor attempts to create an atmosphere in which the client can freely explore himself and his problems. The client-centered therapist reflects what the client says back to him, usually without interpreting it.

clinical psychology: the branch of psychology concerned with testing, diagnosing, interviewing, conducting research and treating (often by psychotherapy) mental disorders and personality problems.

cloning: the artificial means of reproducing organisms genetically identical to the donor organism by using cells from the donor.

clustering: tendency to store new information in classification schemes based on past experience.

cognitive appraisal: intellectual evaluation of situations or stimuli. Experiments suggest that emotional arousal is produced not simply by a stimulus but by how one evaluates and interpets the arousal. The appropriate physical response follows this cognitive appraisal. *See* labeling-of-arousal.

cognitive dissonance: People are very uncomfortable if they perceive that their beliefs, feelings, or acts are not consistent with one another, and they will try to reduce the discomfort of this dissonance.

cognitive psychology: the study of how individuals gain knowledge of their environments. Cognitive psychologists believe that the organism actively participates in constructing the meaningful stimuli that it selectively organizes and to which it selectively responds.

comparative psychology: the study of similarities and differences in the behavior of different species.

computer simulation: a technique used to study human thinking. If a computer can be programmed to solve problems in the same way humans apparently solve them, the computer's program can be used as a theoretical outline of human thought.

concept learning: the acquisition of the ability to identify and use the qualities that objects or situations have in common. A class concept refers to any quality that breaks objects or situations into separate groupings.

concrete-operational stage: A stage in intellectual development according to Piaget. The child at approximately seven years begins to apply logic. His thinking is less egocentric, reversible, and the child develops conservation abilities *(see)* and the ability to classify.

conformity: the tendency of an individual to act like others regardless of personal belief.

conscience: a person's sense of the moral rightness or wrongness of behavior.

conservation: refers to the child's ability to understand laws of length, mass, and volume. Before the development of this ability, a child will not understand that a particular property of an object (e.g. the quantity of water in a glass) does not change even though other perceivable features change.

conservative focusing: a strategy in learning in which only one attribute is concentrated on at a time. *See* focus gambling.

contact comfort: the important component in loving relationships that derives from the mother-infant relationship in which the infant is comforted by touching the softness of the mother.

control group: a group used for comparison with an experimental group (see.) All conditions must be identical for each group with the exception of the one variable (independent) that is manipulated.

convergent thinking: the kind of thinking that is used to solve problems having only one correct answer, (as contrasted with divergent thinking, see.)

corpus callosum: nerve fibers that connect the two halves of the brain in humans. If cut, the halves continue to function although some functions are affected.

correlation: a measurement in which two or more sets of variables are compared and the extent to which they are related is calculated.

correlation coefficient: the measure, in number form, of how two variables vary together. They extend from −1 (perfect negative correlation) to +1 (perfect positive correlation.)

creativity: the ability to discover or produce new solutions to problems, new inventions, or new works of art. Creativity is an ability independent of IQ and is open-ended in that solutions are not predefined in their scope or appropriateness (as contrasted to problem-solving; see.)

credibility: the degree of believability and trustworthiness of a source of information.

critical period: a specific stage in an organism's development during which the acquisition of a particular type of behavior depends on exposure to a particular type of stimulation.

cross-sectional study: a research technique that focuses on a factor in a group of subjects as they are at one time, as in a study of fantasy play in subjects of three different age groups. See longitudinal study.

cutaneous sensitivity: the skin senses: touch, pain, pressure and temperature. Skin receptors respond in different ways and with varying degrees of sensitivity.

D

defense mechanism: a way of reducing anxiety that does not directly cope with the threat. There are many types, denial, repression, etc., all of which are used in normal function. Only when use is habitual or they impede effective solutions are they considered pathological.

delusion: a false belief that persists despite evidence showing it to be irrational. Delusions are often symptoms of mental illness.

demand characteristics: what the subject in an experiment thinks the experimenter wants from him.

dementia praecox: old name for schizophrenia (see.)

democratic leader: a group leader who participates in group projects and encourages group decision making rather than giving orders.

dependence: reliance on others. Dependency needs are those needs for satisfaction that a person actually cannot, or feels he cannot satisfy by himself.

dependent variable: those conditions that an experimenter observes and measures. Called "dependent" because they depend on the experimental manipulations.

depression: a temporary emotional state that normal individuals experience or a persistent state that may be considered a psychological disorder. Characterized by sadness and low self-esteem (see.)

descriptive evidence: evidence from uncontrolled studies that allows one to assess the degree of relationship between variables but provides little insight into which variables are the cause and which the effect; naturalistic observation and case study approach. See experimental evidence.

developmental psychology: the study of changes in behavior and thinking as the organism grows from infancy to death.

deviation, standard and average: Average deviation is determined by measuring the deviation of each score in a distribution from the mean and calculating the average of the deviations. The standard deviation is used to determine how representative the mean (see) of a distribution is.

diffusion of responsibility: As the number of witnesses to a help-requiring situation—and thus the degree of anonymity (see)—increases, the amount of helping decreases and the amount of time before help is offered increases.

discrimination: the ability to tell whether stimuli are different when presented together or that one situation is different from a past one.

displacement: the process by which an emotion originally attached to a particular person, object, or situation is transferred to something else.

distal stimuli: physical events in the environment that affect perception.

divergent thinking: the kind of thinking that characterizes creativity (as contrasted with convergent thinking, see) and involves the development of novel resolutions of a task or the generation of totally new ideas.

DNA: See gene.

double bind: a situation in which a person is subjected to two conflicting, contradictory demands at the same time.

dreams: the thoughts, images, and emotions that occur during sleep. Dreams occur periodically during the sleep cycle and are usually marked by rapid movements of the eyes (REM sleep). The content of dreams tends to reflect emotions (sexual feelings, according to Freud) and experiences of the previous day. Nightmares are qualitatively different from other dreams, often occuring during deep or Stage 4 sleep.

drive: a need or urge that motivates behavior. Some drives may be explained as responses to bodily needs, such as hunger or sex. Others derive from social pressures and complex forms of learning, for example, competition, curiosity, achievement. See motivation.

drug dependence: a state of mental or physical dependence on a drug, or both. Psychoactive drugs (see) are capable of creating psychological dependence (anxiety when the drug is unavailable,) although the relationship of some, such as marijuana and LSD, to physical dependence or addiction (see) is still under study.

drug tolerance: a state produced by certain psychoactive drugs in which increasing amounts of the substance are required to produce the desired effect. Some drugs produce tolerance but not withdrawal symptoms, and these drugs are not regarded as physically addicting.

E

early experience: The early experience of an individual provides the foundation for later personality development. Different theories place different weights on the importance of early experience. Freudians hold that early experiences are usually decisive. The term is also used in studies of behavior of non-human subjects where personality is not the issue.

effectance motive: the striving for effectiveness in dealing with the environment. The effectance motive differs from the need for achievement in that effectance depends on internal feelings of satisfaction while the need for achievement is geared more to meeting others' standards.

ego: a construct to account for the organization in a person's life and for making the person's behavior correspond to physical and social realities. According to Freud, the ego is the "reality principle" that is responsible for holding the id *(see,)* or "pleasure principle" in check.

egocentrism: seeing things from only one's own point of view; also, the quality of a child's thought that prevents him from understanding that different people perceive the world differently. Egocentrism is characteristic of a stage that all children go through.

eidetic imagery: technical term for "photographic memory," the total recall of a visual field. Eidetic imagery occurs in a small part of the population and is mainly found in children, who lose the capacity at puberty.

elaborated code: according to Bernstein, the kind of formal language used in writing, lecturing, or other formal situations, available only to the middle-class child.

Electra complex: a term used by Freud to describe a girl's erotic desire for her father and accompanying resentment of her mother.

electroshock therapy: a form of therapy used to relieve severe depression. The patient receives electric current across the forehead, loses consciousness, and undergoes a short convulsion. When the patient regains consciousness, his mood is lifted.

empathy: the ability to appreciate how someone else feels by putting yourself in his position and experiencing his feelings. Empathy is acquired normally by children during intellectual growth.

empiricism: the view that behavior is learned through experience.

encounter groups: groups of individuals who meet to change their personal lives by confronting each other, discussing personal problems, and talking more honestly and openly than in everyday life.

equilibration: According to Piaget, the child constructs his understanding of the world through equilibration. Equilibration consists of the interaction of two complementary processes, assimilation (taking in input within the existing structures of the mind, e.g. putting it into mental categories that already exist) with accommodation (the changing of mental categories to fit new input that cannot be taken into existing categories) and is the process by which knowing occurs. One's developmental stage affects how one equilibrates.

ethnocentrism: the belief that one's own ethnic or racial group is superior to others. Ethnocentrism is often a component of prejudice *(see.)*

ethology: the comparative study of animal behavior patterns as they exist in nature (as contrasted with an experimental approach,) founded by Konrad Lorenz.

experiment: procedures executed under a controlled situation in order to test a hypothesis and discover relationships between independent and dependent variables.

experimental control: the predetermined conditions, procedures, and checks built into the design of an experiment to ensure scientific control; as opposed to "control" in common usage, which implies manipulation.

experimental evidence: evidence from studies where conditions are carefully controlled and measurements taken so that cause-and-effect relationships between the independent and dependent variables can be inferred. *See* descriptive evidence.

experimental group: in a scientific experiment, the group of subjects that is usually treated specially, as opposed to the control group *(see,)* in order to isolate just the variable under investigation.

experimental psychology: the branch of psychology concerned with the laboratory study of basic psychological laws and principles as demonstrated in the behavior of animals.

experimenter bias: how the expectations of the person running an experiment can influence what comes out of the experiment. Experimenter bias can affect the way the experimenter sees the subjects' behavior, causing distortions of fact, and can also affect the way the experimenter reads data, also leading to distortions.

extrasensory perception (ESP): the range of perceptions that are "paranormal," (such as the ability to predict events, reproduce drawings sealed in envelopes, etc.)

F

factor analysis: a branch of mathematical statistics used by psychologists in constructing tests and interpreting their scores to discover correlations *(see)* and the factors that make up a complex trait such as intelligence or personality.

fading: the loss of an image when the eye is focused on it because the eye (retina) becomes fatigued by constant stimulation. *See* retina.

feedback: experiencing the consequences of one's actions, as when impulses from the body return to a control center in the brain where they are processed and contribute to further control. *See* biofeedback.

fixed-action pattern: movement that is characteristic of a species and does not have to be learned.

focus gambling: a strategy used in learning in which more than one attribute is concentrated on or changed at one time.

forgetting: the process by which material that once was available is no longer available. Theory exists that forgetting occurs because memories interfere with one another, either retroactively (new memories block old) or proactively (old memories block new); that forgetting occurs when the cues necessary to recall the information are not supplied, or when memories are too unpleasant to remain in consciousness. *See* repression.

formal operational stage: According to Piaget, the stage at which the child develops adult powers of reasoning, abstraction, and symbolizing. The child can grasp scientific, religious, and political concepts and deduce their consequences as well as reason hypothetically ("what if . . . .")

frustration: a feeling of discomfort or insecurity aroused by a blocking of gratification or by unresolved problems. Several theories hold that frustration arouses aggression *(see).*

functional autonomy: a concept of motivation *(see)* described by Allport suggesting that after a behavior has been repeatedly aroused, it may develop autonomy (control of itself) and continue long after the original motive is gone.

functionalism: an early school of psychology stressing the ways behavior helps one adapt to the environment and the role that learning plays in this adaptive process.

G

gate-control theory: the theory of pain proposed by Wall and Melzack stating that pain signals are sent from the body to the spinal cord and brain through a dynamic process that is controlled by a series of gate-like mechanisms in the body's pain-signaling system.

gene: the unit of heredity that determines particular characteristics; a part of a molecule of DNA. DNA (dioxyribonucleic acid) is found mainly in the nucleus of living cells where it occurs in threadlike structures called chromosomes. Within the chromosomes each DNA molecule is organized into specific units that carry the genetic information necessary for the development of a particular trait. These units are the genes. A gene can reproduce itself exactly, and this is how traits are carried between generations. The genotype is the entire structure of genes that are inherited by an organism from its parents. The environment interacts with this genotype to determine how the genetic potential will develop.

general adaptation syndrome (GAS): the way the body responds to stress, as described by Hans Selye. In the first stage, an alarm reaction, a person responds by efforts at self-control and shows signs of nervous depression (defense mechanisms, fear, anger, etc.) followed by a release of ACTH. In stage 2, the subject shows increased resistance to the specific source of stress and less resistance to other sources. Defense mechanisms may become neurotic. With stage 3 come exhaustion, stupor, even death.

general intelligence: a term postulated by Spearman, called *g*, to represent a supposed general ability at the heart of intelligence.

generalization: the process by which learning in one situation is transferred to another, similar situation. It is a key term in behavioral modification and classical conditioning *(see.)*

genetics: the study of the transfer of the inheritance of characteristics from one generation to another.

genotype: the underlying genetic structure that an individual has inherited and will send on to descendants. The actual appearance of a trait (phenotype) is due to the interaction of the genotype and the environment.

Gestalt psychology: a movement in psychology begun in the 1920s, stressing the wholeness of a person's experience and proposing that perceiving is an active, dynamic process that takes into account the entire pattern ("gestalt") of the perceptual field (as opposed to behaviorism or associationism; *see.*)

glia: cells in the central nervous system that regulate the chemical environment of the nerve cells. RNA is stored in glial cells.

grammar: the set of rules for combining units of a language.

group dynamics: the study of the interaction in groups, how individuals are influenced by groups and their leaders.

group therapy: a form of psychotherapy aimed at treating mental disorders in which interaction among group members is the main therapeutic mode. Group therapy takes many forms but essentially requires a sense of community, support, increased personal responsibility, and a professionally trained leader.

groupthink: the deterioration of judgment, efficiency, morality, and reality testing that may result from pressures within a group.

guilt feelings: those feelings of psychological discomfort or distress that a person experiences because he thinks he has done something wrong.

gustation: the sense of taste. Theory suggests that the transmission of sense information from tongue to brain occurs through patterns of cell activity and not just the firing of single nerve fibers. Also, it is believed that specific spatial patterns or places on the tongue correspond to taste qualities.

H

hallucination: a sensory impression reported by a person when no external stimulus exists to justify the report. Hallucinations are serious symptoms and may be produced by psychoses *(see.)*

hallucinogen: a substance that produces hallucinations, such as LSD, mescaline, etc.

halo effect: the tendency for first impressions to color subsequent impressions.

hedonism: the belief that pleasure is life's highest good. Also used to describe the stage in a child's moral development when what is "right" is the same as what gives the child pleasure.

hippocampus: part of the cortex of the brain governing memory storage, smell, and visceral functions.

homeostasis: a set of processes maintaining the constancy of the body's internal state, a series of dynamic compensations of the nervous system. Many processes such as appetite, body temperature, water balance, heart rate are controlled by homeostasis.

homosexuality: sexual interest in, or sexual contact with one's own sex.

hormones: chemical secretions of the endocrine glands that regulate various body processes (e.g. growth, sexual traits, reproductive processes, etc.)

humanism: branch of psychology dealing with those qualities distinguishing humans from other animals.

hypnagogic imagery: images that appear in a twilight state of consciousness and are not consciously generated.

hypnosis: a trancelike state marked by heightened suggestibility and a narrowing of attention which can be induced in a number of ways. Debate exists over whether hypnosis is a true altered state of consciousness and over to what extent strong motivating instructions can duplicate so-called hypnosis.

hypochondriasis: a state of excessive concern with and complaints about one's physical condition.

hypothalamus: a part of the brain that acts as a channel that carries information from the cortex and the thalamus to the spinal cord and ultimately to the motor nerves or to the autonomic nervous system *(see,)* where it is transmitted to specific target organs. These target organs release into the bloodstream specific hormones that alter bodily functions.

hypothesis: A hypothesis can be called an educated guess, similar to a hunch. When a hunch is stated in a way that allows for further testing, it becomes a hypothesis.

I

iconic memory: a visual memory. Experiments suggest that in order to be remembered and included in long-term memory, information must pass through a brief sensory stage. Theory further suggests that verbal information is subject to forgetting but that memorized sensory images are relatively permanent.

id: According to Freud, a component of the psyche present at birth that is the storehouse of psychosexual energy called *libido,* and also of primitive urges to fight, dominate, destroy. The id is hedonistic *(see)* and operates by the "pleasure principle."

identification: the taking on of attributes that one sees in another person. Children tend to identify with their parents or other important adults and thereby take on certain traits that are important to their development.

illusion: a mistaken perception of an actual stimulus.

imitation: the copying of another's behavior; learned through the process of observation. *See* modeling.

imprinting: the rapid, permanent acquisition by an organism of a strong attachment to an object (usually the parent.) Imprinting occurs shortly after birth.

incentive: a goal toward which an organism may be motivated.

independent variable: what the researcher arranges to happen beforehand through experimental manipulation.

inhibition: restraint of an impulse, desire, activity, or drive. People are taught to inhibit full expression of many drives (for example, aggression or sexuality) and to apply checks either consciously or unconsciously. In Freudian terminology, an inhibition is an unconsciously motivated blocking of sexual energy. In Pavlovian conditioning *(see,)* inhibition is the theoretical process that operates during extinction, acting to block a conditioned response.

insight: a sudden perception of useful or proper relations among objects necessary to solve the problem.

insight therapy: a general classification of therapy in which the therapist focuses on the patient's underlying feelings and motivations and devotes most effort to increasing the patient's self-awareness or insight into his behavior. The other major class of therapy is action therapy *(see.)*

instinct: an inborn pattern of behavior, relatively independent of environmental influence. An instinct may need to be triggered by a particular stimulus in the environment, but then it proceeds in a fixed pattern. The combination of taxis (orienting movement in response to a particular stimulus) and fixed-action pattern (inherited coordination) is the basis for instinctual activity. *See* fixed-action pattern.

instrumental learning: often used as a synonym for operant conditioning *(see,)* a basic learning process in which a behavior that is followed by a positive consequence will increase in probability and frequency and a behavior followed by a negative consequence will decrease. Behaviors may be acquired, maintained, or eliminated in this way.

intelligence: a capacity for knowledge about the world. This is an enormous and controversial field of study, and there is not agreement on a precise definition. However, intelligence has come to refer to higher-level abstract processes and may be said to comprise the ability to deal effectively with abstract concepts, the ability to learn, and the ability to adapt and deal with new situations. Piaget defines intelligence as the construction of an understanding. Both biological inheritance and environmental factors contribute to general intelligence *(see.)* Children proceed through a sequence of identifiable stages in the development of conceptual thinking (Piaget). The degree to which factors such as race, sex, and social class affect intelligence is not known. Many different tests have been designed to measure intelligence.

intelligence quotient (IQ): a measurement of intelligence originally based on tests devised by Binet and now widely applied. Genetic inheritance and environment affect IQ, although their relative contributions are not known. IQ can be defined in different ways; classically it is defined as a relation between chronological and mental ages *(see.)* Measured IQ is a good predictor of school performance, yet the best way to measure intelligence is still subject to considerable debate.

interpersonal attraction: a basis for love, in combination with affectionate behavior.

interstimulus interval: the time between the start of the conditioned stimulus and the start of the unconditioned stimulus in Pavlovian conditioning *(see.)*

intra-uterine environment: The environment in the uterus during pregnancy can affect the physical development of the organism and its behavior after birth. Factors such as the mother's nutrition, emotional and physical state significantly influence offspring. The mother's diseases, medications, hormones, stress level all effect the pre- and post-natal development of her young.

introspection: reporting one's internal, subjective mental contents for the purpose of further study and analysis. *See* structuralism.

K

key stimuli: certain environmental cues that trigger specific behavior patterns.

L

labeling-of-arousal: Experiments suggest that an individual experiencing physical arousal *(see)* that he cannot explain will interpret his feelings in terms of the situation he is in and will use environmental and contextual cues.

laissez faire leader: a type of group leader who makes few suggestions and allows great freedom to group members.

language: a set of abstract symbols used to communicate meaning. Language includes vocalized sounds or semantic units (words, usually) and rules for combining the units (grammar.) There is some inborn basis for language acquisition, and there are identifiable stages in its development that are universal.

language acquisition: Linguists debate how children acquire language. Some believe in environmental shaping, a gradual system of reward and punishment. Others emphasize the unfolding of capacities inborn in the brain that are relatively independent of the environment and its rewards.

latency period: according to Freud, the psychosexual stage of development during which sexual interest has been repressed and thus is low or "latent" (dormant.)

leadership: the quality of exerting more influence than other group members. Research suggests that certain characteristics are generally considered essential to leadership: consideration, sensitivity, ability to initiate and structure, and emphasis on production. However, environmental factors may thrust authority on a person without regard to personal characteristics.

learned helplessness: Theory suggests that living in an environment of uncontrolled stress reduces the ability to cope with future stress that *is* controllable.

learning: the establishment of connections between stimulus and response, resulting from observation, special training, or previous activity. Learning is relatively permanent.

libido: According to Freud, libido is psychosexual energy and is stored in the id *(see.)* This energy may go into sexual activity or become transformed (sublimated) in other activities, such as the arts.

linguistics: the study of language, its nature, structure, and components.

locus of control: the perceived place from which come determining forces in one's life. A person who feels that he has some control over his fate and tends to feel more likely to succeed has an internal locus of control. A person with an external locus of control feels that it is outside himself and therefore that his attempts to control his fate are less assured.

longitudinal study: a research method that involves following subjects over a considerable period of time (as compared with a cross-sectional approach; *see,*) as in a study of fantasy play in children observed several times at intervals of two years.

love: affectionate behavior between people, often in combination with interpersonal attraction. The mother-infant love relationship strongly influences the later capacity for developing satisfying love relationships.

M

manic-depressive reaction: a form of mental illness marked by alternations of extreme phases of elation (manic phase) and depression.

maternalism: refers to the mother's reaction to her young. It is believed that the female is biologically determined to exhibit behavior more favorable to the care and feeding of the young than the male, although in humans maternalism is probably determined as much by cultural factors as by biological predisposition.

mean: the measure of central tendency, or mathematical average, computed by adding all scores in a set and dividing by the number of scores.

meaning: the concept or idea conveyed to the mind, by any method. In reference to memory, meaningful terms are easier to learn than less meaningful, unconnected, or nonsense terms. Meaningfulness is not the same as the word's meaning.

median: In a set of scores, the median is that middle score that divides the set into equal halves.

memory: involves the encoding, storing of information in the brain, and its retrieval. Several theories exist to explain memory. One proposes that we have both a short-term (STM) and a long-term memory (LTM) and that information must pass briefly through the STM to be stored in the LTM. Also suggested is that verbal information is subject to forgetting, while memorized sensory images are relatively permanent. Others see memory as a function of association—information processed systematically and the meaningfulness of the items. Debate exists over whether memory retrieval is actually a process of reappearance or reconstruction.

mental age: a person's present level of mental functioning as compared to others and as measured by an intelligence test. *See* chronological age.

mental disorder: a mental condition that deviates from what society considers to be normal.

mnemonic device: a specific, well-learned strategy used to aid in remembering items. A person devises a mental image or verbal device relating two or more items.

mode: in a set of scores, the measurement at which the largest number of subjects fall.

modeling: the imitation or copying of another's behavior. As an important process in personality development, modeling may be based on parents. In therapy, the therapist may serve as a model for the patient.

models: individuals whose behavior a person imitates. Live individuals such as parents and peers, as well as cartoon or film characters may serve as models.

moral dilemma: a situation or problem that requires a moral decision or judgment about right and wrong.

morality: the standards of right and wrong of a society and their adoption by members of that society. Some researchers believe that morality develops in successive stages, with each stage representing a specific level of moral thinking (Kohlberg.) Others see morality as the result of experiences in which the child learns through punishment and reward from models such as parents and teachers.

motivation: all factors that cause and regulate behavior that is directed toward achieving goals and satisfying needs. Motivation is what moves an organism to action.

motor unit: one spinal motoneuron (motor nerve cell) and the muscle fibers it activates. The contraction of a muscle involves the activity of many motoneurons and muscle fibers. Normally we are aware only of our muscles contracting and not of the process producing the contraction, although biofeedback *(see)* can train to people to control individual motor units.

N

narcotic: a drug that relieves pain. Heroin, morphine, and opium are narcotics. Narcotics are often addicting.

neuron: a nerve cell. There are billions of neurons in the brain and spinal cord. Neurons interact at synapses *(see)* or points of contact. Information passage between neurons is electrical and biochemical. It takes the activity of many neurons to produce a behavior.

neurosis: any one of a wide range of psychological difficulties, accompanied by excessive anxiety (as contrasted with psychosis, *see.)* Psychoanalytic theory states that neurosis is an expression of unresolved conflicts in the form of tension and impaired functioning. Most neurotics are in much closer contact with reality than most psychotics.

nonverbal behaviors: gestures *(see,)* facial expressions, and other body movements. They are important because they tend to convey emotion. Debate exists over whether they are inborn or learned.

norm: an empirically set pattern of belief or behavior. Social norm refers to widely accepted social or cultural behavior to which a person tends to or is expected to conform.

normal: sane, or free from mental disorder. Normal behavior is the behavior typical of most people in a given group, and "normality" implies a social judgment.

O

object permanence: according to Piaget, the stage in cognitive development when a child begins to conceive of objects as having an existence even when out of sight or touch and to conceive of space as extending beyond his own perception.

objective responsibility: refers to a type of moral judgment in which wrongness is judged by the actual damage done. *See* subjective responsibility.

Oedipus complex: the conflicts of a child in triangular relationship with his mother and father. According to Freud, a boy must resolve his unconscious sexual desire for his mother and the accompanying wish to kill his father and fear of his father's revenge in order that he proceed in his moral development. The analogous problem for girls is called the Electra complex *(see.)*

olfaction: the sense of smell. No general agreement exists on how olfaction works though theories exist to explain it. One suggests that the size and shape of molecules of what is smelled is a crucial cue. The brain processes involved in smell are located in a different and evolutionarily older part of the brain than the other senses.

operant conditioning: the process of changing, maintaining, or eliminating voluntary behavior through the consequences of that behavior. Operant conditioning uses many of the techniques of Pavlovian conditioning *(see)* but differs in that it deals with voluntary rather than reflex behaviors. The frequency with which a behavior is emitted can be increased if it is rewarded (reinforced) and decreased if it is not reinforced, or punished. Some psychologists believe that all behavior is learned through conditioning while others believe that intellectual and motivational processes play a crucial role.

operational definitions: If an event is not directly observable, then the variables must be defined by the operations by which they will be measured. These definitions are called operational definitions.

organism: any living animal, human or subhuman.

orienting response: a relatively automatic, "what's that?" response that puts the organism in a better position to attend to and deal with a new stimulus. When a stimulus attracts our attention, our body responds with movements of head and body toward the stimulus, changes in muscle tone, heart rate, blood flow, breathing, and changes in the brain's electrical activity.

outgroups: any groups of people, usually ethnic or racial minorities, that are perceived as foreign, inferior, or different. Outgroups are often seen in a stereotyped *(see)* fashion that serves to reinforce prejudice *(see.)*

P

Pavlovian conditioning: also called classical conditioning, Pavlovian conditioning can be demonstrated as follows: In the first step, an *unconditioned stimulus* (UCS) such as food, loud sounds, or pain is paired with a neutral *conditioned stimulus* (CS) that causes no direct effect, such as a click, tone, or a dim light. The response elicited by the UCS is called the *unconditioned response* (UCR) and is a biological reflex of the nervous system (for example, eyeblinks or salivation). The combination of the neutral CS, the response-causing UCS, and the unlearned UCR is usually presented to the subject several times during conditioning. Eventually, the UCS is dropped from the sequence in the second step of the process, and the previously neutral CS comes to elicit a response. When conditioning is complete, presentation of the CS alone will result in a *conditioned response* (CR) similar but not always the same as the UCR.

perception: the field of psychology studying ways in which the experience of objects in the world is based upon stimulation of the sense organs. In psychology, the field of perception studies what determines sensory impressions, such as size, shape, distance, direction, etc. Physical events in the environment are called distal stimuli while the activity at the sense organ itself is called a proximal stimulus. The study of perceiving tries to determine how an organism knows what distal stimuli are like since proximal stimuli are its only source of information. Perception of objects remains more or less constant despite changes in distal stimuli and is therefore believed to depend on relationships within stimuli (size *and* distance, for example.) Perceptual processes are able to adjust and adapt to changes in the perceptual field.

persuasion: the process of changing a person's attitudes, beliefs, or actions. A person's susceptibility to persuasion depends on the persuader's credibility *(see,)* subtlety, and whether both sides of an argument are presented.

phenotype: the physical features or behavior patterns by which we recognize an organism. Phenotype is the result of interaction between genotype (total of inherited genes) and environment. *See* genotype.

phobia: a neurosis consisting of an irrationally intense fear of specific persons, objects, or situations and a wish to avoid them. A phobic person feels intense and incapacitating anxiety. The person may be aware that his fear is irrational, but this knowledge does not help.

pituitary gland: is located at the base of the brain and controls secretion of several hormones: the antidiuretic hormone that maintains water balance, oxytocin which controls blood pressure and milk production and ACTH *(see)* which is produced in response to stress, etc.

placebo: a substance which in and of itself has no real effect but which may produce an effect in a subject because the subject expects or believes that it will.

pleasure center: a powerful center of reinforcement in the brain. Electrical stimulation of the brain *(see)* is pleasurable to the animal if applied at certain points in the hypothalamus.

prejudice: an attitude in which one holds a negative belief about members of a group to which he does not belong. Prejudice is often directed at minority ethnic or racial groups and may be reduced by contact with these perceived "others."

prenatal development: development from conception to birth. It includes the physical development of the fetus as well as certain of its intellectual and emotional processes.

preoperational stage: the developmental stage at which, according to Piaget, come the start of language, the ability to imitate actions, to symbolize, and to play make-believe games. Thinking is egocentric in that a child cannot understand that others perceive things differently.

problem solving: a self-directed activity in which an individual uses information to develop answers to problems, to generate new problems, and sometimes to transform the process by creating a unique, new system. Problem solving involves learning, insight *(see)* and creativity *(see.)*

projective test: a type of test in which people respond to ambiguous, loosely structured stimuli. It is assumed that people will reveal themselves by putting themselves into the stimuli they see. The validity of these tests for diagnosis and personality assessment is still at issue.

propaganda: information deliberately spread to aid a cause. Propaganda's main function is persuasion.

proximal stimulus: activity at the sense organ.

psychic overload: a term used to describe the human inability to process inputs from the environment when they come too rapidly or when there are too many of them.

psychoactive drug: a substance that affects mental activities, perceptions, consciousness, or mood. This group of drugs has its effects through strictly physical effects and through expectations.

psychoanalysis: There are two meanings to this word: it is a theory of personality development based on Freud and a method of treatment also based on Freud. Psychoanalytic therapy uses techniques of free association, dream analysis, and analysis of the patient's relationship (the "transference") to the analyst. Psychoanalytic theory maintains that the personality develops through a series of psychosexual stages *(see)* and that the personality consists of specific components energized by the life and death instincts.

psychodrama: a form of group therapy in which a person (the protagonist) is asked to act out his conflicts as if in a play. Others present may be enlisted to play significant people in the protagonist's life.

psycholinguistics: the study of the process of language acquisition as part of psychological development and of language as an aspect of behavior. Thinking may obviously depend on language, but their precise relationship still puzzles psycholinguists, and several different views exist.

psychology: the science of the behavior of organisms.

psychopath: Someone with a psychological disorder who acts antisocially but feels no guilt about that behavior. (Contrast with neurosis.)

psychosexual stages: According to Freud, an individual's personality develops through several stages. Each stage is associated with a particular bodily source of gratification (pleasure.) First comes the oral stage when most pleasures come from the mouth. Then comes the anal stage when the infant derives pleasure from holding and releasing while learning bowel control. The phallic stage brings pleasure from the genitals, and a crisis (Oedipal, *see*) occurs in which the child gradually suppresses sexual desire for the opposite-sex parent, identifies with the same-sex parent and begins to be interested in the outside world. This latency period lasts until puberty, after which the genital stage begins and mature sexual relationships develop. There is no strict timetable, but according to Freudians, the stages do come in a definite order. Conflicts experienced and not adequately dealt with remain with the individual.

psychosis: the most severe of mental disorders, distinguished by a person being seriously out of touch with objective reality. Psychoses may result from physical factors (organic) or may have no known physical cause (functional.) Psychoses take many forms of which the most common are schizophrenia and psychotic depressive reactions, but all are marked by personality disorganization and a severely reduced ability to perceive reality. Both biological and environmental factors are believed to influence the development of psychosis, although the precise effect of each is not presently known. *See* neurosis.

psychosomatic disorders: a variety of body reactions that are closely related to psychological events. Stress, for example, brings on many physical changes and can result in illness or even death if prolonged and severe. Psychosomatic disorders can affect any part of the body.

psychotherapy: treatment involving interpersonal contacts between a trained therapist and a patient in which the therapist tries to produce beneficial changes in the patient's emotional state, attitudes, and behavior.

R

reality therapy: a form of treatment of mental disorders pioneered by William Glasser in which the origins of the patient's problems are considered irrelevant and emphasis is on a close, judgmental bond between patient and therapist aimed to improve the patient's present and future life.

redundancy: refers to the highly predictable nature of speech and its quality of providing repeated clues about what is likely to come next.

rehearsal: the repeating of an item to oneself and the means by which information is stored in the short-term memory (STM.) Theory suggests that rehearsal is necessary for remembering and storage in the long-term memory (LTM.)

reinforcement: the process of affecting the frequency with which a behavior is emitted. A reinforcer can reward and thus increase the behavior or punish and thus decrease its frequency. Reinforcers can also be primary, satisfying basic needs such as hunger or thirst, or secondary, satisfying learned and indirect values, such as money.

reliability: consistency of measurement. A test is reliable if it repeatedly gives the same results. A person should get nearly the same score if the test is taken on two different occasions.

repression: a defense mechanism *(see)* in which a person forgets or pushes into the unconscious something that arouses anxiety *(see.)*

restricted code: according to Bernstein, the ungrammatical, colloquial speech that we all use most of the time but which is the only form of speech available to the lower class child. *See* elaborated code.

reticular formation: a system of nerve fibers leading from the spinal column to the cerebral cortex *(see)* that functions to arouse, alert, and make an organism sensitive to changes in the environment.

retina: the inside coating of the eye, containing two kinds of cells that react to light: the rods which are sensitive only to dim light and the cones which are sensitive to color and form in brighter light. There are three kinds of cones, each responsive to particular colors in the visible spectrum (range of colors.)

risky shift: Research suggests that decisions made by groups will involve considerably more risk than individuals in the group would be willing to take. This shift in group decision depends heavily on cultural values. *See* cautious shift.

rod: part of the retina *(see)* involved in seeing in dim light.

RNA (ribonucleic acid): a chemical substance that occurs in chromosomes and that functions in genetic coding. During task-learning, RNA changes occur in the brain.

role playing: adopting the role of another person and experiencing the world in a way one is not accustomed to.

role taking: the ability to imagine oneself in another's place or to understand the consequences of one's actions for another person.

Rosenthal effect: the tendency of a person's expectations to affect others' performance to meet his expectations in a way that creates a self-fulfilling prophecy *(see.)*

S

schizophrenia: the most common and serious form of psychosis *(see)* in which there exists an imbalance between emotional reactions and the thoughts associated with these feelings. It may be a disorder of the process of thinking.

scientific method: the process used by psychologists to determine principles of behavior that exist independently of individual experience and that are untouched by unconscious bias. It is based on a prearranged agreement that criteria, external to the individual and communicable to others, must be established for each set of observations referred to as fact.

selectivity: Theory suggests that the brain "tunes in" certain messages and rejects others, thus reducing the load on the perceptual system.

self-actualization: a term used by humanistic psychologists to describe what they see as a basic human motivation: the development of all aspects of an individual into productive harmony.

self-esteem: a person's evaluation of himself. If a person "likes himself," feels he can control his actions, that his acts and work are worthy and competent, his self-esteem is high.

self-fulfilling prophecy: a preconceived expectation or belief about a situation that evokes behavior resulting in a situation consistent with the preconception.

semantic differential: a technique devised by Charles Osgood to measure word meaning *(see.)* Subjects rate specific words on scales such as hot-cold, good-bad, and the pattern of responses indicate the word's subjective meanings.

senses: an organism's physical means of receiving and detecting physical changes in the environment. Sensing is analyzed in terms of reception of the physical stimulus by specialized nerve cells in the sense organs, transduction or converting the stimulus' energy into nerve impulses that the brain can interpret, and transmission of those nerve impulses from the sense organ to the part of the brain that can interpret the information they convey.

sensitivity training: aims at helping people to function more effectively in their jobs by increasing their awareness of their own and others' feelings and exchanging "feedback" about styles of interacting. Sensitivity groups are unlike therapy groups in that they are meant to enrich the participants' lives. Participants are not considered patients or ill. Also called T-groups.

sensorimotor stage: According to Piaget, the stage of development beginning at birth during which perceptions are tied to objects which the child manipulates. Gradually the child learns that objects have permanence even if they are out of sight or touch.

sensory deprivation: the blocking out of all outside stimulation for a period of time. As studied experimentally, it can produce hallucinations, psychological disturbances, and temporary disorders of the nervous system of the subject.

serial position: The order in which items in a list are learned affects the ease with which they are remembered. Experiments show that the first (primacy effect, *see*) and last few items (recency effect, *see*) are learned with the fewest errors and suggest that the beginning and end are learned first. Further, items at the beginning are learned with slightly fewer errors than items at the end.

sex role: the attitudes, activities, and expectations considered specific to being male or female, determined by both biological and cultural factors.

shaping: a technique of behavior shaping in which behavior is acquired through the reinforcement of successive approximations *(see)* of the desired behavior.

Skinner box: a piece of laboratory equipment, designed by B. F. Skinner, for conditioning behavior. Stimuli are controlled and reinforcements can be provided for given behaviors.

sleep: a periodic state of consciousness marked by four brain-wave *(see)* patterns. Dreams *(see)* occur during relatively light Stage 1 sleep. Sleep is a basic need without which one may suffer physical or psychological distress.

sleeper effect: the delayed impact of persuasive information. People tend to forget the context in which they first heard the information, but they eventually remember the content of the message sufficiently to feel its impact.

social contact: the interaction of individuals or groups. It is believed that more frequent contact tends to reeducate, to reduce perceived differences between people and thus diminish stereotyping *(see)* and prejudice *(see.)*

social contract: an agreement among group members establishing their rights, limits, and obligations.

social-emotional leader: a type of group leader who is more interested in maintaining cohesiveness and good feeling in the group than "task leaders" who supervise productivity.

social influence: the process by which people form and change the attitudes, opinions, and behavior of others.

socialization: a process by which a child learns the various patterns of behavior expected and accepted by society. Parents are the chief agents of a child's socialization. Many factors have a bearing on the socialization process, such as the child's sex, religion, social class, and parental attitudes.

social learning: learning acquired through observation and imitation of others.

social psychology: the study of individuals as affected by others and of the interaction of individuals in groups.

sociogram: a map or diagram which shows the interaction among group members. A sociogram of a group might show who is most preferred and who least preferred, for example.

species-typical behavior: behavior patterns common to members of a species. Ethologists state that each species inherits some patterns of behavior (e.g. birdsongs.)

Stanford-Binet Intelligence Scale: tests that measure intelligence from two years through adult level. The tests determine one's intelligence quotient *(see)* by establishing one's chronological and mental ages.

stereotype: the assignment of characteristics to a person mainly on the basis of the group, class, or category to which he belongs. The tendency to categorize and generalize is a basic human way of organizing information. Stereotyping, however, can reinforce misinformation and prejudice *(see.)*

strategy: an organized sequence of responding designed by the subject to discover a rule defining a concept. *See* conservative focusing, focus gambling.

stress: pressure that puts unusual demands on an organism. Stress may be caused by physical conditions but eventually will involve both. Stimuli that cause stress are called stressors, and an organism's response is the stress reaction. A three-stage general adaptation syndrome *(see)* is hypothesized involving both emotional and physical changes.

structuralism: an early school of psychology that stressed the importance of conscious experience as the subject matter of psychology and maintained that experience should be analyzed into its component parts by use of introspection *(see.)*

subjective responsibility: refers to a type of moral judgment in which wrongness is judged according to one's intention rather than actual damage done. *See* objective responsibility.

subliminal stimuli: stimuli that do not receive conscious attention because they are below sensory thresholds. They may influence behavior, but research is not conclusive on this matter.

successive approximations: a technique of behavior shaping of rewarding situations that are more and more similar to the desired behavior.

suggestibility: the extent to which a person responds to persuasion *(see.)* Hypnotic susceptibility refers to the degree of suggestibility observed after an attempt to induce hypnosis *(see)* has been made.

superego: According to Freud, the superego corresponds roughly to conscience *(see.)* The superego places restrictions on both ego *(see)* and id *(see)* and represents the internalized restrictions and ideals that the child learns from parents and culture.

surrogate: substitute or stand-in. Many studies have tried to determine the effect of surrogate mothers on the offspring's emotional, social, and intellectual development.

synapse: a "gap" where individual nerve cells (neurons) come together and across which chemical information is passed.

syndrome: a group of symptoms that occur together and mark a particular abnormal pattern.

systematic densensitization: a technique used in behavior therapy to eliminate a phobia *(see.)* The symptoms of the phobia are seen as conditioned responses of fear, and the procedure attempts to decondition the fearful response until the patient gradually is able to face the feared situation.

T

taxis: an orienting movement *(see)* in response to particular stimuli in the environment. A frog, for example, always turns so its snout points directly at its prey before it flicks its tongue.

territoriality: the tendency of animals to adopt a possessive attitude toward a particular area and to repel intruders from it. Psychologists debate whether territoriality is innate or learned.

theory: a very general statement that is more useful in generating hypotheses *(see)* than in generating research.

therapeutic community: the organization of a hospital setting so that patients have to take responsibility for helping one another in an attempt to prevent patients from getting worse by being in the hospital.

token economy: a system for organizing a treatment setting according to behavioristic principles. Patients are encouraged to take greater responsibility for their adjustment by receiving tokens for acceptable behavior and fines for unacceptable behavior. The theory of token economy grew out of operant conditioning techniques *(see.)*

tranquilizers: psychoactive drugs *(see)* which reduce anxiety.

transposition: the ability of a subject to learn to respond to a relationship among stimuli (for example, the larger of two stimuli), rather than to one characteristic. Studies suggest that transposition learning increases with age.

U

unconscious: in Freudian terminology, a concept (not a place) of the mind. The unconscious encompasses certain inborn impulses that never rise into consciousness (awareness) as well as memories and wishes that have been repressed *(see.)* The chief aim of psychoanalytic therapy is to free repressed material from the unconscious in order to make it susceptible to conscious thought and direction. Behaviorists describe the unconscious as an inability to verbalize.

V

validity: the extent to which a test actually measures what it is designed to measure.

variable: any property of a person, object, or event that can change or take on more than one mathematical value.

visual cliff: a structure used to test for the presence of depth perception. A subject is placed on a glass platform on which there is a severe visual drop on one side.

W

Wechsler Adult Intelligence Scale (WAIS): an individually administered test designed to measure adults' intelligence, devised by David Wechsler. The WAIS consists of eleven subtests, of which six measure verbal and five measure performance aspects of intelligence. *See* Wechsler Intelligence Scale for Children.

Wechsler Intelligence Scale for Children (WISC): similar to the Wechsler Adult Intelligence Scale *(see,)* except that it is designed for people under fifteen. Wechsler tests can determine strong and weak areas of overall intelligence.

withdrawal: social or emotional detachment; the removal of oneself from a painful or frustrating situation.

index of names

Achievement Motive, The, 357
Adamson, R.E., 302–303
Adelson, J., 272
Aderman, D., 53
Adler, Alfred, 329, 363–364
Adler, C., 611
Adorno, T.W., 124
Allen, T.W., 276
Alexander, B.K., 70
Alexander, M., 596
Allport, Gordon W., 137, 256, 264, 365
Allyn, J., 161
Ames, Adelbert, 401
Approval Motive, The, 363
Ardrey, Robert, 62, 532
Aristotle, 8, 76, 110, 172, 366
Aronfreed, J., 83
Aronson, E., 114
Asch, Solomon E., 144, 260
Aserinsky, Eugene, 556
Atkinson, J.W., 357, 362
Atthowe, J.M., Jr., 176
Auden, W.H., 247
Austin, George, 373–374
Australian Aboriginal, The, 489
Authoritarian Personality, The, 124
Ayllon, T., 470

Back, Kurt W., 182
Baer, Donald, 479
Bales, Robert, 148
Baker, J.G., 465, 470
Baker, R.W., 417
Bandura, A., 67
Bandura, A., 81
Bankart, C.P., 490
Baratz, J.C., 239, 240
Barber, Theodore S., 42
Barber, T.X., 318, 324–325
Bardwick, J.M., 97, 98, 99
Baron, J., 321
Barstow, C.A., 629
Barter, J.T., 221
Basedow, R. Herbert, 489
Basmajian, J.V., 608
Baumal, E., 255
Bayley, N., 194
Beach, B.R., 303
Beach, Frank A., 105
Becker, Howard S., 44, 45
Beethoven, Ludwig van, 208
Bekésy, Georg von, 544, 546
Bell Jar, The, 221
Bem, D.J., 142
Benedict, Ruth, 62

Ben-Horen, P., 561
Bennett, E.L., 511
Bennett, K.S., 355
Bennis, W.G., 145
Berko, J., 232
Berkowitz, L., 53, 68
Berlyne, D.E., 410
Bernstein, Basil, 242–243
Berzins, J., 340
Berzonsky, M., 275
Bettelheim, B., 130
Betz, B., 338–339
Bever, T.G., 235
Beyond Freedom and Dignity, 462, 478
Binet, Alfred, 188–189
Biondo, J., 159
Birch, H.G., 250, 251, 353
Bird, E., 469
Birdwhistell, Ray L., 295
Black, K.N., 237
Blake, William, 627
Blank, M., 277
Bleuler, Eugene, 209
Blum, G.S., 252
Bohdanecky, Z., 577–578
Bodily Changes in Pain, Hunger, Fear, and Rage, 484
Bodmer, W., 199
Bousfield, W.A., 434
Bower, G.H., 434
Bower, T.G.R., 396
Bowne, G., 596
Braid, James, 315
Brain Mechanisms and Intelligence, 570
Breger, Louis, 258, 260
Brehm, J.W., 162
Breland, K. and M., 466
Brener, J., 606
Breuer, Josef, 328
Brogden, W. and J., 451, 452
Brown, Claude, 634
Brown, H. Rap, 62
Brown, R., 432
Bruner, Jerome, 269, 304, 372–374, 376
Bryan, J.H., 51
Bucher, V.M., 592
Budzynski, T.H., 611
Bugelski, R., 126
Burke, R.L., 145
Burton, N.G., 234
Butler, J.M., 332
Butterfield, W.H., 473
Byrne, D., 114, 418
Byrne, J.V., 562

Calhoun, J.B., 65, 66, 67
Calley, Lt. William, 73
Campbell, D.T., 401
Camus, Albert, 218, 220
Cannon, Walter B., 350, 484, 489
Carlson, P., 333
Carmichael, L., 524
Carnegie, Dale, 324
Carroll, J.B., 238
Carter, J.H., 146
Cartwright, D.S., 339
Casagrande, J.B., 238
Cattell, J. McK., 409
Cattell, Raymond B., 256
Cavalli-Sforza, L.L., 199, 200
Chafetz, P., 274
Chamove, A., 110
Chapman, D.W., 359
Chess, S., 250, 251
Chevalier, J.A., 509
Chinsky, J.M., 303
Chomsky, Noam, 228–229, 478–479
Civilization and Its Discontents, 48
Cohen, D.J., 262, 340, 405
Cohen, L.B., 415
Cole, M., 380
Coleman, S.R., 448
Coleridge, Samuel Taylor, 627
Collins, M.E., 131
Columbus, Christopher, 204
Combs, A.N., 261
Concerning Memory, 424, 425
Conezio, J., 437
Confucius, 146
Connors, C.K., 625
Conover, C., 274
Coons, W.H., 174
Cooper, R.M., 196
Cowan, J.E., 467
Crandall, V.C., 36
Crowne, Douglas P., 362–363
Cutter, E., 451, 452

Dallenbach, K.M., 431
Darbyshire, M., 469
Darley, J., 52
Darlington, R.B., 50
Darwin, Charles, 9, 10, 11, **284–285,** 518
da Vinci, Leonardo, 536
Davis, Kingsley, 105
Davison, L., 288
Deaux, K., 100
Delgado, José, 587, 591, 593, 596, 600
Dement, W., 556, 557, 559
Denenberg, V.H., 487, 510, 511
Descartes, René, 8
Deutsch, M., 131
de Valois, R.L., 539

Dewey, John, 10–11
Diamond, M.C., 511
Dilger, W.C., 521
Diuk, Juan, 163, 164
Diven, K., 216
Dobzhansky, T., 501
Doors of Perception, The, 626
Dopp, A., 112
Doppelman, L.F., 625
Dostoyevsky, F., 89
Dove, Adrian, 204
Duncker, Karl, 302, 387
Dweck, C., 277
Dylan, Bob, 88

Ebbinghaus, Hermann, **424– 425,** 431, 443
Edison, Thomas, 208, 404
Edwards, A., 562
Efron, D., 291
Eibl-Eibesfeldt, I., 527–528
Eidelberg, E., 629
Eimas, P., 230
Einstein, Albert, 62, 404
Eisenberg, L., 625
Ekman, P., 290
Elements of Psychophysics, The, 424
Elkind, D., 274, 281
Epstein, W., 236
Erdelmann, B., 51
Erikson, Erik, 252, 253
Erikson, Leif, 204
Erlenmeyer-Kimling, L., 195
Ertl, John, 204–205
Evans, F.J., 320, 563
Experimental Studies of Apparent Movement, 386
Eysenck, H.J., 337

Fairweather, G.W., 176, 179
Fantz, R.L., 415
Fechner, Gustav, 424
Feldman, M.P., 476
Feldman, H., 637, 634
Feldman, R.S., 467
Festinger, L., 161, 162
Fiedler, F.E., 148, 339
Fifer, G., 201
Fischer, Bobby, 208
Fisher, C., 562
Fisher, S., 625
Flavell, J.H., 303, 304
Fleck, S., 213
Fode, K.L., 42
Fodor, J.A., 235
Ford, Clellan S., 105
Franklin, Benjamin, 314
Fraser, B., 465
Freedman, J.L., 434
Freeman, Jo, 96
French, John R. P., Jr., 496
Frenkel-Brunswik, E., 125

Freud, Sigmund, 13, 48, 62, **92–93**, 140, 172, 217, **246–247**, 251, 404; and dreaming, 562; and hypnosis, 315, 324, as therapist, **328–329**
Frey, Max von, 548
Friedman, Meyer, 497
Fromm, Erich, 111, 161
Frosch, W.A., 627

Gardner, B.T., 233
Gardner, R.A., 233, 559–560
Garton, W.H., 612
Gay, J., 380
Gaylin, Willard, 515
Gazzaniga, M.S., 573
Geller, Uri, 405
Gelman, R., 417
Genghis Khan, 363
Genovese, Kitty, 51
Gibb, Cecil, 146
Gibson, E.J., 394, 395
Gibson, James J., 393
Ginsburg, B.E., 505
Glasser, William, 342–343
Glick, J., 380
Glucksberg, S., 303
Goldman, B., 353
Goldsby, Richard, 200
Goodnow, Jacqueline, 373–374
Gore, P.M., 55
Gormezano, I., 448
Green, A.M., 615
Green, E.E., 612, 615
Greer, Germaine, 97, 127
Guilford, J.P., 192, 193, 306
Gurdon, John, 514–515
Gustafson, L., 563
Gynther, M.D., 454

Haber, R.N., 436, 437
Hack, M., 412
Haigh, C.V., 332
Hall, C.S., 562
Hall, G. Stanley, 329
Hall, K., 626
Halpin, A.W., 146
Hardyck, J.A., 127
Harlow, H., 70, 105, **108–109**, 110, 111, 112, 220, 300, 301
Hart, I., 254
Hartshorne, Hugh, 77–78
Haughton, E., 470
Havemann, Ernest, 343
Heath, R., 598, 601
Hebb, D.O., 213, **354**, 501, 542, 579
Hein, A., 397
Held, R., 397, 398
Helmholtz, Hermann von, 537, 538, 539
Hering, Ewald, 538, 539
Herodotus, 151

Heron, W., 542, 543
Herskovits, M.J., 401
Hess, E.H., 23, 525–526
Hess, Walter Rudolf, **586–587**, 589, 591
Hess. J.L., 487
Hewitt, L., 220
Heyns, R.W., 362
Hilgard, E., 316, 317, 322, 324
Hinkle, L.E., 486
Hippocrates, 250
Hitler, 363
Hoebel, B., 594
Hoffman. M.L., 85
Holt, B.G., 356
Holt, Robert, 614
Homzie, M.J., 453
Hopkins, H.K., 626
Horner, M.S., 98, 100
Hovda, R.B., 585
Hovland, Carl I., 124, 154–155, 157, 427
Hubel, D.H., 542
Hudgens, G.A., 511
Hull, Clark, 348–349, 372, 375–376, 378
Hunsperger, R.W., 592
Huxley, Aldous, 627
Hyden, H., 579–580

Inhelder, B., 272
Ittelson, W.A., 401
Ivey, M., 97, 99

Jackson, George, 73
Jackson, Philip, 308
Jacobs, Jane, 65
Jacobson, E., 605
Jacobson, L.F., 36
Jaffa, M., 353
James, William, 10, 62, 286, 318, 404, 405, 409, 622, 636
Janis, Irving, 143, 150, 151, 161, 162, 173
Janowitz, M., 130
Jarvik, L.F., 195
Jarvik, M.E., 577–578
Jenkins, J.G., 431
Jenkins, R.L., 220
Jensen, A.R., 198
Jensen, V., 469
Johnson, H., 612
Johnson, L.C., 559
Jones, Ernest, 329
Jones, S.C., 37
Jordan, H.A., 351
Joslyn, W.D., 112
Joyce, James, 434
Jung, Carl, 329, 404
Juscqyk, P., 230

Kagan, J., 95

Kahn, E., 562
Kahn, R.J., 625
Kallman, Franz, 212
Kamiya, J., 605, 609, 614
Karnes, M.B., 197
Katz, Daniel, 122, 124
Kaufman, C., 253
Kehoe, B., 469
Keith-Spiegel, P., 221
Kelman, Herbert C., 157, 479
Kendler, H.H. and T.S., 378
Kennedy, Sen. Edward, 147
Kennedy, J.F., 143, 159
Kennedy. W.A., 197
Kinsey, Alfred C., 105
Kirtner, W.L., 339
Klee, Paul, 328
Kleinman, R.A., 606
Kleitman, Nathaniel, 556–557
Koch, Sigmund, 182
Koestler, Arthur, 404, 478
Koffka, Kurt, 12, 387
Kogan, N., 142, 306–307
Kohlberg, Lawrence, **78–80**, 88, 89, 269, 272
Kohler, Ivo, 399
Kohler, Wolfgang, 12, **298–299**, 387
Konrad, K.W., 412
Kopp, R., 577–578
Korchin, S.J., 492, 509
Kortlandt, Adriaan, 233
Kraepelin, Emil, 208–209
Krasner, L., 176
Krebs, D., 56
Krebs, R.L., 80

Laborit, Henri, 622–623
Laing, R.D., 38, 119, 224–225
Landauer, T.R., 435
Lashley, K.S., 570, 571
Latane, B., 52
Lazarus, R.S., 188
Leckart, B.T., 355
Lesser, G.S., 201
Lettvin, J.Y., 540
Levine, M., 376
Levine, S., 488, 509, 511
Lewin, Kurt, 12, **140–141**, 148, 154, 387
Lewis, M., 94
Licklider, J.C.R., 234
Lieberman, Morton, 183
Lim, D.T., 319
Linder, D., 114
Litt, E. 156
Locke, John, 372
Lorenz, Konrad, 23, **518–520**, 521, 525, 529
Lovaas, O.I., 474–475
Lowell, E.L., 357
Luh, C.W., 432
Lumsdaine, A.A., 161, 162
Luria, A.R., 411, 439

McClelland, David, 357, 358, 360–361
Maccoby, E.E., 412
McConnell, James, V., 369, 582–583
MacCulloch, M.B., 476
MacDonald, A.P., Jr., 159
McDonald, F.J., 81
McGhee, P.E., 36
McGlashlin, T.H., 320
Macker, C.E., 50
MacKinnon, D.W., 307
McNair, D.M., 625
McNeill, David, 232
McNeill, D., 432
Madell, T.O., 417
Manchild in the Promised Land, 634
Mann, L., 173
Manosevitz, M., 504–505
Marler, P., 523
Marlowe, David, 362–363
Martin, G.L., 469
Maslow, Abraham, 108, 260, 365–366
Matson, Floyd, 15
May, Mark, 77–78
May, Rollo, 260
Mead, Margaret, 98, 404
Merei, F., 146
Merton, Robert, 34
Mesmer, Friedrich Anton, **314–315**, 328
Messick, Samuel, 308
Meyer, Adolf, 209
Meyers, G.M., 561
Miles, A., 179
Miles, Matthew, 183
Milgram, Stanley, **58–59**, 63, 66, 67
Miller, D.R., 252
Miller, G.A., 429–430
Miller, George, 304, 434
Miller, Neal E., 126, 594, **604–605**
Milner, B., 574
Milner, P., 594
Mir, D., 591
Mitchell, Edgar, 405
Mitchell, G., 110
Mone, L.C., 174
Mordkoff, A., 288
Moreno, Jacob L., 170
Morris, Desmond, 532
Moss, H.A., 95
Mulholland, and brainwave research, 605, 609
Müller, Johannes, **536–537**, 547, 548
Murdock. B.B., 437
Murstein, Bernard I., 119
Mussen, P., 54

Nader, Ralph, 166

Namath, Joe, 147
Napoleon, 363
Newcomb, T.M., 158, 159
Newell, A., 304–305
Newman, E.B., 389–390
Newman, Oscar, 533
Nichols, J.R., 632
Nietzsche, 48
Nixon, Richard M., 16, 166
Noble, C.E., 425–426

O'Connell, D., 563
Odbert, H.S., 256
Olds, J., 594
O'Neil, R., 272
Organization of Behavior, The,
579
Origin of Species, 9, 284
Orne, Martin, 39, 40, 320, 325,
563
Ottinger, D.R., 508
Overmeier, J.B., 489

Paivio, A., 427
Panitch, D., 37
Parker, Dorothy, 94, 95
Paul, G., 335
Pavlov, Ivan, 11, 446–447
Peacock, E.P., 174
Peale, Norman Vincent, 324
Penfield, W., 437–438, 576, 597
Perkins, C.C., 440
Peterson, L.E., 436
Peterson, M.J., 436
Pfaffmann, C., 546–547
Pfeifer, W., 487
Physiological Psychology, 8
Piaget, Jean, 78, 80, 81, 203,
229, 237, **268–269,** 270–271,
272, 274, 280–281
Pierce, A.H., 39
Plath, Sylvia, 221, 222
Pollock, C.B., 68
Powell, Adam Clayton, 154
Praft, R.J., 415
Pribram, Karl, 304, 576–577
Principles of Behavior, 348
Pritchard, R.M., 542
Psychological Abstracts, 20

Randi, James, 405
Rapaport, C., 321
Rappaport, M., 626
Rayner, R., 450
Rebelsky, F., 274
Reston, James, 552–553
Riess, B.F., 527–528
Rivera, M., 591
Robbins, E.S., 627
Roberts, G.G., 237
Robinson, B.W., 596
Rock, Irving, 400–401

Rogers, Carl, 48–49, 260, 330,
331, 342
Roget, Peter, 627
Rokeach, Milton, 127, 128,
132, 134
Roosevelt, Eleanor, 147
Rosenblum, L., 253
Rosenhan, D.L., 225
Rosenman, Ray H., 497
Rosenthal, Robert, 35, 36, 40,
42
Rosenzweig, M.R., 511
Ross, D., 67
Ross, S.A., 67
Ross, W., 340
Rotter, J.B., 55
Rubenstein, Richard, 478
Ruch, Floyd, 265
Ruff, G.E., 492
Rush, Benjamin, 623
Russell, Bertrand, 113
Rutherford, E., 54
Rutledge, E.G., 453

Saltzstein, H.D., 85
Salzinger, K., 467
Salzinger, S., 467
Sarbin, T.R., 319
Sargent, J.D., 612
Schachter, S., 286–287, 353
Schaeffer, B., 474–475
Scheff, Thomas, 45
Schultz, Johannes, 605
Scoville, W.B., 574
Seay, B., 70
Segall, M.A., 401
Selfridge, J.A., 429—430
Seligman, Martin, 456, 457,
489
Selye, Hans, **484–485,** 497
Senke, M.G., 112
Shakespeare, 161, 294
Shaw, J.C., 304
Sheldon, William H., 250
Sherif, M., 144
Shor, R., 563
Shuey, A.M., 198
Silverman, J., 626
Simmons, J.E., 508
Simmons, J.Q., 474–475
Simon, H.A., 304
Simon, Theophile, 189
Singer, J.E., 286–287
Sinsheimer, Robert, 514
Siqueland, E.R., 230
Skinner, B.F., 12, 228, **461–**
462, 467, **478–479**
Sloan, Alfred P., 151
Slobin, D.I., 231
Slye, E.S., 559
Smith, M.B., 127
Smith, M.D., 448
Smock, C.D., 356
Smolev, S.R., 475

Smythe, P.C., 427
Snow, C.P., 404
Sokolov, E.N., 410
Solomon, F., 277
Solomon, K.C., 172
Solomon, M.L., 172
Spearman, C., 191
Spence, K.W., 453
Sperry, R.W., 573, 574
Spiegel, D.E., 221
Spiesman, J.C., 288
Staats, A.W., 473
Standing, L., 436, 437
Stanish, B., 465
Steele, B.F., 68
Stein, D.D., 127
Steinbeck, John, 434
Stellar, Eliot, 351–352
Stern, M., 627
Stern, Wilhelm, 189
Stevens, S.S., 389–390
Steward, F.C., 514
Stockwell, F.E., 426
Stoner, J.A., 142
Stoyva, J.M., 611
Stratton, G.M., 399
Study of Thinking, A, 373
Stumpf, Carl, 41
Swaback, D.O., 221
Szasz, Thomas, 39, 224–225

Tajfel, H., 129
Tamura, M., 523
Tart, C.T., 628
Taylor, C., 261
Taylor, R.L., 70
Taynor, J., 100
Teitelbaum, P., 594
Test, M.A., 51
Thomas, A., 250–251
Thomas, William Isaac, 34
Thompson, W.R., 507–508
Thorndike, E.L., 299, **460–461**
Three Faces of Eve, The, 211
Thurstone, L.L., 192
Tinbergen, Niko, 519
Titchener, Edward, 9, 11, 409
Todd, D., 221
Tolman, E.C., 349
Tompkins, Silvan, 289
Townsend, Robert, 146
Traub, A.C., 561
Treiman, D.M., 488
Tryon, R.C., 502
Tubbs, W.E., 576
Turner, S.H., 440

Ungar, Georges, 583

Valins S., 115, 116
Varela, J.A., 164
Veroff, J., 362, 364

Vigorito, J., 230
Vitro, F.T., 85
Vogel, G.W., 561
Volkman, J., 359

Walden II, 462, 478
Walder, L.O., 68
Walk, R.D., 394, 395
Wall, Patrick, 553
Wallace, W.A., 440
Wallach, H., 392
Wallach, M.A., 142, 306–307
Walters, E.D., 612, 615
Watson, D., 255
Watson, John B., 11, 12, 450,
570
Wechsler, David, 190
Weil, Andrew, 637
Weisberg, R.N., 303
Weiss, J.M., 492, 494
Weisz, A.E., 70
Weizmann, F., 415
Wertheimer, Max, 12, 140,
386–387, 393
Wertheimer, Michael, 396
White, R.W., 359
White, Sheldon, 281, 379
Whitehorn, J., 338–339
Whorf, Benjamin, 237–238, 242
Wiesel, T.N., 542
Wilkes, A.L., 129
Williams, C.D., 474
Winer, B.J., 146
Wogan, M., 338
Wolff, H.G., 486
Wollstonecraft, Mary, 94
Wolpe, J., 336, 343
Woolf, Virginia, 434
Work in America, 497
Wundt, Wilhelm, 8, 9, 11, 208
408–409

Yalon, Irvin, 183
Young, R.K., 132
Young, Thomas, 538
Yuille, J.C., 427

Zarrow, M.X., 487, 511
Zebley, S.P., 351
Zeller, A.F., 432–433
Zigler, Edward, 119
Zimbardo, Philip, 59, 64, 72,
321
Zubek, J.P., 196

general index

A-B distinction, in therapist personalities, 339–340
abnormal behavior, 208; modified by conditioning, 469; *see also* mental disorders
academic achievement: language vital to, 243; overemphasis on, 119
accommodation, *see* equilibration
acetylcholine (ACh), and brain functions, 589
achievement: and locus of control, 35–39; and male roles, 98, 99–100; as motivation, 357–358
acrophobia, 215
ACTH, **484**, 485, 487, 491, 511
action therapies, *see* psychotherapy, types
active testing, in concept learning, 376, 377, 382
acupuncture, 404, **552–553**
adaptation: and functionalism, 10–11; to inverted visual field, 399–400; of species-typical behaviors, 518
adaptive responses, to stress, 492–493
addiction, 628
Adlerian psychotherapy, 339
adolescent deviance, 45, 175
adrenal glands: 491; and fear, 484
adrenaline: 497, 507, 508; in studies of arousal, 286
adrenocorticotropic hormone, *see* ACTH
advertising: 163–164, **166–167**; effectiveness of, 167; and female sex-roles, 101; as social influence, 161
affective defense reaction, in cats, 592
affective disorders: 209; and suicide, 221–222
affective response, in psychodrama, 172
affiliation, need for (n-Aff), 360–362
afterimages: in color vision, 538; and sensory deprivation, 543
age regression, under hypnosis, 316
aggression: **62–73**, 131; brain-stimulation of, 595–596; and deprived upbringing, 112; and frustration, 127; and overcrowding, 65; and power, 364; in prisoners, 72; in psychopaths, 219; and sex differences, 95–96; against stereotypes, 127; and territoriality, 532–533
alarm reaction, to stress, 485
alcohol: as addictive, 629; and attention paying, 420–421
alienation: and suicide, 221, 222; and need for therapy, 342
all-or-none law, and neuron discharge, 589
alpha waves: 564, 609; control of, 614–615
altered consciousness: 637; hypnotic state as, 319–320, 324–325
altruistic behavior, 48

American Psychiatric Association, 104, 105
American Psychological Association: 4, 108; divisions of, 8; purpose of, 7
American Sign Language (ASL), and chimps, 233
Ames room, 401
amnesia: 215, 578; and hypnosis, 316; of sleep-acquired material, 564
amphetamines, 630–631
anal phase, in psychosexual development, 246
animal behavior: 284, 518–533; problem solving in, 298
animism, in cognitive development, 271, 275
anonymity, 59, 64–65
antihistamines, and anxiety, 622–623
anti-Semitism, and anxiety, 130, 131
antisocial behavior: 218–220; and crowding, 59
anxiety: 92–93, 258, **482–497**; absence of, in psychopaths, 219; and achievement motivation, 358; and biofeedback, 611; chronic, 484; and female sex-roles, 99, 100; and menstrual cycle, 98; and novelty, 356–357; and pain, 553; prejudice as reductive of, 130; in therapists, 338; and therapy, 173, 333–334
anxiety hierarchies, in systematic desensitization, 334, 336
anxiety reactions, type of neurosis, 215
apathy, of bystanders, 52–53, 58
approach-avoidance behavior, 356–357
approval, need for, as motivation, 362–363
arousal: and cognitive appraisal, 287–288; and interpersonal attraction, 115; as motivational factor, **353–355**, 362, 368; and perception of emotions, 286
artificial intelligence, 382–383
aspiration, *see* level of aspiration
assimilation: in cognitive development, 270; of cultural groups, 291–292
association: and meaningfulness, 426; and memory organization, 434; and moral development, 83–85; of stimuli, 446, 457
associationism, 372
associative learning, 198
attention: **406–421**; defined, 408; as reinforcer for disruptive behavior, 473; and variations in stimuli, 414–416
attitude research, 158
attitudes: 34; defined, 154, and learning in children, 277–278; relationship to behavior, 162, 166
authoritarian leadership, 140
authoritarian personality: 124–125; origins of, 254–255
authority: abuse of, in prisions, 72–73; and ethnocentrism, 126; and hurtful behavior, 63–64; respect for, as moral stage, 79
authority figures, coping with, 179
autistic children, conditioning of, 474–475
autogenic training, 605, 611
autohypnotic effect, 553
autokinetic effect, 144, 393–394

autonomic functions, control of, with biofeedback, 606
autonomic nervous system (ANS): **491**, 604; changes in, with OR, 410; and stress or anxiety, 484, 490, 491
average deviation, in statistics, 25–26
avoidance behavior, 456–457

backward conditioning, 448, 449, 456
Barber Suggestibility Scale (BSS), 316, 318–319
barbiturates, 629, 630–631
basilar membrane, in ear structure, 544–546
Bass Scale of Acquiescence, 625
bedwetting, 566
behavior: as component of morality, 76; genetic factors in, 502, 503–508, **516–533**; psychology as science of, 4, 348
behavior acquisition, and conditioning, 464–469
behavior control: 26, 462; and subliminal stimuli, 418, 420
behavior genetics, as field of study, 502
behavior modification: **478–479**; described, 463; painful, when justified, 475; and therapy, 343; in token economy, 465
behavior therapy: 330; and operant conditioning, 463; types of, 333
behavioral development, factors in, 501
behavioral engineering, 462
behavioral responses, during sleep, 563–564
behavioral technology, and Skinner, 478
behavioral theories of personality, 261–262
behaviorism: **11–12**, 13, 348, 520; and cognitive processes, 460, 478; and Pavlovian conditioning, 456–457; and Skinner, 461–462
Binet-Simon scale, 189
biochemical changes, and memory, 579–580
biofeedback: **602–619**; applications of, in medicine, 618–619; defined, 604; and epilepsy, 610; and self-awareness, 614–616
biological clocks, 567
biological needs, and drives, 348
black English (BE), 239–240
blood circulation, control of, through biofeedback, 606–607, 611–612
brain damage, in strokes, 601
brain development, in enriched environments, 511–512
brain, human: experiments with hemispheres of, 311, **571–574**; and food-intake regulation, 352; and problem solving and creativity, 310–311; reticular formation of, and arousal, 354; sensory parts of, 549, 550; topography of, 572
brain mapping, 586
brainstem, 586, 588–589
brain stimulation (ESB): **584–601**; and behavior, 590–596; defined, 586; and medicine, 601; and social behavior, 595–596, 600–601

brain storage: 568–583; defined, 570; molecular basis for, 579–580
brain structure, and sleep regulation, 558
brain surgery, and memory retrieval, 439
brainwaves: 310–311; and biofeedback, 605; in hypnosis, 314; and OR, 410; rhythmic components of, 609
built-in behavior: 516–533; defined, 518; and maturation events, 524–530

cardiovascular disease, and stress, 496–497
castration fear, 217
catatonic stupor, 211
categorical storage, in memory organization, 373, 434–435
catharsis: 172; in early therapies, 328
cautious-shift hypothesis, 143–144
central nervous system (CNS), 410, 604, **607**
central cues hypothesis, and hunger, 351–352
central tendency, in statistics, 25, 27
cerebellum: 588–589; functions of, 571, 572
cerebral cortex, 570, **588–589**, 624
cerebral hemispheres, 573–575, 582
cerebrum, 571, 572
chaining, in operant conditioning, 467–469
character disorders, 333
chemotherapy, see drug therapy
child abuse, **68–69**; 220
child psychology, 268–269, **372–383**
childhood experience: 252–253; and later aggressiveness, 68, 70; and stress, 486, 487
childhood sexuality, in Freudian therapy, 328
children's thinking, 266–281, 418
chimpanzees, and language acquisition, 232–233
chlorpromazine, 622, **623**
chorda tympani, taste nerve, 547
chromosomes, 500
chronological age (CA), 188, 190
chunking, and memory organization, 434, 443
circadian cycle, 567
classical conditioning, 218; see also Pavlovian conditioning
claustrophobia, 215
Clever Hans, 40–41
client, in non-directive therapy, 49
client-centered therapy: **48–49**, 330–331; consequences of, 333; example of, 331; major task of, 331; and personality variables, 339–340; and psychoanalysis, 330
clinical psychology, 4, 6
cloning, and genetic engineering, 514
closure, as perceptual principle, 388
clustering, and memory organization, 434
coefficient of correlation, 25, 30
cognitive appraisal: of arousal states, 287–288; and stress reduction, 288
cognitive development: 266–281; educational implications of, 280–281; environ-

mental theories of, 274–275; and language acquisition, 236–237; and moral development, 78–83, 88
cognitive dissonance: 134, 136, 166; and persuasion, 162–163
cognitive psychology: 78, 370–383; and language learning, 232; origins of, 299
Coleman Commission Report, 36, 200
color blindness, 538
color vision: 538–544; in dreams, 562
compensation, as defense mechanism, 259
competitiveness, as personality trait, 54
compulsive neurosis, 215
computer-simulation: 155; and intelligence, 382–383; of problem solving, 304–305
concept learning: 370–383; defined, 372; developmental changes in, 378–380, and problem solving, 376
concrete operational stage, in cognitive development, 270, 272, 274
conditioned response (CR): 446, 448; and childhood learning, 448; extinction of, 453; higher-order, 451–452
conditioned stimulus (CS), 446
conditioning: 375–376, **444–457, 458–479**; and anxiety reaction, 216; classical, see Pavlovian conditioning; in language learning, 231–232; in moral development, 85; of neurotic behavior, 216; and personality, 261; and psychopathic behavior, 219; see also operant conditioning
cones, in vision, 538
conformity: and group decision-making, 144; and helping behavior, 51–52; and hostility, 260; and locus of control, 160
conscience: and moral development, 79; and psychopaths, 219–220; as superego, 247
consciousness: altered forms of, 622, 636–637; characteristics of, 10; ego as, 247; ignored by behaviorism, 11; as a process, 10
conservation, in cognitive development: 272, 274, 417–418; testing for, 276
conservative focusing, as concept-learning strategy, 374
contact comfort, 109, 118
content analysis, 156
continuous reinforcement, 471
control group, defined, 21
controlled environment, and conditioning, 462
conventional morality, as Kohlberg stage, 77, 79–80
conversion reactions, in neurosis, 215
corpus callosum, 310, 571, 575
correlation coefficient, 25, 27, 30, 31
correlation, of IQ tests, 191–192, 195
counseling: 6; and T-groups, 145; see also therapy for individuals
counterpropaganda, and persuasion, 161–162
courtship behavior: innate in birds, 518; and key stimuli, 527–528

creative personalities, 307–308
creative urge, in Freudian theory, 62
creativity, see problem solving and creativity
credibility: 157, 166; and persuasion, 161
critical period, and built-in behavior, 525
critical period, and built-in behavior, 525
cross-cultural studies: of expressions, 284; cross-cultural validity: of facial expressions, 290–291; of moral stages, 80, 88
cross-sectional studies, of intelligence, 194
crowding, and stress, 58–59, 65–67, 496
cultural bias, in IQ tests, 204–205
cultural expectations: and gestures, 291–292; and male role preference, 98; and sex-role differences, 93, 95–96
curiosity, and motivation, 349, **355–357**
cutaneous sensitivity, 548

daydreaming, in problem solving, 298
decision-making, in groups, 140–143
defense mechanisms: 215; and anxiety, 258–259; and neurosis, 217; types of, 259
defensive reaction (DR), 410–411, 420
deferred imitation, in cognitive development, 271
delayed gratification, in Freudian theory, 247
delusions, 209, 211
dementia praecox, 209
democratic leadership, in groups, 140
denial, as defense mechanism, 259
dependence: and female sex-role, 95–96, 101; and helpfulness, 54–55; and personality development in monkeys, 253; of women, 94
dependent variable, 21, 25, 27, 29
depression: 215; electroshock therapy for, 330; and personality, 253; and suicide, 208, 221–222; treatment of, in groups, 170; type of neurosis, 215
deprivation: and aggression, 68–70; and mental abilities, 199; as motivation, 348–349; and personality development, 253; and sexual inability, in monkeys, 112; and violence, in monkeys, 70–71
depth perception, innateness of, 394–395
descriptive evidence, 20, 23
destructive urge, in Freudian theory, 62
developmental psychology: **6**, 378–380; and language, 229; Piaget's influence on, 269; in studies of children, 78
deviant behavior, and self-fulfilling prophecies, 45; see also mental disorders
dialects, equality of, 238–240
diencephalon, stimulation of, 586
dieting, 368–369
diffusion of responsibility: 51–53; in group decisions, 142
discipline, and moral development, 85–86, 88
discrimination: and adult sex roles, 100–102; and IQ tests, 205; in operant con-

ditioning, 475–476; of similar stimuli, 454; *see also* prejudice
discrimination learning, 301, 375, 376, 377
displaced guilt, 51
displacement: as defense mechanism, 217, 259; and development of prejudice, 126–127
dissonance reduction hypothesis, 162–163
distal stimulus, defined, 386
DNA (deoxyribonucleic acid), 500, 579
dominant hemisphere, in brain function, 571
domination, and sex-roles, 98
double-bind: 100; in drug therapy, 624; and schizophrenia, 214
dream deprivation, 560
dreams: 554–567; in color, 562; defined, 556; importance of, 561; interpretation of, 562
drives: 348–350; sensitivity to, 352
drug abuse, 629, 632
drug dependence, and personality, 628–634
drugs: effect on attention, 420–421; facts about, 630–631; psychological dependence on, 628, 630–631, 632; and rehabilitation, 178
drug therapy, 329, **622–626**
drug tolerance, 629

early experience: and adult personality, 68–69; and aggression, 68–69; and moral development, 85; and species-typical behavior, 523–524
ECS, *see* electroconvulsive shock
ectomorphic somatotype, and personality, 250
education: and language, 243; and Piaget's theories, 269, 280–281
EEG, *see* electroencephalograph
effectance motive, 359
ego, or reality principle, 246–247
egocentrism, in cognitive development, 271, 272, 274
egotism, distinguished from egocentrism, 271
eidetic imagery, 439
Electra complex, 93, 246
electroconvulsive shock (ECS), 577, 578
electroencephalograph (EEG), 314, 556, 609
electromyograph (EMG), 608, 611, 612
electroshock, in conditioning, justified, 475
electroshock therapy (EST), described, 329
emotion, signs of: 282–295; defined, 284; and lie detector, 295
emotional behavior: and hormones, 97–98; stimulation of, 591–592
emotional deprivation, and psychopathology, 220
empathy: in client-centered therapy, 331; and helpfulness, 50, 53–54, 55, 56; and psychopaths, 220
encounter groups: 49, 145, 182–183; in

business, 182; casualty rate in, 182–183; damage done by, 183; in prisons, 182; as therapy, 343
endomorphic somatotype, and personality, 250
engrams, 570
enriched-environment, and brain development, 511–512
environmental basis, of psychoses, 213–214
environmental factors: in cognitive development, 274–275; in development, 501; in intelligence, 196
environmental properties, and perception, 389–394
epilepsy: control with biofeedback, 610; and ESB, 597–598
equilibration, in cognitive development, 270
ESB (electrical stimulation of the brain): 592; and pleasure, 593–594; as reinforcer in operant conditioning, 594
ethnocentrism, 126, 254
ethology, 285, 518–533
evolution: 284; and genetic engineering, 514–515
expectations: and behavior, **36–37**, 411; influence of, in research, 39–40
experimental evidence, 21
experimental psychology, 4, 6
experimental subjects, submissiveness of, 39–40
experimenter bias, 15, 35, **40–44**; remedies for, 42
extinction: of behavior through conditioning, 473–474; of conditioned responses, 453–454
extrasensory perception (ESP): 404–405; and biofeedback, 616
eye-hand coordination, 397

facial expressions, and emotion, 289–290
factor analysis, 192, 256
fading, of stabilized retinal images, 543
familiarity: and language structure, 234–235; in perceptual organization, 401
family dynamics, and schizophrenia, 213–214
feedback: in cognitive development, 276; in concept learning, 376; and emotional arousal, 286; in operant conditioning of autonomic functions, 605; and perceptual capacity, 397; in sensitivity groups, 145; and stress response, 494
feeding center, of brain, 352, 594–595
fixation, at psychosexual stages, 246, 251–252
fixed-action patterns: 518; in humans, 530
Flanagan Tests of General Ability, 37
"focus gambling," as concept-learning strategy, 374
food intake, regulation of, 352
forgetting, 424–443
formal operational stage, in cognitive development, 270, 272

forward conditioning, 448, 449
free association, in psychoanalysis, 434
Freudian psychotherapy, and neurosis, 217
Freudian slip, 329
Freudian theory: inadequacy of, 93; and love, 109; origins of, 92–93
frontal lobes, and memory functions, 576–577
frustration: and aggressive behavior, 124; of gratification, and personality abnormalities, 246; prejudice as reductive of, 130
functional autonomy, of motives, 365, 368
functional-fixedness, and problem solving, 302–303
functionalism, in psychology, 8, **9–11**, 13
functional psychosis, 209–210

galvanic skin response (GSR), 216, 321, 410
GAS, *see* general adaptation syndrome
gastrointestinal effects, of stress, 490, 492
gate-control theory, of pain, 553
gene, defined, 500
general adaptation syndrome (GAS), 485
generalization, of conditioned stimuli, 450
genes and their nurture: 498–515; defined, 501
genetically determined behavior, 516–533
genetic differences: and homosexuality, 105; and stress reactions, 487–489
genetic engineering, 514–515
genetics: 500; and intelligence, 195–196; and psychoses, 212
genital stage, in Freudian theory, 246
genotype: 488; defined, 500
Gestalt psychology, 12, 13, 299, **386–387**
gestures, 284, 291–292
glial cells, and brain storage, 579–580
gradient of density, and distance perception, 393
grammar: of children's language, 229–234; and language learning, 232
gratification: in dreams, 562; and Freudian theory, **246–247**; and hedonism, 88
group behavior: 138–151; defined, 140
group dynamics, 12, 138–151, 170
group marriages, 118–119
group pressure: and attitude-change, 166; and wrong decisions, 144–145
Group Semantic Differential (GSD), 145
group therapy, *see* therapy in groups
groupthink, 143, 150–151
GSR, *see* galvanic skin response
guilt: absence of, in psychopaths, 219; and defense mechanisms, 258–259; as motivation for helping others, 50–51
gustatory sense, 546–547

habituation: and attention to stimuli, 410; in infants, 230
halfway house, as therapeutic community, 178
hallucinations: 209, 211; and hypnosis,

315; in sensory deprivation, 543
hallucinogens, 622, 627, 630–631
halo effect, 36
Head Start Program: 277; failure of, 199
hearing: and pain threshold, 545; theories of, 544–546
heart disease, and stress, 496–497
hedonism: in Freudian theory, 246; as moral stage, 79, 88
helping others: 46–59; defined, 48
hemispheres, of human brain: 310–311; separation of, 571–574
heredity: 498–515; and mental disorders, 212; and personality, 250
Hering theory, of color vision, 538, 541
heroin addiction, 632–634
hierarchical trees, and memory, 434–435
hierarchy of human needs, 365
hippocampus: 571, 572; and memory, 574–576
hoarding, as genetic, 503–505
Hogan Empathy Scale, 56
homeostasis, and stress, 484
homosexuality: 45, **104–105**; and conditioned aversion, 476; and Freudian theory, 92–93; and genetic differences, 105; as mental disorder, 104; as learned behavior, 105
hormones: 487; and arousal, 286; in prenatal environment, 507; and sex-differences, 97–98
hostility, as defense mechanism, 258–260
humanism, 15
humanistic psychology, and personality, 260–261
hunger: 350–353; and obesity, 368–369; source of feeling of, 350–351
hurting others, 60–73; see also aggression, violence
Hutterites, 178
hyperactive children, and drug therapy, 625–626
hyperphagia, 352
"hypersanity," mental illness as, 225
hypertension, biofeedback control of, 619
hypnagogic imagery, and biofeedback, 614–615
hypnosis: 312–325; defined, 314; medical applications of, 325; and role playing, 319; skeptics of, 318–319
hypnotic susceptibility: 315–317; and age, 316; and punishment, 317; and personality, 317
hypochondriasis, reduction of, 174
hypothalamus: 491, **587**, 588–589; and depressants, 624, 625 and "hunger contraceptive," 368–369; and hunger regulation, 352; and overeating, 586; and pleasure centers, 594; and sleep, 558; and stress, 484, 491
hypothesis testing, in concept learning, 376–377, 382
hysteria, treatment of, 328

iconic stage, in memory, 436

id, or pleasure principle, 246–247
identification: as defense mechanism, 259; and prejudice, 125–126
identity crisis, 253
imitation: of behavior, 51; and hurtful behavior, 67–68; in language learning, 231–232; and moral behavior, 81–83, 88; of neurotic behavior, 216–217
imprinting: 23, 519–520; and critical periods, 525
inbred strains, 503
incentives, see motivation
individual therapy, see therapy for individuals
induction, in parental discipline, 86
infant development: environmental effects on, 509–512; and independence, 111; and sexuality, 92
inferiority complex, 364
information processing, 156, 299, 304, 382–383
information storage, in brain, 577–580
inhibitions, and sexuality, 92–93
innate ability: to use language, debated, 229–234; and perceptual capacity, 394–396
innateness, of gestures and expressions, 284
innate releasing mechanism, 518, 522
IQ (Intelligence Quotient): 188, of identical twins raised apart, 195
IQ tests: 25; and brainwave monitoring, 204–205; and creativity, 306–307; cultural bias in, 204–205; history of, 189; in mental patients, 174; as predictor of success, 205; scoring of, 190; and teacher expectations, 37; and tutoring, 277
insanity, 209, 225, 328
insight, 298, 305
insight therapy, 330
insomnia: and biofeedback, 618; in nightmare-prone people, 566
instinctive behavior, see built-in behavior
instrumental learning, 181, 228, 461
intellectualization, as defense mechanism, 259
intelligence: 186–205; artificial, 382–383; and creativity, 306–307; defined, 188; and deprivation, 199; ethnic patterns in, 201; genetic factors in, 195–196; multifactor hypothesis of, 192; Piaget's definition of, 270; racial differences, 197–198; sexual differences in, 201; and socio-economic factors, 199–200; stability of, 193–194; two-factor hypothesis of, 191–192
intelligence quotient, see IQ
Interaction Process Analysis (IPA), 148
intermittent reinforcement, in conditioning, 471
International Psychoanalytic Association, 13
interpersonal attraction: 108, 114, 154
interpersonal relationships: and need-for-affiliation, 362; and suicide, 221
interstimulus interval, 448

intrapsychic conflict, and dream content, 562; and personality, 258
intrapsychic events, and neurosis, 217
intra-uterine environment, 501; and post-natal behavior, 505–506
introjection, as defense mechanism, 259
introspection, as method in psychology, 8–9, 408, 409
intuition: and artificial intelligence, 383; and brain functions, 310–311; in scientific method, 17
investigator bias, see experimenter bias
IT Scale for Children, 96–97

key stimuli, and fixed action patterns, 518, 522, **527–528**
Kpelle, tribe in Liberia, 380
"Kraepelin era," in psychiatry, 208

labeling concept, 44–45
labeling, of emotions, 285–287
labels: in concept learning strategies, 379; and functional-fixedness, 303
laissez-faire leadership, 140
language: **226–243**; and brain hemispheres, 310; in chimpanzees, 232–233; in cognitive development, 271; in concept learning, 379–380, 382; defined, 228; and dialects, 238–240; formal, or "elaborated code," 243; grammatical structure of, 234–236; innate capacity for, debated, 229–234; and linguistic relativity, 238; and mental processes, 236–240; and problemsolving, 303; redundancy as feature of, 234; syntactical structure of, 236; and thought, 242–243
language acquisition, 228, **229–234**, 380; and cognitive development, 236–237
language-acquisition-device (LAD), 229–230
"language center," in brain, 310, 574
language-skills: in cognitive development, 276–277; and preschool education, 243
latency period, in sexual development, 92, 246
lateral geniculate nucleus (LGN), 539, 540
law of effect, Thorndike's, 461
leadership styles: 140, 142, **146–148**; and results of group effort, 141
learned helplessness, and stress, 489–490
learning: and attention, 410, 417–418; as component of behavior, 348; of concepts, 370–383; and curiosity, 355; and insight, 298; and operant conditioning, 460; and orienting response, 411; Pavlovian conditioning as, 446, **456–457**; of perceptual responses, 396; and serial-position effect, 427–428; in sleep, 563–564
learning sets, 300–301
learning theory, and language, 228
Least Preferred Coworker (LPC) scale, 148
level of aspiration, and motivation, 358–359

levels of moral development, 79–80
libido, 246
lie detector, and emotion, 295
limited-retrieval, of memories, 431–432
linguistic relativity, 238, **242–243**, 380
linguistics, 228–229, 235
Little Hans, 217
locus of control (LC): defined, 36; external, 36, 85; and helpfulness, 55; internal, 36; as personality dimension, 255–256; and social influence, 159–160; testing for, 36
Logic Theorist (LT), 305
logical reasoning: and brain hemispheres, 310, 571–574; as mental ability, 192
longitudinal studies, of intelligence, 194
long term memory (LTM), **436–437**, 442, 570
love: 106–119; defined, 108; and hate, 119; and learning, 109; and physiological arousal, 115–116; in psychopaths, 219
love withdrawal, in parental discipline, 86
LSD, 622, 627, 630–631

maintenance motives, 350–357
male role preference, 96–97
manic-depressive psychosis, 209, 211
manipulation: in advertising, 167; of behavior, 462
marijuana, 420, 622, 628, 630–631
Marlowe-Crowne Social Desirability Scale, 363
Maslow's hierarchy of needs, 365
mass media: and advertising, 166–167; and social influence, 154
masturbation, 105, 246
maternal behavior:and offspring development, 511; as partly learned, 70
maternal stress, and prenatal development, 507–508
maternalism, 110–111
mathematics, in psychology, 25–31; 348–349
maturation, and built-in behavior, 524–530
maturational events, in development, 231
maze-bright and maze-dull rats, 196, 502
mean, statistical, defined, 25, 27
meaningfulness: and memory, 425–427; and rate of learning, 426–427, 437
median, statistical, defined, 25, 27, 28
medicine, uses of biofeedback in, 618–619
meditation, 637
memory: **422–443**, 568–583; access to, 615; and brain physiology, 568–583; and chunking, 434; and clustering, 434; cues for, 431–432; defined, 424; and intelligence, 188; and interference, 432; and meaningfulness, 425–426; organization of, 433–437; and repression, 432–433; time-dependence of, 577–579; two-stage theory of, 436–437; verbal factors in, 425–429
memory aids, 442–443
memory loss, after electroshock therapy, 330

memory transfer, 582–583
mental age (MA), 188, 190
mental disorders: 206–225; as alternative form of consciousness, 225; as culturally relative, 224–225; defined, 208; and group therapy, 170–183; and psychoactive drugs, 624–626; and subtle reinforcement, 471
mental hospitals: group therapy in, 174–175; overload problem in, 175; vs. therapeutic communities, 177–178; token economies in, 176–177
mental illness: attitudes towards, 38–39; in Hutterite communities, 178; individual treatment of, 328–329; and labeling, 45; as myth, 224; see also mental disorders
mental patients, preconceptions about, 44
meridians, in acupuncture, 552
mescaline, 622, 627, 630–631
mesmerism, 314
mesomorphic somatotype, and personality, 250
microsurgery, and cloning, 514–515
migraine relief, with biofeedback, 611–612, 618
mind expansion, and drugs, 627
Minnesota Multiphasic Personality Inventory (MMPI), 174, 247–248, 338
mnemonic devices, 440
mode, statistical, defined, 25, 27, 28
modeling: in behavior therapy, 333–334; and helping behavior, 51–52; in moral development, 82–83; of neurotic behavior, 216; and personality, 261
models: and aggressive behavior, 67–68; in moral development, 81–82
modes of consciousness, physiological basis of, 310–311
Montessori classroom, 197, 273
"mood questionnaire," 53
moral autonomy, 89
moral dilemmas: defined, 79; use in research, 79–81
morality: 74–89; components of, 76; defined, 77
moral stages, Kohlberg theory of, 78–80
morphine, 629, 630–631
motivation: 346–369; and attention, 411; and brain stimulation, 594–595; cognitive, 349; defined, 348; and level of arousal, 353–355
motives, hierarchy of, 365–366; 368
motor activities, in cognitive development, 271
motor behavior, stimulation of, 591
motor units, and biofeedback, 608–609
Muller-Lyer illusion, 401, 402
multifactor hypothesis, of intelligence, 192
multiple personality, as neurosis, 211
m value, 426

n-Ach, see need for achievement
n-Aff, see need for affiliation
naive instrumental hedonism, as moral stage, 79

n-App, see need for approval
narcolepsy, and ESB, 598
narcotics, 629, 630–631
National Commission on Marijuana and Drug Abuse, 421
natural selection, 9, 518, 519
nature-nurture question, 196
need for achievement (n-Ach), and motivation, 357–359
need for affiliation (n-Aff), and motivation, 360–362
need for approval (n-App), 362–363
need for power, (n-Power), 363–365
neurons, 570, 571, 579–580, 582, 589
neuroses: 208; and defense mechanisms, 258; major types of, 215; and psychoanalytic treatment, 217
nicotine, properties of, 629, 630–631
nightmares, 562–563, 566
nondirective therapy, see client-centered therapy
nonverbal communication: 294–295; of emotions, 288–289
normal behavior, in personality theories, 208, 260–262
novelty: and curiosity motivation, 355–356; excess, and anxiety, 356–357; of stimuli, and attention, 414–415
n-Power, see need for power
NREM sleep, 562, 566
nyctophobia, 215

obedience to authority, 63–64, 72
obesity, 368–369
object permanence: and cognitive development, 271; and language learning, 237
objective responsibility, 81–83
objectivity, in interpretation, 35
obsessive-compulsive reactions, 215
occupational therapy, 174
Oedipus complex: 92, 172, 246; and neurosis, 217; resolution of, 92
olfaction, 548, 550
operant conditioning: 218, 458–479; of autonomic functions, 605; defined, 460; ESB as reinforcer in 594; and neurosis, 216; distinguished from Pavlovian, 460; techniques, 464–469; and voluntary behavior, 604
operational definitions, 18
opinion: defined, 154; manipulation of, 160–162
optical illusion: 389, 401; Ames room as, 401; cultural susceptibility to, 401–402
OR, see orienting response
oral personality, 252
oral stage: in Freudian theory, 246; in infant development, 109
organic psychoses, 209–210
orgasm, and Freudian theory, 93
orienting response (OR): 410–411, 420; and built-in behavior, 518; and learning, 411
outgroups, and prejudice, 125, 126, 137
out-of-body experience, and ESP, 405

overcrowding: and hurtful behavior, 65–67; and psychic overload, 66; in rat populations, 66
overlearning, as memory technique, 442

pain: 545; and acupuncture, 553; and hypnosis, 320–321
paranoid schizophrenics, and drug therapy, 626
paranoid states, 209, **211**
parapsychology, 404–405
parental demands, and child abuse, 69
parental identification: and prejudice, 124–125; and sex role development, 94–95
parental rejection, and psychopaths, 219–220
passive learning: and associationism, 372; of concepts, 375–376; in education, 281
patient attributes, and therapy success, 339–340
pattern coding, in sensory transmission, 546–547, 548
Pavlovian conditioning: 444–458; and autonomic nervous system, 604; backward, 448, 449; defined, 446; and phobias, 450; simultaneous, 448, 449
peer groups, influence of, 110, **158**, 362
penis envy, 93
percentile, in IQ test scores, 190
perception: 384–405; defined, 386
perceptual capacity, innateness of, 394–396
perceptual organization: 391–394; laws of, 387–388; and visual images, 543
perceptual wholes, and Gestalt psychology, 387
perfect pitch, 398
permissiveness, of parents, 94
personal space, 533
personality: 244–265; and achievement motivation, 358; constitutional theories of, 250, and creativity, 306, 307–308; defined, 246; and drug dependence, 628–634; and heredity, 250; of high-IQ children, 307; and hypnotic susceptibility, 317; and need traits, 362–363; and prejudice-maintenance, 130–131; and social deprivation, 253; somatotype theory of, 250
personality change: in group therapy, 174; in psychodrama, 173
personality conflict, and identity, 253
personality development, 80, 246, **247–253**
personality integration: function of prejudice in, 131; and success of therapy, 340
personality inventories, 247, 264–265
"personality sphere," 256
personality traits: 254–257; and effectiveness of therapy, 337–340; of helpful people, 54–59; and response to drugs, 625; and sex, 93
persuasion: 154, 161–167; effectiveness of, 154–155; and locus of control, 159–160; and manipulation, 167; and subtlety, 161; techniques of, 161–164, 166

phallic stage, 246
phenotype, 501
phobias: and behavior therapy, 333; as classically conditioned, 216, 450, 457; cure of, with biofeedback, 619; as neurotic reaction, 215; and Oedipus complex, 217
photographic memory, 439
phrenology, 250
pituitary gland, 484, 487, 491
placebos: 624, 625; in hypnosis experiments, 320; and psychosomatic disorders, 325
planaria, and memory transfer, 582–583
pleasure center, and ESB, 594
positive reinforcement, in behavior therapy, 333, 463
postconventional morality, 79, 88–89
power, and motivation, 363–365
power assertion, in parental discipline, 86
precognition, and ESP, 405
prejudice: 120–137; and anxiety reduction, 130; and belief similarities, 127–128; defined, 122; development of, 125–126; racial, 34, 136–137
premoral level, of moral development, 79–80
prenatal environment, 501, 503–508
prenatal maternal anxiety, 507–508
preoperational stage, 270–271, 304
primacy effect, in verbal learning, 428
prisons, and social breakdown, 72–73
privacy, invasion of, 264–265
proactive memory interference, 431
problem solving: and brain hemispheres, 310; concept learning as, 376; and creativity, 295–311
projection, as defense mechanism, 259
projective tests, of personality, 174, 249
propaganda, and social influence, 161
proximal stimulus, defined, 386
proximity, as perceptual principle, 388
psychedelic drugs, 325, 420; see also hallucinogens
psychic overload: 66; and aggression, 67
psychoactive drugs: 420, **620–637**; defined, 622
psychoanalysis: 246, 330; dissatisfaction with, 342; effectiveness of, 337
psychoanalytic theory: 13, **246–247**, 258; negative orientation of, 261; and morality, 76
psychodrama, 170, 171–172
psychokinesis, and ESP, 405
"psycholexicon," 256, 257
psycholinguistics, 229; see also language
psychological punishment, and moral development, 85
psychology: defined, 4; as "hard" science, 348; subfields of, **5**, 6–7
psychometric tests, 179, 247
psychopathic behavior, 208, 218, 333
psychoses, 208, 209–210
psychosexual energy, or libido, 246
psychosexual stages, in personality development, 246–247, 251–252

psychosomatic illness: 325, 496; and biofeedback, 611; and stress, 485
psychotherapy: in groups, 170; humanistic, 49; individual, 172; types of, 330–335; see also therapy for individuals
"psychotic," as label, 214
psychotic behavior: and chemical or hormonal causes, 212–213; and conditioning, 471; and ESB, 598; negatively reinforced, 475
puberty, and sexuality, 92
punishment: distinguished from negative reinforcement, 464; and elimination of unwanted behavior, 474–476; and locus of control, 84–85, 255–256
punishment and obedience orientation, as moral stage, 79
puzzle boxes, in operant conditioning, 461, 464

Q-sort technique, 332, 339
quality-coding, in color vision, 538

random sampling technique, 31
range, in statistical analysis, 27
rapid eye movements, see REMs
Raskolnikov Regression, 89
rationalization, as defense mechanism, 259
reaction formation, as defense mechanism, 259
reactive depression, type of neurosis, 215
reality therapy, 342–343
recency effect, in learning, 428
red nucleus, and brain stimulation, 593
redundancy: as language feature, 243; in verbal learning, 428–429
reference groups, and aspiration, 359
reflex arc, 11
regression: as defense mechanism, 259; in moral development, 88–89
rehearsal, in memory process, 436–437
reinforcement: in concept learning, 375–376; defined, 463; in language learning, 228, 232; in mental hospitals, 176; in operant conditioning, 460; schedules of, 471
rejection, of infants, 70
relaxation, and biofeedback, 611
REM deprivation: 560–561; and psychotics, 561
REMs (rapid eye movements), 556–559
REM sleep: and age, 560; after sleep deprivation, 559
repression: 92–93, 126; as defense mechanism, 258–259; of unpleasant memories, 432–433
research, ethical issues in, 21
retention, see memory
reticular formation: and arousal, 354; and pain, 553; and sleep, 558
retinal images, inversion of, 399
retroactive memory interference, 431, 443
retrograde amnesia, 578
reverberating circuits, in memory, 579

reversal shift, in concept learning, 378
risky-shift, in group decision-making, 142
RNA (ribonucleic acid): 500, and brain storage, 579
role-playing: as basis of hypnosis, 319; in psychodrama, 173
role-taking, and moral development, 80, 86
Rorschach inkblot test, 174, **248–249**
Rosenthal effect, 35

salivation, and Pavlovian conditioning, 446
satiety center, in hypothalamus, 352
scatter diagram, 30, 31
schismatic marriages, and schizophrenics, 214
"schizoid," defined, 212
schizophrenia: **209**, 211, 214; and drug therapy, 623, 626; sleep research on, 567; and therapist-patient relationship, 338–339
scientific method, 15–19
secondary psychopaths, 219
selective filtering, and attention, 412
self-actualization: **260**, 331–332; and Maslow's hierarchy of needs, 365
self-awareness: 332; and biofeedback, 614–616; and encounter groups, 182
self-fulfilling prophecy: 32–45; defined, 34; and mental patients, 38; and schizophrenia, 214–215; and "tracking" in schools, 204
self-management, by mental patients, 177–179, 181
self-stimulation, and human behavior, 597–598
semantic differential, 426
senile dementia, 209
sense receptors: and brain functions, 589; listed, 537; and OR, 410
senses: 534–553; defined, 536
sensitivity-training groups: 145, 148, 170; as therapy, 343
sensorimotor measures, of mental ability, 188
sensorimotor stage, in cognitive development, 270–271
sensory deprivation: **40**, 543; consequences of, 357
sensory inputs, attention to, 408–421
sensory integration, 396
sensory preconditioning, 450–451
Sequential Tests of Educational Progress, 306
serial-position effect, in learning, 427–428
sex differences: and expectations, 38; and discrimination, 100; in intelligence, 94; in personality, 93
sex drive, 105
sex roles: and attitudes, 126; development of, 92–93, **94;** preferences for, 96–97
sexual behavior: as learned, 105; and overcrowding, 66
sexual deviance, 218
sexual inability, and deprivation, 112

sexual inhibitions, 92–93
sexual responses, and brain stimulation, 595
sexual symbolism, in dreams, 562
sexual taboos, and Freudian theory, 93
sexuality: 90–105; defined, 92
shaping, of behavior: 465–467; and biofeedback, 605; in operant conditioning, 461–462
shock therapy, *see* electroshock therapy
short term memory (STM), 436–437, 442, 570
significance, statistical, 25
sign language, and chimpanzees, 233
simultaneous conditioning, 448, 449, 456
Skinner box, 462, 594
skin senses, 548
sleep: 554–567; body movements during, 558; defined, 556; stages of, 557–558
sleep deprivation, 559–560
sleep learning, 563–564
sleeper effect, in credibility, 157
sleepwalking, 215, 566
smell (olfaction), 548–550
sneezing, and behavior modification, 479
social behavior: and brain stimulation, 595–596; early theory of, 34
social contract stage of moral development, 79
social deprivation, 112–113, 118
social influence: 152–167; defined, 154; sources of, 156–157; susceptibility to, 157–159
social learning: and moral development, 76, 80–86; and neuroses, 216–217; and psychoses, 213–214
social learning theory, and personality, 261–262
social psychology, 4, 6, 34, 140
socialization: and homosexuality, 105; and love, 111–113; and sex role differences, 94–97
socioeconomic status: and intelligence, 199–200; and language problems, 243; and power motivation, 364
sociogram, 170
sociopaths, 218
somatotype theory, 250
species-typical behaviors, 518, 521, 522–524
speech-shaping, and operant conditioning, 467
split-brain operations, 311, **571–574**
stage theory: in cognitive development, 269–270; in moral development, 78–80, 86
standard deviation, 26, 27, 29–30
Standard English (SE), 239–240
Stanford-Binet Intelligence Scale for Children (SBIS), 190, 277
Stanford Hypnotic Susceptibility Scale (SHSS), 315, 316
statistics, use of, in psychology, 24–31
stereognosis, 574, 575
stereopsis, 396
stereotypes, 122–125, 129

STM, *see* short term memory
strategy: in classification, 373–374; in concept learning, 378–379; in problem solving, 303–304
stress: 482–497; and biofeedback control, 611; from crowding, 58–59; defined, 484; gastrointestinal effects of, 490, 492; and heart disease, 496–497; prenatal effect on offspring, 507–508; in sensory-deprivation experiments, 40
stress reactions: 484; genetic factors in, 487–489; variation in, 490–494
stroboscope, 386
structuralism, in psychology, **8–9**, 13
subjective responsibility, 81–83
subliminal advertising, 167
subliminal stimuli, and learning, 418
successive approximation, and shaping, 465, 466, 605
suicide: 208, **220–222**
superego, 246, 247
surrogate mothers, 109, 111
Synanon, as therapeutic community, 179
synapse, 579, 589
systematic desensitization: as behavior therapy, 333–334, 335; effectiveness of, 336

T-groups, 145; *see also* encounter groups
tachistoscope, 436
tactile sensation, 400–401
taste (gustation), 546–548
taxis, 518
television, and models of violent behavior, 68
temporal lobe, and memory, 439, 574–576
territoriality, 532–533
thalamus: in color vision, 539; and sleep and dreaming, 558
Thalidomide, 506–507
Thematic Apperception Test (TAT): 98, **248–249**, 258, 260; examples, 361–362; and motivation, 357
therapeutic communities, 170, 177–178
therapist attributes, and success, 337–338
therapy for individuals: 326–343, 611–614; defined, 328; different types of, 329–335; effectiveness of, 335–337; new forms of, 342–343
therapy groups, vs. encounter groups, 145
therapy in groups: 168–183; defined, 170; types of, 171; uses of, 170
theta waves, and biofeedback, 615–616
thinking: convergent, 306; creative, 306–308; divergent, 306; in problem solving, 298–311
Thorndike's law of effect, 461
three-component theory, of color vision, 538
tip-of-the-tongue (TOT) phenomenon, 432
toilet training, and dependence, 111
token economies: **175–176;** as behavior therapy, 333; as operant conditioning, 464–465

"tracking" in schools, and self-fulfilling prophecies, 204
tranquilizers: 622, **623**; in therapy, 329
transcendental meditation, 325
transduction, of sensory input, 537
transposition, 12, 380
traumatic events: and personality, 253; and stress, 484, 485
traveling-wave hypothesis, of hearing, 544–546
trial-and-error learning, 299, 461
trophotropic relaxation, 611
two-factor hypothesis, of intelligence, 191
two-stage theory, of memory, 436–437

ulceration, and stress, 485, 490, **492**, 494
unconditioned response (UCR), 446
unconditioned stimulus (UCS), 446
unconscious mind: in Freudian theory, 247; and mental disorder, 217, 328
undirected thought, creativity as, 306

urban crowding, 58–59, 65–67

validity, as criterion of IQ test, 190
Valium, 625
variables, statistical, 21, 25, 27, 29
variance, 27, 30
ventromedial nucleus, and food-intake, 352
verbal behavior, *see* language
verbal learning, 425–429
verbal memory, and retrieval, 431–432, 437
vestibular apparatus, and balance, 546
"vigilance function," of reticular formation, 354
violence: 62, 119; and television models, 68
virtual images, and perception, 396
vision, 538–544
visual cliff, 394–395, 397
visual field, inversion of, 399–400
visual-motor coordination, 397–398

voice synthesizer, 230
voodoo death, 489

Washoe, 233
Wechsler Adult Intelligence Scale (WAIS), 174, 190
Wechsler Intelligence Scale for Children (WISC), 190, 306
Whorfian hypothesis, 238, 242, 380
withdrawal, 209, 211, 221
withdrawal symptoms, 629–632
women's liberation, 97, 159
word association tests, 208

yin and *yang*, 552
Young-Helmholtz theory, of color vision, 538, 541

zoophobia, 215

credits

Graphics

Unit 1: 3—Laurie Fendrich Danford. 5, 6, 7, 8—*A Career in Psychology* published by the American Psychological Association. Reprinted by permission. 9 (top left)—The Bettmann Archive. (top right)—Brown Brothers. 10(top left)—The Bettmann Archive. (top right)—Harvard University Archives. 11—Pictorial Parade, Inc. 12—Johns Hopkins University Archives. 13—Clark University Archives. 16—*A Career in Psychology* published by the American Psychological Association. Reprinted by permission. 17—From *Herblock Special Report* (W. W. Norton and Company, Inc., 1974). 18—Copyright © 1974, reprinted by permission of *Saturday Review/World* and Randy Glasbergen. 20—*Psychology Encyclopedia*, The Dushkin Publishing Group, Inc. 21—From the *APA Monitor*, September/October 1974. Copyright © 1974 by the American Psychological Association. Reprinted by permission of the APA and Konicek-Kaufman.

Unit 2: 33—Joe Smith, Craven & Evans. 34—The Department of Special Collections, The University of Chicago Library. 35—Brown Brothers. 38—Adapted from Jones, S. C., & Panitch, D., "The self-fulfilling prophecy and interpersonal attraction," *Journal of Experimental Social Psychology*, 7 (1971), 356–366. 41—Laurie Fendrich Danford.

Unit 3: 47—Joe Smith, Craven & Evans. 48—John T. Wood, Center for the Studies of the Person. 53 (left)—Tania D'Avignon. (right)—Adapted from Aderman, D. & Berkowitz, L., "Observational Set, Empathy, and Helping," *Journal of Personality and Social Psychology*, 14 (1970), 141–148. 55—Gore, P. M. & Rotter, J. B.,

"A personality correlate of social action." *Journal of Personality*, 1963, 31, 58–64. 56—Dick Swanson/Black Star.

Unit 4: 61—Joe Smith, Craven & Evans. 65 (bottom left)—Zimbardo, P. G., "The human choice: individuation, reason and order vs. deindividuation, impulse, and chaos." In *Nebraska Symposium on Motivation*, 1969, Vol. 17. Lincoln, Nebraska: University of Nebraska Press, 1970, pp. 237–307. 65 (bottom right)—Brown Brothers. 66—From Calhoun, J. B., "Population density and social pathology." *Scientific American*, February 1962, 206, 139–148. Copyright © 1962 by Scientific American, Inc. All rights reserved. 67 (top left)—Photoworld, Inc. (bottom left)—Charles Moore/Black Star. 69—UPI Photo. 70—Laurie Fendrich Danford.

Unit 5: 75—Joe Smith, Craven & Evans. 76 (bottom left)—Brown Brothers. (bottom right)—From *Herblock Special Report* (W. W. Norton and Company, Inc., 1974). 77—UPI Photo. 82, 84—Laurie Fendrich Danford.

Unit 6: 91—Joe Smith, Craven & Evans. 92—Pictorial Parade. 95—The Bettmann Archive. 99—Reprinted from *Psychology Today* Magazine, February 1972. Copyright © Ziff-Davis Publishing Company. 100, 101—Copyright © 1972 by the New York Times Company. Reprinted by permission. 104—Robert Crandall.

Unit 7: 107—Joe Smith, Craven & Evans. 108—University of Wisconsin-Madison News Service. 109, 111, 112—University of Wisconsin-Madison, Department of Psychology. 113—Tania

D'Avignon. 116—Charles Contis.

Unit 8: 121—Joe Smith, Craven & Evans. 122—University of Michigan. 123 (top left)—Frank Siteman/Stock, Boston. (top right—Illka Hartmann. (middle left)—Frank Siteman/Stock, Boston. (middle right)—Illka Hartmann. (bottom left)—Illka Hartmann. (bottom right)—Frank Siteman/Stock, Boston. 124—Adapted from Hovland, C. & Sears, R., "Minor studies in aggression: VI. Correlation of lynchings with economic indices," *Journal of Psychology*, 1940, 9, 301–310. 126—Glinn/Magnum. 128—Stephen Shames/Black Star. 129—Henry S. Levy and Son, Inc. 130—Patterson/Stock, Boston. 133—Rockeach, M., "Long-range experimental modification of values, attitudes, and behavior," *American Psychologist*, 26, (1971), 453–459. Reprinted by permission.

Unit 9: 139—Joe Smith, Craven & Evans. 140—M.I.T. 147 (top left)—Pictorial Parade, Inc. (top right)—Ken Regan/Camera Five. (bottom right)—Pictorial Parade, Inc.

Unit 10: 153—Joe Smith, Craven & Evans. 154—Yale University Archives, Yale University Library. 155—The Bettmann Archive. 159—Biondo, J. & MacDonald, A. P., Jr., "Internal-external locus of control and response to influence attempts," *Journal of Personality*, 1971, 407–419. Copyright © 1971 by the Duke University Press. 163 (left & right)—American Cancer Society.

Unit 11: 169—Joe Smith, Craven & Evans. 170—Moreno Institute, Inc. 171, 174—Flyspecks, Inc. 178—Burri/Magnum.

Unit 12: 187—Joe Smith, Craven & Evans. 188—The Bettmann Archive. 189—Courtesy, Irving Lorge, Robert Thorndike, and Houghton-Mifflin Co. 193—From *The Nature of Human Intelligence* by J. P. Guilford. Copyright © 1967 by McGraw-Hill Inc. Used with permission of McGraw-Hill Book Company. 194—Bayley, N., "Behavioral correlates of mental growth, birth to 36 years," *American Psychologist*, 1968, 23, 1–17. Copyright © 1968 by the American Psychological Association. Reproduced by permission. 195—Erlenmeyer-Kimling, L. and Jarvik, L. F. "Genetics and intelligence: a review," *Science*, 1963, 142, 1477–1479. Copyright © 1963 by The American Association for the Advancement of Science. 196—Cooper, R. M. & Zubek, J. P., "Effects of enriched and restricted early environments on the learning ability of bright and dull rats," *Canadian Journal of Psychology*, 1958, 12, 159–164. 198—Kennedy. W. A., "A follow-up normative study of Negro intelligence and achievement," *Monograph of the Society for Research in Child Development*, 1969, 34, 1–40. Copyright © 1969 by The Society for Research in Child Development, Inc. 199—Robert Crandall. 200—Adapted from Lesser, G. S., Fifer, G. & Clark, D. H., "Mental abilities of children from different social class and cultural groups," *Monograph of the Society for Research in Child Development*, 1965, 30, No. 4.

Unit 13: Joe Smith, Craven & Evans. 208—Culver Pictures, Inc. 209—*Based on Diagnostic and Statistical Manual of Mental Disorders* (Washington: American Psychiatric Association, 1968). 210—Waldman/Magnum. 212—Kallman, F. J., *Heredity in Health and Mental Disorder*. New York: W. W. Norton & Co., Inc. 213—Joe Smith/Craven & Evans. 214—Stanton/Magnum. 215—Fox, L., *Psychology as Philosophy, Science and Art*. (Pacific Palisades, Calif.: Goodyear Publishing Company, 1972) pp. 87–88. 218—Adapted from Cleckley, H., *The Mask of Sanity* (St. Louis: C. V. Mosby, 1964). 222—Shneidman, E. S. & Faberow, N. L., *Some Facts About Suicide*. Washington, D. C. PHS Publication, No. 852, U.S. Government Printing Office, 1961.

Unit 14: 227—Joe Smith, Craven & Evans. 228—Lee Lockwood/Black Star. 230—Eimas, P., Siqueland, E. R., Juscqyk, P., & Vigorito, J., "Speech perception in infants," *Science*, January 1971, 303–306. Copyright © 1971 by the American Association for the Advancement of Science. 231—McNeill, D., "Developmental Psycholinguistics." In Smith, F., & Miller, G. A., (Eds.,) *The Genesis of Language*. Cambridge, Mass.: M.I.T. Press, 1966, 15–84. 233—Courtesy of R. A. Gardner & B. T. Gardner. 235—Burton, N. G., & Licklider, J. C. R., "Long-range constraints in the statistical structure of printed English," *American Journal of Psychology*, 1955, 68, 650–653. Published by University of Illinois Press. Reprinted by permission. 239—Adapted from Baratz, J. C., *Child Development*, 40, (1969), 889–901; and Seymour, D. Z., "Black English," *Intellectual Digest*, 2 (1972), 78–80.

Unit 15: 245—Joe Smith, Craven & Evans. 248 (left)—Copyright © 1948 by the Psychological Corporation. All rights reserved as stated in the manual and catalog. (right)—*Psychology Encyclopedia*, The Dushkin Publishing Group, Inc. 249—Reprinted by permission of the publishers from Henry A. Murray, *Thematic Apperception Test*, Cambridge, Mass.: Harvard University Press, Copyright 1943 by the President and Fellows of Harvard College, 1971 by Henry A. Murray. 250—Charles Contis. 251—Thomas, A., Chess, S., & Birch, H. G., "The Origin of personality," *Contemporary Psychology: Readings from Scientific American*. (San Francisco: W. H. Freeman & Company, 1971) 340–357. 252—Adapted from Blum, G. S. & Miller, D. R., "Exploring the psychoanalytic theory of the 'oral character,'" *Journal of Personality*, 20 (1952) 287–304. 255—Franken/Stock, Boston, 257—Cattell, R. B., *The Scientific Analysis of Personality* (Baltimore: Penguin Books, 1965).

Unit 16: 267—Joe Smith, Craven & Evans. 268—Yves de Braine/Black Star. 271—Laurie Fendrich Danford. 273—Cambridge Montessori School. 275—Dianne Smith.

Unit 17: 283—Joe Smith, Craven & Evans. 284—The Bettmann Archive. 285—John Murray. 287—From "Emotion" by George Mandler in *New Directions in Psychology* by Roger Brown, Eugene Galanter, Eckhard H. Hess, and George Mandler. Copyright © 1962 by Holt, Rinehart, and Winston, Inc. Reprinted by permission. 289—Manos/Magnum. 290—Laurie Fendrich Danford. 291—Tania D'Avignon.

Unit 18: 297—Joe Smith, Craven & Evans. 298—*Psychology Encyclopedia*, The Dushkin Publishing Group, Inc. 299—Hess/Three Lions, Inc. 301—Harlow, H. F., "The formation of learning sets," *Psychological Review*, 1949, 56, 51–65. Copyright © 1949 by the American Psychological Association. Reprinted by permission. 302 (left)—*Psychology Encyclopedia*, The Dushkin Publishing Group, Inc. (right)—Laurie Fendrich Danford. 307—Wallach, Michael, and Kogan, Nathan, *Modes of Thinking in Young Children*. Reprinted by permission of Holt, Rinehart and Winston, Inc.

Unit 19: 313—Joe Smith, Craven & Evans. 314—The Bettmann Archive. 315—Weitzenhoff, A. M., & Hilgard, E. R., *Stanford Susceptibility Scale Form A and B*. Palo Alto, Calif.: Consulting Psychologists Press, 1962. 317—Hilgard, Ernest, *Hypnotic Susceptibility*. New York: Harcourt, Brace, Jovanovich, Inc., 1965. 319—Adapted from T. X. Barber, *Hypnosis: A Scientific Approach*. Copyright © 1969 by Litton Educational Publishing Company, Inc. 320—McGlashlin, T. H., Evans, F. J., and Orne, M. T., "The nature of hypnotic analgesic and placebo response to experimental pain," *Psychosomatic Medicine*, 1969, 31, 227–246. 321—Pictorial Parade, Inc.

Unit 20: 327—Joe Smith, Craven & Evans. 328—Pictorial Parade, Inc. 330—Drawing by Frascino; Copyright © 1972 *The New Yorker* Magazine, Inc. 332—Daniel Thaxton. 337—J. Wolpe, "The systematic desensitization treatment of neuroses," *The Journal of Nervous and Mental Disease*, 132 (1963), 189–203.

Unit 21: 347—Joe Smith, Craven & Evans. 348—Yale University Archives, Yale University Library. 351—Adapted from Mook, D., "Oral and postingestional determinants of the intake of various solutions in rats with esophageal fistulas," *Journal of Comparative and Physiological Psychology*, 1963. Copyright © 1963 by the American Psychological Association. Reprinted by permission. 352—Adapted from Stellar, E., "Hunger in man: comparative and physiological studies," *American Psychologist*, 1967, 22, 105–117. Copyright © 1967 by the American Psychological Association. Reprinted by permission, 354—Adapted from Hebb, D. O., "Drives and the CNS (Conceptual Nervous System)." *Psychological Review*, 1955, 62, 243–254. Copyright © 1955 by the American Psychological Association. Reprinted by permission. 356—Adapted from Smock, C. D., & Holt, B. G., "Children's reactions to novelty; an experimental study of 'curiosity motivation.'" *Child Development*, 1962, 33, 631–642. University of Chicago Press. 360, 361—Adapted from McClelland, C. C., *Assessing Human Motivation*. Copyright © 1971 General Learning Corporation. Reprinted by permission. 365—Adapted from data on "Hierarchy of Needs" from *Motivation and Personality* by A. H. Maslow (Harper & Row, 1954).

Unit 22: 371—Joe Smith, Craven and Evans. 372—Harvard University News Office. 373—Adapted from Bruner, J. S., Goodnow, J. J., & Austin, G. A., *A Study of Thinking*, New York: Wiley, 1956. Copyright © 1956 John Wiley & Sons, Inc. 375—Adapted from Hull, C. L., "Quantitative aspects of the evolution of concepts," *Psychological Monographs*, 1920, 28, (Whole No. 123). Copyright © 1920 by the American Psychological Association. Reprinted by permission. 377—Adapted from Levine, M., "Hypothesis behavior by humans during discrimination learning," *Journal of Experimental Psychology*, 1966, 71, 331–338. Copyright © 1966 by the American Psychological Association and reprinted by permission. 379—Adapted from Kendler, H. H., & Kendler, T. S., "Vertical and horizontal processes in problem solving," *Psychological Review*, 1962, 69, 1–16. Copyright © 1962 by the American Psychological Association. Reprinted by permission.

Unit 23: 385—Joe Smith, Craven & Evans. 386—Omikron. 387—Muybridge, Eadweard. *Daisy Jumping a Hurdle*, 1886. Plate 640 from *Animal Locomotion*. Photogravure, $10 \times 12^{1}/_{8}$". Collection, The Museum of Modern Art, New York. 338 (top left)—John Urban. (top right)—From "A Factorial Study of Perception" by L. L. Thurstone. Copyright © 1974 by the University of Chicago. (middle left & bottom left)—*Psychology Encyclopedia*, The Dushkin Publishing Group, Inc. (bottom right)—John Urban, 389—Reprinted by permission of *Saturday Review/World* and Junco. 390 (top left)—*Psychology Encyclopedia*, The Dushkin Publishing Group, Inc. (bottom right)—Laurie Fendrich Danford. 391—Adapted from Stevens, S. S., & Newman, E. B., "The localization of actual sources of sound," *American Journal of Psychology*, 1936, 48, 297–306. 392 Charles Contis. 393 (top left)—Wallach, H., "Brightness constancy and the nature of achromatic colors," *Journal of Experimental Psychology*, 1948, 38, 310–324. Copyright © 1948 by the American Psychological Association. Reprinted by permission. (bottom right)—Gibson, James J., *The Perception of the Visual World*, 1950. Reprinted by permission of Houghton Mifflin Company, Boston. 395 (top right)—Monkmeyer Press.

396—Laurie Fendrich Danford. 398—Adapted from Held, R., & Hein, A., "Movement produced stimulation in the development of visually guided behavior," *Journal of Comparative and Physiological Psychology*, 1968, 56, 872–876. Copyright © 1968 by the American Psychological Association. Reprinted by permission. 400 (top left)—Monkmeyer Press. (top right)—Siteman/Stock, Boston. 402—Segall, M. H., Campbell, D. T., & Herskovits, M. J., "Cultural differences in the perception of geometric illusions," *Science*, Vol. 139, 769–771, February 22, 1963. Copyright © 1963 by the American Association for the Advancement of Science.

Unit 24: 407—Joe Smith, Craven & Evans. 408—The Bettmann Archive. 413, 416—Laurie Fendrich Danford.

Unit 25: 423—Joe Smith, Craven & Evans. 424—The Bettmann Archive. 426—Adapted from Cieutat, V. J., Stockwell, F. E., & Noble, C. E., "The interaction of ability and amount of practice with stimulus and response meaningfulness (m, m) in paired-associate learning," *Journal of Experimental Psychology*, 1968. Copyright © 1968 by the American Psychological Association. Reprinted by permission. 427—Adapted from Paivio, A., Yuille, J. C., & Madigan, S. A., "Concreteness, imagery, and meaningfulness values for 925 nouns," *Journal of Experimental Psychology*, 1968, 76, Monograph Supplement No. 1, Pt. 2, 1–25. Copyright © 1968 by the American Psychological Association. Reprinted by permission. 428—Adapted from Hovland, C. I., "Experimental studies in rote learning theory, III. Distribution of practice with varying speeds of syllable presentation," *Journal of Experimental Psychology*, 1938, 23, 172–190. Copyright © 1938 by the American Psychological Association. Reprinted by permission. 429, 430—Adapted from Miller, G. A., & Selfridge, J. A., "Verbal context and the recall of meaningful material," *American Journal of Psychology*, 1950, 63, 176–185. Published by the University of Illinois Press. Reprinted by permission. 433—Adapted from Luh, C. W., "The conditions of retention," *Psychological Monographs*, 1922, 31, No. 142. Copyright © 1922 by the American Psychological Association. Reprinted by permission. 435—Adapted from Bower, G. H., "Organizational factors in memory," *Journal of Cognitive Psychology*, 1970, 1, 18–46. 438—Bower, Gordon, "Analysis of a mnemonic device," *American Scientist*, 58, No. 5, 1970. Reprinted by permission of *American Scientist*: New Haven, Connecticut. From the Simone Withers Swan Collection, New York.

Unit 26: 445—Joe Smith, Craven & Evans. 446—Culver Pictures, Inc. 447—Laurie Fendrich Danford. 449 (top)—Tania D'Avignon. (bottom). 452—Adapted from Brogden, W. J., & Culler, E., "Experimental extinction of higher-order responses," *American Journal of Psychology*, 1936, 47, 663–667.

Unit 27: 459—Joe Smith, Craven & Evans. 460—Teachers College, Columbia University. 461—*Psychology Encyclopedia*, The Dushkin Publishing Group, Inc. 462 (top left)—Monkmeyer Press. (bottom right)—Hugh Rogers/Monkmeyer Press. 466—Copyright © 1971 by Richard H. Normile, Ph.D. and Kathryn L. Normile. Reprinted with permission. 468—*Psychology Encyclopedia*, The Dushkin Publishing Group, Inc. 472 (bottom right)—Adapted from CRM, *Psychology Today: An Introduction*, first edition, Del Mar, Calif.: Communication Research Machines, Inc. Based on Reynolds, G., *Operant Conditioning*, Glenview, Illinois: Scott, Foresman and Company. 475—Lovaas, O. I., Schaeffer, B., & Simmons, J. Q., "Building social behavior in autistic children by use of electric shock," *Journal of Experimental Research in Personality*, 1 (1965). Reprinted by permission of Academic Press, Inc.

Unit 28: 483—Joe Smith, Craven & Evans. 484—Pictorial Parade, Inc. 485—From *Introduction to Psychology* by Clifford T. Morgan and Richard A. King. Copyright © 1971 by McGraw-Hill, Inc. Used with permission of McGraw-Hill Book Company. 487—Moon/Stock, Boston. 488—Adapted from Levine, S. & Treiman, D. M., "Differential plasma corticosterone response to stress in four inbred strains of mice," *Endocrinology*, 1964, 75, 642–644. J. B. Lippincott Company. 493 (top left)—Jerry Irwin/Black Star. (bottom right)—Pictorial Parade, Inc.

Unit 29: 499—Joe Smith, Craven & Evans. 500—*Psychology Encyclopedia*, The Dushkin Publishing Group, Inc. 501—From Hebb, D. O.: *A Textbook of Psychology*, 3rd Edition. (Philadelphia: W. B. Saunders Company, 1972), p. 128. 502—University of California, Berkeley. 504—*Psychology Encyclopedia*, The Dushkin Publishing Group, Inc. 505—Reprinted from *Psychology Today* Magazine, August 1970. Copyright © 1974 Ziff-Davis Publishing Company. 507, 510—Victor Denenberg.

Unit 30: 517—Joe Smith, Craven & Evans. 519 (top left)—Thomas McAvoy, Time/Life Picture Agency. (top right)—Nina Leen, Time/Life Picture Agency. 521 (bottom right)—Eibl-Eibesfeldt, *Ethology, The Biology of Behavior*. (New York: Holt, Rinehart & Winston, 1970.) Reprinted by permission. 522 (top left)—National Wildlife. (bottom) and 523—From *The Behavior of Lovebirds* by William C. Dilger, January 1962. Copyright © 1962 by Scientific American, Inc. All rights reserved. 526 (top)—Reprinted by permission from Hess, E. H., *Science*, 1959, 130, 134. Copyright © 1959 by the American Association for the Advancement of Science. (bottom)—*Imprinting*, by E. Hess. Copyright © 1973 by Litton Educational Publishing, Inc. Reproduced by permission of Van Nostrand Reinhold Company. 528—Eibl-Eibesfeldt, *Ethology, The Biology of Behavior*. (New York: Holt, Rinehart and Winston, 1970.) Reprinted by permission.

Unit 31: 535—Joe Smith, Craven & Evans. 536 (bottom left)—Culver Pictures, Inc. (bottom right)—The Bettmann Archive. 537—*Psychology Encyclopedia*, The Dushkin Publishing Group, Inc. 539—Risa Glickman, Craven & Evans. 540—*Psychology Encyclopedia*, The Dushkin Publishing Group, Inc. 541—John Condon, Time/Life Picture Agency. 542, 545, 547, 548, 549, 550—*Psychology Encyclopedia*, The Dushkin Publishing Group, Inc.

Unit 32: 555—Joe Smith, Craven & Evans. 556—University of Chicago Library. 558 (bottom left)—*Psychology Encyclopedia*, The Dushkin Publishing Group, Inc. (top right)—Grass Instruments Company, Quincy, Mass. 560—*Psychology Encyclopedia*, The Dushkin Publishing Group, Inc.

Unit 33: 569—Joe Smith, Craven & Evans. 570—Fabian Bachrach. 572—*Psychology Encyclopedia*, The Dushkin Publishing Group, Inc. 573—From "The split brain in man" by Michael S. S. Gazzaniga. Copyright © August 1967 by Scientific American, Inc. All rights reserved. 575—Risa Glickman, Craven & Evans. 578—Kopp, R. Bohdanecky, Z., & Jarvik, M. E., "Long temporal gradient of retrograde amnesia for a well-discriminated stimulus," *Science*, 1966, 153, 1547–1549. 580—Risa Glickman, Craven & Evans.

Unit 34: 585—Joe Smith, Craven & Evans. 586—Wide World Photos, Inc. 587—Dr. Jose M. R. Delgado. 588, 589—*Psychology Encyclopedia*, The Dushkin Publishing Group, Inc. 590—Dr. E. R. Lewis, University of California, Berkeley. 591—Risa Glickman, Craven & Evans. 592—Authenticated News International. 597—John Loengard, Time/Life Picture Agency.

Unit 35: 603—Joe Smith, Craven & Evans. 604—Courtesy The Rockefeller University. 605—Franken/Stock, Boston. 607—*Psychology Encyclopedia*, The Dushkin Publishing Group Inc. 608—Basmajian, J. V., "Control and training of individual motor units," *Science*, Vol. 141, 440–441, Fig. 2, August 2, 1963. Copyright © 1963 by the American Association for the Advancement of Science. 609—Owen Franken/Stock, Boston. 613—Risa Glickman, Craven & Evans. 615—New York Cyborg.

Unit 36: 621—Joe Smith, Craven & Evans. 622—UPI Photo. 623—The Bettmann Archive. 625—Risa Glickman, Craven & Evans. 630, 631—From *Today's Education: NEA Journal*, February 1971. 633 (top)—Brown Brothers. (bottom)—Hanulak/Magnum.

Text

95—"Indian Summer" from *The Portable Dorothy Parker*; Copyright © 1926, 1954 by Dorothy Parker. All rights reserved. Reprinted by permission of The Viking Press, Inc. 233—Emily Hahn, "Washoese," *The New Yorker*, December 11, 1971. 247—W. H. Auden, "In Memory of Sigmund Freud," from *Collected Poetry of W. H. Auden*, New York: Random House, Inc., 1945. 331—Carl Rogers, *Client-Centered Therapy*, Cambridge, Mass.: The Riverside Press, 1966. 336—From *Patients View Their Psychotherapy* by H. H. Strupp, R. E. Fox, and K. Lessler. Copyright © 1969 by The Johns Hopkins Press, reprinted by permission. 434—From *The Beatles Illustrated Lyrics* by Alan Aldridge. Copyright © 1969 by Alan Aldridge Associates (Ltd.), London. A Seymour Lawrence Book/Delacorte Press. Used by permission of the publisher.

Charts and diagrams by Flyspecks, Inc. and Dushkin Publishing Group, Inc. except where otherwise noted.

Photograph for cover and part opening pages viii, 184, 344 and 480 by A. Devaney, Inc., N. Y.

Cover design by Kirchoff/Wohlberg, Inc.

acknowledgments

My role in the earlier version of this text was both to write and to orchestrate contributions made by a number of other psychologists. My major concern for the book was that it sample studies that were both relevant and up-to-date. With this in mind, I asked these psychologists to expand our basic outline and to abstract specific studies for the units of their specialties. The following people contributed in this way: John Aiken, Martin Bass, Stephen Bender, Michael Brosnan, John Brown, Carl Castore, Kay Deaux, Richard Dimond, David Feldman, Mark Fineman, Barry Fritz, Janet Gillmore, Charles Hart, Richard Heslin, Jonathan Hess, C. Donald Heth, Stewart Kiritz, Dennis Krebs, Joel Lubar, Gregory Martin, John Muller, Steven Reiss, Gail Roberts, David Ryugo, Freya Sonenstein, Robert Sorkin, Irene Stephens, Gerald Tolchin and Anthony Vandenpol.

The original edition was written during a sabbatical spent in Connecticut in a large beach house. Among those who worked with me there were psychologists Roland Siiter, Peter and Brenda Bankart, Mark Friedman, and historian William Donnelly.

When a unit was finished, we sent it to a reviewer. These included: Justin Aronfreed, T.X. Barber, S. Howard Bartley, Donn Bryne, James Calhoun, Eve Clark, William Dember, Victor Denenberg, Paul Ekman, Norma Hahn, Ernest R. Hilgard, Lois Hoffman, David Hothersall, Stephen C. Jones, Joe Kamiya, David Martin, James McGaugh, Edward J. Murray, Theodore Newcomb, Freda Rebelsky, Loren A. Riggs, Edgar Schein, Joseph Speisman, Tom Trabasso, Wilse Webb and Jay M. Weiss. These reviewers were exceptionally helpful, pointing out many ways for improvement in the content, flow and readability of the original manuscript.

The illustration program throughout the text is the result of considerable research and effort by many individuals. I'm particularly pleased with the drawings at the beginning of each unit, which were the product of many interesting hours spent with psychologist Mitchell Robin and illustrator Joe Smith.

To all of these individuals who gave of their time and knowledge, I extend once again my appreciation.

Joseph Rubinstein

the study of psychology staff

Rick Connelly	Publisher
Susan Friedman	Editor
Barbara Blum	Director of Production and Design
Laurie Danford	Designer/Staff Artist
Don Burns	Designer
Addie Kawula	Production Assistant
Maureen Luiszer	Permissions

This book was set in 10/12 Palatino on the Linotron 505 by Black Dot, Inc., Crystal Lake, Illinois.

The text was printed sheetfed offset lithography and bound by Kingsport Press, Inc., Kingsport, Tennessee.

Text paper is Finch Westfield Offset, furnished by Pratt Paper Co., Boston, Massachusetts.

The cover material is Corvon 120, furnished by Wyomissing Corporation, Reading, Pennsylvania.

The cover was printed in offset lithography by Kingsport Press, Inc., Kingsport, Tennessee.